shakespearean criticism

"Thou art a Monument without a tomb,
And art alive still while thy Book doth
    live
And we have wits to read and praise to
give."

*Ben Jonson, from the preface
to the First Folio, 1623.*

Mr. WILLIAM
SHAKESPEARES

COMEDIES,
HISTORIES, &
TRAGEDIES.

Publifhed according to the True Originall Copies.

Martin Droeʃhout ʃculpʃit London.

LONDON

Printed by Iſaac Iaggard, and Ed. Blount. 1623.

Frontispiece to the First Folio (1623). By permission of the Folger Shakespeare Library.

ISSN 0833-9123

Volume 42

shakespearean criticism

Yearbook 1997

A Selection of the Year's Most Noteworthy Studies
of William Shakespeare's Plays and Poetry

Advisers

Ralph Berry, *University of Ottawa*
Graham Bradshaw, *Chuo University*
William C. Carroll, *Boston University*
S.P. Cerasano, *Colgate University*
Sidney Homan, *University of Florida*
MacDonald P. Jackson, *University of Auckland*
Randall Martin, *University of New Brunswick*
T. McAlindon, *University of Hull*
Yasuhiro Ogawa, *Hokkaido University*

GALE

DETROIT · LONDON

STAFF

Michelle Lee, *Editor*

Dana Ramel Barnes, *Contributing Editor*

Aarti Stephens, *Managing Editor*

Susan M. Trosky, *Permissions Manager*
Kimberly F. Smilay, *Permissions Specialist*
Steve Cusack, Kelly A. Quin, *Permissions Associates*
Sandy Gore, *Permissions Assistant*

Victoria B. Cariappa, *Research Manager*
Jeff Daniels, Tamara C. Nott, Tracie A. Richardson,
Cheryl L. Warnock, *Research Associates*
Phyllis Blackman, Corrine Stocker, *Research Assistants*

Gary Leach, *Graphic Artist*
Randy Bassett, *Image Database Supervisor*
Robert Duncan, Michael Logusz, *Imaging Specialists*
Pamela A. Reed, *Imaging Coordinator*

This book is printed on acid-free paper that meets the minimum requirements of American National Standard for Information Sciences—Permanence Paper for Printed Library Materials, ANSI Z39.48-1984.

Library of Congress Catalog Card Number 86-645085
ISBN 0-7876-1987-6
ISSN 0883-9123

Printed in the United States of America
Published simultaneously in the United Kingdom
by Gale Research International Limited
(An affiliated company of Gale Research)
10 9 8 7 6 5 4 3 2 1

Gale Research

Contents

Preface vii

Acknowledgments ix

v

Romances and Poems

Preface

*S*hakespearean Criticism (SC) provides students, educators, theatergoers, and other interested readers with valuable insight into Shakespeare's drama and poetry. A multiplicity of viewpoints documenting the critical reaction of scholars and commentators from the seventeenth century to the present day derives from the hundreds of periodicals and books excerpted for the series. Students and teachers at all levels of study will benefit from *SC,* whether they seek information for class discussions and written assignments, new perspectives on traditional issues, or the most noteworthy analyses of Shakespeare's artistry.

Scope of the Series

Volumes 1 through 10 of the series present a unique historical overview of the critical response to each Shakespearean work, representing a broad range of interpretations. Volumes 11 through 26 recount the performance history of Shakespeare's plays on the stage and screen through eyewitness reviews and retrospective evaluations of individual productions, comparisons of major interpretations, and discussions of staging issues. Beginning with Volume 27 in the series, *SC* focuses on criticism published after 1960, with a view to providing the reader with the most significant modern critical approaches. Each volume is ordered around a theme that is central to the study of Shakespeare, such as politics, religion, or sexuality.

The *SC* Yearbook

SC compiles an annual Yearbook, collecting the most noteworthy contributions to Shakespearean scholarship published during the previous year. The essays are chosen to address a wide audience, including advanced secondary school students, undergraduate and graduate students, and teachers. Each year an advisory board of distinguished scholars recommends approximately one hundred articles and books from among the hundreds of valuable essays that appeared in the previous year. From these recommendations, Gale editors select examples of innovative criticism that represent current or newly developing trends in scholarship. The 33 essays in the present volume, *SC-42,* the *1997 Yearbook,* provide the latest assessments of the Shakespeare canon.

Organization and Features of the *SC* Yearbook

Essays are grouped on the basis of the genre of the Shakespearean work on which they focus: Comedies, Histories, Tragedies, and Romances and Poems. An article examining the relationship between pastoralism and *The Winter's Tale,* for example, appears in the Romances and Poems section of the yearbook.

- Each piece of criticism is reprinted in its entirety, including the full text of the author's footnotes, and is followed by a complete **Bibliographical Citation.**

- The *SC Yearbook* provides a **Cumulative Index to Topics.** This feature identifies the principal topics in the criticism and stage history of each work. The topics are arranged alphabetically, and the volume and starting page number are indicated for each essay that offers innovative or ample commentary on that topic.

Citing the *SC Yearbook*

Students who quote directly from the *SC Yearbook* in written assignments may use the following general forms to footnote reprinted criticism. The first example pertains to material drawn from periodicals, the second to material reprinted from books.

[1]Michael Neill, "Unproper Beds: Race, Adultery, and the Hideous in *Othello,*" *Shakespeare Quarterly,* 40 (Winter 1989), 383-412; reprinted in *Shakespearean Criticism,* Vol. 13, Yearbook 1989, ed. Sandra L. Williamson (Detroit: Gale Research, 1989), pp. 327-42.

[2]Philip Brockbank, "*Julius Caesar* and the Catastrophes of History," in *On Shakespeare: Jesus, Shakespeare and Karl Marx, and Other Essays* (Basil Blackwell, 1989), pp. 122-39; reprinted in *Shakespearean Criticism,* Vol. 13, *Yearbook 1989,* ed. Sandra L. Williamson (Detroit: Gale Research, 1991), pp. 252-59.

Suggestions Are Welcome

The editors encourage comments and suggestions from readers on any aspect of the *SC* series. In response to various recommendations, several features have been added to *SC* since the series began, including the topic index and the sample bibliographic citations noted above. Readers are cordially invited to write, call, or fax the editors: *Shakespearean Criticism,* Gale Research, 27500 Drake Rd., Farmington Hills, MI 48331-3535. Call toll-free at 1-800-347-GALE or fax to 1-313-961-6599.

Acknowledgments

The editors wish to thank the copyright holders of the excerpted criticism included in this volume and the permissions managers of many book and magazine publishing companies for assisting us in securing reproduction rights. We are also grateful to the staffs of the Detroit Public Library, the Library of Congress, the University of Detroit Mercy Library, Wayne State University Purdy/Kresge Library Complex, and the University of Michigan Libraries for making their resources available to us. Following is a list of the copyright holders who have granted us permission to reproduce material in this volume of *SC*. Every effort has been made to trace copyright, but if omissions have been made, please let us know.

COPYRIGHTED EXCERPTS IN *SC*, VOLUME 42, WERE REPRODUCED FROM THE FOLLOWING PERIODICALS:

Cahiers Élisabéthains, v. 51, April, 1997 for "*Pro Patria Mori*: War and Power in the Henriad" by Jean-Christophe Mayer; v. 52, October, 1997 for "Shakespeare at Work: 'Attributed Dialogue'" by E. Pearlman. All rights reserved. Both reproduced by permission of the publisher and the respective authors.—*ELH*, v. 64, Fall, 1997. Copyright © 1997 by The Johns Hopkins University Press. All rights reserved. Reproduced by permission.—*English Literary Renaissance*, v. 27, Autumn, 1997; v. 27, Winter, 1997. Copyright © 1997 by English Literary Renaissance. Both reproduced by permission of the editor.—*English Studies*, v. 78, January, 1997; v. 78, July, 1997. Copyright © 1997 Swets & Zeitlinger. Both reproduced by permission.—*Essays in Criticism*, v. XLVII, January, 1997 for "What are Shakespeare's sonnets called?" by Katherine Duncan-Jones. Reproduced by permission of Oxford University Press (Oxford) and the author.—*Journal of English and Germanic Philology*, v. 96, July, 1997. Reproduced by permission.—*Literature/Film Quarterly*, v. 25, 1997. © copyright 1997 Salisbury State College. Reproduced by permission.—*Modern Philology*, v. 94, May, 1997 for "Losing the Map: Topographical Understanding in the *Henriad*" by David Read. © 1997 by The University of Chicago. Reproduced by permission of the University of Chicago Press and the author.—*Papers on Language & Literature*, v. 33, Spring, 1997. Copyright © 1997 by The Board of Trustees, Southern Illinois University at Edwardsville. Reproduced by permission.—*Shakespeare Quarterly*, v. 48, Spring, 1997. © The Folger Shakespeare Library, 1997. Reproduced by permission of *Shakespeare Quarterly*.—*Shakespeare Survey: An Annual Survey of Shakespeare Studies and Production*, v. 50, 1997 for "Marlowe's *Edward II*: Penetrating Language in Shakespeare's *Richard II*" by Meredith Skura; v. 50, 1997 for "Hamlet's Ear" by Philippa Berry; v. 50, 1997 for "Household Words: *Macbeth* and the Failure of Spectacle" by Lisa Hopkins; v. 50, 1997 for "'Voice Potential': Language and Symbolic Captiol in *Othello*" by Lynne Magnusson. © Cambridge University Press, 1997. All reproduced with the permission of Cambridge University Press and the respective authors.—*Studies in English Literature, 1500-1900*, v. 37, Spring, 1997. Copyright © 1997 William Marsh Rice University.—Reproduced by permission of *SEL Studies in English Literature 1500-1900*.—*Studies in Philology*, v. XCIV, Spring, 1977; v. XCIV, Fall, 1997. Copyright © 1997 by the University of North Carolina Press. Both reproduced by permission of the publisher.—*Theatre Journal*, v. 49, May, 1997. © 1997 by The Johns Hopkins University Press. Reproduced by permission of The Johns Hopkins University Press.

COPYRIGHTED EXCERPTS IN *SC*, VOLUME 42, WERE REPRODUCED FROM THE FOLLOWING BOOKS:

Berger, Jr., Harry. From "Food for Words: Hotspur and the Discourse of Honor" in *Making Trifles of Terrors: Redistributing Complicities in Shakespeare*. Edited by Peter Erickson. Stanford University Press, 1997. © 1997 by the Board of Trustees of the Leland Stanford Junior University. Reproduced with the permission of the publishers, Stanford University Press.—Carlisle, Carol J. and Patty S. Derrick. From "*The Two Gentlemen of Verona* on Stage: Protean Problems and Protean Solutions" in *Shakespeare's Sweet Thunder: Essays on the Early Comedies*. Edited by Michael J. Collins. University of Delaware Press, 1997. © 1997 by Associated University Presses, Inc. All rights reserved. Reproduced by permission.—Cunningham, James. From "Marxist Criticism: Cultural Materialism, and the History of the Subject" in *Shakespeare's Tragedies and Modern Critical Theory*. Fairleigh Dickinson University

Comedies

The Homoeroticism of Duke Vincentio: "Some Feeling of the Sport"

Carolyn E. Brown, *University of San Francisco*

Shakespeare's *Measure for Measure* has been a source of critical contention for centuries. Rosalind Miles, for example, claims that the play "holds today an unassailable position as chief 'problem'" among Shakespeare's plays that have been labeled as such.[1] David Lloyd Stevenson argues that part of the complexity and the discomfort of the play derives from Shakespeare's "forcing us to adjust to a level of apprehension of motives for human actions which lie far deeper than we are usually willing to go."[2] While all of the protagonists are psychologically intricate, it is the enigmatic Duke Vincentio whose motives require and yet seem to defy the deepest probing and who, consequently, has contributed to earning *Measure for Measure* the unenviable designation as the most outstanding problem play of Shakespeare. Don D. Moore claims that Duke Vincentio is "probably the most controversial Duke in all of Shakespeare."[3] His governmental decisions and administration of justice evoke critical debate and consternation. But what is equally disturbing for critics is his sexual nature and the sexual nuances of his actions, which have resisted critical explanation.

Although critics have long seen *Measure for Measure* as focusing on the relationship between mercy and justice in effective rule, the play has also been shown to be about sexuality. In fact, some critics argue that it is the predominant concern of the play. Marilyn French, for example, argues that "it is not just authority (justice) which is tried in *Measure for Measure:* it is sexuality itself that is on trial."[4] Eric Partridge calls *Measure for Measure,* along with *Othello,* "Shakespeare's most sexual, most bawdy plays."[5] Derek Traversi notes that the play shows a "preoccupation with the flesh"; Robert Rogers concurs by claiming that the play is "well stoked with libidinal fire."[6]

To help us probe the sexual motives of his psychologically complex protagonists—Angelo, Isabella, and the Duke—Shakespeare parallels them, creating what critics have called a "triumvirate," who share striking similarities.[7] They can be evaluated by "measuring" one against the other. Angelo and the Duke, in fact, betray so many similarities that they have been viewed as doubles.[8] All three, for example, live religiously austere, almost reclusive lives, devoted to cerebral and meditative pursuits; they find sexual vices abhorrent and believe the perpetrators of such "sins" should be subjected to the "blow of justice" (II.ii.30); and they attempt to suppress or "rebate and blunt" (I.iv.60) their fleshly desires until they are defunct.[9] Yet despite the

protagonists' dedication to sexual abstinence, the play focuses on the passions, one of the main themes being the impossibility of eradicating the libido. The play illustrates that it is "impossible to extirp [carnality] quite" (III.ii.98) and that "blood, thou art blood" (II.iv.15). Shakespeare creates a subtext in his protagonists, one in which they harbor an undeniable sexual nature beneath the saintly surface. Their unsuccessful repression creates an erotic undercurrent in the characters and a battle between virtuous intentions and sometimes unconscious lurid desires: the "so learned and so wise" "slip so grossly, both in the heat of blood / And lack of temper'd judgement afterward" (V.i.468, 470-71). Marvin Rosenberg describes the phenomenon as a "saintlike, angelic seeming that covers healthy, passionate, sometimes frightening mortal impulses."[10] Angelo himself describes the conflict as "heaven [being] in my mouth" and "in my heart the strong and swelling evil / Of my conception" (II.iv.4, 6-7). The play, then, studies the incongruity between ideal and reality, between virtuous seeming and flawed humanity, as Shakespeare allows us to probe "what may man within him hide, / Though angel on the outward side" (III.ii.264-65).

The subtext of a disturbed sexuality that lies hidden under an angelic exterior comes to the surface in Angelo and to a lesser degree in Isabella, and it has received substantial critical analysis. Isabella "seems" a woman of high moral rectitude, devoted to becoming a "bride of Christ." But critics note that she betrays a submerged passionate nature that contorts her most virtuous actions into sexually charged acts—often tinged with erotic masochism.[11] While she pleads for her brother's life, for example, her repressed sexual nature compels her to seduce Angelo with a sexual tenor to her words. By the play's end, she becomes partially cognizant of her latent eroticism when she acknowledges that she is responsible for some of Angelo's arousal: "I partly think / A due sincerity govern'd his deeds / Till he did look on me" (V.i.443-45). Angelo's sexuality, however, has received the most critical disapprobation because he is placed in a position that allows his covert libidinous nature to surface. While professing to be sexually pure and seeming to be a saint, Angelo harbors a latent sexuality that betrays signs of sadism and that compels him to warp his governmental power into a way of gratifying his physical needs.[12] He tries to maneuver Isabella into a compromising situation, corrupting his power into a means of making Isabella repay his promise to reprieve her brother with her sexual favors. Angelo becomes guilty of "Bidding the

1

law make curtsey to [his] will, / Hooking both right and wrong to th'appetite, / To follow as it draws" (II.iv.174-76). By the play's end, Angelo proves himself to be a poor ruler, divested of self-respect and the regard of Vienna's subjects.

One of the major differences between the Duke and his doubles, though, is that while admitting to his perplexing and sometimes troubling nature, critics have not been as condemnatory toward the Duke as they have been toward Isabella and especially Angelo, nor have they detected such prurient motivations in him. In fact, while the Duke's similarities to Angelo and Isabella intimate comparable subterranean desires, the Duke has long been seen as a providential, benevolent figure, a tribute to monarchial rule. Yet even some of the Duke's supporters cannot always dismiss the sense of shadiness and illicit sexuality that lurks around the Duke's most sterling actions. Like Angelo and Isabella, the Duke reveals a sexual subtext to his language and actions, especially his planning of the bedtrick, for which he has been compared to a pander.[13] One of the reasons, however, that the Duke has not received the critical censure that Isabella and Angelo have received is his latent sexuality is more submerged and more difficult to probe than that of his doubles and remains largely subtextual. His saintly surface, furthermore, is more difficult to puncture because he maintains it so expertly. Consequently, the analyses of the Duke always seem incomplete, for, as Janet Adelman contends, the Duke is linked with a "sexuality that is itself hidden and devious" and makes "us uncomfortably aware of the possibility of hidden sexual impulses in sacred guises."[14]

I propose to uncover a part of this hidden sexuality, exploring a facet of the doubling between Angelo and the Duke that has not been examined and illustrating how consummately the Duke conceals his desires and actually manages to enhance his ducal image in the process of fulfilling his libido. Angelo helps us to comprehend the perplexing Duke, since qualities only intimated in the Duke's character are more clearly delineated in Angelo. While the Duke appears to be a divine agent, God's representative on earth, Shakespeare presents him as merely human and a "seemer," more ruled by his desires than his wisdom. Like Angelo, he uses his political privilege to fulfill his desires and bid "the law make curtsey to [his] will," for I propose that the close associations between Angelo and the Duke consist of more than a similar nature. I contend that the Duke's "closeness" to Angelo indicates his veiled sexual attraction for the young deputy and that the Duke misuses his power to maneuver Angelo into a compromising situation, just as Angelo does to Isabella, in order to gain Angelo's gratitude and, ultimately, his affections.

One of the reasons that Shakespeare makes the Duke's homoerotic attraction to Angelo and his misuse of

power more concealed than the latent desires of Angelo and Isabella is political. That is, Shakespeare is addressing topical concerns about sovereign mismanagement and favoritism that plagued the Jacobean court, for the play has been shown to have a historical context. Catharine F. Seigel states that there is "fairly general agreement that Shakespeare intended Duke Vincentio to suggest the reigning monarch himself," and Herbert Howarth concurs that the "court audience would have been alive to potential resemblances" between the governmental actions and character of the fictional Duke Vincentio and those of the real King James I.[15] While some critics see the play as reflecting the more admirable qualities and political policies of James I and view Shakespeare as intending his play to flatter James and monarchial rule,[16] James was a controversial and, for the most part, an unpopular king. In fact, in 1607 the Venetian ambassador to England, Nicolo Molin, suggested that James was "despised and almost hated," and scholars note that the "general delight with which James's accession had been attended" was so "shortlived" that it dissolved within the first two years of his reign.[17] Contemporary writers, moreover, did not refrain from addressing some of the concerns and criticisms about Jacobean governmental rule. Sir Ralph Winwood, for example, describes the disrespect shown to James on the stage: "The players do not forbear to present upon their stage the whole course of this present time; not sparing either king, state, or religion."[18] Arthur Wilson alludes to the "strange Monstrous Satyrs against the King's own Person, that haunted both Court and Country, which express'd, would be too bitter to leave a sweet Perfume behind him."[19] Some scholars argue that Shakespeare in *Measure for Measure* is not serving solely as a proponent for Tudor rule but that he is, in fact, one of those players who offers "satyr" against his unpopular and controversial king and highlights various problems of the Jacobean court.[20] One controversy of James's reign, however, has been overlooked as a concern that Shakespeare is addressing: a ruler's use of his power to fulfill his sexual desires and to reward and protect his favorites.

In addressing topical controversies, Shakespeare had to be cautious that he did not offend those in power, especially since it is recorded that the play was performed before James during the Christmas festivities of 1604. He accomplishes this by couching his depiction of a flawed monarch within an overall framework of praise. In spite of its problematical stature, *Measure for Measure* is a play with a comedic thrust that depicts a ruler's omniscient and omnipotent handling of his subjects. By having his duke offer honorable explanations for his actions, Shakespeare places the compliment in the Duke's professed motivations and in a plot line in which "all's well that ends well"—a source for some of the critical approval of the Duke as a providential figure. And, indeed, Shakespeare presents his duke as having many admirable governing qualities, especially in comparison to Angelo, who makes a disastrous attempt to "duke it." The play uses the comedic framework to celebrate an effective ruler, who ultimately proves himself severe but just and merciful and who benefits the state, overseeing the well-being of his subjects. On the other hand, Shakespeare lodges the censure in the subtext, which, unlike that in the doubles of Angelo and Isabella, does not as readily come to the surface. One of Shakespeare's subversive intentions, then, is to debunk the royal theory about the divinity of rulers (one of which James was markedly fond). He presents his duke as an adept ruler, but he also humanizes him, giving him peccadilloes, emotional needs, and a propensity to fulfill these needs through less than honorable means.

Shakespeare shows that, unlike Angelo, who makes one political blunder after another in salving over his indiscretions, the Duke proves himself a more accomplished, successful ruler, astute at the necessary art of image making. One of the reasons, therefore, for the perception of the Duke as a providential figure is that he skillfully fashions the image. And one of the reasons that *Measure for Measure,* despite its troubling aspects, maintains its comedic nature is that the Duke cultivates a festive surface. Shakespeare portrays his duke as human and, thus, as imperfect as any of his subjects, but he also makes him a shrewd leader, in many senses reminiscent of Niccolò Machiavelli's Prince: he rules not so much with virtues but with a great deal of ingenuity, being "so prudent as to know how to avoid the infamy of those vices that would take his state from him."[21] Shakespeare offers not an idealized, but a pragmatic, at times cynical, view of leadership, showing that good governing skills need not be based on an impeccable character but on the appearance of such. Unlike James who showed political acumen in creating spectacles to glorify himself but whose early and irretrievable decline of his reputation illustrates he was not skillful enough, Shakespeare's ruler consummately disguises his flaws and projects an image of righteousness. One of the reasons that *Measure for Measure* has received the designation of the most problematical play of Shakespeare is that it tackles such politically sensitive and scandalous topical issues that they must be broached delicately and allusively, never fully articulated lest Shakespeare be accused of censure of his own ruler, monarchy in general, and the royal theory about the divinity of earthly rulers.

It was in large part King James's questionable behavior with male favorites—behavior that he publicly established first in Scotland and then in England—that contributed to his reputation as king plummeting so rapidly and to the production of offensive satires and dramatic productions. Robert Ashton states that in the opinion of many of his contemporaries "the king's passion for male favorites was the greatest and most disastrous of his vices" and was "widely satirised, ridi-

culed and attacked by a wide variety of contemporary observers."[22] In a written declaration from the nobility, James was warned that his policies with his favorites were causing his "good fame" to fall into "decay, and his crown and authoritie to be putt in questioun."[23] James's contemporaries, as well as modern day historians, conjecture that the relationships were sexual in nature, that his "relations with the handsome young male favourites whom he found so necessary to him were at least tinged with homosexuality."[24] Thomas Birch clearly alludes to this tenor when he calls the young men James's "male hareem."[25] The king's embarrassingly blatant displays of affection in public made it difficult for his subjects not to notice. Francis Osborne describes the disgraceful situation:

> And these . . . his favourites or minions . . . like burning-glasses, were daily interposed between him and the subject, multiplying the heat of oppressions in the general opinion. . . . The love the king shewed was as amorously convayed, as if he had mistaken their sex, and thought them ladies. . . . Nor was his love, or what else posterity will please to call it . . . carried on with a discretion sufficient to cover a lesse scandalous behaviour; for the kings kissing them after so lascivious a mode in publick, and upon the theatre, as it were, of the world, prompted many to imagine some things done in the tyring-house, that exceed my expressions no lesse then they do my experience: And therefore left floting upon the waves of conjecture, which hath in my hearing tossed them from one side to another.[26]

M. de Fontenay, the envoy of Mary Stuart to James when he was king of Scotland, wrote that one of the king's "defects which may possibly be harmful to the conservation of his estate and government" is that "he loves indiscreetly and obstinately despite the disapprobation of his subjects"—an allusion to his public displays of affection for male companions.[27] David Calderwood refers to anonymous "contumelious verses made in contempt of [James], calling him Davie's sonne, a bougerer, one that left his wife all the night *intactum.*"[28] James himself intimated his lack of interest in women by admitting that he married his wife not for reasons of love but for reasons of state and by proclaiming when he set sail to bring home a wife—Anne of Denmark—that he "could have abstained langer" from relations with women.[29] Certainly, James was notorious for his "contempt for the female character."[30]

The scandal and public outcry became inflamed when James's sexual proclivities interfered with his governing decisions. James went off on unexplained absences, often revolving around leisurely hunting expeditions, and usually left his rule in the hands of incompetent favorites or "minions," as they were called. They were typically given the highest and most powerful positions at court, such as that of the Lord Chancellor, and were virtually omnipotent, exercising more power than the king himself, who was usually physically, if not mentally, disengaged. William Robertson claims the favorites had "devolved upon [them] the whole regal authority" and they exercised "the whole management of affairs."[31] Sir Edward Peyton speaks in a much more exasperated tone: "What shall I say more? Did not King James his minions and favourites rule the kingdom in the person of the king?"[32] His subjects objected to the "lightning advance to power" of these unqualified favorites, who had little to commend them except a "fair face and a graceful form," and hunting skills.[33] These subjects saw learned men being overlooked. One contemporary, Gundamore, sardonically condemned the conferral of undeserved power and titles by claiming that James made "privy counsellors sage at the age of twenty-one," a position of knowledge that most men could not attain until the age of sixty.[34] That these young men were unqualified and did not deserve the prestigious positions lavished on them was indicated by their abuse of the unlimited power. For example, the earl of Arran, James's second favorite in Scotland, was the most abusive. James left "all his affairs to be managed by the Earl of Arran," who introduced a "regime of fierce and brutal terrorism."[35] Characterized as "of a prowd and arrogant mynd [who] thoght no man to be his equall," he "execute[d] his office with all spedie regour" and became hateful for his oppressions, while James "remained an unconcerned spectator of these enormities."[36]

James lavished the young men with power because he "was able to deny them nothing."[37] The rumors spread that he gave these young men power and positions as a way to show his affection for them and to win their attentions. Contemporary Anthony Weldon claims it was distressing "what a slave King James was to his favourites," who "had that exorbitant power over the king."[38] James showered the young men with generosity in order to buy their affections. He heaped on them "profuse guiftes"—"money, jewels, honours, titles, lands"—none of which they deserved.[39] Francis Osborne complains that "the setting up of these golden calves cost England more then Queene Elizabth [sic] spent in all her wars."[40] But the abuse of power continued when James protected his favorites for crimes they had committed—favoritism that provoked much contumely and dissension. James was most severely condemned for protecting his favorites, for treating their crimes with "impunitie and oversight," for allowing these "enemeis of the truthe [to be] favoured and overlooked."[41] He excused his favorites, as well as the friends of his favorites, of all degrees of crimes, including murder. And he expected his efforts to be appreciated and reciprocated. For example, after James saved one of his favorites from prosecution for murder and treason and, as a result, incurred the anger of his subjects, he wrote to the favorite, informing him of how much he had endangered his life and reputation for him in order to make the young man feel obligated to him: "Bethink

you how I have 'incurred skaith and hazarde for your cause, and presentlie quhat estait I ame in for it.'"[42] While many historians consider this as James's most well-known offense, and while many scholars argue that *Measure for Measure* contains a historical context, none explores the possibility that Shakespeare is addressing a similar situation. I contend that Shakespeare is exploring monarchial vices similar to, but less blatant than, those of King James and is examining the general issue of monarchial moral turpitude, an issue that was hotly debated during James's reign.

At the play's beginning, Shakespeare begins the subtext by making his duke's behavior potentially scandalous. Because Shakespeare has the Duke and Angelo appear together in only two scenes—the opening and closing scenes—we can easily be misled into thinking that their relationship is slight and unimportant. But the fact is that their relationship is central to the action. Almost everything the Duke does relates back to his elusive scheme that focuses on Angelo, and in the disguise of a friar he keeps himself well informed of Angelo's behavior by spying on Angelo's reign. Angelo is never far from his thoughts or his view. The Duke's first questionable act centers on his removing himself from his ducal position and naming Angelo as his replacement. Shakespeare makes his duke's actions deliberately unsettling by having the Duke seem irresponsible in mysteriously surrendering all of his power and lodging it in an inappropriate choice. And, certainly, scholars have been stymied in looking for convincing explanations for such behavior.

Shakespeare underscores the impropriety of his duke's actions by introducing the character Escalus, the undisputed choice as a replacement—sagacious and experienced. Shakespeare's having the Duke cavalierly overlook the appropriate choice in favor of the inappropriate Angelo—a young, harsh, inexperienced, and untested neophyte—only complicates the issue and impresses us with a possible case of favoritism. The Duke himself admits that he gives Angelo preferential treatment: "We have with special soul / Elected him our absence to supply" (I.i.17-18). He has "elected" or personally preferred Angelo over Escalus. Angelo is "special" or the Duke's favored choice,[43] and for this he receives extra recognition and privileges. Shakespeare continues to hit his audience with the Duke's improper choice by having even Angelo himself recognize that he is not qualified, that he needs more experience before such an extravagant boon is laid at his feet: "Let there be some more test made of my metal, / Before so noble and so great a figure / Be stamp'd upon it" (I.i.48-50). The Duke is profligate in his conferral of privileges on Angelo. He appoints him the most powerful man in the land with the prerogative to make life and death decisions: "In our remove, be thou at full ourself. / Mortality and mercy in Vienna / Live in thy tongue, and heart" (I.i.43-45). Shakespeare, furthermore, suggests that Angelo is an inappropriate choice by having this replacement subsequently misuse and abuse his power. Shakespeare makes us feel uncomfortable with a ruler who chooses a harsh, unqualified man to rule because he "favors" him and who merely watches once Angelo channels this harshness into a prohibitive rule.

Shakespeare, moreover, has the Duke treat and speak of Angelo in unusual, perplexing ways. The Duke is intensely interested, if not fixated, on Angelo, admitting to this young man that he has so closely "observe[d]" the "character in [his] life" that he could his "history / Fully unfold" (I.i.27-29). Later, the Duke proves the validity of this statement, for he informs Isabella about all of the intimate details of the engagement between Angelo and Mariana and about Angelo's ultimate betrayal (III.ii.212-43). He knows everything about Angelo's past. The Duke is particularly interested, though, in one aspect of Angelo's life—his sexual history—and whenever he speaks of him, he inevitably refers to Angelo's libido or his suppression of it. While Shakespeare allows the Duke's language to and about Angelo to be read in formal and appropriate terms, he also suffuses it with a subtext that strikes us as markedly familiar. Richard A. Levin claims that the "Duke's attitude to Angelo is intimate in an odd way in Act 1."[44] The Duke refers to Angelo lovingly, as the choice of his heart: he claims he has "drest him with our love" (I.i.19). He says he has chosen Angelo with "special soul" (I.i.17), the "soul" designating an emotional involvement, and "special" suggesting an intimate relationship.[45] In fact, the Duke appears with Angelo in only two scenes—Act I, Scene i and Act V—and in both he requests to take Angelo's hand, which can be simply a diplomatic formality and yet it can suggest a desire for physical closeness.

In Act V, Shakespeare has his duke continue to use language that seems unusually intimate, as the Duke alludes to how dearly he holds Angelo in his "soul" (V.i.6) or his heart. He addresses Angelo as "cousin," a term that can denote merely a political term of address or on a subtextual level can suggest closeness if it is used "as a term of intimacy, friendship, familiarity."[46] He later speaks of Angelo being "so near us" (V.i.123) as though he always wants Angelo to be in close proximity to him and touching him, as when he holds his hand, a sign that he ultimately wants to be "near" him or emotionally and physically close with him.[47] He alludes to Angelo's being "lock[ed]" in his "covert bosom" (V.i.11), to holding Angelo dearly in his heart and desires.[48] When in Act V Angelo asks the Duke permission to question the witnesses, the Duke grants him permission "with [his] heart" (V.i.238), reinforcing an affection for Angelo and speaking almost as if he is giving him his heart. The Duke's loving references to the deputy suggest that Shakespeare is subtextually alluding to his duke having intimate feelings for the young man and that these feelings are related to his giving Angelo his ducal power.

But Shakespeare has his duke openly profess sanctioned motivations. In Act I, scene iii, the Duke gives a fuller accounting of his actions, a scene which begins in *medias res* and in which the Duke and Friar Thomas are having a conversation. The Duke is attempting to explain his absence in Vienna and his conferral of power on Angelo. He repeatedly attests to the worthiness of his motivations, helping to establish the comedic tone of the play. He goes on to offer no less than four reasons for making Angelo his replacement, all of which, while elusive, seem reputable and well-meaning: he wants to reinstate judicial order in Vienna, which out of benign neglect he has "let slip" (I.iii.21); he intends for Angelo to "unloose this tied-up justice" (I.iii.32) for him because Angelo is severe; he assigns Angelo the job in order to avoid appearing tyrannical and "too dreadful" "to strike and gall [his subjects]/For what [he] bid them do" (I.iii.34, 36-37); and he alludes to his suspicions about the authenticity of Angelo's extreme virtue and his intention to subject Angelo to some kind of test: "Hence shall we see / If power change purpose, what our seemers be" (I.iii.53-54). On a principal level of meaning, Shakespeare presents his duke as a wise leader and an astute judge of character, who dedicates himself to rectifying his mistakes and making Vienna a better state. Although his means may be questionable, he ultimately accomplishes his worthy governmental mission, which he also intends to bolster his political stature. He is presented as a shrewd ruler in that he lets Angelo do the unenviable job of reestablishing order in his kingdom so that his own "nature [will] never in the fight / To do in slander" (I.iii.42-43). The Duke's professed motivations, then, are obscure but benign and politically astute.

But the Duke is doing much more than he openly professes, for as Janet Adelman puts it, "We never quite have full confidence in his motives: from the start, they seem both contradictory and obscure."[49] The Duke's giving Angelo his full power serves his private sexual needs as well. In Act I, scene iii, Shakespeare continues to weave the sexual subtext, having his duke intimate his feelings for Angelo and his illicit reasons for giving Angelo his position. The Duke is responding to a query that Friar Thomas has posed to him, an inquiry that Shakespeare does not allow us to hear:

> No. Holy father, throw away that thought;
> Believe not that the dribbling dart of love
> Can pierce a complete bosom. Why I desire
>   thee
> To give me secret harbour hath a purpose
> More grave and wrinkled than the aims and
>   ends
> Of burning youth.
>
> (I.iii.1-6)

Throughout the scene, the primary level of the Duke's words supports the comedic tenor, with the Duke asserting the purity of his character and motivations and projecting a godly image. By not permitting us, however, to be privy to the Friar's "thought[s]" about the Duke's motivations, Shakespeare continues to shroud his duke's actions in mystery and to make us piece together bits of information and make inferences in order to break through to the subtextual level. While we do not know the exact nature of the Friar's inquiry or the "thought" that the Duke tells him to "throw away," Shakespeare allows us to gather the essence of it from the Duke's response. Since the Duke is denying a sexual nature in himself and a sexual tenor to his scheme with regard to Angelo, we are allowed to conjecture that the Friar is suspicious of the Duke's motives, as Shakespeare has made his audience suspicious as well, and that the Friar suspects the Duke's actions are sexual in nature. It would seem the Friar has made the following insinuations: the Duke does not have such a "complete bosom" or the Duke is not as immune to sexual desires as he professes; and the Duke has been hit by Cupid's "dart of love" or has felt the "sexual sting of amorous passion"[50] and found a love interest. The Duke's denial also suggests that the Friar has intimated his suspicions about the Duke's motivations being less "grave and wrinkled" or cerebral than the Duke alleges and being, instead, about "aims and ends / Of burning youth"—a sexually loaded phrase. Partridge clarifies that the word "end" "has, for centuries, been used in bawdy innuendo to mean 'penis'" and that "burn" can refer to being "inflame[d] with love."[51] The Friar seems to have suggested that he suspects the Duke not only has an active libido (that his "end" is not "wrinkled" or defunct but "burning" or aroused) but also has an interest in the "ends" of "youth"—a reference to an erotic interest in young men. Partridge contends that "youth" is "often used in Shakespeare" with a sexual overtone, referring to "'youth with its sexual curiosity and amorous ardour.'"[52] And while "youth" can be unspecified with regard to gender, it can be used to refer specifically to "a young man between boyhood and mature age,"[53] and the Duke's terminology suggests this meaning.

These suspicions may be more than idle speculation. Although Shakespeare does not specify the exact nature of the relationship and does not develop the character of Friar Thomas, it seems that the Friar and the Duke are well acquainted: the Duke himself claims that "none better knows than" (I.iii.7) the Friar about his personal habits. The Friar speaks with some personal knowledge of the ruler. Shakespeare has the Duke inadvertently attest to homoeroticism when he later defends himself against Lucio's sexual imputations: he proclaims he is not guilty of "servicing" women, for he was not "much detected for women; he was not inclined that way" (III.ii.118-19). And the Duke does not woo any women during the play.

By throwing us into the middle of a conversation that draws our attention to the Duke's defensiveness about sexual allegations, Shakespeare, moreover, allows that there is some validity to them since the Duke is so intent on denial. We are confronted with overreaction on the Duke's part as he tries repeatedly to repudiate even a tinge of sexuality in himself and his plans—as if he fears the Friar has hit too close to home. Although he offers to give "more grave" reasons for his actions, he is unable to explain himself and unable to forget the Friar's ostensible imputations on his character, to which he keeps returning:

> My holy sir, none better knows than you
> How I have ever lov'd the life remov'd,
> And held in idle price to haunt assemblies,
> Where youth, and cost, witless bravery keeps.
> (I.iii.7-10)

He continues to try to clear his character, claiming he is more saintly than sexual, denying that he "haunts" places where "witless[ness]" might take place, where people might lose rational control of their actions. Once again, he denies that he seeks out "youth." Shakespeare deliberately makes words such as "cost" and "bravery" ambiguous in order to conceal his subtext. But "bravery" can refer to "beaus, gallants, or grandees," and "cost" can refer to a price paid for something.[54] Given the previous sexual innuendo in the Duke's defenses, the Duke may be denying the Friar's intimation that he frequents places of sexual excess where young men's attentions can be purchased for the right price.

Although the Duke professes to be explaining his actions, he goes on to cleanse not only his own character of sexual desire but also that of Angelo, whom he characterizes as chaste, "a man of stricture and firm abstinence" (I.iii.12):

> Lord Angelo is precise;
> Stands at a guard with Envy; scarce confesses
> That his blood flows; or that his appetite
> Is more to bread than stone.
> (I.iii.50-53)

His delineation of Angelo does not emphasize the deputy's governing capabilities—qualities that seem pertinent for the circumstances—but only Angelo's sexlessness. The Duke's defensiveness suggests that the Friar has cast doubts upon not only the Duke's chastity but also Angelo's professions of abstinence and that he suspects that the Duke's intentions toward Angelo are sexual in nature—imputations that the Duke is intent on denying. The Duke denies that he and Angelo have sexual stirrings beneath the pure exterior—as if he fears the opposite is true. The Duke's defensiveness, evasiveness, and uneasiness suggest that his motives are not only too personal and improper for him to articulate but also perhaps not fully conscious.

While Shakespeare does not have his protagonist neatly delineate his secret reasons for leaving his kingdom in the hands of Angelo, he gives us hints in the Duke's language if we are willing to search into the subtext. Friar Thomas's apparent suspicions, the Duke's defensiveness, his favoritism toward Angelo, and his intimate references to Angelo—all of these suggest that the Duke's latent motives are sexual and that they relate to desires for "youth" and one "youth" in particular—Angelo—on whom the Duke's discussion pivots. While the Duke's repeated delineations of Angelo's sexual repression are meant to vindicate the deputy's character, they also reveal more about the ruler's motives than he is made to realize. They indicate the Duke's fixation on Angelo as a sexual being and his own inability to awaken Angelo's appetite. The Duke's description of Angelo as "scarce confess[ing] / That his blood flows; or that his appetite / Is more to bread than stone" (I.iii.51-52) suggests that the Duke has confronted Angelo and tried to get him to admit to his sexuality but that Angelo has denied the advances, has refused to "confess" that he is sexual. Shakespeare allows for the reading that the Duke's harping on Angelo's sexual frigidity denotes his frustration at not being able to get this man even to admit to his libido- one that Shakespeare suggests may excite the Duke.

When the Duke first addresses Angelo in Act I, scene i, Shakespeare makes his language cryptic and puzzling, as the Duke advises his replacement about his "virtue":

> Thyself and thy belongings
> Are not thine own so proper as to waste
> Thyself upon thy virtues, they on thee.
> Heaven doth with us as we with torches do,
> Not light them for themselves; for if our
>   virtues
> Did not go forth of us, 'twere all alike
> As if we had them not. Spirits are not finely
>   touch'd
> But to fine issues; nor nature never lends
> The smallest scruple of her excellence
> But, like a thrifty goddess, she determines
> Herself the glory of a creditor,
> Both thanks and use.
>
>   (I.i.29-40)

By having his language evoke biblical images and contain sententious words of advice, Shakespeare allows on a primary level for his duke to be seen as a knowledgeable ruler of superior moral rectitude, lecturing a less experienced and flawed young man. Shakespeare, however, also allows for a less obvious and less noble meaning. Like a shrewd ruler, the Duke is skillful at cloaking his suspicious actions—especially the most inappropriate—in religious garb. He, in fact, seems to be trying to convince Angelo to drop his abstinence and become sexually active. What is so

suspicious is that he does not give Angelo, who has no governing experience, any specific advice about the duties of a ruler, despite the fact that he is about to delegate all of his power to this neophyte. His advice is personal and is delivered in a personal manner with the familiar pronoun "thy." The Duke focuses on Angelo's private life and, specifically, the "uses" to which Angelo puts his "torch." His redundant reproofs bear striking resemblances to those in *Venus and Adonis* and in Sonnets 1, 4, 6, and 9, which advise a self-absorbed, narcissistic young man to engage in sex. He exhorts Angelo to put his "torch" or penis to "use" in sexual intercourse. The Duke advises him to realize his "natural" desires and engage in "touching" or sexual contact. In telling Angelo "thyself and thy belongings / Are not thine own so proper as to waste / Thyself upon thy virtues, they on thee," he advises this young man that he should not "waste" himself on himself—a possible reference to masturbation—but that he should go beyond his onanism and look for erotic gratification outside of himself. Enlisting a *carpe diem* theme, he urges Angelo to stop wasting himself by being reclusive. The imagery of coining often having sexual import in Shakespeare,[55] the Duke advises Angelo to be like a good borrower, who does not hoard his coins but profits himself by putting them in circulation, by putting himself in circulation. Certainly, the language has a subtextual erotic tenor and seems like strange advice to a governmental replacement—advice that should be more about governing procedures than about personal proclivities. Shakespeare intimates that the Duke is frustrated because Angelo has made himself sexually inaccessible to him and that his duke is trying to convince a young man to light his "torch," become sexual, and stop denying him sexual favors.

The Duke later refers to his "plot" (IV.v.2), and he may very well have an elaborate scheme in mind to accomplish his "mission"—one that involves misusing his sovereign prerogative. In Act I, scene i, he places Angelo in a tempting position by giving him "full," limitless power and by instructing him to do whatever he wishes, to interpret the law as he sees fit, to punish or forgive whomever he wants: "Your scope is as mine own / So to enforce or qualify the laws / As to your soul seems good" (I.i.64-66). In speaking of Angelo's latent desires at lines 29-40 and in giving him political power at the same time, the Duke correlates Angelo's achieving sexual pleasure with his administration of power. The Duke, in other words, subtly links Angelo's power with putting his "torch" to "use." The Duke, in fact, goes so far as to intimate that Angelo can abuse his power, especially since the Duke will not be present to monitor his behavior and Escalus is only a "secondary," who must follow Angelo's orders: "Nor need you, on mine honour, have to do / With any scruple" (I.i.63-64). The Duke urges Angelo to be unscrupulous. Shakespeare implies that the Duke gives Angelo power for less public, sanctioned reasons and that he means to trap his replacement into confessing to his latent eroticism: "Hence shall we see / If power change purpose, what our seemers be" (I.iii.53-54). The word "purpose" is elusive, and given the sexual subtext of the play and of the Duke's language in particular, it can refer to genitals or sexual appetite.[56] Shakespeare is suggesting that the Duke gives Angelo unconditional power and instructs him not to worry about being ethical as a way to prod Angelo into abusing his power for sexual satisfaction. His scheme is to trap Angelo into showing that his sexlessness is mere "seem[ing]." And Angelo does ultimately abuse his power for sexual advantage, forcing Isabella to submit to his desires or lose her brother. Since the Duke cannot get Angelo to loosen the restraints on his affections and respond to the Duke's attentions by directly appealing to him, he uses duplicity to wheedle Angelo into a tempting position and into admitting, in spite of himself, that "his appetite / Is more to bread than stone" (I.iii.52-53).

The Duke sets Angelo up for failure: Angelo is inexperienced, yet the Duke gives him "full" power; he refuses to provide Angelo even an iota of advice, yet he leaves him to decide "matters of needful value" (I.i.55). Angelo's inevitable failure serves several illicit purposes. It allows the Duke to puncture Angelo's pride in his virtue and infallibility and, thus, forces the deputy to drop his "precise[ness]" and "stricture" and admit to his flawed nature. It also makes Angelo obligated and vulnerable to the Duke for not living up to the Duke's belief in him and for not successfully executing the duty the Duke gave him. The Duke does not test the strength of Angelo's virtue, as he states, but induces Angelo to drop his virtue. His "purpose" involves proving that Angelo is no angel, that he is a flawed human and a "motion generative," and that he is, thus, capable of sexually responding to the Duke.

Shakespeare also has his duke in Act I, scene i lavish Angelo with power as a way to impress Angelo with his regard for him and to make Angelo grateful to him. The Duke lets Angelo know he is doing a special favor for his deputy because Angelo is his "choice" (I.i.51): "Old Escalus, / Though first in question, is thy secondary" (I.i.45-46). He informs Angelo that he does not really deserve the "honor," as the Duke calls it, that Escalus should have received it, but that he has broken some protocol because of a preference for Angelo. He, furthermore, impresses Angelo with the greatness of his gift to him. The Duke repeatedly tells him that he gives him free reign to do whatever he wants and that he gives him his greatest gift of his kingdom. Certainly, such an extravagant boon makes the recipient beholden to the giver. The Duke has "drest [Angelo] with our love" or dressed him in his ducal robes as a way to win Angelo's "love." And yet Shakespeare and the Duke disguise this sexual scheme behind a professed honorable plan to rectify the judicial chaos of the kingdom and to test a "seemer"—to which the Duke

is also dedicated and at which he succeeds. He preserves his image as a "fond father" of his people and dedicates himself to protecting his reputation, concealing his illicit motivations and misuse of power, and maintaining a comedic surface.

The other character who has suspicions about the Duke's profession of sexual sterility and his "plot" is Lucio, who claims that he knows "the very nerves of state" (I.iv.53), or that he is an insider, privy to the most intimate details of state and of the Duke in particular. Lucio voices some of the suspicions that the more reputable Friar Thomas seems to entertain, a similarity that gives more credence to Lucio's words. In fact, Act I, scene iii and Act III, scene ii are similar in that the Duke is defensively reacting to imputations on his character, the major difference being that Shakespeare allows us to hear Lucio's words whereas he does not allow us to be privy to Friar Thomas's. Lucio suggests that he knows what the Duke is up to and that the Duke and his plan are not as "wise" (III.ii.134) as he publicly proclaims. Rather than believing that the Duke has purely governmental concerns in mind, Lucio claims his ruler is engaging in "a mad, fantastical trick" (III.ii.89) or an elaborate, personal scheme of his own. Although Lucio's language is incorrigibly laced with bawdy innuendoes, he, nonetheless, echoes the Friar's apparent suspicions about the Duke— that his "withdrawing" and his intentions toward Angelo are sexually oriented. He repeatedly describes the Duke, Angelo, and the scheme in sexual terms as though the three are interrelated. His words surfeited with sexual innuendo, he openly proclaims what Friar Thomas only intimated—that the Duke is sexual: "He had some feeling of the sport; he knew the service" (III.ii.115-16). The Duke's defensiveness and overreaction to Lucio's depiction, like the Duke's overreaction to Friar Thomas's words, indicate that Lucio has come too close to some hidden, delicate truth that the Duke would rather suppress.

Lucio claims that he speaks knowingly and that his portrayals of the Duke are not idle gossip but based on close acquaintanceship and observation of his ruler: he repeatedly maintains that he was an "inward" (III.ii.127) of the Duke and "knows" (III.ii.129, 145, 148, 155) and "loves" him (III.ii.145). Undoubtedly Lucio shows signs of being a braggart and of taking creative license with the truth. But Shakespeare allows for some personal basis from which Lucio speaks. Lucio's numerous references to the Duke's sexual proclivities and the confident manner in which he asserts them suggest that he has intimate knowledge of the Duke himself, that he knows of the Duke's desires because he has experienced them himself. With the words "inward," "knows," and "loves," Shakespeare suggests a friendship or even an intimacy between Lucio and the Duke. The word "inward" denotes intense feeling or sexual intimacy, and "knows" refers to carnal knowledge.[57]

Such nuances allow for the reading that Lucio is an old favorite—as he proclaims—who knows the "very nerves of state" or the secret desires of his ruler, and whom the Duke is replacing with a younger, more pleasing favorite. When Lucio speaks evasively about knowing "the cause of [the Duke's] withdrawing" (III.ii.129), he can be referring to more than the Duke's removal from Vienna and his position as duke; he can mean the Duke's "withdrawal" or drawing away his affections from him in favor of another.[58]

Shakespeare leaves the crucial issue elusive as to whether Lucio recognizes the Duke and vice versa. Such equivocation permits him to allow for the reading that one or both characters recognize the other and that Lucio is trying to make a special plea to the Duke. If Lucio is read as being a rejected favorite who recognizes the Duke in disguise, then his harping on Angelo's character is more than idle gossip or slander. Lucio's numerous disparaging references to Angelo throughout Act III, scene ii indicate his resentment and jealousy toward the Duke's new choice and his hurt at being jilted. All of his derisive characterizations of Angelo focus on the same point: Angelo is sexually undersirable and frigid. Lucio mockingly calls Angelo "a motion ungenerative" (III.ii.108)—a sexless "thing"—and an "ungenitured agent" (III.ii.167-68)—a creature without genitals.[59] Lucio means his derogatory references to Angelo's sexual frigidity and the contrary portrayal of the Duke as a sexually potent figure to convince the Duke that he should turn his affections away from Angelo as an unsuitable companion. Lucio, in other words, is trying to persuade the Duke to turn away from Angelo and, instead, redirect his affections to himself—an "inward" who "love[s] him." When he states that he "would the Duke we talk of were returned again" (III.ii.166-67), Lucio means more than he wishes the Duke would return to Vienna and save Claudio's life: on a subtextual level he is also wishing that the Duke would "return" to him, a more suitable choice as a companion than the icy, cold Angelo, who will never return the Duke's affections. He underscores his constancy in that even though the Duke has "withdrawn" from him and rejected him for another, he claims he will "stick" or remain faithful and continue to "serve" him: "I am a kind of burr, I shall stick" (IV.iii.177).[60]

Certainly, with Lucio's depiction of a salacious duke, Shakespeare continues to make his audience uneasy about the Duke's character. In portraying Lucio as a problematic character, Shakespeare creates perplexity for his audience, who do not know how much credence to put in Lucio's words. While Shakespeare does not permit us put complete trust in his words, Lucio's wit, intellectual acuity, and often correct assessment of other characters allow for there to be some validity to what he says, especially since his hunches about the Duke's actions and his delineation of his character often

seem well founded. Shakespeare, therefore, uses Lucio to enrich the subtext and to expand the sexual element of the Duke. But Lucio also helps Shakespeare to maintain the tribute to the Duke and monarchial rule, for ultimately Shakespeare makes Lucio—given to irreverence, gossip, bawdy innuendo, exaggeration, and subterfuge—far from a trustworthy voice. He permits us to discount Lucio's words and, instead, believe the Duke, who defends himself against Lucio's imputations by proclaiming himself "a scholar, a statesman, and a soldier" and accusing Lucio of being "mistak[en]," "envious," and "malic[ious]" (III.ii.137,142, 144).

Upon overhearing Isabella's revelation to her brother of Angelo's perfidious proposal that she sacrifice her virginity to him to save Claudio's life, the Duke devises the scheme of the bedtrick. The critical controversy that surrounds the Duke's plot betrays the fact that the bedtrick is part of the disturbing subtext. If read on this level, the bedtrick can be seen as the Duke's way of remaining loyal to Angelo, not Lucio, as Shakespeare impresses on us the Duke's consistent efforts to shelter Angelo from danger and the serious consequences of his actions. Shakespeare suggests that his duke devises the bedtrick not only to save Claudio but also to shield Angelo, preventing him from committing a heinous crime of bartering with Isabella for sexual favors in exchange for her brother's safety and, instead, having him consummate his legal bond to Mariana. More importantly, though, the bedtrick helps the Duke perfect his "purpose and plot" with regard to Angelo. His interference ensures that Angelo has the opportunity to abuse his power and satisfy his desires and that he is trapped into revealing his sexuality. The Duke arranges an opportunity to get conclusive proof that Angelo's "blood flows," that his sexlessness is mere "seem[ing]." Mariana, moreover, poses no threat to his plans, for Angelo, obviously, is not in love with Mariana. His union with her was not one of passion but of financial security, and when the dowry disappeared so did Angelo. He has no romantic feelings for her and has not seen or spoken to her for five years. In fact, Angelo may actually dislike Mariana, for the Duke calls Mariana Angelo's "old betrothed but despised" (III.ii.272). Moreover, the Duke's later proposing to Isabella, a woman for whom he has shown no love interest, is a way for him to keep Angelo separated from a woman to whom the deputy is attracted and to keep Angelo for himself.

Shakespeare's bedtrick in *Measure for Measure* also evokes a note of pruriency, which has been difficult for many critics to ignore, and it is quite different from other instances of it. In *All's Well That Ends Well,* for example, we hear none of the specifics of the bedtrick, none of the sordid details, and the exchange happens before we know it—much removed from our hearing or sight. But in *Measure for Measure,* the Duke vitally and gratuitously involves himself in arranging sex for others. Critics note that Shakespeare makes his duke become so questionably and excessively involved in the clandestine arrangements that the Duke resembles Pompey the bawd, with whom Shakespeare juxtaposes the Duke as if to suggest a strange connection. What is so shocking is his planning and delineating the bed scene in titillating detail. Shakespeare has the bedtrick enhance the subtextual reading of the Duke by suggesting that his ruler indulges voyeuristic tendencies, enjoys hearing of others' sexual activities, and derives pleasure from imagining and planning sex for others[61]—and all while he is executing his governmental duties.

Shakespeare is using the bedtrick as a means to dramatize yet again general concerns about a sovereign's misuse of power to involve himself in the most intimate aspects of his subjects' lives. James arranged marriages and sexual liaisons for his favorites and, in fact, was not threatened by these unions or rendezvouses: "while he was bitterly jealous of his favorites' male friends, he always showed himself willing and indeed eager to arrange advantageous marriages for them."[62] He continued his relations with the men even more intensely after the favorites entered into marital bonds, and he used the passionless marriages as fronts for intimate encounters with the young men, as he tried to quell suspicions about his sexual orientation. He admitted that he married to dispel the suspicion of impotency in him, "as gif I were a barran stock; thir reasons, and innumerable others hourly objected, moved me to heasten the treatie of my marriage"—an oblique reference to rumors about his intimacy with young men.[63]

James's promoting others' sexual activities was not something that his contemporaries praised or even modern day biographers treat with much acceptance. Rather it was a source of embarrassement. James intimately involved himself in the heterosexual intrigues of his male companions. When, for example, one of James's first male favorites in England—the earl of Montgomery—decided to marry Lady Susan Vere at the close of 1603, the king took the whole matter on himself, arranging the ceremony and reconciling the couple's families to the surprise event. This could be attributed to solicitude, but what cast a dark shadow on such intervention was James's obsession with the actual sexual relations of the newly married couple. Otto Scott, for example, describes James's strange behavior: "The king supervised and beamed during the marriage of his favorite, the earl of Montgomery, to Lady Susan Vere; the following morning he rushed to their bedchamber to learn the details of their first night, lolling familiarly between them"—a story that quickly became a source of gossip.[64] Contemporary Sir Dudley Carleton in a letter to Mr. Winwood obliquely suggests a peculiar aspect to the king's behavior in the newlyweds' bedroom: "They were lodged in the Councill Chamber, where the King, in his Shirt and Night-Gown,

gave them a *Revelee Matin* before they were up, and spent a good time in or upon the Bed, chuse which you will believe."[65] In November of 1603, the king did something similar, behavior that he indulged in so often that it became a pattern for him: he intimately involved himself in the union of the young Lady Margaret Stewart and the aged earl of Nottingham, prying for details about Nottingham's ability to consummate the marriage. Queen Anne, James's wife, alludes in a letter addressed to James to the indelicacy and inappropriateness of James's involvement in Lady Margaret and the earl of Nottingham's sex life:

> The last part of your letter you guessed right that I would laugh. Who would not laugh both at the persons and at the subject, but more at so well a chosen Mercury between Mars and Venus? You know that women can hardly keep counsel. I humbly desire your Majesty to tell me how it is possible that I should keep this secret, that have already told it, and shall tell it to as many as I shall speak with; and if I were a poet, I would make a song of it, and sing it to the tune of 'Three fools well met.'[66]

Later in his reign, he took a major interest in arranging marriages for his children, especially his daughter, Elizabeth. After attentively supervising the courting and marriage of his daughter to Frederick, he visited them the morning after the ceremony. A modern biographer, David Willson describes the odd behavior of the king: "with shocking pruriency he questioned Frederick minutely about what had happened during the night." Robert Ashton also describes the event: "James was passionately devoted to his daughter, though the salacious pruriency which impelled him to visit the newlyweds in bed and question them in detail about the events of their wedding night—a practice which the king indulged on other similar occasions—shews [*sic*] him in one of his least attractive lights." Antonia Fraser, likewise, records the disturbing behavior: his visiting the newlyweds brought out "that faintly ludicrous side in his public behaviour which his rather pathetic curiosity towards the sexual relationships of others only enhanced."[67] What the king was doing amounted to spying on the newlyweds, even if he was doing it secondhand by having them describe the scene so that he could envision it in his mind. These strange predispositions indicate that the king took vicarious pleasure in planning and hearing about the sexual relations of others, that he had voyeuristic tendencies—libidinous interests that he concealed under the guise of fatherly solicitude for his subjects and that he often fulfilled through misuse of his governmental prerogative.

While Shakespeare with the bedtrick again creates some unsettling scenes for his audience, and most likely for James himself, he glosses them over with a more obvious harmonious surface. As numerous scholars have clarified, the bedtrick was an established and popular dramatic device during this time, and, thus, Shakespeare hides his covert meaning within conventions. The Duke, moreover, again professes the most honorable intentions: the bedtrick allows him to "redeem [Claudio] from the angry law" (III.i.200-201); it permits him to do Mariana "a poor wronged lady a merited benefit" (III.i.199-200); and it prepares for the Duke to "scale" "the corrupt deputy" (III.i.255-56). While the Duke's methods may be unsettling, Shakespeare makes the results good. Shakespeare also shows the Duke to be a consummate politician, shrewd enough to turn his most questionable actions into a means of enhancing his own image as a solicitous, loving father of his people—somewhat reminiscent of King James's talent.

On a subtextual level, though, the Duke's actions continue to be sexually loaded as he seeks more than a voyeuristic relationship with Angelo. Act V contains the consummation of the Duke's submerged scheme to trap Angelo into becoming his new favorite and into returning his affections. The play ends much as it began, with the Duke acting as enigmatically as in Act I. The play comes full circle or full "measure," and we can "measure" the last act by the first one. In Act V the Duke duplicates his actions of Act I, scene i: once again he surrenders his power and leaves the scene to assume his priestly garb; again he names Angelo as his replacement and gives him his full power; again his actions can seem irresponsible and tinged with favoritism as he leaves the least appropriate man—Angelo—in charge; and once more his actions all pivot around Angelo. The Duke's motivations, likewise, are as problematical as they are at the play's beginning and have caused scholarly debate and consternation. Again Shakespeare maintains the pleasing comedic surface by having the Duke attest to holy and virtuous intentions for the most questionable actions, such as lying to Isabella and making her think her brother is dead: "I will keep her ignorant of her good, / To make her heavenly comforts of despair / When it is least expected" (IV.iii.108-10). That the Duke's professed spiritual explanations for his behavior are so strained, however, indicates a subtext in which he is concealing less savory motivations. His lying to Isabella is geared more to persuading her to condemn publicly Angelo of rape, to "accuse him home and home" (IV.iii.143), than to giving her "heavenly comforts." He also arranges to have Mariana accuse Angelo of seducing her. Such maneuvers allow him to put Angelo in a distressing situation, and he has several salacious reasons for doing so.

While the Duke's praise of Angelo in Act V serves as dramatic irony and is meant to activate the deputy's guilt and to trap him into revealing his perfidy, it is gratuitous and indicative that something else is transpiring. The Duke creates an opportunity to impress Angelo with his devotion to him. He is excessively kind and complimentary to Angelo. Shakespeare has

the Duke inform Angelo that he "favours" him, that he regards him as a "favorite": "let the subject see, to make them know / That outward courtesies would fain proclaim / Favours that keep within" (V.i.15-17). The Duke declares that he will show him "outward courtesies," that he will publicly lavish him with his generosity and material rewards,[68] in order to gain his "in[ner]" "favours" during more private times, a reference to sexual favors.[69] He proceeds to allude to all of the material ways he can benefit Angelo, referring to the "more requital" (V.i.8), to the forthcoming perquisites. He tells Angelo that his worthiness "deserves with characters of brass / A forted residence 'gainst the tooth of time / And razure of oblivion" (V.i.12-14). The hyperbolic promise tantalizes Angelo with boundless wealth, with "characters of brass" or copper and bronze coins or money in general.[70] The "characters of brass" also refer to public acclaim. The "forted residence" entices Angelo with promises of lands and estates. In tempting Angelo with promises of wealth, fame, and material possessions, the Duke is trying to buy the affection of a young man, who has been withholding his sexual attention from him.

The Duke, in fact, proceeds to treat his deputy with great privilege. The Duke's creating a seemingly dire situation for Angelo, in which his character is being impugned, allows the ruler to impress the young man with his belief in him and his dedication to protecting him. He repeatedly and excessively defends him against what he terms unfounded accusations, attesting to Angelo's "integrity" (V.i.110):

> think'st thou thy [Angelo's accusers'] oaths,
> Though they would swear down each
>   particular saint,
> Were testimonies against [Angelo's] worth and
>   credit,
> That's seal'd in approbation?
>   (V.i.241-44)

The Duke suggests that even if the accusations were well founded and could convict saints, and even if Angelo were guilty of the charges, he would safeguard Angelo, over whom he has placed a "seal" or an impenetrable protective covering.[71] He instructs Angelo that he has nothing to worry about since the Duke will not "permit / A blasting and a scandalous breath to fall / On him so near us" (V.i.124-26). His closeness or preference for his deputy compels him to see that no danger comes his way and to resort to any tactics to ensure his well-being. And, indeed, the Duke proves true to his word, for he shows himself willing to distort justice by making Angelo judge of his own case: "Come, cousin Angelo, / In this I'll be impartial: be you judge / Of your own cause" (V.i.167-69). The declaration is highly ironic, for the Duke is being far from impartial in allowing the guilty party to control his own trial. As in Act I, scene i, he shows his devotion and preference for Angelo by giving him all of his power and allowing Angelo to behave unethically if he wishes. Once again, he does him a special favor.

He also encourages Angelo to behave poorly and to conceal the truth. The Duke's finding Isabella and Mariana guilty himself before handing them over to Angelo and his own insulting behavior as Friar Lodowick encourage the deputy to punish his victims "to [his] height of pleasure" (V.i.239). The Duke's actions again parallel those of the first scene, for in both scenes the Duke prompts his deputy to abuse his power. As he does in Act I, scene i, the Duke prods Angelo to behave shamefully so that the deputy will be more at his mercy, more in need of forgiveness when his crimes are revealed. These tactics are largely geared to making Angelo feel "sealed" (V.i.244) to the Duke, to feel bound or obligated to him[72] for his kindness and his patronage during scandalous times. Shakespeare makes us sense that the Duke puts a "seal" on Angelo and maneuvers him so that he can claim possession of him as his favorite.[73]

As soon as the Duke has been divested of his disguise, Angelo admits his wrongdoing and guilt. Although Angelo readily admits to his faults, the Duke presents him as a vile criminal who "would'st deny" (V.i.411) his crimes if not trapped into doing otherwise. The Duke proceeds to reveal Angelo's abuse of his power, never clarifying that he set Angelo up to do exactly that. His public humiliation of Angelo makes his deputy, deprived of the last shred of pride, drop his sanctimonious pose and admit to his flawed humanity. The Duke's arranging for Isabella and Mariana to accuse Angelo of a libidinous nature forces Angelo to "confess" "that his appetite is more to bread than stone." That his sexuality is revealed in public prevents Angelo from ever denying it. The Duke's preceding tributes to Angelo's virtue and his avowals of unwavering belief in his deputy's goodness are meant partially to increase Angelo's devastation at not living up to the Duke's expectations and disappointing his ruler. The Duke so vilifies, shames, and mortifies Angelo that his spirit is broken and he wants only to die—a desperate condition that makes Angelo vulnerable and resigned to the Duke's plans for him. The Duke ensures that Angelo can no longer claim his superiority—either ethically or sexually. He is just as, if not more, marred and sexual as others. He can no longer hold himself at a distance from others—especially not from the Duke.

Despite Angelo's avowal of guilt, the Duke continues with what seems like needless and heartless deception: he lies to Isabella yet again and reassures her of her brother's death, makes Mariana believe her new husband must die, and ominously and repeatedly pronounces the death sentence on Angelo: "An Angelo for Claudio; death for death"; "We do condemn thee to the very block / Where Claudio stoop'd to death";

"Away with him to death"; "He dies for Claudio's death" (V.i.407, 412-13, 427, 441). Shakespeare has his duke create a horribly frightening scene, protracting the misconception about Claudio's death and making everyone believe he will carry out the execution of Angelo, which he secretly never intends to enforce. The Duke lets the scene get to a pitch of desperation and morbidity and only at the last moment miraculously produces Claudio and announces that Angelo is "safe." The Duke's scaring and impressing on Angelo his looming death and his vileness make Angelo feel forever duty-bound and grateful to the Duke when he forgives him his sins and saves his life. Keeping his scheme cloaked in mystery, he never lets Angelo know that he was carefully trapped or that Angelo's life was never in real danger. This level of meaning presents a ruler who is willing to hurt anyone, including the innocent participants who helped him perfect his scheme and including the object of his desires, in order to satisfy his personal needs.

The Duke exercises absolute power, making himself judge and jury, conducting a trial that conceals more than it reveals the crimes and the criminal. Shakespeare allows for a subtextual reading in which his duke uses the judicial process to serve his private desires and to protect Angelo, rather than to reveal the truth. The Duke underscores what he does for his deputy: "Methinks I see a quickening in his eye. / Well, Angelo, your evil quits you well. / Look that you love your wife: her worth, worth yours" (V.i.493-95). The Duke's telling Angelo that his "evil quits [him] well" indicates that the Duke misuses justice in order to protect his favorite, for Angelo's "evil" pays off or benefits him in the end. He saves Angelo's reputation by marrying him to the woman with whom he has slept; he "quit[s]"—absolves or delivers—him of his abuse of power and his attempts to conceal that abuse; and he "quicken[s]" him or gives him life again, rescuing him at the last minute from the hands of death. Within the word "quit" is couched the Duke's primary intention. "Quit" meaning to repay or requite a person for a favor,[74] the Duke performs this elaborate maneuver to make Angelo feel he owes him for his very life. Earlier Shakespeare alludes to the game the Duke is playing when he has Angelo tell the Duke, "You make my bonds still greater" (V.i.9). The Duke is trying to establish a bond—a strong union—between himself and Angelo, a sense of commitment, one based on an obligation or duty.[75] Angelo is trapped by the "bonds" of gratitude and shame and is in "bonds" or the shackles and chains of obligation.[76] The Duke, on the other hand, is excessively harsh to Lucio, refusing to forgive him completely for his supposed slander. That the Duke pursues Lucio for slander and yet forgives Angelo for what many see as more serious offenses underscores his severity toward Lucio and his favoritism toward Angelo. That his actions seem extreme also indicates that he is capitalizing on an opportunity to rid himself of an unwanted "inward," of whom he has grown tired. Despite his professions of constancy and love, Lucio is discarded in favor of a younger companion.

Shakespeare, then, allows his duke to be read as abusing his power in order to gratify his desires. Shakespeare lodges a subversive and politically dangerous message in his subtext, suggesting that rulers are not godly agents (and the present king of England, in particular) but, rather, fleshly humans, more in touch with the earth than the heavens. What Shakespeare's subtext presents is an undermining of a divine monarch, for Shakespeare's monarch is influenced by questionable, personal, and perhaps not fully conscious motives—a theme that would have had special import to Shakespeare's audience, who were subject to a sovereign with similar problems of governmental mismanagement.

But to recognize only this level of meaning and to see Shakespeare as merely censuring his duke for being a flawed leader, ruled primarily by his latent homoerotic feelings for Angelo, misses the complexity and multiplicity of Shakespeare's message and characterization. If the Duke is "moulded out of faults" and is "a little bad" (V.i.437, 439), he is also "very good" at governing, and all of his actions in Act V serve other purposes as well—more political in nature. The last act is also the Duke's greatest moment: he proves himself to be a powerful leader and a consummate politician. Although the Duke has ulterior motives and uses his governmental prerogative to please his private needs, and although he does questionable, selfish acts, he sees that harmony prevails and his actions benefit his subjects, and for this he can be called a "good" ruler. It is the Duke's intervention and his overview of the action, in fact, that prevent the play from veering toward tragedy several times. Working behind the scenes, he preserves the comedic thrust and maintains the surface harmony. Shakespeare and the Duke himself allow his actions to be read in more favorable terms: he saves Claudio's life and marries the young man to his beloved; he prevents Angelo from accomplishing the perfidious schemes of raping Isabella and killing Claudio; he traps Angelo into revealing his baseness and recognizing his limitations and makes him suffer for his crimes, despite the fact that the deputy is his "favorite"; he forces Angelo ultimately to do good and keep his promise of marriage to Mariana; he traps Lucio into revealing his scandalous nature and punishes him for taking liberties with the Duke's reputation, which the Duke shows to be an egregious crime not to be tolerated in a stable government; he looks out for Isabella's happiness and preserves her brother's life and teaches this rigidly doctrinaire woman the value of true forgiveness; and he himself joins in the festive, celebratory atmosphere of the ending by proposing to abandon his reclusive lifestyle and enter into the social contract of marriage. All of these actions temper the sexual subtext and make the Duke an effective ruler.

He also proves to be a cunning politician: he sets Angelo up to gratify his desires and conceals his "vices" so well that they pose no threat to his public image; and he portrays himself as a god figure, unseen but always overseeing his subjects' welfare. Shakespeare presents Act V as not only a means for the Duke to maneuver Angelo into a compromising situation but also a stage production, created and choreographed by his duke to accentuate his grandeur. In Act V, he twice allows events to deteriorate to the extent that evil is defeating goodness so that he can miraculously transform at the last moment from a poor friar into a glorious ruler, who sets things right and reveals a breathing Claudio, whom he seems to have brought back from the dead. The Duke shows himself to be like God—severe but loving—and grants mercy to all. He arranges for himself to shine for his divinity, wisdom, sternness, and benevolence in comparison to Angelo, whom he has shown to be the poorest of rulers. The Duke uses Angelo as a foil, assigning his deputy the difficult and unpopular task of rectifying his ruler's mistakes and guaranteeing Angelo's failure. He publicly displays the deputy's base nature and corrupt governing skills in order to underscore by contrast his own divine image and superlative skills. Angelo shows reverence for the image that the Duke has so expertly chiseled: "I perceive your Grace, like power divine, / Hath looked upon my passes" (V.i.367-68).

The Duke is adept at concentrating on the glorious ends rather than the dubious means. He, for example, makes Angelo look like the sinner and disguises the fact that he has done something quite similar in warping the law to satisfy his libido. He, moreover, discredits Lucio, with some help from the incorrigible prankster himself, who may have spoken more correctly of the real Duke than anyone recognizes: Lucio contends that "the greater file of the subject" are "deceived" (III.ii.134, 120) in the Duke, believing in the external image of wisdom, when he "knows" that the true Duke, who has "crotchets in him" (III.ii.124), would have "dark deeds darkly answered" (III.ii.171) and "had some feeling of the sport" (III.ii.115-16). The shrewd Duke recognizes that people who know too much and can tarnish the finely polished image must be forever silenced. He puts the final polish on the image when he proposes marriage to Isabella, whom he has not wooed and in whom he has shown no sexual interest. The proposal permits him to conceal his homoerotic proclivities and his desire for Angelo, in particular, behind a front of a socially sanctioned union.

It is the Duke's skill at bringing good out of bad and, ironically, at being so good at disguising the bad, which often resides in himself, that the play, although tottering on tragedy several times, ends as a comedy and a tribute to the Duke's miraculous powers and his successful "ends." Shakespeare's Duke proves to be an effective leader in that he ultimately works for the good of his people and accomplishes admirable deeds, yet he is fox-like enough to know when to resort to cunning methods to maintain his power and position and conceal his less honorable actions. In Machiavelli's words, he knows "how to get around men's brains with [his] astuteness."[77] The play is a troublesome comedy, however, in that Shakespeare sometimes permits us to puncture the image and to see the flawed underside, to detect the Duke's less savory motivations, and to question his means of achieving impressive ends. As scholars note, the festive ending is marred by the relative silence of the Duke's subjects—Claudio, Mariana, Angelo, and particularly Isabella, whom Shakespeare does not have definitively accept the Duke's marriage proposal—and by the severe fate of Lucio, whom Shakespeare has made scandalous yet likeable. The subdued ending reinforces the troublesome nature of the play and of the Duke in particular. It reflects the questionable means behind the Duke's impressive ends— the painful lies; the scheming deceptions; the humiliating public shattering of reputations; the frightening threats of death; the unnecessary suffering; and the illicit motivations. The play is problematical in part because Shakespeare gives us glimpses of what the Duke may "within him hide / Though angel on the outward side."

Notes

[1] Rosalind Miles, *The Problem of "Measure for Measure"* (London: Vision, 1976), 13.

[2] David Lloyd Stevenson, *The Achievement of Shakespeare's "Measure for Measure"* (Ithaca: Cornell University Press, 1966), 131.

[3] Don D. Moore, "Three Stage Versions of *Measure for Measure*'s Duke: The Providential, the Pathetic, the Personable," *Explorations in Renaissance Culture* 12 (1986): 59.

[4] Marilyn French, *Shakespeare's Division of Experience* (New York: Ballantine, 1981), 182.

[5] Eric Patridge, *Shakespeare's Bawdy* (1947; repr. New York: Routledge, 1990), 46.

[6] Derek A. Traversi, *An Approach to Shakespeare,* 3rd ed. (New York: Doubleday, 1969), 364; Robert Rogers, *A Psychoanalytic Study of the Double in Literature* (Detroit: Wayne State University, 1970), 74.

[7] Richard A. Levin, "Duke Vincentio and Angelo: Would 'A Feather Turn the Scale'?" *SEL* 22 (1982): 262.

[8] Rogers, 72-74; Herbert Weil, Jr., "Form and Contexts in *Measure for Measure*," *Critical Quarterly* 12 (1970): 62; French, 190; Levin, 260.

[9] All textual quotations of *Measure for Measure* are taken from the Arden edition, ed. J. W. Lever (London: Methuen, 1976).

[10] Marvin Rosenberg, "Shakespeare's Fantastic Trick: *Measure for Measure*," *Sewanee Review* 80 (1972): 53.

[11] For a discussion of Isabella's sexuality, consult the following: Arthur C. Kirsch, "The Integrity of *Measure for Measure*," *ShS* 28 (1975): 96; Harriet Hawkins, "'The Devil's Party': Virtues and Vices in 'Measure for Measure,'" *ShS* 31 (1978): 107; Richard P. Wheeler, *Shakespeare's Development and the Problem Comedies* (Berkeley: University of California Press, 1981), 112; Northrop Frye, *The Myth of Deliverance: Reflections on Shakespeare's Problem Comedies* (Toronto: University of Toronto Press, 1983), 21; Carolyn E. Brown, "*Measure for Measure*: Isabella's Beating Fantasies," *American Imago* 43 (1986): 67-80.

[12] Angelo's sadism is explored by Hawkins, 108; and Wheeler, 109.

[13] The Duke's sexuality is discussed by the following: Janet Adelman, "Mortality and Mercy in 'Measure for Measure'" in *The Shakespeare Plays: A Study Guide* (San Diego: University Extension, University of California, San Diego & the Coast Community College District, 1978), 106-7; Bernard J. Paris, "The Inner Conflicts of *Measure for Measure*: A Psychological Approach," *Centennial Review* 24 (1981): 266, 273; Wheeler, 154; Levin, 264; Carolyn E. Brown, "Erotic Religious Flagellation and Shakespeare's *Measure for Measure*," *ELR* 16 (1986): 158-62.

[14] Adelman, 107.

[15] Catharine F. Seigel, "Hands off the Hothouses: Shakespeare's Advice to the King," *Journal of Popular Culture* 20 (1986): 81; Herbert Howarth, "Shakespeare's Flattery in *Measure for Measure*," *SQ* 16 (1965): 30.

[16] Consult, for example, the following: Thomas Tyrwhit, *Observations and Conjectures Upon Some Passages of Shakespeare* (Oxford: Oxford University Press, 1766); George Chalmers, *A Supplemental Apology for the Believers in Shakespeare-Papers* (London: T. Egerton, 1797); Charles Knight, *Studies in Shakespeare* (London: C. Knight, 1849); Elizabeth Marie Pope, "The Renaissance Background of *Measure for Measure*," *ShS* 2 (1949): 66-82; David Lloyd Stevenson, "The Role of James I in Shakespeare's *Measure for Measure*," *ELH* 26 (1959): 188-208, now included in David Lloyd Stevenson, *The Achievement of Shakespeare's "Measure for Measure"*; Josephine Waters Bennett, *"Measure for Measure" as Royal Entertainment* (New York: Columbia University Press, 1966); Brian Rose, "Friar-

Duke and Scholar-King," *English Studies in Africa* 9 (1966): 72-82; J. W. Lever, "Introduction," Arden edition of *Measure for Measure,* xlviii-li; Leonard Tennenhouse, "Representing Power: *Measure for Measure* in Its Time" in *The Forms of Power and the Power of Forms in the Renaissance,* ed. Stephen Greenblatt (Norman: University of Oklahoma Press, 1982), 139-56; Jonathan Goldberg, *James I and the Politics of Literature: Jonson, Shakespeare, Donne, and Their Contemporaries* (Baltimore: Johns Hopkins University Press, 1983); Jonathan Dollimore, "Transgression and Surveillance in *Measure for Measure*" in *Political Shakespeare,* ed. Jonathan Dollimore and Alan Sinfield (Manchester: Manchester University Press, 1985), 72-87.

[17] "Report on England presented to the Government of Venice in the year 1607, by the Illustrious Gentleman Nicolo Molin, Ambassador there" in *Calendar of State Papers and Manuscripts, relating to English affairs, existing in the Archives and Collections of Venice, 1603-1607* (London: Longman, Green, Longman, Roberts, & Green, 1864), 513; G. B. Harrison, *A Jacobean Journal: Being a Record of Those Things Most Talked of During the Years, 1603-1606* (London: George Routledge & Sons, 1946), viii.

[18] *Memorials of Affairs of State in the Reigns of Queen Elizabeth and King James I Collected Chiefly from the Original Papers of the Right Honourable Sir Ralph Winwood,* 3 vols. (London: T. Ward, 1725), 2: 54.

[19] Arthur Wilson, *The Life and Reign of James, the First King of Great Britain,* in *A Complete History of England: with the Lives of all the Kings and Queens Hereof,* ed. White Kennett, 3 vols. (London: B. Aylmer, 1706), 2: 792.

[20] Howarth, 29-37; Roy Battenhouse, "*Measure for Measure* and King James," *Clio* 7 (1978): 193-215; Charles Swann, "Lucio: Benefactor or Malefactor?" *Critical Quarterly* 29 (1987): 55-70; and Craig A. Bernthal, "Staging Justice: James I and the Trial Scene of *Measure for Measure,*" *SEL* 32 (1992): 247-69—all argue that Shakespeare is instructing King James on the proper relationship between mercy and justice, in which James displayed considerable interest and of which his own administration was defective. Swann and Cynthia Lewis, "'Dark Deeds Darkly Answered': Duke Vincentio and Judgment in *Measure for Measure,*" *SQ* 34 (1983): 271-89, contend that Shakespeare is addressing the controversy over James's neglect of state and his abdication of political responsibilities. Swann also contends that the play examines James's unpopular assumption of unlimited power over his subjects and the Parliament. Marilyn L. Williamson, "The Comedies in Historical Context," in *Images of Shakespeare: Proceedings of the Third Congress of the International Shakespeare Association, 1986,* ed.

Werner Habicht, D. J. Palmer, and Roger Pringle (Newark: University of Delaware Press, 1988), 188-200, believes that the play looks at the political debate within Parliament and the public about the legal regulation of personal conduct. Seigel, 81-88, argues that Shakespeare uses his play to address the conflict over the state of the stews in the suburbs of England. Anthony B. Dawson, "*Measure for Measure,* New Historicism, and Theatrical Power," *SQ* 39 (1988): 328-41, and Bernthal contend that Shakespeare is demysticizing James's rule by having the Duke duplicate the King's reliance on histrionic showmanship in governmental actions.

[21] Niccolò Machiavelli, *The Prince,* trans. Harvey C. Mansfield, Jr. (Chicago: University of Chicago Press, 1985), 62.

[22] Robert Ashton, *James I by his Contemporaries* (London: Hutchinson, 1969), 106.

[23] "A Declaration of the Just and Necessar Causes Moving us of the Nobilitie of Scotland, and Others the King's Majestie's Faithfull Subjects, to Repaire to His Hienesse' Presence" in David Calderwood, *The History of the Kirk of Scotland,* 10 vols. (Edinburgh: Wodrow Society, 1843), 3: 653.

[24] G. P. V. Akrigg, *Jacobean Pageant or the Court of King James I* (Cambridge: Harvard University Press, 1962), 14.

[25] Thomas Birch, ed. *The Court and Times of James the First,* 2 vols. (London: Henry Colburn, 1849), 1: viii.

[26] Francis Osborne, "Traditional Memoyres on the Raigne of King James the First," in *The Secret History of the Court of James the First,* ed. Sir Walter Scott, 2 vols. (Edinburgh: James Ballantyne, 1811), 1: 74-75.

[27] M. de Fontenay, Envoy of Mary Stuart to King James VI, "Letter to Mary's secretary, August 15, 1584," in *Historical Manuscripts Commission: Manuscripts of the Marquess of Salisbury preserved at Hatfield House, Hertfordshire (1883-1965),* 24 vols. (London: n.p., n.d.), 3: 60.

[28] Calderwood, 5: 171.

[29] "Proclamation to his Subjects" in Sir Edward Peyton, "The Divine Catastrophe of the Kingly Family of the House of Stuarts," in *The Secret History of the Court of James the First,* 2: 333.

[30] William Robertson, *The History of Scotland During the Reigns of Queen Mary and of King James VI,* 2nd ed., 2 vols. (London: A. Millar, 1759), 2: 172.

31 Ibid., 105, 260.

32 Peyton, 352.

33 Birch, 1: viii.

34 Peyton, 364.

35 David Harris Willson, *King James VI and I* (New York: Oxford University Press, 1967), 48, 47.

36 *The Historie and Life of King James the Sext* (Edinburgh: James Ballantyne, 1825), 185, 188; Lucy Aikin, *Memoirs of the Court of King James the First,* 2nd ed., 2 vols. (London: Longman, Hurst, Rees, Orme, and Brown, 1822), 1: 16.

37 Aikin, 1: 60.

38 Anthony Weldon, "The Court and Character of King James," in *The Secret History of the Court of James the First,* 1: 311, 332.

39 Caroline Bingham, *The Making of a King: The Early Years of James VI and I* (New York: Doubleday, 1969), 198.

40 Osborne, 276.

41 Calderwood, 5: 471, 454.

42 "Letter of James VI to Huntly, 2 October 1596" in *The Warrender Papers,* ed. Annie I. Cameron, Publications of the Scottish History Society, 3rd ser. 19 (Edinburgh: Edinburgh University Press, 1932), 2: 299-300.

43 *The Compact Edition of the Oxford English Dictionary,* 2 vols. (New York: Oxford University Press, 1971), *special,* adv., c 1 (hereafter cited as *OED*).

44 Levin, 259.

45 *OED, special,* 2b.

46 Ibid., *cousin,* 5.

47 Ibid., *near,* adv.1, 2c; adv.2, 3; a., 2.

48 Ibid., *bosom,* sb., 6. Partridge suggests that "bosom" can have the sexual undercurrent of genitals (69); and James T. Henke, *Renaissance Dramatic Bawdy (Exclusive of Shakespeare): An Annotated Glossary and Critical Essays,* 2 vols. (Salzburg: Universitat Salzburg, 1974), 2: 96, glosses "bosom" as sexual intimacy. Given the sexual undercurrent to his words of "covert bosom," the Duke can be alluding to having Angelo "lock[ed]" in intercourse with him.

49 Adelman, 106.

50 Partridge, 97.

51 Ibid., 99, 74.

52 Ibid., 223.

53 *OED, youth,* 6.

54 Ibid., *bravery, 5; cost,* sb., 2.

55 Partridge, 81.

56 Frankie Rubinstein, *A Dictionary of Shakespeare's Sexual Puns and Their Significance,* 2nd ed. (London: Macmillan, 1989), 207-8.

57 Partridge, 131. Rubinstein argues that "inward" can more specifically elicit "anal puns" (135-36).

58 *OED, withdraw,* 13. The word "withdrawing" can have a more bawdy designation of the "withdrawal" of a penis during or after intercourse.

59 Lever, 89.

60 "Stick like burrs" is proverbial and can mean to cling in fidelity. Pandarus in *Troilus and Cressida* wittily uses the saying to express the faithfulness of Cressida and his other kin: "They are constant being one. They are burs. They'll stick where they are thrown" (III.ii.119). In *Henry IV, Part II,* Shakespeare also enlists the word "stick" to mean remaining firm and steadfast (*OED* 7): "The knave will stick by thee. I can assure thee"; "I'll stick by him" (V.ii.66; 68). With the word "stick" containing a possible bawdy innuendo of copulation (Rubinstein, 255-56), Lucio can be intimating that he will continue to serve the Duke sexually.

61 Critics of the play have commented on the Duke's voyeuristic tendencies and vicarious pleasure in other characters' sexual activities, especially in arranging sex for Angelo and Mariana during the bedtrick: Adelman, 107; Paris, 273; Wheeler, 132; Levin, 265; and Carolyn E. Brown, "The Wooing of Duke Vincentio and Isabella of *Measure for Measure:* 'The Image of It Gives [Them] Content,'" *ShS* 22 (1994): 189-219.

62 Caroline Bingham, *James I of England* (London: Waidenfeld & Nicolson, 1981), 125.

63 "Proclamation to his Subjects," in Peyton, 333.

64 Otto Scott, *James I* (New York: Mason/Charter, 1976), 276.

65 *Memorials of Affairs of State in the Reigns of Queen Elizabeth and King James I Collected Chiefly from the Original Papers of the Right Honourable Sir Ralph Winwood,* 2: 43.

[66] "Letter from Queen Anne to King James VI, 1603" in John Hill Burton, *The History of Scotland: from Agricola's Invasion to the extinction of the last Jacobite insurrection,* 2nd ed., 7 vols. (London: William Blackwood & Sons, 1873), 5: 384-85.

[67] Willson, 286; Ashton, 87-88; Antonia Fraser, *King James VI and I* (New York: Alfred A. Knoff, 1975), 34.

[68] *OED, courtesy,* 2.

[69] Partridge glosses "favours" as sexual parts (104); Henke glosses it as "pleasure derived from copulation" (150).

[70] *OED, brass,* 3a, 3b.

[71] Ibid., *seal,* 5.

[72] Ibid., 1c; 1e.

[73] Ibid., sb.², 1h.

[74] Ibid., *quit,* 10.

[75] Ibid., *bond,* 7, 6b.

[76] Ibid., 1.

[77] Machiavelli, 69.

Source: "The Homoeroticism of Duke Vincentio: 'Some Feeling of the Sport'," in *Studies in Philology*, Vol. XCIV, No. 2, Spring, 1997, pp. 187-220.

The Two Gentlemen of Verona on Stage: Protean Problems and Protean Solutions

Carol J. Carlisle, *University of South Carolina*
Patty S. Derrick, *University of Pittsburgh*

In the theater, as in the study, *The Two Gentlemen of Verona,* possibly Shakespeare's earliest comedy, has traditionally been one of his least popular plays. By our present count, there have been just twenty-four productions of it on the London stage since Shakespeare's time, and seven of these were first seen elsewhere.[1] At Stratford-upon-Avon there have been only ten since the annual Festivals began there in 1879. Most of the productions in these two major centers have been in the twentieth century, the greater number in the second half. The play has also been produced three times by the BBC, twice on radio and once on television. In New York, as one would expect, *Two Gentlemen* has had a much slighter stage history than in London,[2] and at the "other Stratford" in Ontario it has had just four productions in a forty-year history. Curiously enough, however, a surprising number of British provincial theaters and American regional or festival companies have been willing, at least once or twice, to tackle the problems of this "flawed but endearing play."[3]

Two Gentlemen does have its charms, but they are largely offset by its peculiar weaknesses. To evoke its magic, a production must overcome these weaknesses or somehow turn them to advantage. Although the same basic problems have confronted producers of the play in all post-Shakespearean periods, some have loomed larger at one time than at another because of differing social and theatrical conventions, and the solutions that actors and directors have found for them have therefore varied considerably. Since such solutions (or attempted solutions) have influenced interpretation of the play, not singly but in varying combinations, it is best to consider them within the contexts of particular productions. Accordingly, we shall discuss here some salient productions from each period *in toto,* giving our fullest attention to seminal ones and occasionally mentioning others to illustrate trends.

First, the problems. For the average reader, *Two Gentlemen,* with its formula-ridden plot, outdated conventions, sketchily drawn characters, and absurd conclusion, is probably too simplistic and too incredible to be very interesting; at the same time, it may have an oddly disturbing effect since the apparent simplicities prove, on examination, too slippery to catch hold of with assurance. This combination of characteristics is not a hopeful one for effective stage production.

The dramatic action of *Two Gentlemen* is largely illustrative of either faithfulness or disloyalty to the potentially conflicting ideals of heroic friendship and courtly love—impossibly rarefied ideals for everyday human life, as the action demonstrates, yet far better than none at all.[4] The concept of ideal friendship, grounded in a medieval blend of classical and scholastic ideas with the lore of blood brotherhood, was prominent in Elizabethan retellings and dramatizations of old tales like *Titus and Gisippus,* glorifying two men of equal endowments and mutual interests who were so united in love that each became the other's *alter ego*—a relation that could transcend love between the sexes.[5] The ideals and conventions of courtly love, a Renaissance descendant of medieval literature portraying love as an all-consuming power and the lover as humble "servant" to a religiously worshipped lady, were found in the Petrarchan lyrics and the romances of the Renaissance, including Jorge de Montemayor's *Diana,* the source (direct or indirect) of Shakespeare's Julia-Proteus plot.[6] Although love and friendship are ageless, these particular concepts had lost their familiarity before any post-Shakespearean revival of *Two Gentlemen;* thus, the heroes' language and actions might well seem a little strange to later audiences. But, even within the context of their own world, Valentine and Proteus are hard to take seriously as romantic heroes.

The naive Valentine is (or becomes) a devotee of both ideals. He exalts Proteus's merits (2.4.62-74), identifies his friend with himself (2.4.62), and feels Proteus's treachery as if his own right hand had turned against his heart (5.4.67-68). Originally he scorns love as an underminer of manly accomplishments, but, once he meets Silvia, he becomes the conventional courtly lover: he recounts the sufferings inflicted by the "mightly lord" Love (2.4.128-42); he resorts to outrageous hyperbole in praising Silvia (2.4.151-53, 156-63) and shows his veneration of her in terms like "heavenly saint," "divine," and "sacred" (2.4.145, 147; 3.1.212); he calls her "myself" and says that without her, his "essence," he will "cease to be" (3.1.172, 182-84). In the courtly game of Milan's aristocratic society, a lady may have publicly acknowledged "servants," whose chivalrous devotion need not be—though it can be—erotically inspired. Valentine becomes Silvia's "servant" in both senses. Though fleetingly aware that Silvia has usurped Proteus in his thoughts (2.4.172-73), he never questions that each of them is his very "self" or wonders what would happen if love and friendship should collide. He persuades Silvia to accept his friend as a "servant" socially, never suspecting that he will make an amorous claim as well.

18

Proteus, though less idealistic than his friend, is obviously attached to Valentine at first, and he is passionately in love with Julia. He knows all along, however, that his emotions are in conflict: thus he simultaneously approves and rejects his father's command to join Valentine in Milan, since he must leave Julia to do so (1.3.90-91). When he falls in love with Silvia, Valentine's lady, he notes the loss of "zeal" toward his friend as well as toward Julia; he adopts an amusingly pragmatic attitude, promising to master his new passion if he can, but vowing to win Silvia for himself if he cannot (2.4.192-214). His sophistry in rationalizing infidelity to both friend and love (2.6.1-32) is almost disarmingly juvenile, but with self-love as guide, he plunges into ever-increasing treachery. His villainy causes little concern, however. He cuts a poor figure in wooing "holy" Silvia, and he is plainly enmeshing himself in a tightening net.

The crux of the play occurs when the demands of love and friendship finally clash, and Valentine, after his long absorption in love, chooses friendship without the blink of an eye—without, in fact, showing any recognition that he is making a choice. Faced with the shocking evidence of Proteus's treachery, quickly followed by a brief speech of repentance, he instantly pardons his friend, and to demonstrate the restoration of his affection, surrenders to Proteus his own claim to Silvia's love (5.4.77-83). The only response to this astonishing offer is Julia's swoon, and the disclosure of her real identity is sufficient to restore the heroes to their abandoned true-loves. Conflict has not been resolved, just ignored.

Some scholars defend Valentine's offer by associating it with the noble self-sacrifices of the friendship tradition or the "courtly virtue of Magnanimity."[7] But if Shakespeare means the audience to sympathize and admire, he does little to elicit this reaction. He hints at no motive for Valentine, no sense of regret over losing his "essence," no sign of consideration for Silvia herself. Even worse, dramatically speaking, he gives Silvia no response when her ideally constant lover proposes to turn her over to her would-be ravisher (indeed no speech at all for the rest of the play). To treat her as a passive "prize," aside from giving the actress a thankless task and (in modern times) offending feminist sensibilities, would contradict the effect of her previous speeches and actions—defying her father's will about Thurio, going after Valentine, denouncing Proteus. Muriel Bradbrook, once a "prize" adherent, later suggested a different interpretation: Valentine, holding Silvia by one hand, "invites" the kneeling Proteus to kiss the other, as he offers him "all that *was* [not is] mine in Silvia." What he offers is not Silvia herself, but reinstatement as her courtly servant, a position which he and Proteus had formerly shared but from which he has now risen to be Silvia's betrothed.[8] Although the interpretation of Valentine's words seems

too subtle for the theater, the suggestion is appealing. Another "Elizabethan" interpretation—one which has actually been tried on the stage—construes Valentine's offer as a "courteous gesture that will give Proteus a chance to be his best self" by declining it. To implement this, Valentine must signal his real purpose somehow, most easily by exchanging meaningful looks with an approving Silvia.[9]

Read and played without sophistication, however, the climactic scene seems to cast ridicule on all three members of the love triangle: on Valentine, whose mechanical adherence to one code makes him an unwitting traitor to another or (for spectators unacquainted with these codes) whose sudden shift in attitude suggests a more-than-Protean instability; on Proteus, whose clever scheming has led only to disgraceful exposure; and even on Silvia, the paragon for whom three men have striven, who finds herself forsaken by the winner. Only Julia, who loves not an ideal but a particular man, who loves him steadfastly, if foolishly, despite his well-known flaws, escapes absurdity.

These effects are partly the result of unskillful plot development, but there are hints that the two gentlemen at least—idealist as much as villain—were meant to appear comic. One hint is the comic exposure of Valentine himself in an earlier scene, caught by the Duke with a rope ladder under his cloak. Another is the incongruous behavior of that other idealist, Sir Eglamour, whose valor, wisdom, and compassion are praised by Silvia (4.3.11-13), but who takes to his heels when confronted by the outlaws, leaving Silvia unprotected (5.3.6-7). Most notable is Shakespeare's use of the comic servants to comment on or reflect their masters' behavior: Speed satirizes Valentine's romantic excesses (2.1.18-32, 42-78), and Launce unwittingly parodies the aristocrats' behavior in several passages—for example, his account of the family farewell (2.3.1-32), which exaggerates to absurdity the pathos of Proteus and Julia's parting.

It has been suggested that *Two Gentlemen,* which presents many problems as romantic comedy, makes perfect sense when considered as burlesque.[10] There are burlesque elements, certainly; but, although Shakespeare sometimes ridicules his young friends and lovers, he does not ridicule friendship or love. To turn the whole romance into burlesque is to lose some of the play's qualities that can be particularly attractive in performance: the lyricism, the passion (often moving, despite the exaggeration), and the youthful spirit, which makes the adolescent lovers appealing without obscuring their follies and vices. Shakespeare's method, so notable in later comedies, of balancing romance with deflating humor yet without destroying its charm, seems to have been attempted in this early play, though less firmly and skillfully: it is hence more puzzling in its effect and more difficult to translate into theatrical terms.

In addition to major problems in interpretation and tone, there are minor ones in simple "factual" matters due to confusing or inconsistent references: to "Verona" and "Padua" in passages seemingly related to Milan: to an Emperor who turns out to be a Duke; to two different Sir Eglamours, only one of whom actually appears on the stage; and so on. These are comparatively easy to deal with, but the mere listing of an Eglamour among Julia's suitors has occasionally colored the representation of the one we see, a sworn celibate who befriends Silvia. There are also failures in dramatic technique, such as an undue reliance on monologue and duologue, the latter even when a number of characters are on the stage.[11] Casual readers may overlook such lapses until the end, when they are suddenly shocked by Silvia's silence; in the theater, however, even the minor awkwardnesses must be dealt with in some way.

The three earliest productions of *Two Gentlemen* that can be described with any confidence tried to cure the play's ills by radical textual revisions; the third used, in addition, a more potent medicine. Being closely related, they can be discussed together: (1) David Garrick's production at Drury Lane, using an adapted text by Benjamin Victor, introduced on 22 December 1762—the first production of the play now known, though there had probably been one in the 1590s; (2) John Philip Kemble's production at Covent Garden, using his own version (based on Victor's but with alterations), first seen on 20 April 1808; and (3) an "operatic" production at Covent Garden, opening on 21 November 1821, with libretto by Frederick Reynolds and music by Henry Bishop—the text evidently based on Kemble's but with extensive cuts to make way for the interpolated songs and for new passages of dialogue to justify them.[12] (Two other London productions of this period, seen just four times in all, may have had texts closer to Shakespeare's, but the evidence is sparse.)[13]

Some of the changes that Victor made and Kemble adopted were typical of that period's theatrical editing of Shakespeare: cuts (mainly in out-of-date wordplay and some indecorous references) and rearrangement of scenes to tighten structure and suit the convenience of the scenic stage. But their other alterations were more drastic. In addition to numerous verbal substitutions, there were many new passages, some to clarify motives left obscure by Shakespeare, others to fill gaps in his action, to strengthen or modernize characterization, to give greater prominence to the comic roles, or to bolster a new interpretation. The rearrangements and amplifications of scenes did give the play a greater sense of coherence and drive, but at the sacrifice of Shakespeare's subtler dramatic effects: for instance Launce's monologue about his family's farewell was no longer paired with Julia and Proteus's parting, and Julia's decision to follow Proteus, now placed immediately after his departure, was no longer in ironic

juxtaposition with Proteus's determination to win Silvia. Among Victor's additions were two scenes for the comic players; Kemble retained (with a softening touch) the first one, in which a badly frightened Launce and a phlegmatic Crab are captured by outlaws, but not the second, in which a disguised Speed plays a callous joke on Launce. Reynolds evidently followed Kemble's lead.

The characters most affected by Victor's additions were Lucetta and Thurio, each of which was economically but effectively remodeled into a contemporary stage type. Shakespeare's Lucetta, a lively but sketchily drawn waiting woman of the Nerissa type, became a pert, intriguing chambermaid, who vowed that Julia shouldn't "think . . . to carry on even an honourable intrigue" without her (Victor, 9); Jane Pope, known for her saucy and hoydenish roles, was Garrick's Lucetta. Kemble returned to the original version of this character, but he followed Victor in giving a new personality to Thurio—that of an affected devotee of the arts, absurdly vain of his ability to write sonnets, set them to music, and sing them himself. In one passage, Thurio, instead of joining the search for Silvia, lingers to practice his new song; when he hears that Proteus has already galloped off, he promises to "gallop after him—fal, fal, fal": he exits singing and, one imagines, "galloping" mincingly (48). On the stage this character may have become progressively more ridiculous: Garrick's Thurio, Joseph Vernon, a gifted singer as well as an actor of some comic parts, is depicted in a contemporary engraving as an elegant figure gracefully posing with a lute (he sang "Who is Silvia?" himself); in Kemble's production, John Liston, famous for his "vain, rich, cowardly, stupid" characters, probably repeated his parodies of the *corps de ballet's* dancing, which he had recently used successfully as Caper in a farce by J. T. Allingham; William Farren, in the Reynolds-Bishop production, reportedly made Thurio a "sportive coxcomb," and a drawing of him in the character, wearing an elaborate, finicky costume and holding a looking-glass, suggests that he did heavily emphasize Thurio's vanity and foppishness.[14] One character that Victor left as he found it was Eglamour. Kemble, however, smoothed out the Shakespearean wrinkles: to avoid confusion, he substituted "Altamont" for "Eglamour" in Julia's list of suitors, and to redeem Silvia's friend Eglamour from the ironic inconsistency between reputation and deed, he had him fight manfully and, after being struck down and left for dead, revive in time for the denouement.

The most important changes, however, affected the interpretation of the whole play. Evidently the adaptors saw nothing comic in Valentine's worship of Silvia but found his climactic offer to Proteus incredible; accordingly they concentrated upon the love story, elaborating the relationship of Valentine and Silvia by additional passages (for example, mutual declarations of love in Act 2 and a tender reunion after Silvia's rescue from Proteus). They completely reformed the climactic scene: Valentine, instead of forgiving Proteus immediately, threatened him with death; this precipitated Julia's swoon and, ultimately, the revelation of her identity; Silvia, not Valentine, joined the hands of Proteus and Julia, then persuaded Valentine to be reconciled to his friend. Victor ended the play by having the reformed Proteus speak a moralizing couplet, which Kemble expanded into seven lines, ending with "A lover must be constant to be bless'd." The love interest must have suffered when stately, fifty-year-old Kemble played Valentine: he was heroic and, in his best scene (the last) very energetic, but, according to the *Morning Chronicle* (22 April 1808), "cold and unimpressive" where love was the "immediate impulse."

The operatic production went well beyond its predecessors in expedients for popularizing *Two Gentlemen:* its revised and much-cut text was embellished with a great deal of music and spectacle. In addition to a newly-set "Who Is Silvia?", there were an overture and eleven elaborately-arranged vocal pieces—solos, duets, glees, choruses, and a grand finale. The words for the new songs were based, with considerable freedom, on passages from other Shakespearean works, mostly sonnets and other poems, but also four plays. The music was obviously more important than the drama, though Maria Tree, a good Shakespearean actress as well as a fine mezzo-soprano, seems to have given an effective portrayal of Julia despite the slender text. None of the male characters except the outlaws had singing parts, and none except John Liston as Launce got much attention from reviewers. Most of the praise went to the two heroines and a young singer who played the interpolated role of Julia's page. The staging was extravagant, with "wonders of scenery and machinery." Especially "gorgeous" was the final scene of Act 4, set in the Great Square of Milan, with grotesque groups of dancers and merrymakers celebrating Carnival. It featured a series of spectacles, notably a huge model of Cleopatra's galley and "an artificial mountain transformed into the Temple of Apollo, by the singular process of conflagration." This "noble pageant," half an hour long, would seem irrelevant to the play, but apparently the distractions of Carnival enabled Silvia and Eglamour to leave Milan unnoticed.[15]

This was the first popular production of *Two Gentlemen:* Garrick's had been seen only six times, Kemble's only three, but the operatic version had twenty-nine performances in its first season and six in its second— an excellent record at that time. Audiences obviously preferred less of the play (even in revised form) and more of the embellishments. As the *Examiner* explained, the passages omitted for the sake of music and spectacle were not "*dramatically* beautiful," and there was nothing a modern audience appreciated less than mere blank-verse recitation.

The first documented production of *Two Gentlemen* that restored Shakespeare's text was William Charles Macready's, which premiered at Drury Lane on 29 December 1841.[16] "Restoring," of course, did not mean returning to Shakespeare's complete text or strictly adhering to his arrangement of scenes. Macready took the usual liberties in both respects. In fact, he cut more lines than either Victor or Kemble, his most noticeable omissions being the whole of 3.2, in which Proteus hypocritically advises Thurio how to woo Silvia (though he transferred seven of its lines, with some verbal changes, to 4.2), and the most vulgar passages of Launce's monologue about Crab's misbehavior. In making structural changes, however, he was more sensitive to the dramatic consequences than the adaptors had been. For example, he preserved the ironic relationship between Julia's plan to join Proteus and the latter's defection to Silvia.

Textual restoration, as Macready understood it, consisted of purifying the original text from "the gross interpolations that disfigure it": in this case, ridding it of all the adaptor's additions and refraining from making any new ones.[17] In preparing his version of *Two Gentlemen,* he came close to this ideal: he cut out all previous accretions to Shakespeare's text; he made far fewer verbal changes within the lines than his predecessors had done; and he added only one full line of his own. But he not only purged the text, he also restored the long-abandoned lines in which Valentine forgives Proteus and offers him "all that was mine in Silvia" (5.4.83). This revived emphasis on friendship reflected a current interest of Macready's: later in the same season he produced Gerald Griffin's *Titus and Gisippus,* a blank-verse dramatization of the old story.

Macready's comparatively slight changes in characterization were made through cuts rather than additions: for example, he made Eglamour seem more consistent by omitting Silvia's praise of his valor rather than by making his behavior conform to it. Several cuts made the two heroes appear in a somewhat better light, but performance, more than textual changes, revealed his interpretation of these roles.

As Valentine, Macready was a noble hero—frank, kindly, warm-hearted. (At forty-eight he was too old for Shakespeare's inexperienced, slightly ridiculous idealist, but he would have rejected that interpretation anyway.) He and James R. Anderson, a "gallant" Proteus, "more picturesque than villainous," played well together; they were better, according to one critic, in their "manly cordiality" as friends than in their "boisterous ardor" as lovers. Another critic found fault with Macready, however, for his "overly-fervid" demonstration of friendship when bidding farewell to Proteus; his "perilous sighs" seemed too emotional for male friends in England's "'cauld clime.'" Young Miss Fortescue, as Julia, was the center of the audience's sympathetic attention, charming them with her warmth, passion, and pathos. Robert Keeley, a fine comedian, played Launce effectively despite his missing vulgarities. Thurio, though now deprived of a chance to sing and caper, was by tradition a fop; Compton created a new identity by combining "foppishness" with "surliness."[18]

The difficult climactic scene was played like this: As Proteus advanced on Silvia, threatening rape, Valentine rushed forward, sword in hand, commanding him to "let go." Proteus drew his own sword and was about to attack, but when he recognized his opponent, he dropped it and staggered back in horror. The actors froze in their positions, creating the effect of a "fixed group" by an artist or sculptor, before Proteus fell to his knees and begged for forgiveness. The applause was "tumultuous." Proteus's horror-struck attitude, which epitomized his shocked self-conviction, seemed to one critic "worth a life's repentance." Idealizing the encounter as a work of art gave the moment of first remorse a symbolic importance, countering, as much as possible, the commonplace demands of probability. Valentine's rebuke was "delivered with manly grace, which was enhanced by the generosity of his forgiveness." Not everyone was reconciled to his offer of Silvia, but critics made surprisingly little objection—perhaps because Miss Ellis's dignified but cold Silvia aroused little sympathy. What did she *do?* We have only a negative clue: the remark that she had not yet mastered "the mystery of by-play."[19]

Among the most effective features of this production were the artistic scenes of characters in Renaissance dress moving against carefully-detailed, authentic-looking Italian backgrounds. Macready had chosen the year 1500 as the approximate time of the story and had consulted the antiquarian authority Colonel Hamilton Smith about the costumes. He had new scenery painted (less common for legitimate plays than for opera at that time) with emphasis on specific, identifiable places. For example, the opening scene, in which Valentine parts from Proteus, was located not simply on "A Street in Verona" (as in Kemble's promptbook), but before the "Tombs of the Scaligeri," and there were several views of the Duke's place, with differing Milanese landmarks in the distance—the Duomo in one, the City Gate in another, and so on.[20] Reviewers approved the "attention to the local scenery and uses of the period," and they praised the "succession of beautiful and animated pictures," noting that the decor, rather than "overlay[ing] the drama," was "in fine keeping with [its] effects."[21]

Audiences and critics were enthusiastic. The latter praised not only the production but (equally complimentary to it) the play itself. The *Argus,* which called *Two Gentlemen* "charming," said that it was "so admirably got up and so deliciously acted" that it produced "a quiet and continual succession of pleasurable sensa-

tions." For the *Times* critic, the atmosphere of "Southern warmth" evidently turned what were usually-considered flaws into part of the play's charm: excessive use of conceits became the "freshness and recklessness" with which *concetti* are "sprinkle[d]" over everything, and the lack of strong characterization hardly mattered with this "company of graceful sonneteers." Such reviews were a pleasant change from some earlier ones, which had condemned the play as dull and not worth reviving.[22] The new appreciation seemingly reflected not only the appeal of the Italian Renaissance decor and the fine acting, but also—for the *Morning Chronicle*'s critic, at least—the liberating effect of the rediscovered Shakespearean text. Macready's revival, he wrote, was "in the simple form" intended by Shakespeare, something that had been previously misunderstood by adaptors and managers. Neither an elaborate work of art nor "a collection of . . . stage effects," it is a "careless, graceful, romantic piece" from Shakespeare's earliest years. Treated that way, "what beauty, what inimitable grace, what freshness and buoyancy" it had! The audience could laugh, sigh, and sympathize with the characters without bothering very much about "character": they need not even feel unhappy about Proteus's perfidy, for it was "clear from the first that everything must come right in the end."

Macready's production had thirteen performances—as many as all preceding ones put together, except for those of the "opera." Unimpressive as the number sounds, it was a very good showing for a minor Shakespearean play at that time. For *Two Gentlemen* without textual or musical embellishments it was remarkable. This production, whose promptbook was used again by Charles Kean (New York, 1846; London, 1848), established the theatrical use of Shakespeare's text with few, if any, additions and often, though not always, with Valentine's offer intact. Stage versions of later years would vary in the amount of liberty taken with the original text (Augustin Daly's in 1895, for example, was heavily edited), but they would, on the whole, conform more closely to it, not less so, than Macready's did.

The next productions of particular interest were William Poel's, important for radical innovations in staging. Unlike the other directors in this study, Poel gave his attention not to making the play more stageworthy, but to revealing its own qualities, which were currently obscured by elaborate sets, artificial breaks in the action, and slow, overly-emphatic speech. His search for "some means of acting Shakespeare naturally and appealingly from a full text"[23] led him back to the original staging as he envisioned it—continuous action on a thrust platform and rapid speech accented only on key words. His involvement with the New Shakespere Society was an early example of cooperation between stage and study. Although Poel was at first ridiculed, his influence and that of more flexible followers revolutionized Shakespearean production.

Not counting a dramatic reading in 1892, Poel directed two London productions of *Two Gentlemen,* both for the Elizabethan Stage Society: at the Merchant Taylors Hall on 28 November 1896 and at His Majesty's Theatre on 20 April 1910 during Beerbohm-Tree's annual Shakespeare Festival. (Each was repeated at other locations). For both he used a conservative text, with no changes except occasional cuts (the only notable ones being the references to Eglamour's running away), and he tried to create the theatrical conditions of Shakespeare's day.[24] The costumes were authentically Elizabethan, if not always appropriate to character and situation: the women wore ruffs and farthingales, the gentlemen's clothes were based on some sixteenth-century frescoes in the Hall of the Carpenters' Company, and the outlaws' on a costume design for a halberdier in the Fishmongers' Pageant of 1609. (A semi-military group, the outlaws marched with banner and trumpeter.)

The first production was not successful, largely because the "stage," an open space at the upper end of a large hall, was too flat to allow good visibility and the amateur actors had difficulty making themselves heard. The second one, however, though seen only once in London, was, in Robert Speaight's opinion, one of Poel's "most important contributions to the Elizabethan Revival." Poel had an apron built out over the orchestra pit of Tree's theater, thus gaining something like a platform stage. The acting seems to have been generally good. Critics approved the distinct enunciation and the use of the old pronunciation when the verse required it; they also noticed some "Elizabethan" gesture. One of Poel's eccentricities, occasionally casting women in men's parts (a reverse reminder of the boy-actress), was used successfully in this production: Valentine and Panthino were reportedly played well by actresses, though Valentine (Winifred Rae) was chided by her director for lack of "virility." Individual performances were less impressive, however, than the mood or atmosphere created by the whole group. Thus Speaight recalled the "innkeeper nodding over his lantern," not as an example of the actor's art, but as one of the production's "beauties which lingered in the memory," and the *Times* mentioned the "'right' Shakespearian" fooling of the "two clowns" without naming the actors or noting any details of performance. In this production, declared the latter, the "puerile complications and improbabilities" of the plot, which would have been "more glaring" in a realistic setting, "became of little account," and the play's best qualities were clearly brought out—the "verve of its dialogue, the lyric beauty of many of its passages," and "the atmosphere of warm, romantic amorism."

During virtually the next half-century, productions of *Two Gentlemen,* in both London and Stratford, generally used Elizabethan costumes, or something like them, though at least one used medieval Italian de-

cor; the settings varied from pictorial to simplified and suggestive. But on 22 January 1957 Michael Langham broke the trend with a production at the Old Vic set in the early nineteenth century, the first *Two Gentlemen* at either major center in a period later than Shakespeare's.[25] The acting text was Shakespearean except for a good many cuts, occasional brief changes in wording, and some (not many) additional lines. Valentine's famous offer in the last act was retained. Changes in interpretation were effected mainly through innovative decor and greatly amplified stage business.[26]

A vaguely Italian permanent set, suggestive of a garden in neo-Gothic style, had flower-entwined pillars, ivy-covered ruin, and, in the foreground, a small, ornate structure, from whose high window Silvia looked down in the serenade scene; different backcloths indicated changes of location. The "mock-Regency" costumes pleased both eye and fancy with their romantic flair—the gentlemen in brightly-colored jackets, close-fitting trousers, caped coats, and velour top hats, the ladies in full-skirted dresses with lace parasols. Valentine and Proteus, "attractively posturing juveniles," looked like Byron and Shelley. The outlaws (stretching chronology) resembled the Pirates of Penzance.[27] The Romantic period, closer to the present than the Renaissance, yet remote enough to evoke a "make-believe" atmosphere, seemed to most critics an inspired choice: it sorted well with the play's sighings and swoonings, its poetic fervor and idealism, and its Byronic philandering. Turning the two gentlemen into "a couple of bucks" heightened the absurdities of the plot and, at the same time, "almost conjured away" one's impatience with them. Reviewers disagreed about the amount of burlesque Langham used, but most thought he managed it delicately (at least, until the climax): as one of them remarked, his production succeeded because the play's "naively young but passionate poetry . . . survive[d] the drastic treatment."[28]

The acting created the effect of irony balanced with sympathy. Robert Gale, a Valentine of "dashing 'true-blue' simplicity," was both lovelorn and valorously spirited. Keith Michell as the Byronic Proteus was "so fiercely driven by passion" as to be "unaware that he was turning into a knave"; at times he seemed "astonished at his own behavior," his attitude varying from humorous ruefulness to "Keatsian melancholy." Barbara Jefford's "shiningly sincere" Julia was praised for "genuine fire and eloquence." Ingrid Hafner's Silvia, though comparatively colorless, was a lovely-looking, nobly-bred heroine. Dudley Jones gave a "brisk" performance of the word-mongering Speed. Robert Helpmann, with comic precision and "ingratiating audience-contact," portrayed Launce as a squeaky-voiced, vacant-looking, but likable Cockney, "funny with pathos." A clever yellow Labrador named Duff was "engagingly miscast" as that dirty dog Crab:

he "shook hands," carried parcels, and behaved so decorously as to belie his master's vulgar account of him (all its vulgarities intact).[29]

The most notable aspect of Langham's production was its constant and ingenious use of stage business which, though not implied by Shakespeare's text, seemed to grow naturally out of it. It endowed the most archaic verbal conceits with a modern spirit, and it often won laughs with the ironic touches it gave to the speaker's words. Since the actors rarely said anything without doing something too, they gave the illusion of a fuller, faster-moving plot than the play actually has. Among other embellishments were an artist painting Silvia's portrait, archery practice, and dancing in the candlelit palace garden. Stage business, combined with distinctive costumes, was also used to "develop" minor characters: Antonio, apparently a country squire, came in with bag and gun, fresh from hunting; Thurio, vain as ever but now a "superannuated rake," was shown being shaved; the Duke, wearing a splendid uniform with epaulettes, strode about, smoking cigars and seeming "always on the edge of sending a gunboat to subdue rebellious tribesmen." Eglamour was uniquely reinterpreted: the "two Eglamours" were combined into one, an ineffectual but dapper old beau, who first courted Julia in Verona, then turned up at Milan, paying his addresses to Silvia. (Chaste devotion to a dead lady was not mentioned.) Stage business, added to scenes where Eglamour did not originally appear, carried out the new interpretation; at one point he was visually paired with Thurio—two silly old fops together.[30] The portrayal, as the *Guardian* suavely remarked, was "not quite perhaps what Shakespeare meant," but it "fitted well in this 'Vanity Fair' treatment of the tale."

The most striking use of stage business, however, was in the climactic scene, where it gave a new explanation of Valentine's notorious offer. Proteus's rescue of Silvia was heard offstage (not merely referred to, as in Shakespeare), with Proteus demanding Silvia's release and, when an outlaw refused, threatening force. The outlaws having fled, Silvia hurried on stage, closely pursued by Proteus, armed with a pistol and followed in turn by Julia-as-Sebastian. Silvia, trying to escape from Proteus, who had gained hold of her, succeeded in taking the pistol from his pocket and, presumably pointing it at him, broke loose and backed away from him, down the shallow steps. He wheeled down after her, took the pistol away, and threatened to force her; he then swung her to him, laying the pistol down for freer action. When Valentine advanced from behind a rock, ordering, "Villain, let go . . . ," Proteus released her, exclaiming, "Valentine!" Silvia fell in a faint, and Valentine and Julia knelt to help her. Julia stayed with her as Valentine confronted Proteus and denounced him. At one point Proteus put his hand on his old friend's shoulder, but Valentine ignored this overture. Proteus, after begging forgiveness, picked up the pis-

tol; Silvia, who had revived, took cover behind a pillar, Julia (drawn toward Proteus?) behind Valentine. Proteus, however, was bent on suicide, not murder. Valentine hastily forgave him, then, taking the pistol from him, made his offer of Silvia "on the spur of an emotional moment."

Critics joined in the audience's merriment over the transformation of Shakespeare's puzzling finale into nineteenth-century melodrama—"a sort of abridged version of . . . 'The Corsican Brothers.'" Nothing could "finally disguise" Valentine's lunatic forbearance, wrote one, "but the players' confidence survived the inevitable laughter"; another said that the mask of light romance, which had been kept in place until now, dropped under the strain of this scene, and "the repressed burlesque [burst] out." The tongue-in-cheek response was, no doubt, exactly what Langham wished. His "brilliant" solution to the problem of Valentine's offer was praised as the best example of his inventive talent.[31]

Langham's successful treatment of the play influenced both critical attitudes and some later productions. Its springlike gaiety was remembered and favorably contrasted with the autumnal mood of Peter Hall's production (Stratford-upon-Avon, 1960), with its decor in the deep, rich tones of an Italian Old Master. And its long-lived influence was felt in Richard Digby Day's productions (Open Air Theatre, Regent's Park, London, summers of 1968 and 1969) with their nineteenth-century costumes, their light-hearted lyricism, and their sharply-defined minor characters (including some anachronistic ones—outlaws in Robin Hood suits and Sir Eglamour in cobwebbed armor like an ancient Quixote).[32]

Among the most interesting of other productions with latter-day settings was Robin Phillips's contemporary *Two Gentlemen* at the Royal Shakespeare Theatre, Stratford-upon-Avon, 23 July 1970 (revived in December for a brief run at the Aldwych in London). Its permanent set, which served for both Verona and Milan (and for the forest, with the help of dangling ropes and dappled light), depicted a scene at an Italian resort, featuring a miniature swimming pool with real water; the lovers were wealthy, golden-tanned adolescents, wearing trendy leisure clothes and huge sunglasses. Antonio, a cigar-smoking tycoon, or perhaps a Mafia boss, doffed his monogrammed beachrobe for a quick swim; the Duke, who sometimes appeared in an academic gown, looked like a vice chancellor of a university. The outlaws were hippies, and Eglamour was an aging scoutmaster, dressed in bare-kneed uniform, who arrived on a bicycle, brought along his camping gear and ordnance map, and laid a bridge across the pool for Silvia to escape on. Launce (Patrick Stewart) was a dour, North-Country workman, dressed in black, who stood apart, a grave, unmoved observer of the others' follies.

The production reflected the current emphasis on a search for identity—it began and ended with an echo-song "Who is Silvia? Who is Valentine? Who is Proteus? Who is Julia?"—and also a modern concern with psychological motivation. Proteus, more cerebral than the handsome, athletic Valentine but relatively puny physically, seemed to be moved to treachery by envious admiration and a sense of his own inadequacy. Simply as interesting characters, the lovers were well played: Peter Egan's Valentine, sincere and naive, a little conceited but maturing under the influence of love and its troubles; Ian Richardson's Proteus, "coldly impassioned," subtle, and self-aware; Helen Mirren's Julia, "delightfully spirited and endearing," at times a "tigress" or "whirlwind," at times an agonized adolescent, sucking her thumb for comfort; Estelle Kohler's Silvia, a graceful socialite, but capable of taking the initiative and acting with spirit. The reconciliation scene was effectively played: as he wound up his expression of forgiveness, Valentine kissed Silvia; then, crossing to Proteus, he ended "And that my love may appear plain and free" (5.4.82) by kissing him. The crucial line that followed ("All that was mine in Silvia I give thee") evidently meant, "The love I have given to Silvia I also give to you." Even so, the play ended on an uncertain note, as Valentine spoke its final line with a doubtful pause before the last word, "One feast, one house, one mutual—happiness." The sound of a cuckoo underlined the ambiguity.

Some critics deplored the effects of the modernization: "incongruities," substitution of irony for lyricism, loss of the lovers' innocence, sacrifice of serious Shakespearean themes. (Once again the Langham production of 1957 was wistfully recalled as the contrasting ideal.) Others insisted that the play had gained by the contemporary treatment of timeless truths. Most reviewers, however, like most audiences, simply enjoyed the production.[33]

An unusual amount of experimentation with *Two Gentlemen* has taken place in North American regional and festival theaters: the play has had settings, for example, in Little Italy of 1900; on a 1920s campus of "Millen University," where Valentine had an athletic scholarship; and in a farcical Wild West, with Silvia doubling as a teasing Mae West and the disguised Julia wearing a ten-gallon hat over her enormous beehive hairdo. It has been given in the style of circus, *commedia dell'arte,* vaudeville, and a combination of all these.[34] In 1984 the American Repertory in New York even revived Kemble's 1808 adaptation.

Among other experiments have been several musical ones. The most famous was the award-winning "rock musical" (which also used other popular rhythms like jazz and Latin American dance), directed by Mel Shapiro from his and John Guare's text, Guare's lyrics and Galt MacDermot's music. It was produced in the summer of 1971 for Joseph Papp's New York Shakespeare Festival in Central Park, had a successful run at the St. James, Broadway, in 1971-72, and was revived (with a different cast) at the Phoenix, London, in 1973. This *Two Gentlemen* was much more, and much less, than an adaptation. Fewer than 450 Shakespearean lines survived, some of them from sonnets and other plays, and a good many new lines were added, besides those of the numerous songs (nearly forty, finally). Some striking character changes produced a pregnant Julia, a lusty Silvia who hated to be idealized, a tough-looking Duke in dark glasses who was a sleazy politician as well as a tyrant, an Eglamour (Silvia's old boyfriend) who had been drafted into the army, a Lucetta who paired off with Thurio, and metadramatic servants (Launce and Speed) who bemoaned the plight of the working man with no time for love and wished to be a "hot lover . . . like the kids in the play." There were references to contemporary concerns—war, abortion, the environment. A racially mixed cast made the point of brotherhood. But the chief emphasis was on the songs, the dances, the mood of lively abandon—and the theme of love, love, love. It was a long way from Shakespeare, but it had some of the same youthfulness, vitality, and, in its own way, innocence.[35]

Some modern directors have attacked the problem of antifeminism in *Two Gentlemen,* usually by reinterpreting Valentine's offer so as to remove its callousness toward Silvia. As we have seen, Robin Phillips tried this solution, yet a critic of his production remarked that this play could "provoke a demonstration by the Women's Liberation Movement." Some North American productions have simply made the offer ridiculous, for example by using double-takes or having the men walk off together and then turn to see with comic dismay the women leaving in the other direction. The most effective expedient, however, has been to involve Silvia in the forgiveness of Proteus.[36]

The *Two Gentlemen* that best illustrates this method— the Royal Shakespeare Company's latest production of the play—also offers examples of other strategies for bringing audience and play together. Directed by David Thacker, it opened at the Swan Theatre in Stratford-upon-Avon on 6 April 1991, transferred to the Pit at the Barbican in October 1992, and later went on tour with a largely different cast, finally closing at the Haymarket Theatre in London in January 1994.[37] Its most obvious features, the choice of period and the related use of music, proved interpretive as well as entertaining. The play was set in the 1930s, when "Coward dressing gowns . . . Lonsdale evening dress and Wodehouse tennis gear" were fashionable—a period whose combination of elegance and shallowness revealingly reflected the same qualities in the play's characters. The atmosphere was established during the quarter-hour before the play began: a palm-court orchestra, ensconced in a bandstand, played hit-parade songs by George Gershwin, Cole Porter, Irving Berlin, and others, while couples in evening wear danced downstage. Between the scenes of the play, a blonde *chanteuse* crooned songs like "Blue Moon," "Night and Day," and "Love Is the Sweetest Thing"—all "cunningly chosen to point and counter-point the action." The evocation of a past distinctly different from today, yet familiar as Bertie Wooster on TV, brought the audience into tune with the play. As Benedict Nightingale explained in the *Times:* "When lovers appear in doublet and hose, we expect them to behave in conventionally romantic ways. Transpose them to places we more easily associate with youthful skittishness and folly, and they can seem perfectly plausible." The actors never mocked or patronized their characters, but their innocent yet artificial world was one whose adolescent passions might well be the subject of fun. The tone was close to Shakespeare's own. Interestingly, a critic who disapproved of the chosen setting—an unusual response—admitted that a post-Shakespearean period makes sense but preferred the early nineteenth century, with a Byronic Proteus. Langham's production and its imitators were hard to forget.[38]

Another notable feature of the production was its success in giving Shakespeare's sketchily drawn characters some sense of development or depth. Valentine (Richard Bonneville), though never profound, progressed from "an awkwardly ingratiating lover" to "an impressively bold one." Even Thurio (Henry Guy) was no mere fop or "silly-ass wooer," but "a stilted prig desperately trying to hide his intellectual and emotional limitations"; unlike the Thurios with literary pretensions, he was depressed by Proteus's suggestions that he woo Silvia with poetry. As usual in modern productions, however, the chief interest was in Proteus (Barry Lynch) and the motivation for his treachery. Here the use of potentially symbolic stage business was striking, though the interpretation depended on the spectator's own bent. The introductory scene showed the two friends in adolescent horseplay, wrestling on the floor, which, for some viewers, would inevitably connote latent sexuality. Paul Nelsen, who was struck by the strange mixture of devotion and rivalry he saw here, has described Lynch's Proteus in some detail, emphasizing the actor's "subtext." For Nelsen, this Proteus was "sullen . . . and Iago-like," and his treacherous actions stemmed from ambiguous feelings toward Valentine rather than erotic desire for Silvia. This dark interpretation was not widely shared, however. Some critics, indeed, saw a boyish charm in Lynch's Proteus: they found him "likeable and inexperienced," even "more naive and impressionable" than Valentine, before he became obsessed with Silvia. And one critic noticed a "curious sense of baffled innocence" (much in line, we think, with Shakespeare's text) even as he argued his way into treachery. Yet there was also something in the actor's manner—a "nervous intensity," a slight instability, a "disturbing little flicker of a smile"—

that suggested, even to sympathetic viewers, introversion and suppressed emotion. Lynch's psychological suggestiveness obviously did not clarify Proteus's motivation, but it did result in an intriguing portrayal.

The other roles were acted well, but there was nothing unusual about them psychologically. Julia (Clare Holman) had a "jaunty boyishness" as Sebastian but also a touching pathos; Silvia (Saskia Reeves) was cool, elegant, but determined. Richard Moore's shuffling, bowler-hatted Launce, with his "hangdog dignity" and deftly executed "takes," was, with his lugubrious-looking lurcher, Woolly, among the memorable pleasures of the production. Small parts were given sharp or colorful touches: the wisecracking Speed (Sean Murray) in his cheap suit had the personality of a traveling salesman; the Duke (Terence Wilton), an amateur cook, zestfully dismembered a lobster.[39]

The use of symbolic stage pictures was most effective in the climactic scene of the final act: Valentine stopped Proteus from raping Silvia by wrestling him to the ground, "echoing, now in desperate earnest, the playful rough-housing of act one." The parallel visually marked the change that had occurred in the relationship, with perhaps a suggestion that the comradely closeness had always included some potential hostility.[40] The actual violence might be interpreted as cathartic. When the change from conflict to reconciliation occurred, the pictorial elements remained strong. After Valentine's denunciation, spoken with "a moving sense of heartfelt grief," there was a lengthy pause before Proteus bowed his head, knelt, and made his short speech of confession. Critics were generally impressed by the poignancy of Lynch's acting here: he "[caught] very well the conflicting emotions of Proteus's final onset of guilt," "flesh[ing] out the character's woefully underscripted moment of shame most realistically." (Nelsen, however, questioned Proteus's sincerity, and indeed, as Smallwood has explained, Lynch's interpretation varied from one performance to another, according to whether he let "that enigmatic flicker of a smile" appear.) The most difficult part of the scene—and the most illuminating example of pictorial acting—followed. As Proteus begged forgiveness, Silvia stood beside him, facing Valentine, and silently but eloquently seconded the plea by her attitude and expression; as Valentine pardoned his friend, she crossed over and stood with him while he offered Proteus "all that was mine in Silvia"—meaning, perhaps, a share in "the mutual love and trust" between himself and Silvia. The exact interpretation of the words was not important; what mattered was Silvia's participation in the forgiveness and the gift of restored love.

Response to this production was joyously enthusiastic. A number of critics, both journalists and scholars, praised Thacker's handling of the difficult climax: his approach made "such perfect sense" that the "'crux' was not evident," and the "near-impossible" scene became both "riveting" and "plausible." But even critics who still found the ending either "risible" or "outrageous" applauded the production. As for the audiences, in Smallwood's euphoric words, "Shakespeare's so-called failure, his apprentice work, his unplayable flop, became the hit of the season."[41]

Reviewing these theatrical attempts to popularize *Two Gentlemen,* one sees some salient trends. Rewriting the text to improve it, never successful, has long since been abandoned, though using it as a framework for new creations has occasionally resulted in popular productions (opera, rock musical). In every age nonverbal elements have been determining factors in making the play's simplicities attractive or, alternatively, in creating the impression of additional depth and development. Extra music has been used, not just in outright musicals, but in a good many regular productions. Decor and style of performance have often been important, especially when a new look has revealed certain aspects of the play more clearly than before— for example, Macready's meticulous Italian sets at a time when stock scenery often sufficed for Shakespeare, Poel's return to simple Elizabethan staging for an audience accustomed to visual illusion, and Langham's evocation of the Byronic period when Elizabethan productions had become the norm. The search for novelty has led to a variety of unusual and inventive treatments. It seems, indeed, that some directors have been willing to undertake this play largely because its reputation for unpopularity serves as a license to experiment without giving much offense. Other things being equal, however, the most effective productions have been those whose staging had some special affinity with the youthful mixture of passion, artifice, lyricism, and folly in the play itself.

In all periods there has been a noticeable attempt to give life and color to Shakespeare's minor characters. In early productions certain roles were transformed into contemporary stage types by textual additions, and even after the adaptations had been discarded, some influence from the memory of previous portrayals probably remained, at least for Thurio. About the middle of the present century, directors began, through inventive use of decor and stage business, to give more distinctive personalities to other mainly functional characters. The types of roles assigned to them have, of course, been suitable to the chosen setting, but they have also reflected the interests and concerns of the period when the production occurred. Eglamour's transformations are particularly interesting in this respect: he has moved from Kemble's perfect knight, to Macready's coward, to Poel's representative of spiritualized love, to modern portrayals as a figure of fun—an elderly beau, an anachronistic Don Quixote, a childish dogooder. Directors have never quite known what to do with Eglamour, but their different ways of dealing

with this absurd but poignant figure reveal him as a touchstone for a production and its time.

Some interesting analogies are found in the climactic scene as staged in otherwise dissimilar productions, widely separated in time. In the earliest ones, using adapted texts with a heavily revised climax, Silvia persuaded a formidably reluctant Valentine to forgive her would-be ravisher; in the latest one (Thacker's), using Shakespeare's version with a more amenable Valentine, she silently did the same. A closer parallel links Macready's production, using a restored text, with Thacker's: in both, Proteus froze for a long moment after Valentine's denunciation, his attitude and facial expression suggesting the emotions he felt at the sudden disclosure of his treachery; in both, the stage picture helped to fill in what was lacking in the short repentance speech.

One aspect of the play noticed by modern scholars, the satirical and parodic function of Launce and Speed, has often been overlooked in the theater. Indeed, some reviewers have remarked that Launce, entertaining as he is, has nothing to do with the main part of the play.[42] The Phillips production called attention to his metadramatic function with a Launce silently brooding over the antics of his social superiors, but although one critic was impressed by this conception of the play's "dark angel," another thought it was merely pretentious. Less blatant was the extra stage business in Thacker's production that showed Launce making clownish use of facilities designed for more elegant purposes (like putting dogfood in the Duke's fruitbowl); thus, as Robert Smallwood observed, "mov[ing] in the hinterland between the audience and the fiction."[43] While less scholarly reviewers, writing to deadlines, did not notice the implications, that hardly matters. Provided Launce is not allowed to overwhelm the romance completely, it is just as well simply to laugh at him, responding unconsciously to his subversive ironies and leaving anything more to afterthoughts.

A notable recent change is the increasing interest in the two gentlemen themselves. In 1808, Leigh Hunt wrote that they came and went, talked or were silent, without exciting sympathy for the one or contempt for the other; in 1842, reviewers commended Macready for taking such a slight role as Valentine in the interests of art.[44] Proteus has always been condemned, of course, though he has frequently seemed less villainous on the stage than in the study; in more recent times Valentine, too, has been denigrated. But some stage productions, in dealing with the problems of Proteus's motivation and Valentine's callousness, have so developed these characters that their central importance in the play goes unquestioned. While the friends' relationship has not reflected the *alter ego* conception (indeed, quite the opposite), Shakespeare himself shows a reality that does not conform to Valentine's ideal.

Again and again over the years some reviewer of a successful production has asked why *Two Gentlemen* has been so neglected; then it has been neglected again for awhile. Today, however, the play is becoming better known in the theater. With Thacker's production to brighten its reputation, with revivals by regional companies to test its wilder possibilities, and with the BBC's stylized work of television art to be viewed on demand, this trend will probably continue. *Two Gentlemen* will always be a special challenge, though. All dramatic productions are collaborations between author and theater—director, actors, designers, and so on. In productions of this play, Shakespeare's collaborators are more than usually responsible for a significant part of the "text."

Notes

1 This does not include any with amateur actors, except for William Poel's—too important to leave out.

2 Even counting a rock musical, we know of only five full-length productions (one of which had a single performance) in New York; three of these were later seen in London. Short entertainments based on *Two Gentlemen* included two skits (one with black minstrels) and a farce. See George C. D. Odell, *Annals of the New York Stage,* 15 vols. (New York: Columbia University Press, 1927-49), 8:219; 11:549; 12:104, 312.

3 Charles Spencer's phrase, in his review of David Thacker's production, *The Daily Telegraph,* 19 April 1991.

4 Other concerns (education, the courtly code of behavior, the qualities essential to a gentlemen), though important, do not impress a spectator as driving impulses of speech and action for the major characters. Kurt Schlueter, in the introduction to his edition, *The Two Gentlemen of Verona,* The New Cambridge Shakespeare (Cambridge: Cambridge University Press, 1990), 2-6, gives a good, condensed discussion of the play's themes. In addition to the scholarly articles he cites, see Ann Jennalie Cook, "Shakespeare's Gentlemen," *Shakespeare Jahrbuch* (West) (1985): 9-27.

5 Gervase Mathew, "Ideals of Friendship," *Patterns of Love and Courtesy: Essays in Memory of C. S. Lewis,* ed. John Lawlor (Evanston: Northwestern University Press, 1966), 46-50; Laurens J. Mills, *One Soul in Bodies Twain: Friendship in Tudor Literature and Stuart Drama* (Bloomington, Indiana: Principia Press, 1937), 259 et passim; Geoffrey Bullough, ed. *Narrative and Dramatic Sources of Shakespeare,* 8 vols. (London: Routledge and Kegan Paul, 1957-75), 1: 204.

6 Bernard O'Donoghue gives a good review of courtly love's various features and its influence on English Renaissance literature, in *The Courtly Love Tradition,* Literature in Context (Manchester: Manchester University Press; Totowa, New Jersey: Barnes and Noble, 1982), 5-6, 15. He defends the term "courtly love" against modern attacks (14).

7 See Mills, 258; Muriel C. Bradbrook, *Shakespeare and Elizabethan Poetry: A Study of His Earlier Work in Relation to the Poetry of the Time* (New York: Oxford University Press, 1952), 151.

8 Bradbrook speculates that the play was written for a private performance by boy actors. See "Love and Constancy in *The Two Gentlemen of Verona,*" *Shakespeare in His Context: The Constellated Globe.* The Collected Papers of Muriel Bradbrook, vol. 4 (Totowa, N.J.: Barnes and Noble, 1989), 47-49, 55. In *Shakespeare and Elizabethan Poetry* (152) she had declared that Silvia "should not react at all. She is the prize, for the purpose of argument, and must not call attention to herself. . . ."

9 Camille Wells Slights, "*The Two Gentlemen of Verona* and the Courtesy Book Tradition," *Shakespeare Studies* 16 (1983): 27. A 1974 production had already used a similar interpretation. See note 36.

10 See, for example, William Rossky, "*The Two Gentlemen of Verona* as Burlesque," *English Literary Renaissance* 12 (1982): 210-19.

11 For the "minor oddities" in the play, see Clifford Leech's introduction to his edition, *The Two Gentlemen of Verona,* The Arden Edition of the Works of William Shakespeare (London: Methuen, 1969; University Paperback, 1986), xv-xxi. For a discussion of its technical failures, see Stanley Wells, "The Failure of *The Two Gentlemen of Verona,*" *Shakespeare Jahrbuch* 99 (1963): 162-66.

12 Discussion of the Victor and Kemble versions will be based on these published texts: (1) [Benjamin Victor, adaptor], *The Two Gentlemen of Verona. A Comedy Written by William Shakespeare. With Alterations and Additions. As it is performed at the Theatre-Royal in Drury Lane* (1763; London: Corn-market, 1969); and (2) John Philip Kemble, *John Philip Kemble's Promptbook of William Shakespeare's* Two Gentlemen of Verona. *Revised by J. P. Kemble.* In Vol. 9 of *John Philip Kemble's Promptbooks,* ed. Charles H. Shattuck, 11 vols. (Charlottesville: University Press of Virginia, for the Folger Shakespeare Library, 1974). Reynolds's dramatic text has not been preserved, but words of the interpolated songs, along with Bishop's music, are available in a rare volume: Henry R. Bishop, *The Overture, Songs, Duetts, Glees & Chorusses. In Shakespeare's Play of the* The Two Gentlemen of Verona. *as Performed at the Theatre Royal, Covent Garden. The Words Selected entirely from Shakespeare's Plays, Poems & Sonnets. The Music Composed (with excep-*

tion of Two Melodies) . . . by Henry R. Bishop . . . (London, [1821]). The songs, together with reviews, give a good idea of the operatic production. For Reynolds's probable use of Kemble, see Schlueter, 31-33.

[13] These were a single performance at Covent Garden, 1784, and a first attempt by Kemble, at Drury Lane, 1790. Although stage historians have said that these used the original text, or the original with slight alterations, Schlueter argues persuasively (22, 24, 25) that the alterations were probably more substantial than previously supposed.

[14] Vernon: Engraving by J. Roberts, published for Bell's Edition of Shakespeare, 7 March 1776 (copy in the Folger Shakespeare Library; also reproduced by Schlueter, 20). Liston: Jim Davis, *John Liston, Comedian* (London: Society for Theatre Research, 1985), 104; 16-18. Leigh Hunt, in *Examiner,* 24 April 1808: 266-67, accused Liston of turning Thurio into Caper. Farren: *Morning Herald* 30 November 1821; contemporary drawing published by J. Smart, London, 29 January 1822 (copy in the Folger Shakespeare Library).

[15] Reviews used in discussing music and spectacle: *Times,* 30 November 1821 ("noble pageant"); *Morning Post,* 30 November; *Morning Herald,* 30 November ("artificial mountain"); *Examiner,* 2 December. Relevance of spectacle: Kemble's version, the basis for Reynolds's, ended Act 4 with Silvia and Eglamour preparing to flee.

[16] Discussion of Macready's production is based on his promptbook (Folger Shakespeare Library PROMPT Two Gent. 11) and the following reviews: *Morning Chronicle,* 30 December 1841; *Morning Herald,* 30 December; *Morning Post,* 30 December; *Theatrical Observer,* 30 December; *Times,* 30 December; *Spectator,* 1 January 1842: 9-10; *Argus,* 1 January; *Athenaeum,* 1 January: 19; *Theatrical Journal,* 8 January: [9]-10; *The Age,* 9 January: 5-6.

[17] *The Diaries of William Charles Macready,* ed. William Toynbee, 2 vols. (London: Chapman and Hall, 1912) 2: 18-19.

[18] *Athenaeum* ("gallant"); *Morning Chronicle* ("more picturesque"); *Spectator* ("manly cordiality"); *Morning Herald* ("overly fervid"); *Times* ("foppishness and surliness").

[19] CONFRONTATION: Promptbook, 254 and opp.; *Times* ("fixed group" and applause); *Morning Chronicle* ("a life's repentance"); *Theatrical Observer* (rebuke and forgiveness). NOT RECONCILED: *Times.* SILVIA: *Spectator* (dignified); *Times* and *Theatrical Journal* (cold); *Morning Herald* (lack of byplay).

[20] Details of scenery are based on a printed flyer that was handed out at the theater, a copy of which is bound with Macready's promptbook in the Folger Library. Apparently the Reynolds-Bishop production had also used some localized Italian scenes, but with less correctness in both place and detail. See Schlueter, 33.

[21] Quoted phrases are, in sequential order, from *Theatrical Observer, Athenaeum, Times,* and *Morning Chronicle.* The only dissenting voice, as far as we know, was from *John Bull,* 10 January 1842, which praised the scenery but said the costumes were "in some particulars almost grotesque, and as a whole apparently hardly in unison." "Historically accurate" costumes did sometimes strike viewers as strange, but the appropriateness and harmony attributed to Macready's decor by other critics were characteristics generally associated with his productions. See Alan Downer, *The Eminent Tragedian* (Cambridge, Massachusetts: Harvard University Press, 1966), 225-26; 252.

[22] See, for example, *Morning Chronicle* 22 April 1808 and *Examiner* 24 April 1808: 266-67.

[23] Quoted by Robert Speaight, in *William Poel and the Elizabethan Revival* (Cambridge, Massachusetts: Harvard University Press, 1954), 90.

[24] See Poel's promptbook for *The Two Gentlemen of Verona,* now in the Theatre Museum, London. Though obviously made for the 1896 production, it was almost certainly used for both. For descriptions of the first production see reviews in the *Times,* 30 November 1896, and *Sunday Times,* 29 November; also George Bernard Shaw, *Our Theatres in the Nineties,* 3 vols. (1932: London: Constable, 1948), 2: 284; and Speaight, 119-20 (note his quotation from a favorable article by the French director Lugné-Poe). Our description of the second production is based mainly on Speaight, 120-22, and *Times,* 21 April 1910: 12, but see also *Sunday Times,* 24 April 1910: 6.

[25] A production using modern dress had been seen much earlier in the provinces, at the People's Theatre, Newcastle, on 17 May 1930. See *Observer* (London), 18 May, and *Shields Daily News,* 19 May 1930.

[26] Discussion of Langham's production is based on his promptbook, now in the University of Bristol Theatre Collection, and the following reviews, clippings of which are found in the Shakespeare Library, Birmingham Reference Library: Stephen Williams, *Evening News,* 23 January 1957; *Times* 23 January; J. C. T. [Trewin], *Birmingham Post,* 23 January; Anthony Carthew, *Daily Herald,* 23 January; Alan Dent, *News Chronicle,* 23 January; Patrick Gibbs, *Daily Telegraph,* 24 January; D. H., *Bristol Evening Post,* 24 January; Philip Hope-Wallace, *Manchester Guardian,* 24 January; A. M., *Stage,* 24 January; Patrick Keatley, *Montreal Star,* 26 January; *Western Independent,* 27 January; W. G. McS., *Scotsman,* 28 January; *Daily Worker,* 29

January; *Punch,* 30 January; Derek Grainger, *Financial Times,* 23 January; George Scott, *Truth,* 1 February; P. R., *Kensington News,* 1 February. See also Richard David, "Actors and Scholars: A View of Shakespeare in the Modern Theatre," *Shakespeare Survey* 12 (1959): 76-87.

[27] SETTING: *Times, Punch, Western Independent, Daily Telegraph.* COSTUMES: Men—*Montreal Star, Times, Western Independent;* Women—*Financial Times;* Byron and Shelley—*News Chronicle.* Outlaws: *Birmingham Post.*

[28] QUOTED PHRASES: *News Chronicle* ("make-believe"); *Scotsman* ("bucks," etc.); *Daily Worker* (the rest). AMOUNT OF BURLESQUE: *Daily Herald* (much); *Birmingham Post* ("shiver[ed] on the knife edge"); *Stage* (resisted the temptation); *Daily Worker* (just the right touch). RESERVATIONS ABOUT THE REGENCY TREATMENT: *Stage;* Richard David, 85.

[29] VALENTINE: *Kensington News.* See also *Times* and *Punch.* PROTEUS: *Times, Punch, Financial Times, Kensington News.* JULIA: *Times, Evening News.* (*Kensington News* deplored her boisterousness, but *Financial Times* said she later muted it.) SILVIA: *Stage, Truth* (colorless); *Bristol Evening Post* (lovely); *Kensington News* (nobly-bred). SPEED: *Times;* see also *Kensington News.* LAUNCE: *Financial Times* ("comic precision," "squeaky"), *Stage* ("audience-contact," vacant expression), *Evening News* (Cockney), *Punch* ("funny with pathos"). CRAB: *Bristol Evening Post* ("engagingly miscast"), *Daily Herald* ("shook hands").

[30] EXTRA STAGE BUSINESS: *Daily Worker* (reinterprets archaic conceits, passion survives treatment); *Times* (ironic touches); *Financial Times* (action always accompanies speech; archery, artist, dancing); *Stage* (many realistic touches). ANTONIO: promptbook, 14, 16. THURIO: quoted phrase from *Daily Telegraph;* shaving scene, promptbook, 92. DUKE: *Punch.* See also *Kensington News* and *Daily Telegraph.* EGLAMOUR: see descriptive phrases in *Daily Worker* and *Manchester Guardian;* stage directions in promptbook, especially in 1.2 (8) and in 2.4 (30, 32, 34—Eglamour and Thurio retire upstage together when Proteus arrives).

[31] ACTING OF CLIMAX: See stage directions in the promptbook, pp. 95-100. One vital stage direction is lacking—Proteus' actually pointing the pistol at himself,—but the implications of the stage directions, together with Patrick Gibbs's reference to Proteus's suicide attempt (*Daily Telegraph* review), leave no doubt about the performance. The quoted phrase is from Gibbs. CRITICS' RESPONSE: *Manchester Guardian; Financial Times; Bristol Evening Post; Daily Telegraph; Truth.*

[32] HALL: *Education,* 15 April 1960. DIGBY DAY: *Times,* 18 July 1968; *Daily Mail,* 18 July 1968; *Birmingham Post,* 20 July 1968 and 4 June 1969 (Eglamour). Putting Eglamour in armor might have been inspired by the bearded and helmeted Eglamour of Hall's production.

[33] This discussion is based on the promptbook, in the Shakespeare Centre Library, Stratford-upon-Avon (see stage directions, opp. 123 for climactic scene), and on the following reviews, many from the *Two Gentlemen* clippings, Birmingham (see note 26): Irving Wardle, *Times,* 24 July 1970 (decor, Antonio, Eglamour, Proteus, some disapproval), but see more positive review in *Times,* 25 December 1970; B. A. Young, *Financial Times,* 24 July (Julia, Silvia); Pearson Phillips, *Daily Mail,* 24 July (Julia, Valentine); *Evening Standard,* 24 July (Julia); J. C. Trewin, *Birmingham Post,* 24 July (decor, deplores Eglamour); Harold Hobson, *Sunday Times,* 26 July (Launce [enthusiastic], Proteus, production shows ancient truths); Wendy Monk, *Stage and Television,* 30 July 1970 (decor, Eglamour, Silvia, loss of innocence, preference for Langham): J. A. P., *Warwick Advertiser,* 31 July (Eglamour, Julia, approves modern treatment); W. T., *Nottingham Evening Post,* 24 July (Eglamour, outlaws, loss of innocence); *Oxford Mail,* 25 July (incongruities, Launce [negative]); Neville Miller, *South Wales Evening Argus,* 25-26 July (Valentine, Silvia, approves "fable on the uncertainties of adolescence"); Eric Shorter, *Daily Telegraph,* 23 December 1970 (serious content "jettisoned") *Glasgow Herald,* 28 December 1970 (theme subtly underlined); Peter Thomson, "A Necessary Theatre: The Royal Shakespeare Season 1970," *Shakespeare Survey* 24 (1971): 120-21 (decor, Antonio, Eglamour, Launce [dubious], psychological analysis, Proteus, Silvia).

[34] These settings were, in the order of their mention, for productions at the Champlain Shakespeare Festival, 1977, at the Pittsburgh Public Theater, 1981, and by the Acting Company on tour, 1990-91. A circus setting and style were combined with Byronic romanticism by the San Diego National Shakespeare Repertory in 1980; the *commedia* style was used at the Odessa Globe Shakespeare Festival (Texas) in 1977, the Utah Shakespeare Festival in 1983 (for some scenes and characters), and the Kentucky Shakespeare Festival in 1988 (in adapted and modernized form); a combination of vaudeville with other styles was used for the heavily burlesqued production of the Acting Company in 1990-91.

[35] John Guare and Mel Shapiro, *The Two Gentlemen of Verona. Adapted from the Shakespeare Play . . . Lyrics by John Guare, Music by Galt MacDermot* (New York: Holt, Rinehart and Winston, 1973). For details of both American and British productions, see reviews by Walter Kerr in *New York Times,* 12 December 1971,

Foster Hirsch in *Educational Theatre Journal* 24 (1971): 194, and Irving Wardle in *Times,* 27 April 1973.

[36] PHILLIPS: Milton Shulman, *Evening Standard,* 23 December 1970. DOUBLE TAKES: Alabama Shakespeare Festival, 1991. MEN GOING OFF TOGETHER: started to do so, Folger Theatre Group, 1977; did so, Great Lakes Shakespeare Festival, 1978. SILVIA'S APPROVAL: At the Oregon Shakespeare Festival, 1974, the offer was made as a ruse, conceived by Valentine and Silvia. In the BBC television production, 1983-84, although the camera focused solely on Valentine and Proteus during the offer, Silvia had silently shown approval of forgiveness before that. For varying interpretations of the BBC scene, see Patty S. Derrick, *"Two Gents:* A Critical Moment," *Shakespeare on Film Newsletter* (December 1991): 1, 4.

[37] The promptbook for this production was lost after the provincial tour had ended; if it is found, it will be housed in the Shakespeare Centre Library, Stratford-upon-Avon. Reviews used in discussing the production are: Benedict Nightingale, *Times,* 19 April 1991 and 15 October 1992; John Peter, *Sunday Times,* 21 April; Michael Billington, *Guardian* 19 April; Rex Gibson, *Times Educational Supplement,* 3 May: 25; Paul Nelsen, *Shakespeare Bulletin* 9, no. 4 (Fall 1991): 15-17; Thomas Clayton, "The Climax of *The Two Gentlemen of Verona:* Text and performance at the Swan Theatre, Stratford-upon-Avon, 1991," *Shakespeare Bulletin* 9, no. 4 (Fall 1991): 17-19; Robert Smallwood, "Shakespeare at Stratford-upon-Avon, 1991," *Shakespeare Quarterly* 43 (1992): 350-53. Also passages from the following, as quoted by Clayton from the *London Theatre Record,* 9-22 April 1991: Paul Taylor, *Independent,* 19 April; Claire Armistead, *Financial Times,* 19 April; Carole Waddis, *What's On,* 19 April; Charles Spencer, *Daily Telegraph,* 19 April; Rod Dungate, *Tribune* 3 May.

[38] SETTING AND MUSIC: *Times,* 19 Apr. ("Coward dressing gowns," "cunningly chosen,"); Smallwood, 351, and *Sunday Times* (appositeness of period to play); Nelsen, 15 (prelude of music, etc., reference to Masterpiece Theatre); *Times Educational Supplement* (musical interludes); *Guardian* (dislikes interludes, prefers nineteenth-century setting).

[39] VALENTINE: *Times,* 1992. Thurio: *Times,* 1992; Smallwood, 351-52. PROTEUS: Clayton ("likeable"); *Financial Times* ("naive"); Smallwood, 351 ("puzzled innocence," "disturbing . . . smile"); *Times,* 1991 and 1992 (intensity, secrecy, passion); *Independent* ("nervous intensity"); *Sunday Times* (slightly unstable). JULIA AND SILVIA: Smallwood, 351; *Guardian* (Julia, "jaunty"); *Sunday Times* (considers both women warm,

lively); Nelsen, 16 (emphasizes "deconstruction"). LAUNCE: Smallwood, 352 (detailed description); *Sunday Times* ("hangdog dignity"). SPEED: Smallwood, 352. DUKE: *Sunday Times; Times,* 1991; Nelsen, 17. Note that the second *Times* review was for the revival at the Barbican; descriptions of Valentine, Proteus, and Thurio are similar to those in the original review but fuller, possibly reflecting further development in the acting.

[40] A similar parallel had been used the previous year in the Acting Company's touring production (U.S.A.), but, in our opinion, the unrestrained burlesque of the production as a whole canceled out (at least for the average spectator) any serious effect beyond a momentary shock. See, however, Jean Peterson's interesting review in *Shakespeare Bulletin,* 9, no. 1 (Winter, 1991): 33-34.

[41] CLIMAX AND ENDING: Nelsen, 16 ("echoing . . . act one," "outrageous"—he still considered the women victims); *What's On* ("great poignancy"); *Guardian* ("conflicting emotions"); *Independent* ("flesh[ing] out"); Clayton, 18 (description of Silvia's actions, abstruse interpretation of Valentine's offer, "crux" not evident); Smallwood, 352-53 (description of scene, Lynch's smile, simple interpretation of offer—the one we accept); *Tribune* ("near-impossible," "riveting," "plausible"); *Sunday Times* (previous skeptic persuaded by actors); *Daily Telegraph* ("risible"); HIT OF THE SEASON: The popularity continued next season at the Barbican in London. By the end of the tour, however, the production had evidently lost its sparkle. See Jeremy Kingston, *Times,* 16 December 1993.

[42] *Manchester Evening News,* 20 April 1938; *Times,* 3 April 1958; Peter Lewis, *Daily Mail,* 18 July 1968.

[43] PHILLIPS: Harold Hobson, *Sunday Times,* 26 July 1970 (approves "dark angel"); *Oxford Mail,* 25 July 1970 (pretentious). THACKER: Smallwood, *Shakespeare Quarterly* 43 (1992): 352.

[44] HUNT: *Examiner,* 24 April 1808: 266. ABOUT MACREADY: *Argus,* 1 January 1842: 10; *Theatrical Journal,* 8 January 1842: [9].

Source: *"The Two Gentlemen of Verona* on Stage: Protean Problems and Protean Solutions," in *Shakespeare's Sweet Thunder: Essays on the Early Comedies,* edited by Michael J. Collins, University of Delaware Press, 1997, pp. 126-54.

Gender Trouble in *Twelfth Night*

Casey Charles, *University of Montana*

The emergence of queer studies in the academy has led to many influential rereadings of Renaissance works, including those of Shakespeare.[1] While *Twelfth Night* continues to be one of the major textual sites for the discussion of homoerotic representation in Shakespeare, interpretive conclusions about the effect of same-sex attraction in this comedy are divided, especially in light of the natural "bias" of the heterosexual marriages in act 5.[2] The relationship between Antonio and Sebastian has proven the most fertile ground for queer inquiry; for example, Joseph Pequigney recently has set out, in New-Critical fashion, to prove the "sexual orientation" of these two characters as unquestionably "homosexual" in a play whose "recurring theme" is "bisexuality."[3] Although Pequigney's observations are refreshing as well as important, "The Two Antonios and Same-Sex Love" unproblematically applies contemporary constructions of sexual identity to an early modern culture in which the categories of homo- and bisexuality were neither fixed nor associated with identity. In fact, as I will argue, *Twelfth Night* is centrally concerned with demonstrating the uncategorical temper of sexual attraction.

The other main focus of queer study in this drama continues to be the relationship between the Countess Olivia and the cross-dressing Viola/Cesario, though critics, tellingly, have discussed the lesbian erotics that are integral to the first three acts of the play much less often.[4] In her recent *Desire and Anxiety: The Circulation of Sexuality in Shakespearean Drama*, Valerie Traub has acknowledged the lesbian overtones of the erotic scenes between Olivia and Viola as part of what she calls the play's "multiple erotic investments"; but her careful and ground-breaking study warns us that Viola's homoerotic investment is not celebrated in the play and concludes that *Twelfth Night* is less "comfortably" open in its representation of the "fluid circulation" of desire than *As You Like It*.[5] In my view, the Olivia-Viola affair is more central to *Twelfth Night* than previously has been acknowledged. This centrality—along with the homoerotics found in relations between Antonio and Sebastian as well as between Orsino and his page—establish same-sex erotic attraction as a "major theme" in the play, to use Pequigney's shopworn term. But this theme functions neither as an uncomplicated promotion of a modern category of sexual orientation nor, from a more traditional perspective, as an ultimately contained representation of the licensed misrule of saturnalia.[6] The representation of homoerotic attraction in *Twelfth Night* functions rather as a means of dramatizing the socially constructed basis of a sexuality that is determined by gender identity.

Judith Butler's critique of the notion that there are fixed identities based on the existence of genital difference provides a useful model for understanding how *Twelfth Night* uses the vagaries of erotic attraction to disrupt paradigms of sexuality. In *Gender Trouble,* Butler argues that the cultural meanings that attach to a sexed body—what we call gender—are theoretically applicable to either sex. Initially, Butler questions the idea that there is an essential, prediscursive subjectivity that attaches to the biology of either male of female, arguing that the "production of sex *as* the prediscursive ought to be understood as the effect of the apparatus of cultural constructions designated by *gender.*"[7] In other words, what she calls the law—the cultural, social, and political imperatives of social reality—actually produces and then conceals the "constructedness" that lies behind the notion of an immutable, prediscursive "subject before the law" (2). Her attack on the concept of biological inherence is followed by an equally strong indictment of the "metaphysics of gender substance"—the unproblematic claim that a subject can choose a gendered identity, that the self can "be a woman" or a man (21).

In *Bodies That Matter,* Butler's subsequent work, she partially retreats from this position of radical constructivism, returning to the sexed body by shifting the terms of the debate from the "construction" of "gender" through an interpretation of "sex" to an inquiry into the way regulatory norms "materialize" the sexed body, both in the sense of making it relevant and fixing or "consolidating" it. The reiteration of norms simultaneously produces and destabilizes the category of sex, creating "terrains" and "sedimented effects" that influence the way we understand the sexed body. Even as the process of materialization creates boundaries, surfaces, and contours by which sex is established as heterosexually normative, these strategies of materialization simultaneously expose the exclusions and "gaps" that are the constitutive instabilities inherent in these norms.[8] *Bodies That Matter* seeks to

> understand how what has been foreclosed or banished from the "proper" domain of "sex"—where that domain is secured through a heterosexualizing imperative—might at once be produced as a troubling return, not only as an *imaginary* contestation that effects a failure in the workings of the inevitable law, but as an enabling disruption, the occasion for a radical rearticulation of the symbolic horizon in which bodies come to matter at all.

[23]

In both *Gender Trouble* and *Bodies That Matter* the primary way that the categories of sex are both established and disrupted is through a process of what Butler calls "performativity," the means by which the norms of sex are naturalized and substantiated simply by their continual pronouncement as foundational and ideal—by the sheer weight of their repetition. Yet because this reiteration necessarily creates erasures that are the very cites of deconstructive possibilities, the interrogation of those exclusions is one strategy by which the symbolic hegemony of sexuality can be challenged.[9] Although performativity is primarily a discursive practice derived from the notion of the performative in rhetoric, Butler acknowledges cross-dressing as a performative practice in which the "sign" of gender is parodically reiterated in a potentially subversive way. The performance of cross-dressing can be disruptive, Butler argues, to the extent it "reflects the mundane impersonations by which heterosexually ideal genders are performed" (231) or "exposes the failure of heterosexual regimes ever fully to legislate or contain their own ideals" (237).

Within the context of early modern theatrical culture, Shakespeare's *Twelfth Night* functions as a dramatic critique of the ideal norm of imperative heterosexuality in three interrelated ways. First, the effects of Viola's cross-dressing point to the socially constructed nature of gender in Shakespeare's play. Secondly, Shakespeare's drama interrogates the exclusionary nature of the constructed categories of sex and challenges the symbolic hegemony of heterosexuality by producing representations or "citations" of same-sex love between Viola and Olivia as well as Antonio and Sebastian. Lastly, I will argue that the final act, through a series of improbable turns of plot and phrase, exposes the failure of heterosexual "regimes ever fully to legislate or contain their own ideals."

I. The Renaissance Context: "I, poor monster" (2.2.33)[10]

The early modern English theatre, unlike its counterparts in other European countries, maintained the practice of using all-male acting companies to perform the parts of both men and women. Thus, an element of what Butler calls the "denaturalization" of gender difference is built into the structure of Elizabethan stage convention, and Shakespeare's *Twelfth Night,* like many other plays of the period, dramatizes the consequences of this ambiguity by casting its heroine Viola, played by a boy, as a character who cross-dresses as the male page Cesario.[11] In the doubly androgynous role of male actor playing a woman playing a man, Viola/Cesario must literally perform the role of the male; her success before the aristocratic Orsino and Olivia consequently points to the constructedness and performative character of gender itself. In other Renaissance critical venues, the concept of performance in social roles has been discussed convincingly by Stephen Greenblatt as

"self-fashioning" and by others in relation to the role of the courtier in Castiglione's famous treatise.[12] Shakespeare's *Twelfth Night* is arguably about the fashioning of gender. This staging of gender imitation by Viola, the performance of her gender performance, uses her disguise and her identity with her brother Sebastian as vehicles to demonstrate that erotic attraction is not an inherently gendered or heterosexual phenomenon.[13] The homoerotic and cross-gendered disruptions that ensue, finally, operate within a world that is properly named Ill-lyria in order to demonstrate how the phenomenon of love itself operates as a mechanism that destabilizes gender binarism and its concomitant hierarchies. Lovers like Olivia, Orsino, Malvolio, and Antonio construct fantasies that turn the objects of their affection into something more than they are, thereby disrupting the boundaries of compulsory heterosexuality and class-consciousness through the performance of these imaginary fantasies.

Butler's postmodern promotion of gender trouble and its application to Shakespeare's dramatization of sexual identity finds historical support in Renaissance conceptions of masculinity and femininity that, by most accounts, were much less essentialized than today's fixed categories of woman and man. Arguably more patriarchal, more homophobic, and more misogynist than contemporary western culture, the polarized rhetoric of sixteenth- and seventeenth-century Europe nevertheless masks a decided anxiety about what is feared to be the actual fluidity of gender.[14] Studying the pseudomedical treatises of the period, commentators like Thomas Lacquer have argued convincingly that sixteenth-century anatomists viewed female genitalia as merely an inverted male penis and testicles.[15] Renaissance scientist Johann Weyer, for example, states, "although women are feminine in actuality, I would call them masculine in potentiality," indicating the degree to which women were thought of as merely incomplete males, capable on certain traumatic physical occasions—a particularly tall hurdle or heated liaison—of springing forth a penis.[16] What Weyer refuses to admit, in spite of evidence to the contrary from the physician Ausonius, is that men, given the proper circumstances, could as it were suck in their genitalia and become women. "[N]ature always adds, never subtracts," Weyer insists, "always thrusts forth, never holds back, always moves toward the more worthy, never toward the less" (346). Weyer's phobic response to the possibility of reciprocated interchange between men and women, his resort to ethics to uphold his science, is a telling sign that the barriers between masculine and feminine in Renaissance discourse were considerably more blurred than they are today. Although Greenblatt has argued that this homology between the sexes was almost always presented within the rhetorical context of a patriarchal ideology, the possibility of women becoming men and to a lesser extent men becoming women was a real one for the physiologic consciousness of the Elizabethan, who upon viewing the final scene of *Twelfth Night* saw just how interchangeable sex as well as gender were.[17]

The English Renaissance popularity of both the all-male stage companies and plays about gender switching reflects a social and cultural fascination with the subject who symbolized the bodily cite of this gender ambiguity: the hermaphrodite—strictly speaking, a person who possesses both male and female sexual organs, but more broadly defined as an androgynous subject with both male and female characteristics. Ann Rosalind Jones and Peter Stallybrass have argued that Renaissance discussions of hermaphroditism reveal that all attempts to fix gender during this period were essentially "prosthetic," that gender in the Renaissance was "a fetish" that played "with its own fetishistic nature" unhampered by the essentializing claims of medicine and biology in the nineteenth century.[18] Their view is usefully contrasted to that of Greenblatt, whose essay on *Twelfth Night* focuses finally on the way the discourse of androgyny is recuperated into a masculine ethos that supports a patriarchal gender hierarchy.[19] The views of these critics are not, however, mutually exclusive; anxiety over the "prosthetic" nature of gender difference could well have produced the exaggerated rhetoric of misogyny and male superiority common in Renaissance discourse. In a play like Jonson's *Epicoene,* for example, representations of the ambiguity of gender in the silent woman exist in conjunction with the rhetoric of antifeminism in speeches by Truewit and Morose. When Sir Edward Coke, the foremost English jurist of the Renaissance states in his *Commentaries* that "every heir is either a male, or female, or an hermaphrodite, that is both male and female," he is acknowledging the degree to which official discourse sanctioned what Trumbach calls the "third sex."[20] But when the same jurist states that hermaphrodites are required by law to follow either a masculine or female role exclusively, his injunction manifests an official desire to place that third term within a juridical binarism that reduces gender to the binary of sex.

The figure of the hermaphrodite, both on and off the stage, gives Renaissance culture a more ready and accepted focus for the questioning of the ideology of gender, even though the rhetoric of that ideology remains more strident. The Renaissance preoccupation with hermaphrodites in medical discourse accompanies social concerns about transvestites walking the streets of London like Moll Cutpurse or the ingle in Middleton's "Microcynicon," as well as in political concerns about queens who were kings (Elizabeth) and kings who were queens (James I).[21] At the outset, however, we must be careful about readily ascribing erotic motivation or sociological categories to these transgender experiences. Cross-dressing was and is undertaken by different subjects for different reasons.[22] Woman as diverse as Mary Frith (Moll Cutpurse) and

Lady Arabella Stuart passed as males out of economic and social necessity because of the limited public roles for women, while the male ingle in Middleton and the roaring girl walk the streets of London presumably for homoerotic as well as economic reasons. By contrast, an androgynous sixteenth-century portrait of Francois I as Minerva met with approval primarily because the influential philosophy of neoplatonism portrayed the soul as ideally androgynous.[23] Women passed as men and men as women for political and social reasons not necessarily attributable to what we now call homo- or heterosexuality.

Viola's metatheatrical cross-dressing takes place within the transvestite context of the Elizabethan stage convention of all-male repertory companies like the Lord Chamberlain's Men, who were the formal successors to the traveling players that roved the countryside in Tudor England as well as other presumably more rotten states like Denmark. Theatrical transvestism—still extant in Asia—arises out of a configuration of social and economic variables that must be distinguished from nontheatric cross-dressing, though most certainly the restricted freedom of women plays a decided part in both. Scholars have questioned why Elizabethan England and not other European states followed the custom of young male actors playing women's parts. Lisa Jardine has argued that the boy actors, by arousing homoerotic passions for the predominantly male audience in late-sixteenth-century England, presented an unthreatening version of female erotic power. In agreement, Stephen Orgel claims that "homosexuality in this Puritan culture appears to have been less threatening than heterosexuality" because it avoids "a real fear of women's sexuality."[24] These explanations shed less light on the historical development of English stage convention than on the growing controversy over the moral implications of this stage practice in the face of the increased secular and religious power of Puritanism.[25] As early as 1579, Stephen Gosson in the *School of Abuse* accuses the theatre of being "effeminate" and effeminizing.[26] In *Th' Overthrow of Stage-Plays,* Dr. John Rainoldes, citing the injunction in Deuteronomy 22.5 against cross-dressing, condemns the wearing of female dress by boy players as "an occasion of wantoness and lust."[27] By 1633, William Prynne's *Histrio-mastix* proclaims transvestism to be a wickedness "which my Inke is not black enough to discypher." "Players and Play haunters in their secret conclaves play the Sodomites," he announces.[28] As Barish and others have documented, Malvolio and the Puritans finally were "reveng'd on the whole pack" of actors when the theatres were closed in 1642.[29]

The continued enjoyment of all-male repertory companies as well as the insertion of Puritans and cross-dressers into plays by Heywood, Shakespeare, Jonson, Middleton, and Ford evidence how the English theatre became both a literal and figurative staging ground for debates over early modern sexuality. Shakespeare's *Twelfth Night,* first staged in 1601, dramatizes this debate by incorporating it into the heart of its plot.[30] Viola, after her initial introduction as a would-be eunuch, describes herself in her soliloquy as a "poor monster," a Renaissance appellation reserved for unnatural prodigies, including hermaphrodites.[31] Sir Toby will later in jest call her a "firago"—a virago or female warrior (3.4.279). Once Viola realizes the effect of her "disguise" on Olivia, she calls her transvestism "a wickedness, / Wherein the pregnant enemy does much," anticipating Prynne's rhetoric (2.2.26-27). "Could this enemy be Satan?" commentators have conjectured.[32] Instead of blaming herself as the deceiver, Viola displaces the mischief of her disguise on to the device of transvestism itself, which is "pregnant"—ready to hatch—the "wantoness and lust" that serve as the signifiers of same-sex desire in the Renaissance. Viola's surprise and concern over the effect of her deception demonstrates the relational nature of transvestism: it functions as a behavior the motivations for which may wholly differ from the erotic effect it produces on those who confront it.

Viola's androgynous performance as a woman playing a man, like the position of the young men playing women's parts on the Elizabethan stage in general, upsets the restriction of erotic attraction to heterosexual binarism in part because that dualism is collapsed in a single subject. As Viola is a man, her "state is desperate for her master's love," but as Viola is a woman, Olivia's sighs for her must prove "thriftless," under the social condemnation of same-sex love (2.3.35-38). She not only upsets essentialist constructs of gender hierarchy by successfully performing the part of a man as a woman, but in her hermaphroditic capacity as man and woman, I will argue, she also collapses the polarities upon which heterosexuality is based by becoming an object of desire whose ambiguity renders the distinction between homo- and hetero-erotic attraction difficult to decipher. The theatrical convention of crossdressing and the androgyny it comes to symbolize thus challenge the regulatory parameters of erotic attraction through the vehicle of performance, a performance that shows gender to be a part playable by any sex.

Critics have struggled recently to determine the degree to which such theatrical gender trouble affected the social fabric of Renaissance England. Although the plethora of antitheatrical diatribes from 1570 to 1633 would appear to signal a strong reaction among some circles to the influence of the popular theatre, the critical social question has tended to revolve around the circumscribed role of women in the Renaissance in relation to Shakespeare's depiction of strong directorial female characters who cross-dress, such as Portia, Viola, and Rosalind. While Catherine Belsey and Phyliss Rackin argued first that "stage illusion radically subverted the gender division of the Elizabethan world,"

new historicists like Stephen Greenblatt and Howard have more recently made claims that the Globe operated as a world in itself, a place of stage and licensed misrule, which had less effect on the diminishing power of women in Renaissance England.[33] Even if the popular performance of Shakespeare's comedies did not coincide with social change for women in late-sixteenth-century England, this lack of coincidence does not necessarily warrant a conclusion that the Elizabethan theatre was socially ineffectual. If the relative power of woman *was* diminished in Renaissance England, the causes of that reduction were as much due to religious and political forces as they were to mechanisms of cultural appropriation.

The larger debate over whether cultural representation has the capacity to subvert and influence social reality or is usually contained by a political matrix that limits its power is not only raging today over questions of pornography and violence on television, but is important for purposes of *Gender Trouble* and *Twelfth Night* because both Butler and Shakespeare rely upon performance as a theoretical means of shaking the foundations of the metaphysics of binarism and gender hierarchy. If that performance is contained or circumscribed within the saturnalia or "green world" of comedic convention, its social and political utility is mitigated. Although the effects of literary discourse are rarely as pronounced as the slue of suicides that followed the publication of *The Sorrows of Young Werther* or the gang fights that took place outside the movie houses after *Boulevard Nights,* Shakespeare's transvestite comedies are safely counted as part of a discursive explosion concerning questions of gender and sexuality, an explosion that included texts as disparate as Sidney's *New Arcadia,* James I's *Letters,* and Marston's satires. In his antitheatrical tract *Histrio-mastix,* Prynne claims that the popular theatre not only promoted sodomitical practices among the theatregoers, but also encouraged effeminacy and sodomitical practices in the general population as well.[34]

For a stage production in Elizabethan England to occur under the purview of an autocratic and censorious monarchy does not mean that the terms of that play's representation necessarily replicate the terms of that matrix of political power. Ironically, the historicist quest to determine whether Shakespeare's plays or other texts actually produced social trends is finally dependent for its conclusions on an examination of texts themselves—diaries, cases, speeches, satires, and last but not least plays. Monique Wittig theorizes that language is a set of acts repeated over time that produce reality effects that are eventually perceived as "facts."[35] The text and the play *Twelfth Night* is an act of language both as it was performed in the Globe in 1601 and as it is read by undergraduates preparing to cast or ignore votes on anti-gay rights initiatives. When Shakespeare's play represents gender and sex in a certain way, it is engaging, from the viewpoint of textual materialists like Wittig, in an act of domination and compulsion, a performative that creates a social reality by promoting a certain discursive and perceptual construction of the body. Historicists in search of containment narratives that reinstate a monolithic patriarchy are not only engaging in what Butler calls the determinism behind a universal, hegemonic notion of masculine domination but also forgetting that Shakespeare's play is part of a contemporary canon of literature that the academy is requiring students to read and take seriously—nothing being more serious than Shakespeare's sexual comedies. Which is not to say that women in Renaissance England—or now for that matter—were free of social, political, and religious oppression; yet to extrapolate from this historical trend that Shakespeare's play was and is largely ineffectual or recuperated or contained by larger social and political forces is, I think, an argument that both overlooks the implications of our own inescapable historicity as contemporary readers and fails to consider fully the ways in which textual power operates through complicated, contradictory methods.

Shakespeare's comedies are sometimes read teleologically for reasons that are as ideological as they are aesthetic. Whether under the rubric of a renewal of normality or of patriarchal containment, the categorical heterosexuality that act 5 hastily produces as the solution to the erotic problems explored in the bulk of the play has become the definitive statement of *Twelfth Night's* perspective, while the possibility of interpreting the conclusion as an ironic retraction in keeping with the medieval tradition remains less appealing to the modern reader. When C. L. Barber suggests that Shakespeare's festive comedies use the sexual and social upheaval of conventional saturnalia in order to renew the meaning of normal sexual relations, he may be overlooking the possibility that Shakespeare's play is as much about the unconventional treatment of erotic attraction in the development of the drama as it is about the conventional romance ending in marriage, as much about Viola fending off Olivia's unknowingly lesbian protestations as about Orsino's decision to marry his page once she retrieves her female habit from the sea captain in the last act.[36]

II. "I am the man" (2.2.24)

If part of the problem with the recent criticism of *Twelfth Night* comes from a proclivity on the part of some to reduce the concerns of gender studies to the us-against-them binarism of traditional feminism, Shakespeare's play arguably introduces patterns of homoerotic representation in order to disrupt that binarism and to show how gender identities that uphold such duality are staged, performed, and "playable" by either sex. Viola/Cesario is the primary performer: she is that strange androgynous "monster," that eunuch/castrato/

page or "script" who, through her gender ambiguity, retunes the music of love that has fallen out of key under the belated courtly scripts that the Count and Countess banally reenact in Illyria. Like the drag queen Butler discusses in *Gender Trouble,* Viola/Cesario demonstrates a parodic awareness of the three contingent dimensions of her corporeality: her anatomical sex as a boy actor, her gender identity in the drama as a woman washed ashore, and her gender performance as the page Cesario in the employ of the sexist Orsino.

Cesario points to himself as actor or performer in the metadramatic comments he makes in his first encounter with Olivia in act 1, scene 5. Having reluctantly been asked to woo the countess on behalf of the man she loves, Cesario initially feels conflicted about delivering the "speech" he has "penned" and "conned" (1.5.174-75). When Olivia asks where he has come from, Cesario replies, "I can say little more than I have studied, and that question's out of my part" (1.5.179-80). When he admits to Olivia that he is not what he plays, the metaphor of theatricality in this scene continues in even greater earnest. Cesario is alluding, in his staginess, to more than the fact that he is a she in this drama; he is reminding us, when he tells us that he took "great pains" to study his "poetical" "commission," that he is an actor playing a part, a boy actor playing the part of a woman playing a part of a man (1.5.190, 195-96). Given the common Elizabethan bawdy pun on the word "parts" as sexual genitalia, this confluence of meaning between the theatrical and the sexual has particular significance for *Twelfth Night's* staging of the performative homology between the two. When Olivia presses Cesario to divulge his identity ("What are you?" [1.5.215]), he cryptically tells her that what he is and what he would be are "as secret as maidenhead," pointing primarily to his gender identity as Viola in the drama but also alluding to the male virginity that Sebastian will admit to in the final act when he tells Olivia she will marry a man and a maid (1.5.218-19). The boy actor's and Cesario's maiden*head* is also Viola's maiden*hood;* the part he plays depends on the hiding of the nature of his private part(s).

Even though Cesario goes out of his text in 1.5 when he lifts the veil of his rival Olivia with jealous interest and commends her unparalleled beauty, his growing interest in Olivia reminds us that Viola is now adlibbing as Cesario and that this impromptu performance, which points to her servant's role as disguise, is in many ways more endearing than the stiff delivery of an identity-bound young man. In fact, improvisation allows Cesario/Viola to enact her third role as agent of her master: the boy actor playing a woman playing a male page who is asked to act out the passion of his master. "If I did love you in my master's flame" (1.5.268), Cesario proclaims, as he warms up to his poetic performance, he would

Make me a willow cabin at your gate,
And call upon my soul within the house;
Write loyal cantons of contemned love,
And sing them loud even in the dead of
   night;
Halloo your name to the reverberate hills,
And make the babbling gossip of the air
Cry out "Olivia!"

[1.5.273-77]

In this performative address, in which the poet speaks the loyal canton s/he has written, Viola/Cesario is the antithesis of Patience on a monument. In Viola's role as a self-conscious male mediator between man and woman, s/he becomes a better—a more eloquent, persuasive—man than the man s/he represents. In fact, Cesario plays his part so well that Olivia immediately catches the plague of lovesickness, a sickness which, from the point of view of gendered identity in the play, casts her as an unwitting lesbian. The upshot of this self-reflexive gender confusion is a layered combination of ironic plays on performance that self-consciously point to boy actor/Viola/Cesario/Orsino's agent's uncanny ability to *be* what he *does,* to adopt his identity through imitation, through an art that not only outdoes nature, but shows nature herself to be art. The "babbling gossip" of the natural element air in its reverberate identity as Echo will take on the poetic artifice of the singing poet, crying out, "Olivia." Echo is a fitting mythological analogue for the imitative Viola/Cesario, whose performative roles as actor and agent make her a master of reverberation.

When Olivia falls in love with the page we know to be a woman, she realizes that the imaginary fantasy of love has taught her that "ourselves we do not owe [own]" (5.1.314-15), that the self is not an entity within the control of an ego-identity. The unorthodoxy of a countess's infatuation with a servant is enough to prove to Olivia that she has, as a result of her passion, fallen into "abatement and low price," but the dramatic nexus between social degradation and homoerotic attraction— not without its historical analogues—is an even more troubling development. Alan Bray and others have identified the relationship of servant/master as one of the social arenas in which homoerotic interaction commonly took place.[37] Admittedly, Cesario/Viola is not Olivia's servant, but Cesario's ostensible estate is well below that of the Countess, and she takes liberties, such as the gift of her ring, which would not be expected to occur between social equals. Although until recently most scholarship in Renaissance homoerotics has dealt almost exclusively with male-male relationships, there is no reason to believe that lesbian practices were not equally as common within the protected hierarchal environment of the domestic household. In fact, erotic practices between women may have been less threatening and more overlooked within domestic spheres. Not only was sex between women

not explicitly prohibited under the 1533 sodomy statute enacted by Henry VIII (in force until 1967), but women were also confined within the household to a much greater degree than men.[38] Condemned by St. Paul in Romans 1:26 and Aquinas in his *Summa,* lesbian sexual practice continued to be an egregious offence outside of England, as Greenblatt has demonstrated in his discussion of the hanging in France of Marie le Marcis for falsely impersonating a man and marrying a woman. Yet even on the Continent, where women were condemned for homosexual practice until before the French Revolution, records of premodern persecutions remain scarce.

The relative dearth of lesbian prosecutions in early modern Europe is indicative of a history even more hidden than that of male homosexuality.[39] The combination of a crime too nefarious to name and a set of perpetrators officially silenced and obedient within a predominantly patriarchal culture has made lesbian history a "blank," a closet within a closet, that scholars are only now beginning to attempt to reconstruct.[40] Cultural representation of relations between women have recently garnered some attention. The Fiordispina-Bradamante episode in Ariosto's *Orlando Furioso* and Philoclea's love of the apparently Amazon Zelmane in the *New Arcadia* are well-known examples from the romance tradition, while Donne's "Sappho to Philaenis" and Katherine Philip's Restoration love poetry are English verses that must be counted as part of this presumably lost tradition.

Jorge de Montemayor's *La Diana,* a sixteenth-century Spanish romance translated into English by Bartholomew Yong in 1598, is an important analogue to Shakespeare's *Twelfth Night,* which contains more than one episode of same-sex love between women cast under the narrative rubric of transvestite performance.[41] In Book Two of *La Diana* Felismena disguises herself as the page Valerio when her beloved Don Felis is sent to the Portuguese court by his father. After enlisting in the service of her unwitting Don Felis, Valerio/Felismena adopts the same role as Viola/Cesario, wooing another woman on behalf of the man she loves and causing that woman, Celia, to fall in love with her instead. In this more tragic rendering of the Italian stage comedy *Gl'Inganni* (1562), Montemayor, unlike Shakespeare, decides not to create a Sebastian-like clone to meet the romance convention of reconciliation. Instead Celia—the Olivia counterpart—dies heartbroken when she learns that the male page with whom she has fallen in love has a stronger affection for his male master than herself. The performance of gender in the story of Felismena leads finally to a suicide that presumably arises out of an assumption by Celia of a male homoerotic relationship that undermines her own unwitting lesbian love for Felismena. *La Diana,* by some accounts the most fashionable Spanish book in England at the close of the sixteenth century, establishes a prose precedent for the representation of erotic relations between women through the mechanism of transvestite performance.[42]

In a theatrical forum more public and regulated than the spheres of private circulation and limited publication of early domestic fiction and poetry, Shakespeare's representation of same-sex attraction between women must even more cautiously use indirection to find direction out. In her discussion of the homoerotics of Shakespearean comedy, Valerie Traub has argued that the limitation of the consequences of theatrical cross-dressing to the evocation of male homoeroticism ignores the ambiguities that transvestism creates and reinstates the restriction of gender binarism into the discussion of homoerotics.[43] Women were in attendance at the Globe, and there is no reason to ignore female homoerotics as part of the disruptions that cross-dressing explores. The gender ambiguity of Viola/Cesario in fact sets the stage for the representation of a plethora of desires: homoerotic attraction between Orsino and Cesario, heterosexual attraction between Orsino and Viola, and lesbian attraction between Viola and Olivia. The last relationship is in many ways the most compelling and time-consuming in the play.[44] Ostensibly, the passion that Olivia finds herself unable "to hide" by means of "wit or reason" is directed at a young man, but dramatic irony tells us that her hidden passion is for a maid (3.1.153-54). When, after their first encounter, Olivia sends Cesario her symbolic ring for him to slip his finger into, Cesario/Viola, in her famous soliloquy, suddenly realizes, "I am the man: if it be so, as 'tis, / Poor lady, she were better love a dream" (2.2.24-25). Viola is acknowledging that her performance as a man has out-manned every other suitor of Olivia in Illyria, but she also realizes that this performance has led to a homoerotic attraction more socially and legally untenable than an illusory dream. Olivia is not entirely to blame for this sudden attraction, as Traub has pointed out.[45] Viola/Cesario, whose original inclination was to stay with the Countess, has gone out of her text in their first meeting, taking the liberty of lifting Olivia's veil, and playing the part of her wooer with more fervency than expected. "But if you were the devil," Cesario exclaims upon seeing her face, "you are fair" (1.5.255).

In her soliloquy that follows their first meeting, Viola/Cesario unquestionably blames the wickedness of her disguise and the frail nature of women for this instigation of bi-gendered passion, but this retreat into essentialism is undermined by Viola's unnatural status as boy actor, female character, and male page, which demonstrates that although frailty may be the name of woman, the name of woman is applicable to both sexes in this play:

> My master loves her dearly
> And I, poor monster, fond as much on him,
> And she, mistaken, seems to dote on me:

> What will become of this? As I am a man,
> My state is desperate for my master's love,
> As I am a woman (now alas the day!)
> What thriftless sighs shall poor Olivia
>   breathe?

> [2.2.32-39]

Viola/Cesario is the poor hermaphroditical monster or, in another context, the master/mistress who has stirred the homoerotic passion of Olivia by incorporating the polarities of sexual and gender difference into the unity of her maddening disguise, thereby representing gender tropes in a manner that de-forms, de-naturalizes, and de-constructs their oppositional status. The dear fondness and doting, moreover, is not altogether gender specific; it occurs among all three in this love triangle. When Viola attempts to articulate the "knot" of her predicament, she finds that her gendered figures of speech are subject to ironies that unsettle the heterosexual bent of her identity as the lover of Orsino. Editors insist that "desperate" in this context means "hopeless," but when Cesario tells us that as a man he is desperate for his master's love, the male homoerotic irony of such a statement again problematizes her desire to be sincere in her heterosexual identity. As a woman, she laments, even pities, the profitless sighs that Olivia must undergo both in her mistaken doting on a page and in her capacity as a woman in love with another woman in a world where such behavior was literally unheard of.

Despite Cesario's protestations, Olivia continues her amorous assault until the end of the play, unwilling to take no for an answer. In act 3, the haughty Olivia is willing to ask Cesario what he thinks of her:

> Viola: That you do think you are not what you are.
> Olivia: If I think so, I think the same of you.
> Viola: Then think you right; I am not what I am.
> Olivia: I would you were as I would have you be.
> Viola: Would it be better, madam, than I am?
> I wish it might, for now I am your fool.
> [3.1.141-45]

In dramatic context, Viola is attempting to fend off Olivia by telling her that she is not really in love as she thinks she is because Cesario is not in fact a man; however, in textual isolation this witty repartee functions as a profound if unsystematic critique of gender identity as a boundary to licit love. Viola assumes that Olivia's love would vanish if she knew Cesario's true sex, but the persistent Countess reminds the heroic androgynene that s/he too thinks s/he is someone s/he is not, thinks s/he is not in love with Olivia when in fact the pity s/he shows her is a form of love. When

Cesario almost steps out of his part and admits with Iago-esque frankness that he is not what he is, the text again shifts into its self-reflexive gear, reminding both audience and reader that subjectivity is constructed by epistemology; it does not exist in some pre-Cartesian substance that instantly assigns a bedrock of transcendent traits to either female or male. Mistaking Sebastian for Viola, Feste will later remind the audience of the fiction of gender identity: "Nothing that is so, is so," he surmises, as he looks at Viola's identical male twin (4.1.8-9). His sly critique of what Butler calls the "metaphysics of gender substance" continues in his role as Sir Topas, the Pythagorean curate, in act 4. "'That that is, is,'" the learned cross-dressing Sir Topas proclaims, "I, being Master Parson, am Master Parson" (4.1.14-15). Feste's mock tautology points to the performative nature of what we assume to be ontological essence. This jester turned sermonizer is who he is because he *plays* who he is; in the same way Viola can be the male Cesario by transvestite performance.

Similarly, who Viola/Cesario is or is not, as a subject, is as much a figure of Olivia's and Viola's imaginations as it is a stable, gendered identity, the revelation of which will undo some mistaken affection (4.2.15-16). The dialogue that Olivia and Cesario have in act 3 not only dramatizes the instability of the subject as a determinate entity that exists outside of social interaction but also shows how the performative self is further complicated by the fictions or fantasies played out in the imaginary mental constructions of those in love. When Olivia tells Cesario that she wishes he were the reciprocating lover she would like him to be, she is divulging the way in which lovers, by reason of their imaginary dreams, act as agents in the disruption of normative identity politics. Put simply, the lover, like Olivia, turns the object of her love into something more than he or she is.[46] Olivia's amorous thinking reshapes this male servant into the gentleman of her dreams, while in fact that gentleman is a woman—a Viola whose anagrammatic name shapes the reverberate echoes that feed the Countess's narcissism. Cesario recognizes that Olivia's amorous strategy is turning him or her into a fool, that her narcissistic aggressivity is the consequence of an emotion that both disrupts determined notions of subjectivity while simultaneously transferring its own ideal notions of self on to the object of love.

Yet surely, critics have argued, the identity and gender trouble produced by Viola's disguise is largely undermined by her ultimately heterosexual aim; after all, the object of her desire is Orsino.[47] Butler herself warns that heterosexuality can augment its hegemony through the denaturalization of cross-dressing, when those denaturalizing parodies work to "reidealize heterosexual norms *without* calling them into question."[48] Unlike Moll Cutpurse or even Portia, Viola, Jean Howard argues, does not use her disguise to gain power, but only to secure her position as a dutiful wife. She never

actually challenges patriarchy.[49] By privileging intentionality over action or what Butler calls performance, these important objections to my line of argument assume that the subversive effects of Viola's disguise are vitiated by the sexual orientation of the character Viola, while it is my position that the language of the play questions the metaphysics of orientation and intentionality, replacing them with a concept of performativity.

Even if Viola does not actively challenge patriarchy in her erotic goal, she nevertheless questions its validity in her disguised wooing of her master in act 2, scene 4. In discussing earlier scenes, both Bruce Smith and Pequigney have commented upon the homoerotic overtones of Orsino's sudden infatuation with his new domestic servant, to whom he "unclaps . . . the book even of [his] secret soul," delighting in Cesario's "smooth and rubious" lips and "shrill and sound" voice, which he calls a "small pipe" comparable to a "maiden's organ" (1.4.31-33).[50] This ambiguous affection for his male servant sets the stage for their discussion of the differing capacities of male and female amorous longing in act 2. When asked by Orsino, Viola/Cesario admits that she is in love with a "w oman," but one close to the Count in "years" and "complexion" (2.4.26-28). When Orsino complains that no woman's heart is capacious enough to hold the passion that a man feels, Viola/Cesario challenges him by passionately telling her own story in the third person: "My father had a daughter lov'd a man / As it might be perhaps, were I a woman, / I should your lordship" (2.4.107-9). The ironies of gender that inform the performative layers of this scene render Orsino's sexist construction of love highly suspect. As a servant, Cesario boldly challenges his master's complacent speculation even as Viola is reiterating the strength of her own passion under the risk of revealing her disguise. But this scene critiques Orsino's assumptions not merely by contrasting traditional female patience to male boasting; both those positions are thrown into question by the posture of Viola's performativity—by the very fact that she is commanding the discursive space of this scene. Her impersonation of herself in her autobiographical history, her objectification of herself as quiet, allegorical Patience on a monument is a *verbal* tour de force ironically iterated by a woman. Viola reveals her concealment, impatiently describes her patience and thereby points to the constructedness of both Orsino's and her own depictions of gender paradigms. Meanwhile, as the boy Cesario tells the story of his sister who is himself, Orsino continues to fall in love with his/her "masterly" speech (2.4.22). This scene thus challenges patriarchy not by reidealizing the heterosexual norms of passion-vowing males and patiently passive females, but by calling those constructions into question through portraying the cross-dressing female as a figure who deconstructs the categories of gender by ironically reiterating them in a context that depicts their reversal.

III. "I do adore thee so, / That danger shall seem sport" (2.1.46)

In counterpoint to the ironies and ambiguities that closet the lesbian subtext in the main courtship of *Twelfth Night,* the representation of male homoeroticism in this comedy is by contrast glaring and ultimately inexplicable. Metaphors of adoration, devotion, and passionate oblation saturate the heated but highly stylized rhetorical interactions between Sebastian, the twin brother of Viola, and Antonio, the erstwhile pirate, who redeems Sebastian "[f]from the rude sea's enrag'd and foamy mouth" and gives his life back to him, adding thereto his "love, without retention or restraint / All his in dedication" (5.1.76-80). Neither the Ciceronian tradition of male friendship nor attention to the intensity of homosocial male bonding in the Renaissance can explain away Antonio's melancholia. He is prepared, we learn, to spend three months with his foundling after rescuing him, prepared to risk his life to follow Sebastian to Illyria (where he is wanted on criminal charges) prepared to give this young man his purse, and prepared finally to intercede on his behalf in the midst of a duel: "I do *adore* thee so," Antonio states, "That danger shall seem *sport,* and I will go" (2.1.46-47; emphasis mine). Like Olivia, Antonio has "exposed himself pure for love"—an exposure doubly dangerous because its gendered object represents an unmentionable anathema to the religious and judicial laws that officially condemned such homoerotic behavior. To put this notable pirate's passion in perspective, we need turn no further than the pages of *Billy Budd* to find a trace of the sodomitical practices that traditionally have been ascribed to men at sea. In the seventeenth century, according to B. R. Burg, English sea rovers and buccaneers were renowned for their sodomitical behavior.[51] Antonio may be a part of this historical tradition, while at the same time he may be another one of Shakespeare's male characters—Horatio, Enobarbus, Patroclus, Antonio in *The Merchant of Venice,* to name a few—who are devoted to other males.

Antonio disrupts normative constructions of gender by enacting his homoerotic passion in a character that is the most traditionally "masculine" in the play. He is aggressive, bold, eloquent, faithful, uncompromising—traits which are ironically alignable with his counterpart Olivia and also ironically employed in the service of a homoerotic rather than heterosexual compulsion. Some critics recently have argued that male homoerotics were not associated with effeminacy until later in the seventeenth century, Antonio's machismo being a case in point.[52] Whatever the validity of this point of social history, Antonio exists as a direct foil to the hopelessly sycophantic but presumably heterosexual courtier, Sir Andrew Aguecheek. Although Antonio's histrionic intensity is tempered by little or none of the gender irony ascribable to Viola, the play's dramatic representation of him as one of the most heroic and intense characters in the drama points to an alternative domain of cultural intelligibility in which the significations of heterosexual masculinity are repeated within a context that directly subverts the rigid codes of heterosexual practice.

The relationship between Antonio and Sebastian even subverts some of the accepted parameters of homoerotic practice in the Renaissance. Although Pequigney calls it "the classic relationship, wherein the mature lover serves as guide and mentor to the young beloved," this facile reading overlooks a number of factors that make this homoerotic relation strangely unclassic, tellingly noncategorical.[53] Alan Bray has tried recently to delineate the difference between the often-similar rhetoric of male friendship and sodomy in the English Renaissance. He concludes that the passionate discourse of male friendship did not imply sexual practices as long as the interlocutors were both assumed to be gentlemen, their relationship personal not mercenary, and their interaction not disruptive of the social order.[54] Despite Orsino's epithets "notable pirate" and "salt-water thief" (5.1.66), Antonio denies his piracy, bears himself as a gentleman consistently, and is known for his fame, honor, and kindness. Antonio's loaning of his purse to Sebastian is an act of generosity, not payment. Although the sea-captain is presumably of lower social standing than Sebastian, the play does not provide sufficient evidence that their interaction is unnatural or disruptive of the social order. Antonio's homoerotic attraction contains few of the social clues of the sodomite that Bray outlines.[55] What *is* unusual in this relationship is that Antonio, although of lower social status than Sebastian, is the more powerful and principled figure, a circumstance that places their connection outside the scope of the usual master/servant, teacher/student matrices that social historians indicate as potentially homoerotic.[56] Similarly, though critics assume Antonio to be older and more experienced than Sebastian because of his sea-battle experience, the play does not make the age difference between the two so discernible that this relationship falls squarely within the man/boy paradigm often associated with homoeroticism in this period.[57] Nor, finally, can this couple be subsumed under accepted categories of gender binarism. Although Antonio's more intense ardor and Sebastian's possibly homoerotic name might lead to assumptions about their masculinity and femininity, both are proven swordsmen; and, ironically, the resistant Sebastian is the character who readily adopts a heterosexual role when he accepts Olivia's marital offer.[58] Even in its depiction of same-sex love, *Twelfth Night* departs from patterns that would subsume homoeroticism under entrenched gender stereotypes. The dramatization of the marginal erotic relationship of Antonio and Sebastian carefully avoids a rendition that reinstates the excluded outside of homoeroticism as a simplified reflection of heterosexual roles within a same-sex context.

IV. "Thou hast put him in such a dream, that when the image of it leaves him he must run mad" (2.5.193-94)

Like Olivia's love for Cesario/Viola, Antonio's love for Sebastian partakes in a psychological enactment of fantasy that functions as an inward performance of gender trouble. Mistaking Viola for her twin brother in act 3, "even in a minute" Antonio has his faith undermined by the confused Cesario (3.4.370-72), who is unable to return Antonio's purse because he does not have it. In his crestfallen state, Antonio announces that he has done "devotion" to Sebastian's "image" with a "sanctity of love," but that this "god" has proved a "vile idol" unworthy of Sebastian's handsome features (3.4.374-75). Antonio's passionate disenchantment—reminiscent of Othello's—is based on a mistaken interpretation of objective reality, and like the amorous image-making that preceded it, his recasting of Sebastian into the image of a deceiving "devil" partakes of the same process of transference that marked his process of falling in love. He turns his lover into something more than he is through a mentality that seeks finally the attention of the idol that he has created, fashioned, and enacted in the realm of his imaginary fantasy. Although his bitterness is played out within the comedic context of his mistaking a "girl" for his "boy," his virulent disappointment stands in marked contrast to his unexplained silence in the play's final act, when his beloved Sebastian has cavalierly married and when, from a contemporary point of view, Antonio would seem to have more reason to protest. Silence is often the most telling form of disappointment.

Antonio and Olivia's transformation of their lovers into something more than they are is indicative of a larger pattern in *Twelfth Night* that employs the process of love as an agency in the disruption of gender binarism and social hierarchy. The internalized fantasy of the lover—whereby an Orsino turns Olivia into a Petrarchan goddess or a Malvolio turns her into a Duchess of Malfi—lays the foundation for the legitimization of a social and gender upheaval under the rubric of what Antonio calls the "witch-craft" of love (5.1.74). Orsino sets the stage for this disruption in his opening words:

> O spirit of love, how quick and fresh art thou,
> That notwithstanding thy capacity
> Receiveth as the sea, nought enters there
> Of what validity and pitch so'er,
> But falls into abatement and low price,
> Even in a minute! So full of shapes is fancy,
> That it alone is high fantastical.
>
> [1.1.9-15]

At once capacious and enveloping, love is at the same time ephemeral and destined to disappointment, primarily because of its dependence on an internal fantasy for its sustenance. In Shakespeare's usage, "fancy" connotes both the operation of "love" and "fantasy" or

imagination. The quick and giddy shapes that the lover's imagination generates and transfers on to the object of affection render that object vulnerable to the "abatement and low price" that the realities of compulsory heterosexuality and diverging desire reaffirm in the proverbial fifth act of Shakespeare's comedies. Yet the capacity to create and "perform" those "shapes"—the ability of Olivia to turn Cesario into the perfect lover, of Antonio to idolize Sebastian—remain the fragile but crucial catalysts for the promotion of gender trouble.

Few who read this final scene, upon which much criticism depends, are not troubled by the solutions to the erotic problems that the plot has engendered. For Traub, *Twelfth Night*'s conclusion seems "only ambivalently invested in the 'natural' heterosexuality it imposes," while Pequigney challenges the accepted interpretation that Sebastian has rejected his male lover because he has taken a wife.[59] Olivia's ready acceptance of her beloved's twin as her husband and Orsino's equally mercurial capitulation to his male page who awaits her change of attire add to the delightful but troubling improbability. These unlikelihoods, whether explained as dramatic plot convention or a return to normalcy, expose "the failure of heterosexual regimes ever fully to legislate or contain their own ideals."[60]

Twelfth Night attempts to resolve this trouble by playing on the concept of identity in so far as it means *sameness* as opposed to *individuality*. If the major portion of Shakespeare's plot employs the tropes of performance to show how gender is a melodramatic act rather than an inherent trait of the individuated ego, the ending of the play reaffirms this conclusion by producing a male that is, for all intents and purposes, the same or identical to a female.[61] Viola/Cesario is not only a female successfully playing a male, but her success is confirmed by her fungibility with her twin brother. The reunion of Viola with Sebastian comes after he opportunely is betrothed to an Olivia who mistakes him for Cesario. Seeing Cesario and Sebastian on stage together for the first time, Orsino exclaims "one face, one voice, one habit, and two persons / A natural perspective that is, and is not!" (5.1.214-15). The identity of this twin brother and sister does more than provide a convenient Terencian plot device to untie the erotic knot that the play has created up to this point; this sameness also points to the way in which the essentialism of a "natural perspective" is not always divided into gendered binarism. Nature herself has produced an unnatural perspective that reveals the constructedness of essentialist notions of gender by depicting the collapse of difference. Echoing Troilus's famous speech during his eavesdropping of a Cressida that is and is not, Orsino sees a nature that is capable of copying itself exactly in spite of the natural sex difference between brother and sister that we expect. In the identity of Sebastian and Viola, the play's denouement stages a critique of binarism, a parodic subversion of the dichotomies between female and male, homo- and heterosexual.[62] The result of the appearance of these identical twins in the final act is a decided disruption of the stability of sexual and gender difference and the sense of individuated identity it fosters. Sebastian tells Olivia that even though she would have been contracted to the maid Viola if he had not fortuitously appeared, she is now "betroth'd both to a maid and a man" (5.1.261). He is not only assuring her that he is himself a virgin, but he is also making wanton with the meaning of the word "maid" as a young woman. Sebastian is a character whose similar appearance to his sister gives him a decided resemblance to a maid, but whose identity with Cesario allows him to play the part of a man. Even in this concluding marriage scene, therefore, the play's language produces destabilizing configurations of gender.

The prosthetic nature of gender's supposed inherency is dramatized even further by the role that costume plays in this concluding scene. Once Cesario discloses herself as Sebastian's twin sister, Orsino decides he wants a share in the "happy wrack" of this collapse of gender identity by capitalizing on Cesario's previously proclaimed love for a woman like him; but he continues to address her as "boy" and "Cesario":

> For so you shall be while you are a man;
> But when in other habits you are seen,
> Orsino's mistress and his fancy's queen.
>
> [5.1.385-87]

Like Clerimont in Jonson's *Epicoene,* who uses his "ingle" at home when his mistress is unattainable, Orsino settles for a marriage with his male page. For Orsino, Viola can only establish her true identity by recovering her maiden's weeds from the captain she left in act 1, who now for some reason is under arrest at the behest of Malvolio. Consistent with the import of Renaissance sumptuary laws that regulated dress among classes as well as sexes—laws championed by Malvolian moralists like Gosson and Stubbes—Orsino's final statement indicates, albeit playfully, that Viola will *be* a man until she adopts the "habit" of female attire, until her appearance conforms to the mundane trappings that are the foundations of gender identity. Her gender is dependent upon a factor as easily change-able as her weeds are *pret-a-porter.* Ironically, that attire is still unrecovered at the close of this final scene, as Orsino walks off stage with his Cesario.

While the wonderful discoveries of act 5 make for a tidy if contrived romance ending, below the surface of these marriage knots, with their diluted flavor of an-drogyny, lies an entanglement that transcends the free-dom these characters may gain from a mild subversion of normative gender relations. What is particularly trou-bling about the ending of *Twelfth Night*—and particu-larly important from a perspective beyond the neces-sary upheaval of entrenched gender politics—are the ways in which gender performance in this play, al-though successful in questioning identity, does not necessarily give these characters what they want.[63] The dismantling of the automatic collapse of sex and gen-der in this play, even when successful, does not bring the subject to a new metaphysical substance, to a new place of performative stability. Although Viola achieves her goal of marrying Orsino, the man she is betrothed to has, minutes before, agreed to sacrifice her for the love of Olivia. Arguably Sebastian is satisfied with his surprise catch of the Countess, but his reaction to the appearance of his friend Antonio on the scene gives the audience pause: "Antonio! O my dear Antonio, / How have the hours rack'd and tortur'd me / Since I have lost thee!" (5.1.216-18). How can Olivia have satisfied her desire by mistakenly marrying the enchant-ing Cesario's seeming copy, a stranger as passionately attached to a pirate as herself? The homoerotic ele-ment of the play, while troubling and disruptive in its dramatic development, may not have the power in this final scene to overcome fully the symbolic dictates of compulsory heterosexuality, at least from a perspec-tive of formal kinship relations. Yet even if homoeroti-cism triumphed in *Twelfth Night* and Viola walked off stage arm-in-arm with Olivia and Sebastian with An-tonio, the problems of the irrationality of desire and the instability of identity would not vanish. Desire is not erased by the successful disruption of gender bound-aries; it continues to haunt the subject despite the per-formance of the most fantastic of love's imaginings. Yet the interminable nature of desire and the fantasies of love that are desire's dialectical counterpart serve as important catalysts for the subversion and displace-ment "of those naturalized and reified notions of gen-der that support masculine hegemony and heterosexist power" through strategies of gender trouble.[64]

Notes

[1] See for example, Alan Bray, *Homosexuality in Re-naissance England* (London: Gay Men's Press, 1982); Bruce R. Smith, *Homosexual Desire in Shakespeare's England: A Cultural Poetics* (Chicago: University of Chicago Press, 1991); Gregory W. Bredbeck, *Sodomy and Interpretation: Marlowe to Milton* (Ithaca: Cornell University Press, 1991); Jonathan Goldberg, *Sodome-tries: Renaissance Texts, Modern Sexualities* (Stanford: Stanford University Press, 1992); Valerie Traub, *De-sire and Anxiety: The Circulation of Sexuality in Shake-spearean Drama* (New York: Routledge, 1992); *Queer-ing the Renaissance,* ed. Jonathan Goldberg (Durham: Duke University Press, 1994).

[2] Some important scholars find the subversive elements of the play to be contained within patriarchal struc-tures: see Stephen Greenblatt's conclusion in "Fiction and Friction," in *Shakespearean Negotiations: The Circulation of Social Energy in Renaissance England*

(Berkeley: University of California Press, 1988), 66-93; Jean E. Howard, "Crossdressing, The Theatre, and Gender in Struggle Early Modern England," *Shakespeare Quarterly* 39 (1988): 418-40; and most recently Michael Shapiro, *Gender in Play on the Shakespearean Stage: Boy Heroines and Female Pages* (Ann Arbor: University of Michigan, 1994). Other scholars find the play more transgressive: see Catherine Belsey, "Disrupting Sexual Difference: Meaning and Gender in the Comedies," in *Alternative Shakespeares* (New York: Methuen, 1985); and Phyliss Rackin, "Androgyny, Mimesis, and the Marriage of the Boy Heroine on the English Renaissance Stage," *PMLA* 102 (1987): 29-41.

[3] Joseph Pequigney, "The Two Antonios and Same-Sex Love in *Twelfth Night* and *The Merchant of Venice*," *English Literary Renaissance* 22 (1992): 201, 209.

[4] For a discussion of the implications of crossdressing see, Howard, "Crossdressing"; Rackin, "Androgyny"; Belsey, "Disrupting Sexual Difference"; and Lisa Jardine, "Twins and Transvestites: Gender, Dependency, and Sexual Availability in *Twelfth Night*," in her *Erotic Politics: Desire on the Renaissance Stage* (New York: Routledge, 1992), 27-36, as well as her more complete study, *Still Harping on Daughters: Women and Drama in the Age of Shakespeare* (Brighton: Harvester, 1983).

[5] Valerie Traub, *Desire and Anxiety,* 130, 141.

[6] See C[esar] L[ombardi] Barber, *Shakespeare's Festive Comedy* (Princeton: Princeton University Press, 1959).

[7] Judith Butler, *Gender Trouble: Feminism and the Subversion of Identity* (New York: Routledge, 1990), 7.

[8] Judith Butler, *Bodies That Matter: On the Discursive Limits of "Sex"* (New York: Routledge, 1993), 9-10.

[9] See Butler, *Bodies That Matter,* 12.

[10] Shakespeare, *The Arden Edition of the Works of William Shakespeare: Twelfth Night,* ed. J[ohn] M[aule] Lothian and T[homas] W[allace] Craik (London: Routledge, 1975).

[11] In *Gender in Play* (221-23), Shapiro lists eighty-one English dramas during a period from 1570 to 1642 that portray heroines in male disguise.

[12] See Stephen Greenblatt, *Renaissance Self-Fashioning: From More to Shakespeare* (Chicago: University of Chicago Press, 1980); Frank Wigham, "Interpretation at Court: Courtesy and the Performance-Audience Dialectic," *New Literary History* 14 (1983): 623-39. For the concept of performativity in Shakespeare generally, see Emily C. Bartels, "Breaking the Illu-

sion of Being: Shakespeare and the Performance of Self," *Theatre Journal* 46 (1994): 171-85.

[13] My argument here and elsewhere is indebted to Catherine Belsey's discussion of the play's questioning of conventional models of gendered interaction in "Disrupting Sexual Difference," 16-17.

[14] See Ann Rosalind Jones and Peter Stallybrass, "Fetishizing Gender: Constructing the Hermaphrodite in Renaissance Europe, in *Body Guards: The Cultural Politics of Gender Ambiguity,* ed. Julian Epstein and Kristina Straub (New York: Routledge, 1991), 80-111.

[15] Thomas Lacquer, *Making Sex: Body and Gender from the Greeks to Freud* (Cambridge: Harvard University Press, 1990), 8-10.

[16] Weyer, Johann, *Witches, Devils, and Doctors in the Renaissance: De praestigii daemonum* (Binghamton: Medieval and Renaissance Texts and Studies, 1991), 345-46.

[17] Greenblatt, "Fiction and Friction," 78.

[18] Jones and Stallybrass, "Fetishizing Gender," 105-6.

[19] Greenblatt, "Fiction and Friction," 92-93.

[20] Edward Coke, quoted in Randolph Trumbach, "London's Sapphists: From Three Sexes to Four Genders in the Making of Modern Culture," in *Third Sex, Third Gender: Beyond Sexual Dimorphism in Culture and History,* ed. Gilbert Herdt (New York: Zone, 1994), 119.

[21] In her speech to the troops at Tilbury, Elizabeth states, "I have the body but of a weak and frail woman; but I have the heart and stomach of a king" (*The Norton Anthology of English Literature: Volume One,* 6th ed. [New York: Norton, 1993], 999). James's romantic letters to his favorites Somerset and Villers are evidence of his homoerotic tendencies; see his *Letters of King James VI and I* (Berkeley: University of California Press, 1984). In this regard, note the Renaissance popularity of the story of Edward II and his fateful attachment to Gaveston in works such as Marlowe's *Edward II* and Michael Drayton's *Piers Gaveston (1593).*

[22] See Vern L. and Bonnie Bullough, *Cross-Dressing, Sex, and Gender* (Philadelphia: University of Pennsylvania Press, 1993); Marjorie Garber, *Vested Interests: Cross-Dressing and Cultural Anxiety* (New York: Routledge, 1992).

[23] See Edgar Wind, *Pagan Mysteries of the Renaissance* (New Haven: Yale University Press, 1958), 212-14.

[24] Jardine, *Still Harping;* Stephen Orgel, "Nobody's Perfect: Or Why Did the English Stage Take Boys for Women," *South Atlantic Quarterly* 88 (1989): 26.

[25] Bullough, *Crossdressing,* 98.

[26] Stephen Gosson, *The School of Abuse,* quoted in Laura Levine, "Men in Women's Clothing: Anti-theatricality and Effeminization from 1579-1642," *Criticism: A Quarterly for Literature and the Arts* 28 (1982): 131.

[27] John Rainoldes, *Th' Overthrow of Stage-Plays* (Middleburgh, 1599), quoted in Jardine, *Still Harping,* 9.

[28] William Prynne, *Histrio-mastix: The Player's Scourge or Actor's Tragedy* (New York: Garland, 1974), 75-76.

[29] See Jonas Barish, *The Antitheatrical Prejudice* (Berkeley: University of California Press, 1981).

[30] For another dramatization of the controversy over theatrical cross-dressing, see the puppet show in the final act of Jonson's *Bartholomew Fair.*

[31] See Ambroise Paré, *Of Monsters and Prodigies,* in *The Workes of Ambrose Parey,* trans. Thomas Johnson (London, 1634). For the eunuch controversy, see Keir Elam, "The Fertile Eunuch: *Twelfth Night,* Early Modern Intercourse, and the Fruits of Castration," *Shakespeare Quarterly* 47 (1996): 1-37.

[32] See Lothian and Craik's Introduction to the *Arden Edition of Twelfth Night,* 26-27.

[33] See Rackin, "Androgyny," 58; Howard, "Crossdressing," 439.

[34] Prynne, *Histrio-mastix,* 208-14.

[35] Monique Wittig, *The Straight Mind and Other Essays* (Boston: Beacon, 1992), 26; see also Butler, *Gender Trouble,* 115.

[36] Barber, *Festive Comedy,* 245.

[37] Alan Bray, *Homosexuality,* 74; Jardine, "Twins," 28.

[38] See James M. Saslow, "Homosexuality in the Renaissance: Behavior, Identity, and Artistic Expression," in *Hidden from History: Reclaiming the Gay and Lesbian Past,* ed. Martin Duberman, Martha Vicinus, and George Chauncy, Jr. (New York: Meridian, 1989), 95.
[39] See Judith C. Brown, *Immodest Acts: The Life of a Lesbian Nun in Renaissance Italy* (Oxford: Oxford University Press, 1986); Louis Crompton, "The Myth

of Lesbian Impunity: Capital Laws from 1270-1791," in *Historical Perspectives on Homosexuality,* ed. Salvatore J. Licata and Robert P. Peterson (New York: Haworth, 1981), 11-25.

[40] For recent scholarship, see Brown, *Immodest Acts;* Lillian Faderman *Surpassing the Love of Men* (New York: Morrow, 1981) and *Playing with Gender: A Renaissance Pursuit,* ed. Jean R. Brink, Maryanne C. Horowitz, and Alison P. Condert (Urbana: University of Illinois Press, 1991).

[41] For an even more developed lesbian subplot in *La Diana* than the analogue to *Twelfth Night,* see the story of Selvagia and Ismenia in Book One (Jorge de Montemayor, *A Critical Edition of Yong's Translation of George of Montemayor's Diana and Gil Polo's Enamoured Diana,* ed. Judith M. Kennedy [Oxford: Clarendon, 1968]).

[42] See Dale B. J. Randall, *"The Troublesome and Hard Adventures in Love:* An English Addition to the Bibliography of *Diana,"* *Bulletin of Hispanic Studies* 38 (1961): 154-58.

[43] Traub, *Desire and Anxiety,* 121.

[44] Shapiro, *Gender in Play,* 151-54.

[45] Traub, *Desire and Anxiety,* 130.

[46] In *The Four Fundamental Concepts of Psycho-Analysis,* trans. Alan Sheridan (New York: Norton, 1981), Jacques Lacan remarks that narcissistic gratification is love's primary motivation. Comparing the processes of analysis to the interaction of lovers, he concludes that the lover turns the beloved into a *subject supposed to know,* someone who can answer all his questions about what he wants (267). This transference is actually undertaken by the lover as a strategy of narcissism, in which the beloved, flattered by the lover, eventually recognizes and pays attention to the beloved (253). This imaginary and narcissistic fantasy called love necessarily seeks to close off the unconscious and the lack that is desire. The motto of the lover in approaching the beloved is always "in you more than you," a phrase that summarizes this process of imaginary overestimation for purposes of avoiding desire (263).

[47] See Howard, "Crossdressing," 431.

[48] Butler, *Bodies,* 231.

[49] "Despite her masculine attire and the confusion it causes in Illyria, Viola's is a properly feminine subjectivity; and this fact countervails the threat posed by her clothes and removes any possibility that she might permanently aspire to masculine privilege and prerogatives" (Howard, "Crossdressing," 432). For Howard the truly

transgressive female in the play is Olivia, but she is "punished, comically but unmistakably" by her love for Viola/Cesario (432). But what characters do not fall into "abatement and low price" because of their erotic attraction in this play? Howard's reading of *Twelfth Night* usefully illustrates one way in which the concerns of feminism can collide with the aims of gender studies, in so far as the latter attacks power through parodic deconstruction of its categories while the former seeks to work within those categories of power by searching for women who gain masculine "privilege."

⁵⁰ See Smith, *Homosexual Desire,* 151; Pequigney, "The Two Antonios," 207.

⁵¹ B[arry] R[ichard] Bury, "Ho-Hum, Another Work of the Devil: Buggery and Sodomy in Early Stuart England," in *Historical Perspectives on Homosexuality,* ed. Salvatore J. Licata and Robert P. Peterson (New York: Haworth, 1981), 69-78.

⁵² See Trumbach, "London's Sapphists," 133; Traub, *Desire and Anxiety,* 134.

⁵³ Pequigney, "The Two Antonios," 204.

⁵⁴ Alan Bray, "Homosexuality and the Signs of Male Friendship in Elizabethan England," *History Workshop Journal* 29 (1990): 10-11.

⁵⁵ Admittedly, one of the historian's main points is that these clues were growing more and more ambiguous at the end of the sixteenth century.

⁵⁶ Bray, *Homosexuality in Renaissance England,* 74.
⁵⁷ See Saslow, "Homosexuality," 94.

⁵⁸ The "homoeroticization" of St. Sebastian is evident in Renaissance art and carried forward in Derek Jarman's recent film. See, for example, Antonio and Piero de Pollaiuolo, *The Martyrdom of St. Sebastian* (1496?), National Gallery, London.

⁵⁹ Traub, *Desire and Anxiety,* 138; Pequigney, "The Two Antonios," 206.

⁶⁰ Butler, *Bodies,* 237.

⁶¹ See Karen Grief, "Plays and Playing in *Twelfth Night,*" *Shakespeare Survey* 34 (1981): 121-30.

⁶² Although Greenblatt ("Fiction and Friction") argues that the sameness is a maleness since both characters are dressed as men at the end of the play, Viola's central performance throughout the play has already shown that clothes do not necessarily make the man, that masculinity is a role played most successfully by a woman.

⁶³ See Barbara Freedman, "Separation and Fusion in *Twelfth Night,*" in *Psychoanalytic Approaches to Literature and Film,* ed. Maurice Charney and Joseph Reppen (Cranbury: Associated University Press, 1978), 96-119.

⁶⁴ Butler, *Gender Trouble,* 34.

Source: "Gender Trouble in *Twelfth Night,*" in *Theatre Journal,* Vol. 49, No. 2, May, 1997, pp. 121-41.

Male Magic: *A Midsummer Night's Dream*

Irene Dash, *Hunter College of the City University of New York*

And with the juice of this I'll streak her eyes,
And make her full of hateful fantasies.
II.i.257-58

Whether in the fantasy world of the forest or the equally fantastic world of Athens on a midsummer night, this play reveals how power, particularly political power, impinges on and shapes women's lives. Ranging from queens—Hippolyta, a character taken from mythology, and Titania, belonging to the fairy world—to youthful Athenian maidens in love, to a parodic heroine in an entertainment for the Duke's guests, these characters illustrate women's varied reactions to the imposition of power. One seems to adjust; one discovers new facts about herself; one serves as a lens for looking at the larger world; and one significantly reveals the tragic dimensions of the loss of power. Least mortal and yet seeming in her speeches and attitudes to mimic the mortal world, the fairy queen illustrates most clearly the loss of self—the abdication of autonomy—that may follow a woman's being victimized, even by fairy power.

In developing the early emotional relationship between her and Oberon, the fairy king, Shakespeare seems to have drawn on the world around him for models. Thus when Titania refuses to comply to Oberon's demands, he vows in pique and jealousy to "streak her eyes" with magic juice "and make her full of hateful fantasies" (II.i.257-58). Moreover, moments before he carries out his threat, he becomes more explicit:

Be it ounce, or cat, or bear,
Pard, or boar with bristled hair,
In the eye that shall appear
When thou wak'st, it is thy dear:
Wake when some vile thing is near.

(ii.30-34)

In fact, she does wake and call some "vile thing" her "dear." How then do we interpret this? Is it the act of magic that forces her to "fall in love" with an ass, or at least with a character who has been temporarily transformed into an ass? Or are we to accept much of the criticism that suggests her erotic desire for the ass reflects her true nature—the nature of woman? Does Titania at this moment "awaken from her dream," look at the monster, and desire him, as Jan Kott (228) suggests? Or is she basically still dreaming, hypnotized by a magic spell, never awakening until Oberon, later in the play, having achieved his purpose, removes that magic juice and Titania, chastened but also transformed

from the outspoken character of the early scene, looks with loathing at the ass she embraced?

Although her disagreement with Oberon lies at the heart of the play, Titania does not enter until the beginning of the second act. Instead, Shakespeare first introduces other women more clearly caught in situations of political or social subordination than the fairy queen: specifically Hippolyta, the captive Amazonian queen; Hermia, the rebellious Athenian daughter; and Helena who, in her complete self-denigration, illustrates more indirectly the impact of patriarchal power on women. Interweaving a third plot strand culminating in the performance of "Pyramus and Thisbe," the comedy also provides a dual vision of women in patriarchy near the play's close. Parodying the tragic results of arbitrary parental power, this play-within-a-play in its metadramatic dimension offers insights into the mainly silent women, now married, in the audience.

Artistically, the dramatist weaves a complex multifaceted plot that exposes the political and domestic challenges confronting women while creating situations that throw us into the world of comedy. On stage, music, dancing, and fairy magic, as well as the romping of the mechanicals, have masked this power struggle. In criticism, the lure of the poetry, the concept of "topsy turvy," the illusion of dreams, and theories of mythology have often tended to blur any interest in the domination of women. Some critics have even proposed that the play was written specifically for a wedding although none has yet been found.

In fact, *A Midsummer Night's Dream* opens with anticipation of a wedding although it hardly reveals clearcut delight by both participants, Hippolyta and Theseus, the Duke of Athens, her captor but also her bridegroom:

Now, fair Hippolyta, our nuptial hour
Draws on apace. Four happy days bring in
Another moon; but O, methinks, how slow
This old moon wanes! She lingers my desires,
Like to a step-dame, or a dowager,
Long withering out a young man's revenue.

(I.i.1-6)

His reference to "happy days" and the final fulfilling of his desire meets a noncommittal response from the bride. Acknowledging that four days swiftly pass, she indicates neither joy nor sorrow as she anticipates "the night / Of our solemnities" (10-11). Her ambiguous answer leads Theseus to search further. Still the host, if also the victor, he sends his master of the revels on an errand to:

> Stir up the Athenian youth to merriments,
> Awake the pert and nimble spirit of mirth.

He would have his bride be merry. Continuing, he relies on a strange metaphor to reinforce his invitation to joyous celebration:

> Turn melancholy forth to funerals:
> The pale companion is not for our pomp.
>
> (12-15)

Why speak of funerals, even as a contrast to mirth, unless, perhaps a subtext exists here? Although "pale companion" defines the personified "melancholy," contextually the words seem linked to Hippolyta, addressed in the very next word:

> Hippolyta, I woo'd thee with my sword,
> And won thy love doing thee injuries;
> But I will wed thee in another key.
>
> (16-18)

Is he apologizing for his earlier role? She fails to reply. His speeches suggest a shift in perception of woman from enemy to lover to wife, with the implication of woman's submission to man. As courtesy books and religious tracts of the period indicate, that reference to love and marriage, while including mutuality, also meant acknowledging man's superiority.[1]

This first scene, particularly the opening entrance and the elliptical conversation between Theseus and his bride, have allowed for a range of interpretations on stage because of Hippolyta's silence. Directors and actor-managers have long manipulated both the action and audience attitude toward a character or a situation during such silences. Writing of this phenomenon recently, particularly as it affects productions, one critic observed:

> Hippolyta's silence is open not because Shakespeare lacked the skill to give her words but because he did not exercise that skill, did not employ the power of his "poet's pen" to give her silence precisely fixed meanings and effects. (McGuire, 17)

McGuire then cites examples from four productions since 1959. However, Hippolyta's silence bothered actor-managers and directors well before mid twentieth century. Because her role is so brief (she does not appear again until act 4) some, like David Garrick in *The Fairies* (1755), have cut her lines although she is physically present and combined Theseus's two speeches into a single long address.[2] Other eighteenth-century versions—like the two different *Pyramus and Thisbes*—

are even skimpier, retaining only the comic characters and the fairies while jettisoning both Hippolyta and Theseus.[3] Earlier, during the Restoration, comic interludes, separated from the larger overall scheme, and abbreviated versions held the stage, culminating in the opera *The Fairy Queen* (1692), from which Hippolyta disappeared.[4]

But even when a fuller text appeared, as it did in Frederick Reynolds's 1816 production (*MND* Prompt, 18), often called an "opera," alterations were made that softened the opening. Some occurred in the text itself, as, for example, when Reynolds not only retained the conversation between the victor and his bride, but elaborated on it. In this version, Theseus's fourth act directive to a forester to provide "the music" of the "hounds," as entertainment for Hippolyta (IV.i.110), is attached to that opening promise to wed her in "another key" (I.i.18), an attempt to strengthen the attractiveness of the bridegroom.[5]

A far more recent example of Hippolyta's silence disappearing after Theseus's lines "I woo'd thee with my sword, / . . . But I will wed thee in another key" occurs in the 1935 Max Reinhardt film where he transposes the sequence of speeches. In the film, Theseus's lines precede, rather than follow, Hippolyta's single speech and therefore evoke her immediate and soothing comment "Four days will quickly steep themselves in night; / Four nights will quickly dream away the time" (7-8). Nor can Reinhardt's film be looked upon as a single aberration. Rather, the German director provides an important link between stage and screen, having produced the play eleven times (beginning in 1905) prior to making the film in 1934.

Free of the confining limits of the stage, he could, as film director, waft his viewers from one location to another, jumping from a distant scene to a close-up of a particular character. In a section of the film script later discarded, Reinhardt not only appears to have been testing the breadth of this comparatively new medium but also offers insights into the finished film. The script also reflects the director's penchant for interpretation. In quick succession, it carries us aboard Theseus's ship, drops us in the land of the Amazons, and involves us in the battle between Theseus and Hippolyta through visuals that act as prologue to the text. Broad shots of the sea and the distant castle of the Amazons are interwoven with close-ups of the two major figures. We read of Theseus standing on the prow of the ship, "a glamorous figure in shining armor, against the dark background of the sail" and of Hippolyta standing with a large wild dog at her side as she "sternly watch[es] the approaching ship" (*MND* Warners, 1934).[6] Stern Hippolyta is contrasted with glamourous Theseus. Finally, when he appears on land followed by his staff, she takes up armor and weapons and shoots at him. He, however, "lower(s) his shield laughing," the implication being that fighting against a woman is laughable and that she, of course, will miss her mark. Eventually, they end up in hand to hand battle, "shield against shield," his shield flat upon hers, pressing it backward. The sequence continues:

2. H[ippolyta].'s knee bending, interlocking with Theseus' leg

3. Th[eseus].'s shoulder pressing H[ippolyta].'s shoulder downward. . . .

5. H[ippolyta].'s head and shoulders going backward.

6. Th[eseus].'s arm across H[ippolyta].'s shoulder, knocks the helmet from her head. H[ippolyta].'s long hair falls about her shoulders.

7. H[ippolyta].'s head bends backward. Th[eseus].'s head comes into picture triumphantly.[7]

There we have the classic picture of the implied rape-seduction scene although as the opening of *A Midsummer Night's Dream* clearly indicates, Theseus waits to wed Hippolyta.[8] What remains of this sequence is a clue to a point of view and to the play's early moments.

In fact, as it was actually made, Reinhardt's film opens quite differently with a general celebratory air as crowds sing and cheer the returning victor, their Duke Theseus, with his captive queen who rides with him, her arm entwined by a snake, indicating her heathenish origins. . . . Later that snake will merely be a pattern on a "civilized" dress she wears. The strange look on her face during that opening entrance as well as her action in a subsequent scene probably owe their origins to this discarded "script." In the later scene, dressed like a lady, Hippolyta sits alone in a large open colosseumlike semicircular area surrounded by large columns (a Hollywood approximation of Athens) and looks wistfully across the water. Is she recollecting her former glory and envisioning again the burning towers she left behind? Moments later, Theseus enters and kisses her hand. . . . Her reaction seems to suggest that she feels a thrill at his kiss. The rape-seduction undercurrent first suggested by their hand-to-hand battle when her helmet fell off is sustained here.

In contrast, Liviu Ciulei's stage production, fifty years later, dramatically emphasized Hippolyta's role as a captive in that opening scene. Brought on stage where everyone is wearing white, Hippolyta enters in dark army garb. Moments later, screened from audience view by her captors, she is basically stripped, her clothes thrown into the fire—all except her boots, which she contines to wear—perhaps symbolically suggesting that some remnant of her former self remains—a remnant that allows her to express her hostility, by stamping

her heels as an accompaniment to her sardonic laughter. Otherwise, she is redressed in a white gown. Someone holds a mirror to her. She turns away. When Theseus enters, there is laughter at his lines, as he says, "But I will wed thee in another key." She simply turns around, and sits, her physical stance exuding hostility.

Many versions simply eliminated this character, thus excising the frame and problems of interpretation, but also insights into how one queen eventually handles the humiliation of defeat. In her next appearance she has adopted an attitude of congeniality, quipping with Theseus about his knowledge of hounds. Moreover, in her final scene she takes on an even more complicated role as the only speaking woman in a world of men.

Out of the theater, the Hippolyta and Theseus relationship evoked still another reaction. Margaret Fuller, the midnineteenth-century American feminist essayist, in her outspoken work *Woman in the Nineteenth Century,* wrote: "Only a Theseus could conquer before he wed the Amazonian queen." Fuller compared Theseus to Hercules, who "wished rather to rest with Dejanira, and received the poisoned robe as a fit guerdon."[9] Whether or not Fuller had the historical story in mind, or Shakespeare's play, she nevertheless does offer an alternative perspective on the play's first nineteen lines.

Hippolyta then fades into the background as another woman enters who must wrestle with her fate. Hermia is dragged in by her angry father, Egeus, who would have the laws of Athens enforced against her because she wishes to marry Lysander, the man of her choice, rather than Demetrius, her father's choice, although, as most critics agree, little difference exists between the suitors. As Muriel Bradbrook has observed, Shakespeare contributed to the development of comedy by breathing life into his characters through language. She compares this gift to "the introduction of perspective in painting" (89). Accepting her analysis, we realize that the similarity between the young men is intentional and meant to highlight Egeus's unreasonableness. "I am . . . as well deriv'd as he," protests Lysander, the suitor who is "belov'd of beauteous Hermia":

As well possess'd; my love is more than his;
My fortunes every way as fairly rank'd.
(I.i.99-104)

But the father refuses to listen, insisting that he "may dispose of" his daughter as he wishes, "either to this gentleman [Demetrius] / Or to her death" (42-44). Nor does Theseus, who only moments earlier had pledged to wed Hippolyta "in another key" from that of conqueror, offer much hope to the young woman. Supporting her father, the ruler warns of the price of disobedience: "Either to die the death, or to abjure / For ever the society of men" (65-66).

Life in a nunnery, a retreat for Isabella in *Measure for Measure,* has little appeal for Hermia. It denies her normal sexuality. Moreover, she is a young woman in love. However, Theseus, the voice of political power, continues, unconcerned about her reactions. Spelling out the meaning of the law, he details the young woman's choices:

> Therefore, fair Hermia, question your desires,
> Know of your youth, examine well your
>   blood,
> Whether (if you yield not to your father's
>   choice)
> You can endure the livery of a nun,
> For aye to be in shady cloister mew'd,
> To live a barren sister all your life,
> Chaunting faint hymns to the cold fruitless
>   moon.
>
> > (*MND*, I.i.67-73)

"Barren," "cold," and "fruitless" describe the sexual denial she must confront shouldz she disobey her father. Theseus presents a frightening alternative for her. Taking the father from Roman comedy, Shakespeare creates a comic scene with undercurrents of possibly tragic dimension.

But sections of this speech as well as of Egeus's complaints against Lysander disappeared from the stage. Gone are such accusations against Lysander as "thou has given her rhymes, / And interchanged love tokens"; sung at her window "verses of feigning love"; seduced her "With bracelets of thy hair, rings, gauds, conceits"; and, finally, "Turned her obedience, which is due to me, / To stubborn harshness."[10] Only Egeus's demand for the privilege of the father remained—the right to "dispose of her" as he saw fit or to call for the death penalty. Although retaining this harsh sentence, those who excised lines had effectively diminished the speech's intensity through abbreviation.

Gone too from the stage are the closing lines of Theseus's admonition to Hermia defining the obligations of a daughter:

> To you your father should be as a god
> One that composed your beauties; yea, and
>   one
> To whom you are but as a form in wax
> By him imprinted and within his power
> To leave the figure or disfigure it.
>
> > (47-51)

The image here, specifically the threat to "disfigure," disturbed critics and editors as early as the eighteenth century. William Warburton, for example, sought to change the last line, finding Theseus's statement inappropriate for comedy. In contrast, Samuel Johnson, always one to favor the text over

any change of language, defended the word although still bothered by the meaning:

> I know not why so harsh a word should be admitted with so little need, a word that, spoken, could not be understood, and of which no example can be shown. The sense is plain, "you owe to your father a being which he may at pleasure continue or destroy." (Yale Johnson, VII, 136)

If that rather chilling ultimatum contributes to the portrait of a powerful ruler asserting the ideas of his society, stage productions, by omitting the last three and a half lines of Theseus's speech, frequently altered the image. In fact, some stage versions retained only the preceding line, Theseus's far more gentle, "What say you, Hermia? Be advis'd, fair maid" (46).[11] Because the interaction of characters helps define them, a weakened portrait of Hermia results from the combination of excisions in Theseus's and Egeus's speeches. Facing less opposition, she need be less defiant. Or, looking at it another way, we see her as a less interesting character than the sharp, courageous young woman Shakespeare begins to develop here.

Illustrating just how complex this text is and how it may be read and reread for the stage, some twentieth-century directors have translated the relationship between the two women at this moment on the stage as one of bonding: Hermia, who faces an anguished choice, and Hippolyta, who stands on the sidelines, listening. And here too promptbooks offer evidence. Beerbohm Tree's, for example, indicates the Amazonian queen's sympathy for the younger woman by directing: "Hyp[polyta] leads Herm[ia] to seat" (*MND* 7, interleaf facing p. 4). In Liviu Ciulei's production, the bonding takes another form. Since Hippolyta's strong personality had been developed at the play's opening, here she sneeringly laughs at Theseus's ultimatum, a clear comment on his actions and on the irony of his earlier words to her, "But I will wed thee in another key" (I.i.18). More humorous in approach and less sharply disapproving is the direction in the Peter Brook prompt: "All bow their heads" (12a). Brook dramatizes the rift between Theseus and Hippolyta by having them exit to opposite sides of the stage, "pausing at doors to look at each other." These twentieth-century directors found their cues in the text and responded, not with excision but with a new awareness of the play's subtlety and of the possibilities that staging might permit.

If Hermia's tragic fate is briefly understood by Hippolyta, the play quickly moves back to the world of comedy as the two lovers left alone on stage not only bemoan their fate but also engage in a conversation in which neither is hearing what the other says. Comforting his love, Lysander cites historical parallels of similarly fated lovers; Hermia, not listening, overflows with anger and frustration:

> *Lys* The course of true love never did run
>   smooth;
> But either it was different in blood—

He begins, but she interrupts:

> *Her* O cross! Too high to be enthralled to
>   low!

Alternating lines, they continue:

> *Lys* Or else misgraffed in respect of years—
> *Her* O spite! Too old to be engaged to
>   young!
> *Lys* Or else it stood upon the choice of
>   friends—
> *Her* O hell! To choose love by another's
>   eyes!
>
>   (I.i.134-40)

The stichomythic pattern of the duet captures the intensity of the lovers' feelings, but also the humor of their reactions as each finds solace from a different verbal outpouring.

Nevertheless, the exchange disappeared from acting texts for over a hundred years.[12] Although the excision at first seems inexplicable, George Bernard Shaw's comments on an Augustin Daly production offer a partial answer. Unaware of how much Daly's version owed to his predecessors, and indignant over his mauling of the text, Shaw attributes the excision to Daly's uncomfortableness with Hermia's "Oh hell," then notes the impact of the cuts. Humorously he writes:

> Mr. Daly, shocked, as an American and an Irishman, at a young lady using such an expression as "Oh hell!" cuts out the whole antiphony, and leaves Lysander to deliver a long lecture without interruption from the lady. (*Our Theatres,* I, 180-81)

This "long lecture without interruption" also further denies audiences the partial portrait, later to be developed, of Hermia. Unsurprisingly, the lines disappeared from the Garrick-Colman and Reynolds operatic versions since these works concentrated on songs loosely connected with one another by speeches, rather than on short exchanges. But the absence of Hermia's frustrated expression from the later stage versions is surprising.[13]

Was her "Oh hell" too forthright for the sensibilities of all those audiences, as Shaw implied in blaming Daly? A glance at the *Variorum,* strong in nineteenth-century criticism, suggests other, literary reasons, as well. Coleridge, for example writes:

> There is no authority for any alteration,—but I never can help feeling how great an improvement it would be, if the two former of Hermia's exclamations were

omitted—the third and only appropriate one would then become a beauty, and most natural. (Coleridge [101], quoted in the *Variorum,* 18)

Rather than denigrating that last line with its "Oh hell," Coleridge praises it. Obviously, Hermia's annoyed exclamations bothered him more than the simple comment on the unfairness of choosing love "by another's eyes." Less generously, Halliwell, another critic of the time, believed Lysander's speech "would be improved by the omission of all of Hermia's interpolations" (18). Moreover, to support his opinion, he cited the editions of Dodd and Planché which actually deleted Hermia's lines.[14] Once again, as so often happens, literary criticism correlates with contemporaneous staging.

Why did her short speeches offend so? Was Lysander's single uninterrupted speech more appropriate? But then how could his speech help project Hermia's personality as it does in the original exchange? Stylistically, those clipped single lines suggest the exasperation and intensity of the young woman we are to meet later on in the forest. Moreover, the patter, or duet, of these two lovers complements the long heavy speeches of Egeus and Theseus, taking us back into the comic, romantic world of the play.

As critics have often noted, conflict between father and daughter arises here as it does in so many other of Shakespeare's plays, and here too the strength of the daughter is created by showing her resistence to her father's pressure; her lines in this duet are important. Shaw's review of Daly's production suggests a further effect of the "alternating lines" spoken by the "two star-crossed lovers"; he believes the alternating pattern sets "the whole scene throbbing with their absorption in one another" (133). It also explodes with their differing responses to the same situation.

Although a strong, self-confident, if frustrated, young woman emerges through the language here, not all of her lines reinforce this portrait. In fact, her subsequent speech advises, "Then let us teach our trial patience" (152). Between her two speeches, she has listened to Lysander's litany of lovers who, throughout history, have faced problems. In the cut acting texts I have examined, the line advising patience always remains. What a different Hermia we experience. The language has been modulated, the humor of the exchange lost, and the outspoken young woman tempered.

Artistically, too, a change occurs. No verbal echoes will sound for the audience when, a few lines later, Hermia and her best friend, Helena, indulge in a similar pattern of alternating lines. Nor will the audience hear how their conversation mimics and yet differs from that of the lovers. The repetition of the pattern, comic in its shift of topic, also defines and contrasts the young women. Helena pines for Demetrius. Hermia would most willingly relinquish him. Unlike the earlier duet, this one concentrates on each young woman's attitude towards Demetrius. Rhyming couplets mark their exchange of confidences, and again acting texts excise:

> *Her.* I frown upon him; yet he loves me still.
> *Hel.* O that your frowns would teach my
>   smiles such skill!
> *Her.* I give him curses; yet he gives me love.
> *Hel.* O that my prayers could such affection
>   move!
> *Her.* The more I hate, the more he follows
>   me.
> *Hel.* The more I love, the more he hateth me.
>   (194-199)

Differing in their appeal to Demetrius, the women differ in their sense of self, Hermia confident with two adoring males, Helena disconsolate that the youth she loves has eyes only for her friend. Physically they differ too: Hermia being small and dark, at one point called "puppet" (III.ii.286), "dwarfish" (295), and an "Ethiop" (257); Helena being tall and lanky—"a painted maypole" (296). She is also probably fair.

Throughout this scene, Hermia exhibits a sardonic sense of humor, not only in her exclamations after her father leaves with Theseus, but even in her exchanges with her less confident friend. And once again, some texts delete Hermia's attempt to console her friend:

> Before the time I did Lysander see,
> Seem'd Athens as a Paradise to me;
> O then, what graces in my love do dwell,
> That he hath turn'd a heaven unto a hell!
>   (I.i.204-7)[15]

Although meant to emphasize the problems Hermia faces, the lines referring to "Lysander's graces" making Athens a hell also have a built-in irony. Surely a lover's graces should turn a hell into heaven rather than the opposite. Although differing from Theseus's comment to Hippolyta on altering their relationship from excombatants to lovers, Hermia's words here suggest a similarly thin and tenuous line between heaven and hell, springing from love.

Of the exchange, Samuel Johnson wrote:

> Perhaps every reader may not discover the propriety of these lines. Hermia is willing to comfort Helena, and to avoid all appearance of triumph over her. She therefore bids her not to consider the power of pleasing, as an advantage to be much envied or much desired, since Hermia, whom she considers as possessing it in the supreme degree, has found no other effect of it than the loss of happiness.
>
> (Johnson, *The Plays,* 1:98)

The comment also appears in a footnote in the Phelps promptbook (*MND* 13, 314). Since this was an 1805 printed text used for an 1861 production, it suggests that the lines were not only challenging in the eighteenth century but continued to be relevant in the nineteenth. When they disappear, as often occurs, they erase a problem for interpreters, but also an insight into Hermia's capacity for humor and sympathy.

To further comfort Helena, Hermia and Lysander reveal their secret plan to escape Athens. In soliloquy at the scene's close, Helena confesses her response. She will divulge the news of their flight to Demetrius, hoping to win his favor. Bemoaning her fate in rhymed couplets, she begins:

> How happy some o'er other some can be!
> Through Athens I am thought as fair as
>   she,
> But what of that? Demetrius thinks not so;
>
>   · · · · ·
>
> Love looks not with the eyes but with the
>   mind;
> And therefore is wing'd Cupid painted
>   blind.
>   (227-35)

But Helena does not think herself as fair as Hermia. Thus this reference to Cupid suggests a rather confused young woman. Continuing for twenty-six lines, the soliloquy ranges from analyses of love to a discussion of Hermia's strengths to a lament for the speaker's own plight:

> For ere Demetrius look'd on Hermia's eyne,
> He hail'd down oaths that he was only mine;
>   (242-43)

She therefore resolves, "I will go tell him of fair Hermia's flight" (246), expecting a kind response. Here too excisions mar the portrait. Sometimes the lines are absent from printed acting versions; sometimes sections are crossed out or blocked for cutting.[16] As a result only the bare plot outline of this section remains, subtleties in characterization being lost.

Later, in the forest, the dramatist further develops the young women's personalities. There the popular Hermia, speaking with confidence, gently reprimands her lover, while the rejected Helena subjects herself to further humiliation, frustratingly following the man she loves. Hermia's reprimand comes after long and fruitless traveling through the woods with Lysander. Escaping Theseus's ultimatum, they seek refuge with the young man's aunt, beyond the range of Athens' law. Weary with wandering, Hermia would rest; Lysander then admits he has lost his way in the enchanted forest:

We'll rest us, Hermia, if you think it good,
And tarry for the comfort of the day.

(II.ii.37-38)

Appreciating the idea, she then counters:

Be't so, Lysander. Find you out a bed;
For I upon this bank will rest my head.

(39-40)

But he would have it otherwise. In fact, the lines indicate the action that has just occurred on stage as she chooses her sleeping site. A minidebate then ensues:

Lys. One turf shall serve as pillow for us
    both,
One heart, one bed, two bosoms, and one
    troth.
Her. Nay, good Lysander; for my sake, my
    dear,
Lie further off yet; do not lie so near.

(41-44)

The adapters once again cut. Garrick's abbreviated musical version provides a record of the cuts in this speech, and, to some extent, sets the pattern for what subsequently occurred. The first eight lines of the exchange between the couple are retained (lines 35-42), followed by a duet (25). Then come lines not Shakespeare's, but believed to be composed by Garrick, which appear in a handwritten insert (*MND* 6).[17] In that version Hermia exhibits proper womanly fear:

Now my Lysander, on that bank repose,
That if perchance my woman's fears shou'd
    seek
Protection in thy love and brav'ry,
I may not call on love and thee in vain.

(*MND* 6, insert 21; Garrick, 25)

Lysander responds with the promise of protective care. The Garrick lines also appear in the Reynolds printed text (*MND* 8, 18). Later the pattern of excision continues although without the new, added material. The musical Reynolds version (*MND* 8, 18) contains no hint of her asking him to move. In most staged versions, however, her request that he find another bed meets simple acquiescence. Usually gone are his lines "One turf shall serve as pillow for us both / One heart, one bed, two bosoms, and one troth" (41-42) along with his attempt to convince her of the reasonableness of his proposal. Gone too is Hermia's perceptive "Lysander riddles very prettily. . . . / But, gentle friend, for love and courtesy, / Lie further off, in humane modesty" (53, 56-57).[18] Amusing, her response in Shakespeare's play highlights her realistic awareness of the physical attraction between lovers. Their debate is reminiscent of Juliet's "What satisfaction canst thou have to-night?" (*Romeo and Juliet*, II.ii.126) when Romeo

protests, "O, wilt thou leave me so unsatisfied" (125). In both cases, the dramatist suggests that confidence in the loyalty of her lover does not blur each young woman's recognition of the reality of the sexual drive.

Unlike Hermia, her friend Helena nurtures no such fear. Groveling for some affection, she trails Demetrius. "I love thee not; therefore pursue me not" (188), he dictates. But Helena, like Emilia in *Othello* so many plays later, has divulged the secret of Hermia and Lysander's flight in order to win a boon:

I am your spaniel; and, Demetrius,
The more you beat me, I will fawn on you.
Use me but as your spaniel; spurn me, strike
    me,
Neglect me, lose me; only give me leave,
Unworthy as I am, to follow you.

(II.i.203-7)

Nor do Demetrius's threats to her virginity (217-19) bother her. Rather they allow her to assert her confidence in his character. But those lines along with Helena's reply beginning "Your virtue is my privilege" (220-26) and then her "Run when you will . . ." (230-34) disappear from the stage in many promptbooks.[19]

By cutting Helena's lines here and elsewhere, those versions tended to obscure the perceptiveness of Shakespeare's sketch of a young woman who is filled with self-doubt and self-hatred.[20] In fact, Shakespeare's insight here, although theatrically developed and placed in a comedic setting, has a contemporary counterpart in Kate Millett's more serious analysis of the lack of self-love that flourishes in women and minorities. She describes this as

group self-hatred and self-rejection, a contempt both
for herself and for her fellows—the result of that
continual, however subtle, reiteration of her inferiority
which she eventually accepts as a fact. (56)

Helena appears to have internalized this attitude. In an excellent essay on the play, David Marshall asks a relevant question concerning Helena. "Are we to be pleased by the success of Helena's subjection of herself?" (548), he wonders, challenging the idea that this is "one of Shakespeare's happiest comedies."[21] Actually, by the time we reach this section of the play we become aware of the various ways in which the women have been dominated by men—bridegroom, father, ruler, and rejecting suitor.

However, we have not yet met the strongest and seemingly freest woman character in *A Midsummer Night's Dream:* Titania, the fairy queen, who so delights us at her first entrance and later raises questions about women's roles. Is she the victim of male power, male irrationality, trickery, or jealousy? Is she merely a fairy? Or does she illuminate the feelings and attitudes of women reacting to dominating male behavior?

At its opening, act 2 stresses the conflict between her and Oberon, the fairy king. Quickly we learn the source of their dissension: control over an "Indian boy" at the time in her possession but desperately desired by Oberon. Representatives of king and queen, Puck and a fairy quickly sketch in the conflict, each hoping the other party will relinquish the field. "But room, fairy! here comes Oberon" (II.i.58), announces Puck. "And here my mistress. Would that he were gone!" (59) retorts the fairy. And then, king and queen enter. Do they make a grand entry from either side of the stage, magically from the air, with a train of followers, or simply alone?

The scene has allowed for a tremendous range of interpretations, some concentrating on the two principals, some surrounding them with troops of followers, many including the Indian Prince. Nonexistent in the play and seeming to symbolize Oberon's drive for dominance over Titania—or perhaps his jealousy of her—the prince materializes into an actual character. Not listed in the dramatis personae, he takes on a life of his own in nineteenth- and early twentieth-century productions, including the Reinhardt film. Although mystery surrounds him in the text—we don't know his age, his size, or his exact identity, except as he is described variously by Puck, Titania, and Oberon—he acquires theatrical substance on stage, frequently wearing a turban or carried in on a golden cushion.[22]

Suggesting the importance of this character to the relationship between the fairy king and queen are the stage directions written in pencil on the interleave to Kean's prompt:

> *Fairies enter dancing round Titania. 2 Bodies of Oberon's Train,—enter separately, . . . then 2 parties of Titania's—chorus first, who make an avenue of boughs, then a second troop of smaller fairies trip down through them,—on tiptoes—and run back thro avenue,—down L[eft] then round avenue and follow Titania with Indian Boy tripping down through avenue,—Oberon entering same time down slote, R[ight] (MND 9, interleaf facing p. 21).*

In another production, a dance of twelve fairies precedes Titania's entry "in a car drawn by swans" and accompanied by the Indian Prince. Paralleling their entry, Oberon descends to meet them (*MND* 20, verso of interleaf facing p. 12). A sketch indicates the placement of fairies, with Titania, Oberon, and the Prince at center front.

The presence of an actual prince also allows the director editorial commentary as he emphasizes the differ-

ent functions of men and women, father and mother. Thus Titania is usually portrayed in a maternal relationship with that young child whereas Oberon is presented as giving the youth space and training for manhood. Consider, for example, the Reinhardt film where the young prince is practically smothered by attention from Titania's fairies and elves whereas later he is free to accompany Oberon. Even in criticism, this reference to the prince colors the perspective. C.L. Barber, for example, writing of Titania's later development, considers her giving up of the child as a maturing process. But one may question whether or not it is the child, as an actual person, or the symbolic importance of the debate between Titania and Oberon and its later outcome that is really at issue in the play especially since the prince's exclusion from the text helps stress the equality between king and queen.

Before turning to their actual verbal sparring, I want to cite other theatrical factors that further vitiated the strength of the debate, attracting eyes to the stage and ears to the music rather than attention to the words. I refer to the persistence of lavish musical accompaniments to productions. In fact, whether it was coincidence or not, the mid-nineteenth-century productions—beginning with that of Elizabeth Vestris and Charles Mathews in 1840, which included Mendelssohn's music—were highly successful and included more of the text than had previously appeared on stage. Discussing that production, one commentator suggested, "It would be an unpardonable mistake to any future performances . . . to omit . . . Mendelssohn's music" (*MND*. *NCP 18—, p. 6).[23] In Reinhardt's film, fairies, accompanied by the orchestral sounds of Mendelssohn's music, dance in on a cloud that spirals around a tree. Later productions, like that of the famous Old Vic Company in 1954 that featured Robert Helpmann and Moira Shearer, both professional dancers, as Oberon and Titania, also testify to the pervasiveness of a musical tradition and the emphasis on dance for the two principal fairies. . . .

Finally, along with the music and the young prince, one stage property worked its magic on the audience: the mushroom from which Puck eventually emerged. The young Ellen Terry as Puck, for example, lay hidden in such a mushroom in Kean's production, springing into view as the mushroom rose. Following Kean's lead, Daly's Puck, hidden by a mushroom, was discovered when a fairy's wand brushed a plant (1888, *MND* 5, p. 32). Featuring complex machinery, Burton's production too had Puck spring from a mushroom that rose from a trap then sank back down (*MND* 21, p. 15 and facing interleaf).[24] The rival Barry production featured a different but equally enticing, entry for Puck:

> *A romantic Landscape, through which is seen a stream of water. (By moonlight.) A bush in the c[enter]. MUSIC—A troop of Fairies are discovered*

grouped. A Fairy touches the bush with her wand, it opens and Puck comes out; the bush disappears through the stage.

(MND 20, Act 2, p. 11)

Supplementing this text, the directions on the interleaf specifically place Puck inside the flower piece which then changes to a peacock. Accompanied by music, "the first fairy trips on from [the side entrance] . . . round the flower" waving the wand. "The flower opens and discovers Puck in a Peacock Car (with wand)." More music sounds as Puck descends from the car. Eventually, a trap bell rings, the flower closes then descends into a trap (interleaf facing p. 11).

I cite these extensive productions because they characterize what occurred on stage once the fuller text was presented. Whether this was because of the accompaniment of Mendelssohn's music or because the combination of the text with that music appealed so strongly to Victorians we do not know. Clearly, however, language and the verbal conflicts between men and women characters, whether fairy or not, were overshadowed by productions. Nor do the many references to a full text, as in the case of Phelps's production, which boasted of having omitted only three hundred lines, alter the general impression of the acted play. If these varied staged versions seemed to promise new perspectives, they failed to deliver; they still concentrated on the magic and wistfulness of the dream. Moreover, extant promptbooks testify to a disproportionate number of excisions of lines that blur Shakespeare's portrayal of the inequities that women faced whether in the real or unreal fairy world.

For it is in the unreal world of the fairies that the dramatist most clearly questions the patriarchal structure. Despite the extravagance of their entrances in different productions, Oberon's and Titania's opening lines sound more like those of humans than of fairies or otherworldly beings: "Ill met by moonlight, proud Titania" (60), asserts proud Oberon. We then encounter the queen of the fairies whom Shakespeare has endowed with dramatic and evocative poetry. Unlike the other women thus far presented, Titania has a sure sense of self-worth and an independence of spirit. Hippolyta was presented as defeated but enigmatic, Hermia as a challenge to the rules of her society, and Helena as a self-doubting person, questioning her own worth. But in Titania Shakespeare offers a portrait of a queen, someone reliant on no one but herself for her power. Her answer to Oberon in her opening lines rings with contemporaneity:

What, jealous Oberon? Fairies, skip hence—
I have forsworn his bed and company.

(61-62)

Why need a fairy assert she has "forsworn" another fairy's bed? Since when do fairies discuss such mundane matters? Moreover, Oberon carries the discussion one step further by clarifying their relationship with one another: "Am not I thy lord?" (63) he asks. "Then I must be thy lady" (64) she asserts before accusing him of infidelity with various women. In his recent book *Road to Divorce: England 1530-1987,* Lawrence Stone notes that until recently—but particularly in the early period covered by this book—"all women of childbearing age" were in a state of "constant anxiety about their bodies. They worried about whether they were pregnant" (8) and about such things as the possibility of dying in childbirth, of coming to term, and of having a well child. Titania, being a fairy, has no such worry although her conflict with Oberon has to do with the child of a mortal who died in childbirth. "His mother was a vot'ress of my order" (123), explains Titania. "For her sake do I rear up the boy; / And for her sake I will not part with him" (136-37). Moreover, in recent studies of women's writings of the period, we become aware not only of women's quest for divorce and of the problems they faced in confronting their husbands but also of the real fears attending childbirth (Otten).

Titania's opening lines to Oberon may well have had specific resonances for Shakespeare's audience. The phrase "separation from bed and board" was applied at the time to a legitimate form of divorce, whether "as'de facto' grants of permission to remarry" or merely following church ordinance that allowed a form of divorce but forbade remarriages (Stone, L., 304). Although Titania, of course, had no particular plans to "remarry," her language mimics that of the time, with, however, a twist—an assertion of her rights vis-à-vis an adulterous husband. Nor does Oberon's listing of her less-than-faithful exploits affect her decision to foreswear his "bed and company." According to Stone, the pattern changed in the 1640s and 50s, which may explain an altered reaction to this section of text. He writes:

> The 1640s and 1650s were a period of disorganization and institutional chaos in the church. The ecclesiastical courts ceased to function in the early 1640s and in 1646 church control over marriage was abolished, authority being shifted in theory to secular authorities. But the bulk of the population seems either to have found ways to be married clandestinely by the old rituals of the Church of England, or were married by non-conformist clergy of their own religious persuasion, or reverted to marriages by verbal contract. As a result of this confusion, when the ecclesiastical courts were restored in 1660 they found themselves faced with an unprecedented torrent of petitions for separation which had been pent up for over a decade. (308)

Interestingly, what Shakespeare is doing here is using the vocabulary of divorce without presenting the actual situation. Moreover, unlike the usual separation between husband and wife of the time, this separation is instituted by the wife. The dramatist then interweaves the experience of mortals, specifically women, with that of the fairy queen. During the nineteenth century, the line referring to "bed and company" was often deleted. It disappeared from the Charles Kean printed text (*MND 9*) and was crossed through in the Beerbohm Tree prompt (*MND 7*). On the other hand, Garrick and Colman retained this line (*MND 19*) although slashing so much material on either side to make room for musical airs that the line's implications probably had little effect on the audience. In that text, the accusations by fairy king and queen refer merely to their specific favorites within the context of this play—Titania's preference for Theseus and Oberon's for the "bouncing Amazon" (70).

However, Titania's full speeches, although couched in "fairy terms," offer insights into the imperfect relationship between men and women. Describing the conflict between her and Oberon, she begins by mentioning jealousy:

> These are the forgeries of jealousy;
> And never, since the middle summer's spring,
> Met we on hill, in dale, forest, or mead,
> By paved fountain or by rushy brook
> Or in the beached margent of the sea,
> To dance our ringlets to the whistling wind,
> But with thy brawls thou hast disturb'd our
>   sport.
>
>   (II.i.81-87)

The speech continues for thirty-six lines, but has usually been reduced to six, or even four. The remnant simply accuses Oberon of disturbing the gatherings of the fairies with his "brawls" whenever the two have met (87). As critics have frequently noted, the speech gives us a sense of Titania's breadth and sensitivity, connecting her with an Eden or a classical world of the gods, or even with nature deities of rustic sixteenth-century England. She refers to the effect of the dissension between her and Oberon on the elements, "The ox hath . . . stretched his yoke in vain, / The plowman lost his sweat . . . / The fold stands empty in the drowned field / And crows are fatted with the murrion flock" (93-97). Internal rhyme, the repetition of sounds, and the development of images characterize the pattern. Her concern for the maintenance of the rhythms in the animal world extends to the human world as well. She decries the effect of their arguments on the normal flow of the seasons and on human life.

> The human mortals want their winter here;
> No night is now with hymn or carol blest.
> . . . . The spring, the summer
> The childing autumn, angry winter, change
> Their wonted liveries; and the mazed world
> By their increase, now knows not which is
>   which.
>
>   (101-14)

Images of nature's gifts and blights vie with one another, investing her speech with cosmic concerns beyond merely trading accusations with Oberon. When, later, she explains why she will not relinquish the child, she describes his mother, with whom she laughed and "gossip'd."[25] Titania's lines—"we have laugh'd to see the sails conceive / And grow big-bellied with the wanton wind" (128-29)—suggestively describe the pregnant woman herself. They too disappear, the verbal inferences coming too close to nature, pregnancy, and women's physical appearance.[26] Whittling down the lines narrows this portrait of Titania; she then more closely parallels Oberon who in this section has only brief comments.[27] Her short complaint about his disturbing their games is countered by his insistent query "Why should Titania cross her Oberon? / I do but beg a little changeling boy, / To be my henchman" (119-21). Reinhardt's film cuts even further. None of Titania's lines remain except her response to Oberon's request for the changeling boy: "Set your heart at rest; / The fairy land buys not the child of me" (121-22). The scene's focus changes to the Indian boy.

Even when they retain practically all of the text, however, productions may alter the power of Titania's lines by stage directions, as did Peter Brook's in the wonderfully unisex-looking work. The performance had an exuberance and originality that captivated audiences. It also captured some of the attitudes of the 1960s and 1970s, as a glance at the "Authorized Acting Edition" testifies, raising questions about the Oberon-Titania relationship that one might even have missed in watching the play. Here, for example, is a detailed description of what went on during this scene of their first meeting which begins with Titania's crossing down stage center and kneeling (23a) before Oberon when she refers to their brawls. Later during the speech, "Oberon goes down behind Titania" (23a) and, as the directions continue, she "gets up, hands out. Oberon puts hands around her waist with wand" (24a). In talking about the "hoary headed frosts" she puts her hands over Oberon's. And at the lines "and the mazed world / by their increase now know not which is which" (24b) the stage direction reads, "Oberon's hands on Titania's breasts, with wand. Titania's arms out" (24a). As the scene continues, one sees more of physical sexual interaction between them until finally at her decision not to give him the boy, she pushes Oberon away. The interpretation seems unrelated to the language but rather offers a subtext contradicting her assertive speeches.

The comments accompanying the promptbook offer a partial explanation of this treatment of Titania. Brook had chosen to double the roles of Titania/Hippolyta and Oberon/Theseus. Alan Howard, who played Oberon/Theseus, discusses the point of view towards the relationship between his roles and the joint Titania/Hippolyta role:

At the beginning of the play, Theseus/Oberon is worried about the moon being gone and that his desires are, in consequence, bottled up. And Hippolyta/Titania says: "Don't worry. Another moon will come in. Wait, and it will all be fine again." *Her kind of intensity is toward her knowledge of herself as a woman . . . in terms of whatever it is that women do that men don't.* Theseus/Oberon has somehow got to explain his case. (41, emphasis added)

Howard's comment indicates a perception of Titania as inexplicable "other" although her language clearly expresses her dismay at the destructiveness of their conflict. Oberon simply isn't listening. What is exciting about the play, however, is the way Shakespeare seems to be applying what he has been hearing, or observing, in the real world to this fantasy couple, embedding a contemporaneity within an otherworldly framework.[28]

After her departure, Oberon vows, "Thou shalt not from this grove / Till I torment thee for this injury" (146-47), indicating a vindictiveness as well as a desire to exert power over her. And here, perhaps because of the implication of equality suggested first by the conversation between the fairy and Puck and later by the confrontation between Oberon and Titania, we are unprepared for the trick he plays on her. Shakespeare's audience, however, may well have expected it, since Titania was behaving like the rebellious, dominant, independent wife who, according to Stone, might be breaking the code of the social group "concerning sexual or power relations within the family" (3). "Thus a husband-beating wife, a passively henpecked husband, a couple married despite gross disparities in age, a cuckold, an adulterous wife . . . were all liable to be treated to . . . humiliating demonstrations of public disapproval" (3). Titania suffers just such a "humiliating demonstration" later on when she falls in love with the first thing that she sees upon awakening, a mortal with an ass's head—the "translated" Bottom.

By endowing the situation with such human qualities and giving Titania wonderful lines, however, the dramatist may also be questioning the justice of Oberon's action especially where he seems to be motivated by revenge. When he directs Puck to fetch the magic herb called "love-in-idleness" (II.i.168), the fairy king explains:

> The juice of it on sleeping eyelids laid
> Will make or man or woman madly dote
> Upon the next live creature that it sees.
>
> (170-72)

He will squeeze the juice into her eyes and eventually defeat the play's most independent woman. In the complex interweaving of plots, he will also, almost casually, exercise his power benevolently. Although some critics have perceived Oberon as an even-handed ruler who insists on establishing a certain kind of obedience to his rule, his actions here seem arbitrary and tinged with jealousy. When later on he acts more generously towards Helena, attempting to change her fate from that of cast-off woman to desired one, Oberon's actions seem to come almost as an afterthought to his more driven desire for revenge on Titania.

Having sent Puck on his way, Oberon, alone in the forest, sees Demetrius and Helena approaching. "I am invisible," he announces to his audience, as Hamlet's and Banquo's ghosts do not; rather on-stage characters provide the clues to the emptiness of the space even while the invisible character appears on stage. Alan Dessen discusses the implications of this "not seeing" or blindness of characters on stage as often metaphoric for the blindness or inability of the characters on stage to see and understand (130-55). Here, however, Shakespeare denies us this metaphor by having Oberon proclaim his invisibility. The dramatist, skilled in embedding stage directions in his text, chooses, instead, to characterize Oberon through this more direct statement, possibly with the aim of literalizing him, just as the mechanicals, later on, so carefully literalize their actions.

Observing Helena trailing Demetrius, the fairy king reacts with sympathy to her plight; he would have Demetrius sue for her love. The magic herb holds the key. What are we to make of Oberon's reaction here? If Titania is aggressive in rejecting him, Helena is aggressive in pursuing Demetrius. Ironically, Oberon, who would have the fairy queen exhibit the kind of self-abasement practiced by Helena, expresses great sympathy for the mortal woman and later sends Puck to find the Athenians while the fairy king himself will anoint Titania's eyes. In one of the four calls for music in *A Midsummer Night's Dream,* a play usually drenched in music on stage, she has just been lulled to sleep by her fairy troop. "Come, now a roundel and a fairy song. . . . sing me now asleep" (II.ii.1,7), Titania directs, becoming vulnerable to Oberon's scheme. Meanwhile, Puck, having sought Athenians in the forest and found only the sleeping Hermia and Lysander, squeezes the magic juice into the eyes of the wrong man.

Now Helena, the rejected Helena, is forced to face a new role—that of the chosen one, the pursued one, when Lysander, upon being awakened, expresses his undying love for her. This is difficult for a woman whose self-image has already been shaped. Speaking in soliloquy moments before his sudden and inexplicable pursuit, she weighs her virtues and strengths and finds them nonexistent. She compares herself first with Hermia then indulges in close self-analysis:

How came her eyes so bright? Not with salt
  tears;
If so, my eyes are oft'ner wash'd than hers.
No, no; I am as ugly as a bear;
For beasts that meet me run away for fear.
Therefore no marvel though Demetrius
Do, as a monster, fly my presence thus.

                      (92-97)

Helena doesn't like what she sees. Although the speech continues developing her profile, it too, like so many earlier speeches by the women, frequently loses its subtlety and color through excision.[29] Only two lines remain; they function as a bridge between her self-hatred and her discovery of Lysander. The full speech, however, explains her astonishment at his actions, and her inability to find any excuse for them. Lacking any sense of self-worth, she is bewildered. The play, however, provides a rationale. According to Lysander, one needs maturity to appreciate Helena's worth. "Reason" must be the guide:

  The will of man is by his reason sway'd;
  And reason says you are the worthier maid.
                      (115-16)

He then expands on this, explaining, "Things growing are not ripe until their season, / so I, being young, till now ripe not to reason" (117-18). The scene also permits the dramatist to differentiate further between the two young women because even in these mere sketches, he assigns specific qualities to each. But once again major chunks of text are cut for the stage, eliminating all but the most obvious differences—the women's varying appeals to men.[30]

Illustrating the effectiveness of the magic juice, the brief scene between Helena and Lysander in its complete form anticipates the sharp reaction Titania will experience. Because so much criticism has interpreted the fairy queen's later actions when under the juice's spell as truly representative of her underlying feelings, one could test the validity of such a theory by applying it to Lysander, the first to be transformed. Does he really mean it when, responding to Helena's reminder of his love for Hermia, he refers to his former love scornfully as "the surfeit of the sweetest things" (137) and undesirable? Since he later returns to her, one must believe that this is merely his manner of coping, under the spell's influence.

Although some critics consider Oberon's potion a symbol of love, as it applies to Titania it appears to be more a symbol of power, or at least of revenge for her failure to release the child. In direct response to her unwillingness to acquiesce to his demand, Oberon induces the spell:

  The next thing then she waking looks upon
  (Be it on lion, bear, or wolf, or bull,

On meddling monkey, or on busy ape),
She shall pursue it with the soul of love.

                (II.i.179-82)

No handsome youth or prince charming but rather a list of animals is intended as her fate. In fact some promptbooks—for the 1856 [*MND* 9] and Tree 1900 [*MND* 7] productions—excise these references to animals. In Garrick's production, she is never seen "enamor'd of an ass" (IV.i.77). Instead, the audience must rely on Puck's report:

  My mistress with a patched fool is in love.
  Near to her close and consecrated bower
  This clown with others had rehearsed a play
  Intended for great Theseus' nuptial day.
  When, starting from her bank of mossy down,
  Titania waked, and straightway loved the
    clown.
    (III.i.2-7; Garrick in Pedicord, III:176)

References to the ass have disappeared; the substitute terms "patched fool" and "clown" soften Titania's fate.

Through the complex interweaving of plot strands in which fairies, tradesmen, and high-born characters from the world of Athens intermingle, Shakespeare can raise questions about women's roles. The dramatist draws on the third group, the mechanicals, for the "ass" who will humiliate, humble, and subdue the fairy queen. Entering the enchanted forest to rehearse their play, "Pyramus and Thisbe," these comic characters, hoping to perform before the Duke on his wedding day, inadvertently participate in Oberon's trickery. Reacting variously to the idea of performing—some with trepidation about learning the words, others protesting assignment of their roles—one in the group plunges into the adventure. He would play every role. Quickly we become acquainted with Nick Bottom, the weaver, who would shout like a bear and weep like a woman. He will, eventually, bray like an ass, a role not in their skit, but one he will take on in his unexpected adventure with the fairy queen.

Doomed to awaken "when some vile thing is near" whom she will take for her love, Titania hears the braying Bottom—anointed with an ass's head by Puck—and marvels at his musicality. She finds his music beautiful and his person appealing. But then she has been blinded by Oberon's magic spell. In the Ciulei production, she reacts to that juice by screaming as if hit by lightning. Few productions, however, dramatize the evil inherent in this type of magic. Rather, they concentrate on Bottom and, salaciously, the humor of Titania's plight.

More than anywhere else, it is in the effect of Oberon's trick on Titania, however, that one feels the tragedy for the women and the insights the dramatist gives us into the ways in which patriarchy manipulates women's options. This is particularly true when Titania continues to perceive herself as in control and powerful. During her first meeting with Bottom, the enchanted Titania praises his wisdom as well as beauty and musical skill, declaring that she loves him. When he wants only to leave the wood, she warns:

> Out of this wood do not desire to go;
> Thou shalt remain here, whether thou wilt or
>   no.
> I am a spirit of no common rate;
> The summer still doth tend upon my state.
>
> (III.i.152-55)

The lines underscore the ironic contrast between her perception of herself and her actual situation. Like Lysander, she is trying to cope. Some versions eliminate her reference to power: "whether thou wilt or no." In many texts, her whole last speech, beginning "Come wait upon him; lead him to my bower," is excised. Thus audiences do not know that she entertains him in her bower, or that the moon, "when she weeps, weeps every little flower, / Lamenting some enforced chastity" (199-200). As a result, the full implication of Oberon's trick on Titania is lost to the audience.[31]

Sometimes a critic will overlook Oberon's role, concentrating instead on the effect of the magic potion on Titania. Jan Kott, for example, not only stresses the eroticism and harshness embedded in the text but also translates this eroticism in terms of the fairy queen. To him, her invitation to Bottom exemplifies woman's passion and hidden desire, rather than illustrating the male (Oberon's) exercise of power. Analyzing the staging of those scenes between Titania and Bottom, Kott also decries the tendency to play them for laughs rather than present them as black humor, an "English kind of humour, 'humeur noir', cruel and scatological, as it often is in Swift" (228). Most revealing, however, is Kott's final comment about the scene, as he describes Titania:

> The slender, tender and lyrical Titania longs for animal love. Puck and Oberon call the transformed Bottom a monster. The frail and sweet Titania drags the monster to bed, almost by force. (228)

This is the effect of the magic juice. Kott continues his male fantasy—the fantasy of women "never wanting to admit" to themselves that they really like being raped. In fact, Kott inverts this:

> This is the lover she wanted and dreamed off (sic); only she never wanted to admit it, even to herself. Sleep frees her from inhibitions. The monstrous ass is being raped by the poetic Titania, while she still keeps on chattering about flowers. . . . Of all the characters in the play Titania enters to the fullest

extent the dark sphere of sex where there is no more beauty and ugliness; there is only infatuation and liberation. (228)

Obviously to Kott, beauty and ugliness vanish before infatuation and liberation.

Fuseli's eighteenth-century illustration captures much of the implied eroticism in this scene although it differs in point of view from Kott's. . . . In the painting, dominated by the two major characters, a large nude male figure, topped by a donkey head with large ears and sitting crossed legged with his arms clasping his knees, is being caressed by Titania, her nude breast amply visible beneath the outstretched arm around his head. Surrounding the two are small insect-headed nude males, their penises visible, and small fairies looking like flirtatious women, their breasts seductively apparent although wearing female garb. While Fuseli indicates the eroticism in the scene, bringing in the whole forest and suggesting, too, the male appetite, Kott concentrates only on Titania, perceiving her as a voracious female. Neither acknowledges the idea of her being tricked.

C. L. Barber provides a totally different perspective. To him, the Titania scenes with Bottom reveal a "growing up," as I mentioned earlier:

> It is when the flower magic leads Titania to find a new object that she gives up the child (who goes now from her bower to the man's world of Oberon). So here is another sort of change of heart that contributes to the expression of what is consummated in marriage, this one a part of the rhythm of adult life, as opposed to the change in the young lovers that goes with growing up. (*FC* 137)

Again the question arises of whether Titania experiences a "change of heart" or is victimized by Oberon and therefore no natural growth occurs, merely a change depriving her of her former sense of self.

Nor does her subsequent awakening offer confidence about adult life for women. Deluded, she courts the ass-headed Bottom, taking him to her bower. Meanwhile Oberon plans his next move:

> I'll to my queen and beg her Indian boy;
> And then I will her charmed eye release
> From monster's view, and all things shall be
>   peace.
>
> (III.ii.375-77)

But shall they be at peace? Or worse, shall Titania's spirit have been broken? In *The Taming of the Shrew,* Kate says, "My tongue will tell the anger of my heart / Or else my heart concealing it will break" (IV.iii.77-78). Shakespeare recognizes the effect on the human heart of bottling up resentment.[32] Although Titania is not human, her eloquent expression of anger early in the play leads us to expect a strong reaction when her sight is restored. But no such response occurs. Instead, she cares neither about the Indian boy, nor the trick that has been played on her, but only about the humiliation of having been in love with an ass. Are we to think of her as resembling the nonhuman witches in *Macbeth* whose deeds do not upset them? Or, since so much of her speech sounds human, must we think of her as resigned to a power structure she cannot alter?

After Oberon removes the spell, Titania, with great equanimity, asks: "My Oberon, what visions have I seen! / Methought I was enamor'd of an ass" (IV.i.76-77). Nor does Oberon try to soften the answer. "There lies your love" (78), he asserts, pointing to the transformed Bottom. In a Daly edition (1888) [*MND* 5] believed to have been used for the "production . . . tour of 1895-96," Oberon's "There lies your love" (77) is accompanied by the stage direction *"sneering" "Puck titters"* (61), reinforcing a sense of Oberon's power, his delight in having played this trick on her, but more importantly, of a director's point of view. Undoubtedly he reflected the attitudes of his time. Unfortunately, as we keep discovering, this delight in seeing a strong woman bested is not confined to a bygone age.

Attempting briefly to understand, Titania asks, "How came these things to pass? / O, how mine eyes do loathe his visage now!" (78-79). But Oberon offers no direct answer. Instead, he orders Puck to "take off this head" [the ass's head] (80). Then, continuing to exert his power over Titania, the fairy king directs:

> Titania, music call, and strike more dead
> Than common sleep of all these five the
> sense.
>
> (81-82)

She complies: "Music, ho, music, such as charmeth sleep!" (86). Finally, as they fly off together, she once more returns to the subject of Bottom:

> Come, my lord, and in our flight,
> Tell me how it came this night
> That I sleeping here was found,
> With these mortals on the ground.
>
> (99-102)

But we never know if she receives an answer.

Although little has been written about Titania's character disintegration from a fiery, concerned fairy to a compliant partner, her change and lack of any clearly defined personality in the last scenes illustrate, on the one hand, the destructiveness of Oberon's action and, on the other, an inconsistency in characterization. Too

easily the richness of her personality as well as her intensity vanish. Writing of the "linguistic and dramatic complexities and contradictions" in the play, Jay Halio observes that

> [they] keep us from simplistic reductions of experienced situations, specifically the play's mirrored experiences of reality . . . and force us out of . . . an artificial prison that R. P. Blackmur has . . . described as a tendency to set artistic unity as a chief criterion of excellence. (145)

Borrowing from Halio but concentrating on how language defines and sometimes creates ambiguities concerning characters, particularly the female characters, I find in Titania either an inconsistency or a tragic transformation. Since this is a comedy one must consider the former as more likely. Examining an early nineteenth-century musical version of the play that attempts to inject sentimental logic to the Oberon-Titania relationship, reconciling the behavior of Oberon through some staging and language, one realizes that Shakespeare probably intentionally allowed the ambiguity in characterization to stand. Reynolds's 1816 version provides an easy alternative. Oberon speaks:

> I'll to my Queen, and beg her Indian boy!
> Not, not so much from love of him, as her,
> I court this contest,—I'd put her to the trial—
> If she refuse, I know her love is on the
> wane;—
> But, if she yield! Ah! that she may! and
> still—
>
> (Prompt *MND* 18, 8 p. 40)

Music then is played. *"(Clouds descend and open.—A Fairy is discovered, who chaunts the following lines)"*

> *Fairy.*   Oberon!
> *Oberon.*   Appear!
> *Fairy.*   Oberon! no more despair!
> Titania wafts him to your care!
> Borne by each propitious gale,
> From India's shores her gallies sail.
> Nor storms, nor quicksands can they meet,
> For Zephyrs fan the Fairy fleet!
> And silv'ry seas the treasure bear,—
> The Boy!—The Indian Boy is near!
> *(Clouds begin to ascend again.)*
>
> (p. 40)[33]

This finale of act 2 in the Reynolds play confirms the portrait of an Oberon driven by love rather than jealousy and of a Titania who, on her own initiative, relinquishes the boy.[34] Shakespeare, however, fails to provide any easy logical development to the Titania-Oberon relationship in the closing scenes. In fact, the difference between this version and Shakespeare's play reminds one of the difference between Cibber's *Rich-*

ard III and Shakespeare's, between simple blacks and whites as compared with an extraordinary range of greys, between directness and ambiguity.

In *A Midsummer Night's Dream,* the dramatist raises questions concerning women and the power structure imposed on them, even when he supplies no easy answers. Having showed us Titania in her strength, he seems to turn to other concerns, returning her to her fairy role. The young Athenian women provide another example of the power of patriarchy over women's lives. Never confused in their affections for the two young men, Hermia and Helena gain insights into themselves and into the unpredictability of male behavior as a result of their experiences in the forest. Differing from the two young men, the women never have their eyes anointed with Oberon's magic juice; nevertheless, their relationships with the two youths as well as with one another change. Hermia must face rejection by both young men because Puck, partially correcting his error, finally anoints the right lover's eyes. Suddenly both Demetrius and Lysander are amorously pursuing Helena. Desired by both youths, she believes neither. Nor does her earlier passion for Demetrius convince her of his sincerity at this moment. She accuses them of mocking her. Disbelief, anger, and hurt mark her words: "Can you not hate me, as I know you do, / But you must join in souls to mock me too?" (III.ii.149-50).

Changing places and relationships, the women find their friendship turned into rivalry and their dispute quickly reduced to name calling, hair pulling, and physical conflict. Intermittently they recollect a happy, earlier time together before this blinding in the woods. Much cutting of lines, however, reduces this section to the outline of the contest between the men, diminishing any sharp character definition of the women. Large sections of Hermia's reprimand to Demetrius disappear. Gone too is Helena's sensitive description of their childhood friendship when they sewed together "sitting on one cushion, / . . . As if our hands, our sides, voices and minds / Had been incorporate. So we grew together, / Like to a double cherry, seeming parted" (205-9). Much later Shakespeare would develop this recollection of an early innocent friendship ruined by sexual jealousy, transmuting it into a description of the friendship between two men, Leontes and Polixenes in *The Winter's Tale.* Seldom heard on the stage, Helena's lines again individualize her, as she accuses her friend of conspiring with the men. Characteristically, Hermia counters with anger and frustration.

Because both suitors are fiercely pursuing Helena, Puck must lead them "Up and down, up and down," (396) to keep them apart, and because the role has its own magic, the scenes in the forest with the blinded lovers allow for farce, action, and humor. The two men pursue one another in the wood while Puck blankets it with fog and mimics each man's voice to mislead and confuse his opponent. Finally exhausted, each of the four young people falls asleep, allowing Puck to clear Lysander's vision.

The dramatist then switches focus from the youths to their elders. Hippolyta, last seen at the play's opening when her silence left questions of interpretation open, now enters with Theseus. Discord seems to have vanished. But here, unlike the Titania-Oberon exit when the fairy queen seemed so muted and transformed, the Amazon queen exhibits sparks of individuality as she jokingly debates the relative merits of Theseus's hounds. Stumbling on the sleeping young lovers, the older couple, upon awakening the youths, discovers two matched pairs. Oberon had never removed the magic juice from Demetrius's eyes; he will no longer pursue Hermia. Theseus's perspective alters. Rather than being the rigid, unbending Duke of Athens, he overrules Egeus's sentence on Hermia. Confused and uncertain, the couples leave the forest.

Bottom then awakens, the ass's head removed, and the spell lifted. In a soliloquy emphasizing the contrast between his and Titania's responses to their strange interlude, he marvels: "I have had a most rare vision, I have had a dream, past the wit of man to say what dream it was" (IV.i.204-6). His speech, as we know, parodies St. Paul's I Corinthians ii.9 ff. If Bottom's vision has been expanded, Titania's has been destroyed. Looking at him, she had reacted with revulsion. Thus, again, the victimization of a woman is implied.

As the play moves towards its denouement, the roles of the women characters have begun to shrink or change. Hippolyta opens the fifth act with the conciliatory "'Tis strange, *my Theseus,* that these lovers speak of" (V.i.1, emphasis added). Her term of address, like Titania's lines when she flies away with Oberon, reveals acceptance of her position although as the scene develops she is the one woman who constantly speaks out. Hermia and Helena, so vocal earlier, are strangely silent during the bridal entertainment hosted by Theseus. In contrast, the young bridegrooms, Lysander and Demetrius, along with Theseus speak a good deal, deriding the entertainment by Bottom and his friends. Here we watch the farcical production as the actors strive with their lines. The prologue begins the performance:

If we offend, it is with our good will.
That you should think, we come not to offend,
But with good will.

(V.i.108-10)

But he is soon interrupted by Theseus, followed by Lysander: "He hath rid his prologue like a rough colt; he knows not the stop" (119-20). Hippolyta too contributes: "Indeed he hath play'd on this prologue like a child on a recorder—a sound, but not in government" (122-24). Trying to outdo one another, the commentators keep interrupting the action as Pyramus exclaims against his fate:

> O grim-look'd night! O night with hue so
>   black!
> O night, which ever art when day is not!
> O night, O night! alack, alack, alack
>   (170-72)

As the play-within-a-play progresses and both Pyramus and Thisby commit suicide in a case of mistaken supposition, much like the deaths of Romeo and Juliet, the interruptions come more often and are more incisive. Whether it is Hippolyta protesting, "I am a-weary of this moon. Would he would change!" (251-52) of a character portraying moon, or Theseus's response, "It appears . . . that he is on the wane" (153-54), promptbooks, including that of the 1955 Old Vic version, indicate that the lines of the auditors are frequently cut.[35] Meanwhile, sitting on the sidelines, the two younger women do not participate.

Is it an accident that for so long, in the early years, it was *Pyramus and Thisbe* or other abbreviated versions that were produced?[36] Abstracted from its place in the context of *A Midsummer Night's Dream, Pyramus and Thisbe* was merely a farcical commentary on lovers who die for love, having been hindered by their parents from uniting. But as part of the larger whole, the play-within-a-play not only mocks the intensity of the Athenian lovers and the price of love, but also highlights, through this distancing lens of metadrama, the submissiveness (or at least silence) expected of women in marriage.

Perhaps aware of the implication of the young women's silence, Augustin Daly, having given the role of Helena to his favorite actress, Ada Rehan, reassigned many of the interrupting lines to the women. Altering the text and countering its implication of the silent women, Daly gave several of the lines of the commentators to Helena and Hermia, but primarily to Helena, creating in her an assertive personality. Specifically, the exchange on the moon is assigned to Helena and Hermia, as is another exchange between Hippolyta and Theseus. In fact, Daly's reassignment of lines spotlights the freedom of speech that Hippolyta, of all the women in the play, has gained. Did Shakespeare give her these lines because she was, even if won in battle, a former queen and Amazon? Or was the assignment based on her role as Theseus's wife? Hermia and Helena's last speeches occur in the fourth act when, delighted to have been united with the men of their choice, each marvels at the outcome, Helena still treasuring Demetrius, whom she has "found . . . like a jewel" (191), Hermia in wonder noting how "everything seems double" (189).

Of all the women characters, Titania has changed the most, accepting her role as Oberon's handmaid. Re-

turning with the fairies, she sings and blesses the newly married couples' beds. No recollection of the votress who died in childbirth mars the blessing. Nor is the Indian boy ever mentioned again. As Stevie Davis observes:

> When Oberon reclaims his rule, and Theseus leads the characters into the reasserted status quo of the final Act, the issue of the changeling child is laid aside, the mother forgotten, as the play closes around the artisans' comedy it contains. But a reader may not forget nor really forgive the misappropriation of the boy-child by the law of the fathers, nor is the haunting music of Titania's elegy contradicted by a preferable ethic or emotion. (127-28)

Shakespeare's portraits of women here raise questions about the validity of the political and social structures that limit women's actions. At other times the dramatist challenges accepted notions by creating women characters, such as those in *All's Well That Ends Well,* who are more capable, clever, and intelligent than their male counterparts. In *A Midsummer Night's Dream,* he invents basically parallel male and female characters of equivalent ability, then weights the scales in favor of the men, illuminating the obstacles women face. Having presented the issues lightly, he then moves on to conventional theatrical treatment in the ending.

Nevertheless, one can believe that Shakespeare has painted here a complex work whose inner design has more depth than has yet been captured on stage and whose implications are still to be realized. Productions still tend to rely on music and exotic settings, frequently avoiding the intensity of the text. As John Simon wrote of a production in 1988 at the Public Theatre in New York, decrying its lack of lyricism, "What has been added is a lot of samba, bossanova, and Brazilian ambiance that often clashes with what is spoken." In that late twentieth-century production by A. J. Antoon, an important contemporary director, the text still seems to have been secondary to music and setting.

Perhaps an argument for the play's still untapped potential lies in the example of the recent revival of *Carousel* of which one critic wrote: "*Carousel* will be 50 next year, but as of this morning it is the freshest, most innovative musical on Broadway" (Richards). Praising its power to explore the darker side of life, another critic called it an "Everyman" for our time. Whatever *A Midsummer Night's Dream* might have been planned for in its own time—whether a wedding; a simple entertainment, a vibrant piece of stagecraft to amuse even those who were being examined—in its language, in its questioning of societal values, and in its brief portraits of several women suffering at the whim of a power structure they did not devise, the play holds the potential for being an "Everywoman" for our time, briefly exploring the "darker side of life." On the other hand, it remains for a work like *Hamlet* to focus more closely on that darkness—on the confusions that face women as well as men in their search for a clearer path in a patriarchal world.

Notes

[1] Such popular works as Vives's *Instructions of a Christian Woman* and Whately's *A Bride-bush,* although slightly later in time (1617), address the obligations of the bride. *Love* appears on this list. In speaking of marriage and its obligations, he speaks of mutuality, at least obliquely:

> 6. The mutuall therefore (that wee may speake of them in order) are requyred both of man and wife, though not in an equall measure of both. For in all these common duties, the husband should bee most abundant, knowing that more of every grace is looked for from him, then from the weaker vessell. Wee call them not therefore common or mutuall, because both should have a like quantity of them; but because both must have some of all, and the husband most of all. And for these common duties, you must know in generall, that whatsoever is requyred of all men and women, generally towards other, by the Law of Christianity and Charity, as they bee men and neighbors; the same is in an higher degree and larger measure requyred from the husband toward the wife, and from her to him. (6)

Unfortunately he then writes of persuasion of a wife to yield to the husband's authority, although earlier he wrote of love being a very important ingredient in the relationship.

> Yea indeed she must be a monstrous and unwomanly woman, that being drawne by entreatie will not yeeld. Authority is like the arts of Logick and Rhetoricke, that must in speaking be used, and yet concealed: and then they most prevaile when being used, they are least seene. . . . Men that ride horses have a wand and a spurre, both; they will rather set forward their horses with the whisk & sound, or perhaps little touch of the smal stick, then with the sharpnesse of their iron spurre. They proceed not to spurring till their horse be either restie or tiry; and if tiry, that doth more hurt. So the husband should governe his wife, & provoke her to accomplish his will with quiet, pleasing and insinuating termes, rather than open and expresse, much lesse violent commandings, unlesse shee bee more then ordinarily unruly. Christ beseecheth his Church most an end, which hee might with most right command. (29)

Having finally finished writing of the duties of the husband, Whately then turns to the duties of the wife:

> The whole duty of the wife is referred to two heads. The first is, to acknowledge her inferiority: the next,

to carry her self as inferiour. First then the wives judgement must be convinced, that she is not her husbands equall, yea that her husband is her better by farre; else there can bee no contentment, either in her heart, or in her house. If shee stand upon termes of equality, much more of being better than he is, the very root of good carriage is withered, and the fountaine thereof dryed up. (36)

[2] *The Fairies* (1755) was billed as an opera. It "is made up from the first four acts only, of Shakespeare's play" and does not include references to Bottom and his troop. It also includes twenty-eight songs added to the text. Some are from the play, some from other plays or other sources, such as Milton's "L'Allegro." It was a success (Stone, *MND,* 469-72). In 1763 a version of *A Midsummer Night's Dream,* attributed variously to Garrick and Colman but which Stone faults Colman for, appeared for one night and failed. It was subsequently followed by *A Fairy Tale,* which consists of two short acts, "centering about the Oberon-Titania dispute and includes Bottom and his fellows" (Stone, *MND,* 480-81). For a complete discussion of the adaptations variously attributed to David Garrick and George Colman, see Stone, *"A Midsummer Night's Dream";* and Pedicord and Bergmann, eds. *The Plays of David Garrick,* vol. 4, 420-31. Depending upon which version I am discussing, I refer either to Garrick or Garrick-Colman as the adaptors.

[3] The first *Pyramus and Thisbe,* adapted by Richard Leveridge, 1716, contained their early scenes of planning as well as the actual play-within-a-play; the second, adapted by John Frederick Lampe, 1745, retained only the fifth-act production but omitted the court personnel (Hogan, I.339). Departing further from Shakespeare's *A Midsummer Night's Dream,* but adopting its adventures of the workmen, Charles Johnson, in 1723, inserted a "Pyramus and Thisbe" comic segment into his version of *As You Like It* calling his work *Love in a Forest* (Hogan, I.339). We are not here dealing with Shakespeare's *A Midsummer Night's Dream,* merely with bits and pieces.

[4] Generally, but inconclusively, attributed to Elkanah Settle, its music definitely written by Henry Purcell, *The Fairy Queen* was a lavish production costing £3000 (*LS,*1:lv). Its closing was capped by a dance with "twenty-four Chineses" (Odell, 1:194).

[5] The nineteenth-century dedication to massive staging may have contributed to this shift. According to Gary Jay Williams the transposition of text and the scenic effects may also reflect the general celebration of empire at the time, with Theseus as the triumphant victor.

[6] Reinhardt here drew on his 1927 stage production at the Century theater, in New York, in which Hippolyta appears with a group of large dogs.

[7] These are some of the numbered "shots" in the script.

[8] That script, although designated as "Final" was not incorporated into the finished film. Nor has any copy of this visual sequence of film—a first reel—been found. Robert H. Ball, in seeking to document this same information, found, in 1971 that "no indication of reels until 15 reel version" existed. This comment appears on a chart he made of the different versions, identifying them as "R=Reinhardt; K=Kenyon + McCall; 15=15 reel dial; 12=12 reel dial." In addition, his K list has "(marked 'Final')" and corresponds exactly with the material I found in the Warner Brothers archives at Princeton. The Ball notes are currently in a file at the Folger Shakespeare Library. It also contains an earlier correspondence between Ball and Joel Swensen at Warner Brothers in 1947. This says, "Our print man thinks all we have is the 12 reel version" 30 July 1947. An earlier letter from Henry Blanke, at Warner Brothers in California, to Joel Swensen, states, "As far as I can recall, the 15 reel version of *A Midsummer Night's Dream* ran all over the country, except that very much later on a certain re-issue it was cut down to 12 reels. However, neither the 15 nor the 12 reel version will completely correspond with the script as many sequences contained in the script were eliminated—as is usually the case in motion pictures—before their release. So the closest thing to go by or to get a comparison to the script would be the dialogue sheets that were put out with the original 15 reel version." The letter is dated 14 July 1947.

[9] The full text of Fuller's comment is:

> In every-day life, the feelings of the many are stained with vanity. Each wishes to be lord in a little world, to be superior at least over one; and he does not feel strong enough to retain a life-long ascendency over a strong nature. Only a Theseus could conquer before he wed the Amazonian queen. Hercules wished rather to rest with Dejanira, and received the poisoned robe as a fit guerdon. The tale should be interpreted to all those who seek repose with the weak. (43)

[10] Aside from having been eliminated from the Garrick-Colman and Reynolds versions, the references also disappeared in whole or part from the printed acting texts of the nineteenth and twentieth centuries such as French's (*MND* 20), Charles Kean's edition (*MND* 9), Augustin Daly's (*MND* 5), and from the typescript of Henry Jewett's for a 1915 production (*MND* 12). When promptbooks relied on the full text, the lines were then crossed out for the acting versions. Among the latter were the recording of the Burton performance of 1854 (*MND* 21), the Beerbohm Tree production of 1900 (*MND* 7), and the Samuel Phelps production of 1861 (*MND* 13). The Reinhardt film retains only a small section of the speech.

[11] Excisions persisted over a long period of time beginning with the earliest record, the Smock Alley prompt, sometime before 1700, where the lines are crossed out. Garrick eliminated them from his preparation copy of 1763. They do not appear in Reynolds's 1816 version, are crossed out in Charles Kean's (*MND* 9) and eliminated by Daly in 1888 as well as by Herbert Beerbohm Tree for the 1900 production (*MND* 7), to name just a few characteristic productions.

[12] Literally, the lines (136-49) were not printed in the French acting texts (*MND* 15, *MND* 20) and Charles Kean's text of 1869 (*MND* 9). In the Burton text of 1854 (*MND* 21), the lines appear but are then crossed through.

[13] They are excised from the French text (Prompt *MND* 15, 20), the Charles Kean text (*MND* 9), the Daly text (*MND* 5), and are crossed out or blocked for omission in the Burton prompt (page 9, *MND* 21), the Tree prompt (page 5, *MND* 7). In the Phelps prompt (page 311, *MND* 13), it is more difficult to be certain of whether or not the section was excised since there are two different sets of markings here—some in brown ink, others in pencil. This section has a penciled bracket on the left. Since another passage immediately above it on the page has been crossed through, the question remains of whether this passage was in fact excised.

[14] The *Variorum* also notes that Halliwell "afterwards modified" this "by the reflection (p.36, folio ed.) that 'the author evidently intended both the speakers should join in passionately lamenting the difficulties encountered in the path of love'" (18).

[15] Having removed this section from the printed text, the Kean book (prompt *MND* 9) indicates even further excision, penciling out still more of the beginning of this exchange between the two women. It is also excised from the Phelps promptbook (*MND* 13). Earlier, Garrick, who had cut the lines of the speech, nevertheless retained the character of Helena here whereas Reynolds, despite his promise to restore more of the play in 1816, eliminated her completely from the scene.

[16] The excisions occur in the following prompts: *MND* 9, *MND* 20, *MND* 21, *MND* 15, and others.

[17] The handwriting has been identified as Garrick's. See also Stone article on *A Midsummer Night's Dream,* discussed in note 2.

[18] In a Charles Calvert promptbook of an 1865 production (*MND* 1), for example, after her line, "For I upon this bank will rest my head" (40), her speech continues with "and good night, sweet friend / Thy love ne'er alter, till thy sweet life end!" (60-61). Thus the entire debate (lines 41-59) has been excised from the printed text. Kean too (*MND* 9) follows this format. Tree (*MND*

7) crosses out text, retaining only one line of Lysander's—"One turf shall serve as pillow for us both," (41)—and then, once again, Hermia's "Nay good Lysander; for my sake" (43) precedes the jump to the conclusion "so far be distant, and good night, sweet friend: / Thy love ne'er alter till thy sweet life end!" (60-61). Lysander's innocuous "Amen" and the few brief lines of good night precede their finally falling off to sleep, which closes this section of the scene. Phelps's book, too (*MND* 13), cuts the debate. Gone is Lysander's sophisticated argument in favor of one bed, along with her "Lysander riddles very prettily . . ." (42, 43b-56a). Daly, too (*MND* 5), includes Lysander's "One turf . . ." (41-42) and Hermia's brief response "Nay good Lysander . . ." (43-44) then jumps to line 60, "So far be distant; and good night sweet friend. / Thy love ne'er alter, till thy sweet life end!" (60-61).

[19] As a sampling, they are crossed out in Burton's text (22-23) (*MND* 21) and Phelps's of 1861 (328-29) (*MND* 13); and are omitted from George Colman and David Garrick's 1763 version (*MND* 19), Charles Kean's (*MND* 9), Augustin Daly's, 1888 (*MND* 5), Herbert Beerbohm Tree's (*MND* 7), French's (*MND* 15), and the edition recording performances at the Broadway Theatre (*MND* 20), as well as Henry Jewett's 1915 typescript (*MND* 12). Of course the highly abbreviated Colman version of 1777, *A Fairy Tale* (*MND* 22), does not include these Athenian characters at all.

[20] Seldom the subject for criticism, Helena has the largest percentage of lines (10.4) and words (11.2) of any woman character in the play although Hermia has more speeches (9.5 percent to Helena's 7.14). Hermia's fewer lines (7.5 percent) and words (7.9 percent) suggest the difference in the pattern of the women's speeches. Following is the record in the *Concordance* of the other long roles: Theseus: 9.5 percent speeches, 10.9 percent lines, 10.7 percent words; Bottom 9.9 percent speeches, 9.7 percent lines, 10.3 percent words; Oberon 5.7 percent speeches, 10.2 percent lines, 9.9 percent words. Spevack, *Concordance* 1:666-713.

[21] Many fine references appear in this article, including one to Gayle Rubin's "The Traffic in Women." Marshall asks questions: "How are we to take Demetrius' recovery from the 'sickness' of abandoning Helena and loving Hermia since it is just as much the product of enchantment as Lysander's abandonment of Hermia and love for Helena? Are we to be pleased by the success of Helena's subjection of herself to Demetrius or Titania's sudden and manipulated surrender to Oberon? What about Hippolyta's marriage to the soldier who vanquished her? . . . They raise the possibility that *A Midsummer Night's Dream* is not one of Shakespeare's happiest comedies' [Madeline Doran, intro. in Penguin *Complete Works*] but rather a 'most lamentable comedy' (I.ii.11-12) and 'very tragical mirth' (V.i.57)" (548).

Marshall also takes exception to C. L. Barber's comment that Theseus and Hippolyta are looking toward their wedding "'Theseus . . . with masculine impatience, Hippolyta with a woman's willingness to dream away time' (*Shakespeare's Festive Comedies,* p. 128)" (548). Marshall asks how Barber knows this since the language doesn't say it. "I don't know how Barber manages to assign genders to these feelings" (548).

Of David P. Young's comment (*Something of Great Constancy: the Art of "A Midsummer Night's Dream"*, New Haven: Yale University Press, 1966, 109), "It is appropriate that Theseus, as representative of daylight and right reason, should have subdued his bride-to-be to the rule of his masculine will. That is the natural order of things (p. 99)," Marshall comments, "This *may* have been the ruling ideology in the sixteenth century or in 1966—I don't see that it has ever been the *natural* order of things—but it is not necessarily the ideology of *A Midsummer Night's Dream*" (550).

[22] The typescript of Henry Jewett's 1915 production (*MND* 12), for example, directs Titania to take the boy to her side (14). In the elegant Daly version, when Titania enters, her "attendant fairies . . . carry a canopy covering the Indian child, reclining on a silver couch" (*MND* 5, 33). In this cut version, there is even the printed stage direction, "Oberon orders his attendants to advance, and he dashes toward the couch to seize the child. He tears aside the curtains, and finds that it has disappeared" (34). Crossed out in pencil by a later manager, the action dramatizes the hostility between king and queen although simplifying the portraits.

[23] The comment is by Thomas Hailes Lacy for the 1840 text. Actually Mendelssohn first wrote the overture for an 1827 revival in Berlin (Campbell, 546). However it was the Vestris production, claiming to present the play "almost as Shakespeare wrote it, for the first time since 1642," that was such a huge success (Campbell, 546). According to Odell, no version this close to Shakespeare's had appeared since Davenant's in the seventeenth century (II.204). Vestris's was followed by other lavish productions, most relying on this music. Only Phelps eschewed the music.

[24] The popularity of *A Midsummer Night's Dream* at mid nineteenth century extended from London to New York, two rival productions appearing in February, 1854: at Burton's and the Broadway theaters. Both claimed Mendelssohn's music.

[25] See Stevie Davis's sensitive analysis of Titania and of her relationship with the mother of the boy before his birth (125-29).

[26] See the following promptbooks: *MND* 5, *MND* 9, *MND* 20, *MND* 21, *MND* 13, *MND* 15. Although, according to Allen, "all but 300 lines of the original"

were excised by Phelps, in prompt *MND* 13, believed to be a record of his production, huge chunks of Titania's speeches were cut. In fact only the first seven lines (81-89) remain of the speech beginning "These are the forgeries of jealousies." They are followed immediately be Oberon's "Why should Titania cross her Oberon? / I do but beg a little changeling boy, / To be my henchman" (119-21). A single line is cut from his speech. Again Titania's description of the boy's mother is also crossed through. Thus, the "restoration" hardly affects the lines of Titania. In II.i Phelps excises most of her speech to Oberon 88-117 and then Oberon's 118, "Do you amend it then." Again the actor-manager excises "When we have laugh'd to see the sails conceive . . . did die," 128-35.

27 Crossed out in Burton's text (*MND* 21), and in Samuel Phelps's (*MND* 13), her lines disappear from the Kean printed text (*MND* 9), the Daly text (*MND* 5), and others.

28 Marilyn Williamson refers to the need to be aware of the historical contexts in which the plays were written. Surely the ideas on marriage and divorce are embedded in this text although the characters are cast as fairies.

29 Circled for excision from *MND* 6 (by Garrick), therefore gone from 1763 text (*MND* 19), and from Reynolds's 1816 text (*MND* 18); Burton (*MND* 21) 1854; (*MND* 9); Daly (*MND* 5); the lines are circled for excision in Phelps *MND* 13. Also excised from typescript of Jewett's, 1915 (*MND* 12).

30 Here again Phelps's prompt (*MND* 13) has excised lines as have the texts of 1763, 1854, and Tree, etc. The whole section referring to "reason" in Lysander's speech has also been eliminated from the 1856 printed text (*MND* 9); most of the lines have been excised from Jewett's 1915 typescript (*MND* 12) and from Daly's 1888 text (*MND* 5); finally, the section has been crossed out in the 1853 (*MND* 13) and 1854

versions (*MND* 21), Tree's in 1900 (*MND* 7) (and probably other contemporaneous ones that I did not examine).

31 Kean (*MND* 9). He emphasizes her unique role as "a spirit of no common rate" and retains only the first line (152) of the quote, following it immediately with "For I do love thee," a variant on the text's "And I do love thee" (156). In that version, neither Bottom nor the audience is told of her power to keep him from leaving.

32 See chapter 3, "Challenging Patterns," in Irene Dash's *Wooing, Wedding, and Power: Women in Shakespeare's Plays,* 33-66.

33 In Prompt *MND* 8, this section has been crossed through in pencil.

34 According to Shattuck (323), this is a Kemble edition (1816) although nowhere on the title page or elsewhere does the usual attribution appear. Some of the alterations, however, do appear in later acting versions.

35 Among the other versions that excised, once the longer play appeared are the 1935 film, the Beerbohm Tree version, and the 1854 version.

36 According to Hogan (II.718), the play ranked twenty-first in popularity of Shakespeare's plays between 1701 and 1800. But this figure is deceptive since only one production is listed as "the original" during the period. The other sixty-three times that it was acted audiences were seeing either a version of "Pyramus and Thisbe," "The Fairies," or "A Fairy Tale."

Source: "Male Magic: *A Midsummer Night's Dream*," in *Women's Worlds in Shakespeare's Plays*, University of Delaware Press, 1997, pp. 67-107.

The Gastric Epic: *Troilus and Cressida*

David Hillman, *Tavistock Centre, London*

Ignorance *in physiologicis*—that damned 'idealism.'
Friedrich Nietzsche, *Ecce Homo*[1]

1. *The Matter of Troy*

Why did Shakespeare write *Troilus and Cressida*? Why, that is, did he turn his attention to a story that was so overdetermined as to have become, by the end of the sixteenth century, little more than a compilation of clichés? The Trojan story was enormously popular during the decades preceding composition of the play,[2] and the most obvious motive suggested by this popularity is the play's commercial potential (written by an already-famous playwright, reworking material that was all the rage in contemporary London). While this motive is called into question by the Epistle attached to the play's Quarto in the second state,[3] the pervasiveness and mass appeal of the matter of Troy was, I believe, nevertheless a decisive factor in Shakespeare's choice of this subject. For in placing these endlessly reiterated, rhetoricized, and textualized heroes onstage, he could not help but embody them;[4] and the limning of these "unbodied figure[s]" (1.3.16) in flesh and blood presented a perfect opportunity to wrestle with the issue that, I will argue, lies at the very heart of the play: the relation between language and the body out of which it emanates. Both within the play and in the cultural milieu that produced it, *Troilus and Cressida* enacts a restoration of words, and of the ideals created out of them, to their sources inside the body.

The play thrusts both its protagonists and the audience back into the body, recorporealizing the epic of the Trojan War. The story's unparalleled canonicity created heroes of a deeply textual nature, protagonists who by Shakespeare's time had become little more than, in Rosalie Colie's words, "rhetorical and proverbial figure[s]."[5] The play's "dependence on a prodigious literary and rhetorical legacy" entangles it (as most critics of the play agree) with issues of citationality and originality.[6] When Shakespeare turns to the legend, he places the relationship between origins and citations at the core of his play. He does this by reintroducing, as it were, the substance or "matter" of the body to the "Matter of Troy." Indeed, the very word *matter*, often associated in Shakespeare with the interior of the body, recurs no fewer than twenty-four times in the play.[7] The missing "matter" that Shakespeare reintroduces into the story is that of the truth of the body, which has been displaced over countless reiterations by something like pure citationality. "[T]ir'd with iteration" (3.2.174), the heroes' identities have become

ever further removed from their material sources: the pun on *tir'd* (attired/tired) implies the increasing distance from the body, as if each retelling adds a layer of covering—a cover story—to the protagonists' flesh, with the overdetermined citationality that constitutes the "starv'd . . . subject" (1.1.93) of Troy rendering it disembodied, "pale and bloodless" (1.3.134). ("*Troy*," apostrophizes Spenser's Paridell, "[thou] art now nought, but an idle name."[8]). By the time Shakespeare comes to write the play, these post-Homeric heroes have all become "Words, words, mere words, no matter from the heart" (5.3.108).

Troilus and Cressida has often been described as being "consciously philosophical," as coming "closer than any other of the plays to being a philosophical debate."[9] There is little physical action in the play; mostly there are rhetorical arguments about degree, about honor, about time and value. Yet the play is compulsively body-bound; from start to finish, its language is replete with imagery of the body's interior, the ebb and flow of its humors looking out at every joint and motive of the text. There is, I think, a powerful connection between the play's intellectuality and its unyielding corporeality, a link that can perhaps be best elucidated by glancing briefly at what Friedrich Nietzsche says about the relations between philosophy and physiology. Entrails, for Nietzsche, are inherently anti-idealizing, undercutting metaphysics and transcendent aspirations of any kind: going *into* the body lies at the opposite pole from going *beyond* it. As Eric Blondel writes, "it is in order to contrast an abominable truth to the surface of the ideal that Nietzsche speaks of entrails."[10] Idealization usually involves a turning away from or repression of the messy truth of the body—toward what Agamemnon calls, in *Troilus and Cressida*, "that unbodied figure of the thought" (1.3.16)—or, alternatively, a conception of the body as a perfect, finished surface.[11] But while the exterior of the body is easy enough to idealize, its interior has a rather more offensive, unsavory reality, as Nietzsche repeatedly points out: "What offends aesthetic meaning in inner man—beneath the skin: bloody masses, full intestines, viscera, all those sucking, pumping monsters—formless or ugly or grotesque, and unpleasant to smell on top of that!"[12]

Reminding us of the existence of this monstrous "inner man" is, throughout Nietzsche's work, a way of revealing the reality *beneath* thoughts, systems, ideals. In "On Truth and Lie in the Extra-Moral Sense," for instance, Nietzsche points out the irony involved in the fact that "the urge for truth" is so often a product of our "proud, deceptive consciousness, far from the coils of the intestines, the quick current of the blood stream, and the involved tremors of the fibers. . . ."[13] Excavating the body is thus for Neitzsche—the "physiologist of morals"[14]—a foundational act of skepticism; in his view any hermeneutic undertaking must begin from the body—and, moreover, from its interior, which is why he speaks of the "hard, unwanted, inescapable task" of philosophy as a kind of vivisection; Socrates, for example, is "the old physician and plebeian who cut ruthlessly into his own flesh, as he did into the flesh and heart of the 'noble.'"[15] This, too, is what Nietzsche means when he speaks of "philosophizing with a hammer": "*sounding out idols. . . .* For once to pose questions here with a *hammer*, and, perhaps, to hear as a reply that famous hollow sound which speaks of bloated entrails—what a delight. . . ."[16] The hammer here is one that can both "sound out" the interior (like a tuning-fork) and, if necessary, smash through to this interior (like a sledgehammer).

I offer this brief reading of Nietzsche's conceptualization of entrails as a potentially instructive analogue to my reading of *Troilus and Cressida*, for both are uncompromising when it comes to revealing the distance between our proudly deployed language and the body's internal reality. Bloated entrails are a dominant image in the play; as Patricia Parker has recently argued, "the inflation or bloating that affects both bodies and words in *Troilus* also affects its presentation of its epic theme, matter, or argument, repeatedly said to represent an overheld or inflated value."[17] In foregrounding the physiological processes taking place within its protagonists' tumid bodies, the play "sounds out" the Homeric idols, the epic heroes at the very source of European culture; it finds at the center of their beings little more than disease and raw appetite, representing them all, more or less, as "idol[s] of idiot-worshippers" (5.1.7). "[M]ad idolatry" (2.2.57) is a subject repeatedly addressed by the play, which, we could say, depicts a kind of "Twilight of the Idols"—ending, as it does, as "the sun begins to set, / . . . [And] ugly night comes breathing at his heels" (5.8.5-6). The play uses a turn to the interior of the body to debunk time-honored ideals—to reveal the "Most putrefied core" (5.8.1) of the heroic ethos.[18] It depicts "the veins of actions highest rear'd" (1.3.6) in the most literal sense of "veins"; even Hector's honorable soldiership is—in his own words—no more than "th'vein of chivalry" (5.3.32) on a good day. In *Troilus and Cressida* the twin ideals of heroism-in-war and idolism-in-love are exploded, in no small part through the attention directed to the "polluted" insides of the body, "more abhorr'd / Than spotted livers in the sacrifice" (5.3.17-18).

The idea that the play evinces a general disgust with corporeality was for many years practically undisputed; and indeed the vast majority of the play's references to the body insist on its internally diseased and utterly corruptible state. My argument here runs not so much "against the hair" (1.2.27) of these interpretations as *under* it; for to take this as a rejection of corporeality as such does little more than reproduce Thersites's bitter invective against the body—echoing his perspective rather than interpreting it. The main thrust in *Troilus and Cressida* is a turn not against but back toward the body, in the same way that Nietzsche's philosophy embraces corporeality with all its "formless or ugly or grotesque" aspects.

Shakespeare's response to the endless reiteration of the legend of Troy is simultaneously a response to the major genealogical project of Tudor mythographers— the tracing of the ancestry of the British nation to the Trojan War, a teleology culminating in the glories of the Elizabethan nation. But, as I am describing it, it was not so much this genealogy that Shakespeare was interested in as in a kind of Nietzschean genealogy, an enterprise of (re) linking words, and the values and ideals constructed out of them, to their bodily origins, to "the basic text of *homo natura.*"[19] Shakespeare's attempt to restore materia to the Matter of Troy constitutes a powerful countermovement to this founding narrative of English nationalism—as if to say that this narrative does not delve *far enough*.[20] That is: while Tudor mythographers sought a heroic site of origin in the Trojan epic, Shakespeare's skeptical satire seeks the origins of the legend of Troy *in* the bodies of its heroes.[21]

The implied repudiation of the idealizing narrative of Elizabethan nationalism simultaneously suggests a radical rereading of the progress-bound idea of time on which this history relies. *Troilus and Cressida* comes closer to a view of history as reiterative or circular in its perpetual return to human physiology as the source of action. The play, in fact, thematizes the question of what the perspective of time does to historical events. Time here is repeatedly personified—an all-consuming scavenger, a thief snatching at scraps of history with which to cram up his thievery, a vulture pouncing on the leftovers of every human deed. And as "raging appetite" is imagined as the origin of both the love plot and the war plot, this same appetite is figured as the terminus of all action, the universal wolf which last eats up itself.

Shakespeare's anti-mythologizing return to the body could be described as nostalgic, though it is anything but idealizing. It is in a sense a turning away from his medieval and early modern sources and back toward Homer, whose epic never for a moment flinches from describing the horror of the human body's utter destructibility. Both the *Iliad* and *Troilus and Cressida*—to quite different ends, to be sure—present the human being as "a bundle of muscles, nerves, and flesh" subjected relentlessly to "force, that is, in the last analysis, to matter."[22] It is this restoration of the body—a restoration of the heroically repressed, or the unveiling of what we might call the entrails of epic—which produces the play's ubiquity of corporeal images.

The return, as it happens, is simultaneously an etymological return, since the very name *Ilium* means, in Latin (in the plural form of *ile*), "intestines, guts." The play can thus be described as not only a genealogical excavation but also, in true Nietzschean fashion, a philological one. And (in case Shakespeare's "small Latine" did not extend this far) we might note that *Ilium* and *Ilion* (the two forms of the Homeric designation for Troy used alternately in the play) are—and were in the sixteenth century—alternative anatomical names for the largest part of the intestinal tract, the part affected in the apparently then-common disease called "iliac passion": bloating of the intestines.[23] If Tudor historiography traced the birth of the British nation to Ilium, Shakespeare traces "Ilium" back to the body. In this sense—and speaking hyperbolically—the entire play can be said to take place within one large, bloated intestine.

2. *The Satirist and the Cannibal*

The ending of the Trojan legend, we might here recall, is inseparably linked to the idea of full intestines—to the Trojan horse, that is, with its bellyful of silent Greek warriors—a proverbial symbol of guile throughout the English Renaissance.[24] Writers of the period persistently figured the potential for deceit as a potential gap between words and the bodies out of which they emerge. A story particularly popular in early modern England was Lucian's version of the tale of Momus and Hephaestus. In *Hermotimus, or Concerning the Sects*—a satire of all manner of philosophical schools and pretensions—Lucian relates the story of how Momus, mocker of the gods, judged a competition among Athena, Poseidon, and Hephaestus. To settle a quarrel among the three gods over which of them was the best artist, Momus is appointed to judge their creations; Athena designs a house, Poseidon a bull, Hephaestus a man. "What faults he found in the other two," writes Lucian, "we need not say, but his criticism of the man and his reproof of the craftsman, Hephaestus, was this: he had not made windows in his chest which could be opened to let everyone see his desires and thoughts, and if he were lying or telling the truth."[25]

Lucian—"the Merry Greek," as he was known to sixteenth-century Englishmen[26]—was a philosopher whose caustic, disillusioned perspectivism may well have influenced *Troilus and Cressida* directly (the epithet "merry Greek" is used twice in the play[27]); Shakespeare's comic satire shares with him a disenchantment with ideals, a deeply relativist attitude to questions of value, and a level of scoffing unparalleled elsewhere in the canon. But my interest here lies less in Lucian's influence on Shakespeare than in the way Momus's tale succinctly highlights a tendency that is central to satire in general and to *Troilus and Cressida* in particular. Momus's criticism of Hephaestus's man exemplifies a desire shared, in one form or another, by many skeptics and satirists: the desire to puncture pretense by revealing the body's innards. This skeptical impulse often takes the form of a desire to see into, or to open up, the body of the other. *Troilus and Cressida* partakes of this satirical tradition of figuring the puncturing of deceit and delusion as a puncturing of the body. The skepticism evinced by the play is itself described within the play in just such terms: "[D]oubt," says Hector, "is call'd / The beacon of the wise, the tent that searches / To th'bottom of the worst" (2.2.15-17).[28]

Such a penetrative impulse stems from an imagination of the interior of the body as capable of concealing an ulterior truth, a fantasy of the possibility of absolute knowledge of the other.[29] In "The Inside and the Outside," Jean Starobinski discusses the origins of such a corporeal schema in its archetypal form. Turning back to Homer's *Iliad*—"one of the first poetic documents in which the censure of duplicity is given full and emphatic voice"—Starobinski quotes Achilles's rebuke to Agamemnon ("For hateful in my eyes, even as the gates of Hades, is that man that hideth one thing in his heart and sayeth another") and comments: "the doubling, the splitting which causes *one thing* to be hidden and *another* said . . . takes on spatial dimensions: what goes unsaid is actively hidden in the heart, the space of the inside—the interior of the body is that place in which the cunning man dissimulates what he doesn't say."[30] The *Iliad* is, to be sure, a particularly effective place to look for such corporeal dimensions, as the exegeses of Bruno Snell and R. B. Onians have made abundantly clear: "emotional thoughts, 'cares', were living creatures troubling the organs in one's chest," writes Onians in elucidating the inseparability of body, mind, and soul in Homer.[31] But the bodily schema Starobinski points to has been too tenacious over the centuries to be dismissed either as a manifestation of primitive or archaic thought or as merely a convenient metaphor.[32]

The explicitly somaticized nature of the urge to puncture deceit and delusion was never more evident than during the English satire-vogue of the final decade of the sixteenth century, a vogue to which *Troilus and Cressida* was Shakespeare's main contribution.[33] "The Satyre should be like the *Porcupine*, / That shoots sharp quils out in each angry line, / And wounds the blushing cheeke," wrote Joseph Hall; and John Marston described the "firking satirist" as "draw[ing] the core forth of imposthum'd sin."[34] The strong corporealization of the satiric impulse owes much to the materialistic habits of early modern thought (and to the centrality of the practice of anatomy in particular); throughout this period, whether the trope is one of injury, anatomical dissection, or medical purgation, both the penetrative drive and the target of this drive—the bodily interior of the satirized object—are practically explicit.[35]

"The Gods had their *Momus, Homer* his *Zoilus, Achilles* his *Thirsites*," writes the melancholy anatomist Robert Burton in his discussion of satirists and caluminators, adding that the "bitter jest . . . pierceth deeper then any losse, danger, bodily paine, or injury whatsoever."[36] *Troilus and Cressida's* chief satirist, "rank Thersites," pierces each and every one of the play's protagonists with his "mastic jaws" (1.3.73). As this last phrase indicates, the penetrative drive of satire can appear at the same time as an impulse to devour the object under attack—it often manifests itself in a specifically oral form of aggression; as Mary Claire Randolph writes, "Renaissance satirists frequently picture themselves as . . . sinking their pointed teeth deep in some sinner's vitals."[37] This idea of oral sadism is a recurrent theme of satirists; it is often figured as a compulsion to bite. Marston, for example, writes that "Unless the Destin's adamantine band / Should tie my teeth, I cannot choose, but bite"; and Burton, quoting Castiglione, says of satirists that "*they cannot speake, but they must bite.*"[38] To say that the aggressive impulse of "byting" satire is predominantly oral is to approach redundancy (as Milton points out in dismissing Joseph Hall's "toothlesse Satyres": it is "as much as if he had said toothlesse teeth.")[39] But there is in satire, over and above this oral aggression, an urge to devour—an urge, moreover, specifically directed at the human body. The satirist typically fantasizes not only penetrating the other's body but devouring it, as if entering this body is a concomitant of being inhabited by it. The derivation of the word *satire*—from the Latin *satura*, meaning "full, satiated"—points to this cannibalistic drive; as Walter Benjamin writes, in his essay on Karl Kraus: "The satirist is the figure in whom the cannibal was received into civilization." And, he adds, "the proposal to eat people has become an essential constituent of his [the satirist's] inspiration."[40] The projective mechanism of satire, in this view, makes it both embody and thematize a cannibalistic urge, an urge epitomized by the delicious ending of one of the earliest Menippean satires, Petronius's *Satyricon*, where the rich Eumolpus bequeaths his wealth to his friends "on one condition, that they cut my body in pieces and eat it up in sight of the crowd."[41]

The misanthropic cannibalism of satire is glimpsed in *Troilus and Cressida's* relentless use of imagery related to food, eating, and digestion.[42] And while this alimentary obsession has often been noticed, a distinct pattern emerges when we examine its figurative trajectory through the course of the play.[43] The outline is one of more or less linear progression, from the early talk of culinary preliminaries ("[T]he grinding . . . the bolting . . . the leavening . . . the kneading, the making of the cake, the heating of the oven, and the baking"

[1.1.18-24]; "the spice and salt that season a man . . . a minced man; and then to be baked with no date in the pie" [1.2.259-62]; the "bast[ing]" in one's "own seam" or grease [2.3.186]) and of "tarry[ing]," "starv'd" (1.1.15, 93), before the meal; followed by the promises of "tast[ing]" on the "fin'st palate" (1.3.337-38, 389), the readiness of the "stomach" (2.1.127), the "raging appetites" (2.2.182), and the preparation of "my cheese, my digestion" (2.3.44); then the "imaginary relish" (3.2.17) leading up to the meal itself, associated as it is with sexual consummation ("Love's thrice-repurèd nectar" [3.2.20]); and thence to the "full[ness]" (4.4.3; 4.5.271; 5.1.9) and "belching" (5.5.23) of engorgement, of having "o'er-eaten" (5.2.159)—and the ensuing nausea, associated with the "spoils" (4.5.62), the rancid leftovers, the "lees and dregs" (4.1.63), the "orts [i.e., refuse] . . . / The fragments, scraps, the bits, and greasy relics" (5.2.157-58). In view of this, it would not be going too far to call *Troilus and Cressida* a bulimic play, one that evokes in its audience (as has often been noted in a general way) a reaction akin to the figurative nausea of the imagistic trajectory delineated above. The play, in fact, begins with a "disgorg[ing]" (Pro. 12) and proceeds through overeating to its anticathartic ending in Pandarus's stomach-turning Epilogue. The Prologue has referred to the ensuing action as "what may be digested in a play" (Pro.29), and—in spite of the Arden editor's rather severe gloss ("*Not* part of the food imagery of the play")—there is, I think, an implication of the nauseating effect of this "unwholesome dish" (2.3.122) on the digestive systems of its spectators.[44] What should also be noted here is that the lion's share of the imagery of food and eating in the play is cannibalistic—that is, it consistently imagines the object of alimentary consumption as a human being. The play thus places its spectators in the position not only of diseased "traders in the flesh" (5.10.46) but also of uneasy "eaters of the flesh"—of cannibals: little wonder that it was apparently "neuer stal'd with the Stage" in Shakespeare's time, and that audiences still find it somewhat unpalatable.

The notion of cannibalism is implicit, too, in the play's repeated evocation of images of self-consumption. The connection between the two is remarked on in Sir Thomas Browne's *Religio Medici*: "We are what we all abhorre, *Anthropophagi* and Cannibals, devourers not onely of men, but of our selves; and that not in an allegory, but a positive truth; for all this masse of flesh which wee behold, came in at our mouths: this frame wee looke upon, hath beene upon our trenchers; In briefe, we have devoured our selves."[45] The most prominent image of self-consumption in the play is of course Ulysses's speech on appetite, which "Must make perforce an universal prey, / And last eat up himself" (1.3.123-24)—a phrase that Kenneth Palmer calls an "image . . . of cannibalism as the last consequence of disorder";[46] but the disorder can take any of several forms (e.g., "He that is proud eats up himself" [2.3.156];

"lechery eats itself" [5.4.35]), so that, in this play at least, self-consumptive cannibalism appears pervasive. The entire project—comprising Shakespeare's relation to his sources, the audience's relation to the play, and the characters' relation to each other—is implicitly cannibalistic.

Forcing the idea of cannibalism on the audience entails, among other things, forcing it to come to terms with the corporeality—the very flesh—of the protagonists of the story. It is Thersites, above all, whose constant punning obsessively returns language to the body's internal "matter." Thersites even appears to know (and this is typical of the play's proleptic style) that he himself is destined to become, quite literally, a disembodied figure of speech, the rhetorical figure of "the standard rhyparographer" (or filth-painter).[47] When threatened by Ajax with "I shall cut out your tongue," he replies: "'Tis no matter" (2.1.112-13). Thersites's pun takes the material organ of speech to be immaterial, construing Ajax's "tongue" in its entirely figurative meaning (i.e., speech), and thus constituting himself, in one sense, as pure citation. (The irony, of course, is that the *actor* playing Thersites must use his material tongue to say these words, thereby revealing the odd status of the body in *Troilus and Cressida*: the play both depicts and—in its reiteration of the tale—enacts the body's displacement by speech even as it reverses this displacement by both foregrounding the role of the body and embodying the tale on stage.) Thersites's quibbling ways with the word *matter* begin earlier in the same scene: "Agamemnon—how if he had boils, full, all over, generally? . . . And those boils did run—say so—did not the general run then? Were not that a botchy core? . . . Then would come some matter from him: I see none now" (2.1.2-9). With his first words in the play, Thersites, whose every third thought is of the body's putrefaction, points punningly to the gap between the substance of the body and the argument of words; as Patricia Parker explains, "The 'head and general,' supposed to be a source of ordered and reasoned argument, the generation of 'matter' for discourse as well as the hierarchical embodiment of order itself, is in this play only a 'botchy core,' the source of 'matter' in an infected body politic."[48] Here, though, Thersites's "Then would come some matter from him: I see none now" announces a *lack* of "matter" at the core of Agamemnon, thereby hinting, synecdochically, at a lack at the heart of the entire legend of Troy. The story's hero, Achilles, is figured in *Troilus and Cressida* as "a fusty nut with no kernel" (ll. 103-4); Ajax is a "thing of no bowels" (l. 52); and Agamemnon himself should be—and, in this play, is clearly not—a "great commander, nerves and bone of Greece, / Heart of our numbers" (1.3.55-56). Troy itself, with the death of Hector, is deprived of interior matter: "Come, Troy, sink down! / Here lies thy heart, thy sinews, and thy bone" (5.8.11-12).

Critics of *Troilus and Cressida* tend to discuss its two salient imagistic strands—those of disease and of eating—separately. But the two are repeatedly interwined in the play: they are twin manifestations of a pervasive "appetite"—"an appetite that I am sick withal" (3.3.237). We could say that as hunger is taken metaphorically for all beginnings of desire, disease is understood synecdochically as the terminus of all desire—hence the play's ending with Pandarus's bequeathal of his "diseases" to the audience's already "aching bones" (5.10.57, 51).[49] Nor is the disease imagery in the play solely a matter of syphilitic or venereal sickness, associated with a narrow (sexual) definition of desire:

> Now the rotten diseases of the south, the guts-griping, ruptures, catarrhs, loads o' gravel i'th'back, lethargies, cold palsies, raw eyes, dirt-rotten livers, whissing lungs, bladders full of impostume, sciaticas, lime-kilns i'th'palm, incurable bone-ache, and the rivelled fee-simple of the tetter, take and take again such preposterous discoveries!
>
> (5.1.16-23)

Thersites's cursing, while specifically attacking homosexual activity ("preposterous discoveries"), encompasses a dozen kinds of illness, most of which have nothing to do with sexuality but are rather the result of quite diverse forms of appetite. Disease and alimentary imagery are linked, first, by their relation to internal physiology and, second, by their relation to appetite in the broadest sense of the term. This is why the idea of self-consumption recurs so often in the play: appetite contains—or wills—its own end. For the play seems to me to conceive of appetite as something very like Nietzsche's "will to power"—an insatiable, appropriative urge that, for all its myriad manifestations, finds its sources in the physiology of each and every organism:

> Then everything includes itself in power,
> Power into will, will into appetite,
> And appetite, an universal wolf,
> So doubly seconded with will and power,
> Must make perforce an universal prey,
> And last eat up himself.
>
> (1.3.119-24)

The deflation of the ideals and of the high-flown rhetoric of these epic heroes centers on this idea of an insatiable, pervasive, polymorphous appetite. The Renaissance's hierarchy of desires, from the merely appetitive to the spiritual, is here portrayed as completely reducible to its lowest common denominator; it is only the arbitrary imposition of degree that stops this collapse. And it is this reduction of all forms of desire to the urge for food—the refusal to separate sexual, martial, and alimentary forms of desire—which makes the play so cannibalistic.

I am suggesting that we think of desire in *Troilus and Cressida* in a very broad scope. Catherine Belsey has recently argued that the play "shows a world where desire is everywhere. . . . Desire is the unuttered residue which exceeds any act that would display it, including the sexual act."[50] As Troilus himself puts it, "desire is boundless"—boundless, that is, not only in aspiration but in origin. Troilus's famous lament—"This is the monstruosity in love, lady: that the will is infinite, and the execution confined: that the desire is boundless, and the act a slave to limit" (3.2.79-82)—has too often been taken to imply little more than that all lovers fall short of their aims. But desire, the entire play seems to be saying, is not only unsatisfiable in relation to its objects—it is insatiable (or, to use Belsey's language, "excessive") at its very source; it is a "slave to limit" not only in that it can never fulfill its aims but also in that it must, perforce, *choose* these aims, these objects, though in and of itself it is "infinite." The various manifestations of desire here—alimentary, martial, amorous, hetero- and homosexual, mimetic—are all conceived of as just that: manifestations of some absolutely voracious and polymorphous physiological drive. All these expressions of desire are merely its protean forms, "Dexterity . . . obeying appetite" (5.5.27).

The theme of alimentary appetite appears everywhere in the very fabric of the play. As in Nietzsche, the alimentary process is here a central metaphor for any manifestation of a will to power; eating and digestion appear indiscriminately as tropes for the play's two main themes of love and war: the "generation of love" is figured as "eat[ing] nothing but doves" (3.1.127, 123), the origin of the "factious feasts" (1.3.191) of bellicosity as having a "stomach" to the war (3.3.219; 2.1.127; 4.5.263). This is not, I think, simply a matter of an interpretive reduction to the level of physiology; it is a way of understanding human activities and processes *metaphorically*. To describe the "spirit," Nietzsche—like Shakespeare in *Troilus and Cressida*—turns to the body: "The spirit," he writes, "is more like a stomach than anything else":

> This inferior being [the stomach] assimilates (*assimiliert*) whatever lies in its immediate vicinity, and appropriates it (property initially being food (*Nahrung*) and provision for food), it seeks to assimilate (*einverleiben*) as many things as it can and not only to compensate itself for loss: this being is greedy (*habsüchtig*).[51]

The "raging appetites" (2.2.182) of both Greeks and Trojans figure the insatiability of this process; their actions, again and again, constitute a display of "the will of the weak to represent *some* form of superiority."[52] *Troilus and Cressida*'s depiction of the endlessly shifting shapes that desire can take (the *folie circulaire* of heterosexual activity expressing itself as martial activity expressing itself as homosexual activity, and so on[53]) ultimately means that the protagonists "lose distinction" (3.2.25) between these shapes, as the spectators, by the end of the play, lose any sense of distinction between Greeks and Trojans, "hot" (3.1.125) lovers and "hot" (4.5.185) warriors: just about any of them could be described as wearing "his wit in his belly and his guts in his head" (2.1.75-76).[54] Nor, at this level, is there a differentiation between male and female: entrails (in this play) are conspicuously ungendered; nowhere is "matter" linked (as it is, for instance, in *Hamlet*[55]) to *mater*, the maternal. All difference is, to use Nietzsche's term, "assimilate[d]"—"consum'd / In hot digestion of this cormorant war" (2.2.5-6)—even, it seems, the distinction between comedy and tragedy. The play displays an indifference to, or at least a profound skepticism about, the many forms of desire, including their generic concomitants; as Valerie Traub points out, "*Troilus and Cressida* declines to differentiate types of desire."[56] It is almost, as Joel Fineman puts it, "as though in *Troilus and Cressida* Shakespeare had turned against desire itself,"[57] exposing its ostensibly distinct manifestations as inextricable from each other at their source. The endlessly "dext[rous]" forms of desire seem to amount, in the end, to little more than "the performance of our heaving spleens" (2.2.197), the "pleasure of my spleen" (1.3.178), "a feverous pulse" (3.2.35), "the hot passion of distemper'd blood" (2.2.170), "The obligation of our blood" (4.5.121), "bawdy veins" (4.1.70), "too much blood and too little brain" (5.1.47), and so on; this approaches Nietzsche's "the coils of the intestines, the quick current of the blood stream, and the involved tremors of the fibers." Metaphors all, in a sense, but nonetheless figuring the distance between the deep sources of human motivation and their manifestations in rhetoric and action:

> However far a man may go in self-knowledge, nothing however can be more incomplete than his image of the totality of *drives* which constitute his being. He can scarcely name even the cruder ones: their number and strength, their ebb and flood, their play and counterplay among one another, and above all the laws of their *nutriment* remain wholly unknown to him. . . . Our moral judgements and evaluations too are only images and fantasies based on a physiological process unknown to us, a kind of acquired language for designating nervous stimuli.[58]

It is precisely the question of "the laws of their *nutriment*"—and of the "ebbs and flows" (as Agamemnon puts it) of the body's "humorous predominance" (2.3.132, 131)—that the play opens up.

Such a view goes some way toward explaining the strangeness of the play, the fact that *Troilus and Cressida* is so difficult to discuss profitably in terms of "character" or coherent "character development." The play seems almost perversely to flout any attempt to perceive full subjectivity in its dramatis personae; these are, without exception, flattened out, reduced to caricatures compared with their Homeric or Chaucerian predecessors.[59] As Shakespeare recorporealizes the story, he (quite uncharacteristically) "decharacterizes"[60] its heroes; they become little more than "ciphers" in the "great accompt" (*Henry V*, Pro. 17) of the Trojan legend. As Matthew Greenfield points out, "the play works through two related theories of human behaviour, one physiological (humors) and the other psychological (emulation, or what René Girard calls 'mimetic desire'). Both are theories of damaged agency, of compulsive, involuntary action."[61] There is something entirely stripped-down, rather than fully rounded, about all the play's characters; Carol Cook speaks of "the play of drives" depicted here.[62] The unflinching nature of this vision can, again, be viewed as a return to Homer, to the "geometrical rigor" of what Simone Weil has called "the poem of force."[63] The entire spirit of the play drags any metaphysical or psychological pretensions back down to earth; indeed, the very word *spirit* is used repeatedly in *Troilus and Cressida* with strong overtones of its physiological sense (as the vital substance that inhabits the body's vessels).[64] In radically shifting our view of these heroes of the Western world, in its materialist reduction of motivation to something like the corporeal "will to power," *Troilus and Cressida* profoundly addresses the question of the relation between language and the body.

3. Cannibalism and Silence

> Let him who has something to say come
>   forward and be silent!
>   Karl Kraus, "In these Great times"[65]

For all its grand rhetoric—or perhaps, more accurately, as a necessary concomitant to this rhetoric—*Troilus and Cressida* reveals an extreme distrust of (not to say disgust with) language. If the play leaves one with a sensation of satiety with words, it is likely that this sensation was one that Shakespeare, in coming to write the play, was himself unable to avoid. Many writers of the period comment on this dilemma, several of them using a specifically oral metaphor: George Whetstone declares that "the inconstancie of Cressid is so readie *in every mans mouth*, as it is needlesse labour to blase at full her abuse"; Montaigne writes that "There is nothing, liveth so *in mens mouthes* as . . . *Troy, as Helen* and her *Warres*"; Burton describes the story's popularity vividly, in a phrase that evokes the play's nausea: "our Poets steale from *Homer, he spewes, . . . [and] they licke it up.*"[66] Perhaps it was this sense of verbal surfeit which impelled Shakespeare to turn the Trojan legend into material for satire, *satura*; such a sense may in fact be an inherent component of satire— oral satiety turned to oral sadism. Burton, in his discussion of satirists and calumniators, warns against "fall[ing] *into the mouthes* of such men . . . for many are of so petulant a spleene, and have that figure

Sarcasmus so often *in their mouthes*, so bitter, so foolish, as Baltasar Castilio notes of them, that *they cannot speake, but they must bite.*"[67] Confronted with a glut of retellings of the legend of Troy, Shakespeare may indeed have found, when he turned his attention to the writing of *Troilus and Cressida*, that he could not speak without biting; hence, perhaps, the play's turn toward cannibalism.[68]

This difficulty in speaking without biting perfectly figures the perplexed relation between language and the body in *Troilus and Cressida*; and for early modern Europeans the idea of cannibalism has a recurrent stake in interrogating this problematic matter. We are speaking here of a period of crisis in the understanding of this relation, a period during which print technology and the exhaustion of the humanist project of "fattening up" language—to name just two factors—had resulted in a profound dissatisfaction with the hollowed-out discourses of European culture. It is at times of cultural crisis such as this, as Elaine Scarry has argued, that "the sheer material factualness of the human body will be borrowed to lend . . . cultural construct[s] the aura of 'realness' and 'certainty.'"[69]

The cultural construct of cannibalism was used in a similar way. Here I would like to turn briefly to Montaigne, whose "motivated confrontation of the philosophical and the anatomical"[70] recalls *Troilus and Cressida*'s linking of the two, and whose essay "Of the Cannibals" can provide us with some illuminating parallels to the play's staging of these issues. Both these texts portray attitudes toward love and war as exemplifying a society's ethical value. Montaigne displaces the idea of savagery back onto European civilization, describing his own countrymen's behavior as far crueler than that of the New World's cannibals; in the process of this displacement, as Michel de Certeau explains, "the word 'barbarian' . . . leaves behind its status as a noun (the Barbarians) to take on the value of an adjective (cruel, etc.)."[71] From one perspective, *Troilus and Cressida*'s trajectory is a diametric inversion of Montaigne's: instead of revealing and ratifying the deeply ethical imperative underlying the culture of cannibal society (and thereby assimilating the latter to "civilization"), it defamiliarizes (or disassimilates) the epic ethos, infusing it with a "cannibalism" that is seen as "savage strangeness" (2.3.128). The former society's "noble and generous"[72] heroism-in-war (the heroism of the victim) and polygamy-in-marriage (based on the love of the wives) are precisely inverted in Shakespeare's barbarism-in-war (the antiheroism of the perpetrator, exemplified by Achilles's butchering of Hector) and cuckoldry-in-marriage (based on the infidelity of the women— both Cressida and Helen). Yet the play ends up in more or less the same place as "Of the Cannibals," proclaiming the "barbarism" (5.4.17) of the heroes of the *Iliad*—the cradle of its own European culture.

Both texts evince a profound dissatisfaction with what Montaigne called, in the title of another essay, "the vanity of words."[73] But Montaigne's (idealized) savage culture is everything that Shakespeare's (debased) European culture is not. Where the former, as de Certeau brilliantly shows, "is founded upon . . . a heroic faithfulness to speech [which] produces the unity and continuity of the social body," the latter's "Bifold authority" (5.2.143) emphasizes the antiheroic faithlessness of language, fragmenting any vestige of social—and, ultimately, individual—unity. Why is cannibal speech so reliable? Because it is "sustained by bodies that have been put to the test":[74] "These muscles," sings the cannibal prisoner before he is eaten, "this flesh, and these veines, are your owne."[75] Why is the speech of Shakespeare's Greeks and Trojans so unreliable? Because it contains "no matter from the heart."

The enigma of the relation between body and speech lies at the very center of both Montaigne's and Shakespeare's texts. Both are concerned with the question of the corporeal source of words, a question about the veracity or duplicity of voice. It is this turn from bodily source to disembodied discourse—the trope of voice—which is the target of much skeptical and satirical attack. Skepticism questions the accuracy of the connection between words and things; here, more specifically, it is the matter of the coherence of the link between the source of things (words, desires) within the body and their emanation in discourse that is at issue. Montaigne's cannibals have no need of skepticism, no use for it, since they are materially inhabited by the body of the other, and this inhabitation guarantees the quality of the link between language and corpus. Cannibalism, here, is a fantasy of speech as "a thing inseparate" (5.2.147) from the body. It is in this sense that what is taken into the body—the gastric—can be imagined as an antidote to the speech—the rhetoric—that leaves it: both Montaigne's cannibals and Shakespeare's protagonists are, in a sense, what they eat.

Montaigne's cannibal society is "a body in the service of saying. It is the visible, palpable, verifiable *exemplum* which realizes before our eyes an ethic of speech."[76] Shakespeare's *Troilus and Cressida* holds out no such hope of "faithful and verifiable speech."[77] But where Montaigne offers, as an alternative to the morally depleted discourses of early modern Europe, a new "ethic of speech," Shakespeare offers no hope of a language guaranteed by the body. Instead he offers the only other possible alternative: an ethic of silence. In the context of the play's outpouring of alternately high-flown, empty rhetoric and scurvy invective, one character stands out in his utter wordlessness: Antenor. A. P. Rossiter, the only critic (as far as I know) who comments on his existence, calls him "Shakespeare's one strong silent man."[78] Onstage on at least five separate occasions, mentioned by those around him a dozen times, he utters not a single syllable throughout. In his

silence he is strikingly at odds with his traditional role: Homer, for example, calls him "strong in talking," and Caxton says of him simply that he "spacke moche."[79] His speechlessness in Shakespeare, then, is quite deliberate, a kind of rebuttal of the nauseatingly "cramm'd" (2.2.49) rhetoric circulating in and around the play. (And Shakespeare's knack for squeezing meaning out of the names he is given may be at work here, for *Antenor* can be related readily enough to the Greek privative *an-* ["not" or "without"] prefixed to *tenor* ["the male voice"].)[80] If *Troilus and Cressida* as a whole shares with Montaigne a skeptical, Pyrrhonic sense of pervasive relativism, Antenor's tenacious muteness may be imagined as a Pyrrhonic commitment to aphasia, a "silence, / Cunning in dumbness" (3.2.130-31).[81]

Leaving behind (like Pyrrho) no textual trace of his voice, Antenor is the embodiment onstage of what de Certeau calls the "(t)exterior [*hors-texte*]"[82]—the space carved out by Montaigne for the figuration of the perfect corporeality of the savage. In his mimetic immediacy, Antenor literally fills this space of the "*hors-texte*." If *Troilus and Cressida* "thematizes the relationship between the mimetic and the citational,"[83] Cressida, upon being "changed for Antenor" (4.2.94), becomes the purely citational to his purely mimetic. She is his precise opposite: "unbridled" (3.2.121) in her language, "glib of tongue" (4.5.58), she has betrayed herself from the outset by having "blabb'd" (3.2.123) to Troilus. She becomes, in the end, a figure of pure textuality—even her body, in Ulysses's mocking description of her, is a text: "Fie, fie upon her! / There's language in her eye, her cheek, her lip—/ Nay, her foot speaks; her wanton spirits look out / At every joint and motive of her body" (4.5.54-57). Her faithlessness is figured as the faithlessness of language itself: "I will not keep my word" (5.2.98). She is, we could say, the "whore-text" to Antenor's "*hors-texte*"— "right great exchange" (3.3.21) indeed.

Antenor, the man of silence, exists only as body, the word made flesh. His is an "art of *silence*"[84] which offers the only real space of alterity to the surfeit of degraded language with which he is surrounded, both inside and outside the play. "Compact, severe, with as much substance as possible, a cold sarcasm against 'beautiful words'"—this is how I imagine him.[85]

I imagine, too, that the actor who played Antenor originally was Shakespeare himself—his own silent, sly escape from the overwhelming citationality of his material. A playwright, though, cannot long remain silent. Shakespeare's great tragedies, written in the years following *Troilus and Cressida*, portray repeated—and often failed—attempts to recover the possibility of a meaningful language, a place for words that retain their integrity with the bodies from which they emerge, a way to heave the heart into the mouth— to love, without being silent.

Notes

I would like to thank Stanley Cavell, G. Blakemore Evans, Elizabeth Freund, Marjorie Garber, Jeff Masten, Ruth Nevo, and the members of the Harvard Renaissance Colloquium for their helpful and generous comments at various stages of the writing of this essay.

[1] Friedrich Nietzsche, *Ecce Homo,* trans. Walter Kaufmann (New York: Vintage Books, 1967), 241.

[2] According to J.S.P. Tatlock, "no traditional story was so popular in the Elizabethan Age as that of the siege of Troy and some of its episodes" ("The Siege of Troy in Elizabethan Literature, Especially in Shakespeare and Heywood," *PMLA* 30 [1915]: 676-78). For a good sense of how many competing versions of the legend were in circulation at the time, see Robert Kimbrough, *Shakespeare's "Troilus and Cressida" and its Setting* (Cambridge, MA: Harvard UP, 1964), 24-46; and Geoffrey Bullough, ed., *Narrative and Dramatic Sources of Shakespeare,* 8 vols. (New York: Columbia UP, 1957-75), 6:83-221.

[3] According to the Epistle of *The Famous Historie of Troylus and Cresseid* (1609), the play was "neuer stal'd with the Stage, neuer clapper-clawd with the palmes of the vulgar" (¶2). All quotations from *Troilus and Cressida* follow the Arden text of the play, edited by Kenneth Palmer (London and New York: Methuen, 1982). Quotations from other plays by Shakespeare follow the *Riverside Shakespeare,* ed. G. Blakemore Evans (Boston: Houghton Mifflin, 1974).

[4] The very fact of putting these heroes onstage, in the inescapably embodied media of the theater, must have brought into sharp focus the disjunction between the rhetorical (and disembodied) and the mimetic (and corporeal). "I am half inclined," wrote Samuel Taylor Coleridge about the play, "to believe that Shakespeare's main object, or shall I rather say, that his ruling impulse, was . . . to substantiate the distinct and graceful profiles or outlines of the Homeric epic into the flesh and blood of the romantic drama" *(Coleridge's Writings on Shakespeare,* ed. Terence Hawkes [New York: Capricorn Books, 1959], 248-49). On this topic, see especially Harry Berger Jr.'s "Text vs. Performance in Shakespeare: The Example of *Macbeth,*" *Genre* 15 (1982): 49-79.

[5] Rosalie Colie, *Shakespeare's Living Art* (Princeton, NJ: Princeton UP, 1974), 326.

[6] Elizabeth Freund, "'Ariachne's Broken Woof': The Rhetoric of Citationality in *Troilus and Cressida*" in *Shakespeare and the Question of Theory,* Patricia Parker and Geoffrey Hartman, eds. (New York: Methuen, 1985), 19-36, esp. 21. Linda Charnes's "'So Unsecret to Ourselves': Notorious Identity and the Material Subject in Shakespeare's *Troilus and Cressida*" (Shakespeare Quarterly 40 [1989]: 413-40) similarly stresses issues of citationality in the play.

[7] For occurrences of the word *matter* in *Troilus and Cressida,* see *The Harvard Concordance to Shakespeare,* comp. Marvin Spevack (Cambridge, MA: Belknap Press of Harvard UP, 1973), 798. On *matter* as bodily substance—and, more specifically, pus—see Alexander Schmidt, *Shakespeare-Lexicon: A complete dictionary of all the . . . words . . . in the works of the poet,* 2 vols. (Berlin: Georg Reimer, 1874-75), 2:700-701; and Elaine Scarry, ed., *Literature and the Body: Essays on Populations and Persons* (Baltimore: Johns Hopkins UP, 1988), xxii.

[8] Edmund Spenser, *The Faerie Queene,* ed. Thomas P. Roche Jr. (Harmondsworth, UK, and New York: Penguin, 1978), 514.

[9] S. L. Bethell, *Shakespeare and the Popular Dramatic Tradition* (London: Staples Press, 1944), 98; L. C. Knights, *Some Shakespearean Themes* (London: Chatto and Windus, 1959), 58. Cf. R. J. Kaufmann's comments in "Ceremonies for Chaos: The Status of *Troilus and Cressida,*" *ELH* 32 (1965), 139-59, esp. 145.

[10] Eric Blondel, *Nietzsche: The Body and Culture* (Stanford, CA: Stanford UP, 1991), 220. My understanding of Nietzsche's use of the physiological metaphor is indebted to Blondel's excellent analysis, as well as to Elizabeth Grosz's essay "Nietzsche and the Stomach for Knowledge" in *Nietzsche, Feminism, and Political Theory,* Paul Patton, ed. (London and New York: Routledge, 1993), 49-70.

[11] This idealized, closed, opaque corporeal model has been described by Mikhail Bakhtin as the "classical" body, in contrast with the open, flowing, "grotesque" body that foregrounds its orifices and protuberances (Mikhail Bakhtin, *Rabelais and His World,* trans. Hélène Iswolsky [Cambridge and London: MIT Press, 1986], esp. 18-30); Shakespeare's play adds to this binary a third model—the "abject" body whose interior organs and physiology are represented. For while *Troilus and Cressida*'s bodies are grotesque, it is not so much their orificial or protuberant status that makes them so as their internal ebb and flow, the diseased status of their visceral interiors.

[12] Nietzsche, *The Will to Power,* quoted here from Blondel, 220.

[13] Nietzsche, "On Truth and Lie in the Extra-Moral Sense" in *The Portable Nietzsche,* ed. and trans. Walter Kaufmann (New York: Viking Press, 1954), 42-50, esp. 44.

[14] The phrase is taken from Georg Stauth and Bryan S. Turner, *Nietzsche's Dance* (Oxford: Basil Blackwell, 1988), 17.

[15] Nietzsche, *Beyond Good and Evil: Prelude to a Philosophy of the Future,* trans. Walter Kaufmann (New York: Vintage Books, 1989), 137 and 138: "By applying the knife vivisectionally to the chest of the very *virtues of their time,* they [philosophers] betrayed what was their own secret: to know of a *new* greatness of man" (137).

[16] Nietzsche, *Twilight of the Idols or, How One Philosophizes with a Hammer* in The Portable Nietzsche, 463-563, esp. 465.

[17] Patricia Parker, *Shakespeare from the Margins: Language, Culture, Context* (Chicago: U of Chicago P, 1996), 224. Parker stresses the association of bodily swelling with rhetorical tumidity in the play.

[18] The phrase has sometimes been taken as a symbol for the entire play; Eric Mallin's comment is particularly apt: "Hector discovers that the ideal has become entirely flesh, a corrupted thing" ("Emulous Factions and the Collapse of Chivalry: *Troilus and Cressida,*" *Representations* 29 [1990]: 145-79, esp. 168).

[19] Nietzsche, *Beyond Good and Evil,* 161. Graham Bradshaw comments on this genealogical project in his excellent chapter on *Troilus and Cressida* in *Shakespeare's scepticism* (Ithaca, NY: Cornell UP, 1987), 126-63. Though Bradshaw addresses primarily questions of the construction of principles of value, his project shares with mine some basic assumptions about the play.

[20] Cf. Matthew Greenfield's comment in "Undoing National Identity: Shakespeare's *Troilus and Cressida*" (unpublished paper presented at the 1995 annual meeting of the Shakespeare Association of America, Chicago): "The work of *Troilus and Cressida* is not to provide England or Elizabeth with a genealogy but rather to undo the genealogies created by other mythmakers" (5). In *Troilus and Cressida,* wrote Tucker Brooke, Shakespeare was, "however subconsciously, anatomizing the England of the dying Elizabeth" ("Shakepeare's Study in Culture and Anarchy," *Yale Review,* n.s. xvii [1928]: 571-77, esp. 576).

[21] There is an analogous reversal in that the normative *end* of the Trojan story is in the belly of the Trojan horse; Shakespeare makes the belly the origin rather than the culmination of the tale. Troy and the belly are again linked—rather oddly—in Phineas Fletcher's *The Purple Island* (Cambridge, 1633), where the "vale" of the belly is described as "A work more curious, then which poets feigne / *Neptune* and *Phoebus* built, and pulled down again [i.e., Troy]" (20).

[22] These quotations are from Simone Weil's description of Homer's epic in Weil, *The Iliad, or, The Poem of Force,* trans. Mary McCarthy (Iowa City: Stone Wall Press, 1973), 6 and 33. Cf. Sheila Murnaghan, "Body and Voice in Greek Tragedy," *Yale Journal of Criticism* 1 (1988): 23-43: "No reader of the *Iliad* fails to be impressed by the poem's vivid accounts of the body materializing as it is severed from the animating *psyche,* or spirit" (24).

[23] For this etymology, see the *Oxford English Dictionary,* s.v. *Ileum, Ilion,* and *Ilium;* and A. Ernout and A. Meillet, *Dictionnaire Etymologique de la Langue Latine (*Paris: Klincksieck, 1959), 308 ("ilia, -ium . . . *parties latérales du ventre*"). For the anatomical data, see, for example, Thomas Vicary, *The Anatomie of the Bodie of Man* (London, 1548; rpt. London: Early English Text Society, 1888), 65.

[24] On the symbolic significance of the Trojan horse, see Robert Durling, "Deceit and Digestion in the Belly of Hell" in *Allegory and Representation: Selected Papers from the English Institute, 1979-80,* Stephen J. Greenblatt, ed. (Baltimore: Johns Hopkins UP, 1981), 61-93, esp. 74.

[25] Lucian of Samosata, *Hermotimus, or Concerning the Sects,* trans. K. Kilburn (Cambridge, MA: Harvard UP, 1959), 297-99.

[26] On the familiarity of Lucian to Elizabethan readers, see Douglas Duncan, *Ben Jonson and the Lucianic Tradition* (Cambridge: Cambridge UP, 1979), 82-96. Prominent allusions to Momus's tale appear in Francis Bacon's *The Advancement of Learning* (1605), where Bacon refers to "that window which Momus did require: who seeing in the frame of man's heart such angles and recesses, found fault there was not a window to look into them" (Bacon, *The Advancement of Learning,* ed. William Aldis Wright [Oxford: Clarendon Press, 1900], 228-29); and in Robert Burton's *Anatomy of Melancholy* (1621), where Burton observes, "How would *Democritus* have beene moved, had he seene the secrets of [men's] hearts? If every man had a window in his brest, which *Momus* would have had in *Vulcans* man. . . . Would hee, thinke you, or any man else say that these men were well in their wits?" (Burton, *The Anatomy of Melancholy,* ed. Thomas C. Faulkner et al., 3 vols. [Oxford: Clarendon Press, 1989-94], 1:55-56). On *Troilus and Cressida* as a Pyrrhonist play, see especially Robert B. Pierce, "Shakespeare and the Ten Modes of Scepticism," *Shakespeare Survey* 46 (1994): 145-58, esp. 151-52.

[27] At 1.2.110: "she's a merry Greek indeed"; and at 4.4.55: "A woeful Cressid 'mongst the merry Greeks." Cf. Troilus's comment "Were it a casque compos'd by Vulcan's [i.e., Hephaestus's] skill, / My sword should bite it" (5.2.169-70).

[28] A "tent" in this context is a surgeon's instrument for opening and probing a wound. Cf. Thersites's (typically somatizing) answer to Patroclus's "Who keeps the tent now?": "The surgeon's box or the patient's wound" (5.1.10-11).

[29] For more on this fantasy in Shakespeare's plays, see my "Visceral Knowledge: Shakespeare, Skepticism, and the Interior of the Early Modern Body" in *The Body in Parts: Fantasies of Corporeality in Early Modern Europe,* David Hillman and Carla Mazzio, eds. (New York: Routledge, 1997), 81-105.

[30] Jean Starobinski, "The Inside and the Outside," *The Hudson Review* 28 (1975): 333-51, esp. 336; Starobinski slightly modifies the translation of A. T. Murray in *The Iliad,* Loeb Classical Library, 2 vols. (London: Heinemann, 1930-34), 1:405.

[31] Richard Broxton Onians, *The Origins of European Thought about the Body, the Mind, the Soul, the World, Time, and Fate* (Cambridge: The University Press, 1951), 86; Bruno Snell, *The Discovery of the Mind in Greek Philosophy and Literature,* trans. T. G. Rosenmeyer (New York: Dover, 1982), 1-22. See also Murnaghan, 23-24; and Jean-Pierre Vernant, "Dim Body, Dazzling Body" in *Fragments for a History of the Human Body, Part One,* Michel Feher, ed. (Cambridge, MA: MIT Press, 1989), 18-47, esp. 29-30.

[32] The idea of an inherent connection between truth and entrails is at least as old as the practice of haruspices—or, in the case of human entrails, anthropomancy. In both Old and New Testaments, as Elaine Scarry has shown, "the interior of the body carries the force of confirmation [of belief]" (Scarry, *The Body in Pain: The Making and Unmaking of the World* [New York and Oxford: Oxford UP, 1985], 215).

[33] Throughout this brief discussion of satire, I generalize about a wide field of material. The specific examples, which I take to be representative of the genre, can do no more than gesture toward this field. For more on early modern English satire, see especially Mary Claire Randolph, "The Medical Concept in English Renaissance Satiric Theory," *Studies in Philology* 38 (1941): 125-57; O. J. Campbell, *Shakespeare's Satire* (London and New York: Oxford UP, 1943); and Alvin Kernan, *The Cankered Muse: Satire of the English Renaissance* (New Haven, CT: Yale UP, 1959).

[34] *The Collected Poems of Joseph Hall,* ed. Arnold Davenport (Liverpool: The University Press, 1949), 83; John Marston, *Antonio and Mellida, Part One* in *The Works of John Marston,* ed. A. H. Bullen, 3 vols. (London: John C. Nimmo, 1887), 1:50. Cf. Marston's description of the satirist as a kind of barber-surgeon, lancing the sores of the world: "Infectious blood, ye gouty humours quake, / Whilst my sharp razor doth incision make" (*The Scourge of Villanie,* in Bullen, ed., 3:339).

[35] Direct injury is usually figured either as biting or as scourging; but even in the latter case, the aim, as often as not, is to get beneath the skin: "Each blow doth leave / A lasting scar, that with a poison eats / Into the marrow" (Thomas Randolph, *The Muses' Looking Glass,* quoted here from Mary Claire Randolph, 150). Kernan writes that "gross, sodden, rotting matter is the substance of the satiric scene" (11).

[36] Burton, 1:337-41, esp. 337 and 339.

[37] Mary Claire Randolph, 153. The combination of impulses delineated here hints at what we might think of as a strongly preoedipal component to the satirist's aggression; Melanie Klein describes the first year of life as full of "sadistic impulses directed, not only against its mother's breast, but also against the inside of her body: scooping it out, devouring the contents, destroying it by every means which sadism can suggest"; so, too, the projective mechanisms crucial to this stage of life are central to the operation of satire. The satirist's oral sadism can be thought of, from this perspective, as an exacerbated version of this primary infantile position (Melanie Klein, "A Contribution to the Psychogenesis of Manic-Depressive States" in *Love, Guilt, and Reparation, and Other Works, 1921-1945,* Vol. 1 of *The Writings of Melanie Klein* [London: Hogarth Press, 1975], 1:262-89, esp. 282).

[38] Marston, *The Scourge of Villanie,* in Bullen, ed., 3:355; and Burton, 1:337-38.

[39] *The Works of John Milton,* Frank Allen Patterson, gen. ed., 18 vols. (New York: Columbia UP, 1931-38), 3:329. "Byting" comes from the title of Joseph Hall's first collection, "Of Byting Satyrs."

[40] Walter Benjamin, *Reflections: Essays, Aphorisms, Autobiographical Writings,* ed. Peter Demetz, trans. Edmund Jephcott (New York: Harcourt Brace Jovanovich, 1978), 260-61. Despite the popular Elizabethan notion that the word *satire* came from the Greek satyr, the correct Latin etymology was not unknown at the time. See, e.g., Thomas Drant, *A Medecinable Morall* (London, 1566), A2ʳ (cited in Hallett Smith, *Elizabethan Poetry: A Study in Conventions, Meaning, and Expression* [Cambridge, MA: Harvard UP, 1952], 217), where the etymology of satire is traced to both the Greek and the Latin sources, as well as to the Arabic for a glaive (i.e., a lance or spear). See also *The Oxford Dictionary of English Etymology,* ed. C. T. Onions (Oxford: Clarendon Press, 1966), 790.

[41] Petronius Arbiter, *Satyricon* in *Petronius,* trans. Michael Heseltine (London: William Heinemann; New

York: MacMillan, 1913), 321. Swift's *A Modest Proposal* is English literature's most overt example of the satiric urge to eat people.

[42] See Caroline Spurgeon, *Shakespeare's Imagery and What it Tells Us* (Cambridge: The University Press, 1936), 320-24.

[43] There are, of course, images that don't fit into this trajectory, which is impressionistic rather than rigorous.

[44] On the way *Troilus and Cressida* "work[s] to extend the logic of the play from the relations among characters to the relations between characters and audience," see Harry Berger Jr., "*Troilus and Cressida*: The Observer as Basilisk" in *Second World and Green World: Studies in Renaissance Fiction-Making,* John Patrick Lynch, ed. (Berkeley: U of California P, 1988), 130-46, esp. 141.

[45] Sir Thomas Browne, *Religio Medici* in *The Works of Sir Thomas Browne,* ed. Geoffrey Keynes, 6 vols. (London: Faber and Gwyer, 1928), 1:48.

[46] Palmer, ed., 130n.

[47] Colie, 343-44. Kimbrough adds that "an Elizabethan audience would have recognized [Thersites] as a walking, talking figure of speech" (39). Shakespeare, however, seems to have associated Thersites less with language than with the body: "Thersites' body is as good as Ajax' / When neither are alive" (*Cymbeline,* 4.2.252-53). Cf. Burton's comment that all men "are in brief, as disordered in their mindes, as *Thersites* was in his body" (34).

[48] Patricia Parker, *Literary Fat Ladies: Rhetoric, Gender, Property (*London and New York: Methuen, 1987), 89.

[49] Is, for instance, "the open ulcer of [Troilus's] heart" (1.1.53) the source or the result of his love for Cressida?

[50] Catherine Belsey, "Desire's excess and the English Renaissance theatre: *Edward II, Troilus and Cressida, Othello*" in Susan Zimmerman, ed., *Erotic Politics: Desire on the Renaissance Stage* (London and New York: Routledge, 1992), 84-102, esp. 93. Carol Cook's "Unbodied Figures of Desire" (*Theatre Journal* 38 [1986]: 34-52) relates desire not so much to the subject's body in the play as to its objects' corporeality.

[51] Nietzsche, *The Will to Power,* quoted here from Blondel, 219 and 218.

[52] Nietzsche, *The Genealogy of Morals,* trans. Walter Kaufmann and R. J. Hollingdale (New York: Vintage Books, 1967), 123.

[53] Charnes's account of these complex circulations in the play is ingenious: "We might posit the circuit thus:

possession of Helen generates desire for war, desire for war generates desire for Helen, desire for Helen generates mimetic desire, mimetic desire generates competitive identification between Greek and Trojan men, competitive identification generates homoerotic aggression, homoerotic aggression generates desire for more war, and finally, desire for more war reproduces desire for Helen" (437).

[54] The phrase comes from Cornelius Agrippa and, interestingly, is used by Burton side by side with a reference to cannibalism: "To see a man weare his braines in his belly, his guts in his head, . . . or as those *Anthropophagi,* to eat one another" (1:53).

[55] See my "*Hamlet,* Nietzsche, and Visceral Knowledge" in *The Incorporated Self: Interdisciplinary Perspectives on Embodiment,* Michael O'Donovan-Anderson, ed. (Lanham, MD: Rowman and Littlefield, 1996), 93-110.

[56] Valerie Traub, *Desire and Anxiety: Circulations of sexuality in Shakespearean drama* (London and New York: Routledge, 1992), 84.

[57] Joel Fineman, "Fratricide and Cuckoldry: Shakespeare's Doubles" in *Representing Shakespeare: New Psychoanalytic Essays,* Murray M. Schwartz and Coppélia Kahn, eds. (Baltimore: Johns Hopkins UP, 1980), 70-109, esp. 100.

[58] Nietzsche, *Daybreak: Thoughts on the Prejudices of Morality,* trans. R.J. Hollingdale (Cambridge: Cambridge UP, 1982), 74-76.

[59] See especially Colie's comment about the characters "refusing altogether to conform to the conventions of psychological illusionism" (326). Cf. Bethell, 102. This is where I part ways with Linda Charnes's powerful account of the play: it is not, I think, part of Shakespeare's enterprise here to take on "the task of giving mimetic spontaneity to, and representing viable subjectivity in" his Homeric characters (417)—quite the contrary.

[60] The term is taken from Stephen Roderick's "Et Tu, Jello," *Boston Magazine* 87, no. 5 (1995): 66.

[61] Greenfield, 10; Greenfield quotes René Girard's "The Politics of Desire in *Troilus and Cressida*" in Parker and Hartman, eds., 188-209.

[62] Cook, 40.

[63] Weil, 15.

[64] See especially the Prologue's "expectation, tickling skittish spirits" (l.20); Troilus's "spirit of sense" (1.1.58), echoed by Achilles's "most pure spirit of sense" (3.3.106); Ulysses's "her wanton spirits look

out / At every joint and motive of her body" (4.5.56-57); and Achilles's "That I may give the local wound a name, / And make distinct the very breach whereout / Hector's great spirit flew" (4.5.243-45). Bradshaw calls *spirit* "a word to watch in this play"; beginning with the Prologue, the play "release[s] the perjorative senses the word spirit may have. These are many and include the clinical senses in humors psychology" (130). On the role of the "spirits" in humoral theory, see especially Gail Kern Paster, "Nervous Tension: Networks of Blood and Spirit in the Early Modern Body" in Hillman and Mazzio, eds. On premodern conceptions of "spirit" as a vapor or liquid inhabiting the body (and as "seed"), see Onians, 480-89, esp. 480-85.

[65] Karl Kraus, In *These Great Times* (Montreal, Quebec: Engendra Press, 1976), 70-83, esp. 71.

[66] George Whetstone, *The Rocke of Regard* (1576), quoted here from Bullough, ed., 6:97; Michel de Montaigne, "Of the worthiest and most excellent men" in *The Essayes of Michael, Lord of Montaigne,* trans. John Florio (1603), ed. Israel Gollancz, 6 vols. (London: J. M. Dent, 1897), 4:327-38, esp. 330; and Burton, 1:11. Emphasis added in all three quotations.

[67] Burton, 1:337-38 (emphasis added except for the last phrase, which is italicized in the original). Perhaps we should think here of Shakespeare as attempting to displace his own anxieties about assimilating or digesting these "massively overdetermined" characters onto his audience; cf. Freund's observation: "Homer and Chaucer are sufficiently rich fare to daunt the digestion of even as voracious a literary imagination as Shakespeare's; and one cannot overlook the rancid flavor of o'ereaten fragments, scraps and greasy relics dominating a text which abounds in food imagery" (21).

[68] One way of understanding this turn is as a return to a pre-verbal state—to infancy (speechlessness)—as a concomitant of the infantile oral sadism and projective mechanisms described above in relation to satire: cf. Klein's view of infantile sadism (see n. 37, above).

[69] Scarry, *The Body in Pain,* 14.

[70] Gary Shapiro, "Jean-Luc Nancy and the Corpus of Philosophy" in *Thinking Bodies,* Juliet Flower MacCannell and Laura Zakarin, eds. (Stanford, CA: Stanford UP, 1994), 52-62, esp. 60. On the bodiliness of Montaigne's skepticism, see Victoria Kahn, *Rhetoric, Prudence, and Skepticism in the Renaissance* (Ithaca, NY: Cornell UP, 1985), 115-51.

[71] Michel de Certeau, *Heterologies: Discourse on the Other,* trans. Brian Massumi (Minneapolis: U of Minnesota P, 1986), 72. My understanding of Montaigne's essay is indebted to de Certeau's powerful reading of it.

[72] Montaigne, "Of the Cannibals" in *Essayes,* 2:32-54, esp. 226.

[73] Montaigne, 2:51. On the slipperiness of language in the play, see in particular C. C. Barfoot, *"Troilus and Cressida:* 'Praise us as we are tasted,'" *SQ* 39 (1988): 45-57: *"Troilus and Cressida* leads us to the conclusion that we can no more trust our heroes, or even our anti-heroes, than we can trust our words" (55).

[74] De Certeau, 73.

[75] Montaigne, 2:51.

[76] De Certeau, 75.

[77] De Certeau, 75.

[78] A. P. Rossiter, *Angel with Horns: Fifteen Lectures on Shakespeare,* ed. Graham Storey (London and New York: Longman, 1961), 151.

[79] *The Iliad,* 3:148; Bullough, ed., 6:194. It is perhaps not surprising to find that the only character to escape his predetermined citational identity is Antenor, the figure of pure mimesis.

[80] I thank Jeff Masten for this observation. *Troilus and Cressida,* as we have seen, includes several such denominative jokes—"Ilium" and "Ilion," "the Matter of Troy," and the scatological play with the name "Ajax" (a jakes or privy) come to mind.

[81] Silence is not, however, invariably an honorable way out of the degradation of language in *Troilus and Cressida.* Ajax's silent treatment of his compatriots in Act 3 is held up to merciless ridicule by Thersites: "Why, a stalks up and down like a peacock, a stride and a stand; ruminates like an hostess that hath no arithmetic but her brain to set down her reckoning; bites his lip with a politic regard. . . . He's grown a very land-fish, languageless, a monster. . . . Why, he'll answer nobody: he professes not answering; speaking is for beggars" (3.3.250-53, 262-63, 267-68): clearly, not all languagelessness stems from an *ethic* of silence.

[82] De Certeau, 73.

[83] Charnes, 429.

[84] Nietzsche, *Ecce Homo,* 311. Sir Francis Bacon uses the same phrase—"the art of silence"—in *De Augmentis,* where he relates the story of Zeno, who, having remained silent throughout an audience with a foreign ambassador, told the latter to "'Tell your king that you have found a man in Greece, who knew how to hold his tongue'" (Bacon, *The Works of Francis Bacon,* ed. James Spedding et al., 14 vols. [London: Longman, 1868-90], 5:31).

[85] Nietzche, *Twilight of the Idols* in *The Portable Nietzsche,* 556.

―――――――――

Source: "The Gastric Epic: *Troilus and Cressida*," in *Shakespeare Quarterly*, Vol. 48, No. 3, Spring, 1997, pp. 295-313.

Slavery, English Servitude, and *The Comedy of Errors*

Maurice Hunt, *Baylor University*

Both critics and editors of *The Comedy of Errors* reveal a notable uncertainty over the social status of the Dromio brothers. Taking their cue from the designations of Shakespeare's text, they refer to the twins sometimes as slaves, sometimes as servants, and occasionally as bondmen. Their uncertainty would perhaps be unimportant were physical violence not an issue. *The Comedy of Errors* is remarkable for the extent of the physical beatings given the Dromios as well as for the commentary on it. This is especially true when the pertinent episodes are compared with their sources in Plautus' *Menaechmi* and *Amphitruo*. The rough treatment of the Dromios and their ambiguous servant/slave status reflect similar features of Elizabethan servitude. In *The Comedy of Errors,* Shakespeare constructs the Dromios so as to condense the potential slavishness of sixteenth-century English service. The playwright's focus on de facto slavery widens to encompass the institution of marriage and the individual's ordering of his or her inner faculties. Implicitly Shakespeare poses a dramatic question: do the reunions and festive releases celebrated at the end of *The Comedy of Errors* include a remedy for slavery, whether of the social, marital, or existential variety?

Assembling the relevant passages into a whole reveals the emphasis Shakespeare gives past and present beatings of the Dromios. In the first major error of the play, Dromio of Ephesus mistakes Antipholus of Syracuse for his master and urges him to hurry home to his cooling dinner and his angry wife, Adriana. Antipholus of Syracuse's bafflement increases when this Dromio professes ignorance of the money that Antipholus gave the other Dromio for safekeeping. Because Dromio of Syracuse often jests to relieve his master's melancholy, Antipholus of Syracuse imagines that Dromio of Ephesus is joking: "I am not in a sportive humour now: / Tell me, and dally not, where is the money?" (1.2.58-59).[1] Dromio replies in terms of the beating he expects to receive: "I from my mistress come to you in post; / If I return I shall be post indeed, / For she will scour your fault upon my pate" (1.2.63-65). Dromio of Ephesus' anxiety stems from a blow he received earlier that afternoon. "The clock hath strucken twelve upon the bell," he informs Antipholus of Syracuse; "My mistress made it one upon my cheek; / She is so hot because the meat is cold" (1.2.45-47).[2] Household beatings apparently are a customary part of Dromio of Ephesus' life. When Antipholus of Syracuse, exasperated over Dromio of Ephesus' repeated denial of any knowledge concerning the disputed "thousand marks," threatens to "break that merry sconce of yours" (1.2.79), Dromio darkly jests:

> I have some marks of yours upon my pate;
> Some of my mistress' marks upon my
>   shoulders;
> But not a thousand marks between you both.
> If I should pay your worship those again,
> Perchance you will not bear them patiently.
>
> (1.2.82-86)

Most Elizabethans would have regarded Dromio's final utterance as ominously subversive: the man threatens to beat his master. That Dromio makes this threat obliquely in the context of punning jests does not lessen its seriousness. One might object that the Dromios' jests accompanying threats of beating prevent auditors from taking the characters' physical abuse as a serious issue of *The Comedy of Errors*. Rather than insulating the play from a troubling topic, the Dromios' jokes represent their habitual strategy for coping with their resentment over their ill-treatment. Freud did, after all, confirm for the twentieth century a fact that Shakespeare intuitively grasped—that disruptive puns mask a good deal of aggression, even hostility. Eamon Grennan claims that the Dromios, "as perpetrators of puns, repeatedly compensate for their social bondage by their linguistic freedom. Doing so they draw attention to the counterpoint between the conventional fixity of society, which victimizes them, and the natural fluidity of language, which is their weapon of comic revenge."[3] The linguistic anarchy resulting from the Dromios' puns substitutes for the social revolution traditionally desired by subjugated men and women.

Antipholus of Syracuse defuses the inflammatory charge of Dromio's joke by reminding him of his abject social status: "Thy mistress' marks? what mistress, slave, hast thou?" (1.2.87). Despite textual references to the Dromios as servants, they are typically called slaves in *The Comedy of Errors*.[4] T. W. Baldwin noted that, "for the ancients, 'Dromio is a slave's name in Terence, Lucian, and in a comedy extracted by Athenaeus.' Dromio appears in Lucian's *Timon* as the 'Stock name for a slave.'"[5] Grown angry, Antipholus of Syracuse beats the slave Dromio: "What, wilt thou flout me thus unto my face / Being forbid? There, take you that, sir knave" (1.2.91-92). "What mean you, sir? for God's sake hold your hands," a fearful Dromio replies: "Nay, and you will not, sir, I'll take my heels" (1.2.93-94). Shakespeare's initial identification of the Dromios as slaves occurs within the context of physical violence. Antipholus of Syracuse's "I'll to the Centaur to go seek this slave" (1.2.104) echoes two verses later in Adriana's remark "Neither my husband nor the slave return'd" (2.1.1). The repeated emphasis upon the Dromios' status as slaves immediately after the beating of act I fixes the sociopolitical value of subsequent thrashings in the play.

Returning to his mistress Adriana, Dromio of Ephesus stresses his bodily abuse:

> *Adr.* Say, didst thou speak with him? knowst thou his mind?
>
> *Eph. Dro.* Ay, ay, he told his mind upon mine ear,
> Beshrew his hand, I scarce could understand it.
>
> *Luc.* Spake he so doubtfully, thou couldst not feel his meaning?
>
> *Eph. Dro.* Nay, he struck so plainly I could too well feel his blows; and withal so doubtfully, that I could scarce understand them.
>
> (2.1.47-54)

Adriana equates this beating with the condition of slavery. When Dromio of Ephesus complains—"So that my errand due unto my tongue, / I thank him, I bare home upon my shoulders; / For in conclusion, he did beat me there"—she commands "Go back again, thou slave, and fetch him home" (2.1.72-75). Dromio's reply evokes a Christian context that doctrinally repudiates the corporeal violence associated with slavery:

> *Eph. Dro.* Go back again, and be new beaten home?
> For God's sake, send some other messenger.
>
> *Adr.* Back slave, or I will break thy pate across.
>
> *Eph. Dro.* And he will bless that cross with other beating;
> Between you I shall have a holy head.
>
> (2.1.76-80)

Dromio of Ephesus' repetition here of his earlier phrase "for God's sake" (1.2.93) and the wordplay latent in his notion of blessing a "cross"—a crucifix/an inscribed wound—"with other beating" strengthen the ironic Christian frame for negatively appraising his master's thrashing of him. "Am I so round with you, as you with me, / That like a football you do spurn me thus?" Dromio painfully questions; "You spurn me hence, and he will spurn me hither; / If I last in this service you must case me in leather" (2.1.82-85).

Later beatings of the Dromios match early pummelings both in their extent and magnitude. Dromio of Syracuse receives his twin's painful reward when he denies knowledge of having spoken of a mistress and dinner to his master (2.2.7-62). "Think'st thou I jest?" Antipholus of Syracuse exclaims, "hold, take thou that, and that" (2.2.23). Beaten, Dromio cries, "Hold sir, for

God's sake" (2.2.24), repeating the Christian talisman for the third time in the play. "Was there ever any man thus beaten out of season," Dromio laments, "When in the why and the wherefore is neither rhyme nor reason" (2.2.47-48). Dromio of Ephesus finds only in the welts left by blows a language of protest equal to his bewilderment. "That you beat me at the mart I have your hand to show," he tells Antipholus of Ephesus: "If the skin were parchment and the blows you gave were ink, / Your own hand-writing would tell you what I think" (3.1.12-14). Concerning the sixteenth-century Spanish practice of branding Aztec slaves, the Franciscan monk Motolinia wrote, "They produced so many marks on their faces, in addition to the royal brand, that they had their faces covered with letters, for they bore the marks of all who had bought and sold them."[6] Similarly Vasco de Quiroga noted, "They are marked with brands on the face and in their flesh are imprinted the initials of the names of those who are successively their owners . . . so that the faces of these men who were created in God's image have been, by our sins, transformed into paper" (p. 137). Admittedly, the comic structure of *The Comedy of Errors* cannot easily support the tragic weight of these facts. Nevertheless, the slavish Spanish practice and resulting commentary on it provide the closest contemporary analogue to Dromio of Ephesus' transformation of his slave's body into a book indicting its insensitive inscribers. In the Dromios' reiterated pleas to the Antipholus twins to hold their hands "for God's sake," Shakespeare's play reproduces the tension in the Spanish commentary between the injustice of slavery and Christian precept. Antipholus of Ephesus' unfeeling reply to the implied question of what the "hand-writing" on Dromio's body makes him think is the terse remark, "I think thou art an ass" (3.1.15)—an animal ordained to bear. "Marry, so it doth appear," Dromio sadly agrees, "By the wrongs I suffer and the blows I bear; / I should kick, being kick'd, and being at that pass, / You would keep from my heels, and beware of an ass" (3.1.15-18) Once again, the slave's final utterance sounds the muted note of rebellion.

As regards the beatings of the Dromios and their arresting complaints, the variations that Shakespeare plays upon his sources are significant. The slave Messenio is never beaten in Plautus' *Menaechmi*. In fact, his master Menechmus Sosicles gratefully frees him at play's end for having proved that Menechmus Epidamnum is his long-lost brother. In *Amphitruo,* the slave Sosia complains about his hard life and he is eventually beaten.[7] But the administrator of the thrashing is not his master Amphitryon but the god Mercury, who has disguised himself as Sosia in order to help Jupiter seduce Amphitryon's wife Alcmena. Plautus never dramatizes a master's physical abuse of his slave.[8]

Antipholus of Ephesus administers the final beating of a slave in *The Comedy of Errors* when his own Dromio brings him a rope's end instead of money for the master's bail (4.4.8-37). In reply to Antipholus' enraged judgment "Thou art sensible in nothing but blows, and so is an ass," Dromio of Ephesus soberly generalizes the disturbing impression of the unjust treatment of slaves in this play: "I am an ass indeed; you may prove it by my long ears. I have served him from the hour of my nativity to this instant, and have nothing at his hands for my service but blows. When I am cold, he heats me with beating; when I am warm he cools me with beating; I am waked with it when I sleep, raised with it when I sit, driven out of doors with it when I go from home, welcomed home with it when I return, nay, I bear it on my shoulders as a beggar wont her brat; and I think when he hath lamed me, I shall beg with it from door to door" (4.4.25-37). Dromio's conclusion resonates with a significance far larger in its implications than the meaning of the local thrashings that the slaves receive for their several errors of mistaken identity. Nevertheless, the physical violence that the audience has witnessed and the many threats that it has heard justify both the seriousness and the length of Dromio's complaint.

These impressions challenge the different attempts of commentators to integrate the beating of the Dromios and the requisites of comedy. Gwyn Williams believes that Antipholus of Syracuse's occasional contact with Dromio of Syracuse saves the master's sanity, enabling him "to work off some of his mental anguish in the physical drubbings he administers."[9] For many critics, the beating of the Dromios drains off potentially tragic emotions, keeping the play a light comedy. In this vein Ruth Nevo argues that the Dromios, "fated to miscarry and constantly belaboured by their irate masters, function to defuse by laughter the dire personal threat of traumatic non-entity, or total chaotic non-being."[10] "Even the beatings of the Dromios are not excessive," Alberto Cacicedo pronounces, "given Antipholus' position in a foreign and, as he has been warned, hostile town."[11] For William Babula, masters pounding slaves in *The Comedy of Errors* illustrate the anxious side effect of the single element present in all of the play's characters—their fear of destructive change.[12] When critics seek motivation for the beatings in the makeup of character rather than in the imagined requirements of genre and dramatic ambience, they generally note references in the play to the choleric humours of the Antipholus twins.[13]

Harry Levin has judged that the number of beatings that the Dromios receive "is a matter of farcical convention rather than social custom."[14] *The Comedy of Errors* has often been termed a farce; and farce, as Eric Bentley has reminded us, "is notorious for its love of violent images."[15] By this logic, Shakespeare's decision to become a farceur committed him to representing physical violence, essentially non-meaningful abuse. J. Dennis Huston has asserted that the charac-

ters of *The Comedy of Errors* "entertain us by threatening and inflicting upon one another violence that does not hurt," while Barbara Freedman has maintained that the Dromios, "well-meaning but thickheaded . . . are the true butts of farce—doomed to be beaten but never to know why."[16] "By status the Dromios of Shakespeare's play are the slaves of Latin comedy," Kathleen Lea notes, "but in behavior and misfortunes they are the servants of the Commedia dell'arte . . . beaten as regularly as any Zanni."[17]

In these accounts farcical convention fully explains the abuse of the Dromios. Nevertheless, contrary to Levin's opinion, analysts of farce generally agree that farce and social custom are inextricably linked. David Wiles has claimed that "Plautine farce is conceived as myth," as a "collective creation which allows the community to sound out possibilities and impossibilities created by the social code."[18] This sounding out as a rule entails social criticism. Jessica Davis has demonstrated that farce represents "the continual impulse to rebel against convention," which according to Bentley is frequently the rigid, imprisoning institution of puritanical marriage.[19] Farce may function best, Leslie Smith concludes, "in a repressive or convention-ridden society."[20] Albert Bermel asserts that from Aristophanes to Chaplin, farce has always possessed the "power of revelation," the force of illuminating social satire and political commentary. Comparing farce to comedy, Bermel argues that the didactic power of farce originates in its distorted picture of life as "more bitter, more cruel, more downright unfair."[21] Concerning existential and social injustices, "the dislike that farce arouses has stronger components of violence and contempt. Therefore, [farce] more tellingly reflects and echoes the corruption, treachery, hypocrisy, brutality, and injustices of life."[22]

II

All this is to say that the beating of the Dromio brothers in the farcical *Comedy of Errors* may amount to contemporary social commentary. "Beaten at nearly every turn of the plot by the contending Adriana and Antipholi, the besieged Dromios," according to Donna Hamilton, "literalise the language of violence . . . not evenhandedly (Adriana suffers no injury) but in such a way as to display hierarchy senselessly victimizing the disempowered."[23] In other words, the beating of the Dromios may represent Shakespeare's veiled criticism of certain Elizabethan social injustices. Hamilton, however, believes that the physical abuse in *The Comedy of Errors* allegorizes "the language of violence that had become a staple of the puritan and anti-puritan tracts and treatises" of the Marprelate controversy (pp. 59-85). Nevertheless, interpretation in this respect does not need to be so symbolically specific. The physical abuse of servants and their virtual enslavement were widely remarked features of late Elizabethan life. The mistreatment of the Dromios in *The Comedy of Errors* calls attention to common inequities of Shakespeare's age.

It is not common knowledge that slavery, strictly defined, was proposed several times during the Tudor period and in fact briefly implemented on two occasions. The Edwardian Vagrancy Act of 1547 made branding and slavery the punishment for sturdy beggary.[24] Moreover, under the Vagrancy Act of 1572, Justices of the Peace could banish incorrigible rogues from England or condemn them to unending servitude in the galleys (p. 166). Still, something in the English temperament made undisguised, institutionalized slavery repugnant. The Act of 1547 was thought to be too severe and was repealed within two years of its passage. (In 1557, however, civil disorder provoked interest in reviving the statute condemning vagabonds to slavery.)[25] Likewise, evidence that JPs availed themselves of the slavery clause of the Act of 1572 is virtually nonexistent, even though the penalty remained on the books. Englishmen such as Sir George Peckham argued that American Indians taken in war should be made slaves.[26] Yet the English never adopted the early sixteenth-century Spanish practice in this respect. What is remarkable here is not so much that English statutes of slavery were proposed and then either repealed or neglected as that in the sixteenth century they were repeatedly formulated and that the ancient practice was so often on people's minds.

If slavery, strictly defined, did not become part of Elizabethan life, virtual de facto enslavement did. Of special interest is the custom among the English gentry and aristocracy of child-giving and fosterage. Patricia Fumerton has shown that both natural and foster parents thought of children in this system as essentially material gifts that could avert clan warfare and promote political alliances and stability.[27] Fostered children were also thought of as investments that might reap future monetary rewards for both offspring and natural parents (in skills or arts learned, in potential mates met, in prime social connections made).[28] In this sense, the materialized child is a personally unrecompensed worker for a master's profit (the foster and especially natural parent's)—a condition that at least one eminent Elizabethan poet likened to slavery. Fumerton has demonstrated that in Book VI of *The Faerie Queene*, Edmund Spenser allegorically criticizes fosterage in the tragedy of the shepherds captured by brigands: "Here the individual is not subsumed in a larger whole but lost in a murky confusion of 'things.' Here living beings are not passed along in an expanding circle of exchange but treated in a self-restricting cycle of profit: sold as 'slaves . . . for no small reward, / To marchants, which them kept in bondage hard, / Or sold againe' (6.10.43)" (pp. 63-64). It will be recalled that in *The Comedy of Errors* Egeon speaks of having bought the Dromios as infants to serve his sons, "for their parents were exceeding poor" (1.1.56-

57). Through the conceit of impoverished parents selling their children (illegal in Elizabethan England), Shakespeare joins a chorus criticizing the abuse of labor inherent in fosterage.

Virtual enslavement also resulted from the uniquely English practice of placing children, generally from the time they were twelve or thirteen to the age of twenty-one or even twenty-four, in other people's homes to act as servants. According to Keith Wrightson, teenaged servants gained valuable working experience, enjoyed opportunities to save which might never come again, and as they reached their 20s had the chance to look out for opportunities for permanent settlement and marriage.[29] Shakespeare's alternative references to the Dromio slaves as servants—see note 4—invited Elizabethans to think of these characters as closely bound attendants.[30] In this respect John Lyly's *Mother Bombie* (1590, publ. 1594) set a precedent. In this comedy Lyly conflates slavery and English servitude in the character Dromio, who has been regarded as either an inspiration for or an analogue to his namesakes in *The Comedy of Errors.* Lyly's Dromio is essentially a page-servant (he is listed as a "boy" in the play's dramatis personae). But Dromio's master Memphio implies that he is a slave when he says that the boy will be "forever set at liberty" if he can arrange a marriage between Memphio's son and Stellio's daughter (1.1.79-82).[31] Dromio confirms this impression when he declares that his fellow page Risio's "knavery and my wit should make our masters that are wise fools, their children that are fools beggars, and us two that are bond free" (2.1.6-8). As the *OED* makes amply clear, a sixteenth-century synonym for "bondman" was "slave." Both A. Harriette Andreadis and Violet Jeffrey have noted the incongruity of slave-keeping in rural Rochester, the English setting of *Mother Bombie.*[32] For Andreadis, Dromio's bondman status "seems a deliberate attempt on the part of the dramatist to maintain an aura of Romanness" in a play partly inspired by the comedies of Plautus and Terence (p. 21). While this explanation may suffice for Lyly (whose veiled social commentary does not address proletarian injustices), it fails to account satisfactorily for Shakespeare's blending of service and slavery in his Dromios. Despite Wrightson's definition of the benefits of sixteenth-century English service, Elizabethan servitude and husbandry approached the condition of slavery and could on occasion be confused for it. Lyly's placing a slave named Dromio in an English setting may have simply made Shakespeare more aware of the slavishness of English servitude.

Dromio of Ephesus' summary speech of physical abuse refers to service, not slavery: "I have served him from the hour of my nativity to this instant, and have nothing at his hands for my service but blows" (4.4.28-30). The only commentator on *The Commedy of Errors* to broach this dimension of the play is Wolfgang Riehle, who states that "there is also a grim reality (and a 'corrective' purpose) behind the comic confusions between the Antipholi and the Dromios. These servants have good cause to fear that their masters may 'break' their 'pates,' because as Thomas Platter observed [in 1599]: 'England is the servant's prison, because their masters and mistresses are so severe.' The Elizabethan physician Dr. Napier mentions in his notebooks the tragic misfortune of a servant whose 'pate' was indeed broken by his master, whereupon he fell into a state of madness from which he never again recovered."[33] E. M. W. Tillyard considered Antipholus of Syracuse's beating of his Dromio as one of several "very human touches" that make farce and romance recognizable as ordinary life in a small English town.[34] Elizabethan and Jacobean records reveal that the community could be any town in England. They indicate the contemporary relevance of the pervasive violence against slavishly held servants in *The Comedy of Errors*.

If slavery is defined as labor without material recompense, then many English servants were basically enslaved. Annual contracts between the *paterfamilias* and a servant placed in his household called for the paying of wages above and beyond room and board. Nevertheless, these wages were often either never paid or outrageously shorted. Ann Kussmaul has shown that farmers in Shakespeare's age "docked shillings, even six-pences, to deny servants their settlements."[35] Because the "minimum age for which wages were specified in Quarter Sessions assessments varied from ten to twenty for men, and from twelve to sixteen for women," very young servants might never receive wages for their labor (p. 37). Servants often collected no annual wages until they completed their multiyear term of service (p. 38). Even then, the number of cases that Susan Amussen has tabulated wherein "the concerns of villagers are evident in their response to masters who withheld wages or belongings at the end of a servant's employment" indicates the slavishness of English servitude.[36] Compounding this problem were the conspicuous neglect and physical abuse suffered by many youthful servants.

Kussmaul quotes the servant Richard Mayo's complaint of being "'laid in some cold out-house, or meanest Loft, of a Poor Cottage, to have the leavings of coarse fare there'" (p. 40). Amussen has chronicled through case studies the often fatal plight of neglected servants: "Sara Patrick of Wickmere demanded an inquest when her daughter, Rebecca Russells, who had been a servant of William Hower and his wife, was found dead after being 'hardly kept.' . . . In 1610, William Childerhouse of Saham Toney had gone to the house of John Tennant at the request of William Wright and reported that, 'about Christmas time last past . . . he did see William Wright's daughter being the said Tennant's servant laid in a barn in a little straw covered with flaggs, the said servant at that time very sick of the Pox . . . And it seemed to him and to

many . . . at that time that the said Wright's daughter was very carelessly looked to and provided for by . . . her said Master.'"[37] Since (by Wrightson's conservative estimate) eighty-five percent of servants in Shakespeare's age were illiterate (pp. 190-91), court records of physically abusive masters rather than letters and diaries testify to the sexual exploitation and beating of servants. If one judges the larger number of complaints that were never written down by those forced into court by sympathetic neighbors and, on occasion, by the aggrieved servant him-or herself, violence against servants was fairly common in the sixteenth and seventeenth centuries.[38] William Marshall's horsewhipping "a 'puny' lad" can stand for a depressing host of other examples of masters' cruelty (Kussmaul, p. 46). One could object that my argument tends to normalize social pathology, that the claim that Elizabethan servants were abused and virtually enslaved comes almost exclusively from our knowledge of the prosecution and correction of these conditions. Certainly many English servants were well-treated (although the figure is impossible to estimate). Yet the sheer number of reports of abuse and the logic that would support a far greater total of unreported cases of violence imply a problem of significant social magnitude. Original audiences of *The Comedy of Errors* almost certainly included servants—and perhaps some enlightened masters—for whom the beating of the Dromios was not a laughable subject.

For the great mass of Elizabethan laborers, the Statute of Artificers of 1562/63 and related legislation created employment conditions resembling slavery. Sixteenth-century English workers could not freely dispose of their labor unless they owned property valued at 40 shillings per annum, stood to inherit property worth at least this value, or owned goods appraised at £10. Craft masters might ask for and compel the labor of persons under age thirty who had completed apprenticeship in a trade. Persons between the ages of twelve and sixty without an agricultural holding who were neither bound apprentices nor practitioners of a craft could be forced to work as farm laborers, even by householders with only half a plowland in tillage.[39] Refusal to do so entailed the punishment for vagrancy—whipping. Those compelled to labor had to accept badly deflated wages controlled to the taskmaster's advantage by Justices of the Peace.[40] In 1572, Kussmaul notes, parishes began to bind the children of beggars as apprentices until they were twenty-four, in the case of men, and eighteen in the case of women (p. 166). Laborers were required to work from five in the morning until seven or eight at night from mid-March to mid-September; during the rest of the year, they were forced to work from daybreak to nightfall. Only two-and-a-half hours a day could be taken for eating, drinking, and rest.[41] Furthermore, it was stipulated that workers could not leave their employment without their employer's written consent. While the Statute of 1562/63 and associated legislation were designed to benefit England by insuring an adequate supply of corn and foodstuffs and by eliminating the evils of idleness and vagrancy (which were thought to be the sources of social unrest and outright rebellion), they in effect enslaved tens of thousands of needy men, women, and children. Despite D. C. Colman's claim that the regulations of the Statute were either ignored or sporadically enforced,[42] both Kussmaul and Amussen argue that their enforcement in the sixteenth century was more uniform than has been supposed.[43] The oppressive conditions of Elizabethan service and husbandry make the bondage and ill-treatment of the Dromios realistic elements in a comedy of illusions.

If the Dromios are slaves of their masters' passions, then the masters themselves must in one sense be considered slaves—slaves of their emotional selves. R. A. Foakes implies as much when he asserts, "each Dromio applies the term 'ass' in relation to the beatings he is made to suffer, and to the way he is made to seem a fool; but the idea of being a beast operates more generally in the play, reflecting the process of passion overcoming reason, as an animal rage, fear, or spite seizes each of the main characters" (p. xlv). By this criterion, most of the characters of *The Comedy of Errors,* especially Antipholus of Ephesus, are slaves at one impassioned moment or another. Enslaved to his baffled anger over his wife's, courtesan's, and bondman's incomprehensible replies to his commands and explanations, Antipholus of Ephesus in his rage appears mad (and thus a candidate for binding). Bound, he is reduced to a slave's status (graphically suggested by Dromio's binding at the same time as his master's). In this case Shakespeare translates an inner bondage into a stage image suggestive of actual slavery.

Judged by Foakes's criterion, almost every important character in Shakespeare's plays could be called a "slave of passion." The phrase complicates the analysis of slavery in *The Comedy of Errors,* partly because it introduces the notion of figurative rather than literal enslavement (and risks confusing the two ideas). Calling a Shakespeare character a "slave of passion" evokes the specter of a sixty-year-old critical approach to Shakespeare's tragedies identified with Lily Campbell.[44] Nevertheless, in *The Comedy of Errors* Shakespeare does extend his exploration of slavery from the literal to the figurative, and a shift in methodology becomes necessary to register this expansion. Thus far, the methodology of this essay could be called New Historical; in what follows it becomes formalistic. Still, literary history provides a ground for formal analysis of figurative enslavements in *The Comedy of Errors.* Throughout the English Renaissance writers such as Thomas Rogers, Thomas Wright, and Robert Burton used the terms "service" and "slavery" as metaphors for the relationship between reason and the passions in ways not described by Campbell.

III

Concerning the passion named Oblectation ("a certain binding, or inclination of the mind, to a pleasure gently and sweetness mollifying the mind"), Rogers remarks in *The Anatomie of the Minde* (1576) that "with this vice was Sardanapalus so brought into slavery, that he could not be one minute without pleasure."[45] As regards Envy, Rogers judges that "not only those two lights and examples of vertue, Themistocles, and Aristides were brought into misery, but also the whole state of Athens into perpetuall slavery" (p. 46). In *The Anatomy of Melancholy* (1621), Burton concludes that "we are slaves and servants the best of us all. . . . *Alexander* was slave to feare, *Caesar* of pride, *Vespasian* to his money . . . *Heliogabalus* to his gut, and so of the rest. Lovers are slaves to their mistresses, rich men to their gold, Courtiers generally to lust and ambition, and all slaves to our affections, as *Evangelus* well discourseth in *Macrobius,* and *Seneca* the Philosopher, *assiduam servitutem extreman & ineluctabilem,* he calls it, a continuall slavery, to bee so captivated by vices, and who is free?"[46] Even as sixteenth- and seventeenth-century writers used forms of the word "slavery" to describe passion's rule of reason, so they carefully employed the word "service" to denote passion's proper subordination. "Hereupon the Philosophers and Fathers," Wright notes in *The Passions of the Mind* (1601), "perceiving what commodities these passions afforded to a virtuous soul, with divers similitudes declared their service. . . . By this Discourse may be gathered that Passions are not only not wholly to be extinguished . . . but sometimes to be moved and stirred up for the service of virtue, as learnedly Plutarch teacheth."[47]

These and other passages in Elizabethan and Jacobean texts undergird Shakespeare's depiction of figurative self-enslavement in *The Comedy of Errors.* As a rule, this kind of enslavement in Shakespeare's plays requires a catalyst outside the self. Othello becomes a slave of passion when he allows himself to become the debased and eventually dehumanized agent for effecting another's will—Iago's. This causal relationship is instructive. When characters in *The Comedy of Errors* such as Adriana and Egeon get caught in social institutions wherein their agency in conforming to another's will makes them feel dehumanized, they act like slaves, becoming the victims of their own rage or sorrow. In their operation in the play, patriarchal marriage and rigorous, talionic law transform characters into figurative bondmen and bondwomen.

Doctrinally the wife's subordinate role in patriarchal marriage involves servitude, not slavery. When Luciana portrays the male-dominated natural hierarchy forming a rationale for patriarchal marriage (2.1.15-25), Adriana shrewdly retorts, "This servitude makes you to keep unwed" (2.1.26). Yet Adriana's marriage is far from ideal, and she pointedly articulates the slavishness lurking in the wife's servitude. Luciana's reminder that "A man is master of his liberty" (2.1.7) prompts Adriana to ask, "Why should their liberty than ours be more?" (2.1.10). Already feeling unjustly constrained, Adriana is told that her husband "is the bridle of your will" (2.1.13). When she replies, "There's none but asses will be bridled so" (2.1.14), she invokes one of the play's metaphors for enslavement. In Act 3, Dromio of Syracuse fearfully explains that Nell, the greasy kitchen wench, has claimed him as her betrothed husband: "To conclude, this drudge or diviner laid claim to me, called me Dromio, swore I was assured to her, told me what privy marks I had about me, as the mark of my shoulder, the mole in my neck, the great wart on my left arm, that I, amazed, ran from her as a witch" (3.2.138-43). Dromio's words comically make explicit a troubling aspect of Adriana's marriage to Antipholus of Ephesus, that of the spouse as no more than material goods laid claim to. Even as slaves may be known and valued by the marks upon them (the scars of whippings usually), so wives may be (although theirs are mainly congenital). Such marks determine contested ownership in both cases. The material transferability of Adriana is underscored by her recollection that Solinus, the Duke of Ephesus, "made" Antipholus "lord of me and all I had" by means of "important letters" (5.1.137-38).[48] The proprietary marks on the wife's body threaten to become slavish realities when enraged Antipholus of Ephesus commands his Dromio to buy a rope by which he will whip her for having locked him out of his house (4.1.15-18). At this moment, Adriana's condition approaches that of her slave Dromio.

Like patriarchal marriage, talionic law can enslave both agent and victim. That the Ephesus of the play is a fallen city is implied by Egeon's opening speech: "Proceed, Solinus, to procure my fall, / And by the doom of death end woes and all" (1.1.1-2). Ephesians and Syracusans are essentially slaves in that their lives may be bought and sold. When Ephesians, "wanting guilders to redeem their lives" (1.1.8), died in Syracuse, Solinus and the synod of Ephesus retaliated in kind, making execution the penalty for any Syracusan caught in their city, "unless a thousand marks be levied / To quit the penalty and to ransom him" (1.1.21-22). Elizabethans most likely detected the eye-for-an-eye spirit of Old Testament Law informing the codes of Shakespeare's Ephesus and Syracuse. Since Egeon's "substance, valued at the highest rate, / Cannot amount unto a hundred marks" (1.1.23-24), he is condemned to death. Egeon basically becomes a slave when he is converted into material goods and cruelly "sold" (to death) when he is found lacking. But this occurs only because Ephesians and Syracusans have generally become slaves to talionic legalism and the compounded passion of hatred that it engenders.

In one of his dramatic sources, Plautus' *Amphitruo,* Shakespeare could have seen how the world view of a society potentially enslaves its members. In Plautus' comedy Sosia suggests that the gods enslave anyone who does not dutifully worship them.[49] Sosia connects a slave's beating not with his master's irascibility but with his own impiety:

> It's a beating for me. Damn, if
> I haven't gone and completely forgot
> to thank the gods for my safe arrival.
> Now I'm really in the soup.
> If the immortal gods decide
> to give me my just desserts,
> then I'm really done for,
> my face would be pounded to a pudding,
> seeing how ungrateful I've been
> and after all they've done for me.
>
> (p. 46)

Mercury later beats Sosia partly because the god resents having been compelled to turn himself into a slave. Concerning his disguise as Sosia, Mercury laments, "Yesterday I was free and genial; / Today, alas! I am a menial" (p. 46). Plautus adopts a conventional ancient perspective when he depicts a god slavishly using a mortal because Jupiter is slavishly using the lesser deity. But it is in completely stealing mortal identities that the Plautine gods most slavishly use men and women. By assuming Amphitryon's identity to satisfy his lust for Alcmena, Jupiter not only abuses Amphitryon's wife, begetting the child Hercules; the god also underscores the fact that the husband is a slave in the sense that he has no ownership of the self or its products. This degrading condition potentially applies to any mortal whose being a god may wish to appropriate and, under that guise, selfishly deceive another person. In this sense ancient men and women were the gods' slaves. Not even the most intimate details of identity were spared. Jupiter has even duplicated Amphitryon's scar on his right arm (pp. 98-99).[50] These are the implications in Plautus' *Amphitruo* that accentuate the suggestion in *The Comedy of Errors* that the metaphysical principles of a community can figuratively enslave its members.

Does Shakespeare resolve the problem of slavery in *The Comedy of Errors*? In the *Menaechmi,* the slave Messenio, shouting "Io Tryumphe," receives his freedom for having proved to his master Menechmus Sosicles that Menechmus Epidamnum is his twin brother.[51] Likewise, the following words of Dromio of Ephesus concerning his master suggest his enfranchisement: "Within this hour I was his bondman, sir, / But he, I thank him, gnaw'd in two my cords; / Now I am Dromio, and his man, unbound" (5.1.289-91). Dromio's punning jest turns upon the difference between bondman (slave) and unbound man (servant), but neither Antipholus brother in the remaining dialogue of the play explicitly liberates his slave. Significantly, Dromio of Ephesus speaks the play's final words, which convey the idea of human equality: "We came into the world like brother and brother, / And now let's go hand in hand, not one before another" (5.1.425-26). But Dromio directs these words to his twin, not to his master; and the Dromios have had to wait their turn to exit as the lowest denominators in a social hierarchy that privileges Duke Solinus, Emilia the Abbess, and Egeon to depart first; the Antipholus brothers second; and the menial Dromios alone last of all (5.1.403-26). The ending of *The Comedy of Errors* reflects the typical Shakespearean strategy of a radical idea suggested within the endorsement of a conventional social paradigm.

For Aristotle, slavery was with few exceptions an irremediable condition, since slaves by nature lack reason—humankind's defining trait: "'those, therefore, who are as much inferior to others as are the body to the soul and beasts to men, are by nature slaves. . . . He is by nature slave who. . . . shares in reason to the extent of apprehending it without possessing it ([*Politics*] 1254b).'"[52] By this measure, the Dromios exuberantly qualify for enfranchisement, for their clever punning jests, in which they often get the better of their masters, depend for their coining on the quick faculty of reason. Dromio of Syracuse's puns, delivered in an exchange with his master (2.2.35-109), transparently reflect a syllogistic, even Scholastic, method and work to "erode the conventional master-slave relationship" (Grennan, pp. 67-68). At the end of this raillery, the bedazzled, slower-witted Antipholus of Syracuse has forgotten his rage against Dromio. As the sixteenth-century wore on, the question for European colonizers of the New World was whether supposedly natural slavery violated New Testament teachings about the brotherhood of all men and women.[53] That the problem was resolved in favor of Christianity decades before the writing of *The Comedy of Errors* is relevant to our analysis of this play.

Recently Arthur Kinney, drawing upon the motifs and dramaturgy of the miracle and morality plays, has documented the pervasiveness of Christian ideas in *The Comedy of Errors*.[54] James Sanderson pointed toward Kinney's exegetical reading when he argued that Patience is a virtue whose cultivation by the characters of *The Comedy of Errors* "helps make possible . . . the creation of a right understanding of oneself and others, and the eventual enjoyment of those ministrations of a benign Providence which . . . brings clarification out of bafflement, happiness out of adversity, life out of death" (p. 605). It is true that forms of the words "patience" and "impatience" occur in the context of all three beatings of the Dromios. But patience is not a virtue expressly voiced by the Antipholus brothers at play's end. If Shakespeare suggests a Christian solution to the problem of slavery in *The Comedy of Errors,* certain ideas in Paul's Epistle to the Ephesians, another major source of Shakespeare's play, hold more promise.

In Ephesians, Paul anticipates Shakespeare's tendency to include statements of equality within a larger affirmation of hierarchy. "Servants, be obedient vnto them that are *your* masters," Paul admonishes, "according to the flesh, with feare and trembling in singlenesse of your hearts as vnto Christ, Not with service to the eye as men pleasers, but as the servants of Christ, doing the will of God from the heart. With good will, serving the Lord, and not men, And know yee that whatsoever good thing any man doth, that same shall he receive of the Lord, whether *he be* bond or free. And yee masters doe the same things vnto them, putting away threatning: & know that even your master also is in heaven, neither is there respect of person with him" (6.5-9).[55] Paul's final command posits universal brotherhood and undermines without overthrowing his tacit acceptance of slavery and its institutionalization in the first part of the passage. (The Geneva Bible's phrase "whether *he be* bond or free" acknowledges that the literal translation of the first word of the passage is "Slaves" rather than "Servants"). The method resembles the process of Paul's admonition to husbands and wives, the biblical text widely considered to comment authoritatively on the inequities of Adriana's and Antipholus of Ephesus' marriage: "Giving thankes alwayes for all things vnto God even the father, in The Name of our Lord Iesus Christ, Submitting your selves one to another in the feare of God. Wives, submit your selves vnto your husbands, as vnto the Lord. For the husband is the wives head, even as Christ is the head of the Church, and the same is the saviour of *his* body. Therefore as the Church is in subiection to Christ, even so *let* the wives *bee* to their husbands in every thing. Husbands, love your wives, even as Christ loved the Church, and gave him selfe for it" (Ephesians 5.20-25). The sacrament of marriage mystically incorporates man and wife in a transformation of patriarchal Christianity.

In a recent study of femininity and English Renaissance drama, Karen Newman denies the message of equality in the above-quoted Pauline text: "throughout the writings on marriage, man is figured as the head, woman as the body; they are one flesh, a Renaissance commonplace. But the union is not equal in that the male term—head, mind, and by analogy here Christ—has a positive value, while the female term has sometimes merely a lesser value, sometimes a more directly negative value. Women are bodies, associated with nature."[56] This interpretation ignores several nuances of the biblical text. Paul's admonition, "Husbands, love your wives, even as Christ loved the Church, and gave himself for it" entails a self-sacrificial passion—a love so selfless that the head risks all for the life of the body (of which it is in fact part). As read by Reformation protestants, Paul's admonition "Submitting your selves one to another in the feare of God" implied the mutuality of companionate marriage, a give-and-take in which comforting roles between husband and wife shift often, out of Christian love for the spouse and the daily necessities of married life.[57] At the finest moments of married love, the head and the body indistinguishably fuse in a sanctified one flesh—a fact that Adriana clearly understands. Concerning Antipholus of Ephesus' abandonment of her and turning to the courtesan, she rhetorically asks,

> O, how comes it,
> That thou art then estranged from thyself?—
> Thyself I call it, being strange to me,
> That undividable, incorporate,
> Am better than thy dear self's better part.
> Ah, do not tear away thyself from me;
> For know, my love, as easy mayst thou fall
> A drop of water in the breaking gulf,
> And take unmingled thence that drop again
> Without addition or diminishing,
> As take from me thyself, and not me too.
>   (2.2.119-29)

Outraged Adriana can perhaps be excused for the one fault in her argument—that she in her married chastity is "better than thy dear self's better part." Essentially, however, her characterization of the one flesh of marriage reproduces the blurred difference in the verses following Paul's central injunctions. "So ought men to love their wives, as their own bodies: he that loveth his wife, loveth himself. For no man ever yet hated his owne flesh, but nourisheth and cherisheth it, even as the Lord *doeth* the Church. For we are members of his body, of his flesh, and of his bones" (Ephesians 5.28-30). For later ages, the egalitarian burden of these Pauline passages humanized patriarchal marriage, precluding slavish treatment of the wife, without destroying the Judeo-Christian hierarchical mindset.[58]

Concerning Adriana's and Antipholus of Ephesus' marriage, Alexander Leggatt has judged that "one curious feature of the ending is that, while the problems of the marriage have been thoroughly aired, there is no explicit reconciliation between husband and wife. The director may contrive a forgiving embrace, but nothing in the text requires it."[59] (One suspects, however, that the rough physical trials that Antipholus of Ephesus has endured in the course of the play have softened him a bit.) Adriana and Antipholus do not necessarily have to embrace, however, for the radical anti-enslavement message of the Pauline direction on marriage to comment relevantly on *The Comedy of Errors.* For informed playgoers, pertinent passages in Ephesians operate as a subtext in Shakespeare's play, providing a corrective for the enslavement of servants, spouses, and parts of the self even when dramatic characters do not expressly voice and act out the texts. Plautine comedies like Shakespeare's usually include an adaptation of the *cognito* of New Comedy, the discovery that a girl is not a slave or courtesan but of higher birth that makes her marriageable. In *The Comedy of Errors,* the *cognito,* which is multiplied among Egeon

and Emilia the Abbess and their sons and slaves, extends to members of the audience attuned to the resonances of the Ephesian scripture that extensive dramatic allusion has evoked; they discover the source of the mindset for self-enfranchisement and the unslavish treatment of others in an on-going patriarchal society.

Confronted finally with the visual spectacle of identical twins, Duke Solinus, asking which Antipholus brother is "the natural man / And which the spirit" (5.1.333-34), posits the notion of a single two-part organism within a biblical context of the Old and New Adam. His utterance, "One of these men is *genius* to the other" (5.1.332) essentially amounts to a rhetorical question. Only when he is freed from his enslavement to the natural man, the man of vicious passion and of an eye-for-an-eye, can the spiritual man of grace and charity assume his rightful place of guide. Barbara Freedman has called our attention to an overlooked passage in Ephesians that illuminates this dimension of the play. Alluding to the union of Jews and Gentiles in the body of Christ, Paul argues, "For he is our peace, which hath made of both one, and hath broken the stoppe of the partition wall, In abrogating through his flesh the hatred, *that is,* the Law of commaundements *which standeth* in ordinances, for to make of twaine one newe man in himselfe, so making peace, And that he might reconcile both vnto God in one body by *his* crosse, and slay hatred thereby" (2.14-16).[60] Such a passage provides a gloss on Shakespeare's suggestion of the reconciliation of warring selves in "one newe man." Initially, this new man is Solinus himself, whose gracious release of Egeon from his enslavement to the *lex talionis* starts a series of events that include the liberation of other characters from various figurative but nevertheless painfully real bondages. This release occurs because Solinus is moved to free himself from the retributive law of his city. The heartrending spectacle of long-suffering members of Egeon's and Emilia's family rediscovering one another liberates the Duke from an enslaving iron law. Recognizing Egeon, Emilia exclaims, "Whoever bound him, I will loose his bonds, / And gain a husband by his liberty" (5.1.339-40). But only Solinus can annual a secular law. "These ducats pawn I for my father here" (5.1.389), Antipholus of Ephesus proclaims; "It shall not need," Solinus replies, "thy father hath his life" (5.1.390). In terms of my subject, the gratuitousness of Egeon's release is crucial. Deeply moved by what he has seen and heard, Solinus without expectation of reward enfranchises first himself and then Egeon, whose new freedom makes possible both Emilia's release from the long bondage of the priory and the nun's empty life and the Antipholus brothers' freedom from tragedy in their sudden joy. The thirty-three years that Emilia mentions as the term of her travail recalls Christ's traditional age when he was released from the slavery of this life. Providence has managed apparently fortuitous events and errors to promote, even compel, the dissolution of several kinds of figurative enslavement.

Still, providence leaves unaltered the rigid hierarchy of a society in which the Dromios remain slaves and husbands the masters of their wives.[61] R. A. Foakes reminds us that Shakespeare's comedies often have as their end "a re-establishment of responsibility among individuals in a society in the light of a test undergone, or a penance endured, or acceptance of moral bondage in the full understanding of what this means" (p. l). The import of the passages in the Pauline Ephesians that Shakespeare's allusions evoke facilitates for play-goers—if not fully for the characters of *The Comedy of Errors*—an "acceptance of moral bondage in the full understanding of what [bondage] means" in a patriar-chal society. Presumably that involves purging, when-ever possible, slavishness from servitude.[62]

Notes

[1] *The Comedy of Errors,* ed. R. A. Foakes, The Arden Shakespeare (London, 1962). All quotations are taken from this edition.

[2] In "'Time's Deformed Hand': Sequence, Consequence, and Inconsequence in *The Comedy of Errors,"* *Shake-speare Survey 25* (1972), pp. 81-91, Gãmini Salgãdo remarks that "the servants, in their hithering and thither-ing and the 'strokes' they collect at either end become veritable travelling clocks being constantly reset" (p. 86). In this view the "strokes" of beating testify to the disruption of the regular "strokes" of time in *The Com-edy of Errors.*

[3] Eamon Grennan, "Arm and Sleeve: Nature and Cus-tom in *The Comedy of Errors,"* *Philological Quarterly 59* (1980): 150-64, esp. 159.

[4] Following Rowe, Foakes in his list of dramatis per-sonae terms the Dromios "servants to the Antipholus twins" (p. 2). Luciana's command, "Dromio, go bid the servants spread for dinner" (2.2.187), makes the nomination seem plausible, as does Dromio of Syra-cuse's judgment, "Thither I must, although against my will; / For servants must their masters' minds fulfil" (4.1.113-14). Moreover, Egeon calls Dromio of Syracuse his master's "attendant" (1.1.127). Anti-pholus of Syracuse's repeated reference to his Dromio as a "villain"—1.2.19, 96; 2.2.163; 3.1.6, 43; 4.4.22—conveys the sense of villenage, that is to say, social and economic bondage. Adriana and Egeon name Dromio of Ephesus a "bondman" (5.1.141, 289). Nevertheless, the nine references to the Dromios as "slaves" make this term their primary identifier in *The Comedy of Errors.*

[5] T. W. Baldwin, *On the Compositional Genetics of "The Comedy of Errors"* (Urbana, 1965), p. 220. Shakespeare may have been indebted to Terence via John Lyly's *Mother Bombie* (1590, publ. 1594), in which a bondman named Dromio appears. According

to Foakes, Lyly took the name from "Dromo, given to a slave in several of the comedies of Terence" (p. xxi).

[6] Tzvetan Todorov, *The Conquest of America: The Question of the Other,* trans. Richard Howard (1982; rpt. New York, 1984), p. 137.

[7] Plautus, *Amphitruo, Amphitryon: The Legend and Three Plays,* trans. James H. Mantinband (Chapel Hill, 1974), pp. 39-108, esp. 45-46, 50, 57-60.

[8] This is the conclusion of Erich Segal, *Roman Laugh-ter: The Comedy of Plautus,* 2nd ed. (New York,1987), pp. 138-54. Segal cites Mercury's cuffing of Sosia in *Amphitruo* as the *only* certain instance in all of Plautus' plays of a slave's onstage physical abuse (p. 153). In Chapters 4 and 5, "From Slavery to Freedom" (pp. 99-136) and "From Freedom to Slavery" (pp. 137-69), Segal argues that the absence of slave-beating and the manumission of the slave in Plautine drama reveal its Saturnalian nature, its topsy-turvy inversion of the normal orders and tough realities of Roman society (evoked in the comedies by the obsessive *talk* of beat-ing, torturing, and crucifying slaves [pp. 138-42]). It is highly unlikely that Shakespeare would have been aware of the Saturnalian inversions of Plautus' plays if only because the historiography necessary for recover-ing the festive context of their performance had not yet been developed.

[9] Gwyn Williams, "*The Comedy of Errors* Rescued from Tragedy," *Review of English Literature* 5:4 (1964), 63-71, esp. 65.

[10] Ruth Nevo, *Comic Transformations in Shakespeare* (London, 1980), p. 28.

[11] Alberto Cacicedo, "'A formal man again': Physi-ological Humours in *The Comedy of Errors,*" *The Upstart Crow* 11 (1991), 24-38, esp. 28.

[12] William Babula, "'If I dream not': Unity in *The Comedy of Errors,*" *South Atlantic Bulletin* 38 (1973), 26-33.

[13] Cacicedo 26. While Cacicedo makes this claim only for Antipholus of Ephesus' character, Wolfgang Riehle, in *Shakespeare, Plautus, and the Humanist Tradition* (Cambridge, MA., 1990), pp. 59-61, delineates the equally choleric character of Antipholus of Syracuse and correctly describes the similar temperaments of the twin masters. In "Patience in *The Comedy of Er-rors,*" *Texas Studies in Literature and Language* 16 (1975), 603-18, James L. Sanderson states that "the pummeling of the brothers Dromio sometimes strikes modern audiences as a not-very-funny comic cliché from a socially primitive era, a cheap ploy to earn guffaws of an unfeeling if not barbaric audience. In reality, however, Shakespeare has charged these at-

tacks with meaning; they are the outward and visible signs of imperfections of character, of lapses from rational control and surrender to the passions in short, manifestations of impatience" (p. 608).

[14] Harry Levin, "Two Comedies of Errors," *Refractions: Essays in Comparative Literature* (New York, 1966), pp. 128-50, esp. 139.

[15] Eric Bentley, *The Life of the Drama* (1964; rpt. New York, 1965), p. 219.

[16] J. Dennis Huston, *Shakespeare's Comedies of Play* (New York, 1981), p. 18; Barbara Freedman, *Staging the Gaze: Postmodernism, Psychoanalysis, and Shakespearean Comedy* (Ithaca, NY, 1991), p. 88. Freedman's claim that the Dromios "never question the angry beatings they receive" (p. 88) simply is not true.

[17] Kathleen M. Lea, *Italian Popular Comedy: A Study of the Commedia Dell'Arte, 1560-1620* (Oxford, 1934), 2.438.

[18] David Wiles, "Taking Farce Seriously: Recent Critical Approaches to Plautus," *Farce,* ed. James Redmond (Cambridge, 1988), pp. 261-71, esp. p. 269.

[19] Jessica M. Davis, *Farce* (London, 1978), p. 22; *The Life of the Drama,* p. 229.

[20] Leslie Smith, *Modern British Farce* (Totowa, NJ: Barnes and Noble, 1989), p. 14.

[21] Albert Bermel, *Farce: A History from Aristophanes to Woody Allen* (1982; rpt. Carbondale, 1990), pp. 44-45.

[22] Bermel, p. 45. In the words of this cultural historian, farce satisfies "our desires for political and social leveling" (p. 46).

[23] Donna B. Hamilton, *Shakespeare and the Politics of Protestant England* (Lexington, 1992), p. 78.

[24] Roger B. Manning, *Social Protest and Popular Disturbances in England, 1509-1640* (Oxford, 1988), p. 165. Also see C. S. L. Davies, "Slavery and Protector Somerset: The Vagrancy Act of 1547," *Economic History Review* 19 (1966), 533-49.

[25] Margaret G. Davies, *The Enforcement of English Apprenticeship, 1563-1642,* Harvard Economic Studies 97 (Cambridge, MA, 1956), p. 4.

[26] Loren E. Pennington, "The Amerindian in English Promotional Literature, 1572-1625," *The Westward Experience: English Activities in Ireland, the Atlantic, and America 1480-1650,* ed. K. R. Andrews, N. P. Canny, and P. E. H. Hair (Liverpool, 1978), pp. 175-94, esp. p. 182.

[27] Patricia Fumerton, *Cultural Aesthetics: Renaissance Literature and the Practice of Social Ornament* (Chicago, 1991), pp. 29-66.

[28] Miriam Slater, *Family Life in the Seventeenth Century: The Verneys of Claydon House* (London, 1984), pp. 132-38.

[29] Keith Wrightson, *English Society 1580-1680* (New Brunswick, NJ, 1982), pp. 113-14.

[30] Shakespeare's various textual names for the Dromios have led critics—in a usually unexamined manner—to refer in their writings to the characters now as servants, then as slaves. This inexactness in analysis is illustrated by Harold Brooks, "Themes and Structure in *The Comedy of Errors,*" *Early Shakespeare,* ed. John Russell Brown and Bernard Harris (1961; rpt. New York, 1966), pp. 55-71, esp. pp. 62-63.

[31] John Lyly, *Mother Bombie,* ed. A. Harriette Andreadis (Salzburg, 1975), p. 73.

[32] Andreadis, pp. 20-21; Violet Jeffrey, *John Lyly and the Italian Renaissance* (1928; rpt. New York, 1969), p. 113.

[33] Riehle, p. 11. This critic believes that "the ultimate reason for this violence against servants seems to be the extreme political and social conservatism as represented above all by the Protestant William Tyndale who held that like an ox or a horse, a servant is part of a man's possessions" (p. 11, n51).

[34] E. M. W. Tillyard, *Shakespeare's Early Comedies* (New York, 1965), pp. 55-56.

[35] Ann Kussmaul, *Servants in Husbandry in Early Modern England* (Cambridge, 1981), pp. 47-48.

[36] Susan D. Amussen, *An Ordered Society: Gender and Class in Early Modern England* (Oxford, 1988), p. 160.

[37] Amussen, pp. 159-61, esp. p. 160. Numerous other case studies of the physical abuse of Elizabethan and Jacobean servants appear in Carl Bridenbaugh, *Vexed and Troubled Englishmen, 1590-1642* (1967; rpt. New York, 1968), pp. 90-91; and Michael MacDonald, *Mystical Bedlam: Madness, Anxiety, and Healing in Seventeenth-Century England* (Cambridge, 1981), pp. 86-88.

[38] See esp. Kussmaul, pp. 44-48. Regarding masters' violence against servants in Shakespeare's age, MacDonald notes that "proving physical abuse must have been difficult, as the severity of the court records suggests. Similarly, a young woman who had been sexually abused had to choose between the disgrace of

admitting that she had lost her virginity and her desire for revenge: many of those who were lucky enough not to become pregnant must have preferred silence. Only one of the eight young women whose masters were reported to have abused them is known to have prosecuted her employer" (p. 88).

[39] Margaret Davies, p. 273; Christopher Hill, *Change and Continuity in Seventeenth-Century England* (Cambridge, MA, 1975), p. 222.

[40] According to Hill, the Statute of 1562/3 "had the effect of depressing wages and lowering the status of all wage-labourers in town and country" (p. 222).

[41] *Tudor Economic Documents,* ed. R. H. Tawney and Eileen Power (London, 1924), 1, 324.

[42] D. C. Colman, "Labour in the English Economy of the Seventeenth Century," *Economic History Review* 8 (1956), 280-95, esp. 291.

[43] Kussmaul, p. 166; Amussen, pp. 48-49.

[44] Lily B. Campbell, *Shakespeare's Tragic Heroes: Slaves of Passion* (Cambridge, 1930).

[45] Thomas Rogers, *A Philosophicall Discourse Entitled, The Anatomie of the Minde* (1576), p. 7.

[46] Robert Burton, *The Anatomy of Melancholy,* ed. Nicholas K. Kiessling, Thomas Faulkner, Rhonda L. Blair (Oxford, 1990), II, 173. Burton also explains that history shows that literal enslavement brings on melancholy and makes the imprisoned morbidly passionate (I, 341-44).

[47] Thomas Wright, *The Passion of the Mind in General,* ed. William W. Newbold (1601; rpt. New York, 1986), p. 101.

[48] Antipholus of Ephesus confirms Adriana's words when, speaking to the Duke, he bitterly refers to her as "she whom thou gav'st to me to be my wife" (5.1.198).

[49] The following quotations of *Amphitruo* are taken from the Mantinband text.

[50] While this detail is part of the interpolated scene written in imitation of Plautus by the fifteenth-century Cardinal Hermolaus Barbarus, it remains true in spirit to a classical understanding of the gods' ways with mortals.

[51] *The "Menaechmi" of Plautus,* trans. William Warner, *The Narrative and Dramatic Sources of Shakespeare, Volume I, Early Comedies, Poems, "Romeo and Juliet,"* ed. Geoffrey Bullough (London, 1957), pp. 13-39, esp. pp. 37, 39.

[52] In Todorov, p. 152.

[53] This tormenting question was memorably set and conclusively resolved by the Spanish priest Bartolomé de las Casas, as John D. Cox explains in *Shakespeare and the Dramaturgy of Power* (Princeton, NJ, 1989), pp. 1-21. Also see Todorov, pp. 134-39, 160-61.

[54] Arthur F. Kinney, "Shakespeare's *Comedy of Errors* and the Nature of Kinds," *Studies in Philology* 85 (1988), 29-52. But cf. Jonathan V. Crewe, "God or The Good Physician: The Retired Playwright in *The Comedy of Errors,*" *Genre* 15 (1982), 203-23, esp. 208. Kinney likens the mistreatment of the Dromios to the "knockabout farce" in miracle plays on Cain and Abel, with both these plays and the episodes in *The Comedy of Errors* providing relief between the "serious treatments of the fall (and 'death') of Adam (needing, like Egeon, to be saved in the person or representative of Christ) . . . and the high seriousness in showing how Christ's love conquered travail and sin (as with the increasing seriousness of the final scenes of Shakespeare's play)" (p. 42).

[55] Quotations of Ephesians are taken from the 1602 (3rd) edition of *The Geneva Bible,* ed. Gerald T. Sheppard (New York, 1989).

[56] Karen Newman, *Fashioning Femininity and English Renaissance Drama* (Chicago, 1991), p. 16.

[57] Companionate marriages of Reformation protestantism and their new mutuality are described by Juliet Dusinberre, *Shakespeare and the Nature of Women* (London, 1975), pp. 77-128; by Ian Maclean, *The Renaissance Notion of Woman* (Cambridge, 1980), pp. 19-20; and by Carol Thomas Neely, *Broken Nuptials in Shakespeare's Plays* (New Haven, 1985), pp. 8-10.

[58] Nevertheless, in *The Comedy of Errors* Shakespeare subtly qualifies hierarchical thinking, especially as it authorizes the husband's absolute mastery of his wife. Luciana's portrayal of an Elizabethan cosmos in which every creature for the sake of universal order has a master, the wife her husband (2.1.15-25), possesses an authoritative ring. The same may be said for the Abbess' later rebuke of Adriana for usurping her subordinate place by jealously railing against her husband so as to make him vulnerable to the madness of rage (5.1.68-86). (Still, Adriana's rebuke of Antipholus has been in response to a violation of marriage, "Some love [for the courtesan] that drew him oft from home" [5.1.56]. Adriana's "clamours" chiefly take the form of telling her husband that his promiscuity is "vile and bad" [5.1.67]—an evil, in other words. It is surprising—and a bit contradictory—that the head of a religious order should sharply condemn a wife for railing partly meant to be morally redemptive.) Luciana's world picture is exclusively natural; if Elizabethans did not

need nurture—all the effects of civilization (such as the egalitarian messages of the sacrament of marriage and the epistle to the Ephesians)—to rectify their fallen natures, Luciana's natural hierarchy might constitute a model worthy of emulation. (If humankind were no more than fish or "winged fowls" [2.1.18], she might have a point relevant to the conduct of its mating). Luciana's unmollified hierarchical thinking underlies her personally discreditable advice to the twin she supposes is Antipholus of Ephesus—that he remain Adriana's master by secretly satisfying his lust for courtesans and so supposedly not paining his ignorant wife (3.2.1-28). Luciana's belief that "We [women] in your motion turn, and you may move us" (3.2.24) recalls, by its allusion to the movement of the spheres, her earlier argument for cosmic hierarchy. Yet heard as part of her morally questionable advice, the opinion and the absolute male mastery in marriage that it entails suffer. Likewise, the Abbess' rebuke in act V is undercut by Luciana's rejoinder, "She never reprehended him but mildly, / When he demean'd himself rough, rude and wildly; / Why bear you these rebukes and answer not?" (5.1.87-89). Obviously Luciana has a double standard: unquestioning compliance to the husband/master's will for wives in general and a considerable egalitarian latitude, subject to negotiation, for herself as imagined wife and for an unhappy wife for whom she cares a great deal. All of these ironies, while not overturning the social hierarchy of patriarchal marriage, validate the humanizing of the model implied in the Ephesian subtext of *The Comedy of Errors.*

[59] Alexander Leggatt, *Shakespeare's Comedy of Love* (London, 1974), p. 8.

[60] Quoted in Freedman, p. 101.

[61] Nevertheless, the visually stereotyped slave of the play is neither Dromio twin but Dr. Pinch, "This pernicious slave" (5.1.242) according to Antipholus of Ephesus. "A hungry lean-fac'd villain," "A mere anatomy, a mountebank, / A thread-bare juggler and a fortune-teller, / A needy-hollow-eye'd-sharp-looking-wretch" (5.1.238-41). Dr. Pinch illustrates the worst kind of slavery in the play: bondage to an inflated self-conception based upon the practice of bankrupt arts such as fortune-telling, sorcery, and exorcism. It is the failure of these arts that has wasted Pinch and given him a beggarly appearance. Pinch—not the Dromios—perceptibly typifies the condition of slavery in *The Comedy of Errors.* Shakespeare thus in act 5 provides a benchmark that allows playgoers to realize that the Dromios are not *abject* slaves. One senses that the witty play of their minds would always preclude the Pinch kind of enslavement to debilitating egoism and dogma.

[62] Richard Strier, David Evett, and Judith Weil improved this paper through their constructive criticisms of an earlier draft, presented at the 1993 Shakespeare Association of America meeting. For another account of slavery in an English Renaissance play, see Carolyn Prager, "The Problem of Slavery in *The Custom of the Country,*" *Studies in English Literature* 28 (1988), 301-17.

———————

Source: "Slavery, English Servitutde, and *The Comedy of Errors,*" in *English Literary Renaissance*, Vol. 27, No. 1, Winter, 1997, pp. 31-56.

"Errors" and "Labors": Feminism and Early Shakespearean Comedy

Ann Thompson, *Roehampton Institute*

Most feminist critics have simply ignored *The Comedy of Errors* and *Love's Labor's Lost:* the bibliographies on these plays in the pioneering anthology, *The Woman's Part* (1980), are minimal,[1] and the number of items specifically devoted to them in the Garland Annotated Bibliography of *Shakespeare and Feminist Criticism* (1991) is still very low.[2] On one level, feminist critics are simply perpetuating the general critical neglect of the earliest works in the canon, whatever the genre, which is disappointing in itself if one had entertained hopes that something genuinely new was happening in Shakespeare criticism. It is indeed quite baffling that plays like *Titus Andronicus* and the *Henry VI/Richard III* tetralogy have not attracted more attention, with their strong but demonized women (Tamora, Joan of Arc, Margaret). The only exception amongst the early comedies has been, predictably enough, *The Taming of the Shrew,* which has been rediscovered and reread with, as it were, a vengeance.

I do not propose to attempt to appropriate *The Comedy of Errors* and *Love's Labor's Lost* for feminism, nor to attack them for not making themselves available for this kind of appropriation. Rather, my emphasis is on how these texts raise issues that are of real interest to feminist critics. One part of my project is to collect and survey such work as has been done so far. The other part is to consider lines of investigation that might be undertaken in the future.

A particular reason for critical neglect in the case of *Errors* an inconstant throughout the play by the mistaken-identity plot, while the men in *Love's Labor's Lost* are ridiculed in the same way in the scene (5.2.79-483) where they make love to the wrong (masked) ladies. In both plays (again, as in the other comedies and in *Romeo and Juliet*), the men make extravagant vows or declarations of affection that are treated skeptically by the women. In 3.2 of *The Comedy of Errors,* Luciana rejects the advances of Antipholus of Syracuse, reminding him of his marriage vows to her sister (which were of course made by Antipholus of Ephesus). In *Love's Labor's Lost,* all four young men begin by vowing not to see women at all, but they quickly break their vows and resort to sophistry for "some salve for perjury" (4.3.285). Not surprisingly, they have difficulty at the end in convincing the women that they are serious.

There are some specific feminist discussions that are relevant here. Deborah T. Curren Aquino has argued that the women in the early plays, though not yet dominant forces like Rosalind in *As You Like It,* possess highly developed survival skills that make them more adaptable and resourceful than the men.[3] She concentrates especially on their verbal skills, demonstrating how the women in *Love's Labor's Lost* outsmart and outmaneuver the men, while Adriana at the end of *The Comedy of Errors* reasons logically with the Duke, in contrast to her emotional, irrational husband. Aquino also argues that the female characters are more practical and more efficient.

Irene G. Dash, in a chapter on *Love's Labor's Lost* in her book *Wooing, Wedding and Power: Women in Shakespeare's Plays,* specifically champions the Princess as a strong, self-assertive woman: "original in her thinking, she is unafraid and undominated".[4] She points out that this character has been the victim of editorial and stage tradition: Pope cut many of her lines in his 1723 edition, and Johnson in 1765 voiced a general disapproval:

> In this play, which all editors have concurred to censure, and some have rejected as unworthy of our poet, it must be confessed that there are many passages mean, childish, and vulgar; and some which ought not to have been exhibited, as we are told they were, to a *maiden queen.*[5]

It was this 'vulgarity' (of which I shall have more to say below) that led to the part of the Princess being much abbreviated on stage; as elsewhere in her book, Dash proves the stage tradition to have been more sexist than the text. Dash is also refreshing in her analysis of the critical tradition, demonstrating how the Princess has been consistently ignored or underestimated by writers who take it for granted that Rosaline, who is Berowne's amorous partner, must also be his intellectual foil. Such critics then prove, to their own satisfaction, that Rosaline does not seriously rival Berowne in this area, conveniently ignoring the princess, who arguably does.

There is a slight problem of essentialist naivety in these discussions, as when Dash writes that "the exchange between [the Princess] and Boyet illustrates the dramatist's remarkable insight into the mind of a woman and his ability to create, as Pope observed, characters as 'Individual as those in Life itself'."[6] Nevertheless it is true that even at the end of the play these women remain independent, at least temporarily, refusing the men the closure of immediate marriage.

A male feminist critic, Peter Erickson, has explicitly contrasted the ending of *Love's Labor's Lost* with that of *As You Like It,* where the men's control is reaffirmed and the women are rendered nonthreatening. In that play, Rosalind explicitly submits to male power, saying to both her father and her husband "To you I give myself, for I am yours" (5.4.116-17). Moreover, the Epilogue reminds the audience that the performer of the heroine's role is not really a woman at all: as Erickson puts it, "Not only are women to be subordinate; they can, if necessary, be imagined as nonexistent."[7] The formal awkwardness of the ending of *Love's Labor's Lost* perhaps renders it aesthetically inferior to *As You Like It,* but from the viewpoint of sexual politics the later play does not represent an unqualified advance.

The ending of *The Comedy of Errors* is significant among the early or middle comedies due to the prominence of the mother. Feminist and other critics have recently explored some of the missing mothers in Shakespeare in essays such as Coppélia Kahn's "The Absent Mother in *King Lear*"[8] and Stephen Orgel's "Prospero's Wife."[9] Kahn has also written on *The Comedy of Errors* in her book *Man's Estate: Masculine Identity in Shakespeare,* where she focuses on the identity crisis in the play and its relation to the sea:

> In [*The Comedy of Errors* and *Twelfth Night*], the fear animating the identity crisis is the fear of losing hold of the self; in psychoanalytic terms, the fear of ego loss. Often it is expressed as the fear of being engulfed, extinguished, or devoured in the sea or in some oceanic entity.[10]

Another psychoanalytic critic, Ruth Nevo, explores the same idea, finding the sea an:

> archetypal symbol of vicissitude in human life—yes; but "oceanic," it will be recalled, was Freud's term for those fantasies of merging, union and dissolution which are rooted in yearnings for the primal symbiosis of infant and mother.[11]

Both critics quote the words of Antipholus of Syracuse:

> I to the world am like a drop of water,
> That in the ocean seeks another drop,
> Who, falling there to find his fellow forth
> (Unseen, inquisitive), confounds himself.
> So I, to find a mother and a brother,
> In quest of them (unhappy), ah, lose myself.
> (1.2.35-40)

Antipholus' search for his mother represents a nostalgia for a lost state of bliss—the undifferentiated union of mother and child. The fantasy of merging with another human being is also a nightmare of losing one's own identity. The ultimate reunion with the identical twin (as also in *Twelfth Night*) both satisfies the longing for a return to some kind of original union and reestablishes individual identity by resolving the confusions that have built up.

There is a curiously strong emphasis on the act of giving birth both at the beginning and at the end of *The Comedy of Errors.* In the opening scene, Egeon describes how he had been obliged to leave his wife when she was "almost at fainting under / The pleasing punishment that women bear" (1.1.45-46) and how she subsequently became "A joyful mother of two goodly sons" (50), adding

> That very hour, and in the self-same inn.
> A mean woman was delivered
> Of such a burthen male, twins both alike.
> (1.1.53-55)

In the final scene, the Abbess, revealing herself to be the long-lost mother, celebrates:

> Thirty-three years have I but gone in travail
> Of you, my sons, and till this present hour
> My heavy burthen [ne'er] delivered.
> (5.1.401-3)[12]

However, the actual dramatic role of the mother here is to criticize her daughter-in-law, Adriana, and especially to tell her that her husband's blatant infidelity is her own fault—indeed that her jealousy may have driven him mad. She interrogates Adriana at some length, leading her on to incriminate herself by admitting to a more extreme form of jealous behavior than she has in fact practiced. This is perhaps the most remarkable example of the double standard in the entire canon: is it possible to imagine someone scolding Othello in this way and telling him that he should have put up with his wife's infidelity quietly?

Moreover, although the mother is present in this scene, the main emphasis is on the reunions of the male twins. Janet Adelman has even argued that both *The Comedy of Errors* and *Love's Labor's Lost* are not primarily concerned with marriage at all but with male identities, male bonding, and male friendship, all of which are potentially threatened by women and marriage.[13]

This threat to male relationships perhaps underlies the wildly shifting attitudes to women displayed by the men in both plays. They veer from worshipping them as quasi-divine beings to despising them as mere sensual animals. Their language about women ranges from romantic lyricism to bawdy innuendo and downright obscenity. This is most obvious in *Love's Labor's Lost* when, in 4.3, the men produce extravagant sonnets in praise of their mistresses. Longaville, for example, speaks of the "heavenly rhetoric of [Maria's] eye" (58) and claims,

A woman I forswore, but I will prove,
Thou being a goddess, I forswore not thee.
My vow was earthly, thou a heavenly love;

(4.3.62-64)

On which Berowne comments,

This is the liver-vein, which makes flesh a
  deity,
A green goose a goddess; pure, pure
  [idolatry].

(4.3.72-73)

Nevertheless, Berowne's own subsequent "salve for perjury" is much in the same style, arguing that it is the women who are the true inspiration of all learning:

For when would you, my lord, or you, or you,
Have found the ground of study's excellence
Without the beauty of a woman's face?
From women's eyes this doctrine I derive:
They are the ground, the books, the academes,
From whence doth spring the true Promethean
  fire.

. . . . .

For where is any author in the world
Teaches such beauty as a woman's eye?

. . . . .

For when would you, my liege, or you, or
  you,
In leaden contemplation have found out
Such fiery numbers as the prompting eyes
Of beauty's tutors have enrich'd you with?

. . . . .

From women's eyes this doctrine I derive:
They sparkle still the right Promethean fire;
They are the books, the arts, the academes,
That show, contain, and nourish all the world,
Else none at all in aught proves excellent.

(4.3.295-351)

Yet Berowne has begun the scene with a very negative description of his own experience of being in love, "I am toiling in a pitch—pitch that defiles" (2-3), and has spoken harshly of his choice:

And among three to love the worst of all,
A whitely wanton with a velvet brow,
With two pitch-balls stuck in her face for
  eyes;
Ay, and, by heaven, one that will do the deed
Though Argus were her eunuch and her guard.

(3.1.195-99)

The play provides no justification for this attack on Rosaline's morals: it is just assumed (as in *The Taming of the Shrew* at 2.1.294-96) that a spirited or outspoken woman must be unchaste.

The "war against the affections" undertaken by the men in the opening scene of *Love's Labor's Lost,* although supposedly a general one against "the world's desires" and involving devotion to study as well as abstinence from food and sleep, quickly turns out to focus exclusively on the vows about women and the threat they pose to the all-male utopia. The first item Berowne reads from the paper he is about to sign is "That no woman shall come within a mile of [the] court. . . . On pain of losing her tongue" (1.1.119-24). While women are, as usual, stereotyped as talkative, it is the men's language in this play that is actually out of control—explicitly so at 4.3.270 when, during the competitive praising of mistresses, Berowne says of Rosaline (apparently forgetting her pitch-ball eyes) "I'll prove her fair, or talk till doomsday here."

Of course the utopia is doomed. From the beginning, Costard the "clown" has pointed out "it is the manner of a man to speak to a woman. . . . Such is the simplicity of man to hearken after the flesh" (1.1.209-18). The country wench Jacquenetta finishes the play two months pregnant with Don Armado's child. There seems to be a class differentiation here, with the lower-class characters accepting the basic facts of life in a way the higher-class characters find difficult, but the play does not simply endorse the lower classes. Berowne's own put-down of Rosaline quoted above ends with a class-insult: "Some men must love my lady, and some Joan" (3.1.205). Don Armado is anxious to justify his love by the precedents of "great men" such as Hercules and Samson (1.2.65-76), and Berowne also cites Solomon, Nestor, and Timon (4.3.165-68). Both class and gender hierarchies are evoked by the patronizing analogies of the king and the beggarmaid (1.2.109-17 and 4.1.64-66) and that of Jove turning mortal for love of a woman (4.3.115-18). There is a comparable class differentiation in *The Comedy of Errors,* where the greasy kitchen wench is a joke and her pursuit of Dromio of Syracuse a parody of courtship. She is "a very beastly creature" (3.2.88), "a mountain of mad flesh" (4.4.154).

Women of all classes are identified with "flesh," the body, sexuality—what Lear is later to call "the sulphurous pit" (4.6.128). In *The Comedy of Errors,* they are also seen as witches and devils: the Courtesan is addressed as "Satan" by Antipholus of Syracuse, who tells his servant she is worse than the devil—"she is the devil's dam" (4.3.48-51). They subsequently call her "fiend" and "sorceress" (64-66)—this is again reminiscent of the way Kate is demonized in *The Taming of the Shrew* (for example, at 1.1.66, 105, 121-25). The supposed threats to male identity of enchantment and physical transformation are also specifically associated with women at the end of *The Comedy of Errors,* when the Duke says "I think you all have drunk of Circe's cup" (5.1.271).

The other way that women turn men into beasts is of course through infidelity: they give them cuckolds' horns. This is an obsessive theme in both tragedy and comedy in this period. Coppélia Kahn points out that it depends on three things:

> First, misogyny, in particular the belief that all women are lustful and fickle; second, the double standard, by which man's infidelity is tolerated, while woman's is an inexcusable fault; and third, patriarchal marriage, which makes a husband's honor depend on his wife's chastity.[14]

The Comedy of Errors contains Shakespeare's longest and most explicit discussion of the double standard. In 2.1, Adriana, whose husband is being unfaithful to her, asks, "Why should their [that is, men's] liberty than ours be more?" (10), to which her sister Luciana replies with a general chain-of-being argument:

> The beasts, the fishes, and the winged fowls
> Are their males' subjects and at their controls:
> Man, more divine, the master of all these,
> Lord of the wide world and wild wat'ry seas,
> Indu'd with intellectual sense and souls,
> Of more pre-eminence than fish and fowls,
> Are masters to their females, and their lords:
> Then let your will attend on their accords.
> (2.1.18-25)

This is the same appeal to cosmic/civic order (as opposed to theological decree) used by Kate at the end of *The Taming of the Shrew.* Later in the scene, Luciana, like the Abbess in 5.1, scolds Adriana for her "self-harming jealousy" (102) and advises patience. When Luciana is courted by Antipholus of Syracuse, whom she takes for Adriana's husband, Antipholus of Ephesus, she accepts the double standard while rejecting his advances:

> If you did wed my sister for her wealth,
> Then for her wealth's sake use her with more
>   kindness:
> Or if you like elsewhere, do it by stealth,
> Muffle your false love with some show of
>   blindness:
>
> . . . . .
>
> Tis double wrong, to truant with your bed,
> And let her read it in your looks at board:
> (3.2.5-18)

Feminist critics have differed in their use of this material. Juliet Dusinberre cites the debate as evidence

that in real life women *were* arguing for their rights within marriage,[15] while Lisa Jardine sees Adriana's articulateness in defense of women as ironically underlining the actual helplessness of a wife: when the wronged wife does (albeit unwittingly) finally shut her husband out of the house, he sends for a "rope's end" to beat her with (4.1.16).[16]

Another relevant aspect of women-as-flesh is the whole issue of verbal obscenity in these plays. People who encounter Shakespeare as readers of edited texts are to some extent protected from the high level of obscenity in his work by squeamish editors who have traditionally passed over certain phrases or simply labeled them *"double entendres"* or "sexual *equivoques"* without further explanation. Similarly, in the theater, audiences have been protected by cuts justified in the past by propriety and in the present by obscurity. As Irene Dash says of the chief heroine in *Love's Labor's Lost,* "the remarkably outspoken Princess [is] infrequently heard."[17] Unlike their editors and producers, Shakespeare's female characters are frank and direct about sex: the Princess and her women in *Love's Labor's Lost,* twice described as "mad wenches" (2.1.257 and 5.2.264), give as good as they get in terms of bawdy repartee, despite occasional criticisms, as when Berowne says to Rosaline "Your wit's too hot" (2.1.119), or when Margaret comments to Boyet and Costard "Come, come, you talk greasily; your lips grow foul" (4.1.137).

Nevertheless, verbal obscenity is most likely to be directed *against* women in these plays, given the association between the female and sexuality in general. Without quite descending to the reductionism of Launce in *The Two Gentlemen of Verona* ("This shoe with the hole in it is my mother" [2.3.17-18]), both plays seem obsessed with the physical aspects of sex and with female genital parts: women constitute a "lack," both in the Freudian sense and as a literal absence from the Elizabethan stage. The itemized or fragmented *blazon,* or catalog of a woman's physical beauties, is parodied in the description of the kitchen maid in *The Comedy of Errors* (3.2), where both the master (supposedly in a state of romantic infatuation with Luciana) and the man relish the comedy of listing the woman's "parts" in increasingly grotesque physical detail, much as the qualities of Launce's mistress are cataloged in 3.1 of *The Two Gentlemen of Verona.* The extravagant eulogy of women's eyes in 4.3 of *Love's Labor's Lost* (quoted above) follows on from the fantasy elaborated by Longaville, Dumaine and Berowne:

> *Long.* Look, here's thy love, my foot and her
>   face see.
> *Ber.* O, if the streets were paved with thine
>   eyes,
> Her feet were much too dainty for such tread!

Dum. O vile! Then as she goes what upward lies
The street should see as she walk'd overhead.

                                        (273-77)

Women's eyes are impossibly idealized as part of the display of erotic attraction, while men's eyes are devoted to "vile" voyeurism.

Despite the dangers of falling back into the more naive forms of character-criticism, I think there is still a case for feminist critics to explore further the roles allocated to women in *The Comedy of Errors* and *Love's Labor's Lost.* We don't need to "identify" with them, or argue that they are "just like real women," in order to analyze the ideology of femininity that is represented within the text by such things as women's function within courtship, the double standard regarding infidelity, and so forth. Similarly, we don't need to treat the plays as documentary dramas about Elizabethan England to allow them to spark off investigations of such relevant social and historical issues as witchcraft, royal marriages, class relations between men and women, and illegitimate births.

We should continue to build on work already done on the reproduction of these texts, both in the theater and in the classroom or study. The editorial tradition might also be investigated, since it too has arguably been more antifeminist than the texts it presents and interprets. It has neglected many of the issues that feminists might be interested in and has at times displayed a casual misogyny in its commentary, especially on obscene passages. Gary Taylor has even argued that sexism has determined male editors' responses to a textual crux in *The Comedy of Errors.*[18] We do, happily, have some feminist criticism of these plays: can we have a feminist production or a feminist edition?

Notes

[1] Carolyn Ruth Swift Lenz, Gayle Greene, and Carol Thomas Neely, eds., *The Woman's Part: Feminist Criticism of Shakespeare* (Urbana: University of Illinois Press, 1980). The bibliography lists just one item on *The Comedy of Errors,* an essay by C. L. Barber published in 1964. It manages three items on *Love's Labor's Lost,* though one of them dates from 1953.

[2] Philip C. Kolin, *Shakespeare and Feminist Criticism: An Annotated Bibliography and Commentary* (New York: Garland Publishing Company, 1991). In the Play/Poem index, *The Comedy of Errors* and *Love's Labor's Lost* have the lowest numbers of references among the comedies, significantly fewer than those to *The Taming of the Shrew* and (even) *Two Gentlemen of Verona.*

[3] Deborah T. Curren Aquino, "'Toward a Star that Danced' Woman as Survivor in Shakespeare's Early Comedies," *Selected Papers from the West Virginia*

Shakespeare and Renaissance Association 11 (1986): 50-61. See also Louis A. Montrose, "'Sport by Sport O'erthrown': *Love's Labor's Lost* and the Politics of Play," *Texas Studies in Language and Literature* 18 (1977): 528-52.

[4] Irene G. Dash, *Wooing, Wedding, and Power: Women in Shakespeare's Plays* (New York: Columbia University Press, 1981), 15.

[5] Ibid., 15

[6] Ibid., 23

[7] Peter Erickson, *Patriarchal Structures in Shakespeare's Drama* (Berkeley: University of California Press, 1985), 35.

[8] Coppélia Kahn, "The Absent Mother in *King Lear,*" in *Rewriting the Renaissance,* ed. Margaret W. Ferguson, Maureen Quilligan, and Nancy J. Vickers (Chicago: University of Chicago Press, 1986), 33-49.

[9] Stephen Orgel, "Prospero's Wife," *Representations* 8 (1984); 1-13. See also my own essay "'Miranda, Where's Your Sister?': Reading Shakespeare's *The Tempest,*" in *Feminist Criticism: Theory and Practice,* ed. Susan Sellers (Harvester Wheatsheaf: Hemel Hempstead, 1991), 45-55.

[10] Coppélia Kahn, *Man's Estate: Masculine Identity in Shakespeare* (Berkeley: University of California Press, 1981), 197.

[11] Ruth Nevo, *Shakespeare's Other Language* (London: Routledge, 1987), 46-47.

[12] There is a discrepancy about dates here. In 1.1, Egeon says that his son left home to look for his brother when he was eighteen years old (1.1.125) and that he himself took up the search after "five summers" (132). In 5.1., he claims he last saw his son "but seven years since" (321). Theobald emended the Abbess's figure to "twenty-five," but modern editors assume these inconsistencies will not be noticed by audiences or even readers, and they therefore leave them alone.

[13] Janet Adelman, "Male Bonding in Shakespeare's Comedies," in *Shakespeare's Rough Magic,* ed. Peter Erickson and Coppélia Kahn (Newark: University of Delaware Press, 1985), 73-103.

[14] Coppélia Kahn, *Man's Estate,* 121.

[15] Juliet Dusinberre, *Shakespeare and the Nature of Women* (London: Macmillan, 1975), 77-82.

[16] Lisa Jardine, *Still Harping on Daughters* (Brighton: Harvester Press, 1983), 44-47.

[17] Irene Dash, 14.

[18] Gary Taylor, "Textual and Sexual Criticism: A Crux in *The Comedy of Errors,*" *Renaissance Drama* 19 (1989): 195-225.

———————

Source: "'Errors' and 'Labors': Feminism and Early Shakespearean Comedy," in *Shakespeare's Sweet Thunder: Essays on the Early Comedies*, edited by Michael J. Collins, University of Delaware Press, Winter, 1997, pp. 90-101.

Histories

Food for Words: Hotspur and the Discourse of Honor

Harry Berger, Jr., *University of California, Santa Cruz*

In *Richard II,* Thomas Mowbray, the Duke of Norfolk, having been accused of grievous crimes and challenged to judicial combat by Henry Bolingbroke, addresses the following piece of ceremonial bluster to the throne:

> However God or Fortune cast my lot,
> There lives or dies true to King Richard's
>   throne,
> A loyal, just, and upright gentleman.
> Never did captive with a freer heart
> Cast off his chains of bondage and embrace
> His golden uncontroll'd enfranchisement,
> More than my dancing soul doth celebrate
> This feast of battle with mine adversary.
> Most mighty liege, and my companion peers,
> Take from my mouth the wish of happy
>   years;
> As gentle and as jocund as to jest
> Go I to fight: truth hath a quiet breast.
>
> (1.3.85-96)

Such ritual self-representation has the obvious purpose of turning the speaker as completely as possible into a conventional icon, of emptying out his particularity so that he may fully embody and signify the discourse of honor. It is insurance against potential detraction should he be defeated. Its value is commemorative: in what may be his last performance the speaker designs his own death mask, speaks his own epitaph, tries to preempt the honor-giving function by stamping his ritualized *idea* on the future. The speech concludes not with one but with two rhymed couplets—double insurance. The message Mowbray intends is that he has already been enfranchised, that he is inwardly untouched by the "chains" of falsehood and corruption that bind him, and therefore that his truth, his probity, can't be affected by the outcome. Everything in this speech, however, strains against this message, qualifies it, contradicts it.

The initial strain is felt in the parallelism of the first two lines: his lot will be cast by God if he lives but by Fortune if he dies. This distinction may serve the rhetorical purposes of his message, but it is, to say the least, theologically difficult, and it is an evasive modification of the juridical logic that governs trial by combat, in which to lose is to be judged guilty by God. Another strain is suggested by Mowbray's insistence that he is true to "King Richard's *throne*"; his effort in 1.1 discreetly to distance himself from complicity with Richard insinuates a distinction into this phrase: truth to the throne may not be identical with truth to Richard. Mowbray is implicated in the Gloucester murder as well as in other unpalatable Ricardian projects. After he deflects blame for the murder from himself to Richard he goes on gratuitously to mention his participation in another failed ambush directed at John of Gaunt (1.1.133-41). Since nothing more is said about this episode we are left to wonder whether that was another Ricardian project, and the speculation only increases our sense of the snarled factional networks, the deep divisions, papered over by the ritual formulas that shape the language and actions of these public scenes.

Given the conventional demands of ceremonial speech, Mowbray's assertion of complacent conscience need not be belied by the catachrestic violence of his wild figural dance. Such a dance is expected to fulfill the pastoral function of ritual without succumbing to the deadly iterability of the clichés of self-praise. The function is pastoral because it is a simplified and artificial procedure that conspicuously excludes and therefore alludes to the complicated network of motives, purposes, and interests to which it responds. Yet because of his unhappy relation to this network Mowbray's defense of his probity and freedom from guilt is compromised from the start. He is not only placed in a false position; he is also in a no-win situation. He would be disgraced if Bolingbroke were to defeat him, but were he to win he would uphold the disgraced regime that taints him by association, and he would validate the king he had all but accused of murder (1.1.132-34). Furthermore, it seems clear to everyone involved that both Richard and Bolingbroke are using him as a factor, an expendable decoy, to further their own designs. For all these reasons the very assertion of truth, autonomy, and quiet conscience must be assumed to jeopardize the self-esteem of any speaker whom we imagine to cherish those values, and the phrase "truth hath a quiet breast" takes on ominous vibrations: given the situation Mowbray finds himself in, there can be no truth in words. He thus welcomes the feast of battle as a liberation from the silenced truth of the network in which he is hopelessly entangled. He throws himself into it as an escape from the effeminizing—because (in his case) castrating—battle of words, "the trial of a woman's war" (1.1.48), in which he has been forced to defend his honor in terms that can only further compromise it. There is no escape from this bondage except in the enfranchisement his language orgiastically solicits and anticipates: death. "Take from my mouth the wish of happy years": not only "I wish you many happy years" but also "let me not wish for happy years";

"let me die now." Mowbray's dilemma is a harbinger, a proleptic epitome, of the dilemma that faces Hotspur in *1 Henry IV.*[1]

. . . . .

The discourse of honor lurches like a sick horse toward the field it pastures and sickens on—the field beneath which problems of gender, speech, and gift exchange twist along in rhizomes whose bad fodder crops up everywhere. Harry Percy alias Hotspur rides into the field on that same horse, but misperceives the poor critter as his roan, his throne, and foolishly—or dashingly—disregards one of the symptoms of what ails it: it is, he says, "a crop-ear" (2.3.70). My topic in this essay is Hotspur's crop-eared dash toward death. More specifically, I am interested in Hotspur's talk and in things mucking about among the rhizomes of his language that the speaker seems not to hear, or not to want to hear. But before following Hotspur into the field, I want to set the stage for his entry by describing the field itself.

One of the many fine moves Pierre Bourdieu makes in *Outline of a Theory of Practice* is to map the discourse of honor onto Mauss's famous account of the discourse of the gift. In that account, Mauss writes that to give "is to show one's superiority, to show that one is something more and higher, that one is *magister. . . .* To accept without returning or repaying more is to face subordination, to become subservient, a client, a debtor," for "charity wounds him who receives, and our whole moral effort is directed toward suppressing the unconsciously harmful patronage of the rich alms-giver"—the patronage, for example, of such figures as the Christian Father and the Jewish Mother, both of whom, taking a page from King Lear's book, continually remind their children that "I gave you all."[2] In the course of sketching out what may be called a "gift-act theory," Bourdieu chooses for his first example the game of honor and goes on to offer a conspectus of its strategies and misfires, which, he claims, conform to "a logic of challenge and riposte."[3]

This move is interesting because the dialectic of honor is more than a casual example of the dialectic of the gift. To superimpose challenge-and-riposte on gift-and-return is to bring out the ambivalence in each (the aggressiveness of giving, the generosity of the challenge) and in fact to suggest that the two form a reversible fabric, each side the inner lining of the other. Bourdieu insists that the logic of honor is inherent in the more general practices of gift exchange: just as a gift "is a challenge which honors the man to whom it is addressed, at the same time putting his point of honor . . . to the test," so a challenge is a gift because it credits its recipient "with the dignity of a man of honor."[4] This general view of the relationship, however, fails to engage the particular difference that distinguishes the special discourse of honor from the contribution its logic makes to the ambivalence of gift exchange. For gift-giving as Mauss discusses it may be aggressive and challenging, but it needn't be *discussed* by anyone but the anthropologist. The semiotics of gift exchange can operate with only nonlinguistic signs; the periodic deposit and removal of material objects (mineral, vegetable, animal, human) could conceivably take place in total silence. Not so the discourse of honor, which entails a linguistic component because it is not a closed or circular interaction but always subtends the arbitration and authority of a third party.

If two men meet in the forest, draw their swords over a point of honor, and one falls, but nobody hears him, has the other won honor? Not unless he returns to tell the tale, and the tale is accredited, and it reaches the right ears. *Percipi est esse*—and therein hangs a problem. Aristotle noted that while many think honor to be the *telos* of the political life, it is too superficial to be the final good because "it appears to depend on those who confer it more than on him who receives it."[5] According to Bourdieu's account, when the claimant to honor challenges others to recognize his claim, he may be said to confer honor on them because the challenge credits them with the capability of "playing the game of honor" and obligates them to respond. But since the challenge is a request, it also confers *power* on them. Even if the honor-seeker feels he deserves the gift, it remains a gift for which he incurs an obligation. Thus the struggle between honor-seekers and honor-givers generates the need on both sides for strategies that control the flow of power and indebtedness.

The coupling of honor and gift exchange goes back at least as far as Aristotle, who says that "a gift is at once a giving of a possession and a token of honor." This remark may be coupled with another in which he indicates that honor itself is a gift, and with still another in which he notes of the "great-souled man"—who above all others prizes and deserves honor—that he "is fond of conferring benefits, but ashamed to receive them, because the former is a mark of superiority and the latter of inferiority." This suggests a problem, because if honor is a benefit conferred, shouldn't the great-souled lover of honor be ashamed to receive it, especially since he knows himself to be superior and "is justified in despising other people"?[6] Aristotle secures the great-souled man from this dilemma by arguing that he will be justified in feeling he receives "only what belongs to him, or even less, for no honor can be adequate to the merits of perfect virtue, yet all the same he will deign to accept their honors, because they have no greater tribute to offer him."[7] His gift to them will be to honor them with the opportunity to signify, however inadequately, what he already possesses. This helps him go on despising them, which is as it should be.

A similar view appears in *Leviathan,* where, characteristically, Hobbes bares its fangs:

> To have received from one, to whom we think ourselves equal, greater benefits than there is hope to requite, disposeth to counterfeit love; but really secret hatred.... For benefits oblige, and obligation is thraldom; and unrequitable obligation perpetual thraldom; which is to one's equal, hateful. But to have received benefits from one, whom we acknowledge for superior, inclines to love; because the obligation is no new depression: and cheerful acceptation, which men call *gratitude,* is such an honor done to the obliger, as is taken generally for retribution.[8]

Hobbes seems to assume that hierarchy preconditions the different responses of equals and unequals, but if his language doesn't actually destabilize the assumption, it lends it a certain bite. *Retribution,* for example, is a strong term for the gratitude that is the honor *done to* the obliger; it is a power word, and he uses it again in chapter 15 in a punitive sense to denote justified revenge. Is the donee's repayment, his discharging of the debt, a form of requital? "The obligation is no new depression": the donee is already depressed, pressed down; this inferiority is what valorizes his gratitude; he isn't expected to make a more substantial repayment; the donation reaffirms his need and inferiority, as does the honor his cheerful acceptation pays the donor. Perhaps, then, generosity is the donor's revenge. But why should this be?

Hobbes suggests why this should be in his discussion of honor: "The *value,* or WORTH of a man, is . . . his price; that is to say, so much as would be given for the use of his power: and therefore is not absolute; but a thing dependent on the need and judgment of another. . . . And as in other things, so in men, not the seller, but the buyer determines the price. For let a man, as most men do, rate themselves at the highest value they can; yet their true value is no more than it is esteemed by others" (1.10). This is the theme that, as D. J. Gordon has shown, is central to *Coriolanus.*[9] If obeying and honoring confer power, those who obey and honor *have* power, which they both exercise and alienate when they obey and honor. It may be that in the terms of this master-slave dialectic, the more depressed they are, the more gratitude and honor they pay out, the more power they alienate, the more power they have. But what is the value of the honor one receives from those he considers his inferiors, those he relies on to reaffirm his superiority? It may be that in the overall scheme of *Leviathan* this dialectic promotes anxiety in the natural person who becomes the preeminent artificial person when authorized by his subjects to represent them as their sovereign.

Aristotle is no less political than Hobbes in his approach to honor, but Hobbes is more sensitive to the abstract and mediated forces of commodity exchange embedded in (but in his time much closer to the surface of) the concrete exchange systems of what may be called logocentric hierarchy. As C. B. Macpherson paraphrases Hobbes's view, honor, "regarded subjectively by the recipient, is the difference between his own estimate and the market estimate of his value. But honor, regarded objectively, corresponds to the market estimate that both establishes his actual power and is established by his actual or apparent power."[10] One buys power or protection by paying out honor, and, as Hobbes asserts, the problem for the hero is that it is a buyer's market. This is because honor can't be taken or stolen or produced for self-consumption. It has to be borrowed, sold, or won; lent, bought, or ceded. As Ulysses puts it in *Troilus and Cressida,* the honor-seeker "Cannot make boast to have that which he hath, / Nor feels not what he owes but by reflection," and the pun on *owes* has real bite to it.

Early in Part One of *Henry IV,* the king calls Hotspur "the theme of honor's tongue, / Amongst the grove the very straightest plant, / Who is sweet Fortune's minion and her pride" (1.1.80-82). All the dilemmas of Hotspur's version of the discourse of honor are inscribed in these words. Honor is the theme of Hotspur's tongue, but since the honor-seeker's discourse is necessarily incomplete and solicits others' tongues, Hotspur is perforce the theme of honor's tongue. This chiasmic predicament is complicated by the fact that there has always been a troubled relation between the honor-seeker's tongue and his valor. It was so in warlike Sparta, from which we get the word and concept *laconic.* It was so in the wild American West, whose soft-spoken six-shooting heroes enjoyed actions louder than words. Enshrined in the films of the 1930s in such oversized, tight-lipped, woolly-mouthed fantasies as Gary Cooper and Randolph Scott, they asserted their special virtue by responding to the demands of civil life and civil or uncivil women with the antirhetoric of *awshucksism.* Who can fail to imagine John Wayne nasally twanging out Mowbray's

> 'Tis not the trial of a woman's war,
> The bitter clamor of two eager tongues,
> Can arbitrate this cause betwixt us twain . . . ?

He would have warmed to this, but the eighteen lines of eager tonguework Mowbray follows it with would have made him nervously toe the hoof-imprinted dirt. Our heroes show themselves aware of the ancient tradition of the *miles gloriosus.* The counterfeit warrior is the one who talks too much; the real one proves his courage by letting his gun and other people do his talking for him.

Paul Jorgensen's study of "the theme of the misplaced soldier" in Shakespeare and his contemporaries throws a certain amount of light on the man of valor's chief problem: "it is only on the battlefield that he is thoroughly at ease."[11] So, if Hotspur says, "I profess not talking," and if Coriolanus says, "When blows have made me stay, I fled from words," Jorgensen thinks this must be because they lack the polish needed to cope with a wordy world run by courtly and lawyer-like operators. But this explanation fails to account for the copiousness of speech with which Hotspur professes not talking, and for the rhetorical power of Coriolanus's wordy flight from words. The story has to change as soon as we recognize that these warrior heroes run away, not from what they do poorly, but from what they do too well—and in Hotspur's case, from what he does so enthusiastically that, when he encounters someone like Glendower who reflects back to him an inflated version of his own bombast, he becomes irritable and embarrassed.

I would argue against Jorgensen, then, that Hotspur's courage (and, in a different way, Coriolanus's) is inseparable from his weakness, and that it is more than battle courage. It is the ability to endure situations of verbal encounter that continually threaten him with disclosure of the weakness he fears. The language that speaks through him is a minefield, because it represents him as both rhetorically self-indulgent and disdainful of rhetorical self-indulgence. He deserves the honor he wants if only for his courage in traveling over linguistic terrain he doesn't control or trust. That terrain is "overcharg'd with double cracks," so it's a good thing he is devoted to his horse. Deep fears and defenses wound the language that represents Hotspur. His speech both dramatizes and problematizes his cardinal virtue by treating it as the transformation of a latent desire of flight, and fear of weakness, into war-like valor and aggressiveness.

The outlines of the problem can be more firmly set by noting that in the tradition which made Aristotle's ethics influential, the sphere of action allocated to the virtue of courage is narrowly circumscribed, and circumscribed in such a way as to create difficulties for its representation in Shakespeare's version of theatrical drama. From a Shakespearean standpoint, Aristotle begins well when, after defining courage as the virtue that observes "the mean in respect of fear and confidence," he states that "the things we fear are . . . broadly speaking, evil things." But the notion of evil is then simplified by the following line of argument: courage is displayed in response to fearful things; the courageous man willingly faces the most fearful things; "the most terrible thing of all is death"; not every kind of death gives an opportunity for courage—drowning and disease, for example, don't qualify as appropriate occasions; the noblest test for courage is the noblest form of death, that is, death in battle. "And this conclusion is borne out by the principle on which honors are bestowed in republics and under monarchies." Hence, the courageous man "will be he who fearlessly con-

fronts a noble death, or some sudden peril that threatens death; and the perils of war answer this description most fully."[12]

Aristotle's subsequent discussion of courage is entirely confined to warfare. Were Shakespeare interested in dramatizing this version of courage he would confront the obvious difficulty that battles are not the easiest things to stage, and that audiences would tend to be diverted from the hero's display of martial courage to the actor's display of acrobatic dexterity, thus from warfare to choreography. Jorgensen addresses this problem in the first chapter of *Shakespeare's Military World*, mounting an astute defense of what had previously been judged a dramaturgical weakness, Shakespeare's "physical staging of warfare." He argues that if Shakespeare differed from some of his contemporaries in his greater scorn of "stage realism" and his more "restricted battle display," it was from choice rather than from the limited "martial resources of the stage" (2-3). Shakespeare chose to appeal to the auditory rather than visual imagination "either through actual sound or through a stylized, connotative rendering of it in dialogue" (3). "With his actual military music" of drums, trumpets, and alarms as well as with his "rhetorical 'music,'" he sought to transport

> his audience from the immediate experience of battle—in which sounds, cannon, and blows have a precise, uncolored meaning—to a superior level of imaginative participation. On this level, not the mind's eye but the mind's ear is appealed to principally as a substitute for a full display of warfare. Remoteness . . . is an essential quality of both the martial discourse and the martial music. And the ear, more susceptible than the eye to the suggestiveness of distant and imminent events, is impressed both by the "sad harmony" of rhetoric and by a skillfully connotative use of drum and trumpet. (34)

The evidence Jorgensen adduces suggests a different and to my mind better generalization than the one his first sentence articulates. For example, he shows how the "persistent 'Low alarums'" in the last scenes of *Julius Caesar* underscore "Caesar's Nemesis-like pursuit of Brutus—but with an ultimate clarification in terms of military function" when "the identity of the Nemesis becomes prosaically clear with the arrival of the victorious enemy, whose presence on stage is far less impressive than the suggestiveness of their distant drums" (32-33). Similarly, Jorgensen remarks the increasing tension produced in the last scenes of *Macbeth* "by the cumulative effect of drums . . . and . . . alarms," and observes that "Macduff, like Octavius Caesar, may be a prosaic instrument of Nemesis, but not so the relentless music with which—in a more than military sense—he encompasses his victim" (33-34). What both these examples suggest is that Shakespeare first elicited "a superior level of imaginary participation" by appealing to the ear, and that the subsequent stage appearance of the victors seemed anticlimactic by contrast. And this is a significant pattern, evident in many plays, including the *Henriad:* the visualization onstage of battles and other external moments of conflict resolution is *represented* as unsatisfactory, as the reductive displacement of inner self-division to outward circumstances.

From Jorgensen's discussion, then, I force this hypothesis: Shakespeare uses the power of auditory effects to arouse a sense of foreboding and premonition that makes the stage realization the effects anticipate seem inadequate as "objective correlatives." We could say, in fact, that "objective" in Eliot's phrase means "inadequate" in the value system of Shakespearean dramaturgy. This isn't only because in "the immediate experience of [staged] battle . . . sounds, cannon, and blows have a precise, uncolored meaning," whereas in "martial discourse" they are more distanced and suggestive—more seductive, as Othello and Desdemona found: "She'd come again, and with a greedy ear / Devour up my discourse" (1.3.149-50). The "precise, uncolored meaning" is itself a meaning. It signifies that insufficient and premature closure has been imposed on latent meaning ("some other grief") by the process of displacement that allows theatrical ending to coincide with dramatic judgment. The effect is not to dispel but, on the contrary, to intensify our bewilderment, skepticism, foreboding, sadness, or terror.

"The music at the close" only reanimates the fearful and mysterious power of Shakespearean speech so that Desdemona's tremulous question remains the auditor's: "what does your speech import? / I understand a fury in your words, / But not the words" (4.2.31-33). And this is the perplexity that Shakespearean language continually inscribes in the speakers it represents: "what does my speech import? / I understand a fury in my words, / But not the words." When the fury is channeled outward in physical violence, the perplexity continues to vibrate. Shakespeare's final *Exeunts* order us out of the theater because the unfinished business they leave us with cannot be transacted here. It is as if, after all the buildup, physical battle *au fond* tests nothing more significant than skill in fencing and counterfeiting; as if the represented violence is no more "serious" an expression of the "inward wars" than the choreography that mimes it. That is not where Shakespeare's heroes kill and die. They kill and die in their language, and we have to follow the lethal traces down into its burrows and rhizomes.

What stage death offers the hero is an escape from this verbal dying into the rest that is silence. What it offers the audience is something like a critique of this commitment to stageable closure as an escape from meaning. When the hero finally faces the test of battle and arrives at the wished-for haven where he can find judg-

ment and prove his truth; when he is on the verge of escaping from his bondage to words, woman, civil life, and perhaps life itself, his drive toward transcendence may be betrayed, diminished, by the very convention of theatrical closure to which he has committed himself. Having displaced his inward wars to swordplay, he becomes vulnerable to a critique that may have arisen accidentally, as a by-product of theatrical constraints, but that offers thematic possibilities to a writer who wants to raise questions about such a displacement. The critique occurs when presentation overpowers and interprets representation, that is, when the agility of actors putting on a fencing exhibition preempts the mind's eye and occludes the symbolic valency of the fictional conflict.

This critique speaks to the ethical limits of such notions as Aristotle's circumscribed concept of courage, the courage that thinks to prove itself by facing death in battle as "the most terrible thing of all." What that notion fails to consider may be suggested by glancing at the following qualification, in which Aristotle limits the range of the term according to the doctrine of the mean: "to seek death in order to escape from poverty, or the pangs of love, or from pain or sorrow, is not the act of a courageous man, but rather of a coward; for it is weakness to fly from troubles, and the suicide does not endure death because it is noble to do so, but to escape evil."[13] But the interest, pathos, and poignancy of Shakespeare's warrior-heroes is produced by ignoring this distinction.

. . . . .

In the language of *1 Henry IV* the politics of honor, the politics of speech, and the politics of gender are closely interrelated. To begin with some textualized representations of woman, consider the passage in which Gadshill boasts that he is the accomplice of those who

> pray continually to their saint the commonwealth, or rather not pray to her, but prey on her, for they ride up and down on her, and make her their boots.
>
> *Cham.* What, the commonwealth their boots? Will she hold out water in foul way?
>
> *Gads.* She will, she will, justice hath liquored her: we steal as in a castle, cock-sure: we have the receipt of fern-seed, we walk invisible. (2.1.79-86)

In this pathologically overstated piece of irreverence, the thrills of political, legal, and religious violation are reduced to that of sexual violation. The commonwealth is feminized and canonized in the mode of Petrarchan parody—as the idealized object of erotic worship who is simultaneously the source, enemy, and target of sexual desire. Manly power and risk-taking are exaggerated in a phallic fantasy the rhetoric of which centers on the victimization of a woman and on the idea of preying on one's very source of protection. Gadshill's idyllic society of thieves is held together homosocially by what is imaged as a gang rape. The victim is not only violated but also "liquored"—corrupted either by bribery or by drink—and thus easier to penetrate.

An earlier analogue to this passage appears in Falstaff's famous play on *body/bawdy/beauty/booty*:

> Marry then sweet wag, when thou art king let not us that are squires of the night's body be called thieves of the day's beauty: let us be Diana's foresters, gentlemen of the shade, minions of the moon; and let men say we be men of good government, being governed as the sea is, by our noble and chaste mistress the moon, under whose countenance we steal. (1.2.23-29)

The paradox in the last phrase is that those who steal under Diana's sylvan authority also steal under her face; they are thieves as well as squires of the night's body, beauty, and booty.[14] Manhood and male bonding are defined in terms of the conventional strategy, first idealizing and then violating the power, authority, or body of woman. Falstaff's idealization is itself motivated by the Prince's equally one-sided derogation: "clocks the tongues of bawds, and dials the signs of leaping-houses, and the blessed sun himself a fair hot wench in flame-colored taffeta" (1.2.8-10). When Falstaff replies, "we that take purses go by the moon" (13-14), he is not exactly changing the subject from prostitution to robbery, since purse-taking is an image that accommodates robbery to the metaphor of sexual violation. The point of Harry's insult to Falstaff is his susceptibility to the lusts of the flesh that make him an easy mark for women. Falstaff gets the point, and parries it a few speeches later: "is not my hostess of the tavern a most sweet wench?" (39-40). But his Diana speech is also a riposte: "when you are king, let my immersion in the life of sack, whores, and thievery to which you (so righteously) consign me be romantically mystified as a form of service to the goddess to whose chaste countenance these very things are anathema. And let you be that goddess."

This is "pretty daring" talk, as Dover Wilson observes, because it glances at the Virgin Queen.[15] The speech is also daring because Falstaff offers Harry the role of Diana. And it is even more daring because of the double pun in the last phrase: (1) "we *steal* (a) under her authority but also (b) right under her nose"; (2) "we *go stealthily* not only (a) under her authority but also (b) under her face." Meaning 2b is the most outrageous because it is sexual, and because it places Falstaff in the position of Actaeon. If Diana's foresters are men, they must be hunters *of* as well as *for* the goddess.[16] As Falstaff's five repetitions of "when thou art king" in this scene indicate, he is dogging his Diana now: lay-

ing bare the real project behind Harry's madcap role and goading Harry into exposing it himself, but also—and more compellingly—daring Harry to turn the verbal dogs back on their fat master.

The Actaeon myth figures explicitly and importantly in *Twelfth Night, A Midsummer Night's Dream,* and *The Merry Wives of Windsor.* Leonard Barkan has shown how *Merry Wives* articulates the comic aspects of the theme: the attempt to overmaster woman results in being mastered by woman; phallic aggression produces emasculation.[17] In this direct form, the Actaeon theme does not enter into the concerns of *1 Henry IV.* Its comic and farcical reduction in *Merry Wives* is a consequence of full detextualization, which transfers the dispersed nodes of textual meaning to the dramatic and theatrical surface, where the dangers are explicit and controlled. In *1 Henry IV,* however, the traces of the myth produce a more sinister network of resonances. From his first words to his final rejection, Falstaff knowingly presents himself to Harry as a target, persistently probes beneath the madcap role to lay bare aggressive motives that Harry tries to conceal even from himself. In doing this, of course, he is asking for punishment and eliciting the gestures of negation or rebuttal that will add up to the ultimate rejection.

. . . . .

> By heaven, methinks it were an easy leap
> To pluck bright honor from the pale-fac'd
>   moon . . .
>
> (1.3.199-200)

With these lines Hotspur declares his candidacy for membership in Falstaff's Actaeon Club. The assault on the moon draws some of its energy not only from its echo of Falstaff's passage but also from a hunting image Hotspur has just unleashed:

> O, the blood more stirs
> To rouse a lion than to start a hare!
> *North.* Imagination of some great exploit
>   Drives him beyond the bounds of patience.
>   (1.3.195-98)

Some light on Hotspur's heroic frenzy and its Actaeonic implications is thrown by Barkan's comments on *Gl' Eroici Furori:*

> From the dedication to Sir Philip Sidney to all Bruno's sonnets which his dialogues analyze, it becomes clear that the conventional behavior and attitudes of the romantic lover are requisite for the visionary experience, *even if the true enthusiast must purge the purely sexual aspect of his love. The enthusiast is first a lover, and Bruno builds his visionary structure upon the foundation of Neoplatonic amorous furor.*[18]

It is the repression and displacement indicated by the italicized phrases that strike me as relevant to the Hotspurian discourse of honor. Erotic desire for woman is transformed into aggressive desire for honor. The linking term, *purge,* encodes a process in which the source of the "sexual aspect" is displaced outward to woman, and woman is violated either by the hero's direct assault or by his flight. The return and triumph of the repressed, which is inscribed in the fate of Actaeon, is also inscribed in Hotspur's language, and the consequent anxiety this language betrays is evident in his very first speech.

Henry's curt dismissal of Worcester at the beginning of 1.3, and his unbending attitude about Hotspur's prisoners, could not but be calculated to incense the Percys. The end of the play's first scene makes it clear that he looks forward to this confrontation, and that he had arranged it *before* his crusade speech. If he assumes that Hotspur is already infected by "his uncle's teaching," as Westmoreland claims (1.1.95), what he does in 1.3 can only be expected to aggravate the infection and strengthen Worcester's hand. We judge Henry's contribution to be even greater when we realize, early in 1.3, that Hotspur is not yet infected, and that although Worcester has clearly been up to something, Hotspur hears for the first time that Richard had proclaimed his brother-in-law, Mortimer, heir to the throne.

Against this background the emphasis in Hotspur's long speech explaining his denial of prisoners becomes more interesting for what it reveals about the speaker's basic motivation. He is chiefly concerned to document the source of his irritation in the behavior of the foppish messenger sent by the king. His caricature of a supercilious court butterfly conflates effeminacy with squeamishness, as in "neat and trimly dress'd, / Fresh as a bride-groom," "perfumed like a milliner," "With many holiday and lady terms," "a popinjay," "talk so like a waiting gentlewoman" (1.3.32-54). G. R. Hibbard sums it up thus: "Scorn and impatience ring through the entire passage. The images are precise, reductive, and, some of them, *admirably designed* to bring out the womanish qualities the soldier sees in the courtier. . . . Brusque, impetuous, impatient, direct, and courageous, Hotspur makes all this side of his nature evident in his first speech."[19] The italicized phrase betrays a certain diffuseness of reference that is no doubt occasioned by Hibbard's titular theme, the making of *Shakespeare's* dramatic poetry. Presumably the praise is directed toward the author rather than his character. But what if we ask whether the images are designed for the stated purpose by Hotspur: is he to be admired along with Shakespeare? Why? Hibbard's general objective often leads him to ignore crucial issues of motivation that would lend his judgments more weight.

Paul Jorgensen comes closer to the problem when he notes that Henry's accusation places Hotspur "in the defensive position habitual to the Elizabethan soldier," and that his apology reflects stereotypical features of the debate between the soldier and the courtier.[20] Hotspur is indeed apologetic, but not quite in the sense intended by Jorgensen. His speech is no less finicky than the finickiness he contemns. Judging by the extravagance of his rhetoric, the dandy whose "womanish qualities" irritated him on the battlefield continues to irritate him now. It is as if he is still compelled to decontaminate himself by a speech act that aims primarily at contrastive self-definition. Hence I think the verb in Hibbard's last clause should be taken more forcefully than he apparently intends it: "Hotspur *makes* all this side of his nature evident," that is, with self-dramatizing emphasis.

There are specific reasons for this emphasis. Hotspur enters the play already on the defense. His utterance is a response to Henry's demand for the prisoners taken at Holmedon, but far from being an aggressive refusal, it is conciliatory, even apologetic. "My liege, I did deny no prisoners," Hotspur begins, and then goes into a long diatribe against the messenger who carried the king's demand to the battlefield. His "bald unjointed chat" so irritated Hotspur that he answered inattentively ("I answer'd indirectly"), and he begs the king not to let the messenger's "report / come current for an accusation / Betwixt my love and your high majesty" (1.3.64-68). This conciliatory tone is not at all what we had been led to expect at the end of 1.1, where Henry and Westmoreland complained of "young Percy's pride" and of Worcester's bad influence, which makes Hotspur "prune himself, and bristle up / The crest of youth against your dignity" (91, 97-98). Hotspur's response is even more surprising in view of the law of arms mentioned in editorial footnotes, which is that Hotspur was entitled to keep all the prisoners he took except those of royal blood. If we suppose this is something Shakespeare not only knew but expected his audience to know, it is still not clear whether it is something they are expected to take note of as a motivational factor. There seems to have been no law that gives the king the right to the prisoners, so even if we ignored the other convention and the question remained moot, we could still see Henry's demand as an aggressive act, and perhaps as a challenge to Hotspur's honor. Why, then, shouldn't Hotspur treat it as such? A closer glance at the circumstances preceding and surrounding his speech will bring out the difficulty of his position.

Taking note of the law-of-arms convention about prisoners sharpens our sense of what motivates Henry's aggression. It reinforces a particular reading of the strategies he pursues in the first and third scenes of the play. His sending a messenger to Holmedon to make an issue of the prisoners; his setting up and eagerly awaiting the confrontation that, as the end of the first scene makes clear, he had arranged well *before* making his crusade speech (so that his frustration at having to call the crusade off is patently a pretense); his dismissal of Worcester and his angry deportment thereafter—these moves seem intended to provoke the Percys into an uprising that he can later be in the position to blame them for, as at the end of 1.1 when he implies that Hotspur is responsible for his having to cancel the crusade that he proposed primarily in order to be able to blame the cancellation on Hotspur. In all this he is deploying the tactics of the language game—the victim's discourse—various forms of which dominate the *Henriad:* stirring up trouble, disclaiming responsibility for it, targeting oneself as its victim.[21]

Hotspur does not make an issue of the denial of prisoners. But why does he downplay it? The reason is suggested at 1.3.76-79, when Henry accuses him of having at some point denied his prisoners,

> But with proviso and exception,
> That we at our own charge shall ransom
>   straight
> His brother-in-law, the foolish Mortimer.

Since Hotspur never disputes this allegation, it suggests that he has come into the scene aware of several things that may well be disquieting to the theme of honor's tongue, especially if one assumes (as I do) that Hotspur is genuinely devoted to this theme.

First, Hotspur could not deny prisoners unless they had previously been demanded, and Henry's aggressiveness by itself constitutes a challenge that must be met. But the possibility of a clean and honorable response has already been severely jeopardized. For, second, even if his initial words in the play ("My liege I did deny no prisoners") are true, at some moment between his encounter with the messenger and the uttering of those words he decided to deny prisoners. Hence the utterance is evasive, and the narrative that follows it may be felt as a diversionary tactic. Third, since that encounter took place he acquired a not fully determinable amount of information about what happened to Mortimer, and we can imagine that this affected his decision. That is, it may not have been on principle that he decided to withhold prisoners but in order to have some leverage in forcing Mortimer's ransom. Fourth, however much or little he knows about Mortimer's defeat, the information he gets from Henry is enough to suggest that it has already weakened Hotspur's position. For he's come to his meeting with Henry prepared to do something he may consider shameful in order to save his wife's brother. To say "I did deny no prisoners" in this situation could be construed as an anticipatory gesture of placation by someone preparing to breach the code—yield up prisoners that were his by right—in order to bargain for his brother-in-law's release.

This helps us contextualize the gender-coded weakness he displaces to the messenger. I read it as representing the sense of weakness aroused in the speaker himself by the utterance of this speech. Isn't there the slightest taint of cowardice and courtly sycophancy in his willingness to appease the king and prepare for the exchange? Doesn't the very function of this speech—what motivates it—subvert its rhetorical emphasis and reawaken the apprehension of moral and political impotence it fends off?

From this standpoint, the figure of the messenger becomes the locus at which two opposed yet cooperating vectors of symbolic power collide: he represents the king's aggressive attempt to insult Hotspur, but he also represents Hotspur's repressed acknowledgment that—in making this elaborate apology—he may be insulting and compromising himself. All this renders more important and problematical Hotspur's relation to the shadowy figure of Mortimer. Having engaged his honor in Mortimer's behalf, he has ceded partial control of it to someone on whose behavior his reputation now depends. And the apparent reason for this commitment can only increase his vulnerability: he is bound to Mortimer through Lady Percy. I shall return to this dilemma after considering one more feature of Hotspur's first speech.

The messenger offends Hotspur not only by his appearance and style, his disdainful comments, and his demand for prisoners, but also by something else. Hotspur complains that as he listened "Breathless and faint, leaning upon my sword" (31), the messenger rattled on about "guns, and drums, and wounds," and finally about what a pity it was that

> This villainous saltpeter should be digg'd
> Out of the bowels of the harmless earth,
> Which many a good tall fellow had destroy'd
> So cowardly, and but for these vile guns
> He would himself have been a soldier.
> This bald unjointed chat of his, my lord,
> I answer'd indirectly . . .

>   (59-65)

Why should this complaint disturb Hotspur? Shouldn't we expect him to agree with the messenger about "these vile guns" that might well diminish the military value of the sword he leans on?

The messenger's point, Kittredge writes, "was that warfare is no longer a glorious thing, as it was in the old days of hand-to-hand fighting before gunpowder was invented."[22] There are enough references to guns in the play (pistols, calivers, heavy-ordnance, powder) to remind us of the wishful archaism of Hotspur's attachment to the golden age of chivalry prior to the violation of mother earth. The clean heroics of single encounter is by no means obsolete, for example, the possibility that "Harry to Harry shall, hot horse to horse, / meet and ne'er part till one drop down a corse"

(4.1.122-23). But it is circumscribed by the presence of more effective and less personal forms of warfare and instruments of death. Perhaps Hotspur's sympathy with the messenger's complaint is another reason for his irritation and decontamination. He never speaks of guns in his waking hours—only in his dreams (2.3.64).

The issue I am raising here is not, however, the familiar historical topic of the influence of technological change on sociopolitical change. I am not directly concerned with the way the decline of chivalry, the crisis of the aristocracy, may be represented in the portrayal of Hotspur's commitment to a threatened discourse of honor. Rather my emphasis is on another theme intrinsic to that discourse and to the ideal of manhood it expresses: the hero's need to have power over and to die his own death; to invent or choose it, to aim all his actions toward that consummation; to meet and stage his death in a public ritual that will inscribe it on the future and thus triumph over it.

Against this ideal, the play opposes two ignominious forms of death that are, appropriately, most often mentioned by Falstaff: the scaffold and "molten lead." In their different ways, both are threats to manhood. The fear of hanging, the image of an elevated body that suddenly drops toward mother earth (sometimes from a horse) and goes limp, gives focus to the pervasive anxiety that nourishes the villain's bravado. Hanging, in addition, suggests emasculation in a pointedly ironic form, since it produces—as an exception to the limpness of the rest of the corpse—an erect penis, which, like the supplementarity of a Priapean dildo, symbolizes the power it wants. The erection represents the power of another. To be hanged is to lose one's power over one's death, to be made the helpless site and spectacle of another's power. The other ignominious death is produced by a similar shift of phallic potency from the manly hero and his sword: death by firepower—basilisk, cannon, or culverin—is the wholesale anonymous death that is the fate of "pitiful rascals . . . good enough to toss, food for powder . . . they'll fill a pit as well as better" (4.2.64-66).

Although Hotspur does not mention guns again, there is a passage in 3.1 that testifies by its hyperbolic distortion to his abiding respect for the destructive force imprisoned in earth's bowels. It's true that in the following speech he is only chiding Glendower by attributing the shaking of the earth not to fear of the Welsh blowhard but to a bad case of gas. Nevertheless, his retort is itself shaken by fascination for the constrained violence that erupts from the image:

> O, then the earth shook to see the heavens on
> fire,
> And not in fear of your nativity.
> Diseased nature oftentimes breaks forth
> In strange eruptions, oft the teeming earth

Is with a kind of colic pinch'd and vex'd
By the imprisoning of unruly wind
Within her womb, which for enlargement
striving
Shakes the old beldam earth, and topples
down
Steeples and moss-grown towers.

                                        (3.1.22-30)

The energy with which Hotspur depicts the grotesque body is carnivalesque. I imagine these lines fired off with the tart and testy exhilaration of a speaker who enjoys sending up the seismic flatulence of his interlocutor's rhetoric. But the caricature, like everything else about Hotspur, is overcharged with double cracks. Glendower embarrasses him because, however inflated his rhetoric and however absurd his pretensions, *they* caricature *Hotspur's,* as in a distorting mirror. He combines the excesses of the *miles gloriosus* with the musico-magical aspirations of a comic Prospero in so bizarre a fantasy of power as to betray the lack of self-mastery that makes him an easy mark. Yet the flatus Hotspur criticizes is a flatus that shakes his own language. The speech is itself a scapegoating violation of the maternal principle, to which it displaces vulnerability and impotence, incontinence and imminent rupture, the threat of having one's body possessed, concussed, by aliens that blow it apart—all the dangers that produce the fears that make the courage worthy of the honor the hero desires.

Glendower is good for laughs, but his role in the play's economy of honor gives him a special kind of power, the power of weakness. The most seductive appeal to erotic desire as well as the most direct gesture of emasculation both come from Wales. The seduction is conveyed in a form that accentuates its alienation from and by the rigid, self-protective warrior ethos: it is uttered in a foreign tongue by Glendower's daughter. As a doting father, he fears her grief and at first wants the warriors to sneak away to battle in order to avoid "a world of water shed" (3.1.90). But he then submits to her desire and translates her invitation in lilting cadences:

> She bids you on the wanton rushes lay you
> down,
> And rest your gentle head upon her lap,
> And she will sing the song that pleaseth you,
> And on your eyelids crown the god of sleep,
> Charming your blood with pleasing heaviness.
>   (207-11)

A truly Spenserian enticement, evoking the helpless Cymochles in Phaedria's lap, the helpless Verdant in Acrasia's, and also Shakespeare's more skittish Adonis with Venus. Glendower mobilizes cosmic harmonies and heavenly steeds in the service of a languor the dangerous allure of which even Hotspur grudgingly acknowledges, and resists with awkward jokes. It is entirely consistent with the uncompromising claims made by the Welsh *other* that, as Westmoreland reported in 1.1, after Glendower captured Mortimer and "butchered" a thousand of his soldiers, the Welsh-women mutilated the soldiers' corpses in "beastly shameless transformation" (44). Seductive enervation and violent dismemberment: these Cymochlean and Pyrochlean extremes represent the twin threats to manly autonomy inscribed in the male fantasy of feminine power. The reported maenadic explosion suggests not only an externalization of the male nightmare but also a futile gesture of revenge on the worse "part of valor" by those who momentarily overcame their discretion, those whom the homoerotic flight to the battlefield has marginalized and dispossessed. In this warrior community Welsh is "the discourse of the other." The extremes over which Glendower presides—the extremes that he himself exemplifies in his grotesque doubleness as a cosmic braggadocio and his daughter's pliable advocate—have the same symbolic force. They speak to fears that male fantasy tries to dispel by blaming them on the power of the frailty named Woman. And that frailty sometimes tries to strike back. Westmoreland's report can serve as a brief reminder that war between men is a form of war against woman. It is a perverse and futile expression of the desire, the lack, attending the more permanent state of bereavement of which Hotspur's banished wife complains in 2.3.

. . . . .

Hotspur's problematic relation to firepower is suggested in the first mention of his name, when Westmoreland describes his fight with the Douglas:

> On Holy-rood day, the gallant Hotspur there,
> Young Harry Percy, and brave Archibald,
> That ever valiant and approved Scot,
> At Holmedon met, where they did spend
> A sad and bloody hour;
> As by discharge of their artillery,
> And shape of likelihood, the news was told.
>
> (1.1.52-58)

The first five lines imply single combat, but the sixth line renders that uncertain. Although Humphreys notes that *artillery* formerly referred to "any missiles in war"—arrows, for example—and was "not confined to gunfire," the messenger's remarks about guns at Holmedon render this gloss gratuitous. The line allows us to wonder whether Westmoreland's previous statement refers literally to single combat or synecdochically to two armies. When we subsequently learn that Douglas has been "discomfited" and that "Ten thousand bold Scots, two and twenty knights" lie "Balk'd in their own blood" (67-69), we may also wonder about the nature of the artillery responsible for such mayhem.[23] The issue is somewhat clouded by the earlier reference

to the barbaric Glendower's butchery of a thousand of Mortimer's soldiers: *butchered* (42) could well suggest manual warfare, though it does not have to (mention of Glendower's "rude hands" in the previous line prompts the suggestion), but at any rate the "beastly shameless transformation" wrought by the Welshwomen may comment on the meaning of the wholesale slaughter of anonymous men.

These issues are reawakened when Hotspur, in 1.3, defends Mortimer against Henry's charge that the latter "wilfully betray'd / The lives of those that he did lead to fight" against Glendower, "Whose daughter, as we hear, the Earl of March / Hath lately marry'd" (80-84). Hotspur's response is marked by the same impulse to decontamination that shaped his account of the messenger. The claim that Mortimer was seduced into treason by the offer of marriage—a claim at least partly borne out by subsequent disclosures—touches off another apology, and one that further betrays the speaker's anxiety:

> He never did fall off, my sovereign liege,
> But by the chance of war: to prove that true
> Needs no more but one tongue for all those
>   wounds,
> Those mouthed wounds, which valiantly he
>   took,
> When on the gentle Severn's sedgy bank,
> In single opposition hand to hand,
> He did confound the best part of an hour
> In changing hardiment with great Glendower.
> Three times they breath'd, and three times did
>   they drink
> Upon agreement of swift Severn's flood,
> Who then affrighted with their bloody looks
> Ran fearfully among the trembling reeds,
> And hid his crisp head in the hollow bank,
> Bloodstained with these valiant combatants.
> Never did bare and rotten policy
> Color her working with such deadly wounds,
> Nor never could the noble Mortimer
> Receive so many, and all willingly:
> Then let him not be slander'd with revolt.
>
> (1.3.93-111)

The speech is extraordinary because Hotspur is describing an encounter he had not seen—and one that may not even have taken place. This fantasy, in which Mortimer becomes the heroic Hotspurian loser, may well be an imaginative replay of Hotspur's own "sad and bloody hour" of battle with Douglas, and if it is, it isolates that conflict by framing it as single encounter and pushing the rest of the fray—the "artillery" and the ten thousand victims—into the background. What prompts this suggestion is the analogy to Hotspur's ignoring the "thousand . . . people butchered" by Glendower. Such conspicuous exclusion renders his account more problematic.

It is already problematic because he uses it to protect himself, along with Mortimer, from the stigma of shameful fear, effeminate cowardice, that Henry tries to mark him with by association. His language continues to be nagged by the rhetoric of decontamination, and the continuity is marked by the echo of the foppish messenger in the figure of the Severn as crisp-headed coward. Hotspur sends "him" cringing to the sheltering lap ("hollow bank") of blood-stained mother earth, and goes on to feminize "bare and rotten policy" by way of parrying the charge that Mortimer "fell off" for the sake of a woman and succumbed to the base condition of which the messenger's "fresh" appearance had reminded Hotspur: "a bridegroom." Henry's first reference to Mortimer had clearly put Hotspur on the defensive: "His brother-in-law, the foolish Mortimer" (1.3.79). Since it is Hotspur's marriage that links him to Mortimer and exposes him to the vagaries of Mortimer's behavior, Mortimer's purported vulnerability and folly reflect his own.

This is partly why Mortimer's wounds *do* speak with Hotspur's tongue, and why that odd revision, "those mouthed wounds," is so telling. The wounds are mouthed because they eat—or are penetrated by—the sword and because they would speak of honor if they had tongues. But because honor's tongue is the tongue of another, the hero's wounds are mute and their mouths mutilated. The defeated hero is doubly emasculated, his heroic autonomy twice breached. The implications of the figure are more explicit in *Coriolanus* and *Julius Caesar*. The Third Citizen says that if Coriolanus "show us his wounds and tell us his deeds, we are to put our tongues into those wounds and speak for them" (2.3.5-8). The metaphor associates stabbing, sexual penetration, licking (to eat or heal), and a surgical probe or *tent* with the giving of voices/votes that affirms Coriolanus's right to the consular honor. In *Julius Caesar*, Antony describes Caesar's wounds in a figure that reminds one of Lavinia's—or any well-behaved woman's—mouth: "like dumb mouths, [they] do ope their ruby lips / To beg the voice and utterance of my tongue" (3.1.260-61). Honor's phallic tongue is what wounds, like women, lack and long for.

Hotspur is more comfortable with the idea of eating swords fed by an enemy than with the idea of feeding "on cates" served up by a friend (3.1.157). The friend happens to be Glendower, whom he finds as tedious as "a railing wife" (154), and "cates"—delicacies—happens to echo the name of his wife. Yet the appetite for swords makes the hero dependent on and vulnerable to the enemy who feeds him. If he finds the prospect of violation and dismemberment by the sword nourishing, it is because "the voice and utterance" of honor can be begged only by exposing oneself to the risk of the ultimate emasculation: the loss of life and speech. Thus Hotspur, dying, grieves that Harry has *"robb'd"* him of his youth and "proud titles," and that "the earthly

and cold hand of death" lying on his tongue cuts him off before he can "prophesy"—which means, perhaps, before he can put his own tongue into his wounds (5.4.76-84). The word *robb'd* briefly discharges into this moment the meanings generated in earlier episodes by the incessant play on threats to manhood—cowardice, victimization, the ignominy of hanging—inscribed in the activities of purse-snatching and pocket-picking. Even the noblest death may be no better than the casual by-product of robbery unless redeemed by honor's tongue. Since winner and loser are equally affected by this logic, Harry redeems both their honors by finishing Hotspur's sentence and letting "my favors hide thy mangled face" (5.4.95). Perhaps it is because he is doing himself a favor that he then somewhat oddly says, "I'll thank myself / For doing these fair rites of tenderness" (96-97).

The discourse of honor allows the hero to enjoy the foretaste and reiterate the promise of whatever may be redeeming in that death. It is a continuous incantation soliciting the tongue that can heal the final wound, and for these reasons the hero loves the talk that defers it. But talk is cheap, incurs debts, and the more the hero talks the greater will be the need to discharge the obligation not by victory but by death. The way of Tamburlaine must be avoided, the way of Sarpedon espoused. Hotspur keeps talking to the end, and at the last moment starts a new sentence that he won't be able to finish in order to leave space in the wound for Harry's tongue. The rationale behind this heroic *ars moriendi* was inadvertently prefigured in an earlier utterance: "I thank him that he cuts me from my tale, / For I profess not talking" (5.2.90-91). Later, it finds its way into Falstaff's mouth: "The better part of valor is discretion" (5.4.119); one meaning of *discretion* is "cutting off."[24]

Returning to the Hotspur / Mortimer relation, we have no information on the basis of which to ascertain what happened (or why it happened) before Mortimer "Was by the rude hands of that Welshman taken" (1.1.41), nor can we ascertain under what conditions he accepted a wife from the same hands. The latter fact is expressed by Henry as hearsay (1.3.83), and since Hotspur doesn't challenge the statement it must be assumed that he is fully aware of it even as he insists that Mortimer "never did fall off . . . / But by the chance of war," and goes on to elaborate a chivalric fantasy "to prove that true." Yet the links between these two events remain mysterious. We needn't assume that Hotspur knows more about those links than we do and is therefore lying. Much more interesting is the assumption that he doesn't know and that what he says is what he would like to believe. But if that is the case, if he knows only as much as Henry knows, then we are entitled to feel that his chivalric defense against Henry's interpretation may be breached by doubt—and it will be well to remember this later, when Mortimer fails to show up at Shrewsbury. Hotspur's own honor would be threatened if Henry's interpretation were true and Mortimer proved to be a traitor for love. More immediately, the honorableness of his discourse is threatened for the same reason. The defense of Mortimer is a reckless move, and puts Hotspur at a disadvantage. He commits himself with high-rhetorical ardor to an interpretation that may be false. Henry directly challenges his account: "Thou dost belie him, Percy, thou dost belie him, / He never did encounter with Glendower," and thrusts home with "Art thou not asham'd?" (1.3.112-16). After he storms out and Worcester returns, Hotspur's report of the heated interchange is evasive:

> He will forsooth have all my prisoners,
> And when I urg'd the ransom once again
> Of my wife's brother, then his cheek look'd
>   pale,
> And on my face he turn'd an eye of death,
> Trembling even at the name of Mortimer.
>
> (138-42)

This is not at all how the conversation went: Hotspur's account of the battle is deleted and replaced by the second clause above, which reports something he did not explicitly say. The deletion argues a kind of willed forgetfulness of the extravagant claims he made on Mortimer's behalf, claims he is as yet powerless to verify. The extravagance may be read as an anxious reaction to his powerlessness, and his choleric response to Henry's exit speech seems all the more defensive in the light of the evasive report that follows it. "Art thou not asham'd?": perhaps he is, or fears to be; Henry seems to have more success managing Hotspur's sense of shame than he does in his parallel project of managing Harry's. Here he may have opened up a wound.

When Worcester returns, however, he pours balm into that wound by mentioning Mortimer's claim to the crown. We should expect this news to relieve Hotspur because it legitimizes his political and verbal activity on behalf of someone who, it now turns out, defected not only for love but also for reasons of state. And indeed, he seizes this opportunity to regain his equilibrium. Relief pours out in the form of a long speech devoted primarily to heaping shame on "you" who helped the usurper to the throne. Worcester had given him the cue: for Richard's deposition and murder "we in the world's wide mouth / Live scandaliz'd and foully spoken of" (151-52)—slander as mastication; the blatant beast; another source of mouthed wounds. Worcester appeals to Hotspur's sense of shame—his *we* reaches out toward his nephew—but in his long response Hotspur gradually narrows the referential focus of his offsetting *you* and evades Worcester's reach by himself assuming the role of appellant. The last half of his speech is directed specifically to his father and uncle, as the parenthetical line below (172) makes clear:

> O, pardon me, that I descend so low,
> To show the line and the predicament
> Wherein you range under this subtle King!
> Shall it for shame be spoken in these days,
> Or fill up chronicles in time to come,
> That men of your nobility and power
> Did gage them both in an unjust behalf
> (As both of you, God pardon it, have done)
> To put down Richard, that sweet lovely rose,
> And plant this thorn, this canker Bolingbroke?
> And shall it in more shame be further spoken,
> That you are fool'd, discarded, and shook off
> By him for whom these shames ye underwent?
> No, time yet serves wherein you may redeem
> Your banish'd honors, and restore yourselves
> Into the good thoughts of the world again:
> Revenge the jeering and disdain'd contempt
> Of this proud King, who studies day and night
> To answer all the debt he owes to you,
> Even with the bloody payment of your deaths:
> Therefore, I say—
> *Wor.*   Peace, cousin, say no more.
>
> (1.3.165-85)

Hotspur's last eight lines trigger a vivid recollection of the end of Harry's "I know you all" soliloquy in the previous scene. The effect of superimposing the two passages, and their respective scenarios, is to increase our sense that Hotspur, like Harry, is selectively emphasizing a not fully justifiable line of argument by way of fending off another that is more reprehensible. In other words, he situates his appeal entirely within the discourse of honor and says nothing about the dishonor that would attend another insurrection against a ruler who—however dubiously he won the crown—was formally invested: "that same greatness," as Worcester had said, "which our own hands / Have holp to make so portly" (1.3.12-13). In doing this, Hotspur joins both Henry and Harry in playing the familiar game of disclaiming responsibility and pleading victimization. He unpacks this argument from the hints conspiratorially dropped by Worcester and Northumberland (143-52) and gives it back to them as a justifying spur to rebellious action—a spur, really, to revenge for the shames doubly heaped on them. But at the same time, by insisting that the responsibility and dishonor are theirs, not his, he directs the argument *against them.*

As my previous discussion has suggested, Hotspur's opposition to the king is rooted in a sense of personal affront which is exacerbated by the suspicion that he may be complicit in compromising his own honor. Here that opposition is inseparably bound to a new one: his competition with his senior kinsmen. He uses this speech event not merely to begin to "redeem" his banished honor, but to do so by dissociating himself from their shame. The force of this move is increased by its reverberation of the more familiar analogue that the verbal echoes of the "I know you all" soliloquy evoke:

Harry's dissociating himself from his father. And as the soliloquy looks forward to the Great Day of his glittering reformation, so Hotspur begins his race along the *cursus honoris* with the express intention of wearing "Without corrival all her dignities" (205).

On the other side, Worcester and Northumberland are obviously less interested in honor than in power and safety (in the power that will make them safe). Worcester's "Peace, cousin, say no more" is comical in part because he has already laid plans for the redemption of honors, and in part because having deliberately set Hotspur's discourse machine in motion he has a hard time shutting it off. The elder Percys need Hotspur to "face" their uprising, and if we bear this in mind we may be curious about their employment of Mortimer's claim, which had never been mentioned before, either in this play or in *Richard II.* Whether it is genuine or not—and we may as well assume that it is—is less important than the use they are putting it to as a political appeal to the legitimacy of the cause and a personal appeal to Mortimer's brother-in-law. The conspiratorial manner in which they broach the topic gives it an unpleasant smell, and the question is whether there is any indication that the smell reaches Hotspur's nose. They are using Mortimer to line their own enterprise, and using Hotspur to line Mortimer's. Does his language reveal any awareness of this?

The phrase I just used is borrowed from Lady Percy who, in 2.3, after expressing concern over Hotspur's recent behavior, says, "I fear my brother Mortimer doth stir / About his title, and hath sent for you / To line his enterprise" (82-84). This is hardly a complimentary way to put it: she fears Mortimer has sent for him as for his factor or tailor. In the words Hotspur uses to show his kinsmen their "line and predicament," she fears he is being sent for as one of "the agents, or base second means" (1.3.163). Lady Percy's phrasing expresses a hint of disapproval directed at Mortimer for being the possible cause of Hotspur's anxiety, but if we hear it with Hotspur's ears we may feel that it only increases his anxiety at the position he finds himself in. For it is possible that he is aware of lining his wife's brother's enterprise at some cost to his own chivalric autonomy and self-respect, and his responses to Lady Percy in 2.3, which I discuss below, play back over his performance in 1.3. Mortimer's subsequent behavior, which suggests that uxoriousness (and perhaps cowardice?) may have caused his failure to show up at Shrewsbury, puts the whole of the enterprise in a bad light, and revives the questions that may have disturbed Hotspur in the early part of 1.3.

Taking all this into consideration, one can't but wonder about the variety of dubious circumstances that hedge Hotspur in from the beginning and wound his sense of honor. From the moment he opens his mouth he appears trapped, like Mowbray, in "chains of bond-age" to political, psychological, and social circumstances, not to mention the military specter of "vile guns." They jeopardize his honor, his manhood, and his chivalric autonomy. He tries by his speech to silence these truths, defend against them, and preserve the discourse of honor in its purity. But his language, inscribed within truth's "quiet breast," continues to disclose them. Even his castigation of Worcester and Northumberland betrays an attempt to ignore the more reprehensible aspects of the action to which he commits himself, as well as a self-defeating attempt to compete with his allies in the race for honor. During the remainder of the scene, these doubts about his own condition give themselves away both in compensatory outbursts of bravado and in deliberately irritating behavior, which—with a wry and self-mocking awareness—he displays as if asking his kinsmen to rebuke him.

After Hotspur's rhetoric arcs excitedly up toward the moon, it comes back down to earth with a set of figures whose idiomatic vividness has a peculiar effect:

> But I will find him when he lies asleep,
> And in his ear I'll holla "Mortimer!"
> Nay, I'll have a starling shall be taught to speak
> Nothing but "Mortimer" . . .
> All studies here I solemnly defy,
> Save how to gall and pinch this Bolingbroke:
> And that same sword-and-buckler prince of Wales,
>
> . . . . .
>
> I would have him poison'd with a pot of ale!
> *North.* Why, what a wasp-stung and impatient fool
> Art thou to break into this woman's mood,
> Tying thine ear to no tongue but thine own!
> *Hot.* Why, look you, I am whipp'd and scourg'd with rods,
> Nettled, and stung with pismires, when I hear of this vile politician Bolingbroke.
>
> (1.3.219-22, 225-30, 233-38)

Hotspur at his most winning playfully vents and deflates his anger. There is self-mockery in the kind and level of punishment he devises—in the threat to turn starling teacher and pester Henry like a popinjay (cf. 3.1.253-54 and 1.3.49), and in the tonal drop from "solemnly defy" to "gall and pinch." It is not so much that he is charming as that he is being charming, begging his auditors' indulgence and apologizing for his own so that he can go on indulging himself, can go on savoring his minor grievances and revenges like a small boy who has been shamed and is bent on getting even. Yet his language acknowledges both his low tolerance for such grievances and his high tolerance for the speech they enable. To scale them down to the level of galls, pinches, beatings, and stings is to admit he has been making more of them than he should. But even as he apologizes to his auditors for his performance, and even if it is an enabling apology, he seems willfully, perversely, to give them—and here I borrow Portia's phrase—a vantage to exclaim on him.

In the speech action of this scene, as in the battle action later, Hotspur (like Harry) stacks the odds against himself and maximizes his commitment to the role of underdog. This relation of interlocutory disadvantage dramatizes one of the self-subverting aspects of the discourse of honor. He presents himself to his uncle and father, his paternal "corrivals," as a naughty headstrong boy who in effect resigns to them the responsibility of tolerating him, checking him, and guiding him, just as he leaves it up to them to find the battlefield he longs for and to aim him toward it. His dependence on them, his obligation to them, and his consequent lack of self-sufficiency are immediately present and active in the conversational protocol he establishes. To assume such a position is to enhance the authority of the fathers he intends to surpass in the race for honor. He relies on his corrivals to help him achieve the goal of wearing honor's dignities without corrival. The irony of Northumberland's subsequent defection is that it gives Hotspur what he wants. Does it give Northumberland what he wants?

The question may not be answerable, yet it is reasonable to ask it in a tetralogy centered on a set of father-son conflicts that reverberate, overlap, and speak to each other. Weak fathers like Gaunt, York, Henry, and Northumberland may be forgiven for flinching from their sons, and from the shame or guilt of small and great betrayals. But of course the plays don't ask us to get into the business of forgiving, as if we had any right to the voyeuristic power of divine judgment. All they ask us to look into is whether the fathers can forgive themselves.

A good case can be made that in *Richard II* Gaunt's manhood and honor are threatened both by his son's behavior and by his response to it. What about Northumberland? There isn't much to go on. His brief responses to Hotspur reveal only irritation. But if we listen to Hotspur with *Northumberland's* ears, or lend him *ours,* we may feel that he is being upstaged, challenged, by the son who speaks of plucking all honor for himself while using his father as a factor. The final replies of father and son to Worcester's instructions poignantly drive home the contrast between them:

> *North.* Farewell, good brother; we shall thrive,
>   I trust.
> *Hot.* Uncle, adieu: O, let the hours be short,
>   Till fields, and blows, and groans applaud our
>   sport.
>
>   (1.3.294-96)

Hotspur looks forward eagerly to the crowds cheering him on the day of the big game. But his father's "I trust," the last words he speaks in the play, hangs weakly and indecisively at the end of a line whose faltering rhythm prepares us for his absence from the future scene of his son's heroics. The father who began the scene interceding for his son, ends it edging away from him.

Until fields and blows and groans applaud his sport, Hotspur finds a substitute outlet in words. His speech drives to an aggressive climax in his violent assault on the moon, a passage that reverbs Falstaff's stealthier attack on "our noble and chaste mistress" and is echoed in Gadshill's attack on Saint Commonwealth. These passages reinforce each other and are all the more significant for being merely incidental to what seems to occupy their speakers' attention. Here, at line 199, is what Hotspur says:

> By heaven methinks it were an easy leap
> To pluck bright honor from the pale-fac'd
>   moon,
> Or dive into the bottom of the deep,
> Where fathom-line could never touch the
>   ground,
> And pluck up drowned honor by the locks,
> So he that doth redeem her thence might wear
> Without corrival all her dignities:
> But out upon this half-fac'd fellowship!

"An oration in Ercles' vein," says the Arden editor: a touch of heroic frenzy. But there is more to it than rant, and it is more than a conventionally hyperbolic expression of chivalric ardors. Several of Hotspur's previous phrases in the scene are echoed: the pale-cheeked king "high in the air," "the downtrod Mortimer," the redemption of "banish'd honors," and the threat of drowning all converge, and some are transsexualized, in the chaste mistress of the moon who rules the deep. They discharge into that figure the value of the Enemy who threatens and challenges, and who provides honor with its occasion because she withholds it as if to "wear / Without corrival all her dignities."

What the figure virtually says is that to desire and pursue honor is to dishonor a woman and a goddess— to violate her, to cause her to drown, to make her pale with fear and anger. (However irrelevant it may be, an image of the drowned Ophelia crosses briefly over my sense of this passage.) The rude force of "pluck up . . . by the locks" casts a dim light on "redeem," especially since what will be redeemed is a corpse. Honor, the ultimate prey of the desire for honor, is identified with, expressed in, the perpetration of dishonor and shame on its possessor. If to receive honor as a gift from others is to be diminished, emasculated, reduced to a minion, then the gift must be refused so that honor may be taken by force.

Hotspur's imagined violation is also a self-violation. There is a suggestion of transvestism in the image of honor's redeemer wearing *her* dignities. It is as if his language refuses to let him defeminize himself, as if the woman who withholds honor stubbornly resists his violence. Honor as the lunar goddess is the ultimate figure of *danger* in the romance sense—the Spenserian *daunger*. Like Belphoebe, she protects the rights of women against the assaults of their male corrivals. Hotspur clearly means *corrival* to refer to his male peers, but in the figure, *corrival* refers to "her." "Half-fac'd" echoes "pale-fac'd" and can describe the figure of the moon, which, whether half or full, is flat, like the image stamped on a coin. So long as Hotspur shares honor with "her," so long as her pale face is partnered to his half-face, he remains impure, incomplete, merely half a man. To castigate and destroy the "noble and chaste mistress" within is the precondition for surpassing other males in honor.

．．．．．

Act 2, scene 3, is a short scene, running to only about 120 lines. It begins with a prose soliloquy in which Hotspur testily responds aloud to the letter of an anonymous correspondent who writes that he is going to pass up the invitation to join the uprising against the king. Hotspur's wife then walks in and spends 27 lines of blank verse complaining about how she has been ignored by her husband and worrying about the obsession with warfare that makes him talk in his sleep. The remaining interchanges between them feature his affectionate but nervous diffidence and her frustrated demands for more love and information. I conclude with some comments on this scene because in it is distilled the essential warfare between the claims of honor and those of gender within Hotspur's language.

The opening soliloquy reads so like a dialogue carried on by the speaker with himself as well as with his correspondent that it has been interpreted by Robert Merrix and Arthur Palacas as an unsuccessful effort at self-reassurance. They attribute the "signs of inner conflict" revealed by his language to his "doubts about the rebellion," doubts which they think he silences "with a combination of argument, exhausting wordiness, and irrational tirade. Even in the face of the possibility that the letter's author will 'to the King and lay open all our proceedings,' Hotspur finally concludes, 'Hang him, let him to the King! we are prepared. I will set forward tonight.'"[25] But is this his only fear, or doesn't he also worry that the rebels' enterprise may succeed? Recall his impatience with "half-fac'd fellowship" in 1.3 and the irritability projected from his expressions of concern for honor. The impatience extended to the details of plotting, which he had wanted to leave up to his elders; they would work out the logistics and he would then ride off and reap the rewards:

Hot. I smell it. Upon my life it will do well!
North. Before the game is afoot thou still
  let'st slip.
Hot. Why, it cannot choose but be a noble
  plot;

．．．．．

In faith it is exceedingly well aim'd.

(1.3.271-76)

He is now aware that he may have proved his father right by "letting slip" when he exposed the plot to the correspondent whose "fear and cold heart" might lead him to turn informer. What is interesting about this is that although he blames himself for his folly, his words hardly betray any depth of guilt: "O, I could divide myself, and go to buffets, for moving such a dish of skim milk with so honorable an action" (2.3.32-34). The self-accusation is lightheartedly irritable, and it is implicitly affirmative insofar as his own discretion proceeds from a rash willingness to take chances (in divulging the plot to potential allies—or informers?) that is more honorable than the correspondent's cautious scruples. The same pattern of contrastive definition is at work here as was evident in his fulminations against the effeminate courtier. If, as Merrix and Palacas observe, the very anonymity of the correspondent "demonstrates dramatically that Hotspur's ravings and defenses are . . . the unsolicited product of his own turmoil,"[26] then the charge of effeminate cowardice may conceivably displace the fear—the fear of fear—inscribed in the discourse that speaks through him.

It is thus questionable that Hotspur's anxiety is to be attributed solely to his "doubts about the rebellion," or that those doubts are silenced by the end of the soliloquy. Yet he anticipates new danger in an oddly positive tone of conviction: "You shall see now in the very sincerity of fear and cold heart will he to the King. . . ." This could be read as the utterance of the naughty "lack-brain" boy who has acted as his father suspected he might, and who expects—not without satisfaction—to get what he deserves. But it could also—if more obscurely—be read as another expression of the wish to be an underdog: to give the secret away will increase the danger and hence the excitement and honorableness of the action. It is as if the soundness of the plot detracts from honor. His anger at the writer's cowardice may well conflict with a touch of fretfulness over the careful plotting that allies him with so many corrivals, and threatens to diminish his share in "so honorable an action."

The impatience of "Hang him, let him to the King, we are prepared: I will set forward tonight" is thus the product of an unresolved clash of motives; it is given a competitive edge by his previous statement that some of his corrivals have "set forward already" (2.3.28-29).

But as a way of concluding the soliloquy it is also another gesture of escape to the enfranchisement of "fields, and blows, and groans"—escape from the tug of conflicting motives and from such logistical nettles or pismires as the precautions of plotting. The situation I analyzed in my reading of 1.3 suggests to me that in addition to the contradictions internal to the discourse of honor, Hotspur's behavior in the circumstances entangling him in Mortimer's affairs could only intensify his uneasiness. Thus I deduce that in the soliloquy he summons up and welcomes the politicomilitary doubts Merrix and Palacas describe—summons them up to provide the trifling galls and pinches with which he diverts himself from other fears. "*Enter* Hotspur *solus, reading a letter*": the soliloquy is itself a single encounter against an absent foe whose "craven scruple" reflects those fears in conveniently parodic and displaced form. Having routed the foe in speech he can rush off to the battlefield before being attacked by second thoughts.

Before dwelling with too long a face on Hotspur's uneasiness I think it is important to appreciate the keenness with which the soliloquist enjoys this verbal encounter. The rhythms of the language make it easy for actors performing the soliloquy to move audiences to laugh not merely at the speaker's expense but in sympathetic enjoyment of his rhetorical exuberance. By the very vivacity of his utterance the actor can secure our approval of, for example, the scornful common sense of "'tis dangerous to take a cold, to sleep, to drink," and can induce us to applaud the memorable riposte that counters it, "but I tell you, my lord fool, out of this nettle, danger, we pluck this flower, safety" (2.3.8-10). The speaker means to distinguish the ultimate risk-taking Danger from quotidian sources of vulnerability, and the gallantry of the sentiment combines with its aphoristic form to elicit our assent. Nevertheless, the language resists this meaning. The syntax confuses the two kinds of danger because "nettle" is another minimizing figure, and "pluck this flower"— which recalls "pluck bright honor"—is a self-defeating image of the fragile, transient safety sought by fleeing from dangers to Danger. This resistance uncovers something deeper and more abiding in Hotspur's language, something engendered not simply by his uncertainty about the rebellion but by a fundamental ambivalence in the discourse of honor to which he commits himself. Merrix and Palacas make good use of the trope of proleptic parody to show how Hotspur's uncertainty is foregrounded by comparison with the prior performance of Gadshill in 1.2: "Whereas Gadshill's defensiveness arises from an attempt to set his challenger [the Chamberlain] straight, Hotspur's much more intense disputations, voiced on a stage empty of everyone but himself, are directed against himself."[27] I imagine Hotspur trying to set himself straight but not fully persuading himself—imagine an edge of self-parody in his romantic posturing, a sense of being trapped in, embattled

by, the bravery of a discourse he loves but has doubts about. If it is dangerous to sleep and drink, it is also dangerous to speak.

And it is indeed dangerous to sleep, as we learn when Lady Percy enters:

> O my good lord, why are you thus alone?
> For what offence have I this fortnight been
> A banish'd woman from my Harry's bed?
> Tell me, sweet lord, what is't that takes from thee
> Thy stomach, pleasure, and thy golden sleep?
> Why dost thou bend thine eyes upon the earth,
> And start so often when thou sit'st alone?
> Why hast thou lost the fresh blood in thy cheeks,
> And given my treasures and my rights of thee
> To thick-ey'd musing, and curst melancholy?
> In thy faint slumbers I by thee have watch'd,
> And heard thee murmur tales of iron wars,
> Speak terms of manage to thy bounding steed,
> Cry "Courage! To the field!" And thou hast talk'd
> Of sallies, and retires, of trenches, tents,
> Of palisadoes, frontiers, parapets,
> Of basilisks, of cannon, culverin,
> Of prisoners' ransom, and of soldiers slain,
> And all the currents of a heady fight.
> Thy spirit within thee hath been so at war,
> And thus hath so bestirr'd thee in thy sleep,
> That beads of sweat have stood upon thy brow
> Like bubbles in a late-disturbed stream,
> And in thy face strange motions have appear'd,
> Such as we see when men restrain their breath
> On some great sudden hest, O, what portents are these?
> Some heavy business hath my lord in hand,
> And I must know it, else he loves me not.
>   (2.3.38-65)

The first thing we learn from this is that whatever bothers Hotspur antedates the reception of the letter (unless he is imagined to have spent fifteen days talking back to it), and we can assume that it affected the response expressed in his soliloquy. Perhaps wounded honor is part of the problem: the word *banish'd* works like a mnemonic trigger connecting the violation of his wife's rights to the violent effect on him of his concern to "redeem / . . . banish'd honors." When she refigures "beads of sweat" to "bubbles in a late-disturbed stream," the image matches and recalls Hotspur's "drowned honor" (1.3.203), and it also recalls his fantasy of the disturbance that "affrighted" the Severn (1.3.103). These echoes filter back into "currents of a heady fight" and trigger another recall, Worcester's "current roaring loud" along with Hotspur's "If he fall in, good night, or sink, or swim" (1.3.185-94). In this context of recollective allusion, "prisoners' ransom" and "soldiers slain" evoke not only Hotspur's generic martial anticipations but also specific backward references to Henry's demand and to the carnage in Wales for which his wife's brother may have been responsible.

To read Lady Hotspur's speech this way is to go beyond the information available to the speaker, to see that the "portents" are also retrospects, and to place a different construction on "heavy business." At the same time it is also to validate the interpretive intuitions displayed in her two comparisons in lines 59-63. Above all it is to listen with Hotspur's ears, not hers, for she knows less than he does. Doubtless this befits a woman's place, and the very accuracy of her woman's intuition might well motivate him to keep her in it. Her insight may cut too deep, her mirror reflect back to him a true image of the heavy business that he may want *not* to know as much as she wants to know it. She reveals the intimacy and demands the rights of a second self, and perhaps the demand itself has the force of "some great sudden hest," since to share in half-faced partnership with a wifely corrival could only widen the breach in his honor and manhood. He can't redeem "drowned honor" or pluck honor from the pale-faced king without at the same time banishing—plucking honor from—his wife. Yet this might confront him with another problem.

"And I must know it, else he loves me not": that importunate "hest" could be bothersome just because he does love her—there can be no other way to read the playful affection and banter that mark their two scenes together. She speaks to him with the frankness, sympathy, and confidence of one assured in his love and therefore perplexed by his recent transformation. If we respond to this, it complicates our sense of the "heavy business" that besets him. For the business comes to include the demands she makes on him not only generally as his wife but also here and now, in this speech, and this adds a more immediate source to those that keep the spirit within him "so at war." Her questions mingle anxiety for his welfare with anxiety over her own frustrated claims on him, while her description mingles the marks of the distraught lover with the marks of fear. But what love, and what fear? Is it the love and fear of "iron wars" that rob him of his "golden sleep" and her of her "treasures" and "rights"? That bend him "thick-ey'd" toward Henry's "thirsty . . . soil," the man-eating mother (1.1.5-6), or toward the "lean earth" the sweating Falstaff lards (2.2.103-4)? And what does the cry she reports mean? Is it only the leader's cry to his soldiers, or is it self-directed? And if self-directed, does it mean that he has to summon up courage to go to the field, or that going to the field—seeking the solace of "all the currents of a heady fight"—will give him the courage he needs? But courage, then, to defend against what fear if not that of

"Thy stomach, pleasure, and thy golden sleep," if not that of "my treasures and my rights of thee"? Or is there another fear, another reason why he would feel threatened by the words with which the watcher at his bed anxiously reflects his anxiety back to him?

The first of the "tales of iron wars" she reports fits comfortably within the chivalric paradigm: lines 50-51 suggest the clean heroics of single encounter, of "Harry to Harry, hot horse to horse." But she then goes on to report his tale of the messier warfare "Of basilisks, of cannon, culverin." It is as if, once the dreamer galloped into the field, he was confronted not by another Harry but by the hungry mouths of heavy ordnance and by the ultimate impotence, the prospect of a death he has no power to make his own—more pointedly, the prospect articulated by the fop who so irritated him on the battlefield with talk of "these vile guns" that "many a good tall fellow had destroy'd" (1.3.62-63), and whose connection with Henry and the question of prisoners is marked by Lady Hotspur's linking the sleeper's talk of guns to his talk "Of prisoners' ransom, and of soldiers slain." Behind this veil of references lurks the problematic figure of Mortimer and thus the even more problematic bond to Mortimer through Lady Hotspur, whose subsequent expression of concern ("I fear my brother Mortimer . . . / . . . hath sent for you / To line his enterprise," 82-84) touches on the network of constraints and accommodations that have compromised Hotspur's honor from the start.

As a bearer of messages from Hotspur's troubled dreamland, this messenger can only add to the anxieties and vulnerabilities her account reflects. We can imagine why he would be eager neither to have her know what he betrays in his sleep nor to have the betrayal mirrored back to him so that he is forced to recognize fears and terrors his waking words never acknowledge. Doesn't all this give a more poignant edge and urgency to the self-defeating impulse to flight inscribed in "out of this nettle, danger, we pluck this flower, safety"? Poignant, I mean, for both of them, for her as well as for him. His response is powerfully evasive. He says nothing to her in reply but instead turns away and calls a servant:

> What ho!
>   Is Gilliams with the packet gone?
> *Serv.* He is, my lord, an hour ago.
> *Hot.* Hath Butler brought those horses from
>   the sheriff?
> *Serv.* One horse, my lord, he brought even
>   now.
> *Hot.* What horse? A roan, a crop-ear is it not?
> *Serv.* It is, my lord.
> *Hot.*   That roan shall be my throne.
> Well, I will back him straight. O Esperance!
> Bid Butler lead him forth into the park.
>   (1.3.66-73)

He has betrayed his fear to his wife in his sleep, he flinches both from her reflecting it back to him and from her claims on him, and he begins to move rapidly away from that surveillance and self-dividing confrontation toward *Esperance.* The Percy motto, "Esperance ma comforte," seems reducible here to "Horse is my stay," especially the horse that carries him away from his wife. Is there any reason why the text contains that apparently gratuitous epithet, "crop-ear"? Animal ears are cropped as a sign of identification, human ears as a sign of punishment. Hotspur's expression becomes less gratuitous when we situate it in the set of references that include a horse named Cut (2.1.5) and Gadshill's gelding (2.1.33, 94). "Cut" signifies either a curtal or a gelding, a horse that has been symbolically or literally castrated. If horses can represent their masters, then perhaps "Cut" speaks to the sense of powerlessness and apprehensiveness expressed by the Carriers who, in 2.1, utter a version of the victim's discourse, and perhaps Gadshill's gelding comments on what lies underneath and bears up the aggressive machismo of his rhetoric in that scene. Applying the same logic to Hotspur, "crop-ear" may conceivably suggest something about his wounded mode of audition, his diffident response to the articulateness of the claims, the sympathy, the careful observation, that threaten to make his wife his loving corrival. His affection for her is apparent in all their exchanges, hence if the crop-eared horse on which he plans to escape from her is identified as his, it may hint at a motive of self-punishment in his flight. But to admit this symbolism is to trot out a telling inconsistency: why should the equine instrument of his flight from the fear of emasculation itself be marked as a symbol of what he flees from?

. . . . .

"What is it carries you away?" Hotspur's wife asks, and when he answers, "my horse, my love, my horse" (2.3.76-77), it may occur to us that his horse performs the same function as his galloping speech, a perpetually unfinished rush of self-representation interrupted only by the death it dooms him to. If there is an Icarian and also an Actaeonic futility inscribed in Hotspur's speech it is because this scene as a whole reveals that from the moment Hotspur opens his mouth he appears trapped in "chains of bondage" to political, psychological, and social circumstances that jeopardize his honor, his manhood, and his chivalric autonomy. He tries by his speech to silence these truths, defend against them, and preserve the discourse of honor in its Artemisian purity. But his language continues to defeat him. "That roan shall be my throne": his only throne will be his crop-eared roan. There is as much desperation and futility as there is determination in this utterance. He is king over himself only when he rides the horse that carries him away from his wife toward "golden"—or leaden—"uncontroll'd enfran-

chisement." Although the discourse of honor carries him away from the weakness he fears, it continually reproduces the weakness in the rhetorical transports that seduce his tongue. When he claims "I profess not talking," when he shows uneasiness about poetry, singing, and lovemaking, he is in flight from his own vulnerabilities. Behind this obvious point is a more significant one: the language assigned to Hotspur is shot through with the awareness that the accents of honor are inseparable from those of the weakness and uncontrol that the discourse of honor marks as dishonorable or shameful. The hero loves and fears what Mowbray dismissively calls "the trial of a woman's war" as much as he loves and fears the only fate that will justify it and put an end to it.

Notes

[1] All quotations from *1 Henry IV* in this and subsequent chapters are from *The First Part of King Henry IV,* ed. A. R. Humphreys, The Arden Shakespeare, 6th ed. (1960; repr. London: Methuen, 1974).

[2] Pierre Bourdieu, *Outline of a Theory of Practice,* trans. Richard Nice (Cambridge: Cambridge University Press, 1977), 4-15; Marcel Mauss, *The Gift: Forms and Functions of Exchange in Archaic Societies,* trans. Ian Cunnison (New York: Norton, 1967), 72-73, 63.

[3] Bourdieu, *Outline,* 1off.

[4] Ibid., 12, 11.

[5] Aristotle, *Nicomachean Ethics* 1.5.4 (1095b), trans. H. Rackham, Loeb Classical Library (London: Heinemann, 1945), 14-15.

[6] Aristotle, *Rhetoric* 1.5.9 (1361a), trans. J. H. Freese, in *The "Art" of Rhetoric,* Loeb Classical Library (London: Heinemann, 1947), 53; *Nichomachean Ethics* 4.3.22, 24 (1124b), pp. 221-23.

[7] *Nichomachean Ethics* 4.3.17 (1124a), p. 219.

[8] Thomas Hobbes, *Leviathan,* ed. Michael Oakeshott (Oxford: Basic Blackwell, 1960), 65 (1.11).

[9] D. J. Gordon, "Name and Fame: Shakespeare's *Coriolanus,*" in *The Renaissance Imagination: Essays and Lectures by D. J. Gordon,* ed. Stephen J. Orgel (Berkeley: University of California Press, 1980), 203-19, esp. 210-13.

[10] C. B. Macpherson, *The Political Theory of Possessive Individualism* (Oxford: Clarendon Press, 1962), 38.

[11] Paul A. Jorgensen, *Shakespeare's Military World* (Berkeley: University of California Press, 1956), 240, 296.

[12] *Nichomachean Ethics* 3.6.6 (1115a27), p. 155.

[13] Ibid., 3.7.13 (1116a13-15), pp. 161-63.

[14] The filaments of the Actaeon myth curling about this cluster are too wispy and discontinuous to nurture into a thesis. They nevertheless have a certain interest. At 3.3.155-56, Harry calls Diana's fat forester an "embossed rascal," and this denotes a young lean deer as well as a fat swollen rogue (Arden notes). See also Harry's "Death hath not struck so fat a deer today" at 5.4.106. The first passage is connected with the pocket-picking episode, while the second is shortly followed by Falstaff's stabbing the dead Hotspur in the thigh. Both, then, are connected with castration symbolism. The "rascal" as both rogue and victim, predator and prey, man and deer, puts forth a tenuous trailer toward the chaste mistress of the pale-faced moon when Hotspur's threat to pluck bright honor from that figure places him in Actaeon's position. For a wonderful discussion of the implications of this theme, see Leonard Barkan, "Diana and Actaeon: The Myth as Synthesis," *English Literary Renaissance* 10 (1980): 317-59, esp. 349ff.

[15] J. Dover Wilson, ed., *The First Part of the History of Henry IV* (Cambridge: Cambridge University Press, 1958), 120.

[16] That Diana should have men as companions is itself outrageous. Is Diana a man in drag? Are her foresters dressed as women? Is Diana secretly "a fair hot wench"?

[17] Barkan, "Diana and Actaeon," 351-52.

[18] Ibid., 343; my italics.

[19] G. R. Hibbard, *The Making of Shakespeare's Dramatic Poetry* (Toronto: University of Toronto Press, 1981), 175-76; my italics.

[20] Jorgensen, *Shakespeare's Military World,* 240-41.

[21] The game appears frequently in Shakespeare. It is the game played by Prospero and by Lear and Gloucester and by the Duke of Vienna as well as by Richard II, Henry, and Harry.

[22] *The First Part of "King Henry the Fourth,"* ed. George Lyman Kittredge (Boston: Ginn, 1940), 117. See also Ullrich Langer, "Gunpowder as Transgressive Invention in Ronsard," in *Literary Theory/Renaissance Texts,* ed. Patricia Parker and David Quint (Baltimore: Johns Hopkins University Press), 96-114; pp. 104-6 are especially relevant to this discussion.

[23] We may also wonder about the disproportion between 10,000 "bold Scots" and 22 knights. Does Henry mean to imply an equitable distribution—22 aristocrats = 10,000 commoners?

[24] See Paul A. Jorgensen, "Valor's Better Parts: Backgrounds and Meanings of Shakespeare's Most Difficult Proverb," *Shakespeare Studies* 9 (1976): 152. Jorgensen comments on the relation of this pun to "the defense of threatened manhood in the passage and in Falstaff's entire career" (153), and one need only add that Falstaff, the source of the pun, is making a similar comment about himself.

[25] Robert P. Merrix and Arthur Palacas, "Gadshill, Hotspur, and the Design of Proleptic Parody," *Comparative Drama* 14 (1980-81): 303.

[26] Ibid., 302-3.

[27] Ibid., 303.

Source: "Food for Words: Hotspur and the Discourse of Honor," in *Making Trifles of Terrors: Redistributing Complicities in Shakespeare,* edited by Peter Erickson, Stanford University Press, 1997, pp. 251-87.

Speaking Freely about Richard II

Paula Blank, *College of William & Mary*

And formally, according to our law,
Depose him in the justice of his cause.
King Richard II (I.iii.29-30)[1]

The deposition of Shakespeare's Richard II has been controversial since the play's original publication, and critics have generally concurred that the omission of "the Parliament Sceane, and the deposing of King Richard"[2] in Elizabethan editions of the play was a result of censorship. Whether or not the playwright himself was complicitous in the act is still uncertain.[3] In this essay I will make the case that Shakespeare's *Richard II* explores the practice of self-censorship, whether or not Shakespeare self-censored the notorious "scene of the crime"; that Shakespeare's version of Richard's story brings specific sixteenth-century notions of "free speech," concerning the relationship of the king to his Parliaments, to bear on the problem of writing, and rewriting, the deposition of the king. The discourse on censorship that the play encodes, in fact, centers on other "depositions" which are subject to suppression in the text. *Richard II* exploits not one but two meanings of the word "deposition," and the politically vexed matter of divesting the monarch's power is bound, dramatically, to the depositions or formal testimony brought against him in trials throughout the play.[4] Deposing both literary and historical sources in the justice of Richard's cause, Shakespeare ultimately incriminates writing itself—including his own account of Richard's story—in the distortion and suppression of evidence.

That *Richard II* is centrally preoccupied with legal rhetoric and legal procedures has been noted before,[5] but the reasons for this preoccupation have not been fully considered. Shakespeare transformed the deposition scene itself into a *cause célèbre*, a trial in which sentence is passed on the accused (in Holinshed, the commons called for such a trial only after Henry's coronation).[6] But the sense that the play as a whole will concern itself with judgment and judicial protocol is established from the very beginning. *Richard II* opens with a trial, as two lords, Thomas Mowbray and Henry Bolingbroke, accuse each other of high treason before the king. In the course of this proceeding, Bolingbroke charges Mowbray with, among other crimes, the murder of Thomas of Woodstock, Duke of Gloucester, the king's uncle. Later, at the start of Act IV, scene i—the so-called deposition scene—Bolingbroke, now presiding as judge, hears further testimony in the Gloucester case. It is no coincidence that this hearing forms part of the same scene of judg-ment that culminates in Richard's deposition: The Gloucester case is key to understanding Shakespeare's cross-examination of the case of Richard, and the nature of the "testimony" preserved in the various records that transcribe his reign.

The scattered references to the Woodstock murder in *Richard II* have long been held to be vague and inconclusive. Mowbray's response to Bolingbroke's accusation, in particular, is difficult to follow: "For Gloucester's death, / I slew him not, but to my own disgrace / Neglected my sworn duty in that case" (I.i.132-34). J. Dover Wilson called Mowbray's words "embarrassed and ambiguous," and dismissed the question of Gloucester's death as "a minor strand in the texture of the play."[7] E. M. W. Tillyard also charged Mowbray with obscurity and concluded that Shakespeare "leaves uncertain the question of who murdered Woodstock."[8] It has also been suggested that Shakespeare glossed over the details of Gloucester's death because he treated the material as "already read," relying on his audience's knowledge of one of his sources, the anonymous play *Woodstock,* to fill in the details he left out.[9] I will argue that there was much more at stake than dramatic economizing here, that the very obscurity of the testimony brought forward in the Gloucester case is a clue that something has been censored. From the opening scene of the play, *Richard II* reveals the way that incriminating testimony is suppressed, testimony that bears, directly, on the "case" of the king. Indeed, the relegation of the Gloucester murder to a "subplot"—enacted both within the play and its critical reception—is one verson of the censorship the play examines.[10]

There seems to be no question that the Gloucester "subplot" of *Richard II* derives from an anonymous play, *Woodstock,* written sometime in the early 1590s. A. P. Rossiter, in his edition of this source, has marshalled the evidence: parallel phrases, adapted passages, analogous characterizations.[11] Shakespeare's John of Gaunt, who refers to "my brother Gloucester, plain well-meaning soul" (II.i.128), seems to have had this Woodstock in mind, rather than the man Holinshed described as "hastie, wilfull and given more to war than to peace."[12] Rossiter makes much of how far the author of *Woodstock* departed from the Tudor histories in his creation of "Plain Thomas"—as he is called throughout the work. This Thomas is "plain" both in style of dress (which sets him apart from the foppery of Richard's court) and in a characteristic directness of speech. Yet for all his innovations, the author of *Wood-*

stock surely found grounds for such a portrayal in the chronicles. Holinshed notes how the dukes of Lancaster and York attempted to contain Richard's displeasure with Gloucester: "to deliver the kings mind of suspicion, [they] made answer, that they were not ignorant, how their brother of Glocester, as a man sometime rash in woords, would speake oftentimes more than he could or would bring to effect, and the same proceeded of a faithfull hart, which he bare towards the king." In Holinshed, Gloucester's tendency to be "rash in woords" brings him into increasing conflict with the king: "Upon this multiplieng of words . . . in such presumptuous maner by the duke against the king, there kindeled such displeasure betwixt them, that it never ceassed to increase into flames, till the duke was brought to his end." The other dukes, apparently, warn him in vain of this: "the duke of Lancaster and Yorke . . . reprov[ed] the duke of Glocester for his too liberall talking, uttering unadvisedlie woords that became not his person."[13] It is clear that the author of *Woodstock* concurs at least this far with Holinshed—that Gloucester's "too liberall talking" was a chief cause of his downfall.

The title character of the anonymous *Woodstock,* moreover, sees it as both his right and his obligation to speak "plainly" before the king. Woodstock characterizes Richard as a man "wounded with a wanton humour, / Lulled and secured by flattering sycophants" (I.i.144-45)[14] and takes every opportunity to reprimand the king for his moral profligacy. At Richard's wedding in Act I, Woodstock interrupts the festivities to warn the new queen of her husband's flaws, and despite Richard's protests, Woodstock insists: "Nay, nay, King Richard, fore God I'll speak the truth!" (I.ii.23). As Richard's abuses worsen, Woodstock returns with greater persistence to his self-appointed role: "I'm Thomas, by th' rood / I'll speak the truth" (I.iii.34-35); "Scoff ye my plainness, I'll talk no riddles, / Plain Thomas will speak plainly" (I.iii.115-16). Though he is confident in his claim that his "tongue hath liberty to show / The inly passions boiling in [his] breast" (I.iii.213-14), his "plainness" turns, for Richard, from provocation to a threat:

Wood. Ye have done ill . . .
King:　　Ha, dare ye say so?
Wood: Dare I? Afore my God I'll speak King
　　Richard
Were I assured this day my head should off:
I tell ye Sir, my allegiance stands excused
In justice of the cause. Ye have done ill.
The sun of mercy never shine on me
But I speak truth.

　　　　　　　　　　　　　　　　　(I.iii.167-73)

When the king can no longer turn a deaf ear to Woodstock's "plain speech" ("Plain Thomas, I'll not hear ye" [II.ii.144]), he plots with his favorites to murder him. As he is captured and led offstage, Woodstock is determined to talk on: "Good heaven . . . forgive me,

pray ye forbear a while / I'll speak but one word more, indeed I will" (IV.ii.207-8). The King, however, has the last word, as he commands that his uncle be brought to silence: "Stop's mouth I say: we'll hear no more" (IV.ii.206).

Woodstock dies in this play a martyr, the victim of the king's efforts to conceal—from himself, in part—the truth of his crimes. Woodstock, however, is only the chief among many such martyrs in the work; in fact, the play follows the widespread efforts of the king and his favorites to apprehend any and all "privy whisperers against the state" (IV.iii.4). The court has unleashed a band of tax collectors[15] who double as spies for the crown, among them one Simon Ignorance, the Bailey of Dunstable who, along with his brother Ignoramus, manages to gather a list of over seven hundred such "whisperers" over the course of the play. Those who speak out against the king's blank charters are immediately accused of treason: "Why suffer ye their speech? To prison hie! / There let them perish: rot, consume, and die!" (IV.iii.47-48). A Serving-man and a Schoolmaster muse that "the country's so full of intelligencers that two men can scarce walk together but they're attached for whisperers" (III.iii.161-63). The Schoolmaster, however, believes he has found a way to write that will pass the censors; taken out of context, any single line of his verse seems innocent enough:

Blank charters they are called
A vengeance on the villain,
I would he were both flayed and bald:
God bless my lord Tresilian.[16]

　　　　　　　　　　　　　　　　　(III.iii.176-79)

But when Ignorance, overhearing the verses, apprehends him, the Schoolmaster tries in vain to defend his self-censored compositions. Ignorance goes on to condemn a man for whistling, as the Bailey explains to the culprit: "There's a piece of treason that flies up and down the country in the likeness of a ballad, and this being the very tune of it, thou hast whistled treason" (III.iii.230-32).

Woodstock concerns, in large part, the risks of "too liberall talking"; it is a tragedy (and, at times, a dark comedy) whose central subject may well be the brutality of the Tudor laws against seditious libel.[17] The fourteenth-century act that had defined treason as compassing or imagining the death of the monarch was reissued, in 1534, to encompass treasonous words against the king. (In fact, the older law had often been interpreted this way, but now the link between seditious words and treasonous intent was made official).[18] According to one historian of the period, the surveillance of "privy whispering" imagined in *Woodstock* was lived: "The Privy Council actively pursued its loose-mouthed subjects, and its register from 1540 to about 1570 is filled with reports about sedition, seditious libel, and rumour-mongering."[19] And the penalties for such crimes were harsh: in 1546 John Wyot, a carpenter, was set on a pillory with his ear nailed to it "the same to remain till he should himself either cut it off or pull it off" for uttering "lewd words" against the king. By Mary's reign, the author of a seditious work could be punished by losing his right hand; by 1581, the same author would face capital punishment. In one famous case of 1605, it was determined that slander was not only an infraction of state law but also an offense against the law of God—and, moreover, that it constituted no defense to say that the offending words were true.[20]

Yet despite the crown's efforts to coerce silence throughout the play, the "truth" about *Woodstock*'s Richard survives—not only the truth about the oppressiveness of his reign, but also, more urgently, his brutal murder of the play's hero. The author of *Woodstock* lays the blame for many of Richard's abuses on his favorites—Bushy, Bagot, and Greene among them—but the king himself is never absolved of his share of the guilt for the murder. Richard's henchman recognizes the harm this truth could do to the monarch: "So we must give it out [that Woodstock died a natural death] or else King Richard / Through Europe's kingdoms will be hardly censured" (V.i.281-82). Shakespeare's Duke of Lancaster refuses to avenge his brother's death:

> God's is the quarrel, for God's substitute,
> His deputy anointed in His sight,
> Hath caus'd his death, the which if
>   wrongfully,
> Let heaven revenge, for I may never lift
> An angry arm against His minister.
>
> (I.ii.37-41)

Woodstock's Lancaster, however, insists on it:

> We will revenge our noble brother's wrongs;
> And force that wanton tyrant to reveal
> The death of his dear uncle: harmless
>   Woodstock,
> So traitorously betrayed.
>
> · · · · ·
>
> If he be dead, by good King Edward's soul
> We'll call King Richard to a strict account
> For that and for his realm's misgovernment.
>
> (V.iii.2-5;19-21)

Indeed, as Rossiter points out, *Woodstock* advances no Carlisle to defend the king at the end of the play, and the idea of the divine right is rarely invoked at all on Richard's behalf.[21] *Woodstock* ends with the defeat of the favorites, and although Richard is left out of the final recriminations on the murderers of the duke, the king awaits heavenly revenge for his crime:

> O my dear friends, the fearful wrath of heaven
> Sits heavy on our heads for Woodstock's
>   death.
> Blood cries for blood; and that almighty hand
> Permits not murder unrevenged to stand.
> Come, come, we yet may hide ourselves from·
>   worldly strength;
> But Heaven will find us out, and strike at
>   length.
>
> (V.iv.47-52).

Rossiter suggests that the author of *Woodstock* made an effort to "avoid too open a conflict with orthodoxy,"[22] that is, with the Tudor doctrine of passive obedience. Yet *Woodstock* stands as testimony that Richard's efforts to avoid the world's "censure" ultimately fail, for his crime is openly avenged by the "liberall" text of the play itself.[23]

The anonymous *Woodstock* is a far more important source for Shakespeare's *Richard II* than critics have acknowledged. *Woodstock* speaks both through what remains of it in *Richard II,* and through what Shakespeare left out or modified. Shakespeare's use of *Woodstock* reveals, in fact, a great deal by its half-silences—strategies of self-censorship which, by laying the procedures of self-censorship bare, manage to expose the "truth" about Richard as well as the dangers of representing that truth too openly. And *Richard II* ultimately goes much farther than *Woodstock* in its dramatization of the king's fear of what was said about him, holding Richard himself responsible not only for the erasure of evidence, but also for having a hand in the rewriting of the official record of his rule.

Like *Woodstock,* Shakespeare's primary source, Holinshed's *Chronicles* was clear enough about Richard's responsibility for the murder of Gloucester. The historian states outright that Richard ordered Mowbray to have him killed. Mowbray, however, delayed the execution of that order "wherby the king conceiued no small displeasure, and sware that it should cost the earle his life if he quickly obeied not his commandement." Mowbray thus "in maner inforced" had the duke suffocated or strangled (Holinshed isn't sure on this point).[24] Holinshed also establishes the idea that Mowbray's crime, as far as Richard was concerned, had to do with something he allegedly said, some seditious libel concerning the king. Before making his accusations before the king, Bolingbroke brings the matter to the parliament: "In this parlement holden at Shrewsburie, Henrie, duke of Hereford, accused Thomas Mowbraie duke of Norfolke of certeine words which he should utter in talke had betwixt them, as they rode togither latelie before betwixt London and Brainford; sounding highlie to the kings dishonor. And for further proofe thereof, he presented a supplication to the king."[25] Before Richard, however, Bolingbroke does not mention the conversation he had with Mowbray on the way to Brainford, charging him only with the murder itself. Yet Richard finds Mowbray guilty of libel: "Thomas Mowbraie, duke of Norfolke, bicause he had sowen sedition in the relme by his words, [shall] likewise avoid the realme, . . . *never to returne* againe into England, nor approch the borders or confines thereof *upon paine of* death."[26] We never learn what Mowbray said that was "sounding highlie to the kings dishonor," what sedition he had sown in words. It seems likely, however, that Holinshed's Mowbray was convicted for revealing (or threatening to reveal) Richard's part in the murder.

Shakespeare, as I have already noted, has been charged with ambiguity in the Gloucester case, despite the unqualified certainty of his sources. But although Richard makes no formal confession in the play, Shakespeare isn't ambiguous at all on this point, though it is instructive that some critics have failed to observe all the corroborating evidence the playwright provides. It is true that the first scene of the play seems to transform the Gloucester case—historically, a closed book—into a mystery. Richard appears to be uninformed about the scene about to be played before him, asking Gaunt if he knows whether Bolingbroke "appeal[s] the Duke on ancient malice, / Or worthily, as a good subject should, / On some known ground of treachery in him" (I.i.9-11). He makes a grand show of his impartiality towards the litigants:

> Then call them to our presence; face to face,
> And frowning brow to brow, ourselves will
> 　hear
> The accuser and the accused freely speak.
> 　　　　　　　　　　　　　(I.i.14-16).

Later he asserts that impartiality again, along with another invitation to speak freely:

> He is our subject, Mowbray: so art thou
> Free speech and fearless I to thee allow.
> 　　　　　　　　　　　　　(I.i.122-23)

The king's proffer of "free speech"—recalling the issue of "liberall" speech in Shakespeare's sources—is central to understanding the "mystery" of Gloucester's murder, and the nature of Mowbray's testimony in this scene.

The right to "free speech" is not a wholly anachronistic notion, as we might suppose; the phrase was already in use in the sixteenth century, in reference to a well-established and yet bitterly contested parliamentary privilege. Freedom of speech seems to have been first requested explicitly by the Commons during parliamentary debates in the reign of Henry VIII. But by the end of the 1540s, according to one recent historian, the Common's insistence on freedom of speech had already become "proverbial."[27] Early journals recording the parliaments of Queen Elizabeth relate the ritual request of the Speaker:

> And lastly [Sir Thomas Gargrave] came, according to the usual form, first, to desire liberty of access for the House of Commons to the Queen's Majesty's presence upon all urgent and necessary occasions. Secondly, that if in anything himself should mistake or misreport or overslip that which should be committed unto him to declare, that it might without prejudice to the House be better declared, and that his unwilling miscarriage therein might be pardoned. Thirdly, that they might have liberty and freedom of speech in whatsoever they treated of or had occasion to propound and debate in the House.[28]

As part of the "usual form," the monarch "freely" granted these privileges to parliament. But throughout most of her reign, Queen Elizabeth sought to restrict the last of these, and nearly every session of Parliament touched on issues that the queen wished to bar from debate. In 1576 Peter Wentworth delivered his impassioned address on the matter: "Sweet is the name of liberty, but the thing itself a value beyond all inestimable treasure. . . . The inestimable treasure is the use of it in this House. . . . in this House, which is termed a place of free speech, there is nothing so necessary for the preservation of the prince and state as free speech, and without, it is a scorn and mockery to call it a Parliament House, for in truth it is none, but a very school of flattery and dissimulation."[29] For all the Commons' insistence, however, Elizabeth ultimately ruled that all "matters of state" (including her marriage, the royal succession, questions of religion and foreign policy) could not be raised in the House unless she had granted explicit license to do so, as was reported by the lord keeper to the Commons in 1593: "her Majesty granteth you liberal but not licentious speech, liberty therefore but with due limitation. . . . It shall be meet therefore that each man of you contain his speech within the bounds of loyalty and good discretion."[30] Shakespeare appears to slight the fact that the most serious political threats facing Richard also came from his parliaments (although Northumberland acknowledges the will of the Commons when, at Richard's deposition, he begins by reminding the assembled courtiers that the trial was being held at their request: "May it please you, lords, to grant the commons' suit?" [IV.i.154])[31] Shakespeare's Richard, however, refers to the "usual" way Tudor monarchs addressed their parliaments when he grants his assembled subjects free speech, while still, like his Tudor successors, placing implicit limits on what they dared to say.

The privilege of speaking freely is also tied, in *Richard II,* to the charge of speaking truly before the king. At the lists, before their judicial duel, Mowbray and Bolingbroke follow the official procedure for giving testimony, as Richard indicates: "And formally, according to our law, / Depose him in the justice of his cause" (I.iii.29-30). In accordance with that law, the men are charged with speaking the truth before they do battle:

> In God's name and the King's, say who thou
>   art
>
> . . . . .
>
> Speak truly on thy knighthood and thy oath,
> As so defend thee heaven and thy valor!
> (I.iii.11,14-15).[32]

Although the appellants are not required to make a comparable oath at Richard's court, it is important to note that they choose to speak "for the record" none-theless. Bolingbroke asks that his words be entered in the heavenly "plea roll": "heaven be the record to my speech" (I.i.30).[33] And he promises to inflict a fitting self-violence if he fails to speak truly:

> Ere my tongue
> Shall wound my honor with such feeble
>   wrong,
> Or sound so base a parley, my teeth shall tear
> The slavish motive of recanting fear,
> And spit it bleeding in his high disgrace,
> Where shame doth harbor, even in Mowbray's
>   face.
> (I.i.190-95)

But despite these ritual oaths, it becomes clear they are merely paying lip service to what was, in its most generous interpretation, a mere formality. Mowbray, for one, deliberately hedges in responding to Boling-broke's accusations. For convenience, I cite his words again here:

> For Gloucester's death,
> I slew him not, but to my own disgrace
> Neglected my sworn duty in that case.

According to Rossiter, Mowbray's words only make sense in the context of *Woodstock,* where Gloucester had charged Richard's murderer[34] with informing him of any threats to his life. For Rossiter, in other words, Mowbray is claiming to have neglected his duty to pro-tect Gloucester.[35] Alternatively, Mowbray may be refer-ring to his sworn duty to Richard, and the fact that he postponed the murder in direct contradiction to Richard's command.[36] Neither reading, however, acknowledges the likelihood that the earl means to be evasive on this point, that his words deliberately deflect interpretation. He had already hinted that he cannot do otherwise: as he turns to make his own accusations against Bolingbroke, he prefaces his words this way:

> I [can]not of such tame patience boast
> As to be hush'd and nought at all to say.

> [But] the fair reverence of your Highness
>   curbs me
> From giving reins and spurs to my free
>   speech,
> Which else would post until it had return'd
> These terms of treason doubled down his
>   throat.
> (I.i.52-57).

This seems to be an appeal to decorum, his fear of offending the king with the harshness of his charges against Bolingbroke. But in the context of the king's granting the right to "free speech," there is also a hint here that Mowbray cannot or will not speak openly before the king. Mowbray repeatedly expresses a wish that the king wouldn't hear what he has to say:

> O, let my sovereign turn away his face,
> And bid his ears a little while be deaf,
> Till I have told this slander of his blood
> How God and good men hate so foul a liar.
> (111-14).

Larry Champion has suggested that Mowbray, for all his hedging, manages to implicate the king as ulti-mately responsible for the murder. When Richard urges him to give up the quarrel, Mowbray protests, "My life thou shalt command, but not my shame" (166), and hints that the king should assume responsibility for the crime: "Take but my shame, / And I resign my gage" (175-76).[37]

But if he had not done so already, Shakespeare surely makes plain the truth of Mowbray's indictment of Richard by continuing Act I with a scene in which John of Gaunt explicitly names Richard as the per-petrator of the crime: "for God's substitute, / His deputy anointed in His sight, / Hath caus'd his death" (I.ii.37-39). Later, in Act IV, we learn that Boling-broke knows the truth as well: "Now Bagot, freely speak thy mind, / What thou dost know of noble Gloucester's death, / Who wrought it with the King" (IV.i.2-4). We can only guess at Bolingbroke's mo-tives for leaving the king out of his accusations, in the opening scene; whether he means to provoke the king, or protect him, is hard to determine from the text. But the indirectness of Bolingbroke's charge is, like the ambiguity of Mowbray's self-defense, surely a deliberate effort to put "reins" on the free speech neither man dares to deliver. Despite the rights formally granted to his petitioners, and the formal act of deposition that encourages—indeed requires—free speech, it is clear that neither one of Richard's subjects speaks freely at all. Both Mowbray and Bolingbroke deliberately suppress what they know of Richard's role in the plot against Gloucester. If Shakespeare makes the opening of his play seem mysterious, it is only to expose the process by which the truth is forced into hiding.

Richard, no doubt, fears Mowbray's deposition in the opening scene. That much seems clear when, breaking off the duel, he determines to banish him from England forever: "The hopeless word of 'never to return' / Breathe I against thee, upon pain of life" (I.iii.152-53). It is easy to understand why Mowbray, considering what he has done on the king's behalf, is not prepared for the word that Richard breathes against him: "A heavy sentence, my most sovereign liege, / And all unlook'd for from your Highness' mouth" (154-55). Mowbray aptly describes his exile as a kind of linguistic imprisonment, because that is precisely what Richard means it to be:

> The language I have learnt these forty years,
> My native English, now I must forgo,
> And now my tongue's use is to me no more
> Than an unstringed viol or a harp,
> Or like a cunning instrument cas'd up,
> Or being open, put into his hands
> That knows no touch to tune the harmony.
> Within my mouth you have enjail'd my
> tongue,
> Doubly portcullis'd with my teeth and lips,
> And dull unfeeling barren ignorance
> Is made my jailer to attend on me.
>
>   . . . . .
>
> What is thy sentence then but speechless
> death,
> Which robs my tongue from breathing native
> breath?
>   (I.iii.159-69, 172-73).

Richard's sentence is, indeed, a "speechless death" for the man who, should he speak more freely, threatens to expose a dangerous truth in open court. Mowbray's "jailor"—"dull unfeeling barren ignorance"— is surely an intertextual play on the Ignorance who apprehended plain speakers in *Woodstock,* another self-censoring revision of Shakespeare's source. Richard's subjects learn, in this scene, that "the breath of kings" (I.iii.215) is more powerful than their own, that the king's words can will speech or silence. Gaunt bemoans his complicity in his son's fate in exactly these terms: "[Y]ou gave leave to my unwilling tongue / Against my will to do myself this wrong" (I.iii.245-46).

Shakespeare's John of Gaunt seems to represent one of his most radical departures from *Woodstock* as well as from Holinshed, who portrayed him as a fierce and ambitious man. Shakespeare's self-appointed prophet determines, with his dying breath, to "undeaf" Richard's ear with the truth:

> O but they say the tongues of dying men
> Enforce attention like deep harmony.

> Where words are scarce, they are seldom
> spent in vain,
> For they breathe truth that breathe their words
> in pain.
>
>   (II.i.5-8)

But this Gaunt, in fact, is not wholly original in his conception, for he seems to have inherited the outspoken character of Thomas of Woodstock, as he appears in Shakespeare's anonymous source. The idea that Shakespeare drew Gaunt after the model of Woodstock has been argued elsewhere.[38] But what must be emphasized here is the literary procedure by which one character who lives (that is, is represented) in a text resurrects one who is dead and buried (that is, unrepresented); how, both within the text of Shakespeare's play and "between" the texts of *Woodstock* and *Richard II,* Gaunt's transformation marks the return of his repressed brother. It is no coincidence that it is Gaunt who, alone in Shakespeare's play, openly accuses Richard of the murder.[39] Although he alludes to it indirectly at first ("O had thy grandsire with a prophet's eye/ Seen how his son's son should destroy his sons" [II.i.104-5]) he comes out with it at last:

> O, spare me not, my brother Edward's son,
> For that I was his father Edward's son,
> That blood already, like the pelican,
> Hast thou tapp'd out and drunkenly carous'd.
> My brother Gloucester, plain well-meaning
> soul,
> Whom fair befall in heaven 'mongst happy
> souls,
> May be a president and witness good
> That thou respect'st not spilling Edward's
> blood.
>
>   (II.i.124-31)

Through Gaunt, Gloucester is put forward as legal precedent and chief witness in the case against Richard, although he has no actual voice in the play.

Gaunt is also a vocal champion of the divine right of kings (so was Woodstock in Shakespeare's source). As the play's most reliable witness, Gaunt may seem to tip the play's scales of justice in favor of upholding Richard's rule, despite his abuses as king. But if Shakespeare's Gaunt seems to maintain Richard's divine right to rule, he nonetheless removes that right—at least rhetorically. Had Edward III, the great patriarch of the royal family, foreseen Gloucester's murder, Gaunt suggests, "From forth thy reach he would have laid thy shame, / Deposing thee before thou wert possess'd, / Which art possess'd now to depose thyself" (II.i.106-8). Richard, Gaunt asserts, ought to have been deposed before he ever possessed the crown, a paradox that suggests that Richard's deposition, in Gaunt's view, is already a foregone conclusion.[40] Gaunt's son, by implication, has nothing to do with Richard's fall; in his retroactive prophecy, Richard's successor is denied agency in the event. Gaunt's famous elegy to a national paradise lost works to the same effect. His allusion to England as an "other Eden" and "demi-paradise" evokes the original Eden lost through disobedience. Yet, oddly, Gaunt does not pursue the analogy all the way. The obvious parallel he might have drawn—that once again, a paradise will fall through disobedience (that is, rebellion)—is averted. The fall of this Eden, according to Gaunt, is occasioned by Richard's "farming" the nation, for his abuses against the state. Tellingly, Gaunt's death is announced as speechlessness: "His tongue is now a stringless instrument, / Words, life and all, old Lancaster hath spent" (II.i.149-50). His death reminds Richard's subjects of the need for secrecy, and the rebels who plot against Richard become privy whisperers:

> Ross: My heart is great, but it must break
>   with silence,
> Ere't be disburdened with a liberal tongue.
> North: Nay, speak thy mind, and let him ne'er
>   speak more
> That speaks thy words again to do thee
>   harm!
>
> (228-31)

Gaunt's story recapitulates, in part, the Woodstock story; under this cover, Shakespeare recalls the suppression of "liberal tongues" that dared to speak freely in his source.

But the truth about Richard, for all the apparent ambiguity, is evident enough in Shakespeare's version of his story. Richard has broken the law, and, in doing so, undermines his own right to rule, at least according to a constitutionalist stand on the nature of the monarchy.[41] York, as many have noted, makes an analogous case:

> Take Hereford's rights away, and take from
>   Time
> His charters and his customary rights; . . .
> Be not thyself; for how art thou a king
> But by fair sequence and succession?
>   (II.i.195-96, 198-99)

Yet at the official arraignment of Richard in Act IV, scene i, the proceeding in which legal grounds for the deposition of the monarch are brought forward, Richard seems, for some readers, to emerge as the victim rather than the perpetrator of a crime. On close scrutiny, however, the scene upholds Richard's conviction. Bolingbroke, having assumed Richard's role as arbitrator, does not begin straightaway with the deposition, but rather, crucially, by reopening the Gloucester case. As I mentioned earlier, Richard's guilt is taken as a matter of course here; what Bolingbroke seeks to discover is who actually served as Richard's hench-

man, "[w]ho wrought it with the King, and who perform'd / The bloody office of his timeless end" (IV.i.4-5). Once again, free speech is granted: "Now, Bagot, freely speak thy mind" (1); "I know your daring tongue / Scorns to unsay what once it hath delivered" (8-9). Yet the circumstances of Gloucester's death seem to become even more remote, more inaccessible as the scene plays on. Bagot accuses Aumerle, who denies it; Fitzwater rises to second the charge. Surrey charges Fitzwater with slander; Bolingbroke determines to recall Mowbray from exile to "enforce his trial" all over again. But Mowbray, Bolingbroke learns, is dead, and for lack of sufficient evidence, Bolingbroke leaves the matter under gage, and the issue is never (openly) raised again in the play. The scene seems designed to further the confusion over the Gloucester case, to suggest that the truth—given the death of a chief witness—will never be known. No doubt, the conflicting testimony given by the appellants in this scene has contributed to the illusion that Shakespeare never assigns blame in the case.

But the confusion the scene creates, the gesture it offers of deferring judgment, is a ruse, designed precisely to distract readers from the one truth that remains, however deeply it is buried in the record of the play: Richard's guilt in the murder of his uncle. Act IV, scene i, is the scene of Richard's trial—a trial which *begins* by reopening the case of Gloucester's murder before it proceeds to the deposition. The so-called "deposition scene" begins, in other words, by rehearsing (though not freely) the testimony in the prosecution of Gloucester's murderer. The truth about Richard is thus established long before the only official legal action taken against him in the play. Shakespeare insists that we judge Richard's deposition in the context of all the "depositions"—albeit unofficial—given in the earlier part of the play.

To be sure, Richard's dethronement is immediately preceded by Carlisle's impassioned plea for Richard's divine right to rule, condemning those who would seek to judge God's anointed: "Would God that any in this noble presence / Were enough noble to be upright judge / Of noble Richard! / . . . What subject can give sentence on his king? / And who sits here that is not Richard's subject?" (IV.i.117-19, 121-22). What might have passed as a legal deposition is, in Carlisle's view, a usurpation, a crime against God and God's deputy. But there is further evidence that Shakespeare aims to discredit the perspective that Carlisle shares, most of all, with Richard. Shakespeare's departures from Holinshed in this scene, for example, are instructive. In his chronicle, Holinshed describes the formal accusations presented by Parliament "to the end the commons might be persuaded, that he was an vnprofitable prince to the common-wealth, and worthie to be deposed." Holinshed's Richard actually insists on reading the thirty-three articles aloud before the assembled court: "for the more suretie of the matter, and for that the said resignation should have his full force and strength, himself therefore read the scroll of resignation."[42] Shakespeare's Richard, however, refuses to read the list of his crimes, saying that he will read, instead "the very book indeed / Where all my sins are writ, and that's myself" (IV.i.274-75). For some commentators, this is proof enough that "[n]either Richard nor Shakespeare is willing to comply" with the deposition,[43] that the playwright, no less than the king himself, cannot condone the act. Janet Clare speculates that Shakespeare's version of the scene may be evidence of self-censorship, in that he deliberately suppressed the fact that Richard publicly confessed to misgoverning the realm.[44] But Richard's refusal to read the paper before him is not necessarily evidence of the king's innocence. Shakespeare shows us that Richard, after all, can hardly be taken as as a reliable judge in his own case. Rather than reading the record of his crimes, Richard proposes to read himself, and what he sees— the "brittle glory" that shines in the "flatt'ring glass" (IV.i.287, 279)—bears little resemblance to the Richard seen in the earlier part of the play. Richard is a bad reader as well as a bad judge; or rather, Richard cannot adequately judge because he cannot accurately read the text of his own life. What is more disturbing, however, is the way that Richard's tendency to misread himself becomes endemic to the play as a whole as it draws to its conclusion.

There has long been critical admiration for the "poet-king so much enchanted by the resources, limitations, and ambiguities of language [that he] . . . never stoop[s] to prose."[45] It seems somehow fitting that this "born poet" easily reimagines himself as text, as the subject of narrative. No sooner does he foresee imminent defeat at the rebels' hands, in Act III, than Richard begins to write his own story, and to include it along with stories like his own:

> Let's talk of graves, of worms, and epitaphs,
> Make dust our paper, and with rainy eyes
> Write sorrow on the bosom of the earth.
>
> . . . . .
>
> For God's sake let us sit upon the ground
> And tell sad stories of the death of kings:
> How some have been depos'd, some slain in
> war,
> Some haunted by the ghosts they have
> deposed,
> Some poisoned by their wives, some sleeping
> kill'd,
> All murthered—
>   (III.ii.145-47, 155-60)

He refers to his own "sad story" again as he bids his queen farewell, entreating her to tell it to others:

> In winter's tedious nights sit by the fire
> With good old folks and let them tell thee tales
> Of woeful ages long ago betid;
> And ere thou bid good night, to quite their
> griefs,
> Tell thou the lamentable tale of me,
> And send the hearers weeping to their beds.
>
> . . . . .
>
> And some will mourn in ashes, some coal-
> black,
> For the deposing of a rightful king.
>   (V.i.40-45, 49-50)

For all Richard's undeniable gifts with language, he is in one sense no better at writing than at reading, for the "lamentable tale" he sketches here, again, has little to do with his story as represented in the text of Shakespeare's play. The fact that Richard is a gifted poet is surely not grounds for his moral (or legal) acquittal. Richard III is a brilliant actor, but no less a villain, however entertaining or attractive; Richard II may be a "born poet," but he is still, in the judgment of the play, a king who is justifiably deposed. There is no reason to assume that Shakespeare identified rhetorical might with right. Indeed, Shakespeare suggests that Richard's linguistic abilities make him (like Richard III) all the more dangerous, in the long-run of history. It is surely no coincidence that Richard becomes "poetic" after he is deposed: Readers who remember Richard as the flawed but sensitive "poet king" fall prey to the trap that Richard himself, in Shakespeare's account, sets for posterity. The king who begins the play by censoring his subjects' testimony aptly ends by attempting to censor the larger "testimony" in the prosecution of his reign.

The story Shakespeare tells in *Richard II* is as self-reflective as its protagonist, for the play is preoccupied with the way stories are written and rewritten, and the fate of "truth" in the transaction. Shakespeare's own relationship to competing versions of Richard's story may well have, in part, inspired these concerns;[46] but the conditions of writing in early modern England no doubt made these issues even more urgent. The play continually alludes to the instability of texts, of stories that can be rewritten and revised. One such "story," the scriptural account of the Fall, is retold several times over the course of *Richard II.* In Gaunt's original version, the "second Fall" is occasioned by Richard's mismanagement of England. The gardeners stress horticulture over scripture, but ultimately concur in Gaunt's judgment that Richard is ultimately responsible for the "garden" going to seed:

> O, what pity is it
> That he had not so trimm'd and dress'd his
> land
> As we this garden!

. . . . .

Superfluous branches
We lop away, that bearing boughs may live;
Had he done so, himself had borne the crown,
Which waste of idle hours hath quite thrown
    down.

                              (III.iv.55-57, 63-66)

Yet the Queen, overhearing them ("O, I am press'd to
death through want of speaking!" [III.iv.72])[47] retells
the story so that Richard is no longer to blame, but
rather the victim of others' wrongdoing:

What Eve, what serpent, hath suggested thee
To make a second fall of cursed man?
Why dost thou say King Richard is depos'd?
Dar'st thou, thou little better thing than earth,
Divine his downfall?

                              (III.iv.75-79)

Generations of readers after Richard's Queen would
reread the "Fall" represented in the play with the same
nostalgic revisionism. But perhaps the most important
narrative that is translated over the course of the play
is the story of Cain's murder of his brother Abel. At
the start of *Richard II,* Bolingbroke sets the mark of
Cain on the man who

[L]ike a traitor coward,
Sluic'd out [Gloucester's] innocent soul
    through streams of blood,
Which blood, like sacrificing Abel's, cries,
Even from the tongueless caverns of the earth,
To me for justice and rough chastisement.

                              (I.i.102-6)

At the end of the play, as many have noted, Bolingbroke
transfers that mark to the man who has murdered Richard: "With Cain go wander thorough shades of night,
/ And never show thy head by day nor light" (V.vi.43-
44). There is no reason to doubt that Bolingbroke, who
openly assumes the guilt for Richard's murder, rightly
assumes the identification that once belonged, exclusively, to Richard. But the danger in this translation is
that the new version of the story—with King Henry as
Cain and Richard as Abel—threatens to expunge the
earlier version altogether. The murdered Gloucester,
though "tongueless," still cries out for retribution;
Richard is still Cain, even if he is legitimately transcribed as Abel in the newest account of his story. It
is easy enough to forget the earlier version, but it is
precisely this kind of erasure that the play, on a closer
reading, recovers.

Shakespeare has often been credited with impartiality
in his judgment of his characters, and his apparent
even-handedness in identifying both Richard and King
Henry with Cain may seem to corroborate this idea.

But the notion that Shakespeare refused to pass judgment on either Richard or Bolingbroke, or that he made
them accomplices in the same crime, seriously misrep-
resents the way the testimony of the play itself is brought
forward and then self-consciously revoked. The early
part of the play, when Richard is still king, bears witness to his numerous crimes; Richard is implicated,
repeatedly, in his own deposition. Shakespeare also radically limits the role of the favorites—even the author of
Woodstock, no great partisan of Richard's, foregrounded
their evil influence on the young king—and isolates
Richard as his own worst enemy.[48] The king reads his
deposition as a violent crime: We hear him continually
speak of himself as a murdered king when only his
dethronement is in question. But, once again, this is
Richard's (mis) reading of the event, and not Shakespeare's. The reason it is so easy to accept Richard's
version of his deposition is because Richard *is* ultimately
murdered so that, with hindsight, his rendition of the
event passes for prophecy, for a truth yet to be revealed.
But the fact that Richard is the victim of a violent crime
at the end of the play does not, retroactively, make his
deposition a crime as well, and reading this way, again,
only underscores the dangers of revision.

Bolingbroke, too, undergoes a "revision" over the
course of the play. His motives at the start are only
vaguely represented, and it is far easier to assign his
guilt with the benefit of hindsight, that is, when we
know him not just as the man who deposed Richard
but as Richard's murderer. King Henry, after all, expresses remorse only for the murder of Richard; only
then does he fear recriminations:

Exton, I thank thee not, for thou hast wrought
A deed of slander with thy fatal hand
Upon my head and all this famous land.

                              (V.vi.34-36)

And Henry, as Shakespeare knows, has reason to fear
the deed as a "slanderous" one, an act that future generations will use—rightly or wrongly—to rescript the
story of Henry's rise to power. By the end of the play,
moreover, it seems that this process has already begun.
Richard's own version of his story, the "sad tale" he
entreats his former subjects to tell over and over, already threatens to rewrite everything that has come
before, to pass over an original account in favor of his
own rendition of the past. York rehearses the "story"
of the procession of the two cousins through London,
a retelling of a scene Shakespeare does not let us witness firsthand. York explicitly describes the scene as a
"dramatized" one; the two men are viewed by their
countrymen "[a]s in a theatre" (V.ii.23). In his account,
Richard already appears as a martyr, a second Christ
on his march to Golgotha:

[D]ust was thrown upon his sacred head,
Which with such gentle sorrow he shook off,

His face still combating with tears and smiles,
The badges of his grief and patience,
That had not God, for some strong purpose,
  steel'd
The hearts of men, they must perforce have
  melted.

                           (V.ii.30-35)

Richard, of course, favored this identification as well, but his reign—as represented in this play—hardly sustains such an analogy. By *1 Henry IV*, Richard will be remembered as a "sweet lovely rose" (I.iii.175) supplanted by a cankerous usurper, but the sources of this "memory," too, can already be traced here.

The greatest threat that *Richard II* potentially posed to Shakespeare's own queen was not the deposition (or dethronement) of the monarch represented there, but rather the "depositions" or testimonials offered against him throughout the play. This threat survives even the excision of the "deposition scene" itself; this single act of censorship (or self-censorship) cannot contain it. Nor is Richard's "trial" contained by the bounds of Act IV, scene i. The legal framework of *Richard II*—initiated by the opening "courtroom" drama—is never abandoned as the play progresses; rather, the play as a whole forms the site where depositions are given, and judgment is passed. Despite the weight of the evidence against its protagonist, *Richard II* recapitulates the way that testimony—the truth about Richard[49]—is ultimately suppressed in favor of a lie that Richard himself is instrumental in promulgating. The Gloucester case, especially, speaks powerfully against reading Richard's dethronement as a "lamentable tale," whatever follows later in the play. The near-suppression of the Gloucester case, so crucial in the larger case of Richard, is just one example of the way that the play manages to leave traces of evidence even as it practices self-censorship. In the sixteenth century, it may well have been inevitable that a writer, like the Schoolmaster in *Woodstock,* would develop strategies to forestall censure. But *Richard II* goes further, revealing the way that "telling tales" is, inevitably, bound up in procedures of censorship, in acts of judgment that, by their very nature, sentence something or someone to silence. Shakespeare's *Richard II* is, after all, one more revision, one more "record" of depositions taken two hundred years before the playwright's time. Yet by exposing the complicity of writing in the practice, the play offers hope that the truth will out, however suspect the record. Edward, the young Prince in *Richard III*, held out exactly the same hope, almost as if he foresaw his fate—to be smothered on command of the king:

But say, my lord, it were not regist'red,
Methinks the truth should live from age to
  age,
As 'twere retail'd to all posterity,
Even to the general all-ending day.[50]

Notes

[1] All quotations from *Richard II* refer to *The Riverside Shakespeare,* ed. G. Blakemore Evans (Boston: Houghton Mifflin, 1974).

[2] The publisher of the Fourth Quarto of 1608 advertised these additions on the title page.

[3] Janet Clare, for example, has suggested that Shakespeare may have had a hand in suppressing the scene not only in published versions of the play but in Elizabethan performances as well. See "The Censorship of the Deposition Scene in *Richard II,*" *The Review of English Studies,* 41 (1990), 89-94. Leeds Barroll, on the other hand, has challenged the assumption that this scene was suppressed; he argues that it may have simply been added to the later quartos by the playwright. See "A New History for Shakespeare and his Time." *Shakespeare Quarterly,* 39 (1988), 441-64, esp. 447-49.

[4] Marjorie Garber has noted several meanings of "deposition" that are in play in *Richard II,* including "the lowering of Christ's body from the cross—Richard's view of the event" (*Shakespeare's Ghost Writers: Literature as Uncanny Causality* [London: Methuen, 1987], p. 20). Jonathan Goldberg, pursuing Garber's insight further, suggests that Richard, in refusing to read the document detailing his crimes in Act IV, scene i, marks written depositions—and by implication, all writing—as "rebel texts." For Goldberg, Richard is logocentric, in the Derridean sense, in his suppression of writing in favor of the primacy of speech. See "Rebel Letters: Postal Effects from Richard II to Henry IV," *Renaissance Drama,* 19 (1988), 3-28, esp. 3-10. While I agree that Richard aims to suppress certain "depositions" in the play, these may be either spoken or written forms of testimony; moreover, I believe the play implicates Richard in the "rewriting" of his realm (that is, in the repression and revision of certain testimony) rather than in the repression of all "textuality."

[5] See, for example, Donna Hamilton's "The State of Law in *Richard II,*" *Shakespeare Quarterly,* 34 (1983), 5-17, and W. F. Bolton's "Ricardian Law Reports and *Richard II,*" *Shakespeare Studies,* 20 (1988), 53-65.

[6] "On wednesdaie following, request was made by the commons, that sith king Richard had resigned, and was lawfullie deposed from his roiall dignitie, he might haue iudgement decreed against him, so as the realme were not troubled by him, and that the causes of his deposing might be published through the realme for satisfieng of the people: which demand was granted"; in Allardyce Nicoll and Josephine Nicoll, eds., *Holinshed's Chronicle: As Used in Shakespeare's Plays* (London: J. M. Dent, 1927), p. 43.

[7] The first is quoted in Larry Champion's "The Function of Mowbray: Shakespeare's Maturing Artistry in *Richard II,*" *Shakespeare Quarterly,* 26 (1975), 3-7, 6. The second comes from *Richard II,* ed. J. Dover Wilson (Cambridge: Cambridge Univ. Press, 1961), p. lxviii.

[8] E. M. W. Tillyard, *Shakespeare's History Plays* (New York: Macmillan, 1946), p. 261.

[9] A. P. Rossiter makes this case in the preface to his edition of Shakespeare's anonymous source, *Woodstock: A Moral History* (London: Chatto and Windus, 1946), p. 48.

[10] I am indebted to Annabel Patterson's *Censorship and Interpretation: The Conditions of Writing and Reading in Early Modern England* (Madison: Univ. of Wisconsin Press, 1984) for her discussion of the ways in which "'literature' in the early modern period was conceived in part as the way around censorship" (p. 63) and for detailing some of the self-censoring strategies employed by Renaissance writers.

[11] Rossiter, pp. 47-53.

[12] Nicoll and Nicoll, p. 24.

[13] Nicoll and Nicoll, pp. 25-26.

[14] All quotations from *Woodstock* are taken from A. P. Rossiter's edition.

[15] As in Shakespeare, this Richard "farms the realm" by issuing blank charters that license his favorites to collect funds, at will, from his subjects.

[16] Tresilian, who does not appear in Shakespeare's play, is a lawyer whom Richard advances to the status of Lord Chief Justice in *Woodstock.* Tresilian continually reinterprets the law to his own advantage.

[17] For a detailed discussion of these laws, see John Bellamy, *The Tudor Law of Treason* (London: Routledge & Kegan Paul, 1979); for a more general discussion of treason and libel in the period, see Penry Williams, *The Tudor Regime* (Oxford: Clarendon Press, 1979), pp. 375-94.

[18] Bellamy, p. 27; Williams, p. 376.

[19] Williams, p. 391. Bellamy asserts that "traitorous words were really the centre-piece" of the legislation of 1534 (p. 31).

[20] Williams, pp. 390-91.

[21] Rossiter, p. 31. In fact, only Woodstock himself invokes the Tudor doctrine of passive obedience in the play, just before he is apprehended by the king and his favorites: "But he's our king: and God's great deputy; / And if ye hunt to have me second ye / In any rash attempt against his state, / Afore my God, I'll ne'er consent unto it" (IV.ii.144-7). But the fact that he is subsequently murdered by Richard casts doubt on the legitimacy of the doctrine. Even Woodstock is sympathetic with the plight of those who rebel against the king: "Afore my God I cannot blame them for it: / He might as well have sent defiance to them. / O vulture England, wilt thou eat thine own? / Can they be rebels called, that now turn head?" (III.ii.82-85).

[22] Rossiter, p. 28.

[23] David Bevington's edition of Shakespeare's works cites *Woodstock* as issuing "almost a call for open rebellion against tyranny" (*The Complete Works of Shakespeare,* 4th ed. [New York: HarperCollins, 1992], Appendix 2, p. 37).

[24] Nicoll and Nicoll, p. 24.

[25] Nicoll and Nicoll, p. 20.

[26] Nicoll and Nicoll, pp. 28-29.

[27] G. R. Elton, ed. *The Tudor Constitution: Documents and Commentary* (Cambridge: Cambridge Univ. Press, 1962), p. 255.

[28] Elton, p. 261.

[29] Elton, p. 263.

[30] Elton, pp. 266-67.

[31] See Bryce Lyon, *A Constitutional and Legal History of Medieval England* (New York: Harper & Row, 1960), pp. 491-95 for a summary of Richard's struggles with Parliament; in Lyon's account, the deposition was the final solution for a king who "conceived of himself as an absolute monarch unrestricted by law or by parliament" (p. 494).

[32] See Henry Charles Lea, *The Duel and the Oath* (Philadelphia: Univ. of Pennsylvania Press, 1974), esp. pp. 116-79, for a history of judicial battles and the oaths that commenced them.

[33] Bolton discusses several references in the play to the official legal record or "plea rolls" of the fourteenth century (in use through Shakespeare's day), p. 53.

[34] In *Woodstock,* a man named Lapoole corresponds with Shakespeare's Mowbray.

[35] Rossiter, p. 48.

[36] C. G. Thayer, *Shakespearean Politics: Government and Misgovernment in the Great Histories* (Athens: Ohio Univ. Press, 1983), p. 16.

[37] Champion, pp. 5-6.

[38] Rossiter, p. 50.

[39] A. L. French ("*Richard II* and the Woodstock Murder," *Shakespeare Quarterly,* 22 [1971], 337-44), has argued that Richard shows increasing hostility towards Gaunt in the early acts of the play because of his knowledge of the murder. That hostility, French claims, culminates in Richard's seizure of Gaunt's property, an act which should rightly be understood as one of revenge. French suggests that the Gloucester subplot is central to the play because it underlies all the action up through the end of II.i. I argue that it continues to be central to the play as a whole.

[40] It is possible that Shakespeare would have expected his audience to understand Gaunt's prophecy as treasonous. In the sixteenth century, Bellamy notes, prophecies foretelling the death or deposition of the king were often interpreted as "imagining" or compassing the king's death (p. 52).

[41] See Lyon, p. 503, for a concise discussion of the historical legality of Richard's deposition. Anthony Tuck reminds us that the historical Gloucester was closely associated with the constitutionalist challenge to the idea of divine right, that is, with a belief in the parliament's right to depose a king:

> Gloucester's political attitudes were formed not only by considerations of prestige and self-interest, however, but also by a view of government and of the relationship between the king and the law which was common and traditional among men of his class. . . . [H]e and Bishop Arundel, presenting an address from the whole parliament, insisted upon the king's obligation to rule in accordance with the laws of the kingdom and the advice of the magnates, contrasting this ideal with the king's stubborn adherence to unwise council and to his own will in government. The final and most telling point of their speech was their assertion that the community had the right to depose a king if he refused to be governed and ruled by the laws of the kingdom and the advice of the lords. (p. 103)

See Tuck, *Richard II and the English Nobility* (New York: St Martin's Press, 1974). I am suggesting, throughout this essay, that Shakespeare supported the constitutionalist position.

[42] Nicoll and Nicoll, p. 44.

[43] Phyllis Rackin, *Stages of History: Shakespeare's English Chronicles.* (Ithaca: Cornell Univ. Press, 1990), pp. 129-30.

[44] Clare, p. 93.

[45] Herschel Baker, preface to *Richard II,* in *Riverside Shakespeare,* p. 803.

[46] As Henry Ansgar Kelly has demonstrated (*Divine Providence in the England of Shakespeare's Histories* [Cambridge, Mass: Harvard Univ. Press, 1970]), Shakespeare's sources (including Holinshed and, perhaps, Daniel's *Civil Wars* and *The Mirror for Magistrates*) were hardly in agreement about Richard or the reasons for his fall from power.

[47] The Queen is probably referring to the "customary penalty in England for refusing to plead guilty or not guilty before a court; i.e. for remaining silent" (*Riverside,* p. 826n.) If so, it is interesting to note that the Queen, too, participates in the play's preoccupation with legal questions of "free" and enforced speech.

[48] Despite several comments about the evil influence of the favorites in Shakespeare's play (the gardeners, for example, charge them with corruption), Bushy, Bagot, and Greene are portrayed in a surprisingly agreeable light here. They are kind to the queen in II.i. and almost noble in defeat in III.i.

[49] I do not, by this, mean to privilege any particular *version* of Richard's deposition as the "true" one, in some absolute sense. I do believe, however, that Shakespeare marks "rewriting" in *Richard II* as a distortion of evidence (i.e., a distortion of what was originally "evident"), whether or not the "truth" itself is ever recoverable.

[50] III.i.75-78. In this scene, Prince Edward is asking his uncle to verify the story that Julius Caesar built the tower. But his concern for the survival of the truth, with or without written corroboration, pertains just as well to Richard III and his "plots."

Source: "Speaking Freely about Richard II," in *Journal of English and Germanic Philology*, Vol. 96, No. 3, July, 1997, pp. 327-48.

Shakespeare's *King Richard III* and the Problematics of Tudor Bastardy

Maurice Hunt, *Baylor University*

Granted Queen Elizabeth's touchiness concerning the subject of royal bastardy, Shakespeare ran a risk in *King Richard III* by focusing questions of bastardy in such a way that they invite comparison with problematical details of bastardy in the Tudor succession. The queen's life-long association with bastardy makes Shakespeare's emphasis surprising.[1] Analysis of Tudor bastardy reveals the emergence of a paradigm of illegitimate legitimacy (or legitimate illegitimacy), a composite reproduced in the discourse on royal bastardy in *King Richard III*. The ambiguous melding of legitimate illegitimacy that allowed Elizabeth, her half-sister and half-brother, and her grandfather to side-step challenges to their right to rule (or potentially to rule) reappears in the play in the rationale that Richard of Gloucester uses to dispossess his nephews and seize the crown. Nevertheless, Shakespeare's dramaturgy finally exonerates rather than undercuts the Tudor monarchy. In the play the growth of bastardy into a metaphor for a certain illegitimacy of human nature transforms the dramatic debate into one of everyman's existential legitimacy or illegitimacy. In this respect, a figurative bastard is much worse than a ruler of moral character who may (or may not) be a bastard in the technical sense of the word. The legitimately born "bastard" Richard and the pious, ethical Henry, Earl of Richmond, who is tainted with bastardy in the play (as he was in life), illustrate this paradoxical idea.

Understanding the problematical history of Tudor bastardy becomes a prerequisite for fully appreciating the representation of royal illegitimacy in *King Richard III*. Charges of bastardy afflicted the Tudors before and even during the historical times depicted in *King Richard III*. Henry VII's paternal grandfather, Owen Tudor, and Catharine of Valois, the widow of Henry V, fell in love and had three sons (Edmund, Jasper, and Owen); but the parents may never have married. This ambiguity invited the stigma of bastardy. Because the boys were the children of a former queen of England, those guarding the rights of the minor Henry VI such as Humphrey, Duke of Gloucester regarded the children as a threat and so branded them illegitimate. Still, King Henry VI countenanced Owen Tudor's sons, making them royal half-brothers. Edmund Tudor—Henry VII's father—in 1453 at age twenty-three became the Earl of Richmond. Concerning this recognition, Eric Simons speculates, "whether [King Henry VI] and his Council were now convinced that [the young men's] parents had been truly married at their birth, or whether they considered it politically advis-

able to remove the stigma of bastardy from the royal half-brothers, cannot be said" (6). In 1459-60, an act of Parliament affirmed the legitimacy of Edmund, Jasper, and Owen Tudor, chiefly because of their father's Lancastrian services during the Wars of the Roses (Simons 5-6). Nevertheless, the taint of bastardy continued to surround the births of certain progenitors of the founder of the Tudor monarchy—Henry VII.

Henry VII's maternal great grandfather, John Beaufort, Earl of Somerset, was—in Simons's words—"technically a bastard" (6). King Henry IV had specifically excluded the Beauforts from the order of succession. The kingship claim of Edmund Tudor's son, Henry, Earl of Richmond, depended principally on the young man's descent from Catharine of Valois and from Edward III's son John of Gaunt via Lady Margaret Beaufort, granddaughter of John Beaufort (Given-Wilson and Curteis 18). Yet we have seen that both of these routes included the quicksand of original bastardy charges. After the final Lancastrian defeat at Tewkesbury and the ascension of the York King Edward IV, Henry and his uncle Jasper Tudor sought refuge in France. In January 1485, the new king Richard III "obtained the outlawry of the Earl of Richmond and the Countess of Richmond, his mother" (Simons 26). In June 1485, Richard, waiting for Henry Tudor's imminent invasion, at Nottingham issued a proclamation declaring that Henry "'is descended of bastard blood both of the father's side and of the mother's side, for the said Owen his grandfather was bastard born, and his mother was daughter unto John duke of Somerset, son unto Dame Katherine Swynford, and of her in double adultery begotten, whereby it evidently appeareth that no title can or may be in him, who fully intendeth to enter this realm purposing a conquest'" (Given-Wilson and Curteis 159).

Richard labored incessantly to resurrect the skeleton in the Tudor closet. Just prior to Henry's second, successful departure from France with an invasionary force, Richard hysterically proclaimed that "Henry and his followers were 'open murderers and extortioners,' and imputing dishonour to his grandmother [Catharine of Valois], Henry himself a bastard of both families, an accusation of which his countrymen must by now have been growing weary" (Simons 33). The question of Tudor bastardy was sufficiently alive that Henry, after Richard's defeat, felt compelled to authorize his claim to the throne partly "by right of the formal legitimization of his birth previously established in an earlier session of Parliament" (Simons 67).

Henry VIII's reign again raised the specter of Tudor bastardy. Long-running accusations of illegitimacy blasted the lives of three of his four children surviving infancy—those of Mary, Henry (later Duke of Somerset and Richmond), and of course Elizabeth. Only the future Edward VI, the son of Jane Seymour, escaped unscathed. Mary's case is perhaps the most pathetic. On 20 April 1534, "all the craftes in London were called to their halls, and there were sworne on a booke to be true to Queene Anne and to beleeve and take her for lawfull wife of the Kinge and rightfull Queene of Englande, and utterlie to thinke the Ladie Marie, daughter to the Kinge by Queene Katherin, but as a bastarde, and thus to doe without any scrupulositie of conscience" (Wriothesley 1:24). Mary Tudor remained an official bastard throughout much of Henry VIII's and all of Edward VI's reigns, until 1553 (after her ascension to the throne) when Parliament declared Henry VIII's divorce from Katharine of Aragon illegal and Mary legitimate.

Mary was usually kept during her father's lifetime far from court, forced to follow with less pomp Elizabeth and Edward in royal processions. Even though she was a proclaimed bastard, Mary followed Edward in the line of succession in her father's will. However, in January 1553, Edward, with only a few months to live, "drew up . . . an elaborate 'device,' directing the succession in the event of his own death without heirs, to the descendants of his aunt Mary by Charles Brandon, Duke of Suffolk. Both his sisters he excluded on the grounds of their illegitimacy" (Loades 15). The descendants of Edward's aunt Mary included the Ladies Catharine, Mary, and Jane Grey. Later the device was tampered with to exclude Frances Grey and make Jane Grey, who represented in early 1553 an unpopular radical protestantism, the royal heir (Loades 16). What allowed Edward VI and his protestant adherents to override the strong legality of Henry VIII's will in the matter of succession so as to bar Mary from the crown was the persisting cancer of her bastardy. Nevertheless, after Edward's death, Mary Tudor squelched Lady Jane Grey and her allies. Henry VIII's will—not Mary's birth—dictated her right to the throne. According to David Loades, "it was not the [legitimacy] of Mary Tudor's birth which was proclaimed in July 1553 but the force of her father's will, and of the statute which authorised it" (17). Only by stacking Parliament could Mary legitimize herself. But as history repeatedly demonstrated from the time of Owen Tudor in the mid-fifteenth century to the present day of 1553, this legislative method for "proving" (or "disproving") legitimacy had transparently become the tool of political opportunists, often of the crassest stripe. This fact made it easier for protestants, both at home and abroad, to continue to insist upon Mary's bastardy and thus upon her usurpation of the throne.

For a period of Henry VIII's reign, a legitimate male royal bastard was deemed a better heir to the crown than either one of two reputed female royal bastards. Henry, surnamed Fitzroy, was described as "a base sonne of our soveraigne King Henrie the Eight, borne of my Ladie Taylebuse, that time called Elizabeth Blunt" (Wriothesley 1:53). King Henry affectionately lavished honors on his first male offspring surviving childhood, making him at age six a Knight of the Garter and later Duke of Norfolk. Henry married his publicly acknowledged bastard to Lady Mary, daughter of the Duke of Norfolk. On 26 July 1525, Henry the base son became Admiral of England; two years later he assumed the wardenship of the marches toward Scotland. The lieutenancy of Ireland constituted a final recognition of young Henry's worth. This preferment prompted contemporary and later observers of Henry VIII's reign to conclude that the king "procured the Act of Parliament empowering him to bequeath his crown in order that he might settle it upon young Henry in the event of his having no male issue by Jane Seymour" (Wriothesley 1:53). Likewise, H. Maynard Smith judges that King Henry's making his bastard Duke of Richmond involved the question of succession, "for Richmond had been the title of his grandmother, Lady Margaret Beaufort, through whom the Tudors derived their claim to the throne" (7). Henry VIII's ultimate intentions with regard to his base son were never known; young Henry died on 22 July 1536, and legitimate Prince Edward was born on 12 October 1537. In many respects, the figurative legitimacy that King Henry created for his orthodox bastard problematizes the bastardy foisted upon his more legitimately born bastard daughters Mary and Elizabeth.

Since Shakespeare presented *King Richard III* during the reign of Elizabeth (the queen may in fact have seen one or more performances of the play), the complex problem of her illegitimacy becomes important for certain aspects of royal bastardy staged in the tragedy. Henry VIII covertly married Anne Boleyn near the end of January 1533; he had been living openly with her since 1531, after he sent Katharine of Aragon from the court. Conceived while Henry was still married to Katharine (Cranmer in mid-1533 declared Henry's marriage to Katharine null), Elizabeth was born only seven months after Henry's and Anne's secret marriage. On 11 July 1533, at Charles V's insistence, Pope Clement VII "issued a bull declaring that Henry was unlawfully cohabitating with Anne Boleyn, and that any child born of their union would be illegitimate" (Ridley 22). But Henry stubbornly insisted that Mary was a bastard and Elizabeth the true heir to the throne until God sent him a son. The Act of Succession of March 1534 required citizens on demand to swear that the children of Henry and Queen Anne were the legitimate heirs of the crown. But considerable grumbling and protest arose; for many of Henry's subjects, "Catherine was still 'the Queen' and Mary 'the Princess.' Anne was 'the concubine,' and Elizabeth 'the little bastard'" (Ridley 23).

On May Day 1536, Anne's arrest purportedly for having committed adultery with five men and for having planned to kill Henry suddenly authorized the murmurings about Elizabeth's baseness. Now Henry's opponents could argue that Elizabeth was not only a bastard but was most likely not even a royal bastard. The New Act of Succession of July 1536 legally bastardized Elizabeth and Mary, chiefly so that the expected children of Henry and Jane Seymour would have no rival claimants to the monarchy. Henry and Cranmer found a basis for declaring the king's marriage to Anne Boleyn illegal: Henry had had sexual intercourse with Mary, Anne's sister, before he carnally knew his future queen. Nevertheless, the official bastardizing of Elizabeth did not preclude her from a place in Henry's will, after Prince Edward and his issue, after the children that King Henry might have by Katharine Parr, and after Mary and her issue.

Elizabeth remained an official bastard throughout Mary's reign, especially once the new queen proclaimed in October 1553 that she was the legitimate daughter of Henry's lawful marriage to Katharine of Aragon. Even though Elizabeth's bastardy prevented Philip II of Spain from considering her a potential wife, once he was married to Mary, he favored Elizabeth, continually seeking a Catholic husband for her—mainly because Mary Queen of Scots had married the Dauphin of France and thus posed a succession threat in England that the presence of a married Catholic Elizabeth could obstruct. As Mary's savage reign wore on, tampering with Henry VIII's will to exclude the official bastard from succession became less and less advisable. Catholic efforts to protect base-born Elizabeth's royal status thus reflect the continuing problematics of Tudor bastardy, which from its inception paradoxically conflated legitimacy and illegitimacy.

Mary's death on 17 November 1558 gave Elizabeth rule of England, and the new queen quickly revealed her hidden protestantism. During the Parliament of 1559, a decision was made that would prove momentous for later sixteenth-century literary depictions of Elizabeth and the issue of royal bastardy. Elizabeth's counselors advised her *not* to repeal the Act of 1536 which bastardized her, or to proclaim her biological legitimacy. "This was done largely on the advice of Sir Nicholas Bacon, the Lord Keeper of the Great Seal. He argued that as Elizabeth was in any case entitled to succeed to the crown under Henry's will, there was no point in reopening old controversies by looking into the events of 1536. Instead Parliament quickly passed a bill which enabled Elizabeth to succeed to her mother's property, notwithstanding any forfeiture imposed by law or by previous statutes" (Ridley 85-86).

In effect, this decision made at the beginning of Elizabeth's long rule kept her bastardization official throughout her lifetime. It remained a major weapon in the unflagging campaign of her adversaries against the "bastard" queen and her "illegitimate" government. One noteworthy example can stand for the hundreds, even thousands, of accusations of bastardy directed against Queen Elizabeth until her death in 1603. In 1588 Cardinal William Allen, leader of English Catholics abroad, published in Antwerp in English a book titled *An Admonition to the Nobility and People of England and Ireland Concerning the Present Wars,* which was intended for distribution in England after the Spanish Armada had landed there. As was often the case, Elizabeth was unsuccessful in her attempts to suppress Allen's treatise and punish the European publisher and printer. In this book Allen "denounced Elizabeth [as] the issue of the 'incestuous copulation' of her 'supposed father' Henry VIII, with an 'infamous courtesan' Anne Boleyn" (Ridley 282). Similar blackenings of Elizabeth's character determined the compensatory nature of many literary depictions of the queen, including those of Edmund Spenser.[2]

If certain members of Elizabethan audiences of *King Richard III* sought a sixteenth-century context for understanding Shakespeare's staging of royal bastardy in *King Richard III,*[3] memorable scenarios of illegitimacy from Henry VIII's reign supplied it. In act III, charges of bastardy become Richard of Gloucester's weapon for destroying the right of his nephews to the crown. Richard tells his henchman Buckingham to "infer the bastardy of Edward's children" (III.v.74)[4] when speaking to the Mayor and citizens of London. So ambitious is Richard for the kingship that he additionally is willing to taint his brother Edward, his mother, and nearly himself with illegitimacy. "Nay, for a need," Richard instructs his tool Buckingham,

> thus far come near my person:
> Tell them, when that my mother went with
>   child
> Of that insatiate Edward, noble York
> My princely father then had wars in France,
> And by true computation of the time
> Found that the issue was not his-begot;
> Which well appeared in his lineaments,
> Being nothing like the noble Duke my
>   father—
> Yet touch this sparingly, as 'twere far off;
> Because, my lord, you know my mother lives.
>   (III.v.84-93)

After Buckingham returns from speaking to the Mayor and Londoners, Richard asks him, "Touch'd you the bastardy of Edward's children?" (III.vii.4). "I did," Buckingham replies,

> . . . with his contract with Lady Lucy,
> And his contract by deputy in France;
> Th' unsatiate greediness of his desire,
> And his enforcement of the city wives;

His tyranny for trifles; his own bastardy,
As being got, your father then in France,
And his resemblance, being not like the Duke.
Withal I did infer your lineaments—
Being the right idea of your father,
Both in your form and nobleness of mind.

                                        (III.vii.5-14)

Concerning this passage, Antony Hammond, the editor of the Arden text of the play, notes that verses 5-6, 8, and 11 of this scene do not appear in the 1597 Quarto of *King Richard III* (245). As a possible reason for the loss, Hammond cites an opinion appearing in the 1908 New Variorum edition of the play, that the lines may have been "deleted in deference to Elizabeth I's feelings, the charges being similar to those brought against her father" (245-46).

The evocation of Henry VIII in this respect becomes quite explicit in Shakespeare's play. At the time Edward IV married Elizabeth Woodville (Grey), he was apparently engaged to both Elizabeth Lucy and Bona of Savoy through a dynastic contract made in France. Edward could be said to have had marital precontracts with the latter two women. "The ecclesiastical theory of pre-contracts which prevailed before the Reformation was the source of great abuses. Marriages that had been publicly acknowledged, and treated for a long time as valid, were often declared null on the ground of some previous contract entered into by one or other of the parties. In this way Henry VIII, before putting Anne Boleyn to death, caused his marriage with her to be pronounced invalid by reason of a previous contract on her part with Percy, Earl of Northumberland" (Shakespeare, *New Variorum* 255-56). Edward's mother, the Duchess of York, was evidently aware of a precontract, or even a secret marriage, between her lascivious son and Lady Lucy, "for she urge[d] it as one of several grounds of objection to her son's marriage with Elizabeth Woodville: 'It must needs stick as a foul disparagement of the sacred majestie of a Prince . . . to be defiled with bigamy in his first marriage'" (Shakespeare, *New Variorum* 256). For Elizabethan playgoers, the notion of a king's "simultaneous" marriages or betrothals later bastardizing his children would have evoked the recollection of a similar archetype in the troublesome reign of Henry VIII.

This evocation was not simply academic for Shakespeare's contemporaries. If Edward IV's marriage to Elizabeth Woodville was illegitimate, then their daughter Elizabeth was a bastard. And since she became Henry VII's wife, the possible illegitimacy of Edward IV's marriage to Elizabeth Woodville further called Henry VIII's pedigree into question. "When Henry VII became king, and married the daughter of Edward IV and Elizabeth Woodville, any allusion to the precontract [with Lady Lucy] was treated as disloyal" (Shakespeare, *New Variorum* 255). Interestingly, Richard's

and Buckingham's accusations against Edward IV stand in Shakespeare's play; no character refutes them, or even makes an attempt to do so. At this point, one might counterclaim that the accusations stand not because characters necessarily think that they are true but because wary nobles and citizens refuse to commit themselves politically through speech in the rapidly destabilizing, treacherous atmosphere of the court and city. The assembled citizens do refuse to assent to Buckingham's pro forma rehearsal of the bastardy argument. But we shall see that their silence is only temporary. Later analysis of the latter part of act III, scene vii will show Richard's and Buckingham's bastardy charges against Edward and his children prevailing with the Mayor and citizens, breaking the people's silence, and giving Richard almost immediate access to the throne.

The source of Shakespeare's representation of King Edward IV's precontracts and "bigamy" was Sir Thomas More's *History of King Richard III* (pub. 1557) (Candido, "More" 139). More originally wrote this work in Latin and English in or near 1513, when he was still strongly supportive of Henry VIII. Ironically, a book written by an advocate of Henry VIII would one day become the source of a stage depiction potentially critical by analogy of the king and embarrassing to his daughter. Analysis of More's *History* sharpens the critical commentary on Henry VIII latent in Shakespeare's dramaturgy. More emphasizes Elizabeth Grey's widowhood as the basis for the Duchess of York's claim that marriage to her would be bigamous: More's Duchess tells Edward, "'wheras ye only widowhed of Elizabeth Gray though she wer in al other thinges conuenient for you, shold yet suffice as me semeth to refrain you from her mariage, sith it is an vnsitting thing, & a veri blemish, & highe disparagement, to the sacre magesty of a prince, y^t ought as nigh to approche priesthode in clenes as he doth in dignitie, to be defouled w^t bigamy in his first mariage'" (62). In canon law, bigamy included marriage to a widow, especially by ecclesiastical clerks. "'And as for ye bigamy,' More reports Edward as replying, 'let ye Bishop hardely lay it in my wai, when I come to take orders. For I vnderstand it is forbidden a prieste, but I never wiste it yet y^t it was forbidden a prince'" (64). Edward had sired at least two illegitimate children—a son, Arthur Plantagenet, definitely by Elizabeth Lucy, and a daughter, Elizabeth, perhaps by Elizabeth Lucy. The girl was born about the time of Edward's marriage to Elizabeth Woodville Grey. More's Edward boasts to his mother, "'That she is a widow and hath already children, by gods blessed Ladye I am a batcheler & have some to: & so eche of vs hath a profe yt neither of vs is lyke to be barain'" (64). Because of the story of Edward's precontract with Elizabeth Lucy and the Duchess's accusations, the bishops refused to marry Edward and the widow. They relented only after Elizabeth Lucy publicly equivocated on the matter of the precontract.

Few literate playgoers of the 1590s were unfamiliar with Henry VIII's argument that his marriage to the widow of his brother Prince Arthur—Katharine of Aragon—ought to be considered bigamous and thus null and void. Mary was bastardized upon this pretext. The issue enmeshes Elizabeth too. If Henry VIII's marriage to Katharine of Aragon was not bigamous, then Elizabeth was a bastard. This possibility remained a primary Catholic argument for the queen's illegitimacy and—until 1572—for Mary Stuart's right to the throne. Shakespeare triggers the above-described Henrician associations by making the bigamy of More's text part of his play.

How this happens deserves further analysis. In act III, scene vii, Richard and Buckingham perform a previously agreed upon dialogue designed to place Richard on the throne (III.vii.94-246). Because of "the corruption of a blemish'd stock" (III.vii.121)—Edward IV's and his sons' imputed bastardy—the crown "as successively from blood to blood" and "right of birth" ought to be Richard's (III.vii.134-35). Or so Richard and Buckingham argue. After Richard hypocritically rejects Buckingham's royal overtures, his fellow Machiavel develops his earlier speech to the Mayor and citizens:

> You say that Edward is your brother's son:
> So say we too—but not by Edward's wife.
> For first was he contract to Lady Lucy
> (Your mother lives a witness to his vow),
> And afterward by substitute betroth'd
> To Bona, sister of the King of France.
> These both put off, a poor petitioner,
> A care craz'd mother to a many sons,
> A beauty-waning and distressed widow,
> Even in the afternoon of her best days
> Made prize and purchase of his wanton eye,
> Seduc'd the pitch and height of his degree
> To base declension and loath'd bigamy.
> By her, in his unlawful bed, he got
> This Edward, whom our manners call the
>   Prince.
> More bitterly could I expostulate,
> Save that for reverence to some alive
> I give a sparing limit to my tongue.
>   (III.vii.176-93)

Alluding to a gloss in the *New Cambridge Shakespeare* edition of the play, Hammond enlarges More's definition of bigamous widowhood by generalizing that "marriage with a widow was bigamy according to canon law" (254). The charge made by the Ghost of Hamlet's father—that Claudius's marriage to the widow Gertrude is adulterous, thus incestuous—constitutes evidence for Hammond's judgment. If the sacrament of marriage made man and wife one flesh, after the first marriage there could be no other. A wife could not share her flesh twice in a lifetime. This, too, was one of Henry VIII's arguments that his

marriage with Katharine of Aragon was bigamous and his child of that union a bastard.

Thus far we have been exploring the Tudor echoes in the first two of the four verses deleted from III.vii.5-14 in the 1597 Quarto of *King Richard III*. The third excised verse—"and his enforcement of the city wives"—strengthens Edward IV's association with bastardy and with Henry VIII. By all accounts, Edward was a lecher, dallying with his subjects' daughters and wives, including the notorious Jane Shore (Given-Wilson and Curteis 4-5). In the script he sketches for Buckingham, Richard says, "Tell them how Edward put to death a citizen / Only for saying he would make his son / Heir to the Crown" (III.v.75-77). Evidently several royal "sons" throughout the city compete with the two princes for succession. "Moreover, urge his hateful luxury," Richard counsels Buckingham,

> And bestial appetite in change of lust,
> Which stretch'd unto their servants, daughters,
>   wives,
> Even where his raging eye or savage heart
> Without control lusted to make a prey.
>   (III.v.79-83)

Richard thus suggests that the king's bastardizing certain families in his realm somehow connects with (or derives from) the reputed bastardy of himself and his supposedly legitimate sons. His begetting bastards on other women in this context justified labeling the princes bastards. Or so Richard's rhetorical logic runs.

Considered in the context of the associations with Henry VIII already evoked, this dimension of Edward's bastardy intensifies the linkage. King Henry had a notoriously roving eye, and his carnal relations with Anne Boleyn and other women before he had extricated himself from the marriage of the moment were popular knowledge. It was Henry VIII's "bastardizing" lust that partly made both Mary and Elizabeth illegitimate as subsequent "marriages" blighted the girls' mothers and their origins. The resonances here are sufficiently disturbing that the verses missing in the 1597 Quarto, which were presumably part of the playhouse script, may have been cut because of the shadow they cast upon Henry and Elizabeth. By saying that Elizabeth Grey "Made prize and purchase of [Edward's] wanton eye, / Seduc'd the pitch and height of his degree / To base declension and loath'd bigamy" (III.vii.186-88), Buckingham reprises the charges of Henry's and Anne's enemies, that the king's wanton, courtesan-like woman had harnessed the king's giant libido and consequently disinherited Katharine of Aragon and bastardized her child Mary. And it was Anne's supposedly promiscuous nature and spotted reputation that made Elizabeth a bastard in the minds of some of her antagonists. That Henry should have gotten Jane Seymour pregnant before he had found convenient reasons for ridding himself of Anne in order to marry her merely repeated the scenario that had bastardized Mary (Bowle 200-1). This time, however, Elizabeth was its victim.

The illegitimate legitimacy (or legitimate illegitimacy) that disturbed the Tudor succession marks the family romance of Edward IV. The disruptive role of bastardy in Henry VIII's life strikingly reprises its place in the mid-fifteenth-century York kingship as depicted by Shakespeare. That Shakespeare should portray unworthy Richard using mainly bastardy charges evocative of problematical Tudor illegitimacy in a bid for the crown was a bold, potentially reprehensible stroke throughout the 1590s. Buckingham urges Richard "to draw forth your noble ancestry / From the corruption of abusing times / Unto a lineal, true-derived course" (III.vii.197-99). Richard agrees to be crowned legitimate king only after Buckingham threatens,

> Yet know, whe'er you accept our suit or no,
> Your brother's son shall never reign our king,
> But we will plant some other in the throne
> To the disgrace and downfall of your House.
>   (III.vii.213-16)

Admittedly, this dialogue is a set-up between two Machiavels; nevertheless, it convinces the Lord Mayor—speaking for the silent citizens—that Richard should be king (III.vii.200, 236). When Buckingham concludes by exclaiming, "Long live Richard, England's worthy King," citizens and Mayor alike pronounce "Amen" (III.vii.239-40). One might object that the citizens' validation of Buckingham's royal salute to Richard—their saying "Amen" to his "Long live Richard, England's worthy King!"—may reflect their prudent fear rather than the persuasiveness of Buckingham's argument. A wary silence signified their reception of Buckingham's initial presentation of the bastardy charges. In the present case the citizens most likely take their cue from the Lord Mayor, whose affirmation of Richard's right to the throne rings with conviction (III.vii.200). The Mayor's spoken endorsement of Richard apparently encourages—perhaps obligates is a better word—the citizens to voice their obedience. Thus for all practical purposes, Richard's and Buckingham's use of bastardy charges places the crown within Richard's grasp.

As he plots the deaths of his nephews, Richard continues to stress their supposed illegitimacy:

> Foes to my rest, and my sweet sleep's
>   disturbers,
> Are they that I would have thee deal upon.
> Tyrrel, I mean those bastards in the Tower.
>   (IV.ii.72-74)

Interestingly, Richard's conversation with his assassin reveals the weakness of his own belief that bastardy publicly disqualifies his nephews from succession. He believes that he must have them murdered to keep them off the throne. Ironically, Richard's insecurity about his right to the kingship moves him to grovel before Edward IV's wife in order to gain her daughter in marriage before Henry does. Richard seeks to unite with a member of the family that he previously bastardized but who now represents a legitimizing match; if Henry Tudor were to marry her, he would powerfully blend the white Yorkist and red Lancastrian roses. Richard's desperate matrimonial begging amounts to a potentially just punishment for his political use of bastardy to win the crown. In a humiliating fashion, he ultimately feels compelled to reverse the bastardy charges he once made.

Nevertheless, Richard continues to use his favorite method of foisting bastardy upon rivals so as to consolidate his political power. In the final instance, this rival is the future Henry VII. Even though bastardy figured strongly in Henry VII's origins, explicitly implying that Queen Elizabeth's grandfather was a bastard would have been highly objectionable, almost certainly self-destructive for the playwright. In *King Richard III,* the taint of bastardy surrounding the Earl of Richmond gets displaced onto his troops. The effect, however, is to associate him distinctly with illegitimacy (since he is their head). During his battle oration at Bosworth Field, Richard tells his soldiers that the "scum of Bretons" in Richmond's ranks will, if victorious, "distain" Englishmen's "beauteous wives" (V.iii.314-23)—will, that is to say, make bastards the children of Richard's troops. "If we be conquer'd, let men conquer us!" (V.iii.333), Richard concludes,

> And not these bastard Bretons, whom our
>   fathers
> Have in their own land beaten, bobb'd, and
>   thump'd,
> And in record left them the heirs of shame.
> Shall these enjoy our lands? Lie with our
>   wives?
> Ravish our daughters?
>   (V.iii.334-38)

No one has provided a satisfactory historical or political explanation for Richard's calling the Bretons, the men of Brittany, bastards. One could argue that Richard calls them bastards simply because he has become fixated upon bastardy during his rise to the crown. More likely, however, is the motive of associating Henry Tudor with illegitimacy. Richard deploys his obsession with bastardy so as to signify the political illegitimacy of the Earl of Richmond. If Henry wrests the crown from Richard, a multitude of English families will include bastards. Political bastardy will lead to widespread biological bastardy. Or so Richard's argument concludes. The bastard Bretons, if triumphant, will spread their bastardy by fathering illegitimate children on the losers' wives. In this conception, politically illegitimate Henry Tudor becomes the wellspring of bastardy in its most basic sense. Richard never directly challenges but in truth defers to, even respects, the principle of legitimate succession. He "never questions the right of Clarence to take the crown before him . . . nor the right of Edward's son; he accepts his place in the hierarchy even as he works to undermine hierarchy in general" (Carroll 213). Once he is on the throne, Richard, despite his murderous methods, becomes the genealogically legitimate holder of the scepter and the humane Richmond technically a usurper (Carroll 215-18; Reese 55; Hodgdon 103; Gurr 40-43, 46).[5] "Richard is, after all, descended from the third son of Edward III," James P. Hammersmith remarks, "whereas the Earl [of Richmond] is descended from the fourth" (35). This suggestion of usurpation further strengthens the overtones of illegitimacy surrounding Richmond.

Nevertheless, tracing the development in *King Richard III* of bastardy into a metaphor for human corruption tends to absolve the original Tudor monarch of the charge. Richard's willingness to impute adultery to his mother opens the door to questions about his own legitimacy, a risk that reveals his potentially self-destructive loathing of his imagined physical "baseness." Jenny Teichman has copiously illustrated Western writers' tendency to portray bastardy in terms of physical deformity and violent rages. On both counts, Shakespeare's Richard III fits the profile. Francis Bacon in his *Essayes* implicitly equates bastardy and physical defects when he judges that "Deformed Persons, and Eunuches, and Old Men, and Bastards, are *Envious:* For he that cannot possibly mend his own case will doe what he can to impaire anothers" (28). Physically twisted, resembling the shape of neither his mother nor his father, Richard feels like a bastard, even though he is by all accounts legitimately born.[6] Self-disgustedly, Richard feels himself to be illegitimately legitimate (or legitimately illegitimate). Several critics have compared Shakespeare's characterizations of Richard and the bastard Edmund of *King Lear.* "Edmund's bastardy works in the same way as Richard's crookedness," John F. Danby argues. "Richard resents both his shape and his position of contemptuous ridicule. He will react therefore against God and man. With both Richard and Edmund we feel that their resentment is understandable" (64). Danby notes that both Richard and Edmund become "sincere" hypocrites who sardonically unmask the hypocrisies of those seemingly sincere (such as respectively Edward IV and the Earl of Gloucester) (60-62). Both Richard's and Edmund's sense of dispossession and social alienation drives them to displace rivals who have more legitimate claims to lands and inheritance. Richard's repeatedly voiced defiant credo of the "self alone" is the ethos of the early modern stage bastard, especially the memorable bastard Edmund.[7] For William C. Carroll, "the connection be-

tween Richard and Edmund . . . is that for both characters the principle of 'lineal glory,' the 'form' and 'order of law,' is both the principle which denies them and so must be annihilated, and the principle which will define them and so is constantly desired" (214). This connection focuses the curious fact of Richard's deferral to the principle of legitimate succession that was documented in the previous paragraph. Now we can say that Richard's recognition of legitimate succession could amount to a compensation for his feeling of being a figurative bastard. Richard protects himself from this negative emotion by projecting bastardy onto his imagined rivals, including Edward, his nephews, and the Bretons (including Richmond).

Richard's struggle with a powerful feeling of personal illegitimacy takes several forms. Buckingham reports that in his address to the Mayor and citizens,

> Withal, I did infer your lineaments—
> Being the right idea of your father,
> Both in your form and nobleness of mind.
> (III.vii.12-14)

Sycophantic Buckingham correctly guesses that Richard wants to hear reported his physical attractiveness in comparison to Edward's supposed ugliness. Buckingham makes Richard's obsession with bastardy serve as the occasion for easing Richard's apparent anxiety about his deformation and thus for ingratiating himself with his master. If Edward is a bastard, he must be ugly—"base"—and thus Richard must be handsome by comparison. Or so this parasitic subtext runs. Because of Richard's mother's purported bastardizing of Edward and Edward's subsequent bastardizing of his "sons," "the noble isle," Buckingham concludes, "doth want her proper limbs" (III.vii.124). Shortly thereafter Richard's accomplice flatters his master's "gracious self" (III.vii.130). This conflation equates England with physical deformity and royal legitimacy with gracious physique, supposedly the being of Richard who would cure the realm of the debilitating effects of others' bastardy.

Despite these ministrations, Richard continues to feel illegitimate. His frantic negotiations for a legitimizing marriage with Elizabeth, the daughter of his brother Edward and Elizabeth Woodville, partly derives from his barren marriage to Anne. He has no heirs to succeed him. The historical Richard and Anne Neville in fact had a son Edward (1473-84), Earl of Salisbury (1478) and Duke of Cornwall (1483). Furthermore, Richard, according to Sir Thomas More, "had at least two bastard children, Catherine Plantagenet and John of Pomfret or John of Gloucester" (211). (Also see Given-Wilson and Curteis 8, 160-61). More notes that Richard pledged his only lawful son to marry Buckingham's daughter, if Buckingham would help make him king (44). Shakespeare in *King Richard III* omits all mention of Richard's legitimate and illegitimate children. His barrenness in the play becomes an additional jealous motive for his smearing Edward's sons with bastardy. If he cannot (or does not) have any sons, then (in his mind) the sons of his brother Edward cannot (will not) be legitimate—that is to say, authentic.

Taken as a whole, Richard's cruelty and faults stamp him a defective person, a human *manque*. The Earl of Richmond in his oration to his troops calls Richard a "base, foul stone, made precious by the foil / Of England's chair" (V.iii.251-52). In this pejorative context, the word "base" catches the overtones of figurative bastardy inherent in Richard's own dehumanized conduct and his tacit self-appraisals and condenses them in the mouth of his adversary. Legitimate Richard's figurative bastardy (or baseness) by contrast makes other Yorkists and especially Henry Tudor who have been either labeled or associated with bastardy appear less culpable, even—in the Earl of Richmond's case—non-blamable. This dramatic strategy provides the basis for the play's concluding emphasis upon Tudor fertility and legitimacy. During his onstage nightmare, Richard hears the ghosts of his two murdered nephews tell sleeping Richmond, "Live, and beget a happy race of kings" (V.iii.158). Ironically, Shakespeare's audience, hearing this speech, might recollect that this "race" would include as many queens as kings, both of whom would have their happiness blighted at one time or another by the frost of bastardy. Yet this recollection concerns the unknown future of the play's characters. In this play the founder of the Tudor dynasty proudly proclaims his political legitimacy (through a powerful conjunction that—dramatically at least—overbears and mutes future questions about his biological legitimacy).

> O now let Richmond and Elizabeth,
> The true succeeders of each royal house,
> By God's fair ordinance conjoin together,
> And let their heirs, God, if Thy will be so,
> Enrich the time to come with smooth-fac'd
>   peace,
> With smiling plenty, and fair prosperous days.
>   (V.v.29-34)

Phyllis Rackin has argued that "the problem of illegitimacy" in the cycle of Shakespeare's dramatized history "is never fully resolved until the end of *Richard III,* when the Lancastrian Henry VII turns to a woman to secure a crown he has won in battle, announcing that he will unite the warring factions by marrying the Yorkist princess Elizabeth. The best efforts of three generations of kings and their suffering subjects and the struggles of three generations of men killing each other in battle can never resolve the problem of royal legitimacy. It can only be resolved in marriage, with the incorporation of the necessary female ground of all patriarchal authority—in this case the Princess Eliza-

beth" (163-64). The stigma of bastardy that Richard, like a lightning rod, deflects from Richmond onto himself in Shakespeare's play prepares the way for Rackin's conclusions and makes them more persuasive.

For one brief moment, divine legitimacy in the formulation of Shakespeare's Richmond characterizes the origins of the Tudors, offsetting the many later political accusations of bastardy within the royal "race." Shakespeare's creation of a scapegoat figurative bastard in *King Richard III* must have made Richmond's claims nostalgically believable. Shakespeare later (most likely in 1594 or 1595) positively portrayed illegitimacy in the character of Philip the Bastard in *King John,* a figure who Ronald Stroud has shown gains a metaphoric legitimacy by comparison with the moral shifting of less honest courtiers.[8] Shakespeare formulates this dramaturgy of *King John* in *King Richard III* when the moral bastardy of "legitimate" Richard and the hypocrites of the Yorkist court defines the moral integrity of the "bastard" Henry Tudor. Despite the generally negative cultural representation of bastardy during Shakespeare's lifetime (Elton 131-35; Hyland 6-9; Neill; Macfarlane 73, 77),[9] the playwright in *King Richard III* found a novel way to evoke the problematics of Tudor bastardy in order to de-emphasize its seriousness. That a censor may have ordered the erasure of key verses of this evocation suggests that the approach may have been appreciated by only a segment of Shakespeare's audience.

Notes

I want to thank my former Baylor University student Jessica Watson for stimulating my interest in the topic of bastardy in *King Richard III* and for suggesting several resources for researching the subject of this essay.

[1] Shakespeare's emphasis upon bastardy in a history play such as *King Richard III* is, *per se,* not surprising. Rather, I am claiming that, considered in light of Queen Elizabeth's distaste for public allusions to the topic of Tudor bastardy, Shakespeare's evocation of the subject in *King Richard III* is surprising. A number of recent commentators have demonstrated that bastardy becomes a major issue in many of Shakespeare's history plays. See especially, Candido, "Blots, Stains, and Adulteries"; Manheim (and less centrally several other essays in Curren-Aquino); Kerrigan 40-44; Rackin 53-54, 66, 76, 184-91; and Neill 275, 278-79, 283-84, 287-88.

[2] In the April Eclogue of *The Shepheardes Calender,* the poem in praise of Queen Elizabeth, Spenser wrote, "For shee is *Syrinx* daughter without spotte, / Which *Pan* the shepheards God of her begot: / So sprong her grace / Of heavenly race, / No mortall blemishe may her blotte" (*Yale Spenser* 72-73). While Elizabethan

writers often mythologized King Henry VIII as the protean, all-powerful god Pan, Spenser's identification of Anne Boleyn with Syrinx is a bit unusual. Pan—Henry VIII—made a kind of immortal music—the miraculous child Elizabeth—through playing the reed that Syrinx had become. In this reading, Syrinx—Anne Boleyn—sacrifices her life so that she and Pan can make something wondrous. While the phrase "without spotte" mainly attaches to Elizabeth, it also modifies Syrinx, suggesting by its ambiguous syntactical position that Elizabeth's legitimacy proceeds from her pure mother. "No mortall blemishe may . . . blotte" Elizabeth because she came of a clean "heavenly race." Spenser's recreation of Elizabeth's virginal conception reappears in Book III of *The Faerie Queene,* wherein the sun's rays innocently beget a prototype of Elizabeth—Belphoebe—within the body of sleeping Chrysogene (III.vi.1-28). Chrysogene/Anne Boleyn in the myth thus preserves her "chaste bodie" (III.vi.5.8), such that, as regards Belphoebe/Elizabeth, "her whole creation did her shew / Pure and vnspotted from all loathly crime / That is ingenerate in fleshly slime" (III.vi.3.3-5). Spenser's adaptation of the motif of the Annunciation suggests the imaginative degree protestant apologists were willing to go to defend Elizabeth from innuendoes of bastardy and sexual corruption in her origin.

[3] In the past sixteen years, commentators on Shakespeare's *King John* and the plays of the First and Second Tetralogies in steadily increasing numbers have demonstrated the relevance of sixteenth-century English personages, doctrines, and events for their interpretations. See for example Trace; Richmond; Greenblatt; Wilson; Williamson; Marcus 51-96; Jackson; McCoy; Belsey; and Poole. One of the original authorizations for giving aspects of Shakespeare's history plays early modern readings was Queen Elizabeth's pronouncement that Shakespeare's company's playing *Richard II* on the eve of the Essex Rebellion especially identified her with King Richard (Kastan 468-69, 473).

[4] All quotations of *King Richard III* refer to the Arden text edited by Antony Hammond. When Richard commands Buckingham to stigmatize Edward's offspring, Robert Ornstein refers to the "time-honored custom for usurpers to bastardize those they overthrow" (26).

[5] "Yet it is the bloody butcher himself, Richard, who most clearly aligns himself with the ideology of loyal and 'natural' succession; and it is the re-sacramentalized emblem of 'ceremonious' order, Richmond, who intervenes when the 'chair' of state is *not* 'empty,' when the 'empire' is not 'unpossess'd'" (Carroll 218).

[6] Neill remarks that around "the 'rudely stamped' Richard of Gloucester['s] . . . monstrous birth and physical deformity hang metaphoric suggestions of the very

bastardy with which he stigmatizes his own nephews. . . . In *3 Henry VI,* V.5.115, [Richard] and his brothers are denounced by Queen Margaret as 'the bastard boys of York' in a context where York's patronage of the usurper Cade (a counterfeit Plantagenet) and appearance at the head of an Irish army associates the Yorkist faction with illegitimacy of all kinds" (283). For the early modern English notion that bastardy often revealed itself in the bastard's monstrous shape, see Neill's analysis of Volpone's "family" and the character of Thersites in Shakespeare's *Troilus and Cressida* (287, 289-92).

[7] Neill asserts that 'the stage bastard repeatedly insists on his own self-begotten sufficiency in overreaching language that insolently travesties the divine 'I am'" (284). Richard shares many character traits with the stage bastards Edmund and Faulconbridge of *King John.* These include a proneness to tease or scoff, cynical commentary—often expressed in an aside—on the dramatic action, a darkly comic or ironic sense of humor and theatrical style of behavior and speech as responses to a sense of illegitimacy (Van de Water 141-43; Rackin 53-54); self-congratulatory double-entendres, soliloquies suggestive of superior intellectual complexity, a fondness for spoken interruptions, expostulations, defiances, mockeries, and expressions of incredulity (Porter 139); and a penchant for Machiavellian policy, made attractive by a large capacity for personal charm (Danby 58-80). Richard shares these and other characteristics with the Shakespearean stage bastard represented by Edmund and Faulconbridge partly because all three figures ultimately derive from the Morality Vice.

[8] Clearly, Shakespeare depicts the brave bastard Faulconbridge, who grows into an understanding and appreciation of moral truth during the course of the events of *King John,* as more qualified to rule England than the problematical but yet more legitimate John and Arthur, the former progressively unscrupulous and confused and the latter pious but frightened and ineffectual in his childhood. See the analysis of Herschel Baker in *The Riverside Shakespeare* 766-67; Manheim; and Rackin 184-91.

[9] Peter Laslett has statistically demonstrated with reference to historical English bastardy ratios that there was "an illegitimacy wave in the latest decades of the sixteenth and the earlier decades of the seventeenth century" (233). Also see Ingram 157-59. For confirmation of this increase and an account of its probable socioeconomic origins within the disorderly popular culture of the 1590s, see Levine and Wrightson 158-75. The marked increase in bastardy rates that occurred while Shakespeare was writing for the theater may have played a role in his emphasis upon illegitimacy in *King Richard III,* other history plays, and several comedies and tragedies.

Works Cited

Bacon, Sir Francis. "Of Envy." *The Essayes or Counsels, Civill and Morall.* Ed. Michael Kiernan. Cambridge, MA: Harvard UP, 1985. 27-31.

Belsey, Catherine. "The Illusion of Empire: Elizabethan Expansionism and Shakespeare's Second Tetralogy." *Literature and History* N. S. 1.2 (1990): 13-21.

Bowle, John. *Henry VIII.* Boston: Little, 1964.

Candido, Joseph. "Blots, Stains, and Adulteries: The Impurities of *King John.*" Curren-Aquino 114-25.

————. "Thomas More, The Tudor Chroniclers, and Shakespeare's Altered Richard." *English Studies* 68 (1987): 137-41.

Carroll, William C. "'The Form of Law': Ritual and Succession in *Richard III.*" *True Rites and Maimed Rites: Ritual and Anti-Ritual in Shakespeare and His Age.* Ed. Linda Woodbridge and Edward Berry. Urbana: U of Illinois P, 1992. 203-19.

Curren-Aquino, Deborah, ed. *"King John": New Perspectives.* Newark: U of Delaware P, 1989.

Danby, John F. *Shakespeare's Doctrine of Nature: A Study of "King Lear."* 1948. London: Faber, 1957.

Elton, William R. *"King Lear" and the Gods.* 1966. Lexington: UP of Kentucky, 1988.

Given-Wilson, Chris, and Alice Curteis. *The Royal Bastards of Medieval England.* 1984. London: Routledge, 1988.

Greenblatt, Stephen. "Invisible Bullets: Renaissance Authority and Its Subversion." *Shakespeare's "Rough Magic": Renaissance Essays in Honor of C. L. Barber.* Ed. Peter Erickson and Coppélia Kahn. Newark: U of Delaware P, 1985. 276-302.

Gurr, Andrew. "Richard III and the Democratic Process." *Essays in Criticism* 24 (1974): 39-47.

Hammersmith, James P. "The Melodrama of *Richard III.*" *English Studies* 70 (1989): 28-36.

Hodgdon, Barbara. *The End Crowns All: Closure and Contradiction in Shakespeare's History Plays.* Princeton: Princeton UP, 1991.

Hyland, Peter. "Legitimacy in Interpretation: The Bastard Voice in *Troilus and Cressida.*" *Mosaic* 26.1 (1993): 1-13.

Ingram, Martin. *Church, Courts, Sex and Marriage in England, 1570-1640.* Cambridge: Cambridge UP, 1987.

Jackson, Gabriele Bernhard. "Topical Ideology: Witches, Amazons, and Shakespeare's Joan of Arc." *English Literary Renaissance* 18 (1988): 40-65.

Kastan, David Scott. "Proud Majesty Made a Subject: Shakespeare and the Spectacle of Rule." *Shakespeare Quarterly* 37 (1986): 459-75.

Kerrigan, John. "*Henry IV* and the Death of Old Double." *Essays in Criticism* 40 (1990): 24-53.

Laslett, Peter, and Karla Oosterveen, and Richard M. Smith, ed. *Bastardy and Its Comparative History.* Cambridge, MA: Harvard UP, 1980.

————. "The Bastardy Prone Sub-society." Laslett, Oosterveen, and Smith 217-46.

Levine, David, and Keith Wrightson. "The Social Context of Illegitimacy in Early Modern England." Laslett, Oosterveen, and Smith 158-75.

Loades, David. *The Reign of Mary Tudor: Politics, Government and Religion in England, 1553-58.* London: Longman, 1991.

Macfarlane, Alan. "Illegitimacy and Illegitimates in English History." Laslett, Oosterveen, and Smith 71-85.

Manheim, Michael. "The Four Voices of the Bastard." Curren-Aquino 126-35.

Marcus, Leah. *Puzzling Shakespeare: Local Reading and Its Discontents.* Berkeley: U of California P, 1988.

McCoy, Richard C. "'Thou Idol Ceremony': Elizabeth I, *The Henriad,* and the Rites of the English Monarchy." *Urban Life in the Renaissance.* Ed. Susan Zimmerman and Ronald F. E. Weissman. Newark: U of Delaware P, 1989. 240-66.

More, Saint Thomas. *The Complete Works of St. Thomas More: "The History of King Richard III."* Ed. Richard S. Sylvester. The Yale Edition of The Complete Works of St. Thomas More 2. New Haven: Yale UP, 1963.

Neill, Michael. "'In Everything Illegitimate': Imagining the Bastard in Renaissance Drama." *The Yearbook of English Studies* 23 (1993): 270-92.

Ornstein, Robert. *A Kingdom for a Stage: The Achievement of Shakespeare's History Plays.* Cambridge, MA: Harvard UP, 1972.

Poole, Kristen. "Saints Alive! Falstaff, Martin Marprelate, and the Staging of Puritanism." *Shakespeare Quarterly* 46 (1995): 47-75.

Porter, Joseph A. "Fraternal Pragmatics: Speech Acts of John and the Bastard." Curren-Aquino 136-43.

Rackin, Phyllis. *Stages in History: Shakespeare's English Chronicles.* Ithaca: Cornell UP, 1990.

Reese, M. M. *The Cease of Majesty: A Study of Shakespeare's History Plays.* London: Edward Arnold, 1961.

Richmond, Hugh M. "*Richard III* and the Reformation." *JEGP* 83 (1984): 509-21.

Ridley, Jasper. *Elizabeth I: The Shrewdness of Virtue.* New York: Viking, 1987.

Shakespeare, William. *King Richard III.* Ed. Antony Hammond. London: Methuen, 1981.

———. *A New Variorum Edition of Shakespeare: "The Tragedy of Richard The Third."* Ed. Horace Howard Furness, Jr. Philadelphia: Lippincott, 1908.

———. *The Riverside Shakespeare.* Ed. G. Blakemore Evans et al. Boston: Houghton, 1974.

Simons, Eric N. *Henry VII: The First Tudor.* New York: Barnes, 1968.

Smith, H. Maynard. *Henry VIII and the Reformation.* London: Macmillan, 1962.

Spenser, Edmund. *The Faerie Queene.* Ed. A. C. Hamilton. London: Longman, 1977.

———. *The Yale Edition of the Shorter Poems of Edmund Spenser.* Ed. William A. Oram et al. New Haven: Yale UP, 1989.

Stroud, Ronald. "The Bastard to the Time in *King John.*" *Comparative Drama* 6 (1972-73): 154-66.

Teichman, Jenny. *Illegitimacy: An Examination of Bastardy.* Ithaca: Cornell UP, 1982.

Trace, Jacqueline. "Shakespeare's Bastard Faulconbridge: An Early Tudor Hero." *Shakespeare Studies* 13 (1980): 59-69.

Van de Water, Julia C. "The Bastard in *King John.*" *Shakespeare Quarterly* 11 (1960): 137-46.

Williamson, Marilyn L. "'When Men are Rul'd by Women': Shakespeare's First Tetralogy." *Shakespeare Studies* 19 (1987): 41-59.

Wilson, Richard. "'A Mingled Yarn': Shakespeare and the Cloth Workers." *Literature and History* 12.2 (1986): 164-80.

Wriothesley, Charles. *A Chronicle of England During the Reigns of the Tudors.* Ed. William D. Hamilton. Westminster: J. B. Nichols, 1875. 2 vols.

Source: "Shakespeare's *King Richard III* and the Problematics of Tudor Bastardy," in *Papers on Language & Literature*, Vol. 33, No. 2, Spring, 1997, pp. 115-41.

Pro Patria Mori: War and Power in the Henriad

Jean-Christophe Mayer, *Université Paul-Valéry—Montpellier III*

Now for our consciences: the arms are fair
When the intent of bearing them is just.
                              1 Henry IV, 5.2.87-88

The words of the Archbishop of Canterbury in the opening scene of *Henry V* are strangely thought-provoking: 'List his discourse of war, and you shall hear / A fearful battle rendered you in music.' (1.1.44-45)[1] Looking beyond Henry's undeniable talents as an orator, one might wonder if it is the quality of Shakespeare's language that sometimes brings to the surface hitherto unsuspected feelings of patriotism in the minds of even the most sceptical of individuals. Kenneth Branagh's 'post-Falklands' film of *Henry V*—shot in a period when the mood of the nation had largely veered to condemnation of armed conflict—still causes us to side and empathize with the victor at one point or another, either consciously or less so.[2] Only a taste for *Concordia discors* can explain why the sound of drums is such sweet music to our ears. Indeed, Shakespeare's history plays seem to provide the natural terrain for a confrontation of opposites. G.K. Hunter defines the genre as 'involving both warmth of identification with the nation and the national story and also a colder analysis of political behaviour.'[3] The Archbishop of Canterbury's incitement poses a further problem in that it highlights the relationship between the language of power—of the sovereign in this case—and the resulting human conflict. War and power, in their numerous permutations and variations, are notions which underpin much of the political journey of those who wield the royal sceptre in the Henriad. As it is most likely that 'the basic unit of Shakespeare's theatre was the single play,' the present study will concentrate on the resonances of these notions in the three plays without—one hopes—implying any overall plan or purporting to sound the depths of the dramatist's creative mind.[4]

. . . . .

Shakespeare's opening gambit in *1 Henry IV* relies upon the King's dubious distinction between civil war and a so-called holy war which would unite the nobility around a common religious enterprise—the crusade. After trying to exorcise the horrid ghost of 'civil butchery' (1.1.5-9), Henry sets out to convince his listeners that some comflicts *can* be holy. Mystification and mysticism merge as Henry paints a pretty picture of war, daubed in the colours of religion and soldiery:

The edge of war, like an ill-sheathèd knife,
No more shall cut his master. Therefore, friends,

As far as to the sepulchre of Christ—
Whose soldier now, under whose blessèd cross
We are impressèd and engaged to fight—
Forthwith a power of English shall we levy,
Whose arms were moulded in their mothers'
  womb
To chase these pagans in those holy fields
                              (1.1.17-24)

Ironically, the only response Henry obtains is Westmorland's news of further civil war. Mortimer's men have been defeated by the Welsh and savagely massacred. Divested of its holy garb, war reveals its vilest aspects again, while the vocabulary used by Westmorland echoes Henry's own description of civil conflict: 'butcherèd' (42), 'beastly', 'shameless' (44). War is inhuman and its violence unspeakable: ' . . . as may not be / Without much shame retold or spoken of.' (45-46) The holy project, which is already 'twelve month old' (28) is postponed indefinitely.

It is worthwhile to remind ourselves of the crucial political role played by the Crusade in the Middle Ages. Henry's predicament stems from his inability to unite men around a common cause. The notion of homeland, or *patria,* is not firmly established. It is troublesome to ask men to die for a cause which, particularly under the influence of Augustinian thought, was construed at best as secondary: the only *patria* deserving human sacrifice was the *patria aeterna,* the Celestial City. The Crusade allowed the sacrifice of human lives as it was a defensive war, waged *pro defensione (necessitate) Terrae Sanctae.* In the the course of the thirteenth century, however, the notion of 'Holy Land' began to be equated with that of 'homeland'. Thus, gradually, any war could bear the title of crusade. Because the religious and the secular spheres were not clearly distinct in medieval times, a war waged against the King was a war against the Church and hence against the Holy Land. In this period secular power increasingly borrowed a sacredness belonging to the Church. The State, for instance, competed with the Church to become a *corpus mysticum.* Death *pro patria* was thus a sacrifice for the *corpus mysticum* of the State, which was as worthy as the Church's own *corpus mysticum.*[5]

Henry IV depicts the State at a somewhat embryonic stage. The sovereign still needs the Crusade in order to unify the kingdom and mask the basic horror of war. In *Henry V* a further stage is reached, seemingly. The mystique of the Crusade to the Holy Land is no longer useful for the State has developed its own mystique. In other words, Henry IV is at pains to achieve the fusion of two traditional roles played by medieval kings: the role of the *thiudans,* or sacred person, and that of the *reiks,* the warrior ruler, 'a person of rank in whom one-man authority is invested but one in whom sacred personal connotations are minimal.'[6]

The necessity of war is far from established by the ruling powers in *1 Henry IV.* The State's all-encompassing warring demands fail to reach certain spheres of society. The tavern scenes in particular are deliberately set outside the linear historical time of human conflicts. The opening lines of 1.2. are revealing. Sir John's question about 'the time of day,' is promptly turned into an irrelevance by Hal: 'What a devil hast thou to do with the time of the day?' (6) The reality of the conflict is, for a while, only allowed to *filter through* to the tavern world. Sir John is the prism through which history is turned into what it really is—a grotesque masquerade. The outside world has become a mere narrative:

> *There's villainous news abroad. Here was Sir John Bracy from your father; you must to the court in the morning. That same mad fellow of the North, Percy, and he of Wales that gave Amamon the bastinado, and made Lucifer cuckold, and swore the devil his true liegeman upon the cross of a Welsh hook* [. . .] (2.5.336-41)

The war finally takes over as Hal announces at the end of the scene: 'We must all to the wars.' (547) The King of Misrule's health deteriorates thereafter and the characters are at once caught in an irrevocable string of events leading to war. It is profoundly ironical that Sir John, the Prince of Disorder, interprets war as another type of disorder which is destructive to his person: 'And now I live out of all order, out of all compass.' (3.3.18-19)

But power itself is in deep crisis. The power of arms is the sole source of legitimacy and sovereignty. The feudal war lords were the makers of Henry's power and the King's greatness amounts to the sum of their good will, as Worcester arrogantly points out: 'And that same greatness too, which our own hands / Have holp to make so portly.' (1.3.12-13) The insolence of Hotspur, full of tales of knightly prowess, widens the gap between the values of war and those of politics ('policy'): 'Never did bare and rotten policy / Colour her working with such deadly wounds.' (1.3.107-108) 'This vile politician Bolingbroke' (239), 'this king of smiles' (244)—to quote Hotspur again—is fighting the battle for the definition and independence of his office. Like Richard II—who made untenable absolutist claims to power—Henry strives to place political power on a different ground than the battlefield. Having replaced Richard II at the helm, Henry has yet to gain 'the means of self-authorization.'[7]

In 3.2 Henry expounds to Hal his concept of politics. The maintaining of power for Henry involves the necessary manipulation of appearances. One is even entitled to borrow heavily from religion and make use of the half-hidden and of false miracles:

> *Thus did I keep my person fresh and new,*
> *My presence like a robe pontifical—*
> *Ne'er seen but wondered at—and so my state,*
> *Seldom but sumptuous, showed like a feast,*
> *And won by rareness such solemnity.*
>
>   (3.2.55-9)

If this strategy is the sure path to power, it does not for all that guarantee the durability of such power. Death, and indeed violent death, is the old enemy of kings. Henry cannot afford to put his office at risk by waging war like the feudal lord he once was. When forced to fight at last, he transfers his political craftiness to the battlefield. In disguising his true self, Henry manages to transform war into a semblance. The king (or rather his lookalikes) is everywhere and nowhere. The essence of kingship seems for a brief moment to be almost without reach of the bloody sword of war:

> DOUGLAS: [. . .] *What art thou*
>   *That counterfeit'st the person of a king?*
> KING HENRY:
>   *The King himself, who, Douglas, grieves at heart*
>   *So many of his shadows thou hast met*
>   *And not the very King.*
>
>   (5.4.26-30)

The innate danger in Henry's successful strategy is that kingship will disperse itself in its many shadows. Henry has momentarily defeated war and death but the underlying question in Douglas's words could be: is the real king real? Sir John points out that illusion is the price to pay for life. Sir John, the very counter-image of power, sheds indirect light upon the mechanisms of conservation of power: 'Counterfeit? I lie, I am no counterfeit. To die is to be a counterfeit, for he is but the counterfeit of a man who hath not the life of a man.' (5.4.113-16) In order to survive the fat knight has played a practical joke on war. But so has Henry, who runs an ultimate risk if his strategy comes full circle. As David Scott Kastan perceptively writes, 'the theatre [. . .] works to expose the mystifications of power. Its counterfeit of royalty raises the possibility that royalty is a counterfeit.'[8] The last line of *1 Henry IV*—spoken by the king—confirms the political malaise which continues to affect the ruling power of the realm in spite of its momentary victory over feudal lords whose existence is closely linked to military might. The conflict between war and power is not resolved: 'Let us not leave till all our own be won.' (5.5.45)

. . . . .

The King is remarkably absent from *2 Henry IV* until the third act where—clad significantly in a dressing gown—he appears somewhat weary. The rebels hold the stage and while they are gradually given more space the question of their lawfulness arises. The banner of 'Rebellion' is not one that is prone to rally the more hesitant, Morton points out (1.1.193-4). But legitimacy can be swiftly acquired. Newly dressed in mystic attire, feudal conflicts bear close resemblance to Holy War, outward legitimacy being one of the prerequisites of a well-established power. Henry is not the only privileged user of the concept. A Holy War has also the obvious advantage that it is willed by God and not by men, which in fact conceals remarkably well underlying political motives. Morton tells how religion has effected this transformation:

> [. . .] *But now the Bishop*
> *Turns insurrection into religion.*
> *Supposed sincere and holy in his thoughts,*
> *He's followed both with body and with mind,*
> *And doth enlarge his rising with the blood*
> *Of fair King Richard, scraped from Pomfret*
> *stones;*
> *Derives from heaven his quarrel and his*
> *cause*
>
> (1.1.199-205)

The name of Richard II is now part and parcel of what is historically preestablished and may be used to disguise rebellious 'innovations.' Rebellion, legitimacy and treason are words which are caught in the incessant linguistic exchanges of the play and may signify their complete opposite. Semantics in many ways is only an epiphenomenon—the force that moulds words and coins new meanings is military might. Yet, because the power of arms is unsure, meaning always fluctuates. What is certain, and what Morton demonstrates, is that, to quote Robert Ornstein:

> [. . .] in rebellion, as in most human enterprises, nothing succeeds like success. A successful rebel, John Harrington shrewdly observed, is no rebel at all: 'Treason doth never prosper; what's the reason? / For if it prosper, none dare call it treason.' This cynical epigram is not the gospel according to Machiavelli—it represents good, though maliciously phrased, Tudor theology: God defends the right of whoever wins.[9]

Thus, defending the right of a so-called worthy cause is not something that men easily consent to. Samuel Daniel, looking at the reign of King John, made a similar observation. His analysis of human psychology is acute: 'men beeing content rather to embrace the present, though wrong, with safety, then seeke to establish anothers right, with the hazard of their owne confusion.'[10]

2 Henry IV is an unsure linguistic universe, in which values constantly vary in their meaning. Rumour in the play's Induction appears on stage as an allegorical character. Pierre Sahel's astute analyses of rumour in *Henry VIII* may also serve to describe the unhealthy world of *2 Henry IV:* "Within the play, rumour is not necessarily either true or false—it simply exists. It evolves, circulates [. . .]. heedless of communicating any precise message, sometimes coactive with what is unreal, sometimes co-joining with something. [. . .] There is a constant interaction between events and reports. Rumour may seem to create reality."[11]

It is no surprise that the notion of war itself becomes affected by the relativity of truth. Despite their indignant claims, the motivation behind the characters' use of armed conflict is unclear. In 1.3 the rebels try to rationalize the aims of the conflict. Lord Bardolph argues that it is crucial to limit the part played by chance in their project: 'For in a theme so bloody-faced as this, / Conjecture, expectation, and surmise / Of aids uncertain should not be admitted.' (22-4) The Archbishop of York then displays his knowledge in the mechanisms of power by describing Bolingbroke's rise to the throne (87-100). The ironic outcome of the scene, however, is summed up in a parting comment by Hastings: 'We are time's subjects, and time bids be gone.' (110) The evidence gathered from this scene indicates that the rebels are not in control of the very historical process they initiated.

War is irrevocably estranged from its overall political, or strategic, objectives. The prospect of new armed conflict even fails to rally former followers. Northumberland, in 2.3.67-8, suddenly decides to retire to Scotland: 'I will resolve for Scotland. There am I / Till time and vantage crave my company.' The rebels are time-servers and it is very quickly obvious that war is synonymous with personal ambition. 4.1 is a case in point. When the Archbishop of York, Thomas Mowbray, Lord Hastings and Coleville meet Westmorland and then Prince John for a parley, the sum of their grievances does not turn out to be so impressive. York pompously but rather perfunctorily hands over to Westmorland a list of grievances (166-7), paradoxically accusing 'time,' a few lines later, to have turned him into a rebel to the Crown: 'The time misordered doth, in common sense, / Crowd us and crush us to this monstrous form' (259-60).

The result of the perversion of warlike values—and one might say almost the finishing touch—is Prince John's betrayal of the traitors, at the end of the same scene, when after the mock reconciliation of the rebels and of the King's party, the Prince proceeds to their arrest. Honour—a word much used, perhaps overused, by the rebels—has no place in a context of warfare. John's sophistry wears the respectable garb of religion, as the 'Holy War' argumentation is brought back into fashion: 'God, and not we, hath safely fought today.' (347) The supreme irony of course is that there has been no fighting—war amounts to a subtle rhetorical device. There is something unsavoury in the way the characters manipulate moral values, so much so that the prevalent imagery in the play is often related to disease and illness. War is associated to disease. Falstaff, in 1.2, sheds some light upon their possible relationship. Apparently suffering from gout (or indeed 'pox'), but forced to play his part in the war, the plump surfeited knight claims: 'I have the wars for my colour, and my pension shall seem the more reasonable. A good wit will make use of anything. I will turn diseases to commodity.' (247-50) Falstaff is a counter-image to the State and his ailment a symptom of more general matters. The conflict is the perfect way for him to transform a personal illness into one seemingly inflicted by the disciplines of war. In the same way, but in a broader perspective, the war aptly conceals the malady of the body politic. Falstaff is hence one who knows how to feed and thrive on the illness of the State.

The continuous disrespect of the fat knight towards authority finds its counterpart in the barons' discontentment. What better illustration, furthermore, of this *intestine* war than Falstaff's celebrated appendix: his belly. The rebellious belly is a familiar threat to the commonwealth. The imagery is borrowed from the field of organicist theories of the State. Unlike the belly in the tale told by Menenius in *Coriolanus*—against which all the other members of the body rebel—Falstaff's unruly appendix represents a latent threat to the State with which it is implicitly at war. Francis Bacon in the essay entitled *Of Seditions and Troubles* warns that:

> This same *multis utile bellum* is an assured and infallible sign of a state disposed to seditions and troubles. And if this poverty and broken estate in the better sort be joined with a want and necessity in the mean people, the danger is imminent and great. For the rebellions of the belly are the worst. As for discontentments, they are in the politic body like to humours in the natural, which are apt to gather a preternatural heat and to inflame.[12]

Falstaff's official role in 3.2 is to lead a recruitment board and enlist men for the war. The scene verges on the burlesque as the men in question turn out to be all affected by some disease—whether real or imaginary. The onomastics of their names bears witness to the degenerate state of the kingdom and of its future army (Mouldy, Feeble, Wart). Bullcalf, with his rather sturdy-sounding name, seems fit for service and yet even he claims to be affected by illness: 'O Lord, sir, I am a diseased man.' (176) Interestingly, his disease is related to his having served the sovereign: 'A whoreson cold, sir; a cough, sir, which I caught with ringing in the King's affairs upon his coronation day,

sir.' (178-80) Moral disease is not uncommon either among the potential recruits. Mouldy and Bullcalf bribe Bardolph and Falstaff into giving them their freedom again. In this context, Feeble's patriotic comments have an indisputable ironic ring to them: 'By my troth, I care not. A man can die but once. We owe God a death. I'll ne'er bear a base mind. An't be my destiny, so; an't be not, so. No man's too good to serve's prince.' (232-5) The subtle dialectics of war and money have only just begun.

But how can this war be justified? War, it seems, is organically necessary to the body politic as a means to purge it from its diseased humours. The Archbishop of York in 4.1 borrows from organicist theories of the State in order to legitimize the rebellious uprising. His use of a field of imagery that can be perceived as traditional officializes a rather dubious political stance:

> [. . .] *we are all diseased,*
> *And with our surfeiting and wanton hours*
> *Have brought ouselves into a burning fever,*
> *And we must bleed for it—of which disease*
> *Our late King Richard, being infected, died*
> (54-8)

According to the Archbishop, the surfeited belly of the State should diet. War is the only way 'To diet rank minds, sick of happiness, / And purge th'obstructions which begin to stop / Our very veins of life.' (64-6)

What the Archbishop does not quite make clear is that the real cause of these disorders is not so much organic and natural as quite simply political. Conflicts of ambition arise when power is enfeebled. Samuel Daniel's Archbishop of Canterbury in *The Civile Wars* believes that the sovereign's health commands the state of the commonwealth: '*Our Health is from our head:* if that be ill, / Distemp'red faint, and weake, all the rest will.'

The semiotic expression of the crisis affecting the seat of power is the King's bed in 4.3. Its very horizontality smacks of illness and ultimately of death. The bed is the place where power is often a prey to worry and insomnia; but when the sovereign has given himself over to sleep, it is also the place where power is the most vulnerable, the most exposed to overthrow. Henry is ill and—as he gradually leaves the realm of the living—he becomes naturally more distanced. The dying man's recurring thoughts about the Crusade acquire otherwordly colours. This earthly world is no place for his Holy War; he will soon be fighting it in another world: 'We will our youth lead on to higher fields, / And draw no swords but what are sanctified.' (3-4)

Henry's distance is a source of clear-sightedness for him also. The King admits that his power—if not acquired by theft—was originally the result of a transaction: 'And now my death / Changes the mood, for what in me was purchased / Falls upon thee in a more fairer sort.' (327-9) More importantly, Henry exposes war for what it is: a political stratagem. To establish the State on firm ground, he advises Hal to 'busy giddy minds / With foreign quarrels, that action hence borne out / May waste the memory of the former days.' (342-4)

The use of 'foreign quarrels' in politics is one which both statesmen and political thinkers have emphasized and more often than not recommended. The last words of those who belong to the lower social orders in the play are significant. The Lord of Misrule and his companions have been defeated by the forces of political order. Prince Hal has awakened from his disorderly dream and 'ten mile' now have to separate him from his most unruly subjects. Further conflict—this time with France—looms near. Pistol, as he is about to be carried off to prison with his companions and probably from thence to the French wars, reiterates what could be a motto: 'Si fortuna me tormenta, spero me contenta.' (5.5.94) Hope ('spero') is precisely the stuff politics is made of. Francis Bacon noted that:

> Certainly the politic and artificial nourishing and entertaining of hopes, and carrying men from hopes to hopes, is one of the best antidotes against the poison of discontentments. And it is a certain sign of a wise government and proceeding when it can hold men's hearts by hopes, when it cannot by satisfaction; and when it can handle things in such manner as no evil shall appear so peremptory but that it hath some outlet of hope [. . .].

A well-orchestrated war mystique offers the illusory prospect of hope and glory, casts aside civil dissensions and unites the people around their newly-respected sovereign. The author of the *Art of War,* Niccolo Machiavelli, argues that war should be the Prince's main concern and occupation as it is so tied up with the nature of his office:

> A Prince then ought to have no other ayme, nor other thought, nor take anything else for his proper art, but warr, and the orders and discipline thereof: for that is the sole arte which belongs to him that commands, and is of so great excellency, that not only those that are borne Princes, it maintains so; but many times rayses men from a private fortune to that dignity. And it is seene by the contrary, that when Princes have given themselves more to their delights, than to the warres, they have lost their States; and the first cause that makes thee lose it, is the neglect of that arte; and the cause that makes thee gaine it, is that thou art experienc'd and approv'd in that arte.[13]

These recommendations capture the mood of the play's conclusion. Rumours of war creep up again but no reasons whatsoever are given—only that conflict seems inevitable. The horrors of civil strife are not dispelled yet but Prince John announces war with France with a measure of excitement and perhaps a little too much lightness:

> *I will lay odds that, ere this year expire,*
> *We bear our civil swords and native fire*
> *As far as France. I heard a bird so sing,*
> *Whose music, to my thinking, pleased the*
> * King.*
> *Come, will you hence?*
>
> (5.5.103-07)

The ritualistic drums of war are close at hand as Henry prepares a Holy War that will be closer to home, unlike his father who fell both tragically and ironically short of a more distant project: 'In that Jerusalem shall Harry die.' (4.3.369)

. . . . .

Moody Prior's appraisal of *Henry V* is one which does not give much importance to the political intricacies of the play. It is at once disconcerting and slightly misleading:

> It [*Henry V*] celebrates in its hero a national ideal that bends the facts of history to the services of a concept which is out of touch with the realities of power and which in consequence evades experience and eludes expectation. In the perspective of the plays which preceded it, *Henry V* appears as a theatrically handsome fulfillment of an obligation, performed with skill but without deep conviction.[14]

That the play is 'out of touch with the realities of power' is a statement that can and will be severely qualified. It is perhaps a little hasty also to be so dismissive about the play and to call it 'a theatrically handsome fulfillment of an obligation', that is to say an obedient version of history destined to please the ruling powers. That playwrights and Shakespeare in particular had to take into account the wills of their Royal Patrons is an evidence which does not require to be demonstrated at length by critics—whether their vantage point is New Historicism or not. There is some sense in David Norbrook's remark that 'There is no need for twentieth-century readings to be more royalist than the King's Men.'[15] All the more so as—one might add—criticism of the play's 'jingoism' was well-established since the nineteenth century.[16]

Conservative views of *Henry V* stem no doubt from the fact that the play does *outwardly* make use of what might be called a mythology of war naturally highlighting all of its heroic aspects. The Prologue to the play and the choruses serve that cause. But the dialogue that they begin with the audience is in fact far from straightforward. Despite its epic style and mythological references, the Prologue's chorus formulates an almost immediate apology. Its sole desire is admittedly to portray war in the most faithful of ways. Its apparent frustration is due to the supposed limitations of the medium of representation—theatre:

> *Can this cock-pit hold*
> *The vasty fields of France? Or may we cram*
> *Within this wooden O the very casques*
> *That did affright the air at Agincourt?*
>
> (Prologue, 11-14)

Yet, these are merely rhetorical questions. The real questions may be elsewhere. On the eve of the battle of Agincourt, the chorus expresses the same type of apology. In this speech, the more noble aspects of war do not get their due—but is this not deliberate?

> *And so our scene must to the battle fly,*
> *Where O for pity, we shall much disgrace,*
> *With four or five most vile and ragged foils,*
> *Right ill-disposed in brawl ridiculous,*
> *The name of Agincourt. Yet sit and see,*
> *Minding true things by what their mock'ries*
> *be*
>
> (Act 4, Chorus, 48-53)

Art is about choice and the 'battle scenes' have certainly been carefully selected according to symbolic or indeed critical criteria, as we shall demonstrate. If Agincourt does not receive the same treatment as in the chronicles, it is perhaps because war does not deserve such an elevated treatment. As William Babula put it, 'Shakespeare is not limited by his theatre, he has chosen to present Agincourt in the worst way possible.'[17]

There is of course no direct criticism of war in the play, nor should we seek explicit condemnations of so complex a phenomenon in a work of art. What there is, however, is much debate about it. It is probably not by chance that a comic character, the Welsh Captain Fluellen, turns out to be the main proponent of a view of warfare that can only be called ideal, mythic, or indeed bookish. In 3.6 Fluellen makes references in his heroic similes to half-legendary figures of the Greco-Roman world: 'The Duke of Exeter is as magnanimous as Agamemnon.' (6-7), while Pistol is 'as valiant a man as Mark Antony.' (13-14) Gower warns him that he might be slightly misled in his romanticized view of war: 'But you must learn to know such slanders of the age, or else you may be marvellously mistook.' (80-82) It soon appears that Fluellen sees the world through the spectacles of part-legendary literary history. He is so well-read or well-versed that he is quite unaware that warfare is more inclined towards the breaking of its own rules than towards the observance of regulations: ' . . . there is no tiddle-taddle nor pibble-babble in Pompey's camp. I warrant you, you

shall find the ceremonies of the wars, and the cares of it, and the forms of it, and the sobriety of it, and the modesty of it, to be otherwise.' (4.1.71-5) Henry remarks knowingly that Fluellen's beliefs are 'a little out of fashion.' (4.1.83)

As in *Henry IV* war seems to creep up on the characters unawares. In 1.1 there is a sudden acceleration of historical time towards war which is unexplained and to some extent irrational. But some wars, to quote Bacon, are not founded on clear rational causes: 'Neither is the opinion of some of the Schoolmen to be received, *that a war cannot justly be made but upon a precedent injury or provocation.* For there is no question but a just fear of an imminent danger, though there be no blow given, is a lawful cause of war.' What is more irrational than 'fear', even if purporting to be just? In more ways than one, this first scene renders 1.2 perfunctory. Even before the Archbishop of Canterbury's Salic Law speech and the diplomatic incident of the 'Paris balls' the fate of the kingdom is sealed.

What Shakespeare helps to unveil in this first scene is the collusion between Church and State when dealing with matters of war. Before Henry appears on stage he is portrayed and eulogized by the Archbishop of Canterbury and the Bishop of Ely. Political power is glorified by religion:

> CANTERBURY: [. . .] *Yea, at that very moment*
> *Consideration like an angel came*
> *And whipped th'offending Adam out of him,*
> *Leaving his body as a paradise*
> *T'envelop and contain celestial spirits.*
> *[. . .]*
> *Hear him but reason in divinity*
> *And, all-admiring, with an inward wish*
> *You would desire the King were made a*
> *prelate*
>
> (1.1.28-41)

The fact that the king is referred to as a 'prelate' should not surprise us for the terminology has an historical justification. In the medieval understanding of the word 'Church' were comprised both the clergy and the laity. Thus, to talk of conflicts between the Church and the State is, by and large, an anachronism. 'Clergy and laity were epitomized in priests and kings and focalized as priesthood (*sacerdotium*) and kingship (*regnum*).'[18] The Church and the State had not yet become independent bodies. The only distinction made was that the sovereign remained—theoretically—a minister of the priests and their subordinate, as John of Salisbury demonstrated with vigour:

> The sword is therefore accepted by the prince from the hand of the Church, although it still does not itself possess the bloody sword entirely. For while

it has this sword, yet it is used by the hand of the priest, upon whom is conferred the power of bodily coercion, reserving spiritual authority for the papacy. The prince is therefore a sort of minister of the priests and one who exercises those features of the sacred duties that seem an indignity in the hands of priests.[19]

In this way, Henry has to obtain the Church's consent before he wages war on France—hence the Salic Law speech. This, as has been suggested, is the theory. From the thirteenth century onwards these conceptions started to change gradually. In case of war in particular the sovereign acquired special powers and an unprecedented degree of autonomy. The king was no longer bound by the law, or 'saying of the law'—the *jurisdictio* aspect of his office. In becoming in times of crisis the *gubernator* (the holder of the tiller), the sovereign gained prestige, independence as well as sacredness:

> It was on their expertise in statecraft, in the *arcana imperii* or secrets of power, in judging the fluctuations of times and seasons, events, circumstances, and human wills, that outstandingly successful rulers . . . based their claim to a mysterious and quasi-divine authority. The sphere in which they operated was that of the inscrutable providence of God, and success in that sphere seemed providential; it argued that they were divinely commissioned to exercise power. But the statecraft of pure policy was detached from either jurisdiction or legislation, for it had nothing to do with the establishment and maintenance of rules of law. It was a mysterious, in a sense an irrational, art of coping with the unique, the contingent, and the unforeseen, at the point where all hope must be abandoned of bringing things under legal control.[20]

With the help of the Church, Henry is about to become one of these successful rulers. If the prelates contribute to the making of the sacred image of the sovereign, they are fully aware of the political strategy which the King is using. The priests have rationalized the workings of power. Ely knows that ' . . . the Prince obscured his contemplation / Under the veil of wildness' (1.1.64-5) and that sudden changes and apparent miracles mask a well-calculated process. Canterbury is quite plain regarding the matter:

> *It must be so, for miracles are ceased,*
> *And therefore we must needs admit the means*
> *How things are perfected.*
>
> (68-9)

The dialogue between the two churchmen takes on thereafter a far more prosaic tone. The Church is about to be dispossessed and urgent action needs to be taken to prevent this. What in fact we discover as the scene unravels is that the Church has concluded a deal with Henry:

> CANTERBURY: *For I have made an offer to his majesty,*
> *Upon our spiritual convocation*
> *And in regard of causes now in hand,*
> *Which I have opened to his grace at large:*
> *As touching France, to give a greater sum*
> *Than ever at one time the clergy yet*
> *Did to his predecessors part withal.*
>
> (76-82)

War, both for the clergy and for Henry, is a transaction and a diversion. Henry exorcises the ghost of civil dissension by uniting the nation around his 'holy' person while the Church funds the King's campaign in order to keep the better part of its possessions. The clergy will also help legitimize the war by establishing Henry's so-called claim to the French throne. War thus involves a whole nation in the realization of private interests, which have more in common with the world of commerce than with that of diplomacy or politics.

Henry's is clearly not a just war. In the light of Augustine's writings, who coined the concept, his war could be regarded as downright theft: 'to make war on one's neighbours and from them to move on against the rest, crushing and subduing peoples who have given no offence, out of mere lust for dominion—what else can this be called except brigandage on a grand scale?'[21] Erasmus in *The Education of a Christian Prince* states that monarchs have a natural tendency to wage war for war's sake and certainly not for any humane or moral reason: 'All monarchs are cut from the same cloth. Some busy themselves with collecting the sinews of war; some, with generals and machines; but hardly any plan for the betterment of human life, which is the basis of everything else and which applies with equal importance to everybody.'

War, it seems, has to play its necessary part in the making of Henry. Might is right, as Samuel Daniel explicitly pointed out about Henry's father, Bolingbroke: 'Thou neuer proov'dst the Tenure of thy right / [. . .] / Till now: and, now, thou shew'st thy selfe Chiefe Lord, / By that especial right of kings; the *Sword*.' War is also the moment when the Sword acquires a measure of autonomy from the Church and when the sacredness of the prelate is irresistibly transferred to the sovereign. Tamburlaine's companions, Usumcasane and Theridamas express this idea unambiguously. If acquiring power in the terrestrial city is the ultimate goal of life on this earth, then a King—on his own political terrain—is superior to God:

> USUMCASANE: *To be a King, is halfe to be a God.*
> THERIDAMAS: *A God is not so glorious as a King,*
> *I thinke the pleasure they enjoy in heaven*
> *Can not compare with kingly joyes in earth.*
>
> (2.5.56-9)[22]

Far from the political ideals of Augustine and Erasmus, the particular portrayal of warfare in *Henry V* shows that the ethics which existed at the outset of the play still prevail. The battle of Agincourt is only glimpsed at in the play. But what glimpses we get as in 4.4— one of the only scenes which contain any fighting— are on the mock-heroic mode. Pistol, in a position of superiority, uses grandiloquent terms, which would get him a part in a comic version of *Tamburlaine,* to subdue a French gentleman. Being offered some money by the Frenchman in exchange for his life, the English 'hero' accepts the deal: 'Tell him, my fury shall abate, and I the crowns will take.' (46) This micro-picture of Agincourt reiterates the simple truth that war is nothing else than a transaction verging on theft imposed by the mightiest on the weakest. Shakespeare's Agincourt says much about the real ethics of warfare. Politics and piracy are akin even in the most civilized of cultures. Jean Bodin in his *Republic* draws a parallel between pirates and some modern statesmen:

> [. . .] et quoy qu'ils ['les chefs des pirates'] semblent vivre en amitié et société, partageans egalement le butin, comme on disoit de Bargule et de Viriat, neantmoins cela ne doit estre appellé société, ny amitié, ni partage en termes de droit, ains conjurations, voleries, et pillage: car le principal poînct, auquel gist la vraye marque d'amitié, leur defaut, c' est à sçavoir, le droit gouvernment selon les loix de nature.[23]

The ultimate transaction of course—which is perhaps not an act of piracy but a gigantic confidence trick— is the one which Henry tries to conclude with God on the eve of Agincourt. 'Five hundred poor have I in yearly pay / Who twice a day their withered hands hold up / Toward heaven to pardon blood.' (4.1.295-7) Repentance for Henry has a price and victory is as much bought as fought for.

Rose Zimbardo's statement that *Henry V* is "full of warfare, yet empty of conflict" should be qualified if not altogether reversed.[24] *Henry V* is full of latent unresolved political conflict revolving around the notion of war for instance, and yet, it is empty of warfare, as one observes when one tries to list the few scenes which actually depict warfare as such.

On the eve of the battle of Agincourt, when the mood ought to be reconciliatory, the King, in disguise, decides to pay a visit to the more humble members of his army. What he uncovers in so doing is misunderstanding and a patent absence of faith in the rightfulness of the common cause. Henry is here testing the limits of his political power. Despite the medieval notion that the king derived his authority from God—*rex dei gratia*—, "there was no absolute secular monarchy in this period, perhaps because the necessary means of communication and control were lacking."[25] Spreading the Good Word to the lower orders is thus a means of consolidating the royal basis of power. Henry's monarchy is at an intermediary and still rather fragile stage in its transition towards more absolutist tendencies. However hard Henry tries to lend a sympathetic ear to his subjects, his enterprise is doomed to failure from the start. Absolutism—even in its nascent form—entails the subjection of the individual; it is not a system which takes into account the freedom of its subjects. As the medieval historian Henry Myers explains:

> Before monarchy as a European institution could become truly constitutional, it had to develop sufficiently absolutist tendencies to dispose of feudal competition. Only later, after experiencing abuses of absolute monarchy and after absorbing the fact that a medieval balance of estates was neither possible nor desirable, could political theorists stop equivocating about the need for institutions to insure that kingship would indeed be the embodiment of the people's will and interest which medieval political theorists from John of Salisbury through Sir John Fortescue had made it out to be.

The mood at the outset of the scene is not particularly conflictual. Henry underlines the very humanity of the king when divested of the attires of power: 'I think the King is but a man, as I am. [. . .] All his senses have but human conditions. His ceremonies laid by, in his nakedness he appears but a man, and though his affections are higher mounted than ours, yet when they stoop, they stoop with the like wing.' (101-07) Shakespeare's Henry is not far from other popular kingly characters such as Peele's Edward I, Heywood's Edward IV, or the monarchs of *George a Greene.* Yet this is where the parallel stops for Henry encounters hostility in the ranks of his own soldiers. The popular and perhaps populist dream of the happy meeting of king and subject is radically shattered. Henry cannot be solely the private man he once was. The essence of authority is more complex and the roles he has to play cannot be severed. As Anne Barton suggests, Shakespeare "used Henry's disguise to summon up the memory of a wistful, naive attitude toward history and the relationship of subject and king which this play rejects as attractive but untrue: a nostalgic but false romanticism."[26]

Henry's notions of 'just cause' and 'holy war' are in fact totally alien to the lower ranks. Even the King's private self is unable to sway his sceptical subjects:

> KING HARRY: [. . .] *Methinks I could not die anywhere so contented as in the King's company, his cause being just and his quarrel honourable.*
>
> WILLIAMS: *That's more than we know.*
>
> BATES: *Ay, or more than we should seek after. For we know enough if we know we are the King's subjects.* (125-30)

Undertones of civil dissension are also to be felt. Williams conjures up a vivid and accusing picture, resembling a medieval *danse macabre,* in which the severed limbs of soldiers come back to haunt the King's conscience on Judgement Day. This is a particularly interesting picture as what is symbolically portrayed here is the dismemberment of the traditional body politic. The members revolt refusing to show solidarity to the common cause of the body. What is more, these severed members form—re-member—a new body of reproach and sufferance:

> But if the cause be not good, the King himself hath a heavy reckoning to make, when all those legs and arms and heads chopped off in a battle shall join together at the latter day, and cry all, 'We died at such a place'—some swearing, some crying for a surgeon, some upon their wives left poor behind them, some upon the debts they owe, some upon their children rawly left. I am afeard there are few die well that die in a battle, for how can they charitably dispose of anything, when blood is their argument? (133-42)

What this picture brings to the fore at the same time is the realistic effects of war—the butchery which ensues. The irony is that a creature of flesh and blood, identical to them, is sending soldiers to their deaths in the name of a cause which is far from clear. The argument used by Williams stems from a definition of power which is dangerously radical. Power—stripped of its mysticism—is precisely what people have given over to a person of flesh and blood. And it is for this person that people accept to lose their lives. This view, which has the potential of considerably undermining the sacred aura of authority, is well expressed in the writings of Étienne de La Boétie:

> [. . .] et tout ce degast, ce maleur, ceste ruine vous vient non pas des ennemis, mais certes oui bien de l'ennemy, et de celui que vous faites si grand qu'il est, pour lequel vous alles si courageusement a la guerre, pour la grandeur duquel vous ne refuses point de presenter a la mort vos personnes: celui qui vous maistrise tant n'a que deus yeulx, n'a que deus mains, n'a qu'un corps, et n'a autre chose que ce qu'a le moindre homme du grand et infini nombre de vos villes, sinon que l'avantage que vous luy faites pour vous destruire. . . . comment a il aucun pouvoir sur vous que par vous? Comment vous oseroit il courir sus, s'il n'avoit intelligence avec vous?[27]

But Henry's spurious personal logic strives to cover up any such dissonances. The King, responding to Williams in a long didactic speech, actually reveals himself as a cunning logician, if not a 'trickster-king,' as Phillip Mallett has nicknamed him.[28] 'The King is not bound to answer the particular endings of his soldiers, the father of his son, nor the master of his servant, for they purpose not their deaths when they propose their services,' says Henry (154-7). Service is part of the contract but death is not, according to the sovereign. Death is God's domain and violent death is a form of moral punishment. This is certainly a bizarre form of Christian logic: 'Now, if these men have defeated the law and outrun native punishment, though they can outstrip men, they have no wings to fly from God. War is his beadle. War is his vengeance. So that here men are punished for before-breach of the King's laws, in now the King's quarrel.' (165-70) Henry's subtle sophistry makes war and death a godly business totally disconnected from its political cause, i.e. 'the King's quarrel.' Henry is unable to accept responsibility for the massacre he has wilfully prepared. As W. L. Godshalk put it, 'the subtle politics of non-responsibility are Henry's forte.'[29]

'Every subject's duty is the King's, but every subject's soul is his own. Therefore should every soldier in the wars do as every sick man in his bed: wash every mote out of his conscience,' adds Henry (175-8). The King continues to separate duty to the ruler from religious ethics, that is, duty to the King of kings. In his current predicament, it is an advantageous argument. Yet, it is in contradiction with his earlier claims that his war with France *is* a holy war, and that the King's quarrel *is* God's quarrel, in other words that ethics are not distinct from reason of State. The nature of the so-called contract which binds King and subject is no longer clear. 'The Crown,' writes M. M. Reese, 'which is the symbol of majesty, is the higher self of every subject, calling him to great deeds and sacrifice.' He adds: 'The cease of majesty occurs when king and subject no longer realise their partnership in greatness.'[30] What Reese calls 'greatness' is certainly a moot point for it smacks of royal mystique, but the conclusion to be drawn from his comments is that Henry cannot honestly claim to reconcile absolutist demands with the peoples' right.

When one looks beyond the King's set piece on the vanity of royal pomp ('ceremony'), a colder lesson in politics appears:

> *No, not all these, thrice-gorgeous ceremony,*
> *Not all these, laid in bed majestical,*
> *Can sleep so soundly as the wretched slave*
> *Who with a body filled and vacant mind*
> *Gets him to rest*
>
> (263-7)

The running of a state is a relentless task and behind the mystical veil sovereignty is as much earned by action as it is outwardly sustained by words. Tamburlaine's private thought on the essence of his power is a good illustration of this truth: ' . . . for all my byrth, / That Vertue solely is the sum of glorie, / And fashions men with true nobility.'

But what of peace in *Henry V?* The end of war naturally reflects the preexistent divide between king and subject. For the more lowly, peace comes with a sense of personal loss. 'History,' as Nicholas Brooke wrote, 'has no place for tragedy.'[31] Pistol's 'Nell is dead / I'th'spital of a malady of France.' (5.1.77-8) War, not unlike Nell's venereal disease ('a malady of France', significantly), has been a shameful business. Pistol returns to England to be a thief and a bawd.

In contrast, 5.2 depicts the English and French nobles seemingly reunited as a happy family. War for them has been a 'family business' almost: 'Peace to this meeting, wherefor we are met. / Unto our brother France and to our sister, / Health and fair time of day,' are Henry's opening words in the scene (1-3). The scene has also decidedly more prosaic aspects. If war was based on transaction, peace, one hastens to add, is no different. 'You must buy that peace,' says Henry to the Duke of Burgundy (70). Katherine, the French princess, is a commodity that will be part of the bargain: 'She is our capital demand' (96). The difficulty for Henry is now to change from the warrior-king that he was into the royal suitor that he must be. This change is part of the comic aspect of the scene. But it can only be an incomplete change for the two roles are impossible to reconcile fully. A few discordant notes are sounded in the midst of the romantic comedy. Henry cannot completely rid himself of the language of commerce: 'Give me your answer, i'faith do, and so clap hands and a bargain. How say you, lady?' (129-31) Nor can he at times make us forget the bitter role he played in the war: '[. . .] I could lay on like a butcher,' he warns Katherine (141-4). As for Burgundy, his part in the transaction could be equated with that of a bawd—'Is she not apt?', asks the good Duke (!) (283) As Pistol would have it, war may turn men into bawds.

Henry V's Epilogue brings only incomplete resolution. This is not the war to end all wars—far from it. The reason is that 'Henry's reign, one could argue, *is* war itself—its masterpiece being Agincourt.'[32] Naturally, Henry's legacy is more war. His issue will have a baneful lot, even if, for a fleeting moment, 'the world's best garden he achieved.'' (7) The sword will have more blood—blood that will be spilt when the long-postponed and dormant civil war of *Henry V* finally breaks out. From a stage history point of view, this prediction is already an artistic truth ('Which oft our stage hath shown' [13]).

. . . . .

That war is not a necessary but rather an *inevitable* ill amounts to a truism which is not worth debating. However, the conclusion that might be drawn after examining the plays of the Henriad is that, if any justification for human conflict is required, it should be sought in the realm of politics rather than in that of religious ethics. The suggestion that some wars *can* be just should be, as Erasmus points out in *the Education of a Christian Prince,* somewhat qualified:

> Some princes deceive themselves that any war is certainly a just one and that they have a just cause for going to war. We will not attempt to discuss whether war is ever just; but who does not think his own cause just? Among such great and changing vicissitudes of human events, among so many treaties and agreements which are now entered into, now rescinded, who can lack a pretext—if there is any real excuse—for going to war?

The greatest deception of all—which Erasmus does not mention, perhaps precisely out of political prudence—lies in the constantly renewed ability of the ruling powers to substitute the ideal for the real. Is this to disguise the uneasiness caused by the inescapable separation of ethics and politics in the modern world? What remains clear is that deception seems to be the only means to justify the concept of death *pro patria.*

Notes

[1] All references to Shakespeare's plays are taken from: William Shakespeare, *The Complete Works,* eds. Stanley Wells and Gary Taylor (Oxford: Clarendon Press, 1986).

[2] Some would have us think that these effects were intended and that the film is an echo of the Thatcherite imperialistic show of strength and its accompanying militaristic patriotism during the Falklands war: "the Falklands war bequeathed to British culture a decidedly ambiguous interest in war, not entirely unconnected with the characteristic emotions of patriotism." Branagh himself, in his interpretation of Henry, has been viewed as an icon of the Thatcherite self-made man: "Branagh too talks like a winner, and *Henry V* offers him better than any other play in the repertoire what might be called a yuppy dynamic, a mythology of success and self-definition rather than struggle." (Graham Holderness, *Shakespeare Recycled: The Making of Historical Drama* [London and New York: Harvester, 1992] 201, 202). This is a path which is perhaps too easy to follow—one which, at all events, the present article will not tread.

[3] G. K. Hunter, 'Religious Nationalism in Later History Plays,' in Vincent Newey and Ann Thompson, eds., *Literature and Nationalism* (Liverpool: Liverpool UP, 1991): 88.

[4] G. K. Hunter, 'Shakespeare's Politics and the Rejection of Falstaff,' *Critical Quarterly* 3.1 (1959): 234. Hunter adds convincingly that "the requirement to keep details of the whole cycle in mind seems to take the

plays out of the theatre, or at least to imply a coterie audience-response more proper to Bayreuth than the Globe." (234-5)

[5] The argument is borrowed from Ernst Kantorowicz's more complex analyses in: 'Pro Patria Mori in Medieval Political Thought,' American Historical Review 56 (1951): 472-92. Pro Patria Mori—which serves as the title of this article—is taken from Horace's second Roman Ode (III,2).

[6] Henry A. Myers, Medieval Kingship (Chicago: Nelson Hall, 1982) 4-5. The subsequent reference to this book is to pages 297-8.

[7] Leonard Tennenhouse, Power on Display, The Politics of Shakespeare's Genres (New York and London: Methuen, 1986): 83.

[8] David Scott Kastan, 'Proud Majesty Made a Subject: Shakespeare and the Spectacle of Rule,' Shakespeare Quarterly 37.4 (1986): 464.

[9] Robert Ornstein, A Kingdom for a Stage, The Achievement of Shakespeare's History Plays (Cambridge: Harvard UP, 1972): 26-7.

[10] Alexander B. Grosart, ed., The Complete Works in Verse and Prose of Samuel Daniel, vol. 5 (New York: Russell, 1963) 30. Subsequent references to Samuel Daniel are respectively taken from: vol. 2, 96 and 155.

[11] Pierre Sahel, 'The Strangeness of a Dramatic Style: Rumour in Henry VIII,' Shakespeare Survey 38 (1985): 150.

[12] Francis Bacon, The Essays, ed. John Pitcher (Harmondsworth: Penguin, 1985) 103. Subsequent references to Francis Bacon are respectively extracted from pages 106 and 117.

[13] Niccolo Macchiavelli, Nicholas Machiavel's Prince [Facsimile reprint of the 1640 English translation] (Amsterdam and New York: Da Capo P, 1968): 111.

[14] Moody E. Prior, The Drama of Power, Studies in Shakespeare's History Plays (Evanston: Northwestern UP, 1973): 341.

[15] David Norbrook, "What Cares these Roarers for the Name of King?: 'Language and Utopia in The Tempest' in Gordon McMullan and Jonathan Pope, eds. The Politics of Tragicomedy, Shakespeare and After (London: Routledge, 1991): 24.

[16] For a detailed account of this type of criticism see Zdenek Stribrny, 'Henry V and History,' in Arnold Kettle, ed. Shakespeare in a Changing World (London: Lawrence, 1964): 85.

[17] William Babula, 'Whatever Happened to Prince Hal? An Essay on Henry V,' Shakespeare Survey 30 (1977): 55-56.

[18] Walter Ullmann, Medieval Political Thought (Harmondsworth: Penguin, 1970): 17.

[19] John of Salisbury, Policraticus: Of the Frivolities of Courtiers and the Footprints of Philosophers, ed. and trans. Cary J. Nederman (Cambridge UP, 1990): 32.

[20] J.G.A. Pocock, The Machiavellian Moment: Florentine Political Thought and the Atlantic Republican Tradition (Princeton UP, 1975): 28.

[21] Quoted in Andrew Gurr, 'Henry V and the Bees' Commonwealth,' Shakespeare Survey 30 (1977): 62. Subsequent quotations from Erasmus are taken from the same article, pages 63 and 64.

[22] Christopher Marlowe, Tamburlaine Part I in The Complete Works of Christopher Marlowe, ed. Fredson Bowers, vol. 1 (Cambridge: Cambridge UP, 1973). The subsequent reference made to Tamburlaine is from the same edition, 5.1.188-90.

[23] Jean Bodin, Les six livres de la République, vol. 1 (Paris: Fayard, 1986): 30.

[24] Rose A. Zimbardo, 'The Formalism of Henry V,' in Anne Paolucci, ed., Shakespeare Encomium, The City College Papers I (New York: Enterprise Press, 1964): 16.

[25] Antony Black, Political Thought in Europe 1250-1450 (Cambridge: Cambridge UP, 1992): 137.

[26] Anne Barton, 'The King Disguised, Shakespeare's Henry V and the Comical History,' in Joseph G. Price, ed., The Triple Bond, Plays, Mainly Shakespearean, in Performance (University Park and London: Pennsylvania State UP, 1975): 99.

[27] Étienne de La Boétie, De la servitude volontaire ou Contr'un, ed. Nadia Gontabert (Paris: Gallimard, 1993): 87.

[28] Phillip Mallett, 'Shakespeare's Trickster-Kings: Richard III and Henry V,' in Paul V.A. Williams, ed., The Fool and the Trickster, Studies in Honour of Enid Welsford (Cambridge: Brewer, 1979): 64.

[29] W.L. Godshalk, 'Henry V's Politics of Non-Responsibility,' Cahiers Élisabéthains 17 (1980): 12.

[30] M.M. Reese, The Cease of Majesty, A Study of Shakespeare's History Plays (London: Arnold, 1961): 109.

[31] Nicholas Brooke, 'Reflecting Gems and Dead Bones: Tragedy versus History in *Richard III*,' *Critical Quarterly* 7.2 (1965): 126.

[32] My translation. 'Le règne de Henri c'est, pourrait-on dire, la guerre même et son chef-d'œuvre, c'est Azincourt.' Pierre Sahel, 'Henri V, Roi idéal?,' *Études Anglaises* (1975): 3.

Source: "*Pro Patria Mori*: War and Power in the Henriad," in *Cahiers Élisabéthains*, Vol. 51, April, 1997, pp. 29-44.

Shakespeare at Work: 'Attributed Dialogue'

E. Pearlman, *University of Colorado, Denver*

Here is some familiar dialogue from *The First Part of King Henry the Fourth:*

> *Hotsp.* Fie vpon this quiet life, I want worke.
> *Lady.* O my sweet *Harry,* how many hast thou kill'd to day?
> *Hotsp.* Giue my Roane horse a drench. Some fourteen, a trifle, a trifle.

In this carefully drawn domestic picture, the Percies, husband and wife, engage in tense but affectionate banter. Kate is all admiration, while Hotspur is unaccountably aloof—less interested in his wife than he is attracted by a favorite horse and by the "worke" of warfare. He is also more than a bit megalomaniacal, airily dismissing a morning's murderous exercise as a mere "trifle."

Although these lines may sound authentic, they are quite obviously a counterfeit, for neither Hotspur nor his lady ever speaks such words *in propria persona.* In actual fact, what happens is that playful Prince Hal amuses his friend Poins with a piece of extremely accomplished mimicry:

> Prin. I am not yet of *Percies* mind, the Hotspurre of the North, he that kills me some sixe or seauen dozen of Scots at a Breakfast, washes his hands, and saies to his wife; Fie vpon this quiet life, I want worke. O my sweet *Harry* says she, how many hast thou kill'd to day? Giue my Roane horse a drench (sayes hee) and answeres, some fourteen, an houre after: a trifle, a trifle.

(I.4.97-102; TLN 1065-71)[1]

The conversation between Kate and Hotspur is, therefore, dialogue that is not spoken by the characters in question but instead consists of lines that are improvised and then attributed to them by the prince. In this fabrication, Hal plays (and therefore plays at being) both Hotspur and Kate. As Hal imagines the Percy family, Kate is doting and submissive, Hotspur thrasonical. By placing Hotspur's lines in the prince's mouth, Shakespeare can succinctly delineate not only Hal's envy but also his admiration for his great antagonist. The prince's mimicry is persuasive because the dialogue that Shakespeare has so adroitly wrought sounds almost like real Percy as it might be transmitted by an equally real Hal. It is all so effortlessly achieved that the playwright's remarkable artistry remains both unobtrusive and unacknowledged.

"Attributed dialogue" of the sort that Hal employs is a sophisticated playmaking technique that Shakespeare adopted and refined over the course of his career. It must be confessed that Shakespeare did not know how to make use of attributed dialogue when he took his first tentative steps as a playwright. Except for an occasional moment in which an otherwise anonymous messenger reports some second-hand news, the earliest plays seldom exploit this device—and they certainly never do so with the ingenuity of Hal's impersonation of the Percies. (The only regular appearance of attributed dialogue in the apprentice plays is the clownish monologue in which the latter development of this technique may very well have its roots.) What, then, are the general characteristics of attributed dialogue, and how did Shakespeare learn to put this technique to good use?

In essence, attributed dialogue configures a relationship between the speaker, a ventriloquist, and another character (or characters) who serves as a foil to him. So in Hal's satirical excursus on Hotspur and Kate in *1 Henry IV,* Hal is the ventriloquist and Hotspur and Kate the foils who become the targets of his mockery.

By the second half of the 1590s, when he was engaged in the great venture of the second series of history plays, Shakespeare had devised some fairly subtle strategies to manage the relationship between the two figures. For example, in the naturalistic but carefully crafted sentence "Giue my Roane horse a drench (sayes hee) and answeres, some fourteen, an houre after: a trifle, a trifle," the phrases that Hal ascribes to Hotspur are separated and discontinuous. They appear as three distinct units of direct quotation. In the interstices Hal has inserted phrases ("[sayes hee] and answeres" and "an houre after") that are designed to characterize the object of his satire. By breaking the sentence ascribed to Hotspur into punctuated segments, Shakespeare contrives it so that the focus remains on Hal the narrator. Hotspur—the Hotspur of Hal's invention, that is—is therefore both controlled by Hal and subordinated to him.

In so representing the conflict between Hal and Hotspur, Shakespeare uses a technique akin to classic fiction's "suspended quotation."[2] If a nineteenth-century novelist were to write about Harry Percy, she might tell her tale in this way:

> "Give my roan horse a drench," cried Hotspur. He waited a few moments. "Some fourteen," he murmured. A short while later he added, almost negligently, "a trifle, a trifle."

A suspended quotation is a rhetorical device that serves to maintain the continuity of the "authorial" voice. By bringing to bear such descriptive terms as "cried," "murmured," and "almost negligently," the narrator enters the story as the omniscient guide—, or moralist perhaps, or social critic—, who regulates, or attempts to regulate, the responses of her readership. In a similar way, Hal also suspends (so to speak) Hotspur's quotation by interspersing parenthetical modifiers. And he does so for aims similar to those of the novelist: the great Boar's Head scene in which these lines appear engages Hotspur only tangentially but takes as its principal subject the education of the prince—so that Hal begins by unconscionably tormenting the lowly drawer Francis but eventually takes a step or so toward reconciling himself to the inevitability of his future kingship. Honoring the priorities of the scene as a whole, Shakespeare suppresses (syntactically speaking) the northern youth, the foil, in order to enfranchise the ventriloquist prince.

In *1 Henry IV,* the ingenious exploitation of attributed dialogue is not confined to this speech alone. The prince's impersonation of Percy, it will be remembered, comments directly on a preceding event—an extended conversation between Kate and Hotspur. In that scene, Hotspur had been both abrupt and negligent ("How now Kate, I must leaue you within these two hours" [II.3.34-35; TLN 884]), engrossed by things military, and even ("That Roane shall be my Throne" [67; TLN 920]) preoccupied with a favorite horse. (Hal's knowledge of the Percy household is so intimate that it almost seems as though he has been eavesdropping at the tiring-house door.) The domestic scene is also, and surely not inadvertently, another of those in which Shakespeare employs attributed dialogue to great advantage—although this time it is dialogue of a different species than that invented by Hal. In this case, Kate is the ventriloquist who repeats by light of day the words she has heard Hotspur mutter in the course of his agitated sleep:

> In my faint-slumbers, I by thee haue watcht,
> And heard thee murmore tales of Iron Warres:
> Speake tearmes of manage to thy bounding
> Steed,
> Cry courage to the field. And thou hast talk'd
> Of Sallies, and Retires; Trenches, Tents,
> Of Palizadoes, Frontiers, Parapets,
> Of Basiliskes, of Canon, Culuerin,
> Of Prisoners ransome, and of Souldiers slaine,
> And all the current of a headdy fight.
>   (44-52; TLN 895-903)

While Hal improvises his pillorying of the Percies, Kate (an audience is to presume) reports on phrases that she has heard in Hotspur's own mouth. Unlike Hal's account, hers is delivered as indirect discourse. Hotspur, exclaims his loyal but neglected lady, has told "tales of Iron Warres." Yet Kate never reveals the particular tales that Hotspur has recited. Hotspur murmured "of" various "tearmes of manage," "of" "Prisoners ransome," and "of" "Souldiers Slaine." But even though his words are given only indirectly, an audience hears not Kate's but Hotspur's intonations. Kate remains invisible and subordinated to the image of Hotspur that she begets; only the partitive "of" forestalls her complete obliteration. In an expression such as "Speake tearmes of manage to thy bounding Steed,/ Cry courage to the field," the patterns of reported speech replicate Hotspur's idiom, not Kate's; "bounding steed" is perfect Percy, while "Cry courage to the field"—which might even be repunctuated as "Cry 'courage' to the field"—is so energetic an outcry that Kate's intervention can scarcely be detected. The litany of military terms—"Sallies, Retires, Trenches, Palizadoes, Parapets, Basiliskes"—comprises the technical vocabulary of warfare, and is therefore far wide of what is later affirmed to be Kate's customary style—an idiom mocked by Hotspur as a "protest of Pepper Ginger-bread" only suitable to "Veluet-Guards, and Sunday-Citizens" (III.1.253-4; TLN 1801-02). While Hal, speaking others' lines, retains his prominence, Kate (saving the crucial "of") fades into little more than a translucency through which the dazzling Harry Percy may shine.

An equally accomplished use of "attributed dialogue" occurs a few scenes further on in the play, when, the tables turned, Hotspur himself becomes for a brief moment the agent who speaks in the vocabulary and rhythms of the Welsh guerrilla Owen Glendower. "He angers me," blurts Hotspur, unable to rein in his disdain for marcher superstition,

> With telling me of the Moldwarpe and the
> Ant,
> Of the Dreamer *Merlin,* and his Prophecies;
> And of a Dragon, and a finne-lesse Fish,
> A clip-wing'd Griffin, and a moulten Rauen,
> A couching Lyon, and a ramping Cat,
> And such a deal of skimble-skamble Stuffe,
> As puts me from my Faith.
>   (146-153; TLN 1678-85)

Reciting the great magician's roll call of mythical creatures, Hotspur momentarily speaks English with a Welsh or Glendowerian lilt—or, at least, he does so up until the irascible irruption of "skimble-skamble Stuffe," in which both iterative compound and sibilance celebrate his momentary recapture of the rhetorical initiative. It is not long after that the out-talked Hotspur is reduced to recapitulating his own irritable grunts of the previous evening: "I cry'd hum, and well, goe too,/ But mark'd him not a word" (156-7; TLN 1689-90). Shakespeare portrays with great precision a clash of idioms in which the braggart mage chases the braggart soldier from the field of language.

There is also a superbly climactic instance of attributed dialogue at the end of the play, when Hotspur, having been defeated in single combat by the prince, finds himself unable to bring his own sentence to completion:

> O, I could Prophesie,
> But that the Earth, and the cold hand of
>   death,
> Lyes on my Tongue: No *Percy.* thou art dust
> And food for [. . .]
> *Prin.* For Wormes, braue *Percy.*

A prince whose competition with Percy has earlier led him to mimic his rival's speech finds it easy to imitate it still one last time; an audience that has witnessed so many instances of attribution can therefore be confident that Hotspur's thoughts are revealed in Hal's words. Hal triumphs not in woes only but in words also.

Attributed dialogue in *1 Henry IV* and in the plays written after it can be both sophisticated and complex. In the earlier dramas, on the other hand, its occasional manifestations are on the whole flat and monochromatic. A representative instance: Talbot describes (in *1 Henry VI*) his mistreatment at the hands of the ignoble French.

> With scoffes and scornes, and contumelious
>   taunts,
> In open Market-place produc't they me,
> To be a publique spectacle to all:
> Here, sayd they, is the Terror of the French,
> The Scar-Crow that affrights our Children so.
>   (I.4.39-43; TLN 506-10)

The lines attributed to a generic and unparticularized citizenry do very little more than exemplify the scorn that Talbot has already described. Another uncomplicated kind of attributed dialogue appears in *Richard III* when the doomed George of Clarence relates a neoclassical dream of foreboding; in the process he includes a series of attributed Senecan sentences, prominent among them those of the ghost of Henry VI's son Edward, who

> came wand'ring by,
> A shadow like an Angell, with bright hayre
> Dabbel'd in blood, and he shriek'd out alowd
> *Clarence* is come, false, fleeting, periur'd
>   *Clarence,*
> That stabb'd me in the field by Tewkesbury:
> Seize on him Furies, take him vnto Torment.
>   (I.4.52-7; TLN 888-93)

A more promising early instance of attributed dialogue occurs when hapless Lady Anne recalls her initial reaction to Richard's offer of marriage:

> O, when I say I look'd on *Richards* Face,
> This was my Wish: Be thou (quoth I)
>   accurst,
> For making me, so young, so old a Widow:
> And when thou wed'st let sorrow haunt thy
>   Bed:
> And me thy Wife, if any be so mad,
> More miserable, by the Life of thee,
> Then thou hast made me, by my dear Lords
>   death.
>   (IV.1.68-74; TLN 2550-6)

Anne's actual words were slightly less vivid; she had in fact prayed of Richard that "If euer he haue Wife, let her be made/ More miserable by the death of him,/ Then I am made by [the death of] my young Lord, and thee" (I.2.26-28; TLN 200-02). Overlooking an opportunity to create stereoptic effects, Shakespeare did not further explore the tension between the words Anne assigned to her earlier self and the words she had actually spoken.

Attributed dialogue, it is clear, becomes a potentially powerful device when Anne reports on Anne, Hal on Hotspur or Hotspur on Glendower—that is, when both the ventriloquist and the foil are well known to the audience. It is less suggestive when Talbot tells of "the French" or Clarence quotes the words of a wraith-like Edward. In the earliest plays, such attributions as Shakespeare contrives are generally of the less challenging sort. With rare exception the audience hears only the words of characters with whom it is otherwise unfamiliar: characters who are 'projected' by the speaker and who are not embodied on the stage.[3] An instance: when, in *The Two Gentlemen of Verona*, Launce tells how Crab disgraced himself in the company of "three or foure gentleman-like-dogs, vnder the Dukes table" (1835-6), Shakespeare gives his clown the opportunity to perform four different staccato voices in rapid succession; all, to be sure, are anonymous:

> [Crab] had not bin there (blesse the marke) a pissing while, but all the chamber smelt him: out with the dog (saies one) what cur is that (saies another) whip him out (saies the third) hang him vp (saies the Duke).
>
>   (IV.4.17-21; TLN 1837-40)

And then Launce proceeds to re-enact a conversation between himself and the dog-disciplinarian:

> I hauing bin acquainted with the smell before, knew it was Crab; and goes me to the fellow that whips the dogges: friend (quoth I) you meane to whip the dog: I marry doe I (quoth he) you do him the more wrong (quoth I) 'twas I did the thing you wot of: he makes me no more adoe but whips me out of the chamber. . . .
>
>   (21-7; TLN 1841-6)

The various speakers (saving the clown himself) appear just this one time and exist only as they are projected by Launce. Launce's monopolylogue is a marvel of colloquial exuberance in which vulgar ethical datives ("goes me," "makes me no more adoe") jostle against pious but ill-aimed euphemisms ("hauing bin acquainted," "the thing you wot of"). Launce is a superb anecdotalist and a splendid stand-up comedian, but as an attributer of dialogue, he still has much to learn before he will be capable of competing with Kate or Hotspur or Hal.

In *The Merchant of Venice,* written four or five years later than *Two Gentlemen,* Shakespeare employed attributed dialogue in inherited ways but also in new and adventurous reconfigurations. An example of old-fashioned attribution occurs when Launcelot Gobbo, working in the clownish tradition of Launce and Dromio, speaks the words of the types of morality figures who a decade earlier might have appeared on stage in their own persons. (It is characteristic of the early Shakespeare, incidentally, to attribute dialogue to abstractions; other examples occur in *Richard III,* when one of Clarence's murderers converses with 'conscience,' and in *King John,* when the Bastard Faulconbridge parodies polite conversation in the form of a discourse between 'question' and 'answer': "O sir, sayes answer, at your best command,/ At your employement, at your seruice sir" [I.1.196-7; TLN 207-08]). In *The Merchant of Venice,* young Launcelot Gobbo might easily pass for a cousin of old Launce:

> Certainely, my conscience will serue me to run from this Iew my Maister: the fiend is at mine elbow, and tempts me, saying to me, *Iobbe, Launcelet Iobbe,* good *Launcelet,* or good *Iobbe,* or good *Lancelet Iobbe,* use your legs, take the start, run awaie: my conscience saies no; take heede honest *Launcelet,* take heed, honest *Iobbe* or as afore-said honest *Launcelet Iobbe,* doe not runne, scorne running with thy heeles. . . .

> (I.2.1-8; TLN 568-75)

Yet unlike the inarticulate dog-whipper, the "fiend" at Gobbo's elbow has developed his own sputtering and repetitive style; when he exhorts Launce to defect, he makes use of three separate but similar locutions: "use your legs, take the start, run awaie." Before he concludes, Gobbo manages to add still another voice to his monopolylogue, for in addition to fiend and conscience, he plays himself in the act of debate with the two abstractions: "wel, my conscience saies Lancelet bouge not, bouge saies the fiend, bouge not saies my conscience, conscience say I you counsaile well, fiend say I you counsaile well . . ." (16-20; TLN 583-6). But even in this very capable show, "fiend" and "conscience" speak in the familiar vernacular *copia* of the clowning from which they descend—nor does Shakespeare make an effort to generate real individuality of speech or to create complex links between ventriloquist and foil.

Yet in the very same play, cheek to jowl with Gobbo's traditional performance, the technique of attributed dialogue takes a great forward leap. One of Shylock's most familiar speeches deserves to be looked at afresh for its unprecedented and exceedingly deft deployment of attributions:

> Signior *Anthonio,* many a time and oft
> In the Ryalto you haue rated me
> About my monies and my vsances:
> Still haue I borne it with a patient shrug,
> (For suffrance is the badge of all our Tribe.)
> You call me misbeleeuer, cut-throate dog,
> And spet vpon my Iewish gaberdine,
> And all for vse of that which is mine owne.
> Well then, it now appeares you neede my
>   helpe:
> Go to then, you come to me, and you say,
> *Shylocke,* we would haue your moneyes, you
>   say so:
> You that did voide your rume vpon my beard,
> And foote me as you spurne a stranger curre
> Ouer your threshold, moneyes is your suite.
> What should I say to you? Should I not say,
> Hath a dog money? Is it possible
> A curre should lend three thousand ducats? or
> Should I bend low, and in a bond-mans key
> With bated breath and whispering
>   humblenesse,
> Say this: Faire sir, you spet on me on
>   Wednesday last:
> You spurn'd me such a day; another time
> You cald me dog: and for these curtesies
> Ile lend you thus much moneyes.
>   (1.3.102-25; TLN 434-56)

Preserving the outward shell of traditional clowning but reforming its content, Shylock performs as both ventriloquist and foil in order to act out a dialogue of his own device. Mulling over (in a kind of past imperfect tense) the abuses of "many a time and oft" that so rankle him, he returns Antonio's own words, rendered both directly ("You call me misbeleeuer, cut-throate dog") and indirectly ("you haue rated me/ About my monies and my vsances"), against their speaker. He imagines phrases with which he might reply to Antonio's proposals ("Should I not say,/ Hath a dog money?"). Shylock answers both Antonio's recalled and imagined words with affected astonishment, and he casts his response in what might be called a reported conditional: "What should I say to you? Should I not say,/ Hath a dog money? Is it possible/ A curre should lend three thousand ducats?"

Shylock's longish speech moves rapidly, in large part because of its imaginative use of various species of attributed dialogue. For example: the two lines "Go to then, you come to me, and you say,/ *Shylocke,* we would haue your moneyes, you say so" are quite ingeniously constructed. Shylock rails against the irreconcilable contradiction between Antonio's principles and his practices (that is, between his hatred of usury and his hunger to borrow). His impersonation of Antonio—"*Shylocke,* we would haue your moneyes"—distills to its essence the Christian merchant's hypocrisy. When the moneylender puts his own name in Antonio's mouth, he implies that Antonio lays claim to some sort of intimacy with him—or at least he suggests that the Venetian would be willing to mortify his scruples for the sake of personal advantage. But the fraudulent intimacy of "Shylocke . . ." is immediately overthrown by the domineering "we would haue. . . ." The regal plural—the "we"—utterly belies whatever claim to personal relationship "Shylocke . . ." makes. The verb itself—"would have"—is exceedingly peremptory; in Shylock's ventriloquy, Antonio cannot be permitted a gracious or mannerly locution such as "Shylock, I would beg," or "Shylock, I seek to borrow." The incongruity between the hypocritical "Shylock . . ." and the utterly imperious "we would have your moneyes" generates the derisive irony—irony so caustic that it allows abominable manners to be characterized as "curtesies"—on which the entirely of the speech pivots. "Shylocke, we would haue your moneyes" carries such great moral weight in part because of its position of emphasis, embedded as it is within two lines of entirely unadorned, unornamented demotic monosyllables. It is introduced by "Go to then, you come to me, and you say" and subtended by a realistic if hypermetrical growl—"you say so"—that expresses Shylock's astonishment (whether feigned or genuine is impossible to establish) at Antonio's presumption. The entire speech, a truly masterful achievement, is fluent and natural; although they are engulfed and concealed by the flood of Shylock's passion, its subtle but revolutionary technical innovations deserve notice.

Why does the playwright lean so heavily on attributed dialogue at this particular juncture? Much has to do with the way Shylock is portrayed. The materialist moneylender is neither theorist nor philosopher; Shakespeare grants him little or no capacity for abstract thought or generalization. Shylock can only comprehend the past by recalling, or re-imagining, or reproducing phrases that have been (or might have been) spoken. The dialogue that Shylock recollects and renders is therefore in its own way as physical and material as other concrete markers of his character—the three thousand ducats, the knife, the pound of flesh, the turquoise. In this unpleasant speech Shakespeare appeals equally to the compassion and to the bigotry of his audience; he employs an unobtrusive but very accomplished technique to lay bare the process by which Antonio's poisonous words provoke (although they do not excuse) Shylock's intransigent villainy.

Shylock's counterpoint of voices may serve to direct attention to other illustrous instances of attributed dialogue in *The Merchant of Venice.* A notable use: the consecutive and cleverly juxtaposed episodes in which first Shylock's words are reported by Solanio and then, immediately afterward, Antonio's are reported by Salerio. According to Salerio (although why he should be privy to so intimate a matter is mysterious), Antonio has instructed Bassanio, his attractive young protege, to pursue Portia assiduously. Antonio is reported to have said (and Salerio cites the exact words), "Slubber not businesse for my sake Bassanio, / But stay the very riping of the time" (II.8.39-40; TLN 1094-5). Moreover, Antonio is said to have added (once again in Salerio's redaction):

> And for the *Iewes* bond which he hath of me,
> Let it not enter in your minde of loue:
> Be merry, and imploy your chiefest thoughts
> To courtship, and such faire ostents of loue
> As shall conueniently become you there.
> (41-4; TLN 1097-101)

These high and ennobling sentiments appear just after another narration composed almost entirely of attributed dialogue. The two speeches are clearly designed to be considered in tandem, not only because both are instances of attribution but also because Solanio (to whom Shylock's words are given) is as empty a vessel as his counterpart Salerio. In deliberate contrast to Antonio's impossibly fastidious and elevated exhortation, Shylock's sentences are ludicrous and degraded. Solanio tells his tale:

> I neuer heard a passion so confusd,
> So strange, outragious, and so variable,
> As the dogge *Iew* did vtter in the streets;
> My daughter, O my ducats: O my daughter,
> Fled with a Christian, O my Christian ducats!
> Iustice, the law, my ducats, and my daughter;
> A sealed bag, two sealed bags of ducats,
> Of double ducats, stoln from me by my
>   daughter,
> And iewels, two stones, two rich and precious
>   stones,
> Stolne by my daughter: iustice, finde the girle,
> She hath the stones vpon her, and the ducats.
> (12-22; TLN 1067-77)

As frivolous as it may be to dispute the ascription of fictional speech, and with all due respect for Solanio's solemn testimony, it must nevertheless be doubted whether Shylock ever said any such thing. Solanio asks the audience to believe that Shylock railed in the Venetian streets not in his own well-developed idiom, but in clownspeak—in the language of Launce or Launcelot Gobbo. "O my Christian ducats," although amusing, is not Shylockian—it is very obviously the embroidered fibbery of an interventionist reporter.

Moreover, the trope on which the speech rests is an elongated equivocation in which bags stand for the scrotum and stones are testes—and while it is not surprising that Shylock should be unconscious of his own metaphor, he does not elsewhere sustain a figure—let alone a bawdy one—at such length. Solanio speaks not in the voice of Shylock, but as a generic jealous *senex* with whom the stereotype of the Jewish usurer has been forcibly conflated. Shakespeare sacrifices Shylock's particularity of language to crude punning because it is the clowning itself that is his purpose; the playwright wants to provoke as well as to legitimatize an Elizabethan audience's howls of triumph. It is just as well that the speech is attributed rather than enacted, because in Shylock's own mouth the lines would strain credibility and the nasty guffaws that are the speech's aim might thereby be defeated.

Once Shakespeare had achieved fluency with attributed dialogue, he created a number of characters who were virtuosi at the art. Hostess Quickly, for example, is not only a prodigious attributer but she is also the queen of the suspended quotation. It is not unusual, in fact, for her to suspend far more than she quotes: "I was before Master Tisick the Deputie, the other day: and as hee said to me, it was no longer agoe then Wednesday last" (*2 Henry IV* I.4.78-80; TLN 1112-14), she begins, and then breathlessly reports Tisick's words:

> Neighbour *Quickly* (sayes hee;) Master *Dombe,* our Minister, was by then: Neighbour *Quickly* (sayes hee) receiue those that are Ciuill; for (sayth hee) you are in an ill Name: now hee said so, I can tell whereupon: for (sayes hee) you are an honest Woman, and well thought on; therefore take heede what Guests you receiue: Receiue (sayes hee) no swaggering Companions. There comes none heere. You would blesse you to heare what hee said. No, Ile no Swaggerers.

> (80-8; TLN 1114-21)

Quickly's disorderly consciousness teems with parenthesis and digression and interjection and reminiscence, but she is an indifferent ventriloquist and the boundary between her own words and those of her foil is easily breached. As a result an audience may come to suspect that Master Tisick exists nowhere but in her own addled imagination. In a later play, incarnated once again, she employs attributed dialogue even in so crucial a context as the death of Falstaff:

> How now Sir *Iohn* (quoth I?) what man? be a good cheare: so a cryed out, God, God, God, three or foure times: now I, to comfort him, bid him a should not thinke of God; I hop'd there was no neede to trouble himself with any such thoughts yet.

> (*Henry V* II.3.17-21; TLN 939-44)

Even if its technical brashness is not immediately apparent, it is nevertheless a very daring moment. Shakespeare allows Quickly to report not only her own expressions but also the words of one of literature's most talkative characters—one whose habits of speech are extremely familiar—and yet the only phrase poor moribund Falstaff is allotted is the thrice-repeated moan, "God, God, God." At the same time, the Hostess's self-quotations, suspensions, and misadvised compassion are so unobtrusively and naturally rendered that they do not obscure the larger resonances of her narrative.

In the second half of his career. Shakespeare was still capable of inventing new varieties of attribution. An innovation in the art occurs when Hamlet, a frequent attributer, describes how Horatio and the other watchers of the night might use hints and suggestions to violate their oaths of secrecy. They should not betray him, instructs Hamlet, by standing

> With Armes encombred thus, or thus, head
>   shake;
> Or by pronouncing of some doubtfull Phrase;
> As well, we know, or we could and if we
>   would,
> Or if we list to speake; or there be and if
>   there might,
> Or such ambiguous giuing out. . . .
>   (1.5.173-7; TLN 869-73)

The embedded phrases, 'well, we know,' 'we could and if we would,' 'if we list to speake' 'there be' and 'if there might' are, exactly as Hamlet claims, not specific but typical. There is a similar but even more daring use of exemplary attribution in *Timon of Athens,* where a series of imaginary or projected persons are realized and then almost immediately discarded. Flavius the steward has been sent to Timon's friends to seek relief. "They answer," says Flavius, his heap of fragments the achievement of a supremely confident playwright,

>   in a ioynt and corporate voice,
> That now they are at fall, want Treasure[,]
>   cannot
> Do what they would, are sorrie: you are
>   honourable,
> But yet they could haue wisht, they know not,
> Something hath been amisse; a Noble Nature
> May catch a wrench; would all were well; tis
>   pitty.
>   (II.2.200-05; TLN 885-90)

As monopolylogue, this passage is a lineal (but highly evolved) descendant of Launce's defence of Crab.

This survey of the maturing of attributed dialogue would be incomplete if it failed to consider Shakespeare's single most suggestive instance of the art. In *Othello,* Iago "proves" Desdemona's infidelity:

> I lay with *Cassio* lately,
> And being troubled with a raging tooth,
> I could not sleepe. There is a kinde of men,
> So loose of Soule, that in their sleepes will mutter
> Their Affayres: one of this kinde is *Cassio:*
> In sleepe I heard him say, sweet *Desdemona,*
> Let vs be wary, let vs hide our Loues,
> And then (Sir) would he gripe, and wring my hand:
> Cry, oh sweet Creature: then kisse me hard,
> As if he pluckt vp kisses by the rootes,
> That grew vpon my lippes, laid his Leg ore my Thigh,
> And sigh, and kisse, and then cry cursed Fate
> That gaue thee to the Moore.
>   (TLN 2061-73; III.3.419-31)

Iago attributes three telling phrases to Cassio: "sweet *Desdemona,/* Let us be wary, let vs hide our Loues," "oh sweet Creature," and "cursed Fate/ That gaue thee to the Moore." Because he knows that Othello is maddened by jealousy, Iago makes only a half-hearted effort to counterfeit Cassio's style of speech. "Sweet creature" sounds like the Cassio who so admires Desdemona, but the apostrophe "cursed Fate" sacrifices mimicry to melodrama. Iago's impersonation of Cassio does not consist of these phrases only; it is supplemented by what might be called 'attributed acts.' According to the fabrication, Cassio grips Iago's hand, kisses him, lays his leg over his thigh, sighs and kisses again. The coupling of attributed speech and attributed action creates the illusion that Iago totally metamorphoses himself into his foil. He imagines the Florentine lieutenant so vividly that it almost seems as though he inhabits his body.

What renders this particular instance of attributed dialogue so pregnant is Iago's malignant versatility: he plays not only the part of Cassio but that of Desdemona as well, and by doing so acts out both the male and female roles in sexual conjunction. In Iago's sentence, "And then (Sir) would he gripe, and wring my hand," the "he" is Cassio, the "my" is Desdemona. More precisely, the "he" is Iago/Cassio, the "my" Iago/Desdemona. So that while the fantasy overtly renders a vision of Cassio and Desdemona in bed, it also subsumes two other pairs of lovers: Iago and Desdemona and also Iago and Cassio. As a consequence, Iago does far more than simply attribute a handful of sentences to Cassio. The dream he has invented expresses a desire to *be* and at the same time to *penetrate* the two characters who are closest to Othello: the Moor's wife Desdemona and the lieutenant whom he continues to love even after he cashiers him. It becomes clear that when Iago pretends to

be Desdemona, he betrays a desire to share a bed with Othello himself and therefore to supplant both Cassio and Desdemona in the general's heart (as he succeeds in doing at the climax of this aptly nicknamed "seduction scene").

Iago's simultaneous identification both with Cassio and with Desdemona generates a long menu of irregular sexualities. It enacts both narcissism and masturbation, for it depicts Iago in the act of making gleeful love to himself: the leg that is thrown over Iago's thigh is his own. It is certainly homoerotic, in the sense that Iago imagines himself and Cassio as the two backs that comprise this particular beast. It is also multiply adulterous. Without question, it generates a *menage à trois* consisting of Iago, Cassio, and Desdemona. And over and above its polymorphous sexuality is the scene's horrid alloy of sadism and voyeurism. Although he is repulsed by the idea that he might degenerate into a supervisor, grossly gaping on, Othello finds himself in just the position he most fears when he attends to Iago's cruel invention. Shakespeare has employed the art of attributed dialogue so skillfully that he has succeeded in cramming almost all of the play's important characters and a nice selection of perversions into Cassio's crowded bedchamber. The horrors served up in this wicked but accomplished speech make the tragic loading of the bed with which the play ends seem by comparison pure and antiseptic.

Still another outgrowth of this technique—let it be called "putative" or "anti"-attribution—makes a first appearance in *King Lear.* Regan twice demands to know how Lear could have escaped to Dover. Gloucester, tied to the stake and bearing the course, at long last turns on his accusers; he brings his exhilarating response to conclusion with these crucial and imaginative words:

> If Wolues had at thy Gate howl'd that sterne time,
> Thou should'st haue said, good Porter turne the Key:
> All cruels else subscribe: but I shall see
> The winged Vengeance ouertake such Children.
>   (III.7.66-9; TLN 2135-8)

Gloucester imagines what Regan "should"—the auxiliary has the force of "must"—have said. On so cold a night she 'should' have welcomed even wolves to her fire. Gloucester is utterly wrong, of course; Regan would never do any such thing. Nor would she even employ so congenial an adjective as "good" to a servant; it is, after all, only a few seconds afterward that she calls Gloucester a "dogge" and the servant who stands up to Cornwall a "pezant." Neither the politeness nor the sentiment is in her vocabulary. It is difficult to imagine a more succinct demonstration of the contrast between Gloucester's good heart and the daughter's wickedness than the five words the beleagured old man wishes to put in Regan's mouth.

A second exceedingly proficient instance of attributed dialogue appears in this same play. An anonymous Gentleman describes Cordelia's reaction to the discovery that Goneril and Regan have abused her father; he represents Cordelia in terms that are both pictorial and highly artificial. The Gentleman sometimes borders on the allegorical: "patience and sorow [strive[4]]/ Who should expresse her goodliest" (IV.3.16-17; TLN 2110-11); he further implies that Cordelia is a natural force who manifests herself as "Sun shine and raine at once" (18; TLN 2112). In addition, the Gentleman draws upon the metaphysical tradition: tears fell from Cordelia's eyes "as pearles from diamonds dropt" (22; TLN 2116). Even more hyperbolically, he depicts Cordelia as if she were a goddess of mercy who "shooke, /The holy water from her heauenly eyes" (30-1; TLN 2125). Although the Gentleman clearly delights in his own baroque exuberance, when he attributes dialogue to Cordelia he becomes simplicity itself:

> Faith once or twice she heau'd the name of
>   father
> Pantingly forth as if it prest her heart,
> Cried sisters, sisters, shame of Ladies sisters:
> *Kent,* father, sisters, what ith storm ith night.
>   (26-9; TLN 2120-3)

According to the otherwise extravagant Gentleman, Cordelia cannot muster a complete sentence. She is capable only of sobs: "Sisters," "sisters"; "shame of ladies"; "sisters"/ "Kent," "father" "sisters," "what, in the storm?" "in the night." Embedded as they are within the Gentleman's rhetorical overplus, Cordelia's unadorned phrases and monumental restraint seem even more truly heartfelt.

Of all Shakespeare's works, it is *Macbeth*—a play of foul whisperings, rumors, reports understood and misunderstood, and prophesy—in which attributed dialogue is deployed most extensively. Shakespeare brings to bear skills honed over the course of two decades of concentrated experimentation and technical achievement. Paraphrase, the narratives of projected persons, and the indirect and direct discourse of both real and supernatural beings are effortlessly integrated into the dialogue. It is truly an art that hides art—and yet an alert student may easily peer through the scrim to admire the craftsman at work:

> Your Children shall be Kings.
> You shall be King.
> And *Thane* of Cawdor too: went it not so?
> Toth' selfe-same tune, and words.
>   (I.3.86-8; TLN 188-91)

> But I haue spoke with one that saw him
>   die:
> Who did report, that very frankly hee
> Confess'd his Treasons, implor'd your
>   Highnesse Pardon,
> And set forth a deepe Repentance.
>   (I.4.3-6; TLN 283-6)

> *Whiles I stood rapt in the wonder of it, came Missiues from the King, who all-hail'd me Thane of Cawdor, by which Title before, these weyward Sisters saluted me, and referred me to the comming on of time, with haile King that shalt bee.*
>   (I.5.5-9; TLN 353-6)

> Still it cry'd, Sleepe no more to all the
>   House:
> *Glamis* hath murther'd Sleepe, and therefore
>   *Cawdor*
> Shall Sleepe no more: *Macbeth* shall sleepe no
>   more.
>   (II.2.40-2; TLN 698-700)

> The Spirits that know
> All mortal Consequences, haue pronounc'd me
>   thus:
> Feare not *Macbeth,* no man that's borne of
>   woman
> Shall ere haue power vpon thee.
>   (V.3.4-6; TLN 2218-21)

When Lady Macbeth sleepwalks, her dreamworld is saturated with attributed speech that is distorted by the madness through which it has been filtered:

> Wash your hands, put on your Night-Gowne, looke not so pale: I tell you yet againe *Banquo's* buried; he cannot come out on's graue. . . . To bed, to bed: there's knocking at the gate: Come, come, come, come, giue me your hand: What's done, cannot be vndone. To bed, to bed, to bed.
>   (V.1.57-9, 61-2; TLN 2153-5, 2157-9)

This familiar and exceedingly able simulation of emotional torment leans upon Shakespeare's trials with Launce and Shylock and Iago; it could not possibly have taken its particular and glorious shape if the playwright had not served an arduous apprenticeship in the craft and art of attributed dialogue.

Notes

[1] Quotations from Shakespeare's plays are drawn from the facsimile of *The First Folio of Shakespeare* ed. Charlton Hinman (New York: Norton, 1968) and are identified by Hinman's through line numbering (TLN) as well as by the lineation in *William Shakespeare: The Complete Works* ed. Alfred Harbage (Baltimore: Penguin, 1969).

[2] This novelistic technique is studied in detail by Mark Lambert in *Dickens and the Suspended Quotation* (New Haven: Yale UP), 1981.

[3] See E. Pearlman, "Shakespeare's Projected Persons," *Style* 28 (1994), 31-41.

[4] Q streme. This scene does not appear in the Folio. *King Lear* citations and TLN numbers are drawn from *The Complete King Lear 1608-1623,* prepared by Michael Warren. Part 2, *The First Quarto (1608) in Photographic Facsimile* (Berkeley: California UP, 1989).

―――――――――

Source: "Shakespeare at Work: 'Attributed Dialogue'," in *Cahiers Élisabéthains*, Vol. 51, October, 1997, pp. 39-52.

Losing the Map: Topographical Understanding in the *Henriad*

David Read, *University of Missouri, Columbia*

What is, on a map, only a physical position (neither more or less important than any other) acquires intensity of meaning by the superimposing of spiritual senses over the physical one; the undifferentiated physical fact has to aspire to spiritual meaning in order to become important.

(G. K. HUNTER)[1]

Recently words like 'geography', 'cartography', 'topography', and 'mapping' have begun appearing regularly in literary criticism, often with only a distant metaphorical relation to the scholarly and practical disciplines from which they were borrowed. A critic might write about the "map" or the "grid" of a particular text or cultural event, but would not want to be pressed too hard on the specific technical dimensions of the equation. While maps are certainly readable as texts, few literary texts have proven readable as maps in any very illuminating way, and "the geography of literature" is likely to remain largely a figure of speech. Even so, I believe that there is considerable value in taking the connections between geography and literature seriously, and that these connections can be quite helpful in the understanding of, among other things, William Shakespeare's history plays. In what follows I will argue that notions of physical orientation in the world are crucial to Shakespeare's presentation of the main characters in the second tetralogy, and especially to their presentation as historical actors. This quality of orientation is in itself neither ethical nor political, but appears at the threshold of both of those spheres of activity—a threshold where "a place in the world" and "a place in history" come close to meaning the same thing.

Hotspur

Among the various indications of Hotspur's flawed character in *King Henry IV, Part 1,* one of the most telling is his mental lapse during the conference with Worcester, Mortimer, and Glendower at the beginning of act 3, scene 1: "a plague upon it! / I have forgot the map" (lines 5-6).[2] The scene depicts a crucial moment in the alliance between the Percys and the Mortimers against Henry IV, and the stage business surrounding the map provides concrete evidence of the critically unfixed quality of Hotspur's thinking and leadership. It turns out that he has spoken too soon, for the map has not been left behind; Glendower, as befits his claim to be a magician, conjures it up only a moment after Hotspur has cursed its absence—though perhaps it was lying under Hotspur's nose all along.

This map has no precedent in Shakespeare's sources for the scene; characteristically, Shakespeare has taken Holinshed's bland remark that Lord Percy, the earl of March, and Glendower "divided the realme amongst them, causing a tripartite indenture to be made and sealed with their seales"[3] and transformed the general idea into some strikingly effective stage business. The map's immediate significance is that it stabilizes in a visible way the plans, motives, and internal relations of the rebel leaders, literally giving shape and line to the future course of the rebellion.[4] As Mortimer says at the beginning of the scene, "These promises are fair, the parties sure" (line 1), and the map itself, with its strict disposition of the land into three parts, is an emblem of this fairness and certainty: "The Archdeacon hath divided it [i.e., England] / Into three limits very equally" (lines 71-72).

The principal characters in the scene nonetheless devote much of their energy to transgressing, or, more aptly, forgetting, the evenhanded limits to the rebels' cosmos that seem to be implied in the lines of the map. Glendower brags that the world has become less stable by virtue of his presence in it: "at my birth / The frame and huge foundation of the earth / Shak'd like a coward" (lines 15-17). Hotspur promptly associates Glendower's boasts with the "strange eruptions" of "Diseased nature" and attributes the "birth-quake" to Mother Nature's having had a bad case of gas (lines 26-31). The dialogue in the early part of the scene alternates between Glendower's claims to have exceeded the normal boundaries—"These signs have mark'd me extraordinary, / And all the courses of my life do show / I am not in the roll of common men" (lines 40-42)—and Hotspur's vigorous efforts to draw him back within them:

> *Glend.* I can call spirits from the vasty deep.
> *Hot.* Why, so can I, or so can any man,
> But will they come when you do call for
>   them?
>
> (Lines 52-54)

Yet, later in act 3, scene 1, the fabulist and the pragmatist have switched places; it is Hotspur who wants to deny the boundaries, over Glendower's objections. In this instance the boundaries Hotspur denies are actually those on the map:

> Methinks my moi'ty, north from Burton here,
> In quantity equals not one of yours.
> See how this river comes me cranking in,

And cuts me from the best of all my land
A huge half-moon, a monstrous cantle out.

> (Lines 95-99)

Hotspur now favors a literal "turning" from the normal order of nature and the map's representation of that order:

I'll have the current in this place damm'd up,
And here the smug and silver Trent shall run
In a new channel fair and evenly.
It shall not wind with such deep indent,
To rob me of so rich a bottom here.

> (Lines 100-104)

Glendower at this point assumes the position of conservative skeptic earlier occupied by Hotspur and appeals to the common understanding, as it were, of the nature of rivers like the Trent: "Not wind? It shall, it must, you see it doth" (line 105). What Hotspur and Glendower "see," of course, is the map's schematic rendering of the Trent, which apparently offers as irrefutable evidence of the river's winding as would be offered by a visit to the Trent itself.

Mortimer and Worcester try to resolve this strange contretemps, Mortimer by inviting Hotspur to "mark" how the river's winding "runs me up / With like advantage on the other side" (lines 107-8) in a topographical balancing of contraries, Worcester by suggesting an engineering solution: "a little charge will trench him here, / And on this north side win this cape of land, / And then he runs straight and even" (lines 111-13). What Mortimer and Worcester attempt to discover within the lines of the map is the prospect of reciprocity and equity in the future course of the rebellion—which is to say that the map has become for them a picture of history in the making, space standing in for time. Yet their aspirations for an "orderly" rebellion are undercut by the nature of the solution that Worcester proposes: to resolve the difficulties raised by this alliance, an explosion will be required. The explosive possibilities are, indeed, already in evidence:

Hot. I'll have it so, a little charge will do it.
Glend. I'll not have it alt'red.

> (Lines 113-14)

This apparently serious impasse resolves itself, however, into a kind of sparring sustained by two parties who simply desire to be contrary to one another and thus refuse to occupy fixed positions. When Glendower abruptly capitulates, Hotspur just as quickly appears to lose interest in the disposition of the land:

Glend. Come, you shall have Trent turn'd.
Hot. I do not care. I'll give thrice so much
  land
To any well-deserving friend;

But in the way of bargain, mark ye me,
I'll cavil on the ninth part of a hair.

> (Lines 134-38)

In his preoccupation with his personal honor, Hotspur here seems unaware of the way in which his language implies a transvaluation of the land—both the proprietary holdings of the Percys and England in general—from a primal source of power, a radical basis for his own actions, into mere currency, a thing to be given easily but also to be bargained with for one's own profit.[5] In making this transvaluation, Hotspur falls under a characterization which has lately been made of quite a number of Shakespearean characters, including several in *King Henry IV, Part 1,* but has rarely been made of him. For all his reliance on the archaic trappings of chivalry, Hotspur proves to be another modern man.

At this point in the scene the map is set aside, and Shakespearean commentators tend to set it aside as well, perhaps with a passing note on the scarcity of references to maps in the plays and the even greater scarcity of actual maps—the other significant example being, of course, the map of Lear's ill-fated kingdom.[6] But students of the plays may do well to keep Hotspur's map in mind not only as an emblem of a certain kind of slippage between the metaphorical and the concrete but also as an index of a specific version of modernity, a version connected with a set of human concerns that I would categorize as topographical.[7] Hotspur's difficulty in finding the map (and in finding it to his liking) points to a larger crisis in his relationship with the objects portrayed on the map. The crisis is one of "alienation from the land," but with a rather different meaning than that phrase generally carries in contemporary critical discussion. The phrase does retain some of its usual economic connotations in the way I apply it here; the sixteenth-century context of enclosures, rural unemployment, and masterless men remains quite relevant to the dramatized situations of *King Henry IV, Part 1,* and the other plays in the tetralogy.[8] At the same time, however, I would argue that the character of this alienation is a question as much of immaterial as of material considerations. Hotspur has lost or abandoned his sense of place, his connection to the land as a presence which is simultaneously concrete and conceptual, a network of tangible, visible topoi around which meanings accumulate and which thus serve to orient the person in time as well as in space, to locate the person as a historical being.

This displacement plays out in act 3, scene 1 in terms of Hotspur's fundamental inability to communicate with those other individuals who also claim the right to occupy a space on "the map." Though Hotspur's fortunes are crucially tied to those of the inhabitants of the marches and borderlands, he winds up his argument with Glendower by celebrating his own scorn, if not ignorance, of all things Welsh:

Hot. Who shall say me nay?
Glend. Why, that will I.
Hot. Let me not understand you then,
Speak it in Welsh.

(Lines 116-18)

Shakespeare further stresses the rebels' difficulty in locating themselves upon a common ground of language during the interlude with Mortimer, Lady Mortimer, and Glendower that helps to conclude the scene; as Mortimer says, "This is the deadly spite that angers me: / My wife can speak no English, I no Welsh" (lines 190-91). These three characters may gesture toward a mutual language of love (or music) that will free them from the curse of Babel, but the excessiveness of Mortimer's own description of his plight— hinging upon "deadly spite" and anger—and the desperate note in his response to Lady Mortimer's Welsh imprecations—"O, I am ignorance itself in this!" (line 210)—suggest that the perils here are as much ethical and political as they are romantic. Despite the dreamy lyricism of this passage in the play, and despite the warmth of Hotspur's bawdy exchanges with his wife at the end of the scene, act 3, scene 1 in its entirety presents a sharply drawn tableau of a rebellion on the verge of collapsing irretrievably from within, its principals having lost the ability to perform any genuinely meaningful action in the history world of the play.

The pathos of this loss is quite evident at the end of act 5, when Hotspur, mortally wounded, cries, "O Harry, thou hast robb'd me of my youth! / I better brook the loss of brittle life / Than those proud titles thou hast won of me" (5.4.77-79). More than anything else, Hotspur laments the fact that he must surrender to Hal his right to a historical identity and instead make an ironic return to the land as dust and food for worms. Hal dwells on this very irony in his soliloquy over Hotspur's corpse:

> When that this body did contain a spirit,
> A kingdom for it was too small a bound,
> But now two paces of the vilest earth
> Is room enough.

(Lines 89-92)

Hotspur may use his dying breath to proclaim that "time, that takes survey of all the world, / Must have a stop" (lines 82-83), yet time does not stop with the end of Hotspur's life. His final grasp at a role in history—"O, I could prophesy"—is denied by "the earthy and cold hand of death" (lines 83-84), a force inseparably linked with the "two paces of . . . vilest earth" that he will finally come to occupy.

Prince Hal

That Hal should deliver Hotspur's eulogy (after first putting himself in a position to do so) is inevitable for all the obvious dramatic and thematic reasons; indeed, the contrast between Hotspur and Hal as "leaders of men" is one of the ancient commonplaces of Shakespeare criticism. However, the poles of that contrast have gradually shifted along with trends in twentieth-century criticism, so that a typical recent version has Hotspur in his familiar role as a scion of outmoded "feudal values," while Hal comes to represent some of the more unsettling aspects of the exercise of art, politics, and commerce in the modern capitalist state: his "authority" is linked in sinister ways with "the ambiguous figures of actor, Machiavel, and merchant."[9]

In many respects I agree with this characterization of Hal, but, as I have hinted above with regard to Hotspur, there is another way of reading the contrast which renders it considerably more complex. For Hal, despite his many transformations in the course of the tetralogy, is always unshakably "placed" within England. The knowledge suggested by the assertion "I know you all" that introduces Hal's best-known soliloquy (1.2.198) is perhaps less a matter of quasi-divine omniscience than of a tacit but long-standing familiarity with the land's inhabitants, both great and small. The soliloquy ends, of course, with Hal's confident assertion that he will become an actor in (and of) history, "Redeeming time when men think least I will" (line 217).

This "landedness" emerges as well at moments of the play that carry less of an immediate thematic charge. It is detectable in Hal's bragging to Poins in act 2, scene 4 about his proficiency in the language of tinkers, a speech which also displays Hal's intensely local consciousness: "They take it already upon their salvation, that though I be but Prince of Wales, yet I am the king of courtesy . . . and when I am King of England I shall command all the good lads of Eastcheap" (lines 9-11, 13-15). In act 3, scene 2, King Henry may accuse Hal of having "lost . . . [his] princely privilege / With vile participation" and by wearying all eyes (except Henry's) with his "common sight" (lines 86-88), yet this "participation" which Henry so much despises also indicates a quasi-organic relationship with England itself. That relationship manifests itself most curiously in the passing remarks which the king and Hal exchange about Shrewsbury's weather at the beginning of act 5:

> *King.* How bloodily the sun begins to peer
> Above yon bulky hill! the day looks pale
> At his distemp'rature.
> *Prince.* The southren wind
> Doth play the trumpet to his purposes,
> And by his hollow whistling in the leaves
> Foretells a tempest and a blust'ring day.

(5.1.1-6)

While King Henry merely observes the weather, Hal interprets it, speaking as if he understood the wind's ominous "purposes," which run parallel to his own. The king's words inevitably recall Hal's promise to "imitate the sun" (1.2.197), and the implicit identification between Hal and the "southren wind" is reinforced by its "rhyming" with the language of Hal's earlier promise to his father concerning Hotspur: "the time will come / That I shall make this northren youth exchange / His glorious deeds for my indignities" (3.2.144-46). Hal can speak in an oracular way about the southern wind because he is himself a metaphorical wind from the south, visiting a tempest on his enemies from the north. In a sense, Hal is only speaking his mind here—a mind with a climate much like England's own.

A similar sort of metaphorical connection occurs in *King Henry IV, Part 2,* after Hal has ascended the throne. As he reinstates the chief justice in act 5, scene 3, he attempts to explain the sea change (as it were) in his character:

> The tide of blood in me
> Hath proudly flow'd in vanity till now;
> Now doth it turn and ebb back to the sea,
> Where it shall mingle with the state of floods,
> And flow henceforth in formal majesty.
>
> (Lines 129-33)

Here Hal likens himself explicitly to a body of land, and perhaps more specifically to London itself, so dependent on the tidal movements of the Thames. The new King Henry emerges as the personification of his grandfather's deathbed vision of the ideal England, and as a kind of repatriation of the "land" (both physical and conceptual) lost during Richard II's reign.

Hal's embodiment of the land extends, of course, beyond England into Wales; from one play to the next the audience witnesses the identity of Wales as a nation and people gradually being subsumed into Hal's identity as prince and monarch. Just before his duel with Hotspur, Hal links himself with "one England" which cannot "brook a double reign / Of Harry Percy and the Prince of Wales" (5.4.66-67). The historical record provides Shakespeare with a notable poetic confirmation in the fact that Glendower and his troops never take the field at Shrewsbury—deferring, as it were, to Hal as the "true" representative of Wales: the country which Hotspur treats as so unambiguously foreign a land is, in however specious a sense, Hal's homeland. Both Glendower and Hal can "speak" for Wales, but Hal speaks with more authority (from the perspective of the history plays, at least), and thus displaces Glendower as a dynamic force in the drama.

Shakespeare picks up the matter of Hal's putative Welsh lineage again in *King Henry V,* through the character of Fluellen, who, in addition to providing Shakespeare with the opportunity for regaling his

audience with some coarse ethnic humor, serves to display the empathy between the Welsh and their "Prince," as when Fluellen and Henry discuss wearing the insignia of the leek:

> *K. Hen.* I wear it for a memorable honor;
> For I am Welsh, you know, good
> countryman.
> *Flu.* All the water in Wye cannot wash your
> Majesty's Welsh plood out of your body, I
> can tell you that.
>
> (4.7.104-8)

Fluellen has already invoked the Wye with similar intent while making his comical case for King Henry as a latter-day "Alexander the Pig" and Monmouth as the new Macedon. In arguing his point, Fluellen directs Gower to some interesting sources of evidence:

> if you look in the maps of the orld, I warrant you sall find, in the comparisons between Macedon and Monmouth, that the situations, look you, is both alike. There is a river in Macedon, and there is also moreover a river at Monmouth. It is call'd Wye at Monmouth; but it is out of my prains what is the name of the other river; but 'tis all one, 'tis alike as my fingers is to my fingers, and there is salmons in both. (4.7.22-31)

Fluellen's speculative "maps of the orld" differ from Hotspur's map in that they will (he thinks) lead the viewer toward a sense of the sameness of things: "'tis all one." For the comparison that Fluellen proposes is essentially a matter of typology:[10] Monmouth is to Macedon as the Wye is to the anonymous Macedonian river as Henry incorporates Alexander as the King of England incorporates the Prince of Wales. Henry's "one England"—Henry as the one England—begins to resemble a microcosm of the whole known world, past and present.

Henry V

Indeed, Henry does behave in *King Henry V* as though the known world belongs to England and England belongs to him. His actions in the play have their impetus in his lengthy discussion with the bishops about "Salique land" in act 1, scene 2—a scene which, while it may be unduly tedious for modern audiences, must surely have had a significant degree of topical interest for its initial viewers.

The wooing scene at the end of the play is perhaps more dubious than tedious, but Henry's relationship with the land (a land which now incorporates France) remains close to the surface:

> *Kath.* Is it possible dat I should love de
> ennemie of France?

K. Hen. No, it is not possible you should love
the enemy of France, Kate; but in loving me,
you should love the friend of France; for I
love France so well that I will not part with
a village of it: I will have it all mine. And,
Kate, when Fance is mine and I am yours,
then yours is France and you are mine.

Kath. I cannot tell wat is dat.
K. Hen. No, Kate? I will tell thee in French . . .
(5.2.169-77)

Henry's French may be no better than Katherine's
English, but it is nonetheless a kind of French—the
kind an English king would speak. However awkwardly
the French and English languages approach one another in *King Henry V,* their meeting betokens a larger
assimilation: "thy speaking of my tongue, and I thine,
most truly falsely, must needs be granted to be much
at one" (lines 190-92).

The most obvious sort of assimilation here is represented by the impending betrothal of Henry and
Katherine, yet even Henry's love-talk reveals his more
general and more crucial affiliations:

take me by the hand, and say, "Harry of England,
I am thine"; which word thou shalt no sooner bless
mine ear withal, but I will tell thee aloud, "England
is thine, Ireland is thine, France is thine, and Henry
Plantagenet is thine" . . . (Lines 236-40)

The structure of this speech becomes suggestive when
the phrase "of England" is treated as carrying a defi-
nite possessive meaning: England possesses the king,
who in turn possesses Katherine "of France." Once
France becomes part "of England," then Henry can
assign to Katherine a nominal ownership which begins
with England and ends with Henry himself. But this
last is like a series of concentric circles within a primum
mobile: England moves the cosmos, with Henry per-
vading that cosmos from center to periphery.

The entire scene may seem overdrawn, yet it does bring
a subtle sort of closure to the narrative of placement
and displacement which runs through the tetralogy. Just
before the betrothal, Henry muses to the French king
over the transformative power of love:

. . . you may, some of you, thank love for my
blindness, who cannot see many a fair French city
for one fair French maid that stands in my way.

Fr. King. Yes, my lord, you see them perspectively:
the cities turn'd into a maid; for they are all girdled
with maiden walls that war hath [never] ent'red.
(Lines 316-23)

The word "perspectively" has usually been associated
with some form of the optical tricks or the trompe

l'oeil techniques that became so popular in the sixteenth century: a painting of a woman that resolves, on
closer examination, into an urban landscape. The word
may also suggest simply a shift in perspective, the
transformation of an object from one set of dimensions
into another, as in a map. Katherine becomes a visual
representation of the territory which Henry now controls—a distinctly ominous development, as feminist
readings of the history plays suggest,[11] but also a final
confirmation of Henry's ability to make sense of and
to use the "map" of the land placed before him.[12]

Shakespeare's presentation of Henry V does, often
enough, suggest a deep-seated ambivalence about his
character; one has only to consider the always open
question of the banishment of Falstaff at the end of
King Henry IV, Part 2. But this question hinges in
large part on the sense, shared by both audiences and
critics, that Falstaff is "close to the land," an authentic
vestige of the English countryside and its folkways.
While Falstaff's language and peculiar *energeia* may
suggest this, his overall role in the plays does not. He
may claim in act 2, scene 4 of *King Henry IV, Part 1,*
that banishing "plump Jack" would be like banishing
"all the world" (lines 479-80), but audiences and readers already know about his weakness for hyperbole;
moreover, such a claim fails to localize Falstaff in any
way. For while he may be a knight, Falstaff appears
not to be "landed"; he is a transient being, with no
specific habitation other than the Boar's Head Tavern.
Falstaff does "come down to earth" with his false death
at Shrewsbury, where, as the stage directions indicate,
Hal "spieth Falstaff on the ground." But Falstaff cannot stay put; he "riseth up," refusing to be "Embowell'd"
(5.4.111), and (significantly) he takes Hotspur's corpse
with him. After deciding to pretend that he has himself
killed Hotspur, he says, "Nothing confutes me but eyes,
and nobody sees me" (lines 126-27). The words are
patently ironic—the audience, of course, sees Falstaff
the entire time—but beyond the reflexive theatricality
of the remark there lies a sense that Falstaff, for all his
great size, is (like a fairy in the daylit world) an invisible being—invisible, at least, within the world of fact.
Falstaff cannot lose his place because he has no place
to begin with. Thus Hal can treat Falstaff at the end of
King Henry IV, Part 2, as if Falstaff lived only within
Hal's nighttime dreams but not within any actual "ten
mile" radius of the king, wherever the king should
happen to reside on English soil (5.5.49-51, 65).

In the quality of his "residence," then, Henry is delivered to the Elizabethan audience as a central moral and
historical referent: he is the king who comprehends the
land, in both of the important senses of comprehension, and thus represents an idealized feudal relationship between ruler and nation—"nation" understood
not so much as polity or people but as a macrocosm of
the manor, with Henry as lord and the people as tenants of an extensive but thoroughly domesticated prop-

erty. Shakespeare's Henry may perch on the cusp of modernity, but he also offers the Elizabethan audience a nostalgic dream-vision of the medieval king, at home in the world because he is the world.

We can note as well in Shakespeare's presentation of Henry an interesting variation on the familiar idea of the king's two bodies, the transient, physical "body natural" and the eternal, immutable "body politic."[13] In *King Henry V,* the identification between the body of the king and the "body" of the nation is so close that the loss of the one is in effect the loss of the other, as is suggested by the brief summary of Henry VI's reign at the close of the play, in which the Chorus equates the gradual dissolution of monarchical authority with the physical disintegration of England and its borders: "Henry the Sixt . . . did this king succeed; / Whose state so many had the managing, / That they lost France, and made his England bleed" (act 5, epilogue, lines 9-12). The sense of the possessive pronoun in line 12 is ambiguous; "his" appears to refer to "Henry the Sixt," but it forms part of the rhyme with line 10 ("this king succeed" / "his England bleed"). "This king" is carefully aligned with "his England," so that the nation remains identified with Henry V even after his death. The troubles of Henry VI's reign are metaphorical wounds in the corpse of the late king, whose demise signals a hiatus in the ability of the English monarch to act effectively in history.

Henry IV

Henry V's charisma in the tetralogy—whether that charisma is construed as positive or negative—is closely connected with his aura of uniqueness. This aura emanates less from his personality or his accomplishments than from his ability to occupy a particular symbolic position in the historical narrative more securely than anyone else on the stage: he is the supremely oriented historical actor ("herein will I imitate the sun"). Unlike Hotspur, he need not worry about losing the map, because he carries the map within himself. His sense of direction is privileged, in every sense, and he is the only character in Shakespeare's historical universe who maintains this privilege from first to last. As such, he has the rather opaque quality that accompanies any figure of nostalgia; a being neither wholly anticipated nor subsequently duplicated in history, he seems not quite human.

The moral distance between Henry V and Henry VI was brutally obvious—we might say too obvious—to both Shakespeare and his audience; but Shakespeare was also interested in limning the distance between Henry V and his father. Henry IV, too, is deeply concerned with orienting himself properly within the world and within history, but his capacity to do so is more like Hotspur's than like Hal's. This is not so much because Henry and Hotspur both fall under a long shadow of usurpation

and rebellion, but rather because they are both placed outside the world they wish to inhabit in ways that the political action of the plays never makes fully explicit. Henry IV, for one thing, has never entirely overcome the onus of exile laid upon him by his unfortunate predecessor. After Richard banishes the two contestants in *King Richard II,* Henry (i.e., Bullingbrook) demands of Mowbray that he confess his treason, for "had the King permitted us, / One of our souls had wand'red in the air" (1.3.194-95); the death of one of the parties to the duel would have forestalled either confession or pardon. But exile—even in its mitigated version—reduces Bullingbrook to a similar state of wandering, as he himself confesses to Gaunt a few moments later: "Must I not serve a long apprenticehood / To foreign passages, and in the end, / Having my freedom, boast of nothing else / But that I was a journeyman to grief?" (lines 271-74). Bullingbrook's use of metaphor here is telling: exile is a form of servitude which does not culminate in a firmer sense of identity or purpose.

The uncertainty of exile overshadows even Bullingbrook's moments of triumph in *King Richard II.* His reentry in act 2, scene 3 begins with a query about local geography:

> *Bull.* How far is it, my lord, to Berkeley now?
> *North.* Believe me, noble lord,
> I am a stranger here in Gloucestershire.
>
>   (2.3.1-3)

Interestingly enough, Hotspur also has trouble "locating" Berkeley Castle in *Henry IV, Part 1,* when he attempts to explain his hatred of Bullingbrook to Northumberland:

> In Richard's time—what do you call the
>   place?—
> A plague upon it, it is in Gloucestershire—
> 'Twas where the madcap duke his uncle
>   kept—
> His uncle York—where I first bow'd my knee
> Unto this king of smiles, this Bullingbrook—
>   'Sblood!
> When you and he came back from
>   Ravenspurgh—
> *North.* At Berkeley castle.
> *Hot.* You say true.
>
>   (1.3.242-50)

To Bullingbrook and Northumberland, as to Hotspur, the region surrounding Berkeley Castle presents itself as alien, but Bullingbrook is "a stranger here" in a sense that transcends the merely parochial. When, later in the scene, he boldly attempts to reclaim his inheritance—"As I was banish'd, I was banish'd Herford, / But as I come, I come for Lancaster" (lines 113-14)—we remain aware of something chimerical in Bullingbrook's character, a fundamental doubt concerning the title which should properly belong to him. The rhetorical questions he directs to York seem to remain suspended, not entirely answerable: "Will you permit that I shall stand condemn'd / A wandering vagabond, my rights and royalties / Pluck'd from my arms perforce— and given away / To upstart unthrifts? Wherefore was I born?" (lines 119-22).

This problem of establishing location—of things, names, purposes—culminates in Exton's murder of Richard, an act inspired, ironically enough, by the same sort of question:

> *Exton.* Didst thou not mark the King, what
>   words he spake?
> "Have I no friend will rid me of this living
>   fear?"
> Was it not so?
> [*1.*] *Man.* These were his very words.
> *Exton.* "Have I no friend?" quoth he. He
>   spake it twice, and urg'd it twice together,
>   did he not?
> [*1.*] *Man.* He did.
>
>   (5.4.1-6)

At the close of the play, Exton tries unsuccessfully to provide Henry with a locus, an unambiguous center from which the question "Where is the King?" could receive a clear answer: "Great King, within this coffin I present / Thy buried fear. Herein all breathless lies / The mightiest of thy greatest enemies, / Richard of Burdeaux, by me hither brought" (5.6.30-33). Henry, though, is unwilling to "come home" in such a way; appropriately, he punishes Exton by passing on to him the burden of exile: "With Cain go wander thorough shades of night / And never show thy head by day or night" (lines 43-44). At the same time, Henry plans to provide a more legitimate locus for himself by undertaking the most solemn and sacred of all homeward journeys in the western world: "I'll make a voyage to the Holy Land, / To wash this blood off from my guilty hand" (lines 49-50).

At the beginning of *King Henry IV, Part 1,* however, Henry is forced to admit that "this our purpose now is twelve month old" (1.1.28). It is also clear in his initial speech that Henry thinks of the Holy Land not only as the general site of a crusade but as a physical place, to be experienced concretely as such:

> Forthwith a power of English shall we levy . . .
> To chase those pagans in those holy fields,
> Over whose acres walk'd those blessed feet
> Which fourteen hundred years ago were nail'd
> For our advantage to the bitter cross.
>   (Lines 22, 24-27)

This is less the language of the crusader than of the penitent pilgrim, tracing the footsteps of Christ along the Via Dolorosa, aspiring to tread the same ground that Christ had trod.[14] In Henry's case, however, the act of pilgrimage is never entirely separable from the ethic of the crusade; like so many other Christian monarchs, Henry wishes to transform Jerusalem from a city on the periphery of the European world to a city at the center of the *oikumenê* as well as at the center of the believer's consciousness. By restoring Jerusalem in this way, Henry will, he hopes, achieve the sort of historical fulfillment that seems perpetually to elude him in England.

Whether consciously or not, Henry is also participating in the medieval tradition that literally placed Jerusalem at the center of the map, and that figured significantly in what might be called the geographical imagination of Europe. The pictorial beginnings of this tradition are in the so-called T-O maps, which date from at least the time of the sixth-century bishop Isidore of Seville, who included one in his *Etymologiae.* These maps present an archetypally—and, one might add, typologically—well-ordered world, a circle divided into three parts (Europe, Africa, and Asia) by a "T" laid on its right side and composed of the Nile, the Don, and the Mediterranean, the last forming the leg of the T. In Isidore's map the three parts reflect not only the conventional continental divisions but Noah's disposition of the world among his sons Shem, Ham, and Japhet in the tenth chapter of Genesis.[15] By roughly A.D. 1100, Jerusalem has come to occupy the point at which the lines of the T join to form a cross.[16]

There are, of course, no T-O maps on display in the *Henriad;* but this ancient picture of a bounded world, organized simply and providentially around an immutable center, is eminently serviceable in suggesting the "mental map" that Henry carries with him.[17] The vision of a holy city at the heart of a static world offers at least the hope of a serene antithesis to the dynamic but uncentered realm over which he struggles to rule.

That Henry is thinking in such terms is clear both at the close of the scene, when he repeats to Warwick, Surrey, and Blunt his long-standing wish—"And were these inward wars once out of hand / We would, dear lords, unto the Holy Land" (lines 107-8)—and earlier as well, when Henry prays for a map of sorts to guide him: "O God, that one might read the book of fate, / And see the revolution of the times / Make mountains level, and the continent, / Weary of solid firmness, melt itself / Into the sea . . ." (lines 45-49). Henry desires a book that will render graphically both the past and future of the world he now inhabits. Unlike the Holy Land of the T-O map, the land in the book of fate is a disordered one, expanding, contracting, and finally dissolving; the closer analogy would be to Hotspur's "revolutionary" map, with its shifting boundaries and altered river course. Henry differs from Hotspur, though, in drawing a moral lesson—albeit an entirely disheartening one—from his study of the "terrain" of human action: "The happiest youth, viewing his progress through, / What perils past, what crosses to ensue, / Would shut the book, and sit him down and die" (lines 54-56). Clearly, Henry is preparing for the hour when he will shut the book on a land with which he has never managed to identify himself.

That hour arrives in act 4, scene 5, during which Henry's chronic sense of dislocation finds its ironic denouement. Shakespeare provides a potent visual emblem within the scene, when Henry wakes from his fitful sleep to ask, "Where is the crown? who took it from my pillow?" (line 57). The question may strike us as slightly comical, suggesting as it does that Henry's notion of himself as king is dependent on an entirely portable "prop"—a prop which is now in another room, resting for the moment on his son's head. His suspicions about Hal's motives give rise to the fear that under Hal England will lose all its familiar boundaries, reverting to a prehistoric feral state: "O thou wilt be a wilderness again, / Peopled with wolves, thy old inhabitants!" (lines 136-37).[18] Yet Henry's assessment of his own reign, which he delivers to Hal in a speech that effectively functions as a deathbed confession, is suffused with the king's understanding of his own refusal to honor the proper boundaries: "God knows, my son, / By what by-paths and indirect crook'd ways / I met this crown . . ." (lines 183-85). His concluding advice to Hal is extraordinary in its cynicism, suggesting a continuing consciousness that, all along, the "wilderness" and the "wolves" have merely been concealed from view by a thin veneer of civility:

> . . . all [my] friends, which thou must make
>   thy friends,
> Have but their stings and teeth newly ta'en
>   out;
> By whose fell working I was first advanc'd,
> And by whose power I well might lodge a
>   fear
> To be again displac'd; which to avoid,
> I cut them off, and had a purpose now
> To lead out many to the Holy Land,
> Lest rest and lying still might make them look
> Too near unto my state.
>
> (Lines 204-12)

Here, at last, Henry acknowledges the threat of displacement in the most pragmatic terms; it is a threat he not only fears but has exploited for his own purposes.

In this account the most penetrating irony is that Henry's journey to the center of the world would actually have been an attempt to de-center the consciousness of his own subjects, to blur and confuse the bounds of Henry's reign over England. In order to preserve his rule, Henry has paradoxically sacrificed the possibility of finding the center of his "state" in England itself. And he

advises Hal to follow a similar course, without acknowledging—for when did Henry ever seem aware of it?—the close identification that already exists between Hal and the land, and Hal's gift not only for finding but for enlarging his own "center."

Shakespeare adapts Henry's dying words from Holinshed, but those words are nonetheless symbolically charged, as Henry discovers that the only Jerusalem he will ever reach is one altogether close to home:

> *King.* Doth any name particular belong
> Unto the lodging where I first did swound?
> *War.* 'Tis called Jerusalem, my noble lord.
> *King.* Laud be to God! Even there my life
>   must end.
> It hath been prophesied to me many years,
> I should not die but in Jerusalem,
> Which vainly I suppos'd the Holy Land.
> But bear me to that chamber, there I'll lie,
> In that Jerusalem shall Harry die.
>
> (Lines 232-40)[19]

At this moment Henry could say, as Edmund does at the end of *King Lear,* "The wheel is come full circle, I am here" (5.3.175). Henry has indeed arrived at a specific place—just as Hotspur finds his "two paces of the vilest earth"—but it is not the place he thought to occupy. His final dislocation takes two distinct forms: not only does Jerusalem come uncentered on Henry's mental map of the world, but the locus of the monarchy, Westminster itself, suddenly shows itself as foreign terrain—for Henry has never known the name of the presumably familiar chamber in which his reign will conclude.

The Border of History

> Welcome destruction, blood, and massacre!
> I see (as in a map) the end of all.
>
> (*King Richard III* 2.3.53-54)

Shakespeare's audience watched the plays of the second tetralogy in theaters that retained the conventional shape of a map of the world; the theater called The Globe would make the connection explicit.[20] Shakespeare himself made dramatic use of the notion of the theater as a metaphor of the *oikumenê* in the prologue to *King Henry V:* "Suppose within the girdle of these walls / Are now confin'd two mighty monarchies, / Whose high, upreared, and abutting fronts / The perilous narrow ocean parts asunder" (prologue, lines 19-22). The prologue invites the audience to suppose, in effect, a tripartite world—the third part, of course, being taken by the audience.

The center of this world is occupied by the protagonist of the drama; in the plays of the second tetralogy, that protagonist is drawn from history. The audience witnesses the struggle of that figure to maintain position as the rightful occupant of that space. This is one of the central tropes of dramatic presentation; historical drama provides the additional element of the protagonist struggling to hold a "place" in history. Only Hal/ Henry V controls this place successfully within the tetralogy. And while the Elizabethan audience might savor this achievement, they would also be aware of its anomaly—that this one figure is surrounded by many others who aspire to occupy the center of the world's stage but can never quite seem to find it, and instead stand in danger of falling from the stage altogether.

The loss of a locus is equivalent to the loss of historical being; it is a loss revealed in failures of both action and language. This double loss can be sensed in Shakespeare's presentation not only of Hotspur but of Henry IV; the king's final exit to "Jerusalem" in *King Henry IV, Part 2,* signals both his personal demise and the end of his usefulness as an actor in either drama or history. The audience's pleasure in Henry V's triumph as a figure of history is tempered by awareness that the stage is more commonly traversed with uncertain footsteps by exhausted—and exhaustible—figures like his father, and Hotspur.

The appropriate genre for such figures is tragedy—a genre which, in Shakespeare's hands, closely resembles that of the history play, but with a crucial shift in emphasis. The protagonists of the late tragedies are those who claim the dramatic and historical center but either cannot locate or cannot occupy that fixed place except, paradoxically, in death: Othello, multiply alienated, deprived of his customary military duties, and finding too much time on his hands in Cyprus; Hamlet, never entirely at home in Denmark, delivering his boldest affirmation of identity—"This is I, / Hamlet the Dane!" (*Hamlet* 5.1.257-58)—literally at the edge of the grave; Macbeth, who finds the very land itself turning against him at the end of the play; and Antony, disoriented in Egypt, in a drama distinguished by its extraordinarily rapid shifts in setting. Most plangently, there is Lear, who divides his kingdom into a "tripartite world" by way of a map, but who (along with the audience) comes to see "the shape and stability of the kingdom replaced by vagaries of movement and motive, and Lear's map itself, by an unmapped wilderness of lust, ambition, and deceit."[21]

The causes of Shakespeare's great turn toward tragedy at the end of the sixteenth century are exceptionally complex; here I would only offer the observation that this turn appears to involve a significant shift in Shakespeare's presentation of the ability of his protagonists to orient themselves within the places they are said to inhabit. The plays of the second tetralogy revolve, however elliptically, around an essentially pastoral vision of a monarch who achieves an ideal consonance with the land of England, and thus an iconic status in history. The tragedies that emerge from Shakespeare's pen during the waning, difficult years of Elizabeth's reign and the turbulent early years of James's suggest, albeit indirectly, that this vision of "terrestrial harmony" belongs to the past and cannot be reclaimed, since the more recent protagonists of history, and especially those who rule, have proven inadequate to its pursuit.

Notes

[1] G. K. Hunter, "Elizabethans and Foreigners," *Shakespeare Survey* 17 (1964): 38. Hunter's article remains an excellent introduction to Elizabethan ideas about the larger world.

[2] My text for the plays is G. Blakemore Evans, ed., *The Riverside Shakespeare* (Boston, 1974); all references use this edition and cite the text according to act, scene, and line.

[3] The relevant passage from Holinshed is in Geoffrey Bullough, *Narrative and Dramatic Sources of Shakespeare,* 8 vols. (London, 1957-75), 4:185.

[4] In a speech partly drawn from the First Folio version of *King Henry IV, Part 2,* Lord Bardolph also aspires to "map out" the revolt in order to ensure its orderly progress; at the same time, and unlike Hotspur, he understands the necessity of laying the "model" against one's "estate," the material resources that are actually available for the enterprise (1.3.41-57). We might say, in linguistic terms, that Bardolph is aware of the perilous gaps that can open up between signs and referents. The same recognition eludes Hotspur.

[5] In *Stages of History: Shakespeare's English Chronicles* (Ithaca, N.Y., 1990), Phyllis Rackin focuses on the occurrence of this sort of transvaluation in *King Richard II,* best captured in John of Gaunt's speech at act 2, scene 1, lines 57-64, where Gaunt's ironically quibbling use of the word "dear" "reduces the incommensurable value of what is loved to the commercial value of an expensive commodity. . . . The enduring, immanent value of land and sea (*real* estate) has been replaced by the fluctuating, mediated value of the market, represented by legal documents ('inky blots and rotten parchment bonds')" (p. 101). I would suggest, though, that Hotspur's map is not this sort of "legal" document; it represents something much more archaic and much closer to the immanent value of land and sea.

[6] Spevack cites thirteen uses of "map" by Shakespeare, including two uses in comedies, three in tragedies, one in a "romance," and six in histories; see Marvin Spevack, *The Harvard Concordance to Shakespeare* (Cambridge, Mass., 1973), p. 788. For a gnomically presented but fascinating discussion, see Frederick T. Flahiff, "Lear's

Map," *Cahiers Élisabéthains* 30 (1986): 17-30. Though different in its style and specific preoccupations from my own efforts here, Flahiff's article is close to mine in its general approach to the geographical dimension of Shakespeare's plays.

7 The cultural uses of topography have—perhaps not surprisingly—received a good deal more attention in the social sciences than in the humanities. Especially noteworthy is the work of the geographer Yi-Fu Tuan; see, for example, his *Topophilia: A Study of Environmental Perception, Attitudes and Values* (Englewood Cliffs, N.J., 1974), *Space and Place: The Perspective of Experience* (Minneapolis, 1977), and *Landscapes of Fear* (New York, 1979). For a sweeping historical survey of many of the issues that Tuan addresses theoretically, see Clarence J. Glacken, *Traces on the Rhodian Shore: Nature and Culture in Western Thought from Ancient Times to the End of the Eighteenth Century* (Berkeley, 1967). A very accessible (and lavishly illustrated) primer on the conceptual dimensions of cartography is provided by David Turnbull in *Maps Are Territories: Science Is an Atlas* (1989; Chicago, 1993); see also two essays by J. B. Harley, "Meaning and Ambiguity in Tudor Cartography," in *English Map-Making, 1500-1650: Historical Essays,* ed. Sarah Tyacke (London, 1983), pp. 22-45, and "Maps, Knowledge, and Power," in *The Iconography of Landscape: Essays on the Symbolic Representation, Design and Use of Past Environments,* ed. Denis Cosgrove and Stephen Daniels (Cambridge, 1988), pp. 277-312. Among literary-critical works that make an approach to these topics, see John Gillies, *Shakespeare and the Geography of Difference* (Cambridge, 1994), which examines Hotspur's map briefly (pp. 46-47); Steven Mullaney, *The Place of the Stage: License, Play, and Power in Renaissance England* (Chicago, 1988), pp. 1-25, esp. pp. 17-18; and Richard Helgerson, *Forms of Nationhood: The Elizabethan Writing of England* (Chicago, 1992), pp. 107-47.

8 On the shifting demographics of the late Elizabethan period, see Keith Wrightson, *English Society, 1580-1680* (New Brunswick, N. J., 1982), pp. 121-48.

9 Rackin, pp. 77, 80. For particularly influential contemporary accounts of the "modern" Hal, see Stephen Greenblatt, *Shakespearean Negotiations: The Circulation of Social Energy in Renaissance England* (Berkeley and Los Angeles, 1988), pp. 40-65, and Mullaney, pp. 76-87.

10 Gillies describes this "form of geographic moralisation" as "typo-geographic"; see his short comment on Fluellen's speech (p. 48).

11 As in, for example, Karen Newman, *Fashioning Femininity and English Renaissance Drama* (Chicago, 1991), pp. 97-108, and Rackin, pp. 167-76.

12 The most extended discussion of the analogy between "land" and "woman," and of male exploitation of this relation, is Annette Kolodny's *The Lay of the Land: Metaphor and History in American Life and Letters* (Chapel Hill, N.C., 1975).

13 For a recent historicist account of the political implications of Henry V's corporeality, see Claire McEachern, *The Poetics of English Nationhood, 1590-1612* (Cambridge, 1996), pp. 83-137, which bears particularly on the dynamics of the wooing scene.

14 Medieval pilgrims were evidently preoccupied with the notion of Christ's feet touching the ground of Palestine, probably out of a perception that the effort to retrace His steps would allow for a kind of physical sympathy with Christ's person ("I walk as He walked") which would otherwise be difficult to achieve. Mandeville accordingly invokes Christ's feet in his very first sentence (*The Travels of Sir John Mandeville,* trans. and intro. C. W. R. D. Moseley [Harmondsworth, 1983], p. 43).

15 See C. Raymond Beazley, *The Dawn of Modern Geography: A History of Exploration and Geographical Science from the Close of the Ninth to the Middle of the Thirteenth Century (c. A.D. 900-1260),* 3 vols. (London, 1901), 2:576-79, 627-33. See also Hunter (n. 1 above), pp. 38-39, and, for the T-O's connection with Noah's division of the world among his sons, Flahiff, pp. 25-26. Stephen Greenblatt discusses the T-O map and the tradition of Jerusalem as center in relation to Mandeville's *Travels* in *Marvelous Possessions: The Wonder of the New World* (Chicago, 1991), pp. 41-43.

16 Beazley, p. 578. Beazley believes the earliest example of a T-O map with Jerusalem at the center is one belonging to St. John's College, Oxford, dated 1110; he speculates that the map was crudely copied from a Byzantine original brought to western Europe after one of the early crusades.

17 In England the T-O map survived into the sixteenth century and even later; E. G. R. Taylor cites an example in an anonymous manuscript *Cosmographia,* transcribed in 1530 for Henry VIII's library though probably produced by a London monk around 1510 (see her *Tudor Geography 1485-1583* [London, 1930], pp. 13-14); and Hunter identifies a very late example used to illustrate John Cayworth's *Enchiridion Christiados,* a Christmas masque, published in 1636 (p. 246n).

18 The danger of the encroaching wilderness makes itself felt in *King Henry IV, Part 1,* as well, whenever the "matter of Wales" is invoked. In the English popular imagination, Wales, along with the surrounding

border region, was de facto a wilderness whose human inhabitants were only a few steps removed from the wolves. Shakespeare introduces this idea in the first scene of the play (1.1.44-46). It is the Prince of Wales in the history plays who bears the responsibility for domesticating the country which is nominally his; thus when Fluellen praises the king as a "countryman" in *King Henry V* (4.7.111), the implication is that this domestication has occurred.

[19] On Henry's desire to reach Jerusalem, as this evolves from *King Richard II* to *King Henry IV, Part 2,* see James Black, "Henry IV's Pilgrimage," *Shakespeare Quarterly* 34 (1983): 18-26.

[20] For a discussion of the more recondite dimensions of this equation, see Frances A. Yates, *Theatre of the World* (Chicago, 1969). See also Gillies (n. 7 above), pp. 70-98.

[21] Flahiff (n. 6 above), p. 19.

Source: "Losing the Map: Topographical Understanding in the *Henriad*," in *Modern Philology*, Vol. 94, No. 4, May, 1997, pp. 475-95.

Marlowe's *Edward II:* Penetrating Language in Shakespeare's *Richard II*

Meredith Skura, *Rice University*

In an often-quoted judgement, Charles Lamb noted that Shakespeare's *Richard II* took hints from, but 'scarce improved' on, 'the reluctant pangs of abdicating Royalty' in Marlowe's *Edward II.* But was Shakespeare in fact trying to 'improve' on Marlowe when he created his own 'weak king' in *Richard II?*[1] Or was he doing something else? This paper re-examines Shakespeare's play as a more complicated response to *Edward II* that reveals dynamic tensions between the two playwrights. Bertolt Brecht's modern response to Marlowe in his 1922 *Edward II* provides a useful introductory comparison. Brecht seems to have been drawn to Marlowe's play not so much for its political as for its personal relevance, in particular for its portrayal of the doomed bond between Edward and Gaveston—the kind of bond Brecht had just written about in *The Jungle.* Brecht was indeed trying to improve on, or at least to outdo, Marlowe's bleak play. With a 'savage pessimism', he rewrote Marlowe to create a world where, as his Edward says, 'There is nothing in life besides the touch of men's bodies, and even that is minimal and vain.'[2] What interests me about Brecht's play however is that it is not only about the difficult closeness between two men but—as adaptation, collaboration, and partly cribbed translation—it is also the product of such closeness. *Edward II* was the first of the collaborative ventures that were to serve Brecht so effectively as catalysts for creativity throughout his career.

On the face of it, Shakespeare's response to Marlowe seems to have been quite different from Brecht's. He was interested in the politics of *Richard II,* not the touch of men's bodies in *Edward II;* and, even politically, the difference between Shakespeare's and Marlowe's plays has always seemed far more striking than the similarity. Where Marlowe reduces politics to personal appetite and a struggle for power, Shakespeare transcends the personal, contextualizing abdication in a universe that makes moral and political sense. Where Marlowe's play is full of sex and violence, Shakespeare's is almost devoid of both. For one thing, Edward II's passion for Gaveston seems to have left no trace on Richard's relationships. Edward's favourites (and Richard's favourites in the anonymous *Woodstock* (*c.* 1592), which Shakespeare also knew), all but disappear in *Richard II.*[3] For another, Edward's extraordinary pain at losing Gaveston is paralleled only by Richard's regret that his roan Barbary now serves the new king Bolingbroke so willingly and by his abstract complaint that 'love to Richard / Is a strange brooch in this all-hating world' (5.5.65-6). As for violence, no one has found any trace of Edward's appalling murder

in *Richard II.* In fact Shakespeare, offered a choice of deaths in Holinshed, could have scripted a passive starvation or even suffocation for Richard; but instead he chose to make his king die fighting. Edward's death is devastatingly physical as the world bears in on him in the form of a burning spit thrust up his fundament; but Richard's death allows him to escape the world of bodies altogether ('Mount, mount, my soul . . . / Whilst my gross flesh sinks downward' [5.5.111-12]).

I shall argue, however, that Shakespeare was more influenced than we have realized by the erotic passion and erotic violence associated with male friendship and male rivalry in Marlowe. Both Edward's love for Gaveston and his erotically suggestive death affect the portrayal of Richard, his friends, and his (often premature) visions of death. Marlowe's love and death have been ousted from Shakespeare's plot by the more languid 'pangs' of abdication, but they return in Shakespeare's language, or rather in what Ruth Nevo has called Shakespeare's 'other language', the unconscious effects that words and verbal images create as they circulate between Marlowe and Shakespeare.[4] They imply less about Richard's sexuality than about his subjectivity—less about whom he loves than about who he is—but their quiet presence is particularly important in *Richard II,* because it helps fill in the gaps of a plot that is so undermotivated in places that critics have had to postulate a missing 'part I' in order to understand why Richard attacks Bolingbroke at the beginning of the play, and they have had to postulate neurosis in order to understand why Richard abdicates even before Bolingbroke claims the throne at the end of the play. In what follows, I will first single out aspects of Marlowe's *Edward II* that were important to Shakespeare insofar as they left their mark on his other plays; and then I will suggest how such material might fill in the missing gaps of *Richard II* as well, even though it is supposed to have been eliminated from that play. Finally, I will suggest that Shakespeare's response to *Edward II* may help us understand new dimensions of dramatic collaboration on the early modern stage.

What Shakespeare saw in Marlowe's Edward II: Twins and rival twins

Sex and violence per se have hardly been neglected in Marlowe's play. Critics no longer either discreetly ignore Edward's homosexuality or mention it only to condemn it; indeed, the erotic implications of Edward's death have become increasingly important to our understanding of the play.[5] And yet I am not sure that we appreciate the range of fantasies in this play if we stop short after specifying the gender of Edward's lover or the particular orifice implicated in their coupling. One can certainly see why Edward's Queen Isabel refers to him and Gaveston bitterly as 'Jove and Ganymede' (or why the barons cite as models Hylas and Hercules, and other famous male lovers). But Edward and Gaveston also compare themselves to the heterosexual Hero and Leander, Jupiter and Danae, and Actaeon and Diana. In fact, Edward and Gaveston in this play are very different from the Jupiter and Ganymede whom Marlowe had actually staged in his earlier *Dido, Queen of Carthage*. The difference is important: in *Dido*, Jupiter and Ganymede are canny, in control—and comically unequal. The couple in this play are tragic. Edward's dotage is far more serious than Jupiter's; and even Gaveston, opportunistic as he is, loves Edward. Edward's love for Gaveston is actually like the heterosexual dotage Marlowe portrays in the rest of *Dido*, between Dido and Aeneas, or like the dotage he draws on for Edward II's lines[6]—like Margaret and Suffolk's love in Shakespeare's *Henry VI, Part One*, or like Andrea's love for Bel-Imperia in Kyd's *Spanish Tragedy*. In any case, more than its classification as 'homosexual' or 'heterosexual',[7] what matters in Marlowe's play is not only the actual 'object' of Edward's love but Edward's—and Marlowe's—narratives (or fantasies) about that object and about love.

Marlowe's narrative of love involves not only love but friendship—and even rivalry. It needs to be read in the context, not only of Jupiter and Ganymede or Hero and Leander, but also of the twinning that Bacon, Montaigne, and Elyot see as prerequisite for ideal friendship. (A friend is 'another I', Elyot writes; 'another himself', says Bacon; they 'entermixe and confound themselves one in the other', says Montaigne.)[8] Gaveston, Edward says, 'loves me more than all the world' (1.4.164); but instead of simply loving back, Edward responds with an 'almost manic desire'[9] to be 'another Gaveston' (1.1.142-3) and to 'knit' his soul to Gaveston.[10] In addition, Edward's love is defined partly by its difference from his other relationships—to his father and the barons, and to his rival Mortimer. Edward II is not only a 'weak king' but also a bad boy, one of the Elizabethan prodigals whom Richard Helgerson saw moving out of the old school plays and into Elizabethan prose fiction, and who had leapt up onto the contemporary stage with Prince Hal in *The Famous Victories*.[11] Like all prodigals, Edward is matched against a straight man or "'good' son" and Mortimer plays this role in Edward's story. If Gaveston is Edward's mirror, Mortimer is his reversal; if Gaveston is his twin, Mortimer is his 'rival twin'. Edward is thus defined not only by his twin, the man he wants to be, but also by his rival, the man who wants to be him and take his place.

We might see in this doubling a Girardian structure of rivalry between Edward and Mortimer, that is, a social truth about division between competitors trying to create difference between them in order to avoid the terrible truth of similarity.[12] In this reading Mortimer seems to be defined by sheer difference from Edward—rational where Edward is passionate, macho where Edward is effeminate—but the two men turn out after all to be alike, two versions of egocentric wilfulness, undistinguished twins who take turns being 'good' or 'bad', but who are finally defined simply by being on opposite sides and competing for the same place. Similarly, we might see a political structure in the subsequent rivalry between Gaveston and Mortimer, whereby each calls forth one of 'the king's two bodies' in Tudor doctrine, or one side of 'the king's twin nature', as Anne Barton calls it, the vulnerable human king versus the divinely protected warrior king.[13] But for the moment I want to focus on the psychological rather than the political or social repercussions of the fact that Marlowe's Edward has both a twin and rival twin, so that he himself is split into two: Gaveston's Edward and Mortimer's Edward, lover's Edward and rival's. The presence of *both* pairings situates *Edward II* among examples of what Bruce Smith calls 'the myth of combatants and comrades', which, he argues, shaped so many early modern texts.[14] Read this way, Gaveston and Mortimer, twin and enemy twin, can be seen as two different faces of Edward's relationships to other men, possibly even to the one other man who counts most, Gaveston. Edward's death at Mortimer's hands, in fact, *has* been read as a nightmare version of Edward's love for Gaveston, in which the twin (Gaveston) is not only replaced by the enemy twin (Mortimer) but metamorphosed into a satanic version of the enemy (Mortimer's tool, Lightbourne) who promises to 'comfort' but comes to kill (5.5.2)—and whose attack transforms sodomy into rape.[15] Passionate love calls forth passionate hatred; hatred, if it is strong enough, ignites a kind of love. Edward's death can be read as punishment—a homophobic society's idea of poetic justice—but it may also be an inevitable fulfilment, just as Romeo's and Juliet's deaths were. This kind of self-consuming love is death.

In this reading, what Marlowe portrays is not only a kind of sexuality but a divided subjectivity inseparable from it, one construed differently from any in Marlowe's earlier plays. Marlowe's earlier heroes, Tamburlaine, Barabas, and Faustus, were singular. Giants in a world of undifferentiated pygmies, they may have had friends, like Tamburlaine's Theridimas, though none as important as Edward's Gaveston; or they may have had rivals, like Faustus' Mephistopheles, though none with his own story like Mortimer's. But none of the earlier protagonists shared his plot with both friend and rival. It has been suggested that Marlowe learned the new balance in *Edward II* from Shakespeare's multiply heroed *Henry VI* histories; but in his play Marlowe makes the leap from mono-hero, not all the way to multitude, nor even just to doubleness, but to *double doubleness*. Marlowe could have found single pairs of opposing rivals elsewhere in Tudor theatre, where not only prodigal and thrifty sons but good and bad kings often acted out conflicting moral principles onstage. And he could have found single pairs of mirroring friends—perhaps even in Shakespeare's *Two Gentlemen of Verona*. But when Marlowe gave Edward not only a rival twin but a mirroring twin, he multiplied and internalized division. He crossed moral ambiguity with emotional ambivalence and made drama a newly subtle instrument for exploring both social and psychological complexity.

This is where Shakespeare's earlier borrowing is relevant. Doubleness and twinship are precisely what's at stake in Shakespeare's very first response to *Edward II*. Two verbal echoes of Marlowe's play had turned up before *Richard II* in the unlikely setting of *The Comedy of Errors*,[16] which is close to *Edward II* in time (*c.* 1592) but seemingly in nothing else—although Marie Axton provides a connection when she argues that *The Comedy of Errors* was also an exploration of the theme of the king's two bodies.[17] The echoes indicate still deeper affinities, however, once we read Marlowe's play as a twin play about two men who loved one another so well that Edward could say, 'I am Gaveston' and call Gaveston his brother, and once we remember that Shakespeare's play is about an identical twin separated since birth and longing to be reunited with his brother.

Marlowe shows the darker side of twinship when Edward's rival, Mortimer, steals his identity as king and husband. In Shakespeare's play, twin and rival are located in the same person, but the dark rivalry is still present. If Antipholus longs for his lost brother, he also steals that brother's identity as citizen and husband, ensuring, however inadvertently, that the ghoulish Dr. Pinch, his wife's 'minion', attacks him. As Pinch arrives to capture Antipholus, Antipholus cries out, 'What, will you murder me?' (*Errors* 4.4.107)—just as Edward II does when his murderer arrives in Marlowe's play. Though Harold Brooks, who pointed out this echo, did not, he could have argued for Marlowe's further influence here in the fact that what Pinch wants to do is to have Antipholus 'bound and laid in some dark room' (*Errors* 4.4.92), which turns out to be 'a dark and dankish vault' (*Errors* 5.1.246), the sort of 'room' one would find in Edward II's medieval castle rather than in Antipholus' bourgeois home. Later, in a second Marlovian echo, Antipholus gets back at Pinch by throwing 'puddled' mire on him (5.1.173), that is, by inflicting on him one of the humiliations that Edward had suffered in Marlowe's play. Shakespeare's allusion to Edward's torture, though inappropriate to describe what is really happening to Antipholus, does convey his fearful fantasy about what's happening to him. Apropos of what is frightening about twinning, it is interesting to note that Pinch not only questions Antipholus' identity by confusing him with another man but goes even further to tie him to another man, leaving

> . . . me and my man, both *bound together*,
> Till, gnawing with my teeth my bonds in
>   sunder,
> I gain'd my freedom.
>
> (5.1.249-51)[18]

For Antipholus, in other words, losing your identity and being thrown into a vault is associated with being so closely—and literally—tied to another man that you have to gnaw your way free. Once before, Antipholus had been literally tied to his servant, when both were bound as infants to the mast that floated them to safety. That earlier tie saved his life (*Errors* 1.1.79-82); but Shakespeare is never certain about whether it is good or bad to be so closely tied to someone that he is your 'glass' (your spatial double (*Errors* 5.1.417)), as Dromio calls his brother, or your 'almanac' (your temporal double (*Errors* 1.2.41)), as Antipholus calls Dromio.

The violent images from Marlowe's *Edward II* left traces elsewhere in the Shakespeare canon. An echo of Mortimer's threat to Edward crops up, for example, in *Henry IV, Part One,* when Hotspur rages at King Henry IV for refusing to ransom Mortimer:

> He said he would not ransom Mortimer . . .
> But I will find him where he lies asleep
> And in his ear I'll holla "Mortimer!"
>   (*1 Henry IV* 1.3.217-20)

As Edmond Malone pointed out, Hotspur's lines echo Mortimer's rate at Edward's similar refusal to ransom Mortimer Senior in Marlowe's play:

> If he [Edward] will not ransom him
> I'll thunder such a peal into his ears
> As never subject did unto a king.[19]
>   (*Edward II* 2.2.127)

It might be argued that Shakespeare remembered the Marlovian lines here simply because he too was writing about 'ransoming Mortimer'.[20] But perhaps it was more than Mortimer's name Shakespeare recalled from Marlowe, and Mortimer's assault specifically on Edward's ears may also have caught the playwright's attention. In any case Marlowe's villain turns up again in what is perhaps the most famous of all Shakespearian lines about ears. It appears in *Hamlet,* another story about brothers who were rival twins, though not actual twins.[21] There, Old Hamlet's Ghost describes his own death in an attack that had first been conjured up by Mortimer's hired assassin, Lightbourne, in *Edward II*. As the Ghost tells it, while he was sleeping in his orchard Claudius stole

With juice of cursed hebenon in a vial,
And in the porches of my ear did pour
The leperous distilment, whose effect
Holds such an enmity with blood of man
That swift as quicksilver it courses through
The natural gates and alleys of the body.
                         (*Hamlet* 1.5.62-7)

In Marlowe's play, Lightbourne boasts:

'Tis not the first time I have kill'd a man.
I learn'd in Naples how to poison flowers;
To strangle with a lawn thrust down the throat
Or pierce the windpipe with a needle's point;
Or whilst one is asleep, to take a quill
And blow a little powder in his ears;
Or open his mouth and pour quicksilver down.
And yet I have a braver way than these.
                         (5.4.29-36)[22]

Here Lightbourne lists six kinds of undetectable penetration through four orifices, and tantalizes us with hints of yet a 'braver' one. Shakespeare condenses Lightbourne's last two possibilities in Claudius' similarly deadly-but-undetectable attack on Old Hamlet.

Marlowe's play is present elsewhere in *Hamlet* as well, in the prince's famous 'To be—or not to be' soliloquy. What calls Hamlet's thoughts back from suicide in that speech is the sudden thought of the 'undiscover'd country, from whose bourn / No traveller returns' (*Hamlet* 3.1.79-80), the same territory ('countries yet unknown') which Mortimer defiantly claims he is going to 'discover', just before he is hanged for killing King Edward (*Edward II* 2.6.24). Hamlet has little in common with Mortimer, but perhaps Shakespeare associated the two men because he associated the two versions of death by penetration, which the one revenged and the other perpetrated.

In other words, both Edward's passion for Gaveston and his death had already left traces in Shakespearian plays before *Richard II* and they would do so again afterwards.

Edward II: In Richard II

It may seem nonetheless that neither Edward's passion nor his violent death by penetration has any part in *Richard II*. Richard's trio of minions is unimportant and erotically neutral compared to Edward's Gaveston— it is hard to imagine Richard wishing to be 'another Bushy' or 'another Bagot', for example. Unlike Gaveston, these friends are just friends, although Bolingbroke nonetheless accuses them of coming between Richard and his Queen in bed.[23] Yet these friends are far more important to Richard than would first appear. In fact, it is the thought of his friends' betrayal and news of their death that marks the turning point of

Shakespeare's play—the moment at which Richard first collapses and gives up all hope. As Richard Harrier puts it, 'The impact of their deaths seems to penetrate Richard as no other event has as yet been able to do . . . some secret depth of the King has been sounded.'[24] In his speech at this point—which Harrier calls Richard's 'real abdication'—the words Richard chooses are extremely revealing.[25] To signal his defeat, Richard gives the first of Shakespeare's 'kings-are-just-people-after-all' speeches. It is like King Henry V's claim that 'the king is but a man, as I am' (*Henry V* 4.1.101-2) or King Lear's recognition that he is not 'ague-proof', or even like the related claims made by outsiders like Jewish Shylock ('Hath not a Jew eyes?') or female Emilia in *Othello* ('And have we not affections? / Desire for sport? and frailty, as men have?' 4.3.101-2). But the specific evidence that Richard cites to prove his common humanity is unusual and none of the others cites it. While they invoke the five senses and the affections that make them human, Richard invokes as well his need for friends:

For you have but mistook me all this while.
I live with bread like you, feel want,
Taste grief, *need friends*—subjected thus,
How can you say to me, I am a king?
         (*Richard II* 3.2.174-7; italics added)

The need for friends, which thus 'subjects' Richard, is precisely the need he tries to deny in a brief moment of bravado when he first comes face to face with Bolingbroke: You think that 'we are barren and bereft of friends', he says,

Yet know, my master, God omnipotent,
Is mustering in his clouds, on our behalf,
Armies of pestilence
                         (3.3.84-7)

By 'friend', Richard may simply mean an ally or supporter, as Burleigh did in the list of Edward II's friends and enemies that he drew up at about the same time Shakespeare was writing *Richard II*. But 'friend' was a many-faceted word, and so was the relation it designated: Jonson used it to refer to men he cared about deeply, and Marlowe used it to refer to Gaveston. I think that Richard's newly recognized need for friends is personal as well as political. He cannot think of himself as a king unless, unlike Henry V banishing Falstaff, he needs no friends—or unless he has friends who will never leave him needy, who love him more than all the world, as if they were another Richard. I don't want to claim that Richard's friends are his doubles, as Gaveston was for Edward. But like Gaveston they do serve as Richard's flattering mirror; and their subterranean role in his life may give yet another meaning to the literal mirror that intrudes into Richard's abdication scene. There, bereft of all friends, Richard has to call for a mirror to see 'what a face I have / Since it is bankrupt of his majesty' (4.1.266-7). And when it reflects his face unchanged, he thinks immediately of those false friends:

> O flatt'ring glass,
> *Like to my followers* in prosperity,
> Thou dost beguile me.
> (*Richard II* 4.1.279-81; italics added)

Here Richard, like the poet in Shakespeare's Sonnet 62, compares the mirror's literal reflection of his face to the very different 'self' he had seen reflected in the glass of his friend's face.[26] When he shatters the mirror[27] he shatters the fantasy of perfect friendship as well as shattering the image of himself. Richard's famous echo of Marlowe's *Doctor Faustus* in this speech—with himself playing Helen's face as well as Faustus asking, 'Was this the face . .?'—bears out the importance of male devotion to Richard's sense of himself. 'Was this face the face', he asks, 'That every day under his household roof / Did keep ten thousand men?' (4.1.281-3).[28] If Helen's face could send forth a thousand men, Richard's had power to keep ten times that number with him.[29] Finally, in a last reversal of his feeling about friends, when Richard does begin to accept his defeat, he sweetens it by embracing it as a 'sworn brother'; 'The truth of what we are shows us but this', he tells the Queen,

> . . . I am sworn brother, sweet,
> To grim Necessity, and he and I
> Will keep a league till death. Hie thee to
>   France
> And cloister thee in some religious house.
> (5.1.20-3)

This is the truth of 'what we are': Richard banishes the Queen to a solitary cloister, but he imagines his own death as a transcendent brotherhood.

Marlowe's Edward is not only passionate about his friend and sworn brother Gaveston but is also engaged in a passionate as well as political rivalry with Mortimer for Queen Isabel. By contrast there seems to be no overt sexual rivalry in Shakespeare's plot; Bolingbroke is simply Richard's political enemy. Nonetheless, a more personal rivalry is suggested when we hear, for example, that one way in which Richard has alienated Bolingbroke was by preventing Bolingbroke's French marriage (*Richard II* 2.1.167-8), or that Richard resents Bolingbroke for having made a divorce between Richard and his queen (*Richard II* 5.1.72-3).[30] More strikingly, the England for which the two men compete is herself a woman, 'a teeming womb of royal kings' (*Richard II* 2.1.51),[31] whom both men image as their own with a passion that has helped make this play seem so much more universal and profoundly patriotic than Marlowe's. In one sense they fight over the Queen as well, insofar as she figures England when

she appears in a real, if allegorical, bit of England's green garden, strangely prescient about 'some unborn sorrow ripe in Fortune's womb' (2.2.10). Assimilating the womb to herself, she calls Greene 'the midwife to my woe', herself 'a gasping new-deliver'd mother', and Bolingbroke 'my sorrow's dismal heir' (2.2.62, 65). Not only has England's 'teeming womb of royal kings' produced Bolingbroke as well as Richard, but the human Queen too has Bolingbroke in her womb. In the Queen's prophecy, Bolingbroke and Richard are not only cousins but rival twins, as Murray Schwartz calls them,[32] two brothers fighting for space in the same womb.[33] John Barton's famous production of the play emphasized this twinning between Richard and Bolingbroke by having Richard Pasco and Ian Richardson alternating as Richard and Bolingbroke—and by having Richard stare through the empty frame of his shattered mirror at Bolingbroke's face.[34] But any production reveals the similarity between Richard's and Bolingbroke's will to power and shows each to be similarly possessive of the motherland each sees as his birthright.

Richard's opening attack on Bolingbroke also suggests a more passionately personal rivalry between these enemies than he admits. It becomes clear, for example, that something else is going on besides judicial process or even power politics in the 'chivalrous design of knightly trial' (1.1.81) that Richard stages in the opening scenes of the play. That 'something else' emerges as soon as the trial is over, when Richard, alone with Aumerle, for the first time drops his royal mask. With a 'threatening sneer', as Peter Ure calls it, he tells Aumerle what he really intended by banishing his kinsman Bolingbroke:

> He is our cousin, cousin, but 'tis doubt,
> When time shall call him home from
>   banishment,
> Whether our kinsman come to see his friends.
> (1.4.20-2)

Editors disagree about what Richard is referring to in the line about 'friends'. No 'friends' have been mentioned before, nor any merely personal antipathy to Bolingbroke. But I think we may hear in Richard's lines a whisper of Iago's malignity in the opening scene of *Othello*, when he hints to Roderigo about his plan to ruin both Othello's marriage and Othello's new alliance with Cassio. In any case, only now do we begin to suspect that getting rid of Bolingbroke may have been Richard's 'darker purpose' in staging the tournament in the first place. Then, within a few lines, Richard goes on to sneer at Bolingbroke's courtship of 'an oyster wench' and the common people, 'as were our England in reversion his' (1.4.35),[35] and his motives become still clearer: Richard is not just worried that Bolingbroke wants to steal the crown; he is afraid that the English want him to do so. He is jealous of Bolingbroke's popularity, of his 'friends', perhaps of his father, Gaunt, who would rather have Bolingbroke in England than support Richard by banishing him.

Not only is Richard jealous of what others feel about Bolingbroke; he may feel it himself. Deborah Warner's recent production made more, perhaps, of the erotic tie between Richard and Bolingbroke than the text does,[36] but some of Richard's lines suggest a masochistic attraction between them. Especially after his defeat, Richard sounds at times as if he were embracing Bolingbroke like his sworn brother Necessity—as if Bolingbroke's triumph over Richard was as erotically tinged as Lightbourne's triumph over Edward in Marlowe's play. At the end of the play, for example, in an exchange paralleling his earlier remarks to Aumerle about Bolingbroke's banishment, Richard tells his one loyal groom what he feels about Bolingbroke's return. When the Groom talks about Richard's fickle roan Barbary, whose back Bolingbroke had so easily usurped at the coronation, Richard makes the horse into a symbol of fickle England. Then he bitterly interrupts himself mid-simile to unfold a more personal and erotic metaphor. The horse, he realizes, 'Wast born to bear', but

> I was not made a horse,
> And yet I bear a burthen like an ass,
> Spurr'd, gall'd, and tir'd by jauncing
>   Bolingbroke.
>
>   (5.5.92-5)

Shakespeare usually associates horses with heterosexual dominance—Petruchio taming Kate ('Women are made to bear and so are you' (2.1.200)), Iago telling Brabantio that his daughter is 'cover'd with a Barbary horse' (1.1.11), or even Cleopatra's longing ('O happy horse, to bear the weight of Antony' (1.5.21)). But Edward II's fate in Marlowe's play may help explain where Richard found this equine image of male humiliation and sexual submission (it is not in Holinshed). Edward had had to bear the real burden of Lightbourne smothering him, and he was spitted rather than being merely 'spurr'd, gall'd, and jaded';[37] but the resemblance is there.

The groom who brings Richard news about the roan Barbary, the one loyal follower left, may also derive partly from Marlowe's play. Holinshed and Daniel had briefly mentioned a loyal Gascoigne, Jenicho, who wore Richard's badge (the symbolic 'hart') long after other men had defected; but that Jenicho had come and gone much earlier in the story. Shakespeare makes his version of Jenicho more important by sending him to Richard just before he dies—just at the point when Marlowe had sent Lightbourne to Edward. In other words, Shakespeare uses the true friend, Jenicho, who comes 'to look upon my sometime royal master's face' (5.5.75), to counter Marlowe's false friend, Lightbourne, who comes to spur, gall, and jade for real.

I think that Shakespeare may have recalled Edward's death even earlier than in Richard's speech about his roan Barbary, as early in fact as when Richard's friends first betray him. Consider the famous speech where Richard fantasizes about his own death by a different sort of penetration:

> . . . for within the hollow crown
> That rounds the mortal temples of a king
> Keeps Death his court, and there the antic
>   sits,
> Scoffing his state and grinning at his pomp,
> Allowing him a breath, a little scene,
> To monarchize, be fear'd, and kill with looks;
> Infusing him with self and vain conceit,
> As if this flesh which walls about our life
> Were brass impregnable; and, humour'd thus,
> Comes at the last, *and with a little pin,*
> *Bores through his castle wall, and farewell*
>   *king!*
>
>   (*Richard II* 3.2.160-70; italics added)

To be sure, Edward's death is not the primary source for this fantasy.[38] There were many visual and verbal emblems of Death lurking behind a king, or behind a lady looking into her glass, which could have served as models. Here, too, Death makes the foolish king think *he* can kill with looks before he discovers that death is not only already inside him—the skull beneath the skin—but outside too, looking on contemptuously, waiting to kill him when he is least ready. But M. M. Mahood suggests also a dramatic source for this speech, in the morality plays when Death enters with his dart and taunts the king before finally striking.[39] It was Marlowe who had probably provided Shakespeare with the most recent version of a morality play Death, when Lightbourne came to kill the king in *Edward II*.[40] Though Lightbourne had a spit rather than Death's dart, what Richard imagines Death doing in Shakespeare's play is exactly what Edward saw Lightbourne doing in Marlowe's play: teasingly promising comfort but really waiting 'to kill with looks': 'These looks of thine can harbour naught but death; / I see my murder written in thy brows', says Edward (*Edward II* 5.5.72-3).

It may seem a long way from Lightbourne's spit to Richard's little pin. Today we think of a pin as a trivial thing, and Shakespeare usually did too, as in Queen Isabel's offer in *Richard II* to change 'My wretchedness unto a row of pins' (*Richard II* 3.4.26). In fact, Richard's pin may seem more like Lightbourne's insidious 'needle's point' to pierce a windpipe than like Lightbourne's spit. But Richard's pin is not so trivial as he teasingly encourages us to think. For in one line the 'little' pin changes into something much more formidable when it 'bores through [the king's] castle wall'. The 'castle wall' refers literally to what Richard has just called 'this flesh which walls about our life'

(3.2.167), and what Bolingbroke in a similarly depressed moment had called 'this frail sepulchre of our flesh' (1.3.196). But the figuration of body as castle wall also evokes the solid mortar or timber of real castle walls, through which no little pin could bore. *This* little pin in other words is not only an inconsequential sewing implement but also a hefty 'pynne auger' or ax (*OED* 5), a carpenter's tool as listed in Warwickshire inventories.[41] When Death 'bores through' the castle wall, therefore, he is not merely sticking a pin into it—as, for example, Supervacuo threatens to do when he tells his ambitious brother, 'here is a pin / Should quickly prick your bladder' (*Revenger's Tragedy* 3.1.14-15).[42] Instead, Death is drilling the pin or screwing it in.

Is there any evidence in Shakespeare's play that the sexual implications of Death's 'pin' are being activated here as were the implications of Lightbourne's spit? That, as Venus puts it when the bore's tusk gores Adonis in Shakespeare's poem, 'death's ebon dart' has been mistook for 'love's golden arrow'? (*Venus and Adonis* lines 931-3). Elsewhere on the early modern stage the pin offers many possibilities for sexual innuendo. Autolycus knows this in *The Winter's Tale* when he offers the country lovers 'pins and poking sticks' for sale, hawking them with a song that has 'dildo' for its burthen. Marston knows it when he refers to the 'itch allaying pin'.[43] But the pin in this play is more than a fleeting anatomical metaphor, because it joins a network of potentially erotic penetrations—of bodies, castles, and country—all of which converge to convey the fragility of Richard's world.

In the play's opening scene, for example, when Bolingbroke attacks Mowbray verbally, and again at the lists, the language transforms verbal gestures into physical penetrations:

BOLINGBROKE With a foul traitor's name stuff I
    thy throat.

                             (1.1.44)

MOWBRAY [I return] These terms of treason
    doubled down his throat

                             (1.1.57)

and

    Now swallow down that lie

                             (1.1.132)

Far from eroticizing it, Richard has an almost phobic response to such offered violence, which he repeatedly invites only to frustrate. Bolingbroke accuses Mowbray of sluicing out Gloucester's 'innocent soul through streams of blood' (*Richard II* 1.1.103); but Richard avoids such violence at all costs. Instead, he wants to do the impossible, to kill the spirit but not the body:[44]

Let's purge this choler without letting blood—
This we prescribe though no physician:
Deep malice makes too deep incision . . .
Our doctors say this is no month to bleed.
            (*Richard II* 1.1.153-7)

Later in the play the Gardeners' words will recall Richard's fatal refusal to 'let blood', when they describe Richard's bad government in similar terms, as a refusal to 'trim . . . and dress . . . his land' as they do their garden:

. . . We at time of year
Do wound the bark, the skin of our fruit-trees,
Lest, being over-proud in sap and blood,
With too much riches it confound itself.
            (3.4.57-60)

Of course, as Freud said famously of cigars, sometimes an incision is just an incision; but with such repugnance for incisions and wounds, such a need for wholeness, such inability to see that any good can come from violation of the walled self either in battling or in breeding, no wonder Richard images himself as a besieged castle, like the female Virtues in *The Castle of Perseverance,* or like a heroine in medieval romance.

Richard's death fantasy is realized, in a fashion, at Flint Castle, to which he withdraws in defeat after his death soliloquy. When Bolingbroke marches on Flint and hears that 'The castle royally is mann'd' by Richard against his entrance, he corporalizes the castle (and perhaps also *un*mans or 'womans' it) and makes it into a displacement of the fearful body hiding inside. Demanding entrance, Bolingbroke tells Northumberland to

Go to the rude ribs of that ancient castle,
Through brazen trumpet send the breath of
    parle
Into his ruin'd ears.
           (*Richard II* 3.3.31-4)[45]

The ears here are important, but a lower orifice is suggested when Richard is forced to let Bolingbroke into his 'base court'.

Richard's actual death takes place in Pomfret castle, which is also—though only for a moment—corporealized. In Pomfret's prison Richard finds himself alone as the Duchess of Gloucester had been earlier, when she withdrew desolate to die in her home, Plashy, with its 'unpeopled offices, untrodden stones' (1.2.69). It is a measure of Richard's growth by this point that not only does he try, unlike the Duchess, to 'people' his prison with his thoughts (5.5.9); he even imagines tearing a passage out through Pomfret's 'flinty ribs' (5.5.20), as he would never have imagined doing when Bolingbroke marched on Flint Castle's 'rude ribs' earlier.[46]

The besieged castles associated with Richard are part of a larger pattern in which England too is besieged. At the imagistic centre of the play is Gaunt's emotional figuration of England walled in by the sea,[47] a 'fortress built by Nature for herself', a 'blessed plot' which is now threatened by both internal and external violation: internal because leased out to tenants and overrun with 'caterpillars', and external because invaded by the Irish from the north and by Bolingbroke from the south. Whether coded male or female or both or neither, these multiple images of enclosures ruptured create a sense not only of England and her castles but also of the human subject as a besieged structure, bounded but always vulnerable to eruptions from inside as well as to penetration from without. And sometimes, disturbingly, it is hard to tell the difference—as with Bolingbroke himself, who both invades from the outside, from France, and from the inside, from the Queen's womb; or, even more insidious, as with Richard's flattering friends who are so close, Gaunt says, they 'sit within thy crown' (2.1.100). Or with Death, whom Richard imagines both inside the hollow crown that rounds the temples of a mortal king, and outside, waiting to bore through with his pin.

Finally, the Marlovian reverberations of Death's pin recall Edward's death not only in Richard's death fantasies but perhaps also in Richard's strikingly odd reference to love in prison just before his loyal Groom arrives: 'love to Richard,' he says meditatively, 'is a strange brooch in this all-hating world' (*Richard II* 5.5.65-6). Richard may simply mean here that love is a strange 'breach' or 'break' in the normally loveless routine of things.[48] But most editors think Richard means that love is a rich 'brooch' or jewel worn usually in one's hat.[49] As such, the brooch is an appropriate emblem for the only remnant Richard has left of Gaunt's England, that 'precious stone set in the silver sea' (*Richard II* 2.1.46), the only equivalent he has ever had to the 'jewels', or friends, whom Bolingbroke had grieved to leave behind when he was banished (1.3.267, 270). But there is more to Richard's brooch. A brooch can also be a 'badge' of livery, like Richard's badge which the loyal Jenicho kept wearing in Holinshed and which Richard's loyal Groom perhaps wore as well. And, I would add, by mentioning love as 'a strange brooch' Shakespeare may have been thinking of the brooches that were commonly offered as love-gifts, like the brooch Ganymede demands from Jupiter instead of Juno's wedding necklace in Marlowe's *Dido, Queen of Carthage:*

> I would have a jewel for mine ear,
> And a fine brooch to put in my hat, [he says]
> And then I'll hug with you a hundred times.
>   (*Dido* 1.1.46-8)

Marlowe's Edward, you remember, having showered jewels on Gaveston, offers Lightbourne a jewel (though not a brooch) to save his life—the very jewel that Isabel had sent to him in prison. And finally, if I may speculate on one last implication of Richard's metaphor, a brooch was of course fastened with a pin. For Richard, in other words, Death comes with a little pin and bores through your skull, but love is a strange brooch pinned in your hat.

Ultimately, in *Richard II* the violation of a safely bounded subject, along with the broken mirror, the broken ceremony, and the broken word are all made more significant by being associated with the mythic fall of Edward III's demi-paradise. They transcend the merely physical violation in Marlowe's play. But my point in the comparison with Marlowe is that they could not be so powerful if they did not also reproduce the sheer physicality of Edward's relation to Gaveston and its violation at the end of Marlowe's play.

The Marlovian echoes suggest that *Richard II,* otherwise so focused on kingship and on the relation between providence and politics, language and power, is also about the lesser concerns that Shakespeare—unlike Marlowe—is supposed to have ignored. It is also about bodies and emotions, about needing friends, about friends turning into enemies, and about the darker pleasures of enmity. This is not the whole truth about *Richard II,* by any means; but, like the offstage murder of Gloucester, we need to know about it in order to understand the rest.

I think, however, that the Marlovian echoes—and the fact that they are so muffled—tell us not so much about the play as about Shakespeare and the way he saw his rival, Marlowe. We already know that Marlowe was Shakespeare's 'provocative agent', in an exchange that was sometimes combative and sometimes comradely.[50] But I think we still have much to learn about a working relationship so close that Forker sees it 'approaching symbiosis' (20), particularly if we examine it in the context of *Edward II,* which is a story about symbiosis.[51] Such an examination can cast light not only on these two plays but also on the widespread process of dramatic collaboration on the early modern stage, and on the meanings, unconscious as well as conscious, that collaboration may have had for writers.

In other words, perhaps Shakespeare, like Brecht, chose Marlowe's *Edward II* as a model for his Richard not only to 'improve on' its portrayal of Edward and the pangs of abdication but also to rework its portrayal of Edward and Gaveston. Brecht's overt 'collaboration' with Marlowe foregrounds Edward's friendship with Gaveston. Shakespeare's 'original' play erases Richard's friendships from *Richard II,* perhaps as part of an effort to erase Marlowe. If so, it is interesting that Marlowe's presence remains strong in Shakespeare's play.[52] Richard's death may seem nothing like Edward's—'Mount, mount, my soul . . . / Whilst my gross flesh sinks downward' (5.5.111-12); but his last words re-call Faustus' unsuccessful dying effort to 'leap up to my God', before he asks, despairing, 'Who pulls me down?' and cries out in 'erotic self-surrender and hor-rified revulsion' as he yields to the embrace of his demon lover: 'Ah, Mephistopheles.'[53] Shakespeare's Richard seems to leave behind the erotic violence in Edward's love for Gaveston or Edward's death, but he may have simply sublimated it instead.[54]

Notes

[1] On Lamb and critical discussion since Lamb, see Charles Forker's introduction to *Edward the Second: The Revel Plays* (Manchester and New York, Manches-ter University Press, 1994), pp. 36-41; on Michael Manheim, 'The Weak King Dilemma in Plays of the 1590s', *Renaissance Drama,* n.s. 2 (1969), 71-80.

[2] Savage pessimism' is Richard Beckley's phrase, in 'Adaptation as a Feature of Brecht's Dramatic Tech-nique', *German Life and Letters,* n.s. 15 (1962), pp. 274-84, 277. On the play's political implications and its place in Brecht's political career, see John Willett and Ralph Manheim, eds., introduction to *Bertolt Brecht Collected Plays* (London, Methuen, 1970), pp. xii-xiii; and John Fuegi, *The Essential Brecht* (Los Angeles, Hennessy and Ingalls, 1972), pp. 26ff. On the impor-tance of Edward and Gaveston's relationship to Brecht, see Louise J. Laboulle, 'A Note on Bertolt Brecht's Adaptation of Marlowe's *Edward II*', *Modern Lan-guage Review,* 54 (1959), pp. 214-20; and Eric Bentley, introduction to *The Works of Bertolt Brecht* (New York, Grove Press, 1966), p. vii and passim.

[3] Glynne Wickham, 'Shakespeare's *King Richard II* and Marlowe's *King Edward II*', in *Shakespeare's Dramatic Heritage: Critical Studies in Medieval, Tu-dor, and Shakespearean Drama* (London, Routledge & Kegan Paul, 1969). Quotations from *Richard II* and other Shakespeare plays which follow are from the Arden editions.

[4] Ruth Nevo, *Shakespeare's Other Language* (New York, Methuen, 1987).

[5] In the 1970s critics talked about gender identity in the play; recent discussion is more often devoted to sexual orientation and object choice in the play, and to early modern attitudes toward same-sex love. For discussion of gender identity in the play, see, e.g., Barbara J. Bains, 'Sexual Polarity in the Plays of Christopher Marlowe', *Ball State University Forum,* 23 (1982), 317; and Sara Munson Deats, '*Edward II;* A Study of Androgyny', *Ball State University Forum,* 22 (1981), 30-41; for dis-cussion of sexual orientation, see, e.g., Purvis Boyette, 'Wanton Humor and Wanton Poets: Homosexuality in Marlowe's *Edward II*', *TSE,* 12 (1977), 33-50; and Wickham, 'Shakespeare's *King Richard*'.

[6] Forker, 34. Shakespeare may have drawn on Mar-lowe's portrayal of Edward and Gaveston, reappropri-ating them for heterosexuality in *Richard II* (for Rich-ard and Isabel) and in *Antony and Cleopatra.* Jonathan Goldberg argues strongly against reducing homosexu-ality to a form of or substitute for heterosexuality (*Sodometries. Renaissance Texts and Renaissance Sexu-alities* (Stanford, Calif., 1992), p. 121). But the echoes across the gap between the two playwrights—and the two orientations—are certainly there.

[7] Or 'presexual', like love between parent and child. Shakespeare, for example, may have heard Edward's lament for Gaveston as parental; it later provided him with a voice for two famous bereaved parents—for Constance in Shakespeare's *King John,* when her son Arthur dies, and for Lear in *King Lear* when he loses Cordelia. Edward: 'I shall never see / My lovely Pierce, my Gaveston again.' Constance: 'Never, never / Must I behold my pretty Arthur more.' Lear's familiar words hardly need quoting: 'Never, never, never, never, never.'

[8] Sir Thomas Elyot, *Boke Named the Governour (1531),* 'Amity or Friendship', ed. Croft (London, 1880), p. 119. (Elyot goes on to tell about 'Titus and Gisippius', who were 'one in form in personage', as well as in affection, will, and appetites, and had 'so confederated themselves, that it seemed none other, when their names were declared, but that they had only changed their places, issuing (as I might say) out of the one body, and entering in to the other' (134). Bacon, *Essays* (1857), p. 265; Montaigne, tr. Florio, vol 1, p. 202.)

[9] Josie Slaughter Shumake, *The Sources of Marlowe's Edward II* (Ph.D. diss., University of South Carolina, 1984), p. cxiii.

[10] Edward's tragedy, in fact, is that he found himself not by being King but by being Gaveston. David H. Thurn speaks of the couple's imaginary 'unity, iden-tity and totality in a structure of reflection', 'Sover-eignty, Disorder, and Fetishism in Marlowe's *Edward II*', *Renaissance Drama,* 21 (1990), 115-41. Claude J. Summers says that Gaveston is 'a mirror in which the king sees reflected his own possibilities of selfhood', and identifies a pattern of sight imagery associated with mirroring in the play ('Sex, Politics, and Self-Realiza-tion in *Edward II*', in *'A Poet and a Filthy Play-Maker': New Essays on Christopher Marlowe* (New York, 1988), p. 233). Forker expands this argument with telling details from the text, observing for example that Ed-ward defines his existence in terms of attachments ('take my heart in rescue of my friends' (4.7.66-7)).

[11] Edward's youth in Holinshed actually has much in common with Hal's. Both are wanton, self-indulgent, and misled by minions as well as harlots; both were warned by venerable fathers about their companions. The difference is that Edward never reforms.

[12] On Girard's 'mimetic desire', see his *Violence and the Sacred* (1977). See also Joel Fineman's Girardian reading of Shakespeare, 'Fratricide and Cuckoldry: Shakespeare's Doubles', in *Representing Shakespeare: New Psychoanalytic Essays,* ed. Murray M. Schwartz and Coppélia Kahn (Baltimore and London, 1980), pp. 70-109.

[13] Ernst Kantorowicz, *The King's Two Bodies* (1957); Anne Barton, 'The King Disguised: Shakespeare's *Henry V* and the Comical History' (1975), in *Essays, Mainly Shakespearean* (Cambridge, 1994), p. 220.

[14] Bruce R. Smith, *Homosexual Desire in Shakespeare's England* (Chicago and London, 1991).

[15] The merging of sexuality and aggression in Edward's murder is paralleled by a similar mix in Gaveston's response to Edward's love: 'I think myself as great / As Caesar riding in the Roman street / With captive kings at his triumphant car' (1.1.171-3). Here 'Tamburlaine's sadism returns as love', says Schumake (cxxii).

[16] Harold F. Brooks, 'Marlowe and the Early Shakespeare', in *Christopher Marlowe,* ed. Brian Morris (New York, Hill and Wang, 1968), pp. 178-9.

[17] Marie Axton, *The Queen's Two Bodies: Drama and the Elizabethan Succession* (London, Royal Historical Society, 1977), pp. 101-2.

[18] Cf. Kent's view of adulterers as rats that 'bite the holy cords a-twain / Which are t'intrise t'unloose' (2.2.75).

[19] Richard S. M. Hirsch points out a second Marlovian echo just a few lines later in the same scene of *Henry IV,* taken from the same scene in *Edward II.* This time it is a nasty wish on Edward's part toward his enemies:

> EDWARD II Would Lancaster and he had both
> carous'd
> A bowl of poison to each other's health.
> *(Ed II 1.3.230-3)*

Hotspur takes up the wish for his own enemy twin, Hal: 'I would have poison'd him with a pot of ale' (*1 Henry IV* 1.3.233). ('A Second Echo of *Edward II* in I.iii of *'1 Henry Four'*, *N&Q,* 22 (1975), 168.)

[20] Although he had to confuse his Mortimers before the threat could make any sense in the context of Henry IV and Hotspur.

[21] Fineman describes them in these terms in 'Fratricide'.

[22] William Dinsmore Briggs, *Marlowe's Edward II* (1914), p. 194; John Bakeless, *The Tragical History of Christopher Marlowe* (Cambridge, Mass., 1942), pp. 11, 209.

[23] Some editors dismiss Bolingbroke's accusation as a thoughtless carry-over from *Edward II*—the archetypical 'mere verbal echo'; others take it as evidence for a sexual relation between Richard and his flatterers. Forker sees it as Bolingbroke's Machiavellian invention to help justify his murder of the flatterers (38-9).

[24] Harrier, 'Ceremony and Politics in *Richard II*', *Shakespeare: Text, Language, Criticism; Essays in Honor of Marvin Spevack,* ed. Bernhard Fabien and Kurt Tetzeli von Rosador (Hildesheim, Zurich, and New York, Olms-Widman, 1987), pp. 80-97.

[25] Richard has three soliloquies of defeat: here when he returns from Ireland to deal with the rebels, then *during* the official abdication at Flint, and finally in prison in the tower.

[26]
> But when my glass shows me myself indeed
> Beated and chopped with tanned antiquity,
> Mine own self-love quite contrary I read . . .
> 'Tis thee, myself, that for myself I praise,
> Painting my age with beauty of thy days.
> (Son. 62, 9-11, 13-14)

[27] At the equivalent moment in Marlowe's play, Edward tears up Mortimer's written name. Edward, that is, attacks his enemy and holds on to his faith in his friends. Richard is more cynical.

[28] Ure notes that Richard's speech probably echoes Holinshed's account of Richard's 'noble housekeeping' ('For there resorted dailie to his court above ten thousand persons that had meat and drink there allowed them' (508/1/8)). But this rational connection is supplemented by the Faustus echo, which suggests that the tie between Richard and the men he kept was also like the erotic tie between Helen and the men she 'launched'. The allusion to Helen may also lead back indirectly to Marlowe's Gaveston, who, as Forker reminds us, was called a 'Greekish strumpet' (39).

[29] What has not been noticed is that Richard may already have put himself into a well-known woman's position even earlier in the mirror scene, when he offers to 'submit' to Bolingbroke:

> I'll give my jewels for a set of beads,
> My gorgeous palace for a hermitage;
> My gay apparel for an almsman's gown;
> My figur'd goblets for a dish of wood;
> My sceptre for a palmer's walking staff;
> My subjects for a pair of carved saints.
> (3.3.146-52)

In the old *King Leir* play Cordella meets the Gallican king disguised as a Palmer and offers to give up her royal estate to marry him:

My mind is low ynough to love a Palmer,
Rather then any King upon the earth . . .
Ile hold thy Palmers staffe within my hand,
And think it is the Scepter of a Queene.
Sometime Ile set thy Bonnet on my head,
And thinke I weare a riche imperiall
  Crowne,
Sometime Ile help thee in thy holy prayers,
And thinke I am with thee in Paradise.
               (692-3, 698-703)

There is something of Cordella in Richard's perversely loving submission to Bolingbroke.

[30] Wangh, 'A Psychoanalytic Commentary on Shakespeare's *The Tragedie of Richard the Second*', *Psychoanalytic Quarterly,* 37 (1968), 212-38.

[31] Murray Schwartz, 'Anger, Wounds, and the Forms of Theater in *King Richard II:* Notes for a Psychoanalytic Interpretation', *Assays,* 2 (1982), 115-29.

[32] Schwartz, 'Anger, Wounds', 120. Richard's entire struggle with Bolingbroke is framed by Bolingbroke's two references to the rival brothers Cain and Abel, in connection first with Richard's murder of Gloucester and then with Bolingbroke's murder of Richard (1.1.104; 5.6.43).

[33] As did the unborn twins in Plautus' *Amphytruo,* one of Shakespeare's sources for *The Comedy of Errors.* Wayne Koestenbaum's *Double Talk: The Erotics of Male Literary Collaboration* (New York and London, 1989, p. 11) notes images of a shared womb among twentieth-century collaborators, and cites as an example *Dead Ringers,* the film about twin gynaeco logists sharing the single womb of a patient-lover who thinks there is only one of them.

[34] See Miriam Gilbert's review essay, '*Richard II* at Stratford: Role-Playing as Metaphor', in *Shakespeare: The Theatrical Dimension,* ed. Philip C. McGuire and David A. Samuelson (New York, 1979), pp. 85-102.

[35] Perhaps Richard here is recalling Bolingbroke's parting dig, when banished, with his pious but quietly overweening farewell: 'Then, England's ground, farewell; sweet soil, adieu, / My mother and my nurse that bears me yet' (1.3.306-7).

[36] See, e.g., Alan Riding's review, 'A Female Richard II Captivates the French', *New York Times,* 27 January 1996.

[37] Perhaps Shakespeare was also recalling some scabrous horseplay in the morality plays when the devil carried the Vice off to hell on his back. 'Now here's a courteous devil, that for to pleasure his friend, will

not stick to make a jade of himself', as Miles says of a similar devil come to take him away (*Friar Bacon* 15.53-5).

[38] Nineteenth-century commenters identified the origins of this passage in 'the spirit of the numerous medieval paintings and designs on the subject of death'. Matthew W. Black, note to line 3.2.163-73, *The Life and Death of King Richard the Second,* New Variorum Edition, ed. Matthew W. Black (Philadelphia and London, 1955).

[39] M. M. Mahood, *Shakespeare's Wordplay* (London: Methuen, 1957), p. 85.

[40] See David Bevington, *From Mankind to Marlowe,* on *Edward II*'s morality play structure.

[41] Hilda Hulme, *Explorations in Shakespeare's Language.* It was powerful but small. Cf. *Coriolanus* downplaying his wound as something that could fit into an 'auger's bore' (*Cor.* 4.6.87). Janet Adelman suggests that Richard's attitude toward death's pin in fact depends on its ambiguous size—on the way in which a seemingly little thing can be strong enough to do such damage.

[42] Black compares Shakespeare's 'little pin' with the possibly derivative lines in *The Faithful Friends* (1620), which return the pin to its traditional role by likening 'the King's intrancet' to 'a bag / Blown with the breath of greatness', so that 'a little pin / Prick but the windy outside, down falls all / And leaves naught but emptiness' (2542-8).

[43] Frankie Rubinstein cites several instances of sexually charged pins in *A Dictionary of Shakespeare's Sexual Puns and Their Significance* (London and Basingstoke, 1984, p. 194), and there are others. See, e.g., Heywood's *4 P's* for jokes about a wife's pincushion, wide pincase, and so on.

[44] Like Brutus trying to deal with his love/hate relationship to his rival Caesar.

[45] When he first returned to England from Ireland, Richard had imagined himself the attacker ferreting out a hidden Bolingbroke, as does the sun 'dart[ing] his light through every guilty hole' (*Richard II* 3.2.43); but the roles are now reversed.

[46] If Bolingbroke and Richard corporealize castles, Isabel performs the reverse transformation when she architecturalizes her body by speaking of it as a house for a 'guest of grief' (*Richard II* 2.2.7) instead of 'so sweet a guest / As my sweet Richard' (8-9); and later of Richard's body as a 'beauteous inn' where grief is lodged, while triumph is become an 'ale-house' guest, in the vulgar house of Bolingbroke (5.1.13-15). Richard similarly describes himself as a container for grief

('an unseen grief that swells with silence in the tortur'd soul' (4.1.295)); and the Duchess of Gloucester reduces Edward II's sons to seven fragile 'vials of his sacred blood' (*Richard II* 1.2.12)—one of which Richard broke, and another of which will be broken when 'Richard's sacred blood is spilt' at the end.

[47] The ideal of an England bound in by walls was not just Shakespeare's; it appears as one of the magical achievements sought—unwisely—in both Marlowe's *Dr Faustus* ('I'll have them wall all Germany with walls of brass' (B Text, 1.1.88)), and Greene's *Friar Bacon and Friar Bungay* (ii. 30).

[48] Cf. Black, note to 5.4.67; Ure, note to 5.5.66.

[49] A dandyish affectation gone out of style by the time Shakespeare mocked it in *All's Well That Ends Well.*

[50] Nicholas Brooke, 'Marlowe as Provocative Agent in Shakespeare's Early Plays', *Shakespeare Survey 14* (1961), pp. 34-44; Brooks, 'Marlowe and the Early Shakespeare'; Muriel Bradbrook, 'Shakespeare's Recollections of Marlowe', *Shakespeare's Styles,* ed. Philip Edwards, Inga-Stina Ewbank, and G. K. Hunter (Cambridge, 1980); Marjorie Garber, 'Marlovian Vision/ Shakespearean Revision', *Research Opportunities in Renaissance Drama* 22 (1979), 3-10; James Shapiro, *Rival Playwrights: Marlowe, Jonson, Shakespeare* (New York, 1991), pp. 75-132.

[51] And in the context of *Richard II,* which seems in so many ways to be a bridge for Shakespeare between older Marlovian and newer styles of language, of rhetoric, and of dramaturgy.

[52] It has been pointed out that besides *Edward II, Tamburlaine* is echoed (and mocked) in 1.1 and 1.3; and that *Doctor Faustus* is quoted in Richard's abdication speech.

[53] Wilbur Sanders, *The Dramatist and the Received Idea. Studies in the Plays of Marlowe and Shakespeare* (Cambridge, 1968), p. 242.

[54] This essay has benefitted from the comments of Alan Grob, Janet Adelman, and James Lake, each of whom read and responded to early drafts, as well as from questions posed by members of the psychoanalytic seminar at the Shakespeare Association of America (1996) and by audience respondents at the Shakespeare Institute at Stratford (1996).

Source: "Marlowe's *Edward II*: Penetrating Language in Shakespeare's *Richard II,*" in *Shakespeare Survey: An Annual Survey of Shakespeare Studies and Production,* Vol. 50, 1997, pp. 41-55.

The Famous Analyses of *Henry the Fourth*

David Willbern, *State University of New York, Buffalo*

One of the earliest criticisms of Shakespearean character is Maurice Morgann's well-known but rarely read "Essay on the Dramatic Character of Sir John Falstaff," published in London in 1777 as a bold defense of the corpulent and witty knight against the charge of cowardice.[1] Morgann assumed that Shakespeare's characters were like people and that Falstaff was like an historical person, with a history and an inner life that corresponded to common human nature, which he termed "certain first principles of character," and who therefore could be understood and judged through the critic's emotional responses to that nature, which he called "mental Impressions" as opposed to rational "Understanding." Since then both Falstaff and his fellow sportsman, Prince Hal, have attracted scrutiny from traditional character critics like A.C. Bradley, L.L. Schucking, and J.I.M. Stewart, and psychoanalytic critics like Ernst Kris.[2] My plan in this chapter is less to review various analyses of characters in *Henry IV, Part One* than to sketch categories of psychoanalytic interpretive strategies that have been deployed in the effort, and then to consider the large issue of psychological versus (new) historical or cultural approaches.[3] I find four major categories of psychoanalytic explication: (1) *structural*, (2) *oedipal*, (3) *pre-oedipal or object-relational*, and (4) *linguistic or semiotic*.

The first, or structural view, is an early approach that considers the play as a kind of intrapsychic allegory, analogous to medieval *psychomachia*. The Freudian model of id/ego/superego can be mapped onto characters in the play, roughly as follows: The id is represented (or symbolized, in this terminology) by Falstaff and Hotspur, figures of unrestrained appetite and uninhibited reaction. The superego is symbolized by King Henry as a judgmental, restrictive father, the basis for an internal imago or ego-ideal based on an introjected paternal image. The King's rebukes sound early in the play and are echoed in Prince Hal's famous soliloquy, "I know you all . . . ," in Act One (1.2.195-217), a rationalizing monologue that presents self-rebuke as self-justification, promising future reformation and reconciliation with the father. The ego is embodied by Prince Hal, the gradually heroic son who learns to mediate among the demands of impulse, restraint, and his various social worlds (tavern, court, battlefield).

Within this structural design, the psychological progress of the play can be seen to enact a gradual working-through and accommodation of id and superego to the framework of the ego; it is, by this design, a process of maturation. This progress occurs over the course of the play, but the interplay of the three elements or agencies can be seen in the initial tavern scene (1.2), where Hal plays at being Falstaff, then announces in soliloquy that he knows better and rebukes the "unyok'd humor" of his friends.[4]

Such a psychoanalytic reconfiguration may seem old-fashioned and allegorical, relying on Latinate Freudian terms that, after these many years, creak when flexed, and unexamined assumptions about symbolism and dramatic representation. Still, a benefit of this style of reading is that it is *pre-characterological*, that is, it does not get caught up in personality-analyses of those reified linguistic complexes conventionally identified as "characters." In some ways this primitive mode of psychoanalytic reading is close to more recent methods that will be addressed later.

The second, or oedipal view focuses on the various father-son conflicts in the play, primarily re-enacted in terms of King Henry's initial wish to replace Hal with Hotspur (1.1.85-89) and Hal's rejection of his filial role and his symbolic replacement of King Henry with Falstaff. The primal scene of these reversals is the role-playing in the tavern (2.4), where Hal dethrones the King and repudiates Falstaff. These oedipal displacements turn the father into a comic scapegoat figure who is eventually sacrificed (Falstaff), while the figure of the rebellious son is displaced onto a character (Hotspur) who is sacrificed for the sake of resolution of conflict and the reunion of father and son, dramatized at the end of *1 Henry IV* by Prince Hal fighting with and for the King, and at the end of *2 Henry IV* by Prince Hal becoming King and banishing Falstaff.[5]

The oedipal reading is dramatically privileged by the play, and made manifest at least in terms of contests between fathers and sons. Through a series of rivalries, alliances, and victories, a proper new balance or filiation is achieved, so that Hal can attain the position of prince as support for his father before he eventually succeeds him. The success of the oedipal project, in short, culminates in a relatively untroubled succession. However, just as the structural reading reasonably assumes the virtue of psychic coherence and mature development, I suggest that most conventional readings of Hal's glorious progress toward heroic monarchy in *Henry V* are fueled by an unexamined complicity in the oedipal project that the plays dramatize. We can largely thank feminist readers, as well as psychoanalytic critics—such as C. L. Barber, Coppélia

Kahn, Richard Wheeler, and Peter Erickson—for helping to de-idealize this unacknowledged masculine identification.

The third, pre-oedipal or object-relational interpretive strategy considers the play's primary dyad of Hal-Falstaff as reconfiguring a more intimate familial bond than father-son, that is, the mother-child relation. As many critics have noted, *1 Henry IV* is notably without effective female presences. There are no manifest mothers, and wives are either mute (Mortimer and his Welsh wife share no language)[6] or muted (see Hotspur's playful yet cruel neglect of Kate). Mistress Quickly is subordinate to Falstaff, who plays both host and guest. It is Falstaff, virtually, who assumes the maternal role, becoming an all-providing source of food, fun, discourse, and self-reflection. He is an androgynous, magical figure, a hall of mirrors for Hal to play in. Falstaff's relation to his world is basically childish; he seeks instant gratification for primitive impulses like eating, drinking, and sleeping. One way to imagine the character is as a big infant (although wondrously precocious in speech) who focuses solely on the sources of his own pleasure (primarily oral—his next cup of sack) or on opportunities to display his magnificent narcissism.[7]

Hal's fondness for the world of Falstaff and the tavern hence represents a wish to reconstitute a simpler, basic bond of mother and child, wherein each mirrors the other. Falstaff is a buffer between Hal and the world, a wall of flesh that encloses him from the demands of harsh reality. W. H. Auden describes Falstaff as a presocial being, whose rotundity brings together mother and child and is therefore fantastically self-sufficient.[8] Hal's rejection of Falstaff thus becomes a rejection of the seductions of childishness, the irresponsibilities of narcissism and instant gratification. Hal grows up by growing beyond the child within himself. The repudiation, however, is only superficial. Hal incorporates his relation to Falstaff, so that, as Wheeler puts it, "Falstaff sustains Hal at a deep level comparable to the power of dreaming to keep intact the essential knowledge of the infantile past."[9]

In an important new analysis of the figure of Falstaff, Valerie Traub deepens and extends previous psychoanalytic criticism of the Hal-Falstaff dyad to include "a projected fantasy of the pre-oedipal *maternal* whose rejection is the basis upon which patriarchal subjectivity is predicated." Using Bakhtin's idea of the grotesque, carnivalesque body, and precise textual details, she refashions "Falstaff" in terms of the female reproductive body and suggests similarities between his magical language and Kristeva's "semiotic." Traub's analysis also extends the social realm of the play—its symbolic politics—beyond evident issues of adult masculine rivalry and succession and into questions of the repression of infantile connections to maternal dependence.[10]

Combining the oedipal and object-relational approaches produces a view of the character of Falstaff as a fantastic, substitute, familial environment: brother, father, child, and mother. The tavern then becomes a *playground* of wishes (and fears) within which Hal can enact various fantasies (of stealing, killing, lying) and styles of being (controlling, submitting, pretending). It is an arena of innocent acts, a safehouse, or *playhouse,* that offers refuge from the dangerous and bloody world of civil war that surrounds it. The opening lines of the play characterize this world:

> No more the thirsty entrance of this soil
> Shall daub her lips with her own children's
>   blood.
> No more shall trenching war channel her fields,
> Nor bruise her flow'rets with the armed hoofs
> Of hostile paces.
>
>   (1.1.5-9)

The image of a devouring and abused maternal figure is thus evoked at the start of the play, but only through denial: "No more. . . ." The insistent absence of manifest female power in *I Henry IV* and throughout the second tetralogy is telling. These opening lines hark back to sanctioned images of a maternal England from *Richard II* (for instance, Gaunt's nostalgic evocation of "this blessed plot, . . . this teeming womb of royal kings / Fear'd by their breed and famous by their birth" [2.1.40 ff]). The appropriation of a benign, creative version of this ground by Falstaff permits Hal a magical playspace within which he can marginally encounter but largely bypass the world of women, as Kahn has noted.[11] In *I Henry IV* this world is either repressed or fantastically transformed; but what is repressed will return. *Hamlet* is the most significant site of this return of repressed femininity, yet it is suggested at the end of this play, as I will show.

The fourth, linguistic or semiotic approach focuses on the question of *identification* as a mode of human development. Psychologically and socially, the ways we represent ourselves publicly are learned in the context of primary childhood identifications within our families. As small but telling examples, consider personal vocal intonation, or handwriting. Our voices mimic those we hear; our handwriting is unique yet derivative, based on imitating parents, teachers, and other ego ideals. In handwriting each of us can see the singular sign of our individuality—it legally identifies us—that also carries indelible traces of its sources.[12] The linguistic approach thus resituates the structural, since Hal's project is to move among various identifications—with Falstaff, Hotspur, and Henry—and to select aspects of each that he can amalgamate in order eventually to define himself as "the true prince." It also resituates the oedipal, since identification has ambivalent motives: (1) becoming like (liking), and (2) taking over (incorporating, replacing).[13]

These examples of voice and handwriting are over-determined, for Shakespeare portrays the process of identification in *I Henry IV* literally in linguistic terms, that is, in terms of the rhetorical styles of his central characters. Prince Hal is expert at imitating the terms and tropes of Falstaff and Hotspur, and later the King. When he arrives in the play, he speaks the language of Falstaff as well as that character himself. Rhetorically, the first "Falstaff" in the play is performed by the Prince.

> *Falstaff.* Now, Hal, what time of day is it, lad?
> *Prince.* Thou art so fat-witted with drinking of old sack, and unbuttoning thee after supper, and sleeping upon benches after noon, that thou hast forgotten to demand that truly thou wouldest truly know. What a devil hast thou to do with the time of the day? unless hours were cups of sack, and minutes capons, and clocks the tongues of bawds, and dials the signs of leaping-houses, and the blessed sun himself a fair hot wench in flame-color'd taffata; I see no reason why thou shouldst be so superfluous as to demand the time of the day.
>
> (1.2.1-12)

This linguistic mimesis is exact in terms of comparisons and metaphors, but it is identification with a difference. Hal's insistence on the passage of time, his criticism of Falstaff's habits (he simultaneously expands and deflates the character as delimited by the pleasure principle), and the pun in "blessed sun" all point to his later repudiation of both style and character.

Hal similarly mimics and places Hotspur in his brief foray into an imitation of that character:

> I am not yet of Percy's mind, the Hotspur of the north, he that kills me some six or seven dozen of Scots at a breakfast, washes his hands, and says to his wife, "Fie upon this quiet life! I want work." "O my sweet Harry," says she, "how many hast thou kill'd today?" "Give my roan horse a drench," says he, and answers, "Some fourteen," an hour after, "a trifle, a trifle."
>
> (2.4.101-8)

This parody is in prose, perhaps because Hal's own verse will need the tropes of ambition and bravery when he achieves the princely goal. But Hal catches Hotspur's unrealistic fantasies of simplistic aggression, his need (like Falstaff) for an appreciative audience, and his tendency to think about his horse when responding to his wife (see 2.3.89-102).

Falstaff and Hotspur are exemplary stylists of one figure of speech, hyperbole. Hotspur is an hyperbolist of linear ambition, an overreacher; Falstaff is an hyperbolist of all-inclusive rotundity and comparison. Hotspur drives aggressively at his topic with figures;

Falstaff surrounds it with similes. Hotspur seems to be pursuing some grandiose heroic identity; Falstaff is instantly ready to re-compose his descriptions of himself in terms of some other person, thing, or possibility. To use a mythological parallel, Hotspur has Mercury's speed, Falstaff his mutability.[14]

The most poignant instance of Hal's mimetic appropriation of his rival's language is at the moment of Hotspur's death, when Hal literally completes his last line: "No, Percy," Hotspur says to himself, "thou are dust, / And food for—/ For worms, brave Percy," Hal continues. "Fare thee well, great heart" (4.4.85-87). The moment merges two styles of identification: affection and aggression, sharing and taking. Hal takes Hotspur's last breath and substitutes his own in order to speak Hotspur's last word, an honorable theft that authentically replaces what was taken ("worms" is surely the word Hotspur would have said; the trajectory of thought and language requires it).

In a word, Hal's project in the play is to find, take, or make his own language—or more precisely that language with which he can identify in such a way as to become "the true prince." The most dramatic moment of this discovery or production is the scene of Hal's magnanimous and mature speeches over the fallen bodies of Hotspur and Falstaff on the battlefield. Here is the inception of his own "authentic" discourse, his "winning of his own" (the final line of the play) in language.[15] Before this dramatic moment, however, Hal enters another register of language at the begining of Act Five, when King and Prince cooperate to produce a verse description of the new day:

> *King.* How bloodily the sun begins to peer
> Above yon bulky hill! the day looks pale
> At his distemp'rature.
> *Prince.*   The southren wind
> Doth play the trumpet to his purposes,
> And by his hollow whistling in the leaves
> Foretells a tempest and a blust'ring day.
> *King.* Then with the losers let it sympathize,
> For nothing can seem foul to those that win.
>
> (5.1.1-8)

This shared poetic construct (the two voices co-produce line three) is a linguistic emblem of what Kahn calls the "reciprocal validation of each other as father and son, king and prince."[16] The validation is tempered, however, by Erickson's inference that "neither father nor son can securely know exactly who the other is because of his theatrical sense of himself."[17] This little poem-within-the-play thus serves well as an indicator of characters (both Henry's and Hal's) and climactic evidence of Hal's achievement of the language of a prince, properly subservient to his father. The lines echo beyond character, however, and beyond the dramatic moment into the domain of the play of language. Psychoanalytic attention should disclose these echoes. The rhetorical set-piece description of the dawning of day on the battlefield coalesces at least two central themes: the manifest theme of oedipal resolution and emerging harmony between father and son, and the latent theme of repressed relations with a maternal image.

King Henry opens the set-piece with a regal observation: "How bloodily the sun begins to peer / Above yon bulky hill! The day looks pale / At his distemp'rature." The King's conventional identification with the sun, the royal eye of day, extends to his projection of his own anger into the hot blood of the dawn's distemperature. Prince Hal joins in, literally in mid-line, to accompany the paternal observation. His forecast deflates the royal appearance of the sun by shifting the trumpet of regal annunciation to "hollow whistling," and his imagery also suggests the question of his own heroic actions to come. Will he "play the trumpet" to his father's purposes, or whistle in the leaves (perhaps with Falstaff)? King Henry ignores any subtleties in Hal's comment, however, and closes the speech with a conventional battlefield homily about the blessings of victors.

This moment of masculine martial harmony occurs on the site of another scene, the literal ground of authority on which the staging of masculine conflicts and resolutions will occur. Typically, a Shakespearean pun discloses this scene. The appearance of the bloody "sun/ son" above the "bulky hill" echoes Hal's previous description of himself (to Henry) "wearing a garment all of blood":

> I will redeem all this on Percy's head.
> And in the closing of some glorious day
> Be bold to tell you that I am your son.
> When I will wear a garment all of blood,
> And stain my favors in a bloody mask,
> Which wash'd away shall scour my shame
>   with it.
> And that shall be the day, when e'er it lights,
> That this same child of honor and renown,
> This gallant Hotspur . . .
>
>   (3.2.132-40)

As Watson and Traub have noted, this imagery promises a magical regeneration of the Prince through a fantasy of birth. Watson situates the moment in a series of autochthonous Caesarean births of the hero, including Glendower, Richard III, Macbeth, and Coriolanus. Traub notes that the fantasy provides the newborn son with a bloody baptism that washes away any maternal connection, so that Hal becomes "his father's son and his nation's hero."[18] One motivation for this fantasy of masculine birth and its implicit rejection of maternity lies in previous metaphoric evocations of violent mother-child interactions (as Watson

notes): "No more the thirsty entrance of this soil / Shall daub her lips with her own children's blood. . . . " Yet the new day that Hal prophesies (the dawn of the bloody sun) rises over this same ground of maternal presence and power. The very ground of masculine authority, then, the "bulky hill" whose soil will once again "daub her lips with her own children's blood" in the ensuing battle, adumbrates the ubiquitous yet invisible primordial female presence in the play, a type of *mons martialis* (whose dangerous confusion of sexes may reciprocate Falstaff's comic version of androgyny). Against the notice of evident feminine/ maternal absence in *I Henry IV*, then, can be placed the deeper observation that the maternal ground is both nowhere and everywhere.[19] As Janet Adelman puts it, in a distillation of her theory of Shakespearean tragic ambivalence:

> The problematic maternal body can never quite be occluded or transformed: made into a monster or a saint, killed off or banished from the stage, it remains at the center of masculine subjectivity, marking its unstable origin. For the contaminated flesh of the maternal body is also home: the home Shakespeare's protagonists long to return to, the home they can never quite escape.[20]

Shakespeare's dramatization in *Henry IV, Part One* of the linguistic production of masculine styles of speech and action provokes useful questions in terms of contemporary theories of the historical origins and psychological structure of identity. Masculine identity as displayed in this play enacts itself generally through contest and cooperation among men, and particularly through careful linguistic identifications. Hal finds and situates himself through sequential identifications with Falstaff, Hotspur, and King Henry; he knows them all. Yet the climactic identification with the father that apparently culminates and completes heroic masculine identity occurs on the site of a repression—the buried relation to the mother, the bulky hill that supports the sport of heroes.

Theoretical Interlude

This dramatic moment in *I Henry IV* impinges on a central question in current psychoanalytic theory. Does primary identity emerge from a series of linguistic identifications whose continual repetition it requires in order to maintain or re-create itself? Or does identity rest on the solid, repressed ground of a preverbal relation? Is identity primarily theatrical, whereby we each play the trumpet to an other's purpose, or is it genuine, the expression of a self from which we truly proceed? Is the self a series of defensive poses, temporary enactments within particular social contexts, a *dramatis persona* we maintain from one discontinuous moment to another? Or is there a core "true self" from which we speak, write, act, and otherwise present ourselves?

Such a self recuperates a primitive connection to a matrix of identity—the mother-infant relation as felt and learned in early childhood. We are approaching, from other angles, the primary question of Hamlet's *"that* within," in terms of psychoanalytic theories of the origins of ego, self, subject, or (for lack of a better term) character.

At this point I will embark on a brief theoretical interlude, to define terms and to fashion the argument. This interlude is relevant to Shakespeare's plays only if one supposes that mimesis, identification, and representation—in terms of language and performed behavior—are relevant to the plays, or if one considers that the question of Hamlet's "that within" might be clarified by psychological concepts.

Very briefly, let me rehearse some general psychoanalytic ideas about human development. Over time, and uniquely for the human animal this is a very extended time, the interaction of innate psychobiological processes (similar to the species but unique to the individual)—call it *nature*—and social modes of caretaking (similar to the culture but unique to the individual caretaker)—call it *nurture*—produces patterns of behavior that form the characteristic blueprint of the person, her or his "character." These characteristic patterns inform psychic and emotional structure, unconsciously. As we grow, experience, and learn, we retain images, memories, and styles—not simply out of who we are "inside" or from whom we encounter "outside"—but from the interactions of inside and outside. These internalized representations of relationships form a template that informs how we feel, think, speak, and act. The primary dispute in current post-Freudian theory is between those who think that this internal template of unconscious identifications is grounded in a core emotional relation (the infant-mother dyad of object-relations) and those who think that the template is a distorting mirror of imaginary identifications (Lacanian psychoanalysis).

A brief sketch of key terms will be useful here: the Freudian *ego,* the object-relational *self,* and the Lacanian *subject.* As Freud described it in *The Ego and the Id* (1923), the ego is a boundary concept, a "frontier creature," analogous to the skin.[21] As such it is a managing agent or interface between internal energies (somatic events, affects) and external reality. In its defensive modes it may seek withdrawal or magical modification of stimuli, but its goal is the integration of outside and inside in a manageable synthesis. In the gradual development of such boundary maintenance, a perceptible and negotiable difference between inside and outside, "me" and "not-me," self and object world, is produced. The ego is the agent or process of this negotiation. Object-relations theory extends this basic Freudian idea of boundaries into a notion of the relational *self* as a style of managing needs, demands, and wishes in the context of an other person (mother) or environment (family, society). Over the course of time, a history of internal relations is experienced, practiced, and established, which produces an idiomatic, individual epistemology, in terms of the environment the person comes to expect. As Christopher Bollas puts it: "The concept of self should refer to the positions or points of view from which and through which we sense, feel, observe and reflect on distinct and separate experiences in our being. One crucial point-of-view comes from the other who experiences us."[22] For Lacan, as I understand him, the impingement of the other's perspective is structurally less benign. (Of course there is plenty of room in the object-relations model for malign impingement and a distorted self, but this would be categorized as pathology.) The Lacanian *subject* is already a pun: both active, thinking agent (though this may be an illusion) and passive victim of domination. Rather than relating across a negotiated distance or absence, the Lacanian subject is faced with a primordial lack, gap, or division from an aboriginal unity ("the imaginary"). The basic organization of the subject is in terms of alienation.[23]

These various concepts, interrelated as they seem, are significantly different. For an object-relations theorist like D.W. Winnicott, an identity of temporary, serial identifications is a skeptical self, a compliant and canny structure of defenses—what he calls a "false self system." It is very like the Lacanian subject, generated by slippery language, constructing an illusory context of relations against a shifting background of irrecoverable loss. As for the ego, that for Lacan is "the sum of the identifications of the subject . . . like the superimposition of various coats borrowed from . . . the bric-a-brac of its props department."[24] The identity that connects to an inner core self, unconscious, expressing a consistent and coherent idiom of being, presents another kind of subject, constructed by object-relations theorists like Winnicott. Lacanians view this self as a nostalgic fiction, a wish and a defense. Winnicottians see it as a ground of being.

The psychological argument, I believe, may be haunted by theology. For the idea of a "true self" is like an article of faith—a residue of the Christian theology of *presence,* a type of psychic Holy Spirit within that relates to a Madonna-like internalized object.[25] Stripped of its adjectival ethic of "true" and "false," Winnicott's ideas of the production of self through a history of repeated transactions with the world (initially the maternal matrix) could be refashioned in other terms, such as "active" or "passive," "aggressive" or "submissive," "managing" or "accommodating." Such modifiers indicate a style of relationship, not a quality of self. By contrast, if the Winnicottian true self is a residue of Christian fictions—an angel in the psyche—then the Lacanian subject is a piece of the devil's work, made of lies and illusions, forever alienated, fragmented, faced with phantoms and lack. Where Winnicott inscribes a Madonna at the source, Lacan reiterates the expulsion from the garden, under the *nom du père*. Between these rival caricatures of theories about the origins of identity, choice is problematic. Shall we be naive or cynical, embraced or estranged, saved or damned? Is there no middle ground?

I think there is. The philosopher and psychoanalyst Heinz Lichtenstein has developed a theory of identity that provides crucial intermediate concepts. Briefly, Lichtenstein theorizes an *instrumental primary identity,* generated through iterative behaviors and emotions, that connects an individual to his or her (maternal) environment in functional terms.[26] We learn how to be *for* an other; we identify with the (unconscious) desires *of* the other *for* us. This primary identification is mimetic in the Winnicottian sense (the recursive mirroring of the mother), and it is derivative in the Lacanian sense (the Desire of the Other). Lichtenstein writes about "the mirroring quality of the infant's sensory responsiveness to the mother's libidinal attachment":

> This mirroring cannot, of course, be understood in terms of any visual perception, but a reflection through touch, smell, and other primitive sensations. What is dimly emerging in this mirror is, at least in the beginning, not a primary love object, but the outlines of the child's own image as reflected by the mother's unconscious needs with regard to the child. In this first, archaic mirroring experience of the child a primary identity emerges which may be called narcissistic. It is not as yet a sense of identity, for that presupposes consciousness. I see in it rather a primary organizational principle without which the process of developmental differentiation could not begin.

> The mother, in contrast to the nonhuman environment, reflects back to the child a configuration of its own presence. I have suggested . . . that this primary identity has the form of an identity theme, i.e., the specific reflection received from the mother conveys to the child a primary identity defined as instrumentality in relation to the mother.[27]

The idea of identity as a belated reflection of an original source achieves splendid evocation in Wallace Stevens's poem, "Description Without Place," which is in my view a precocious postmodern gloss on Hamlet's remarks about seeming and being as well as a poetic illustration of psychoanalytic theories of identity and language.[28] The poem is difficult, and relies on contemporary science (solar position and energy) and philosophy (being and consciousness). It begins by sidestepping Hamlet's paralyzing quandary about the unbridgeable difference between seeming and being.

> It is possible that to seem—it is to be,
> As the sun is something seeming and it is.

> The sun is an example. What it seems
> It is and in such seeming all things are.
>
>   (1-4)

After thus setting a stellar scene of projected and reflected reality, Stevens personifies the agent of reflective energy as "a queen that made it seem / By the illustrious nothing of her name."

> Her green mind made the world around her
>   green.
> The queen is an example . . . This green
>   queen
> In the seeming of the summer of her sun
> By her own seeming made the summer
>   change.
> In the golden vacancy she came, and comes,
> And seems to be on the saying of her name.
>
>   (7-14)

Later in the poem influential *noms du père*—like Nietzsche and Lenin—figure prominently. Initially, however, the source of being and seeming (or their coincidence) is this archaic (m)other who comes on call, literally corresponding to the speaking agent who calls. In the full ambiguity of the term, she *appears.* "Such seemings are the actual ones," the poem continues (17). Even "if seeming is description without place," "it is a sense / To which we refer experience, a knowledge / Incognito"; "it is an expectation, a desire" (99-107). We construct and experience the reality of our lives in terms of this earliest reflection, which is not precisely ourselves nor an illusory replica.

> Description is revelation. It is not
> The thing described, nor false facsimile.
> It is an artificial thing that exists
> In its own seeming, plainly visible,
> Yet not too closely the double of our lives,
> Intenser than any actual life could be,
> A text we should be born that we might read,
> More explicit than the experience of sun
> And moon, the book of reconciliation,
> Book of a concept only possible
> In description, canon central in itself,
> The thesis of the plentifullest John.
>
>   (121-32)

As this penultimate section makes clear, Stevens is writing about the human experience of living a life mediated through language, a language that exists before us and that we learn as new ("a text we should be born that we might read"). Language enables description, a conscious awareness and articulation that intensifies the natural, sensory phenomena of "actual life." The poem ends with a section that praises the particular nature of language ("men make themselves their speech" [139]) while it simultaneously returns human invention to its natural origin: language or description must "be alive with its own seemings, seeming to be / Like rubies reddened by rubies reddening" (151-52). If *being* is natural existence ("actual life"), then *seeming* is consciousness of that existence. Paradoxically, until we seem we cannot fully realize being. Seeming is self-reflection, a secondary enlightenment that mirrors the archaic dawn of existence, in which we are held, warmed, and *shown* "in the golden vacancy" of an archaic maternal matrix. In the final lines of Stevens's poem, the quintessential human verb (*to be*) is reabsorbed into the lustrous reflections of visual similitude and acoustic rhyme (ru*bies*). Are rubies red, or do they only seem to be so within the spectrum of visible light that human eyes require? Absent such light their redness vanishes, but so too does our sight. The redness of rubies is hence a blend of seeming and being, "as the sun is something seeming and it is." Without the primal *lux* that shows us the world, we cannot see it. Without the archaic (m)other that originally describes our place in the world, we cannot experience it as a coherent self.

Hamlet dramatizes the problems of being and seeming from at least two perspectives. From one view the hero is apparently paralyzed by his perception of an unbridgeable gulf between inner self and external representation, and from another he leaps that gulf by casting thought away, trusting in spontaneous reaction. In his book about Hamlet and *Hamlet,* the psychoanalyst André Green observes:

> Dans le deuil qui l'affecte Hamlet oppose les actions qu'on homme peut jouer, c'est-à-dire feindre sans doute, mais surtout représenter au théâtre et ce qu'il a en lui qui dépasse tout ce qui peut se représenter. "Play" et "show": la métaphore du théâtre est en sous-texte.
>
> Voilà donc le paradoxe rencontré par Shakespeare. Donner à jouer, à représenter ce qui dépasse les possibilités de la représentation: la douleur psychique. Toute la pièce va devoir soutenir ce défi. Le langage poétique va servir de médiateur entre le monde intérieur indicible et son extériorisation sur la scène.[29]

> Within the grief that affects Hamlet are opposed the actions that a man could play, that is, feign, undoubtedly, but above all represent in the theater, and what he has within, which goes beyond anything he can represent. "Play" and "show": the metaphor of the theater is in the subtext.

> There is the paradox Shakespeare encounters: to put into play, to represent, that which surpasses the possibilities of representation—psychical pain. The entire play must sustain this challenge. Poetic language will serve as mediator between the inexpressible interior world and its exteriorization on the stage. (my translation)

Caught in the paradox of representing that essential "Hamlet" who cannot be truly enacted, language mediates between intrinsic inarticulation and extrinsic behavior. How does one show what cannot be shown? And if shown, how will it be perceived?

> *Oph.* Will 'a tell us what this show meant?
> *Ham.* Ay, or any show that you will show
>   him. Be not you asham'd to show, he'll not
>   shame to tell you what it means.
>
>   (3.2.143-46)

Display first, criticism after. Both modes of exhibition involve shame. The witty moment gestures toward the problem of interpretation (and its confident inevitability) as well as toward the potentially shameful bodily bases that may underlie both textual and critical display. Yet what Hamlet cannot show through deliberate speech or demeanor he is ultimately able to show through sudden action.

>   Rashly—
> And prais'd be rashness for it—let us know
> Our indiscretion sometime serves us well
> When our deep plots do pall, and that should
>   learn us
> There's a divinity that shapes our ends,
> Rough-hew them how we will—
>
>   (5.2.6-11)

What Hamlet terms "rashness," then "indiscretion," and then "divinity" is a spontaneous expression of an inner state without conscious articulation: unmediated, thoughtless action, show *sans* tell. Considered psychologically, the Hamlet who reacts to Laertes's histrionic display of grief, his astounding "phrase of sorrow," by leaping into Ophelia's grave and claiming, "This is I, / Hamlet the Dane" (5.1.254-58), has moved from an initial assertion of inward authenticity that cannot be shown to a sheer declaration and exhibition of self in action: "*that* within" becomes "*this* is I."[30] This is the moment, tragically short-lived, of Hamlet's assumption of an identity of his own, not one located elsewhere ("I'll call *thee* Hamlet," he said to the Ghost).

"The spontaneous gesture," wrote D.W. Winnicott, "is the True Self in action."[31] For Winnicott, the core self is paradoxically the point of deepest connection and isolation: it is a secret, sacred essence to be expressed through genuine, spontaneous gesture and to be preserved and protected from manipulations and violations from without.[32] For Lacan, on the other hand, the "that within" is a *lack,* a mark of the mourned object that constitutes an always alienated subject. For Winnicott it is a pristine *presence.* As Adam Phillips understands Winnicott (and he does), "the self is by definition elusive, the player of hide and seek."[33] "Hide fox, and all after!" (*Hamlet,* 4.2.30). Hence Hamlet's bold assumption of identity at graveside is also a broad histrionic exhibition; his "show" is both theatrical and authentic. His seeming now fully displays his being. This *complication* (folding together) becomes both the question and the answer for Hamlet's problem of (re)presentation.[34]

"Rough-hew them how we *will.*" Hamlet's remarks in praise of rashness modulate among several registers of unconscious, conscious, and supraconscious. The volitional project of plots is bracketed by the sudden gesture of indiscretion and the final design of divinity. A full appreciation of the term "will" includes this range of motivation and agency. Conscious intention occupies a shifting mid-range along a spectrum that spans unconscious spontaneity (a glimpse of unknown genuineness) and suprapersonal structure, whether understood in vague theological terms, as here, or in psychological and social terms, as in contemporary psychoanalysis.

I insert this theoretical interlude in order to provide current psychoanalytic ideas about identity and its origins as background to corollary arguments in current criticism, not merely about *Henry IV Part One* but about Shakespeare and the Renaissance, and in larger debates about the relation of the personal to the social, or of psychology to history. For instance, Stephen Greenblatt discusses the Henriad in terms similar to a linguistic approach, but draws different inferences.[35] He sees one mode of the plays, especially the two parts of *Henry IV,* as a "'recording' of alien voices," those disempowered or illiterate characters who compose the lower elements of society. Hal studies the language of these others from a position of mastery and contempt. As his brother says in *Henry IV Part Two:* "The Prince but studies his companions / like a strange tongue . . ." (4.4.68-9). Rather than noting a style of identification, however, Greenblatt stresses the construction of difference and cites contemporary sixteenth-century compilations of glossaries of marginal vocabularies, like "cant language." Following his argument of self-fashioning, he then remarks about Hal and the notion of *self:* "Hal's characteristic activity is playing, or, more precisely, theatrical improvisation . . . , and he fully understands his own behaviour through most of the play as a role that he is performing." Greenblatt hence wonders if "such a thing as a natural disposition exists in the play as anything more than a theatrical fiction." For instance, in Falstaff's case even an appeal to "instinct" becomes a histrionic artifice, a rhetorical device.[36]

In its largest form, the argument about natural disposition and socially constructed artifice is an argument about the developmental priority of psychology or history. Greenblatt presents one test case in his essay on "Psychoanalysis and Renaissance Culture."[37] His fundamental argument is that psychoanalytic interpretations of the Renaissance must be "marginal and belated" because psychoanalysis itself, and the concept of self from which it proceeds, are historical developments whose sources can be located in the Renaissance. Psychoanalysis is hence a "product" of the Renaissance and not privileged as an interpreter. One of Freud's primary assumptions—a coherent, continuous and authentic "self"—did not exist or was not assumed in Shakespeare's time. In the sixteenth century, Greenblatt asserts, such an idea of an irreducible physical and psychological self was "irrelevant to the point of being unthinkable."[38] By contrast, he argues, Freudian psychoanalysis credits a "dream of authentic possession," "a primal, creatural individuation" anchored in the personal body, "the fixity, the certainty, of our own body."[39]

As historical evidence, he presents the story of Martin Guerre, the sixteenth-century Frenchman whose identity was claimed by another. The dispute was resolved in a public trial, through communal judgment and legal authorization. The impostor was eventually executed because he laid claim to Martin Guerre's social place. The man's "subjectivity does not any the less exist," Greenblatt acknowledges, "but it seems peripheral, or rather, it seems to be the *product* of the relations, material objects, and judgments exposed in the case rather than the *producer* of the relations, objects, and judgments." Guerre's identity was an effect of external social framing and not of an adduced interior subjectivity; identity was a "placeholder in a complex system of possessions, kinship bonds, contractual relationships." Toward the end of his essay Greenblatt notes a shift in the "body-property-name" relation: "this slow, momentous transformation of the middle term from 'property' to 'psyche.'" In a note he adds that this transformation "is at once a revolution and a continuation: 'psyche' is neither a mere mystification for 'property' nor a radical alternative to it."[40]

The essay is provocative and problematic. Before addressing specific problems, let me suggest that even if the main argument were true, the interpretive pertinence of psychoanalysis to Renaissance culture and texts is not thereby disabled. In the discussion of *Macbeth* (Chapter Six) I posit an *isomorphic* relation between Freud and Shakespeare that uses similarities in their models of psychic structure to elucidate meanings in both. But I do not believe that Greenblatt's argument holds up, for several reasons. First, his reductive restatements of the Freudian ego and his brief oedipal reading of Guerre's case indicate a limited familiarity with psychoanalytic theory. He sketches an analysis of Guerre's anxious sexuality and uncertain masculine identity that precipitated an oedipal rebellion against his father, the failure of which caused him to flee—"classic materials of Freudian speculation," as Greenblatt sees them. His inference that Guerre's flight "abandoned" a social identity while retaining a personal one is not, however, the paradox or problem Greenblatt represents it to be. His argument stresses the biophysiological components of Freudian theory (real aspects, to be sure) and ignores the social, interrelational aspects of identity-formation through identification. The Freudian ego develops simultaneously "from the inside," through its mediation of instinctual derivatives and the pleasure principle, and "from the outside," through its identifications with others and its management of external exigencies (the reality principle).[41] Greenblatt constructs an antagonism between personal body and social place, where Freud theorized a cooperation—troublesome though it was.

Second, in historical terms, why is one sequential arrangement of "body-property-name" so privileged? Why is "property" or "psyche" a middle term? One might rearrange the terms to demonstrate alternative ways of thinking about the interrelations of each, thereby questioning an assumption of priority. Socially, name customarily precedes body, and name is a function of property. Humans are never entirely outside culture, nor did Freud think they were. When the real Guerre's identity was established in a sixteenth-century court, is this an instance of historical difference? Even today identity is established in similar ways. Finally, who could think that individual subjectivity would be the *producer* of social relations and material objects? A solipsist, perhaps, but not a Freudian. In brief, what Greenblatt's version of psychoanalysis lacks is a sophisticated idea of *identification* whereby individual identity is produced through the interrelations of self and others, understood in familial, linguistic, and social contexts.

Yet although Greenblatt's version of psychoanalysis in this essay is reductive, his conclusion recuperates much of its validity and value:

> But if we reject both the totalizing of a universal mythology [of psychoanalysis] and the radical particularizing of relativism, what are we left with? We are left with a network of lived and narrated stories, practices, strategies, representations, fantasies, negotiations, and exchanges that, along with the surviving aural, tactile, and visual traces, fashion our experience of the past, of others, and of ourselves.[42]

This is not a bad definition of psychoanalysis, both in terms of its theory of self and the analytic process. Rather than providing historical precedent to devalue psychoanalysis, I think Greenblatt's essay offers substantial evidence to enrich the theory: indeed, as he asks, to "historicize" it, to amplify its relevance beyond the reductive modes in which it is sometimes employed and adjudged.

The issue of history (or sociology) versus psychology can be further examined by citing another contempo-

rary, nonpsychoanalytic critic, Terry Eagleton, who states, citing Hamlet:

> The self lives an irresolvable division between its desire, which conducts it along an endless chain of inflated signifiers, and its effort at "imaginary" unity with the fixed signified of its social position. As far as Hamlet is concerned, such efforts are hardly worth the trouble.[43]

Compare this statement with Greenblatt's famous Epilogue to *Renaissance Self-Fashioning:*

> But as my worked progressed, I perceived that fashioning oneself and being fashioned by cultural institutions . . . were inseparably intertwined. In all my texts and documents, there were, so far as I could tell, no moments of pure, unfettered subjectivity: indeed, the human subject itself began to seem remarkably unfree, the ideological product of the relations of power in a particular society.[44]

These statements rest on differing yet connected assumptions about the relations of "self" and "society." Eagleton's assumptions lead him to describe a self torn between endless desire and stable unity, where both desire and unity are illusory. The former is an endless series of steps along an ultimately tautological linguistic system, and the latter is a projected integrity of fixed social identity. In the Lacanian terms the passage deploys, the self circulates within the symbolic order while wishing to restore itself to the imaginary. It is a *subjected self,* conducted by desire and not actively desiring—although it may delusively credit the fiction of such an independent agency. The effort is troublesome and possibly futile, a lost cause, a burntout case. This self can find no satisfaction, because it is looking in a narcissistic mirror for a relationship with a genuine other.

Greenblatt's assumptions permit him to describe a less constrained, more complex subject, based on the interrelationship of self and others. He rejects, albeit to some degree regretfully, the fiction of self-creativity or of the individual, subjective production of language or literature. The work of art is a co-production of individual consciousness and the shared social customs and internalized relationships within which individuals develop. For Greenblatt these relationships are the residue of ideology, a product of systems of power. His rhetoric presses toward tragic limitation, whereby pure unfettered subjectivity is shackled by deterministic social forces.

The implicitly Marxist bias of this language can be refashioned, however, to allow the trajectory of the concept to incline another way. For there is a more positive theoretical statement of the interdependence of self and society, or subject and other. That is the domain of object-relations psychoanalysis, where sub-ject and other are originally (re)presented by infant and mother, in a prolonged and productive construc-tion—not of binary oppositions like "self" and "soci-ety," or "desire" and "unity," but of a style of relation-ship that underlies and informs all emotions and ac-tions of the individual as he or she grows out of the maternal and familial arena and enters the wider social world. Persons are thus truly "products of relations," but not necessarily as slaves stamped by ideology or subjects chained to paranoid projections of illusory unity. Object-relations are co-productions, primary at-tachments to and losses of objects (persons and inter-nal representations of persons) that produce the expe-riential reality of self, object, and the relationships that link them.[45] Although psychoanalysis posits a basic and prior human, interpersonal relation, it does not thereby reject the formative functions of what Lichtenstein calls "the nonhuman environment." The special value of the mutually reflective relation is that it offers the child an initial "configuration of its own presence" that gradu-ally enables it to interact with the larger social world.[46]

Large designs of the "history versus psychology" de-bate can thus be found in contemporary criticism of Shakespeare's plays *and* in those plays. Of course, our tendency to discover such issues in Shakespeare is it-self a reflection of our current modes of framing criti-cal questions.[47] Perhaps the relation of "Shakespeare" and "Shakespeare criticism" is analogous to the inter-relation of subject and society. That is, does criticism derive from a clear reading of Shakespeare, so that it reproduces the truth of the texts, or does criticism produce a "Shakespeare" answering to its own current needs? Is criticism a window onto the Bard or a mirror wherein we practice behavior to our own shadows? From my perspective, it's both.

Notes

[1] Maurice Morgann, *Shakespearian Criticism,* ed. Daniel Fineman (Oxford: Clarendon Press, 1972). Fineman's Introduction reviews critical controversies over the status of character in Shakespeare studies up to the mid-twentieth century: see pp. 11-36.

[2] See A. C. Bradley, "The Rejection of Falstaff," *Ox-ford Lectures on Poetry* (1909) (London: Macmillan, 1950); L. L. Schucking, *Character Problems in Shake-speare's Plays: A Guide to the Better Understanding of the Dramatist* (London: Harrap and Co., 1922); J. I. M. Stewart, "The Birth and Death of Falstaff," *Char-acter and Motive in Shakespeare* (New York: Long-mans, 1949); Ernst Kris, "Prince Hal's Conflict," *Psy-choanalytic Explorations in Art* (New York: Interna-tional Universities Press, 1952), pp. 273-88. Kris's seminal essay on the psychoanalysis of a literary char-acter has been reprinted, along with several critiques, in George Moraitis and Sidney Pollock, eds., *Psycho-*

analytic Studies of Biography (New York: International Universities Press, 1987). Most recently, Harold Bloom discovers in Falstaff, alongside Hamlet, the verbal self-consciousness that constitutes modern literary charac-ter itself. See *The Western Canon: The Books and School of the Ages* (New York: Harcourt Brace, 1994), pp. 47-50.

[3] For a summary of psychoanalytic approaches to *I Henry IV* up to 1964, see Norman Holland, *Psycho-analysis and Shakespeare* (New York: McGraw Hill, 1966), pp. 206-10. I will refer to salient items since 1964 in what follows.

[4] A lucid tripartite psychic mapping of *I Henry IV* is by Norman Holland, *The Shakespearean Imagination* (Bloomington: Indiana University Press, 1964), pp. 109-29. The embodiment of uncontrolled wishes and mor-tal mischief in Falstaff relates to the emblem of "Riot" incarnate, and to the psycho-anthropological reading of C. L. Barber in *Shakespeare's Festive Comedy* (Princeton, N.J.: Princeton University Press, 1959), pp. 192-213. The most thorough mapping of Freudian struc-tural categories onto the dramatized *psychomachia* in the *Henry IV* plays is by Robert Watson, *Shakespeare and the Hazards of Ambition* (Cambridge, Mass.: Harvard University Press, 1984), pp. 47-75. Even non-psychoanalytic critics find Freudian terms tempting in this case. M. M. Mahood remarks that Falstaff "repre-sents freedom from all the normal inhibitions, [and] even succeeds in breaking down those of the Lord Chief Justice, that walking embodiment of Freud's censor, to the point where he, too, begins to pun": see *Shakespeare's Wordplay,* p. 29.

[5] The standard oedipal view is by Kris. For a sophis-ticated reading of the process of identity-formation through rivalry with the father, see Coppélia Kahn, *Man's Estate: Masculine Identity in Shakespeare* (Ber-keley: University of California Press, 1981), pp. 69-79. Kahn develops her analysis into a consideration of masculine imitations of the mother-son relation, thus merging into the "object-relations" view I sketch be-low. Harry Berger's work on the displacements of oedipal feelings and representations in *Richard II* uses a kind of family systems theory approach to teasing out latent meanings and relations between characters: see "Psychoanalyzing the Shakespeare Text: The First Three Scenes of the *Henriad,*" in *Shakespeare and the Question of Theory,* ed. Patricia Parker and Geoffrey Hartman (New York: Methuen, 1985), pp. 210-29. Watson amplifies the standard oedipal view to include Hal's identification with paternal power through his defeat of Hotspur: see *Shakespeare and the Hazards of Ambition,* p. 63.

[6] Colin McCabe, in "Toward a Modern Trivium—En-glish Studies Today," *Critical Quarterly* 26 (1984), notes that Mortimer's Welsh wife represents the se-

ductive nonverbal power of female sexuality (pp. 71-72). Phyllis Rackin draws strong analogies between Wales, women, and female sexuality: "the country of the Others, a world of witchcraft and magic, of mysterious music, and also of unspeakable atrocity." See "Genealogical Anxiety and Female Authority: The Return of the Repressed in Shakespeare's Histories," in *Contending Kingdoms: Historical, Psychological, and Feminist Approaches to the Literature of Sixteenth-Century England and France,* ed. Marie-Rose Logan and Peter Rudnytsky (Detroit: Wayne State University Press, 1991), pp. 323-45, p. 332.

[7] The earliest psychoanalytic characterization of Falstaff, as "the pleasure-seeking principle," is by Franz Alexander: "Some Notes on Falstaff," *Psychoanalytic Quarterly* 22 (1933), 592-606.

[8] "A fat man," writes Auden, "is a cross between a very young child and a pregnant mother." See "The Prince's Dog," in *The Dyer's Hand and Other Essays* (New York: Random House, 1948), p. 195. For further discussion of this idea, see Kahn, *Man's Estate,* pp. 72-73, and Richard Wheeler, *Shakespeare's Development and the Problem Comedies: Turn and Counter-Turn* (Berkeley: University of California Press, 1981), pp. 165-67. The most extensive analysis is by Valerie Traub, in *Desire and Anxiety: Circulations of Sexuality in Shakespearean Drama* (London: Routledge, 1992), which is discussed below. In his essay on Falstaff, Morgann (1777) noted "the unaffected freedom and wonderful pregnancy of his wit and humour" (Fineman, ed., *Shakespearian Criticism,* p. 194).

[9] *Shakespeare's Development and the Problem Comedies,* p. 166.

[10] Traub, "Prince Hal's Falstaff: Positioning Psychoanalysis and the Female Reproductive Body," *Shakespeare Quarterly* 40 (1989), 456-74; reprinted as Chapter Two in her book, *Desire and Anxiety.* She also quotes McCabe ("Toward a Modern Trivium"): "Falstaff's body constitutes a polymorphously perverse threat to the possibility of representation." For an account of the social and psychological functions of Elizabethan genealogy and history to support patriarchal structures and marginalize women, see Rackin, "Genealogical Anxiety and Female Authority." Two sentences from this excellent essay are especially pertinent here:

> Patriarchal history was designed to construct a verbal substitute for the visible physical connection between a mother and her children, to authenticate the relationships between fathers and sons, and to suppress and supplant the role of the mother. (p. 324)

> Never present in patriarchal history, women could only be represented, and what they represented was

the material physical life that patriarchal discourse could never completely capture or control. (p. 336)

[11] *Man's Estate,* pp. 72-73.

[12] See Jonathan Goldberg, "Hamlet's Hand," *Shakespeare Quarterly* 39 (1988), 307-27, for an extensive examination of Elizabethan handwriting practices and a theoretical extension to the idea of Hamlet as written character.

[13] See Watson, *Shakespeare and the Hazards of Ambition,* pp. 62-64.

[14] Terry Eagleton notes another difference. "Hotspur is an old-fashioned idealist," he writes, "who desires a language adequate to action and vice-versa; Falstaff has not the slightest wish to integrate the two, but flourishes in the gulf between them." See *William Shakespeare* (Oxford: Blackwell, 1986), p. 17.

[15] For a thorough survey of the different languages in the play, see W.F. Bolton, "Linguistic Variety in *1-2 Henry IV,*" in *Shakespeare's English: Language in the History Plays* (Oxford: Blackwell, 1992), pp. 151-85. Bolton provides many examples of different styles, with some gestures toward characterization, especially of Hal's mimetic appropriations of Falstaff and Hotspur. For cogent remarks on the blending of political, sexual, and linguistic power in the play, and their relation to the project of a national language, see McCabe, "Toward a Modern Trivium."

[16] *Man's Estate,* p. 69.

[17] *Patriarchal Structures in Shakespeare's Drama* (Berkeley: University of California Press, 1985), p. 42.

[18] Watson, *Shakespeare and the Hazards of Ambition,* pp. 57-58; Traub, *Desire and Anxiety,* p. 60.

[19] Watson (*Shakespeare and the Hazards of Ambition,* pp. 48-50) cites Hotspur's reference to "the maidenhead of our affairs" (4.1.59) and quotes his arrogant reply to Glendower's claim that an earthquake announced his birth:

> Oft the teeming earth
> Is with a kind of colic pinch'd and vex'd
> By the imprisoning of unruly wind
> Within her womb. . . .
>
>   . . . . .
>
> . . . At your birth
> Our grandam earth, having this distemp'rature,
> In passion shook.
>   (3.1.26-34)

(Notice the iteration of the term "distemp'rature" in 5.1.3.) In the deep fantasy structure of the language of this play, or the play of this language, the unruly uterine wind of this passage replicates the whistling wind in the regal poem that begins Act Five.

[20] "Man and Wife Is One Flesh: *Hamlet* and the Confrontation with the Maternal Body," in *Suffocating Mothers: Fantasies of Maternal Origin in Shakespeare's Plays* (New York: Routledge, 1992), p. 36.

[21] *Standard Edition,* 19, 3-66; 56.

[22] These ideas are implicit in Winnicott, for instance in "Mirror-Role of Mother and Family in Child Development" in *Playing and Reality* (London: Tavistock, 1970), pp. 111-18. For the explicit restatements by Bollas, see *The Shadow of the Object: Psychoanalysis of the Unthought Known* (New York: Columbia University Press, 1987), pp. 9-10.

[23] Lacan speaks for himself in "The mirror stage as formative of the function of the I as revealed in psychoanalytic experience," in *Écrits: A Selection,* trans. Alan Sheridan (New York: Norton, 1977), pp. 1-7; and "The subversion of the subject and the dialectic of desire in the Freudian unconscious," in *Écrits,* pp. 292-325. I make no claim to full representation of his concept of the subject nor would I undertake to explicate his various schemata. For selective secondary explication, see Kaja Silverman, *The Subject of Semiotics* (New York: Oxford University Press, 1983), pp. 126-93; Ellie Ragland Sullivan, *Jacques Lacan and the Philosophy of Psychoanalysis* (Urbana: University of Illinois Press, 1986), pp. 1-16; and Malcolm Bowie, *Lacan* (Cambridge, Mass.: Harvard University Press, 1991), pp. 186-90.

[24] *The Seminar of Jacques Lacan: Book II: The Ego in Freud's Theory and in the Technique of Psychoanalysis,* ed. Jacques-Alain Miller (New York: Norton, 1988), p. 155.

[25] As Adam Phillips has noted, at crucial moments Winnicott's language harbors religious residues: see his critical biography, *Winnicott* (Cambridge, Mass.: Harvard University Press, 1988), pp. 3, 155 (n. 5), 97, 130.

[26] See Lichtenstein's collected essays, *The Dilemma of Human Identity* (New York: Jason Aronson, 1977), especially "Identity and Sexuality," pp. 49-122, and "Narcissism and Primary Identity," pp. 207-21.

[27] Lichtenstein, "Narcissism and Primary Identity," in *Dilemma of Human Identity,* p. 215, p. 218. The concept of the "identity theme" is elaborated by Norman Holland, *The I* (New Haven, Conn.: Yale University Press, 1986).

[28] Published in *Transport to Summer* (1947) and in *The Collected Poems of Wallace Stevens* (New York: Alfred Knopf, 1965), pp. 339-46.

[29] *Hamlet et* Hamlet (Paris: Ballard, 1982), p. 60.

[30] Freud's version of this ideal developmental and therapeutic moment is: *"Wo es war, soll ich werden"* ("Where it was, I will be"): see *New Introductory Lectures on Psycho-Analysis* (1933), *Standard Edition* 22, p. 80. Lacan notes a telling historical and psychological shift in French idiom: "The *'ce suis-je'* of the time of Villon has become reversed in the *'c'est moi'* of modern man." See "The Function and Field of Speech and Language in Psychoanalysis," in *Écrits,* p. 70. That exemplary adventurer of early modernity, Hamlet, asserts himself at a most propitious historical moment. For a Lacanian reading of Hamlet's spontaneity as an expression of his desire and its relation to chance and change, see William Beatty Warner, "The Case of Hamlet, Prince of Denmark," in *Chance and the Text of Experience: Freud, Nietzsche, and Shakespeare's* Hamlet (Ithaca, N.Y.: Cornell University Press, 1986), pp. 215-98, especially pp. 246-63.

[31] See "Ego Distortion in Terms of True and False Self" in *Maturational Processes and the Facilitating Environment: Studies in the Theory of Emotional Development* (London: Hogarth Press, 1965), pp. 140-52.

[32] See "Communicating and Not Communicating Leading to a Study of Certain Opposites" in *Maturational Processes and the Facilitating Environment,* pp. 179-92.

[33] See *Winnicott,* pp. 138-52.

[34] Recent readings of *Hamlet* paint a much darker picture of this internalized relation to the mother. Adelman's brilliant essay argues that Hamlet's appeal to "an inviolable core of selfhood" that cannot be shown or known is a defense against his fear of contamination by the sullied world that engulfs him. Since the source of this contamination is his fantasy of a debased and threatening maternal body, however, his "that within" also paradoxically marks the unavoidable link to the matter of the mother. See "Man and Wife Is One Flesh," especially pp. 29-30. See also Juliana Schiesari, *The Gendering of Melancholia: Feminism, Psychoanalysis, and the Symbolics of Loss in Renaissance Drama* (Ithaca, N.Y.: Cornell University Press, 1992), for a Lacanian and Kristevan account of Hamlet's melancholy that differs from Adelman's Kleinian and Winnicottian perspective. In a recent dissertation, Marsha Ginsberg links psychoanalytic ideas about melancholy and the maternal to classical, medieval, and early modern sciences of physiology, sexuality, and psychology. See *Reconceiving Melancholy: Gynecological Moles of Difference in Shakespeare's* Hamlet *and* Ri-

chard II (Ph.D. Dissertation, SUNY Buffalo, 1996). Patricia Parker develops an intense and provocative reading of the links between maternal sexuality and "show" in "*Othello* and *Hamlet:* Dilation, Spying, and the 'Secret Place' of Woman," in *Shakespeare Reread: The Texts in New Contexts,* ed. Russ McDonald (Ithaca, N.Y.: Cornell University Press, 1994), pp. 105-46.

[35] "Invisible Bullets: Renaissance Authority and Its Subversion, *Henry IV* and *Henry V,*" in *Shakespeare: New Essays in Cultural Materialism,* ed. Jonathan Dollimore and Alan Sinfield (Ithaca, N.Y.: Cornell University Press, 1985), pp. 18-47.

[36] "Invisible Bullets," p. 33, p. 35.

[37] In *Literary Theory/Renaissance Texts,* ed. Patricia Parker and David Quint (Baltimore: Johns Hopkins University Press, 1986), pp. 210-24; reprinted in Green-blatt, *Learning to Curse: Essays in Early Modern Culture* (New York: Routledge, 1990), pp. 131-45. The thesis is also noted by Joel Fineman in *Shakespeare's Perjured Eye: The Invention of Poetic Subjectivity in the Sonnets* (Berkeley: University of California Press, 1986), p. 47.

[38] "Psychoanalysis and Renaissance Culture," p. 133. Although Greenblatt offers no proof of this assertion, similar claims are made by J. Leeds Barroll in *Artificial Persons: The Formation of Character in the Tragedies of Shakespeare* (Columbia: University of South Carolina Press, 1974), p. 73, pp. 85-88, and Anne Ferry in *The "Inward" Language: Sonnets of Wyatt, Sidney, Shakespeare, and Donne* (Chicago: University of Chicago Press, 1983), pp. 31-70.

[39] "Psychoanalysis and Renaissance Culture," pp. 134-35, p. 138.

[40] "Psychoanalysis and Renaissance Culture," p. 137, p. 141, p. 145 (n. 7).

[41] Freud's most succinct account of the development of the ego is in *The Ego and the Id* (1923), *Standard Edition,* 19, 3-68. He discusses the pleasure and reality principles in "Formulations on the Two Principles of Mental Functioning" (1911), *Standard Edition,* 12, 213-26. For a theoretical essay that refashions Greenblatt's

strictly oedipal model into a process of identification, see Freud, "The Dissolution of the Oedipus Complex" (1924), *Standard Edition,* 19, 173-82.

[42] "Psychoanalysis and Renaissance Culture," p. 138.

[43] *William Shakespeare,* p. 13.

[44] *Renaissance Self-Fashioning: From More to Shake-speare* (Chicago: University of Chicago Press, 1981), p. 256.

[45] Eloquent and subtle restatements of Winnicott can be found in Bollas, *The Shadow of the Object:* see Introduction, pp. 9-10, and "The Self as Object," pp. 41-63. For a review of psychoanalytic literature on the self that does not rely on Lacan or Winnicott, see Otto Kernberg, "The Dynamic Unconscious and the Self," in Raphael Stern, ed., *Theories of the Unconscious,* ed. Raphael Stern (Hillsdale, N.J.: Analytic Press, 1987), pp. 3-25. See also the response by Marcia Cavell in the same volume, pp. 58-63.

[46] Lichtenstein, "Narcissism and Primary Identity," p. 218. For further postmodern elaborations of the question of personal identity as a struggle between inscribed or prescribed "character" and an individual will to originality, enacted through play or a staging of self in Shakespeare, see Linda Charnes, *Notorious Identity: Materializing the Subject in Shakespeare* (Cambridge, Mass.: Harvard University Press, 1993), pp. 1-19. Later she writes that "by deconstructing the legend of Troilus and Cressida, Shakespeare reconstructs theater and drama as a new site not for representing 'identity' but for staging 'kinds of selves'" (p. 102).

[47] A brilliant and thorough analysis of the dispute is offered by Meredith Skura in "Discourse and the Individual: The Case of Colonialism in *The Tempest,*" *Shakespeare Quarterly* 40 (1989), 42-69.

Source: "The Famous Analyses of *Henry the Fourth,*" in *Poetic Will: Shakespeare and the Play of Language,* University of Pennsylvania Press, 1997, pp. 55-63.

Tragedies

Iago's Alter Ego: Race as Projection in *Othello*

Janet Adelman, *University of California, Berkeley*

Othello famously begins not with Othello but with Iago. Other tragedies begin with ancillary figures commenting on the character who will turn out to be at the center of the tragedy—one thinks of *Lear, Macbeth, Antony and Cleopatra*—but no other play subjects its ostensibly tragic hero to so long and intensive a debunking before he even sets foot onstage. And the audience is inevitably complicit in this debunking: before we meet Othello, we are utterly dependent on Iago's and Roderigo's descriptions of him. For the first long minutes of the play, we know only that the Moor, "the thicklips" (1.1.66),[1] has done something that Roderigo (like the audience) feels he should have been told about beforehand; we find out what it is for the first time only through Iago's violently eroticizing and racializing report to Brabantio: "Even now, very now, an old black ram / Is tupping your white ewe" (ll. 88-89).[2]

At this point in my teaching of the play, I normally point to all the ways in which Othello belies Iago's description as soon as he appears; in the classroom my reading of race in *Othello* turns on this contrast as Shakespeare's way of denaturalizing the tropes of race, so that we are made to understand Othello not as the "natural" embodiment of Iago's "old black ram" gone insanely jealous but as the victim of the racist ideology everywhere visible in Venice, an ideology to which he is relentlessly subjected and which increasingly comes to define him as he internalizes it—internalizes it so fully that, searching for a metaphor to convey his sense of the soil attaching both to his name and to Desdemona's body, Othello can come up with no term of comparison other than his own face ("My name, that was as fresh / As Dian's visage, is now begrim'd, and black / As mine own face" [3.3.392-94]).[3] Othello's "discovering" that his blackness is a stain—a stain specifically associated with his sexuality—and "discovering" that stain on Desdemona are virtually simultaneous for him; hence the metaphoric transformation of Dian's visage into his own begrimed face. If Desdemona becomes a "black weed" (4.2.69)[4] for Othello, her "blackening" is a kind of shorthand for his sense that his blackness has in fact contaminated her; as many have argued, his quickness to believe her always-already contaminated is in part a function of his horrified recoil from his suspicion that he is the contaminating agent.[5]

In other words, in the classroom I usually read race in *Othello* through what I take to be the play's representation of Othello's experience of race as it comes to dominate his sense of himself as polluted and polluting, undeserving of Desdemona and hence quick to believe her unfaithful. But although the play locates Othello in a deeply racist society, the sense of pollution attaching to blackness comes first of all (for the audience if not for Othello) from Iago; though Iago needed Brabantio to convince Othello of Desdemona's tendency to deception and the "disproportion" of Othello as her marriage choice, Iago legitimizes and intensifies Brabantio's racism through his initial sexualizing and racializing invocation of Othello. And if the play offers us a rich representation of the effects of racism on Othello, it offers us an equally rich—and in some ways more disturbing—representation of the function of Othello's race *for Iago*. I offer the following reading of that representation as a thought-experiment with two aims: first, to test out the applicability of psychoanalytic theory—especially Kleinian theory—to problems of race, an arena in which its applicability is often questioned; and, second, to identify some of the ways in which racism is the psychic property (and rightly the concern) of the racist, not simply of his victim.

Iago erupts out of the night (this play, like *Hamlet,* begins in palpable darkness), as though he were a condensation of its properties. Marking himself as opposite to light through his demonic "I am not what I am," Iago calls forth a world, I will argue, in which he can see his own darkness localized and reflected in Othello's blackness, or rather in what he makes—and teaches Othello to make—of Othello's blackness.

Iago's voice inducts us into the play: long before Othello has a name, much less a voice, of his own, Iago has a distinctive "I." The matter of Othello, and satisfaction of the audience's urgent curiosity about what exactly Roderigo has just learned, are deferred until after we have heard Iago's catalogue of injuries to that "I" ("I know my price, I am worth no worse a place" [1.1.11]; "And I, of whom his eyes had seen the proof, . . . must be lee'd, and calm'd" [ll. 28-30]; "And I, God bless the mark, his worship's ancient" [l. 33]). Iago's "I" beats through the dialogue with obsessive insistence, claiming both self-sufficiency ("I follow but myself" [l. 58]) and self-division, defining itself by what it is not ("Were I the Moor, I would not be Iago" [l. 57]), in fact simultaneously proclaiming its existence and nonexistence: "I am not what I am" (l. 65). I, I, I: Iago's name unfolds from the Italian *io,* Latin *ego;* and the injured "I" is his signature, the ground of his being and the ground, I will argue, of the play. For Iago calls up the action of the play as though in response to this sense of injury: "Call up her father, . . . poison his delight" (ll. 67-68), he says, like a stage manager, or like a magician calling forth spirits to perform his will; and with his words, the action begins.

The structure of the first scene models Iago's relation to the world that he calls up, for the play proper seems to arise out of Iago's injured "I": it is not only set in motion by Iago's "I" but becomes in effect a projection of it, as Iago successfully attempts to rid himself of interior pain by replicating it in Othello. Othello—and particularly in relation to Desdemona—becomes Iago's primary target in part because Othello has the presence, the fullness of being, that Iago lacks.[6] Othello is everywhere associated with the kind of interior solidity and wholeness that stands as a reproach to Iago's interior emptiness and fragmentation: if Iago takes Janus as his patron saint (1.2.33) and repeatedly announces his affiliation with nothingness ("I am not what I am"; "I am nothing, if not critical" [2.1.119]), Othello is initially "all in all sufficient" (4.1.261), a "full soldier" (2.1.36), whose "solid virtue" (4.1.262) and "perfect soul" (1.2.31) allow him to achieve the "full fortune" (1.1.66) of possessing Desdemona. "Tell me what you need to spoil and I will tell you what you want," says Adam Phillips:[7] the extent to which Othello's fullness and solidity are the object of Iago's envy can be gauged by the extent to which he works to replicate his own self-division in Othello. Split himself, Iago is a master at splitting others: his seduction of Othello works by inscribing in Othello the sense of dangerous interior spaces—thoughts that cannot be known, monsters in the mind—which Othello seems to lack, introducing him to the world of self-alienation that Iago inhabits;[8] by the end, Othello is so self-divided that he can take arms against himself, Christian against Turk, literalizing self-division by splitting himself graphically down the middle.[9] Though Iago is not there to see his victory, we might imagine him as invisible commentator, saying in effect, "Look, he is not all-in-all sufficient, self-sustaining and full; he is as self-divided as I am."[10]

To shatter the illusion of Othello's fullness and presence is also to shatter the illusion of his erotic power; his division from himself is first of all his division from Desdemona and from the fair portion of himself invested in her. If Cassio is any indication, that erotic power is heavily idealized by the Italians:

> Great Jove, Othello guard,
> And swell his sail with thine own powerful breath,
> That he may bless this bay with his tall ship,
> Make love's quick pants in Desdemona's arms
> Give renew'd fire to our extinced spirits. . . .
> (2.1.77-81)[11]

But for Iago it is intolerable: what begins as a means to an end (Iago creates Othello's suspicions about Desdemona to discredit Cassio in order to replace him as lieutenant) increasingly becomes an end in itself, as Iago drives Othello toward a murderous reenactment of sexual union on the marriage bed, even though that reenactment will make Othello incapable of bestowing the position Iago initially seeks. The thrust of his plot toward the marriage bed, even at the cost of his own ambition, suggests that what Iago needs to spoil is on that bed: the fullness and presence signified by Othello's possession of Desdemona, the sexual union that reminds him of his own extinced spirits. For Iago's own erotic life takes place only in his head; though he seems to imagine a series of erotic objects—Desdemona (ll. 286-89), Cassio (3.3.419-32), and Othello himself (in the coded language—"the lustful Moor / Hath leap'd into my seat" [2.1.290-91]—that makes cuckoldry an anal invasion of Iago's own body)—he imagines them less as realizable erotic objects than as mental counters in his revenge plot, and he imagines them only in sexual unions (Othello with Desdemona, Othello with Emilia, Cassio with Desdemona, Cassio with Emilia) that everywhere exclude and diminish him. And in response, he effectively neutralizes the erotic potency that mocks his own lack.

His primary tool in this neutralization is the creation of Othello as "black": and in fact it is Othello as progenitor that first excites Iago's racializing rage. His first use of the language of black and white is in his call to Brabantio: "An old black ram / Is tupping your white ewe." If Cassio needs to make Othello into an exotic super-phallus, capable of restoring Italian potency, Iago needs to make him into a black monster, invading the citadel of whiteness. (The idealization and the debasement are of course two sides of the same coin, and they are equally damaging to Othello: both use him only as the container for white fantasies, whether of desire or fear.) *Your white ewe/you:* Iago's half-pun invokes the whiteness of his auditors via the image of Othello's contaminating miscegenation;[12] true to form in racist discourse, "whiteness" emerges as a category only when it is imagined as threatened by its opposite. Iago's language here works through separation, works by placing "blackness" outside of "whiteness" even as it provokes terror at the thought of their mixture. But the play has already affiliated Iago himself with darkness and the demonic; the threat of a contaminating blackness is already there, already present inside the "whiteness" he would invoke. Iago creates Othello as "black"—and therefore himself as "white"—when he constructs him as monstrous progenitor; and he uses that racialized blackness to destroy what he cannot tolerate. But the trope through which Iago imagines that destruction makes Iago himself into the monstrous progenitor, filled with a dark conception that only darkness can bring forth: "I ha't, it is engender'd," he tells us; "Hell and night / Must bring this monstrous birth to the world's light" (1.3.401-2). This trope makes the blackness Iago would attribute to Othello—like his monstrous generativity—something already inside Iago himself, something that he must project out into the world: as though Iago were pregnant with the monster he makes of Othello.[13]

If the structure of the first scene predicts the process through which Iago becomes the progenitor of Othello's racialized blackness, the trope of the monstrous birth in the first act's final lines perfectly anticipates the mechanism of projection through which Iago will come to use Othello's black skin as the container for his own interior blackness. Cassio uses Othello as the locus for fantasies of inseminating sexual renewal; Iago uses him as the repository for his own bodily insufficiency and his self-disgust. For Iago needs the blackness of others: even the "white ewe" Desdemona is blackened in his imagination as he turns "her virtue into pitch" (2.3.351). How are we to understand Iago's impulse to blacken, the impulse for which Othello becomes the perfect vehicle? What does it mean to take another person's body as the receptacle for one's own contents? The text gives us, I think, a very exact account of what I've come to call the psycho-physiology of Iago's projection: that is, not simply an account of the psychological processes themselves but also an account of the fantasized bodily processes that underlie them. "Projection" is in its own way comfortingly abstract; by invoking the body behind the abstraction, Othello in effect rubs our noses in it.[14]

Let me begin, then, by thinking about the way Iago thinks about bodies, especially about the insides of bodies. For Iago is the play's spokesman for the idea of the *inside,* the hidden away. At the beginning of his seduction of Othello, he defends the privacy of his thought by asking "where's that palace, wherein to foul things / Sometimes intrude not?" (3.3.141-42); no palace is impregnable, no inside uncontaminated. Characteristically, Othello takes this image and makes it his own, reinscribing it in his later anatomy of Desdemona as "a cistern, for foul toads / To knot and gender in" (4.2.62-63). But merely by insisting on the hidden inwardness of thought, Iago has already succeeded in causing Othello to conflate the *hidden* with the *hideous,* as though that which is inside, invisible, must inevitably be monstrous ("he echoes me, / As if there were some monster in his thought, / Too hideous to be shown" [3.3.110-12]).[15] According to this logic, the case against Desdemona is complete as soon as Iago can insinuate that she, too, has—psychically and anatomically—an inside, unknowable and monstrous because it *is* inside, unseen.

If Iago succeeds in transferring his own sense of hidden contamination to Desdemona, localizing it in her body, the sense of the hideous thing within—monstrous birth or foul intruder—begins with him. Seen from this vantage point, his initial alarum to Brabantio ("Look to your house, your daughter, and your bags. . . . Are

all doors lock'd?" [1.1.80, 85]) looks less like a description of danger to Brabantio or Desdemona than like a description of danger to Iago himself. For Iago finds—or creates—in Brabantio's house the perfect analogue for his own sense of vulnerability to intrusion, and he can make of Othello the perfect analogue for the intrusive "foul thing," the old black ram who is tupping your white ewe/you—or, as we later find out, tupping Iago himself in Iago's fantasy, and leaving behind a poisonous residue ("I do suspect the lustful Moor / Hath leap'd into my seat, the thought whereof / Doth like a poisonous mineral gnaw my inwards" [2.1.290-92]).

But even the image of the body as a breached and contaminated "palace" suggests rather more interior structure than most of Iago's other images for the body. Again and again Iago imagines the body filled with liquid putrefaction, with contents that can and should be vomited out or excreted. The three fingers Cassio kisses in show of courtesy to Desdemona should be "clyster-pipes" for his sake (l. 176), Iago says; through the bizarre reworking of Iago's fantasy, Cassio's fingers are transformed into enema tubes, an imagistic transformation that violently brings together not only lips and faeces, mouth, vagina, and anus, but also digital, phallic, and emetic penetration of a body—Desdemona's? Cassio's?—imagined only as a container for faeces. Early in the play, poor Roderigo is a "sick fool . . . Whom love has turn'd almost the wrong side outward" (2.3.47-48); by the end, he is a "quat" rubbed almost to the sense (5.1.11), that is, a pus-filled pimple about to break. The congruence of these images suggests that Roderigo becomes a "quat" for Iago because he can't keep his insides from running out: the love that has almost turned him inside out is here refigured as pus that threatens to break through the surface of his body. In Iago's fantasy of the body, what is inside does not need to be contaminated by a foul intruder because it is already pus or faeces; in fact, anything brought into this interior will be contaminated by it. Iago cannot imagine ordinary eating, in which matter is taken in for the body's nourishment; any good object taken in will be violently transformed and violently expelled. When he is done with her, Iago tells us, Othello will excrete Desdemona ("The food that to him now is as luscious as locusts, shall be to him shortly as acerb as the coloquintida," an emetic or purgative [1.3.349-50]); when Desdemona is "sated" with Othello's body (l. 351), she will "heave the gorge" (2.1.231-32). (Poor Emilia has obviously learned from her husband: in her view men "are all but stomachs, and we all but food; / They eat us hungerly, and when they are full, / They belch us" [3.4.101-3].)

Given this image of the body's interior as a mass of undifferentiated and contaminated matter, it's no wonder that Iago propounds the ideal of self-control to

Roderigo in the garden metaphor that insists both on the rigid demarcation and differentiation of the body's interior and on its malleability to the exercise of will:

> . . . 'tis in ourselves, that we are thus, or thus: our bodies are gardens, to the which our wills are gardeners, so that if we will plant nettles, or sow lettuce, set hyssop, and weed up thyme; supply it with one gender of herbs, or distract it with many; either to have it sterile with idleness, or manur'd with industry, why, the power, and corrigible authority of this, lies in our wills.

(1.3.319-26)

This is not, presumably, his experience of his own body's interior or of his management of it; it seems rather a defensive fantasy of an orderly pseudo-Eden, in which man is wholly in control both of the inner processes of his body/garden and of the troublesome business of gender, and woman is wholly absent.[16] His only explicit representation of his body's interior belies this defense: the mere "thought" that Othello has leaped into his seat (even though he "know[s] not if't be true" [l. 386]) "Doth like a poisonous mineral gnaw [his] inwards." No reassuring gardener with his tidy— or even his untidy—rows here: Iago's "inwards" are hideously vulnerable, subject to a poisonous penetration. Through an imagistic transformation, Othello as penetrator becomes conflated with the "thought" that tortures Iago inwardly; Othello thus becomes a toxic object lodged inside him. (The garden passage simultaneously expresses and defends against the homoerotic desire that here makes Othello a poisonous inner object, insofar as it voices a fantasy of "supply[ing]" the body with one gender rather than "distract[ing]" it with many.[17])

What I have earlier called Iago's injured "I"—his sense that he is chronically slighted and betrayed, his sense of self-division—produces (or perhaps is produced by) fantasies of his body as penetrated and contaminated, especially by Othello. In fact, any traffic between inner and outer is dangerous for Iago, who needs to keep an absolute barrier between them by making his outside opaque, a false "sign" (1.1.156 and 157) of his inside; to do less would be to risk being (Roderigo-like) turned almost the wrong side outward, to "wear [his] heart upon [his] sleeve, / For dawes to peck at" (ll. 64-65).[18] To allow himself to be seen or known is tantamount to being stabbed, eaten alive: pecked at from the outside unless he manages to keep the barrier between inner and outer perfectly intact, gnawed from the inside if he lets anyone in. Iago's need for sadistic control of others ("Pleasure, and action, make the hours seem short" [2.3.369], he says, after managing Cassio's cashiering) goes in tandem with his extraordinarily vivid sense of vulnerability: unable to be gardener to himself, he will sadistically manage everyone else, simultaneously demonstrating his su-

periority to those quats whose insides are so sloppily prone to bursting out, and hiding the contamination and chaos of his own insides.

Roderigo plays a pivotal role in this process. As the embodiment of what Iago would avoid, Roderigo exists largely to give Iago repeated occasions on which to display his mastery over both self and other: in effect, Iago can load his contaminated insides into Roderigo and then rub him to the sense in order to demonstrate the difference between them and, hence, the impermeability of Iago's own insides. Moreover, in managing Roderigo, Iago can continually replenish himself with the fantasy of new objects to be taken into the self: objects over which—unlike the thought of Othello, which gnaws at his inwards—he can exert full control. Obsessively—six times in fourteen lines— Iago tells Roderigo to "Put money in thy purse . . . fill thy purse with money" (1.3.340, 348). We know that Iago has received enough jewels and gold from Roderigo to have half-corrupted a votarist (4.2.189), but we never see Iago taking the miser's or even the spendthrift's ordinary delight in this treasure; detached from any ordinary human motivation, the money accrues almost purely psychic meaning, becoming the sign not of any palpable economic advantage but of Iago's pleasure in being able to empty Roderigo out, to fill himself at will. "Put money in thy purse," he repeats insistently, and then adds, "Thus do I ever make my fool my purse" (1.3.381), as though the emptied-out Roderigo becomes the container that holds the illusion of Iago's fullness. For his repetition signals a compulsive need to fill himself with objects in order to compensate for the contamination and chaos inside: hard shiny objects that might be kept safe and might keep the self safe, objects that could magically repair the sense of what the self is made of and filled with.

Iago's hoarding, his sadism, his references to purgatives and clyster-pipes can be read through the language of classical psychoanalysis as evidence of an anal fixation; in that language the equation of money with faeces is familiar enough, as is the association of sadistic control with the anal phase.[19] Iago's obsessive suspicion that Othello has leaped into his seat, along with his heavily eroticized account of Cassio's dream, similarly lend themselves to a classically psychoanalytic reading of Iago as repressed homosexual.[20] While these readings are not "wrong" within their own terms, they nonetheless seem to me limited, and not only insofar as they can be said to assume a historically inaccurate concept of the subject or of "the homosexual":[21] limited even within the terms of psychoanalysis insofar as they do not get at either the quality of Iago's emotional relationships (his inability to form *any* kind of libidinal bond, his tendency to treat others as poisonous inner objects) or the terrifying theatrical seductiveness of the processes of projection that we witness through him. I want consequently to move from the consideration of libidinal zones and conflicted object choices characteristic of classical psychoanalysis to the areas opened up by the work of Melanie Klein; a Kleinian reading of Iago will, I think, help us to understand the ways in which Iago's imagination of his own interior shapes his object relations as he projects this interior onto the landscape of the play.

In Klein's account the primitive self is composed in part of remnants of internalized objects (people, or bits and pieces of people, taken into the self as part of the self's continual negotiation with what an outside observer would call the world) and the world is composed in part of projected bits and pieces of the self. Ideally, "the good breast is taken in and becomes part of the ego, and the infant who was first inside the mother now has the mother inside himself."[22] Internalization of the good object "is the basis for trust in one's own goodness";[23] "full identification with a good object goes with a feeling of the self possessing goodness of its own" and hence enables the return of goodness to the world: "Through processes of projection and introjection, through inner wealth given out and re-introjected, an enrichment and deepening of the ego comes about. . . . Inner wealth derives from having assimilated the good object so that the individual becomes able to share its gifts with others."[24] And the corollary is clear: if the infant cannot take in the experience of the good breast (either because of his/her own constitutional conditions or because the experience is not there to be had in a consistent way), the bad breast may be introjected, with accompanying feelings of one's own internal badness, poverty, poisonousness, one's own inability to give back anything good to the world.

But, in the words of Harold Boris, a contemporary post-Kleinian analyst of envy, "the infant who cannot, sooner or later, feed the hand from which it feeds . . . is the child who will then attempt to bite it."[25] The infant stuck with a depleted or contaminated inner world will, Klein suggests, exist in a peculiar relation to the good breast: even if it is there and apparently available, the infant may not be able to use it. For if the infant cannot tolerate either the discrepancy between its own badness and the goodness outside itself or the sense of dependency on this external source of goodness, the good breast will not be available for the infant's use: its goodness will in effect be spoiled by the infant's own envious rage. The prototype for Kleinian envy is the hungry baby, experiencing itself as helplessly dependent, empty, or filled only with badness, confronted with the imagined fullness of a source of goodness outside itself: "the first object to be envied is the feeding breast, for the infant feels that it possesses everything he desires and that it has an unlimited flow of milk, and love which the breast keeps for its own gratification."[26] Klein's insistence on the priority of the breast as the first object of envy effec-

tively reverses Freud's concept of penis envy; in Klein's account even penis envy becomes secondary, derivative from this earlier prototype.[27] But Klein's concept of envy turns on an even more startling innovation: for most analysts of infantile destructiveness and rage, the source and target is the frustrating "bad" object—a maternal object that doesn't provide enough, is not at the infant's beck and call, provides milk that in some way is felt to be spoiled; but in Klein's reading of envy, the source and target of rage is not the frustrating or poisonous bad breast but the good breast, and it is exactly its goodness that provokes the rage. Hence the peculiar sensitivity of the envious to the good—and the consequent need not to possess but to destroy it, or, in Klein's terms, "to put badness, primarily bad excrement and bad parts of the self, into the mother, and first of all into her breast, in order to spoil and destroy her."[28] But the breast so destroyed is of course no longer available to the child as a source of good: "The breast attacked in this way has lost its value, it has become bad by being bitten up and poisoned by urine and faeces."[29] Insofar as the infant has succeeded in destroying the good object, he has confirmed its destruction as a source of goodness within himself; hence the peculiarly vicious circle of envy, which destroys all good both in the world and in the self, and hence also its peculiar despair.

We do not, of course, need the help of a Kleinian perspective to identify Iago as envious. His willingness to kill Cassio simply because "He has a daily beauty in his life, / That makes me ugly" (5.1.19-20) marks the extent to which he is driven by envy; in an older theatrical tradition he might well have been named Envy. Here, for example, is Envy from *Impatient Poverty:*

> A syr is not thys a ioly game . . .
> Enuy in fayth I am the same . . .
> I hate conscience, peace loue and reste
> Debate and stryfe that loue I beste
> Accordynge to my properte
> When a man louethe well hys wyfe
> I brynge theym at debate and stryfe.[30]

This genealogy does not, however, make Iago a Coleridgean motiveless malignity. For in Iago, Shakespeare gives motiveless malignity a body: incorporating this element of the morality tradition, he releases through Iago the range of bodily fantasies associated with a specifically Kleinian envy.

Klein describes an envy so primal—and so despairing—that it cannot tolerate the existence of goodness in the world: its whole delight lies not in possessing what is good but in spoiling it. And that spoiling takes place in fantasy through a special form of object-relating: through the violent projection of bits of the self and its contaminated objects—often localized as contaminated bodily products—into the good object. By means of this projection, the self succeeds in replicating its own inner world "out there" and thus in destroying the goodness it cannot tolerate; at the end of the process, in the words of one Kleinian analyst, "There is nothing left to envy."[31] Through the lens of a Kleinian perspective, we can see traces of this process as Iago fills Othello with the poison that fills him.

In Iago's fantasy, as I have suggested, there is no uncontaminated interior space: he can allow no one access to his interior and has to keep it hidden away because it is more a cesspool than a palace or a garden. And there are no uncontaminated inner objects: every intruder is foul; everything taken in turns to pus or faeces or poison; everything swallowed must be vomited out. This sense of inner contamination leaves him—as Klein would predict—particularly subject to the sense of goodness in others and particularly ambivalent toward that goodness. His goal is to make those around him as ugly as he is; but that goal depends on his unusual sensitivity to their beauty. Even after he has managed to bring out the quarrelsome drunkard and class-conscious snob in Cassio, transforming him into a man who clearly enjoys sneaking around to see his general's wife, Iago remains struck by the daily beauty in Cassio's life—at a point when that beauty has become largely invisible to the audience. To Roderigo, Iago always contemptuously denies the goodness of Othello and Desdemona (he is an erring barbarian and she a supersubtle Venetian); but in soliloquy he specifically affirms their goodness— and affirms it in order to imagine spoiling it. Othello's "free and open nature" he will remake as the stupidity of an ass who can be led by the nose (1.3.397-400). He will not only use Desdemona's virtue; he will turn it into pitch, in a near-perfect replication of the projection of faeces into the good breast that Klein posits.

For Iago the desire to spoil always takes precedence over the desire to possess; one need only contrast him with Othello to see the difference in their relation to good objects.[32] Othello's anguish over the loss of the good object gives the play much of its emotional resonance. He imagines himself as safely enclosed in its garnery, nourished and protected by it, and then cast out: "But there, where I have garner'd up my heart, / Where either I must live, or bear no life, / The fountain, from the which my current runs, / Or else dries up, to be discarded thence" (4.2.58-61). When he is made to imagine that object as spoiled—"a cistern, for foul toads / To knot and gender in"—its loss is wholly intolerable to him; even at the end, as he kills Desdemona, he is working very hard to restore some remnant of the good object in her. Although he approaches Desdemona's bed planning to bloody it ("Thy bed, lust-stain'd, shall with lust's blood be spotted" [5.1.36]), his deepest desire is not to stain but to restore the purity of the good object, rescuing it from contamina-

tion, even the contamination he himself has visited upon it. By the time he reaches her bed, he has decided not to shed her blood (5.2.3). Instead he attempts to recreate her unviolated wholeness ("that whiter skin of hers than snow, / And smooth, as monumental alabaster" [ll. 4-5]) in a death that he imagines as a revirgination;[33] in fantasy he cleanses "the slime / That sticks on filthy deeds," remaking her unmarred and unpenetrated, "one entire and perfect chrysolite" (ll. 149-50, 146).

But Iago's only joy comes in spoiling good objects: Othello mourns being cast out from the garnery/fountain that has nourished him; Iago mocks the meat he feeds on (3.3.170-71). His description of the green-eyed monster he cautions Othello against marks the workings of a very Kleinian envy in him:[34] like the empty infant who cannot tolerate the fullness of the breast, he will mock the objects that might nourish and sustain him, spoiling them by means of his corrosive wit.[35] (Or perhaps—in good Kleinian fashion— by tearing at them with his teeth: especially in conjunction with the image of feeding on meat, "mock" may carry traces of *mammock*,[36] to tear into pieces, suggesting the oral aggression behind Iago's biting mockery and hence the talion logic in his fantasy of being pecked at.) Mockery—especially of the meat he might feed on—is Iago's signature: different as they are, Othello, Cassio, and Roderigo share an almost religious awe toward Desdemona; Iago insists that "the wine she drinks is made of grapes" (2.1.249-50), that even the best woman is only good enough "To suckle fools, and chronicle small beer" (l. 160). If "the first object to be envied is the feeding breast," Iago's devaluation of maternal nurturance here is just what we might expect.

But envy does not stop there. As Klein suggests, "Excessive envy of the breast is likely to extend to all feminine attributes, in particular to the woman's capacity to bear children. . . . The capacity to give and to preserve life is felt as the greatest gift and therefore creativeness becomes the deepest cause for envy."[37] If Othello's potency and fullness make him the immediate target of Iago's envious rage, the destruction of Desdemona's generativity has been Iago's ultimate goal from the beginning: "poison his delight," he says; "And though he in a fertile climate dwell, / Plague him with flies" (1.1.70-71). The image half-echoes Hamlet's linking of conception and breeding with the stirring of maggots in dead flesh,[38] for the "fertile climate" that Iago will transform into a breeding ground for plague is Desdemona's generative body. Hence, I think, the urgency with which Iago propels the plot toward the marriage bed ("Do it not with poison, strangle her in her bed, even the bed she hath contaminated" [4.1.203-4]): the ultimate game is to make father destroy mother on that bed in a parody of the life-giving insemination that might have taken place there.[39]

And hence the subterranean logic of Iago's favorite metaphor for that destruction, his monstrous birth. For if Iago enviously devalues Desdemona's generativity (she can only suckle, and only suckle fools; her body will breed only flies), he also appropriates it, and appropriates it specifically through imitation. Here both senses of *mock*—as devaluation and derisive imitation—come together, as Boris's work on envy predicts: "The urge to take charge of the envied object has several components to it. First, of course, is the denuding (an idea) and disparagement (an emotion) of the inherent value of the original. This makes possible what follows, namely the idea that the 'knock-off' (the 'as-if') is in every way the equal of the real thing."[40] In conceiving of his monstrous birth, that is, Iago not only mocks but also displaces Desdemona's generativity by taking on its powers for himself, denying the difference—between her fruitfulness and his barrenness, between her fullness and his emptiness—that he cannot tolerate. Iago's substitution in fact proceeds by stages. When he first invokes the metaphor of pregnancy, he is merely the midwife/observer: "There are many events in the womb of time, which will be delivered" (1.3.369-70). But his triumphant "I ha't" only thirty lines later—"I ha't, it is engender'd; Hell and night / Must bring this monstrous birth to the world's light"—replaces time's womb with his own: as I have already argued, his is the body in which the monstrous birth is engendered, and hell and night have become the midwives.

Through this metaphor, Iago's mental production becomes his substitute birth, in which he replaces the world outside himself[41]—the world of time's womb, or of Desdemona's—with the projection of his own interior monstrosity; thus conceived, his plot manages simultaneously to destroy the generativity that he cannot tolerate and to proclaim the superior efficacy of his own product. Emilia's description of the jealousy Iago creates in Othello—it is "a monster, / Begot upon itself, born on itself" (3.4.159-60)—is not accurate about Othello, but it suggestively tracks Iago's own envy to its psychic sources. If Iago imagines himself enacting a substitute birth, making the world conform to the shape of his envy by undoing the contours of the already-existing generative world, Emilia expresses the wish behind his metaphor: the wish to *be* begot upon oneself, born on oneself, no longer subject to—dependent on, vulnerable to—the generative fullness outside the self and the unendurable envy it provokes.[42] Unable to achieve that end, he will empty himself out on the wedding bed, substituting his own monstrous conception for the generative fullness that torments him, and destroying in the process the envied good object in Desdemona.

And it is just here, in this fantasy, that Othello's blackness becomes such a powerful vehicle for Iago. I have already suggested that Iago's capacity to spoil good objects rests on his capacity to blacken them, and to blacken them through a bodily process of projection. His monstrous birth is from the first associated with the darkness of hell and night; and when, in his conversation with Desdemona, he imagines his invention as his baby, that baby is associated specifically with the extrusion of a dark and sticky substance:

> my invention
> Comes from my pate as birdlime does from frieze,
> It plucks out brain and all: but my Muse labours,
> And thus she is deliver'd. . . .
>
> (2.1.125-28)[43]

Presumably Iago means that his invention is as slow—as laborious—as the process of removing birdlime from rough cloth (frieze), in which the nap of the cloth is removed along with the soiling agent (hence "plucks out brain and all"). But the route to this relatively rational meaning is treacherous: the syntax first presents us with birdlime oozing from his head ("invention / Comes from my pate as birdlime does"), takes us on an apparent detour through the soiling of cloth (the birdlime stuck to the frieze), and ends with the image of his head emptied out altogether ("plucks out brain and all"), as though in a dangerous evacuation. Then, through a buried pun on *conception,* the concealed intermediary term, the evacuation becomes a pregnancy and delivery, displaced from his own body to that of the Muse, who labors and is delivered.

Invention, in other words, becomes the male equivalent of pregnancy, the production of a sticky dark baby. What we have here, I suggest, is the vindictive fantasy of a faecal pregnancy and delivery that can project Iago's inner monstrosity and darkness into the world:[44] initially displaced upward to the evacuated pate, this faecal baby is then returned to its source as his monstrous birth, the baby he has conceived in response to Desdemona's request for praise (2.1.124) and the easy generativity (his own is a difficult labor) that he envies in her. This baby's emergence here marks, I think, both the source of his envy and the exchange that envy will demand: he will attempt in effect to replicate his dark sticky baby in her, soiling her generative body by turning her virtue into pitch,[45] spoiling the object whose fullness and goodness he cannot tolerate by making it the receptacle for his own bodily contents. And he counts on the contagion of this contaminated object: he will turn Desdemona into pitch not only because pitch is black and sticky—hence entrapping—but because it is notoriously defiling;[46] his scheme depends on using Desdemona as a kind of tar baby, counting on her defilement—her blackening—to make Othello "black." In fantasy, that is, Iago uses Desdemona and Othello to contaminate each other; they become for him one defiled object as he imagines them on that wedding bed. But at the same time, Othello plays a special role for Iago: in Othello's black skin Iago can find a fortuitous external sign for the entire process, or, more accurately, a container for the internal blackness that he would project outward, the dark baby that hell and night must bring to the world's light; emptying himself out, Iago can project his faecal baby into Othello, blackening him with his own inner waste.

Iago plainly needs an Othello who can carry the burden of his own contamination; and to some extent the play makes us complicit in the process, as it makes Othello in effect into Iago's monstrous creation, carrying out Iago's "conception" as he murders Desdemona on her wedding bed, enacting a perverse version of the childbirth that might have taken place there. Othello himself seems to recognize that a birth of sorts is taking place, though he does not recognize it as Iago's: preparing to kill Desdemona on that bed, he says that her denials "Cannot remove, nor choke the strong conception, / That I do groan withal" (5.2.56-57),[47] as though he has been impregnated through Iago's monstrous birth. And in fact he has: part of the peculiar horror of this play is that Othello becomes so effective a receptacle for—and enactor of—Iago's fantasies. If Iago imagines himself filled with a gnawing poisonous mineral through what amounts to Othello's anal insemination of him (2.1.290-92), he turns that poison back on Othello: "I'll pour this pestilence into his ear" (2.3.347). This retaliatory aural/anal insemination fills Othello with Iago's own contents, allowing Iago to serve his turn on Othello by doing to Othello what he imagines Othello has done to him. ("I follow him to serve my turn upon him" is sexualized in ways not likely to be audible to a modern audience [1.1.42]. For *turn,* see Othello's later "she can turn, and turn, and yet go on, / And turn again" [4.1.249-50];[48] characteristically, Othello replicates in Desdemona the "turn" Iago has replicated in him.) And "The Moor already changes with my poison," Iago says, adding for our benefit—in case we have not noticed the links between his poisonous conceit and Othello's—"Dangerous conceits are in their natures poisons, / Which . . . Burn like the mines of sulphur" (3.3.330-34).

"The Moor already changes with my poison": the line marks what is distinctive about projection in this play— and distinctively Kleinian. Before Klein, projection was usually understood as a relatively uncomplicated process in which disowned ideas and emotions were displaced onto an external figure. Klein insisted both on the fantasies of bodily function accompanying this process and on the extent to which it is specifically pieces of the self and its inner objects that are thus relocated, with the consequence that pieces of the self are now felt to be "out there," both controlling the object into which they have been projected and subject to dangers from it; Klein renamed this process "projective identification." And her followers have expanded on the concept, stressing the effects of these projected contents on the recipient of the projection, the ways in which the projector can in fact control the recipient. In this version of projective identification, the recipient will not only experience the bits of self projected into him but also enact the projector's fantasy scenarios, hence relieving the projector of all responsibility for them.[49] When Iago imagines Roderigo turned inside out, his body filled with pus, he seems to me to be engaging in something close to garden-variety projection: he is attributing to Roderigo portions of himself, or ideas about himself, that he would like to disown; and, as far as we know, Roderigo does not come to experience himself as pus-filled or inside out. But when Iago imagines filling Othello with his poison, when he imagines (in Klein's formulation) "the forceful entry into the object and control of the object by parts of the self,"[50] he is much closer to a specifically Kleinian projective identification; and, as Klein's followers would predict, Othello really does change with Iago's poison, as he begins to experience himself as contaminated and hence to act out Iago's scenarios.

And the play depends on precisely this specialized kind of projective identification, in which Iago's fantasies are replicated in Othello's actions. When we first meet Othello, he is confident enough about his status and his color that he wishes to be found; he can confidently wish "the goodness of the night" (1.2.35) on Cassio and the duke's servants because blackness has not yet been poisoned for him. But as Iago projects his faecal baby into him, Othello comes more and more to imagine himself as the foul thing—the old black ram— intruding into the palace of Venetian civilization or the palace of Desdemona's body; as Iago succeeds in making Othello the container for his own interior waste, Othello himself increasingly affiliates his blackness with soiling (he becomes "collied" or blackened by passion [2.3.197];[51] his name is "begrim'd, and black" as his face) and with bad interior objects. (In "Arise, black vengeance, from thy hollow cell" [3.3.454], he calls on "black vengeance" to arise as though from within the hollow of himself.)[52] His experience of himself, that is, comes increasingly to resemble what Iago has projected into him; and he begins to act in accordance with that projection, replicating in Desdemona the contagion of projection itself. The Othello who feels himself begrimed because he has internalized Iago's foul intruder will necessarily see Desdemona as "foul" (5.2.201), as a "begrim'd" Diana or a "black weed," and will evacuate his good object as Iago had predicted (1.3.350); by the end of the play, Emilia can call Othello "the blacker devil," Desdemona's "most filthy bargain," "As ignorant as dirt" (5.2.132, 158, 165) because he has so perfectly introjected Iago's sense of inner filth.

Insofar as Iago can make Othello experience his own blackness as a contamination that contaminates Desdemona, he succeeds in emptying himself out into Othello;

and insofar as Othello becomes in effect Iago's faecal baby, Othello—rather than Iago—becomes the bearer of the fantasy of inner filth. Through projective identification, that is, Iago invents blackness as a contaminated category before our eyes, enacting his monstrous birth through Othello, and then allowing the Venetians (and most members of the audience) to congratulate themselves—as he does—on their distance from the now-racialized Othello. Through this process, Othello becomes assimilated to, and motivated by, his racial "type"—becomes the monstrous Moor easily made jealous—and Iago escapes our human categories altogether, becoming unknowable, a motiveless malignity.

But this emptying out of Iago is no more than Iago has already performed on himself: if the projection of his own inner contamination into Othello is Iago's relief, it is also his undoing, and in a way that corroborates both the bodiliness of the fantasy of projection and its dangers to the projector as well as the recipient. Klein notes that excessive use of projective identification results in the "weakening and impoverishment of the ego"; in the words of Betty Joseph, "at times the mind can be . . . so evacuated by projective identification that the individual appears empty."[53] If at the end of the play there is nothing left to envy, there is also no one left to experience envy: Iago's projection of himself into the racial other he constructs as the container for his contamination ends not only by destroying his (and our) good objects but also by leaving him entirely evacuated. Having poured the pestilence of himself into Othello, Iago has nothing left inside him: his antigenerative birth hollows him out, leaving him empty. The closer he is to his goal, the flatter his language becomes; by the end, there is no inside left, no place to speak from. The play that begins with his insistent "I" ends with his silence: from this time forth he never will speak word.

Notes

1 Quotations follow the Arden edition of *Othello,* edited by M. R. Ridley (London: Methuen, 1958). Ridley follows the 1622 quarto, which often differs from the Folio *Othello;* I have noted the differences where they seem significant to my argument. Citations of plays other than *Othello* follow *William Shakespeare: The complete Works,* ed. Alfred Harbage (Baltimore: Penguin, 1969).

2 *Race* is of course a vexed term; many have pointed out that the word *race* gained its current meaning only as it was biologized in support of the economic institution of slavery and that the link between race and skin color is a peculiarly contemporary obsession, that (for example) Irish and Jews might in 1604 have been thought of as racially separate from the English. For a particularly lucid account of the questions surrounding the invocation of race as a category in early modern England, see Lynda E. Boose, "'The Getting of a Lawful Race': Racial discourse in early modern England and the unrepresentable black woman" in *Women, "Race," and Writing in the Early Modern Period,* Margo Hendricks and Patricia Parker, eds. (London and New York: Routledge, 1994), 35-54, esp. 35-40; see also John Gillies, *Shakespeare and the geography of difference* (Cambridge: Cambridge UP, 1994), for the claim that early modern otherness was based on geography rather than on the anachronistic category of race (25). Nonetheless, in Iago's capacity to make Othello's blackness the primary signifier of his otherness—as Boose observes, "once his Ensign has raised the flag inscribing Othello within the difference of skin color, all the presumably meaningful differences Othello has constructed between himself and the infidel collapse" (38)—the text insists on the visible difference of skin color that will increasingly come to define race, perhaps because, unlike religion, it (proverbially) cannot be changed. For a discussion of the significance of visible difference in early modern England, see Kim Hall, "Reading What Isn't There: 'Black' Studies in Early Modern England," *Stanford Humanities Review* 3 (1993): 23-33, esp. 25-27; in her account "science merely takes up already pre-existing terms of difference, such as skin color and features, that have [previously] been combined with physical and mental characteristics" (25).

3 Ridley follows the Folio reading of line 392, since this line occurs in a passage not found in Q1; Q2 (1630) famously reads "Her name" in place of F's "My name," perhaps to rationalize Othello's peculiar association of his name with the fairness of a figure for female virginity. I prefer "My name," partly because it suggests the identificatory dynamics that underlie Othello's love for Desdemona; but either reading points toward Othello's association of the stain on Desdemona's virgin body with the blackness of his own face.

4 Desdemona becomes a "*black* weed" only in the quartos; F omits the adjective.

5 This position was powerfully—and variously—articulated in three classic essays published in 1979-80: Edward A. Snow's "Sexual Anxiety and the Male Order of Things in *Othello,*" *English Literary Renaissance* 10 (1980): 384-412; Stanley Cavell's "Othello and the Stake of the Other" in *Disowning Knowledge in Six Plays of Shakespeare* (Cambridge: Cambridge UP, 1987), 125-42 (originally published in 1979 in *The Claim of Reason* [Oxford: Oxford UP]); and Stephen Greenblatt's "The Improvisation of Power" in *Renaissance Self-Fashioning: From More to Shakespeare* (Chicago and London: U of Chicago P, 1980), 222-54, esp. 232-52. For the association of Othello's blackness specifically with sexual contamination, and Othello's internalization of this association, see especially Snow,

400-402; and Cavell, 136-37. For a fuller reading of the association between blackness and monstrous sexuality in early modern English culture and in *Othello,* see especially Karen Newman, "'And wash the Ethiop white': femininity and the monstrous in *Othello*" in *Shakespeare Reproduced: The text in history and ideology,* Jean E. Howard and Marion F. O'Connor, eds. (New York and London: Methuen, 1987), 143-62, esp. 148-53; for a fuller reading of the ways in which Othello internalizes the Venetian construction of his blackness, see Edward Berry, "Othello's Alienation," *Studies in English Literature 1500-1900* 30 (1990): 315-33. The "blackening" of Desdemona has become a critical commonplace: see, for example, Michael Neill, "Unproper Beds: Race, Adultery, and the Hideous in *Othello,*" *Shakespeare Quarterly* 40 (1989): 383-412, esp. 410; Berry, 328; Ania Loomba, *Gender, race, Renaissance drama* (Manchester and New York: Manchester UP, 1989), 59; Parker, "Fantasies of 'Race' and 'Gender': Africa, *Othello* and bringing to light" in Hendricks and Parker, eds., 84-100, esp. 95; and especially Newman, 151-52, for whom the blackening of Desdemona indicates the convergence of woman and black in the category of monstrous sexuality.

⁶ See W. H. Auden's related account of Iago as practical joker: "The practical joker despises his victims, but at the same time he envies them because their desires, however childish and mistaken, are real to them, whereas he has no desire which he can call his own. . . . If the word motive is given its normal meaning of a positive purpose of the self like sex, money, glory, etc., then the practical joker is without motive. Yet the professional practical joker is certainly driven, . . . but the drive is negative, a fear of lacking a concrete self, of being nobody. In any practical joker to whom playing such jokes is a passion, there is always an element of malice, a projection of his self-hatred onto others, and in the ultimate case of the absolute practical joker, this is projected onto all created things" (*The Dyer's Hand and other essays* [New York: Random House, 1962], 256-57). The emptiness of Auden's practical joker is sometimes associated by later critics with Iago's facility in role-playing; see, e.g., Shelley Orgel, whose Iago gains a temporary sense of self by playing the roles that others project onto him ("Iago," *American Imago* 25 [1968]: 258-73, esp. 272). Greenblatt's Iago "has the role-player's ability to imagine his nonexistence so that he can exist for a moment in another and as another"; but for Greenblatt, Iago's imagined emptiness is less an ontological state than a cover for his emptying out of his victim (235 and 236). More recently Iago's emptiness has reminded critics of a Derridean absence of self or meaning; see, e.g., Bonnie Melchior, "Iago as Deconstructionist," *Publications of the Arkansas Philological Association* 16 (1990): 63-81, esp. 79; or Karl F. Zender, "The Humiliation of Iago," *SEL* 34 (1994): 323-39, esp. 327-28. In Alessandro Serpieri's brilliant semiotic reading, Iago suffers from an "envy

of being" that is the deconstructionist's equivalent of the state Auden describes: "Iago cannot identify with any situation or sign or *énoncé,* and is thus condemned to deconstruct through his own *énonciations* the *énoncés* of others, transforming them into simulacra. Othello is precisely the lord of the *énoncé*" (Serpieri, "Reading the signs: towards a semiotics of Shakespearean drama," trans. Keir Elam, in *Alternative Shakespeares,* John Drakakis, ed. [London and New York: Methuen, 1985], 119-43, esp. 139). In its emphasis on envy and projection, Auden's and Serpieri's work is closest to my own; but see also David Pollard's powerful Baudelairian reading of Iago's emptiness and the sadistic projections through which he attempts to fill it ("Iago's Wound" in Othello: *New Perspectives,* Virginia Mason Vaughan and Kent Cartwright, eds. [Rutherford, Madison, and Teaneck, NJ: Fairleigh Dickinson UP; London and Toronto: Associated University Presses, 1991], 89-96).

⁷ Adam Phillips, "Foreword" in Harold N. Boris, *Envy* (Northvale, NJ, and London: Jason Aronson, 1994), vii-xi, esp. ix.

⁸ For some, Othello is split long before Iago begins his work. In Berry's account, for example, Othello is divided from the beginning by the two contradictory self-images he absorbs from Venice; his failure to escape this limiting framework and hence to "achieve a true sense of personal identity" is a powerful source of tragic feeling in the play (323 and 330). But for critics who read Othello as an early instance of a colonized subject, this "failure" is not personal but systemic: both Loomba (32, 48, and 54) and Jyotsna Singh ("Othello's Identity, Postcolonial Theory, and Contemporary African Rewritings of *Othello*" in Hendricks and Parker, eds., 287-99, esp. 288) position Othello specifically in opposition to what Singh calls "the dominant, Western fantasy of a singular, unified identity" (288). But Iago at least insists that he is the divided one, and Othello initially claims that his soul is "perfect" or undivided; whatever the state to which Othello is reduced, *Othello*—like *The Tempest*—seems to me to encode the fantasy that the exotic other possesses a primitive unitary identity before his induction into a Western-style split self.

⁹ I first read this paper to a very helpful and responsive audience at Notre Dame in November 1994, on which occasion Richard Dutton called my attention to the way in which Othello's self-division is literally played out on the stage.

¹⁰ As Iago's self-alienation passes to Othello, so does his habit of soliloquizing. Soliloquies are usually in Shakespearean tragedy the discourse of self-division: only those whose selves are in pieces need to explain themselves to themselves and have distinct-enough interior voices to carry out the job for our benefit.

Initially Iago's soliloquies formally mark him as fractured in comparison with Othello's wholeness; by the end, Othello is the soliloquizer.

[11] I here depart from Ridley in following F's version of line 80; Ridley and Q1 (1622) give "And swiftly come to Desdemona's arms." Ridley himself finds Q1's version of line 80 "pallid" and thinks Shakespeare probably revised it for F; that he nonetheless rejects the Folio version on the grounds that it is inconsistent with Cassio's character suggests his resistance to seeing just how eroticized Cassio's idealizing of Othello is (xxix-xxx and 52n). In the context of lovemaking, *spirits* is not a neutral term; for its specifically sexual senses, see Stephen Booth, *Shakespeare's Sonnets* (New Haven, CT, and London: Yale UP, 1977), 441-43.

[12] See Neill's powerful account of the ways in which the audience is implicated in Iago's invocation of the horrors of miscegenation, the improper sexual mixture that medieval theologians called adultery (395-99 and 407-9). For Arthur L. Little Jr. the whole of the play constitutes "the primal scene of racism," a forbidden sexual sight/site from which the audience "constructs the significance of race" ("'An essence that's not seen': The Primal Scene of Racism in *Othello,*" *SQ* 44 [1993]: 304-24, esp. 305-6).

[13] The familiar associations of blackness with monstrosity (see, e.g., Newman, 148; and James R. Aubrey, "Race and the Spectacle of the Monstrous in *Othello,*" *Clio* 22 [1993]: 221-38) and specifically with monstrous births (see Neill, 409-10; and Aubrey, 222-27) would probably have made the subterranean connection between Othello and Iago's monstrous birth more available to Shakespeare's audiences than it is to a modern audience.

[14] Projection has classically been invoked as a mechanism in *Othello,* but usually in the other direction, from Othello to Iago; see, e.g., J.I.M. Stewart, *Character and Motive in Shakespeare: Some Recent Appraisals Examined* ([London, New York, and Toronto: Longmans, Green and Company, 1949], 102-5), though Stewart ultimately abandons a naturalistic reading of the play through projection for a symbolic reading of Iago and Othello as parts of a single whole. For somewhat later versions of Iago as Othello's projection, see, e.g., Henry L. Warnken, "Iago as a Projection of Othello" in *Shakespeare Encomium 1564-1964,* Anne Paolucci, ed. (New York: The City College, 1964), 1-15; and Orgel, 258-73. In these accounts projection is loosely used to indicate that Iago expresses unacknowledged doubts or desires in Othello's mind (or, in Orgel's reading, Othello's unacknowledged need for a punitive superego); they generally do not explore the mechanism of projection or consider the degree to which the structure of the play posits Iago—not Othello—as its psychic starting point. For Auden, who reads the play

through Iago as practical joker, projection begins with Iago, not Othello (see n. 6, above); see also Leslie Y. Rabkin and Jeffrey Brown, who read Iago as a Horneyan sadist, assuaging his pain by projecting his self-contempt and hopelessness onto others ("Some Monster in His Thought: Sadism and Tragedy in *Othello,*" *Literature and Psychology* 23 [1973]: 59-67, esp. 59-60); and Pollard, who reads Iago as Baudelairian sadist, filling the world with sadistic projections with which he then identifies to fill his inner emptiness (92-95). Serpieri sees Iago as the "artificer of a *destructive projection*"; in his semiotic analysis, litotes—Iago's characteristic nay-saying figure—becomes the linguistic equivalent of projection, "a figure of persuasion which, by denying, affirms in the 'other' all that—the diabolical, the lustful, the alien—which it refutes or censures in the 'self'" (134 and 142). Attention to the status of "others" has made contemporary criticism particularly sensitive to Othello as the site of Iago's projections rather than as the originator of projection; see, e.g., Parker on "the violence of projection" (100). My account differs from those cited here largely in giving projection a body and in specifying the mechanisms of projective identification at work in the play.

[15] Although Neill emphasizes the hidden/hideousness of the bed rather than of bodily interiors (394-95), my formulation here is very much indebted to his. In the course of her enormously suggestive account of the cultural resonances of the hidden/private in *Othello* and *Hamlet,* Parker comments extensively on the association of the hidden with the woman's private parts, partly via gynecological discourse; see Parker, "*Othello* and *Hamlet:* Dilation, Spying, and the 'Secret Place' of Woman," *Representations* 44 (1993): 60-95, esp. 64-69.

[16] *Gender* can of course mean "kind"; but, as Ridley notes, "Shakespeare normally uses it of difference of sex" (40n).

[17] Ridley notes that "*supply* = satisfy" (40n); for a specifically sexualized use, see *Measure for Measure,* 5.1.210.

[18] "Doves" is the reading in Ridley and Q1; I here depart from it in giving F's and Q2's "dawes."

[19] On the relationship between money and faeces, see Sigmund Freud, "Character and Anal Eroticism" in *The Standard Edition of the Complete Psychological Works of Sigmund Freud,* ed. James Strachey, 24 vols. (London: Hogarth Press and the Institute of Psycho-Analysis, 1953-74), 9:167-76, esp. 171 and 173-74; Ernest Jones, "Anal-Erotic Character Traits," *Journal of Abnormal Psychology* 13 (1918): 261-84, esp. 272-74 and 276-77; Karl Abraham, "Contributions to the Theory of the Anal Character" in *Selected Papers of Karl Abraham* (New York: Brunner/Mazel, 1927), 370-92,

esp. 383; and Otto Fenichel, *The Psychoanalytic Theory of Neurosis* (New York: Norton, 1945), 281. On sadism and anality, see Abraham, "The Narcissistic Evaluation of Excretory Processes in Dreams and Neurosis" in *Selected Papers,* 318-22, esp. 319 and 321; Jones, 268; and Fenichel, 283.

[20] The *loci classici* for this reading are Martin Wangh, "*Othello:* The Tragedy of Iago," *Psychoanalytic Quarterly* 19 (1950): 202-12; and Gordon Ross Smith, "Iago the Paranoiac," *American Imago* 16 (1959): 155-67. Both essays are based on Freud's account of delusional jealousy as a defense against homosexual desire in the Schreber case. For an extension and elaboration of this view, with particular focus on Iago's hatred of women, see also Stanley Edgar Hyman, *Iago: Some Approaches to the Illusion of His Motivation* (New York: Atheneum, 1970), 101-21. Contemporary critics who comment on the homoerotic dynamic between Iago and Othello tend to locate their readings not in this model but in the complex of metaphors that makes Iago's seduction of Othello into an aural penetration and insemination, with a resulting monstrous (and miscegenistic) conception; see, e.g., Coppélia Kahn, *Man's Estate: Masculine Identity in Shakespeare* (Berkeley, Los Angeles, and London: U of California P, 1981), 144-45; and Parker in Hendricks and Parker, eds., 99-100. Parker notes that the imagined penetration is anal as well as aural (99); see also, e.g., Graham Hammill's brief discussion of Iago's anal eroticism, "The Epistemology of Expurgation: Bacon and *The Masculine Birth of Time*" in *Queering the Renaissance,* Jonathan Goldberg, ed. (Durham, NC, and London: Duke UP, 1994), 236-52, esp. 251n.

[21] For historically based arguments against Iago-as-repressed-homosexual, see Jonathan Dollimore, *Sexual Dissidence* (Oxford: Clarendon Press, 1991), 157-62; and Bruce R. Smith, *Homosexual Desire in Shakespeare's England: A Cultural Poetics* (Chicago and London: U of Chicago P, 1991), 61-63 and 75. Both Dollimore and Smith stress the social functions of the male homosocial bond rather than the dynamics of homoerotic feeling partly on the grounds that the homosexual subject is an anachronism in the early modern period. But Shakespeare does not need to have the category of the "homosexual subject" available to him in order to represent Iago as acting out of desires inadmissible to him, including sodomitical desires; and critics who insist that we do away with "the homosexual" as a category sometimes throw out the baby with the bathwater. In "Homosexuality and the Signs of Male Friendship in Elizabethan England" (in Goldberg, ed., 40-61) Alan Bray demonstrates the cultural (nonsexual) uses to which the "bedfellow" could be put; but in order for Smith, for example, to invoke Iago's report of Cassio's "bedfellow" dream to make the argument that Iago is a self-conscious male-bonder rather than a repressed homosexual, he has to ignore

the explicit sexiness of the dream (the hard kisses plucked up by the roots, the leg over the thigh). The dream clearly crosses the line—between male friendship and sodomy—that Bray delineates, more strikingly because Iago need not have included all that sexiness to convey his "information" to Othello; and whether or not the reported dream proclaims Iago a "repressed homosexual," its effect on Othello clearly depends as much on its crossing of that line as on the information that Cassio dreams about Desdemona. As for subjectivity: whether or not the Renaissance shared our sense of the bourgeois subject—in any case, emphatically not the subject as it is construed by psychoanalysis—*Othello* is obsessively about what is hidden away within the person, the inner, private, and unknowable self that might harbor inaccessible desires. For a good summary of these controversies—and a sensible middle position—see Alan Sinfield, *Cultural Politics—Queer Reading* (Philadelphia: U of Pennsylvania P, 1994), 12-14.

[22] Melanie Klein, "Envy and Gratitude" (1957) in *Envy and Gratitude and Other Works 1946-1963* (London: Hogarth Press and the Institute of Psycho-Analysis, 1975), 176-235, esp. 179.

[23] Klein, 188.

[24] Klein, 192 and 189.

[25] Boris, xvi.

[26] Klein, 183.

[27] For an early statement of this position, see Klein, "Early Stages of the Oedipus Conflict" (1928) in *Love, Guilt and Reparation and Other Works 1921-1945* (London: Hogarth Press and the Institute of Psycho-Analysis, 1975), 186-98, esp. 190-91 and 193-96.

[28] Klein, *Envy and Gratitude,* 181.

[29] Klein, *Envy and Gratitude,* 186.

[30] Quoted here from Bernard Spivack's discussion of Iago and the morality tradition in *Shakespeare and the Allegory of Evil: The History of a Metaphor in Relation to His Major Villains* (New York: Columbia UP, 1958), 184.

[31] Betty Joseph, "Envy in everyday life" in *Psychic Equilibrium and Psychic Change: Selected Papers of Betty Joseph,* ed. Michael Feldman and Elizabeth Bott Spillius (London and New York: Tavistock/Routledge, 1989), 181-91, esp. 185.

[32] In Kleinian terms, Othello has reached the depressive position, characterized by the capacity to mourn for the damaged object and to make reparations to it

(see especially Klein, "A Contribution to the Psychogenesis of Manic-Depressive States" [1935] and "Mourning and its Relation to Manic-Depressive States" [1940], both in *Love, Guilt and Reparation,* 262-89 and 344-69); Iago functions from within the more primitive paranoid-schizoid position, with its characteristic mechanisms of splitting and projection/introjection (see especially Klein, "Notes on Some Schizoid Mechanisms" in *Envy and Gratitude,* 1-24).

33 As many have argued: see especially Cavell, 134; and Snow, 392. See also my *Suffocating Mothers: Fantasies of Maternal Origin in Shakespeare,* Hamlet *to* The Tempest (New York and London: Routledge, 1992), 69-70.

34 Iago's words here, like Emilia's at 3.4.157-60, refer explicitly to *jealousy* but nonetheless define the self-referential qualities of *envy*. Although the two terms are sometimes popularly confused, they are distinct in psychoanalytic thought: jealousy occurs in a three-body relationship, derived from the oedipus complex, in which the loss of a good object to a rival is at stake; envy occurs in a pre-oedipal two-body relationship, in which the "good" qualities of the object are felt to be intolerable. Jealousy seeks to preserve the good object, if necessary by killing it; envy seeks to spoil the good object. (For these distinctions, see Klein, *Envy and Gratitude,* 196-99; and Joseph in Feldman and Spillius, eds., 182.) Jealousy is a derivative of envy but is more easily recognized and more socially acceptable (Klein, *Envy and Gratitude,* 198; Joseph in Feldman and Spillius, eds., 182); partly as a consequence, it can sometimes serve as "an important defence against envy" (Klein, *Envy and Gratitude,* 198). This defensive structure seems to me at work both in Iago and in the play at large: in Iago, who repeatedly comes up with narratives of jealousy as though to justify his intolerable envy to himself (tellingly, he uses the traditional language of envy—Spenser's Envy "inwardly . . . chawed his owne maw" in *The Faerie Queene* [I.iv.30]—to register the gnawing effects of jealousy on him); and in *Othello* itself, insofar as its own narratives of jealousy are far more legible and recognizably "human" than the envy represented through Iago and dismissed in him as unrecognizable, inhuman, or demonic.

35 "Mock" has puzzled commentators for years, occasioning five pages of commentary in the New Variorum edition of *Othello* (ed. Horace Howard Furness [Philadelphia: J. B. Lippincott, 1886]). William Warburton (1747) glosses "mocke" (in terms strikingly close to my own) as "loaths that which nourishes and sustains it" (176). With very little plausibility but some interest for my argument, Andrew Becket (1815) transforms "mocke" to *"muck,"* glossing it as to *"bedaub* or *make foul";* two other commentators—Zachariah Jackson and Lord John Chedworth—approved of this emendation

enough to come up with candidates for the monstrous animal that befouls its food, mouse and dragon-fly, respectively (179).

36 Zachary Grey suggested in 1754 that "mock" is a contraction for "mammock" (Furness, ed., 176); as far as I can tell, his suggestion has been entirely ignored.

37 Klein, *Envy and Gratitude,* 201-2.

38 See *Hamlet,* 2.2.181-82.

39 This destruction also has the effect of separating the two figures whose conjunction has haunted Iago's imagination. Klein hypothesizes the combined parent figure as a special target of envy ("the suspicion that the parents are always getting sexual gratification from one another reinforces the phantasy . . . that they are always combined" [*Envy and Gratitude,* 198]); Iago in fact evokes such a fantasy-figure in his initial description of Othello and Desdemona as fused, a "beast with two backs" (1.1.116), always in the process of achieving the "incorporate conclusion" (2.1.258-59) that is always denied him.

40 Boris, 36.

41 My formulation here is partly indebted to Janine Chasseguet-Smirgel's work on perversion, especially anal perversion, which she sees as an attempt to dissolve generational and gender differences in order to defend against acknowledgment of the pervert's own puniness and vulnerability; though she does not draw specifically on Klein's concept of envy, her work sometimes intersects usefully with Klein's. In Chasseguet-Smirgel's reading, Sade's intention, for example, is "to reduce the universe to faeces, or rather to annihilate the universe of differences" ("Perversion and the Universal Law" in Chasseguet-Smirgel, *Creativity and Perversion* [New York: W. W. Norton, 1984], 4). Insofar as perversion attempts to replace God's differentiated universe with its own undifferentiation, it is "the equivalent of Devil religion" (9); the undifferentiated anal universe "constitutes an imitation or parody of the genital universe of the father" (11). While this formulation is suggestive for Iago, I think that Chasseguet-Smirgel is hampered by her Lacanian milieu, with its overvaluation of the phallus and the father's law; Iago is at least as intent on imitating and ultimately replacing the mother's generative function as the father's law.

42 With the kind of psychological intuition that everywhere animates his portrayal of Satan, Milton reworks Emilia's comment: unable to stand the "debt immense of endless gratitude" to the God who has created him (*Paradise Lost,* Bk. 4, l. 52), Satan proclaims himself "self-begot, self-rais'd / By our own quick'ning power" (Bk. 5, ll. 860-61). Klein cites Milton's Satan

as an instance of "the spoiling of creativity implied in envy" (*Envy and Gratitude*, 202).

[43] According to the *Oxford English Dictionary*, birdlime is a sticky substance made out of the bark of the holly tree and smeared on branches to entrap birds; "With the barkes of Holme they make Bird-lyme," cited from Henry Lyte's 1578 *Niewe herball or historie of plantes* (*Oxford English Dictionary*, prep. J. Simpson and E.S.C. Weiner, 2d ed., 20 vols. [Oxford: Clarendon Press, 1989], 2:216). *Holme* is confusing; it is cited as "blacke Holme" in Spenser's *Virgils Gnat* (l. 215), but there apparently refers to the oak, not the holly. In any case, despite the echo of lime, birdlime seems to have been dark, not white.

[44] The equation of faeces with baby is familiar to psychoanalysis; see, e.g., Freud, "On the Sexual Theories of Children," on the cloacal theory of birth ("If babies are born through the anus, then a man can give birth just as well as a woman" [9:205-26, esp. 219-20]); Jones, 274-75; and Susan Isaacs, "Penis-Feces-Child," *International Journal of Psycho-analysis* 8 (1927): 74-76. For fantasies that overvalue the power of faecal creation "to create or destroy every object," see Abraham, "The Narcissistic Evaluation of Excretory Processes," 322; about one of his patients he reports, "That night he dreamed that he had to expel the universe out of his anus" (320).

[45] Oddly, Ridley associates the pitch into which Iago will turn Desdemona's virtue with birdlime without noting its source in Iago's earlier metaphor (88n).

[46] For Shakespeare's reworkings of the proverbially defiling properties of pitch, see, e.g., *Love's Labor's Lost*, 4.3.3; *1 Henry IV*, 2.4.394-96; and *Much Ado About Nothing*, 3.3.53.

[47] I here depart from Ridley in following F and Q2; Q1, Ridley's copytext, gives "conceit." The half-buried metaphor of childbirth is, I think, present in either case, both through the association of "groan"—especially in proximity to a bed—with childbirth (see, e.g., *All's Well That Ends Well*, 1.3.140 and 4.5.10; and *Measure for Measure*, 2.2.15) and through the family relation between *conceit* and Latin *conceptus*, cited in the *OED*; the *OED* also gives "Conception of offspring" as an obsolete meaning for *conceit* with a 1589 instance, though it notes that this usage is "Perhaps only a pun" (3:647-48, esp. 648).

[48] See also "the best turn i' th' bed" (*Antony and Cleopatra*, 2.5.59). For *serve*, see *Lear's* Oswald, "A serviceable villain, / As duteous to the vices of thy mistress / As badness would desire" (4.6.248-50); for *serve my turn*, see Costard's exchange with the king (*Love's Labor's Lost*, 1.1.281-82). For *follow / fallow*, see Parker in Hendricks and Parker, eds., 99, citing Herbert A. Ellis, *Shakespeare's Lusty Punning in Love's Labour's Lost* (1973).

[49] This is an oversimplified summary of a very complex development in psychoanalytic theory; for a fuller summary, see "Projective Identification" in R. D. Hinshelwood's *A Dictionary of Kleinian Thought* (London: Free Association Books, 1991), 179-208; or Elizabeth Bott Spillius's "Clinical experiences of projective identification" in *Clinical Lectures on Klein and Bion*, Robin Anderson, ed. (London and New York: Tavistock/Routledge, 1992), 59-73, esp. 59-64. For Klein's initial development of the concept of projective identification, see *Envy and Gratitude*, 8-11. The development of the concept by her followers has had broad ramifications for clinical work; for a particularly lucid account of some of these, see, in addition to Spillius, Joseph, "Projective identification—some clinical aspects" in *Melanie Klein Today: Developments in Theory and Practice*, Elizabeth Bott Spillius, ed., 2 vols. (London and New York: Routledge, 1988), 1:138-50.

[50] Klein, *Envy and Gratitude*, 11.

[51] *Collied* is conjecturally related to *coaly* by the *OED*, 3:390-91.

[52] Folio gives "hell" for Q1's "cell." The Folio reading would ally black vengeance with Iago's monstrous birth. In either reading, the apparently superfluous hollowness suggests an inner space; as Ridley notes, it occurs, again redundantly, in the reference to a "hollow mine" (4.2.81). Shortly after he calls up black vengeance, and again in 5.2, Othello imagines his revenge swallowing up his victims (3.3.467 and 5.2.76), as though returning them to the interior source of his vengeance.

[53] Klein, *Envy and Gratitude*, 11; Joseph in Spillius, ed., *Melanie Klein Today*, 140.

Source: "Iago's Alter Ego: Race as Projection in *Othello*," in *Shakespeare Quarterly*, Vol. 48, No. 2, Spring, 1997, pp. 125-44.

Hamlet's Ear

Philippa Berry, *King's College, Cambridge*

An alienation from the hypocrisy of a courtly style or decorum in language afflicts Hamlet from his first appearance in the play. The courtly airs or 'songs', the 'words of so sweet breath', the 'music vows', with which he wooed Ophelia are no longer part of his idiom, although he will briefly redeploy them to disguise his true state of mind. In Act 1 scene 2, we meet a Hamlet whose abrupt retreat from social intercourse is not only signalled by his mourning dress, but is also articulated through an intensely satiric relationship to language. This scathing view of the world is articulated in all of Hamlet's language, in his soliloquies and monologues as well as in his dialogues with others; it finds its most effective form of expression, however, in his use of wordplay. Indeed, before the final tragic catastrophe Hamlet's role as malcontent and revenger succeeds not so much by action as by his disordering, through punning, of social constructions of identity. The centrality of the pun to the view of earthly mutability and death which Hamlet gradually elaborates in the course of the play is aptly illustrated by the fact that he puns not only on his own death ('The rest is silence'), but also as he finally accomplishes his task of revenge and kills Claudius, asking 'Is thy union here?' as he forces him to drink the wine that Claudius has poisoned with a pearl or 'union'. Yet the chief interest of Hamlet's quibbling lies not in his semantic puns, which play upon words with two or more meanings, like 'rest' or 'union', but in his richly suggestive use of homophonic resemblances between words, in order to expand their significance. Through these linguistic acts of expansion, Hamlet comments upon particular elements of the tragic narrative, augmenting their apparent meaning by interweaving ostensibly disparate themes and motifs into a complex unity.

In contrast to the use of wordplay as the supreme instance of a dialogic courtly wit which celebrates the shared values of an aristocratic group, it is through an ironic use of iteration, and of the pun in particular, that Hamlet's echoic or quibbling discourse is able to enunciate, albeit obliquely, those hidden meanings which are concealed within the polite language of the Danish court. Hamlet condemns and rejects that courtly playing upon him as a phallic pipe or recorder of which he accuses Rosencrantz and Guildenstern:

> You would play upon me, you would seem to know my stops, you would pluck out the heart of my mystery, you would sound me from my lowest note to the top of my compass; and there is much music,

> excellent voice in this little organ, yet cannot you make it speak. 'Sblood, do you think I am easier to be played on than a pipe? Call me what instrument you will, though you can fret me, you cannot play upon me.
>
> (3.2.352-60)

In contrast to this courtly attempt to play upon or 'sound' him, Hamlet's resonant unsettling of courtly language follows a different tune. For his quibbles remind us constantly of Hamlet's familial displacement, as a son and heir whose place in a masculine genealogy of kings is no longer certain. In these puns, as well as in the tropes which are applied to him by others, we find a curious refiguring of Denmark's 'heir'—a word which, significantly, is only evoked through homophony in this play—in relationship to 'th'incorporal air' (3.4.109).

In his magisterial study of *Shakespeare's Pronunciation,* where he aimed to recover many Elizabethan homonyms which are no longer pronounced alike, Helge Kökeritz concluded that hair-heir-here-hare were four words often pronounced similarly in early modern English; in particular, he noted the likely pun on air-heir in *Hamlet,* together with related puns on hair-heir and heir-here from other Shakespearian plays.[1] Through a common interlingual pun, whereby *mollis aer* (Lat.: soft air) was equated with *mulier,* the Latin for woman, the attributes of air were frequently associated with the female sex in the English Renaissance. But although Shakespeare could apply this pun quite conventionally, to female dramatic protagonists such as Imogen and Cleopatra, he also used it to trope the beloved youth of the *Sonnets;* while Imogen is compared to 'tender air' (5.5.234, 5.6.447-53) and Cleopatra, in her dying, is 'as soft as air' (5.2.306), the beautiful youth who is initially exhorted by the poet to 'bear' his father's memory through procreation is also a 'tender heir' (*Sonnets,* 1, 4). Similarly, Hamlet's airy and echoic utterances emphasize his failure to conform to traditional forms of masculine identity and sexuality; in particular, he rejects the implicit association which runs through the play, between kingship and 'earing' as copulation. Yet the association of his 'air' imagery with a nexus of images related to hearing as well as to fertility serves to remind us that a significantly different use of the ear is central to Hamlet's punning activity, which often appears to imply vocal play on 'ear' as well as 'air' in relation to an unspoken 'heir'. Although Kökeritz did not mention 'ear' in his hair-heir-here-hear combination, elsewhere he noted homonymic play on ear-here, while he also observed that John Lyly puns on ear-hair in *Midas* (4.1.174f.).[2] Hamlet's quibbling language substitutes an echoic or airy form of auditory attention for sexual or procreative modes of (h)earing. The motions of air as wind were often associated by the ancients with a ghostly and uncannily repetitive auditor, the nymph Echo; Abraham Fraunce declared that Echo 'is nothing els, but the reverberation and reduplication of the ayre. *Eccho* noteth bragging and vaunting, which being contemned and despised, turneth to a bare voyce, a winde, a blast, a thing of nothing',[3] while in Ben Jonson's *Cynthia's Revels,* first performed in 1600, the same year as *Hamlet,* Mercury asks Echo to:

> Salute me with thy repercussive voice,
> That I may know what caverne of the earth
> Contains thy airy spirit, how or where
> I may direct my speech, that thou mayst hear.[4]

There are certainly puns in Hamlet's soliloquies, yet punning requires a social context in order to be fully effective; it is therefore an apt instrument of the satirist. It is also one of the ways in which a rhetorical emphasis upon the singular fate of the tragic protagonist, as articulated through soliloquy or monologue, can be juxtaposed with a dialogic form of self-undoing, in a comic discourse which is less focussed on the subjective 'I', and more on the exposure of an illusory social mask. At the same time, as Gregory Ulmer has observed, the pun can often function as a 'puncept', in its formation of new concepts which may hint at another order of knowledge.[5]

Through multiple entendre, unobserved or hidden relationships can be demonstrated, as various homophones reverberate echoically throughout a text. It is above all through his relentless quibbling that Hamlet meditates upon the sexuality of—and within—families. Yet the oblique meanings of his word-play also extend beyond this immediate sphere of familiarity. For Hamlet reintroduces nature, the body and death into the sphere of courtly discourse, reimaging courtly society in terms of an 'overgrowth' within nature, and thereby reassimilating culture into nature. Thus, in a trope used several times in the play, 'rank' as the foul smell and abundant growth of weeds is substituted for social rank: 'things rank and gross in nature / Possess it merely' (1.2.136-7). Similarly, Claudius' kingship is troped as a sexual excess which is also a 'moor' or wilderness, as well as a disturbing racial difference (3.4.66). And in spite of his several misogynistic diatribes, which attribute this degenerative trend in nature to the female body and female sexuality in particular, through his quibbling language Hamlet also tropes himself as having an obscure figurative association with these processes of decay.

In his encounter with his father's ghost, Hamlet is informed of Claudius' twofold poisoning of the ear of Denmark. Claudius has killed Old Hamlet with 'juice of cursèd hebenon', poured 'in the porches of mine ears' (1.5.62-3); furthermore, he has deceived the court as to the nature of the king's death: 'the whole ear of Denmark / Is by a forgèd process of my death / Rankly abused' (1.5.36-8). But Hamlet, the other ear—and other heir—of Denmark, has already begun to hear Claudius' courtly discourse otherwise—or satirically. He is now fully undeceived by his exchange with the airy spirit. In the ghost's imagery of ears there is an implicit quibble upon 'earing' as copulation, since it is through his incestuous marriage, as well as his murderous attack on the royal ear, that Claudius has interrupted the patrilineal transmission of royal power. The usurper's assumed sexual appetite parallels what Hamlet sees as the disorderly disseminating power of nature—with the result that, in Hamlet's eyes, the state of Denmark 'grows to seed', while Claudius is a 'mildewed ear' of corn (3.4.63). It seems, therefore, that the usurper is a chief tare or weed (in Latin, this could sometimes be *aera* as well as the more common *lolium*) in what Hamlet now defines as the 'unweeded garden' of the world; and of course, like Lucianus in *The Murder of Gonzago,* Claudius has literally used 'midnight weeds' to poison or 'blast' (like a strong wind blighting a crop) both Old Hamlet's life and Young Hamlet's inheritance. But while his uncle, as a 'mildewed ear', is associated by Hamlet with the paradox of a degenerative fertility within nature, Hamlet's own wit performs a more oblique and airy form of generation as well as (h)earing. This is inspired not so much by a commitment to the monarchy as the political (h)earing of the state as by a more feminine and aesthetically responsive form of hearing: one which is appropriate to the narration or the performance of tragedy, and which also interprets human suffering as inextricably interwoven with a tragedy within nature.

In Greek tragedy, the role of listener was an important function of the chorus, as the primary auditors and spectators of the tragic events. It is this echoic and choric mode of hearing which is implicitly required by the ghost of Old Hamlet when he describes his murder to his son; like the mythological figure of Echo, Young Hamlet is left to repeat the ghost's final words: 'Now to my word: / It is "Adieu, adieu, remember me"' (1.5.111-12). But this acutely responsive and implicitly feminine mode of hearing is also comparable to that enacted by Dido when she asks Aeneas to tell her of the fall of Troy, for it is Dido's place which Hamlet effectively occupies when in Act 2 he asks the player to give an impromptu performance of Aeneas' tale. And the more feminine faculty of hearing which motivates Hamlet's interest in the drama also appears to involve responsiveness to the mysterious resonance of nature within language; in the last act, he will trope the more discerning members of society as 'the most fanned and winnowed opinions' (5.2.153): in a figure that is probably derived from the winnowing of the soul by wind in the *Aeneid* (6.740), they are like ears of corn which have been separated out from the chaff by the activity of the wind. Similarly, through his ironic quibbling, Hamlet uses his different style of hearing to effect an airy and echoic reordering of the world around him, in a discursive equivalent to winnowing whose spiritual implications are apparent from the traditional affinity of air and wind with spirit as well as breath (from the Latin *spiritus*). A chief result of this reclassification through punning is a reinterpretation of those distorted relations between kin which are integral to the tragedy.

The theme of a kinship which is both rather less than affectionate and also excessive or incestuous is wittily introduced by Hamlet's first paronomasic play on 'kin' and 'kind'. *Adnominatio* or *paronomasia* (or 'prosonomasia', as it was sometimes called in the Renaissance) depends on a slight change, lengthening or transposition of the letters in a word; Henry Peacham defines the trope as 'a certayne declyninge into a contrarye, by a lykelyhoode of letters, eyther added, chaunged, or taken awaye', while George Puttenham describes it as 'a figure by which ye play with a couple of words or names much resembling, and because the one seemes to answere th'other by manner of illusion, and doth, as it were, nick him, I call him the *Nicknamer* chaunged, or taken awaye'.[6]

In response to Claudius' greeting, 'But now, my cousin Hamlet, and my son—', Hamlet murmurs his aside: 'A little more than kin, and less than kind' (1.2.64-5). The quibble aptly suggests the difficulty of finding suitable words to represent Claudius' outrageous transgression of the conventional boundaries of kinship, which is also, Hamlet implies, a subversion of courtly conventions of *gentilité* or kindness. However, Hamlet's subsequent homophonic quibble on 'son', is made to his uncle's face, inspired by Claudius' own indirect pun on son-sun in his query about Hamlet's mourning garb. To Claudius' question: 'How is it that the clouds still hang on you?', Hamlet replies 'Not so, my lord, I am too much i'th' sun' (1.2.66-7). This ironically suggests that whereas another homophone of kin and kind—king—does describe Claudius' situation, through the traditional association of king with sun it is also related to Hamlet's own position, as a son (and heir). The pun spells out more clearly the still unspoken pun on kin and king, allying an excess of kinship (since Hamlet is not Claudius' son, and Claudius has married his brother's wife) with an image of kingship (the sun) that is itself excessive, apparently because its brightness is incompatible with those conventions of mourning dress which (in contrast to Hamlet) the Danish court has signally failed to observe. But beneath its apparent compliment to the king as sun, the quibble also alludes to a potentially unhealthy surplus of sons or heirs; we are reminded that in spite of his mourning attire, as a king's son, Hamlet too has a homophonic

affinity with the sun, and that, like Claudius, he too may have an unexpected generative potential.

The peculiar difference of Hamlet's disseminating activity is made clear in his retorts to Gertrude. Her description of dying as 'common' is allied by Hamlet's ironic iteration with the 'common' or vulgar usage of 'to die', evoking thereby the commonness of another, sexual, dying; similarly, her question, 'Why seems it so particular with thee?' (1.2.75) is converted by Hamlet into a barbed criticism of the King and Queen's courtly semblance of mourning: 'Seems, madam? Nay, it *is,* I know not "seems"' (1.2.76). This ironic differing of 'seems', which additionally hints at the links between courtly seeming and the spilling of generative seed (from the Latin: *semen*), also anticipates the 'enseamèd bed' that Hamlet will later accuse the Queen of copulating in with Claudius. The rejection by Hamlet of sexual activity is also implied in his subsequent reference to a near-synonym for 'seems', when he tells Gertrude that 'I have that within which passeth show' (1.2.85); later, in his quibbling exchange with Ophelia during the play scene, the sexual meaning of 'show' will be stressed. None the less, it is Hamlet's mocking echoes of courtly language which turn the meaning of 'common' or ordinary words back towards the body and sexuality. He will warn Polonius, in a remark which appears to imply his own erotic intentions towards Ophelia: 'Let her not walk i'th' sun. Conception is a blessing, but not as your daughter may conceive. Friend, look to't' (2.2.186-7). Here the use of a semantic pun, or *antanaclasis,* in which the same word (conception) has two different meanings, clarifies the difference of Hamlet's fertilizing powers from those of his uncle; the nephew's sun-like powers seed a legacy or inheritance which operates above all at the level of signs (from the Greek, *semeion*), in the realm of words and ideas. And while he assists conception, as understanding, in women in particular—for the 'conceits' which are attributed to both Gertrude and Ophelia (3.4.104, 4.5.44) are directly or indirectly inspired by Hamlet—this son also 'conceives' much himself. For him, morbid meditations, or 'conceits' concerning natural and human corruption, are themselves part of a (re)generative process. But if, through his quibble on 'conception', the gendered identity of the heir is effectively called into question, what kind of heir is he?

As *The Murder of Gonzago* is about to be performed, Claudius greets Hamlet with 'How fares our cousin Hamlet?' (3.2.89). Hamlet replies with a triple quibble. Redefining 'fares' in terms of sustenance, he simultaneously converts 'fare' to 'air' by *paronomasia,* and he also quibbles thereby on the unspoken 'heir': 'Excellent, i'faith, of the chameleon's dish. I eat the air, promise-crammed. You cannot feed capons so' (3.2.90-1). Although the word 'heir' is only evoked through homophony in the play, this quibble makes explicit the obscure but important connection which runs through the play, between the dispossessed 'heir' of Denmark and 'air'; at the same time, it presents us with the trope of the displaced heir as a 'chameleon' or shape-shifter who is not, he warns Claudius, as stupid as a castrated cock or 'capon': a bird which allows itself to be over-fed for the table. Instead, it seems, Hamlet is mysteriously feeding on himself (as heir/air), in a way which is not only consistent with the mutable identity of the chameleon (a creature which was nourished by air), but which also hints at his affinity with the mysterious singularity of the double-gendered phoenix. And the substance which Hamlet figuratively feeds on is paradoxically full as well as empty, although as 'promise-crammed', its fecundity is associated only with words. Thus while the empty flattery of Claudius to his 'son' is ironically dismissed by Hamlet, his quibble suggests none the less that the airy substance of speech does afford him a curious kind of nourishment, where none might be expected.

This metamorphosis of the heir of Denmark through and in relation to air begins, of course, on the battlements of Elsinore, where, as Hamlet and his companions wait for the ghost to appear, he declares: 'The air bites shrewdly, it is very cold'. To this Horatio replies: 'It is a nipping and an eager air' (1.4.1-2). His words aptly convey the change that has already begun to affect Hamlet, in his assumption of a satiric demeanour, expressed through a mordant or biting wit which is 'eager', or sour. In its later echo by the ghost's reference to the curdling of his blood by Claudius' poison, 'like eager droppings into milk' (1.5.69), this reference to the eager air, ear or heir attributes to Hamlet a property of bitterness which parallels the corrupting effects of Claudius' fratricide. But these images in Act 1 also give a new, auto-erotic dimension to Hamlet's satiric temper. For as he develops a new, biting relationship to the air, as well as to the courtly language (or promises) which fill it, he is also consuming his identity as heir.

In feeding upon himself (as well as others) through his mordant quibbling, Hamlet plays the part of Narcissus as well as Echo. Like the addressee of Shakespeare's *Sonnets,* he can be accused of self-love, or of 'having traffic with thyself alone' (*Sonnets,* 4.9). But in also assuming the implicitly feminine role of the 'tender heir' (as *mollis aer* or *mulier*) who will bear the father's memory (*Sonnets,* 1.4), Hamlet is able to redefine both his father's and his own inheritance verbally or vocally, through his airy conceits. In this respect, his own legacy or inheritance will be twofold: while his 'story' is bequeathed directly to Horatio, who by telling it will preserve his name, it is Fortinbras who will be the ultimate recipient both of that story and of Hamlet's 'dying voice'—which chooses him, perforce, as the future king of Denmark. Significantly, neither man is even a member of Hamlet's kin-group, much less his child. Hamlet thereby refigures inheritance in

terms of a phoenix-like succession to other men (and most importantly, to two rather than to one), as a succession which circumvents the generative obligations of patriliny. And this formation of a different bonding 'between men'—a bonding across rather than within families—is effected by the historical reverberations of Hamlet's echoing voice.

When Polonius refers to Hamlet's replies as 'pregnant', he attributes a feminine or fecund character to his quibbling; similarly, the tropes and puns used by Claudius of Hamlet's melancholy or madness figure it as concealing an airy fecundity which is apparently feminine. The prince is twice imaged as a female bird on her nest in late spring or early summer: 'There's something in his soul / O'er which his melancholy sits on brood' (3.1.167-8);

> This is mere madness,
> And thus a while the fit will work on him.
> Anon, as patient as the female dove
> When that her golden couplets are disclosed,
> His silence will sit drooping
>
> (5.1.281-5)

But a more grotesque, and implicitly masculine, version of this differing of gendered models of generation is later proposed by Hamlet himself when, in his remark to Polonius about the dangers of Ophelia walking 'i' the sun', he defines the sun as a breeder of worms or maggots which eat the flesh, and so accelerate the decay of dead matter: 'For if the sun breed maggots in a dead dog, being a good kissing carrion—' (2.2.182-3). Yet in the myth of the phoenix as reported by Pliny (an account which was often cited in the Renaissance), a worm or maggot plays a central part in the bird's solitary work of regeneration through self-consumption: Pliny tells us that 'from its bones and marrow is born first a sort of maggot, and this grows into a chicken'.[7]

In his reflexive relationship to air, therefore, Hamlet has a superficial resemblance to Narcissus as well as Echo. However, several of the images I have mentioned were connected in Renaissance iconography with Hermes or Mercury, a classical deity whose identity was especially marked by paradox and doubleness. This god, whose emblematic creature was a cock, herald of the dawn, and who was frequently depicted with a pipe as well as his more familiar caduceus, combined his role as a divine messenger and god of eloquence with attributes of trickery, secrecy and concealment; according to Richard Linche in *The Fountaine of Ancient Fiction:* 'Mercurie was often taken for that light of knowledge, & spirit of understanding, which guides men to the true conceavement of darke and enigmaticall sentences'.[8] And Mercury's identification by Macrobius with 'that power [of the sun] from which comes speech' hints at another, solar, aspect of his classical identity, whereby he was associated with the return of fertility to the earth in springtime.[9] The affinity between Mercury and obscure yet meaningful utterances makes it hardly surprising that in *Cynthia's Revels* it is Mercury who temporarily restores the speech of Echo, inviting her to 'strike music from the spheres, / And with thy golden raptures swell our ears' (1.2.63-4). It was this play, in fact, which was the first production of the 'little eyases', or young hawks, whose 'eyrie' was the Blackfriars playhouse: the Children of the Chapel.

Yet Charles Dempsey has recently pointed out, in his reinterpretation of Botticelli's *Primavera*, that it was Mercury as a wind-god (for example, in the *Aeneid*, 4, 223ff.), able to calm harsh winds and storms, and to disperse clouds, who was most explicitly regarded as a god of spring, or *Mercurius Ver*.

> Botticelli shows Mercury dispersing and softening clouds with his upraised caduceus in the *Primavera*, a representation of him that unequivocally identifies him as acting in his archaic persona as a springtime wind god. By this action he ends the season that began with the warming west blowing its regenerative breath over the bare earth, shown as Zephyr and Chloris, and that reaches its fullness in April, the month presided over by Venus.[10]

In the *Primavera*, clusters of seeds swirl about the god's winged sandals, but no act of copulation is associated with this generative process. Instead, Mercury's fertilizing role is implied to supplement rather than complement that of Venus as a goddess of nature. Indeed, although the mythographers are understandably silent on the subject, their curious debates about whether or not Mercury has a beard, together with the emphasis on his youthfulness (in other words, his difference from adult masculinity), created a distinct aura of ambiguity around his sexual identity, as Joseph A. Porter has shown.[11]

The *Primavera* suggests that Mercury enjoys a different and more harmonious relationship with the feminine generative principle within nature from that attributed to figures of masculine generation. In alchemical texts, Mercury likewise emblematized the mysterious changes wrought within nature or matter by a principle of ambiguous gender, sometimes called *Mercurius duplex;* in this literature, 'our Mercury' was analogous to the *spiritus* which was the secret transforming substance within matter, and was variously described as 'divine rain', 'May dew', 'dew of heaven', 'our honey'. Such was its ambivalent character, however, that alchemical Mercury was also identified with that part of matter which, phoenix-like, fed upon itself in order to produce transmutation.[12]

Similarly, Hamlet's puns may indeed articulate a covert but coherent level of meaning, in a Renaissance alchemization of language. While his mercurial messages function to disrupt the fixity of social identities—along with the embassies or utterances of aberrant father figures—they hint too at the existence of a different order, hidden within the visible one. Douglas Brooks-Davies has pointed out that the imagery of Mercury was often appropriated by royalist panegyrics during the Renaissance;[13] yet in Mercury's oblique association with Hamlet, what appears to be figured is the enigmatic difference of a son and heir who is identified with 'th'incorporal air' and its movements, and hence with a grotesque form of verbal as well as vernal regeneration—through worms of maggots. In French, worms are *vers;* this not only links spring—*le ver*—with the worm, but could also suggest an additional pun in Hamlet's discourse of worms: on the putrefying activity of *vers* as verse. This serves to remind us that in spite of a nominal affinity, Hamlet never occupies the solid place of the earthly father; instead he is distinguished by a mutability of identity which implicates him in the more sexually ambiguous spheres of nature and spirit, and identifies him especially with the mobility of air or wind. It is noteworthy in this connection that it is the mercurial bird, the cock (whose castrated equivalent—the capon—Hamlet mentions in his ironic remark to Claudius about eating the air), which by its crowing dispels the apparition of the paternal ghost in the first scene of the play, thereby eliciting allusions to the cock's connection with that other son/sun figure, Christ, with whom the *Mercurius* of the alchemists was indeed often equated (1.1.119-46).

Hamlet's satirical rejection of the generative activity—or 'earing'—which would make a son a father has often been dismissed as misogyny; by this move, however, he confirms his separation from that genealogy of fathers upon which a hereditary (in contrast to an elective) model of kingship depends. And curiously, this is a dislocation which Claudius' assumption of the throne has already initiated. Yet through his mercurial and quibbling language 'of darke and enigmaticall sentences' Hamlet accords the final inheritance of all costly or aristocratic breeding to nature, and 'my lady Worm': 'Here's fine revolution, an we had the trick to see't' (5.1.88-9).

Notes

[1] Helgë Kökeritz, *Shakespeare's Pronunciation* (New Haven, 1953), pp. 90-1, 111. Kökeritz observes that air-heir are punned on by Lyly in *Mother Bombie,* 2.2.24-6 and 5.3.13, and are given as homonyms in Charles Butler, *English Grammar* (1634) and R. Hodges, *A Special Help to Orthographie* (1643). He emphasizes that 'no homonymic pun has been admitted here which has not stood the combined test of phonology and context' (pp. 64-5). See also Margreta de Grazia and Peter Stallybrass, 'The materiality of the

Shakespearian text', *Shakespeare Quarterly,* 44 (Fall 1993), 3, pp. 255-83, where the wordplay in *Macbeth* on air-hair-heir is discussed.

[2] Kökeritz, *Shakespeare's Pronunciation,* p. 111. See also Stephen Booth's comment on 'hearsay' in Sonnet 21, line 13, in his edition of *Shakespeare's Sonnets* (New Haven, 1978).

[3] Abraham Fraunce, *The Third Part of the Countesse of Pembrokes Yvychurch: entituled, 'Amintas Dale'* (London, 1592), p. 15ʳ.

[4] Ben Jonson, *'Cynthia's Revels',* in *The Complete Plays of Ben Jonson,* ed. G. A. Wilkes, vol. 11 (Oxford, 1981), 1.1.104-7.

[5] Gregory Ulmer, 'The Puncept in Grammatology', in *On Puns: The Foundation of Letters,* ed. Jonathan Culler (Oxford, 1988), pp. 164-90.

[6] Henry Peacham, *The Garden of Eloquence* (London, 1577), sig. Kiiʳ; George Puttenham, *The Arte of English Poesie,* eds. G. D. Wilcox and Alice Walker (Cambridge, 1936), pp. 168-9.

[7] Pliny, *Natural History,* trans. H. Rackham (London, 1938), vol. 3, x, ii, p. 294.

[8] Richard Linche, *The Fountaine of Ancient Fiction* (London, 1599), Riʳ-Riᵛ.

[9] Macrobius, *The Saturnalia,* trans. Percival Vaughan Davies (New York, 1969), pp. 114-15.

[10] Charles Dempsey, *The Portrayal of Love: Botticelli's 'Primavera' and Humanist Culture at the Time of Lorenzo the Magnificent* (Princeton, 1992), p. 40.

[11] See Joseph A. Porter, *Shakespeare's Mercutio: his History and Drama* (Chapel Hill, 1988), pp. 32-53.

[12] Charles Nicholl, *The Chemical Theatre* (London, 1980), p. 46.

[13] Douglas Brooks-Davies, *The Mercurian Monarch: magical politics from Spenser to Pope* (Manchester, 1983), passim.

Source: "Hamlet's Ear," in *Shakespeare Survey: An Annual Survey of Shakespeare Studies and Production*, Vol. 50, 1997, pp. 57-64.

The Return of the Domestic in *Coriolanus*

Ann C. Christensen, *University of Houston*

I

Critical responses to *Coriolanus* tend to concentrate on two dominant issues: the political and the maternal. Approaches to the former typically address the play's representation of the polis, the conflicts between patricians and plebeians, and draw on Shakespeare's historical sources of Plutarch, Livy, and Machiavelli as well as contemporary contexts such as the food shortages and Midlands enclosure uprisings of the early seventeenth century.[1] Understandably, maternal issues—from milk to mildness—dominate psychoanalytic and gender studies of the play and focus on Volumnia—her curious attitude towards nurture, her role in forming her son, his responses to "feeding and dependency."[2] Of course, neither approach wholly neglects the other.[3] Stanley Cavell neatly summarizes the two critical strains while noting that both recognize the play's central concern with nurture: "the play lends itself equally, or anyway naturally, to psychological and to political readings: both perspectives are, for example, interested in who produces food and in how food is distributed and paid for. From a psychological perspective . . . the play directs us to an interest in the development of Coriolanus's character. From a political perspective the play directs us to an interest in whether the patricians or the plebeians are right in their conflict."[4] The present study poses a third term, the domestic, to encompass both the political and maternal issues raised by the play, along with feeding and nurture. In *Coriolanus,* home is a place and an idea which localizes the diffuse conflicts in family and state.[5] A category at once more narrow than "politics" and "gender" and more general than "maternal," the domestic accounts for the complex interplay of gender, power, nurture, family, and state by addressing the play's convoluted estimations of "home" and not home. The Shakespearean household houses the family, while serving as a metaphor for the early modern state.[6] By domestic I mean both literal households and the people, objects, and activities associated with the place where one lives; for the purposes of this essay, the category covers both home and homeland, "[t]he country, our dear nurse" (V.iii.110). Because it conveys a sense of location, "domestic" is especially suited to address this play so rich in architectural metaphors and so dependent upon the physical boundaries—city gates and thresholds—of homes, Rome, and Corioli/Antium.[7]

Coriolanus challenges expectations concerning "home" as protected space, the source of familiarity and com-

fort, by constructing public and private in mutually constituting tension—a relation resisted by Marcius, who tries to polarize the spheres in an effort to maintain autonomy.[8] For him there is a reversal whereby "home" is seen as both non-compelling and threatening while "not-home," here enemy territory, demands the hero's involvement and lends him succor. While the domestic is denigrated for laxity, wartime activities are part of the "stirring world" (IV.v.220-1). So Marcius comes to "hate" his "birthplace," in all its connotations of Rome, Volumnia, family life—in short, the domestic—and instead embraces the Volscian towns of Corioli and Antium, his enemy's "hearth" (IV.iv.23-4). His relationship with Rome as both native city and domicile is marked by departure[9]—whether in defense of or in banishment from the city. Even his achieved or promised returns fail to be true "home-comings": after victory at Corioles he defers going home by visiting the patricians "[e]re in our own house I do shade my head" (II.i.184-5); his threatened return to conquer his homeland is aborted at the threshold, "even to / The gates of Rome" (V.vi.75-6), and he is killed as a traitor in the city where he was renamed.

Gail Kern Paster attributes the relative exclusion of private settings from the world of the play to the demands of Roman citizenship, noting that "extreme civic consciousness" pervades even the one obviously domestic scene, I.iii, in which domestic concerns are displaced by grander assertions of civic obligation—breeding sons for warfare.[10] While this context of sacrifice of the personal for the civic certainly informs Shakespeare's depiction of Rome, the hero's recurrent flights from his household and his quest for revenge against his homeland reflect the tensions accompanying the separation of the spheres in early modern England—tensions surrounding the function and authority of domestic space and the necessary reevaluations of work and home, production and consumption, labor and leisure under nascent capitalism. Shakespeare presents English concerns through Rome. The conflicting definitions of the domestic sphere in the play and Marcius's failed attempt to repress domestic ties result in a sense of the deep and materially efficacious interactions between public and private realms of experience.

The relative significance of public and private is challenged from the beginning as Caius Marcius, the "public man," in fact detests "the public" in both senses of the word: the populace from whom he must gain approval, along with his public role of statesman. When faced with the requisite public display of wounds, he offers instead to show them only "in private" (II.iii.74, 161). While he appears always uncomfortable on the public street, Volumnia walks tall among the people of Rome, eventually becoming their "patroness" (V.v.1). The whole project of the early republic itself translates the private to the public through its reliance upon the individual voices of (private) citizens to create (public) assent.[11] Furthermore, it is as his "private friend" that Volumnia convinces her son to abandon his political enterprise, upsetting traditional hierarchies between family and state, private and public, and the places of women and men within these structures.[12] It is, finally, the denial of domestic affiliations that *Coriolanus* exposes to be disastrous because the private and public arenas cannot be separated. A fear that domestic commitments at best distract men from more worthy relationships and activities and at worst destroy them altogether leads Marcius to endorse a false separation of the spheres.

Because Volumnia and her train prevail in V.iii in convincing the hero to abandon his assault on Rome, many readers see the play as a triumph for familial and domestic ties, even if short-lived and hard-won (for her suit proves "most mortal" to him [V.iii.189]): "[M]ilitary commitment, resisting civic pressure, yields to domestic."[13] While such conclusions do emerge from real conflicts in the play, we ought not weigh too heavily the final triumph of mother Rome via mother Volumnia at the expense of masculine military endeavors (or *virtu*) which she (and the play) has all along construed through the prism of the domestic.[14] Coriolanus's efforts to unmake his domestic identity as both Roman citizen and "son, . . . husband, and . . . father" prove fatal (V.iii.102). "Wife, mother, child, I know not. My affairs / Are servanted to others" (V.ii.78-9); "No more infected with my country's love / That when I parted hence" (V.vi.71-2): thus does he claim immunity from the domestic realm which shaped him.

For a play containing arguably only two scenes set in domestic interiors (I.iii and IV.v), it seems to some ironic that the word "home" occurs more frequently in this play than in any other of Shakespeare's plays.[15] A locus so little represented, but so verbally omnipresent, home in fact exerts immense "shaping power" in the play; it functions rhetorically and dramatically to compete for Marcius's (and other warriors') identification. For this reason public men have a habit of dismissing home ties in hyperbolic assertions of commitment to public causes. This tendency is underpinned by the fear that the domestic has a hold on those who attempt to extricate themselves from it. Marcius, for example, recognizes that the domestic economy operates by a system of exchange and cooperation—a notion promoted in seventeenth-century advice manuals, and one anathema to a man determined to act autonomously: "Alone I did it" (V.vi.115).

Janet Adelman describes this fear as one of dependence on the "outside world" in general and on the mother in particular;[16] here precisely is where the domestic mediates between the two spheres, for speakers continually remind us of the centrality of the domestic even as they attempt to diminish its importance.

Each instance of acknowledging that centrality is both undermined and reasserted through flamboyant figurative language. For example, the remembered hospitality rendered by the poor man of Corioles causes Marcius to spare the captive: "I sometime lay here in Corioles / At a poor man's house; he used me kindly. / . . . I request you / To give my poor host freedom" (I.ix.81-2, 85-6). Yet this rare moment of mildness weirdly serves the hero's larger investment in the renunciation of domestic debts. For Marcius's suit so convinces Cominius that he assures him, "Were he [the Volscian host] the butcher of my son, he should / Be free as is the wind. Deliver him, Titus" (lines 87-8).[17] No sooner is this unsolicited vow uttered than Aufidius promises similarly. Echoing the suppression of fraternal bonds, he vows to hunt Marcius: "Where I find him, were it / At home, upon my brother's guard, even there, / Against the hospitable canon, would I / Wash my fierce hand in's heart" (I.x.24-7). The hospitable canon holds greater sway, it seems, when the host is not a member of one's own family. This phenomenon whereby home and non-home change places becomes particularly true when Marcius, banished from his homeland, is welcomed instead at Aufidius's feast though he "[a]ppear not like a guest" (IV.v.6). In Antium Marcius takes on a civil, even polite, demeanor so unlike his arrogance at home (see IV.iv.7, 10, 11). The interchange between him and Aufidius's servingmen is abated by Marcius's assurance that he'll "not hurt [their] hearth" (IV.v.24-5). That his purpose in coming to Antium is to attack his homeland emphasizes that, for Marcius, sparing an enemy's hearth depends on sacrificing one's own. So absolute a separation of the spheres results in tragedy.

II

The play insists on the deep connections between the private and the public evidenced, as Paster observes, in the pervasive language of kinship to convey relations, for example, between patrician and plebe, victor and vanquished, warrior and enemy.[18] Domestic metaphors show how private life inflects public situations, making domestic concerns as prominent as those which are conventionally political. For example, a Roman spy's colloquialism tellingly depicts political conflict in terms of domestic discord: "I have heard it said, the fittest time to corrupt a man's wife is when she's fallen out with her husband" (IV.iii.28-30). A more extended illustration of the relation between the domestic and the public is I.iii, the only women-centered domestic scene in the play, which continually figures personal, familial experience in relation to public action. Imagining that her son were her husband, Volumnia conflates family roles, preferring "Coriolanus's absence on the battlefield to conjugal embraces as she, his mother, rejoiced more in the news of his first glory in battle than in the news of the birth of a boy."[19] The scene goes on both to celebrate and parody domestic life. Child's play is the "mammocking" of butterflies and mimicking of the father; women's needlework is "fine" yet futile; the "manifest housekeepers" such as Penelope and Virgilia, Marcius's stay-at-home wife, are dutiful bores: "You would be another Penelope; yet they say all the yarn she spun in Ulysses' absence did but fill Ithaca full of moths," Valeria teases (I.iii.79-81). For all its conventionality, the women's discourse encompasses public affairs as well as traditional "women's issues." Valeria's news of the army's progress, which she has heard from a senator (lines 92-8), reflects the on-going and vital dialogue between public officials and private citizens. Amidst talk of needlework, children, and the brief wars, the two matrons plan to attend on a "good lady that lies in" (line 74). Here a glimpse of domestic community appears, however momentarily, as both politically astute and tied to reproductive and social life.

This hopeful, even playful, domestic portrait is counterposed by an image of home that is an alien and a threatening landscape in the play. Whereas other Shakespearean tragedies employ foreign or uninhabited space to define the hero's identity and to contrast the human or social landscape, for Marcius there is no such place; as Adrian Poole puts it, there is, "no Dover cliff, no sea, nor even after all a fen in which he could fancy himself as a dragon . . . no empty or 'wild' space in which he could face the strangeness in himself and give it utterance, as Lear and Macbeth do."[20] The wilderness for Marcius—the realm to be denied, renounced, set apart, cast off—is the domestic. Neither the battlefield, for that has been a home to Marcius since youth (I.iii.13-7), nor Antium, for Marcius reenters that city like a developer sizing up his newly acquired property (IV.iv.1-4), the "other" for him is ironically home. In renouncing local affiliations, he indirectly acknowledges the terrifying force behind the domestic. The "puny battle" waged by the Volscians against Marcius at the end appears as a nightmare return of the repressed. It is after all the widows and orphans—the fragments of family—of Antium who dismember Marcius at last. The rabble's wrath originates in these "broken homes."[21]

Volumnia demonstrates, in a different way, the political efficacy of the domestic sphere. Her looming maternal presence classes her with Lady Macbeth and misleads critics as to both the primacy of family bonds as well as their exclusively maternal origin in the play. True, Volumnia places great stock in her identification

with motherhood. Yet she uses this identification in public and political ways throughout the play, blurring the distinctions between family and state. Coppélia Kahn aptly notes Volumnia's tendency to construct herself in terms that "stress her role as bearer and nurturer as to make her [Coriolanus's] creator."[22] She reminds her son that "Thy valiantness was mine, thou suck'st it from me," and establishes his birth and military success as the pinnacles of her own existence: "I sprang not more in joy at first hearing he was a man-child than now in first seeing he had proved himself a man" (III.ii.129, I.iii.15-7). It is also true that Virgilia deploys the same strategy in the supplication scene (V.iii.125-7). But Volumnia's success is rooted in her ability to exploit her highly politicized "maternity" when she kneels before her son in the final act. Her achievement derives from the way she plays upon and threatens to unmake her "private friend[ship]" with Coriolanus, in the way she sees her action as politically urgent.[23]

Adelman imputes the "maternal malevolence" of such Shakespearean characters as Volumnia and Lady Macbeth to "the [early modern] culture's fear of maternal nursery."[24] Such fear and fantasy are aimed at developing forms of domestic economy as well as motherhood: as the ideological separation of the spheres took hold in early modern imaginations, cultural evaluations of space, work, worth, and gender shifted to accommodate the demands of nascent capitalism. In this transitional period anxieties surrounded women's power to sustain families, not only through breast-milk, but through other social forms of authority as well—the everyday running of the household, the supervision of servants, the rearing of children. The proliferation of domestic conduct manuals and sermons on "domestical duties" over the course of the seventeenth century attests to this anxiety.[25] In this play about "the organization of the body politic and about how that body is fed,"[26] household government is crucially implicated by political agents such as tribunes and warriors who threaten to displace domestic experience. *Coriolanus* bodies forth an ambivalent domestic sphere in which gender identities are articulated, affirmed, and challenged. The domestic sphere is uneasily occupied, indeed dominated by women, in both Rome, where the ladies await news from abroad, and Corioli, where widows and orphans survive the wars, and where a peaceful domesticity is decried as a wasteful luxury, "a great maker of cuckolds" (IV.v.220-31). The play's opposition between the civic life of Rome and private households properly inhabited by women, children, and the fickle plebeians appears as a dramatic analog to the nascent bourgeois separation of household and business under construction in early modern England. The ways in which *Coriolanus* deploys "home" rhetorically to define and represent self and other locates in the domestic the intersection of the political and the maternal.

III

The play articulates these cultural tensions by envisaging the domestic sphere alternately as impoverished and potent. "Home" is less a staged locus than an insult in the play, more often used adverbially than nominally.[27] Volumnia herself equates action or productivity with a necessary absence from home when she claims to prefer the noble death of eleven (hypothetical) sons in battle "than [have] one voluptuously surfeit out of action" at home (I.iii.21-3). The congenital phobia of eating in Marcius and Volumnia as well as the consumptive nature of "home" having been ably treated elsewhere, I am concerned with the dual evaluations of "home" as both constitutive force integral to the public sphere and a debilitated, second-best place where only the weak reside: for example, Marcius fights abroad, while the people stay home; Menenius, the notably mild patrician, is a "perfecter giber for the table than a necessary bencher in the Capitol" (II.i.74-6).[28]

The twin offenses of being a Volscian or a homebody register the ambivalence of the domestic. Marcius equates "retire[ment]" or retreat with otherness. "He that retires," challenging his army at the gates of Corioles, "I'll take him for a Volsce" (I.iv.28), eventually bidding the Romans, "Mend and charge home, / . . . we'll beat them to their wives" (lines 38, 41). While most editors gloss "home" as an adverb, meaning "to the utmost," the fact that Marcius's charge yokes "home" with "wives" lends a sexual, and specifically domestic cast to the image. Marcius's invocation of the wives of the enemy—a category of person mentioned frequently in the play (IV.iv.2, II.i.168, V.vi.150)—specifies the association of home with female relations and, like Volumnia's fantasy, shows the preference for manly action against the "voluptuous surfeit" of home-dwelling.

Household objects themselves as well as domestic activities take on a negative cast and seem irrelevant to those of the political world; yet the play's central conflict over the price and availability of corn reminds us of the political valence of ordinary domestic items such as tools and foodstuffs. The first citizen calls the others to action: "Let us revenge this with our pikes ere / we become rakes; for the gods know I speak this in / hunger for bread, not in thirst for revenge" (I.i.20-22). Marcius fails to see the political import of pikes and bread. He refuses the spoils awarded him, and is baffled by the Roman soldiers looting "[c]ushions, leaden spoons, / Irons of a doit" while he himself remains ready for further battle: "My work hath yet not warmed me" (I.v.5-6, 17). To "keep at home" is one way to express surrender, as when Menenius wavers in his campaign to address Marcius in his banishment (V.i.7).[29] The ability of domestic discourse to comprehend the public life in the streets, senate, and on the battlefield appears in Menenius's theory of the value of a hot meal: "He was not taken well; he had not dined" (V.i.50). While Menenius's assumption does not apply to Marcius, we should not fail to notice that the play supports the belief that domestic comforts, including meals, have the positive power to soften and the negative power to emasculate their consumers. Menenius pursues his humors theory, noting that without adequate nourishment,

> We . . . are unapt
> To give or to forgive; but when we have stuffed
> These pipes and these conveyances of our blood
> With wine and feeding, we have suppler souls
> Than in our priest-like fasts.
>
> (lines 52-6)

The "suppler souls" of well-fed householders compare favorably, in Menenius's metaphor, to the rigidity of fasting priests. In this image, home life implies satiety, emotional exchange ("to give or to forgive"), erotic fulfillment, family, and nurture—a vision challenged in the alternative domestic discourses of the play.

As if returning home were a type of "retirement" from politics, the patricians continually command the people home, off the public streets, out of the political fray. So Menenius tells the homely tale of the belly in an effort to send the people home. In the confrontation between the people and Marcius in act III, Menenius and senators alike urge one another home (III.i.230, 234), and Brutus orders Marcius pursued "to his house" and plucked thence while bidding his co-agitator to meet in the market-place: "Go not home" (lines 308, 330). When things get too heated, the tribunes Sicinius and Brutus repeat their wish to dismiss the people home (IV.ii.1, 5, 7) just before Volumnia makes her invidious comparison between the Capitol and "[t]he meanest house in Rome" (IV.ii.40)—a rhetorical foray which Menenius celebrates: "You have told them home" (IV.ii.48). Going home means giving up political action.

In this play, which climaxes in the mutual banishment of citizens and hero (III.iii.117-24), the ejection from home—whether literal or metaphorical—is equally fraught. For example, Marcius verbally alienates the people by expressing his belief that they are barbarians rather than native Romans (III.i.238-40). The ultimate manifestation of this insult is Volumnia's taunt that her son is in fact a Volscian bastard, a point to which I return below (V.iii.178). "Home" then alternately images the Roman and non-Roman, the plebeian and patrician, the familiar and barbaric, weakening surfeit and strengthening nurture.

That the positive values of domestic experience such as comfort, familiarity, and nurture have a place in

Roman civic life inflects the language men use to express public matters. As noted, Marcius tries to deny the authority of the domestic sphere by denying his affiliation with it, "As if a man were author of himself / And knew no other kin" (V.iii.36-7). Yet such a statement depends on the very assertion of kinship, on the inescapable ties to a realm of personal history. In the use of this rhetorical posture he is joined by both Volscian and Roman men. Coriolanus, Cominius, and Aufidius independently cast their military relations in terms of their own wedding days (and nights!) and family ties, thereby acknowledging the crucial power of the domestic aspect of their lives, as they pretend to disown it.[30]

Masculine relations in the Senate and on the battlefield are figured not only as heterosexual (marital) relations, as Adelman has argued, but also in terms of the whole of "private" life.[31] *Coriolanus* flattens out Shakespeare's "division of experience," showing that the public sphere of war and statecraft is meaningless without reference to private, domestic foundations. Just as the debt to a foreign host is seen to supersede paternal protection in Cominius's rhetoric, and just as the compulsion of hate transcends Aufidius's brotherly bonds, so are other domestic relations deployed as ironic standards against which to measure non-domestic commitments. In a quasi-romantic moment of battle, Cominius calls Marcius the "Flower of warriors" (I.vi.32); as they embrace Marcius exclaims:

> O, let me clip ye
> In arms as sound as when I woo'd, in heart
> As merry as when our nuptial day was done
> And tapers burnt to bedward!
>
> (lines 29-32)

Comparing the experience of camaraderie in combat to his courtship and consummation of marriage, Marcius shows how fundamental (and handy) domestic metaphors are in conveying other experiences. The "arms" and "heart" that won Virgilia now serve the state and join him to comrades. By accretion this figural speech establishes the domestic not so much as a vehicle for metaphor but as a realm of experience upon which other, extramural relationships are based.

In similar situations Cominius and Aufidius find rhetorical capital in the invocation of family ties. Cominius responds to the news of his friend's banishment with overwhelming patriotism:

> I do love
> My country's good with a respect more
>   tender,
> More holy and profound, than mine own life,
> My dear wive's estimate, her womb's increase
> And treasure of my loins;
>
> (III.iii.111-5)

This testimonial to public spirit depends on the sanctity of the domestic economy (see "estimate," "increase," "treasure"). Similarly, Aufidius relates his alliance with Coriolanus to his desire for his wife when crossing the threshold into domestic space. Momentarily, this public affiliation supersedes even the essential pleasures of sex, home, marriage:

> Know thou first,
> I lov'd the maid I married; never man
> Sighed truer breath. But that I see thee here,
> Thou noble thing, more dances my rapt heart
> Than when I first my wedded mistress saw
> Bestride my threshold.
>
> (IV.v.114-9)

As if to substantiate his assurance to Marcius, Aufidius welcomes him over his "threshold" and "makes a / mistress of" his guest (IV.v.197-8). Aufidius resubscribes to the code of hospitality once broken by setting Coriolanus "at upper end o' th' / table" (IV.v.195-6). The rendering of political bonds in terms of domestic union furthers the play's insistence that the two spheres are integrated.

This pattern whereby politico-military alliances are forged on the model of domestic bonds is emphasized by the strategic repetition of "threshold"—that potent liminal space between inside and outside, which can be captured in performance.[32] Entryways and gates of all sorts signal transformation in the play as when Caius Marcius enters and emerges bloody from the city gates of Corioles and is renamed for the conquest (I.ix), again when he is reborn under Aufidius's roof as traitor to Rome (IV.v), and differently when Virgilia follows the other women to her husband's encampment (V.iii). Interestingly, the term threshold occurs twice in this play (and only six times altogether in the Shakespeare canon).[33] It is first used by Virgilia in lines already alluded to as she refuses to budge over her threshold onto the public streets (I.iii.71-2). Second, it is uttered at this reunion by Aufidius who remembers his bride entering his threshold—a memory invoked in order to ennoble the present occasion.[34] This word is in each case uttered from within domestic settings as if to suggest that its transformational power originates there. Although these two domestic thresholds of the play are circumscribed spatially (cf. Valeria's judgment of Virgilia, "Fie, you confine yourself most unreasonably" [I.iii.73]) and temporally (Virgilia's self-elected place is in the home *until* her husband's return, Aufidius's domestic identity is chiefly a past-tense construction, remembered "when . . . first" he married), in fact, the private, interior spaces of the play help to define that "world elsewhere" which Marcius seeks.

The repeated attempts to deny the power of domestic space extend to the troubling representations of household inhabitants: Virgilia, whose commitment to keeping house is derided by the older women; the wine-swilling Menenius; the futilely-spinning Penelope. The literal fact that widows and orphans are necessary results of warfare heightens the rhetorical force of unmaking domestic ties, and the play frequently dwells on "broken families."[35] Rather than boast of how many men he has killed, Coriolanus focuses on his destruction and division of families: the wives and boys in Antium, the "widows in Corioles" and "mothers that lack sons" (II.i.168-9).[36] Returning to the city he invaded, Coriolanus addresses Antium with a mixture of pride and fear:

> 'Tis I that made thy widows. Many an heir
> Of these fair edifices 'fore my wars
> Have I heard groan and drop. Then know me
>   not,
> Lest that thy wives with spits and boys with
>   stones
> In puny battle slay me.
>
> (IV.iv.2-6)

In this instance of Shakespeare's keenest irony, it seems unlikely that Marcius doubts the outcome of a "puny battle" waged by housewives and children. Yet he knows he is vulnerable, at the moment unarmed, undefended, unallied. Having denigrated the private citizens of Rome, he arrives here and subjects himself to a foreign version of the same danger. The spit—the same symbolic kitchen tool envisaged in popular iconography and contemporary drama—is indeed potent as the symbolic hub of the household and as a weapon.[37] An ordinary household tool like the pikes, "stiff bats and clubs" of the Roman commoners, the spit can be used for political ends. The fact that a confluence of "widows" and "people" "tear[s] him to pieces," crying vengeance for their families—"He killed my son!— My daughter!—He killed my / cousin Marcus! He killed my father!" (V.vi.119-21)—asserts the real threat the domestic sphere poses to a soldier whose "work" destroys family bonds.

Although the Volscian people kill Marcius, in many ways they constitute the "collective double" of the Romans, and on stage the same actors almost always play both crowds.[38] The people of Rome share their dual representation: they, too, are feminized and domesticated; they, too, pose a real political threat to Marcius. As Adelman notes, "The crowd, then, is both dependent, unmanly, contemptible—and terrifyingly ready to rise up and devour Coriolanus."[39] In II.i, amidst the "Flourish" and "cornets" of Marcius's return, Brutus grudgingly reports on the people's making a spectacle of the victor:

> Your prattling nurse
> Into a rapture lets her baby cry,
> While she chats [chatters about] him; the
>   kitchen malkin pins

> Her richest lockram [cheap linen] 'bout her
>   reechy neck,
> Clamb'ring the walls to eye him.
>
> (lines 195-9)

Brutus's characterization of his own constituents in the lurid detail of their smothering up "walls . . . [s]talls, bulks, [and] windows" signals his disdain for the working classes but also his awareness of their political importance (II.i.199). His description of these working-class women, the nurse and the malkin—both entrusted with domestic nurture—as representatives of the people, serves to identify the crowd with the alternately devalued and empowered domestic sphere.[40] This logic denies the political efficacy of the people, attempting to divorce the domestic sphere from the political machine. Fearful that Marcius's power will slacken "our office," Brutus sets up an opposition between, on the one hand, private citizens like nurses and slatterns, whose presence on the streets is obscene, and, on the other, political leaders like himself who deserve to rule (II.i.211-2).

One act later Marcius similarly figures as inconsequential the "virgin voice / That babies lulls asleep" (III.ii.114-5); he likewise denigrates the speech of harlots, eunuchs, schoolboys, and beggars—all associated with domesticity, sexuality, and powerlessness. The "voice[s]," "tear[s]," and "tongue[s]" of the inactive are incompatible with "[his] throat of war" (line 112). His disdain vents against the plebeians' carnality, contingency, and dependence; he despises their "desire, be it desire for food, for spoils, for a voice, for a vote."[41] Significantly, the desires of the androgynous lower-classes associate them with consumption and with the domestic, from which the hero distances himself. Aufidius's indictment of Coriolanus presents with ironic force the power of the domestic sphere. He reports to the Volscian heads of state:

> He has betrayed your business and given up,
> For certain drops of salt, your city Rome—
> . . . to his wife and mother;
> Breaking his oath and resolution like
> A twist of rotten silk; never admitting
> Counsel o' th' war; but at his nurse's tears
> He whined and roared away your victory.
>
> (V.vi.91-7)

The reigning opposition is here laid bare: the entitlements of war—"your business," "your city Rome," "your victory"—are traded to women for tears, metonyms for the emotional hold of domestic affiliations. The private sphere represented by mothers, wives, nurses, slatterns, and babies is thus seen to be vital to political and military business, and its resurgence to the ruin of Marcius.

When the domestic is seen broadly to encompass not only Volumnia's overbearing motherhood but all forms of nurture, affection, and family relations, the hero's characteristic abstemiousness ("better to starve, / Than crave the hire which first we do deserve" [II.iii.108-9]) is a function of his politically disastrous renunciation of domestic hospitality—the source of comfort and communal feeding. Significantly, it is only among strangers that Coriolanus eats, and by them instated as the foundation of their ritual: Volscian "soldiers use him as the grace 'fore meat, / Their talk at table, and their thanks at end" (IV.vii 3-4), but in his own country, he promised to starve, like his mother, supping upon "anger."

Adelman's reading of Coriolanus's reception into "a safe male world" in Antium contributes to my own sense of the problem of the play: men view women's domestic authority as threats to their own identity and to the workings of the public sphere. She explains: "Here, far from Rome, Coriolanus at last allows his hunger and his vulnerability to be felt, and he is given food . . . But here in Antium, the play moves toward a fantasy in which nourishment may be safely taken because it is given by a male, by a father-brother-twin rather than a mother."[42] In the context of the domestic, then, it is not nourishment per se that Coriolanus rejects, nor only that nourishment dispensed or withheld by his mother, but all the associations of food, nurture, familiarity, and family with the domestic sphere. Seen in this way, the domestic is political.[43]

IV

Given *Coriolanus*'s tendency alternately to enforce and deny domestic identity and family ties, how then can "his nurse's tears" (V.vi.96) ultimately convince the hero to change his mind and spare Rome? The answer is they don't.[44] For all her charming rhetoric of mother-hens and trampled wombs, Volumnia does not win him over simply by invoking familial/filial bonds, but by alloying them with her sense of public, civic duty, thus rendering explicit the mutual dependence of the spheres operating in the play all along. Volumnia equates Rome with domestic nurture: "The country, our dear nurse" (V.iii.110) in an echo of the nurses and dairy maids supporting Marcius on the streets of Rome. In both cases—the Roman matron and the working women—a political force drives the so-called private sphere. As Donald Stauffer notes, "In one sense Rome is not so much a *patria* as a *matria,* like the England of the history plays: 'This nurse, this teeming womb of royal kings.'"[45] Furthermore, as I have argued, Volumnia does understand the political nature of her production of "men-children only" as servants to the state. In act V, she presents an enlarged domestic sphere blurring home and homeland in language more explicit than the metaphors characteristic of her son and other "public men."

The note struck by "nurse's tears" is recognized immediately by both Marcius and Aufidius as uniquely per-

suasive (Marcius has already sent Menenius away with a letter, and has promised to entertain no suits "from the state nor private friends" [V.iii.18]) and, in the present, tense situation, dangerous. Upon the entrance of the embassy of ladies, Marcius worries, "Shall I be tempted to infringe my vow / In the same time 'tis made? I will not" (lines 20-1). This oath, of course, is premature as are his other absolute claims: "But out, affection! / All bond and privilege of nature break!" (lines 24-5). Now his metaphors reverse the usual placement of vehicle and tenor; by comparing his current political position to his past domestic situation—"'O, a kiss / Long as my exile, sweet as my revenge!" (lines 44-5)—Marcius unintentionally acknowledges the relation between his public and private, exiled and domestic selves, but here he privileges the former terms as if to locate himself only as a public man. The latter term, which imposes itself so urgently, so integrally, returns to slay him.

The presence of his family in V.iii and the memory of things Roman together lead him to spare Rome, while he yet clings to his false sense that the spheres of his existence are separate. As Volumnia plays up the familial sentiment of their suit by presenting him his wife and son, "a poor epitome of yours" (line 68), she is ever mindful of the political nature of her plea. She rehearses the family relations in graceful parallel constructions, while charging him with treason:

> Making the mother, wife, and child to see
> The son, the husband, and the father tearing
> His country's bowels out.
>
>   (V.iii.101-3)

This rhetoric of family relation builds to a climax in the singling out of her own "mother's part" to shame him, a "foreign recreant," into compliance:

> There's no man in the world
> More bound to's mother; . . .
> . . . Thou hast never in thy life
> Showed thy dear mother any courtesy, . . .
> . . . thou restrain'st from me the duty which
> To a mother's part belongs.
>
>   (lines 158-68)

These same poses worked before, when, in Derek Traversi's words, she "adds the unique appeal of her maternity": "thou hast said / My praises made thee first a soldier" (III.ii.107-8).[46]

But now, when more than her son's reputation is on the line, namely her own life and the "life of Rome" (V.v.1), which becomes her epithet, Volumnia exploits the interactive relation between home and homeland, spelling out the common domestic grounding of the maternal and political. In a last-ditch effort to move him she gives the same kind of assurance Cominius and Aufidius had extended to him earlier: the assurance that her commitment to country supersedes that to the private life, while simultaneously granting the dependence of public on private life. To this end, she un-mothers herself, and divorces, orphans, and cuckolds Coriolanus:

> Come, let us go.
> This fellow had a Volscian to his mother;
> His wife is in Corioles, and his child
> Like him by chance.
>
> (V.iii.177-80)

Roman and familial identifications are at once threatened in this ironic unmaking of family ties. With the dominant rhetoric of family-disowning established, Volumnia's speech is less a "rebuke," as many contend,[47] or an oath, than a final assertion that Rome and home are inseparable, that domestic ties cannot be escaped. Moments before, she had determined, "So, we will home to Rome, / And die among our neighbors" (lines 172-3), finally yoking together the two words in an inevitable rhyme so far eluded in the play. Thus "his nurse's tears," which convey such political freight as to move Coriolanus to stifle his revenge, are quickly recognized as political acts: "Ladies, you deserve / To have a temple built you" (lines 206-7). Back in Rome the traditionally feminine role of "bring[ing] . . . comfort home" receives its full political weight as Menenius proclaims, "This Volumnia / Is worth of consuls, senators, patricians, / A city full; of tribunes . . . / A sea and land full," and an official welcome to the ladies constitutes a public ritual (V.iv.51-4).

The previous scene at the camp, with its theatrical gestures of kneeling and rising and its formality of speech, dramatically prefigures the public, ritual nature of the women's triumphant return to Rome. Their personal pleas of V.iii combine with their formal commemoration of V.iv and V.v to illustrate the direct relationship between private and public. Nor is V.iii properly a "domestic" one, as many critics surmise. Although it transpires inside (the tent) and although the family unit dominates the foreground, the performance is public. First, Aufidius acknowledges to Marcius that he has "never admitted / A private whisper" on the matter of Rome (V.iii.6-7). Second, Valeria's presence as a kind of public figure (she has access to news before Marcius's family does; she is hailed by him always in formal terms) complicates the assumption of enclosed domesticity here. Finally, Marcius insists on crafting the encounter as a public occasion, exposing the women's suit to Volscian witnesses (V.iii.92-3). Fittingly, then, only after Volumnia's mock dismissal of private ties does her son assent to her "happy victory." This decisive scene succeeds dramatically and rhetorically by insisting on the political nature of family, the private nature of politics.

Domestic objects, relations, and experiences are verbally degraded, denied, or subsumed into political discourse by Marcius and other warriers who claim to love their countries, enemies, or comrades more than their wives. This pattern works to reinforce rather than resist the integral role of domestic life in political arenas. When polarizations of private and public are asserted, as they are by Marcius, the result is ruin: the "puny battle" he had scorned manifests itself in the crowd of Volscians crying "a terrible litany of kinship" in revenge of their broken homes (V.vi.119-21).[48]

V

Critics have properly identified gender and family disturbances in *Coriolanus* in which a potent mother defines manhood through aggression and bloodshed, and warring men align womanhood with a debilitated (and debilitating) domestic sphere. Equally compelling is the play's focus on the political conflicts between classes, states, and forms of government. Yet, as Lisa Lowe has argued, critics tend to see these issues as separate; she affirms that the play "resists the narrow definitions of 'political drama' or 'gender drama.' It . . . directs the reader to consider the ways in which political conflicts take place in the family, and likewise the ways in which gender is not restricted to psychological interrelationships but is inscribed upon civic activities as well."[49] I have shown that the domestic sphere houses, as it were, the political and intrafamilial disturbances of the play which represents home at once as a safe refuge and a coward's retreat, both disabled and threatening, but ultimately politically efficacious. *Coriolanus*'s reversal of conventional notions about home and abroad is in part a response to the growing ideological division between the domestic sphere and the public sphere in early modern England. Through Volumnia's politicization of the maternal roles of feeding and nurturing in the domestic province, and through Marcius's false opposition of domestic relations to public ones, this play challenges traditional associations of household with comfort and warfare with danger, eventually showing that the domestic expands to influence all of public life—from corn riots to public ritual, from warrior bonding to political murder. Furthermore, these dramatizations of "domestic politics" reflect similar if more mundane concerns of Jacobean England articulated in the extensive popular and ecclesiastical literature on household government. This tragedy at once reflects the bourgeois privatization of the domestic sphere and resists the historical polarization by showing the interdependence of private lives and public experience. The mutual influence of mothers and warrior-sons, the metaphoric omnipresence of domestic relations, the power of widows and orphans to exact revenge from wars which exclude them—the circulation of cause and effect between the public and the private spheres attests to the impossibility of drawing hard and fast lines between them. According to Eugene M. Waith the hero cannot be assimilated into a city, whether foreign or domestic; for Paster, Marcius is "unaccommodated man."[50] These formulations of the conflict are underpinned by what I have shown to be Marcius's undomesticated status. Established as a spatial, psychological, and political center in the play, the domestic sphere drives the tragedy, making visible the conflicts surrounding family and power. By repressing his connection to private life, Marcius invites the domestic to return in the form of an angry crowd avenging families, hearths, and homes.[51]

Notes

[1] Some studies of political and economic concerns in *Coriolanus* include Stanley Cavell, "'Who does the wolf love?': *Coriolanus* and the Interpretations of Politics," in *Shakespeare and the Question of Theory*, ed. Patricia Parker and Geoffrey Hartman (New York: Methuen, 1985), pp. 245-72; Michael Bristol, "Lenten Butchery: Legitimation Crisis in *Coriolanus*," in *Shakespeare Reproduced: The Text in History and Ideology*, ed. Jean Howard and Marion F. O'Connor (New York: Methuen, 1987), pp. 207-24; Anne Barton, "Livy, Machiavelli, and Shakespeare's *Coriolanus*," *ShS* 38 (1985): 115-29; David G. Hale, "*Coriolanus*: The Death of a Political Metaphor," *SQ* 22, 3 (Summer 1971): 197-202; Andrew Gurr, "*Coriolanus* and the Body Politic," *ShS* 28 (1975): 63-9; Patricia K. Meszaros, "'There is a world elsewhere': Tragedy and History in *Coriolanus*," *SEL* 16, 2 (Spring 1976): 273-85; and Shannon Miller, "Topicality and Subversion in William Shakespeare's *Coriolanus*," *SEL* 32, 2 (Spring 1992): 287-310. In an essay to which I am indebted, Lisa Lowe surveys recent studies of the play in terms of their discrete emphases on political or gender issues; see "'Say I play the man I am': Gender and Politics in *Coriolanus*," *KR* n.s. 8, 4 (Fall 1986): 86-95, 86-90.

[2] Janet Adelman, "'Anger's my meat': Feeding, Dependency, and Aggression in *Coriolanus*," in *Representing Shakespeare: New Psychoanalytic Essays*, ed. Murray M. Schwartz and Coppélia Kahn (Baltimore: Johns Hopkins Univ. Press, 1980), pp. 129-49. See also Coppélia Kahn, "The Milking Babe and the Bloody Man in *Coriolanus* and *Macbeth*," in *Man's Estate: Masculine Identity in Shakespeare* (Berkeley: Univ. of California Press, 1981), pp. 151-92; Madeline Gohlke Sprengnether, "Annihilating Intimacy in *Coriolanus*," in *Women in the Middle Ages and the Renaissance: Literary and Historical Perspectives*, ed. Mary Beth Rose (Syracuse: Syracuse Univ. Press, 1986), pp. 89-112; Richard Wheeler, "'Since first we were dissevered': Trust and Autonomy in Shakespearean Tragedy and Romance," in *Representing Shakespeare*, pp. 150-69.

[3] Lowe anticipates my argument that the "separate spheres" of gender and politics so delineated in the criticism ought to be reexamined for their relation to each other (p. 86).

[4] Cavell, pp. 246-7.

[5] William Shakespeare, *Coriolanus*, in *The Complete Pelican Shakespeare*, ed. Alfred Harbage, rev. edn. (New York: Viking, 1969; rprt. 1977). Further references to the play are to this edition and will be cited parenthetically by act, scene, and line number.

[6] In representing the family in terms of a "little commonwealth," Shakespeare follows such contemporary political theorists as Jean Bodin, whose *Six Bookes of a Commonweale*, trans. Richard Knowles (London: G. Bishop, 1606) explored the analogous relationship between "a Familie and a Commonweale" (p. 746). See William W. E. Slights, "Bodies of Text and Textualized Bodies in *Sejanus* and *Coriolanus*," *MRDE* 5 (1991): 181-93, 193, n. 31.

[7] G. Wilson Knight, I think, was the first to point out the imagery of bricks, walls, and stone in the creation of a city at war with itself; see *The Imperial Theme: Further Interpretations of Shakespeare's Tragedies Including the Roman Plays* (1931; rprt. London: Methuen, 1951), p. 155. For further discussions of building imagery, see Gail Kern Paster, "To Starve with Feeding: The City in *Coriolanus*," *ShS* 11 (1978): 123-44, 130-2.

[8] For a discussion of domestic space, see Gaston Bachelard, *The Poetics of Space*, trans. Maria Jolas (Boston: Beacon Press, 1969), esp. pp. 7, 17.

[9] Adrian Poole observes in Marcius the desire for frequent separations from Rome. See *"Coriolanus"* (Boston: Twayne, 1988), p. 75.

[10] Paster, p. 128. Richard Wilson observes Marcius's separation of his work from his domestic identity in "Against the Grain: Representing the Market in *Coriolanus*," *SCen* 6, 2 (Autumn 1991): 111-48, 115.

[11] Annabel Patterson explicates the workings of consent and assent in the parliamentary selection process of Stuart England and in republican Rome. See *Shakespeare and the Popular Voice* (Cambridge MA: Basil Blackwell, 1989), pp. 128-9.

[12] For a history of the gendering of public and private, see Jean Bethke Elshtain, *Public Man, Private Woman: Women in Social and Political Thought* (Princeton: Princeton Univ. Press, 1981).

[13] Harry Levin, "Introduction to *Coriolanus*," in *The Complete Pelican Shakespeare*, pp. 1212-5, 1213.

[14] See Donald A. Stauffer, *Shakespeare's World of Images: The Development of His Moral Ideas* (1949; rprt. Bloomington: Indiana Univ. Press, 1966), pp. 252, 263.

[15] Poole, p. 34.

[16] Janet Adelman, *Suffocating Mothers: Fantasies of Maternal Origin in Shakespeare's Plays, "Hamlet" to "The Tempest"* (New York and London: Routledge, 1992), pp. 151 and 152.

[17] Clifford Chalmers Huffman recognizes the echo between Cominius's image and the Volscians' rending of Marcius. See "Coriolanus and His Poor Host: A Note," *Etudes Anglaises* 35, 2 (April-June 1982): 173-6, 173, n. 2.

[18] Paster, p. 134.

[19] Paster, p. 133.

[20] Poole, p. 80.

[21] The BBC version of the play directed by Elijah Moshinsky (originally aired 21 April 1984 in Britain and 26 March 1984 in the U.S.) disappointingly dramatizes Marcius's death as a combination of assisted suicide and assassination by Aufidius, with the Volscian senate calmly seated in the background. None of the ranting accusations by the people are voiced and Marcius and Aufidius share the repeated chant of "Kill, kill."

[22] Kahn, p. 159.

[23] In the tent scenes, Coriolanus repeatedly discounts the power of persuasion by "private friends" (V.i.24; V.iii.18).

[24] Adelman, "'Anger's,'" p. 98. See also her revision of the essay in *Suffocating Mothers*, pp. 134, 147.

[25] For a survey of the popular literature of household government in the period, see Susan Cahn, *Industry of Devotion: The Transformation of Women's Work in England, 1500-1660* (New York: Columbia Univ. Press, 1987). See William Gouge, Of *Domesticall Duties* (London, 1622; rprt. Norwood NJ: W. J. Johnson, 1976).

[26] Cavell, p. 246.

[27] Poole adds that "the word [home] represents less a place than a direction, more an adverb than a noun" and cites other usages of the expression (p. 35).

[28] On the importance of food, see Maurice Charney, "The Dramatic Use of Imagery in Shakespeare's *Coriolanus*," *ELH* 23, 3 (September 1956): 183-93; Adelman, *Suffocating Mothers*, esp. pp. 147-52; Paster, pp. 135-8; and my unpublished dissertation, "Private Supper / Public Feast: Gender, Power, and Nurture in Early Modern England" (Univ. of Illinois, 1991).

[29] A similar instance occurs when a messenger warns Sicinius, "Sir, if you'd save your life, fly to your house" (V.iv.34).

[30] See M. W. MacCallum, *Shakespeare's Roman Plays and Their Background* (London: 1910; rprt. Russell and Russell, 1967), p. 569.

[31] Adelman, "'Anger's,'" pp. 138-9.

[32] For a brief discussion of doorways in the BBC production of this and other plays, see Susan Willis, *The BBC Shakespeare Plays: Making the Televised Canon* (Chapel Hill: Univ. of North Carolina Press, 1991), p. 138.

[33] Poole, p. 83.

[34] Poole discusses "threshold" and Marcius's disdain for barriers, gates, and walls (pp. 83-4).

[35] Often "normal" family configurations are replaced by images of bastardy and cuckoldry. See, for example, IV.v.221-33 and IV.vi.82-4. Even Virgilia, who is seen by many as the symbol of "family values," threatens the Roman people with the extinction of their families—an "end of thy posterity" (IV.ii.26).

[36] A remorseful Aufidius remembers Coriolanus in the last lines of the play: "Though in this city he / Hath widowed and unchilded many a one . . . Yet he shall have a noble memory."

[37] In *The Comedy of Errors,* the wrath of a neglected wife results from the overdone meat falling from the spit, and Luce, the kitchen maid, threatens to emasculate a male love object, Dromio, by making him turn the kitchen spit.

[38] Ralph Berry, "Casting the Crowd: *Coriolanus* in Performance," *Assaph* 4 (1988): 119-20.

[39] Adelman, *Suffocating Mothers,* p. 155.

[40] In this speech Brutus emphasizes the private and enclosed nature of women ("our veil'd dames") and priests: "Seld-shown flamens, / Do press among the popular throngs" (II.i.204, 202-3). On the topic of the gendered representations of the crowd, see Adelman who argues that they are imaged as both phallic aggressors ("stiff bats and clubs") and feminized hungry mouths ("'Anger's,'" pp. 130, 137-8). Patterson treats the people's alleged fickleness, also a "feminine" vice (p. 129).

[41] Zvi Jagendorf, "*Coriolanus:* Body Politic and Private Parts," *SQ* 41, 4 (Winter 1990): 455-69, 462.

[42] Adelman, "'Anger's,'" p. 139.

[43] Although I agree with Adelman's explication of the scene, I depart from her conclusion for reasons which should be clear: "Since his mother will not feed him, Coriolanus will find in Aufidius the only nourishment that can sustain him; and insofar as Aufidius is his alter-ego, he, like his mother, will sup upon himself" ("'Anger's,'" p. 139).

[44] Most readings of Volumnia's embassy assume that "[i]n the deciding moment, [Marcius's] resolve turns upon his boyish relations with his mother" (Stauffer, p. 262). See also Leonard Tennenhouse, "*Coriolanus: History and the Crisis of Semantic Order,*" *CompD* 10, 4 (Winter 1976-77): 328-46, 341-2; Knight, pp. 155-65; Traversi, pp. 277-80; Adelman, "'Anger's,'" p. 143. Charles K. Hofling disagrees with most other interpretations and argues that the hero's ties to his wife and child come to supplant those to Volumnia. See "An Interpretation of Shakespeare's *Coriolanus,*" *American Imago* 14 (1957): 425-7.

[45] Stauffer, p. 252.

[46] Traversi, p. 253.

[47] MacCallum, p. 554.

[48] Paster, p. 134.

[49] Lowe, pp. 94-5.

[50] Eugene M. Waith, "The Herculean Hero," in *The Herculean Hero in Marlowe, Chapman, Shakespeare, and Dyden* (New York: Columbia Univ. Press, 1962), rprt. in *William Shakespeare's "Coriolanus,"* ed. Harold Bloom (New York: Chelsea House, 1988), pp. 9-31, p. 30; Paster, p. 126.

[51] I wish to thank Carol Thomas Neely and Richard Wheeler for their generous yet keen criticism in reading earlier versions of this essay.

Source: "The Return of the Domestic in *Coriolanus,*" in *Studies in English Literature, 1500-1900*, Vol. 37, No. 2, Spring, 1997, pp. 295-316.

Marxist Criticism: Cultural Materialism, and the History of the Subject

James Cunningham, *Trinity College, Carmarthen, Wales*

In his primer *Marxism and Literary Criticism* (1976), Terry Eagleton defines Marxism as "a scientific theory of human societies and of the practice of reforming them."[1] Marxist criticism, he states, "analyses literature in terms of the historical conditions which produce it" (vi). The business of this criticism is "to understand ideologies—the ideas, values and feelings by which men experience their societies at various times," some of the ideologies of the past being accessible only in literature. An understanding of ideologies, it is argued, helps clarify the process of social control and "contributes to our liberation" (viii). Ideologies, as socially generated and historically relative ways of apprehending reality, are understood to reflect and underpin the status quo; or, as Eagleton puts it in a more sophisticated study, ideologies are "modes of feeling, valuing, perceiving, and believing which have some kind of relation to the maintenance and reproduction of social power."[2] Not every Marxist critic would accept Eagleton's formulation, but his definition of ideology is consistent with the practice of most of the critics who have written on Shakespeare's tragedies from a Marxist viewpoint, and when the expression "the Marxist" is used in the following account it is in the restricted sense of those who have contributed significantly to the Shakespearean debate. Jonathan Dollimore and Alan Sinfield, for example, consider ideology to be "composed of those beliefs, practices, and institutions which work to legitimate the social order."[3] In common with many Marxist theoreticians, Eagleton, Dollimore, and Sinfield conceive of ideologies not as "a set of false beliefs capable of correction by perceiving properly," but as "the very terms in which we perceive the world."[4] Ideology works to maintain existing power relations and mitigate class conflict by providing a system of apparently natural forms of consciousness that actually interpret reality in particular ways and inhibit alternative interpretations.

The relationship between literature and ideology is a stress-point in Marxist theory, and only an outline can be given here. It would be theoretically consistent with Marxism to hold that literature merely reflects ideological distortions of reality and thereby helps to sustain the established order. A more fruitful approach for the literary critic, however, is exemplified by Ernst Fischer's *Art Against Ideology* (1969), which argues that art disrupts ideologies, yielding insights into social realities. This view has been given impetus by the theories of Louis Althusser, whose refinements to the concept of ideology have made possible the formulations of the Shakespearean critics cited above. Althusser's model of reading provides a theoretical defense of the view that literature is not merely a reflection of ideology. Althusser argues that the view of reality immanent in a text is always incomplete, because the conceptual apparatus of the writer cannot render a comprehensive account of the relations between the phenomena of which he writes. A competent reader will therefore approach a text as a psychoanalyst approaches a patient's symptoms, reading beyond what is stated, into the gaps and incongruities, and elucidating what the text evades in the light of a more coherent and exhaustive intellectual framework. Such a "symptomatic reading" will give access to "a different text, present as a necessary absence of the first."[5] Althusser uses this model to explain Marx's superimposition of new theory on the silences and fissures in earlier economic theories. His analysis problematizes the relations between author and text, text and reality, and he tries, by operating in the textual interstices, to reconstruct the intellectual constraints within which the work was produced.

Althusser's version of the text is echoed in Pierre Macherey's influential study *A Theory of Literary Production* (1966; 1978 translation). Like Althusser, Macherey expounds an anti-unitary and anti-intentionalist view of the text. A literary work, he contends, is not "created by an intention" but "produced" under certain conditions.[6] The writer cannot transcend his social consciousness, but the tensions in his society's apprehension of reality will be discernible in the work's "incompleteness" or "de-centredness" (79). This "formlessness and imperfection" must be recognized as the consequence of the work's presentation of ideology in literary form. Ideology processed in literature loses its normal invisibility; literature "constructs a determinate image of the ideological, revealing it as an object rather than living it from within." Ideology is "put to the test of the written word, the test of that watchful gaze in which all subjectivity is captured, crystallised in objective form" (131). The critic, in exploring the internal discontinuities of the text and their relation to the ideological material that has been used to produce it, "must go beyond the work and explain it, must say what it does not and could not say: just as the triangle remains silent on the sum of its angles" (77). The debt to psychoanalysis is evident in Macherey's reference to "the unconscious of the work" (92). With Macherey's notion of writing as production, a new agenda is set for the critic. Interpreting a text in the sense of extricating inherent truths that elude the nonspecialist reader becomes impossible if the text itself marks a problematic rendering of reality. The critic's task is to account for the pathology of the text by employing diagnostic tools not available to the writer. In Macherey's case, this means using Marxism.

The interface between Marxist and poststructuralist theory is a difficult area, raising questions about the compatibility of the two analytical systems, but mention should be made here of the influence of the poststructuralist historian Michel Foucault on Marxist criticism. In a series of studies, Foucault develops the argument that the complex of conventions governing what is thought, said, and written is a function of the power structure.[7] Every culture, he maintains, has an "archive" of permissible discourse that reflects the distribution of power but is beyond the grasp of any individual; it is ideological in the sense that it codifies reality in terms consistent with the maintenance of the existing order, for example by binary oppositions such as "sanity" and "madness." In all our discursive practices, we are compelled to think and express thought by way of the governing codes specific to our social context. As a result, we can never achieve an Olympian understanding of history; in reading the past, we always read ourselves into the text. We can, however, perceive the ideological constraints of Renaissance writing better than the writers themselves because we no longer share their discursive archive.

If Macherey suggests a method for the Marxist critic— and it is one taken up in important critiques by Jonathan Dollimore and Catherine Belsey—liberal humanism provides a target. To the Marxist, liberal humanism denotes the keystone in the ideological arch of Western capitalism: the belief in the individual as a unique essence, autonomous, unified, and capable of knowledge and decision-making; and the accompanying assumption that this is man's natural state, liberated and fostered by capitalism. The Marxist objection to this view of man is that it obscures the social determinants of identity in the interests of a particular social formation, making what is contingent appear natural and inevitable. This suppression of social factors weakens the ethical and political force of humanism: it is merely "the impotent conscience of bourgeois society," trapped in a paradoxical relationship with a system that has "very little time for it at all." It is "a suburban moral ideology, limited in practice to largely interpersonal matters . . . and its valuable concern with freedom, democracy, and individual rights are simply not concrete enough."[8]

The received notion of the value of literature is seen by the Marxist as an arm of liberal humanism, in particular the propositions that literature is life-enhancing, that it reproduces the texture of experience, and that it cultivates the moral sense. The Marxist perceives literature in different terms. As Terry Eagleton puts it, "Literature, in the meaning of the word we have inherited, is an ideology. It has the most intimate relations to questions of social power."[9] He goes on to argue that, from the time of Matthew Arnold onwards, and concurrently with the decline of established Christianity, English literature has served as an element of the power structure, providing "the social 'cement,' affective values and basic mythologies by which a socially turbulent class-society can be welded together."[10] It achieves its quietist effects, Eagleton submits, by perpetuating the myth that the individual is a unique self-regulating agent; by implying that there are universal human values that are more important than any restrictions imposed by social organization; by making possible a literary culture compatible with imperialism; and by allaying frustration through the provision of vicarious fulfilment. For Eagleton, English literature is a "non-subject," since it overlaps with other disciplines to the exclusion of a distinctive methodology and cannot define its subject matter except as the arbitrary selection of books taught. Its methods proliferate unsystematically and are often employed idiosyncratically. Yet, Eagleton contends, while it professes hostility to doctrinaire schools of criticism, orthodox literary criticism ensures self-preservation by an implicit but nonetheless firm regulation of its discourse. Only certain kinds of utterance are permissible as literary criticism, and this internal discipline is enforced throughout the educational system. The university English school, therefore, is, in Althusserian parlance, "part of the ideological apparatus of the modern capitalist state."[11]

Jonathan Dollimore and Alan Sinfield designate their Marxist approach "cultural materialism," a term derived from Raymond Williams. They offer "a combination of historical context, theoretical method, political commitment, and textual analysis." Their use of "cultural" draws on the evaluative and nonevaluative senses of the word, indicating their attitude to high culture as "one set of signifying practices among others."[12] "Materialism" signals a desire to ground cultural artifacts such as Shakespeare's plays in the physical, economic, political, and social circumstances of their production and reception. Dollimore and Sinfield dedicate their critical activity to the transformation of a society that they regard as repressive and exploitative: they aim to elucidate "How Shakespeare has been used to sustain delusions of social unity and subjective freedom in what is in fact a divided, strife-ridden culture."[13]

In this context, the very idea of tragedy is itself ideological. The issue is raised vigorously by Dollimore in *Radical Tragedy* (1984), as he sets out to challenge humanist criticism of tragedy on the grounds that, in sanctifying the suffering of the individual and presenting it as an inevitable part of the human condition, it distracts our attention from the alterable social causes of human misery and therefore has a politically conservative effect. He contrasts this appropriation of the genre with what he sees as the subversive import of Renaissance tragedies. *Radical Tragedy* deals with English tragedies of the late Elizabethan and Jacobean period, including *King Lear, Antony and Cleopatra,* and *Coriolanus,* viewing them as theatrical precursors of the political revolution in the seventeenth century. Building on Macherey's analysis of the relation of literature to ideology, Dollimore argues that his chosen tragedies subvert orthodox belief, not in a transcendent manner, but partially and fitfully. Macherey is cited three times and his theory of literary production juxtaposed suggestively to the Brechtian alienation effect, which, by encouraging in the audience a critical posture towards the representation, challenges the ontological basis of accepted realities and thereby intimates the ideological status of our commonsense view of things. Dollimore also takes his bearings from an analogy, found in Macherey and Eagleton, between the textual processing of ideology and the theatrical production of a play; the production "cannot transcend its text but it may nevertheless interrogate it with critical rigour."[14] The interrogation of ideology may be partly the result of the author's intention, Dollimore adds, but intentional radicalism is less important than those "aspects of that historical process . . . already there in the language, forms, conventions, genres being used."[15] Any conscious social critique by the writer, although not excluded from Dollimore's theory, is subordinated to the concretization of ideology in the linguistic and literary formulas of the day. It is in the theorizing of the articulation and disintegration of ideology that the Macherey model figures in Dollimore's argument, allowing him to speak of the "attempted coherence and actual incoherence" of Jacobean tragedy (68).

Dollimore's interest in the uses to which Shakespeare is put means that he is as much occupied by the critical reception of texts as by his own readings. He bases his political critique of humanism on generalizations about the criticism of the tragedies in what he terms the "recent years," prior to 1984 (189). An examination of his case in relation to *King Lear* will illustrate how Marxist criticism can work on the tragedies. It will also show that Dollimore's version of humanist criticism is overgeneralized and fails to take account of the variety of humanist exegesis that exists alongside the Bradleyan tradition.

Dollimore's readings of Jacobean tragedy bring him into planned confrontation with what he presents as a clear-cut critical orthodoxy. He contends that Christian interpretations of Jacobean tragedy, taking man as the pivot of a providential scheme, have been supplanted by "the humanist view" (188). This continues to place man in a central position, but in a world that balks his aspirations and fails to satisfy his needs. Redemption in such a situation is achieved when adversity seeks out the deepest resources of the human spirit. Tragic

suffering is redemptive, not in a specifically Christian sense, but inasmuch as it reveals man's courage or his capacity for pity. Dollimore teases out two strands of humanism that, he claims, feature in the criticism of tragedy. "Existential" humanism celebrates man's inherent capacity to brave misfortune with dignity. "Ethical" humanism admires the inherent human impulse to pity others, seeing it as part of man's "essential humanity" (194). Dollimore maintains that the Christian residue in critiques based on these species of humanism is evident in their religiose diction, in their essentialism (man as a "quasi-transcendent identity," 190), and in the implied link they forge between suffering, growth, and affirmation of the value of human life. Their sustaining principle Dollimore defines as the "tragic paradox" (189) that in "individual extinction" lies man's "transcendence" (194). This assertion of the Christian infusion into tragic criticism deserves to be taken seriously. The idea of purgatorial suffering is an observable feature in Bradley, Brower, Honigmann, Mehl, and Wilson, who represent, as outlined above, the conservative wing in a broad church. It could not, however, be applied without careful qualification to Mack, Long, or even Lever. Undeterred, Dollimore refers confidently to a supposed consensus that he terms "the humanist theory of tragedy" (156). This version of the critical orthodoxy must, like any other, be premised on selection, exclusion, and the placing of emphasis; how tendentious these are affect the cogency of the case. Instead of accepting Dollimore's sketch-map of the humanist critical terrain, it will be useful to look once again at the landscape.

Philip Brockbank's British Academy Lecture of 1976, "Upon Such Sacrifices," is described by Dollimore as a "sensitive humanist reading" of *King Lear.*[16] Brockbank is said by Dollimore to argue for the importance of Lear's pity in his redemption and renewal. Yet Lear's very empathy with the poor, Dollimore insists, is the product of an experience of dispossession denied most kings; it therefore merely accentuates the division between high and low that is inherent in hierarchical societies. The redemptive value of the King's newfound pity for his subjects must be qualified by our knowledge of the *Lear* society, which is "structured in such a way that to wait for shared experience to generate justice is to leave it too late."[17] Moreover, the argument goes, Lear's pity is assimilated into the solipsism of his own grief and is soon ousted by a desire for vengeance. Dollimore goes on to expound a Marxist reading of the play in which the king is confronted with the social origins of his identity and the power structure on which it depends; dislocation rather than purification takes place. The play is "about power, property, and inheritance," and it demonstrates that human values and in particular the allegedly natural ties of kinship are actually functions of material conditions.[18] Cordelia's frankness is a threat to Lear because it divests the existing order of its ideological niceties. In asking why Regan and Goneril have husbands if, as they claim, they love Lear absolutely, Cordelia applies a corrosive political realism to those filial relations that her sisters have mystified by rhetoric. The other antagonist to the status quo is Edmund, voicing in his "revolutionary scepticism" an understanding of the operation of power, yet ironically bound to assert himself through material advancement in the very regime that he demystifies. Lear and Gloucester, too, continue to measure human importance on a scale of money and possessions, Dollimore argues, and even at the end the survivors "attempt to recuperate their society in just those terms which the play has subjected to sceptical interrogation."[19] The deaths of Cordelia and Lear, however, undermine the efforts to reinstate the discredited social framework.

In the light of this reading, Dollimore complains of Brockbank's "idea that man can redeem himself in and through an access of pity" and declares that "far from transcending in the name of an essential humanity the gulf which separates the privileged from the deprived, the play insists on it."[20] This, coupled with his earlier remark that "Through kind-ness and shared vulnerability human kind redeems itself," makes clear the kind of redemption Dollimore has in mind: it is primarily a spiritual exaltation of Lear himself, his "transcendence" in "extinction."[21] This is the brand of humanism that Dollimore associates with the Bradleyan metaphysic. Certainly the title of Brockbank's paper recalls Bradley's reading of *King Lear,* and in particular the suggestion that Lear's words "Upon such sacrifices, my Cordelia / The gods themselves throw incense" (Folio text, 5.3.20-21)[22] denote a redemptive "renunciation of the world, with its power and glory and resentments and revenges."[23] But in other respects, Dollimore's account, even allowing for customary critical smash-and-grab, is a considerable distortion of Brockbank's argument.

"Upon Such Sacrifices" proposes common elements in sacrifice and tragedy. Brockbank's idea of the sacrificial is derived from Walter Burkert, who points out that sacrifice and tragedy formalize "Human existence face to face with death."[24] In sacrificial ritual, Burkert goes on, the horror of death and of taking life in obedience to divine injunction is alleviated by a ritual emphasis on the fitness, even the willingness, of the victim. Examining the sacrificial resonances set up by *King Lear,* Brockbank contends that sacrifice, in Burkert's terms a ritual confrontation with death, "persists as an elemental if not inescapable process of human consciousness," and that this persistence sheds light on our response to tragedy.[25] Thus, the renewal envisaged by Brockbank is radically different from the equable Christian-humanist version imputed to him by Dollimore. It is located in the audience rather than in the protagonist, is communal rather than individual, and proceeds from a collective encounter with death. Far

from elevating Lear's pity to a redemptive emotion in Lear's case, Brockbank stresses the deconstruction of Lear's ego, the "dissolution of the senses and of the self" (27) that attests to his "fitness for death" (26) as a sacrificial victim. Nor does Brockbank suggest that Lear's pity redeems his social order by mitigating it, and thereby justifying it in principle. He argues that with Lear perishes "the kind of authority once exercised but now played out" (26). The tragic process carries away both the king and the order that once sustained him. If Brockbank's reference to pity as "a condition for the renewal of human life" (27) is unclear, as Dollimore alleges, the point may be elucidated by considering the assertion elsewhere in the lecture that "It is an essential element in the sacrificial experience that life should be renewed, refreshed, reawakened, resurrected" (25). A confrontation with death brings the audience back with a reanimated appreciation of life; the crucial exercise of pity is not *by* Lear, but *for* Lear. The thrust of Brockbank's lecture, properly understood, suggests the partiality of Dollimore's representation of it. True, Brockbank occasionally gestures towards "existential humanism," in his admiration of Cordelia's "invincible independence of spirit" for example (5); equally, he is prepared to explore Christian doctrine and metaphor; but in other ways, his analysis proposes a *Lear* as challenging as anything in *Radical Tragedy.* To reduce Brockbank to a component of a humanist consensus is therefore unjustified, unless that consensus is more generously defined.

Another of Dollimore's candidates for the putative humanist orthodoxy is Clifford Leech. Dollimore reads Leech's observation in *Shakespeare's Tragedies and Other Studies in Seventeenth Century Drama* (1950) that tragic heroes have "the power to endure and the power to apprehend" as an indication of existential humanism, with its accent on a defiantly struggling humanity. In the work cited, there is a wealth of evidence to support Dollimore's view, including the statement that in admiring the hero we are "proud of our human nature because in such characters it comes to fine flower"; there is also, significantly, a Bradleyan reference to "doom-in-the-character."[26] Yet the publication date of Leech's comments means that they hardly help to establish a modern orthodoxy in relation to Dollimore's publication date of 1984. A little more recent is Leech's brief survey of tragic theory, *Tragedy* (1969). This does have some common ground with the earlier work but has moved perceptibly away from essentialism and from Bradley. While the 1950 study argues the exercise of a degree of free will by the tragic protagonist, the 1969 survey describes as "too simple"[27] the idea that an act of will by the hero triggers the tragic sequence of events. Instead, Leech accentuates "the encompassing process" itself (39), the "developing process of event" (38) in which the protagonist is caught. The concept of free will is described as "highly dubious" in relation to tragedy (41). This stress on circumambient conditions, together with Leech's remarks on the ideological nature of the sense of free choice, reflects a concession to the formative power of social process. A complementary shift takes place in Leech's revised account of the tragic effect. The balance of terror and pride, seen in the earlier study as producing stasis and a "quiet close," is now modified by the recognition that "balance does not mean equanimity. Rather it gives to our response its peculiar anguish, its basic sense of puzzlement."[28] There is no facile affirmation here, but a clear acknowledgement that the experience of tragedy resists quietist interpretations. To read Leech historically, then, reveals that his views are not static, not part of a consensual monolith, but subject to change and ready to absorb what appear to be materialist elements.

A similar lack of historical sense mars Dollimore's comments on G. K. Hunter's criticism. Dollimore notes wryly that Hunter, in *Dramatic Identities and Cultural Tradition* (1978), describes the humanist approach as "the modern outlook which sees *King Lear* as the central Shakespearian statement," because it "not only strips and reduces and assaults human dignity" but also shows "the process of restoration by which humanity can recover from this degradation." The operation of essential and existential humanism is clearly visible in Hunter's critique, with its assertion that "the individual mind is seen here as the place from which a man's most important qualities and relationships draw the whole of their potential," and its claim that Lear seeks to "pursue the tenor of his own significance" by steadfastly affirming "his innermost perceptions."[29] Dollimore's quotation of the word "modern" seems intended as an ironic glance at Hunter's remoteness from the real front line of critical endeavor; but the hit is poorly directed, since Hunter's essay "Shakespeare's Last Tragic Heroes," from which the comment in question comes, appeared in 1966 as "The Last Tragic Heroes" in *The Later Shakespeare,* edited by John Russell Brown and Bernard Harris. Dollimore quotes from a reissue of the essay, with minor changes, in Hunter's 1978 collection of essays. Failure to clarify the genealogy of the piece would be allowable if Dollimore intended merely to establish some broad twentieth-century trends, but to prove Hunter is out of touch would require more scrupulous handling of the evidence. Even disregarding the chronology, we are not justified in extrapolating Hunter's approach to Shakespeare's tragedies in general from his observations on *King Lear.* Hunter contends in the same essay that later tragedies such as *Timon of Athens, Macbeth,* and *Coriolanus* insist on "the isolated individual's ultimate powerlessness" and show that the self-will of the tragic heroes evades its social consequences only by being fixed in death. Shakespeare's skeptical view of the protagonists presages the "loss of confidence in the heroic individual" to be found in the final plays.[30]

Hunter's interpretation of *King Lear* should be taken in conjunction with his readings of the later tragedies if oversimplification is to be avoided. Dollimore's humanist consensus again proves a misrepresentation.

Barbara Everett's essay "The New King Lear" (1960) is cited by Dollimore as another product of the existential humanism that, he maintains, has superseded Christian exegeses of the play.[31] Evidence to support Dollimore's view is found in Everett's admiration of the enormous, fate-defying passion with which Lear confronts "a hostile universe," and in her proposition that tragedy serves "to ennoble and illuminate the moment of death."[32] Once more, however, Dollimore neglects the considerable qualification of humanism in the criticism under discussion. Everett is careful to dissociate her critique from any mystification of suffering, tartly defining Bradley's idea of Lear's redemption as a matter of "what happens to Lear's soul outweighing what happens to his body" (328). The suffering of Lear, she argues, is not mitigated by any redemptive learning on his part; learning in Lear's case means admitting the likelihood of future suffering, and Everett suggests that "No moralistic outline that blurs this can be fully satisfying" (335). Moreover, Everett modifies Lear's status as the hero. She points out that his demand for "absolutes of love, of power, and of truth itself" is counterpoised by the play's emphasis on the tragic absolutes of "silence and cessation," which undercut "the idea of the overriding power of heroic and individual experience" (336). Nor does Everett substitute a humanist reconciliation (man with life, man with his own nature) for the Christian reconciliation she rejects. For her, part of the exhilaration of tragedy may be a question of form, the "gaiety of mastery inherent in the creative act," rather than the result of "any cheerful propositions made by tragedy itself" (339). In her willingness to reckon with the negatives of *King Lear* and with a formalistic explanation of the tragic effect, Everett broadens her reading to encompass not only existential humanism but also its qualifiers. The richness of her critique is not captured by Dollimore's selective account.[33]

One of the most recent critical studies referred to by Dollimore, and therefore a particularly useful example of the alleged modern humanist consensus, is J. W. Lever's *The Tragedy of State* (1971), ... According to Dollimore, "existential humanism forms the basis" of Lever's analysis.[34] Dollimore deprecates Lever's centering of the hero's response to events rather than the social milieu in which the characters operate. The comment may be taken as an extreme reaction to the Senecan element in Lever's critique. Lever does in fact take significant account of the social ground from which his chosen tragedies spring and of the social backdrop in each play. If Dollimore finds existential humanism in Lever's definition of certain tragedies as dramas of adversity and stance, it must be made clear that not all of the protagonists are said by Lever to achieve a stance of defiance or Stoical endurance. In his reading of Webster's *The White Devil,* it is Lever's similarity to Marxist criticism that stands out, not his humanism. The characters are seen as "victims of power": guilty or innocent, they stifle in the "suffocating ambience of power and oppression."[35] Even the lavish spectacle of the play, often regarded as peripheral, embodies "the hollow pomps and splendours of greatness" with "calculated irony." This, Lever declares, is a "satirical tragedy," the theme of which is "the debasement of a whole civilization." The White Devil is "not Vittoria Corombona but Renaissance Europe" (86).

There are strong echoes of this analysis in Dollimore's own reading of *The White Devil.* He describes the play's "dominating power structure," which defines the characters as "either agents or victims of power, or both."[36] His proposition that "The crimes of Flamineo and Vittoria reveal not their essential criminality but the operations of a criminal society" is not far removed from Lever's observations on the same theme.[37] As Dollimore likens Flamineo to "the so-called 'alienated intellectuals of early Stuart England,'"[38] he recalls Lever's reference to "a society where declassed intellectuals find the only alternative to the galleys, or gallows, in serving without scruple the desires of their rulers."[39] While Dollimore acknowledges a debt to a 1965 essay by Mark H. Curtis, the other similarities to Lever suggest an additional obligation.[40] Dollimore presses the social analysis further than Lever, but in the end the two are close. The influence of Lever is recognized belatedly by Dollimore in the introduction to the 1989 edition of *Radical Tragedy.* He states that Lever "largely broke with" the tradition articulated by such critics as Bradley, rejecting the principle that tragedy presents an inescapable human condition, and instead seeing "the causes of suffering and conflict in [these] tragedies as contingent rather than necessary, the effect of social and historical forces focussed [*sic*] in state power."[41] The 1989 view is more balanced than that of 1984, and fairer to Lever. At the same time, in its revision of the 1984 verdict on *The Tragedy of State,* it invites us to question Dollimore's assertions about the humanist criticism of tragedy as a whole.

Dollimore's study has since 1984 become an important point of reference in discussions of Jacobean tragedies. If *Radical Tragedy,* in other respects cogent and well documented, is allowed to smuggle in the dubious notion of a narrow and rigid humanist orthodoxy in the post-1950 criticism of the plays in question, justice will not be done to the richness and openness of that criticism. Furthermore, since most of the critical works cited in Dollimore's humanist Establishment appeared before 1970, his construction of the critical orthodoxy must already have been out of date when *Radical Tragedy* was published. Dollimore's weakness is, above all,

a failure to direct his attack precisely. Had he concentrated on neo-Bradleyans such as Brower and Honigmann, his case would have been more persuasive; as it is, it is compromised by being pressed beyond reasonable limits. A more temperate judgment is provided by Dollimore in *Political Shakespeare* (1985). He censures "idealist criticism," which he defines as "that preoccupied with supposedly universal truths which find their counterpart in 'man's' essential nature." While rejecting such criticism for its failure to address history, he does concede that "It would be wrong to represent idealist criticism as still confidently dominant in Shakespeare studies."[42] The verdict here is much more consonant with the evidence, and suggests that the humanist monolith erected earlier may have been no more than a convenient target. The issue at stake here goes beyond good critical manners. If Dollimore's account of humanist criticism is flawed, his estimate of its ideological function is also called into question, and part of the political case of his book is disabled. What is left, however, is a stimulating oppositional reading of a number of tragedies. The theory of Althusser and Macherey enables Dollimore to play up the discordant elements in the dramatic texts, amplifying emergent ideologies in contrast to the dominant, and leaving us with an enhanced awareness of textual complexity and cultural process. This may not realize all the aims of *Radical Tragedy,* but it represents a considerable achievement.

Sharing some ground with Dollimore is Catherine Belsey. In the introduction to her book *The Subject of Tragedy* (1985), she is careful not to exalt the genre. Tragedy, she avers, is "no more . . . than a point of departure" for her Marxist reading of Renaissance literature, and she expresses a desire not to privilege the genre more than the humanist tradition has done already.[43] Nor does she try to construct any tragic canon, preferring instead to range widely through plays not usually categorized as tragedies, and to take in nonfictional texts. Such a catholic approach need hardly wrestle with definitions of tragedy, but one element is singled out. According to Belsey's model of the "interrogative text," which has much in common with Macherey's production model, all fiction may be said to expose ideological flaws by drawing ideologies into narrative, which, as form, thrives on conflict and resistance. Belsey argues that tragedy is particularly telling in this regard because, unlike comedy, it is not impelled towards formal resolution of all conflict and may therefore interrogate the prevailing views of reality without reconciling contradictions. What Macherey provides for Belsey is a poetics of conflict, the laws of the text taking precedence over authorial intention and viewpoint. It is a powerful aesthetic that is elaborated by poststructuralism, ... Marxist and poststructuralist critics contrast the aesthetics of conflict with the aesthetics of unity, seen as central to humanism. This search for unity, they claim, has taken different forms in English studies. Leavis stressed the unity of healthy language and the experience to which it referred, while the New Critics tried to harmonize the ostensibly discordant elements in the text by postulating a tension of opposites. From a Marxist viewpoint, an aesthetic pursuing harmonious integration is seriously flawed because it suggests the organic unity of the word and the world.

Belsey's one concession to the distinctiveness of tragedy is outweighed by the rest of her study. Her main concern is to contest the concept of the unified self. For Belsey, this idea, seminal to humanist ideology and criticism, is a fiction whose historical origins she seeks to expose by contributing to "a history of the subject in the sixteenth and seventeenth centuries" (ix). Behind Belsey's formulations can be detected a number of prominent figures in twentieth-century literary and linguistic theory. The most immediate presence is Althusser, whose "symptomatic reading" has been discussed above. Belsey draws on further aspects of Althusserian theory. In his *Lenin and Philosophy* (English translation, 1971), Althusser explores the relation between ideology and the subject. The individual is seen as the product of social factors rather than a self-determining unified essence. Ideology, however, "centers" the subject, giving it an illusory impression of wholeness and autonomy. Althusser's definition of ideology would include not only the linguistic codification of reality but the whole array of social conventions conferring a spurious self-sufficiency upon the individual. Althusser leans on structuralist theory and therefore ultimately on Ferdinand de Saussure's *Cours de Linguistique Générale* (1916), ...[44] A fundamental point in Saussure's thesis is that individual words can carry meaning only because they are part of a language system. Althusser's theory of the subject may be regarded, on one level, as an expression of social relationships in terms of Saussurean linguistics. It is an application anticipated by the structural anthropology of Claude Lévi-Strauss, whose work on the grammar of myths and other social phenomena locates meaning in the internal relations of the symbolizing system rather than in the individual consciousness. The result is the decentering of the subject, which is no longer seen as the producer of meaning.

Belsey indicates her theoretical position by citing, among others associated with Marxist criticism, Dollimore and Drakakis, Stephen Greenblatt and Jonathan Goldberg, and Foucault. She does not cite, but takes account of, Mikhail Bakhtin, to whom she refers in her *Critical Practice* (1980). The Bakhtin School comprises a group of Soviet scholars whose work is rooted in the Russian Formalism of the 1920s. Operating within a Marxist tradition, they propose that language is the material medium of social interaction and of ideology, thereby disputing the older Marxist view that ideology is an immaterial mental reflection of the socioeconomic base. They insist also on language as a social activity or discourse, which always presupposes some kind of dialogue, some speaker and audience. Their conclusion is that the literary work should be examined as a practice in language proceeding from a certain kind of speaker, in a certain context, with a certain kind of audience in mind. In addition, they stress the capacity of any utterance to mean different things: in a dialogue, the words used by a speaker may carry a different meaning for a listener, so to see language as "dialogic" entails recognizing that the meaning of words is not fixed. Literature highlights this linguistic ambiguity and the conflicting versions of the world that circulate as a result. Bakhtin's study of Dostoevsky, for instance, argues that Dostoevsky initiates a new genre, the "polyphonic novel," in which a number of characters express discrepant world-views not resolved into a unity by the author. Bakhtin does not dismiss the regulatory power of the author as a possibility but sees Dostoevsky adopting a permissive approach to his characters' voices. The genre is seen by Bakhtin as offering new perceptual schemata, for literary genres "enrich our inner speech with new devices for the conceptualization of reality."[45] Special importance is attached to those kinds of literature that subvert or query authority; Bakhtin proposes the category of "carnival literature" to include works derived from popular festivity that play mischievously with social and linguistic convention. The value of this verbal sportiveness to a Marxist critic is to contest the meaning of linguistic signifiers as part of the resistance to institutional power. The ruling interests, the argument runs, attempt to foreclose radical questioning by limiting the meanings of the signifier, while the subversive voice of carnival proclaims the relativity of all perceptions and values. There are points of contact here with C. L. Barber's analysis of Shakespeare's comedy in terms of "the experience of moving to humorous understanding through Saturnalian release."[46]

Belsey's case, then, is the Marxist one that our sense of selfhood is a product of social conditions, not a natural and ineradicable essence that clarifies and fulfils itself in Western capitalist culture. She traces the tentative formation of the idea of selfhood from the medieval morality play through to Restoration drama. The morality, she suggests, is without a stable concept of the subject. Man is presented not as an essential entity but a passive "battleground" for the forces of good and evil (48); man has no ontological unity, but a soul and body in uneasy juxtaposition. There is, Belsey admits, a unified conspectus available to the audience, which, unlike the protagonist, can see human life in the context of heaven and hell, but the human character as depicted in this early antecedent of English tragedy is disjointed.

Belsey argues that the concept of the unified subject crystallizes into orthodox belief during the latter half of the seventeenth century, with "the bourgeoisie [is] installed as the ruling class" (33-34). The Restoration playhouse, with its employment of classic realism and perspective, enshrines the perception of the individual subject in dramaturgical technique and theater design. It is the end of a phase of psychosocial development. But during the period between 1576, when Burbage built the Theatre, and 1642, when the Puritans closed the playhouses, the emergence of the subject may be detected, Belsey maintains, in some of the most celebrated tragedies. Belsey sees the growth of illusionism in the theater as an early stage in the process, a haphazard verisimilitude being grafted onto the emblematic method of the morality play. The resultant hybrid of styles creates an uncertainty of technique that makes the Elizabethan and Jacobean theater profoundly interrogative of its characters' existential status. Thus, Belsey suggests, Hamlet's disquisition on man ("I have of late, but wherefore I know not, lost all my mirth . . . this quintessence of dust"; *Hamlet,* 2.2.297-310) uses the metaphor of the world as a theater and thereby invokes the hierarchical cosmology in which man acts out an allotted part. At the same time, however, Hamlet is given an identity in a specific place and time, which invites the audience to view him as a discrete self-determining entity, a sensitive man recoiling from the evil around him. The ambiguous presentation may be taken to endorse either the reassuring traditional order, in which man is "like an angel," or an almost nihilistic vision of man as the "quintessence of dust." No clear position, Belsey states, is offered to the audience, because the play enacts a "radical uncertainty" about the nature of the self (29). Given the diversity of response to *Hamlet,* Belsey's contention does little to trouble the play's critical tradition. Her interpretation does warn against imposing a false unity on a rebarbative text or character, but so too do much earlier studies, such as L. L. Schücking's *Character Problems in Shakespeare's Plays* (tr. 1922) and E. E. Stoll's *Art and Artifice in Shakespeare* (1935).

Crucial to the evolution of the unified subject in drama, Belsey argues, is the soliloquy, its impression of interiority accentuated by the contemporaneous influence of the iambic pentameter, which, less foregrounded than earlier verse-forms, suggests an inner voice behind the speech. This suggestion is reinforced by a movement in the theater away from allegorical personifications and towards social types; and the clash of good and evil, rendered in soliloquy, creates the illusion of psychomachy within a single consciousness. But Belsey prefers to stress the instability of the subject in soliloquy, arguing that what may seem to represent internal conflict still recalls the morality abstractions rather than evincing a unified individual presence. She observes, familiarly enough, that Marlowe's Doctor Faustus echoes in some of his utterances the voices of the Virtue and the Vice. Similarly, Lady Macbeth's invocation of "spirits / That tend on mortal thoughts" (*Macbeth,*

1.5.39-53) anatomizes her body into crown, toe, blood, and breasts, much as the morality character Everyman acknowledges the separate dramatic figures representing his own Beauty, Strength, and Five Senses. In both cases, Belsey's conclusion is that the "precariously unified" protagonist points to "the contradictory nature of the subject" as then conceived (48, 47). Belsey proceeds to argue that, when such a character soliloquizes in the first person, the effect is to postulate a "true self," corroborated by the physical presence of the actor on stage, but not made fully intelligible in the character's words and behavior. The purpose of humanist criticism, in Belsey's view, is to fill the gap between the stage behavior and the anterior self that is only partly revealed. The assumed truth of self is for Belsey chimerical, the search for it misguided. The tragic hero is an effect of language and dramatic technique, not an embodiment of essential human nature.

If there is no unified self behind the utterances of the tragic hero, then clearly the notion of that hero's advancement in self-knowledge, an important factor in Bradleyan criticism, is called into question. For Belsey, the concern with self-knowledge discloses the ideological nature of tragedy. She charts the growing emphasis during the sixteenth and seventeenth centuries on empirical knowledge gained through individual experience rather than discursive knowledge acquired by deduction from traditional propositions. She concludes that the important place assigned to self-knowledge in humanist criticism testifies to our cultural preoccupation with knowing as a manifestation of selfhood and a qualification for the proper engagement with capitalist consumer society, buying, voting, and exercising a supposedly free choice that is in fact largely illusory. The idea of self-knowledge is also ideologically potent in conferring a spurious freedom on the subject to transcend even its own perceived limits; as Belsey puts it, "The subject of liberal humanism literally knows no bounds" (56). The danger of this, she suggests, is that "In the subject's hopeless pursuit of self-presence politics can safely be left to take care of itself" (54).

Again a case that is coherent on its own terms suffers when individual pieces of evidence are reexamined. Lady Macbeth's invocation of the evil spirits in the first act of *Macbeth* may be taken as an example:

> Come, you spirits
> That tend on mortal thoughts, unsex me here,
> And fill me from the crown to the toe top-full
> Of direst cruelty. Make thick my blood,
> Stop up th'access and passage to remorse,
> That no compunctious visitings of nature
> Shake my fell purpose, nor keep peace between
> Th'effect and it. Come to my woman's breasts,

And take my milk for gall, you murd'ring
   ministers,
Wherever in your sightless substances
You wait on nature's mischief. Come, thick
   night,
And pall thee in the dunnest smoke of hell,
That my keen knife see not the wound it
   makes,
Nor heaven peep through the blanket of the
   dark
To cry 'Hold, hold!'

(1.5.39-53)

Belsey argues that although the figure of Lady Macbeth is indisputably present as a stage personage when she delivers these lines, the subject implied in the speech is elusive. She points out that "It is not the grammatical subject of the actions—the spirits are—and the moment it appears (as 'me') in the third line of the text, it is divided into crown, toe, cruelty, blood, remorse, nature, breasts, milk" (47). This interpretation underplays two linguistic features of the extract. It ignores the nine imperatives, from "Come" to "pall"; and although the understood grammatical subject of these verbs is "you" (spirits), the rhetorical agent of the imperatives is Lady Macbeth, who may therefore be said to reiterate her presence emphatically. In addition, Lady Macbeth's muster-roll of bodily parts could equally be taken as a triumphant affirmation of the controlling subject, harmonizing and bestowing meaning upon the separable but subordinate elements. And is it not special pleading to declare that the routine references to heaven and hell are "reproducing the morality pattern of the human being as a battleground between cosmic forces, autonomous only to the extent of choosing between them" (47-48)?

When assessed in this fashion, Belsey's argument can be seen to rest, at this key point as at others, on the assertion of one interpretation over others equally consistent with the text. It would be possible to subject any of Belsey's varied evidence to the same scrutiny as the above passage, and produce alternative readings. This means that her arguments may claim to be new, but not necessarily any truer than other readings. Her cultural analysis derives considerable impetus from its strenuous pursuit of a clear goal, but ultimately her individual judgments about the meaning of textual extracts are contestable hypotheses. The book distinguishes itself sharply from humanist exegetics by signaling its political concerns: Belsey contrasts her own "substantial political purposes" with "the mysterious aesthetic and moral pleasures" of traditional criticism (10). This self-conscious polemic, suffused with a Foucauldian sense that we construct the past only by reworking representations in the light of our own subject positions, lends vigor to the discourse of *The Subject of Tragedy* but does not in itself guarantee the book's conclusions.

Alan Sinfield, coeditor of *Political Shakespeare,* carries forward some of the concerns of Dollimore and Belsey in his *Faultlines: Cultural Materialism and the Politics of Dissident Reading* (1992). Dissident reading is an interpretation that amplifies the ideologically subversive elements in a text, as do Dollimore's readings in *Radical Tragedy.* Sinfield claims that his procedures offer "a way of apprehending the strategic organizations of texts—both the modes by which they produce plausible stories and construct subjectivities, and the faultlines and breaking points through which they enable dissident reading." This critical activity is placed within an overall program of "relating English teaching and writing to left-wing political concerns."[47]

Sinfield offers a politicized reading of *Othello,* taking up the idea that the subject constructs itself, within ideology, by continuously fashioning and refashioning the story of its life. There are obvious affinities to Belsey here, and to Stephen Greenblatt's work on the idea of selfhood in the Renaissance.[48] Sinfield postulates the ideological conditions within which the characters in *Othello* hammer out their self-defining stories. What he calls the "conditions of plausibility" for these stories are established by the dominant ideologies of Venetian culture, and they include, he suggests, "the notion that Blacks are inferior outsiders" (30). Sinfield argues that Othello is aware of the falsity of this stereotype, at least in the first act of the play. The hero's defense against Brabantio's charge of bewitchment and abduction is said to employ "two main strategies": first, Othello mirrors the Venetians' self-concept by appearing rational and contained in the face of his accuser; secondly, however, in his account of his extraordinary adventures, he appeals to a stereotype of the alien that is at odds with his Venetian sangfroid. Sinfield sees this appeal as conscious and artful: "shrewdly," he suggests, Othello "uses the racist idea of himself as exotic" (30), in order to convince the Senate that he captivated Desdemona by outlandish tales of adventure. In casting himself in this stereotypical role, Othello makes a knowing concession to Venetian racial prejudice. It is a calculated measure, the more finely judged because it involves "granting, in more benign form, part of Brabantio's case" (30).

In explaining Othello's exploitation of Venetian ideology, Sinfield stipulates that no discursively constructed subject can attain "a privileged vantage point outside the dominant" (45). Rather, it is the incongruities within ideology itself that enable it to be interrogated: in the case of Othello, it is paradoxical that the "inferior outsider" has been entrusted with a key military position in Venice. In effect, however, interrogation thus conceived amounts to a ventilation of the dominant structures of perception, and the subject, while thinking within ideology, can think critically about the conventional world-view. Ideology, then, permits a degree of dissident thinking. In fact, Sinfield's vocabulary implies that the subject can be conscious of its own position within ideology: "If ideology is so intricately 'layered,' with so many potential modes of relation to it, it cannot but allow awareness of its own operations." Such awareness is not confined to Othello himself, Sinfield argues, for Emilia, too, in her critique of the double standard in sexual morality, "takes notable steps towards a dissident perception" (46). Sinfield theorizes the workings of ideology in a manner that permits a degree of individual autonomy and self-consciousness. He cites in support Anthony Giddens's analogy between ideology and language: a grammatical sentence is framed within linguistic conventions, but "it is individual and, through its utterance, may both confirm and slightly modify language."[49]

The application of this theory to Othello, whose manipulation of the Senate's prejudice is presumably a kind of informed dissidence, is, however, inadequately documented from the play: the descent of the hero from manipulator of ideology to its victim is implausibly charted. The essay argues that Iago, in the course of deceiving Othello, trades in cultural stereotypes and therefore manufactures plausible lies about Desdemona, Cassio, and Othello himself. As a result, Sinfield observes, "Othello is persuaded of his inferiority and of Desdemona's inconstancy" (31). This is a measure of the extent to which Othello has internalized Venetian ideology, just as, in Stephen Greenblatt's reading of the play, it is an index of the Moor's enthusiastic espousal of Christian doctrine.[50] It seems difficult to square this surrender to cultural norms with the sophisticated appropriation of senatorial expectations that Sinfield finds in 1.3. A convincing version of the case would need to resolve this difficulty by detailed reference to Iago's infiltration of Othello. As it is, the account jumps in the space of a paragraph from the Senate Scene (1.3) to Othello's final speech (5.2), in which he identifies himself with a "base Indian" (5.2.356) and "turbaned Turk" (5.3.362) before taking his own life. Sinfield sees the speech in predictable terms as an example of Althusserian "interpellation," the subject being defined as the juncture of numerous ideological discourses: "Venice hails Othello as a barbarian, and he acknowledges that it is he they mean" (31).

Sinfield's attempt to disengage the play from what he sees as the "reactionary politics" underlying "traditional critical activity" is also unconvincing. On the one hand, he has it that "The easiest way to make *Othello* plausible in Britain is to rely on the lurking racism, sexism, and superstition in British culture . . . We can make [Othello's] gullibility plausible by suggesting that black people are generally of a rather simple disposition" (50). Yet, to explain Othello in this way is to ignore the ostentatious villainy of Iago, the Vice and Machiavel whose deception extends beyond Othello and the gull Roderigo to Cassio, Desdemona, Montano, Lodovico,

and Emilia, thereby making Othello's susceptibility less egregious. Sinfield recognizes the malignity of Iago, but not the degree to which it qualifies any impression of Othello's gullibility; to give due weight to the villain of the piece would be to weaken Sinfield's wider cultural argument; in making a point about modern British culture, he simplifies the play.

Sinfield also examines tragedy as a locus of tension between Calvinist and Stoic ideas. He contends that "The reformed English church, centrally and generally, was Calvinist" rather than Lutheran (143), while "the principal model of tragedy" was Seneca (214). Attempts were made in the sixteenth and seventeenth centuries to accommodate Seneca's tragedies to Christian doctrine, notably by applying a providential overlay to the plays, but some of Seneca's ideas were difficult to reconcile with Calvinism, above all his tendency "to validate Stoic ethics entirely on rationalist grounds, and to show humankind and the universe to be devoid of transcendent purpose" (215). Sinfield concludes that Senecan tragedy "facilitated engagements with religious unorthodoxy" (217).

A raw nerve in Calvinist doctrine, Sinfield suggests, was the predestination of the elect. Theologians debated how far it was compatible with divine mercy and justice; how apparent inconsistencies in the Bible could be resolved; how a distinction could be made between the operation of Providence, in which Calvinists urged believers to rejoice, and the arbitrary strokes of a pagan Fortune or Fate, which invited a Senecan Stoicism as the apt response. *Hamlet* is discussed as a site of this ideological conflict. Sinfield reminds us that the play alludes to Stoicism in Hamlet's praise of Horatio as "A man that Fortune's buffets and rewards / Hast ta'en with equal thanks" (3.2.65-66). The hero himself, however, fails to attain the Stoic ideals of emotional control and dedication to duty, and his development in the play, as Sinfield reads it, is marked by a number of debates on aspects of Stoic philosophy. The "To be or not to be" soliloquy, for example (3.1.58-90), is seen as focusing the Stoic issue of the proper attitude to suicide: it is exalted as a dignified end in extreme circumstances, but condemned if it is a precipitate and cowardly retreat from endurable adversity. In the same vein, Sinfield relates Hamlet's words to Rosencrantz and Guildenstern in the second act ("What a piece of work is a man . . . quintessence of dust," 2.2.304-10) not only to what he calls "optimistic humanism" and Neoplatonic notions of the soul's perfectibility, but to Hamlet's disillusion "at the failure of the Stoic ideal in others and himself" (224).

Sinfield finds the ideological complexities to be most strongly marked in Hamlet's own acknowledgement of divine Providence in the last two acts of the play. At this stage, it is argued, Hamlet "seems to have abandoned his Stoic aspirations" (226), and there is a vivid sense of events bearing the hero along: his impulse to read the orders given to Rosencrantz and Guildenstern, and his speedy revision of the death warrant; his boarding of the pirate ship and subsequent separation from his own vessel; his good treatment by the pirates; his references to "a divinity that shapes our ends" and the "special providence in the fall of a sparrow" (5.2.10, 165). There is an intensive deployment of dramaturgical resources here to negotiate what Sinfield calls "a particularly awkward ideological moment" (227), in which Hamlet's endorsement of Christian Providentialism as opposed to pagan Stoicism must be rendered plausibly. Accepting the governing role of divine Providence in human affairs means, in a Calvinist context, accepting that both good and bad, elect and reprobate, may suffer at God's hands as part of the divine scheme of things. The action of *Hamlet* at this point, therefore, moves towards an aesthetic rather than a philosophical resolution of this intricate theological issue.

Yet Sinfield holds that Hamlet's conversion remains problematic. The hero does not embrace Providence with a good heart, as recommended by those Calvinist divines who "urged . . . that the believer should show his or her delight in God's will by cooperating as far and as eagerly as possible" (228). After his exhilaration at his evasion of Claudius's death sentence and his reunion with Horatio, Hamlet lapses into a weary submission to forces beyond his control, including, preeminently, death, upon whose grisly ironies he dwells in the Graveyard Scene. Sinfield suggests that the "readiness" of which Hamlet speaks at 5.2.168 is a preparedness for death that makes purposeful action impossible. This readiness manifests itself above all in Hamlet's incaution, as he sweeps aside Horatio's misgivings about the fencing match and "competes recklessly with Laertes"; even the killing of Claudius is accomplished "in a burst of passionate inspiration" (228). Stoicism is reinstated as Hamlet's philosophical reference point, Sinfield suggests; but it is an enervated Stoicism that responds to divine determinism with jaundiced passivity. Hamlet, in short, "sees no point, now, in bothering" (229), neglecting even to exercise the rudimentary caution that Calvinist authorities recommended. Sinfield concludes that Hamlet's "slide into Senecan fatalism" (230) embodies precisely the tendency against which Calvin inveighs as he expounds Providentialist doctrine in his *Institutes of the Christian Religion;* the play, therefore, accentuates this theological crux rather than resolving it.

Sinfield's dissident reading, centering on Hamlet's rashness, is suspect because it ignores the connection made in the play between unpremeditated behavior and the hand of God. In 5.2, Hamlet offers rather more than the "sermon tags" noted by Sinfield (226). He reflects that rashness attunes him to divine Providence in a way that considered action does not:

> Rashly—
> And praised be rashness for it: let us know
> Our indiscretion sometime serves us well
> When our dear plots do pall, and that should
> teach us
> There's a divinity that shapes our ends,
> Rough-hew them how we will.

> (5.2.6-11)

Hamlet refers here to his impromptu visit to Rosencrantz and Guildenstern's cabin, where he found the sealed commission from Claudius importing his death. When he describes how he rewrote the document, he stresses again the spontaneity of his behavior:

> Being thus benetted round with villainies—
> Ere I could make a prologue to my brains
> They had begun the play—I sat me down;
> Devised a new commission, wrote it fair.

> (5.2.30-33)

The haste with which he proceeds is seen by Hamlet as a means of aligning himself with Providence, circumventing conscious calculation and thereby swimming with the Providential current. There is certainly no need to see his behavior here as a disillusioned Stoicism. In the same way, his acquiescence in the duel with apparent disregard for his safety represents precisely that alacrity in complying with the divine will that Sinfield claims is absent from the hero. Providentialist discourse may well be queried in the play, but the faultline is by no means as clear as Sinfield suggests.

Even if one accepts Sinfield's argument in relation to *Hamlet,* it is not necessary to endorse his thesis on the centrality of Calvinism to the English Reformation. His declaration that "The reformed English church, centrally and generally, was Calvinist" (143), a "Reformation orthodoxy hardly disputed in the English church before 1600" (153) is supported by a number of primary and secondary sources, but it underestimates the complexity of the reforming process in an uncentralized church organization. Elizabeth, for example, was unreformed in her liturgical tastes, evincing a fondness for Latin and for Catholic harmonics in church music, as well as retaining the notorious silver crucifix in the Chapel Royal. More importantly, she could not impose a settlement uniformly on the English church, but had to accept a series of local compromises negotiated between radical and conservative elements. In any event, the Calvinist discourse cited in the essay is prescriptive, not descriptive of people's actual belief, as Sinfield admits (152).

Sinfield's insistence on the Calvinist orthodoxy is part of his critique of what he terms the "Christian humanism" supposedly dominant in literary studies until the 1970s and characterized by "a genial, moderate (except when under threat), gentlemanly/ladylike attachment to something not too specific, but involving a loose respect for Jesus' Sermon on the Mount and an assumption that 'redemption' will come to people of goodwill" (144-45). Such bland Christianity, Sinfield suggests, reworks Renaissance religion in its own soft-focus image, denying the "violently polarized kind of Christianity" and the "rigors of protestant experience" that are "very likely uncongenial to modern readers" (145). Any attempt to recover Renaissance viewpoints alien to us is commendable, but Sinfield's "Christian humanism" is not exemplified in detail, only Kenneth Muir and Theodore Spencer on Shakespeare being adduced, together with Louis L. Martz on Donne. In view of the difficulties attendant on Dollimore's proposed humanist consensus, it seems reasonable to suspend judgment on Sinfield's until more supporting evidence is provided.

It is also possible to recognize Senecan allusions in *Hamlet* without adopting Sinfield's view that "Seneca was the principal model for tragedy" (214). In aligning himself with T. S. Eliot and John W. Cunliffe on this issue, Sinfield notes that G. K. Hunter "disputes Seneca's importance on thematic grounds—because he believes that early modern drama is distinguished by a strong assertion of 'the redeeming feature of a tragic existence: the gratuitous loyalties, the constancy under pressure, the renewed faith'" (215). Sinfield refers here to Hunter's essay "Seneca and English Tragedy" (1974) but simplifies Hunter's argument considerably.[51] Hunter warns against overestimating Seneca's influence on English tragedy. He argues that it is hard to separate Senecan elements from those derived from the native English tradition. He underlines the permeability of generic boundaries in the Renaissance and the consequent presence of cross-generic influences, in particular that of Ovid. His conclusion is that Seneca must be seen as one factor among others in the intellectual milieu of the Renaissance. The point is not the superiority of one judgment or the other, but that Sinfield does not represent his opponent's thesis accurately. The thematic argument features in Hunter as one of a number of propositions constituting a much larger case. Sinfield, like Dollimore in his account of the humanist criticism of tragedy, seems impelled by his own argumentative momentum to reduce or distort an opposing point of view.

Marxist criticism like that of Dollimore, Belsey, and Sinfield uses texts as points of location for a broader social analysis. The procedure is legitimate when the readings are demonstrably consistent with the textual evidence, but the capacity of texts to sustain multiple interpretations means that any reading is open to dispute. The Marxist theorists Althusser and Macherey themselves enhance our sense of the complexity of texts through their aesthetic of discordance, which brings out the disunity of the literary work. In this context, it is impossible for Marxist criticism to claim absolute validity for its readings or a privileged status for its intellectual apparatus. It commands a place as one more way of talking about texts, and its concern, however laudable, for the oppressed and dispossessed in the modern world does not compel assent to any of its individual exegeses.

Recent history has itself demanded a response from Marxist critics. In his review of *Shakespeare Reproduced,* John Drakakis notes "the paradoxical rise of Marxism as an intellectual position at a time when it is faring badly in the West as a political paradigm."[52] The comment, published in Autumn 1989, predates the collapse of East European communist regimes from 1989 onwards. These events scarcely lend impetus to Marxist intellectual activity, though it is important to distinguish between Marxism as a system of ideas or a means of analysis on the one hand, and the practice of states that purport to embody Marxist principles on the other; between the theory and the practice there is ample room for criticism to operate on the contextualization, reception, and use of Shakespeare. Nonetheless, the political shift in Eastern Europe highlights the need to historicize Marxism, too; as a conceptual framework it is as historically contingent as any other. Dollimore seems aware of this need in his introduction to the 1989 edition of *Radical Tragedy;* he reflects that "contemporary Marxist criticism has as complex and dynamic a relation to the writings of Marx as does contemporary psychoanalysis to Freud, or Christianity to the Old and New Testaments."[53] The relationship is likely to become more complex, and Marxism, including Marxist criticism, more self-qualificatory.

Notes

[1] Terry Eagleton, *Marxism and Literary Criticism* (London, 1976), vii; subsequent page references follow quotations in the text.

[2] Terry Eagleton, *Literary Theory: An Introduction* (Oxford, 1983), 15.

[3] Jonathan Dollimore and Alan Sinfield, "History and Ideology: The Instance of *Henry V,*" in *Alternative Shakespeares,* edited by John Drakakis (London and New York, 1985), 210-11.

[4] Jonathan Dollimore, *Radical Tragedy* (Brighton, 1984), 9.

[5] Louis Althusser, *Lenin and Philosophy and Other Essays* (English translation, London, 1971), 28.

[6] Pierre Macherey, *Pour Une Théorie de la Production Littéraire* (Paris, 1966), translated by Geoffrey Wall (London, 1978), 78; subsequent references in the text.

[7] See, for example, the following works by Foucault (in translation): *Madness and Civilization* (London, 1967); *The Order of Things* (London, 1970); *The Archaeology of Knowledge* (London, 1972); *Discipline and Punish* (London, 1977).

[8] Eagleton, *Literary Theory* (1983), 199, 207.

[9] Ibid., 22.

[10] Ibid., 23-24.

[11] Ibid., 197, 200.

[12] *Political Shakespeare* (1985), vii, viii.

[13] *Radical Tragedy* (1989 ed.), xlviii.

[14] Eagleton, *Criticism and Ideology* (1976), 68.

[15] Dollimore, *Radical Tragedy* (1984), 277, note 12; subsequent references in the text.

[16] *Radical Tragedy,* 191.

[17] Ibid., 192. Dollimore here builds on L. L. Schücking, *Character-Problems in Shakespeare's Plays* (tr. London, 1922), 168.

[18] Ibid., 197.

[19] Ibid., 198, 202.

[20] Ibid., 191, 192.

[21] Ibid., 188, 194.

[22] Quotations from Shakespeare's plays are taken from *William Shakespeare: The Complete Works,* General Editors Stanley Wells and Gary Taylor (Oxford, 1986), compact edition (Oxford, 1988). I am grateful to Oxford University Press for permission to reproduce this material.

[23] A. C. Bradley, *Shakespearean Tragedy* (London, 1904), 289.

[24] Walter Burkert, "Greek Tragedy and Sacrificial Ritual," *Greek, Roman and Byzantine Studies,* 7 (1966), 121.

[25] Philip Brockbank, "Upon Such Sacrifices," 66th British Academy Shakespeare Lecture (Oxford, 1976), 23; subsequent references in the text.

[26] Clifford Leech, *Shakespeare's Tragedies and Other Studies in Seventeenth Century Drama* (London, 1950), 15, 16, 17.

[27] Clifford Leech, *Tragedy,* in the Critical Idiom series (London, 1969), 40; subsequent references in the text.

[28] *Shakespeare's Tragedies,* 18; *Tragedy,* 60.

[29] Hunter, *Dramatic Identities and Cultural Tradition: Studies in Shakespeare and his Contemporaries* (Liverpool, 1978), 251-52.

[30] Ibid., 269.

[31] *Radical Tragedy,* 193.

[32] Barbara Everett, "The New *King Lear,*" *Critical Quarterly,* 2, 4 (1960), 333, 334; subsequent references in the text.

[33] A similar argument could be mounted in relation to Robert Ornstein's *The Moral Vision of Jacobean Tragedy* (Madison, 1960), to which Dollimore also refers.

[34] *Radical Tragedy,* 194.

[35] Lever, *Tragedy of State,* 83, 84; subsequent references in the text.

[36] *Radical Tragedy,* 231.

[37] Ibid., 234.

[38] Ibid., 242.

[39] Lever, 84.

[40] Mark H. Curtis, "The Alienated Intellectuals of Early Stuart England," in *Crisis in Europe 1560-1660,* edited by Trevor Aston (London, 1965).

[41] *Radical Tragedy* (1989 edition), xviii.

[42] *Political Shakespeare,* edited by Dollimore and Sinfield (1985), 4.

[43] Catherine Belsey, *The Subject of Tragedy: Identity and Difference in Renaissance Drama* (London and New York, 1985), 10; subsequent page references in the text.

[44] Ferdinand de Saussure, *Cours de Linguistique Générale* (Paris, 1916), translated by Roy Harris as *Course in General Linguistics* (London, 1983).

[45] Mikhail Bakhtin, *Problems of Dostoevsky's Poetics* (English translation, Michigan, 1973; first published in Russian, 1929), 134.

[46] C. L. Barber, *Shakespeare's Festive Comedy: A Study of Dramatic Form and Its Relations to Social Custom* (Princeton, 1959; 1972 edition), 4.

[47] Alan Sinfield, *Faultlines: Cultural Materialism and the Politics of Dissident Reading* (Oxford, 1992), 9, 8; subsequent references in the text.

[48] See Stephen Greenblatt, *Renaissance Self-Fashioning: From More to Shakespeare* (Chicago and London, 1980), ...

[49] Anthony Giddens, *Central Problems in Social Theory* (London, 1979), cited in Sinfield, *Faultlines,* 33.

[50] See Greenblatt, op. cit., ...

[51] See T. S. Eliot, Introduction, in *Seneca, his Tenne Tragedies,* edited by Thomas Newton (1581; New York, 1967); John W. Cunliffe, *The Influence of Seneca on Elizabethan Tragedy* (Hampden, Conn., 1965). See also G. K. Hunter, "Seneca and English Tragedy," in *Seneca,* ed. C. D. N. Costa (1974), reprinted in G. K. Hunter, *Dramatic Identities and Cultural Tradition*

(1978). Also in *Dramatic Identities,* see Hunter, "Seneca and the Elizabethans: A Case-Study in 'Influence.'"

[52] John Drakakis, review in *Shakespeare Quarterly,* 40 (1989), 342.

[53] Dollimore, *Radical Tragedy* (1989 ed.), xliv.

———————

Source: "Marxist Criticism: Cultural Materialism, and the History of the Subject," in *Shakespeare's Tragedies and Modern Critical Theory*, Fairleigh Dickinson University Press, 1997, pp. 38-63.

The "Noble Thing" and the "Boy of Tears": *Coriolanus* and the Embarrassments of Identity

Burton Hatlen, *University of Maine at Orono*

Tonally, *Coriolanus* is Shakespeare's coolest tragedy. The protagonist does not invite audience identification—if anything, he spurns our sympathy. But the play treats his antagonists no less coolly. As a consequence, audiences and critics have often seen the play as working not so much upon our passions as upon our analytic faculties.[1] But what questions does the play address? In our century, many critics have seen the play as turning on political issues. For some of these critics, the key issue is the struggle, whether in ancient Rome or in Jacobean England, between opposing social classes, noble and plebeian, or the relationship of the "great man" to the people, while other critics have argued that the play problematizes the very concept of the "political." But a second tradition of interpretation has built on psychoanalytic theory to explore Coriolanus' problematic relationship with his mother. And yet a third school of critics has focused on the way the play self-reflexively examines issues of language, especially naming. In this paper, I want to build some bridges among these three schools of interpretation, by focusing on two interrelated issues that seem to me central to *Coriolanus:* the issues of identity and shame.[2]

Identity is born at the interface between the public and the private realms. But because it is ambiguously both personal and social, identity is inherently flawed, vulnerable, and shame represents the (always reluctant) acknowledgment of the problematic status of individual identity. *Coriolanus,* I will argue, demonstrates that identity is not only problematic but "impossible," simply because any form of selfhood is always already implicated in otherness. The play demonstrates the impossibility of identity in at least three ways. On the social level, Coriolanus attempts to define himself as an autonomous individual, only to discover that the self is always dependent upon the social ground on which it stands. Psychologically, Coriolanus struggles to separate himself from his mother, but finally fails. And on the linguistic level, he sets out to name himself, only to fail once again. On all three levels, furthermore, the concrete sign of Coriolanus' failure to become the "author of himself" (5.3.36)[3] is a flood of shame, which thus serves to define the limit of personal identity, the moment when identity dissolves into contradiction. Around the issues of identity and shame, then, all the great themes of *Coriolanus*—political, psychological, linguistic—converge.[4]

II

That *Coriolanus* is Shakespeare's most political play—perhaps his "only great political play"[5]—has become a commonplace of Shakespeare studies. For many commentators, a political play must necessarily be partisan. Thus our century has seen an extended critical debate over whether the patricians (and thus Coriolanus) are "right" and the plebeians "wrong," or vice versa. Eugene Waith, for example, sees Coriolanus and the class he represents as the embodiment of everything truly noble, and he argues that Shakespeare "makes it impossible to respect" the "many-voiced, ceaselessly shifting people."[6] And C. C. Huffman argues that "of all the available possibilities of presenting [the] political situation [dramatized in *Coriolanus*], Shakespeare chooses one consonant with King James's royalist view of it as a rivalry between absolute monarchy and democracy, between rule and misrule, between order and chaos."[7] In contrast, Kenneth Muir sees Shakespeare reworking his source materials to give us "a more favorable idea of the citizens" by emphasizing their "genuine grievances" and their willingness to "forgive Coriolanus' deplorable rudeness to them."[8] This debate goes on—as recently as 1989, for example, Annabel Patterson offered an eloquent defense of the "populist" reading of the play.[9]

But another tradition of political interpretation has emphasized the ways in which *Coriolanus,* rather than choosing sides in the class struggle, dramatizes the very nature of the political itself. This tradition finds its first major spokesperson in A. P. Rossiter, who sees the play as concerned "with the workings of men's wills in the practical management of affairs; with the making (by some), the manipulation (by others) of 'scenes,' emotional eruptions of individual or group will; with all that unstable, shifting, trustless, feckless, foolish-shrewd, canny, short-sighted, self-seeking, high-minded, confused, confusing *matter* which makes up a State's state of mind."[10] Robert S. Miola argues that in *Coriolanus* Shakespeare "exposes the paradoxes inherent in the civilized community, especially those deriving from the differences between private virtue and the public good, or as Aristotle put it, between the good man and the good citizen."[11] And Stanley Cavell has proposed that *Coriolanus* "is not a play about politics, if this means about political authority and conflict, say about questions of legitimate succession or divided loyalties. It is about the formation of the political, the founding of the city, about what it is that makes a rational animal fit for conversation, for civility."[12] Like some other recent commentators[13] I will here attempt to follow up on Cavell's suggestion that *Coriolanus* is about the "creation of the political." But I want to go beyond Cavell and his heirs in one respect, by linking the "creation of the political" to my two key issues, identity and shame.

The political, I will argue, makes possible personal identity: for human beings there is no "self" outside of or prior to the political order. Yet this order also necessarily denies the autonomy of that self to which it gives birth. There is here a fundamental and irreducible contradiction, so fundamental that the political represents not so much a stable "order" as an ongoing dialectical process.[14] In *Coriolanus* the issue of identity is posed first of all as a debate over the question of what it means to be a Roman. Coriolanus, born in Rome of a Roman mother, a soldier in the service of the Roman state, finds himself defined by circumstances of birth and profession as a Roman. But what is a Roman? At the beginning of the play, we see signs of increasing conflict between the two principal social classes in the city, the patricians and the plebeians. Does "Rome" embody itself in one of these social classes or the other? Or is the social conflict itself in some sense constitutive of Rome? Is "Romanness" equally present in each Roman, regardless of social position? Or are some Romans more Roman than others? Conversely, is it possible for some "Romans" to be "un-Roman," as a certain Select Committee of the U.S. House of Representatives once defined some Americans, or the actions of certain Americans, as "Un-American"?[15]

At the beginning of the play Coriolanus sees himself and is seen by others not only as a Roman, but as the very embodiment of *romanitas*. Unflinching courage, absolute devotion to the state, and by implication disdain for a "Greek" predilection for reflection over action—these are the attributes that define the ideal Roman. And these are the values that Volumnia has instilled in her son, as she reveals in her opening exchange with Virgilia:

> *Vol.* To a cruel war I sent him, from whence
> he returned, his brows bound with oak. I
> tell thee, daughter, I sprang not more in joy
> on first hearing he was a man-child than
> now in first seeing he had proved himself a
> man.
>
> *Vir.* But had he died in the business, madam,
> how then?
>
> *Vol.* Then his good report should have been
> my son. . . . [H]ad I a dozen sons, each in
> my love alike and none less dear than thine
> and my good Marcius, I had rather had
> eleven die nobly for their country than one
> voluptuously surfeit out of action.
>
> (1.3.13-25)

After the battle of Corioles, Coriolanus himself sums up this Roman credo to the two Roman generals, Cominius and Titus Lartius: "I have done / As you have done—that's what I can; / Induced as you have been— that's for my country" (1.9.15-17). And Cominius in reply sees Coriolanus as, in effect, the perfect "product" of Rome: "Rome must know / The value of her own" (1.9.20-21).

Yet, paradoxically, Coriolanus' very conception of himself as the quintessence of *romanitas* ends by placing him in opposition to Rome as a concrete historical and social reality. This split within Coriolanus' self-image occurs at the moment when the Roman army retreats before the Volscians, triggering this tirade from Coriolanus:

> All the contagion of the south light on you,
> You shames of Rome! You herd of—Boils
>   and plagues
> Plaster you o'er, that you may be abhorred
> Farther than seen, and one infect another
> Against the wind a mile! You souls of
>   geese,
> That bear the shapes of men, how have you
>   run
> From slaves that apes would beat! Pluto and
>   hell!
>
> (1.4.31-37)

The language here suggests that what we today call "losers" are not only un-Roman but subhuman—a disease, an excrescence on the face of the earth. And significantly, one of our key words, "shame," figures prominently in this speech: if people like *this* are Romans, Coriolanus declares, then he is ashamed to think of himself as a Roman. For insofar as he shares an identity with creatures such as these, then his own identity is infected, plastered over with boils and plagues.

Because Coriolanus' identity as a Roman implicates him with all other Romans, including the common people that he despises, he finds himself in an intolerable situation.[16] His dilemma is most fully dramatized for us in Act 2, scenes 2 and 3, and again in Act 3, scenes 2 and 3. In both these extended episodes Coriolanus struggles with the legal requirement that he present himself before the Roman people and ask for their "voices" before he can assume the office of consul. As a soldier he can—or so he believes—stand alone, but as a politician he is dependent upon the good will of his fellow Romans. The requirement that he appear before the people in a "gown of humility" is only pro forma: if he will go through the motions, the office of consul is his. Twice he overcomes his revulsion and agrees to go through this ritual. And twice at the decisive moment he balks and begins to berate the very people whose votes he needs.

In the first of these incidents, Coriolanus makes it clear that the issue is shame:

> I do beseech you,
> Let me o'erleap that custom, for I cannot
> Put on the gown, stand naked, and entreat
>   them
> For my wounds' sake to give their suffrage
>
> . . . . .
>
>   It is a part
> That I shall blush in acting
>
> . . . . .
>
> To brag unto them, "Thus I did, and thus!"
> Show them th' unaching scars which I should
>   hide,
> As if I had received them for the hire
> Of their breath only!
>
>   (2.2.136-52)

Coriolanus' shame arises in part from a sense that he will be acting a false role: he doesn't *feel* humble, so to put on the "gown of humility" seems hypocritical. But it is also clear that he is ashamed to expose himself, to "stand naked."[17] He wants to hide his scars, not display them. Here we have a simpler, more universal kind of shame. And what is it he fears, if not the revelation that he too is human, a creature of flesh and blood, sharing a common destiny with the ordinary people that he so disdains? And that his actions belong, not to himself, but to the city that has given him his identity?[18]

Our protagonist's self-identification with Rome and his contempt for Rome as an actual historical polity reach a climax in Act 3, scene 3, where the tribunes banish Coriolanus from Rome, and he replies,

> You common cry of curs, whose breath I hate
> As reek o' the rotten fens, whose loves I prize
> As the dead carcasses of unburied men
> That do corrupt my air, I banish you!
>
>   (130-33)

Again we hear Coriolanus' usual note of abuse: these supposed Romans are subhuman creatures, curs, and their very breath breeds infection. He claims ownership not only of the ideal of *romanitas* but of the very air itself. And indeed, if he embodies the quintessence of Rome, then wherever he is, there Rome is: thus his famous bravura gesture, "I banish you!" Yet at this moment—the end of Act 3, traditionally the climax of a five-act play, the point of reversal and the beginning of the falling action—the absurdity of Coriolanus' posture also becomes inescapable. He cannot in fact "be Rome" all by himself. To identify oneself as a Roman means to be part of something larger than oneself. But Coriolanus refuses any longer to see himself as a part of Rome, and what will happen now to his identity?[19]

Coriolanus' final curse upon the city of his birth defines the problem: "Despising / For you the city, thus I turn my back. / There is a world elsewhere" (3.3.142-44). Is there indeed a "world elsewhere"? This is the question that the last two acts of the play will address. And the answer, I believe, is "No. Or at any rate, not the kind of world that Coriolanus wants."[20] The problem is that any "world elsewhere" remains just that: a world. And any world claims rights—*absolute* rights, rights of life and death—over any person who seeks to define an identity in terms of that world. For Coriolanus does not simply go off to live alone, in the splendid isolation of his untarnished ego. Rather he goes off to join forces with his erstwhile enemies, the Volscians. But can the conqueror of Corioles find a new identity as a citizen of that city? The answer is, clearly, "No."

In the last act of the play Coriolanus leads a Volscian army to the gates of Rome and threatens to conquer the city. He does so, however, not as a Volscian, but simply as a hired gun: and in the space between the city of his birth and his new allies, he is in limbo, "a kind of nothing, titleless, / Till he had forged himself a name o' the fire / Of burning Rome" (5.1.13). By defeating Rome, that is, Coriolanus hopes to regain the identity he lost when he left the city of his birth in search of a world elsewhere. Yet as soon as we conceptualize this possibility, we must recognize that such an identity would be a contradiction in terms. No one can, in fact, "conquer" an identity. If he conquers Rome, as his mother tells him, he will destroy once and for all any possibility that Rome will offer him a functional identity:

> if thou conquer Rome, the benefit
> Which thou shalt thereby reap is such a name
> Whose repetition will be dogged with curses,
> Whose chronicle thus writ: "The man was
>   noble,
> But with his last attempt he wiped it out,
> Destroyed his country, and his name remains
> To th' ensuing age abhorred."
>
>   (5.3.142-48)

The referent of the "it" in "wiped it out" is ambiguous. But this ambiguity itself is the most telling detail here, for to destroy "your" country, the very basis of your self, is to annihilate everything, including the self.[21]

When Coriolanus recognizes that he can never recover his Romanness by conquering Rome and accedes to his mother's pleas, his identity simply collapses. Why does he return to Corioles with Aufidius? Surely he knows that the Volscians have never accepted him as one of themselves—that they have simply tolerated him as a mercenary as long as he agrees to do their will? And since he has now decided not to do what they want, surely he must realize that the Volscians will now discard him. He suggests as much to his mother:

> O my Mother, Mother! O!
> You have won a happy victory to Rome;
> But for your son—believe it, O, believe it!—
> Most dangerously you have with him
> 　prevailed,
> If not most mortal to him.

(5.3.185-89)

In the circumstances, Coriolanus' decision to return to Corioles seems tantamount to suicide. With no possibility of finding an identity either in Rome or among the Volscians, he is now condemned to remain "a kind of nothing" forever. Thus it should not surprise us that he surrenders to death without a struggle. Of all Shakespeare's tragic protagonists, Coriolanus is surely the most "heroic," a cool and invincible soldier. Yet in his death he is the most passive—even Lear seizes a sword to kill the slave that was hanging Cordelia. Coriolanus gives himself to the conspirators' swords as if he were already dead—as indeed he is, from the moment when, outside the gates of Rome, his struggle toward an identity collapses under its internal contradictions.

III

On the social level, then, Coriolanus cannot accept himself as a part of Rome, as simply a Roman; but neither can he separate himself from Rome to become an autonomous individual. Either possibility would allow him to establish an identity, but in the circumstances identity becomes impossible for him. Parallel to this struggle for a social identity, Coriolanus is also engaged in a struggle for personal identity. Here the principal issue is his relationship, not to the city, but to his mother Volumnia and to the other members of his family. At times in the play, as when Volumnia persuades her son to stand for consul in Act 3, and as when she persuades him not to conquer the city in Act 5, the city and the mother may seem identical. For Volumnia defines herself as the "perfect Roman mother," and she has deliberately inculcated in her son the Roman ideals summed above. Yet an exploration of Coriolanus' relation to his city demands a socially and politically based interpretive framework, whereas to understand his relationship to his mother we must focus on the psychological dynamics of the relationship between mother and son. In the last two decades a rich tradition of psychological commentary on *Coriolanus* has emerged, stimulated primarily by Janet Adelman's interpretation of the play[22]; and in the discussion that follows I will build upon this tradition.

Volumnia's name invites a psychoanalytic reading of this play, for she is voluminous, all-encompassing, engulfing. She claims to have made her son what he is, and he does not dispute this idea. Defiant toward all other influences, he cannot resist her wishes. But Volumnia "is not a nourishing mother," says Adelman,

who sees "the image of the mother who has not fed her children enough" as central to *Coriolanus* (p. 148). Some later commentators in this psychoanalytic tradition have wondered whether the problem lies not so much in Volumnia herself as in the value system of Roman society,[23] or have read the play as a critique of the ways in which women who are denied an active role in society are tempted to enact a "male" identity through their sons, with disastrous consequences to both mother and son.[24] But no one disputes Adelman's suggestion that Coriolanus' behavior represents a frantic flight from the female: "The rigid masculinity that Coriolanus finds in war becomes a defense against acknowledgment of his neediness; he nearly succeeds in transforming himself from a vulnerable human creature into a grotesquely invulnerable and isolated thing" (p. 149). From a psychoanalytic perspective,[25] Coriolanus' impetuous plunge into the gates of Corioles (metaphorically, the vulva, the "gates of life") and his victorious emergence becomes a violent reentry into the womb and a symbolic rebirth as a purely male being:

> 　　　His sword, death's stamp
> Where it did mark, it took; from face to foot
> He was a thing of blood, whose every motion
> Was timed with dying cries. Alone he entered
> The mortal gate o' the city, which he painted
> With shunless destiny; aidless came off,
> And with a sudden reinforcement struck
> Corioles like a planet. Now all's his

(2.2.107-14)

The new Coriolanus born in this moment is a hard, invulnerable "thing," a "thing of blood," armed with a phallic sword that disseminates death.[26] And in this guise he becomes a portent, even a kind of god.[27]

Coriolanus' attempt to transform himself into a "noble thing"—so Aufidius labels him (4.5.121)—that will be invulnerable to all female influences obviously fails. But why does it fail? For Adelman, the cause lies in unresolved conflicts within Coriolanus himself: "it is the intensity and rigidity of Coriolanus' commitment to his masculine role that makes us suspect the intensity of the fears that this role is designed to hide, especially from himself" (p. 153). But I would argue that the problem lies not simply in the peculiarities of Coriolanus' individual psychological development but in the structure of human selfhood. Volumnia is the matrix out of which Coriolanus is born, the ground and origin of his existence. To deny her is to deny himself. Any final, absolute separation from the mother is in this respect impossible.

The male child may, as revisionist psychoanalytic theory proposes, need to separate himself from his mother to establish a male identity, and this project may be shadowed by a fear of sliding back into a state of undifferentiated unity with the engulfing mother.[28] Yet even if this separation is successful, it can never be absolute: the child, whether male or female, must in some way acknowledge the primordial experience of unity with the mother, a "blissful experience" that lies "buried but active in the core of one's identity."[29] But Coriolanus, an absolutist like all of Shakespeare's tragic protagonists, insists upon an absolute separation. His attempt to achieve such a separation marks him as psychologically flawed, for he is denying the deepest level of his experience. But it is important to recognize that the absolute autonomy to which Coriolanus aspires is also logically impossible: no human being can be the author of himself.

In his attempt to separate himself from his mother specifically and more generally from all manifestations of the female, Coriolanus is unable merely to assert an independent male identity. Instead he seeks out an alternative object of identification, an ideal embodiment of the "hard," thing-like masculine self he aspires toward, and he finds—or invents—such an object of identification in Aufidius.[30] At the first news that the Volscians are in arms, Coriolanus enthusiastically declares,

> They have a leader,
> Tullus Aufidius, that will put you to 't.
> I sin in envying his nobility,
> And were I anything but what I am
> I would wish me only he.
>
> . . . . .
>
> Were half to half the world by the ears and
> he
> Upon my party, I'd revolt, to make
> My wars only with him. He is a lion
> That I am proud to hunt.
>
> (1.1.229-37)

The action of the play does not support Coriolanus' initial picture of Aufidius as his sole worthy opponent, for every time the two fight, Coriolanus wins. In 1.8.15 Aufidius declares himself "shamed" because he needs to be rescued by other Volscians from imminent death at the hands of Coriolanus. And two scenes later we learn that in his shame Aufidius has given up the attempt to "crush" Coriolanus honorably, "in an equal force, / True sword to sword"; instead he will "potch at" Coriolanus some other way, by "wrath or craft" (1.10.13-16). Aufidius is not, then, the coeval that Coriolanus craves. But Coriolanus needs a mirror in which he can see reflected back to him his imagined heroic self, and he has created a fictional Aufidius to meet that need.

Appropriately, when Coriolanus goes off in search of a "world elsewhere," an alternative to the maternal Roma that threatens to engulf him, he moves toward

Aufidius. As he nears his erstwhile rival, his language grows oddly erotic: "My birthplace hate I, and my love's upon / This enemy town" (4.4.23-24). And Aufidius greets Coriolanus in words even more explicitly erotic:

> Let me twine
> Mine arms about that body, whereagainst
> My grainèd ash an hundred times hath broke
> And scarred the moon with splinters. Here I
> clip
> The anvil of my sword, and do contest
> As hotly and as nobly with thy love
> As ever in ambitious strength I did
> Contend against thy valor. Know thou first,
> I loved the maid I married; never man
> Sighed truer breath. But that I see thee here,
> Thou noble thing, more dances my rapt heart
> Than when I first my wedded mistress saw
> Bestride my threshold.
>
> (4.5.111-23)

By the end of the play, Aufidius' "love" of Coriolanus has come to appear distinctly hypocritical. Nevertheless, his extravagant rhetoric in this scene voices an ideal of comradely love between warriors that is clearly at work within Coriolanus himself and that Aufidius admires even as he violates the ideal. In flight from the female—as Aufidius' reference to his wife suggests—the two warriors embrace one another, in something like love. Indeed, this scene is as close as we come in this play to a love scene, as Coriolanus and Aufidius discover in one another the image of their hearts' desire.[31]

Yet there is an inescapable contradiction here, for both Coriolanus and Aufidius seem to be fixated at Lacan's mirror stage, entranced by a "perfect" image of the self.[32] And in both cases, too, the "perfect" self is a warrior self, directed entirely toward triumphing over all rivals. While they may "love" one another, then, Coriolanus and Aufidius cannot "make love." Rather, they can only "make war." Or perhaps more precisely, they can "make love" only by "making war" on each other. Thus in Aufidius' speech, military imagery and erotic imagery interpenetrate. The spear becomes a phallus, which "splinters" against the steely body of the beloved; and conversely, the phallus becomes a sword, which has been sharpening itself against the anvil of the beloved's body, and is now ready to consummate the lover's desire by (mortally) penetrating the loved flesh.[33] Such a "love" can end only in self and mutual destruction—a result graphically dramatized in the final scene, when Aufidius, in what must surely be Shakespeare's strangest stage direction, "stands on" the body of Coriolanus to deliver his final speech. Clearly, Aufidius is still grounding—in the most literal sense—his own identity on Coriolanus. This stage tableau graphically emblematizes the relationship of

Aufidius and Coriolanus throughout the play, for each has been "standing on" the other all along; and if you can create a self only by standing on someone else, sooner or later somebody—and someone necessary to your sense of self—will get crushed.

Thus identification with a masculine mirror image does not offer Coriolanus a way out of his dilemma. Caught between the Scylla of the engulfing mother and the Charybdis of an endless, sterile struggle with the mirror self, Coriolanus' identity simply crumbles.[34] The moment of collapse comes in 5.3, when Volumnia, Virgilia, and Valeria—the three women in Coriolanus' life, mother, wife, and honorary sister—and his son Marcius all kneel before Coriolanus to beg him not to proceed with the conquest of Rome. Our key word, "shame," plays a prominent role in this scene: "Down, ladies!" says Volumnia, "Let us shame him with our knees" (5.3.169). And they do shame him into relenting. If Coriolanus feels shame at this moment, the principal reason seems to be that the action of his mother and the other women have reminded him that his identity is inescapably grounded within his family. Once again, then, shame defines the limit of identity. And while the shaming of Coriolanus may save Rome, it also means, as Coriolanus himself realizes, the end of his life: the women may have won "a happy victory to Rome," but for Coriolanus their victory will be, he prophesies, "most mortal" (5.3.185-89). Shame is a little death, a loss of what the Elizabethans called "honor" or what we have come to call "self-esteem." For an absolutist like Coriolanus, to know shame is to die, and from this point to the end of the play he is, in his own self-conception, already dead.

Why does Coriolanus remain deaf to the appeals of all other Romans, including Menenius his surrogate father, but accede to his mother's pleas? He relents, I would propose, because Volumnia persuades him that to conquer Rome would be tantamount to raping and murdering his own mother:

> thou shalt no sooner
> March to assault thy country than to tread—
> Trust to 't, thou shalt not—on thy mother's
> womb
> That brought thee to this world.
>
> (5.3.122-25)

The image of Coriolanus "treading on" his mother's womb suggests the triumphant goose-step of the conqueror, but the term also carries a potential sexual connotation, as if Volumnia has recognized that Coriolanus is on the verge of raping her.[35] These lines draw together the political and the psychosexual dimensions of Coriolanus' situation. And at the level of abstraction that I have here postulated, mother and motherland are the same: both represent an original ground of identity, a matrix out of which the self

emerges. (Potentially, we could add a third parallel term, "nature"; but nature as ground seems relatively important to this play.[36]) To conquer one's own nation is to destroy the very ground that makes identity possible. Here, in a psychological (and biological) context, we confront a different impossibility: if a man is to become the "author of himself," he must become his own father, which means he must have intercourse with his own mother, which means breaking the primal taboo. It also means undoing time itself, which dictates that the father must be prior to the child. As he collides with these impossibilities, Coriolanus is again overwhelmed by shame: the shame of origins, the shame of knowing that however many men he slaughters and however many cities he burns, he cannot become his own father, but instead will always be his mother's son—the "boy of tears" that Aufidius so contemptuously invokes in the final scene of the play.

IV

As several recent critics have noted, issues of language are also central to *Coriolanus,* along with issues of political power and psychological integrity. Coriolanus himself seems deeply suspicious of language. Unlike virtually all of Shakespeare's other tragic protagonists, he never uses language to explore inward emotional states: he has only one true soliloquy (4.4),[37] and it is primarily about the instability of human social relationships, rather than about Coriolanus' feelings. Coriolanus, Lawrence Danson asserts, demands "wholeness of being," and this demand leads to a "distrust of words, and indeed of all the conventional symbolic means (verbal and gestural) that men have for expressing themselves."[38] Similarly, Leonard Tennenhouse argues that Coriolanus' "abhorrence of public speech and his distrust of words are functions of his obsessive quest for a personal integrity which can only be concretely realized in physical action."[39] This disjunction between words and actions emanates from Coriolanus himself to affect everything that happens in the play. As James L. Calderwood has proposed, words here tend to become meaningless, while meanings become wordless.[40] Both Tennenhouse and Calderwood see this opposition between words and meanings as pointing toward a political crisis[41]: in the absence of a stable relationship between words and things, how do we assess the possibility of truth? But the opposition also becomes constitutive of Shakespeare's dramaturgy in the play, as scene after scene turns on the opposition, as Joyce Van Dyke suggests,[42] between language and gesture—or, as Jarrett Walker, invoking a currently more fashionable critical vocabulary, proposes, between the body and speech.[43]

In a brilliant essay first published in 1964, D. J. Gordon anticipates most of the major themes explored by later linguistically oriented commentators.[44] Gordon recognizes the ways in which, in the vortex that surrounds Coriolanus, words and deeds are divorced, so that "civil life" is defined "in terms of empty, perverted, destructive relationships between speaker and utterance, word and subject, which is between man and man and man and himself." More particularly, Gordon emphasizes the ways in which the semantic crisis in *Coriolanus* becomes a crisis of naming. Coriolanus' deeds, he argues, "must be named" if they are to take on public meaning. Ideally, the "deed, being named, passes into its opposite: voice." But if neither Coriolanus nor we trust the "voices" of the people to name his deeds accurately, then "the relationship between name and thing is disrupted." "In seeking the voices Coriolanus is a subject looking for his name: it is his name that will be uttered. But the search leads him into the gravest danger. He must ask" (p. 213). Naming is crucial to the issue of identity, and in this final section I will follow the clues adumbrated by Gordon and explore the ambiguities that emerge around the names of the protagonist of *Coriolanus:* ambiguities that direct us once again toward the impossibility of identity itself.

Coriolanus is not the only Shakespearean character to experience a change of name in the course of a play. In *Richard II,* for example, Bolingbroke becomes King Henry in the last act.[45] But in no other play does a change of name receive such emphasis within the text, as a crucial transition in the protagonist's life history. In 1.10 the character heretofore identified as Marcius is renamed Coriolanus before our eyes, by his general Cominius:

> Therefore be it known,
> As to us, to all the world, that Caius Marcius
> Wears this war's garland, in token of the
>   which
> My noble steed, known to the camp, I give
>   him,
> With all his trim belonging; and from this
>   time,
> For what he did before Corioles, call him,
> With all th' applause and clamor of the host,
> Caius Marcius Coriolanus! Bear
> Th' addition nobly ever!
>
>   (57-65)

This new name immediately receives public approval, as "All" shout "Caius Marcius Coriolanus!" (66).

I see no evidence to support Lisa Lowe's suggestion that Coriolanus "refuses to accept" this new, "socially conferred name, position, and role."[46] However, he does apparently "blush" at this moment, even as he explicitly accepts the new name:

> I will go wash,
> And when my face is fair you shall perceive
> Whether I blush or no. Howbeit, I thank you.

> I mean to stride your steed, and at all times
> To undercrest your good addition
> To th' fairness of my power.
>
>   (1.9.67-72)

Coriolanus must wash because he is covered with blood: the blood that, in effect, "baptizes" him into this new identity. But his (possible) blush attests to a certain sense of shame that the new identity is external, an "addition," as he himself calls it. The fact that Coriolanus receives and accepts simultaneously a new name and a new horse might also remind us that the new name is external to the self, a kind of "thing" that Coriolanus owns, rather than the name of his "true self." And Lowe is certainly correct when she suggests that this name is "socially conferred." All names are socially conferred, and we have already seen abundant evidence that Coriolanus finds dependence on any kind of Other acutely embarrassing.

Given the problematic status of his new name, should we perhaps adopt the suggestion of Constance Relihan and think of him as "really" Marcius (or Martius, as some editions would have it)?[47] Relihan sets out to "locate the internal nature" of our protagonist's character and suggests that "the best way to begin that search is to return to his given name."[48] But in fact Coriolanus himself prefers his new name to his old one: in the final scene, when Aufidius denies him the name "Coriolanus" and addresses him instead as "Marcius," he is outraged. And the reason he prefers "Coriolanus" is clear: he believes that he has won this name by his own actions. To his mind, Cominius and the soldiers do not "give" him this name. Rather they acknowledge that his feats in battle have made it his "true" name. "Caius Marcius," on the other hand, is not his "true" name but simply his first "given name"— given to him by others (presumably his mother, since he has no apparent father), when he was a helpless child. Furthermore, Relihan's argument assumes that if we work hard enough we will discover our protagonist's "right" name. But I think that Shakespeare's point is quite different. The change of name one act into the play reminds us that all names are "given"—and thus problematic. Names name not identities but relationships.[49] "Caius Marcius" names this man in terms of his relationship to a family system. "Coriolanus" names him in terms of his relationship to a city he has conquered. The first kind of relationship may seem unproblematic to us, but it does not seem so to Coriolanus. The second kind of relationship does not seem initially problematic to our protagonist, but it becomes increasingly so in the course of the play.

"Coriolanus," we must first recognize, derives from the name of a city that our protagonist has conquered. Coriolanus is "of Corioles" in the sense that he has captured the city in battle.[50] (Other successful generals, we might note, have taken their names from battles they have won. Thus Field Marshal Montgomery became Viscount Montgomery of Alamein.) But our protagonist's new name is, as Aufidius cruelly declares in the last scene of the play, stolen: "Ay, Marcius, Caius Marcius. Dost thou think / I'll grace thee with that robbery, thy stol'n name / Coriolanus, in Corioles?" (5.6.92-94). No citizen of Corioles will recognize Coriolanus as being "of Corioles." Thus, ironically, Coriolanus can be "Coriolanus" only in Rome. He is named for "a world elsewhere," but this name is efficacious only when he is at home. When he leaves Rome, his name immediately becomes a serious problem. Arriving at the house of Aufidius, he is scorned by the servants and mutters to himself, "I have deserved no better entertainment / In being Coriolanus" (4.5.10-11). Meeting Aufidius, Coriolanus refuses to give his name. He apparently wants Aufidius to perceive some sort of identity inherent in his face itself, an identity beyond all names. But Aufidius does not recognize the visitor, demanding six times to know his name (4.5.57-69). Coriolanus does finally name himself "Caius Marcius," and then after considerable hesitation he adds "my surname, Coriolanus" (4.5.73). He also acknowledges that among the Volscians that name has become a "witness of the malice and displeasure / Which thou shouldst bear me" (77-78). And in the long speech that follows Coriolanus twice links his own name to the shame that he has inflicted on Aufidius and his people.

When he allies himself with Aufidius, it might seem that the name "Coriolanus" takes on a new meaning: no longer "the conqueror of Corioles," but rather "the servant of Corioles." Yet Coriolanus never entertains this possibility, for he cannot imagine a "true" name won in any other way than through conquest. Thus when he arrives with the Volscian army outside the gates of Rome, he has—to return to some lines that I have quoted previously—become nameless. Interestingly, it is Cominius, the very man who first gave our new protagonist his new name, who now defines his nameless condition:

> "Coriolanus"
> He would not answer to; forbade all names.
> He was a kind of nothing, titleless,
> Till he had forged himself a name o' the fire
> Of burning Rome.
>
>   (5.1.11-15)

The new name that Coriolanus hopes to forge for himself could only be, as Kenneth Burke brilliantly suggests, "Romanus": if the conqueror of Corioles became "Coriolanus," then the conqueror of Rome must become "Romanus."[51] With this new name, it might seem, our protagonist would at last have the identity he needs. He would be "of Rome" in a new and total way. He would *be* Rome, and Rome would *be* him. That, we can now recognize clearly, is what he wants. Yet as I have shown, it is logically impossible for a part to be co-extensive with the whole. And this project

is humanly impossible too. You cannot become one with your homeland by destroying it. You cannot become your own father by raping your mother. "Coriolanus" can never be "Romanus." And that, precisely, is his and everyone else's—for we have here a uniquely pure example of the identity problem we all must live through—tragedy.[52]

When we recognize that it is impossible for Coriolanus to win a new identity by defeating Rome, we can also begin to see why the new identity that he won within the gates of Corioles can only be deeply problematic. Coriolanus believes that he owes this new identity solely to his own heroic actions. "Alone I did it" (5.6.122), he proudly tells the Volscians in the last scene. Yet while he achieves this new identity without the aid of other Romans, he could not have done so if the Volscians had not been there to be conquered. We are here in the territory of Hegel's master/slave dialectic: the slave "needs" the master to tell him who he is, but ironically the master is also dependent on the slave for his very identity as "master."[53] Thus long before he offers his services to the Volscian army, Coriolanus is "of Corioles," belongs to that city in a way that he does not anticipate: he owes his name to Corioles. In accepting that name, he also accepts a dangerous illusion, that the master can rest easy in his identity, without worrying about any lingering resentments on the part of the slave. In its extreme forms this illusion can even beguile the master into thinking that the slave loves his own enslavement. But in fact to accept an identity from the enemy you have defeated is to invite the Trojan horse into the city, as Coriolanus will finally be forced to recognize in the last scene of the play.

In the final scene Aufidius, the mirror in which Coriolanus has hoped to find a true image of his identity, abruptly turns against him. There is a moral here: mirrors often turn out to have agendas of their own. All along, Aufidius has been planning to "potch at" Coriolanus in any way he can, to create a space in which he can expand his own ego, and Coriolanus' failure to carry through the conquest of Rome gives Aufidius his chance. Significantly, Aufidius begins the attack by systematically renaming the man we have become accustomed to call "Coriolanus." Coriolanus comes before the Volscian lords to claim victory in the war, which has, he says, brought "shame to th' Romans" (5.6.82). But when he presents to the lords the peace treaty he has signed with Rome, Aufidius responds with scorn:

> *Auf.* Read it not, noble lords,
>   But tell the traitor, in the highest degree
>   He hath abused your powers.
> *Cor.* "Traitor"? How now?
> *Auf.* Ay, traitor, Marcius.
> *Cor.* "Marcius"?
>
>   (5.6.86-91)

The quotation marks here suggest how problematic all labels of identity have suddenly become. The word "traitor" denies Coriolanus any possibility of a home or homeland, any identity defined in terms of place. And in the next few lines Aufidius denies our protagonist the only name he himself has found even marginally acceptable, the name of the conqueror of Corioles. That name, says Aufidius, was "stol'n." Further, Aufidius declares that Coriolanus has shamed himself and all the Volscians by acceding to his mother's pleas: at this sight, says Aufidius, the "pages blushed at him and men of heart / Looked wondering at each other" (5.6.103-04). And this accusation is immediately followed by the final insult, as Coriolanus appeals to the only god he recognizes ("Hear'st thou, Mars?"), and Aufidius renames our protagonist one last time: "Name not the god, thou boy of tears" (5.6.104-05).

This new name affixes Coriolanus firmly back in a position of dependency. He will be eternally, it seems, the child of his mother, for the boy of tears can never be the author of himself. Thus renamed, Coriolanus can only bluster incoherently, frantically attempting to reclaim an identity that will be acceptable to him. But the best he can do is to place quotation marks around this new label too: "Cut me to pieces, Volsces. Men and lads, / Stain all your edges on me. 'Boy'? False hound!" (5.6.117-18).[54] Paralyzed with rage and shame, Coriolanus offers no effective resistance as the assassins strike him down. But this new label should also serve to remind us how problematic all the other names that Coriolanus has assumed in the course of the play have also been. Coriolanus has set out to become the "author of himself." His linguistic absolutism has persuaded him that there must be a "true" name for each thing: his explicit contempt for politicians and his implicit hatred of poets stem from a sense that such people play with language and thereby separate word from thing. But he has also claimed the right to name himself—how else could he become the author of himself? Immediately we encounter a contradiction. If you can change your name, as Coriolanus does, then all names become relative to the circumstances in which you find yourself. How can we be sure that "Coriolanus" is the "right" name for this man? That he will not go on to conquer another city and take a new name such as "Romanus"?

There are, then, two problems here. First, it turns out that all names are in fact "given." Even if you name yourself, that name becomes real only in the mouths of others. As Gordon points out, Coriolanus must ask the plebeians to speak the word that will name him aright, and thus he is always already dependent on them in a way that is intolerable to him. But even if he could name himself, that act would immediately relativize any name he gave himself. Anyone who has had more than one name must acknowledge that all names are relative, a function of circumstances; and as Aufidius

runs through all the names that he has had, both we and Coriolanus must acknowledge the quotation marks around all of these names. The "true" name, of the sort that Coriolanus demands, is thus impossible. And what does the human being become without a "true" name? When Aufidius greets Coriolanus with love in 4.5, he salutes him, as we have seen, as a "noble thing" (121). At the time, this label seems like an accolade: a celebration of one hero by another. But "noble *thing*"? This word, as it reduces our protagonist to the status of an object, can serve to remind us how the names that enmesh us in a web of relationships alone serve to make us human. Freed from this web, we become simply "things." Is that perhaps what Coriolanus wants? If so, he gets his wish in the last scene, as Aufidius stands on what has become a lump of meat, to deliver the last speech of the play.[55]

V

The system of homologies that I have here described defines all the names that our protagonist assumes, all the identities that he tries to create or that others create for him, as fundamentally contradictory—"impossible." An individual human being cannot become coterminous with the polity into which he is born, or separate himself entirely from it: no man can become his own father, and no man can name himself. "Coriolanus" has no "self" that stands prior to the social and familial and linguistic systems which define his possibilities of existence. Moreover, the plurality of such systems within the play suggests that the issue here is not the state or the family or even language, but relationship itself. The self exists only as a shifting point within a network of relationships. Yet the sole ambition of our protagonist is to become an autonomous being, the author of himself, standing apart from and uncontaminated by any relationship. As it brings into focus this paradoxical, irresolvable dilemma, Shakespeare's final tragedy exposes, with a merciless lucidity, the contradictions of a particular historical moment. As Catherine Belsey has argued, "in the fifteenth century the representative human being has no unifying essence. . . . Disunited, discontinuous, the hero of the moralities is not the origin of action; he has no single subjectivity which could constitute such an origin; he is not a subject."[56] In contrast, "the scenic stage of the Restoration period addressed a unified and unifying spectacle to a series of unified spectator-subjects who, as guardians of the liberties of the people of England, each possessed a degree of sovereignty in the new regime" (p. 26). Belsey argues that Elizabethan drama becomes a site of contestation between the dispersed or discontinuous subject of the medieval period and the unified subject of modernity. And *Coriolanus* offers considerable support to this hypothesis, as it dramatizes the irresolvable conflict between a man who would author of himself (the "self-made man" of the bourgeois epoch) and an older ethos that defines human existence as inescapably relational.

The contradiction between the protagonist's demand for absolute autonomy and the relational character of the world he inhabits can explain both the coldness that repels so many readers of *Coriolanus* and its peculiar power over other readers. As I have tried to demonstrate here, this play systematically works through an essentially logical issue. We are invited to contemplate the contradictions of the protagonist's situation, not his inner life. We may see him as caught up in contradictions that affect all of us—or at least all of us who live in the bourgeois epoch. But it is hard to think of him as a person we might know and love. The perspective that I have here sketched out may also help account for the bleak and abrupt conclusion of the play. At the end of *Coriolanus,* unlike the finales of *Hamlet* or *King Lear,* the stage is not littered with corpses. We are left with only one corpse, Coriolanus'. But we are also left with a sense that nothing has survived the catastrophe: certainly we don't look to Aufidius, as we look to Fortinbras or Edgar, to reestablish a functioning civic order. And indeed we may ask if the civic order has ever really stopped functioning. Does the death of Coriolanus really mean anything to Rome except the disappearance of a threat? The logic of the play has thus carried us not through the death of the protagonist to a revitalization of the community, but simply to an impasse. Selfhood, the creation of an autonomous subjectivity—this is the project of modernity itself. But this project is, Shakespeare coolly demonstrates, impossible. And what then?

Notes

[1] Thus D. J. Enright sees the play as less a tragedy than a debate. See his "*Coriolanus:* Tragedy or Debate," *Essays in Criticism* 4 (1954), 1-19. For Michael McCanles the movement of the play is "as inexorably logical as anything in Shakespeare" ("The Dialectic of Transcendence in Shakespeare's *Coriolanus,*" *PMLA* 82 [1967], 44). And Nicholas Grene describes *Coriolanus* as "the most austere and stringently analytic embodiment of tragic action" in Shakespeare's oeuvre (*Shakespeare's Tragic Imagination* [New York, 1992], p. 250).

[2] My thinking on the question of identity has been influenced by Heidegger, who argues that identity can be conceptualized only as a function of difference. See *Identity and Difference,* trans. Joan Stambaugh (New York, 1974). On the relationship between shame and identity, see especially Helen Merrell Lynd, *On Shame and the Search for Identity* (New York, 1958). For a philosophic exploration of the place of shame in human life, see Bernard Williams, *Shame and Necessity* (Berkeley, 1993), esp. pp. 75-102. Williams argues that shame, by "giving through the emotions a sense of who one is and of what one hopes to be, . . . mediates between act, character, and consequence, and also between ethical demands and the rest of life. Whatever

it is working on, [shame] requires an internalised other . . . whose reactions the agent can respect" (p. 102). For a comprehensive examination of shame in Renaissance culture, and especially in the drama of the period, see Gail Kern Paster, *The Body Embarrassed: Drama and the Disciplines of Shame in Early Modern England* (Ithaca, 1993).

[3] All quotations from *Coriolanus* are from the Harper Collins text (New York, 1992), ed. David Bevington.

[4] Several recent critics have pointed to issues of identity as central to *Coriolanus,* and some have also called attention to the homologies between the social and the psychological strata of the play. Thus Brian Vickers sees the play as "Shakespeare's most detailed analysis of politics, an analysis carried out both at the public level—the formal political manoeuvering between the patricians and the plebeians . . . ; and, at the personal level, within the family, in the relationship between Coriolanus and his mother, Volumnia" (*Shakespeare: Coriolanus* [London, 1976], p. 7). At one point Vickers verges upon a view of the play similar to the one I shall develop here, arguing that Coriolanus "is a character, and his is a situation, which are fully tragic because they exist in a context in which a profound conflict of values renders individual action, and finally existence itself, impossible and pointless" (p. 8). But Vickers does not pursue this insight, choosing instead to defend Coriolanus as the one example of individual integrity in an otherwise degraded world. Christopher Givan, in "Shakespeare's *Coriolanus:* The Premature Epitaph and the Butterfly," *Shakespeare Studies* 12 (1981), clearly recognizes the problematic status of Coriolanus' identity: "His sense of identity precariously wavers between winning and losing, words and deeds, and ultimately between destroying others or destroying himself" (p. 152); but like most critics, Givan assumes that Coriolanus has a "private self" which he "loses" in the course of the play (p. 157). Michael Platt, in *Rome and Romans According to Shakespeare* rev. ed. (Lanham, MD, 1983), pp. 52-184, anticipates some parts of my argument, in emphasizing Coriolanus' attempts "to make himself his own author" (p. 104). Because Coriolanus' life project is the pursuit of honor, says Platt, "he cannot be his own author, since the thing which he aims at is outside himself" (p. 105). Specifically, "the project of Coriolanus to become his own origin, the only condition which would allow him to live free of the city, founders upon the body" (p. 110)—both the body politic (i.e., Rome itself) and the body of his mother. Platt's exploration of the problematics of identity within the *polis* is full and subtle. However, he discusses the psychological and linguistic dimensions of this theme only in passing, and I do not share his conviction that Shakespeare addresses the contradictions of identity within the *polis* only to demonstrate the need for a natural or divine law that will lift us beyond these contradictions (pp.

160-79). Robert N. Watson, in *Shakespeare and the Hazards of Ambition* (Cambridge, MA, 1984), pp. 142-221, develops a subtle and searching reading of *Coriolanus;* but while he calls attention to the contradictions that undermine Coriolanus' quest for an autonomous identity, he does not foreground this issue in the way that I shall do here, and he does not discuss the relationship between identity and shame within the play. Alexander Leggatt's analysis of Coriolanus arrives at a conclusion very similar to mine: "The contradictions of Coriolanus simply tear apart the image of the character the play has created, cancelling each other out and leaving us with nothing" (*Shakespeare's Political Drama: The History Plays and the Roman Plays* [London and New York, 1988], pp. 212-13). And Leggatt argues at length that Coriolanus' attempts to establish "a new, asocial identity" (p. 203) apart from Rome are unsuccessful. However, Leggatt also refers to Coriolanus' "authentic self" (p. 193), in a way that I would reject. Nicholas Grene sees "the issue of identity" as central to all Shakespeare's tragedies, but especially to *Coriolanus:* "Caius Marcius Coriolanus is someone made by his mother, by his city, by his 'deed-achieving honour'; the very process of this making is laid bare. Yet he is also the hero who resists the forces that shape and validate his being in the extremity of his commitment to an absolute idea of selfhood" (p. 269). Grene also notes that "in so far as his identity is not self-created but dependent upon a mixed community of others, it is always vulnerable, always liable to instability" (p. 270). However, Grene does not fully develop this insight in relation to the political, psychological, and linguistic strata of the play. Lars Engle, in *Shakespearean Pragmatism: Market of His Time* (Chicago, 1993), offers a description of the political, psychological, and linguistic strata of the play similar to mine (pp. 172-74). Engle is not primarily concerned with issues of identity, but his argument parallels mine in showing how within this play the operation of a market economy relativizes traditional aristocratic models of heroic identity. In his conclusion Engle declares that "*Coriolanus* offers a key instance of the forced acceptance, by its hero, of both his city and his own identity as economies rather than fixed systems" (p. 194); and this statement suggests how an "economic" reading of the play can arrive at conclusions very similar to mine.

⁵ A. P. Rossiter, *Angel with Horns: Fifteen Lectures on Shakespeare* (London, 1989), p. 251.

⁶ *The Herculean Hero in Marlowe, Chapman, Shakespeare and Dryden* (New York, 1962), p. 16.

⁷ *Coriolanus in Context* (Lewisburg, 1971), p. 180.

⁸ *Shakespeare's Tragic Sequence* (New York, 1979), pp. 172-73.

⁹ *Shakespeare and the Popular Voice* (Oxford, 1989), pp. 120-53. For additional examples of the assumption that *Coriolanus* expresses a contempt for the common people and popular government, see E.C. Petit, "*Coriolanus* and the Midlands Insurrection of 1607," *Shakespeare Survey* 3 (1950), 34-42; W. Gordon Zeeveld, "*Coriolanus* and Jacobean Politics," *Modern Language Review* 57 (1962), 321-34; Willard Farnham, *Shakespeare's Tragic Frontier: The World of His Final Tragedies* (Berkeley, 1963), esp. pp. 227ff; Bertrand Evans, *Shakespeare's Tragic Practice* (Oxford, 1979), esp. pp. 312ff; and Michael D. Bristol, "Lenten Butchery: Legitimation Crisis in *Coriolanus,*" in *Shakespeare Reproduced: The Text in History and Ideology,* ed. Jean E. Howard and Marion F. O'Connor (London, 1987), pp. 207-24. For the belief that the play opens up alternatives to absolutism, see Clifford Davidson, "*Coriolanus:* A Study in Political Dislocation," *Shakespeare Studies* 4 (1973), 263-74; Anne Barton, "Livy, Machiavelli, and Shakespeare's *Coriolanus,*"*Shakespeare Survey* 38 (1985), 115-29; R. B. Parker, "*Coriolanus* and 'th' Interpretation of the Time,'" in *Mirror up to Shakespeare: Essays in Honour of G. R. Hibbard,* ed. J. C. Gray (Toronto, 1984), pp. 261-76; Thomas Sorge, "The Failure of Orthodoxy in *Coriolanus,*" in *Shakespeare Reproduced,* pp. 225-41; Shannon Miller, "Topicality and Subversion in William Shakespeare's *Coriolanus,*" *Studies in English Literature* 32 (1992), 287-310; and Marilyn L. Williamson, "Violence and Gender Ideology in *Coriolanus* and *Macbeth,*" in *Shakespeare Left and Right,* ed. Ivo Kamps (New York, 1991), pp. 147-66. Vickers (esp. pp. 12-18) sees the play as expressing a blistering contempt both for the patricians and for the plebeians. Richard Wilson neatly finesses this issue by arguing that *Coriolanus* "reflects contemporary confusion about representative government." See his "Against the Grain: Representing the Market in *Coriolanus,*" *The Seventeenth Century* 6 (1991), 127. Similarly, Vivian Thomas, in *Shakespeare's Roman Worlds* (London, 1989) argues that "it is a mistake to see the most detached and impartial of writers giving expression to his political sympathies in this play. The energy, vitality and intense conflicts which animate the play create an immediate awareness of class antagonisms and quickly trigger individual prejudice, but only the most bigoted member of the audience can remain impervious to the distortions or excesses of 'their' side" (p. 181). And Virgil Nemoianu, in *A Theory of the Secondary: Literature, Progress, and Reaction* (Baltimore, 1989), contends that Shakespeare deliberately seeks to build our sympathy for Coriolanus, even as he also recognizes that the archaic virtues represented by the protagonist must inevitably give way to the more complex and ambiguous political awareness represented not only by the tribunes but also by Volumnia and Meninius: "Progress is unfolding and explicitation. Progress is a movement towards a contractual and disintegrated condition. . . . *Coriolanus* is thus a tragedy of regret and remembrance. Coriolanus

is doomed to defeat, but this defeat ought to be perceived by the audience as a genuine loss" (p. 41).

[10] Rossiter, p. 240. Rossiter's arguments are, however, anticipated in part by F. N. Lees, who argued in 1950 that the play is grounded in Aristotle's conception of man as a political animal. See "*Coriolanus*, Aristotle, and Bacon," *Review of English Studies* N.S. 1 (1950), 114-25.

[11] *Shakespeare's Rome* (Cambridge, Eng., 1983), p. 165.

[12] "'Who Does the Wolf Love?': *Coriolanus* and the Interpretations of Politics," in *Shakespeare and the Question of Theory,* ed. Patricia Parker and Geoffrey Hartman (London, 1985), p. 262.

[13] See James Holstun, "Tragic Superfluity in *Coriolanus,*" *ELH* 50 (1983), 485-507; and Arthur Riis, "The Belly Politic: *Coriolanus* and the Revolt of Language," *ELH* 59 (1992), 53-75.

[14] My argument that *Coriolanus* sees the relationship of self and society as irresolvably problematical has been anticipated by several critics. See, e.g., Ruth Nevo, *Tragic Form in Shakespeare* (Princeton, 1972), pp. 356-404; Philip Brockbank, "Introduction," in *Coriolanus,* the New Arden Edition, ed. Brockbank (London, 1976), p. 50ff.; and Richard S. Ide, *Possessed with Greatness: The Heroic Tragedies of Chapman and Shakespeare* (Chapel Hill, 1980), pp. 168-97. Terence Eagleton sees *Coriolanus* as "about the conflict of authentic life and social responsibility" (*Shakespeare and Society* [New York, 1967], p. 113). Norman Rabkin argues that Coriolanus, "having accepted his identity and his name as Rome's defender, . . . must . . . reject that identity until nothing is left but his ever more intense sense of personal honor" (*Shakespeare and the Common Understanding* [New York, 1967], pp. 135-36). But once again I would argue that the problem in the play is not so much the hero's "loss of identity" as the inherently contradictory character of identity itself. In "The Other Coriolanus" (*PMLA* 85 [1970], 228-36), Katherine Stockholder recognizes the ways in which Coriolanus' assertion of his ego makes him dependent on others. Leonard Barkan (*Nature's Work of Art: The Human Body as Image of the World* [New Haven, 1975], pp. 95-109) explores the ways in which the play is built around "the multiple commonwealth made single" and "the single individual made multiple" (p. 104). And in *Shakespeare's Rome: Republic and Empire* (Ithaca, N.Y., 1976), Paul A. Cantor discusses the ways in which Coriolanus' sense of himself is bound up with Rome (pp. 105-06). However, Cantor seems to assume that if our protagonist had been a bit more self-aware he could have become the "author of himself" (pp. 107-16). Hans-Jürgen Weckermann has argued that "the main antagonism in the play is . . .

between Coriolanus' self-reliant individualism and the demands of the commonweal" ("*Coriolanus*: The Failure of the Autonomous Individual," in *Shakespeare: Text, Language, Criticism: Essays in Honour of Marvin Spevack,* ed. Bernhard Fabian and Kurt Tetzeli von Rosador [Hildesheim, 1987], p. 336); but Weckermann does not discuss the way this conflict calls into question the concept of personal identity. In his essay Wilson suggests that the protagonist's mistake is his failure to realize that "far from being essential, identity is created by exchange" (p. 124-25).

[15] In "To Starve with Feeding: The City in *Coriolanus*" (*Shakespeare Studies* 9 [1978], 123-44), Gail Kern Paster notes that the word "Rome" appears eighty-eight times in *Coriolanus,* as opposed to only thirty-eight times in *Julius Caesar* and thirty times in *Antony and Cleopatra* (p. 127). I am indebted to Paster's essay, which brilliantly dissects the ways in which "Rome, the symbol of human community, is at once the source of life and the instrument of death, the agent of immortality and the exactor of a sacrifice which diminishes the city's existence in preserving it" (p. 124).

[16] I. R. Browning suggests that the major question this play raises is why Coriolanus "should depend so heavily on public approbation and why he should strive so vigorously to conceal that dependence from others, and possibly from himself too" ("*Coriolanus*: Boy of Tears," *Essays in Criticism* 5 [1955], 25).

[17] Williams points out that "the basic experience connected with shame is that of being seen, inappropriately, by the wrong people, in the wrong condition. It is straightforwardly connected with nakedness, particularly in sexual connections" (p. 78).

[18] Cf. Janet Adelman, *Suffocating Mothers: Fantasies of Maternal Origin in Shakespeare's Plays,* Hamlet *to* The Tempest (New York, 1992), p. 155. See also Zvi Jagendorf, "*Coriolanus*: Body Politic and Private Parts," *Shakespeare Quarterly* 41 (1990), 455-69. Jagendorf sees Coriolanus as "embarrassed by his wounds because, paradoxically, they mark his dependence on the people. Wounds are signs not of what he *is* but of what he has *done*. They tell stories and are interpretable. They are currency in a political economic exchange that breeds votes in return for a certain amount of nakedness and verbal display in the marketplace" (p. 465). Una Ellis-Fermor usefully links Coriolanus' shame at this moment to a sense that he is acting a role ("It is a *part* that I shall blush in *acting*" [2.2.149-50]) and has thereby lost contact with his "true" self (*Shakespeare the Dramatist* [New York, 1961], pp. 70ff). Paster argues that Coriolanus feels shame at this moment because the display of his scars places him on the same plane as a woman (*The Body Embarrassed,* p. 97). On Coriolanus' struggle to deny the woman within him, see also Jane Carducci, "Shakespeare's *Coriolanus*:

'Could I find out / The Woman's part in me,'" *Literature and Psychology* 33 (1987), 11-20; and Coppélia Kahn, "Mother of Battles: Volumnia and Her Son in Shakespeare's *Coriolanus," Differences: A Journal of Feminist Cultural Studies* 4 (1992), 154-70.

[19] On the ways in which "I banish you!" sums up Coriolanus's paradoxical relationship with Rome, see Michael Long, *The Unnatural Scene: A Study in Shakespearean Tragedy* (London, 1976), pp. 76-78. In "*Coriolanus*—A Tragedy of Love" (*English* 40 [1991], 117-34), Paul Dean notes that at this point in the play Coriolanus' identity becomes problematic: "what Acts 4 and 5 show is the searing irony that, whilst Coriolanus' habits of speech and bearing remain what they were, he has changed without knowing it: that, without Rome, he almost ceases to exist; that it was only in Rome, soured and sordid though it was, that he could be fully himself" (p. 124).

[20] "This scene is the decisive test of [Coriolanus'] character and of the binding character of the body politic; Coriolanus cannot leave Rome behind; he cannot banish Rome; there is no world elsewhere; when a man leaves the city of his birth behind he leaves his human nature, too" (Platt, p. 96). On this issue, see also Jonathan Dollimore: "when Coriolanus is exiled from Rome he declares confidently 'There is a world elsewhere.' But it is the world being left which he needs, because it is there that his identity is located" (*Radical Tragedy: Religion, Ideology, and Power in the Drama of Shakespeare and His Contemporaries* [Chicago, 1984], p. 220). Vickers makes a similar point: "Rejected by Rome Coriolanus resolves to live outside society, a drastic transformation for any man. Yet he fails to do so, since he finds that he is not a dragon, that he needs human society and human action" (p. 37). See also Stanley Fish: "The truth is that there is no world elsewhere, at least not in the sense Coriolanus intends, a world where it is possible to stand freely, unencumbered by obligations and dependencies. There are only other speech-act communities, and every one of them exacts as the price of membership acceptance of its values and meanings" (*Is There a Text in This Class? The Authority of Interpretive Communities* [Cambridge, Mass., 1980], p. 218).

[21] Miola points out that in this situation "Coriolanus finds himself in an impossible dilemma: To be Roman is to act and not to act, to conquer and to surrender" (p. 201).

[22] Adelman's analysis of *Coriolanus* has been published in several different versions starting in 1978. I will here cite her most recent revision and elaboration of this analysis, as included in *Suffocating Mothers,* pp. 147-64. Some earlier psychoanalytic readings of the play tried to define the character type represented by Coriolanus, whether "phallic-narcissistic" (Charles

K. Hofling, "An Interpretation of Shakespeare's *Coriolanus,*" in *The Design Within: Psychoanalytic Approaches to Shakespeare,* ed. M. D. Faber [New York, 1970] pp. 290-305) or "authoritarian" (Gordon Ross Smith, "Authoritarian Patterns in Shakespeare's *Coriolanus,*" in Faber, pp. 310-26); other psychoanalytically inclined critics have seen Coriolanus as the instrument of Volumnia's own phallic aspirations (Robert J. Stoller, "Shakespearean Tragedy: *Coriolanus,*" in Faber, pp. 329-39, and—although he avoids a Freudian vocabulary—D. W. Harding, "Women's Fantasy of Manhood: A Shakespearian Theme," *Shakespeare Quarterly* 20 [1969], 252-53), or have seen Coriolanus as in rebellion against the castrating threat of the phallic mother (Emmett Wilson, Jr., "*Coriolanus:* The Anxious Bridegroom," *American Imago* 25 [1968], 224-41). Adelman shifts away from the static character typologies and symbolic equations of earlier psychoanalytic critics, to focus on the dynamics of the mother/son relationship. In this respect she both synthesizes and moves beyond earlier psychoanalytic readings. David B. Barron, in "*Coriolanus:* Portrait of the Artist as Infant," *American Imago* 19 (1962), 171-93, anticipates some of Adelman's insights, but attempts to psychoanalyze Shakespeare. Shuli Barzilai supports my argument, suggesting that Coriolanus' behavior reveals an active death-wish that is "silently pressing for dissolution of the self." See "Coriolanus and the Compulsion to Repeat," *Hebrew University Studies in Literature* 19 [1991], p. 131).

[23] Lisa Lowe, "'Say I Play the Man I Am': Gender and Politics in *Coriolanus,*" *Kenyon Review* 8 (1986), 86-95.

[24] See Page duBois, "A Disturbance of Syntax at the Gates of Rome," *Stanford Literature Review* 2 (1985), 185-208. duBois sees Coriolanus as caught within double binds imposed by his mother: "First, she has said to him, in word or deed: 'Be a man like me, or I will not love you.' Second, in the course of the tragedy, she says 'Disguise who you are, while you expose yourself.' Finally, she threatens, 'Do as I say or I will die'" (p. 191).

[25] Adelman, p. 152; see also Wilson, 227-29; Coppélia Kahn, *Man's Estate: Masculine Identity in Shakespeare* (Berkeley, 1981), pp. 160-61; and Watson, pp. 168-72.

[26] After his triumph within the gates Coriolanus summons the Roman army to follow him back into the battle, and the soldiers "shout and wave their swords" and then lift Coriolanus onto their shoulders to signal their enthusiastic obedience. At this point in the Folio text, Coriolanus says, "O me alone! Make you a sword of me:" (1.6.76). This puzzling line has been variously emended by editors. For me, the line makes most sense if spoken by Coriolanus and punctuated with an exclamation point, so that Coriolanus is here shouting exult-

antly to the soldiers, who have just picked him up and are in effect waving him aloft, "Make *me* your sword!" When so read, the line graphically confirms the transformation of the protagonist into a hard, invulnerable, murderous "thing." On the implications of this line, see Givan, p. 145.

[27] In "Caius Marcus Coriolanus: The Self as Art" (*Shakespeare Bulletin* 5 and 6 [1987], 5-8) Michael Quinn argues that Coriolanus here achieves a transformation into "the fundamentally Homeric martial image of the heroic self" (p. 6). I see this presumed transformation as far more problematical than Quinn's comment would suggest.

[28] For a full discussion of this issue, see Madelon Sprengnether, "Annihilating Intimacy in *Coriolanus,*" in *Women in the Middle Ages and the Renaissance,* ed. Mary Beth Rose (Syracuse, 1986), pp. 89ff.

[29] Robert Stoller, "Facts and Fancies: An Examination of Freud's Concept of Bisexuality," in *Women and Analysis,* ed. Jean Strouse (New York, 1974), p. 358. Quoted by Sprengnether, p. 91.

[30] Watson offers (pp. 206-21) a full and subtle analysis of the "mirror" relationship between Coriolanus and Aufidius. See also Maurice Hunt, "'Violent'st' Complementarity: The Double Warriors of *Coriolanus,*" *Studies in English Literature* 31 (1991), 309-25. Platt notes that Coriolanus is "in need of an 'other' to validate his own existence," and believes he has found such an "other" in Aufidius (p. 101).

[31] See Adelman, pp. 156-57. Stoller ("Shakespearean Tragedy," pp. 335ff), Michael Long (pp. 67-68) and Ralph Berry ("Sexual Imagery in *Coriolanus,*" *Studies in English Literature* 13 [1973], 309) all detect homosexual overtones in the relationship between Coriolanus and Aufidius. Leggatt suggests that "what Aufidius offers is not an alternative" to marriage "but a parody of it." As a result, "the intense excitement of this moment does not last; it is doubtful if Coriolanus himself even feels it" (p. 205).

[32] Jacques Lacan, *Écrits: A Selection,* trans. Alan Sheridan (New York, 1977), pp. 1-7. For Lacan, "the *mirror stage* is a drama whose internal thrust is precipitated from insufficiency to anticipation—and which manufactures for the subject, caught up in the lure of spatial identification, the succession of phantasies that extends from a fragmented body-image to a form of its totality that I shall call orthopaedic—and, lastly, to the assumption of the armour of an alienating identity, which will mark with its rigid structure the subject's entire mental development" (p. 4).

[33] Stoller describes *Coriolanus* as a "play that centers about phalluses and castration. The references to

swords, pikes, lances, staves, darts, war, Mars, charge, beat, wrath, hate, hard, advance, pierce, fight are beyond count. We feel the great social stiffness, the muscular and psychological hardness of this man, who can scarcely help himself from penetrating everyone he meets either with his explosive words or with his weapons" ("Shakespearean Tragedy," p. 330).

[34] Compare Watson, pp. 220-21.

[35] Some years before Adelman's essay, Ralph Berry suggested that "Coriolanus' tragedy is that he cannot forge a new identity without destroying his mother" (p. 301). See also Watson, pp. 174-75, and Riss, pp. 68-69.

[36] Platt comments at length on the absence of any "green world" in this play (pp. 62-67). "Nature" is represented primarily by the butterfly that young Marcius brutally "mammocked."

[37] In 2.2.112-24, Coriolanus speaks some lines while alone on stage; but in these lines he is anticipating what he will say when the plebeians return to speak with him, so the lines are only technically a soliloquy.

[38] *Tragic Alphabet: Shakespeare's Drama of Language* (New Haven, 1974), p. 149. Elizabeth Story Donno also sees Coriolanus as differing from the other characters primarily in his willingness to speak from the heart, in a world where everyone else is guilty of varying degrees of duplicity ("*Coriolanus* and a Shakespearean Motif," in *Shakespeare and Dramatic Tradition: Essays in Honor of S.F. Johnson,* ed. W.R. Elton and William B. Long [Newark, 1984], pp. 47-68).

[39] "*Coriolanus:* History and the Crisis of Semantic Order," *Comparative Drama* 10 (1976), 334.

[40] "*Coriolanus:* Wordless Meanings and Meaningless Words," *Studies in English Literature* 6 (1966), 211-24.

[41] See also Carol M. Sicherman, "*Coriolanus:* The Failure of Words," *ELH* 39 (1972), 189-207.

[42] "Making a Scene: Language and Gesture in *Coriolanus,*" *Shakespeare Survey* 30 (1977), 135-46.

[43] "Voiceless Bodies and Bodiless Voices: The Drama of Human Perception in *Coriolanus,*" *Shakespeare Quarterly* 43 (1992), 170-85. Stanley Fish also sees *Coriolanus* as an examination of the conflict between the claim to self-*author*ship and the claims of the speech-act community, a conflict that comes to a climax in the scene before the gates of Rome: "since it has been his claim and his desire to stand apart from human ties, he cannot now acknowledge them without paying the penalty demanded by the abstraction—the

totally autonomous self—he has set up in their place. Yet at the very moment that he pays the penalty, Coriolanus exposes that abstraction as a fiction. The speech-act community reclaims him as inescapably its own when he provides the strongest possible evidence that he is neither a God nor a machine. He dies" (p. 219).

[44] "Name and Fame: Shakespeare's *Coriolanus*," in *The Renaissance Imagination: Essays and Lectures,* ed. Stephen Orgel (1962, Berkeley, 1975), pp. 203-19.

[45] Macbeth becomes Cawdor but continues to be called "Macbeth."

[46] Lowe, p. 93. Givan also suggests that "'Coriolanus' . . . is only the name that society's leaders have given the hero" (p. 148), and he argues that Coriolanus' acceptance of this new name leads to "the loss of self. . . . He struggles to preserve his identity but, as evidenced by his new name, he allows others to formulate its terms," and the result is "the death of his individual self" (p. 150). For a view closer to mine, see Leggatt (p. 191). See also Grene, who says that the new name "seems acceptable as it defines him by the purest moment of action he has ever achieved, a deed both purely action and purely his own" (p. 270).

[47] "Appropriation of the 'Thing of Blood': Absence of Self and the Struggle for Ownership in *Coriolanus*," *Iowa State Journal of Research* 62 (1988), 407-20.

[48] Relihan, p. 418, fn. 1. Relihan sees Coriolanus as having "very little sense of identity" (p. 408). As a consequence of this lack, she argues, other characters in the play seek to impose on him their conceptions of what he should be.

[49] Cf. Danson: "the bestowing of a name, especially one so intrinsically related to its bearer as 'Coriolanus,' is a social act, defining relationships, going outside of whatever purely inner integrity we can conceive" (p. 151).

[50] My colleague Prof. Tina Passman tells me that the grammatical form of our hero's new name normally implies "the adopted son of." So the enemy city here becomes, paradoxically, Coriolanus' "father," as Rome is his "mother."

[51] "Coriolanus—and the Delights of Faction," in *Language as Symbolic Action: Essays on Life, Literature, and Method* (Berkeley, 1966), p. 91n.

[52] As Grene notes, "the Caius Marcius Romanus which he aims to become is ultimately an impossible projection of the self" (p. 271).

[53] For Hegel's own exposition of this dialectic, see *The Phenomenology of Mind,* trans. by J. B. Baillie (New York, 1967), pp. 228-40. McCanles' "dialectical" reading of *Coriolanus* brings into sharp focus the operation of the master/slave dialectic within the play.

[54] Coriolanus goes on to remind the Volscians of his victory over them at Corioles, and ends "Alone I did it. 'Boy'?" Reuben A. Brower, in *Hero and Saint: Shakespeare and the Gracco-Roman Heroic Tradition* (Oxford, 1971), offers a perceptive analysis of this line: "'Alone' and ' "Boy"?' carry the weight of Coriolanus' whole dramatic career. In 'Alone' we recognize his cult of independence, his integrity, his insistence on being 'Coriolanus.' But we hear also the opposite theme, in a play in which the wholeness of the state is the public ideal, in which metaphors of the body politic keep reminding us that the great natural order is realized in a whole of which the single man is only a part. This is his final denial of nature's bond, only making clearer his real dependence on Rome, his mother, Menenius, and now on the Volscians" (p. 371).

[55] Brockbank suggests that in the play "the dominant dehumanizing word is . . . 'thing,'" and he comments at some length on how this word defines Coriolanus' transformation into "the god, the machine, and the butcher" (p. 51). See also Givan, pp. 145ff.

[56] *The Subject of Tragedy: Identity and Difference in Renaissance Drama* (London, 1985), p. 18.

Source: "The 'Noble Thing' and the 'Boy of Tears': *Coriolanus* and the Embarrassments of Identity," in *English Literary Renaissance*, Vol. 27, No. 3, Autumn, 1997, pp. 393-420.

Household Words: *Macbeth* and the Failure of Spectacle

Lisa Hopkins, *Sheffield Hallam University*

In her epic novel on the life of Macbeth, *King Hereafter,* Dorothy Dunnett suggests that one of the primary reasons for the eventual failure of her hero's kingship is his inability to be perceived as sufficiently charismatic: 'a diverse people in time of hardship need a priest-king. The English know that. Edward is anointed with holy oil: he has the power of healing, they say'.[1] Although Dunnett's Macbeth-figure—an Orkney jarl also known as Thorfinn—is very differently conceived from Shakespeare's, each shares an unfortunate tendency towards the mundane. Most particularly, Shakespeare's hero and his wife both, at certain crucial moments of their lives, strongly favour a low-key, occasionally almost bathetic vocabulary.[2] This aspect of their characterization has been much mocked in the English comic and popular tradition: Bertie Wooster is continually amused by the concept of the cat i' th' adage, and Edmund Crispin's irascible literary detective Gervase Fen, Oxford professor, gives the play very short shrift:

> 'Do!' exclaimed Fen. 'If it were done when 'tis done, then 'twere well it were done quickly.'
>
> 'What is that supposed to mean?'
>
> 'It isn't supposed to mean anything. It's a quotation from our great English dramatist, Shakespeare. I sometimes wonder if Hemings and Condell went off the rails a bit there. It's a vile absurd jingle.'[3]

The point was, perhaps, made most strongly, and most elegantly, by Dr Johnson, fulminating on the 'lowness' of the diction in the 'Come, thick night . . .' speech (though he mistakenly attributes this to Macbeth). He castigates the use of 'an epithet now seldom heard but in the stable . . . *dun* night may come or go without any other notice than contempt';[4] he rhetorically enquires, 'who, without some relaxation of his gravity, can hear of the avengers of guilt *peeping through a blanket?'*; and he asserts:

> sentiment is weakened by the name of an instrument used by butchers and cooks in the meanest employments; we do not immediately conceive that any crime of importance is to be committed with a *knife;* or who does not, at least, from the long habit of connecting a knife with sordid offices, feel aversion rather than terror?

Coleridge concurred so strongly with Johnson's strictures on the inappropriateness of 'blanket' that he suggested that the reading should actually have been 'blank height'—[5] though the quality of his engagement with the play's language in general is perhaps indicated by his remark that, '[e]xcepting the disgusting passage of the Porter, which I dare pledge myself to demonstrate an interpolation of the actors, I do not remember in *Macbeth* a single pun or play on words' (pp. 69-70).

Other responses have been less damning and more interested in teasing out the implications of the imagery. Bradley, characteristically, saw it as evidence of characterization, and (correctly attributing the speeches) believed mundanity of diction to be differentially, and deliberately, employed in the play: he suggested that Lady Macbeth 'uses familiar and prosaic illustrations' as an indication of '[t]he literalism of her mind'.[6] More recently, Paul Jorgensen has observed that the use of the banal is not in fact confined to Lady Macbeth, but is still disposed to regard patterns of speech as symptomatic and revelatory of states of mind, commenting of the 'If it were done . . .' speech that Macbeth 'is still, as in his talk with Lady Macbeth, relying upon shrinking words like *it* (four uses) and *do* (three uses)';[7] and Coppélia Kahn performs a similar manoeuvre when she offers a sustained and ingenious reading of Macbeth's apparently simple use of the word 'cow'.[8] Even Coleridge was prepared to concede that some at least of the play's language might be suggestively, rather than disturbingly, 'low', commenting on 'the appropriateness of the simile "as breath" in a cold climate',[9] and speculating that 'enkindle you unto the crown' might still further underline the play's concern with childlessness by encoding the suggestions not only of 'kind' and 'kin' but of the 'kindling', or engendering, of rabbits (p. 61).

Perhaps most interesting of all, however, are the observations of Walter Whiter on the supposedly prosaic character of the imagery. Responding silently but unmistakably to Johnson, Whiter observes:

> The word *'knife'* (says Mr Malone) has been objected to, as being connected with the most sordid offices; and therefore unsuitable to the great occasion on which it is employed. But, however mean it may sound to our ears, it was formerly a word of sufficient dignity, and is constantly used by Shakespeare and his contemporaries as synonymous [sic] to *dagger . . . Blanket* (Mr Malone observes) was certainly the Poet's word, and 'perhaps was suggested to him by the coarse *woolen* curtain of his own Theatre, through which probably, while the house was yet but half lighted, he had himself often *peep'd.*'[10]

The idea that Shakespeare could have 'peep'd' through a *curtain* at a *half-lighted* Globe which he would have called a *house* clearly owes a very great deal more to eighteenth-century awareness of its own theatrical practices than to any historical awareness of what Elizabethan ones had been; but nevertheless I think Whiter, and Malone before him, have grasped something really central to the play here. Whiter goes on to develop his insights further, declaring that 'Nothing is more certain, than that all the images in this celebrated passage are borrowed from the *Stage*' (pp. 63-4) and commenting that '[t]he peculiar and appropriate dress of TRAGEDY personified is a PALL with a KNIFE' (p. 64).

In Whiter's reading, the ostensible 'lowness' of the diction is, with breathtaking ingenuity, completely recuperated in a register which allows the passage to be perceived as a sustained piece of metatheatricality. Other critics have not been slow to see similar links, ranging from Bradley's remark that Macbeth 'is generally said to be a very bad actor'[11] to Malcolm Evans' comment that 'numerous theatrical references emerge on the "bloody stage" (II.iv.930) of Scotland in the course of the play, culminating in Macbeth's speech on "signifying nothing"'.[12] And Christopher Pye combines elements of both these lines of critical approach, that focusing on the mundanity of the play and that focusing on its theatricality, in virtually the same breath: citing 'a foolish thought to say a sorry sight', he comments on 'the spectacular banality of Macbeth's response',[13] but he also calls the play 'the most spectacular of Shakespeare's tragedies. Like Lady Macbeth and like the inquisitive king [James I] who watches her, *Macbeth* is notable for the disquieting visibility of its mysteries' (p. 145). What I want to argue, however, is that the two elements are, precisely, forced apart by the play's structure so that what we see in *Macbeth* is not in fact, in Pye's suggestive phrasing, 'spectacular banality', but a banality which achieves spectacularity only in metaspectacular terms—a concept which I am, I hope, going to be able to clarify.

Dr Johnson's objection to terms like 'knife' and 'blanket' was, in effect, that they were household words, representing a 'low' diction associated with 'sordid offices'. Walter Whiter counters that all these banal-seeming terms have in fact another meaning in another register, in which they are associated not with the home but with the theatre, and that they are thus actually instances of elevated—and technical—terminology by their association with the classical concept of tragedy; the value-system which Whiter is implicitly working with here is clearly signalled by the typography, which italicizes *Stage* and uses upper case for TRAGEDY, PALL, and KNIFE. However, these theatrical meanings are accessible only on the metatheatrical or extradiegetic level: they are there to be perceived by the audience of the play, but not by its characters. We may conceive of the characters in *Macbeth* primarily as actors on a stage,

but they, with the notable exception of Macbeth himself towards the end of his career, are presented as representations blind to their own status as representations. When Lady Macbeth speaks of knives and blankets, she, at least, can have no access to any ulterior meaning which casts them as the accoutrements of tragedy: to her, as to Dr Johnson, they are only knives and blankets, though to us, as to Walter Whiter, they may be the appropriate props of the role she plays. Moreover, Lady Macbeth is alone: if she herself does not register the metaphorical force of her words, there is no one else present to do so. This is, in fact, a consistent and striking feature of *Macbeth* as a whole. It may well be, as Christopher Pye terms it, 'the most spectacular of Shakespeare's tragedies', but the elements which are most obviously 'spectacular', the episodes centring on the outlandish appearance and supernatural doings of the Weird Sisters, are (even when they are of undoubtedly Shakespearian origin) consistently staged very much for the benefit of the audience alone, and are never perceived by the majority of the characters. After their initial appearance to Macbeth and Banquo jointly, the Weird Sisters are seen only by Macbeth, and so too is the ghost of Banquo, and Lady Macbeth, for all her apostrophizings and invocations of the supernatural, never has any personal contact with it. Most other characters are even less aware than she of the presence of the diabolical and the paranormal in the play: when Malcolm gives the order for the cutting of the branches, he is adhering to a military requirement for camouflage rather than consciously fulfilling a prophecy, and it is doubtful that Macbeth's half-hints about his 'charmed-life' can convey to Macduff any sense of the extent and nature of his dealings with the Weird Sisters (indeed Macduff can refer to them, collectively, merely as an 'angel' [5.7.44]). In short, Macbeth's subjects are consistently denied any sight of the spectacles of horror that have made the play so theatrically celebrated.

This discrepancy between the experiences of Macbeth's on-stage subjects and his off-stage audience serves to reveal the ways in which Shakespeare's Macbeth shares with Dorothy Dunnett's a vulnerability to the accusation that his kingship is insufficiently charismatic and theatrical. In fact, he and Lady Macbeth are, for all their egregious brutality, in some sense the most domestic of couples, making literal and consistent use of household words. In the theatre, it may be customary to present their relationship as an explosively erotic one,[14] but Nicholas Brooke well observes that 'no play of Shakespeare's makes so little allusion to sex'.[15] The element of familiarity and domesticity is strongly highlighted from the very outset of the play. The Weird Sisters may have beards, live on a heath and vanish into thin air, but their conversation is notably marked by features serving to associate it with the normal concerns of women in the home:[16] they use popular terminology like 'hurly-burly',[17] and they discuss household animals like Grey-malkin and Paddock which are, literally, familiar(s). They even talk about the weather. As with their later parodic rituals of food preparation, the alienness of the Weird Sisters is closely inscribed here within degrees of difference and inversion of the normal.

The motif of food preparation, in however distorted a form, is first signalled in the speech of the sergeant who describes the battle, when he relates how Macbeth, fighting Macdonwald, 'unseamed him from the nave to th' chops' (1.2.22). This is the first hint of the Macbeth whom Malcolm will eventually label 'this dead butcher' (5.7.99), and the epithet of butcher is applicable to him both metaphorically and literally, though the elaborate imagery and rhetorical patterning of the sergeant may tend to submerge, for the moment at least, the possibility of a literal reading. His set-piece speech, which deliberately delays the knowledge of success until he has carefully cultivated fears of uncertainty, sits well in Duncan's camp, for Duncan, as we soon learn, is marked precisely by those shows and ceremonies of kingship which will be so notably absent from the court of Macbeth. In marked contrast to the unheralded, unglossed entrance of the Weird Sisters, the sergeant is formally presented to Duncan by Malcolm, who performs a similar function when he announces the arrival of Ross to his father (1.2.45)—surely a ceremonial rather than a factual communication, unless hyper-naturalism desired a short-sighted Duncan here. Duncan, moreover, ends the scene by conferring an honour: Macbeth is to become Thane of Cawdor. The bestowal of favours and titles is a marked feature of Duncan's kingly style, and something which, we see in the closing speech, his son will also practise (could there be here an unusually favourable imaging of James I's notorious open-handedness with knighthoods and other titles?); Shakespeare had already shown in *Richard III* how crucial a tool this could be in retaining support. Macbeth, notably, never does this. There are no nobles of his creation, no henchmen (with the arguable exception of the Murderers) dependent entirely on his continued favour; from the time of the disrupted banquet, he converses only with those conspicuously beneath him, like the doctor, the 'loon', and Young Seyward. Here, as in other areas, there are no outward manifestations of his kingship.

Macbeth can, however, think in terms of the spectacular and the ceremonial. We see this in his first soliloquy:

> (*aside*) Two truths are told
> As happy prologues to the swelling act
> Of the imperial theme—I thank you
>   gentlemen—
> This supernatural soliciting
> Cannot be ill, cannot be good.
>
> (1.3.128-32)

The most marked feature of his language here, however, is the dramatic register shift between his public and private discourses in the early part of the play, before horrid banquetings force disastrously together the arenas of the public and the domestic. To himself, this early Macbeth speaks stirringly, with elaborate metaphors of theatre and performance; but for public consumption, he confines himself to the plain 'I thank you gentlemen', and later apologizes, 'Give me your favour: my dull brain was wrought / With things forgotten' (1.3.150-1). A similar dualism of approach characterizes Lady Macbeth. Alone, she talks of symbolically hoarse ravens; to her servants, she speaks, like a good housewife, of preparation for the king's visit. But perhaps the most marked contrast of this type comes in Macbeth's next soliloquy:

> Go bid thy mistress, when my drink is ready,
> She strike upon the bell. Get thee to bed. *Exit*
>   *Servant.*
> Is this a dagger which I see before me,
> The handle toward my hand?
>
> (2.1.32-5)

The movement from bedtime drinks to imaginary (or supernatural) daggers within the space of two lines tellingly encapsulates the contrast between Macbeth's public and private faces. In public, he is the model of bourgeois marital comfort; but in private, he—and the audience—see strange things. At the same time, though, even Macbeth's inner life displays clear elements of continuity with his outer one, for the dagger of the mind does not only represent the antithesis of the comfort and normality offered by the drink; it also comes from the same world of household objects and food, as is suggested by the lack of any noticeable register shift in the diction, with 'drink' and 'bell' giving place almost seamlessly to 'dagger' and 'hand'. The connection becomes strikingly apparent when Lady Macbeth prefigures the Weird Sisters' parodies of cooking in her preparations for the murder: she makes drinks not only for her husband but for the guards, but she has 'drugged their possets' (2.2.6); and she has 'laid their daggers ready' (2.2.12) not for a meal, but for murder. Her housewifery continues as she soothes her husband's night fears, bids him wear his nightgown (2.2.69), and, above all, adjures him to wash his hands (2.2.45-6)—the domestic ritual that will still be with her in her madness. Her infamous cry of 'What, in our house?' (2.3.89) does not simply strike the bathetic note of her husband's 'Twas a rough night' (2.3.62); it sits perfectly with her public image as 'most kind hostess' (2.1.16). We never see Lady Macbeth out of her own house, and her mental collapse narrows even further the world we perceive her to inhabit, as we are shown her bedchamber. Bradley's comment that '[s]trange and almost ludicrous as the statement may sound, she is, up to her light, a perfect wife'[18] could well have been extended to the argument that she is also, up to her light, a perfect house-wife. The Macbeths are, after all, so apparently innocuous that those about them are notably slow to realize the full horror of their behaviour.

Perhaps the most striking example of this emphasis on the discrepancy between the public and private lives of Macbeth, and the simultaneous, paradoxical, imbrication of both in the domestic, comes at the opening of 1.7. The scene is prefaced by an unusually detailed stage direction:

> *Hautboys. Torches.*
> *Enter a sewer and divers servants with dishes*
>   *and service crossing over the stage.*
> *Then enter Macbeth*
>
> (1.7.s.d.)

This is so elaborate that Brooke elevates it to the status of formal 'dumb-show' (see note), a phenomenon without precedent in Shakespearian tragedy except in the deliberately archaic play-within-the-play in *Hamlet,* and although Brooke points out that the episode 'stresses the evening-time and the obligations of lavish hospitality' it does nothing to advance the narrative. What it does do, however, is make for a particularly startling contrast. Shakespeare brings on stage the whole panoply of the elaborately regulated ritual of the courtly serving of food; he then follows this with the very sequence of repetitive monosyllables which aroused the scorn of Gervase Fen, and which Nicholas Brooke concurs in terming 'notably plain vocabulary'.[19] Superficially, this inverts the contrast between private eloquence and public reticence which characterized Macbeth's earlier soliloquy; but in fact he goes on to launch himself upon one of the most sustained and dense speeches in the play, in the course of which he figures the possibility of murder, and its potential consequences, precisely in terms of food:

> This even-handed justice
> Commends th'ingredience of our poisoned
>   chalice
> To our own lips.
>
> (1.7.10-12)

When Lady Macbeth enters, demanding 'He has almost supped: why have you left the chamber?' (1.7.29) we realize that Macbeth has, indeed, been once again neglecting his public image, causing a feast to be disrupted by his failure to attend to it fully, just as he will on the occasion of the appearance of Banquo's ghost. His wife indeed characterizes his dereliction in terms of improper banqueting when she uses the language of drunkenness and surfeit to describe it:

> Was the hope drunk
> Wherein you dressed yourself? Hath it slept
>   since?

And wakes it now to look so green and pale
At what it did so freely?

> (1.7.35-8)

Typically, the one attempt at public show that the Macbeths do make revolves round cooking: they hold a ceremonial feast. Just as the murder of Duncan violated codes of hospitality, though, so too do their dinner invitations, since they demand compulsory attendance, a fact twice underlined—'Fail not our feast' says Macbeth to Banquo (3.1.27), and Lennox lists a precisely similar crime as one of the reasons for Macduff's downfall:

> But peace—for from broad words, and 'cause
>   he failed
> His presence at the tyrant's feast, I hear
> Macduff lives in disgrace.
>
> (3.6.21-3)

Nicholas Brooke points out that in Holinshed, 'the quarrel with Macduff involves a complicated story about the building of Forres castle which Shakespeare reduced to refusal of an invitation (command) to dinner';[20] the modification may well have been made not only in the interests of dramatic economy but because of its thematic congruence. The clear suggestion that the Macbeths are a couple at whose dinners attendance must be enforced is a powerful and compact device. It neatly measures the length of the journey they have travelled since, in the first act, Duncan deliberately solicited them as host and 'most kind hostess'. Equally, it reinforces the images both of their customary domesticity and of its rapid disintegration, making theirs a nightmare which, even at its most outlandish, retains that most distinctive quality of what Freudian theory on the uncanny has termed the *unheimlich* by relying for its full horror on the distortion of the traditional comforts of home. It is little wonder that the Lord who converses with Lennox should figure the rule of Macbeth precisely in terms of the subversion of the domestic:

> with Him above
> To ratify the work—we may again
> Give to our tables meat, sleep to our nights,
> Free from our feasts and banquets bloody
>   knives.
>
> (4.1.32-6)

Macbeth has not only murdered sleep, he has also perverted the proper consumption of food.

As well as Macduff's decision to boycott it (which in itself ironically recalls Macbeth's earlier failure to attend his own feast, for suggestively similar political reasons), the grand banquet is also devastatingly upstaged by its near-homonym Banquo, the name that we might always have guessed would lurk within the word in this instance, who is, suggestively, imaged by Macbeth almost in terms of a distasteful food item: 'Thy bones are marrowless, thy blood is cold' (3.4.95). The disastrous feast is a common enough feature of Renaissance drama, but it is particularly appropriate in the Macbeths' case, especially since the next time we see Macbeth it is at an eerily similar occasion, the brewing of the Weird Sisters' hell stew, with its foul concoction of ingredients, for 'a devil's-banqueting'.[21] As with so much in the play, however, the cause of the occasion's failure is never apparent to the onlookers. Macbeth's language, especially in the early part of the scene, is infuriatingly riddled with deictic phrases intelligible only to the off-stage audience, not to the on-stage one:

> Which of you have done this?
>
> (3.4.49)

> Thou canst not say I did it—never shake
> Thy gory locks at me.
>
> (3.4.50-1)

> Ay, and a bold one, that dare look on that
> Which might appal the Devil.
>
> (3.4.58-9)

> Prithee, see there—behold, look, lo
>
> (3.4.69)

> Thou hast no speculation in those eyes
>
> (3.4.96)

> Take any shape but that
>
> (3.4.103)

'This', 'it', 'that', 'behold', 'look', 'lo', 'those eyes', and 'any shape but that' can all make sense only in the presence of the referent, but that referent is literally invisible to all others on stage (and it is of course also open to the director similarly to tantalize and titillate the off-stage audience by staging the scene without an actual ghost). Moreover, 'behold', 'look' and 'lo', which Macbeth piles one on top of the other like a demented thesaurus, undo themselves even as they are spoken by their status as near-variants of one another. Their iteration serves only to underline the inadequacy of each on its own: as speech continually glosses itself, with a lack of difference that powerfully reinforces *différance,* we are offered a radical awareness of the slippage between signifier and signified which, even as the deictic is spoken, undermines its ability to show. (Here again, as with the banqueting, we are afforded an ironic prolepsis of the 'show' shortly to be offered by the Weird Sisters).

The whole scene is typical of the experience of Macbeth's subjects: under his rule, they get no visual value for their money. Macbeth himself is a conspicuous

example of his regime's radical failure to validate itself through the performance of spectacles of power: even when he becomes aware of his own role-playing, he denigrates acting, characteristically, with his image of the 'poor player' (5.5.24), and when we hear that his title is ill-fitting 'like a giant's role / Upon a dwarfish thief' (5.2.21-2) the image may well suggest a simple failure to acheive proper costuming for his part. While the spectacle of Banquo's ghost may be one of horror, it is, surely, more frustrating to be so comprehensively denied not only the experience of seeing it, but of hearing any coherent description of it. Certainly the public, performative nature of state punishment at the time would indicate that such sights would be enjoyed, and it is a pleasure that is definitively envisaged as part of Malcolm's regime:

> Then yield thee, coward,
> And live to be the show and gaze o'th'
>   time.
> We'll have thee, as our rarer monsters are,
> Painted upon a pole, and underwrit
> 'Here may you see the tyrant'.
>
> (5.7.53-7)

Just as Duncan had made a public show of the execution of Cawdor, with the full Foucauldian apparatus of proper acknowledgement of guilt by the criminal, so the reign of his son will be inaugurated with spectacle: Macbeth's head is publicly produced (5.7.84-5), and the play's last line is an invitation 'to see us crowned at Scone' (5.7.105).

The latter actions of Macbeth's own reign have been in marked contrast to this. As he is seen talking not to his generals or lords, but only to his doctor and his armourer, the paradoxical homeliness of the 'butcher' in him becomes ever more apparent. Dismissing the English as 'epicures' (5.3.8), he notably identifies himself with simpler produce. He rails at the servant 'The Devil damn thee black, thou cream-faced loon: / Where got'st thou that goose-look?' (5.3.11-12). 'Cream-faced' functions in obvious opposition to 'black', but a simple 'white' would have done so even more strongly; indeed in this sense 'cream', by failing to act as a clear contrast, undoes itself as constituent part of a trope and stakes a claim for a more literal meaning. Particularly in conjunction with 'goose', 'cream' must surely suggest, however momentarily, the simple farm-food from which Macbeth's own actions have so radically alienated him. The images are appropriate, for he is thinking of his 'land' here (5.3.50), and he again sites it in terms of an economy of ingestion when he asks the Doctor 'What rhubarb, senna, or what purgative drug / Would scour these English hence?' (5.3.54-5). It is such images of evacuation and failure to nourish which lead directly to his peculiarly apposite threat to the messenger who informs him that Birnam wood is moving:

> If thou speak'st false,
> Upon the next tree shall thou hang alive
> Till famine cling thee; if thy speech be sooth,
> I care not if thou dost for me as much.
>
> (5.5.38-41)

Macbeth counters his enemies' moving wood, with its obvious connotations of renewed fertility and Maying rites, with branches of his own, twice figured as bearing parodic fruit—first the messenger and then himself—which denies life and nourishment rather than celebrating it.

Macbeth's images of a cream-faced, goose-like messenger who hangs like fruit provides the climax to a strain of cannibalistic suggestion throughout the play. Triply interpellating the messenger as foodstuff, he also recapitulates in 'cream' a recurrent play on figures centring on milk and cows. The first example of this comes in Lady Macbeth's invocation, 'Come to my woman's breasts / And take my milk for gall, you murd'ring ministers' (1.5.46-7). This clearly follows from the request to 'unsex me here' (1.5.40), but it may do rather more than simply develop the earlier idea: Janet Adelman suggests that 'perhaps Lady Macbeth is asking the spirits to take her milk *as* gall, to nurse from her breasts and find in her milk their sustaining poison'.[22] If so, she specifically identifies herself as a food-source, a thing to be eaten. This is soon followed by the most striking and most notorious instance of the image, in Lady Macbeth's infamous lines:

> I have given suck, and know
> How tender 'tis to love the babe that milks
>   me;
> I would, while it was smiling in my face,
> Have plucked my nipple from his boneless
>   gums
> And dashed the brains out, had I so sworn
> As you have done to this.
>
> (1.7.54-9)

Clearly this picture of menstrous motherhood encodes a terrifying ferocity, accentuated by the rapidity of the change from the emotional range of 'tender' to that of 'dashed'. Equally, though, the aggression it registers is directed not only against the putative 'babe', but also, masochistically, against Lady Macbeth herself. The action of plucking the nipple from the gum would be (as anyone who has breastfed knows) deeply unpleasant; it is more usual to insert one's little finger to prise the infant's gums apart so that the nipple can be released gently and (relatively) painlessly. Perhaps more suggestive, though, is the tacit auto-interpellation of Lady Macbeth here as a thing milked—in essence, a cow. This not only returns to the earlier *motif;* it is also closely echoed, as Coppélia Kahn has shown, by Macbeth's lament that 'it hath cowed my better part of man' (5.7.48).[23] In his final dehumanization, Macbeth is unmanned, feminized, and radically identified with his wife, all in one fell swoop; moreover, all this is achieved, neatly, in another of his monosyllabic, literally household words.

This 'cowing' of both Macbeths works in conjunction with other images of cannibalism in the text. Duncan's horses eat each other (2.4.18); prey and predator change places when a falcon is devoured by a 'mousing owl' (2.4.12-13). Like the Weird Sisters' hideous banquet in which parts of babies are eaten, like Macbeth figuring the messenger and his enemies as cream-faced and goose-like, all of these invert conventional categories of eater and eaten, deconstructing boundaries as crucial to civilization as Lévi-Strauss's raw and cooked. In many of them, the thrust, whether covert or overt, is towards imaging humans themselves as, or in terms of, food, as it is also with the 'chops' of Macdonald and with Banquo's 'marrowless' bones;[24] such an undercurrent may even be discernible in Malcolm's assertion that in comparison with himself, the state will esteem Macbeth as a 'lamb' (4.3.54), and it certainly inheres in Macduff's figuring of Macbeth as a 'hell-kite' (4.3.218) and his wife and children as 'chickens and their dam' (4.3.219). All of these offer powerful images of a humanity diminished to either prey or predator, and all of them, again, do so in terms of household words. There is the lamb which could, in other circumstances, be redolent of the pastoral, the chickens which might, but do not, evoke the farmyard, the mousing owl, the geese and the cream which might also belong there,[25] and the chops and bones which could suggest the kitchen. This is, indeed, a plain diction, but its very plainness is what enables it to strike so directly to the deepest fears, and to allow *Macbeth* to root horror in the heart and in the home.

What all these instances of plainness do, however, is work to remove the play from the arena of state affairs and situate the concerns of its main characters, at least, insistently within the realm of the domestic. As such, they doubly indicate the reasons for Macbeth's ultimate failure. The expedience of the use of ceremony in the creation of the royal image, and the seriousness of Macbeth's failure to do so, can perhaps best be appreciated by reinserting the play into the circumstances of its production. Jonathan Goldberg suggests that 'the text of *Macbeth* that we have derives from a court performance'.[26] He also argues that the dramaturgy of the play is profoundly affected by the traditions of court theatre: 'we can come closer to the source of *Macbeth* if we look at the Jonsonian masque that stands somewhere behind the masquelike movement that the play ultimately takes' (p. 254). He suggests, as others have done, that the obvious comparator is Jonson's *The Masque of Queens,* termed by its author 'a spectacle of strangeness',[27] which features an antimasque of twelve witches who boast that they have 'Kill'd an infant, to have his fat' (p. 78). Goldberg terms Jonson's play a 'spectacle of state';[28] Pye uses the same phrase when he argues that 'Macbeth's "rapture" aligns the play with spectacles of state.'[29] But within *Macbeth,* it is not only that the Weird Sisters perform a purely private cabaret; there are no spectacles of state at all. Though the play itself may function as one for its off-stage audience, the experience of the court to which the play is represented will be radically different from the experience of the court which is represented within it. Goldberg suggests of James and Macbeth that 'one king slides into the other' (p. 251), but however true this may be of the rulers, the very act of staging the play performatively undoes any likeness between the self-presentational strategies of the two regimes.

There may indeed, though, be one pertinent point of similarity between the inhabitants of the stage-play world and those of the court which views it. Though we are carefully reminded that James is descended from Macbeth's enemy, Banquo, and has no blood-link with his tyrannical predecessor, the play may perhaps be seen as encoding subtle comment on James's own attitude towards the use of spectacle. Alan Sinfield notes the particular relevance of touching for the King's Evil to the world of the play: 'James himself knew that this was a superstitious practice, and he refused to undertake it until his advisers persuaded him that it would strengthen his claim to the throne in the public eye.'[30] It might also be worth noting that the title of Jonson's *Masque of Queens* overtly declares its affiliation with Queen Anne of Denmark—well known for her passion for the theatre—rather than with the King himself.[31] Were James a sufficiently attentive viewer, he might perhaps draw conclusions from *Macbeth* about the proper use of theatrical display which might lead him to find his own behaviour wanting—except that to do so would probably demand from him a cognitive shift as radical as that which might enable the characters in the play to become aware of their own imbrication in theatricality. If the play can indeed be read as offering such a commentary on the appropriate use of the spectacular, it would then be harking back directly to the didacticism of the morality play, a genre with which the porter scene has already connected it; and in addition to this artistic self-reflexivity, it would also be remarking on the domestic politics of the royal household itself, and pointing up the extent to which, though the language of the home may be plain in diction, it may be complex indeed in terms of resonance and register.

Notes

[1] Dorothy Dunnett, *King Hereafter* [1982] (London, 1992), p. 672.

[2] On the relationship between the two characters' diction, see William Shakespeare, *Macbeth,* edited by Nicholas Brooke (Oxford, 1990), introduction, pp. 14-19.

[3] Edmund Crispin, *Holy Disorders* [1946] (Harmondsworth, 1958), p. 136.

[4] From *The Rambler,* no. 168, 26 October 1751.

[5] Samuel Taylor Coleridge, *Shakespearean Criticism,* edited by Thomas Middleton Raysor, 2 vols. (London, 1960), vol. 1, p. 65.

[6] A. C. Bradley, *Shakespearean Tragedy* [1904], (London, 1974), pp. 312 and 311.

[7] Paul Jorgensen, 'Macbeth's Soliloquy', from *Our Naked Frailties: Sensational Art and Meaning in 'Macbeth'* [Berkeley, 1971], reprinted in Roy Battenhouse, ed., *Shakespeare's Christian Dimension* (Bloomington, 1994), pp. 481-5; p. 483.

[8] Coppélia Kahn, *Man's Estate: Masculine Identity in Shakespeare* (Berkeley, 1981), p. 191.

[9] Coleridge, *Shakespearean Criticism,* p. 61.

[10] Walter Whiter, 'Specimen of a Commentary on Shakespeare' [1794], reprinted in John Wain, ed., *Macbeth: A Casebook,* pp. 63-76; p. 63.

[11] Bradley, *Shakespearean Tragedy,* p. 298.

[12] Malcolm Evans, *Signifying Nothing,* second edition (London, 1989), p. 133.

[13] Christopher Pye, *The Regal Phantasm: Shakespeare and the Politics of Spectacle* (London, 1990), p. 150.

[14] This could, I think, be illustrated from many productions, but a recent and striking example was Philip Franks' November, 1994 production at the Crucible Theatre, Sheffield. Lady Macbeth's backless purple dress was so eye-catching that the actress was featured wearing it, in character, in the Sheffield *Star*'s 'wardrobe' section (usually including only real people), sharing her 'seduction tips'.

[15] *Macbeth,* ed. Brooke, introduction, p. 19.

[16] On the element of domesticity in the representation of the Weird Sisters, see also Naomi Conn Liebler, *Shakespeare's Festive Tragedy* (London, 1995), p. 224.

[17] William Shakespeare, *Macbeth,* ed. Brooke, I.1.3. All further quotations will be taken from this edition and reference will be given in the text.

[18] Bradley, *Shakespearean Tragedy,* p. 316.

[19] *Macbeth,* ed. Brooke, introduction, p. 7.

[20] *Ibid.*

[21] G. Wilson Knight, *The Imperial Theme* (Oxford, 1931), p. 138.

[22] Janet Adelman, *Suffocating Mothers* (London, 1992), p. 135.

[23] Kahn, *Man's Estate,* p. 191.

[24] *OED* cites the first use of 'chop' as a cut of meat as occurring in 1461, in the Paston Letters.

[25] This element would have been even more pronounced when the Cat appeared in the Middleton-authored revisions, which Brooke prints.

[26] Jonathan Goldberg, 'Speculations: *Macbeth* and Source', in *Shakespeare Reproduced,* edited by Jean E. Howard and Marion F. O'Connor (London, 1987), 242-64; p. 251.

[27] Ben Jonson, *The Masque of Queens,* in *Jacobean and Caroline Masques,* Vol. 1, edited by Richard Dutton (Nottingham, 1981), p. 71.

[28] Goldberg, 'Speculation', p. 260.

[29] Pye, *The Regal Phantasm,* p. 156.

[30] Alan Sinfield, '*Macbeth:* History, Ideology and Intellectuals', in *Critical Quarterly,* 28 I:2 (Spring, Summer, 1986), 63-77, reprinted in *New Historicism and Renaissance Drama,* edited by Richard Wilson and Richard Dutton (Harlow, 1992), 167-80; p. 172.

[31] Suggestively, *Sophonisba,* another play with which *Macbeth* is occasionally compared, also focuses on a queen. (Kenneth Muir comments on the comparison in his introduction to the Arden edition [London, 1951], introduction, p. xxii.)

Source: "Household Words: *Macbeth* and the Failure of Spectacle," in *Shakespeare Survey: An Annual Survey of Shakespeare Studies and Production*, Vol. 50, 1997, pp. 101-10.

'And All Things Change Them to the Contrary': *Romeo and Juliet* and the Metaphysics of Language

David Lucking, *Università degli Studi di Lecce, Italy*

While the fact that oxymoron is the most pervasive rhetorical figure in *Romeo and Juliet* is unlikely to escape the notice of any reasonably attentive reader, the significance that is to be attributed to this predominance is by no means equally apparent. Critics have evinced widely varying views as to whether the frequency with which this device recurs is to be regarded as a key to character or to the stage of development attained by Shakespeare's own art at the time of composition, and whether in either case its use is indicative of control of the verbal medium or of domination by it. It has been suggested on the one hand that the predilection for this and other figures is symptomatic of an initial immaturity which the protagonists of the tragedy outgrow through their experience of authentic love,[1] and on the other that it reveals their verbal dexterity and hence their intellectual superiority to the various other characters surrounding them.[2] At a somewhat more distant remove from the play, attention has been directed towards the issue of the playwright's personal commitment to oxymoron, the question, that is, of whether his insistent utilization of this device in *Romeo and Juliet* should not be interpreted as an index of his own rhetorical propensities rather than of any particular trait in his personages. Although many such discussions of the rhetorical fabric of the drama appear to imply that oxymoron is a wholly artificial, self-indulgent, or otherwise inferior device, and that its prevalence betrays a want of taste or judgment on the part either of the characters or of the playwright himself, it has been pointed out by more sympathetic commentators that oxymoron is an eminently suitable choice of figures in a play which seems deliberately concerned to dramatize the paradoxical identity of opposites. Taking my cue from proponents of the latter view, I propose in the following analysis to examine the manner in which oxymoron functions as a sort of figural paradigm for the structural dynamics operating throughout *Romeo and Juliet* as a whole, enacting in terms specific to itself the tensions rendered on a more comprehensive scale at the levels of plot and theme.[3]

That oxymoron should be the rhetorical device most frequently resorted to by Romeo himself is entirely to be expected in view of the premises of the play, and might therefore appear at first to be adequately explicable in those terms alone. Romeo is cast in the role of a lover from the moment we first hear of him, and oxymoron is traditionally regarded to be a congenial figure for people in his plight for the reason that it can function as a sort of verbal correlative to the para-doxes and dilemmas supposed to be intrinsic to their condition. Love is an illness, though an illness of which the victim is unwilling to be cured; the mistress is a tyrant, but a gentle tyrant and perhaps even a docile one; the relationship is sweet and bitter at the same time, a source of simultaneous anguish and delight, and so forth. More particularly, it was part of the stock-in-trade of Renaissance love poets to represent the beloved woman as an enemy undergoing a protracted siege in which the poetry itself was deployed, with greater or lesser expectation of success, as a weapon. Perceived in the light of this metaphor, which depicts the process of wooing as a military campaign of incalculable duration and indeterminate outcome, the poet's mistress assumes the paradoxical character of beloved antagonist, passionately adored even as means are relentlessly sought to subdue her.

What at one level is merely a literary convention, however, contains in *Romeo and Juliet* a significant component of literal truth from the beginning. If love and hate are generally understood to be diametrically opposed forces contending against one another in the human world, in this play they reveal themselves to be potential manifestations of one another. Part of the reason for this is the ambivalence of erotic love as such, what M. M. Mahood describes in her illuminating discussion of the drama as 'the *odi-et-amo* duality of passion',[4] thematized by amatory poets from Catullus to Petrarch. But this ambivalence does not confine itself to the contradictory currents of feeling flowing within the individual psyche alone. The relation between the sexes in *Romeo and Juliet* is in actual fact, and not only metaphorically, implicated in a broader pattern which is overtly conflictual in character, and which is objectified in that perennial enmity between the Capulets and Montagues which constitutes the most fundamental datum of the drama. The connection between violence and eroticism is made apparent as early as the first scene of the play, when two of the Capulet retainers, Samson and Gregory, engage in an exchange of obscene banter that, however fatuous in itself, is representative of a prevalent attitude and so more than a little sinister in implication.[5] Part of the dramatic function discharged by the heavy-handed jesting about maidenheads and naked weapons in which they take such puerile delight is that it invests violence with a sexual connotation from the beginning, the feud between the two houses being conceived among other things as a pretext for rape. Thus when the initial fray begins it is already endued with associations that give literal point to the oxymoronic conjunction of love and hate that will be developed subsequently. Sex is conceived merely as a mode of aggression, the vehicle of love as an instrument of hate.

Inasmuch as the identification of sex and violence underlying the coarse double-entendres of the first scene is implicit also in the extravagantly oxymoronic language that Romeo habitually employs, it affords a possible perspective within which we can evaluate that language. It is not only symptomatic of Romeo's preoccupied state of consciousness that the spectacle of the aftermath of the street brawl should evoke to his thoughts the turmoil of his feelings for Rosaline. What is to be suspected instead is that there is an indissoluble association in his mind between the concepts of love and violence, an association that extends well beyond the poetic convention of the beloved antagonist as such:

> . . . O me! What fray was here?
> Yet tell me not, for I have heard it all.
> Here's much to do with hate, but more with
>   love.
> Why then, O brawling love, O loving hate,
> O anything of nothing first create!
>
> (I.i.171-5)[6]

While it is true that, as critics have frequently remarked, Romeo's revelling in ornate paradoxes of this sort betrays the essential insincerity of his sentiments—or at least their contrived nature, their status as a function of the language used to register them—the darker implications of the situation should not be overlooked. What is perhaps worth observing in this connection is that the object of Romeo's infatuation, Rosaline, is apparently a Capulet herself. So at least we might infer from Capulet's invitation list (which includes 'My fair niece Rosaline' [I.ii.70]) and—lest it be surmised that Verona boasts more than one damsel of this name—Benvolio's confirmatory reminder for Romeo's benefit that Rosaline will be present at the festivities (I.ii.84-5). Even before meeting Juliet, then, Romeo seems almost instinctively to gravitate towards women belonging to the rival household. If this is so, then his initial obsession with what appears to be a totally unresponsive woman, his publicly proclaimed desire to overcome her resolute chastity, might after all have something in common with the aggressive fantasies of the Capulet servants, however circumspectly he cloaks his ambitions in the language of courtly passion. And there would thus already seem to be a dimension of submerged but literal truth to the elaborately wrought paradoxes with which he formulates his feelings.

The close interdependency of love and aggression manifests itself again, though in somewhat different guise, in the feast scene. It is significant that it is in the very moment in which Romeo first glimpses Juliet that Tybalt should conceive the personal animosity that will eventually culminate in the fatal duel between the two men, focussing onto a single individual the generic antagonism he feels for the entire Montague clan. Love and its opposite come into being simultaneously, both kindled by the identical event.[7] But there is more to the matter than this. Enjoined by Capulet to refrain from quarrelling, Tybalt snarls:

> I will withdraw; but this intrusion shall
> Now seeming sweet, convert to bitt'rest gall.
>
> (I.v.90-91)

Here we are no longer in the essentially static realm of oxymoron as an exclusively verbal phenomenon, but in a world in which things are literally transformed into their opposites, in which paradox reveals itself to be an active principle operating in human affairs. Juliet articulates such a dynamic conception of paradox when she learns the name of the young man to whom she has already emotionally committed herself:

> My only love sprung from my only hate.
> Too early seen unknown, and known too late.
> Prodigious birth of love it is to me
> That I must love a loathed enemy.
>
> (I.v.137-40)

Thus hate transmutes itself into love in the private world of Juliet's experience, at the precise instant in which, in the external domain of public events, the quickening of love in Romeo engenders Tybalt's implacable hatred.

Another conspicuous instance of the process whereby things are transformed into their formal opposites appears in the recurrent allusions to light and darkness which in their ensemble constitute one of the dominant image patterns of the play. In this case as well what manifests itself as oxymoron at the strictly verbal level becomes fundamental to the action and thematic development of the drama. The manipulation of words and concepts in such a way that light and darkness each become, or can be represented as, the other, is a linguistic strategy frequently encountered in Shakespeare, assuming notable thematic relevance in such plays as *Love's Labour's Lost* and *Othello*. Often the word *heavy* as a possible antonym to *light* is used to complicate the relation between the two terms still further, at least at the level of linguistic play, and this is what in fact occurs in *Romeo and Juliet* as well. Benvolio's report that he encountered Romeo 'an hour before the worshipp'd sun / Peer'd forth the golden window of the east' (I.i.116-17) prompts the observation on the part of Romeo's father that at dawn

> Away from light steals home my heavy son
> And private in his chamber pens himself,
> Shuts up his windows, locks fair daylight out
> And makes himself an artificial night.
>
> (I.i.135-38)

Under the influence of his sterile infatuation for Rosaline Romeo shuns literal light, preferring to stimulate a night in day, an oxymoronic space in which he can indulge his melancholy without interference. At the same time, Romeo makes the ambivalent relation between light and dark, or black and white, one of the themes of the rather convoluted wordplay in which he engages at every opportunity: 'These happy masks that kiss fair ladies' brows, / Being black, puts us in mind they hide the fair' (I.i.228-9). Perhaps inspired by his example, his companions adopt the same idiom. Benvolio urges Romeo to attend the feast so that he can compare Rosaline with other fair ladies of Verona, promising that if he does so 'I will make thee think thy swan a crow' (I.ii.89). Benvolio's hope is that white will seem black when contrasted with other instances of what Capulet himself has earlier described as 'Earth-treading stars that make dark heaven light' (I.ii.25). And this is of course exactly what happens when Romeo is transfixed by the metaphoric light emanating from Juliet herself, a radiance which to his enraptured vision overwhelms all other sources of illumination. It is ironic that the words with which he registers the impact of this effulgence—'O, she doth teach the torches to burn bright' (I.v.43)—should be those that provoke Tybalt's dark enmity.

Shortly afterwards, having taken refuge in the Capulet garden in order to escape his rowdy companions, the young man who has earlier shrunk from daylight and cultivated an artificial night in day now finds himself being irresistibly drawn towards the source of a spiritual illumination propagating itself through physical darkness. His celebrated solo beginning 'But soft, what light through yonder window breaks? / It is the east and Juliet is the sun!' (II.ii.2-3) is a metaphorical adumbration of the process by which darkness transforms itself into light, a physical night into a spiritual dawn. What is important in this connection is less the fact that 'each of the lovers thinks of the other as light', as Caroline Spurgeon puts it,[8] than that the light that each associates with the other represents the metamorphosis of darkness, and hence a reversal of one of the most fundamental of natural polarities. Juliet, although she is in many respects the more practical and down-to-earth of the two lovers, testifies in her speech to a perception of mystic transformation identical to that of Romeo. As she is awaiting Romeo on the evening of their marriage she summons darkness not only because it ensures welcome privacy but also because it will arrive attended by its own opposite:

> Come night, come Romeo, come thou day in
>   night,
> For thou wilt lie upon the wings of night
> Whiter than new snow upon a raven's back.
> (III.ii.17-19)

What might legitimately be inferred, however, is that if night can be converted into day when it is transfig-

ured by love, then the converse can also occur, and light transform itself into darkness. This is precisely what would seem to happen as the tragic impetus asserts itself with increasing force in the action of the play. When Juliet announces on the morning that Romeo's sentence of exile must begin that it is growing lighter, Romeo replies: 'More light and light: more dark and dark our woes' (III.v.36), and later, after the simulated death of Juliet, the Nurse laments that 'Never was seen so black a day as this' (IV.v.53). There is an ironic anticipation of such a reversal even in the garden scene, for Romeo's observation that 'Her eyes in heaven / Would through the airy region stream so bright / That birds would sing and think it were not night' (II.ii.20-22) presages the lovers' conversation on the morning following their wedding night, much of which revolves around the question of whether a bird heard singing in the garden is a lark or a nightingale, harbinger of day or of night. On this occasion Juliet attempts briefly to duplicate her triumph in the garden, when she seemed for a while to be the arbiter of language and its meanings, attempting desperately to incorporate literal light into her universe of metaphor:

> Yond light is not daylight, I know it, I.
> It is some meteor that the sun exhales
> To be to thee this night a torchbearer
> And light thee on thy way to Mantua.
> (III.v.12-15)

But although Romeo is once again willing to acquiesce in her imaginative appropriation of reality, as he has earlier acquiesced in her imaginative manoeuvre of unnaming him in the garden, he remains aware of the very literal price he will have to pay for succumbing to the seductions of metaphor.

Although the principle governing the events of *Romeo and Juliet* is one of irreconcilable opposition, then, it is a paradoxical opposition the terms of which are, in various ways and for various reasons, interchangeable. In the social sphere, the Montagues are locked in perpetual strife with the Capulets, yet because both families proceed according to the identical rules of conduct, and pay homage to the same value system, their antagonism appears as a largely formal one in which roles can be reversed without in the least affecting the essential structure of the relationship. On the plane of human emotion, love and hate not only generate each other but in certain respects are indistinguishable from each other, so that a character such as Romeo seems uncertain on occasion which of the two he is in fact experiencing. In the world of images darkness can turn into light and light into darkness, while at the level of rhetorical figures formulas such as brawling love and loving hate make perfect sense. It is even arguable that the notorious instability of the play as regards its generic affiliations—the fact that it gestures unmistakably in the direction of comedy before deviating into tragedy—can be subsumed beneath this pattern.[9] If this is indeed the case, then the instructions Capulet issues to his household when he is confronted with what appears to be the lifeless body of his daughter after a night of feverish preparations for her marriage assume a special relevance:

> All things that we ordained festival
> Turn from their office to black funeral:
> Our instruments to melancholy bells,
> Our wedding cheer to a sad burial feast;
> Our solemn hymns to sullen dirges change,
> Our bridal flowers serve for a buried corse,
> And all things change them to the contrary.
>
> (IV.v.84-90)

There is another character who comments in more explicitly philosophical terms on these relationships of irreconcilable but potentially reversible opposition, although the fact that he does so proves in the end to be as much a source of irony as it is of insight. This is Friar Laurence, whose disquisition on the beneficent and baneful properties of the selfsame herbs is a clear statement not only of the simultaneous presence in the same object or phenomenon of radically opposed qualities, but of the propensity of those qualities to transform themselves into their own opposites. The Friar begins, characteristically enough, with yet another identification of apparent opposites, those of the womb and the tomb, and goes on from there:

> The earth that's nature's mother is her tomb:
> What is her burying grave, that is her womb;
> And from her womb children of divers kind
> We sucking on her natural bosom find.
> Many for many virtues excellent,
> None but for some, and yet all different.
> O, mickle is the powerful grace that lies
> In plants, herbs, stones, and their true
>   qualities.
> For nought so vile that on the earth doth live
> But to the earth some special good doth give;
> Nor aught so good but, strain'd from that fair
>   use,
> Revolts from true birth, stumbling on abuse.
> Virtue itself turns vice being misapplied,
> And vice sometime's by action dignified.
>
> (II.iii.5-18)

This speech might be construed as a sequence of expanded oxymora, ranging from uterine tombs and sepulchral wombs to vicious virtue and virtuous vice, but once again rendered dynamic inasmuch as the polarized extremes actually transform themselves into one another: 'Virtue itself turns vice'. The Friar seems to qualify his view somewhat when he goes on to apply his perception of simultaneous contrariety to the moral state of man, offering his version of the metaphor of the two steeds of the soul that Plato develops in the

Phaedrus: 'Two such opposed kings encamp them still / In man as well as herbs: grace and rude will' (II.iii.23-4). The conceptual distinctions operating here are once again rigidly dualistic in character, and in view of what has gone before it might be expected that even 'grace and rude will' might somehow transform themselves into one another as do virtue and vice. In this case, however, the Friar adopts a more orthodox position, rather lamely concluding that 'where the worser is predominant / Full soon the canker death eats up that plant' (II.iii.25-6).

Notwithstanding this apparent reversion to a less complicated vision at least as regards the rival forces contending in the human soul, however, the Friar continues to act on the assumption that opposites can be converted into one another in the world at large, aspiring to be an agent whereby this process can be exploited for the good of all. He agrees to officiate at the marriage of Romeo and Juliet on the grounds that the general principle he has enunciated might apply in this case as well, and that 'this alliance may so happy prove / To turn your households' rancour to pure love' (II.iii.87-8). He is successful in the long term, in the sense that it is the destruction of the lovers through his unintentional agency that ultimately makes possible the reconciliation of the two families, but his triumph is quite obviously an ironic one. And in the meantime he becomes the unwitting means by which other reversals, unforeseen and even more ambiguous, occur. Juliet's early declaration concerning Romeo that 'If he be married, / My grave is like to be my wedding bed' (I.v.133-4) turns out to be no less than perfect truth, a lethal drug is deemed to be 'cordial, and not poison' (V.i.85), the elevation of Juliet's chamber is succeeded by the subterranean depths of her tomb, Romeo wreaks vengeance upon his cousin Tybalt's murderer by killing himself (V.iii.97-101). In an ironic fulfilment of Friar Laurence's metaphorical assimilation of telluric womb and tomb, the Capulet monument is perceived by Romeo as a 'womb of death' (V.iii.45), and although it is at one point described as a 'palace of dim night' (V.iii.107) it is also a temple of light in which Romeo is briefly vouchsafed one final time the epiphany he first experienced in the garden scene:

> A grave? O no, a lantern, slaughter'd youth.
> For here lies Juliet, and her beauty makes
> This vault a feasting presence, full of light.
>
> (V.iii.84-6)

The concealed flaw in the Friar's strategy is that he seeks to accomplish the transformation of one extreme into the other through a process of mediation which, according to his own tacit theoretical premises—which I have been arguing are also the structural premises of the play—is impossible. His intention is to 'turn your households' rancour to pure love' by effecting another conversion of conceptually opposed terms, that of plurality into unity, through the mechanism of a ceremony which will 'incorporate two in one' (II.vi.37). Precisely by assuming the role of agent, however, and envisioning the possibility of a mediating term in the form of a couple who will unite extremes and occupy a middle ground between the two warring families, the Friar is implicitly invoking a principle that is formally extraneous to the oppositional logic he has himself earlier adumbrated in his botanical metaphor. In the Prologue to Act II the Chorus remarks that notwithstanding the various obstacles to the union of Romeo and Juliet, 'passion lends them power, time means, to meet, / Tempering extremities with extreme sweet' (13-14). But tempering extremities would seem to be precisely what is not possible in this play. Opposites can be transformed into one another, but no negotiation between them can occur. As Richard Fly points out in his perceptive discussion of the drama, what appear to be mediatory figures are introduced onto the scene, but they conspicuously fail to fulfil the function they assign themselves, thus leaving the antithetical structure of the situation ironically intact.[10] The attempt to intercede, as Mercutio discovers to his cost—'why the devil came you between us? I was hurt under your arm.' (III.i.104-5)—can have disastrous consequences. Indeed, the pointed elimination of a character whose name would seem expressly calculated to evoke the possibility of intercommunication between disparate realms might be regarded as symbolic of the destruction of the principle of mediation itself,[11] and the 'plague' that he repeatedly calls down on both houses an intimation of the only means through which the conflict between them can ultimately be resolved (III.i.92-110).[12] For as Juliet herself suggests in the desperate comments she addresses at one point to the Friar, the only intermediary that is likely to prove successful in the final reckoning is death:

> Give me some present counsel, or behold:
> 'Twixt my extremes and me this bloody knife
> Shall play the umpire, arbitrating that
> Which the commission of thy years and art
> Could to no issue of true honour bring.
>
> (IV.i.61-5)

Whereas the Friar aspires to be an active agent turning the logic of reversal to his own benign purposes, then, he ends by being no more than an instrument whereby that logic continues inexorably to determine the course of events, until at last it reaches its terminus in the catastrophe with which the play concludes. The deaths of Mercutio, Tybalt, Paris, and Romeo and Juliet themselves are all directly or indirectly attributable to his interference. The play that begins with an unsheathing of Capulet swords that are linked through broad humour to aggressive male sexuality, ends with the sheathing of a Montague dagger in a Capulet breast in what looks suspiciously like a parody of the sexual act: 'O happy dagger. / This is thy sheath. There rust, and let me die' (V.iii.168-9). The initial threat of violence is thus fulfilled, and the oxymoronic conjunction of sex and death actualized in the unfolding of events, precisely through the attempt 'To turn . . . rancour to pure love'. When the Prince enjoins Montague and Capulet to 'See what a scourge is laid upon your hate, / That heaven finds means to kill your joys with love' (V.iii.291-2), he omits to mention that the means that heaven has found is, ironically enough, the loving intervention of the Friar himself.

Various critics have argued that the phrase 'O brawling love' sums up the dramatic movement of *Romeo and Juliet*.[13] I would suggest instead that it is not so much the words as such as the relationship implicit in the figure exemplified by this phrase that reflects both the underlying dynamics and the controlling metaphysics of the play. Oxymoron elides the predicative syntax of such statements as 'The earth that's nature's mother is her tomb', but nonetheless makes the same assertion in compressed form, thereby becoming a sort of linguistic paradigm for the paradoxical coexistence in the same object of opposites.[14] It probably does not very much matter in the end whether we say that oxymoron represents a figurative crystallization of the tensions worked out discursively in the drama, or that the drama constitutes a discursive projection of the tensions contained in encapsulated form within the figure. What does matter is that a play which has often been criticized for its divided inspiration, for an alleged want of congruence between the lyrical and the dramatic impulses at work within it, exhibits on the contrary a remarkably high degree of formal integration, the aesthetic cohesion that results when each element reflects the whole. What unifies the play in all of its aspects is, as I have tried to show, a metaphysics of irreconcilable but reversible opposition, a metaphysics rendered as much in the deployment of language as in the dynamics of plot. If there is a single phrase in the play that summarizes this metaphysics with anything resembling thematic precision, it is perhaps to be found in Capulet's strangely haunting remark, itself ambivalently formulated both as an observation and an imperative: 'And all things change them to the contrary'. It is a poignant but deeply ironic fact that this phrase should be pronounced over the body of a girl who, at once both living and dead, has herself become an incarnate oxymoron, a visible emblem of the conjunction of opposites; a girl who has confronted all the horrors of death in order to attain to a richer life, and who will subsequently be restored to life only in order to die.

Notes

[1] See for instance Harry Levin's assertion that in the course of the drama 'the leading characters acquire together a deeper dimension of feeling by expressly repudiating the artificial language they have talked and

the superficial code they have lived by'. 'Form and Formality in *Romeo and Juliet*', *Shakespeare Quarterly* 11 (1960), 3-11 (this quotation p. 6).

[2] Robert O. Evans for instance argues that 'both Romeo and Juliet are masterful manipulators of figures. It is the measure of their intellects and a mark of the transcendence of the intellectual portions of their souls above the others'. *The Osier Cage: Rhetorical Devices in Romeo and Juliet* (Lexington, 1966), p. 41.

[3] Two previous studies that have approached *Romeo and Juliet* from points of view analogous to my own are Evans, op. cit., especially pp. 18-41, and Joseph S. M. J. Chang, 'The Language of Paradox in Romeo and Juliet', *Shakespeare Studies* 3 (1967), 22-42. Evans argues that 'In a real sense the structure of the play is mirrored in Shakespeare's choice of *oxymoron* as his dominant rhetorical device. The macrocosm (in this case the play) is mirrored in the microcosm (the dominant rhetorical figure). Shakespeare extended, it would seem, the doctrine of correspondence into the very rhetoric of the lines' (p. 32). Chang makes the similar point that 'whether or not we care for oxymorons, their function in the play . . . is development of theme, not character, and to this end they are consistent, using the same polarities despite fluctuations in poetic quality. The effect sought by the use of oxymorons and paradoxes is . . . to indicate the irreconcilable oppositions of love, or, indeed, of life itself' (pp. 23-4).

[4] M. M. Mahood, *Shakespeare's Wordplay* (1957; rpt. London, 1988), p. 61.

[5] The relevance of this exchange to the conventional topos of the 'dear enemy' is touched on by Jill L. Levenson in her paper 'The Definition of Love: Shakespeare's Phrasing in *Romeo and Juliet*', *Shakespeare Studies* 15 (1982), 21-36 (this reference p. 23).

[6] All references to *Romeo and Juliet* are to the Arden Edition edited by Brian Gibbons (1980; rpt. London, 1983).

[7] T. J. Cribb, who believes this play to have been inspired by the tenets of Renaissance Platonism as filtered through the teachings of Ficino, argues that Tybalt actually personifies the principle of hatred, and is therefore the counterpart to Romeo in his character as the embodiment of love. 'The Unity of "Romeo and Juliet"', *Shakespeare Survey* 34 (1981), 93-104. While I regard this to be somewhat schematic, Cribb's interpretation does have the merit of drawing attention to the paradoxical parallelism obtaining between diametrically opposed forces.

[8] Caroline Spurgeon, *Shakespeare's Imagery and What it Tells Us* (1935; rpt. Cambridge, 1965), p. 310.

[9] In his fine Introduction to the Arden Edition of the play Brian Gibbons argues that 'the two modes of tragedy and comedy are opposed, so generating the central dynamic of the action, but there are subterranean connections between them which make an antithetical structure complex like a living organism' (ed. cit., pp. 62-3).

[10] Richard Fly, *Shakespeare's Mediated World* (Amherst, 1976), pp. 3-26. Fly argues that 'the basis of the Friar's faith in the efficacy of human actions is his conviction that a middle ground of moderation exists, which, if conscientiously pursued, will allow for a human control of destiny. He repeatedly expresses his sense of an operative *via media* . . . Thus, he is the most likely person to arbitrate as the clashing extremes of the play close in. Shakespeare means him to represent the only course of action open to the distraught and harried lovers in the play's second half, and his eventual failure should suggest not so much a personal inadequacy as a general inadequacy in the play itself: a recognition that there is finally no viable middle ground in the polarized world of *Romeo and Juliet*' (p. 20). Although I agree with Fly's conclusion, my own view is that, far from being an exponent of the *via media,* the Friar enunciates what is perhaps the most explicit statement that the play contains of the radically dichotomized conception of reality, and that his effort to constitute himself intermediary represents a fatal compromise with that conception.

[11] Mercury is of course the god of boundaries and messenger of the gods. I do not wish to suggest that Mercutio's role in this play is actually mediatory or even potentially so, but only that it is significant that it is the death of a man bearing this name that spells the destruction of any prospect of reconciliation between Romeo and the Capulet family into which he has married. It might be noted that Mercutio's jocular entreaty to Benvolio to 'Come between us, good Benvolio, my wits faints' (II.iv.69) during a duel of wits with Romeo would seem to be a deliberate anticipation of his death in consequence of a bungled attempt at intercession.

[12] In a certain sense Mercutio's malediction does in fact work itself out in the action of the play, since it is the suspicion that he has been exposed to the plague that causes Friar John to be quarantined within a sealed house before he is able to deliver Laurence's letter to Romeo, an accident that contributes to the destruction of the two lovers and (since they apparently have no siblings) to the eventual extinction of their families (V.ii.5-12).

[13] See for instance Chang, who describes the phrase as 'the most succinct statement of the play's action, which is so contrived that for every moment of love, there is one of hatred' (op. cit., p. 24).

[14] The pun can accomplish the same thing in even more radically concentrated form, but depends for its effect on the coincidence in the same word of contrary, or at least contrastable, meanings. This is what in fact occurs in the case of the verb 'die', the final word pronounced by both Romeo and Juliet, the Elizabethan connotation of which turns their deaths into an ironic consummation.

Source: "'And All Things Change Them to the Contrary': *Romeo and Juliet* and the Metaphysics of Language," in *English Studies*, Vol. 78, No. 1, January, 1997, pp. 8-18.

'Voice Potential': Language and Symbolic Capital in *Othello*

Lynne Magnusson, *University of Waterloo, Ontario*

Before Brabanzio complains to the Venetian senators of Othello's marriage, Iago warns Othello that 'the magnifico is much beloved, / And hath in his effect a voice potential / As double as the Duke's'. Brabanzio's words will exert power—the power to 'divorce you, / Or put upon you . . . restraint or grievance' (1.2.12-15). Their power, however, will depend not upon Brabanzio's rhetorical skill but instead upon his social position—that is, both on his aristocratic status ('magnifico') and on the accumulated credit he has with his auditors ('much beloved'). How his speech is received will depend less on what he says than on the social site from which it is uttered. Othello rebuts Iago's position, but he does not dispute Iago's presupposition that linguistic competence counts for less than rank or otherwise attributed status in this matter of 'voice potential': 'My services which I have done the signory', he responds, 'Shall out-tongue his complaints' (1.2.18-19). In the event, Othello's voice does outweigh Brabanzio's, with an unanticipated element affecting the reception of their discourse and the outcome of the scene: that is, the exigency of the military threat to Cyprus.

In 'The Economics of Linguistic Exchanges', the French sociologist Pierre Bourdieu develops a market analogy to explain how utterances receive their values in particular contexts and how, in turn, the conditions of reception affect discourse production. Giving discourse pragmatics a sociological turn, he asks questions critical to the Senate scene and to other situations in *Othello:* whose speech is it that gets recognized? whose speech is listened to and obeyed? who remains silent? and whose speech fails to gain attention or credit? In Bourdieu's account, language in any situation will be worth what those who speak it are deemed to be worth: its price will depend on the symbolic power relation between the speakers, on their respective levels of 'symbolic capital'.[1] The price a speaker receives for his or her discourse will not, however, be an invariable function of class position or relative status, even in a rigidly hierarchical society. Instead, as Othello's positive reception in the context of the Turkish threat suggests, the price will vary with varying market conditions.

Focusing on a reading of the Senate scene (1.3) and other public situations, in this paper I will sketch out the complex and variable linguistic market that shapes and refigures 'voice potential' in *Othello.* Gender, class, race, necessity, linguistic ingenuity and a number of other competing measures enter into the moment-by-moment relations of symbolic power that affect discourse value—that affect, for example, how Brabanzio's charges against Othello or Desdemona's request to accompany Othello to Cyprus are heard. This paper will explore not only discourse reception in *Othello,* but also the force within Shakespeare's play of Bourdieu's hypothesis that a person's discourse production is conditioned by anticipatory adjustments to discourse reception. Finally, I will focus on Iago as a rhetorician and argue for a new perspective on Iago's rhetorical performance in terms of his efforts to manipulate the linguistic market in *Othello.*

In enunciating a sociology of speech in opposition to formal linguistics, Bourdieu argues that 'Language is not only an instrument of communication or even of knowledge, but also an instrument of power. A person speaks not only to be understood but also to be believed, obeyed, respected, distinguished.'[2] One main event in Act I of *Othello* is the contest of voices between Brabanzio and Othello. What is at issue between them is whose voice will be given credit, whose voice will have power to shape the ensuing course of events. This criterion for evaluating a particular discourse is foregrounded even before Brabanzio and Othello enter the Senate chamber, as the Senators endeavour to digest the news of the Turkish fleets: the Duke observes that 'There is no composition in these news / That gives them *credit*' (1.3.1-2; emphasis added). As the discursive contest between Brabanzio and Othello proceeds, the verbal performance of each speaker receives a summary evaluation from the Duke. Whereas Brabanzio's accusation draws the caution that 'To vouch this is no proof' (106), the Duke responds with approval to Othello's colourful account of wooing Desdemona: 'I think this tale would win my daughter, too' (170). Although the Duke apparently evaluates intrinsic features of the linguistic performance of each speaker, it is situational context, as I have already suggested, more than verbal competence that accounts for Othello's profit and Brabanzio's loss.

The carefully staged entrance of senator and general provides a vivid theatrical emblem for the dynamic variation in relative power. First, the significance of the entrance is prepared by the Duke's order to write 'post-post-haste' (46) to Marcus Luccicos, a character not otherwise identified except by his unavailability at this time of crisis. The verification of his absence heightens the importance of 'the man', in Brabanzio's words, 'this Moor, whom now' the Duke's 'special mandate for the state affairs / Hath hither brought' (71-3). A stage direction signals the arrival of a large group of characters, including *'Brabanzio, Othello, Roderigo, Iago, Cassio, and officers'*. The First Senator announces the arrival selectively, singling out 'Brabanzio and the valiant Moor' (47) and relegating to lesser importance those left unnamed. The structure of the Duke's greeting encapsulates the power dynamic of the situation, articulating the priorities of the moment:

> Valiant Othello, we must straight employ you
> Against the general enemy Ottoman.
> *(To Brabanzio)* I did not see you. Welcome,
>   gentle signor.
> We lacked your counsel and your help
>   tonight.
>
> (48-51)

Othello is greeted first; the need for his military skills accounts for his precedence. Brabanzio is greeted in second place, with the conversational repair work nonetheless signalling a recognition of his claim, based on rank, to first place.

This account of how Othello's voice gains ascendancy within the immediate situation in no way exhausts the complexity of the linguistic market depicted in the Senate scene. Another principal speaker whose voice power is at issue in the scene is Desdemona. Answering the Duke's summons, she speaks first to confirm Othello's account of their courtship and later to make a request of her own, to accompany Othello to the war zone. In both cases her speech wins credit, in the first instance solidifying the Duke's acceptance of the marriage and silencing Brabanzio's complaint and in the second instance gaining her permission to go with Othello. In making the request to accompany Othello, Desdemona does show her devotion to Othello, but she also asserts her separate and independent voice, her own claim to have her wish heard even after he has already publicly requested accommodation for her in Venice. Desdemona shows herself by Renaissance standards a bold and self-confident speaker in a setting whose formality and importance would silence most speakers, especially— one might expect—a woman. Her verbal behaviour in the scene and in the play as a whole is not consistent with any simple stereotype of feminine speech, especially not with the Renaissance commonplace concerning silence as woman's eloquence. In her initial appearances in the play, Desdemona is an assured and self-confident speaker. This is not to say that stereotyped gender roles do not come into play here. Consider, for example, Othello's embedded narrative of the courtship as 'mutual' recognition: 'She loved me for the dangers I had passed, / And I loved her that she did pity them' (166-7). What could better exemplify the standard clichés about male and female roles in cross-sex conversation prevalent even today than Othello's account of how he talked and she responded?[3] When Othello told over 'the story of my life' (128), Desdemona 'gave me for my pains a world of sighs'[4]

and 'swore in faith 'twas strange, 'twas passing strange, / 'Twas pitiful, 'twas wondrous pitiful' (158-60). And yet, whatever we are to make of the accuracy of Othello's report, such self-effacing speech behaviour is not Desdemona's predominant manner in the play.

Traditional readings of *Othello* have often focused, as I am doing now, on the complex speech patterns of the characters. In such readings, the *raison d'être* for an utterance is the speaker's character, or essential nature. Dramatic language is said to construct character: whereas in life language expresses character, in his plays Shakespeare shapes language to make it seem that language expresses pre-existing character.[5] In this view, the divergence from received stereotypes of female speech evident in Desdemona's self-assured and eloquent public speaking is to be explained as a particularizing and richly complicating mark of her essential character. But in a play so insistently dialogic as *Othello*—a play so intently focused on how one character's conversational contributions shape and direct the words, thoughts, and actions of another—it seems particularly pertinent to argue a different case, to take up Bourdieu's thesis that '[t]he *raison d'être* of a discourse . . . is to be found in the socially defined site from which it is uttered'.[6] Bourdieu's account of the social production of discourse emphasizes anticipatory adjustment, and offers a fruitful way to account for the speech patterns of Desdemona and other characters in *Othello*.

'[O]ne of the most important factors bearing on linguistic production', Bourdieu argues, is 'the anticipation of profit which is durably inscribed in the language habitus, in the form of an anticipatory adjustment (without conscious anticipation) to the objective value of one's discourse.'[7] What one says, how one says it, and whether one speaks at all in any given situation is strongly influenced, in this view, by the 'practical expectation . . . of receiving a high or low price for one's discourse'.[8] An utterance, then, inscribes an expectation of profit, an estimate of the likelihood that the speaker will be believed, recognized, obeyed. This expectation will not, in most instances, derive solely or even in the main part from an assessment of the immediate social situation; it cannot be entirely accounted for by the immediate relation of speaker to listener. The context of reception which shapes a speaker's linguistic production has a history, and it is that history Bourdieu tries to account for by positing the 'language habitus' of the speaker. That language habitus is a practical memory, built up through the accumulated history of speech contexts in which a speaker has functioned and received recognition or censure. The language habitus is shaped by the history of a person's most sustained social connections, by a person's cumulative dialogue with others.

But let us begin with Desdemona and class. Desdemona does not enter the play as the stereotypical silent and modest woman, but rather as an aristocratic speaker whose discourse is full of the assurance and self-confidence of her class habitus. This can be seen not only in the remarkable ease with which she speaks before the Duke and Senators, but also in the basic facts that she speaks at all and that she initiates speech topics. If we consider how it could be that speech patterns inscribe a speaker's expectation of profit, we need to look not only at the internal constitution of the speeches but also at turn-taking and access to the floor. '[T]he linguist', Bourdieu remarks, 'regards the *conditions for the establishment of communication* as already secured, whereas, in real situations, that is the essential question.'[9] To read the power relations of the scene one needs to observe the access to speech in this formal Senate setting of those who speak. Furthermore, one needs to consider what shapes the silence or non-participation of Roderigo, Cassio, the soldiers—and, most important for the developing action, the silence of Iago. Of course, in a play, considerations apart from those of real life will affect the access of speakers to the floor. The distinction, for example, between major and minor characters within any plot structure will help account for who speaks at length and whose speech is sparing. Nonetheless, one can still reasonably argue that the configuration of speakers Shakespeare represents in the Senate scene primarily reflects the power dynamics of the urgent situation as played out in a formal setting of the kind that regulates speaker access to a very high degree. Desdemona's confidence in her access to the floor, borne out by the Duke's solicitous question—'What would you, Desdemona?' (247)—suggests a history of access, the history of her class habitus.

This discourse history is also emphatically suggested by Desdemona's conversation with Cassio in 3.3 regarding her commitment to mediate on his behalf with Othello. 'Be thou assured' is the opening phrase and repeated motif of her talk:

> *Be thou assured,* good Cassio, I will do
> All my abilities in thy behalf.
>
>   (1-2)
>
>   . . . *Do not doubt,* Cassio,
> But I will have my lord and you again
> As friendly as you were.
>
>   (5-7)
>
>   . . . and *be you well assured*
> He shall in strangeness stand no farther off
> Than in a politic distance.
>
>   (11-13)
>
> *Do not doubt that.* Before Emilia here
> I give thee warrant of thy place. *Assure thee* . . .
>   (19-20; emphasis added)

When she moves Cassio's suit to Othello, her whole manner bespeaks this assurance of a ready acquiescence to her request—her repeated insistence that he set a time to see Cassio, her understated persuasion tactics, her assumption that she has a role to play in Othello's public affairs, her low assessment of the speech act risk involved in making the request, and finally her minimizing of her suit:

> Why, this is not a boon.
> 'Tis as I should entreat you wear your gloves,
> Or feed on nourishing dishes, or keep you
>   warm . . .
>
>   . . . Nay, when I have a suit
> Wherein I mean to touch your love indeed,
> It shall be full of poise and difficult weight,
> And fearful to be granted.
>
>   (77-83)

This assurance is not simply the naïvety of a new wife about her power to sway a husband she scarcely knows. Desdemona's assurance inscribes the history of her prior speech reception, the ease that marks the dominant classes and exempts them from speech tension, linguistic insecurity, and self censoring. The crisis for Desdemona in this play comes as a surprising alteration in how her speech is received, specifically by Othello. The change in speech reception, it is possible to argue, also makes for a change in Desdemona.

If Desdemona's 'voice potential' in the Senate scene and later bespeaks her class habitus, to what extent can be read a history of voice inscribed in Othello's speech? Othello's long speeches in Act 1 can be distinguished partly by their amplitude, by a high degree of elaboration and embellishment. Characteristic are the nominal and adjectival doublets, in some instances marked by syntactic strangenesses bearing some relation to hendiadys:[10] Othello speaks of 'circumscription and confine' (1.2.27), 'the flinty and steel couch of war' (1.3.229), 'A natural and prompt alacrity' (231), 'such accommodation and besort' (237), being 'free and bounteous to her mind' (265), 'serious and great business' (267), 'speculative and officed instruments' (270), 'all indign and base adversities' (273). In what George Wilson Knight called the 'Othello music', there is, E.A.J. Honigmann has suggested, a complicating note of bombast.[11] It is an eloquence that displays its eloquent performance, not—like Desdemona's—an eloquence that bespeaks its adequacy. Apparently at odds with this high performance speech is Othello's familiar disclaimer:

>   Rude am I in my speech,
> And little blessed with the soft phrase of
>   peace,
>
>   . . . . .
>
> And little of this great world can I speak
> More than pertains to feats of broils and
>   battle.

And therefore little shall I grace my cause
In speaking for myself. Yet, by your gracious
    patience,
I will a round unvarnished tale deliver
Of my whole course of love . . .

                                    (1.3.81-2; 86-91)

While I argued earlier that it is not primarily the distinction of Othello's verbal performance that accounts for his voice power in the scene, it is nonetheless untrue that he delivers 'a round', or plain, 'unvarnished tale' (90). Verbal virtuosity, and not plainness, marks his tale. Othello's discourse style, then, blends linguistic insecurity and linguistic effort. Not, as with Desdemona, ease and assurance, but instead some degree of tension characterizes Othello's discourse production. And, by the logic of Bourdieu's hypothesis that discourse production is shaped by anticipated discourse reception, it is not the aristocratic insider who will feel a performance compulsion, an impulse to linguistic overreaching, in the accustomed formality of the senate chamber. Hence we can see how Othello's distinctive speech patterns may have a social motive: a man of great talent without so consistent and homogeneous a history of speech-making and speech reception as the dominant speakers among the Venetians may well overreach in his speech, and a highly formalized, institutionalized setting will increase the likelihood of speech tension.[12] As Bourdieu argues in his efforts to characterize the speech of aspiring groups, 'the greater the gap between recognition and mastery, the more imperative the need for the self-corrections aimed at ensuring the *revaluing of the linguistic product* by a particularly intensive mobilization of the linguistic resources, and the greater the tension and containment that they demand'.[13] This helps to explain why Othello, as a person of colour and an exotic outsider, might— even without making conscious adjustments—tend to mobilize his verbal resources more fully than Venetian speakers of the dominant group. In language terms, what he does is to try harder.

As we have seen, trying harder to produce well-crafted discourse may not always pay off, since a discourse's value depends on the power relations obtaining in a particular market. Not all the characters in the play respond in the same way to a felt gap between the recognition they commonly receive and their verbal mastery. Consider Iago, who early on in the play registers his perception of a gap between recognition and mastery in the assertion: 'I know my price, I am worth no worse a place' (1.1.11). Iago is keenly aware of a gap between his own considerable skills—including his verbal skills—and the limited advantages that readily come his way through their deployment. This shows in the extreme contempt he expresses for the linguistic accents of other characters—a contempt bound up in his recognition that the limited verbal repertoires of some others nonetheless garner them easy profits that

his own greater rhetorical expertise cannot attain. At the start of the play, Iago derides the 'bombast circumstance' (1.1.13) of Othello's talk, but the intensity of his resentment against the speech of others is most strongly illustrated in his reaction to Cassio's conversation with Desdemona upon their arrival in Cyprus. Shakespeare takes great care to draw his audience's attention to the courtier-like politeness of Cassio's speech here and elsewhere. When Iago derogates Cassio's style, delivering sarcastic asides about his gestural and verbal courtesies, he is not, I think, voicing resentment that his lower-class position excludes him from the verbal finesse of a gentlemanly discourse. Iago is a verbal chameleon; he knows how to speak like Cassio. What Iago resents is how easily Cassio's speech gains credit with his auditors, a credit Iago could not earn by employing the same speech patterns. Iago devalues the products of civil conversation not because he cannot replicate them but because he is not socially positioned to receive advantage from them. Cassio, Iago remarks to Roderigo, has 'an eye can stamp and counterfeit advantages' (2.1.243-4). What Iago expresses is a keen awareness that different people can draw different profits from the same discourse—that Cassio's gentlemanly status and good looks make even the very motion of his eyes able to garner an advantage his own finest verbal performance could not attain in situations like the conversation with the aristocratic Desdemona. In *Othello,* Iago is—as many scholars have previously noted—a consummate rhetorician. But he is a rhetorician keenly aware that the prize for best speaker cannot be won with polished verbal skills.

The significant fact about Iago's discourse in the senate scene is that he does not speak. His silence signals his slight chance of profit in that formal public setting. Whether with full consciousness or not, Iago as rhetorician assesses the conditions of the linguistic market in which he operates and chooses tools and timing that will work to gain him profit. Adapting Bourdieu's suggestions, we can generalize that rhetorical mastery consists not merely in the capacity for discourse production but also in 'the capacity for appropriation and appreciation; it depends, in other words, on the capacity . . . to impose the criteria of appreciation most favourable to [one's] own products'.[14] This helps to explain Iago's preference for private conversational settings, for in the less restricted discourse conditions of talk between friends he can more readily capture the floor and win an appreciation for his speech products.

In the concluding movement of this paper, however, I will concentrate on Iago's rhetorical expertise as exercised within the constraints of public occasions, where he exhibits rhetorical strategies substantially different than in conversation. One of his key strategies for public situations is voice mediation. Where his own voice has little chance of success, Iago appropriates other voices to his use. The play opens with Iago commenting on how he (like a typical Elizabethan suitor) negotiated through mediators for the place, lost to Cassio, as Othello's lieutenant: 'Three great ones of the city, / In personal suit to make me his lieutenant, / Off-capped to him; . . . / But he . . . / Nonsuits my mediators' (1.1.8-15). But Iago by no means restricts his tactics of voice mediation to this institutionalized form. Act 1, scene 1 also provides, in the role Iago constructs for Roderigo, a characteristic example of how Iago appropriates the credit of an intermediate voice. In the effort to fire Brabanzio up against Othello, Iago uses his own voice in chorus with Roderigo's. To arouse Brabanzio's emotions, Iago—keeping his personal identity obscure—takes on the voice of a 'ruffian[ ]' (1.1.112), a voice from the gutter, whose lewd conceits prompt Brabanzio to ask, 'What profane wretch art thou?' (116). A ruffian's voice has power in public to stir up trouble, but little chance within the verbal economy of the polite Venetian society to elicit belief. Iago therefore deploys the different accent of Roderigo's voice to the end of shaping Brabanzio's belief. Roderigo speaks as a gentleman, and calls upon Brabanzio to 'recognize' his voice ('Most reverend signor, do you know my voice?' [93]). He calls upon Brabanzio not merely to recognize that it is Roderigo who speaks but also to recognize that the speaker's social status guarantees his credit: 'Do not believe / That, from the sense of all civility, / I thus would play and trifle with your reverence' (132-4). Shrewdly calculating his slight chances of gaining such credit through his own voice in making this public disturbance, Iago appropriates to his own purposes the Cassio-like politeness and the matching status of Roderigo's voice. Iago tells the audience of how he makes 'my fool my purse' (1.3.375), but we never actually see Iago spending Roderigo's money. What we see instead is how he deploys the symbolic capital of Roderigo's voice.

Fundamental, then, to Iago's rhetorical mastery is his manipulation of what Bourdieu claims linguists long ignored: social context, understood here as the conditions for speech profit. While many public occasions tend to restrict his own access to speech and his opportunities for speech profit, Iago is what he ironically calls Cassio—'a finder of occasion' (2.1.242-3). The riotous street scene is his public occasion of choice, the scene in which he most profitably draws speech credit away from others and toward himself. As I have suggested, Bourdieu distinguishes sharply between the communication conditions obtaining in situations of high formality and in situations of lesser formality. In situations of high formality the reproductive role of politeness is most pronounced, scripting in the language of the participants a mutual recognition and acknowledgement of their relative social stations: 'Politeness', as Bourdieu explains it, 'contains a politics, a practical, immediate recognition of social classifications and of hierarchies, between the sexes, the generations, the classes, etc.'[15] In our analysis of the Sen-

ate scene, we have seen how the combination of formal scene and disruptive urgency made for a kind of re-ranking: the urgency of the moment meant that forms of symbolic capital apart from static social rank could more readily take on importance. But the adjustment in power relations was still strictly contained by the formal setting, keeping lesser ranking characters like Iago in their silent—and inferior—places. Lessen the formality and intensify the disruptive urgency of a scene, and Iago can make occasions in which even his speech can prevail over those of higher rank. Provide an outdoor setting, street fighting, darkness—as Iago does both when Cassio is discredited (2.3) and when Roderigo is murdered and Cassio badly hurt (5.1)—and restrictions on speech roles are relaxed or overturned.[16] As the murder scene in 5.1 draws towards its conclusion, Iago himself articulates this principle which has released his speech, at least for a short space of time, from the perpetual obligation to 'recognize' his subordinate relation to others: 'Signor Graziano', he exclaims, pretending only then to make out who his interlocutor is and adjust his language to their prescribed relation: 'I cry your gentle pardon. / These bloody accidents must excuse my manners / That so neglected you' (5.1.95-7). Hence we see that Iago's instruction to Roderigo—'do you find some occasion to anger Cassio' (2.1.266-7)—is as supreme a rhetorical act as any virtuoso speech of persuasion he makes in the play. It is through this construction of a favourable context that Iago can set up a contest of voices in which he is able to secure the floor ('Honest Iago, that looks dead with grieving, / Speak.' (2.3.170-1)) and to disable the voices of his superiors Cassio and Montano ('I pray you pardon me. I cannot speak.' (182); 'Your officer Iago can inform you, / While I spare speech—which something now offends me' (191-2)). Iago has full scope to elaborate his version of reality at extended length before important people. What he seeks and what he gains is not the hearers' simple belief in the facts as he represents them. What he is after is an enhancement of his 'voice potential', or—in Bourdieu's terms—an accumulation of his symbolic capital, which is registered in the personal approbation of Othello's response: 'I know, Iago, / Thy honesty and love doth mince this matter, / Making it light to Cassio' (2.3.239-41). Furthermore, Iago has engineered the loss of Cassio's lieutenancy with—perhaps more important—the loss of his annoying expectation that he can easily profit from the 'show of courtesy' (2.1.102) characteristic of his discourse: 'I will ask him for my place again. He shall tell me I am a drunkard. Had I as many mouths as Hydra, such an answer would stop them all.' (2.3.296-8). A rhetorician able to understand the mechanisms by which the polite Venetian social order, instantiated in its typical speech situations, stops talented voices and gives credit to the incompetent, Iago manages, if only for a short time,[17] his own correction of the gap between linguistic capital and credit.

In this paper, I have used Bourdieu's economic model for linguistic exchange as a heuristic to explore speech reception and speech production in some public scenes of *Othello*. This enabled, first, an examination of how variable power relations affect discourse reception in a particular setting and, second, an account of how the history of a person's speech reception functions together with immediate context to shape speech production. This reading has allowed me to offer a different perspective on the interrelation Shakespeare represents between character and language than is usual in *Othello* criticism—a perspective that links linguistic performance not to essential character but instead to character as the locus of social and power relations. Bourdieu's economic model for linguistic exchange also provided the foundation for assessing Iago's rhetorical artistry, an artistry founded on manipulating speech context, or the conditions for 'voice potential'.

Notes

[1] 'The Economics of Linguistic Exchanges', *Social Science Information,* 16 (1977), 645-68; p. 648. Much of the material in this essay is recirculated as 'Price Formation and the Anticipation of Profit' in *Language and Symbolic Power,* ed. John B. Thompson (Cambridge, Mass., 1991), pp. 66-89.

[2] Bourdieu, 'Economics', p. 648.

[3] For overviews of research on cross-sex conversations, see Deborah James and Sandra Clarke, 'Women, Men, and Interruptions: A Critical Review' and Deborah James and Janice Drakich, 'Understanding Gender Differences in Amount of Talk: A Critical Review of Research', in *Gender and Conversational Interaction,* ed. Deborah Tannen (New York and Oxford, 1993), pp. 231-80 and 281-312.

[4] Here I quote QI's 'world of sighs' instead of F's 'world of kisses'. While still a non-verbal response, the Folio's version gives a significantly different turn to Desdemona's portrayal here. If Desdemona is so forward here with her kisses, it is hard to reconcile with Othello's remark later in the speech that he spoke of his love upon a 'hint' (1.3.165) from her. I am grateful to Paul Werstine for drawing my attention to this variant.

[5] Virginia Mason Vaughan notes critics' fascination with language in *Othello* and the general tendency to relate language patterns to essential character in the Introduction to *'Othello': New Perspectives* (London and Toronto, 1991), pp. 14-15.

[6] Bourdieu, 'Economics', p. 657.

[7] *Ibid.,* p. 653.

[8] *Ibid.,* p. 655.

[9] *Ibid.,* p. 648.

[10] On hendiadys in Shakespeare, see George T. Wright, 'Hendiadys and *Hamlet*', *PMLA,* 96 (1981), 168-93.

[11] G. Wilson Knight, 'The *Othello* Music', in *The Wheel of Fire: Interpretations of Shakespearian Tragedy* (Oxford, 1930), pp. 97-119; E. A. J. Honigmann, "Shakespeare's 'Bombast'", in *Shakespeare's Styles: Essays in Honour of Kenneth Muir,* ed. Philip Edwards, Inga-Stina Ewbank, and G. K. Hunter (Cambridge, 1980), 151-62; pp. 158-9.

[12] Clearly, with Othello, this linguistic overreaching, with its exotic touches, has become a habit that has itself received a positive reception in various settings (e.g., in Brabanzio's household), thus adding a motive beyond linguistic insecurity for Othello to reproduce the style. Hence, this encoded discourse history may even be consistent with a proud and apparently self-assured delivery in 1.3, but it nonetheless anticipates Othello's susceptibility to Iago's persuasions.

[13] Bourdieu, 'Economics', p. 658.

[14] Bourdieu, *Language and Symbolic Power,* p. 67.

[15] Bourdieu, 'Economics', p. 662.

[16] Penelope Brown and Stephen C. Levinson, *Politeness: Some Universals in Language Usage,* 2nd edn (Cambridge, 1987), pp. 95-6 and p. 282, make the point that in situations of urgency and desperation, when maximum efficiency of communication is required, the face-redress work of politeness is unnecessary.

[17] The rough and improvisatory nature of Iago's rhetoric of situation makes his a particularly high risk performance. In the end he loses control of the play's speech outcomes when he fails to anticipate that circumstances very much like those that gained him speech access and credit—a public disturbance coming as the aftermath of street violence—could contribute to Emilia's speaking out against him and being heard.

Source: Lynne Magnusson, "'Voice Potential': Language and Symbolic Captial in *Othello*," in *Shakespeare Survey: An Annual Survey of Shakespeare Studies and Production*, Vol. 50, 1997, pp. 91-9.

Grinning Death's-Head: *Hamlet* and the Vision of the Grotesque

Yasuhiro Ogawa, *Hokkaido University*

In its perennial phase tragedy is a metaphysics of death, death seen preeminently as eternity, silence, that is to say, as mystery. The individual "pass[es] through nature to eternity" (1.2.73) and "the rest is silence" (5.2.358). These memorable phrases from *Hamlet* sound like a resigned acceptance of the common human condition of death, which makes us realize that the concern of tragedy is coming to terms with death—the final mystery. Yet the philosophical acquiescence will come only after *Todesschmerz*—if we may be permitted to appropriate the term coined by a famous thanatologist in analogy with *Welt-schmerz*[1]—is experienced to the utmost in its most agonizing fear and trembling and is made, figuratively speaking, analgesic.

The way *Hamlet* dramatizes this *Schmerz* is impressive; "the subject of *Hamlet* is death"[2] to the extent that this cannot be said of any other Shakespearean tragedy. But the peculiarity of this play in respect to this theme does not so much spring from the single-ness of vision concerning it as from the curious fact that it is a rendering of a particular mode of thinking that is preoccupied with *"being dead."*[3] The thinking is pursued in terms of "the dread of something after death" (3.1.77), and this "something" involves not merely "the soul's destiny" but "the body's" as well.[4] The solicitude for the body's destiny after its shuffling off of the mortal coil takes on an obsession with its imaginary transformation into something loathsome, reeking, and despicable.

Hamlet portrays the dead Polonius as suffering an ignominious fate. According to Hamlet's quaint, cynical imagination, Polonius is now "At supper. . . . /Not where he eats, but where 'a is eaten; a certain convocation of politic worms are e'en at him" (4.3.17-21). The corpse of the late lord chamberlain has fallen a prey to wily fornicating worms. We may callously say that perhaps this is an instance of retributive justice meted out to a Machiavellian of Polonius's caliber. (May not this imagined scene remind us of the one in which Julius Caesar was assassinated by "a certain convocation of politic[al]" men led by Brutus? In *Hamlet,* which is the immediate successor to *Julius Caesar*—these two have always been companion plays— we learn on Polonius's own avowal that, as a university student, he used to play the role of Julius Caesar in dramatic performances mounted by the university [the University of Wittenberg, Hamlet's alma mater?], the Caesar who he expressly adds is to be killed by Brutus [3.2.98-104]. Julius-Polonius is being assaulted by a party of political man-worms.) The pitiable condition is, however, not solely Polonius's. Hamlet makes a generalization.

> Your worm is your only emperor for diet: we fat all creatures else to fat us, and we fat ourselves for maggots. (4.3.21-23)

We fatten ourselves by eating all other living things which we fatten for that purpose, but all this is finally for the ingestion of us as prey by maggots. As far as dietary business goes, "Your worm" is supposed to hold sovereign sway.

Nevertheless, *pace* Hamlet "your worm" cannot be said to be the absolute victor in this process. It will be eaten by a fish, of which Hamlet himself is by no means unaware. Hamlet accompanies the statement by a variation upon the theme.

> A man may fish with the worm that hath eat of a king, and eat of the fish that hath fed of that worm. (27-28)

Dull-witted King Claudius, to whom all these remarks of Hamlet are directed, is stupefied: "What dost thou mean by this?" (29) But is the meaning of this statement so difficult to grasp? It seems to us to be fairly obvious. Let us put aside for a moment "a king" and replace it with "a human being." Then a totally disquieting situation arises: man-eating maggots are eaten by fish, which will in turn be eaten by men. In Shakespeare and other Elizabethan playwrights worms do eat dead human bodies. However, in *Hamlet* the eating does not stop there; it goes on endlessly, forming something like a vicious circle.

Note the uroboric shape the formula takes. The person who initiates this voracious movement finally meets fish-eating men. Through the carnivorous process, the initial person becomes, in the last analysis, part of other people's flesh. What is thrust upon us is virtual cannibalism. If the spectacle of an individual's corpse being devoured by maggots alone must arouse a sense of the grotesque within the minds of the spectators, the eerie sensation will be immensely increased by Hamlet's fantasy of a cannibalistic state of things.[5]

The imaginary situation assumes implications of *lèse-majesté* in case we interpret Hamlet's saying in its original phraseology. For not only an ordinary human being but also a king is subject to the predatory cycle, and it is specifically "a king" to whom Hamlet refers. Hamlet sticks to "a king." In the face of King Claudius, he says, "your fat king and your lean beggar is but variable service, two dishes, but to one table—that's the end" (23-25). At last Hamlet's intent is revealed. What he has been driving at all along is, in his own words, "Nothing, but to show you [Claudius] how a king may go a progress through the guts of a beggar" (30-31). Hamlet's language is dangerously charged. A king is vulnerable to murderous aggression and may be forced to tread the way of all flesh, which will take the form of a procession, an incomparably impoverished one at that, "through the guts of a beggar." A royal progress to be carried out with pomp and circumstance will transmogrify itself into an anti-progress, something unimaginably demeaning. Hamlet's view uncrowns, being radically democratic; it is a perverse version of the notion that death levels all people. Or it may be closer to the mark to say that death creates a sort of festive moment, turning the world upside down. The elevated are superseded by the humble. By the simple process of eating a fish which has incorporated "a king," "a beggar" puts the king under absolute subjugation. He is immeasurably superior to the fish-king.

I resume, man-eating worms will be eaten by fish that will conversely be eaten by men. . . . *Ad infinitum* and *ad nauseam*. The conceit of this circular migration originates in our hero's all-too-curious, idiosyncratic, even pathological habit of thinking—a major factor in making this play markedly different from other Shakespearean tragedies. *Hamlet* establishes a special perspective in which death is viewed as an occasion for bodily putrescence feeding maggots, thus ushering in the obscene natural system of preying among people, maggots, and fish that will include resultant cannibalism. The topic of this "cannibalism feeding on putrefaction" can be best described as "grotesque nonsense."[6]

Another unexpected dimension may lend itself to the sense of the grotesque when those man-eating maggots are correlated with those the sun breeds in a dead dog. Hamlet abruptly broaches the matter:

HAMLET: For if the sun breed maggots in a
  dead dog, being a good
kissing carrion—Have you a daughter?

POLONIUS: I have, my lord.

HAMLET: Let her not walk i' th' sun.
  Conception is a blessing, but as
your daughter may conceive, friend, look to 't.
                                        (2.2.181-86)

In the cryptic and disjointed discourse that might resemble a passage from a metaphysical poem, the extraordinary force derives from Ophelia's being likened to a dead dog that bears maggots. Like the dead dog or "a good kissing carrion," Ophelia will breed; she will breed persons who, when dead, will be food for maggots. (In a Russian cinematic version of *Hamlet* and a Japanese literary work which is a rehashing in a dramatic form of the same play, Ophelia is pregnant.) The ultimate source of conception is traceable to the sun. Conception is far from being a blessing: it entails death that brings about putrefactive cannibalism by mediation of maggots that the sun causes to be bred. Can not the very conception be corruption?—"the sun is a powerful agent of corruption."[7] We recall Hamlet's petulant rejoinder to Claudius: "I am too much i' the sun." (1.2.67). Seeing that Claudius, as a king in Renaissance England, may be made to figure as the sun on earth in the archetypal mystique surrounding kingship that may conceivably have been still a sector of lived ideology at that time, Hamlet's complaint rings perilously defiant.

Hamlet, and through him we, vicariously, inhabits an unredeemed world in which "an ineradicable corruption [inheres] in the nature of life itself,"[8] the world unshunnably impregnated with "the thought of foulness as the basis of life."[9]

At this juncture, we are also reminded of an unusual dialogue that occurs several lines before the passage pertaining to the sun-bred maggots, To Polonius's somewhat ridiculing query, "Do you know me, my lord?" Hamlet answers promptly: "Excellent well; you are a fishmonger" (2.2.173-74). Taken at literal value, this baffling fling leaves a weird reverberation.[10]

These "appalling jokes about worms and maggots"[11] are anticipatory of the Graveyard Scene (5.1), where Hamlet asks the grave-digging Clown about the length of time "a man will lie i' th' earth ere he rot" (164). His curiosity about "the tempo of decay in corpses"[12] is characteristic enough. The information it elicits is forbidding and slightly funny: "Faith, if 'a be not rotten before 'a die—as we have many pocky corses, that will scarce hold the laying in—'a will last you some eight year or nine year. A tanner will last you nine year. . . . His hide is so tann'd with his trade, that 'a will keep out water a great while, and your water is a sore decayer of your whoreson dead body" (165-77). The debate coalesces with the episode of putrefaction that triggers the wry imaginary ecology of the predatory man-maggot-fish-man cycle.

Still, much more horrifying is the gaze of the skull over which Hamlet proceeds to contemplate upon the vanity of all vanities. The gruesomeness of "the skull which has shed the final mask of humanity and wears only the perpetual grin of death"[13] is stunning. Death that the skull emblematizes is itself gruesome. The idea of death that Mathew Winston unfolds in his discussion of black humor is seminal.

Death is the final divorce between body and spirit, the ultimate disjunction in a form that dwells on violent incongruities. Often it is reduced to its physical manifestation, the corpse, which is man become thing; *rigor motris* is the *reductio ad absurdum* of Bergsonian automatism.[14]

The skull is a localization of the corpse that is the product of physical *reductio ad absurdum,* which deathly rigidity partakes of the Bergsonian automatism of the comic.[15]

The gaze of the skull is awfully repulsive, and at the same time it holds irresistible fascination. We may be drawn to the ineffably expressive visage. Its intense visual fixation may make us wonder whether life itself be not the "grave joke of death,"[16] for, being a didactic property of emblematic significance, the skull serves as a grim reminder of the end of all human endeavors. An agonizing intuition seizes us that death has instituted grotesque comedy, or what Mathew Winston prescribes as black humor that dictates the world of human beings who must be finally turned, in absurd reduction, into the grinning skull.

The skull exudes the uncanny, which emanates supposedly from the grin with which it is so inextricably bound up that that particular type of laugh has become its sole epithet. The skull is part of an individual become dead matter and yet this lifeless, nonhuman object, despite its lifelessness and nonhumanness, is apparently intent upon the live, quasi-human gesture of grinning. The grotesque may gestate in this discrepancy. To formularize, the picture of an inanimate object beginning to look like a man or vice versa gives the impression of the grotesque; it shows the reversible concourse of categorically disparate things.

The skull secretes the grotesque because the dead matter is tinged with the illusion of human agency. There is a palpable complexity, which resides in the genesis of the skull. It is not necessarily dead matter *per se.* It is the physical wreck of its former living self. It was originally a human being that has returned to a lifeless object. In this respect, the grin is a resuscitation of the grin that the very human being may have expressed during his lifetime.

It is suggestive that Hamlet is offered by the gravedigging Clown "this same skull . . . Yorick's skull, the king's jester" (5.1.180-81). (How could the gravedigger identify the skull from among the numerous others scattered in the churchyard? But we had better bypass such a question that realism's demand for verisimilitude will raise.) The grinning was presumably Yorick the court jester's professional tact of behavior. In a grinning, seriocomic vein, the king's jester may have hinted darkly at the reality of nothingness, the truth of mortality, the essential vacuity of mundane kingly pomp

and pride when contemplated *sub specie aeternitatis.* We can even imagine a prank of his, his showing up before the king and his courtiers, wearing the mask of a skull. At least Hamlet can think of such a practical joke Yorick was prone to. Talking to the skull of Yorick scoffingly, Hamlet presses him: "Now get you to my lady's chamber, and tell her, let her paint an inch thick, to this favour she must come; make her laugh at that" (192-95). But Yorick has outlived his "flashes of merriment"; "Not one now" is left "to mock your own grinning—quite chop-fall'n" (190-92). "A fellow of infinite jest, of most excellent fancy" (184-85) is dead and has become the skull wearing the eternal grin. "And now how abhorr'd in my imagination it is! my gorge rises at it" (186-88). The grin Yorick wears now proves to be his last . . ."serious joke." We are convinced that "the skull is the first and one of the most important components of Shakespeare's *memento mori* episode."[17] In conjunction with the motif of the Dance of Death that we will examine later, the skull constitutes the Renaissance carryover of medieval *Weltanschauung,* a worldview indigenous to that age of *contemptus mundi,* that is, the contempt of the world.[18]

Hamlet's confrontation with the skull leads to flighty reveries on the vanity of human wishes. His imagination locates "the noble dust of Alexander till 'a find it stopping a bunghole" (203-04):

> Alexander died, Alexander was buried, Alexander returneth to dust, the dust is earth, of earth we make loam, and why of that loam whereto he was converted might they not stop a beer-barrel? (208-12)

The way in which the dead Alexander is reduced to a loamy gadget to stop a beer barrel is undoubtedly ludicrous. "Imperious Caesar" is not exempt from this sort of comic degradation.

> Imperious Caesar, dead and turn'd to clay,
> Might stop ı hole to keep the wind away.
> O that that earth, which kept the world in
>   awe,
> Should patch a wall t'expel the winter's flaw!
> (213-16)

Hamlet's doggerel-like poem narrates jocular metamorphosis that might take hold of Caesar—is this Caesar Julius or Octavius?—in his afterlife, which might be equally the lot of Alexander. These two peerless personages representing the classical Graeco-Roman world are forcibly put to "base uses" (202). Broadly speaking, this is a variety of Lucianic humor brewed in the dialogue with the dead which Rabelais and his most brilliant literary successor Swift loved. In a parodic form of spiritual peregrination in the other world the protagonist encounters historical celebrities who have descended into incredibly undignified circumstances—I am to blame for my deliberate imprecision about details. In the fabulous otherworldly journey that he himself fabricated, Hamlet drops in with the risible ruin of imperious, awe-inspiring Alexander and Caesar. The abject vicissitude that befalls them, presented with gelastic overtones, induces Hamlet's deepest reflection upon the very substance of earthly glory, which is worth contempt. (Such a sentiment would be supposed to be in unison with the mental readiness for the contempt of the world.) Alexander's beer-barrel stopper and Caesar's hole filler are blatantly debasing images indicative of absurd reduction.

Horatio counters Hamlet's overingenious view: "'Twere to consider too curiously, to consider so" (205-6). Possessed of extraordinary capability of such an extreme logic that explodes with irreverent, provocative truth,[19] Hamlet is a veritable Shakespearean fool. It was not for nothing that in his boyhood he saw Yorick as a kind of surrogate father: with nostalgic feeling Hamlet recollects that "He hath bore me on his back a thousand times" (185-86). Our hero is the jester's disciple. He has profound affinity with the latter.

There is, however, one thing that Hamlet finds unbearable about Yorick. Hamlet is obliged to interrupt the remembrance of things past in which he steeps himself, on account of a physical problem that has survived Yorick: "Alas, poor Yorick!" You stink! Disgusted by the stench the skull gives forth, Hamlet hastily puts it down with revulsion. Forces of putrefaction are formidable; universal decay is inescapable for the dead thing. Yorick's skull is now being ravened by microbic worms, emitting insufferable odor. "Alas, poor Yorick!" (184).

As we have seen, it is the grave-digging Clown who has informed Hamlet of the identity of Yorick's skull. Now, who on earth is this strange figure? The gravedigger performs his job nonchalantly, even joyously, crooning a snatch of ballad about sweet bygone love, which leads Hamlet to suspect total absence of "feeling of his business" (65). "Custom hath made it in him a property of easiness" (67-68), Horatio chimes in. Hamlet examines in a derisive manner "the pate of a politician . . . one that would circumvent God," that of an affable, yet vilely wistful "courtier," that of "a lawyer" who, while he was alive, exploited and prevaricated with his display of vertiginous vocabulary, employing such legal jargons as "his quiddities . . . , his quillets, his cases, his tenures, . . . his tricks, . . . his statutes, his recognizances, his fines, his double vouchers, his recoveries . . . indentures . . . conveyances"— all these grotesquely technical words were unable to fend off death and some of them are subjected to our hero's parodic treatment through punning. What astonishes Hamlet is that "the mazzard," "the sconce" of each of these very important persons, receives merciless and disrespectful blows from "a dirty shovel" of

"a sexton's spade," "as if 'twere Cain's jaw-bone, that did the first murder." Indeed, "Here's fine revolution," says Hamlet (75-112). After such a scrutiny, Hamlet speaks to the fellow:

HAMLET: Whose grave's this, sirrah?

I CLOWN: Mine, sir. . . .

HAMLET: I think it be thine, indeed, for thou liest in't.

I CLOWN: You lie out on't sir, and therefore 't is not yours; for my part I do not lie in't and yet it is mine.

HAMLET: Thou dost lie in't, to be in't and say it is thine. 'Tis for the dead, not for the quick; therefore thou liest.

I CLOWN: 'Tis a quick lie, sir, 'twill away again from me to you.

HAMLET: What man dost thou dig it for?

I CLOWN: For no man, sir.

HAMLET: What woman then?

I CLOWN: For none neither.

HAMLET: Who is to be buried in't?

I CLOWN: One that was a woman, sir, but, rest her soul, she's dead.

(117-36)

Paronomastic playing with "lie," "quick," and "man" is involved. Even if it is too much to say that this is a textual conundrum, this is a fairly difficult passage that we cannot hope to decipher completely. A tentative reading will be:

It is a lie to say that a grave belongs to a person who happens to be within it for digging, since it is essentially for the dead, not for the quick [the living], that is, its true tenant is only someone deceased for whom it was dug. On the other hand, one is deceived to think that one has nothing to do with it, since it will be one's inevitable habitation sooner or later. It is a deceptive idea that the living tend to hold, which will be quickly belied to the very living. Here gender does not matter, as man and woman are equally destined for the grave. And strictly speaking, we can not say that a grave is a man's or woman's even though he or she is to be buried in it; the most correct way of putting it is that it is that of "One that was [a man]" or of "One that was a woman." Death forbids the use of present tense for a man's or a woman's being.

The wit combat Hamlet was forced to fight drives him to despair: "equivocation will undo us" (138). Only by going through this exhausting conversation ruled by labyrinthine wordplay do we learn that the grave in question is Ophelia's.[20]

We happen to discover an interesting item in the curriculum vitae of this Clown.

> HAMLET: How long hast thou been grave-
> maker?
>
> 1 CLOWN: Of all the days i' th' year I came to't
> that day that our last king Hamlet overcame
> Fortinbras.
>
> HAMLET: How long is that since?
>
> 1 CLOWN: Cannot you tell that? every fool can
> tell that. It was that very day that young
> Hamlet was born—he that is mad and sent
> into England.
>
> (142-48)

Of all the days, the Clown became a sexton on the very day of the year that the Danish nation reached the apex of glory by the late King Hamlet's defeat of Fortinbras. It is also the day when our Hamlet was born, the prince most immediate to the glorious throne of Denmark. Both Denmark's future and Hamlet's career have been ominously clouded.

Apart from Danish destiny, the days of Hamlet were numbered. On the strength of this state of affairs, G. R. Elliott speculates that "maybe he [the Clown] is Death."[21] Willard Farnham is of the same opinion; what he has to say, recognizing the Clown for what he is, is insightful and profitable:

> And in medieval terms the clown with his spade does what the figure of Death does in the Dance of Death. The Dance traditionally has that figure as a human being already dead who points one of the living the way to the grave. In pictorial representation he is a decaying corpse or a skeleton who comes from the grave and calls, one by one, upon living figures ranging in rank from pope or emperor down to natural fool or innocent child, to prepare for death and follow him. The grave-digging clown in *Hamlet* takes the place of this corpse or skeleton. He occupies a grave he claims as his at the same time that he makes it for Ophelia. In it he is Death itself and from it he can speak to Hamlet of bodily dissolution with grotesque authority. To debate whether the grave he digs is his or Ophelia's is pointless. It belongs to him because it belongs to Everyman, alive or dead. The word-twisting that goes on over whether he "lies" in the grave that he says is his and whether it is for the quick or the dead finally brings a riddling summons from the clown, as Everyman-Death, to Hamlet, whose

tragedy has drawn near to its ending in death: "'Tis a quick lie, sir; 'twill away again from me to you."[22]

The Clown, who lies in the grave and indulges there in a bantering dialogue with Hamlet, is Death ringleading the Dance of Death. It may be said that, as such, he invites Hamlet "to join the dance [that] means to die";[23] he virtually points Hamlet the way to the grave as he is nearing his end at the close of his tragedy. Hamlet's encounter with the Clown may be considered a teleological one. At the end his purpose was fulfilled. This is the be-all and end-all of his life's quest. It seems as though the Clown-Death had been shadowing Hamlet ever since the very day that he came into the world, somewhat in the same way that the "*son of a whore* Death," in a version of the Dance of Death from volume seven of *Tristram Shandy,* perpetually ferrets Tristram out.[24] The Clown-Death has overtaken Hamlet. Hamlet is doomed.

Granted that the Clown is Death in the Dance of Death, it is undeniable that Hamlet himself impersonates Death. He "has above all that preternatural aptitude for mocking each man according to his station and peculiar folly which was the distinguishing mark of Death itself in the Dance of Death."[25] A student of the Dance of Death instructs us that "'Death' in the Dance of Death has been variously styled—'la railleuse par excellence—variée à l'infini mais toujours bouffonne'—and as exhibiting a 'cynisme railleur.'"[26] According to G. Wilson Knight's testimony, Hamlet is not innocent of "the demon of cynicism," "the cancer of cynicism," and "the hell of cynicism."[27] Another Shakespearean scholar concludes that Hamlet's responses are "the jests of Death" and that the diseased wit which is admittedly Hamlet's (3.2.321-22) is "Death's own."[28] Even if "Death is not the only character whose qualities Hamlet has inherited,"[29] it is a preponderant aspect of Hamlet's makeup. Hamlet is a principal persona in this drama of the Dance of Death, a macabre medieval legacy. It may be said that Hamlet plays Death in the status of a jester, albeit officially he has no cap and bells.

In this context Hamlet's "antic disposition" (1.5.172) poses itself. Contrary to the notion that it denotes assumed madness with "antic" being synonymous with "mad, crazy, or lunatic," lexicographical investigation of the word "antic" reveals that the phrase signifies something like "grotesque demeanor" since the most fundamental meaning of the word current at the date Shakespeare composed our play corresponds to "grotesque." The etymological explanation that *The Oxford English Dictionary* (2d ed. on CD-ROM) gives is cogent: "appl. ad. It. *antico,* but used as equivalent to It. *grottesco,* f. *grotta,* 'a cauerne or hole vnder grounde' (Florio), orig. applied to fantastic representations of human, animal, and floral forms, incongruously running into one another, found in exhuming some ancient remains (as the Baths of Titus) in Rome, whence extended to anything similarly incongruous or bizarre: see *grotesque.*" The word "antic" comes from the Italian *"antica"* (*la manièra antica,* i.e., the antique fashion) but in its actual usage, historically it referred to "[*la manièra*] *grottesca,*" literally rendered, "the manner of the grotto." In any theoretical consideration of the grotesque its basic connection with the Italian *"grotta"* in its derivation is unanimously recognized. Hence "antic" as denotative of "grotesque." (We may be given to venture a hypothesis that the "antic" fashion, the ancient way, could have impressed those exposed to it with a sense of regression into the remotest primordial world peopled by phenomenal, phantasmagoric images, where human beings, animals, plants, and even inanimate objects merged in natural confusion and profusion, the world as symbolized, in a manner, by the grotto. In the psychoanalytic language of evolution this immemorial world is translated as the unconscious. In our idiom manifestation of such a regression is grotesque.) Let us further found our argument on the said dictionary, this time for its definition (we want to omit historical illustrations):

"A. *adj.*

1. *Arch.* and *Decorative Art.* Grotesque, in composition or shape; grouped or figured with fantastic incongruity; bizarre.

2. Absurd from fantastic incongruity; grotesque, bizarre, uncouthly ludicrous.

3. Having the features grotesquely distorted like 'antics' in architecture; grinning. *Obs.*"

It is noteworthy that for the adjectival meaning, the *OED* (2d ed.) lists only these three items. The substantive usage perfectly reflects the adjectival one so that we do not think it worthwhile to cite it as a whole. Suffice it to heed the fourth definition: "4. A performer who plays a grotesque or ludicrous part, a clown, mountebank, or merry-andrew." Quotation from a Shakespearean text in its subdivision is more to the purpose:

"b. *transf.* and *fig.*

1593 <u>Shakes.</u> *Rich. II,* iii. ii. 162 There [death] the Antique sits, Scoffing his state, and grinning at his Pompe."

Parenthetical addition of "death" in the quotation is that of the *OED.* Fuller citation of the passage would have made the meaning unmistakable:

KING RICHARD: . . . for within the hollow crown
That rounds the mortal temples of a king
Keeps Death his court, and there the antic sits,
Scoffing his state and grinning at his pomp.

The *OED* supplements the quotation above with reference to a fascinating illustration, which, unfortunately, we could not verify: "1631 A death's head grins like an 'antic.'"

The foregoing perspective is also set forth by Eleanor Prosser in her succinct formulation regarding the usage of the word "antic" in *Hamlet.*

Hamlet's choice of words, "antic disposition," is significant. In Shakespeare's day, "antic" did not mean "mad." It was the usual epithet for Death and meant "grotesque," "ludicrous." The term is appropriated for the grinning skull and the tradition of Death laughing all to scorn, scoffing at the pretenses of puny man.[30]

The term "antic" covers the whole range of the grotesquerie that death gives rise to. It connotes the grinning skull and the traditional motif of the macabre Dance of Death with which our play implodes. Its semantic consideration allows us to apply it to the grave-digging Clown whose speech is replete with grotesque sporting with death.

When it comes to characterization of our hero, the "antic disposition" he decides to put on proves to be a grotesque mask he wears, a mask designed to conceal his true colors and befuddle his enemies with a view to executing his revenge more conveniently. His ludicrous simulation of madness is to be necessarily overshadowed by Death, for whom "antic" as meaning "grotesque" served as the usual epithet in the age of Shakespeare. Hamlet is the titular protagonist of the antic hay that this tragedy is geared to.

The characteristic melancholy, the mythical sorrows of Hamlet that often end up in detracting from his personality, can be deemed a form of such "an antic disposition" (even if it is an involuntary one) redolent of death. Melancholy is traditionally associated with Saturn, which is "symbolic of the sad tranquility of death."[31] Hamlet's brooding melancholy partakes of Saturnian death. If we may go further and attend to a literary convention that Saturn is a patron-god for satirists and to the satiric temper that informs Hamlet to a certain degree, Hamlet's character will be delineated like this: Hamlet as melancholiac and satirist (the satirist in English Renaissance literature was almost invariably a melancholiac) is under Saturn's influence.[32] And that is the price of his being a genius as revealer of dark truths.

The world of *Hamlet* is probably presided over by Saturn, who makes such problematical epiphany in Chaucer's *The Knight's Tale,* which has prompted A. C. Spearing to link the pagan god to the absurd of the sort that Samuel Beckett creates and Jan Kott's literary criticism envisions.[33] Under Saturn the world is "antic" and absurd. Saturn alias Cronos (mistaken, in etymological confusion, for Chronos ["time" in Greek] devouring his own children, drawn by Goya with his consummate artistry) is emblematic of the absurd nature of Time, who blindly annihilates what he has begotten. Time is a bodeful presence suffused with the spirit of death. The melancholy, death-heralding Father Time in Thomas Hardy's *Jude the Obscure* who appears invested with naked allegory is a grotesque composite figure whose actual boyhood is wholly blighted by his untimely physical corrugation and spiritual incorrigible volition of not living. He kills Jude's children as well as himself.

Probably Saturn is identical to Death, and Hamlet's "antic disposition" is ultimately Saturn's machination. . . . Hamlet is Time's fool.

Be that as it may, Hamlet's rage for punning can be taken for manifestation of the same pattern of deportment that we are discussing. A pun can even be personified. "[A pun] is an antic which does not stand upon manners, but comes bounding into the presence," thus Charles Lamb in *Elia,* which the *OED* supplies as another example of the transferential or figurative meaning of the noun "antic," no. 4 (parentheses in the quote added by the *OED*). A pun is an antic, that is, a grotesque, clownish creature who, intruding as a nuisance, breaches courtesy in decent speech. A recidivistic pun-maker, Hamlet can be labeled (or libeled) as pun incarnate. It is fruitful to take a glance at Willard Farnham's idea expressed in his book devoted to the exploration of *The Shakespearean Grotesque:*

> In its grotesqueness the pun is a monstrous union
> of incompatible things that has at times a complexity
> carried beyond doubleness. Its wholeness built of
> incompatibility is prone to be incompatible with and
> defiant of dignity.[34]

An apposite instance may be Hamlet's utterance "I am too much in the sun," which is supposed to comprehend ventriloquistic undertones of "I am too much in the son."[35] The phrases that will exemplify the case are legion. But we want to refrain from analyzing them. Suffice it to remark that in his antic disposition Hamlet is addicted to making the pun that is an antic, that is to say, grotesque figure of speech in its monstrous yoking together of incompatible things, the pun that, like the joke of which it is a prominent component, partially discloses the dark recesses of the human mind.[36]

The skull not only of Yorick but also of the God-circumventing politician, the cannily sycophantic courtier, the tergiversating lawyer, and the grave-digging Clown is equivalent to Death in the macabre Dance of Death and Hamlet himself, who is, as practicer of antic disposition, a character distinguished by the grotesque. *Hamlet* is a gallery of grotesque figures,

the gallery which mirrors the inferno that the world has become, for "through the depiction of grotesque characters" Shakespeare, just like Bosch, "shows us Hell, the Hell of man's making."[37] Anyway, the gallery accommodates other characters than these. For example, Osric. To begin with, his name has an unpalatable resemblance to "ostrich," which sounds, at the least, ludicrous.[38] Farcical naming notwithstanding, he "comes, *like some grotesque angel of death,* to announce to Hamlet his fate, and to announce it in the strangest and most distorted language of all, a language which Hamlet gleefully parodies."[39] Osric was apparently dispatched to Hamlet to claim him on behalf of "this fell sergeant, Death, [who] / Is strict in his arrest" (5.2.336-48).

And Claudius. In mythical terms he is the Serpent that corrupted the Garden of Eden, Gertrude being a fallen Eve. The poison resorted to by him to murder his brother in the garden and his stealthy steps in committing the crime accord with the surreptitious, poisonous wiles that the Archenemy used to tempt Eve and eventually to bring about humanity's fall from paradise. In both cases death has ensued from the malefactory activity. (Is it workable, in an experimental production of the play, to have the Claudius role speak in hissing, sibilant intonation?) The world has now drastically changed from its prelapsarian state. "Something is rotten in the state of Denmark" (1.4.90). Denmark is at present ruled by a king embodying corruption in its multifarious ramifications. If Denmark is, to say nothing of a hell, "a prison" (2.2.243), as Hamlet declares, Claudius has to do with it (we may even suspect that Claudius's reign is that of terror, with his people being forced to live in an incarcerate environment, always insidiously watched, under strictest policing). The world is decisively not what it used to be. Something alarmingly fatal has happened. "Then is doomsday near" (238), so Hamlet thinks. Hamlet's elegiac monologue tells of the world that is now "an unweeded garden, / That grows to seed" "Possess[ed] merely" by "things rank and gross in nature" (1.2.135-37). The paradisiacal garden has degenerated to a garden burdened with rank and gross vegetation apparently endowed with demonic vitality. "That it should come to this!" (137). The world has already, let us dare to say, grotesquely changed. In our view, the grotesque is a sign of the tremendous, catastrophic alteration of the world occasioned by original sin.

But we have to tone it down a bit. What is more interesting about Claudius is the fact that he is frequently the butt of Hamlet's satiric attacks. In Hamlet's opinion or prejudice, Claudius is "a satyr," a lecherous humanoid being, the fabulous hybrid of man-beast in stark contrast with his brother who is comparable to "Hyperion" (140). The distinction is all the more striking, as Hamlet praises, in the interview with his mother, his deceased father hyperbolically, even in mythical apotheosis, itemizing "Hyperion's curls, the front of Jove himself, / An eye like Mars, to threaten and command, / A station like the herald Mercury / New-lighted on a heaven-kissing hill" (3.4.56-59), whereas on the same occasion Hamlet calls his uncle Claudius, vituperatively and ridiculingly, first a "mildewed ear, / Blasting his wholesome brother" and then:

A murtherer and a villain!
A slave that is not twentieth part the tithe
Of your precedent lord, a Vice of kings,
A cutpurse of the empire and the rule,
That from a shelf the precious diadem stole,
And put it in his pocket—. . . .
A king of shreds and patches,—

(64-65, 96-102)

Hamlet even sketches him in the image of the devil. In his denunciation of Gertrude's incestuous remarriage Hamlet exclaims: "What devil was't / That thus hath cozen'd you at hoodman-blind?" (76-77). The devil may refer to Claudius as well as to devilish lust that urged Gertrude to an infamous union. Taking into account these circumstances, Paul Hamill argues that Claudius's deed is reminiscent of "the pranks of Vice on stage and of Death in the Dance of Death," that "in the Dance of Death, when Death steals valuables or plays with crowns, he is thief not only of material goods but of honor and pride—as here Claudius has stolen kingship—of life, and sometimes of grace" and that "finally, this [Claudius] is 'a king of shreds and patches'—a detail that associates him again with death and the devil, both of whom may wear the rags of harlequin."[40] There is a sense in which the enormity of regicide and Cain-like fratricide, "the offense [that] is rank [and] smells to heaven, / [Which] hath the primal curse upon't, / A brother's murther" (3.3.36-38) that Claudius is guilty of is intelligible within the framework of the so-called "allegory of evil" and "comedy of evil."[41] Hamill's conclusion is that Claudius "is a grotesque parody of the first [King Hamlet]."[42] (Renovation of production may be encompassed by having these two parts doubled, which is technically possible since these two persons never appear simultaneously on the stage.) *Hamlet* is a dramatization of the myth of two brothers who are antipodally distinct from each other. Half-brothers Edgar and Edmund (the quasi-alliterative similarity of their names is noticeable), who engaged in mythical sibling rivalry in the Gloucester subplot of *King Lear,* conform to the configuration. The mythical (or melodramatic) composition opens up a horizon of Manichaean opposition between the forces of good and evil, God and the devil.

One of the most salient facets of irony in *Hamlet* is that King Hamlet, who is, again in Hamill's view, "not a god, of course, but a representation of godly perfection in man,"[43] approximates, in his advent to this world, what his extremely inferior brother, who may be termed

his "counterfeit" (3.4.54), supposedly impersonates. The comedic form Hamill supposes for Claudius is inapplicable to King Hamlet. Still the latter appears as the devil and Death. Left uncertain about the true identity of the Ghost, Hamlet's mind misgives him that "The spirit that I have seen / May be a dev'l, and the dev'l hath power / T' assume a pleasing shape, yea, and perhaps, / Out of my weakness and my melancholy, / As he is very potent with such spirits, / Abuses me to damn me" (2.2.598-603). Horatio is sceptical about the intention of the Ghost so that he dissuades Hamlet from following it lest at a certain dangerous spot it should "assume some . . . horrible form" and precipitate him into derangement (1.4.72-74). Death bulks large when King Hamlet emerges as a visitant from the land of the dead. In spite of the critical disagreement as to its true nature,[44] this much can be said, that the Ghost, apparently surrounded with the strange aura of death, is its dreadful messenger, for what he recounts to Hamlet is "his foul and most unnatural murder" (1.5.25) by his own brother and what he enjoins him to do is to revenge it, which is tantamount to slaying the murderer. He is forbidden to, but could, tell the secrets beyond the grave that are suggested with sensational vividness. Pertaining genetically to Senecan revenge tragedy, Hamlet is laden, to a certain degree, with crude, sadistic, horror-inspiring scenes. Horrors of Gothic nature color the play. "Blasts from hell" (1.4.41) are blowing through it.

No less frightful is the revolting physical deformation of King Hamlet because of the "leprous distillment" poured by his brother in "the porches of my ears." The "effect" of the "juice of cursed hebona in a vial . . . / Holds such an enmity with blood of man" that coursing throughout the body,

with a sudden vigor it doth posset
And curd, like eager droppings into milk,
The thin and wholesome blood. So did it
    mine,
And a most instant tetter bark'd about,
Most lazar-like, with vile and loathsome crust
All my smooth body.

(1.5.62-73)

(In view of this striking bodily change that the King has suffered, it is puzzling that nobody seemingly suspected a foul hand in his death.) The story of his death will be reproduced in the play within a play in fulsome reference to "Thou mixture rank, of midnight weeds collected, / With Hecate's ban thrice blasted, thrice infected, / Thy natural magic and dire property / On wholesome life usurps immediately" (3.2.257-60).

The scene of Hamlet's encounter with the Ghost is haunted by apprehension and brain-racking mystery; Hamlet's query is desperate:

O, answer me!
Let me not burst in ignorance, but tell
Why thy canoniz'd bones hearséd in death
Have burst their cerements? why the
   sepulchre,
Wherein we saw thee quietly inurn'd,
Hath op'd his ponderous and marble jaws
To cast thee up again. What may this mean,
That thou, dead corse, again in complete steel
Revisits thus the glimpses of the moon,
Making night hideous, and we fools of nature
So horridly to shake our disposition
With thoughts beyond the reaches of our
   souls?
Say why is this? wherefore? what should we
   do?

                                          (1.4.45-57)

The Ghost, a "dead corse" whose "canoniz'd bones [were] hearséd in death," turns up in a clap, "Making night hideous" and pushing Hamlet off into radical interrogation about the wherefore of this visitation. Hamlet is right, "There are more things in heaven and earth, Horatio, / Than are dreamt of in your philosophy" (1.5.166-67). In your philosophy, that is, in your physics, natural science.

The Ghost is a completely unexpected intruder from "The undiscover'd country, from whose bourn / No traveller returns" (3.1.78-79) and how he could and why he did return from it remain only a mystery in the ultimate sense of the word. Hamlet has been pestered from the very outset by radical uncertainty due to his inability to unveil the Ghost. Is it "a spirit of health, or goblin damn'd"? does it "Bring with [it] airs from heaven, or blasts from hell"? are its "intents wicked, or charitable"? and so on (1.4.40-42). Mystery lingers on till it is finally resolved in the play within a play in which the Ghost's revelation tests true. The interval is permeated with painful insecurity that is almost beyond our hero's endurance. Irresolvable, disconcerting ambiguity exists up to a certain stage, giving birth to perception of the grotesque, as the world is left incapable of rationality and orderly dispensation. Chaos is come again. In the words of Wolfgang Kayser, a major scholar of the grotesque, "what intrudes remains incomprehensible, inexplicable."[45]

And "impersonal," so Kayser adds.[46] Indeed, the neutral, impersonal mode perseveres when it comes to mentioning the Ghost; the Ghost is called "this thing" ("What, has this thing appear'd again to-night?" [1.1.21]), then "this dreaded sight" (25) and thenceforth "it" several times consecutively. Kayser's theory that the grotesque is prescribed as "the objectivation of the 'It,' *the ghostly 'It'*" is strangely relevant here.[47]

The considerable fear with which this nondescript presence strikes the guard prompts an inverted *qui-vive.*

Indeed, the play begins with a question "Who's there?" that Bernardo, coming to relieve the guard, hurls at Francisco, the other sentinel who has been on duty there. Needless to say, it's the other way around; it is Francisco who should have challenged Bernardo. Apart from its being inverted, the question itself is rather gratuitous, for who else should be there but Francisco as someone standing on watch? The inversion and gratuitousness of the question prefigure the fearful secrecy that "the ghostly 'It'" foments.[48]

Confronting himself with the Ghost, Horatio questions it: "What art thou that usurp'st this time of night . . . ?" (46-49). In spite of the personal pronoun "thou," the ominous, sinister quality of the revenant does not mitigate itself. The Ghost and the atmosphere it brings with it, together with the dreadful chill and alienating darkness that govern the scene, can be meaningfully designated as "numinous."[49] What Hamlet experiences on this occasion is . . . a supreme moment that will have far-reaching consequences upon the ontological phase of a man concerned, transforming his being utterly. The chronological sequence of an everyday way of being is disrupted; a crisis comes to Hamlet. Hamlet's "antic disposition" is due to his exposure to such a climactic, timeless moment.

The Ghost "usurp[s] this time of night," yet it is not only a usurper of this specific time of night but of time in general, time itself, for it is the past incarnate who has intruded upon the present and by this intrusion it has infringed the inviolable law of time; it has disintegrated the solid coherence of time. It seems as if the Ghost had been cast up not so much from "the sepulchre" as from the rift of time. . . . "The Time is out of joint" (1.5.188), Hamlet cries out after the Ghost disappears. Kayser tells us that the grotesque amounts exactly to the sense of this sort of out-of-jointness *(Aus-den-Fugensein).*[50] "O cursed spite, / That ever I was born to set it right!" (188-89), Hamlet grieves. It's a shame that Hamlet has to redress the grotesque reality.

The grotesque "contradicts the very laws which rule our familiar world."[51] The Ghost has violated the very law of temporal irreversibility that dictates our everyday reality. Another Kayserian precept that "the grotesque is 'supernatural'"[52] has a singular vibration: the Ghost should be said to be above "nature" (temporality), since by dying it has "pass[ed] through nature to eternity." And that it has not reached "eternity" underscores the paradoxical nature of it. The paradox is parallel to the grotesque. The Ghost occupies an epistemological interstice.

The abrupt apparition of the Ghost surprises Hamlet and others. "Suddenness and surprise are essential elements of the grotesque."[53] Its unexpected emergence that engenders horror, mystery, and the sense of "the time" being "out of joint" causes us to share in "the basic feeling" . . . of surprise and horror, an agonizing fear in the presence of a world which breaks apart and remains inaccessible."[54] The feeling is admittedly indicative of the grotesque.

Listening to the subterranean voice that the Ghost has uttered, Hamlet observes pejoratively: "Well said, old mole! canst work i' th' earth so fast? / A worthy pioneer!" (162-63). The "old mole" is, as Norman N. Holland suggests so perceptively, retrospective of Hamlet's earlier dictum "some vicious mole of nature" (1.4.24) which will court as "the dram of ev'l" (36) the final collapse of integrity in humanity.[55] The Ghost, being an "old mole," is associated with the devil, who, like the subterranean creature mole, is an inhabitant of the netherworld. The Ghost as "worthy pioneer" mines or undermines our familiar world. Being perhaps, metaphorically speaking, *mors ex machina,* it is "an alien force that has taken hold of"[56] Hamlet and, through him, other characters of this play. In the hands of this antic force "they have lost their confidence and their orientation."[57] "The characters are all watching one another, forming theories about one another, listening, contriving, full of anxiety. The world of *Hamlet is a world where one has lost one's way,*" says C. S. Lewis in his celebrated essay on our play.[58] *Angst* predominates in *Hamlet.* "THE GROTESQUE IS THE ESTRANGED WORLD," Kayser asseverates in a capitalized aphorism, which seems to hold true of the world of *Hamlet.*[59]

As in that of *The Tempest,* we see in the world of *Hamlet* that metamorphosis is consequent upon the sea experience. Our hero's sea journey to England leads to a remarkable alteration of his personality. No doubt "a sea-change" (*The Tempest,* 1.2.401) visits him.

This change is qualitatively different from his former self-imposed transformation of character, the "antic disposition" that has embarrassed so irritably those around him. His voyage to a foreign country may have contributed to his heightened awareness of national identity. "This is I, / Hamlet the Dane!" (5.1.257-58), Hamlet asserts, plainly and resolutely, to Laertes and to the rest of Ophelia's mourners.[60] Hamlet has attained this simplest truth about his own self that has been hitherto a cause of existential malaise to himself. Just before the fatal duel Hamlet apologizes sympathetically to Laertes for his "madness," to which he attributes the outrageous deed done to the Polonius family. Hamlet confesses—we should not necessarily take it for a crafty self-justification on his part—that "His madness is poor Hamlet's enemy" (5.2.239). And now Hamlet has vanquished this ruthless opponent. *Terribilità* of the morbid, obsessive vision that "this distracted globe" (1.5.97) of his had created has left him. His passion is spent. He is seized with serene perception:

> . . . there's special providence in the fall of a sparrow. If it be now, 'tis not to come; if it be not

to come, it will be now; if it be not now, yet it will come—the readiness is all. (5.2.219-22)

The redundant, tautological allusion to the maturation or eventuation of the unspecified "it" discloses the self-evident, inevitable property of that which "it" implies. After all is said and done, "the readiness is all." That's why, despite foreboding misgivings, "defy[ing] augury" (219), Hamlet accepts the invitation of the deadly duel that Osric, emissary of Death, delivers him.

In the catastrophic *dénouement,* which is too well known or notorious (in truth, it is too Senecan for the tragedy not to be vitiated as an artistic form), Hamlet meets his death, leaving his beautiful dying words, "the rest is silence" (358). It is as if grace had come, all of a sudden, undeservedly, like a miracle. "In this play, perhaps the noisiest of Shakespeare's tragedies, the shock of silence stuns."[61] The mysterious silence Hamlet confronts is numinous.

The eternal pun-maker Hamlet might have dropped a hint that the "rest" includes repose.[62] It may be paradoxical that this particular *anagnorisis* is conveyed by words. In any event, the recognition is tragic in that it involves the mystery of death as "silence" and, by extension, eternity.[63]

But we must admit that, finally, the vision has been wrested from Death through the unflinching stare at the skull. Given that in the world of Rabelais as elucidated by Mikhail Bakhtin, the grotesque functions as immunization against the fear of death through the essential homogeneity of "comicity" and "cosmicity,"[64] macabre engagement with the skull has domesticated Death for Hamlet. Tristram's antic dance with Death eventuates in its transfiguration into a dance of life in which "he rather confounds Death by no longer fearing him."[65] In Tristram's case, "thus he must dance off; but it is a festive, not a macabre, dance."[66] The *Todesschmerz* that had been rankling in Hamlet's heart seems to have undergone a healing, which has been accomplished only through homeopathic procedure.

By dying in the process of eventually fulfilling the mandatory revenge, Hamlet has to die no more. "Death destroys death," which "was a common conceit" in Elizabethan tragedy.[67] "So shalt thou feed on Death, that feeds on men, / And Death once dead, there's no more dying then," so the poet in *The Sonnets* asserts in a metaphysical concept.[68] "And fight and die is death destroying death," a character in *Richard III* encourages the then crestfallen Richard (3.2.184).

At the moment of his dying, Hamlet requests Horatio to tell a story that will vindicate his career:

> If thou didst ever hold me in thy heart,
> Absent thee from felicity awhile,

And in this harsh world draw thy breath in
    pain
To tell my story.

(5.2.346-49)

Hamlet is in a resigned position to regard death as "felicity" that he persuades Horatio to defer when the latter shows a willingness to commit suicide in order to follow him. Our hero has achieved spiritual maturity; he has reached a completely new stage nurtured even by religious tranquility. A horizon of transcendence is in prospect. "Now cracks a noble heart. Good night, sweet prince, / And flights of angels sing thee to thy rest!" (359-60), Horatio voices a touching epitaph in honor of him.

We should say that throughout the tragedy of *Hamlet* what Herman Melville describes as "the knowledge of the demonism in the world"[69] has been consistently addressed by our hero. "The demonic, that force of chaos which annihilates all order, whether it be religious, social or psychological, and which manifests itself in the whiteness of the whale or the ash heap vision of *Endgame* or any world turned inside out upon itself, is integral to the concept of the grotesque."[70] But as Kayser has the last say in this matter, "in spite of all the helplessness and horror inspired by the dark forces which lurk in and behind our world and have power to estrange it, the truly artistic portrayal effects a secret liberation."

> The darkness has been sighted, the ominous powers discovered, the incomprehensible forces challenged. And thus we arrive at a final interpretation of the grotesque: AN ATTEMPT TO INVOKE AND SUBDUE THE DEMONIC ASPECTS OF THE WORLD.[71]

What Hamlet has performed may be assessed as this invocation and subdual of the demonic residing in the world.

Hamlet is dead. And yet closure of *Hamlet* does not necessarily synchronize with the titular hero's death. Horatio's story of Hamlet remains to be told. As he promises Fortinbras, the Norwegian prince, who pops up at the very end of this tragedy as its final victor, Horatio will give an account

Of carnal, bloody, and unnatural acts,
Of accidental judgments, casual slaughters,
Of deaths put on by cunning and forc'd cause,
And, in this upshot, purposes mistook
Fall'n on th' inventors' heads.

(381-85)

Horatio's recapitulation undoubtedly reflects a weighty side of a tragedy in which our hero has played a principal part. Still, isn't it a rather distorted version? Can it be said to do justice to our hero's potential tragic

stature? Would the recently departed Hamlet be satisfied with it? "The grotesque is more cruel than tragedy"—Jan Kott's perspicacity is tremendous as ever.[72]

In a post-*Hamlet* world tragedy ceases to be viable. (It goes without saying that in a sense the tragedy of *Hamlet* itself is a verdict of death delivered upon tragedy. But that is another matter.) Whether intentionally or not, Horatio will try to deprive Hamlet's story of its (vestigial) tragic quality of pity and terror, consigning it to the genre of revenge play as launched eponymously by Seneca, pervaded with "carnal, bloody, and unnatural acts," from which *Hamlet* has descended in terms of genre. Horatio's future narrative will be an atavistic reproduction of Hamlet's tragic story. There is no denying that "my story" will sustain a kind of *reductio ad absurdum*.

Horatio deconstructs Hamlet's originally tragic story. Now that the parties to the affair have all perished, nobody could possibly interpellate the authority with which he spins the yarn. It is hardly possible for anybody to object to Horatio's authoritative narrative performance. We cannot eradicate a suspicion that "all" those events that he says he can "Truly deliver" (385-86) with the eager Fortinbras and "the noblest" of his court as the "audience" (387) may be easily manipulated in such a way as to be built in the mechanism of consolidation of power that the Norwegian prince will certainly set about. Hamlet's dying voice for Fortinbras regarding the next Danish throne, which Hamlet has also entrusted to Horatio (355-58), together with Fortinbras's own claim of "some rights, of memory in this [Danish] kingdom" (389), will be conducive to the legitimation of power. Fortinbras might capitalize on this opportune story, emphasizing the unspeakable corruption and monstrous atrocity that dominated the bygone regime of "this kingdom," the quondam Danish court, and thus enhancing the justice of his rule of the realm. Horatio, assigned the task of storytelling at the end of the tragedy—etymologically, his name stands for "oratorical recitation"—might be deliberately made to negotiate with the newly established power in a way inauspicious to "my story." "Horatio, I am dead, / Thou livest. Report me and my cause aright / To the unsatisfied" (338-40). Contrary to Hamlet's keenest wish, "my cause" will be irretrievably misrepresented. How sad! Alas, poor Hamlet!

Whatever the case may be, tragedy is over. The final *Hamlet* landscape that an eminent Shakespearean critic depicts is awful. After referring to the "sound" of the "musings and indecision of Hamlet" that "have been a frantically personal obbligato in the Senecan movement of revenge," Thomas McFarland closes his existentialist reading of the play with this statement: "Now at last [the] sound is stilled, *the skulls grin,* and the play moves toward its universal night."[73] The "universal night" that the critic assumes for the play's final tableau could be apocalyptic. Perhaps apocalypse is intrinsically grotesque. And in our modern time we will be exposed to such an apocalyptic scenery. In his enormously provocative and problematical tirade, Lucky in Beckett's *Waiting for Godot,* a grotesque parody of "man thinking" as he is,[74] betraying glossolalia and logorrhea, talks compulsively and ceaselessly about "the skull the skull the skull the skull" that supposedly abounds in the universal graveyard that his visionary reflection reveals our entire world has become. Lucky's antic discourse is, as he himself paradoxically avers at its temporary end, left "unfinished. . . ."[75]

Notes

I have amended the original text of this essay, which appeared in *The Northern Review* (The English Department, Hokkaido University, Hokkaido, Japan) 8 (1980). All Shakespearean references are to *The Riverside Shakespeare,* ed. G. Blakemore Evans (Boston: Houghton Mifflin, 1974). I have taken the liberty of removing all the parenthetical additions that are found in this edition.

In addition to those I have adduced directly in the notes I would like to acknowledge my indebtedness to the following important studies for understanding the grotesque: G. Wilson Knight, "*King Lear* and the Comedy of the Grotesque," in *The Wheel of Fire: Interpretations of Shakespearian Tragedy* (1930; London: Methuen, 1972), pp. 160-76; Robert Eisler, "Danse Macabre," *Traditio* 6 (1948): 187-225; Vivian Mercier, "Macabre and Grotesque Humour in the Irish Tradition," in *The Irish Comic Tradition* (Oxford: Oxford University, 1962), pp. 47-77; Lee Byron Jennings, "The Term 'Grotesque,'" in *The Ludicrous Demon: Aspects of the Grotesque in German Post-Romantic Prose,* University of California Publications in Modern Philology 71 (Berkeley: University of California, 1963), pp. 1-27; Howard Daniel, *Devils, Monsters, and Nightmares: An Introduction to the Grotesque and Fantastic in Art* (London: Abelard-Schuman, 1964); Frances K. Barasch, *The Grotesque: A Study in Meanings* (The Hague: Mouton, 1971); Philip Thomson, *The Grotesque,* The Critical Idiom Series (London: Methuen, 1972); Richard M. Cook, "The Grotesque and Melville's *Mardi,*" *ESQ* 21, 2d Quarter (1975): 103-10; Frederick Busch, "Dickens: The Smile of the Face of the Dead," *Mosaic* 9 (summer 1976): 149-56; Richard M. Cook, "Evolving the Inscrutable: The Grotesque in Melville's Fiction," *American Literature* 49 (January 1978): 544-59; M. B. van Buren, "The Grotesque in Visual Art and Literature," *Dutch Quarterly Review* 12 (1982): 42-53; Geoffrey G. Harpham, *On the Grotesque: Strategies of Contradiction in Art and Literature* (Princeton: Princeton University, 1982).

[1] Jacques Choron, *Death and Modern Man* (New York: Macmillan, Collier Books, 1964), p. 163.

[2] C. S. Lewis, "Hamlet: The Prince or the Poem," in *Studies in Shakespeare: British Academy Lectures,* ed. Peter Alexander (London: Oxford University, 1964), p. 211.

[3] Lewis, p. 212.

[4] Lewis, p. 212.

[5] In his treatment of *Elizabethan Grotesque* (London: Routledge and Kegan Paul, 1980), p. 42, Neil Rhodes mentions the provocative use that Thomas Nashe and François Rabelais made of "grotesque food imagery" for portraiture of the protean body: "sharply aware of the body's capacity for mutation, both Nashe and Rabelais use grotesque food imagery to remind us of the essential similarity between our own flesh and the flesh we feed it with: the devourer is devoured." In our opinion, what amplifies the grotesque ambience is the endless cyclical reciprocation of eating mobilized by death.

[6] Eleanor Prosser, *Hamlet and Revenge,* 2d ed. (Stanford, Calif.: Stanford University, 1971), p. 205.

[7] Richard D. Altick, "*Hamlet* and the Odor of Mortality," *Shakespeare Quarterly* 5 (spring 1954): 168.

[8] M. M. Mahood, "*Hamlet,*" in *Shakespeare's Wordplay* (London: Methuen, 1957), p. 112.

[9] G. Wilson Knight, "The Embassy of Death: An Essay on *Hamlet,*" in *The Wheel of Fire: Interpretations of Shakespearian Tragedy* (1930; London: Methuen, 1972), p. 22.

[10] Eric Partridge, *Shakespeare's Bawdy* (1948; rev. ed., New York: Dutton, 1969), informs us that in the age of Shakespeare, the word "fishmonger" had the bawdy connotation of "a procurer; a pimp." It was synonymous with "fleshmonger," or "wencher," and was apparently made on the analogy of a "whoremonger." Polonius is a Pandarus. As a matter of fact, he looses his daughter Ophelia to Hamlet with a view to sounding the mystery of the prince's behavior. In their confrontation Hamlet bursts out to his former sweetheart in an uncontrollable bout of anger: "Get thee to a nunn'ry. . . . / Go thy ways to a nunn'ry" (3.1.120, 128-29). This is equally an innuendo. Partridge says that "'nunnery' . . . bears the fairly common Elizabethan slang sense 'brothel.'" Hamlet has detected Polonius's scheme. By no means will he be taken in by a whore Ophelia set on by a whoremonger Polonius.

On the other hand, we can take the passage in another sense, quite literally. That is to say, Hamlet is trying to confine Ophelia's disturbing sexuality, darkly associated with death and decomposition through maggots, to an institution where it may be safely contained. As the sight of Celia shitting dumbfounds Swift's ingenuous persona, Ophelia's liability to conception (whose causation may be thought to be her seductive beauty, irresistible carnal attraction) repels and saddens Hamlet. He blames Ophelia ruthlessly, "why wouldst thou be a breeder of sinners?" (120-21). Conception is never a blessing; it is the damnable act of breeding a sinner. Conception as the fruit of sinful sexuality—so it seems to our hero—can be regarded as perpetual reproduction (in the economic sense of the word, as well) of sin, since daughters of Ophelia will successively be breeders of sinners. Procreation is a practice of eternal return.

Defining himself as a sinner, he catalogues a number of his faults, the defects that flesh is heir to. His agony culminates in a self-denunciation: "What should such fellows as I do crawling between earth and heaven?" (126-28). Hamlet thinks of himself as a vile creature crawling between heaven and earth, a kind of reptile wriggling its way on earth, unable to find any meaning for his herpetological existence. (Without much offending the susceptibility on the part of the audience, a Hamlet actor could, if he would, adopt here a grotesque reptilian posture of prostrate crawling.)

With maniacal tenacity Hamlet urges Ophelia: "Get thee to a nunn'ry, farewell. . . . To a nunn'ry, go, and quickly too. . . . To a nunn'ry, go" (136-49). Like any sexually unruly woman, Ophelia must be excluded from a conjugal life. At least Hamlet wants to shun the yoke, for unlike a fool who only is fit for marriage, he is wise enough to know what a "monster" Ophelia will make of him (138-39). The "monster" refers, admittedly, to a cuckold, a man growing horns on his forehead on account of his wife's infidelity. Hamlet is congener with the comic protagonist Panurge in Rabelais's novel who takes such aversion to becoming a *cocu* that he goes on quest for the wondrous means to avoid the infamous destiny and with Othello, who is demonically concerned with "this forked plague" (*Othello,* 3.3.276). Marriage is a civilized institution geared to production of male monstrosities. Many a monster (a grotesque conglomeration of man and beast) dwells in Venice, Iago whispers gleefully to the wretch Othello (*Othello,* 4.1.62-64).

Speaking of marriage, it turns out another species of monster. Taking his leave for his journey to England, Hamlet accosts Claudius:

HAMLET: Farewell, dear mother.
KING: Thy loving father, Hamlet.
HAMLET: My mother: father and mother is man
    and wife, man and wife is one flesh—so,
    my mother.

(4.3.49-52)

The biblical proposition is given an accursed exegesis. It is interpreted to the letter by deploying irrefutable

syllogism, and in the event Claudius is passed off as Hamlet's mother. What an extraordinary and yet funny logic it is! (As we will see in due course, Hamlet is a fool, a talented one at that. Only a fool has propensity for such unpredictable verbal ingenuity. In passing, the fool Hamlet and the whore Ophelia are specular images of their prototypical counterparts in one of the sources of *Hamlet.*) Being a man-wife, Claudius looms up as a double-gendered aberration, an anamorphic case, a teratological phenomenon. . . .

A modern student of depth psychology would find fitting material for his or her study of the so-called primal scene in the fantastic union of Hamlet's father and mother. Enormously offensive is Hamlet's prurient, even voyeuristic depiction of the scene.

Nay, but to live
In the rank sweat of an enseamed bed,
Stew'd in corruption, honeying and making
  love
Over the nasty sty!

(3.4.91-94)

In their sexual life that Hamlet daydreams and actually verbalizes in the presence of his mother, Claudius and Gertrude appear as satyrs (Claudius is, as a matter of fact, called "a satyr" on the same occasion)—mythically conceived beastly figures endued with inordinate lust.

Hamlet has no right to pry into, still less reveal, the most private, secret part of his parents' marital life. Still their marriage causes another disturbance to Hamlet. Their incestuous union seems to have affected a sound family relationship. "My uncle-father and aunt-mother" (2.2.376), once Hamlet so called Claudius and Gertrude, respectively. It is a question of civil register. And how would anthropology deal with this anomaly in kinship structure? How would it resolve this exceptional case of mixed familial appellation? "A little more than kin, and less than kind" (1.2.64-65)—Hamlet's riddling reply to Claudius's greeting words "my cousin Hamlet, and my son" (63) might remain unamenable to facile explanation.

"Empson, *Some Versions of Pastoral,* p. 5: 'There was a performance of *Hamlet* in the Turk-Sib region which the audience decided spontaneously was farce'" (Norman O. Brown, *Closing Time* [1973; New York: Vintage Books, 1974], p. 50).

Or if it is genre that matters, we could surmise that an item on the impressive list Polonius has compiled is eligible for generic nomenclature applicable to our play: "tragical-comical-historical-pastoral" (2.2.398-99). And will this miscegenated qualifier strike us as grotesque?

[11] Prosser, p. 205.

[12] G. R. Elliott, *Scourge and Minister: A Study of* Hamlet *as Tragedy of Revengefulness and Justice* (1951; New York: AMS Press, 1965), p. 164.

[13] Nigel Alexander, *Poison, Play, and Duel: A Study in* Hamlet (London: Routledge and Kegan Paul, 1971), p. 162.

[14] Mathew Winston, "*Humour noir* and Black Humor," in *Veins of Humor,* ed. Harry Levin, Harvard English Studies 3 (Cambridge, Mass.: Harvard University, 1972), p. 283.

[15] Henri Bergson, "Laughter," in *Comedy,* ed. Wylie Sypher (Garden City, N.Y.: Doubleday, Anchor, 1956).

[16] Alexander, p. 163: "one of the most vital moments in the play is when Hamlet, examining the 'chap-fall'n' skull of Yorick, appears to accept that the end of all the playing, and all the painting, must be the last grave joke of death." I have stretched Alexander's idea in my favor.

[17] Harry Morris, "*Hamlet* as a *Memento Mori* Poem," *PMLA* 85 (October 1970): 1037. The skull of Yorick signals that which has been irremediably lost in the passage of time, and it immediately propels Hamlet to retrieve it. What a Shakespeare critic terms "the myth of memory," which is, incidentally, one of the most important themes in Proust's monumental novel *Remembrance of Things Past* (1954) in 3 vols., trans. C. K. Scott Moncrieff and Terence Kilmartin (1981; New York: Vintage Books, 1982), is inscribed in the impassioned episode; see James P. Hammersmith, "*Hamlet* and the Myth of Memory," *E.L.H.* 45 (winter 1978): 597-605: "The issue of time and its relationship to memory in *Hamlet* is raised in its most problematical aspect by the *memento mori,* the skull of Yorick" (p. 597).

[18] For this subject in our play, see D. R. Howard, "Hamlet and the Contempt of the World," *The South Atlantic Quarterly* 58 (spring 1959): 167-75. In it Howard points out "the popularity during Shakespeare's time of the Dance of Death and of *memento mori* devices, both of which reflect contempt of the world," and argues that "motifs in popular and religious art seem to have been employed with a certain mild humor as a popular convention which traditionally, though perhaps not very effectively, reminded men of the brevity of life and the need for repentance" and that "no doubt a certain amount of *Weltschmerz* attached itself to them" (p. 168). Man-devouring worms and the dusty or clayey fate that awaits a person after death, which we will subsequently discuss, are to be fixed in this tradition: "man's body was called worms' meat or food for worms, and his life was likened to dust or ashes, clay, smoke, fire, wax, and so on" (p. 169).

[19] Apropos of logical ultraism, Arthur Clayborough treats Swift in terms of "The Fantasy of Extreme Logic" in his study *The Grotesque in English Literature* (1965; rpt. with corrections, Oxford: Clarendon, 1967), pp. 112-57.

[20] Because of the suspiciousness of her dying, Ophelia is allowed only the "maimed rites" (5.1.219), at which Laertes utters forth imprecations accompanied by a supplication "from her fair and unpolluted flesh / May violets spring!" (239-40). Ophelia's supplicated passage into floral being may remind us of Ovidian metamorphoses which are occasionally marked by the grotesque. But I am not sure whether it has a shade of the Ovidian grotesque. Her "mermaid-like" (4.7.176) death may sound equally Ovidian.

[21] Elliott, p. 164.

[22] Willard Farnham, *The Shakespearean Grotesque: Its Genesis and Transformations* (Oxford: Oxford at the Clarendon Press, 1971), pp. 116-17. The focal scene appears to be imbued with "fear of death and humour." According to Earle P. Scarlett, "The Dance of Death," *The Dalhousie Review* 37 (winter 1958): 384, "the very incongruity of these two things" is characteristic of a design of the Dance of Death.

[23] James M. Clark, *The Dance of Death in the Middle Ages and the Renaissance* (Glasgow: Jackson, 1950), p. 105.

[24] Thomas M. Columbus, "Tristram's Dance with Death— Volume VII of *Tristram Shandy,*" *The University of Dayton Review* 8 (fall 1971): 3-15.

[25] Paul Hamill, "Death's Lively Image: The Emblematic Significance of the Closet Scene in *Hamlet,*" *Texas Studies in Literature and Language* 16 (summer 1974): 258.

[26] Leonard P. Kurtz, *The Dance of Death and the Macabre Spirit in European Literature* (New York: Columbia University, 1934), p. 1.

[27] Knight, pp. 27, 30, and 41, respectively. Incidentally, in respect to inordinate death-consciousness, Knight links Hamlet with Stavrogin in Dostoyevski's *The Possessed* (or *The Devils* (1870-72) (p. 35). When we focus on the problematics of suicide, however, Hamlet appears to be more akin to Kirilov, that extraordinary, superhuman proponent of the philosophy of suicide. Anyway, these three men are coordinated in a triptych; Hamlet shows a striking proclivity for suicidal imaginings, while, like Kirilov, Stavrogin kills himself. As Eleanore Rowe says in a chapter called "Dostoevsky and *Hamlet,*" in her book *Hamlet: A Window on Russia* (New York: New York University, 1976), p. 87, "the theme of suicide seems to evoke Hamlet for Dostoevsky."

To continue the comparison between Hamlet and Dostoevsky, our hero also reminds us of "the underground" man of the Russian writer's creating. Hamlet's correlative to the Dostoevskian "underground" is the "nutshell in [which] I could be bounded, and count myself a king of infinite space—were it not that I have bad dreams" (2.2.254-56). Another name for both Hamlet's "nutshell" and Dostoevsky's "underground" is the "grotto" in our diction: their claustrophile, reclusive way of living is "grotto-esque," that is, grotesque. For exciting discussion of the sympathy between these anti-heroic protagonists, see Stanley Cooperman, "Shakespeare's Anti-Hero: Hamlet and the Underground Man," *Shakespeare Studies* 1, ed. J. Leeds Barroll (1965): 37-63.

[28] Hamill, p. 258.

[29] Hamill, p. 259.

[30] Prosser, p. 151.

[31] Raymond Klibansky, Erwin Panofsky, and Fritz Saxl, *Saturn and Melancholy: Studies in the History of Natural Philosophy, Religion, and Art* (London: Thomas Nelson, 1964), p. 197.

[32] I found the following studies greatly stimulating: Oscar James Campbell, "What Is the Matter with Hamlet?" *The Yale Review* 32 (1942): 309-22; the same author's *Shakespeare's Satire* (1943; rpt., Hamden, Conn.: Archon Books, 1963); Lawrence Babb, *The Elizabethan Malady: A Study of Melancholia in English Literature from 1580 to 1642* (East Lansing: Michigan State University, 1951); Alvin Kernan, *The Cankered Muse: Satire of the English Renaissance* (1959; rpt., Hamden, Conn.: Archon Books, 1976); Robert C. Elliott, "Saturnalia, Satire, and Utopia," in *The Shape of Utopia: Studies in a Literary Genre* (Chicago: University of Chicago, 1970), pp. 3-24; Bridget Gellert Lyons, *Voices of Melancholy: Studies in Literary Treatments of Melancholy in Renaissance England* (New York: Norton, 1971).

[33] *The Knight's Tale* from *The Canterbury Tales,* ed. A. C. Spearing with introduction (Cambridge, Eng.: Cambridge University, 1966). Spearing concludes his introduction with this observation: "The twentieth century can perhaps legitimately see in this fourteenth-century poem a view of the human condition as neither comic nor tragic but absurd—a view of life similar to that expressed by a modern writer such as Samuel Beckett and found in Shakespeare by a modern critic such as Jan Kott. The poem's view of life does not seem to me to be that of orthodox medieval Christianity, nor is it necessarily Chaucer's own total and final view. . . . Perhaps the world is ruled by Saturn: this is the hypothesis into which The Knight's Tale invites us to enter, and it is all the more chal-

lenging and disturbing a poem because its view of human life is not pure but dubious and mixed" (p. 79).

[34] Farnham, p. 61.

[35] Bernard Grebanier, *The Heart of Hamlet: The Play Shakespeare Wrote,* with the text of the play (New York: Apollo Editions [Thomas Y. Crowell], 1960), p. 321, scrutinizes the son-sun quibble, demonstrating six ways of interpreting it.

[36] Sigmund Freud, *Jokes and Their Relation to the Unconscious,* trans. James Strachey (1960; New York: Norton, 1963).

[37] Guy Mermier, "The Grotesque in French Medieval Literature: A Study in Forms and Meanings," *Genre* 9 (1976/77): 381.

[38] Maurice Charney, *Style in* Hamlet (Princeton, N.J.: Princeton University, 1969), p. 69.

[39] Norman N. Holland, *"Hamlet,"* in *The Shakespearean Imagination* (2d ed., Bloomington: Indiana University, 1975), p. 176. Emphasis added.

[40] Hamill, p. 253.

[41] On my mind are the two fascinating Shakespeare tomes: Bernard Spivack, *Shakespeare and the Allegory of Evil: The History of a Metaphor in Relation to His Major Villains* (New York: Columbia University, 1958); and Charlotte Spivack, *The Comedy of Evil on Shakespeare's Stage* (Rutherford: Fairleigh Dickinson University Press/London: Associated University Presses, 1978).

[42] Hamill, p. 253.

[43] Hamill, p. 252.

[44] On the Ghost a great number of studies are available. The following seem to be typical: John Dover Wilson, "Ghost or Devil?" in *What Happens in* Hamlet (1935; rpt., Cambridge Eng.: Cambridge University, 1970), pp. 51-86; Madeleine Doran, "That Undiscovered Country: A Problem concerning the Use of the Supernatural in *Hamlet* and *Macbeth,*" *Philological Quarterly* 20 (July 1941): 413-27; I. J. Semper, "The Ghost in *Hamlet:* Pagan or Christian?" *The Month* (April 1953): 222-34; J. C. Maxwell, "The Ghost from the Grave: A Note on Shakespeare's Apparitions," *Durham University Journal,* n.s. 17 (March 1956): 55-59; Sister Miriam Joseph, "Discerning the Ghost in *Hamlet,*" *PMLA* 76 (December 1961): 493-502; Niels L. Anthonisen, "The Ghost in *Hamlet,*" *American Imago* 22 (winter 1965): 232-49; Eleanor Prosser, "Enter Ghost" and "Spirit of Health or Goblin Damned?" in *Hamlet and Revenge,* pp. 97-117 and 118-43; Robert H. West,

"King Hamlet's Ambiguous Ghost," in *Shakespeare and the Outer Mystery* (Lexington: University of Kentucky, 1968), pp. 56-68.

[45] Wolfgang Kayser, *The Grotesque in Art and Literature,* trans. Ulrich Weisstein (1963; rpt., New York: McGraw-Hill, 1966), p. 185.

[46] Kayser, p. 185.

[47] Kayser, p. 185. Emphasis added.

[48] For description of this paragraph, I am indebted to Harry Levin's excellent study *The Question of Hamlet* (London: Oxford University, 1959). The dominant theme and atmosphere of mystery in our play are ably discussed by: Maynard Mack, "The World of Hamlet," *Yale Review* 41 (September 1951): 502-23 (rpt. in *Tragic Themes in Western Literature,* ed. Cleanth Brooks [New Haven, Conn.: Yale University, 1955], pp. 30-58); Mahood, *Shakespeare's Wordplay;* West, *Shakespeare and the Outer Mystery;* Robert G. Hunter, *"Hamlet,"* in *Shakespeare and the Mystery of God's Judgments* (Athens: University of Georgia, 1976), pp. 101-26; John Arthos, "The Undiscovered Country," in *Shakespeare's Use of Dream and Vision* (London: Bowes and Bowes, 1977), pp. 137-72. Mahood's contention in this respect deserves special attention (pp. 111-12): "To the Elizabethan audience, it [*Hamlet*] must have been primarily a mystery drama in the cinema-poster sense of the word. It is a detective story: almost everyone in it is involved in some form of detection. . . . *Hamlet* is also a mystery play of a deeper kind. It is a mystery play in the medieval sense and its background of a Catholic eschatology keeps us constantly in mind of something after death. Murder and incest are unnatural acts; but behind and beyond the discovered crimes lies an evil which is supernatural. . . . Philosophy, however (as Hamlet tells Horatio), does not comprehend mysteries of this order. Hamlet's own insight into such mysteries sets him apart from friends and enemies alike. Everyone else is concerned in the unmasking of legal crimes. Hamlet alone, surrounded by the politic ferrets of a Machiavellian court, knows that the action in which he is involved is 'not a story of detection, of crime and its punishment, but of sin and expiation.'"

[49] The numinous constitutes the idea of the holy that Rudolf Otto developed in his epoch-making study *The Idea of the Holy: An Inquiry into the Non-rational Factor in the Idea of the Divine and Its Relation to the Rational,* trans. John W. Harvey (1923; rpt., London: Oxford University, 1979). For the germaneness of the numinous with the grotesque, see Carl Skrade, *God and the Grotesque* (Philadelphia: Westminster, 1974), passim. I feel grateful to the late James Luther Adams for having directed my attention to Skrade's interesting book.

[50] This is one of the most vital ideas in Kayser's theory of the grotesque.

[51] Kayser, p. 31.

[52] Kayser, p. 31.

[53] Kayser, p. 184.

[54] Kayser, p. 31.

[55] Holland, p. 172, says: "That fatal revelation is the disease, the rottenness, at the core of the play. Early on, Hamlet speaks of the tragic flaw that a man may have: he calls it 'the dram of e'il,' 'some vicious mole of nature,' and later he calls the Ghost 'old mole.' Indeed, the Ghost is the walking blemish of the land, the figure who proves by his very presence that 'Something is rotten in the state of Denmark.' The Ghost turns this blight, this disease, onto Hamlet himself, so that Hamlet becomes, in the words of the King, 'the quick of the ulcer,' the living, growing part of the disease."

[56] Kayser, p. 15.

[57] Kayser, pp. 14-15.

[58] Lewis, p. 212. Emphasis added.

[59] Kayser, p. 184.

[60] James L. Calderwood finds this self-definition that our hero attains to be of pivotal significance for *Hamlet;* see his study *To Be and Not to Be: Negation and Metadrama in* Hamlet (New York: Columbia University, 1983). Calderwood's Shakespeare volume is one of the major contributions to the study of *Hamlet* in our modern time.

[61] Prosser, p. 238.

[62] I owe this idea to Norman N. Holland, p. 171: "and he [i.e., Hamlet] dies on a pun: 'The rest is silence'—'rest' as either 'repose' or 'remainder.'"

[63] Shakespeare's idealistic view of silence and eternity (as in "Passing through nature to eternity") is not immune to deflating commentary, which is provided by Tom Stoppard in his *Rosencrantz and Guildenstern Are Dead* (New York: Grove Press, 1967):

But no one gets up after death—there is no applause—there is only silence and some second-hand clothes, and that's—death—. (p. 123)

Death followed by eternity . . . the worst of both worlds. It *is* a terrible thought. (p. 72)

Stoppard's dramatic work, whose title is a quotation from *Hamlet* (5.2.371), can be called a meta-*Hamlet* play, living on *Hamlet* and constituting critique of it.

[64] See Mikhail Bakhtin, *Rabelais and His World,* trans. Hélène Iswolsky (Cambridge, Mass.: The MIT Press, 1968). I borrowed the notion of the convergence of "comicity" and "cosmicity" from Farnham, p. 50.

[65] Columbus, pp. 14-15.

[66] Columbus, p. 14.

[67] Theodore Spencer, *Death and Elizabethan Tragedy: A Study of Convention and Opinion in the Elizabethan Drama* (New York: Pageant Books, 1960), p. 155.

[68] William Shakespeare, "The Sonnet 146," in *The Sonnets,* ed. William Burto (New York: New American Library, 1964), p. 186.

[69] Herman Melville, "The Whiteness of the Whale," in *Moby-Dick,* A Norton Critical Edition, ed. Harrison Hayford and Hershel Parker (New York: Norton, 1967), p. 169.

[70] G. Farrell Lee, "Grotesque and the Demonism of Silence: Beckett's *Endgame,*" *Notre Dame English Journal* 14 (winter 1981): 59.

[71] Kayser, p. 188.

[72] Jan Kott, *Shakespeare Our Contemporary,* trans. Boleslaw Taborski, with preface by Peter Brook (London: Methuen, 1965), p. 67.

[73] Thomas McFarland, *Tragic Meanings in Shakespeare* (New York: Random House, 1966), p. 59. Emphasis added.

[74] In reviewing *Waiting for Godot* (17 January 1953), Jacques Lemarchand evaluates Lucky's *tour de force* thinking performance as "a remarkable recital of the parodic, baroque monologue of 'man thinking'": *Samuel Beckett: The Critical Heritage,* ed. Lawrence Graver and Raymond Federman (London: Routledge and Kegan Paul, 1979), p. 92.

[75] Samuel Beckett, *Waiting for Godot* (New York: Grove Press, 1954), p. 29b. For explication of Lucky's monologue see my article "'In the Muddle the Sound-dance': Lucky and His Tirade in Beckett's *Waiting for Godot,*" *Gengobunka-bu Kiyo (Bulletin of the Institute of Language and Culture Studies)* (Hokkaido University, Hokkaido, Japan) 24 (1993): 95-130.

Source: "Grinning Death's-Head: *Hamlet* and the Vision of the Grotesque," in *The Grotesque in Art and Literature: Theological Reflections*, edited by James Luther Adams and Wilson Yates, William B. Eerdmans Publishing Company, 1997, pp. 193-226.

Romances and Poems

What are Shakespeare's sonnets called?

Katherine Duncan-Jones, *Somerville College, Oxford*

The naming, or entitling, of literary works raises questions which range from the abstractly philosophical to the concretely bibliographical. Indeed, this is an area in which such approaches, normally divergent, converge. Some of the metalinguistic problems of naming are amusingly cracked open in Lewis Carroll's *Through the Looking Glass* (1893), where Alice is offered four different names for a song about to be performed by the White Knight. The titles offered by the White Knight in response to Alice's questions range from '*Haddocks Eyes*', 'The name of the song', by way of what the name 'really is', '*The Aged Aged man*', then moving on to what the song 'is called', '*Ways and Means*', and arriving finally at what appears to be the essentialist centre:

> 'Well, what is the song, then?' said Alice, who was by this time completely bewildered.

> 'I was coming to that,' the knight said. 'The song really is '*A-sitting On A Gate*', and the tune's my own invention.'[1]

None of the four names or titles offered by the White Knight incorporates his own name, or indicates his own relationship to the text he performs—which is, of course, a parody of Wordsworth's ramblingly deferred *Resolution and Independence*, also known as *The Leech-Gatherer*—but it is interesting that it is only when he comes to what 'The song really is' that he divulges his own supposed contribution to it, the invention of the tune. In the case of Shakespeare's sonnets, contrariwise, a claim for authorship is incorporated into the title itself, as printed in 1609: 'SHAKE-SPEARES SONNETS. Neuer before Imprinted'. Curiously, although there has been so much discussion of the following leaf, with T. T.'s capitalized dedication of 'THESE. INSUING. SONNETS' to 'Mr. W. H.', the title-page has been relatively little examined. Because of an almost universal assumption by earlier editors and critics that the text is unauthorized, and possibly acquired by Thomas Thorpe in an underhand or even malicious manner, the title has been conventionally viewed as a bare-faced claim to authenticity by a greedy publisher, the crucial words being 'Neuer before imprinted'.[2] Yet at least three external witnesses suggest, conversely, that this may be a text authorized by Shakespeare himself.[3] Thomas Heywood, reprimanding the piratical William Jaggard for his appropriation, not only of two epistles from his own *Troia Britanica*, but also of some of Shakespeare's 'sugred sonnets', previously pirated by Jaggard in 1599, added that 'hee to doe

himselfe right, hath since published them in his owne name'. William Drummond in conversation with Jonson referred to Shakespeare, along with Sir William Alexander, as having lately published his own love poems.[4] And the publisher John Benson in 1640 appears to have believed that it was Shakespeare himself who was responsible for the 1609 text, with which he then proceeded to take great liberties, for he praised the sonnets as being 'of the same purity, the Author himselfe then living, avouched'. If the text is authorized, it follows logically that the title, too, may be as Shakespeare wished it to be. Certainly it is perfectly consistent with the form of the Stationers' Register entry, on 20th May 1609, where it is described as 'a Booke called SHAKE-SPEARES sonnettes'. The absence of any more elaborate, fictive or teasing title—such as *Mistress Emilia and the Two Williams*, say, or *Rose-water Distilled*—is indeed one of the many distinctive and puzzling features of Shakespeare's sonnets, especially if the sequence is compared, as it most often has been, with Elizabethan sonnet sequences of the 1580s and 90s. However, a closer examination of the 1609 volume's title in conjunction with comparable titles in the period produces some interesting analogies.

Today, a two-word title consisting of an author's name in the possessive followed by a noun—what, for short, I will call a 'genitive title'—may often be colloquially applied to major works of reference or scholarship. Scholars allude familiarly to 'North's Plutarch', 'Johnson's *Dictionary*' or 'Cruden's *Concordance*'. This form of title suggests unchallengeable weight and authority, and has generally acquired currency because the work occupies a position which requires frequent citation, and the author's achievement is of such magnitude that it is felt that he should always be mentioned as responsible for it. Titles of this sort are fashioned by the use of readers over a period of time, rather than initiated by the original authors. However, when a genitive title is applied to a work of literary imagination by its author, rather than by appreciative users of it, the effect can be totally different, and may seem both whimsical and egotistical, as in Pam Ayres's *All Pam's poems* (1978). Egotistical whimsicality may also have been a feature of some genitive titles in the period 1570-1620.[5] Such titles often seem to point to some sort of cult of personality by a notorious or popular writer, who may wish—or whose publisher may wish on his behalf—to draw attention to the individuality or persona behind or in the work. The works attributed posthumously to Shakespeare's hostile rival Robert Greene offer some celebrated Elizabethan instances, such as *Greenes Groats-worth of Witte,* 1592; compare also *Greenes neuer too late, Greenes orpharion, Greenes mourning garment,* all published in 1590; *Greenes newes both from heauen and hell,* 1593; the apocryphal *Greenes arcadia,* 1610, and so on. But poets earlier in the period also frequently used the genitive formula. Consider, for instance, the Countess of Pembroke's obscure retainer Thomas Howell, author of *Howell his deuises,* 1581; the musician William Hunnis, *Hunnies recreation,* 1588; or the prolific Thomas Churchyard, with nine or more titles of the genitive type, ranging from *Churchyardes Chippes,* 1575, to *Churchyards Challenge,* 1593. In his only surviving letter Thomas Nashe elaborately mocked *Churchyardes Chippes,*[6] yet it may not have been its whimsical genitive title, but rather its old-fashioned poetic style, that Nashe thought ridiculous, since he called his own last-written work *Nashes Lenten Stuffe* (1599). Lest we should think this a mere catchpenny title devised by the publisher, the aptly-named Nicholas Ling, Nashe opens his second prefatory epistle with a discussion of it:

> *Nashes Lentenstuffe:* and why *Nashes Lentenstuffe?* Some scabbed scald squire replies, because I had money lent me at *Yarmouth,* and I pay them againe in prayse of their towne and the redde herring.[7]

Genitive titles are deployed by many authors of works that we know to have been drawn on by Shakespeare, such as John Florio, *Florio his first fruites,* 1578, and *Florios second frutes,* 1591; or Barnabe Riche, *Riche his farewell . . . ,* 1581; or an obscure work on which I believe Shakespeare may have drawn for the 'Hecuba' scene in *Hamlet* (II. ii), Thomas Fenne, *Fennes frutes,* 1590, which includes a long prosopopoeic complaint poem, *Hecubaes mishappes.* Here the two genitives function quite differently. The whole book, in three sections, constitutes the 'fruits' of Thomas Fenne's intellectual labours; the final item in it, a long poem in fourteeners, offers a vision of Hecuba who, in the manner of *The Mirror for Magistrates,* chronicles her own appalling 'mishaps'. The possibility that a genitive title may refer either to the author or the theme, or both, should be borne in mind when we return to the case of Shakespeare.

Despite this accumulation of examples of genitive titles within Shakespeare's writing lifetime, it is hard to dispel some suspicion that then, as now, such titles, when bestowed on their works by the authors themselves, were a bit vulgar or low-grade. At worst, they can seem ponderously self-advertising, in drawing attention to an otherwise little-known individual, such as the composer Tobias Hume's *Captain Humes poeticall musicke,* 1607. At other times, they can be explicitly comical, as in *Tarltons tragical treatises,* 1578, or *Tarltons jests,* 1613; or Thomas Coryat's *Coryats crambe* and *Coryats crudities,* both 1611.

Could Shakespeare really have devised such an egotistical title for his own precious and long-awaited sonnets, whether pompously or playfully, especially when this formula was so strongly associated with the works of his alleged enemy Robert Greene?

There is one obvious reason why he may have done so. Thomas Heywood's reference to Shakespeare as 'much offended with M. Jaggard' for his attribution to him in print of inauthentic poems in *The Passionate Pilgrim* (1599, 1612) seems to allude also to the subsequent publication of the full sequence of sonnets— 'hee to doe himselfe right, hath since published them *in his owne name*' (my emphasis). If this refers, as it certainly appears to do, to the 1609 quarto, it is extremely apt. Shakespeare's sonnets are doubly or even trebly published 'in his owne name'. Shakespeare's authorship is immediately proclaimed in the genitive title on the title-page. We encounter the assertion of possession and authorship even before we are enlightened as to the genre of poems by (and about?) Shakespeare which are to ensue. This may be contrasted with Jaggard's 'THE PASSIONATE PILGRIME. By W. Shakespeare'—a fanciful title which gives away little or nothing about what is to follow, except for making a false claim for Shakespeare's authorship, five only of its twenty poems being authentic. The title indicates little more than that the poems which follow may concern love or suffering—'PASSIONATE'— while being rambling or various—'PILGRIME'. If the title is intended to suggest that there is a continuous persona—perhaps even a fictionalized projection of William Shakespeare—who makes his amorous pilgrimage through the twenty poems, a quick perusal of its contents will show such a reading to be unsustainable. In the 1609 quarto, in contrast, every single opening is headed, on the verso, SHAKESPEARES, and on the recto, SONNETS. However far we go into the book, we never cease to be reminded that what we are reading is Shakespeare's work: and lest we should think the volume eventually stuffed up with other matter, even the last piece is separately titled, on sig. K1ᵛ, 'A Louers complaint. *BY* WILLIAM SHAKE-SPEARE'. Jaggard's inane and irrelevant title may have irritated Shakespeare almost as much as the ascription to him of lyrics by Griffin, Barnfield, Marlowe and others. It may have provoked him to assert the absolute distinction between Jaggard's piratical little miscellany and his own superb and large-scale sequence by adopting the downright, but truthful, 'SHAKE-SPEARES SONNETS'. Ben Jonson, incidentally, may have had reservations about the egotistical implications of the genitive form of title, although he did deploy it on occasion, as in 'BEN: IONSON / his / VOLPONE' (1607). But there is reason to suspect that it was Jonson himself who intervened, early in 1609, while the work was in the press, to change the title 'BEN: IONSON, *HIS CASE IS ALTERD*', a title that inevitably implied not merely that the play was written by

Jonson, but also that it dealt with his own altered case, to 'A Pleasant Comedy, CALLED: The Case is Alterd . . . Written by Ben. IONSON'.[8]

If it is established that Shakespeare's sonnets should be properly and authentically entitled (in a modernized text) *Shakespeare's Sonnets,* some further consequences follow. Grammatically, for instance, the title, though plural, forms a single unit, and should be referred to in the singular. *Shakespeare's Sonnets* 'is', not 'are' a major non-dramatic text, just as *The Two Gentlemen of Verona* 'is', not 'are'; an early comedy, and *The Merry Wives of Windsor* 'is', not 'are', a mature one. In an index or library catalogue it should appear, not as 'Shakespeare, W., *Sonnets*', but as 'Shakespeare, W., *Shakespeare's Sonnets*'. Larger critical and biographical considerations also ensue, by which some critics will be troubled. In the case of such titles as *Coryats crudities, Greenes neuer too late, Nashes lenten stuffe* or *Tarltons jests,* the genitive is clearly not just possessive, it is also denotative, and in some cases primarily so. That is, these works are not only written or generated by, respectively, Coryat, Greene, Nashe, and Tarlton, they also deal with their personal situations and exploits—Coryat the traveller, Greene the repentant prodigal, Nashe the refugee from London, Tarlton the jester and stuntman. The title *Shakespeare's Sonnets* may imply, analogously, that the poems so labelled concern Shakespeare in some way, as well as being written by him. It may be this further implication, that Shakespeare is not merely responsible for the sonnets as verbal constructs, but is essentially present within them as their principal subject-matter, that has inhibited many scholars from accepting Q's title as authoritative, for it makes some recourse to biographical reference inescapable. Such reference has made generations of Shakespeare scholars deeply uncomfortable, above all those who, like Sir Sidney Lee, worked during the period of the Oscar Wilde trial and its aftermath. Though Lee had originally been a convinced Pembrokian, and then an equally convinced Southamptonite, after the second version of his *DNB* article on Shakespeare in 1898 his attitude hardened, and he fiercely dismissed the notion of personal allusion of any kind. In 1905 he made the reasons for his anti-biographical reading quite explicit:

> A literal interpretation of the poems credits the poet with a moral instability which is at variance with the tone of all the rest of his work . . . a purely literal interpretation of the impassioned protestations of affection for a 'lovely boy', which course through the sonnets, casts a slur on the dignity of the poet's name which scarcely bears discussion.[9]

Lee's vehement insistence[10] that Sonnets 1-126 drew on literary sources alone in celebrating male friendship has set the tone for much twentieth century scholarship and criticism. Even much more recent editors,

such as Ingram and Redpath, Booth, and Kerrigan, have in different ways avoided making any close connexions between *Shakespeare's Sonnets* and Shakespeare's 'life' and presumed personality. For instance, Ingram and Redpath offer only a brief embarrassed comment on

> our general impression, which is that the relationship was one of profound and at times agitated friendship, which involved a certain physical and quasi-sexual fascination emanating from the young friend and enveloping the older poet, but did not necessarily include paederasty in any lurid sense.[11]

Stephen Booth was much more cryptic and even more noncommittal:

> William Shakespeare was almost certainly homosexual, bisexual or heterosexual. The sonnets provide no evidence on the matter.[12]

Working as recently as the mid-80s, John Kerrigan side-stepped the possibility of personal (sexual) reference even more adroitly, speaking of the 'sonnets to the youth' as arising 'out of comradely affection in the literature of friendship', and referring dismissively to

> innumerable crackpot theories about the poet's life and love-life—fantasies in which the Sonnets have played a large part.[13]

Crackpot these theories may be: yet the truth is that the grammatical form of the title, in which it appears that Shakespeare asserts his intimate relationship with his sonnets without the intervention of any visibly fictionalized name or persona, seems positively to invite biographical scrutiny. It must inevitably appear to the first-time reader of the 1609 quarto that, as Sidney's disguised Pyrocles confesses in the 'Old' *Arcadia,* 'The singer is the song's theame'.[14] *Pace* Sir Sidney Lee, such a response is neither inappropriate nor far-fetched. This may be illustrated with reference to one early analogue, and one modern one.

In the sonnet sequence that offers the closest analogy to Shakespeare's in the Jacobean period, the 1605 version of Michael Drayton's *Idea,* Drayton marks the transition from *Englands Heroicall Epistles* with a sonnet which ends:

> Their sev'rall Loves since I before have
>   showne,
> Now give me leave, at last, to sing mine
>   owne.[15]

'Wild, madding, jocund, and irregular' though these sonnets are, Drayton positively invites Jacobean readers to receive them as images of his 'owne' love. Though critics belonging to the Sidney Lee school often claim that personal readings of Renaissance sonnet sequences are a post-Romantic anachronism, Drayton's lines seem explicitly to invite such reading.

A much later parallel is offered by that great American poet John Berryman, who surely intended to proclaim his personal preoccupations, as well as his authorship, when he entitled his 1966 sequence *BERRYMAN'S SONNETS. [NOW FIRST IMPRINTED]*. He dedicated the collection to his publisher, Robert Giroux, a life-long devotee of Shakespeare's sonnets, here cast in the role of 'onlie begetter'. Berryman's next major collection, *HIS TOY, HIS DREAM, HIS REST.* (1968) also reflected his delicate appreciation of Elizabethan genitive titles, which offer a much richer and subtler method than Whitman's of heralding a 'Song of Myself'.

Oddly enough, in *Through the Looking Glass* it is the singer who makes a more lasting impression on Alice than the diversely-titled song that he performs:

> Years afterwards she could bring the whole scene back again, as if it had been only yesterday—the mild blue eyes and kindly smile of the Knight—the setting sun gleaming through his hair, and shining on his armour in a blaze of light that quite dazzled her.[18]

Though the song may 'really be' *A-sitting On A Gate,* Alice receives it as if it were the White Knight's 'song of himself'. *Shakespeare's Sonnets,* too, has very naturally appeared to generations of readers to offer a series of windows or half-open doors through which Shakespeare himself may be glimpsed, or through which his voice can be heard. Perhaps what readers think they have seen or heard has often revealed more about their own expectations or prejudices than about the ultimately unknowable 'Shakespeare' as he constructs a voice within the sonnets. Yet it should be acknowledged that the title of the sequence, as well as its dedication, does seem emphatically to invite such an approach.

There is at least one further way in which the title *Shakespeare's Sonnets* can be interpreted. Within Shakespeare's period there is a whole category of genitive titles of which I have not yet cited instances. These are applied to works in which some special and definitive expertise is asserted, not by posterity, but by the author. Examples are the classic treatise on horsemanship, *M. Blundeuile his Exercises,* 1594; or on falconry, *Lathams falconry,* 1614; or on cookery, *Murrels two bookes of cookerie and carving* (only fourth edition survives, 1631); or on botany and horticulture, John Parkinson's punning *Paradisi in sole paradisus terrestris,* 1629. ('Park' translates Greek 'paradise', an enclosed garden: the name shared by the book and its author alludes to the earthly paradise of a 'park in the sun'). Shakespeare, who by the plague-year of 1609 was undoubtedly a celebrated and authoritative drama-

tist and poet, may have intended to suggest, not only that the 1609 sequence, in contrast to the piratical *Passionate Pilgrim,* was the real McCoy, the long-awaited volume in which his truly authentic sonnet writings were to be found, but also that it was—as it has pretty much proved to be, historically—the absolutely definitive English sonnet sequence. The whole sonnet sequence movement in England had been started off by Sidney's *Astrophil and Stella,* composed in the early 1580s, but not printed until Thomas Newman's pirated quarto in 1591, in which it received a sub-title: 'Wherein the excellence of sweete Poesie is concluded'. For alert readers in 1591 who were aware of the *Defence of Poesy*—not to reach print until 1595—the sub-title may have suggested, 'You've read Sidney's poetic theory, now read his practice, in which he demonstrates conclusively "the excellence of sweete Poesie"'. But for other readers, probably the majority, who had not yet had a chance to read the *Defence,* the suggestion may have been, rather, that Sidney's *Astophel and Stella* (thus entitled) was the consummate, definitive example of the sweet, or sugared, sonnet sequence: it could never be bettered. It can be argued that it was indeed never bettered, until the salty, not sugary, sequence published in 1609. Shakespeare knew *Astrophil and Stella* well, and knew that his audiences did, too, as when he made the amorous Falstaff clod-hoppingly mimic the courtly young Astrophil in *The Merry Wives of Windsor,* III.iii.38. In calling his own sequence, published eighteen years later than Sidney's, and a quarter of a century after Sidney's death, SHAKESPEARES SONNETS, he may have intended to boast, spear-shakingly, that his was indeed the conclusive sonnet sequence of the age, the well-wrought construction of a poetic master-craftsman, the sonnet sequence to end all sonnet sequences. Turn to Blundevile for horsemanship, or Tarlton for jests: but if sonnets are what you want, turn to Shakespeare. *Shakespeare's Sonnets* is not only what the book is *called,* but what it *is.*

Notes

[1] Lewis Carroll, *Through the Looking Glass,* (1893) ed. R. Lancelyn Green, (1971), p. 218.

[2] For counter-arguments and evidence, see Katherine Duncan-Jones, 'Was the 1609 *Shakespeares Sonnets* really unauthorized?', *Review of English Studies,* N.S. 34 (1983), 151-71.

[3] Thomas Heywood, *An Apology for Actors,* (1612), sig. G4; William Drummond, supplementary notes on his conversations with Jonson, printed in *Works,* (1711), 226; John Benson, Epistle prefaced to *Poems: Written by Wil. Shakespeare. Gent,* (1640).

[4] Alexander's sonnet sequence *Aurora* was published in 1604.

[5] I have identified over fifty instances of 'genitive titles' in the *Short Title Catalogue.*

[6] R. B. McKerrow ed., *The Works of Thomas Nashe,* (1958), v. 194-6.

[7] Nashe, ed. cit. iii. 151.

[8] Herford and Simpson eds., *Ben Jonson,* (1927), iii. 95. However, Jonson had used the formula proudly five years earlier, in 'B.ION: HIS PART OF King James his Royall and Magnificent Entertainement', and 'B.I. HIS PANEGYRE . . . ', both 1604.

[9] Sidney Lee ed., *SHAKESPEARES SONNETS being a reproduction in facsimile . . . ,* (1905), 11.

[10] For an amusing account of Lee's unacknowledged turnabout, cf. S. Schoenbaum, *Shakespeare's Lives,* (1970), 506-12.

[11] W. G. Ingram and Theodore Redpath eds., *Shakespeare's Sonnets,* (1964), xi.

[12] Stephen Booth ed., *SHAKESPEARE'S SONNETS,* (New Haven and London 1977), 548.

[13] John Kerrigan ed., *The Sonnets and A Lover's Complaint,* (1986), 55, 74.

[14] W. A. Ringler ed., *The Poems of Sir Philip Sidney,* (1962), OA 32.36.

[15] J. W. Hebel ed., *The Works of Michael Drayton,* (1941), ii. 308.

[16] Lewis Carroll, *Through the Looking-Glass,* ed. cit., 218-9.

Source: "What are Shakespeare's sonnets called?," in *Essays in Criticism*, Vol. XLVII, No. 1, January, 1997, pp. 1-12.

"You speak a language that I understand not": The Rhetoric of Animation in *The Winter's Tale*

Lynn Enterline, *Yale University*

Between Leontes's opening imperative, "Tongue-tied our queen? Speak you" (1.2.28), and the final act, where Hermione as living statue returns to her husband yet says nothing directly to him, *The Winter's Tale* traces a complex, fascinated, and uneasy relation to female speech.[1] A play much noted for interrogating the "myriad forms of human narration"[2]—old tales, reports, ballads, oracles—*The Winter's Tale* begins its investigation of language when Hermione tellingly jests to Polixenes, "Verily, / You shall not go; a lady's 'verily' is / As potent as a lord's" (ll. 49-51), for Leontes's swift turn to suspicion hinges on the power of his wife's speech. Unable to persuade Polixenes to stay, he first expresses annoyance when Hermione is able to do so. Polixenes has just assured his boyhood friend "There is no tongue that moves, none, none i' th' world, / So soon as yours could win me" (ll. 20-21). Nonetheless, it is Hermione's tongue, not her husband's, that wins Polixenes. "You, sir, / Charge him too coldly," she chides Leontes before persuading their friend to stay (ll. 29-30). Leontes therefore shifts quickly from "Well said, Hermione" (l. 33), to churlish acknowledgment of her rhetorical power. He understands her persuasive speech not as obedience to his desire—since he is the one who commanded "Speak you"—but as a force that eclipses his own:

LEONTES   Is he won yet?
HERMIONE He'll stay, my lord.
LEONTES   At my request he would not.
                              (ll. 86-87)

From Hermione's success, jealous deductions quickly follow. Indeed, the first hint that something is amiss in this marriage is this seemingly minor quibble over who speaks to better purpose and who is the better rhetorician. When he later broaches with Camillo Polixenes's decision to stay, Leontes confirms his suspicions on the basis of his own earlier failure to persuade:

CAMILLO You had much ado to make his
     anchor hold,
When you cast out, it still came home.
LEONTES   Didst note it?
CAMILLO He would not stay at your petitions,
     made
His business more material.
LEONTES   Didst perceive it?
                              (ll. 213-16)

Outdone in rhetorical power by his wife. Leontes makes two interpretive moves to reassert control over her

language. First, he reminds Hermione of her answer to his proposal of marriage—in fact, he quotes her words of assent, "'I am yours for ever'" (l. 105)—and calls those words a "better" speech than the one to which Polixenes has yielded. And, second, he reads as evidence of infidelity the conversation he has himself induced between Hermione and his friend: "Too hot, too hot!" (l. 108). Making himself arbiter of Hermione's language, Leontes approvingly quotes the words he prefers while giving a fixed, suspicious meaning to the ones he does not. The scene's pronounced interest in acts of persuasion, one failed and the other successful, produces an odd effect: plunging into Leontes's jealousy, the scene makes his unreasonable emotion appear to be the consequence of this rivalry between male and female speech. As the drama quickly unfolds, we watch the king turn a rhetorical anxiety—why do her words achieve the desired effect where mine do not?—into a sexual one, minimizing his wife's superior rhetorical skill by interpreting it narrowly as the consequence of her erotic power. In Act 5, however, Hermione returns as a theatrical version of Pygmalion's silent statue to the husband who was once so jealous of her tongue. Almost but not quite "tongue-tied," she addresses herself to her lost daughter only. (I will return to her words to Perdita at the end of this essay.) After her theatrical metamorphosis, Hermione does not address the man who doubted her to the brink of annihilation. Having once triggered a terrible response with her voice, she now evades the problem by saying nothing to Leontes.[3]

I am tempted to say Hermione has learned her lesson. But as I hope to show, *The Winter's Tale* defies an intuitive understanding of the difference between speech and silence—or, for that matter, the difference between agency and impotence, male and female, often allied with it. The elaborate Pygmalion fantasy offered in the last scene as a way to resolve the problems inaugurated by Hermione's initially "potent" tongue tells us that before we can begin to hear the full resonance of her concluding silence, we must consider the relationship between, on the one hand, the trope of the female voice in the Ovidian-Petrarchan tradition that Shakespeare inherits and transforms in this play and, on the other, the quite specific rhetorical concerns through which *The Winter's Tale* reads that tradition, turning it into theatrical metacommentary. Any reading of the play's uneasy fascination with the female voice, that is, must take account of the complex literary legacy of Pygmalion's obsession with his mute *simulacrum*. As this silent figure passes from Ovid to Petrarch to Shakespeare, it criticizes even as it perpetuates a mysterious tie between love of art and hatred for women. Narratives of rape and misogyny frame the figure of the animated statue, tranishing the luster of a story that otherwise seems to be about love for beautiful form, visual as well as verbal. The literary legacy of Pygmalion's statue asks readers, therefore, to think again about the consequences of the many kinds, and discourses, of love.

I should preface this analysis by noting that when I speak of a "female voice" in this play, I mean to designate a pervasive and seductive trope—a discursive effect, not a prediscursive fact. Through the sound of the very "female" voice that inaugurates Leontes's jealousy, I will argue, the play distances itself from the king's essentializing effort to dismiss Hermione's rhetorical power by understanding it as erotic power only. Of course the arbitrary force of Leontes's jealous interpretation of his wife's tongue raises troubling questions about the violence latent in such culturally pervasive ideas as those of "male" speech and "female" silence. Because *The Winter's Tale* was written for a transvestite theater, moreover, I do not presume a given—or, more important, an intelligible—phenomenon anterior to the language that gives it shape (for instance, "woman" or "the female subject"). Reading the way in which the voices of Hermione and Leontes affect and implicate each other, I hope to show, tells us that—like Echo and Narcissus or Salmacis and Hermaphroditus—female and male voices in this very Ovidian play are locked in a mutually defining, differential embrace. An analysis of the "female voice" in *The Winter's Tale* is important precisely because it must change our understanding of that term.

Renaissance revisers of the *Metamorphoses* routinely adopt such stories as Ovid's Pygmalion as a way to comment on the medium of their appearance; Shakespeare is no exception. Ovid's own generic experimentation, his rhetorical and poetic self-reflexivity, and his habit of linking oral/aural dilemmas to visual ones encouraged in Renaissance imitators a highly self-conscious practice of borrowing.[4] Erotic stories from the *Metamorphoses* became highly charged reflections on the power (and dangers) of the story's very medium—whether painting, poetry, music, or drama. Such self-conscious visitations prepare us for Shakespeare's much noted—and celebrated—effort to turn Ovid's story of Pygmalion into one about the transforming powers of theatrical representation, about a theater that succeeds where even Orpheus failed: "I'll fill your grave up" (5.3.101). Because the idea of the living statue plays a crucial role in Shakespeare's claims for the theater and in our own critical reception of those claims, it becomes vital that we understand the epistemological and ethical consequences of the rhetoric of animation. For Shakespeare's final invocation of the living statue's "magic"

draws on a story that self-consciously proposes a close yet opaque alliance between aesthetics and misogyny. I will suggest that, in silence as in speech, the female voice in *The Winter's Tale* allows us to interrogate the terms and the limits of that alliance.

I. "SHALL I BE HEARD?"

To apprehend the burden Shakespeare assumes when he has Paulina tell Hermione to "bequeath to death" her "numbness," we must remember the symbolic and libidinal economy that informs the Pygmalion story in the two chief texts that gave it such tenacity as a fiction about voice, masculinity, and desire: Ovid's *Metamorphoses* and Petrarch's *Rime Sparse.* As Leonard Barkan writes, Hermione's metamorphosis enacts "a kind of marriage of Pygmalion and Petrarchanism."[5] In the *Rime Sparse,* Petrarch draws on numerous Ovidian characters to represent his own situation of unfulfilled desire; and in a pair of sonnets that praise Simone Martini's portrait of Laura, he brings Ovid's story of Pygmalion into the cycle as a particularly compelling analogue for his own predicament.[6] Two rhetorical issues are central to both Petrarch's and Shakespeare's versions of Ovid's Pygmalion: the trope of apostrophe and the language of praise or epideixis. By lamenting the picture's silence—"if only she could reply to my words!" (*"se risponder savesse a' detti miei!"*)— Petrarch's apostrophe creates the fiction of his own voice; a second apostrophe accentuates the fiction of a voice and the language of epideixis at once: "Pygmalion, how much you must praise yourself for your image (*"quanto lodar ti dei"*) if you received a thousand times what I yearn to have just once!" (78.11, 12-14).[7] In these concluding lines Petrarch rewrites Ovid's story according to one of the *Rime Sparse*'s controlling signifiers: *lodare.* He thereby refashions Ovid's Pygmalion in his own image, reading him as an artist devoted to *praising* himself for the excellence of his *simulacrum.* Petrarch derives the name Laura from the Latin *laudare* and, according to the *Secretum,* loves the name just as much as he loves the lady herself.[8]

In *The Winter's Tale,* Shakespeare reads the tradition Petrarch's poetry inaugurated in precise rhetorical terms—in terms, that is, of the power of address and of epideixis. Long before staging his own kinds of address to a composite Ovidian-Petrarchan statue ("Chide me, dear stone" or "descend; be stone no more; approach" [5.3.24, 99]), Shakespeare fits the representation of Hermione (and Leontes's relation to her) into a meditation on epideictic speech. Where *The Rape of Lucrece* explores the violent consequences of Petrarchan epideixis—because "Collatine unwisely did not let / To praise" Lucrece to other men (ll. 10-11), rape is the consequence[9]—*The Winter's Tale* gives us a Hermione who, in jest, offers herself as the beloved object of praise:

What? have I twice said well? When was't
   before?
I prithee tell me; cram's with praise, and
   make's
As fat as tame things. One good deed dying
   tongueless
Slaughters a thousand waiting upon that.
Our praises are our wages.

                        (1.2.90-94)

Understood in light of Shakespeare's critique of praise in *The Rape of Lucrece,* Hermione's pose as epideictic object for her husband while in the presence of another man should alert us that the rhetorical competition between Hermione and Leontes may already have entered the troubled world of Petrarchan verbal exchanges gone awry. Indeed, Hermione's very participation in a rhetorical competition with one man to vie for another man's ear alerts us that culturally dominant alignments of gender and rhetoric do not pertain. Her "potent" rhetoric disrupts received expectations for epideictic speech. And so in this play, terrible consequences attend *Hermione*'s speaking, even though Leontes is the character whom her playful remarks about praise might lead us to believe will follow Collatine as ill-fated epideictic rhetorician. Instead of hearing more from Leontes, however, we hear from Hermione; and what she speaks about is her own power of speech. Her balanced syntax hints to the jealous ear that, just as they are matched in her discourse, the two men may be equivalent objects for her exchange: "I have spoke to th' purpose twice: / The one for ever earn'd a royal husband; / Th' other for some while a friend" (ll. 106-8). As if following her lead into the language of payment and exchange, Leontes begins to angle for proof by changing Hermione's equation of the two men into a marketplace where she is *their* commodity: "Hermione, / How thou lov'st us, show in our brother's welcome; / Let what is dear in Sicily be cheap" (ll. 173-75). While the rest of the play may seem to return to expected discursive convention by making Hermione (and her fidelity) the enigmatic object of others' discourse—in praise and in slander—that predicament, we should remember, is initiated in Act 1 by the unexpected power of her persuasive tongue.

The play's most striking debt to the Petrarchan tradition, of course, emerges in the final scene when a stony lady comes to life. Both Ovid and Petrarch use what Kenneth Gross aptly calls "the dream of the moving statue" as an erotic, synesthetic investigation of the status of the human voice and the consequences of rhetorical speech. In both, as in Shakespeare's play, this investigation occurs by way of a meditation on the success or failure of an *address.* In each of the three texts, this address draws our attention to the way that all parties present are implicated in and defined by the verbal event. Before looking more carefully at Petrarch's version of Pygmalion, however, we must first under-

stand the complex connections between rhetoric, voice, and sexuality which he inherited from Ovid's poem.

In the *Metamorphoses,* Pygmalion's wishes come true because he addresses words of prayer to Venus. The story of animation, the event of the statue's motion, offers an erotic version of a rhetorician's dream. The scene's action and considerable dramatic effect (waiting for a statue to move) derives from a pun on the desired end of rhetorical speech. Drawing on the contemporary word for rhetorical power—the power, that is, to "move" (*movere*)—the narrator tells us that in his statue, Pygmalion believes he has an audience who "*wants* to be moved" (X.251).[10] And because the narrator of the story is the grieving Orpheus, yet another compelling fantasy about the voice's power informs the ivory maiden's animation. Shakespeare, too, connects the stories of Orpheus and Pygmalion. After the "statue" moves, Paulina warns Leontes: "Do not shun her / Until you see her die again, for then / You kill her double" (5.3.105-7). Paulina's imperative deftly combines the story of Pygmalion's statue with that of Orpheus's Eurydice by implying two things: like the statue, Hermione has come to life; and because of this animation, she may, like Eurydice, die twice. Indeed, Golding's translation of Ovid's text may have suggested Paulina's wording. For Ovid's version of Eurydice's "twin" death—"*stupuit gemina nece coniugis Orpheus*" (X.69)—Golding renders, "This double dying of his wyfe set Orphye in a stound."[11]

The interwoven stories of Orpheus and Pygmalion seem, at first glance, to propose a familiar hierarchy between male verbal agency on the one hand and female silence and death on the other. Where the sculptor's prayer succeeds, the statue says nothing and has no name; where Orpheus's song momentarily takes over the narrative of the poem—thus predicating Book X of the *Metamorphoses* itself on Eurydice's absence—Eurydice utters a barely audible "*vale*" before "falling back again to the place whence she had come" (X.63). As Petrarch realized, the first (male verbal agency) seems to depend on the second (female silence and death). But trouble soon disturbs this too-sanguine version of male vocal power. Once able to move the inanimate world by "moving his voice in song" ("*hoc vocem carmine movit*" [1. 147]), Orpheus dies because Bacchic (female) noise drowns out his voice: the "huge uproar" of discordant flutes, horns, drums, "and howlings of the Bacchanals" overwhelms the sound of Orpheus's lyre ("*ingens / clamor . . . et Bacchei ululatus*" [XI.15-18]). Once-listening stones turn to weapons, stones now "reddened with the blood of the bard whose voice was unheard" ("*saxa / non exauditi rubuerunt sanguine vatis*" [II. 18-19]). And where Pygmalion succeeds in animating his beloved, his narrator fails. Having won Eurydice only to lose her again through his own action, Orpheus then sings a song in which we hear the story of yet another beloved woman given life through art. Orpheus's *failure* underwrites the story he tells, making the fantasy of the statue's animation part of the wishful *fort-da* game of his impossible desire. These interwoven narratives therefore tell us that power is fleetingly, intermittently, and only phantasmatically granted the male voice. And they tell us, moreover, that his voice may not be the only sound that matters.

Still, we must acknowledge that Eurydice's death and the unnamed statue's silence in the Orpheus-Pygmalion sequence conform to a larger fantasy, first proposed in Book I of the *Metamorphoses,* in which male vocal triumph requires female absence or resistance. Two stories of attempted rape—Apollo's pursuit of Daphne and Pan's of Syrinx—tell the origins of epideictic and pastoral poetry by presenting a rigid sexual division of labor in the production of song. Close on Daphne's heels, the god of poetry fails to persuade and so becomes himself *because* she eludes his grasp.[12] And hard on the heels of that encounter follows Pan's pursuit of Syrinx, an attempted rape that repeats and intensifies the first. Where Apollo's breathing down Daphne's neck becomes the breath of poetry, Pan's breath turns into music as he sighs through the newly immobilized body of Syrinx: "the soft air stirring in the reeds gave forth a low and complaining sound" (*"sonum tenuem similemque querenti"* [I.708]). In the context of this violence, remember that yet other forms of misogyny underwrite the Orpheus-Pygmalion sequence. Grieving for Eurydice, Orpheus "shunned all love of womankind," becoming the "author" in Thrace of "giving his love to tender boys" (*"omnemque refugerat Orpheus / femineam Venerem . . . ille etiam Thracum populis fuit auctor amorem / in teneros"* [X.79-84]).[13] Pygmalion's "disgust" for female sexual behavior repeats his narrator's aversion: having seen the prostitution of the Propoetides, he creates a statue "better than any woman born" (*"qua femina nasci / nulla potest"* [II. 248-49]) to eradicate the "faults that nature had so liberally given the female mind" (*"vitiis, quae plurima menti / femineae natura dedit"* [II. 244-45]). For rejecting women, Orpheus will soon die at the hands of the Bacchantes. Ovid thus twice qualifies Pygmalion's seeming aesthetic triumph, suggesting that it is rooted in misogyny; aversion to women is its inaugural gesture.[14] The Bacchic cry upon seeing Orpheus—"here is the man who scorns us!" (*"hic est nostri contemptor!"* [XI.7])—claims that revenge is the best this erotic-symbolic economy can expect.[15]

Such misogyny was not lost on later writers. In "The Metamorphosis of Pigmalions Image" (1598), John Marston summarizes his reading of Pygmalion concisely:

> Pigmalion, whose hie love-hating minde
> Disdain'd to yeeld servile affection,
> Or amorous sute to any woman-kinde,
> Knowing their wants, and mens perfection.

> Yet Love at length forc'd him to know his fate,
> And love the shade, whose substance he did hate.[16]

As Shakespeare's only other direct reference to the story suggests, he is more than familiar with this "love-hating" tradition. In *Measure for Measure* the phrase "Pygmalion's image" means "prostitute," exactly recalling the reason for Pygmalion's creative act. "What, is there none of Pygmalion's images newly made woman to be had now, for putting the hand in the pocket and extracting [it] clutch'd?" (3.2.44-47).[17] In this version of the story, the fantasy of animation *is* the moment of sexual penetration (i.e., "to make a woman" is to deflower a virgin). Both Shakespeare and his audience were well aware of the sexual and misogynist aspects of the story that are omitted in order to achieve closure in *The Winter's Tale.* If we ignore the negative aspects of the Pygmalion tradition, we foreclose the possibility of thinking about the work and effects of repression in the play's last scene—or, for that matter, about the problem that Ovid's narrative so memorably posed: what, precisely, *is* the relationship between misogyny and art?[18]

In the first three acts Leontes's skepticism places the "truth" of Hermione's body (her innocence or her guilt) beyond the reach of words—beyond the reach, even, of oracular speech. Similarly, the final scene turns to a story in which evasion of the female body is representation's foundational premise: Pygmalion's statue is *not* mimetic; it is "better than any woman born." From this disquieting gap between language and the world, Shakespeare aspires to a mode of representation that can move beyond the impasse. If, as most critics agree, the spectacle of Hermione's pregnancy troubles the play's language from the start (most obviously in Polixenes's opening reference to "nine months"), this spectacle works together with her potent tongue to spark her husband's suspicions. The final scene of animation therefore works to reclaim another, "better" mode of generation than the one that so disturbs Leontes's understanding of the world. In constructing this scene, Shakespeare tries to replace the animating power of the maternal body with the language and visual spectacle of the theater.[19]

The play's implied claim for theatrical power, then, derives from a literary history of aversion to female flesh. But this is not the only story the play tells about its own fiction. I want to suggest not only that Hermione's concluding silence criticizes the symbolic-erotic economy inaugurated in Book I of the *Metamorphoses* and developed in the Orpheus-Pygmalion sequence, but that this economy itself tells us something important about why Hermione's speech is so unexpectedly powerful. It is as if the first half of *The Winter's Tale* were asking of this legacy, what would happen if the stony lady actually did speak back? To understand the play's question, we need only remember that Pygmalion's statue is both nameless and speechless. Or that Eurydice, lost again, says only "farewell" before finally disappearing in death. Although the first book of the *Metamorphoses* initially proposes a sexual division of labor in the creation of poetry and the Orpheus segment adds death to rape as one of the possible roles for women in the process of inventing poetic song, readers may have heard the murmur of a story different from the one that emerges from a focus on the activities of Apollo, Pan, or Orpheus. For in the line I quoted about Pan's music, Ovid leaves unclear exactly *whose* voice is audible in these pipes: "Instead of [Syrinx] he held nothing but marsh reeds . . . and while he sighed in disappointment, the soft air stirring in the reeds gave forth a low and complaining sound" (I.708). Ovid lets us wonder, whose sound is this? The complaint seems as much Syrinx's as Pan's. The female voice troubles the Apollo-Daphne story, too, thus disturbing one of the *Metamorphoses*'s most prominent narratives about the origins of poetry. Where Apollo's "imperfect" rhetoric (*"verba imperfecta"*) fails to persuade her to stay, Daphne's prayer to lose the "figure" that provokes such violence convinces her father to change her shape. Her words possess a persuasive force that Apollo's do not; they inaugurate one of the metamorphoses that are the subject of Ovid's poem. If Book I creates the expectation that the poem will focus on male vocal power, that expectation is soon thwarted. In a series of influential stories, Ovid ventriloquizes numerous women, obliquely yet consistently hinting that these female characters are violated by the very mode of representation available to them. Echo's mimicking voice, Syrinx's complaining reed, Philomela's severed tongue, and, I would argue, Medusa's fearsome face mark female experience in the *Metamorphoses* as a struggle against the restrictive conditions within which they must represent themselves.[20] To return to the case in point: Daphne's metapoetic plea—that she lose her *"figura"*—tells us that the figural quality of language betrays her just as surely as her bodily form makes her vulnerable to Apollo's violence.[21] For when Daphne prays to lose her figure and is turned into a tree, she may not have meant to lose her human form: when used to signify the body rather than language, *figura* designates not only general shape but also a person's beauty.[22] What Daphne means to ask is to become less attractive, but what she actually *says* prompts her father to alter her human figure altogether. The relief brought her by the unintended power of her prayer is just as constricting as the figural language with which she must speak— language that departs "from the straightforward and obvious"[23] and whose obliquity therefore condemns her to be "immobilized" or "stuck fast" with "sluggish roots" (*"pigris radicibus haeret"* [l. 551]). Her voice may *do* more than Apollo's, her words may achieve greater effects, but their action eclipses her

intention. And this sense of violation by language, I believe, forms the basis of Ovid's insistent alliance of the origin of poetry with rape.[24]

This aspect of Ovid's poem—in which female voices such as Daphne's are betrayed by the very words they speak—helps us to understand Hermione's courtroom protest that she stands somehow outside the restrictive terms of Leontes's accusation: "Sir, / You speak a language that I understand not" (3.2.79-80). To the woman who will later be restored to life as a version of Pygmalion's statue, her husband's "language," like his jealousy, violates her sense of herself. Hermione's ensuing remark about the deadly effects of fantasy— "My life stands in the level of your dreams, / Which I'll lay down"—then provokes Leontes's most concise statement of his Pygmalionlike revision of womankind: "Your actions are my dreams" (ll. 81-82). As both Apollo's desire and figurative language ensnare Daphne yet give her voice an unforeseen efficacy, so the collusion between language and male fantasy frames Hermione yet does not utterly deprive her voice of power. *The Winter's Tale* may mark her words as insufficient to tell the truth or command belief, yet it also gives her voice the power to unhinge her husband's sense of the world itself: "Is this nothing? / Why then the world and all that's in't is nothing" (1.2.292-93).

And the corollary aspect of Ovid's poem—in which female voices suggest that male voices are not so powerful as the stories of rape or of animation might lead one to believe—illuminates why Leontes, once he has lost the rhetorical competition with his wife, spends much of the play trying (and failing) to control his own language and the language of others. For Leontes the fact that tongues other than his own can speak becomes an increasing source of irritation. When his lords voice their initial opposition to his accusation of adultery, Leontes snaps: "Hold your peaces" (2.1.139). He then dismisses their comments as an infringement of his power:

> Why, what need we
> Commune with you of this, but rather follow
> Our forceful instigation? Our prerogative
> Calls not your counsels . . .
> We need no more of your advice. The matter,
> The loss, the gain, the ord'ring on't, is all
> Properly ours.
>
> (ll. 161-70)

Leontes always speaks as if his voice alone should be heard. When accusing Hermione, he leans on the implicit power of his own voice: "*I have said* / She's an adult'ress, *I have said* with whom" (ll. 87-88, my emphasis). The mere existence of a king's saying, he believes, should be enough to establish facts. Where Orpheus tried and failed to use his voice to master death, Leontes tries and fails to use the power of his tongue to master truth.[25] In both cases women's bodies become the signifiers of that desire. Leontes, moreover, pairs his sense of his own linguistic prerogative with a declaration designed to preempt all other voices whatsover: "He who shall speak for her is afar off guilty / *But that he speaks*" (ll. 104-5, my emphasis). To Leontes anyone else's discourse is but a further sign of guilt. This is so, I submit, because Leontes, like an Orpheus singing alone in the woods, can bear to hear only the sound of his own tongue.

The king aspires to order all linguistic exchanges in Sicily, but Hermione's voice teaches him that any such ordering properly belongs to no one. Just as she obeys his command, "Speak you," in Act 1 only to challenge Leontes's sense of authority over acts of persuasion, so in Act 2, scene 1, Hermione speaks in obedience to his command with words that prompt Leontes to assert that his voice has again been eclipsed. Although Leontes has just ordered "Away with her, to prison" (l. 103) and his order is obeyed, by the end of Hermione's speech, Leontes protests that he has somehow gone unheard. Hermione addresses herself to the attendant lords in words that obey the king's command and yet seem to him to undermine it:

> HERMIONE . . . Beseech you all, my lords,
> With thoughts so qualified as your charities
> Shall best instruct you, measure me; and so
> The King's will be perform'd!
> LEONTES   *Shall I be heard?*
> HERMIONE Who is't that goes with me?
>   (ll. 112-16, my emphasis)

Hermione cedes the power of action to Leontes's word, but her token of obedience makes that word ring hollow. The act of "go[ing]"—an act that follows the letter of the king's order—begins, in her mouth, to sound like a declaration of alliance: "Who is't that goes with me?" To counter her question, Leontes can do no more than repeat himself as he tries to reassert power over one word: "Go, do our bidding; hence!" (l. 125).

Indeed the play as a whole instructs Leontes that the linguistic marketplace he hopes to master cannot be negotiated by the careful parsing out of what he calls "the loss, the gain." He finds that it cannot be ordered by the logic of equivalence at all: language, in this play, repeatedly exceeds Leontes's demand. Certain that the oracle will prove him right, Leontes finds himself instead proclaimed a "jealous tyrant" (3.2.133-34). Responding to the charge with "this is mere falsehood" (l. 141), Leontes is confronted with the news of Mamillius's death, a death that results from Leontes's having doubted oracular speech. Or so Leontes understands it: "Apollo's angry, and the heavens themselves / Do strike at my injustice" (ll. 146-47). And so Leontes finds himself, like Ovid's Orpheus, brought low by the clamorous noise of a crowd. In Shakespeare's interro-

gation of the fear of losing one's rhetorical power, however, Leontes's distrust of other voices turns into an imaginary scene in which he is encircled by "whisp'ring" gossip rather than Bacchic cries: "They're here with me already, whisp'ring, rounding: / 'Sicilia is a so-forth.' 'Tis far gone, / When I shall gust it last" (1.2.217-19).

It is the tongues of Hermione and Paulina together, however, that most distinctly instruct Leontes in what I take to be the lesson of Orpheus: that power resides only fleetingly in one's voice, even if it be the voice of a poet or a king. In the scene of Hermione's arrest (2.1), the queen notifies her husband, as she did indirectly in the first act, that he cannot bring all language—even his own—under control. Though Leontes may claim that "the matter" and "the ord' ring" of his accusation of adultery is "all / Properly ours," she teaches him otherwise. Once published, Hermione reminds him, a text will go its own way. It can be controlled by no mere speaking:

> How will this grieve you,
> When you shall come to clearer knowledge,
>   that
> You thus have publish'd me! Gentle my
>   lord,
> You scarce can right me thoroughly, then, to
>   say
> You did mistake.
>   (ll. 96-100)

Unable to master the truth by mastering other voices, Shakespeare's Orpheus/Leontes soon finds himself heavily beset by the tongue of Paulina. In her, Leontes contends with a voice that resists all ordering:

> LEONTES   [What] noise there, ho?
> PAULINA No noise, my lord, but needful
>   conference
> About some gossips for your Highness.
> LEONTES   How?
> Away with that audacious lady! Antigonus,
> I charg'd thee that she should not come about
>   me:
> I knew she would.
>   (2.3.39-44)

Like an Ovidian bad penny, Paulina returns to avenge her mistress. "A callat / Of boundless tongue, who," Leontes claims, "late hath beat her husband" (ll. 91-92), Paulina plagues Leontes with her "noise." A domestic version of the Bacchic horde, Paulina has a tongue that no man controls. Thus the harassed Leontes rebukes her husband, "What? canst not rule her?" (l. 46). Paulina, the somewhat softened spirit of a revenging Ovidian woman, goes about her work with a tongue that will, after sixteen years, cure Leontes rather than kill him.

II. "NOT GUILTY"

We have seen that when Shakespeare adopts the imagined scene of speaking to a stony lady as a way to repair the devastation caused by Leontes's jealousy, he turns the conflict between male and female verbal power into a meditation on Ovidian and Petrarchan rhetoric in general and on the role of the female voice in that literary legacy in particular. Before looking more closely at the telling role female voices play in *The Winter's Tale,* however, we must examine the vicissitudes of the voice in the *Rime Sparse,* particularly for those Ovidian characters whom Petrarch borrows as so many figures for his own situation. Like many of his literary contemporaries, Shakespeare frequently juxtaposes Ovidian rhetoric with Petrarchan in order to derive a flexible lexicon of figures for sexual experience, whether erotic or violent. Recall, for instance, that Marcus greets the mutilated Lavinia, Shakespeare's Philomela, with the conventional language of a *blason* in praise of her beauty and talent (*Titus Andronicus,* 2.4.22-47). Similarly, the narrator of *The Rape of Lucrece* sets his critique of Petrarchan epideixis in an explicitly Ovidian context, rewriting the story of Lucretia from the *Fasti* in terms of several other Ovidian characters: most notably, Philomela, Orpheus, and Hecuba. Understanding the *Rime Sparse* and Ovid's presence in it will help clarify why the female voice occasionally exercises such disruptive force in a play that ends with yet another version of Pygmalion's address to his statue.

In Sonnet 78 Petrarch's apostrophe to Ovid's Pygmalion epitomizes the rhetorical and erotic concerns of the *Rime Sparse,* bequeathing strategies, tropes, and effects to one of the most influential modes of Renaissance self-representation, and allowing the poet ample room to compare the relative merits of visual and verbal figuration. Because Petrarch, as a second Pygmalion, cannot make the picture speak, the speaker's desire for words replaces Ovid's scene of desire for a new and improved woman. Words, not sex, become the focus of the poet's longing: "if only she could reply to my words!" From Petrarch's repression of Ovid's bluntly sexual scene, verbal fetishism is born.[26] And so, too, is an imaginary conversation—not between Petrarch and Laura but between Petrarch and Pygmalion ("Pygmalion, how much you must praise yourself for your image . . ."). Laura's muteness, of course, is the necessary condition for this all-male conversation about aesthetic merit. And her silence deeply influenced English Petrarchanism: Barkan recalls Daniel's figure of the "marble brest" and "stony heart" and Marston's distinctly lascivious use of the metaphor. Indeed, the power relations implicit in the convention of the poet pleading with his silent mistress fuel Marston's satire of Petrarchanism: "O that my Mistres were an Image too, / That I might blameles her perfections view."[27]

Despite Marston's telling barb about the erotic advantages of female silence, however, and despite Petrarch's rhetorical turn in Sonnet 78 to speak to another male artist about her silence, the distinctions of power implied by such figures as Pygmalion's statue are not absolute in the *Rime Sparse.* The seemingly silenced female voice does, on occasion, interrupt Petrarchan self-reflection. First, the persona who takes Apollo's story as his own also represents himself as "Echo," exiled by the very language in which he represents his fate. Like Echo or Daphne, the poem's speaker is betrayed by his own speech; in canzone 23 his echoing song angers Laura as Diana, who imprisons the poet in stone (ll. 13, 64-66, 138-40). As with both Ovid's and Shakespeare's reflections on male and female voices, Petrarch's trope of echo implicates the fate of one voice in that of another. The male voice leans on various female voices from Ovid's text in order to define itself.[28] Echo's may not seem the kind of verbal power an aspiring Apollo would want to claim, since it disrupts any sure sense of intention or origin; yet it remains a kind of power nonetheless. Like Echo, the poet is never able to make his pain "resound" sweetly or softly enough so as to persuade ("*né mai in sì dolci o in sì soavi tempre / risonar seppi gli amorosi guai / che 'l cor s'umiliasse aspro et feroce*" [23.64-66]). But such failure finds its Apollonian solace in the aesthetic pleasures of Petrarchan autobiography: "every valley echoes to the sound of heavy sighs which prove how painful my life is" ("*et quasi in ogni valle / rimbombi il suon de' miei gravi sospiri, / ch' acquistan fede a la penosa vita*" [23.12-14]).

Second, though Laura rarely speaks in the *Rime Sparse,* her few words wield authority. As Diana, she utters the taboo against speaking that subtends the cycle: "make no word of this" ("*'Di ciò non far parola'*" [23.74]). Her prohibition enables Petrarch to portray himself as one driven by compulsion to write about what is forbidden. Laura's sentence against his speech becomes, paradoxically, the positive condition for Petrarch's appearance as the speaking subject in exile. Like the undertone in the complaining sound that issues from Syrinx's reed, Laura's spoken taboo is that without which we would not hear Petrarch's voice. Indeed, in the *Rime Sparse* as a whole, Laura's voice, when heard, carries the force of prohibition or revelation. "Soft, angelic," and "divine" ("*in voce . . . soave, angelica, divina*" [167.3-4]), it attracts her lover like "the sound of the sirens" ("*di sirene al suono*" [207.82]). I therefore understand the seeming polarity between male speech and female silence in Petrarch's rendition of the Pygmalion story in light of the larger fantasies about the poet's own symbolic and erotic condition, which give the female voice, though infrequently heard, an unsettling power.[29]

This voice articulates the specific rhetorical concerns that preoccupy Shakespeare as he transforms this

Ovidian-Petrarchan legacy into a figure for the theater. Act 1, scene 2, the scene of rhetorical competition, opens with a brief meditation on the power and limits of a particular speech act: Polixenes complains of the imbalance between "thank you" and the time it takes to say it.

> Nine changes of the wat'ry star hath been
> The shepherd's note since we have left our
> throne
> Without a burthen. Time as long again
> Would be fill'd up, my brother, with our
> thanks,
> And yet we should, for perpetuity,
> Go hence in debt. And therefore, like a cipher
> (Yet standing in rich place), I multiply
> With one "We thank you" many thousands
> moe
> That go before it.
>
> (1.2.1-9)

Leontes's reply, however, only reopens the debt that Polixenes's "I multiply" was meant to close: "Stay your thanks a while, / And pay them when you part" (ll. 9-10). Polixenes's verbal maneuvers open a rhetorically self-conscious play in which Shakespeare continues to test language's power as a mode of action rather than mere vehicle of representation, to search for a kind of voice that can effect the changes of which it speaks. Moreover, the verbal power that Polixenes desires in this scene and Paulina finally stages in the last raises the same question—the question of language's ability to transcend time. As the concluding scene's greater success suggests, Shakespeare asks this question most pointedly through the sound of the female voice—Leontes's less than "tongue-tied" queen and the "boundless tongue" of her faithful Paulina. He does so in such a way, I submit, that the (barely) suppressed undercurrent of illicit sexuality in Polixenes's opening references to nine months and "standing in rich place" comes to define the very notion of time.

Let us examine exactly how this happens. Beginning with Polixenes's desire for words that can discharge a debt—for some kind of verbal action—the play's rhetorical concern is precisely delimited by its often-repeated doublet, "to say" and "to swear." Preoccupied with the inability of any statement to prove Hermione innocent and the concomitant failure of all speech to persuade Leontes of the truth, the first three acts of *The Winter's Tale* continually present us with this pair, "to say" and "to swear." The doublet appears early: in the first scene of rhetorical and sexual competition, Hermione says of Polixenes, "To tell he longs to see his son were strong; / But let him say so then, and let him go; / But let him swear so, and he shall not stay, / We'll thwack him hence with distaffs" (ll. 34-37). Similarly, when Leontes charges Hermione directly, "'tis Polixenes / Has made thee swell thus," she re-

sponds: "But I'd say he had not; / And I'll be sworn you would believe my saying, / Howe'er you lean to th' nayward" (2.1.61-64). This iterated pair of verbs draws a distinction similar to the one made by J. L. Austin in his theory of the difference between constative and performative utterances, between *saying*—words that "'describe' some state of affairs . . . either truly or falsely"—and *swearing*—words in which to say something is "to do it."[30] In *The Winter's Tale* oath-taking and swearing faith take on the peculiar urgency of futility, since neither utterances that aspire to state the truth nor words conventionally designated as actions exercise any force.

Indeed we might say that this pair, saying and swearing, precisely distinguishes the two halves of the play. In Act 3, Paulina is the first woman whose spoken words command belief: "I say she's dead; I'll swear't. If word nor oath / Prevail not, go and see" (3.2.203-4). Before Paulina's oath no proof or belief attended woman's word. For women, according to Leontes, "will say anything" (1.2.131). After Paulina's oath Leontes views female speaking differently: "Go on, go on," he says to her, "Thou canst not speak too much" (3.2.214-15). But just as Leontes invokes the evidence of sight without ever having visual proof—Hermione's adultery "lack'd sight only" (2.1.177)—Paulina's imperative makes the "fact" of Hermione's death, like the "fact" of her innocence, a kind of metatheatrical crime: the one thing the audience *cannot* do is "go and see." The truth of Hermione's body—its innocence and its death—is always held from view; all that remains is the evidence of "word" and "oath." Where neither "word nor oath" allow Hermione to testify to the truth of her innocence, Paulina's oath marks the moment when a woman's words do finally work—but only to testify to a lie. Only a lie—Hermione is dead—establishes the trust in Leontes necessary for her to live as innocent. Only this lie to the audience, moreover, allows Shakespeare the surprise ending of the living statue that claims such powers for the theater.[31] Between Hermione's vain though truthful swearing of innocence and Paulina's successful yet false swearing of death, *The Winter's Tale* uses the female voice to point beyond truth or falsehood, beyond a conception of language as transparent description. Instead it asks us to consider the *effects* of language—particularly female language but also theatrical language—in relation to the fugitive truth of the female body and the "old tale" it tells.[32]

In the courtroom scene, saying and swearing come together at the moment of their failing. The oracle, for instance, is truth-telling's last chance. That telling is supposed to be secured by another performative, for the officers, swearing "upon this sword of justice" that they have been "at Delphos, and from thence have brought / This seal'd-up oracle," open it and read: "'Hermione is chaste, Polixenes blameless, . . . Leontes a jealous tyrant,'" and so on (3.2.124, 126-27, 132-

34). Leontes merely declares, "There is no truth at all i' th' oracle" (l. 140). But in this scene, it is Hermione's voice in particular that puts performative language on trial by stressing its failure and, at the same time, connecting that failure to the central problem of the play. For her commentary on her own speaking, like Paulina's false oath that Hermione is dead, connects the transformation of language into action with the play's two chief preoccupations: the "truth" of the female body and the effects of theatrical representation. Brought forward to testify, Hermione declares her innocence by commenting on her own lack of vocal power. She quotes the one performative for which she longs but which, in this context, will not work:

> Since what I am to say must be but that
> Which contradicts my accusation, and
> The testimony on my part no other
> But what comes from myself, it shall scarce
>   boot me
> To say, "Not guilty."
>
> (ll. 22-26)

Quoting the performative that in her mouth and in this place must misfire, Hermione's meditation on the inefficacy of saying "Not guilty" does two things. First, it constructs Leontes as tyrant for bringing her forth in a courtroom where no words can acquit her. Commenting on her own inability to speak, Hermione claims that her predicament, viewed by a higher, divine witness, "shall make / False accusation blush, and tyranny / Tremble at patience" (ll. 30-32). The necessary misfiring of Hermione's "Not guilty" becomes the verbal event that marks Leontes, against his hopes, as "tyrannous" (l. 5). Second, Hermione's meditation on the necessary failure of her "Not guilty" recalls an earlier "Not guilty." This one is first spoken offstage, but it defines the time of the play as the fallen time of sexuality. In Act 1, Polixenes remembers a prelapsarian idyll of male bonding. Of his boyhood friendship with Leontes he remarks,

> We were as twinn'd lambs that did frisk i' th'
>   sun,
> And bleat the one at th' other. What we
>   chang'd
> Was innocence for innocence; we knew not
> The doctrine of ill-doing, nor dream'd
> That any did.
>
> (1.2.67-71)

Had this edenic state continued, he claims, "we should have answer'd heaven / Boldly, 'Not guilty'; the imposition clear'd, / Hereditary ours" (ll. 73-75). In the decidedly less than innocent time of the play, "Not guilty," though boldly declared, will *not* clear "the imposition." Instead the immediate action of a prelapsarian performative is nullified by the sight of the female body:

> HERMIONE   By this we gather
> You have tripp'd since.
> POLIXENES   O my most sacred lady,
> Temptations have since then been born to 's:
>   for
> In those unfledg'd days was my wife a girl;
> Your precious self had then not cross'd the
>   eyes
> Of my young playfellow.
>
> (ll. 75-80)

Like Leontes's suspicious interpretation of her pregnancy, of course, Polixenes's comments on Leontes's fall from innocence mark Hermione's body as a sign of transgression. But the echoing of "Not guilty" across the play turns the female *voice,* too, into another mark of transgression. For the possibility of saying a "Not guilty" that performs the action of absolution belonged to a world without women. When young men answered to heaven, there was no human convention to be violated and so deprive these words of efficacious action. With a language so natural as that of lambs bleating, heaven automatically witnesses and ratifies all performatives; the one who enters a plea simultaneously delivers his own verdict. Between the two very different circumstances for saying "Not guilty," Shakespeare defines the play's time as one of broken linguistic conventions—conventions broken, moreover, around the question of sexual guilt. Turning what Shoshana Felman calls the scandal of the *"speaking body"* into the scandal of the speaking *maternal* body, Shakespeare sets *The Winter's Tale* in a time when woman's performative "Not guilty" cannot act.[33]

The failure of Hermione's "Not guilty" is implicit in Austin's definition of the performative. As Felman demonstrates of Austin's work, the performative is "defined only through the dimension of failure."[34] That failure is, however, not simple; it produces further effects. If the conventional rules governing a performative utterance are not in effect—if, as Austin writes, when we say "I do" in a marriage ceremony, "we are not in a position to do the act because we are, say, married already"—that does not mean that "I do" will be "void or without effect." Instead, "lots of things will have been done": for instance, "we shall most interestingly have committed the act of bigamy."[35] What other effects, then, follow from Hermione's meditation on the impossibility of saying "Not guilty"? As we have already seen, the inevitable misfiring of her "Not guilty" turns Leontes's court into a mockery, the ruse of a tyrant who has already determined the verdict. Within the fictions of the play and of Leontes's justice, Hermione's refusal to enter a plea defines, by rhetorical means, the extent of the king's tyranny.

But more radically still, the self-reflexivity that defines all performatives reminds us, suddenly, that we are not only in the mock courtroom of a tyrant. We are also in the mock courtroom of a play. Of such a fictive situation, Austin observes that "a performative utterance will . . . be *in a peculiar way* hollow or void if said by an actor on the stage."[36] I do not cite Austin's observation here in order to endorse his distinction between a "non-serious" theatrical use of language and a "serious" or "ordinary" use of language. Jacques Derrida, Barbara Johnson, and Shoshana Felman have amply demonstrated that such a distinction is untenable. But each of these critics argues, as well, that Austin's failed distinction is extremely revealing. When Austin writes that something "peculiar" is at work onstage or in a poem, his choice of words reminds us that his work is "often more fruitful in the acknowledgment of its impasses than in its positions."[37] I recall Austin's unsuccessful distinction, rather, because of the considerable theoretical work on the status of the speaking subject which it has enabled. For Derrida, Austin's attempt to exclude "non-ordinary" poetic or theatrical language from his theory of performative action turns on a foundational belief in consciousness or intention: "the conscious presence of the intention of the speaking subject in the totality of his speech act." Derrida argues that this exclusion allows Austin to avoid acknowledging the "general citationality" or "general iterability" that is the "risk" or "failure" internal to all performative intentions—their "positive condition of possibility." It is not that the "category of intention will disappear," only that intention will no longer "govern the entire scene and system of utterance": "the intention animating the utterance will never be through and through present to itself and its content."[38] Derrida therefore argues that an "absence of intention" is "essential" to performative utterances; and he calls such absence the performative's "structural unconscious."[39] In *The Literary Speech Act,* Felman elaborates the full psychoanalytic resonance of such a phrase, discussing the consequences of the performative's "structural unconscious" for her understanding of the condition of the speaking subject. Reading Austin together with Lacan, she rephrases Lacan's "deliberately superficial" notion of the unconscious in terms of a poststructuralist theory of the failure necessary to performatives. "It is precisely from the *breach in knowledge* . . . that the act takes its performative *power:* it is the very *knowledge that cannot know itself,* that [in the speaking subject] *acts.*"[40]

In order to specify what such a definition of the "structural unconscious" of performative utterances means for Hermione's courtroom speech, we must remember one further comment about what Austin finds so "peculiar" in a performative uttered onstage. As Barbara Johnson succinctly puts it, when Austin tries to distinguish between ordinary language and theatrical language for the purposes of his theory, he is "objecting not to the use of the verb but to the status of its subject." For in a poem or on the stage, "the speaking subject is only a persona, an actor, not a person." A

theatrical performative is "peculiar" insofar as it reveals how all performatives put personae in place of persons. It reminds us that the necessity of speaking *in persona*—intrinsic to the conventionality of all performatives—opens up a difference *within* the speaker.[41] Johnson evokes *Hamlet* to illustrate her point: "the nonseriousness of a performative utterance 'said by an actor on the stage' results, then, not from his fictional status but *from his duality,* from the spectator's consciousness that although the character in the play is swearing to avenge his dead father's ghost, the actor's own performative commitments lie elsewhere."[42]

In the case of the trial scene in *The Winter's Tale,* Shakespeare presents us with an escalating succession of performatives. The series opens with the somber tones of an indictment that, because it is uttered in a play, divides its speaker from himself: "'Hermione, queen to the worthy Leontes, . . . thou art here accused and arraigned of high treason, in committing adultery,'" and so on (3.2.12-14); the messengers follow suit, swearing that they have fetched the oracle and left it unopened ("All this we swear" [l. 130]). And it culminates in an oracular message that should provide the last word by enacting the verdict it announces. In the case of Hermione, who explains why she can and will not utter the words "Not guilty," the play's rhetorical move here is pointedly and internally citational: she repeats Polixenes's phrase, thereby reminding us that he, in turn, was quoting a conventional utterance despite the fantasy of his youth as an originary moment prior to language. Hermione's quotation, then, makes us uncertain of the status of the subject who is giving her voice to these deeply conventional words by elaborately refusing to say them. The conceit of her impossible "Not guilty" tells us that "Hermione" is at once a (persuasive) character terribly wronged by her doubting husband *and* an actor "whose own performative commitments lie elsewhere." Hermione evanescently evokes the action her words cannot achieve if uttered, reminding us that this is so, in part, because we are listening to an actor speak in a play. Hermione's words do pass into action but not the act she intended and certainly not the one that the character "Hermione" could know. What she knows—that these words will fail—and what she does—reveal herself through these words as an actor playing a falsely accused Hermione—do not coincide.

Hermione protests that she has been "proclaim'd a strumpet" and "hurried / *Here to this place, i' th' open air*" to proclaim innocence in vain (ll. 104-5, my emphasis). It is "here" in "this place" that Hermione puts "Not guilty" in quotation marks. Her deictics refer us, within the fiction, to Leontes's mock courtroom. As if underlining the self-reflexive nature of performative utterances, however, they also refer us to the story's frame—to the "here" and now of "this" stage on which Hermione speaks.[43] The disjunction or misfiring that happens in "this place" of the theater is what Felman might call the unconscious action of *The Winter's Tale,* a "knowledge that cannot know itself" and therefore hollows out the speaking subject, Hermione, from within her own voice. Further still, Felman's psychoanalytic view of the import of theatrical performatives suggests that we must examine the relation between the play's unsettling rhetorical performance and its story of sexuality. I have argued that Hermione's "Not guilty," echoing Polixenes's "Not guilty," colors the entire question of performative misfiring through Leontes's obsession with female sexual guilt; only in the prelapsarian world inhabited by male twins do plea and verdict coincide. But if we read Hermione's rhetoric in light of the material conditions of the theater for which her lines were written—the here and now of the English transvestite theater—we are confronted with a division within the speaking subject called Hermione that is peculiar indeed. We are reminded not merely that Hermione is an actor, but that the voice speaking these lines was that of a *boy*-actor playing a falsely accused wife and mother. Leontes's suspicions may reduce Hermione's tongue to her body; similarly, the story attached to the two versions of "Not guilty" may define Hermione's voice through a story about the necessary link between the female body and sexual guilt. But the material practice of the English Renaissance stage, to which the rhetoric of Hermione's speech also refers, would tell a far different story about Hermione's body, one in which the alleged difference between two sexes is in fact a difference within one. The hollowness or duality of "her" voice, then, mirrors a division internal to the play's representation of gender. That is, the metatheatrical echo implicit in the performative and Hermione's deictics reminds us, as I suggested at the opening of this essay, that Shakespeare's representation of a "female" voice—what it can or cannot say and what effects it achieves—is a dramatic trope. It is, quite literally, a "travesty" of womanhood, a femininity-effect rather than a revelation of anything essential to what it continues to call the "female" tongue.

We might understand the tropological status of what counts as female in this play in one further way. As we have seen, what Felman calls an unconscious "breach in knowledge" is marked by the misfiring of "Not guilty." The precise content of this phrase will not let us forget that for Shakespeare a specific sexual story deeply informs what might otherwise seem a strictly rhetorical failure. Indeed, Felman's discussion of the affinities between Austin and Lacan suggests something further about the mysterious female body in *The Winter's Tale.* Through its constant meditation on the failures of its own language to reveal the truth or to act as intended, the play turns the secret of "female" sexuality—the question raised by Hermione's pregnancy—into what Lacan calls the missed encounter. Disjunction defines the subject's mediated, eccentric relation

to "the real." One might say of the play's relation to Hermione what Lacan says of the speaking subject's relation to the real: "Misfiring *is* the object."[44] On such an understanding of the discursive limits to knowledge, we might comprehend what Stanley Cavell aptly calls Leontes's skeptical "annihilation of the world" in other terms—as the vanishing of the maternal body before the joint pressure of language and of fantasy. That is, Shakespeare is exploring the (Cartesian) problem of radical doubt by representing a specific body—the maternal body—as the privileged object that resists the play's knowledge and its verbal action.[45] A psychoanalytic perspective, moreover, reminds us that it is not a philosopher's idea about a deceptive, malignant deity but a husband's idea about a deceptive, pregnant wife which sets the process of skeptical annihilation in motion. Foundational to the way the play rhetorically defines the limits of knowledge, the female body remains, nonetheless, forever fugitive.

III. "BE STONE NO MORE"

The literary figure to whom Shakespeare turns to explore such a vexed relation to the world is Ovid's Pygmalion.[46] For both skepticism *and* projection join hands to fashion Leontes's misery (e.g., "Your actions are my dreams"). On David Ward's persuasive argument for retaining the punctuation of the First Folio and for remembering the contemporary meaning of "coactive" as "coercive" or "compulsory" (and not merely "acting in concert"), Leontes's speech about "affection" is stressing "the *coercive* nature of affection," its "action upon the 'nothing' it generates in the imagination" (as Ward parses it, "Affection . . . Thou . . . Communicat'st with dreams . . . With what's unreal: thou co-active art, / And fellow'st nothing" [1.2.138-42]).[47] In addition, it is through Ovid's Orpheus-Pygmalion sequence—particularly as given the influential contours of Petrarchan linguistic self-consciousness—that Shakespeare can explore the subject's missed relation to that (maternal) object not as a process of doubting alone but as a meditation on the simultaneously productive and aberrant effects of rhetoric—on language conceived not merely as a representation *of* the world but as a mode of action *in* the world. As I suggested above concerning Hermione's vain yet truthful swearing of innocence and Paulina's successful yet false swearing of death, such action, precisely by distinguishing the two halves of the play, turns the relation between the subject and the world of which it speaks into a recurrent misfiring. On the one hand, neither saying nor swearing reestablishes the faith in Leontes required for Hermione to live as herself, outside Leontes's "dreams" or beyond the "language" of male fantasy she "understands not." And on the other, when Paulina's words do have effect, they do their work through a lie. That such misfirings as these or Hermione's impossible "Not guilty" are inaugurated by the mere sight of her pregnant body or the sound of her voice I understand as the symptom of a deeply entrenched—though not necessary or inevitable—collusion between the representational and libidinal economies of patriarchal culture.

When the truth of Hermione is the object of representation, representation fails, drawing attention to the opacity of language rather than the clarity of truth.[48] And when Hermione speaks, something happens that she does not intend: though she intends to persuade Polixenes to stay, her words trigger Leontes's jealousy; though she intends to speak of her innocence, her speech about the failure of "Not guilty" in her case declares her an actor and the scene the space of the theater. That a failed performative still has power to act despite having dislocated language's action from intention becomes vividly clear when the scene ends. For this self-reflexively theatrical trial produces further unintended effects. We hear that Mamillius, "with mere conceit and fear / Of the Queen's speed" in this staged trial, has died (3.2.144-45). And the report of his death becomes, in turn, words with the power to kill: "This news is mortal to the Queen" (l. 148). Hermione's unintended act—the "Not guilty" that produces the effect of theatricality—and the lethal effects that attend the play's reflection on its own fictive enactment darkly underline Shakespeare's attempt to evoke consciously and artistically controlled theatrical effects through Paulina's staging of Pygmalion's statue. That story works through yet another woman's voice to rein in the action of a now-benign theater in which language appears to perform the act it intends: "Music! awake her! . . . descend; be stone no more" (5.3.98-99).

Paulina's imperative to the statue, we should note, is not literally a performative utterance. Rather, her command represents an *idea* about language as performance. Shakespeare inherits this idea from Ovid's Orpheus and calls it "magic": the dream of a voice so persuasive that it can effect the changes of which it speaks.[49] It is the dream of a language that, when it acts, "fills up" the grave, makes good our debt to time. Paulina's spectacle of Hermione-as-statue offers more than a meditation on the desire to see in the theater: it becomes a visual analogue for the play's desire for a truly performative language. The long-awaited verbal event—signaled by such performatives as "Not guilty," the incessant taking of oaths, and the search for oracular truth—finds its culminating visual icon in the event of Hermione's "animation." Drawing on verbal and visual fictions, Shakespeare nonetheless accentuates the power of the voice in Paulina's heavily weighted moment of invocation and, eventually, in the much-desired event of Hermione's speech. Although Leontes declares himself content to be a "looker-on" (l. 85), thus inscribing the audience in the theatrical circuit of his desire, and though Paulina apologizes for the effects of the "sight of my poor image" (l. 57), what

everyone waits to hear is Hermione's voice. As the doubters in Paulina's audience demand, "If she pertain to life let her speak too" (l. 113) and "Ay, and make it manifest where she has liv'd, / Or how stol'n from the dead" (ll. 114-15). The scene, however, both claims and disavows the Orphic power for which it longs. Availing itself of a language at once oral and visual, this theater seems to "steal" Hermione, like Eurydice, "from the dead." At the same time, we hear a warning, through Paulina, that the Orphic story of life, were it "told . . . should be hooted at / Like an old tale" (ll. 116-17).

The acts that words do in the courtroom scene exceed intention and, by so doing, turn the theater into the space of these unpredictable effects. The final scene attempts to control verbal action through Paulina's careful stage management, her magically effective voice. Yet such an attempt may all too easily recall Leontes's disastrous desire to master the world by controlling all language. It therefore does not go unqualified. On the one hand, when Paulina proclaims "descend; be stone no more," a woman's successful voice in *The Winter's Tale* appears to replace Pygmalion's successful prayer to Venus in the *Metamorphoses*. On the other, just as Hermione once reminded her husband that even his own language exceeds his control, so now her voice is the one to remind us that the play's seeming animation is only a fiction. Despite the ruse of death, she has "preserv'd" herself somewhere else (l. 127). Hermione, moreover, says nothing to the man who now longs to hear her speak. She seems poised to speak to him—"Still methinks / There is an air comes from her. What fine chisel / Could ever yet cut breath?" (ll. 77-79)—but does not. Leontes's lines should remind us that throughout the *Metamorphoses* "breath" is the etymological root for Ovid's interest in speaking voices and poetry as "song": Apollo's "breath," the "wind" streaming through Daphne's hair, and the Orphic *"vox"* telling the story of the statue's animation all derive from the narrator's fascination with the vicissitudes of speech, with the uneasy relationship between voice and mind. For the *anima* in animation—meaning "the mind," "consciousness," and "breath"—is derived from the Greek *anemos* for "wind" internal and external to the body.[50] In this image of the chisel that can "cut breath," Leontes signals his, and the play's, desire for a rhetoric of animation, for a theatrical version of the *"l'aura"* or "breeze" that blows through the figures of the *Rime Sparse* or the "breath" that Ovid asks the gods to bestow on his song (I.1-3).

What Hermione does and does not say in this scene tells us something about the cost of that desire. Given the gendered relations of power passed down through literary history as the "air" that seems to "come from her," very much indeed hangs on Hermione's voice. I take the fact of Hermione's silence toward Leontes—

and the fact that, after she moves, Leontes never asks her a direct question—to be Shakespeare's way of acknowledging the problems raised by her voice in the first three acts. Nothing she says to Leontes diminishes the force of his projections; the language she "understand[s] not" limits the field of her possible responses; and any answer she makes must still be read by him, a reading she cannot control. This awareness of the limits that Leontes's fantasy places on the stony lady's possible reply stems, in part, from Shakespeare's understanding that, in Ovid as in Petrarch, the stories of Pygmalion and Narcissus are deeply intertwined.[51] Leontes has, of course, always viewed others through the mediating screen of his own form. Observing his son in Act 1, he begins testing his theory about his wife's guilt according to whether or not Mamillius is his mirror: "Looking on the lines / Of my boy's face, methoughts I did recoil / Twenty-three years, and saw myself unbreech'd" (1.2.153-55). Even Leontes's admission of culpability in the final scene, prompted when he gazes on the "statue," surreptitiously imports Narcissus's story into Pygmalion's. Repentant though he may be, Leontes still reads Hermione as a version of himself: "does not the stone rebuke me / For being more stone than it?" (5.3.37-38). To Leontes even her stoniness is not "hers." If anything of the world is to return to Leontes that does not stand at the level of his dreams, it cannot do so within the reflexively binary terms proposed by Petrarchan rhetoric. Rather, Paulina's intervention tells us that if Hermione is to be restored to Leontes and not fade away again before the force of fantasy and doubt, it is on the condition that she *not* respond to his words only, that she not conform utterly to his language and his desire. Therefore a third party (Paulina) must manage this meeting from outside the restrictive frame of Pygmalion's desirous yet annihilating address.

And finally, what Hermione *does* say—precisely not to Leontes but to her lost daughter—offers a telling index of how constraining have been the terms of that address. What Pygmalion loathes, what his phantasmatic love for his *simulacrum* pushes aside, Ovid tells us, is not simply female sexuality but "the female *mind*" (*"menti / femineae"* [X.244-45]). So one final allusion to the *Metamorphoses* tells us something about that mind. Hermione's allusion prompts a question that seems never to occur to Petrarch: what does *she* want? The shift from Petrarchan autobiography to Shakespearean ventriloquism marks a subtly but crucially different return to Ovidian narrative. In *The Winter's Tale,* Shakespeare animates Petrarchan tropes in order to perform an ethical critique of them, particularly the animating rhetoric of address and its role in Petrarch's story of love and the self. When Shakespeare listens once more to Ovid's female voices, he shifts the emphasis away from the otherness within the self (Petrarch's "exile" of blindness, obsession, and forgetting) to pose, instead, a question: the question of the

other's desire. And for a moment that "other"—the Petrarchan stony lady—has something else in mind than "responding" to the speaker whose apostrophe restricts them both (*"se risponder savesse a' detti miei!"*). What "moved" Hermione, her last words tell us, were thoughts of Perdita. Turning to a daughter who has already coded herself as Proserpina at the moment of dropping her flowers, Hermione models herself on Ceres as a mother unable to forget her lost, though still living, daughter:

> Tell me, mine own,
> Where hast thou been preserv'd? where liv'd? how found
> Thy father's court? for thou shalt hear that I,
> Knowing by Paulina that the oracle
> Gave hope thou wast in being, have preserv'd
> Myself to see the issue.
>
> (5.3.123-28)

Hermione's question to Perdita—"Where hast thou been preserv'd? where liv'd?"—obliquely recalls Ovid's story of violent rape and maternal grief by making her reason for living the hope of reunion with her daughter.

Where the suspicion of female sexual guilt defines the relation between time and language's action in the first half of the play, in this final scene both are redefined by another story—that of rape and maternal grief. Hermione's allusion to Book V of the *Metamorphoses,* of course, echoes the title, place, and time of *The Winter's Tale.* For Ceres's grief over Proserpina's rape brought winter into the world. Golding's translation of that grief brings the story of Ceres closer still to that of the animated statue in Act 5. When the nymph Arethusa tells Ceres why her daughter has vanished, Golding renders Ovid's lines as follows: "Hir mother stoode as starke as stone . . . And long she was like one that in another worlde had beene."[52] It is left to Shakespeare's Hermione to return from that "other world" of stone in order to be reunited with her Proserpina. Alongside Pygmalion's prayer and Orpheus's suppliant song, then, we must also remember Ceres's curse. In Ovid's text we find yet another story, often less well remembered, about a voice that can bring about the changes of which it speaks. Orpheus's mother, the muse Calliope, tells us that when Ceres saw Proserpina's girdle floating on the surface of the pool, she "reproached all the lands loudly, calling them ungrateful . . . but *Sicily above all other lands,* where she had found the traces of her loss. . . . She ordered the plowed fields to fail in their trust and spoiled the seed" (ll. 474-80). Setting his "old tale" of Leontes's winter in Sicily, Shakespeare invokes but finally turns attention away from the fantasy of the animated statue.[53] He thereby suggests that Pygmalion's self-reflexive fantasy so narrowly constricts female speech that there is, quite literally, *nothing* Hermione can say. Yet by recalling Proserpina's rape and Ceres's powerful reproach, he grants her voice a different authority. Her last words to Perdita fleetingly testify to the violence against the female body that subtends such "old" and "sad" tales as that of an animated statue or the first appearance of winter.

Female voices in *The Winter's Tale* acquire an oblique but telling power: the power to point out that, in the Ovidian tradition, stories about poetic authority, creativity, or "voice," however purely "poetic" their claims may seem, nonetheless entail violence against the female body. Not necessarily conscious, that violence continues to emerge in the unlikely circumstance of metapoetic or metatheatrical reflection. Challenging Ovidian-Petrarchan tropes for male vocal power when they thwart Leontes's desire to control speech, the tongues of Hermione and Paulina recall Ovid's rhetorically self-conscious narratives of rape, misogyny, and female vengeance that form the background for Orpheus's descent into the underworld. When Shakespeare returns to Ovidian narrative in this play, therefore, he reminds us that if we isolate Pygmalion's story from Orpheus's, or Proserpina's from Ceres's, we fail to notice the ethical dilemmas woven into the very fabric of Ovid's rhetorical self-consciousness in the *Metamorphoses.* Investigating the causes and effects of rhetorical speech through these seemingly disparate figures, and inviting reflection on the connections between language and sexuality proposed by their interwoven stories, Shakespeare reveals the cost to women of Ovid's foundational tropes for poetic authority. It is in the voices of Hermione and Paulina that we catch something of the sound of that cost. In their voices *The Winter's Tale* stages a cautionary story about the uncanny returns of cultural inheritance, one that attests to the often unconscious—yet no less lethal—consequences of representing such things as love, voice, and beauty in the Ovidian tradition.

A number of colleagues read and commented on this essay with care and acuity. I would like to thank them here: Ian Duncan, Kevin Dunn, Richard Halpern, William Jewett, Wayne Koestenbaum, Larry Manley, Jeff Nunokawa, Patricia Rosenmeyer, and Katherine Rowe. I owe the inaugural idea for this essay to a conversation several years ago with David Marshall.

Notes

[1] Quotations of Shakespeare's plays follow *The Riverside Shakespeare,* ed. G. Blakemore Evans (Boston: Houghton Mifflin, 1974).

[2] William R. Morse, "Metacriticism and Materiality: The Case of Shakespeare's *The Winter's Tale,*" *ELH* 58 (1991): 283-304, esp. 297.

[3] How to read Hermione's silence has been an important question in much criticism of *The Winter's Tale.*

I am particularly indebted to Kenneth Gross, *The Dream of the Moving Statue* (Ithaca, NY, and London: Cornell UP, 1992), 105-9; and Leonard Barkan, "'Living Sculptures': Ovid, Michelangelo, and *The Winter's Tale,*" *ELH* 48 (1981): 639-67.

[4] For an overview, see Barkan, *The Gods Made Flesh: Metamorphosis & the Pursuit of Paganism* (New Haven, CT, and London: Yale UP, 1986). As Barkan comments of "Diana and Actaeon," Titian turns Ovid's story of Actaeon's visual transgression into a painting that comments on the act of looking at a painting. Actaeon, poised "on the threshold," lifts a curtain to gaze on Diana; therefore "the bath almost becomes a picture within a picture. The result is a powerful identification between the viewer and Actaeon as both participate in the visual, the voyeuristic, and the visionary" (200-201). One could make similar comments about the resonance between Petrarch's many allusions to Ovid's stories about the human voice and the characteristic fiction that a lyric poem is a spoken utterance—particularly in light of its favored trope, apostrophe. Such aesthetically self-reflexive allusions to Ovid's *Metamorphoses* are not a purely "Renaissance" phenomenon. On Dante's poetically self-conscious appropriations of Ovidian narrative, for example, see Rachel Jacoff and Jeffrey T. Schnapp, eds., *The Poetry of Allusion: Virgil and Ovid in Dante's "Commedia"* (Stanford, CA: Stanford UP, 1991).

[5] Barkan, "'Living Sculptures,'" 660.

[6] Sonnets 77 and 78. For further discussion of the relationship between Ovid's version of Pygmalion and Petrarch's, see my "Embodied Voices: Petrarch Reading (Himself Reading) Ovid" in *Desire in the Renaissance: Psychoanalysis and Literature,* Valeria Finucci and Regina Schwartz, eds. (Princeton, NJ: Princeton UP, 1994), 120-45.

[7] I have here modified the translation of Robert M. Durling in *Petrarch's Lyric Poems: The* Rime sparse *and Other Lyrics* (Cambridge, MA, and London: Harvard UP, 1976) to capture the rhetorically specific sense of the verb *lodare,* "to praise." Elsewhere in this essay translations of Petrarch are Durling's. Barbara Johnson distinguishes between the two apostrophes in Shelley's "Ode to the West Wind" in a way that is useful for reading Petrarch's two sonnets: the first, emotive "if only" lays stress on the first person, and the second, vocative "Pygmalion" on the second person. The typography of Shelley's poem marks this difference as one between "oh" and "O," a difference Johnson allies with the one between Roman Jakobson's emotive function, or "pure presencing of the first person," and his conative function, or "the pure presencing of the second person" (Johnson, *A World of Difference* [Baltimore and London: Johns Hopkins UP, 1987], 187).

[8] "[N]on minus nominis quam ipsius corporis splendore captus" (Petrarch, Prose, ed. G. Martellotti, P. G. Ricci, E. Carrara, and E. Bianchi [Milan and Naples: Riccardo Ricciardi Editore, 1955], 158). Petrarch's anagrams and puns on laurel derive from Ovid's own verbal wit in the story of Apollo and Daphne (Metamorphoses, I.451ff).

[9] On epideixis and gender in Petrarchanism, see Joel Fineman, "Shakespeare's Will: The Temporality of Rape" in The Subjectivity Effect in Western Literary Tradition: Essays Toward the Release of Shakespeare's Will (Cambridge, MA, and London: MIT Press, 1991), 165-221; and Nancy Vickers, "'The blazon of sweet beauty's best': Shakespeare's Lucrece" in Shakespeare and the Question of Theory, Patricia Parker and Geoffrey Hartman, eds. (New York and London: Methuen, 1985), 95-115.

[10] Quotations of the Metamorphoses follow the text translated and edited by Frank Justus Miller (Cambridge, MA: Harvard UP, 1927), though I have made a few silent emendations to Miller's translations.

[11] The. xv. Bookes of P. Ouidius Naso; entytuled Metamorphosis, translated oute of Latin into English meeter, by Arthur Golding Gentleman (London, 1567), 123ʳ.

[12] The association between the stories of Orpheus and Eurydice and Apollo and Daphne is commonplace. The most influential Renaissance commentator on Ovid's poem, Raphael Regius, claims that Orpheus is Apollo's son, adding that the singer received his lyre from Apollo as a gift (Metamorphoses [Venice, 1556], X.1). The first edition of Regius's commentary appeared in 1492.

[13] Despite the frequent representation of polymorphous desires in the Metamorphoses, Ovid's narrative almost always brings homoerotic moments such as this one back into the orbit of a controlling heterosexual imperative. Thus Iphis's love for Ianthe, which immediately precedes the story of Orpheus, is refracted through a missing penis; the phallus becomes the sign, therefore, that the love of one woman for another is "more mad" than the love of a woman for a bull (IX.668-797). Similarly, although Orpheus may be the "author" of love for boys, that love is represented as the effect of, and only in relation to, his love for his dead wife; the jury of avenging Bacchic women in Book XI then judge his love again as merely the sign of his feelings about women. Because of this frame (and its repetition in the hands of Pygmalion, Orpheus's surrogate), the song in Book X about the many kinds of transgressive love has little to say about male-male eroticism on its own terms.

[14] Harry Berger Jr. recently argued that a gynophobic and misogynist discourse informs Book X ("Actaeon at the Hinder Gate: The Stag Party in Spenser's Gardens of Adonis" in Finucci and Schwartz, eds., 91-119).

[15] Leontes signals an awareness of this punitive possibility. But he does so in the domestic register, containing the threat no sooner than uttered: "Chide me, dear stone, that I may say indeed / Thou art Hermione; or rather, thou art she / In thy not chiding; for she was as tender / As infancy and grace" (5.3.24-27).

[16] John Marston, "The Metamorphosis of Pigmalions Image" in Elizabethan Minor Epics, ed. Elizabeth Story Donno (London: Routledge and Kegan Paul, 1963), 244-52, esp. 244. Citations of Marston follow this edition. On Marston's satire of the language of erotic idealism, particularly in the Petrarchan mode, see William Keach, Elizabethan Erotic Narratives: Irony and Pathos in the Ovidian Poetry of Shakespeare, Marlowe, and Their Contemporaries (New Brunswick, NJ: Rutgers UP, 1977), 134-61.

[17] For a history of this misogynist tradition, see Barbara Rico's "From 'Speechless Dialect' to 'Prosperous Art': Shakespeare's Recasting of the Pygmalion Image," Huntington Library Quarterly 48 (1985): 285-95. Except for the two works I discuss here—the last act of The Winter's Tale and Petrarch's paired sonnets (77 and 78)—the Pygmalion story is generally not a positive one in the Middle Ages or the Renaissance. Misogynist diatribes inform it, and the story of prostitution, too, clings to it: John Marston uses Pygmalion to adjudicate between the "wanton" and the "obsceane" (252), and George Pettie's A Petite Pallace (London, 1586) alludes to the story of the statue in overtly misogynist ways. Jonathan Bate, in a book otherwise dedicated to tracing the minutiae of Ovid's presence in Shakespeare's poetry, oddly dismisses the relevance to The Winter's Tale of the misogynist genealogy in Ovid (Shakespeare and Ovid [Oxford: Clarendon Press, 1993]).

[18] It seems to me no accident that the artist Shakespeare chose for his Pygmalion, Giulio Romano, was known not only as a painter but as a pornographer. The nature of Shakespeare's reference to Romano has been much debated. For a useful summary of the debate as well as an account of a contemporary English conduct book for young women which refers to the excellent work of "Iules Romain," see Georgianna Ziegler, "Parents, Daughters, and 'That Rare Italian Master': A New Source for The Winter's Tale," Shakespeare Quarterly 36 (1985): 204-12. For Romano's notorious, if rarely seen, collaboration with Aretino (the so-called posizioni), see David O. Frantz, Festum Voluptatis: A Study of Renaissance Erotica (Columbus: Ohio State UP, 1989), 46-48 and 119-23; and Frederick Hartt, Giulio Romano (New Haven, CT: Yale UP, 1958), 29. As Hartt points out, Romano's prints, though suppressed, were also

widely copied and widely destroyed; Frantz notes that when Perino del Vaga and Agostino Carracci imitated Romano, they did so in an Ovidian vein, calling their own versions of the *"posizioni"* the "loves of the gods" (123). It is the rumor of Romano's work, rather than an actual copy in England, that seems to me important to Shakespeare's reference.

[19] See Janet Adelman's account of dreams of male parthenogenesis and the problem of the maternal body in this play in *Suffocating Mothers: Fantasies of Maternal Origin in Shakespeare's Plays,* Hamlet *to* The Tempest (New York and London: Routledge, 1992).

[20] For a persuasive reading of the way language violates Philomela as surely as her rape—particularly Ovid's meditation on the severed *"lingua"* (both tongue and language more generally)—see Elissa Marder's recent "Disarticulated Voices: Feminism and Philomela," *Hypatia* 7 (Spring 1992): 148-66. My claim about Medusa lies outside the scope of this essay; I take up her story in greater detail in my next book, *The Rhetoric of the Body in Renaissance Ovidian Poetry.*

[21] *Figura* signifies in both grammatical and rhetorical registers and designates the material aspects of writing as well. It can specify a written symbol or character or refer to the form, spelling, or grammatical inflection of a Latin word; it is also a rhetorical term for trope.

[22] [F]*igura,* definition 3; see *Oxford Latin Dictionary,* 3 vols. (Oxford: Clarendon Press, 1968), 1:700.

[23] [F]*igura,* definition 11, *OLD,* 1:700.

[24] Here we should remember that, according to Ovid, Medusa became the Gorgon because she was raped, and her beheading produced the fountain of poetry. Pegasus arose from the Gorgon's blood, and the Heliconian fountain, in turn, arose from the "beating of his feet" (both the horse's feet and the feet of poetic meter). The origin of poetry's fountain is therefore "the blood of the mother," the raped Medusa (*"vidi ipsum materno sanguine nasci . . . est Pegasus huius origo / fontis"* [V.259-63]).

[25] For an analysis of the role that bodies—especially female bodies—play in the relationship between desire and "the drive to know" in modern narrative, see Peter Brooks, *Body Work: Objects of Desire in Modern Narrative* (Cambridge, MA, and London: Harvard UP, 1993). Leontes's devotion to speaking about the fantasized "truth" of Hermione's body might usefully be considered part of what Brooks calls "epistemophilia," a project in which we tell stories "about the body in the effort to know and to have it" and which results "in making the body a site of signification—the place for the inscription of stories—and itself a signifier, a prime agent in narrative plot and meaning" (5-6).

[26] I adapt the phrase "verbal fetishism" from John Freccero ("The Fig Tree and the Laurel: Petrarch's Poetics" in *Literary Theory/Renaissance Texts,* Patricia Parker and David Quint, eds. [Baltimore and London: Johns Hopkins UP, 1986], 20-32, esp. 22). My understanding of the nature of fetishism in Petrarch and the literary filiation from which it derives differs from Freccero's and is outlined in my "Embodied Voices."

[27] Marston, 246.

[28] Petrarch uses both female and male Ovidian characters to suggest that he is alienated from his own tongue; the story of Actaeon, as well as of Echo and Daphne, appears in canzone 23 for this purpose. For further comment on Actaeon, see my "Embodied Voices." As we have seen, Ovid no sooner proposes the story of male poetic control over language than he dissolves it; this dissolution subtends Petrarch's poetic self-portrait. Although Ovid and Petrarch after him suggest that alienation from one's own tongue is the condition of having a voice—male or female—in both poets the trope of a female voice appears strategically, as the place in the text where one can hear the greatest strain on such cherished illusions about artistic vocal power as those proposed by Apollo, Pan, Pygmalion, and Orpheus. It is the diacritical function of the female voice, its ironic juxtaposition to such ostensibly "male" fantasies, that is important for understanding Shakespeare's representation of the tongues of Hermione and Paulina.

[29] Heather Dubrow has recently argued that we must attend carefully to the complex and often contradictory role of Laura's voice if we are to understand the "relationship among speech, power, and gender" in the *Rime Sparse* and beyond; see her *Echoes of Desire: English Petrarchism and its Counterdiscourses* (Ithaca, NY, and London: Cornell UP, 1995), 40-48, esp. 42.

[30] J. L. Austin, *How to do things with Words,* ed. J. O. Urmson (Oxford: Clarendon Press, 1962), 1 and 6. Austin lists *swear* (along with such other verbs as *promise, give my word, pledge myself*) as part of a class of "commissive" performatives in which conventional phrases are deployed to "commit the speaker to a certain course of action" (156-57). Over the course of his lectures, Austin renders problematic his "provisional" performative/constative distinction; he eventually rejects any absolute dichotomy between the two, finding that constatives may well have a performative aspect (91). My point here is simply to note that in *The Winter's Tale,* Shakespeare is exploring a distinction analogous to Austin's provisional one—between statements that report some state of affairs truly or falsely (in this case, the "state of affairs" in question being Hermione's fidelity) and other, conventional statements (such as "I swear") in which saying and doing explicitly converge. For a study of performatives in Shakespeare with an emphasis on cultural and institutional

authority, see Susanne L. Wofford, "'To You I Give Myself, For I Am Yours': Erotic Performance and Theatrical Performatives in *As You Like It*" in *Shakespeare Reread: The Texts in New Contexts,* Russ McDonald, ed. (Ithaca, NY, and London: Cornell UP, 1994), 147-69.

[31] Since, unlike the audience, the characters in the story *can* "go and see" the dead body of Hermione, Paulina's lie is dramaturgically more complicated than my presentation of it. Leontes describes scenes that the audience does not observe, and his words give playgoers every reason to believe that he will verify for us the fact of Hermione's death: "Prithee bring me / To the dead bodies of my queen and son. / One grave shall be for both. . . . Once a day I'll visit / The chapel where they lie, and tears shed there / Shall be my recreation. . . . Come, and lead me / To these sorrows" (3.2.234-43). Critics have argued that these lines, coupled with Antigonus's report in 3.3 of the appearance of Hermione's spirit, suggest that when Shakespeare wrote Act 3, he still intended to follow his source, in which the dead wife does not return. Whatever Shakespeare's intentions, the play's refusal to clear up ambiguities about Hermione's possible death and resurrection provides a compelling link between the play and the Orpheus/ Eurydice story.

For a discussion of critical responses to the problem of Hermione's death and unexpected revival, see Barbara A. Mowat, *The Dramaturgy of Shakespeare's Romances* (Athens: U of Georgia P, 1976), 77ff and 145, n. 18.

[32] In thinking about the relationship between performativity and sexuality, I have drawn on several important discussions: Judith Butler, *Bodies That Matter: On the Discursive Limits of "Sex"* (New York and London: Routledge, 1993); Shoshana Felman, *The Literary Speech Act: Don Juan with J. L. Austin, or Seduction in Two Languages* (Ithaca, NY: Cornell UP, 1983); Lynne Huffer, "Luce et veritas: Toward an Ethics of Performance," *Yale French Studies* (1995): 20-41; and Johnson, *The Critical Difference: Essays in the Contemporary Rhetoric of Reading* (Baltimore and London: Johns Hopkins UP, 1980).

[33] Felman, 94-96, esp. 94. Analyzing performative language in relation to the stories of Don Juan and of Oedipus, Felman's work is equally telling for the central dilemma of *The Winter's Tale*: the relationship between theatrical representation and the female body or, more generally in Ovidian narrative, between body and voice. Felman writes that "the problem of the human act," in psychoanalysis as well as performative analysis, "consists in the relation between language and body . . . because the act is conceived . . . as that which problematizes at one and the same time the separation and the opposition between the two. The act, an enigmatic and problematic production of the

speaking body . . . , breaks down the opposition between body and spirit, between matter and language" (94). She reminds us of Austin's comment that "in the last analysis, doing an action must come down to the making of physical movements with parts of the body; but this is about as true as . . . saying something must . . . come down to making movements of the tongue" (as quoted in Felman, 94).

[34] Felman, 82. Austin explores the contingent and context-bound nature of any speech act in "the doctrine of Infelicities" (14-24). Jacques Derrida's critique of Austin constitutes a sustained analysis of "the failure" that is an "essential" risk of performative utterances; see Derrida, "Signature Event Context," first published in *Glyph* 1 (1977) and translated by Samuel Weber and Jeffrey Mehlman in *Limited Inc* (Evanston, IL: Northwestern UP, 1988), 1-24.

[35] Austin, 16-17.

[36] Austin, 22.

[37] Derrida, 10.

[38] Derrida, 14 and 17.

[39] Derrida, 18.

[40] Felman, 96.

[41] "If one considers the conventionality of all performative utterances (on which Austin often insists), can it really be said that the chairman who opens a discussion or the priest who baptizes a baby or the judge who pronounces a verdict are persons rather than personae? . . . The performative utterance thus automatically fictionalizes its utterer when it makes him the mouthpiece of a conventionalized authority" (Johnson, *The Critical Difference,* 60). Or one could say, as well, that read rhetorically, the performative utterance may uncover the *theatrical* nature of such "ordinary" social actions.

[42] Johnson, *The Critical Difference,* 60 (my emphasis).

[43] In light of the duality of Hermione's deictics, we might read the specification "i' th' open air" within historical context as well. The stage in London's earliest commercial theaters projected into a yard and therefore placed actors "i' th' open air." On the physical conditions of London's public amphitheaters and private halls, see Andrew Gurr, *Playgoing in Shakespeare's London* (Cambridge: Cambridge UP, 1987), 13-48. Most critics believe the play to have been written for the closed theater of Blackfriars. But a note on the play by Simon Forman tells us that at least one contemporary remembers having seen *The Winter's Tale* performed at the Globe (on 15 May 1611).

44 Jacques Lacan, *Encore* (Paris: Seuil, 1975), 55. On the important difference between the usual misprision of the Lacanian "lack" and the productive process of misfiring, see Felman, 82-84.

45 Stanley Cavell, *Disowning Knowledge in Six Plays of Shakespeare* (Cambridge: Cambridge UP, 1987), 193-221, esp. 214. Cavell is, of course, most concerned with Leontes's doubts about his son and his paternity. But in light of Janet Adelman's work on the play, one is led to wonder, when poised between these two powerful essays, why it is the *maternal* body that sparks Leontes's radical doubt. I would add to Adelman's analysis only that it is Hermione's language—the effects of her voice—as well as her body that unsettle her husband's sense of himself. To Cavell's approach, similarly, I would add only that the play explores the action of Leontes's doubt through the action of both language and thought. For the scandal of what cannot be known—the truth about Hermione—turns, as we have seen, into an interrogation of the power and the limits of theatrical representation as well as of two kinds of discourse: saying and swearing.

46 It is perhaps worth remembering, as Jonathan Bate points out, that Shakespeare's contemporaries understood him to be the inheritor of Ovid. Drawing on the very rhetoric of animation at issue here, Francis Meres observed that "the sweete wittie soule of Ouid liues in mellifluous and hony-tongued Shakespeare" (*Palladis Tamia* [1598], as quoted in *Elizabethan Critical Essays,* G. Gregory Smith, ed. [Oxford: Clarendon Press, 1904], 317). For further comment on Renaissance Ovidianism, see Bate, 1-47; and *Ovid Renewed: Ovidian influences on literature and art from the Middle Ages to the twentieth century,* Charles Martindale, ed. (Cambridge: Cambridge UP, 1988).

47 David Ward, "Affection, Intention, and Dreams in *The Winter's Tale," Modern Language Review* 82 (1987): 545-54, esp. 552. Ward offers a precise discussion of Leontes's "affection" in relation to sixteenth-century faculty psychology, particularly in medical discourse. Looking at discussions in Hooker and Burton, Ward suggests that with this word Leontes is designating a "disease of the mind" linked to the faculty of the appetite rather than to the will or to reason; for Hooker, affection is both involuntary ("Wherefore it is not altogether in our power") and a desire for the impossible, for "any thing which seemeth good, be it never so impossible" (as quoted in Ward, 546). For Shakespeare, Ovid's combined stories of Pygmalion and Orpheus give a distinctive mythographic and erotic turn to the involuntary aspect of affection (revulsion from womankind out of grief or disgust) and its connotation of a desire for the impossible (for art to conquer death).

48 See Howard Felperin, "'Tongue-tied our queen?': the deconstruction of presence in *The Winter's Tale"*

in Parker and Hartman, eds., 3-18. Although I clearly agree with Felperin's emphasis on the play's consciousness of its own failure to refer, it seems to me that, by framing the question in terms of the possibility that Hermione may be guilty, Felperin participates in the very logic he critiques; his reading repeats what it might otherwise analyze—the question of *why* language's misfiring should be represented in cognitive terms as the truth or falsity of the maternal body.

49 Ovid, of course, shared this dream: the final lines of the *Metamorphoses* claim that the poet will live (*"vivam"*), his name survive the "gnawing tooth of time" though his body does not (*"ne cedax abolere vetustas"*), if his poem is "read on the lips of the people" (*"perque omnia saecula fama"* [XV.871-79]). For my understanding of this scene, I am indebted to conversations with Thomas M. Greene on the relationship between poetry and magic. See his essays "The Balance of Power in Marvell's 'Horatian Ode,'" *ELH* 60 (1993): 379-96; and "Poetry as Invocation," *New Literary History* 24 (1993): 495-517.

50 Henry George Liddell and Robert Scott cite Hippocrates for the sense of wind in the body: derived from "ανε-, 'blow, breathe', cf. [Sanskrit], *áni-ti,* 'breathes'" (*Greek-English Lexicon,* 2 vols. [Oxford: Clarendon Press, 1951], 1:132). The primary meaning of *anima* is "breath" or "breathing as the characteristic manifestation of life," and it thus connotes "the characteristic or quality whose loss constitutes death" (*OLD,* 1:132-34). It can also designate "a disembodied spirit, soul, ghost" (132), a hint of which meaning appears, perhaps, when Polixenes asks Paulina to "make it manifest where she has liv'd, / Or how stol'n from the dead" (5.3.114-15). For interesting comments on the ghostly undertone here and at other moments in this scene, see Gross.

51 Since Ovid handled the scene, the link became one of the mainstays of the tradition. The subjective and objective genitive in Marston's title, "The Metamorphosis of Pigmalions Image," for instance, derives its power from this connection. Thus his Pygmalion is enamored less of the statue than of his own reflection in that statue: "Hee was amazed at the wondrous rarenesse / Of his owne workmanships perfection. . . . And thus admiring, was enamored / On that fayre Image *himselfe portraied"* (245, my emphasis). Pygmalion's resemblance to Narcissus was also central to the representation of the lover in the *Roman de la Rose;* for an overview, see Louise Vinge, *The Narcissus Theme in Western European Literature up to the Early 19th Century* (Lund: Gleerups, 1967). I learned to attend to the crucial role that Pygmalion and Narcissus play in the *Rime Sparse* from Giuseppe Mazzotta (*The Worlds of Petrarch* [Durham, NC, and London: Duke UP, 1993]).

52 Golding, 64ᵛ. Ovid uses the simile of turning to stone but says nothing of "another worlde": *"Mater ad*

auditas stupuit ceu saxea voces / attonitaeque diu similis fuit, utque dolore / pulsa gravi gravis est amentia" (V.509-11). For another reading of the import of Ceres's grief for the play, see T. G. Bishop, *Shakespeare and the theatre of wonder* (Cambridge: Cambridge UP, 1996), 125-75.

[53] Golding, too, preserves the detail of Sicily in his translation: "But bitterly aboue the rest she banned *Sicilie,* / In which the mention of hir losse she plainely did espie" (64ʳ). Understanding Hermione as a second Ceres may tell us why Shakespeare makes an otherwise puzzling change of location. Where Greene begins *Pandosto* in Bohemia and later moves to Sicily, Shakespeare *opens* the story of winter in Sicily only to move, in Act 4, to Bohemia's pastoral landscape.

Source: "'You speak a language that I understand not': The Rhetoric of Animation in *The Winter's Tale*," in *Shakespeare Quarterly*, Vol. 48, No. 1, Spring, 1997, pp. 17-44.

Conquering Islands: Contextualizing *The Tempest*

Barbara Fuchs, *Stanford University*

It is an axiom of contemporary criticism that *The Tempest* is a play about the European colonial experience in America. While this perspective has generated enormously enriched readings of the play, it runs the risk of obscuring the complicated nuances of colonial discourses in the early seventeenth century. When is America not America? When it is Ireland, or North Africa, or Europe itself, or the no-man's-land (really every man's *desired* land) of the Mediterranean in-between. Just as the formal literary elements of a text—metaphors, puns, patterns—may signify in multiple ways, context, too, may be polysemous. By exploring other contexts for the insistent colonial concerns of Shakespeare's island play, I hope to show how a multiple historical interpretation can unpack the condensed layers of colonialist ideology. This type of reading depends not only on recent *Tempest* criticism—what one might call the American readings—but on studies of England's colonial role in Ireland. My aim is, first, to provide descriptions of the contemporary colonial contexts in both Ireland and the Mediterranean, which I believe shed light on the play, and, second, to suggest the advantages for political criticism of considering all relevant colonial contexts simultaneously. If, as I will argue, the superimposition of those contexts on the play reflects the way colonialist ideology is "quoted" from one contact zone to another in the sixteenth and early seventeenth centuries, criticism that attempts to trace that ideology will gain from identifying precisely such layering of referents.[1]

My purpose in this essay is not to refute American readings of *The Tempest;* I agree with Peter Hulme that placing New World colonialism at the center of the play has made it a fundamentally more interesting and, at least for twentieth-century readers, a more relevant text.[2] Instead, by highlighting the historical and political dimensions of the contemporary Mediterranean world and England's colonial experience in Ireland, I hope to continue to historicize the colonialist discourse that American readings first brought to the fore. Even in highly suggestive and politically sophisticated readings of *The Tempest,* the Mediterranean often equals the literary, the *Aeneid,* the essentially European, functioning largely as a background to American *newes*[3]—what Hulme calls the first layer of a textual palimpsest.[4] The new transatlantic colonial discourse works itself out against this background of the *Aeneid* and classical Mediterranean travels. Yet this critical privileging of America as the primary context of colonialism for the play obscures the very real presence of the Ottoman threat in the Mediterranean in the early seventeenth-century and elides the violent English colonial adventures in Ireland, which paved the way for plantation in Virginia.

Although twentieth-century historians can speak of the Ottoman Empire in the early seventeenth century as having "passed its peak,"[5] such a perspective was hardly available, as Samuel Chew points out, to contemporary observers of Islam's might.[6] As I hope to show, the sense of an Eastern empire encroaching on Europe pervades Shakespeare's play, making the European "center" of the text simultaneously the origin of colonial adventure and the target of another empire's expansionism. The general absence of Ireland from discussions of colonialism in the play is troubling, particularly since the devastation of a native population and its culture was more deliberate and vicious in England's first plantation than in its later ventures in Virginia. As Paul Brown has suggested, there are strong analogies between Prospero's island and Elizabethan Ireland, which locate them both "between American and European discourse."[7]

. . . . .

> The Irish are the niggers of Europe, lads.
> *The Commitments*

What are we to make of Roddy Doyle's equation—his rather tongue-in-cheek justification for an Irish band's focus on soul music? Doyle has found a parallel between the situation of African Americans within the U.S. and that of the Irish vis-à-vis postimperialist Europe. While his use of the ugly term *niggers* indicates the conflictive nature of such a comparison (in that the register of working-class/colonized solidarity fails to transcend racial prejudice, and in that the comparison problematically erases the presence in Europe of large black immigrant populations), Doyle's comparison also parodies the discursive strategies of quotation which contribute to colonization. By comparing them to another oppressed population, Doyle establishes the right of the Irish to soul; ironically, the colonization of Ireland itself depended largely on strategies of comparison which represented its conquest as a repetition of earlier imperialist ventures to Africa and the Americas. As Nicholas P. Canny has pointed out, the colonization of Ireland functioned as an apprenticeship for England's plantation in the Americas.[8] I propose to focus here on the discursive dimension of this education—what I term colonial quotation.

By *quotation* I mean the references by colonial writers to the works of earlier explorers and planters as well as the larger rhetorical maneuver of assimilating the unknown by equating it with the already-known. Such quotation does not overlap perfectly with the notion of *translatio imperii*—the westward translation of Rome's imperial tradition to the nascent European empires. However, the quoted discourse may use *translatio imperii* as its particular justification.[9] The quotation of colonialist discourse from one instance to the next naturalizes expansion by bringing newly "discovered" lands and people under the conceptual domain of the already-known, the already-digested. Thus this particular kind of intertextuality advances a colonialist ideology.[10]

The equation between prior and ongoing colonial encounters may be achieved by literal textual quotation of authorities, by referring to the colonist's own previous experiences in another territory, or by reading a newly discovered culture as another manifestation of one already othered. Such a strategy underlies the remarkable encounter between Trinculo and Caliban in 2.2 of *The Tempest,* where the European does not know what the man/fish is but certainly knows what to *make of it:* a for-profit display like the multiple "dead Indians" in London fairs: "Were I in England now, as once I was, and had but this fish painted, not a holiday-fool there but would give a piece of silver. There would this monster make a man—any strange beast there makes a man" (ll. 27-30).[11]

The context of exhibition that Trinculo quotes serves to frame the new and bring it under his dominion. The irony, of course, lies in the fact that the man "made" by such exhibition would be not Caliban attaining human status but Trinculo made rich.[12] Although Trinculo claims to "let loose" his earlier opinion when he realizes that Caliban is alive, even calling him an "islander," the framework of exhibition is immediately reinstated by Stephano, who says he would take the monster home to present to a ruler or sell for profit (ll. 67-68, 74-75). Alive or dead, Caliban fulfills the role of spectacular other and, throughout the comic process of recognition by which Stephano and Trinculo discover him, occupies an abject position. His monstrosity corresponds quite neatly to the Europeans' expectations. For Caliban himself, of course, the situation is framed by Prospero's abusive treatment, which has scripted him as victim.

Caliban's cloak plays a central part in this complicated series of misrecognitions and discoveries, especially as a signal of the play's Irish context. The presence of the cloak does not prove such a context, but it suggests how English domination of Ireland might *take cover* in the text under precisely such details. The cloak, I would argue, is the only native artifact allowed Caliban. He first shrouds under it in order to escape detection by

Trinculo, who he fears is a spirit in Prospero's service. Trinculo does discover him and immediately joins him under his "gaberdine" to seek protection from the storm.[13] There Stephano finds the two of them—a curious hybrid creature with four legs and two mouths, recalling Iago's characterization of Othello and Desdemona's marriage as a miscegenistic "beast with two backs." Such unhallowed combinations are precisely the issue here, as Trinculo unwittingly becomes monstrous in Stephano's eyes. Given England's anxiety over distinguishing savage from civilized, islander from colonizer in Ireland, it is possible to read this episode in Shakespeare's text as one of the indices of this colonial adventure.

The English conquest of Ireland was a messy affair. The twelfth-century Anglo-Norman conquest had provided England with a foothold in Dublin and the eastern counties—an area known as the Pale—while large portions of Ireland remained, literally and figuratively, beyond the Pale of English authority.[14] Cruel attempts to control the island during Elizabeth's rule were both enabled and impeded by this earlier conquest. Over the intervening four centuries the Old English settlers had become in cultural terms all but indistinguishable from the Irish, which hugely complicated English attempts to fight the colonial war on cultural turf by proscribing Irish custom, dress, and social institutions. One of the earliest English statutes in Ireland, enacted in 1297, had required the English to "relinquish the Irish dress," while the Statutes of Kilkenny in 1366 had expressly linked English adoption of the "manners, fashion, and language of the Irish enemies" to the decay of "the said land and its liege people, the English language, the allegiance due to our lord the king, and the English laws."[15] By the sixteenth century, despite such separatist legislation, Old English settlers had adopted many Irish ways. The imperfect allegiance of the Anglo-Irish nobility to Elizabeth and to her metropolitan power was reflected in their rather less ambivalent embrace of Irish culture.

The Irish mantle became a particularly loaded signifier of such cultural struggles.[16] In Spenser's *A View of the Present State of Ireland* (1596) the two interlocutors, Eudoxus and Irenius, propose several competing genealogies for such mantles. Irenius states that the Irish have such a custom "from the Scythians," to which Eudoxus responds with a long history tracing the mantle from Jews to "Caldees" and Egyptians, through Greeks and Romans. But Irenius—who is given an extensive last word on the matter—cuts that history short:

> I cannot deny but anciently it was common to most, and yet Sithence disused and laid away. But in this latter age of the world since the decay of the Roman Empire, it was renewed and brought in again by those northern nations, when breaking out of their cold caves and frozen habitation into the sweet soil

of Europe, they brought with them their usual weeds, fit to shield the cold and that continual frost to which they had at home been enured; the which yet they left not off, by reason that they were in perpetual wars with the nations where they had invaded, but still removing from place to place carried always with them that weed as their house, their bed and their garment, and coming lastly into Ireland they found there more special use thereof, by reason of the raw cold climate, from whom it is now grown into that general use in which that people now have it; afterward the Africans succeeding, yet finding the like necessity of that garment, continued the like use thereof.[17]

The mantle—house, bed, and garment—becomes inextricably linked to Irish transhumance, the seasonal movement of people and their livestock in search of pastures, one of the practices that most disturbed the English and which they associated closely with barbarity and "enormities unto that commonwealth."[18] Yet this history looks forward, too, by projecting the mantle from the Irish to the Africans, despite the logic of climatic determinism. Irenius does not deny the mantle a genealogy but simply replaces the history of civil peoples with one of savagery, setting the stage for the kind of colonialist quotation that I shall analyze below.

The discussion of the mantle continues at some length, with Irenius paradoxically providing more examples of the usefulness of such garments the more he seeks to criticize them. The perspective from under the cloak differs greatly from that outside it—as Irenius says, "the commodity doth not countervail the discommodity. . . . for it is a fit house for an outlaw, a meet bed for a rebel, and an apt cloak for a thief."[19] One's appreciation of the mantle, then, will vary radically according to whether one is the persecuted or the persecutor. In Spenser's description the mantle becomes the reified signifier of Irish resistance, which cannot be fully penetrated by English authority, even with English ethnography leading the way. As Jones and Stallybrass argue, "The mantle represents Irishness as the refusal to adopt English order, English social categories, English style."[20] Moreover, as one of the prime signifiers of Irishness, the mantle served to assess the extent to which earlier settlers had "gone native": the adoption of the mantle was presumably the culminating move in such acculturation.[21] It is significant, then, that this problem is carefully avoided in Irenius and Eudoxus's discussion, as the latter moves quickly from the mantle to a warning about English use of the "glib," or long bangs over the eyes:

> Sure I think Diogenes' dish did never serve his master more turns, notwithstanding that he made his dish his cup, his measure, his waterpot, then a mantle doth an Irishman, but I see they be all to bad intents, and therefore I will join with you in

abolishing it. But what blame lay you to then glib? Take heed, I pray you, that you be not too busy therewith, for fear of your own blame, seeing our Englishmen take it up in such a general fashion, to wear their hair so unmeasurably long that some of them exceed the longest Irish glibs.[22]

The Irish glibs, Irenius answers, are "fit masks as a mantle is for a thief." The subject of English mimicry of Irish fashions, however, has once again been carefully avoided. If, as Sir John Davies wrote, the Old English imitating Irish ways are "like those who had drunke of Circes Cuppe, and were turned into very Beasts," the real threat lay not in the power of the witch but in the fact that her colonist victims "tooke such pleasure in their beastly manner of life, as they would not returne to their shape of men againe."[23] The metaphor takes on an interesting resonance if read back into Spenserian allegory in Book II of *The Faerie Queene*. In the Bower of Bliss, Acrasia/Circe's cup threatens not so much the disarmed knight (who can, after all, be disenchanted) as it does Grill, who stubbornly insists on going—and staying—native, famously refusing to be saved back into civilization.

The cultural warfare so well exemplified by Spenser's diatribe was just one front of attack in the English conquest of Ireland. As the violence escalated from the 1560s to the early part of the seventeenth century, anti-Irish rhetoric became ever more virulent, precisely to justify the widening attacks against Irish civilian populations. Ireland did eventually provide large estates for English gentlemen, but only after a bloody and extended struggle such as the English had not expected. Throughout this conflict, Ireland and America were both considered attractive options for expansionist ambitions; when particularly frustrated in their Irish campaigns, colonizers like Humphrey Gilbert and Walter Ralegh turned to America instead. Similarly, when the earliest English settlements at Roanoke proved impossible to sustain, such veterans of the American voyages as Thomas Hariot and John White tried planting in Ireland as an alternative.[24]

The connection between these desirable colonies as expansionist sites was established rhetorically at a number of levels. The description of dress—to return to our discussion of Caliban's cloak—is one of the clearest instances of the quoting of a previous colonial experience in a new plantation. The English often perceived the Americas through an Irish filter. Thus Gabriel Archer described the natives' leggings in New England as "like to *Irish* Dimmie Trouses," and Martin Pring saw natives with "a Beares skinne like an *Irish* Mantle over one shoulder."[25] Even Powhatan's dress was described by one of John Smith's companions as "a faire Robe of skins as large as an Irish mantle."[26] As the comparisons expand beyond costume to other cultural practices, such as "wild" mourning, devil worship, and transhumance—all of which the English believed they had found on both sides of the Atlantic—it becomes easier to see how such comparisons contribute to the "othering" of a culture by assimilating it conceptually to one already subdued, if not conquered.[27] The resulting quotations function as the colonist's mirror image of miscegenation: instead of the confusion of racial boundaries that might actually threaten his dominion, he creates a purely rhetorical union of various colonial subjects. The others are insistently other but similar among themselves. I should stress, of course, that both the similarities and differences quoted belong to a constructed "text" of culture.[28]

Quoting from one colonial context to the other serves to domesticate the new—the American experience—and equate it with the already-advanced plantation of Ireland. Yet the considerable chronological overlap of European colonial experience in Ireland and America makes the temporal sequence more difficult to untangle. Although Ireland's subjection is the primary colonial context for England in the 1590s and early 1600s, that conquest is in turn justified by comparing the English role in Ireland to that of the Spaniards in America.[29] References to previous Spanish conquests introduce a kind of reciprocity in colonialist quoting, with Ireland as the middle term: the English quote the Spanish experience in America in order to justify England's role in Ireland, and then transfer that Irish experience to Virginia. Yet the process of quotation must reach increasingly farther back in history for additional terms to substantiate the comparison. Thus the similarity between the English situation in Ireland and the Spanish *Conquista*—a problematic one considering Elizabethan propaganda against Spain—is reinforced by allusions to the *Reconquista,* or expulsion of the Moors from Spain, to further buttress colonialist apologias. Davies justifies the forcible transplantation of the Irish in Ulster by referring to "the Spaniards [who] lately removed all the Moors out of Grenada into Barbary, without providing them any new seats there."[30] The end of the comparison gives away Davies's conscience: Spain was far more concerned with preventing the return of the Moors expelled from North Africa than with their resettlement. In Ireland what to do with a starving peasant population forcibly removed from its land was a question not easily addressed.

Nicholas Canny finds the main source for the English/Spanish connection in Richard Eden's translation of Peter Martyr's *De Orbe Novo* (1555), which was probably familiar to English notables in Ireland in the 1560s.[31] The Spanish conquest of the Americas became a model for the domination of savage peoples, so that the English comparison of their own role in Ireland to the Spanish conquests became closely imbricated with the construction of the Irish as barbarous. In this colonialist logic, once the Irish were thus char-

acterized, they became appropriate subjects for the same treatment Native Americans had received at the hands of the Spanish. That the English reviled Spanish behavior, disseminating the infamous Black Legend of Spanish atrocities in the Indies, seems not to have impeded use of this model when the Irish situation made it expedient.[32] English characterizations of Irish savagery, based on the natives' supposed paganism and transhumance, proceeded apace: by 1560 Archbishop Matthew Parker could take such descriptions as a given, advocating the establishment of resident clergy in the north of England to prevent the inhabitants from becoming "too much Irish and savage."[33]

In constructing the Irish as savages, the English placed them within a temporal framework in which Ireland existed at a stage of social development long since surpassed by England. Ireland required civilizing by England in much the same way that England had required colonizing by Rome.[34] Sir Thomas Smith engaged in this rather partial relativism when he explained:

> This I write unto you as I do understand by histories of thyngs by past, how this contrey of England, ones as uncivill as Ireland now is, was by colonies of the Romaynes brought to understand the lawes and orders of thanncient orders whereof there hath no nacon more streightly and truly kept the mouldes even to this day then we, yea more than thitalians and Romaynes themselves.[35]

The recognition of one's own past in another by no means implies an acceptance of that other; it instead establishes a temporal dynamic in which that other must be made the same—forcibly brought up to date, so to speak. Here, England has already been civilized, having accepted the imposition of the Roman mold. This shapely civility then authorizes the imposition of a similar rule on Ireland, as *translatio imperii* becomes a kind of *translatio morum.*

English emphasis on the need to civilize the savage Irish partly replaces an earlier model of colonialist justification in which the Old English had argued that the Irish needed to be liberated from the tyranny of their own ruling class but were essentially fit subjects for English law and, indeed, desirable tenants or laborers.[36] It is possible to read these shifting constructions of the colonial subject in the two depictions of islanders in Shakespeare's text. Although Ariel need not be read as the co-opted native, as some modern rewritings of *The Tempest* insist, it *is* possible to view him as the colonizer's fantasy of a pliant, essentially accommodating, and useful subject. Of course, the play's ironic presentation of Prospero's fantasy shows the tensions inherent in this model. Ariel's gratitude is never as complete or as certain as Prospero would wish. Perhaps, the text suggests, a liberated native tends to interpret liberation in terms rather different from those of his or her enlightened liberator. In the lively prehistory of the play, Prospero freed Ariel from Sycorax's tyranny—wonderfully literalized in the pine trunk that bound him; but it is unclear whether subjugation to the new magician on the scene really means more liberty for the sprite.

Caliban, meanwhile, recalls the second model developed by the English to justify colonization: the Irish subject in need of civilizing. Miranda's speech presents the colonizer's story of attempts to civilize the native and locates the supposed intractability of Caliban in his lack of language (1.2.350-61). Consider her description of his inability to express himself:

> I pitied thee,
> Took pains to make thee speak, taught thee
>   each hour
> One thing or other. When thou didst not,
>   savage,
> Know thine own meaning, but wouldst gabble
>   like
> A thing most brutish, I endowed thy purposes
> With words that made them known.
>   (ll. 352-57)

Emphasis on the impenetrability of Caliban's language—even he, according to Miranda, cannot understand it—evokes the English colonizers' frustration with Gaelic as a barrier to their penetration of the territory.[37] But Caliban cannot be "liberated" simply by being taught English. The end of Miranda's speech betrays the unspoken half of the colonialist argument: if the native's "vile race" makes him inherently unsuited to civilization, then violence is justified:

>   But thy vile race—
> Though thou didst learn—had that in't which
>   good natures
> Could not abide to be with; therefore wast
>   thou
> Deservedly confined into this rock,
> Who hadst deserved more than a prison.
>   (ll. 357-61)

Here the duplicitous logic of colonialist ideology is exposed: if one explanation for Caliban's subjection doesn't work, a more essentialist one will be found. Language is more useful than Caliban knows.

My point is not that the elements of colonialist discourse in the text do not apply to the Americas. It would be ridiculous to deny that the English experienced a similar or even greater disorientation when confronted with American languages and cultures than with Gaelic. Instead, I am attempting to display the layering of such contexts in the play, from the basic discourse of savagery developed by the English in Ire-

land to their eventual experiences in the Americas. To read only America in *The Tempest* is to ignore the connections that colonial quotation establishes between England's two main Western plantations, connections perhaps expressed most graphically in the instability of their geographic referents. In the first part of the seventeenth century, Ireland could be, as it was to Bacon, "the second island of the ocean Atlantic," or it could migrate to a completely different conceptual context, as in Fynes Moryson's description of "This famous Island in the Virginian Sea."[38]

· · · · ·

> This Tunis, sir, was Carthage.
>   (2.1.82)

Even within these pages it has not been possible to separate Irish and Mediterranean colonial contexts without postponing the insistent presence of the latter, as the English in Ireland compare themselves to the Spaniards expelling the Moors and the Irish mantle is sighted not only in America but in Africa. Our inability to describe simultaneously the bewildering number of ways in which early modern Europe experienced other civilizations prevents us from uncovering all the connections among those experiences, but a focus on one area of contact should not preclude consideration of others. Ann Rosalind Jones has tried to bring together multiple cultural encounters by exploring the often-made comparison of Vittoria Colombina's Moorish maid Zanche to the Irish in Webster's *The White Devil*.[39] The attribution to Zanche of both Irish and Moorish savagery is particularly evocative if we consider that two terms of the comparison represent, respectively, a newly established Western colony *of* England and an Eastern empire that was a threat *to* England. Such a conflation of attributes in the figure of the Moorish maid may suggest how the English import a gendered discourse into their cultural negotiations with the Moors in order to disable the Islamic threat.

Textual signs of English anxiety about Islamic power in the Mediterranean abound in the play, though critics generally relegate those signs to a literary register. When discussing the marriage of Alonso's daughter Claribel to the king of Tunis, Gonzalo points out that Tunis *is*, in a fundamental way, Carthage: "This Tunis, sir, was Carthage." Critics hastily explain *Carthage*, with its baggage of Virgilian associations, as though the mention of Tunis were self-explanatory.[40] While some recent criticism has explored the early seventeenth-century construction of Islam in the English theater,[41] there are specific textual traces of the imperial Ottoman threat in *The Tempest*. Even though by the 1580s trade was established between England and the Turkish world, the perceived menace of Islam was still great. Writing his *Generall Historie of the Turkes* in 1603, Richard Knolles calls them "the greatest terrour of the world" and advocates the reading of his text because the Ottoman Empire "in our time so flourisheth, and at this present so mightily swelleth as if it would ouerflow all, were it not by the mercie of God."[42] The threat of Islam existed on two fronts: southeastern Europe (which will not concern us here) and the Mediterranean. Knolles shows great respect for Ottoman power on both land and sea: "With the great Ocean [the Ottoman monarch] much medleth not, more than a little in the gulfes of Persia and Arabia: most of his territories lying vpon the Mediterranean and Euxine seas. . . . Now for these seas, no prince in the world hath greater or better means to set forth his fleets than hath he."[43]

During the sixteenth century the Barbary Coast that figures so prominently in Shakespeare's play had come gradually under Turkish power.[44] In fact, Algiers, Sycorax's home before her banishment, had been captured by the Turks in the 1530s. Charles V led an expedition against it in 1541 but without success. Tunis itself had very recently been the site of a European struggle against the Ottoman Empire: captured by the Spanish in 1572, it was reconquered by the Turks in 1574.[45]

Morocco had never been part of the empire, and a substantial diplomatic relationship developed between its rulers and Elizabeth, allied together against both the Spanish and the Turks.[46] After James's peace with Spain, England abandoned its rather fanciful plans for invading Spain with Morocco's help and instead considered invading Morocco. Writing to King James, Henry Roberts suggested that the campaign be carried out with "Irish soldiars and they of the Out Isles," as "the countrey wilbee the better to bee ridd of them, for they bee but idle and will never fall to worke but steale as longe as they remaine in Ireland."[47] Once again the colonized—here proposed as mercenaries—return to English rhetoric as new conquests are envisioned.

The possibility of conquering Morocco, however remote, might account for the representation of non-Turkish Moors, in plays such as Heywood's *Fair Maid of the West,* as embodying a "dangerous but effeminate otherness that finally renders them safely inferior to their European visitors," as Jean Howard puts it.[48] But Howard makes race the main cause of such a representation, minimizing the difference between Turks and Moroccan Moors in terms of an expansionist imperative. I think that the difference in terms of an imperial threat is fundamental: isolated Morocco could be an ally or, treacherously, could be turned into a colony; under the Ottoman Empire the rest of North Africa remained a much greater threat. Thus England's willingness to consider Moroccan Islam a lesser threat than Spanish Catholicism: Morocco was not an expansionist power, or at least not in the direction of Europe.

The perceived threat from the Ottoman Empire itself, however, did not abate, even after the decisive victory

at Lepanto. This 1571 naval battle was hailed as the triumph of Christendom over the Turks, but it was soon clear that the intra-European alliances necessary to mount a credible challenge to Ottoman power would not last. One textual record of the unusual place that Lepanto occupied in the history of the European struggle against Islam is King James's epic poem on the subject, written after the battle and republished when he acceded to the English throne.[49] The poem caught Richard Knolles's attention, and he dedicates his history to James, "for that your Majestie hath not disdained in your *Lepanto* or *Heroicall Song,* with your learned Muse to adorne and set forth the greatest and most glorious victory that euer was by any the Christian confederat princes obtained against these the *Othoman* Kings or Emperors."[50] Perhaps the most interesting signs of the European tensions that made the Lepanto victory unrepeatable appear in James's preface to the reader, where he provides an extensive set of justifications for a Protestant monarch's praise of the Catholic alliance: "And . . . I knowe, the special thing misliked in it, is, that I should seeme, far contrary to my degree and Religion, like a Mercenary Poët, to penne a worke, *ex professo,* in praise of a forraine Papist bastard. . . . " Although the extraordinary circumstances of the battle justify his praise of Don Juan of Austria "as of a particular man," James suggests, the reader should not extrapolate from that praise any sympathy for the Catholic League: "Next follows my invocation to the true God only, and not to all the He and She Saints, for whose vain honors, DON-IOAN fought in all his wars."[51] In James's ambivalent unwriting of the poem's epic praise, we see reflected the fragility of the European unity that had led to the great naval triumph.

In the years after Lepanto, as English trade with the Turks was gradually established, England developed a complex relationship to the Ottoman threat. While a healthy respect for the Turks' imperial might prevailed, Islam (especially in the Moroccan version) also became a term in an elaborate set of rhetorical constructions which played it off against Catholicism as a lesser, or merely equivalent, evil. An observer like Knolles, however, thought that Spain, given its American riches, was the most appropriate power to deal with the Turkish emperor:

> There remaineth only the king of Spaine, of all other the great princes either Christians or Mahometanes (bordering vpon him) the best able to deale with him; his yearely reuenewes so farre exceeding those of the Turkes. . . . [52]

Knolles suggests that the Spanish have the best chance of defeating the Turks but regrets that their resources are spread too thin over their many possessions "for the necessarie defence and keeping of his so large and dispersed territories."[53]

For England the situation vis-à-vis the Turks was further complicated by piracy in the Mediterranean. As the sixteenth century drew to a close, petty piracy gradually replaced large naval encounters.[54] English merchants were prey to Barbary pirates from Algiers or Tunis, but English piracy also flourished, glorified during Elizabeth's reign as privateering against the Spanish and alternately condemned and condoned once peace with Spain had been reached. When English pirates fell out of favor at home, they "turned Turk." Purchas locates the scandalous confusion of Moors and English renegades in Algiers, which he calls "the Whirlepoole of these Seas, the Throne of Pyracie, the Sinke of Trade and the Stinke of Slavery; the Cage of uncleane Birds of Prey, the Habitation of Sea-Devils, the Receptacle of Renegadoes of God, and Traytors to their Country."[55] But the figure of the English renegade seemed threatening, I conjecture, mainly because it shattered the carefully constructed mirroring of Barbary Coast pirates in English privateering. As long as this mirror image was maintained, the English could imagine a role for themselves in controlling the Mediterranean. Once English pirates became, effectively, outlaws and went over to the other side, England was at a disadvantage, having no official expansionist presence in such contested territory. This complicated background of piracy on the sea and traditional Islamic expansionism on land lies behind the Algiers described as Sycorax's birthplace in *The Tempest*, 1.2. Yet even that origin is made more complicated by the location of the main action of the play on an island somewhere between Tunis and Italy.

In some ways the Mediterranean islands themselves were the most volatile territories in the region. Malta had withstood the Turkish assault in 1565, but the Knights of St. John had moved there only when it proved impossible to defend Rhodes. Cyprus, too, was in Turkish hands, as even the victory at Lepanto had proved insufficient to reconquer it. All the islands were especially vulnerable, of course, to pirate raids. Any island imagined in the Mediterranean at the time of the play, then, would be understood to exist in a hotly contested space, permanently threatened by the Ottoman Empire if not directly under its control.

If one focuses on Tunis and the threat it posed to the Christian areas of the Mediterranean, the indecorous marriage that sets the royal party in *The Tempest* on their journey becomes ever more outrageous. If the marriage of Desdemona to Othello is controversial, it could at least be partly redeemed by the fact that Othello the Moor fights against the Turks on the side of Venice. To marry a daughter to the king of Tunis, while perhaps expedient in political terms, is a far more radical move than to pair her off in some convenient European alliance. To Lynda Boose's argument that "the black male-white female union is, throughout this period and earlier, most frequently depicted as the ulti-

mate romantic-transgressive model of erotic love,"[56] I would add that the chastening tragic end of *Othello* cannot be discounted as one vision of such unions. The threat of violence to Christian women from irascible foreign husbands is well chronicled in Knolles, who tells the story of Manto, a Greek lady taken prisoner by the Turks, who marries Ionuses Bassa, an official in Suleiman's army. After an initial interlude of married bliss, Bassa, "after the manner of sensuall men still fearing least that which so much pleased himselfe, gaue no lesse contentment to others also," becomes madly jealous.[57] Manto tries to leave him and return to her country but is betrayed by a eunuch, whereupon her husband kills her. This story could have served as a source for *Othello;* whether or not it did so, it highlights the dangers that Europe imagined for a woman married into the empire of Islam. Such a union would probably be more acceptable in European eyes when (as with Othello fighting for Venice or the Prince of Morocco coming to Belmont to woo Portia unsuccessfully in *The Merchant of Venice*) it involved the domestication of the foreign male rather than the removal of a European woman to North Africa or Asia Minor. As Sebastian points out, rubbing salt in Alonso's wounds:

> Sir, you may thank yourself for this great loss,
> That would not bless our Europe with your
>   daughter,
> But rather lose her to an African,
> Where she, at least, is banished from your
>   eye,
> Who hath cause to wet the grief on't.
>   (2.1.121-25)

The description of Claribel's forced marriage recalls grim accounts of Christians captured by Barbary Coast pirates rather than stories of transgressive romance. Sebastian continues to insist upon the near-sacrificial nature of the union:

> You were kneeled to and importuned
>   otherwise
> By all of us, and the fair soul herself
> Weighed between loathness and obedience at
> Which end o'th' beam should bow. . . .
>   (ll. 126-29)

What does this marriage tell us, then, about the sexual politics of the play as a sublimated arena for imperial struggles? Knolles suggests the reason for the Claribel-Tunis union when he describes Naples as the European border of the Ottoman Empire. Alonso is thoroughly chastised for his decision to marry off his daughter (presumably to contain Islamic attacks on Naples), but the reproaches come from one who wishes him ill and would usurp his crown. The thoroughly negative characterization of the island conspirators somewhat relegitimizes the marriage, since it is mainly Sebastian who condemns it. Yet the most telling reaction to the supposed alliance with Tunis comes when Sebastian and Antonio discuss murdering Alonso for his crown. At this point Claribel entirely replaces her Moorish consort, as her femaleness is used to fix Islam firmly in Africa. When Antonio asks Sebastian who, after Ferdinand, is next in line to the crown of Naples, Sebastian answers "Claribel." Antonio then places Claribel at a further and further remove from the crown by insisting on the impossible distances that separate her from Europe:

> ANTONIO She that is Queen of Tunis; she that dwells
>
> Ten leagues beyond man's life; she that from Naples
>
> Can have no note unless the sun were post—
> The man i' th' moon's too slow—till newborn chins
>
> Be rough and razorable; she that from whom
> We all were sea-swallowed, though some cast again—
>
> And by that destiny, to perform an act
> Whereof what's past is prologue, what to come
>
> In yours and my discharge.
> SEBASTIAN   What stuff is this? How say you?
> 'Tis true my brother's daughter's Queen of Tunis,
>
> So is she heir of Naples, 'twixt which regions There is some space.
> ANTONIO   A space whose every cubit
> Seems to cry out, 'How shall that Claribel
> Measure us back to Naples? Keep in Tunis, And let Sebastian wake.'
>
>   (2.1.244-58)

Sebastian's commonsense rejoinder about "some space" is perfectly reasonable, considering that the distance from Tunis to Naples, as Stephen Orgel points out, is three hundred miles.[58] But what interests me here is the incredible amplification of space that Antonio imagines, as he expands the Mediterranean into an immense ocean. His hyperbole not only makes the crossing impossible but also neatly obscures its possible agents. Although Antonio measures the length of the voyage by a man's lifespan, by the man in the moon's speed, and by the time it takes for a baby boy to reach manhood, the actual man Claribel has married is nowhere to be found in the passage. Presumably, however, the king of Tunis would support his royal consort's claims to a European throne; perhaps his interest in conquering that throne justified the marriage in the first place. Antonio's exclusive focus on the possibility of Claribel's return should thus be read as a strategy for containing the role of Islam in the play. In a perverse metonymy, the European woman, instead of her threatening husband, becomes "Tunis." Unlike "Norway," "Denmark," "Morocco," "Aragon," and other heroic national ap-

pellations, the name of "Tunis" signifies only an infinitely distant Claribel. Much as the Turks in *Othello* are conveniently drowned in a single line of dialogue— "News, friends: our wars are done; the Turks are drown'd" (2.1.202)—in order to allow the domestic action to proceed, Antonio's relocation of Claribel to faraway Tunis and his erasure of her husband define the power struggles within the play as essentially European, regardless of the place where they are occurring. Of course Alonso's party is itself an exception to the supposed impossibility of getting to Tunis. Antonio admits this but points to their being "sea-swallowed" on their return. And yet the very urgency of the conspiracies on the island would indicate that the Italians have little doubt they will eventually return home. The play's containment of "Tunis"—a pressing, contemporary imperial threat—by focusing on Claribel's distance rehearses the earlier containment of a historical empire, Carthage, through the jocund references to "Widow Dido" in 2.1.

In *The Tempest* gender does the work of imperialism rather than of discovery.[59] The containment of the Islamic threat to European sovereignty or Mediterranean expansion plays itself out once again in the peculiar story of Sycorax's banishment from Algiers. This expulsion functions as a screen for European fears of Islamic control of the Mediterranean islands. Sycorax—cast as too awful even for the rough society of Algiers—is banished, as Prospero (whose source for this knowledge is somewhat unclear) tells Ariel, "For mischiefs manifold and sorceries terrible / To enter human hearing" (1.2.264-65). Yet her banishment was a commuted sentence; her life was spared "for one thing she did"—that is, her pregnancy. This ascription of mercy to the Algerians, reflecting European law, effectively replaces the Barbary pirates or Ottoman galleys—whose power so impressed Knolles— with the flimsy bark of sailors on a charitable mission who deposited the pregnant Sycorax on the island. Again, the metonymic reduction of Islam to the figure of the witch is perverse, for what is at stake in the Mediterranean is not the "Satanic" side of Islam— which Sycorax might represent—but its military might. The rewriting of Islamic expansionism into an errand of mercy operates once again through a female figure—a type of containment far more subtle than the effeminization Howard points to in Heywood's play, or even than the commonplace associations of the East with luxury and sensuousness. Here the female figures take the place of the threatening Moors, so that the latter are disarmed at a remove. By indirectly neutralizing the threat of Islam, the text of *The Tempest* prevents any direct engagement with its forces, addressing instead a female version, which is more easily conquered, at least in rhetoric. As the action of the play proves, Sycorax represents a temporary presence rather than an effective Islamic conquest of the island; her son Caliban loses it immediately to the

Europeans. Moreover, this second instance of containment through figuration is presented by Prospero, who, whatever his colonialist failings, clearly represents a center of moral authority in the text. Thus it is not only conspirators who turn to the feminine as a strategy for ensuring European power: Prospero's story emasculates Algerian naval power just as Antonio and Sebastian's fantasies erase the king of Tunis.

The gendered dynamics of Mediterranean containment in the play recall the more common gendered colonialist trope of ravishing a newly discovered land. Clearly this particular island no longer has her maidenhead; she is thoroughly known by Caliban, who was familiar with her secrets even before Prospero arrived, and who showed Prospero "all the qualities o'th' isle" (l. 337). Instead of rhapsodizing the European rape of the island, then, the text provides as counter-metaphor another rape—Caliban's attempt on Miranda—as colonialist justification (ll. 347-48).[60] Caliban's attack on Prospero's daughter once more genders the colonizing impulse; here it is the defense of the European woman that justifies repression of the non-European.

The triad of female figures which I have considered (two of them absent, two largely submissive daughters) thus participates in the text's containment of Islamic expansionism and its more complex espousal of European colonialism. The rhetorical representation of the women, through hyperbole, metonymy, and the anti-metaphor of Miranda's near-rape, performs European imperial goals at the discursive level, and it is only by interrupting that performance through, for example, a consideration of the play's multiple contexts that the illusionism can be examined.

Thus the discursive work of gender functions as yet another set of colonialist strategies. Much like the use of quotation which I identified when discussing the connections between English experiences in Ireland and America, these rhetorical strategies in *The Tempest* make sense only when viewed from the perspective of multiple contexts. Europe's experience of being another empire's goal was closely bound up, temporally, materially, and rhetorically, with its burgeoning experience of empire-building; it is no wonder, then, that the multiple dimensions come together in a text as complex and polysemous as *The Tempest*. By purposely conflating and collapsing these contexts, I have attempted to give a political reading of the play which insists on what Richard Knolles would call "the four parts of the world," in order to prevent Shakespeare's island play from itself becoming isolated somewhere in the Americas.

Notes

I would like to thank Stephen Orgel and Patricia Parker for their kind suggestions for this essay.

[1] I take the term "contact zone" from Mary Louise Pratt's *Imperial Eyes: Travel Writing and Transculturation* (London and New York: Routledge, 1992). Pratt uses this term to replace "colonial frontier," a term "grounded within a European expansionist perspective" (6-7).

In her suggestive "Rogues, Shepherds, and the Counterfeit Distressed: Texts and Infracontexts of *The Winter's Tale* 4.3," (*Shakespeare Studies* 22 [1994]: 58-76), Barbara A. Mowat explores the "infracontexts" of *The Winter's Tale*. In my analysis of *The Tempest*, I will show how such superimposition of contexts serves colonialist ideologies. In discussing what I shall call "colonial quotation," I adhere to a wide definition of intertextuality as a relation between not only literary but also cultural texts. This notion of intertextuality recognizes that, as Roland Barthes argues, "The logic that governs the Text is not comprehensive (seeking to define 'what the work means') but metonymic; and the activity of associations, contiguities, and cross-references coincides with a liberation of symbolic energy" ("From Work to Text" in *Textual Strategies: Perspectives in Post-Structuralist Criticism*, Josué V. Harari, ed. [Ithaca, NY: Cornell UP, 1979], 73-81, esp. 76). Unlike Barthes, I perceive such symbolic energy as driving a particular ideological project.

[2] See Peter Hulme, *Colonial Encounters: Europe and the native Caribbean, 1492-1797* (London and New York: Methuen, 1986), 106.

[3] William C. Spengemann, in *A New World of Words: Redefining Early American Literature* (New Haven, CT, and London: Yale UP, 1994), points out that America "was in fact the source of the genre called 'newes'" (97).

[4] See Hulme, 108-9.

[5] Bernard Lewis, *Islam and the West* (New York: Oxford UP, 1993), 16.

[6] See Samuel C. Chew, *The Crescent and the Rose: Islam and England during the Renaissance* (New York: Oxford UP, 1937), 100.

[7] Paul Brown, "'This thing of darkness I acknowledge mine': *The Tempest* and the discourse of colonialism" in *Political Shakespeare: Essays in cultural materialism*, Jonathan Dollimore and Alan Sinfield, eds., 2d ed. (Ithaca, NY, and London: Cornell UP, 1994), 48-71, esp. 57.

[8] See Nicholas P. Canny, "The Ideology of English Colonization: From Ireland to America," *William and Mary Quarterly* 30 (1973): 575-98.

[9] For one approach to the role of translation in colonization, see Eric Cheyfitz, *The Poetics of Imperialism:*

Translation and Colonization from The Tempest *to* Tarzan (New York and Oxford: Oxford UP, 1991).

[10] In his "Broken English and Broken Irish: Nation, Language, and the Optic of Power in Shakespeare's Histories" (*Shakespeare Quarterly* 45 [1994]: 1-32) Michael Neill suggests how a different form of quotation might serve to *counter* colonialism. If, as he argues, Irish nationalism was produced by the same English nationalism that violently redefined and colonized Ireland, then perhaps the strategy of quotation need not work entirely to the conquerors' advantage.

[11] Quotations of *The Tempest* in this essay follow the Oxford text (ed. Stephen Orgel [Oxford: Clarendon Press, 1987]).

[12] I find Brown's identification of Trinculo with the "footloose Irish" (56) as a masterless barbarian unconvincing, given that Trinculo so clearly occupies the position of colonizer in this episode. This is not to suggest, however, that the text is not staging an anxiety about the *English* masterless classes.

[13] In his introduction, Cheyfitz suggests that this reference to gaberdines links Caliban to the Jews (xii), although the main evidence in the *Oxford English Dictionary* for such a connection derives from Shakespeare's own usage in *The Merchant of Venice* (*Oxford English Dictionary,* prepared by J. A. Simpson and E.S.C. Weiner, 2d ed., 20 vols. [Oxford: Clarendon Press, 1989], 6:302). I would argue that the highly charged discourse about Irish coverings in the period provides a more immediate referent.

[14] For a good summary of this history, see David Beers Quinn, *The Elizabethans and the Irish* (Ithaca, NY: Cornell UP, 1966), or Canny, *The Elizabethan Conquest of Ireland: A Pattern Established 1565-76* (New York: Barnes and Noble, 1976).

[15] The preamble to the Statutes of Kilkenny, excerpts reprinted in A. J. Otway-Ruthven, *A History of Medieval Ireland* (London: Ernest Benn; New York: Barnes and Noble, 1968), 291.

[16] For a suggestive account of the role of the Irish mantle in terms of gender dynamics, see Ann Rosalind Jones and Peter Stallybrass, "Dismantling Irena: The Sexualizing of Ireland in Early Modern England" in *Nationalisms & Sexualities,* Andrew Parker, Mary Russo, Doris Sommer, and Patricia Yaeger, eds. (New York and London: Routledge, 1992), 157-71. Neill also discusses the mantle as a site for English anxieties about the "inscrutable" Irish other (26).

[17] Edmund Spenser, *A View of the Present State of Ireland,* ed. W. L. Renwick (Oxford: Clarendon Press, 1970), 51.

[18] Spenser, 49.

[19] Spenser, 51.

[20] Jones and Stallybrass in Parker et al., eds., 166.

[21] In discussing the contradictory English attitudes toward the mantle, Jones and Stallybrass note that "a miscegenation of clothes returns to haunt the colonizer" when a military supplier in Ireland suggests to Elizabeth that she provide her English troops there with an Irish mantle (Jones and Stallybrass in Parker et al., eds., 168). Although the authors read the episode as a sign of fragile English cultural identity, to adopt the mantle might also be to incorporate the enemy's tricks.

[22] Spenser, 53.

[23] Sir John Davies, *A Discovery of the Reasons Why Ireland Was Never Entirely Subdued* (1612), 182; quoted here from Jones and Stallybrass in Parker et al., eds., 163.

[24] See Quinn, 109ff.

[25] Samuel Purchas, *Purchas His Pilgrimes,* 4 vols. (London, 1625), 4:1647 and 1655.

[26] John Smith, *Works. 1608-1631,* ed. Edward Arber (Birmingham: Privately Printed, 1884), 102; see also page 405.

[27] Although I cannot address it here, such colonial quoting was also used to characterize African peoples newly encountered in the period, comparing them to the Irish.

[28] Colonialism mediates English encounters with its several others, so that observation is never neutral or transparent. As Neill has shown, not only is ocular control essential to English domination in Ireland, but the construction of the Irish as different already brands them with a kind of guilt (26-27 and 6).

[29] For a discussion of such triangulation, see Canny, "The Ideology of English Colonization."

[30] Davies to Salisbury, 8 November 1610, quoted here from Davies, *Historical Tracts* (Dublin, 1787), 273-86, esp. 283-84.

[31] See Canny, "The Ideology of English Colonization," 593-94.

[32] The first translation of Bartolomé de las Casas's *Breve historia de la destrucción de las Indias* appeared in England under the title *The Spanish Colonie* (London, 1583). The English emulation of Spanish behavior is thus exactly contemporaneous with its condemna-

tion. For an account of how this ambiguity played itself out in Ralegh's voyage to Guiana, see Louis Montrose, "The Work of Gender in the Discourse of Discovery" in *New World Encounters,* Stephen Greenblatt, ed. (Berkeley: U of California P, 1993), 177-217.

[33] Matthew Parker, *Correspondence* (1833), quoted here from Quinn, 26.

[34] This strategy for disarming criticism of colonialism has had a long life. Compare Joseph Conrad's evocation of a "primitive" London in *Heart of Darkness* (New York: Signet, 1978): after eulogizing the Thames as the artery of commerce and empire, Marlow says, "And this also has been one of the dark places of the earth" and proceeds to evoke the Roman arrival in Britain (67).

[35] Sir Thomas Smith to Fitzwilliam, 8 November 1572; quoted here from Canny, *Elizabethan Conquest,* 588-89.

[36] See Canny, *Elizabethan Conquest,* 580 and 589.

[37] The English address the threatening incomprehensibility of the natives' language itself through the mechanisms of colonial quotation. The term *hubbub,* originally used to describe an Irish war cry or outcry, migrates to Virginia, where Henry Spelman hears the Indians making a "whoopubb" (Smith, cv). The *OED* itself incorporates the strategies of colonial quotation, defining *hubbub* as "a confused noise of a multitude shouting or yelling; esp. the confused shouting of a battle-cry or 'hue and cry' by *wild or savage races*" (7:459, my emphasis).

[38] Francis Bacon, *The Letters and the Life of Francis Bacon,* 4th ed. (1868), and Fynes Moryson, *An Itinerary* (1617); both quoted here from Quinn, 121-22.

[39] See Ann Rosalind Jones, "Italians and Others: Venice and the Irish in *Coryat's Crudities* and *The White Devil,*" *Renaissance Drama* 18 (1987): 101-19.

[40] See, for example, Robert Wiltenburg, "The *Aeneid* in *The Tempest,*" *Shakespeare Survey* 39 (1987): 159-68; and John Pitcher, "A Theater of the Future: *The Aeneid* and *The Tempest,*" *Essays in Criticism* 34 (1984): 193-215. Orgel does mention Spain's repeated attempts to invade Tunis in the sixteenth century (40).

It must be noted that the imperial name of Carthage itself travels far beyond the classical world. By the seventeenth century Cartagena was the name of both a city in Spain and a Spanish settlement in what is now Colombia. Orgel cites Richard Eden's mention of this West Indies harbor as "Carthago" in *The Decades of the New World* (London, 1555), a translation of Peter Martyr's *De Orbe Novo.*

[41] See especially Lynda E. Boose, "'The Getting of a Lawful Race': Racial discourse in early modern England and the unrepresentable black woman"; Jean E. Howard, "An English Lass Amid the Moors: Gender, race, sexuality, and national identity in Heywood's *The Fair Maid of the West";* and Patricia Parker, "Fantasies of 'Race' and 'Gender': Africa, *Othello,* and bringing to light," all in *Women, "Race," and Writing in the Early Modern Period,* Margo Hendricks and Patricia Parker, eds. (London and New York: Routledge, 1994), 35-54, 101-17, and 84-100.

[42] Richard Knolles, *The Generall Historie of the Turkes,* 2d ed. (London, 1610), A4^v and A6^v.

[43] Knolles, Aaaaaa6^r.

[44] See, for example, Prospero's account of Sycorax (1.2.261-70) and the discussion of Claribel's marriage to the king of Tunis (2.1.68-84 and 244-58).

[45] For a concise summary of these events, see Chew, 551-55.

[46] For a detailed account of the history of Anglo-Moroccan relations, see Jack D'Amico, *The Moor in English Renaissance Drama* (Tampa: U of South Florida P, 1991), 7-40.

[47] Henry De Castries, *Les Sources Inédités de L'Histoire du Maroc* (1918); quoted here from D'Amico, 38.

[48] Howard in Hendricks and Parker, eds., 113.

[49] For the poem's publication history and an account of the battle as the background for *Othello,* see Emrys Jones, "'Othello', 'Lepanto' and the Cyprus Wars," *SS* 21 (1968): 47-52.

[50] Knolles, A3^r.

[51] "Lepanto" in *The Poems of James VI of Scotland,* ed. James Craigie, 2 vols. (Edinburgh: William Blackwood and Sons, 1955), 1:198.

[52] Knolles, Bbbbbb^r.

[53] Knolles, Bbbbbb^r.

[54] See Fernand Braudel's encyclopedic *The Mediterranean and the Mediterranean World in the Age of Philip II,* trans. Siân Reynolds, 2 vols. (London: Collins, 1973), 2:1186-95.

[55] Purchas, quoted here from Chew, 344.

[56] Boose in Hendricks and Parker, eds., 41.

[57] Knolles, 557.

[58] Orgel, ed., 2.1.245n.

[59] I allude to Montrose's discussion of Ralegh in Guiana ("The Work of Gender" in Greenblatt, ed.).

[60] In another variation on this theme, the natives' alleged sexual violence toward the Europeans' intended land was sometimes offered as a colonialist justification, as in Purchas's description of the vulnerable Virginia: " . . . howsoeuer like a modest Virgin she is now vailed with wild Couerts and shadie Woods, expecting rather rauishment then Mariage from her Natiue Sauages . . ." (4:1818).

Source: "Conquering Islands: Contextualizing *The Tempest*," in *Shakespeare Quarterly*, Vol. 48, No. 1, Spring, 1997, pp. 45-62.

Stormy Weather: Derek Jarman's *The Tempest*

Diana Harris and MacDonald Jackson, *University of Auckland*

British filmmaker Derek Jarman died in February 1994. Any comprehensive account of his achievements must include a revaluation of his 1979 screen adaptation of Shakespeare's *The Tempest,* which anticipated many of the distinctive strategies of Peter Greenaway's *Prospero's Books* (1991). Greenaway's film is hi-tech, with lavish crowd scenes and a kaleidoscopic profusion of images created with the aid of the "digital, electronic Graphic Paintbox."[1] Jarman's film was low budget, employing an orthodox mix of "masters, mid-shots and close-ups" (Jarman 194).[2] Yet, in their vastly different idioms, both movies dwell on the original script's obsession with the interaction between life, art, dream, and play, subtly shifting through different planes of reality and representation. In filling the frame each director draws on a rich European artistic heritage. Greenaway recalls Piranesi, Bronzino, Da Messina, Michelangelo, Leonardo da Vinci, Botticelli, Veronese, Rembrandt, Bellini, and others. Jarman playfully alludes to Velázquez's "Las Meninas" and composes candle-lit shots with the balance and beauty of paintings by Caravaggio or De la Tour.

Where Greenaway adds a postmodern self-consciousness about the relations between signifiers and the signified, and the ways in which text, as it is inscribed, conjures a world into being, Jarman's contemporaneity is more "social," the product of an exotic sensibility rather than of a modish intellect.[3] Jarman's films have been widely perceived as "statements of the late-1970s and early 1980s British counterculture, intended for punk and gay audiences" (Vaughan and Vaughan 209), and his version of *The Tempest* certainly re-imagines the play, foregrounding the same-sex relationship between Prospero and Ariel, desentimentalizing the romance of the young lovers, Ferdinand and Miranda, with comedy and burlesque and fun, and emphasizing dream as a Jungian search for self-hood.

Jarman jettisons the bulk of Shakespeare's dialogue and re-orders most of what he keeps. The remains of the play's speeches may be scattered over several film sequences. Gonzalo's amiable garrulousness, for example, is enhanced by being protracted in this way. After Alonso's group arrives on shore in a dinghy, they trek through sandhills toward Prospero's mansion, and Gonzalo's Pollyanna-like chatter as he attempts to cheer the king or expounds his vision of Utopia percolates through three of the sequences showing this journey. We gain the impression that Alonso has an *idée fixe,* about which he cannot stop talking. Shakespeare's long expository monologues, in which

Prospero, in scene ii, tells Miranda of historic grievances, risk an audience's boredom and are thoroughly uncinematic. Jarman avoids tedium by dispersing them over several episodes, extending well into the middle of the film. Like Zeffirelli in his recent *Hamlet,* Jarman repeatedly breaks Shakespeare's scenes into smaller units, which he interweaves. The effect is to compress the time-scheme of a play that is already one of only two in which Shakespeare preserves the Aristotelian unities,[4] and to suggest that several related events are happening at the same time. The film's closing wedding-masque sequence assembles the whole cast and draws all the threads of the plot together.

The opening tempest is itself a challenge to a director. Shakespeare creates it through his dialogue, with the aid of a few primitive sound effects. On the modern stage, designer pyrotechnics and the electronic speaker system are apt to obliterate the words. In the cinema we expect to see a frothing ocean and a masted ship foundering, but may regret the loss of Shakespeare's evocative language and the metaphorical link between the storm and Prospero's inner turmoil. Jarman's solution to the practical problem becomes a key to the main significances of his film. In *Prospero's Books,* Greenaway has Gielgud as Prospero speak all the dialogue. Jarman had toyed with this idea: in his "first cut-up of the text . . . a mad Prospero, rightly imprisoned by his brother, played all the parts" (183). But in the final version it is only during the opening sequence that Prospero (in voice-over) utters other characters' speeches.

Throughout his film, Jarman uses blue filters for outdoor scenes. This establishes a night-time, illusory quality, and the opening shot of sea, sky, and clouds is quickly assimilated into the imagination of Prospero as he dreams in a shadow-haunted gothic castle on the Northumbrian coast.[5] The ship-master's "Bestir" is an urgent, echoing whisper in sleep; the wind of the tempest merges with the exhaling of breath as Prospero tosses and turns on his bed, his face netted under a gauze scarf. The shouts of the storm-tossed sailors become the anxious disembodied utterances of nightmare. "We split, we split!" (I.i.61) is as much a comment on disintegration of the personality as a reference to the breaking up of the vessel. Through Jarman's montage, the dark-blue shots of the lurching ship, crew scrambling along the rigging, and turbulent seas are linked with the mind of the troubled dreamer. The sleeper is conjuring up not only the shipwreck of his enemies but memories of his own maltreatment by them, when, ousted from his dukedom, he was hurried aboard a rotten bark, which was providentially washed ashore upon the island where he now reigns supreme. "The very rats/Instinctively have quit it" (I.ii.147-48), recalls Prospero, when later narrating his ordeals to Miranda; and in Jarman's film a white rat, heralded by a squeak on the soundtrack, scuttles across Prospero's bed. A little later a rat's eye glints momentarily through the gloom. More rodent screeches signal the ship's destruction. As the word "aground" reverberates, Prospero gasps himself awake, sits upright, and stares ahead in horror, to amplified sounds of a wave crashing. Miranda in her bed also stirs, as though implicated in her father's nightmare, but sticks her fingers back into her mouth, and curls up again under the covers.

Jarman's transitions from the sleeping Prospero to the stricken ship are very subtle. The bedroom is mostly shot in full colour, but as he cuts back and forth between indoors and outdoors, or dreamer and dream, Jarman sometimes for a split second shows Prospero and his bed in virtual monochrome, which thus mediates between the two orders of reality. At the end of the sequence, Jarman cuts to a shot of Prospero striding toward his study, where he will evoke Ariel. Jarman thus constructs the first half of a frame that encloses Prospero's, Shakespeare's, and the director's fantasy. Thereafter deep breathing is heard intermittently over the soundtrack to maintain the theme, and lines such as Miranda's "'Tis far off;/And rather like a dream" (I.ii.44-45) and Ferdinand's "My spirits, as in a dream, are all bound up" (I.ii.487) are given prominence.

Heathcote Williams is an unusually youthful Prospero, a forty-something "cross between Heathcliff in grunge and Dr Who" (Harris) with a hands-off approach to parenting. His hair recalls Beethoven. But his study is cluttered with the pseudo-scientific equipment of a Renaissance magician like the German Cornelius Agrippa, the Italian Giordano Bruno, or the Elizabethan adept Dr John Dee: there are mathematical and cabbalistic formulae, astrological diagrams, alchemical symbols, Egyptian hieroglyphs, the runic inscriptions of Agrippa's *Occult Philosophy,* a model of the zodiac, arrays of candles, perspective glasses, and crystal balls. Prospero's wand derives from Dee's *Monas Hieroglyphica,* "which symbolized the unity of spirit and matter" (Jarman 188). The indoors scenes were shot in Stoneleigh Abbey in Warwickshire, and this crumbling Kafkaesqe pile with its gloomy stairwells becomes the natural habitat of a scholar recluse, mad inventor, master of the occult. It is also well stocked with paraphernalia for play, like a Theatre Costume and Properties Hire shop. An alabaster bust resembling Prospero raises our awareness of questions of identity and mimesis.

Like many Shakespeare plays, *The Tempest* looks very different to most modern critics from the way it looked a few decades ago.[6] Instead of Prospero the benign mage, wise ruler over his island kingdom, stand-in for a Shakespeare who was delivering his farewell to the London stage after having emerged from the anguish of his tragic phase into a mood of reconciliation and faith in natural renewal, commentators find a deeply disturbed protagonist, whose tyrannical and repressive urge to control reflects his own inner insecurities, and who represents that vein of British empire-building which robs the indigenous peoples of their native inheritance in the name of civilization. Nineteenth-century critics accepted Prospero's attitude towards Caliban. Recent critics are apt to sympathize with Caliban's impulse to overthrow the oppressor. The patriarch, imposing his will on others, must take a measure of blame even for his subject's attempted rape of Miranda. The play's keynote was once thought to be "forgiveness"; lately it has more often been seen as preoccupied with "power."

Certainly *The Tempest* bears some relation to the Renaissance revenge play. Prospero is like the wronged avenger-hero, who now has his enemies at his mercy. An emotional and psychological struggle within him between passion and reason, vengeance and forgiveness, can introduce "a sense of dramatic conflict necessarily lacking in an action moving at the will of an omnipotent being."[7] Modern critics have explored the conflict within Prospero—and behind him Shakespeare—between his need to see himself as humane, benevolent, and forgiving and his innate aggression, resentment, vindictiveness, and rage.[8] The plot itself moves toward Prospero's recognition that "the rarer action is/In virtue than in vengeance" (V.i.27-28), but his anger surfaces in the verbal details: the threats with which he controls the recalcitrant Ariel and Caliban, his mouth-filling descriptions of the cramps and convulsions to be visited on Stephano and Trinculo, the relish with which he pretends enmity toward Ferdinand. Against his brother Antonio he wields his forgiveness like a shillelagh: "For you, most wicked sir, whom to call brother/Would even infect my mouth, I do forgive/Thy rankest fault—all of them" (V.i.130-32). Jarman brings out Prospero's unacknowledged rancour through some striking images. As he addresses the spellbound Antonio he holds a rapier point just below his treacherous brother's eye. Approaching the sleeping Ferdinand, he raises an axe, as though about to behead him, but smashes it down into the chopping block that Ferdinand is thus implicitly commanded to use. "The concept of forgiveness in *The Tempest* attracted me," wrote Jarman (202), who exposes the strain with which Prospero subdues his animosity and achièves that compassion which Ariel says he would feel were he human: "if you now beheld them, your affections/ Would become tender" (V.i.18-19). Jarman's tricksy spirit utters this key speech as a wistful face peering out of a bundle of straw; his expression registers pleasure as Prospero resolves to forgive.

Toyah Wilcox's Miranda, a neglected child turned adolescent, is obviously used to creating her own entertainment. She invents herself with the help of a fertile imagination and a chest of clothing. Her hairdo, dreadlocks adorned with whisps of thread, is even more outlandish than her father's. She tries on hooped petticoat and bridal veil, blows a handful of feathers from a balcony, and arranges larger ones in her hair. She has the air of a self-absorbed but engaging urchin, with an infectious sense of fun. But she is also a curious, adventurous, sexually awakened young woman. Ariel sets her on the path to marriage with Ferdinand by intoning the wedding-masque verses forecasting fertile union, "Honor, riches, marriage-blessing" (IV.i.106), as he rocks astride her old rocking-horse, his motion lightly hinting at the consummation to come, while the toy itself serves as reminder of the child now poised on the verge of womanhood. In response, she mimes being a princess with airs and graces as she descends a flight of stairs to a xylophone accompaniment, but slips over on her backside and has to start again! Recapitulating Ariel's benediction, she herself recites scraps from the masque during her play-acting. She appears to treat Ariel as a familiar playmate, but he has cast himself in the role of nurse or surrogate mother, supervising her maturation. But she remains a lively teenager with a gleeful chuckle, playing battledore and shuttlecock with Ferdinand before their game of chess.

Miranda has very little fear of Caliban, as portrayed by the blind harlequin Jack Birkett, "The Incredible Orlando." This Caliban is more "mooncalf" than "monster" (Vaughan and Vaughan 210). He is slack-jawed, camp, very physical but hardly a sexual threat to Miranda, who regards him as a voyeuristic nuisance. After her first encounter with him, he flaunts his open flies as she hurries away. Later he bends over and makes farting noises. This merely amuses her. Bald, shambling, baring his ugly teeth in vacant grimaces, he cackles and leers, a drooling natural. He is like a giant baby, so that the bizarre flashback showing him sucking at the breast of his grotesque mother, the hookah-smoking witch Sycorax, seems strangely appropriate. On his first appearance his hands are rummaging in a still-life platter of bruised fruit and stale vegetables in search of a raw egg. Finding one, he breaks it with his teeth and sucks the contents with slavering relish. He lisps and whines and croons. Prospero treats him with sadistic contempt, trampling on his fingers, as though corporal punishment is the only language he really understands. Caliban often seems like the embodiment of some despised element of Prospero's own psyche, an incarnation of the Freudian id; he lurks, motionless, in the background, like some dark shadow-self, while Prospero informs Miranda of past happenings. He is indeed a "thing of darkness" that Prospero must acknowledge as his (V.i.275-76). But he is clothed, as he sweeps the stairs, like an old-time Deep South butler. Drake, Purchas,

or Raleigh might have called him a "mulatto." Racially unclassifiable, this Caliban might be the modern commentators' colonized native of disputed origin. His broad North Country "This island's mine by Sycorax my muvver" (I.ii.331) brings specifically English considerations of class and regionalism into his characterization, and he is vehement in his accusations that Prospero has robbed and enslaved him.

The inset of Sycorax is one of a sharply contrasting pair. With her mountain of naked flesh, lurid lipstick, and short peroxided hair in Medusa ringlets, Caliban's dam looks as though she belongs in the seamiest kind of 1930s Berlin night-club, where Ariel suffers, rather than enjoys, bondage: Sycorax hauls him towards her by a long chain attached to his metal collar, while Caliban watches and sniggers. These images accompany Prospero's reminder to Ariel of the torment from which the mage had freed him. Jarman similarly illustrates Prospero's assurance to Miranda that during their sufferings at sea she was "a cherubim . . . that did preserve me" (I.ii.152-53): through an enchanter's scrying-glass Prospero shows his daughter a curly-headed blonde cherub, smiling as though lifted from some pastel-tinted Shirley Temple postcard; the adoring father, a spruce young aristocrat, beams with pride as she shyly parades in her Sunday best to music-box tinklings. Both flashbacks—to decadence and to innocence—have an air of camp excess that includes a hint of parody, but they are effectively antithetical nonetheless: cherubim as opposed to sorceress, preserver to torturer, virgin to whore.

Ariel (Karl Johnson) is a fascinating counter to Prospero. Dressed in a white boiler-suit and gloves, he is the technician for Prospero's research. This Ariel fits Jan Kott's conception of the character as like "a laboratory assistant working at an atomic reactor" (206). Yet he manages to convey a curiously disengaged quality that makes him more authentically a "spirit" than many conventional Ariels. He is like Prospero's Jungian anima figure—the mysterious "other" who complements him. He seems already to have gone through the angst that plagues Prospero, is more worldly wise, more cryptic, older even, and unsurprisable. He wears a pearl in his left ear-lobe, and, without the least suggestion of stereotypical homosexual mannerisms or the conventional androgyny, he comes across as knowingly and securely gay. His pallor is other-worldly. Spotlighting emphasizes it, especially when Prospero sits in contrasting shadow. The relationship between Prospero and Ariel is ambiguous, homoerotically charged, and sometimes tortuous. The dynamics of power are held in balance, often slipping or oscillating between them. We are aware that master can become slave, and slave can become master. Prospero's dominance is most evident when he pins Ariel behind a glass screen; both Prospero's vision of Ariel and Ariel's of Prospero are shown as consequently blurred. Williams's lines are spoken softly and sensitively, "not bawled across the footlights" (Jarman 194), and Ariel's delivery is flat and impassive, and sometimes droll. He crouches in the long marram grass of the dunes, as he sings (in *Sprechgesang* style) "Full fathom five" to Ferdinand or "Awake, awake!" to Alonso and Gonzalo; the effect is to indicate his affinity with sea, sand, and sky, rather than to hint that he is potentially visible to the courtiers.

Ariel's nervousness about reminding Prospero that he has promised him his freedom is brought out by the way he rehearses his brief rebuke, accompanying his words with hand gestures mimicking the playground power-game "Scissors-Paper-Stone," where the aim is to anticipate the opponent's counter-move. He is curious about Prospero's knick-knacks. Corpse-like himself, he toys with a miniature skull, clicking its jaws as he clicks his own, as though puzzling over what makes him different from mere mortals. When he recounts his escapades with Ferdinand, he appears, greatly diminished in size, as a floating projection on the wall above the mantlepiece in Miranda's bedroom, and at another point he goes to open a door, finds it stuck, glances at Prospero, shrugs deprecatingly, and with a snap of his fingers disappears. This looks almost like a parody of the antics of screen fairy folk, including the BBC Ariel, with his trick exits.[9] In general this Ariel's non-human nature is established in more subtle ways. His first arrival is genuinely spooky: as Prospero repeats his commands, "Come away, servant, come; I am ready now" (I.ii.187), a doorknob turns, chandeliers sway and tinkle, a spider scuttles across a prayerbook open at the communion service, a beaker of red wine (adjacent to "The Thirty-Nine Articles") falls on its side, and Ariel's voice is heard, as at a seance, before he materializes in person in a lightning flash and a clap of thunder. Madam Blavatsky could not have managed a more effective spirit entry. Jarman's cuts back and forth between close-ups and medium or long shots are perfectly calculated to produce the required frisson.

Sometimes you might half wonder whether there is anyone corporeal inside Ariel's overalls. With several other characters there is a contrasting emphasis on the body. The shipwrecked Ferdinand, for instance, wades to shore in blue-filtered light, a male Venus emerging from the waves, and staggers to Prospero's castle, to sleep naked in the straw of Caliban's lair before a blazing fire. There he is discovered by Ariel, who is joined by Prospero, Miranda, and Caliban in turn. After Prospero's feigned threats and accusations, Ferdinand, standing face to a wall, is manacled and made to wear a white uniform, while Caliban grinds out a merry tune on a hurdy-gurdy. The disjunction between the carnivalesque gaiety of the music and the pathos of Ferdinand's humiliation is unsettling. Miranda feels only pity: the next shot shows her weeping as she gently handles a dead butterfly. This aligns her with Shakespeare's other compassionate maidens, such as Marina, who in *Pericles* "never kill'd a mouse, nor hurt a fly" and wept when she "trod upon a worm" (IV.i.77-78).

Judging that "if one deals with unconventional subject-matter, experimental camera work can push a film over into incoherence" (194), Jarman restricted himself throughout to an orthodox repertoire of shots, but his masterly editing creates a remarkable visual poetry, with rhythms that enhance a sense of mystery. The skull-clicking episode, for example, begins with a close-up of a hand swinging a small glass pendulum, cuts to an extreme close-up of a wan-faced Ariel intently staring diagonally downward as he clicks his teeth, tilts slowly down his boilersuited torso to settle on the object of his gaze, the miniature skull whose jaws he opens and shuts, and only then moves to the long-shot overview that reveals Ariel in the foreground with Prospero in the background sitting at a table, each engrossed in his business; the holder of the pendulum turns out to have been Prospero. Ariel drops the skull on the table as Prospero addresses him. Through the ordering of the shots, which reverses the normal progression from master to close-up, we have been made to share Ariel's puzzlement, sense his strangeness, meditate on mortality, and deepen our understanding of the relationship between spirit-servant and sage.

The soundtrack is no less inventive. The whirring of wings may signal Ariel's arrival, departure, or unseen presence. Frogs croak as Alonso's benighted group heads for the castle. The sound of marching feet serves as a backing to Prospero's tale about the usurpation of his dukedom. Seagulls cry as Ferdinand wades ashore or Caliban plods along the strand. An owl hoots as Prospero performs his night-time rituals. Drum beats or a synthesized rolling hum, blending with the sough of wind, intensify foreboding, mystery, or menace.

The comedy surrounding Trinculo and Stephano, escapees from a Butlins Holiday Camp, is reduced to a few giggled phrases, supplemented by visual gags—funny walks and drunken dancing—though the conspiracy against Prospero, like that of Sebastian and Antonio against Alonso, is retained, together with some effective sorcery as punishment, with Ariel in close-up snarling and howling like a bayhound, dwarves screeching and clawing at the offenders like angry cats, and the contents of Prospero's costume room, with its skull-masked dummies, taking on a life of their own. The rocking-horse whinnies and snorts as it pitches back and forth to the soundtrack's excited hunting scene. Later Ariel pants with his tongue hanging out, an exhausted hound, but also resembling an epileptic whose fits confer a psycho-kinetic power. There are also suggestions of postcoital lassitude. Over the whole episode there hangs a vague air of erotic exhilaration. Sex, domination, magic: Jarman's Prospero is no Alister Crowley, but there is more than a smack of eros in his "so potent art."

The plan to murder Prospero is always patently doomed to failure. Events are so arranged that Jarman's Prospero is never distracted into forgetting about it, and he has the clairvoyance to keep track of all his enemies.

The *pièce de résistance* is Jarman's stunning wedding-masque finale, the "vanity of his art," to use Prospero's phrase for his show of spirits (IV.i.41). Alonso and his entourage have finally reached the castle. Warily treading its dark passageways, they hear unexpected sounds: "What harmony is this?" asks Alonso; "Marvellous sweet music!" exclaims Gonzalo (III.iii.18-19). We catch, muffled behind closed doors, the strains of a dance band and the shouts and laughter of convivial party-goers. Turning an engine that resembles some primitive forerunner to the orrery, Ariel weaves cobwebs to symbolically envelop the courtiers and transports them spellbound to the ballroom, which is garlanded in coronation splendour. Before the loving couple arrive—Miranda gorgeously attired as a cross between Scarlett O'Hara and My Fair Lady—Prospero instructs Ariel to go to the king's ship and rescue "the mariners asleep/Under the hatches," waken them and "enforce them to this place" (V.i.98-100). "Presently," urges Prospero, meaning "immediately," and the room is forthwith invaded by the whole ship's company of sailors, miraculously dressed in modern naval uniform as if on leave from H.M.S. Pinafore and dancing a speeded-up hornpipe in a hilarious send-up of chorus-line revues and spectaculars from Gilbert and Sullivan on: Hollywood blockbusters, Esther Williams/Busby Berkley productions, and perhaps the Reinhardt-Dieterle film of *A Midsummer Night's Dream*.[10] It is a joyous celebration of male bonding. In fact it is also a gay in-joke. In his autobiography *Dancing Ledge* Jarman describes a party for Sir Francis Rose, where Jean Cocteau brought twenty-one sailor boys as a gift to Francis for his twenty-first birthday. After the dark-blue outdoor and chiaroscuro indoor scenes, the blaze of light that fills the room is itself invigorating, and the music is witty and cheerful to the point of frenzy. Ariel, MC in white jacket and bow tie, remains an onlooker but seems close to contentment amidst this bevy of sweating men. Shakespeare's nautical concerns are brilliantly fused with Jarman's homoerotic theme. If this *Tempest* is Prospero's dream, the dance routine is the symbolic fulfilment of repressed desire. It is liberating and parodic at the same time. But it is also an apt enough entertainment for a Miranda who has been isolated from humankind and now bubbles over with delight. "How many goodly creatures are there here!" indeed (V.i.182).

Next to appear are Caliban and his fellow conspirators, with Trinculo, dressed as a drag queen, eliciting wolf whistles from the sailor lads. In Shakespeare's play Stephano and Trinculo do in fact don the "trumpery" by which Prospero has diverted them from their murderous scheme, but Jarman gives their frivolity a char-

acteristic twist. Then Ariel's wizardry plucks down a shower of rose petals, which becomes a deluge when supplemented by the contents of the sailors' upturned hats. We view the beaming bride and groom through this confetti, until down the florally carpeted corridor formed by the naval guard of honour walks Iris, Ceres, and Juno rolled into one—Elisabeth Welch, Sycorax's antitype, a black woman in the sophisticated garb of twenties chanteuse, golden as a sunflower. With feathery imitation cornstalks in her hair, she conveys the promise of the harvest goddess and the reminder of pain from the "brave new world": the pain of racial difference in a world of slavery, the pain of sexual relationships in a world of inconstancy. The text of Harold Arlen's "Stormy Weather," in Welch's marvellously soulful rendition, harmonizing music and tempest, resonates with echoes from the rest of the film and from Shakespeare's play:

> Don't know why, there's no sun up in the
>   sky,
> Stormy weather, since my man and I ain't
>   together,
> Keeps raining all the time.
>
> Life is bare, gloom and misery everywhere,
> Stormy weather, just can't get my poor self
>   together,
> I'm weary all the time.
>
> When he went away, the blues walked in and
>   met me,
> If he stays away, old rocking chair will get
>   me,
> All I do is pray the Lord above will let me
> Walk in the sun once more.
>
> I can't go on, everything I had is gone,
> Stormy weather, since my man and I ain't
>   together,
> Keeps rainin' all the time,
> Keeps rainin' all the time.

There is something in "Stormy Weather" for each character to recognize. Caliban hears the sound of slavery and resistance in the classic twelve-bar blues, the sound he unwittingly echoed in his own stumbling slave song, "'Ban, 'Ban, Ca-Caliban" (II.ii.184). Miranda and Ferdinand hear the complexities of lovers' relationships exposed. Ariel acknowledges the pain of losing Prospero: "Since my man and I ain't together/Keeps rainin' all the time." A touching close-up shows a sad and pensive Ariel, forefinger brushing his lips, as those lines are sung. Ferdinand and Miranda reassure each other with a tender kiss.

"Can't get my poor self together": the theme of psychic integration is touched on even here. "I can't go on"—"unless I be reliev'd by prayer" (Epi. 16): Prospero will renounce his magic and retire to Milan "where/ Every third thought shall be my grave" (V.i.311-12). "Everything I had is gone"—"The cloud-capp'd towers, the gorgeous palaces,/The solemn temples, the great globe itself" (IV.i.152-53).

A blues number is the ideal twentieth-century song form to encompass love and hate, vengeance and forgiveness, estrangement and reconciliation; to acknowledge how hard it is to limit desire, proscribe sexuality, exact penitence, or contain suffering. And what song could be more apt to the tempest conjured up by Prospero's so potent art than "Stormy Weather," with its refrain echoing Feste's wistful coda to the reunions and marriages that end *Twelfth Night:* "the rain it raineth every day."

"When he went away, the blues walked in and met me," sings Welch, and the blues have indeed walked in and complicated the jollity. At the end of the song, after Welch's yellow head-dress has momentarily drenched the screen in sunshine, this world is plunged back into blue-black night. Ariel picks his way through the deserted ballroom, which looks, now that the lights are out, oddly like an autumnal woodland dell, littered as it is with confetti, streamers, and faded flowers. He clambers onto the vacant "throne," looks toward Prospero, slumped asleep in a chair, gives a rueful smile, glances sadly about the room, falteringly sings "Merrily, merrily, shall I live now" (V.i.93) in a doleful voice, tiptoes past his master, pausing for one last lingering look, runs up a flight of stairs, and vanishes to the sound of beating wings. It is a poignant moment. The camera focuses on a close-up of Prospero, whose breathing serves as background to his sleep-talking voice-over:

> Our revels now are ended. These our actors
> (As I foretold you) were all spirits, and
> Are melted into air, into thin air . . .
> We are such stuff
> As dreams are made on; and our little life
> Is rounded with a sleep.
> (IV.i.148-58)

Although Jarman maintains an interest in power relations, and the shipwrecked nobles sport the regalia of evangelical imperialism (admiral's cap, scarlet ecclesiastical robes, war medals, military uniform, pendant crucifix), there is, finally, more of "Shakespeare's farewell to his stage" in this film than of "an allegory of colonization." Prospero's release of Ariel and abjuration of his art throb with our knowledge that Shakespeare's genius would soon cease to manifest itself in the creation of new scripts for the London theaters and that his life itself was nearing its end. While the relationship between Prospero and Ariel is at the emotional centre of Jarman's *Tempest,* Miranda's guileless teenage response to Ferdinand's courtship and her

unaffected *joie de vivre* may also touch the heart. Greenaway's *Prospero's Books* bombards the ear and eye with stimuli and teases the intellect, but it remains emotionally sterile. Jarman's movie, though often bizarre, engages the feelings; it is genuinely moving, and the emotions it arouses are essentially those aroused by Shakespeare's play. It captures many key aspects of the original, being particularly deft at hinting at the element of psychodrama involving the central trinity of Prospero, Ariel, and Caliban. It raises questions about body and mind, restraint and liberty, freedom and control, desire and fulfilment; it balances joy and sadness, innocence and experience, hope and despair; above all it powerfully conveys a sense of the shifting boundaries between illusion and reality, waking and dreaming, the playful and the serious, life and art. Jarman's anti-establishment style challengers or mocks "the designs of empire," gender stereotyping, and other forms of ideological policing. But, as every actor of Prospero knows, the speeches that, through their poetic richness, most move an audience are those conveying the playwright-magician's sense of mortality and the impermanence of all earthly things. A memorial to Jarman's mother, as the final frame announces, his *Tempest* stands both as a *memento mori* and as a monument to a filmmaker of idiosyncratic flair.[11]

Notes

[1] Greenaway's term in his book of the film, *Prospero's Books.*

[2] Jarman notes that most American reviews of his *Tempest* "saw it as deliberately wilful, and the *New York Times* mounted an attack which destroyed it in the cinemas there" (206). Frank Kermode slated the film in his review in the *Times Literary Supplement,* 16 May 1980, 553, but granted that "it sustains a mood" and "has a dreamlike, underwater quality, cold, dimly magical."

[3] The sensibility exhibited in Jarman's *Tempest* bears a close relation to that defined by Susan Sontag in her "Notes on Camp" in *Against Interpretation and Other Essays* (London: Eyre and Spottiswoode, 1967): 275-89. "Camp" is not "homosexual," but there is considerable overlap. Recent theorizing of gay literature and film, as by Eve Kosofsky Sedgwick in *Between Men, Epistemology of the Closet,* and *Tendencies,* has potential application to Jarman's films, but our interest in his *Tempest* is as an example of "Shakespeare on screen."

[4] The other is, of course, *The Comedy of Errors.*

[5] Jarman shot exteriors on the Northumberland coast near Banburgh Castle, where the viewer assumes the interiors to be, though they were actually shot in Stoneleigh Abbey in Warwickshire. See Samuel Crowl,

Shakespeare Observed: Studies in Performance on Stage and Screen (Athens: Ohio UP, 1992): 77. Crowl gives a brief, mainly positive, account of Jarman's film.

[6] Two major editions, Frank Kermode's Arden (1954) and Stephen Orgel's Oxford (1987), mark the shift in critical thinking.

[7] Review in *The Times* (London) of Peter Brook's 1957 production, as quoted by Hayman 178.

[8] Especially Bernard J. Paris, "*The Tempest:* Shakespeare's Ideal Solution," in Norman N. Holland, Sidney Homan, and Bernard J. Paris, eds., *Shakespeare's Personality* (Berkeley: U of California P, 1989): 206-25.

[9] However, the BBC/Time Life version of *The Tempest* was released in 1980, after Jarman's film had been made.

[10] The connection with Reinhardt and Dieterle is made by John Collick, *Shakespeare, Cinema, and Society* (Manchester: Manchester UP, 1989): 98-103. Collick discusses Jarman's film in rather different terms from ours. David L. Hirst offers some brief observations in his "Text and Performance" booklet on *The Tempest* (London: Macmillan, 1984): 41-60 *passim.*

[11] We are grateful to Maggie Taylor for allowing us to see her notes taken from the Jarman archives in the British Film Institute, London.

Works Cited

Greenaway, Peter. *Prospero's Books.* London: Chatto and Windus, 1991.

Harris, Diana. "Stormy Weather: Three Screen Adaptations of *The Tempest.*" ANZSA Conference. Perth, Feb. 1994.

Hayman, Ronald. *John Gielgud.* London: Heinemann, 1971.

Jarman, Derek. *Dancing Ledge.* London: Quartet Books, 1984.

Kott, Jan. *Shakespeare Our Contemporary.* London: Methuen, 1964.

Shakespeare, William. *The Tempest. The Riverside Shakespeare.* Ed. G. Blakemore Evans. Boston: Houghton Mifflin, 1974.

Vaughan, Alden T., and Virginia Mason Vaughan. *Shakespeare's Caliban: A Cultural History.* Cambridge: Cambridge UP, 1991.

Source: "Stormy Weather: Derek Jarman's *The Tempest,*" in *Literature/Film Quarterly*, Vol. 25. No. 2, 1997, pp. 90-8.

Virtue, Vice, and Compassion in Montaigne and *The Tempest*

Arthur Kirsch, *University of Virginia*

It has long been recognized that Shakespeare borrowed from Montaigne. Gonzalo's Utopian vision in *The Tempest* (II.i.142-76)[1] is indebted to a passage in Florio's translation of Montaigne's essay, "Of the Cannibals,"[2] and Prospero's speech affirming that "The rarer action is / In virtue than in vengeance" (V.i.20-32) is derived from the opening of Florio's translation of the essay, "Of Cruelty" (2:108). The king's speech in *All's Well That Ends Well* on the distinction between virtue and nobility (II.iii.117-44) appears to be a similarly direct, if less well-known, borrowing from "Upon Some Verses of Virgil" (3:72-3), an essay whose treatment of the polarization of sensuality and affection also has bearing upon *Othello*.[3] Leo Salingar has perspicuously shown that a number of the major themes of *King Lear,* as well as much of its distinctive vocabulary, are drawn from "An Apology of *Raymond Sebond*" and "Of the Affection of Fathers to their Children" as well as other essays;[4] and D. J. Gordon brilliantly demonstrated analogies between the critical stress upon names in *Coriolanus* and Montaigne's essay, "Of Glory."[5] Finally, as Robert Ellrodt has argued, the inward characterizations of Hamlet as well as of many of Shakespeare's other tragic heroes show clear affinities with the dynamics of self-consciousness, "a simultaneous awareness of experience and the experiencing self,"[6] that is fundamental to Montaigne's quest in all his essays to represent what he called "le passage" (3:23), the "minute to minute" movement of his mind.

The Tempest, however, remains the work in which Shakespeare's relation to Montaigne is most palpable and most illuminating. Shakespeare's play, of course, is exceptionally elusive. A variety of models and analogues have been proposed for it—Roman comedy, the Jacobean masque, and voyage literature among them—but it has no single governing source to offer a scaffold for interpretation, and it remains in many ways as ineffable as Ariel's songs. Confronted with such suggestiveness, and in revolt against the apparent sentimentality of traditional readings, the disposition of most critics of the last two decades has been to follow W. H. Auden's lead in *The Sea and the Mirror* (1942-44)[7] and stress ironic and subversive ambiguities in the play as well as its apparently patriarchal and colonialist assumptions.[8]

Shakespeare's demonstrable borrowings from Montaigne in *The Tempest,* which are among the very few verifiable sources for the play, can provide a complementary, and I think more spacious, way of understanding *The Tempest*'s ambiguities. In the absence of a narrative source, Shakespeare's organization of the action, as well as Prospero's, seems unusually informed by the kind of working out of ideas that suggests the tenor of Montaigne's thinking: inclusive; interrogative rather than programmatic; anti-sentimental but humane; tragicomic rather than only tragic or comic, incorporating adversities rather than italicizing them as subversive ironies. The particular constellation of ideas in the play, moreover—the mutual dependence of virtue and vice, forgiveness, compassion, imagination—is habitual in Montaigne.

Of the two clear borrowings from Montaigne in *The Tempest,* Gonzalo's vision of Utopia is by far the most well-known and most discussed, but it is the play's more neglected relation to "Of Cruelty" as well as several associated essays that is more fundamental and that I wish mainly to focus upon in this essay. Montaigne remarks in "Of Cruelty" that "If vertue cannot shine but by resisting contrarie appetites, shall we then say, it cannot passe without the assistance of vice, and oweth him this, that by his meanes it attaineth to honour and credit" (2:110). He elaborates on the same theme in "Of Experience": "Even as the Stoickes say, *that Vices were profitably brought in; to give esteeme and make head unto vertue,* So may we with better reason and bold conjecture, affirme, that Nature hath lent us griefe and paine, for the honour of pleasure and service of indolency" (3:357). He also writes in "Of Experience," in a passage drawn from Plutarch: "Our life is composed, as is the harmony of the World, of contrary things; so of divers tunes, some pleasant, some harsh, some sharpe, some flat, some low and some high: What would that Musition say, that should love but some one of them? He ought to know how to use them severally and how to entermingle them. So should we both of goods and evils, which are consubstantiall to our life. Our being cannot subsist without this commixture, whereto one side is no lesse necessary than the other" (3:352-3).

Such a view of virtue's dependence on vice—paradoxical rather than invidiously binary—is clearly relevant to both the structure and texture of *The Tempest.* Antonio and Sebastian's unregenerate rapaciousness and desperation are contrasted throughout to Gonzalo's beneficence and hopefulness, quite directly during the very speech in which Gonzalo paraphrases Montaigne. Venus is counterpointed with Ceres within the wedding masque, and the conspiracy of Caliban, Stephano, and Trinculo complements as well as disrupts the performance of the masque itself, whose high artifice and graciousness remain in our memory as much as the drunken malice of the conspiracy does in Prospero's. Caliban's own earthiness is constantly in counterpoint to Ariel's spirit—they are conceived in terms of each other.

Similarly, Miranda's celebrated verse, "O brave new world / That has such people in't," is not denied by, but co-exists with, Prospero's answer, "'Tis new to thee" (V.i.183-4). Neither response is privileged: youth and age are as consubstantial in the play as good and evil. Prospero's skepticism is directed toward the court party Miranda admires, not toward her and Ferdinand, whose marriage he himself speaks of with reverence and hope:

> Fair encounter
> Of two most rare affections! Heavens rain
>   grace
> On that which breeds between 'em.
> (III.i.72-4)

The marriage, indeed, is at the heart of Prospero's "project" within the play and is finally associated with the "project" of the play itself, "Which was to please," that the actor playing Prospero refers to in the Epilogue.

Both projects depend upon a union of opposites, of goods and evils, that ultimately suggests transformation as well as symbiosis. At the outset of the action Prospero tells Miranda, when she sees the shipwreck, that there is "no harm done . . . No harm," and that he has "done nothing but in care" of her (I.ii.15-7). His care culminates in Miranda's betrothal, but evolves through her suffering as well as his own, and he associates that suffering with the blessing as well as pain of their exile from Milan. They were driven from the city, he tells her, "By foul play," but "blessedly holp hither" (I.ii.62-3):

> There they hoist us
> To cry to th' sea that roared to us, to sigh
> To th' winds, whose pity, sighing back again,
> Did us but loving wrong.
> (I.ii.148-51)

The same motif is expressed by Ferdinand as he submits to Prospero's rule and works as a "patient logman" (III.i.68), a ritual ordeal that Prospero contrives to make him earn and value the love of Miranda:

> There be some sports are painful, and their
>   labour
> Delight in them set off; some kinds of
>   baseness
> Are nobly undergone; and my most poor
>   matters

> Point to rich ends. This my mean task
> Would be as heavy to me, as odious, but
> The mistress which I serve quickens what's
>   dead,
> And makes my labours pleasures. O, she is
> Ten times more gentle than her father's
>   crabbed,
> And he's composed of harshness. I must
>   remove
> Some thousands of these logs and pile them
>   up,
> Upon a sore injunction. My sweet mistress
> Weeps when she sees me work, and says such
>   baseness
> Had never like executor. I forget.
> But these sweet thoughts do even refresh my
>   labours,
> Most busil'est when I do it.
> (III.i.1-15)

This paradoxical combination of opposites—delight and pain, gentleness and harshness, the quickening of the dead—is analogous to the Christian idea of *felix culpa* that nourished Guarini's conception of the genre of tragicomedy to which *The Tempest* belongs and that is also to be found in the voyage literature frequently associated with *The Tempest*.[9] In "A true reportory of the wreck" off the islands of Bermuda, for example, William Strachey exalted the marvelous beneficence of the shipwreck at the same time that he delineated the vicious dissension among the voyages that developed in Bermuda and later in Virginia, the result, he wrote, of "the permissive providence of God."[10]

The manner in which the possibility of fortunate suffering informs the moral consubstantiality of the action of *The Tempest,* however, suggests the particular force of the process of Montaigne's thought in the play, a process that reaches its climax in Prospero's forgiveness of his enemies, the speech that Shakespeare derived directly from "Of Cruelty." In the ostensibly digressive manner that is typical of him, Montaigne opens the essay with a discussion of virtue, the passage Shakespeare paraphrases in the play. "Me thinks virtue is another manner of thing," Montaigne writes,

and much more noble than the inclinations unto goodnesse, which in us are ingendered. Mindes well borne, and directed by themselves, follow one same path, and in their actions represent the same visage, that the vertuous doe. But vertue importeth, and soundeth somewhat I wot not what greater and more active, than by an happy complexion, gently and peaceably, to suffer it selfe to be led or drawne, to follow reason. He that through a naturall facilitie, and genuine mildnesse, should neglect or contemne injuries received, should no doubt performe a rare action, and worthy commendation: But he who being toucht and stung to the quicke, with any wrong or offence received, should arme himselfe with reason against this furiously-blind desire of revenge, and in the end after a great conflict, yeeld himselfe master over-it, should doubtlesse doe much more. The first should doe well, the other vertuously: the one action might be termed goodnesse, the other vertue. For, *It seemeth that the verie name of vertue presupposeth difficultie, and inferreth resistance, and cannot well exercise it selfe without an enemie.* It is peradventure the reason we call God good, mightie, liberall, and just, but we terme him not vertuous.

(2:108)[11]

Shakespeare's version of this passage occurs in the last act of *The Tempest,* after Ariel tells Prospero of the sufferings of the court party.

Ariel. Your charm so strongly works 'em
That if you now beheld them, your affections
Would become tender.
Prospero. Dost thou think so, spirit?
Ariel. Mine would, sir, were I human.
Prospero. And mine shall.
Hast thou, which art but air, a touch, a feeling
Of their afflictions, and shall not myself,
One of their kind, that relish all as sharply
Passions as they, be kindlier moved than thou
        art?
Though with their high wrongs I am struck to
        th' quick,
Yet with my nobler reason 'gainst my fury
Do I take part. The rarer action is
In virtue than in vengeance. They being
        penitent,
The sole drift of my purpose doth extend
Not a frown further. Go, release them, Ariel.
My charms I'll break, their senses I'll restore,
And they shall be themselves.

(V.i.17-32)

Shakespeare's reliance upon Florio's translation of Montaigne in this speech was first pointed out by Eleanor Prosser in 1965 and now seems self-evident.[12] "Though with their high wrongs I am struck to th' quick / Yet with my nobler reason 'gainst my fury / Do I take part" is clearly indebted in phraseology as well as conception to Montaigne, and "The rarer action is / In virtue than in vengeance" is particularly indebted to Florio's phrase, "performe a rare action," which in the original reads "feroit chose très-belle et digne de louange," "do a fine and praise-worthy thing." These verbal parallels have been generally accepted in Shakespeare criticism, but their larger implications for the characterization of Prospero and for much else in the play have been, I think, almost willfully neglected.[13] A figure of supernatural as well as patriarchal authority, Prospero has godlike attributes, including a disquieting measure of the kind of irritability and wrath that often characterizes the Lord God in the earlier books of the Old Testament, but he learns about his humanity

in the course of the action,[14] and he transforms himself (as well as others) in a way that Montaigne specifically illuminates. His speech on compassion constitutes both an implicit acknowledgment of the difference between God's power and man's, a prologue to the adjuration of his "rough magic" that immediately follows, and an elucidation of the consequent strife that his human virtue entails. Many, if not most, of the traits and actions that in recent years have been thought to falsify Prospero's ostensible motives and to signify his intractably tyrannical, if not colonialist, mentality, are made immediately intelligible by Montaigne's essay. His impatience with his daughter, and with her suitor, the son of his enemy, his "beating mind," his insistent asperity, his marked reluctance in forgiving his brother, and his violence to Caliban: all are ultimately signs of the struggle of virtue that Montaigne describes. Rather than subverting Prospero's "project," they constitute and authenticate it. Touched and stung to the quick in the present as well as in the past, animated by a "furious," if not "furiously-blind desire of revenge," Prospero "in the end after a great conflict, yeeld[s] himselfe master over-it" (2:108). The emotional keynote of the play is precisely this sense of Prospero's labor pains, of the "sea-change," to paraphrase Ariel's luminous song, that he "suffer[s],"[15] of his "groan[ing]" "Under [the] burthen" of his "sea-sorrow" (I.ii.401, 156, 170) to give birth to new and resolved feelings. The action of the play dramatizes this process. The ordeals to which Prospero subjects others on the island are at once recapitulations of his beating memories and images of his effort to overcome them. His interruption of the wedding masque when he remembers Caliban (and perhaps thereby unconsciously expresses the threat of his own sexual desires)[16] is intelligible in just these terms, as is his ultimate and pained recognition that Caliban is native to him, has been made, indeed, partly in his image: "this thing of darkness I / Acknowledge mine" (V.i.275-6). The play's unusual obedience to the classical unities intensifies the sense of Prospero's struggle and is exactly appropriate to the presentation of the minute-to-minute pulsations, *le passage,* of a mind in the throes of accepting and forgiving.

Shakespeare also explores what makes compassion possible in *The Tempest,* and the whole of "Of Cruelty" is germane to this exploration, not just the introductory passage from which Shakespeare directly borrows. In the subsequent argument of the essay Montaigne reiterates the proposition that to be "simply stored with a facile and gentle nature" may "make a man innocent, but not vertuous," a condition "neere unto imperfection and weaknesse," and adds that "the verie names of Goodnesse and innocentie are for this respect in some sort names of contempt" (2:113). He goes on, however, to identify his own temperament with precisely such "a facile and gentle nature," and this identification is the essay's core subject. It is what makes the whole of it coherent, what connects it with "Of the Cannibals," whose essential subject is also cruelty,[17] and what forms the deepest ligament, I think, between both essays and Shakespeare's *Tempest*. "My vertue," Montaigne writes, "is a vertue, or to say better innocencie, accidentall and casuall . . . a kinde of simple-plaine innocencie, without vigor or art." "Amongst all other vices," he continues, announcing the theme of this essay, "there is none I hate more, than crueltie, both by nature and judgement, as the extremest of all vices" (2:115, 117). Montaigne's conjunction of his "innocence" and his hatred of cruelty has wide implications for an understanding of *The Tempest*. Montaigne says that he "cannot chuce but grieve" at seeing a "chickins neck puld off, or a pigge stickt," and "cannot well endure a seele dew-bedabled hare to groane, when she is seized upon by the houndes; although hunting be a violent sport" (2:117). His response is the same to cruelty to human beings. He protests that "Let any man be executed by law, how deservedly soever, I cannot endure to behold the execution with an unrelenting eye," and he condemns the "extreme point whereunto the crueltie of man may attaine," in which men torture others "onely to this end, that they may enjoy the pleasing spectacle." "I live in an age," he continues, "wherein we abound with incredible examples of this vice, through the licentiousnesse of our civill and intestine warres: And read all ancient stories, be they never so tragicall, you shall find not to equall those, we see daily practised" (2:119, 121). The contemporary civil wars in France elicit Montaigne's compassion, but they do not create it. The premise as well as the conclusion of Montaigne's response to cruelty is the recognition of his own inherently sympathetic nature: "I have a verie feeling and tender compassion of other mens afflictions, and should more easily weep for companie sake, if possiblie for any occasion whatsoever, I could shed teares. There is nothing sooner moveth teares in me, than to see others weepe, not onely fainedly, but howsoever, whether truly or forcedly" (2:119).

The discrimination of such compassionate impulses lies close to the heart of Montaigne's definition of himself in the *Essais* as a whole. In an addition made in 1588 to the opening essay of the first volume, when the full direction of the *Essais* must have become clear to him, he announces, "I am much inclined to mercie, and affected to mildnesse. So it is, that in mine opinion, I should more naturally stoope unto compassion, than bend to estimation. Yet is pitty held a vicious passion among the Stoicks. They would have us aid the afflicted, but not to faint, and co-suffer with them" (1:18). This opposition between compassion and detachment, as Jean Starobinski has suggested,[18] is part of the central dialectic of the *Essais*. Montaigne goes on to deprecate his mildness as effeminate and childish, but the Stoic self-sufficiency that at once animates his project and is its ostensible goal is always balanced, in this

essay and in the *Essais* as a whole, by his disposition to sympathize and "co-suffer" with others. One critic has argued that in "[p]utting cruelty first" among vices, ahead even of the seven deadly sins, Montaigne in effect repudiates Christian theology.[19] But that issue is at least open to debate. Montaigne has plenty to say about pride in *Sebond* and elsewhere, and his extraordinary capacity to "co-suffer" with other human beings, remarkable for his age, but not unlike Shakespeare's, can just as aptly and interestingly be understood as an internalization, if not embodiment, of Christian charity.

In *The Tempest,* in any event, cosuffering, compassion, is a tonic chord in the whole of the action, not just the work of Prospero alone. It is revealed throughout the play in the "piteous heart" of Miranda, who is animated by "the very virtue of compassion," as well as in Gonzalo. Gonzalo's "innocence," like Miranda's, is "simple-plaine . . . without vigor or art," and like Montaigne's also, it is composed of a "verie feeling and tender compassion of others mens affliction" (2:117, 119). It is the sight of "the good old Lord Gonzalo" and others in tears, "Brimful of sorrow and dismay" (V.i.14-5), that prompts Ariel's sympathy for the courtiers, and through him, the movement toward compassion in Prospero. "[I]f you now beheld them, your affections / Would become tender," Ariel says to Prospero, "Mine would, sir, were I human" (V.i.18-9). And Prospero answers, as we have seen, that if Ariel, who is but air, can have a "feeling / Of their afflictions," shall not he, "One of their kind," who relishes passions as sharply as they, be "kindlier moved," take the part of "reason 'gainst [his] fury," and find the rarer action in virtue than in vengeance (V.i.21-6).

Prospero, of course, emphatically does not have the innocence that nourishes Miranda's "virtue of compassion," nor does he have the innocent nature of Gonzalo, though he has from the first understood and responded to both. They can forgive instinctively, he cannot. But in this speech, the decisive moment in the action, Prospero is able to emulate them. He speaks of his reason in the struggle of virtue, as Montaigne does, but the speech more importantly suggests another faculty as well. "Kind," as often in Shakespeare, denotes humankind as well as human kindness, and it is in the first instance Prospero's ability to imagine what others feel and to understand what he has in common with them—including, especially, Caliban— that enables him to sympathize with Alonso and to forgive Antonio and Sebastian despite the wrongs that continue to anger him.

It is particularly significant that it should be Ariel, associated throughout the play with Prospero's imaginative power, who prompts this movement, because human imagination is finally the deepest preoccupation of Shakespeare in *The Tempest* and a central filament in Montaigne's thoughts on compassion as well. In an apparent digression in the midst of the discussion of forgiveness in "Of Cruelty," Montaigne suggests that a lack of imagination can *"sometimes counterfeit vertuous effects"* and that the Germans and the Swiss, for example, appear brave in war because they have "scarce sense and wit" to imagine their danger, whereas the "subtiltie of the Italians, and the vivacitie of their conceptions" is so great, that they foresee "such dangers as might betide them . . . far-off" and can provide for their safety even before they actually see the danger (2:114). Montaigne's remark may be ironic, but it is nonetheless to such "sense and wit," such "vivacitie" of imagination, that he relates his own innocence and susceptibility to the suffering of others.

That imaginative susceptibility also subsumes the indictment of the cruelty of European culture in "Of the Cannibals," and it appears as well in interesting ways in another essay, "Of Cato the Younger," in which Montaigne writes,

> I am not possessed with this common errour, to judge of others according to that I am my selfe. I am easie to beleeve things differing from my selfe. Though I be engaged to one forme, I doe not tie the world unto it, as every man doth? And I beleeve and conceive a thousand manners of life, contrarie to the common sort: I more easily admit and receive difference, than resemblance in us. I discharge as much as a man will, another being of my conditions and principles, and simply consider of it my selfe without relation, framing it upon it's owne modell. Though my selfe be not continent, yet doe I sincerely commend and allow the continencie of the Capuchins and Theatines, and highly praise their course of life. I doe by imagination insinuate my selfe into their place: and by how much more they bee other than my selfe, so much the more doe I love and honour them.
>
> (1:243)

Montaigne discusses an analogous imaginative "insinuation" in "Of Diverting and Diversions," where he relates cosuffering to the creation as well as effects of rhetoric and art:

> An orator (saith Rhetorick) in the play of his pleading, shall be moved at the sound of his owne voice, and by his fained agitations: and suffer himselfe to be cozened by the passion he representeth: imprinting a lively and essentiall sorrow, by the jugling he acteth, to transferre it into the judges, whom of the two it concerneth lesse: As the persons hired at our funerals who to aide the ceremony of mourning, make sale of their teares by measure, and of their sorrow by waight . . . *Quintilian* reporteth, to have seene Comedians so farre ingaged in a sorowful part, that they wept after being come to their lodgings: and of himselfe, that having undertaken to move a certaine passion in another: he had found himselfe surprised not only

> with shedding of teares, but with a palenesse of countenance, and behaviour of a man truly dejected with griefe.
>
> (3:59-60)

Quintilian's remark is a commonplace of the period, but Montaigne's mention of it in "Of Diversions" has a special suggestiveness because, like *The Tempest,* the essay associates the virtue of compassion not only with the salutary effects of the imagination but also with its illusoriness.[20] Right after mentioning Quintilian, Montaigne remarks that no cause is needed

> to excite our minde. A doating humour without body, without substance overswayeth and tosseth it up and downe. Let me thinke of building Castles in *Spayne,* my imagination will forge me commodities and afford me meanes and delights where with my minde is really tickled and essentially gladded. How ofte do we pester our spirits with anger or sadnesse by such shadowes, and entangle our selves into fantasticall passions which alter both our mind and body? what astonished, flearing and confused mumpes and mowes doth this dotage stirre up in our visages? what skippings and agitations of members and voice, seemes it not by this man alone, that he hath false visions of a multitude of other men with whom he doth negotiate; or some inwarde Goblin that torments him? Enquire of your selfe, where is the object of this alteration? Is there any thing but us in nature, except subsisting nullity? over whom it hath any power?
>
> (3:61)

In a well-known passage in "An Apology of *Raymond Sebond,"* Montaigne remarks that "We wake sleeping, and sleep waking . . . Our reason and soul, receiving the phantasies and opinions, which sleeping seize on them, and authorising our dreames actions, with like approbation, as it doth the daies. Why make we not a doubt, whether our thinking, and our working be another dreaming, and our waking some kind of sleeping" (2:317).

The same consciousness both of the force of human imagination and of its evanescence in human existence haunts Shakespeare's *Tempest* as well. Caliban expresses it with the greatest immediacy in his moving speech about the magic of the island and of his own dreams:

> Be not afeard, the isle is full of noises,
> Sounds, and sweet airs, that give delight and
>   hurt not.
> Sometimes a thousand twangling instruments
> Will hum about mine ears; and sometimes
>   voices,
> That if I then had waked after long sleep,
> Will make me sleep again, and then in
>   dreaming

The clouds methought would open and show
   riches
Ready to drop upon me, that when I waked
I cried to dream again.

                               (III.ii.133-41)

Prospero conveys a similar apprehension of imaginative impalpability and wonder, in a more metaphysical key, in his famous speech to Ferdinand after the interruption of the masque. He is enraged with Caliban, but in that very process, he incorporates Caliban's dreaming as well as interprets it. "You do look, my son, in a moved sort," he tells Ferdinand,

As if you were dismayed. Be cheerful, sir;
Our revels now are ended. These our actors,
As I foretold you, were all spirits, and
Are melted into air, into thin air,
And, like the baseless fabric of this vision,
The cloud-capped towers, the gorgeous
   palaces,
The solemn temples, the great globe itself,
Yea, all which it inherit, shall dissolve,
And, like this insubstanial pageant faded,
Leave not a rack behind. We are such stuff
As dreams are made on, and our little life
Is rounded with a sleep.

                               (IV.i.146-58)

The *topos* of life as a dream is of course very common in the Renaissance, but its collocation in *The Tempest* with the impalpable realities of the imagination as well as with Prospero's achievement of compassion, suggests the particular matrix of ideas found in Montaigne's essays. If not a source, Montaigne's association of these ideas is an explanation. One tendency in recent criticism of *The Tempest* has been to see Prospero's magnificent speech and the play itself as an expression of Shakespeare's disenchantment with the limitations of theatrical illusion.[21] But Caliban's dreaming and Prospero's incorporation of it in his reflection on the "baseless fabric of this vision" do not so much question the value of the theater, as characterize the dream-like nature of the human experience it imitates; and what the analogues to Montaigne should make clear is that Shakespeare's sense of this insubstantial pageant, of the subsisting nullity both of human existence and of the theater, is not ironic, but the "stuff" of wonder and a motive to charity.

The idea of imaginative insinuation and compassion is given a final, hauntingly expansive, turn in the epilogue to *The Tempest,* when Prospero, still the character but now also an ordinary human being, an actor, asks the audience for applause. He speaks at precisely the moment in a play when we too are midway between our own world and the world of the theater.[22] "Let me not," he says to us,

Since I have my dukedom got,
And pardoned the deceiver, dwell
In this bare island by your spell,
But release me from my bands
With the help of your good hands.
Gentle breath of yours my sails
Must fill, or else my project fails,
Which was to please. Now I want
Spirits to enforce, art to enchant;
And my ending is despair
Unless I be relieved by prayer,
Which pierces so that it assaults
Mercy itself, and frees all faults.
As you from crimes would pardoned be,
Let your indulence set me free.

                               (V.i.323-38)

Jan Kott[23] as well as other critics and directors have wished to place the entire stress in this epilogue on "despair." The emphasis is more naturally placed, if we attend to the syntax, on the "piercing" power of prayer, a phraseology common in Shakespeare but never in this self-consciously theatrical context. Montaigne, very appositely, uses the word "pierce" in his essay, "Of the Force of the Imagination," to describe his vulnerability to the suffering of others: "I am one of those that feels a very great conflict and power of imagination . . . The impression of it pierceth me . . . The sight of others anguishes doth sensibly drive me into anguish; and my sense hath often usurped the sense of a third man" (1:92). The same thought and the same image of piercing inform Montaigne's description of the moving power of poetry, and especially of plays, in "Of Cato the Younger," the essay in which he talks of imaginatively insinuating himself into the place of others. "It is more apparently seene in theaters," he writes, "that the sacred inspiration of the Muses, having first stirred up the Poet with a kinde of agitation unto choler, unto griefe, unto hatred, yea and beyond himselfe, whither and howsoever they please, doth also by the Poet strike and enter into the Actor, and [consecutively] by the Actor, a whole auditorie or multitude. It is the ligament of our senses depending one of another." "Even from my infancie," he concludes, "Poesie hath had the vertue to transpierce and transport me" (1:246).

The religious reverberations of the allusion to the Lord's prayer in Prospero's epilogue may be peculiarly Shakespearean (though Montaigne too repeatedly identifies the verse "forgive us our trespasses" with the virtue of forgiveness), but the correspondences between the sympathetic illusions of the theater and of life, between theatrical imagination and human compassion, are essentially the same as they are in Montaigne. *The Tempest,* of course, calls attention to theatrical imagination not only in its evident meta-theatrical references but also in the distinctive manner in which it moves us. It begins with the depiction of a storm that captures Miranda's imaginative sympathy as well as ours, and then immediately makes us understand that the storm was not real, that it was an illusion of an illusion; and this exponential consciousness of our own imaginative work in the theater informs our response throughout the action. We are thus peculiarly receptive to Prospero's epilogue. For what the actor playing Prospero suggests, in his grave and beautiful plea for our applause, is a recapitulation and crystallization of what the experience of the play itself has all along induced us to feel: that the illusory and evanescent passions of the theater are like those of actual life, and that both can be cosuffered, that the imaginative sympathy which animates our individual responses to the play also binds us together, "our senses depending one of another." He suggests, in a plea which is like a prayer, that an audience's generosity to the fictions of the actors is like mercy itself, and that the com-passionate imaginative ligaments which form a community within the theater can also compose a community, in Montaigne's words, "void of all revenge and free from all rancour" (1:365), outside of it. There is no more spacious and humane a justification of the theater in all of Shakespeare.[24]

Notes

[1] All references to *The Tempest* are to the New Oxford edition, ed. Stephen Orgel (Oxford: Clarendon Press, 1987) and will be cited parenthetically in the text by act, scene, and line numbers.

[2] *Montaigne's Essays,* trans. John Florio, ed. L. C. Harmer, 3 vols. (London: Everyman's Library-Dent, 1965), 1:220. Subsequent references to Montaigne's essays are to this edition and will be cited parenthetically in the text by volume and page number.

[3] For a discussion of Shakespeare's affinities to Montaigne in *All's Well That Ends Well* and *Othello,* see Arthur Kirsch, *Shakespeare and the Experience of Love* (Cambridge: Cambridge Univ. Press, 1981), pp. 121-7, 38-9.

[4] Leo Salingar, *Dramatic Form in Shakespeare and the Jacobeans* (Cambridge: Cambridge Univ. Press, 1986), pp. 107-33. See also Kenneth Muir, ed., New Arden edition of *King Lear* (Cambridge MA: Harvard Univ. Press, 1959), pp. 249-53.

[5] D. J. Gordon, "Name and Fame: Shakespeare's *Coriolanus,*" in *The Renaissance Imagination: Essays and Lectures by D. J. Gordon,* ed. Stephen Orgel (Berkeley and Los Angeles: Univ. of California Press, 1980), pp. 203-19.

[6] Robert Ellrodt, "Self-Consciousness in Montaigne and Shakespeare," in *ShS* 28 (1975): 37-50, 42.

[7] See also W. H. Auden's brilliant interpretation of *The Tempest* in *The Dyer's Hand and Other Essays* (New York: Random House, 1962), pp. 128-34.

[8] For the most comprehensive and elegant instance of contemporary interpretations of *The Tempest,* see Stephen Orgel's introduction to his New Oxford edition of the play, pp. 1-87. For discussions of the subject of colonialism, specifically, see, e.g., Stephen J. Greenblatt, "Learning to Curse: Aspects of Linguistic Colonialism in the Sixteenth Century," in *First Images of America: The Impact of the New World on the Old,* ed. Fredi Chiapelli, vol. 2 (Berkeley and Los Angeles: Univ. of California Press, 1976), pp. 561-80; Francis Barker and Peter Hulme, "Nymphs and Reapers Heavily Vanish: The Discursive Con-texts of *The Tempest,*" in *Alternative Shakespeares,* ed. John Drakakis (London and New York: Methuen, 1985), pp. 191-205; Terence Hawkes, "Swisser-Swatter: Making a Man of English Letters," in *Alternative Shakespeares,* pp. 26-46; and Paul Brown, "'This thing of darkness I acknowledge mine': *The Tempest* and the Discourse of Colonialism," in *Political Shakespeare: New Essays in Cultural Materialism* (Ithaca and London: Cornell Univ. Press, 1985), pp. 48-71. For a full consideration of the scholarship on colonialism and *The Tempest* and a decisively trenchant criticism of it, see Meredith Anne Skura, "Discourse and the Individual: The Case of Colonialism in *The Tempest,*" *SQ* 40, 1 (Spring 1989): 42-69.

[9] See Arthur C. Kirsch, *Jacobean Dramatic Perspectives* (Charlottesville: Univ. Press of Virginia, 1972), pp. 7-15.

[10] See, e.g., William Strachey, "A true repertory of the wreck," Appendix B, *The Tempest,* ed. Orgel, pp. 212-3.

[11] "Il me semble que la vertu est chose autre et plus noble que les inclinations à la bonté qui naissent en nous. Les ame reglées d'elles mesmes et bien nées, elles suyvent mesme train, et representent en leurs actions mesme visage que les vertueuses. Mais la vertu sonne je ne sçay quoi de plus grand et de plus actif que de se laisser, par une heureuse complexion, doucement et paisiblement conduire à la suite de la raison. Celuy qui, d'une douceur et facilité naturelle, mespriseroit les offences receus, feroit chose très-belle et digne de louange; mais celuy qui, picqué et outré jusques au vif d'une offence, s'armeroit des armes de la raison contre ce furieux appetit de vengeance, et après un grand conflict s'en redroit en fin maistre, feroit sans doute beaucoup plus. Celuy-là feroit bien, et cettuy-cy vertuesement; l'une action se pourroit dire bonté; l'autre, vertu; car il semble que le nom de la vertu presuppose de la difficulté et du contraste, et qu'elle ne peut s'exercer sans partie. C'est à l'aventure pourquoy nous nommons Dieu bon, fort,

et liberal, et juste; mais nous ne le nommons pas vertueux: ses operations sont toutes naifves et sans effort" (Michel Montaigne, *Oeuvres Complètes,* ed. Albert Thibaudet et Maurice Rat [Paris: Pléiade-Gallimard, 1962], pp. 400-1).

[12] Eleanor Prosser, "Shakespeare, Montaigne, and the 'Rarer Action,'" *ShakS* 1 (1965): 261-4.

[13] For a notable exception, see John B. Bender, "The Day of *The Tempest,*" *ELH* 47, 2 (Summer 1980): 235-58, 250-1.

[14] See Jack Miles, *God: A Biography* (New York: Alfred A. Knopf, 1995), pp. 240-4, for a suggestive discussion of the changing faces of God Himself in the Old Testament, including in Second Isaiah, the movement, through His participation in human experience, from an inhumane (because first inhuman) God to a God of "loving pity."

[15] For an illuminating explication of Ariel's song and particularly the transformational resonance of the word "suffers," see Stephen Orgel, "New Uses of Adversity: Tragic Experience in *The Tempest,*" in *In Defense of Reading: A Reader's Approach to Literary Criticism,* ed. Reuben A. Brower and Richard Poirier (New York: Dutton, 1962), pp. 110-32, 116.

[16] See Skura, p. 60.

[17] See David Quint, "A Reconsideration of Montaigne's *Des Cannibales,*" *MLQ* 51, 4 (December 1990): 459-89. Quint argues that Montaigne is less interested in investigating the new world in "Des Cannibales" than in criticizing the old and concludes that Montaigne "may not so much create the figure of the noble savage" in the essay "as disclose the savagery of the nobility" (p. 482).

[18] Jean Starobinski, *Montaigne in Motion,* trans. Arthur Goldhammer (Chicago and London: Univ. of Chicago Press, 1985).

[19] Judith N. Shklar, *Ordinary Vices* (Cambridge MA and London: Harvard Univ. Press, 1984), pp. 7-44.

[20] For a discussion from a different perspective of the possible relevance of "Of Diversions" to *The Tempest,* see Gail Kern Paster, "Montaigne, Dido, and *The Tempest:* 'How came that widow in?'" *SQ* 35, 1 (Spring 1984): 91-4.

[21] See, e.g., Alvin B. Kernan, *The Playwright as Magician: Shakespeare's Image of the Poet in the English Public Theater* (New Haven and London: Yale Univ. Press, 1979), pp. 129-59.

[22] See Michael Goldman, *Shakespeare and the Energies of Drama* (Princeton: Princeton Univ. Press, 1972), pp. 147-8.

[23] Jan Kott, *Shakespeare Our Contemporary,* trans. Boleslaw Taborski (Garden City NY: Anchor Books—Doubleday, 1966), pp. 237-85.

[24] An abbreviated version of this essay was presented in a talk at a symposium on "Cultural Exchange between European Nations" in Uppsala, Sweden and published in *Studia Acta Universitatis Upsaliensia Anglistica Upsaliensia 86,* ed. Gunnar Sorelius and Michael Srigley (Uppsala, 1994), pp. 111-21.

Source: "Virtue, Vice, and Compassion in Montaigne and *The Tempest,*" in *Studies in English Literature, 1500-1900,* Vol. 37, No. 2, Spring, 1997, pp. 337-52

The Ending of *Venus and Adonis*

Anthony Mortimer, *University of Fribourg*

For much of *Venus and Adonis* Shakespeare seems careful to avoid direct confrontation with his source for the tale in the *Metamorphoses,* Book X. It is not simply that he omits all the antecedents that Ovid provides (the incestuous union of Cinyras and Myrrha, the miraculous birth of Adonis, the wounding of Venus with Cupid's arrow) and modifies the whole situation by making Adonis resist the advances of the goddess. The striking fact is that most of the frequent Ovidian echoes seem to derive from anywhere in the *Metamorphoses* except the passage which gave him the story in the first place. The sexually aggressive female and the reluctant youth recall Salmacis and Hermaphroditus (IV. 285-388) and, to a lesser extent, Echo and Narcissus (III. 339-510); the Lament of Venus owes little to Ovid's goddess, but a great deal to his long line of desperately eloquent human heroines (including those of the *Heroides*); the episode of Mars and Venus harks back to Book IV (171-89); even the description of the boar takes its details not from the boar of Book X, but from the Calydonian boar of Book VIII. Shakespeare, while happy to plunder the riches of the *Metamorphoses,* is not writing the kind of paraphrase, adaptation or expansion that keeps sending his readers back to the original.[1]

There is, however, one moment when the direct confrontation becomes unavoidable. However much of the Ovidian story Shakespeare might omit and however he might change the relation between the protagonists, the final metamorphosis had to remain: this was the moment his readers had been waiting for and, with Ovid in mind, they would expect a virtuoso performance. Shakespeare's task, briefly put, was to provide a metamorphosis that would rival Ovid's while still conforming to his own rereading of the myth.

The challenge, it must be said, was formidable. Here is Ovid in his most dazzling form and the passage must be quoted in full if we are to appreciate the significance of the Shakespearean revisions.

> 'at non tamen omnia vestri
> iuris erunt' dixit. 'luctus monimenta manebunt
> semper, Adoni, mei, repetitaque mortis imago
> annua plangoris peraget simulamina nostri;
> at cruror in florem mutabitur. an tibi quondam
> femineos artus in olentes vertere mentas,
> Persephone, licuit: nobis Cinyreius heros
> invidiae mutatus erit?' sic fata cruorem
> nectare odorato sparsit, qui tactus ab illo
> intumuit sic, ut fulvo perlucida caeno

surgere bulla solet, nec plena longior hora
facta mora est, cum flos de sanguine concolor ortus,
qualem, quae lento celant sub cortice granum,
punica ferre solent; brevis est tamen usus in illo;
namque male haerentem et nimia levitate caducum,
excutiunt idem, qui praestant nomina, venti.

(*Met.* X. 724-39)

'But all shall not be in your [the Fates'] power. My grief, Adonis, shall have an enduring monument, and each passing year in memory of your death shall give an imitation of my grief. But your blood shall be changed to a flower. Or was it once allowed to thee, Persephone, to change a maiden's form to fragrant mint, and shall the change of my hero, offspring of Cinyras, be grudged to me?' So saying, with sweet-scented nectar she sprinkled the blood; and this, touched by the nectar, swelled as when clear bubbles rise up from yellow mud. With no longer than an hour's delay a flower sprang up of blood-red hue such as pomegranates bear which hide their seeds beneath the tenacious rind. But short-lived is their flower; for the winds from which it takes its name shake off the flower so delicately clinging and doomed easily to fall.[2]

Ovid's conclusion to the story is finely balanced between consolation and regret. Venus establishes an annual ritual (the *Adoniazusae*) to commemorate the death of her lover. She does not have the power to grant him anything like a full-blown apotheosis and she needs to invoke the precedent of Persephone in order to justify the metamorphosis. But she does, at least, bring into being a flower that will continue to embody his beauty and his fragility. The last two lines, with the wonderfully mimetic suspension of the syntax and the final sighing exhalation of *venti*, leave us with the consolation that beauty, in some form or other, will always be renewed and with the regret that its specific incarnations will always prove transient.

In turning to Shakespeare, the first thing we notice is that his Venus is incapable of offering Adonis even the limited form of perpetuation granted in the *Metamorphoses*. Ovid's Venus defies the Fates ('all shall not be in your power') first by creating the ritual and then by performing the metamorphosis. Shakespeare's Venus seems too overcome by events to think of such positive action. There is, first of all, no suggestion of an annual commemoration and this is hardly surprising if we consider the tone of the immediately preceding speech where, under the guise of etiological prophecy, she has pronounced a curse on love and lovers:

> Sith in his prime death doth my love destroy,
> They that love best their loves shall not enjoy.[3]
>
>   (1163-4)

A communal rite of mourning would, after all, be a way of coming to terms with death and a gesture of solidarity that Shakespeare's vindictive Venus, out of love with the world, is in no mood to make or accept.

Even more important is the fact that in Shakespeare the metamorphosis of Adonis appears as a natural miracle which owes nothing to the intentions or powers of the goddess:

> By this the boy that by her side lay killed
> Was melted like a vapour from her sight,
> And in his blood that on the ground lay spilled
> A purple flower sprung up check'red with
>   white.
>
>   (1165-8)

'By this' is typical of the poem's rapid transitions ('At this', 'With this', 'This said') and, as we can see from previous occurrences (175, 877, 973), indicates mere succession with no necessary suggestion of causality—especially since the preceding speech contains no reference whatsoever to metamorphosis. Venus, therefore, has no power over the natural world and the metamorphosis appears less as a consolation for the death of Adonis than as the last stage of the process that takes him from her. A number of details confirm that Shakespeare is, in fact, consciously undermining traditional readings of the myth. Not only is there no indication that Adonis embodies the vegetative and seasonal cycle (an aspect that is, in any case, barely perceptible in Ovid), but even the idea that the flower will somehow perpetuate his beauty is frustrated by the action of Venus herself.

> She bows her head the new-sprung flower to
>   smell,
> Comparing it to her Adonis' breath,
> And says within her bosom it shall dwell,
> Since he himself is reft from her by death.
> She crops the stalk, and in the breach appears
>   Green-dropping sap, which she compares to
>   tears.
>
>   (1171-6)

This gesture, absent in Ovid, is the one she has conventionally attributed to Death ('thou pluck'st a flower', 946), but it also recalls her own attempt to crop the flower of Adonis's virginity and her argument that flowers should be 'gath'red in their prime' (131). By now literalizing her own metaphor Venus inverts its significance. The metaphorical cropping of the youth's virginity would have ensured his perpetuation through offspring; the literal cropping of the flower cuts off any hope of regeneration. In this context, it may well be significant that Shakespeare does not identify the flower. Ovid specifies that, though it resembles the bloom of the pomegranate, it is, indeed, the flower that takes its name from the wind, the anemone (from Greek *anemos*) that his readers could recognize. By omitting to name the flower Shakespeare may be implying that it no longer exists; its beauty, like that of Adonis, has been lost without trace. We remember that Venus had urged on Adonis the reproductive example of 'sappy plants' (165), but here the 'green-dropping sap' of the Adonis-flower falls to the earth like wasted semen.

Shakespeare clearly modifies Ovid by depriving the metamorphosis of its consolatory function. And yet this modification remains in the spirit of Ovid where the metamorphosis usually involves two stages—first the progressive dissolution of the human identity and then the subject's reemergence in a radically simple form reflecting the status to which he or she has been reduced by the story. As Leonard Barkan remarks, 'the artistic effect of metamorphosis is to transform human identities into images'.[4] Thus, to take only one example, the metamorphosis of Arachne (*Met.* VI. 1-145) eliminates all that made her an individual—her lowly birth, her professional pride, her irreverence towards the gods—and makes her simply a spider, the embodiment of skill in weaving. Even where the concluding image is more attractive, as with Daphne transformed into a laurel, admiration at the aesthetic solution is still tempered with a sense of human loss. Shakespeare's Adonis receives the same kind of treatment. Not only is the complex adolescent we have known reduced to a single image of beauty, but, in conformity with his rôle throughout the poem, it is a beauty that will not be reproduced.

Since Venus has not herself performed the metamorphosis, she remains uncertain as to how it should be understood. The radical ambivalence of her gesture in cropping the flower is reflected in a final speech that hovers between a recognition that it is no real perpetuation of Adonis and a desire to cherish it as his child.

> "Poor flower", quoth she, "this way thy
>   father's guise—
> Sweet issue of a more sweet-smelling sire—
> For every little grief to wet his eyes;
> To grow unto himself was his desire,
>   And so 'tis thine, but know it is as good
>   To wither in my breast as in his blood.

"Here was thy father's bed, here in my breast;
    Thou art the next of blood, and 'tis thy right.
Lo, in this hollow cradle take thy rest,
    My throbbing heart shall rock thee day and
        night;
    There shall not be one minute in an hour
    Wherein I will not kiss my sweet love's
        flower".

(1177-88)

The two stanzas complete Venus's rewriting of the story which, omitting all reference to her sexual aggression and his resistance, has already transformed the stubborn young hunter into a marvellous child who, like the child in Virgil's Fourth Eclogue, restores Nature to a prelapsarian harmony where the lamb need no longer fear the wolf and where even the boar only wounds Adonis in a misguided attempt to kiss him (1081-1116). Now the Adonis-flower becomes both a child to be cradled at her breast and the lover that Adonis has never been. Jonathan Bate has argued persuasively that the image of the son who takes his father's place in the mother's bed is an 'adroit variation' on the Myrrha story in Ovid.

> Ovid begins his tale with Adonis as a son issuing from a tree, Shakespeare ends his with a flower issuing from Adonis who thus becomes a father. Shakespeare's Venus acts out an extraordinary family romance. By imaging her lover as a father, she makes herself into the mother and the flower into the fruit of their union. But the logic of the imagery dictates that the flower is her sexual partner as well as her child, for it clearly substitutes for Adonis himself.[5]

The birth of Adonis was the result of an incestuous father-daughter union (Cinyras and Myrrha); Venus exploits his death and metamorphosis to envisage a further incest which is that of mother and son. But even without reference to the Myrrha story, it would still be clear that incest is the only conclusion that can satisfy Venus's desire to possess Adonis both as child and as lover. Throughout the poem she has alternated between bouts of sexual aggression and moments of maternal protectiveness. She concludes with the only image that can reconcile her 'variable passions' (967).

Venus exploits the power that the living usually have over the dead, that of being able to transform them into self-flattering fictions. The Adonis-flower, unlike Adonis himself, cannot answer back to say that he is no longer a child and will not be a lover. But the passage suggests that Venus is not really convinced by her own rhetoric. The consolation involved in seeing the flower as the child of Adonis is undermined by her memory of the Adonis who refused procreation despite her argument that 'things growing to themselves are growth's abuse' (166).

To grow unto himself was his desire,
    And so 'tis thine, but know it is as good
    To wither in my breast as in his blood.

(1180-2)

This, surely, is a recognition that the metamorphosis must be ultimately meaningless. Even cradled at her breast, the flower will still wither and is, therefore, no real perpetuation of Adonis. Only ironically can the flower be made to resemble Adonis by being rendered barren. There is a touch of the same vindictiveness that marked her curse on love. Adonis himself has vanished without trace, and so she condemns the flower to the same extinction. Venus had prophesied that the world and its beauty could not survive the death of Adonis (10-11, 1019-20); that prophecy has obviously not been fulfilled ('The flowers are sweet, their colours fresh and trim', 1079), but she does her best to take revenge for Nature's indifference by cropping whatever beauty comes to hand.

It is, finally, disgust with the world that gains the upper hand over the illusory consolations of the metamorphosis.

Thus weary of the world away she hies,
    And yokes her silver doves, by whose swift
        aid
Their mistress, mounted, through the empty
    skies,
In her light chariot quickly is conveyed,
    Holding their course to Paphos, where their
        queen
    Means to immure herself, and not be seen.

(1189-94)

There is a fine irony in the suggestion that Venus, whose habitual imagery has been so all-embracing, so world-welcoming, (the metaphorical expansion of her body into a deer-park, 229-40) now intends, by immuring herself, to imitate the attitude of Adonis who yearned for 'quiet closure' and the solitude of his bedchamber (781-6). As for the flight, the couplet may, as Roe suggests, contain an echo of Virgil:[6]

> ipsa Paphum sublimis abit sedesque revisit
> laeta suas, ubi templum illi centumque Sabaeo
> ture calent arae sertisque recentibus halant.
>
> *(Aen.* I. 415-7)

> She herself through the sky goes her way to Paphos, and joyfully revisits her abode, where the temple and its hundred altars steam with Sabaean incense and are fragrant with garlands ever fresh.

If Shakespeare is indeed inviting comparison with the Virgilian passage, then our attention is drawn to the difference between the role of the goddess in his poem and her very different status in the epic. Virgil's Venus leaves her son, Aeneas, with words of encouragement after demonstrating her power to protect him; Shakespeare's Venus leaves Adonis whom she regards as the son she has been unable to protect. Aeneas is destined to become the father of a great race; Adonis has no progeny. In the *Aeneid* Venus flies away in a joyful spirit to receive the homage of her worshippers and to be greeted with 'garlands ever fresh'; in *Venus and Adonis* she is 'weary of the world', 'means to immure herself' and carries a flower that will wither at her breast. For Virgil's Venus divinity involves a power to change the world; for Shakespeare's goddess divinity offers, at best, an escape from the world that she cannot change.

There is, of course, also a flight to Paphos in Ovid. After warning Adonis of the dangers of hunting, Venus leaves for Paphos and is recalled in mid-flight by the groans of the dying youth (*Met.* X. 717-20). Thus Ovid's story ends not with Venus abandoning the world, but with her returning to it, accepting her share of grief and offering the consolation of a ritual and a metamorphosis. Shakespeare's Venus has nothing to offer the world except her curse. Ovid's version concludes with a goddess who stands on earth, sharing our common human experience of transience and loss; but Shakespeare's goddess has already been all too human—frustrated, sweating and repeatedly falling to the ground. Being a creature of extremes, she reacts by a rejection of humanity. There is no trace here of the goddess who, according to Heather Asals, undergoes a Neoplatonic education and rises from lust to love.[7] For most of the poem Venus has been descending not ascending the Neoplatonic ladder (see her inversion of the hierarchy of the senses, 433-50), and the sensuality of her last incestuous image does not suggest that she has changed very much. What has changed is that the goddess of love has discovered what it is like to be subject to her own law ('Poor queen of love, in thine own law forlorn', 251) and has not enjoyed the experience. It is precisely because her descent has ended in defeat that her ascent sounds so resentfully definitive.

The comparisons with Virgil and Ovid might lead us to think that *Venus and Adonis* ends with the desolate vision of a world deprived of divine sympathy or protection, overarched by 'the empty skies' and abandoned to the meaningless violence of the boar. But any sense of gloom is surely dispelled by the grace, swiftness and lightness of the imagery. Venus may intend to 'immure herself', but her actual movement is one of aerial and unrestricted freedom. There is, if anything, a sense of relief in seeing the goddess restored to her supernatural element of space and soaring flight, finally released from the gravity that bound her to earth and to the human condition. We respond this way because we too are released from gravity, freed from any temptation to read this ending as the conclusion to a real human tragedy. The burden of pathos that might have been imposed on the reader by seeing Venus as a *mater dolorosa* is lifted by this magical Venus whose

silver doves draw her chariot through the skies. We need not feel too sorry for someone who can so easily shake off the weight of the world and we are, indeed, slyly encouraged to think that her protestations of eternal devotion to the memory of Adonis should be taken with a pinch of salt. We are not told that she will, in fact, 'immure herself, and not be seen', only that she 'means' to do so. Shakespeare does not go as far as Ronsard who reminds us that she will soon replace Adonis with the Phrygian shepherd, Anchises ('Telles sont et seront les amitiez des femmes'), but there is a hint of the same urbane cynicism.[8]

Shakespeare's handling of the conclusion works on two levels: on the one hand, as we have seen, he undermines the positive significance of the metamorphosis as a perpetuation of beauty or as a myth of seasonal regeneration; on the other hand, he clears the atmosphere and lightens the spirit by finally restoring the tale to the realm of fable. And this procedure brings to the surface some of the assumptions that underlie Shakespeare's treatment of his Ovidian source. For all the portentous interpretations of classical myth offered by Renaissance Neoplatonists (some of them still plague criticism of *Venus and Adonis*), the Ovidian revival of the sixteenth century did not necessarily lend itself to solemnity. Though an occasional allegorical gloss might come in useful to deflect censorship, there is little evidence that Lodge, Marlowe, Shakespeare, Drayton and other authors of *epyllia* regarded classical mythology as a repository of universal wisdom. Given the reverence with which modern criticism usually uses the term 'myth', it might be better to speak of the Ovidian stories as 'fables'—fables which did not invite the reader to suspend his disbelief and which, therefore, allowed Renaissance poets to treat potentially serious sexual themes without committing themselves to seriousness. The ending of *Venus and Adonis* is consistent with this attitude. It is designed to distance the reader from the often hilarious but frequently uncomfortable psychological realism of the poem he has been reading. The real and final metamorphosis is that of a frustrated woman and a sullen youth into miraculous apparitions who vanish in the turning of a verse. Adonis is 'melted' from our sight and Venus disappears into 'the empty skies'. The whole poem, so fraught with unresolved tensions, so psychologically convincing, so solidly rooted in our earthly experience, dissolves like the masque in *The Tempest*, freeing us to regard as entertainment the disturbing passions it has entertained.

Notes

[1] For the Ovidian sources of *Venus and Adonis* the most useful modern editions are Hyder Edward Rollins, *The Poems: A New Variorum Edition of Shakespeare* (Philadelphia, 1938) and F. T. Prince, *The Poems,* The Arden Shakespeare (London, 1960). There is a detailed scholarly account of the Ovidian influence in T.W.

Baldwin, *On the Literary Genetics of Shakspere's Poems and Sonnets* (Urbana, Ill., 1950). The most stimulating critical discussion of what Ovid means to *Venus and Adonis* is in Jonathan Bate, *Shakespeare and Ovid* (Oxford, 1993), Chapter Two, 'Sexual Poetry'.

[2] For Latin texts I have used the editions of the Loeb Classical Library with translations by Frank Justus Miller (Ovid) and H. R. Fairclough (Virgil).

[3] All citations are to the *The Poems,* ed. John Roe, The New Cambridge Shakespeare (Cambridge, 1992). Line numbers are given in brackets.

[4] Leonard Barkan, *The Gods Made Flesh: Metamorphosis and the Pursuit of Paganism* (New Haven, Conn., 1986), p. 26.

[5] Op. cit., pp. 58-9.

[6] Op. cit., p. 138.

[7] Heather Asals, '*Venus and Adonis:* The Education of a Goddess', SEL 13 (1973), 31-51.

[8] 'Adonis' in *Ronsard, Oeuvres complètes,* ed. Gustave Cohen (Paris, 1950), vol. 2, p. 33.

Source: "The Ending of *Venus and Adonis,*" in *English Studies*, Vol. 78, No. 4, July, 1997, pp. 334-41.

Pericles and the Wonder of Unburdened Proof

Peter G. Platt, *Barnard College*

2. Gent. Is not this strange?
1. Gent.   Most rare.

At the beginning of act 5 of *A Midsummer Night's Dream,* Theseus and Hippolyta discuss the reports of the lovers from the previous act, and in doing so, they provide an enactment of the two models of wonder that I attributed . . . to Jonson and Daniel. An examination of their speeches will help take us toward an exploration of the Shakespearean marvelous.

Hippolyta begins the discussion by emphasizing the wonder of the stories: "'Tis strange, my Theseus, that these lovers speak of."[1] Interested in downplaying the strangeness of the claims—and separating them from truth ("More strange than true" [2])—Theseus skeptically links lovers with madmen and poets as people who possess "seething brains" (4) and "shaping fantasies" (5), basing their interpretations of the world on imagination—"of imagination all compact" (8)—and apprehension (5), instead of on "cool reason" and comprehension (6). In short, all three create what does not exist, "as imagination bodies forth / The forms of things unknown" (14-15). These are the "tricks" (18) that imagination plays, forcing one to confuse apprehension—or mere perception, implying error—with comprehension—or full understanding, implying truth (19-20). To believe in the imagination, the strange, the wondrous, is to suppose a bush a bear (22).

Hippolyta has more room in her interpretive world for the marvelous. She draws a distinction between the "fancy's images" (25) dwelt upon by Theseus and the "something of great constancy" that is "strange and admirable" (26-27); she seems comfortable with this paradox, Puttenham's "Wonderer."[2] Suggesting that something true or constant can come out of the "minds transfigur'd" (24) by the marvelous events in the forest, she turns a skeptical, Montaignian eye on Theseus's skepticism, suggesting that the marvelous can lead one to previously unimaginable realities. Instead of clouding minds and leading them into error, Hippolyta suggests (as do Patrizi, Montaigne, and Daniel), that the strange and admirable can transfigure minds.

In examining Shakespeare's use of the marvelous, I build on the notions of wonder underlying the work of both fiction and the masque explored in chapters 4 and 5: the link between intellectual and epistemological destabilization on the one hand, and visual, often theatrical, awe on the other. The present chapter, then, explores the significance of wonder to both the philosophical issues raised by and the dramatic strategies of the late plays, before examining *Pericles* within this framework.

This double sense of wonder—an ongoing inquiry and an aesthetic astonishment, both caused by an acceptance of and openness to the previously unimaginable—is crucial to an understanding of the late plays. While recent criticism has tended to focus on "skepticism" or politics, the late plays inevitably move beyond these concerns, and part of this move is a connection with the audience, the importance of which Patrizi's theory of wonder recognizes.[3] Late Shakespeare operates within this framework, in a kind of philosophical and aesthetic contingency, and invites the spectators to engage in—and in some cases to shape—the marvels on the stage before them.[4]

The urge to locate Shakespeare intellectually has led in recent years to several books that address Shakespeare's skepticism.[5] Although different in argument and methodology, these studies share a sense of a tradition of "learned ignorance" that includes Plato, Nicholas of Cusa, Erasmus, Agrippa, and Montaigne (particularly the Montaigne of book 2 of the *Essays,* and even more particularly, of "Apology for Raymond Sebond"). In his important study, Richard Popkin distinguished "Academic" from "Pyrrhonian" skepticism in the third and fourth centuries B.C. and traced the significance of this dualism for the Renaissance and beyond. Popkin makes a distinction between the Academics—who argued, following Socrates's dictum "All I know is that I know nothing," that "no knowledge was possible"—and the Pyrrhonians, who went further and claimed that "there was inadequate evidence to determine if any knowledge was possible . . . ; the Pyrrhonians proposed to suspend judgment on all questions on which there seemed to be conflicting evidence, including the question whether or not something could be known."[6] Cicero was primarily responsible for bringing Academic thought to the Renaissance, and Sextus Empiricus provided the only remnant the Renaissance had—or anyone has—of Pyrrhonian thought. In particular, Sextus had considerable influence on Montaigne, whom Popkin identifies as an intellectual descendant of the Pyrrhonian tradition.[7] One example from "Apology for Raymond Sebond" will have to suffice for many: "Whoever will imagine a perpetual confession of ignorance, a judgment without learning or inclination, on any occasion whatever, he has a conception of Pyrrhonism."[8]

Recently Graham Bradshaw, in attempting to locate Shakespeare's skepticism vis-à-vis Montaigne, set forth ahistorical categories parallel to Popkin's, which he called "dogmatic" and "radical"; he firmly lodges Shakespeare in the latter group, along with Montaigne.[9] James L. Calderwood is more specific about Shakespeare's stance with regard to uncertainty: "Shakespeare's negative mode is more radical and less resolvable. . . . In place of Hamlet's implied ['To be or not to be'] and Aristotle's explicit law of the excluded middle (a thing is either A or not-A) we have Shakespeare's law of the included middle (a thing may be both A and not-A). This is by no means the same thing as saying, with some of the more extreme devotees of indeterminacy, that a thing is neither A nor not-A; nor is it a license to valorize *any* A or any not-A."[10] This notion of "included middle" neatly captures the logic of Shakespearean wonder, and I return to it when considering the couplet from *As You Like It* that forms my title. There is much force, then, in the version of intellectual history that undergirds recent characterizations of Shakespeare as a type of skeptic. Nevertheless, I propose to recast the terminology, with the help of late Montaigne and Patrizi. For I want to argue that Shakespeare adheres far more closely, especially in his late plays, to a philosophy of wonder than to a philosophy of skepticism.[11]

Just as Shakespeare puts philosophical certainty into question, he challenges the conventions of the stage. Ernest B. Gilman notes the connection between the two—epistemology and aesthetics—when he claims that the movement in perspective treatises from Alberti to the seventeenth century was one toward "a more complex and ambiguous relationship between the knower and the knowable."[12] Barbara Mowat, also turning to art theory, bases her terminology on Heinrich Wölfflin's *Principles of Art History* and calls Shakespeare's late drama "open form": "Open form drama, specifically, is that drama in which cause-and-effect patterns are broken, generic conventions abandoned (and with them the easily established point of view, of attitude, that observance of generic conventions made possible), and the dramatic illusion repeatedly broken through narrative intrusion, spectacle, and other sudden disturbances of aesthetic distance."[13] Several critics have suggested that Shakespeare's late plays be thought of as mannerist.[14] Indeed, mannerism, as defined by Arnold Hauser, goes a long way toward helping us link the challenge to certainty that Shakespeare presents both intellectually and theatrically: "Common to mannerism in all the arts are intellectualism and irrationalism, a mingling of the real and the unreal, a predilection for striking contrasts and insoluble contradictions, and a taste for the difficult and paradoxical."[15] Mannerism considers the spiritual "so irreducible to material form," Hauser explains, "that it can only be hinted at (it is never anything but hinted at) by the distortion of form and the disruption of boundaries."[16] Shakespeare's late plays evince just this sort of "distortion of form" and "disruption of boundaries."

It is easy to demonstrate that these late plays evince a dramaturgy that reinforces their intellectual preoccupation with uncertainty. But it is difficult to explain why this development occurred. Biography has never yielded an answer here, and recent political criticism has focused on James's family and power relations but has not sufficiently accounted for the intellectual, supernatural, and theatrical/aesthetic issues that the presence of the marvelous raises in these late plays.[17]

Theater historians are slightly more helpful. G. E. Bentley tentatively suggested many years ago that the dramaturgical change was rooted in the King's Men's acquisition of the private Blackfriars Theater in 1608.[18] Andrew Gurr has urged caution, however, in light of the fact that the same plays were performed both at the outdoor Globe and at the indoor Blackfriars, citing the Globe productions of late plays such as *Pericles* in 1607 and *The Winter's Tale* and *Cymbeline* in 1611: "His Globe plays transplanted to the Blackfriars unchanged, as his Blackfriars plays transplanted to the Globe."[19] Daniel Seltzer notes that while there is clearly something different in tone and structure in the late plays, this "does not mean that the staging which articulated them was necessarily new in any drastic way." He goes on, however, to add that "It would be folly to ignore aspects of private production which, although practicable, are given interesting significance . . . ; the needs of the playwright's art and the development and availability of theatrical facilities answered each other." Not the least of these coincidences of art and facility is what Seltzer calls the "experiments towards joining visual and moral wonder."[20] This joining is particularly significant because visual and philosophical wonder are together so widespread in the last plays.

Shakespeare's use of the romance form—being essentially "nomadic" and "associating itself with an imaginative uprooting, a drive over and across everything settled and planted and built"[21]—also allows for the epistemological and theatrical interrogations of these late works. As a starting point, I use Stanley Wells's definitions of the contentious term "romance": "Romancers delight in the marvellous; quite often this involves the supernatural; generally the characters are larger than life size. All is unrealistic; the logic of chance or fortune governs all."[22] In addition, the romance tradition and form better encompass the late plays than the tradition of tragicomedy, at least as defined by Giambattista Guarini and his literary descendant, John Fletcher. Guarini asserts that the author of tragicomedy "takes from tragedy . . . its pleasure but not its sadness, its danger but not its death," while Fletcher claims that the genre "wants deaths, which is inough to make it no tragedie, yet brings some nere it, which is inough to make it no comedie." Romance, unlike tragicomedy, includes sadness and death, or as Howard Felperin puts it, "Shakespeare's final romances subsume tragedy in the process of transcending it."[23]

And Lee Bliss has distinguished Beaumont and Fletcher's tragicomedy from Shakespearean romance by noting that the former requires "an aesthetic and technical rather than a primarily emotional response. It is not allowed to evoke our participation in mysteries beyond full comprehension."[24]

Foregrounding story, spectacle, and "mysteries beyond full comprehension" instead of character and "a mirror up to nature," Shakespeare's romances experiment with the uncertain and the unreal.[25] In the late plays this experimentation with uncertainty is wedded to an experimental, non-naturalistic form that, in its movement from disorder and confusion toward wonder, resembles the structure of the masque.[26] Focusing on this destabilizing quality of the romances, Robert Knapp has pointed out that they "seem to emphasize difference itself: between art and nature, between experience and innocence, between belatedness and the imaginary unity which it always posits, between diegetic mediation and mimetic sheerness of display."[27]

This notion of Shakespearean romance's recognition of differences brings us back to Calderwood's formulation of Shakespeare's "included middle," and it is here that Montaigne and Patrizi can furnish some contemporary reinforcement. . . . [T]he Montaigne of book 3 of the *Essays,* and particularly "Of Cripples" and "Of Experience," revaluates wonder, making it part of an intellectual project of ongoing inquiry; the marvelous pushes out the boundaries of the known and forces us to open up new epistemological categories: "Wonder is the foundation of all philosophy, inquiry its progress, ignorance its end," and "Its [a spirited mind's] pursuits are boundless and without form; its food is wonder, the chase, ambiguity."[28] Furthermore, as we have seen, Patrizi presents a poetics that recognizes that this late Montaignian notion of wonder can be—should be—the essential quality of aesthetic experience. To be in a play, suspended between the various categories listed by Knapp, is to be in a state of Patrizian wonder, "of believing and not believing. Of believing because the thing is seen to exist; and of not believing because it is sudden, new, and not before either known, thought, or believed able to exist."[29]

Before moving to *Pericles,* let us return briefly to a Montaignian/Patrizian model—Hymen's lines from *As You Like It,* cited as one of my epigraphs and discussed in the preface: "Feed yourselves with questioning; / That reason wonder may diminish" (5.4.138-39). As I note above, these lines highlight the destabilizing relationship between reason and wonder, but they also provide—with their radical ambiguity—an example of Calderwood's "included middle." It could be argued, of course, that the epilogue reveals the triumph of logic and reality, that reason, in the end, diminishes wonder. In this reading, the marvels cease as the character of Rosalind—who has pretended to

be a young man in order to work her magic on Orlando—reveals that, after all (and on the Elizabethan stage this would be the actual case), she has been a young boy all along: "If I were a woman I would kiss as many of you as had beards that pleas'd me" (epilogue, 18-19).

However, I see Shakespeare looking ahead to the late plays, in which his admission and demonstration of his art become essential aspects of his dramaturgy of wonder. The Patrizian *potenza ammirativa,* the capacity that lies in between reason and affect and that allows us to be moved by the incredible, is what Shakespeare is able to evoke in his foregrounding of the artistic act.[30] M. S. Kuhn notes the bawdy (but ultimately aesthetic) pun in the epilogue—"between you and the women the play may please" (17)—and goes on to comment, "In a sexual encounter, there must be a mutual yielding for the love-play to please. At a stage-play the audience must yield its disbelief to be pleased."[31] In late Shakespearean drama, some elements of which are anticipated in *As You Like It,* there exists also the play between wonder and reason, underscored by Shakespeare's self-referentiality and mannerist style, the form that Mowat calls "open" and "startingly anti-Aristotelian"[32] and that ultimately provides wonder for the marveling observer.

My argument so far has focused on several variations on the tension between the rational and the marvelous, . . . I suggest that this pair has a corresponding dualism: the verbal and the visual. The clash between them is personified in the conflict between the rational and verbal Ben Jonson and the marvel-making and visual Inigo Jones. Shakespeare's earliest romance, *Pericles,* begins a foregrounding of this dualism that was to assume a central significance in the late plays. I want to focus first on the prominence of this tension in the speeches of Gower and then look at the symbiotic nature of the verbal and visual in *Pericles* as a whole. For the power of wonder is evinced in speech and action, words and spectacles, and both must be acknowledged—by the characters and by the audience—if new epistemological insights are to be gained and tragedy is to be avoided.

While it has been well established that Shakespeare did not write *Pericles* alone, all of the Gower speeches (save the very last) are linked by a preoccupation with the interaction of speech and spectacle.[33] Indeed, Gower proclaims in his first appearance that he wants "To glad your ear and please your eyes" (1.cho.4). Referring, perhaps, to the lost source of his own *Confessio Amantis,* Gower says that "lords and ladies in their lives / Have read it for restoratives" (7-8), but he concludes his opening speech focusing not on the verbal but on the visual: "What now ensues, to the judgment of your eye / I give my cause, who best can justify" (41-42).

There is a more problematic relation between narrative and spectacle in Gower's speech at the opening of act 2. He summarizes the events of act 1, distinguishing between the wicked and incestuous Antiochus and Pericles, "A better prince and benign lord, / That will prove aweful in deed and word" (2.cho.3-4); Gower suggests that the "aweful"—the wonder-ful—Pericles will unite action and speech. But the division between them is highlighted here. After telling us that the people of Tharsus have built a statue thanking Pericles for saving them from the horrors of famine, Gower informs us that "tidings to the contrary / Are brought to your eyes; what need speak I?" (15-16). What follows is a dumb show that, the stage directions tell us, reveals Pericles' receiving a letter and knighting the messenger who delivers it. Yet Gower returns after the dumb show to explain in detail what we have just seen. As Thomas Bishop has pointed out, "there is a substantial need for Gower's supplementary speech: emblematic truths of the eye are not alone sufficient. . . . The dumb-shows thus function both as a foreshortening of the narrative and as a reminder of the potential of appearances to become screens. . . . Our viewing is now an occasion of difficulty and scepticism, of something remote and requiring interpretation."[34] The deception perpetrated by Antiochus and his daughter taints subsequent viewing—for us and, as we shall see, for Pericles.

And yet the issue gets complicated again at the end of the speech, as Gower does not privilege the verbal. After interpreting the dumb show—in which he relays to us that Antiochus's Thaliard is seeking Pericles in order to murder him—Gower describes Pericles' flight from Tharsus and his ensuing shipwreck. Just before releasing us to watch what happens to Pericles at Pentapolis, Gower says: "And here he comes. What shall be next, / Pardon old Gower—this long's the text" (2.cho.39-40). The Riverside editor glosses "this long's the text" as "the text of my speech is this long and no longer" (1489n.). The Arden edition cites the line as "this 'longs the text," reading "'longs" to mean "belongs to [the play itself]" (41n.).[35] I suggest a third possibility: that "this 'longs the text" is a return to Gower's self-deprecation about the importance of words; "'longs," then, would mean "prolongs." The OED (1.2) confirms this denotation. Although its last citation for this usage is 1500, an outmoded definition would be consistent both with Gower's words and in a play that is generally rich in archaism. In any case Gower's speech in act 2 reveals the complexity of the relation between word and enactment.

This same sense of the mutual dependence of the verbal and visual permeates Gower's speech at the beginning of act 3. After briefly describing the marriage of Pericles and Thaisa, Gower introduces the dumb show, this time recognizing in advance that it will be insufficient: "What's dumb in show I'll plain with speech" (3.cho.14). Yet Gower again does not privilege speech,

and at this point recalls the chorus in *Henry V* as he exhorts the audience to help forge a bridge between the verbal and the visual:

> And what ensues in this fell storm
> Shall for itself itself perform.
> I nill relate, action may
> Conveniently the rest convey,
> Which might not what by me is told.
> In your imagination hold
> This stage the ship, upon whose deck
> The sea-toss'd Pericles appears to speak.
>
> (3.cho.53-60)

It seems particularly appropriate that Gower needs the aid of the audience in an act that will contain such catastrophes and wonders as Thaisa's death and "rebirth" and the birth of Marina.

Both speeches in act 4 also focus on the power of the audience to knit together tale and spectacle. In the first, Gower needs the audience's credence because he is about to thrust the story ahead many years "[on] the lame feet of my rhyme, / Which never could I so convey, / Unless your thoughts went on my way" (4.cho.48-50). After we have seen the attempted murder of Marina and the brothel at Mytilene, Gower returns to "Take our imagination, / From bourn to bourn, region to region" (4.4.3-4): he, "who stand i'th' gaps to teach you, / The stages of our story" (8-9), takes us by means of narrative to Tharsus, where Pericles hopes to see Marina. Knowing that the following dumb show—in which the monument to the "dead" Marina is unveiled to Pericles by Cleon and Dionyza—will need explication, Gower proclaims: "Like motes and shadows see them move a while, / Your ears unto your eyes I'll reconcile" (21-22). Like an emblem theorist, Gower recognizes that the act of perception is complex and relies on a marriage of the visual and verbal. Because the audience has an increased role in making meaning, in achieving wondrous effects, it must not be misled by "motes and shadows." Or, as Gower exclaims after the dumb show, "See how belief may suffer by foul show!" (23). Gower thus encourages the audience to believe even as he exposes the difficulty of belief. Although the feet of his rhyme are lame, Gower senses the danger of misinterpretation that spectacle without language can bring, and he hopes to protect the audience's belief from further suffering.

Gower grants the spectators their power of supposing in his first speech in act 5, but again he asks them both to watch and to listen to the wondrous recognition scene that is about to unfold:

> In your supposing once more put your sight:
> Of heavy Pericles think this his bark;
> Where what is done in action, more, if might,
> Shall be discover'd, please you sit and hark.
>
> (5.cho.21-24)

In Gower's penultimate appearance, the narrator asks the audience to help bring off one final miracle: Pericles' swift arrival at Ephesus, where he will make a sacrifice to Diana and will be reunited with Thaisa: "That he can hither come so soon / Is by your fancies' thankful doom" (5.2.19-20).

Gower's final speech is the only one not to foreground the verbal/visual dichotomy; it acts as a summary and provides a moral for the play. But there is one more invocation of the audience, who, as it will in *The Tempest,* has the responsibility for closing the play: "So, on your patience evermore attending, / New joy wait on you! Here our play has ending" (5.3.101-2). Gower's role, then, is twofold: he provides a narrative framework but also acts as a guide to how the spectators are to see and hear the play. In a drama that begins with a catastrophic fall into knowledge based on a false appearance, a wicked signifier, Gower must lead the audience toward perceptual healing, must help it learn how to accept knowledge that is not wicked, how to believe both in the marvels of a non-naturalistic, anti-Aristotelian theater and in the wonder of a kind of truth. The terrible alternatives are naive credulity—Pericles' first error—or despairing skepticism. How Pericles is led away from this latter *periculum* is the subject of the rest of this chapter.

That Pericles' journey to Antioch is an epistemological catastrophe has been noted by very few, but this is a crucial aspect of the play.[36] Pericles' first description of Antiochus's daughter emphasizes both her visual beauty and the hermeneutical dimension of this encounter for the young prince of Tyre:

> See where she comes, apparelled like the
>   spring,
> Graces her subjects, and her thoughts the
>   king
> Of every virtue gives renown to men!
> Her face the book of praises, where is read
> Nothing but curious pleasures, as from thence
> Sorrow were never ras'd, and testy wrath
> Could never be her mild companion.
>
>   (1.1.12-18)

Significantly, Antiochus's daughter is described as both a marvelous vision and a wondrous text. Indeed, her features conflate the visual and verbal: Pericles tells Helicanus specifically in the next scene that "Her face was to mine eye beyond all wonder" (1.2.75), and here her face is called "a book of praises." After hearing the riddle, he wonders why heaven's eyes, the stars, do not eschew vision altogether if encounters like this one can exist on earth:

>   But O you powers!
> That gives heaven countless eyes to view
>   men's acts,

> Why cloud they not their sights perpetually,
> If this be true which makes me pale to read
>   it?
>
>   (1.1.72-75)

Indeed, the uncovering of the daughter's falseness taints Pericles' confidence in perception and leads to a distaste for the aesthetic: "Here pleasures court mine eyes, and my mine eyes shun them" and "neither pleasure's art can joy my spirits, / Nor yet the other's [Antiochus's] distance comfort me" (1.2.6, 9-10).[37] Like Philoclea in the *Arcadia*—the lover of his possible namesake, Pyrocles—Pericles is exposed to the dark side of the marvelous, and the remainder of the play represents, at least in part, Pericles' journey toward the recovery of cleansed perception and healthy wonder.

As we have seen in the Gower speeches, *Pericles* constantly reminds us of the potential for visual duplicity. The play proper is no exception. Even a seemingly innocent description of pre-famine Tharsus, "whose towers bore heads so high they kiss'd the clouds, / And strangers ne'er beheld but wond'red at" (1.4.24-25), retrospectively resembles what Bishop calls "visual prodigality" when we think of the later actions of Cleon and Dionyza.[38] Further, both the verbal/visual dualism and the problem of hermeneutics are foregrounded in the tournament scene (2.2), as Simonides attempts to decode *imprese* paraded in front of him and Thaisa.[39] And although the fishermen praise their king to Pericles on the latter's arrival at Pentapolis, Simonides sounds very much like Antiochus as he describes the marvelous beauty of his daughter, Thaisa, to the wondering suitors:

>   and our daughter here,
> In honor of whose birth these triumphs are,
> Sits here like beauty's child, whom nature gat
> For men to see, and seeing wonder at.
>
>   (2.2.4-7)

Pericles does not immediately know what we do—that Simonides is different, that he understands the potential threat to perception that vision can pose: "Opinion's but a fool, that makes us scan / The outward habit by the inward man" (56-57). In fact, Simonides finds himself in the awkward position of wondering over Pericles: "By Jove, I wonder, that is king of thoughts, / These cates resist me, he not thought upon" (2.3.28-29).

Yet Pericles' skepticism about fathers and appearances extends to Simonides and the "wondrous fair" (2.5.36) Thaisa; after reading a letter that details Thaisa's love for him, Pericles proclaims doubtfully: "'Tis the King's subtility to have my life" (44). Only when Simonides stages a mini-romance, complete with trials (he pretends to think Pericles a traitor) and a *peripeteia* ("Either be rul'd by me or I'll make you—/ Man and wife" [83-84]), does Pericles put aside his skepticism enough to believe in what he hears and sees. After the death of Thaisa, which shortly follows, he loses this capacity until he encounters a more fully developed drama—staged and performed by his daughter.

The resurrection of Thaisa by Cerimon in act 3, scene 2, is the play's central marvel, one that foreshadows the figurative restoration of Pericles in act 5. Witnessing this wonder and hearing the language used to describe it—"marvel" (21), "most strange" (24), "wondrous heavy" (53), "most strange" (64), "wonder" (96), "rare" (104), "strange" (106), "most rare" (106)—the audience recognizes what Pericles cannot: that there is an alternative wonder, one that saves and transforms perception instead of damning and sullying it. Cerimon—the man who, like Cornelius Agrippa and John Dee, "can speak of the disturbances / That nature works, and of her cures" (37-38)—uses his magical and mystical knowledge to effect the good. Further, there is no doubt of his motives or abilities, the way that there is in Nashe's Agrippa in *The Unfortunate Traveller;* this wonder is thoroughly possible and noble in the world of *Pericles.* And although the First Gentleman declares that Cerimon's career will benefit from this act—"The heavens, / Through you, increase our wonder, and sets up / Your fame for ever" (95-97)—there is never any doubt that this restoration is its own good for the magus.

Let by Gower and privy to the salvation of Thaisa, the audience is further along its journey toward perceptual cleansing than Pericles by act 4. Here we are also able to see Marina in Mytilene, whose skills and education make her "both th'heart and place / Of general wonder" (4.cho.10-11). It is her story that is able to transform men, turning them "out of the road of rutting for ever" (4.5.9). Thus, Lysimachus, himself one of the converted, summons Marina to Pericles' ship at the beginning of act 5, in hopes that she can wrest Pericles from his nihilistic and silent despair.

After singing him a song and asking him to listen to her tale, Marina is greeted violently by Pericles, *"pushing her roughly back"* (5.1.83 s.d.). It is at this point that Marina begins her story, significantly admitting that she knows the dark side of wonderment, learned all too well from her experience in the brothel: "I am a maid, / My lord, that ne'er before invited eyes, / But have been gaz'd on like a comet" (84-86). Still lost in a kind of solipsism, Pericles speaks because he has heard fragments that resonate with events from his own life: "My fortunes—parentage—good parentage—/ To equal mine—was it not thus? What say you?" (97-98). The power of telling has penetrated Pericles' skepticism, but he does not move beyond doubt until he *sees* something in Marina that reminds him of Thaisa:

> Prithee speak.
> Falseness cannot come from thee, for thou *lookest*

> Modest as Justice, and thou *seemest* a palace
> For the crown'd Truth to dwell in. I will believe thee,
> And make my senses credit thy relation
> To points that seem impossible, for thou *lookest*
> Like one I lov'd indeed. . . .
>   (119-25; emphasis mine)

We have not heard Pericles lavish such praise on anyone since Antiochus's daughter. Marina now is the repository of truth that will allow him to "believe" in things seemingly "impossible." And unlike the daughter, Marina is a true wonder, a paradox who is not born "of any shores, / Yet . . . was mortally brought forth, and am / None other than I appear" (103-5) and who "beget'st him that did thee beget" (195). As Hippolyta suggested, truth can emerge from the marvelous, and wonder can transfigure minds.

It is significant, too, that this recovery of a moral referent is figured as something spatial and visual—a "palace"—instead of textual: the daughter in Antioch had been described as the "book of praises." It is not just narrative, then, that transforms, but—as we saw in Daniel—visual wonder as well. Furthermore, although Pericles' reunion with Thaisa is not as central as *The Winter's Tale*'s portrayal of conjugal reunion, it is crucial to this play and comes about because of another visual marvel. His capacity for wonder restored to him by Marina, Pericles is able to experience what no one else on stage can: the theophanic message of Diana that sends him to Ephesus and Thaisa. In a play focusing on the link between the journeys of Pericles and the audience, it is significant that the playgoers are the only other people aware of Pericles' vision.

Wonder for Pericles is not passive awe, however. Just as Gower calls for the active participation of the audience in his speeches, Shakespeare does not let Pericles rest with his knowledge, and indeed, as Dennis Kay has shown, both Pericles' questing for knowledge and the questions of *Pericles* go on beyond the frame of the play.[40] Pericles wants to uncover the truth about his and his family's lives, and the final scene is filled with verbs of recognition and proof: "see" (25), "confirm" (54), "hear" (56, 84), "resolve" (61), "deliver" (64), "shown" (66). And yet this is not the destructive raging after knowledge and certainty that plagues Hamlet, Othello, and Leontes and that Stanley Cavell has called "the burden of proof."[41] Pericles' inquiry takes the form of Montaignian and Patrizian wonder: with uncertainty as a base that allows him to entertain the impossible, Pericles seeks to know what he can. In the process his faith in perception is restored.

Although *Pericles* foregrounds the artistic act less than the other three romances, there is still an embryonic version of what I call throughout this study a "wonder shift." Just as early modern scientists' wonder moves from a general fascination with nature to an appreciation of its minute mechanisms, so Shakespeare's vision of wonder increasingly includes not only wondrous subjects and ideas but also the marvelous mechanics of his dramatic art.[42] To Bishop, the wonder shift in *Pericles* comes in the "skill and sophistication with which the playwright has restored this 'mouldy tale' to new life"; Shakespeare thus "directs our attention, even as we are deeply moved, to the exercise of composition over the materials."[43] This shift, this redirecting of attention, comes for me in the foregrounding of the audience's role.[44] For in late Shakespeare, a phase in many ways ushered in by *Pericles*, the audience experiences—and finally enables—the active, dynamic process of wonder. This is the very process that I have located in Patrizi and Montaigne and that was to become increasingly "Shakespearean." To paraphrase Gower, the spectators' joy attends on their patience—and increasingly upon their capacity for wonder.

Notes

[1] *A Midsummer Night's Dream* 5.1.1. Subsequent citations from the works of Shakespeare, all of which are taken from the Riverside edition, are annotated within the text.

[2] See Puttenham, *Arte of English Poesie,* ed. Willcock and Walker, 225-26.

[3] Thomas Bishop—whose Ph.D. dissertation, *The Uses of Recognition,* shares many of the interests of this study—sees an active audience participation as part of the romance form: romance articulates "through its narrative workings claims and understandings that are part of 'the real,' by means of a particular participation of the audience in the work" (202). For a brief treatment of Shakespearean comedy that begins to explore wonder in a way similar to mine, see Dolora G. Cunningham, "Wonder and Love in the Romantic Comedies."

[4] Stanley Cavell acknowledges the audience's role in the Shakespearean journey beyond skepticism in his essay on *The Winter's Tale* in *Disowning Knowledge* ("Recounting Gains, Showing Losses," 193-221). "A transformation is being asked of our conception of the audience of a play," Cavell writes, "perhaps a claim that we are no longer spectators, but something else, more, say participants": "our capacity for participation is precisely a way of characterizing the method no less than the subject of this piece of theater" (218-20; see also his introduction to this volume, esp. 15-20). On theophanic wonders in the relationship between Shakespeare's foregrounded art and audience participation in the romances, see Knowles, "'The More Delay'd, Delighted.'" More recently Philip C. McGuire has explored uncertainty and audience participation using some of the terminology of quantum physics in his

Speechless Dialect, esp. 122-50. See also Barton, "'Enter Mariners Wet,'" in *Essays,* esp. 202-3.

[5] See Bradshaw, *Shakespeare's Scepticism;* Cavell, *Disowning Knowledge;* Chaudhuri, *Infirm Glory;* Engle, *Shakespearean Pragmatism;* Freedman, *Staging the Gaze;* Levao, *Renaissance Minds;* and Rabkin, *Shakespeare and the Problem of Meaning.*

[6] Popkin, *History of Scepticism,* xiii-xv. For Socrates, see the *Apology* 21b-d, in *Collected Dialogues of Plato,* ed. Hamilton and Cairns, 7-8. For Cicero, see *Academica* 1.4.16, trans. Rackham, 424-25. For a general background to skepticism in the Renaissance, see Carey, *John Donne,* 217-46.

[7] See Popkin, *History of Scepticism,* 18-65. See also Victoria Kahn, *Rhetoric, Prudence, and Skepticism,* esp. 115-51. Gregory Vlastos discusses the irony, complexity, and misinterpretations of this disavowal of knowledge in his *Socrates, Ironist and Moral Philosopher,* 82-86 and 236-42. Vlastos notes the earliest known misreading as that of Cicero (83 n.4). It would seem that, if Vlastos is correct, Socrates is actually closer to the Pyrrhonian position than to the Academic one that was founded on his pronouncement.

[8] Montaigne, "Apology for Raymond Sebond" (2.12), in *Complete Essays,* trans. Frame, 374; and *Essais,* ed. Villey, 505.

[9] Bradshaw, *Shakespeare's Scepticism,* 39.

[10] Calderwood, *To Be and Not To Be,* xiv-xv. This sort of doubleness exists in Longinus as well and is explicated carefully by Paul Fry in his *The Reach of Criticism,* 47-86. On Montaigne's work as an example of this resistance to certainty and resolution—in both theory and practice—see Kahn's chapter on Montaigne in *Rhetoric, Prudence, Skepticism,* esp. 129-51.

[11] Even in his first essay on Shakespearean skepticism, "The Avoidance of Love," Stanley Cavell stresses the importance of wonder to Shakespeare's plays: "a strategy whose point is to break up our sense of the ordinary (which is not the same as a strategy whose point it is to present us with spectacularly extraordinary events) also has claim to be called philosophical: This is perhaps why an essential response in both philosophy and tragedy is that of wonder" (*Disowning Knowledge,* 88). See also Bradbrook, *The Living Monument,* 184-226; and Young, *The Heart's Forest,* 104-91. I should also add that this view of wonder, linked as it is to the epistemological and aesthetic issues I have been exploring throughout, is different from the providential readings of the romances, however useful I may find them. See, for example, Hartwig, *Shakespeare's Tragicomic Vision;* Knight, *The Crown of Life;* Mebane, *Renaissance Magic,* 169-72;

and Peterson, *Time, Tide, and Tempest.* For a fascinating article linking the marvelous in the late plays to fantasy and self-consciously fictive forms of literature, see Semon, "Fantasy and Wonder in Shakespeare's Last Plays."

[12] Gilman, *Curious Perspective,* 14.

[13] Mowat, *Dramaturgy of Shakespeare's Romances,* 99 (see Wölfflin, *Principles of Art History,* esp. chap. 3, 124-54). Douglas L. Peterson makes a similar distinction between the ordinary, probable, and verisimilar found in "mirror comedy," and the extraordinary and marvelous found in "ideal comedy"; see "*The Tempest* and Ideal Comedy," in *Shakespearean Comedy,* ed. Charney, 99-110.

[14] See Greenwood, *Shifting Perspectives.* The term "mannerism" is a deeply problematic one and has caused a great deal of controversy in art history. For a thorough discussion of the concept of mannerism—the history behind it and the debates that surround it—see Mirollo, *Mannerism and Renaissance Poetry,* esp. 1-71. Important general studies include Battisti, *L'antirinascimento,* esp. 19-45; Bousquet, *Mannerism,* trans. Taylor; Shearman, *Mannerism;* and Sypher, *Four Stages of Renaissance Style.* Shearman in particular rejects the notion that there is much of anything intellectual or epistemological in sixteenth-century mannerism. What almost all recent commentators agree upon, however, is that there is a self-consciousness to mannerism, a heightened awareness and foregrounding of form and technique. Although I sense that Arnold Hauser is at least partly right about the intellectual doubt and uncertainty behind mannerism (see below), I use the term primarily in its formal sense.

[15] Hauser, *Mannerism,* 277.

[16] *Mannerism,* 10 (on Shakespearean mannerism, see 112-13). See also Brooke, "Shakespeare and Baroque Art"; Caws, *The Eye in the Text,* esp. 9-10 and 36-37; Hoy, "Jacobean Tragedy and the Mannerist Style"; and Roston, *Renaissance Perspectives,* esp. 239-75.

[17] Although recent, politically oriented Shakespeare criticism has improved upon David Bergeron's influential but overly simplistic *Shakespeare's Romances,* the new historicists have had less success with romances than other Shakespearean genres because their explications of power have not accounted for the power of wonder. In the case of Steven Mullaney's *Place of the Stage,* this omission is curious because Mullaney writes eloquently about wonder cabinets but does not connect these insights to his treatment of *Pericles.* Even those who do address the marvelous do not seem to see its wide-ranging impact. Leonard Tennenhouse limits his vision of the scenes of wonder in the romances to Shakespeare's "strategy for

rewriting the king's body . . . ; the unfolding of disorder within the domestic unit operates to reinscribe this unit within a hierarchy governed by the metaphysics of blood" (*Power on Display,* 182-83). Only Stephen Greenblatt's recent work—*Shakespearean Negotiations* ("Martial Law in the Land of Cockaigne," 129-63); *Learning to Curse* ("Resonance and Wonder," 161-81); and *Marvelous Possessions*—recognizes the epistemological and aesthetic, as well as the political, power of wonder.

[18] See Bentley, "Shakespeare and the Blackfriars Theatre."

[19] Gurr, *Playgoing in Shakespeare's London,* 167-68.

[20] Seltzer, "Staging the Last Plays," in *Later Shakespeare,* ed. Brown and Harris, 128-29, 163.

[21] Frye, *The Secular Scripture,* 186.

[22] Wells, "Shakespeare and Romance," in *Later Shakespeare,* ed. Brown and Harris, 49. Many prefer the term "tragicomedy" to describe Shakespeare's late plays. George Hunter has brilliantly elucidated the importance of Guarini's *Il pastor fido* in shaping the epistemological concerns of late Shakespeare. A crucial characteristic of tragicomedy, according to Hunter, is paradox, "the collision of two opposed attitudes" and "the painful and unbridged gap" between them (*Dramatic Identities,* 153).

[23] Guarini, *Compendium of Tragicomic Poetry,* cited in *Literary Criticism,* ed. Gilbert, 511. Fletcher, "To the Reader," "*The Faithful Shepherdess": A Critical Edition,* ed. Kirk, 15-16. Felperin, *Shakespearean Romance,* 62. For a more general discussion of Shakespearean romance and tragicomedy, see Frank Kermode's introduction to the Arden *Tempest,* lix-lxiii. On the political and social forces that may lie behind the genre of romance, see Jameson, *Political Unconscious,* esp. 103-150.

[24] Bliss, "Tragicomic Romance in the King's Men," in *Comedy from Shakespeare to Sheridan,* ed. Braunmuller and Bulman, 158-59.

[25] See Frye, *A Natural Perspective,* 8, and *Secular Scripture.* See also Knight, *Crown of Life.*

[26] See Frye, *Secular Scripture,* 38, and "Romance as Masque," in *Shakespeare's Romances Reconsidered,* ed. Kay and Jacobs, 11-39.

[27] Robert S. Knapp, *Shakespeare—The Theater and the Book,* 233. See also Patricia Parker's notion of romance as "a form which simultaneously quests for and postpones a particular end, objective, or object" (*Inescapable Romance,* 4).

[28] Montaigne, "Of Cripples" (3.11), in *Complete Essays,* trans. Frame, 788; and "Of Experience" (3.13), in *Complete Essays,* 818.

[29] Patrizi, *La deca ammirabile,* in *Della poetica,* ed. Aguzzi-Barbagli, 2:365 (my translation): "Di credere, perchè la cosa si vede essere; e di non credere, perchè ella è improvisa, e nuova, e non più da noi stata conosciuta, nè pensata, nè creduta poter essere."

[30] A parallel from the Italian Renaissance can be found in the letter from Pietro Aretino to Bernardino Daniello in 1536, describing Michelangelo's work in the Sistine Chapel: "the eyes, in suddenly being raised to those figures, and confounded in *meraviglia,* and confused in such marveling, begin subtly to retrace with their gaze the might of his labors" (cited in David Summers, *Michelangelo and the Language of Art,* 174-75).

[31] Kuhn, "Much Virtue in *If,*" 50. Kuhn is responding to Palmer, "Art and Nature in *As You Like It.*"

[32] Mowat, *Dramaturgy of Shakespeare's Romances,* 98-99.

[33] For a thorough treatment of the authorship issue, see F. D. Hoeniger's Arden edition of *Pericles,* lii-lxiii. More recently see *A Textual Companion,* ed. Wells and Taylor, 556-60. On unity in *Pericles,* see Edwards, "An Approach to the Problem of *Pericles*"; Knight, *Crown of Life,* 32-75; and Pitcher, "The Poet and Taboo," in *Essays and Studies,* ed. Bushrui, 14-29.

[34] Bishop, *Uses of Recognition,* 266-67.

[35] The Quarto reads "this long's the text"; the Third Folio reads "thus long's the text." "This 'longs the text" is an emendation of Theobald's.

[36] See Adelman, *Suffocating Mothers,* 194-96; Bishop's chapter on *Pericles* in *Uses of Recognition,* 237-307; Felperin, *Shakespearean Romance,* 143-76, esp. 148-49; and Pitcher, "The Poet and Taboo."

[37] See Bishop, *Uses of Recognition,* 251.

[38] *Uses of Recognition,* 265.

[39] On this scene and its relationship to Renaissance emblems, see Young, "A Note on the Tournament Impresas in *Pericles.*" Given his role in negotiating the verbal and the visual in act 2, Simonides' name may have significance: according to Plutarch, it was Simonides of Ceos (ca. 556-467 B.C.) who first uttered the famous maxim "Painting is mute poetry, and poetry a speaking picture." See Plutarch, "Were the Athenians More Famous," in *Roman Questions* 346f., trans. Babbitt, 501. See also Hagstrum, *Sister Arts,* 10.

[40] See Kay, "'To Hear the Rest Untold,'" esp. 211-13.

[41] See Cavell, *Disowning Knowledge,* 179-91.

[42] It is helpful to recall the remarks of the Pseudo-Aristotle that I cite earlier (preface, note 13): "Our wonder is excited, firstly, by phenomena which occur in accordance with nature but of which we do not know the cause, and secondly by those which are produced by art despite nature for the benefit of mankind" (*Mechanics,* 847a10ff., in *Complete Works,* ed. Barnes, 2:1299). The cause of the marvel, then, can also induce wonder.

[43] Bishop, *Uses of Recognition,* 306.

[44] What Northrop Frye has said about the role of romance in the recovery of myth can also be applied to the theater: "The first step . . . is the transfer of the center of interest from hero to poet. The second, and perhaps final, stage is reached when the poet entrusts his work to the reader. . . . As we have seen, the message of all romance is *de te fabula:* the story is about you; and it is the reader who is responsible for the way literature functions, both socially and individually" (*Secular Scripture,* 185-86).

Source: "*Pericles* and the Wonder of Unburdened Proof," in *Reason Diminished: Shakespeare and the Marvelous,* University of Nebraska Press, 1997, pp. 124-38.

Emilia's Argument: Friendship and 'Human Title' in *The Two Noble Kinsmen*

Laurie J. Shannon, *Duke University*

The masculinity of ideal friendship in the Renaissance is as proverbial as the "one soul in two bodies" formulation that celebrates it. Extending Cicero's disqualification of women from ideal friendship in *De Amicitia,* Montaigne's influential essay "De l'amitié" argued that women's minds were "not strong enough to endure the pulling of a knot so hard, so fast, so durable" as that composing a friendship based on (masculine) virtue.[1] Writers throughout the Renaissance commonly employed the classical trope of a virtuous friendship between male equals as a counterpoint to the conditions of engagement with a political tyrant. In gender terms, the manly autonomy of friendship virtue and its rule by reason contrasts both with the obedient deference deemed appropriate for women and with an inference of "womanishness" or effeminacy regarding the tyrant, whose subjection to passion and appetitiveness emasculates him in the gendered register of Renaissance moral values.[2] Not without reason did Montaigne describe friendship as "soveraigne Amitie."[3]

Why, then, given these conventions, would Shakespeare and Fletcher collaborate to construct a *female* voice as the advocate of both reasonable rule and a same-sex friendship principle that, doubly revising Montaigne, admits sexuality to the friendship script?[4] Although *The Two Noble Kinsmen* (1613) has generally been read in accord with the conventional privileged place of marriage in dramatic comedy, the play provocatively casts marriage as the expression of unreasoning political power, tainting it as the favored means of a ruler's caprice and as inimical to a subject's self possession or volition. Marriage and unreasonable rule are associated and juxtaposed with the principles of friendship and choice. The play thus construes "human title"—power and authority over the disposition of the self—as a bedraggled prize in a struggle between personal affective autonomy, on the one hand, and an external prerogative understood less as state power than as a personal excess by an unreasoning "tyrannical" ruler on the other.[5] Jacques Derrida describes this opposition between autonomy and heteronomy as a philosophical trademark of "the tradition of a certain concept of friendship."[6] But here, against tradition, a female voice dramatizes friendship and reason, and it is the voice of an Amazon, a figure infinitely more likely in the period to serve as an absolute other beyond reason's pale.[7]

In the following discussion, I suggest that female friendship appears in a specifically social form of female chastity which revises the characteristic masculinity of friendship rhetoric in the period. In *The Two Noble Kinsmen,* Emilia, a votaress of Diana and a lady knight, articulates a commitment to such a chastity of women among themselves. Chastity, envisioned as a bond between women rather than as "single blessedness," in turn, carries political meanings analogous to the autonomy valorized in ideal male friendship.[8] But Emilia's case also extends the range of this principle of self-rule, and so it complicates an already vibrant scholarship considering early-modern sexuality.[9] The drama conceives same-sex associations, including those that are erotic, in a vocabulary of "persuasion" and even "faith."[10] In so doing, *The Two Noble Kinsmen* offers an alternative to the present terms of the historical debate. It reflects neither the anti-identitarian view that same-sex eroticism transpired detached from any means to articulate it, nor the more essentialist view that such eroticism pertained to those whose "nature" prescribed it.[11] Instead, same-sex associational primacy appears as something one might profess or choose, as an espousal of a "faith," or as a "way of life," echoing distantly the vital idea of conscience so resonant in the period.[12]

The construction of a female character's commitment to other women as an argument or position contrasts interestingly with Jonathan Goldberg's investigation of the word "sodometries." Noting its "nonce-word suggestiveness," Goldberg expands on an idea of logics or metrics, citing the term's use "to impugn . . . customs . . . and arguments."[13] Goldberg's assessment of "sodometry" as a period allegation of false logic is neatly reversed in this case of a *female* homoerotics advocated by a reasoning Amazon. For rather than representing a negativized position or a sedition without limits as "sodomy" seems to have done, female association here reprehends a tyranny without limits, admonishing the abuse of absolute power from the established viewpoint of reason.[14] The phenomenon of female friendship, so elusive in the texts of the Renaissance, appears to extraordinary dramatic effect, linking marriage and tyranny and enhancing the otherwise familiar disapprobation the play registers toward absolute (or unreasoning, unbounded, "tyrannical") power.

The non-subordinating relation of friendly equals represented a utopian alternative to the subordination without limits inflicted by the tyrannical ruler. More generally, friendship's "twinned soul" vision of parity represented the sharpest contrast to the politics of vertical difference, authority, or "degree." Gendering friendship female makes available metaphors of chastity to express an urgent rationale for opposition to external powers of incursion—and suggests how the ideal of manly self-possession might profitably be considered a kind of masculine political chastity. This cross-gender identification, in turn, emphasizes the flexibility of gender representations, even to the point of their submission to moral and political categories. Emilia (and all she represents) advocates a position not only on the content of friendship's meanings, but also in the contest over who shall determine them, as she attempts to defend the threatened terrain of the subject's prerogative.

I. Chastity and the Space Of Female Friendship

What are the possible meanings of "chastity" in Shakespeare and Fletcher's historical context? Beyond both a modern conflation of chastity with celibacy and the familiar Renaissance innovation of marital chastity, a third, less regulatory interpretation involves a morally ambitious chastity, a pursuit of integrity and autonomy, which operates like masculine "virtue" and embodies a similar power.[15] Exploring this aspect of chastity, Philippa Berry considers the use of Petrarchan models in poet-courtiers' representations of Elizabeth I, whose own grand improvisation on her choice "to lyve out of the state of mariage" provides the most (in)famous contemporary reference for chastity as a "determynacion."[16] Berry examines the role of Elizabeth as chaste beloved in the development of masculinity through Petrarchan forms, suggesting that

> the most vital aspect of the beloved's role as mediator of a new masculinity, her chastity, had a disturbing habit of eluding or contradicting the significance accorded to it by the male lover as poet or philosopher. It often seemed to connote . . . the survival of a quality of feminine autonomy and self-sufficiency.[17]

Berry's analysis occasionally notes that imaginings of female chastity in Elizabethan literary representation can suggest a female community, allowing that the "quality of feminine autonomy and self-sufficiency" could be troped in the plural. She proposes, for example, that male fear of an active female sexuality presented "the disturbing possibility of woman taking narcissistic, and possibly even homosexual, pleasure in the female body," and that this latter "possible possibility" is suggested by "the recurrence of the figure of the goddess Diana . . . whose association with close-knit communities of women . . . is stressed." Despite this indication, the associative aspects of a chastity figured by Diana's circle are never explored. Berry reads such plural instances in terms of female narcissism, or in terms of Elizabeth's female "community" with her mother, Anne Boleyn, or in terms of a unified feminine sphere, by which the masculine is excluded or civilized.[18] Where these categories fail, Berry defaults to a lexicon of "ambiguity" rather than directly

argue the implications of a self-specified, same-sex association that her texts would seem to offer. She refers to "the theme of sexual ambiguity inscribed in the mythology of Diana"; "when we remember that the primary allegiance of [Sappho] was to women, [her] words . . . could be interpreted as somewhat ambiguous"; Lyly's *Gallathea* is said to involve "somewhat ambiguous subject matter"; and an analogy to Sappho is "a comparison which of course carries the ambiguity I mentioned earlier."[19] Berry's systematic rendering of these textual moments as "ambiguous," stemming perhaps from a too specifically erotic categorization of their meanings, occludes the social dimension of her "feminine sphere" from view. A fuller understanding of Renaissance representations of female chastity, however, requires an account of its frequent configuration as female association, often by reference to Diana and her followers, where a commitment to chastity incorporates a choice for the company of women.

Diana's most resonant presence in sixteenth-century lore is the story narrated in Ovid's *Metamorphoses.*[20] In Ovid's version of her explosive encounter with Actaeon, Diana is discovered in a place sacred and proper to her, in a grotto in its deepest, wooded recess (*"Vallis erat. . . . sacra Dianae / cuius in extremo est antrum nemorale recessu"*).[21] The withdrawn privacy of the spot enhances the sense of Actaeon's transgression when he enters it. The locale is private, indeed, but it is not lonely: Ovid enumerates the activities of Diana's companions, and he lists many of their names (ll. 165-72). When Actaeon bursts upon them, they weave a protective wall around Diana with their bodies (*"circumfusaeque Dianam / corporibus texere suis"* [ll. 180-81]) and guard her (*"comitum turba est stipata suarum"* [l. 186]).[22] Here, in its original version for the Renaissance, Diana's legend locates female chastity in a sacred, enclosed or withdrawn realm and also populates that space with a plural female company.[23] Literary references to Diana preserve the *social* nature of this cult of chastity. An adherent of Diana takes a vow and joins a group, she becomes a "votaress"; Diana's votaries are members of a "company," a "sweet troop"; they belong to a "band."[24] In this plural form, female chastity takes on a volitional character.

Images of Diana and her company are generally situated in the kind of private locale depicted in Ovid, a zone of feminine autonomy physicalized as the grove, the *locus amoenus* or the garden (indeed this spatialization gives female friendship an even more marked sense of place than idealized male friendship enjoyed). In social terms, of course, this seclusion of women within the garden and domestic space has a primarily regulatory purpose.[25] As Georgiana Zeigler argues, there is a developing homology or identification between women and household, chamber, garden, or closet that plays a role in the rise of the idea of the private; she notes the degree to which "the woman's room signifies her 'self'" in Shakespearean drama.[26] As Zeigler's materials indicate, the will to keep women within the domestic sphere also generates an anxiety about their conduct within the women's quarters. The act of seclusion is slightly at odds with the desire to control women's "private" conduct, as the continuous recommendation of activities like sewing and prayer attests.[27] What these literary feminine places begin to suggest is the Foucaultian prospect that the "proper" zone of female persons accorded by the conduct books and gender ideology of the period could take on a "proprietary" sense, affectively and erotically.[28] As we shall see, *The Two Noble Kinsmen* unites the paradigms of plural chastity and female proprietary spaces to surprising effect.

II. Improvisations On the Friendship Form

Much critical consideration of *The Two Noble Kinsmen* has concerned itself with allocating authorship between Shakespeare and Fletcher.[29] Treatments undertaking more thematic interpretation have often utilized an idea of the "naturalness" of marriage to interpret this drama, which, as I will show, could hardly go further than it does to argue that marriage is a (brutally) political institution. As one editor of *The Two Noble Kinsmen* suggests, "perhaps the chief difficulty is that the play seems to compel us to attribute to Shakespeare at the end of his career an apparently partial and distorted attitude to love."[30] Other critics read the play as a representation of the inevitability of such a "distorted" attitude's ultimate defeat. Mary Beth Rose argues that "the best studies of the play have relied on the psychoanalytic conception of individual development to argue . . . that *The Two Noble Kinsmen* concerns . . . the unavoidable process of growth."[31] Barry Weller characterizes marriage, though soberly, in terms of "the inevitability of this institution as both the building block of the social order and the seal of adult sexuality."[32] Rose sees *The Two Noble Kinsmen* as a "representation of neurotic suffering"; in her reading the play equates any resistance to marriage as a celebratory zone for self-fulfillment with "perversity" and an "unnatural recoil from experience and, specifically, from sexual love."[33]

Critical approaches that blend nature, growth, and love with marriage underestimate the power of the theories of friendship in the play, especially since marriage was only just becoming normative as a locus of affectivity.[34] They fail to grapple with the astonishingly negative conception of marriage the drama involves. They also diminish the force and interest of the character Emilia, who walks on stage to dramatize the most explicit case for same-sex association in the period except for what Janel Mueller terms John Donne's "brief for lesbianism" in "Sapho to Philenis." Describing this unprecedented poem as a "what if? imagining," Mueller proposes that Donne fully envisions lesbianism, in both erotic and economic terms, as a utopian resolution of the sexual dilemma in Montaigne's friendship theory.[35] *The Two Noble Kinsmen's* Emilia, by comparison, appears as an advocate of female homoerotics in a contest situation, as a representative of individual, volitional association against the sovereign's power to reorganize one's affective arrangements. In a sense, the play moves female homoerotics from utopia into the realm of political contest, where it remains positively coded as utopian; its apparent defeat by marriage is marked by funerals rather than celebration. Since the power of the sovereign and the imposition of marriage are so morally tainted in *The Two Noble Kinsmen,* Emilia's advocacy is not simply an example of what James Holstun usefully terms "lesbian elegy."[36] For the "inevitability" of a female homoerotics pressed into the past tense is just what Shakespeare and Fletcher qualify and recast as political injustice.

The literary rarity of Emilia's position, its specific political role in the drama, and its connection to female proprietary spaces make *The Two Noble Kinsmen* an extraordinary text. For Emilia's combined dedication to women and to chastity makes the case for chastity as an associative form. This chastity opposes not only tyrannical or coercive marriage, but also tyranny in its plain political sense. While Rose locates the play's conflict between "erotic love and friendship" and Weller instead considers the play to "dramatize the conflict between friendship and marriage," friendship and marriage arguably trope another conflict.[37] This third conflict places non-subordinated affective bonds in opposition to compulsory and hierarchical ones, where relations preferred or chosen counter those compelled by tyrannical compulsion. Thus the primary conflict of the play pits Emilia as a spokesperson for volitional association against Theseus as the agent of imposed marriage. Their contest determines which of the two paradigms will capture "human title."

The prologue to *The Two Noble Kinsmen* signals its source in Chaucer's "The Knight's Tale." The points of deviation, however, are equally interesting, for they all tend to highlight friendship—for both sexes—and to darken marriage and diminish its prestige. In Chaucer's tale, Theseus's marriage to the captured queen of "Femenye" is already completed, not indefinitely deferred as in the drama. The playwrights have also de-emphasized the marriage of Emilia and Palamon, deferring it too beyond the play's borders. The drama enhances Pirithous's presence, giving his friendship with Theseus sufficient weight to counterbalance that of Palamon and Arcite; the kinsmen's friendship is given a new declamatory intensity. Finally, the play vastly expands the role of Emelye into a character who articulates an entirely new, pro-female argument, actively connecting a female preference for chastity with the pursuit of a camaraderie of

women. All these changes weaken the marriage element they adapt from Chaucer while substantiating
the counter-presence of friendship.

The friendship theme is strengthened by Shakespeare
and Fletcher, but it is also made more complex, a fact
previous criticism has not addressed. Indeed, one critic
has asserted that Palamon and Arcite are just "younger
versions of Theseus and Pirithous."[38] The case of
Palamon and Arcite, however, deviates so markedly from
Theseus and Pirithous's model friendship that it must be
considered a parody of the highly-rhetoricized period
ideal. The drama presents the secure friendship of
Theseus and Pirithous by way of others' observation. In
a rich conversation between Hippolyta and Emilia, the
two Amazon sisters analyze both the scope and basis of
this famous friendship. Their dialogue proceeds as
Pirithous leaves them to follow Theseus to war:

> EMILIA: How his longing
> Follows his friend!
> . . . Have you observed him
> Since our great lord departed?
> HIPPOLYTA: With much labor;
> And I did love him for it. They two have
>   cabined
> In many a dangerous as poor a corner,
> Peril and want contending . . .
> . . . Their knot of love,
> Tied, weaved, entangled, with so true, so long,
> And with a finger of so deep a cunning,
> May be outworn, never undone. I think
> Theseus cannot be umpire to himself,
> Cleaving his conscience into twain and doing
> Each side like justice, which he loves best.
>   (1.3.26-47)[39]

The sisters, experienced in war themselves, find this
friendship to be rooted in mutual experience and trial
over time. Emilia subsequently comments on the friendship's sense of "ground" and its "maturely seasoned"
quality (1.3.56). This perspective distinguishes the
Theseus-Pirithous friendship from the rapture of
Montaigne's formulation.[40]

In contrast to this model, Palamon and Arcite articulate their twinning friendship with a youthful excess
that effectively parodies some of Montaigne's declamatory rhetoric. The Jailer's Daughter had observed that
the imprisoned kinsmen (not unlike Donne's lovers in
"The Good-Morrow") "have all the world in their chamber" (2.1.25). Arcite begins to imagine that they can
thrive in confinement:

> And here being thus together,
> We are an endless mine to one another;
> We are one another's wife, ever begetting
> New births of love; we are father, friends,
>   acquaintance;

> We are, in one another, families.
> I am your heir, and you are mine; this place
> Is our inheritance; . . .

> We shall live long and loving.
>   (2.1.132-40)

A few lines before this extravagantly rhetoricized relationship has ended, Palamon asks "is there record of
any two that loved / Better than we do Arcite?" (2.1.166-
67) and concludes in the same self-congratulatory tone
"I do not think it possible our friendship / Should ever
leave us" (2.1.168-69). However, the entire declama-
tion of Palamon and Arcite's friendship notably transpires in the shadow of a captivity that serves as both
its context and its caveat. Unlike Theseus and Pirithous,
the kinsmen envision their friendship both as a haven
from the trial of their virtue in the world and as a bond
vulnerable in the circumstance of liberty. The prison is
a "holy sanctuary" to keep them from corruption
(2.1.125). "Were we at liberty, / A wife might part us
lawfully, or business; / Quarrels consume us . . . A
thousand chances, / Were we from hence, would sever
us" (2.1.142-49). On the contrary, within Renaissance
friendship theory, "neither sovereign's nor father's hate
/ A friendship fix'd on virtue sever can."[41] The kinsmen's
speeches were premature. Montaigne refers to Cicero
on this issue: "Clearly friendships are to be judged by
wits, and ages already strengthened and confirmed."[42]
Compared to Theseus's "knot of love" as Hippolyta
and Emilia had just described it, the kinsmen's friendship is precarious in the extreme.

This precariousness is immediately dramatized as their
love for Emilia registers primarily as a quarrel *between
them* over rights to love her.[43] The collapse of Palamon
and Arcite's friendship falls decisively short of the
right result, according to friendship lore, when two
virtuous friends fall in love with the same woman. The
touchstone to which this dilemma refers is Boccaccio's
story of Tito and Gesippo, a tale circulated further in
Elyot's *Boke Named the Governour*. In Weller's words,
"one friend surrenders his bride to the other, but this
gift creates an asymmetry that, in the second movement of the tale, is presumably rectified when the recipient of the bride offers to die for the donor. The
crises of death and sexual desire test the proposition
that a friend is an 'other self' under extreme conditions."[44] False to form, Palamon and Arcite instantly
pursue their separate interests, and vow instead to take
one another's lives. A "true" friendship would not have
collapsed under this pressure. By the drama's close,
both will sadly question the fatality by which one love
exacts the life of another love.

Theseus himself takes on the role of spokesman for
this sense of fate as an unpredictable external power.
In the final speech of the play, he offers this commentary on the bizarre—and appallingly serious—turn of

events: "Never fortune / Did play a subtler game . . . yet in the passage / The gods have been most equal . . . The gods my justice / Take from my hand, and they themselves become the executioners / . . . O heavenly charmers, / What things you make of us!" (5.4.112-32). Theseus's light tone here belies the spiritual bruises, long faces, and blood that surround him. His claim that outcomes have been effected by fortune or the gods, however, masks his agency in setting up the original "fateful" dilemmas in over-passionate exercises of his unilateral power. Despite these gestures to the role of fate in the drama, the absolute power, the "tyranny," of Theseus remains to be explored.

III. Theseus's Power

In act 1, we find the kinsmen discussing the nature of Creon's power in Thebes. They call him "a most *unbounded* tyrant" and prepare to exile themselves, when the approach of warring Theseus revives their political loyalty to Creon: "we must / With him stand to the mercy of our fates / Who hath bounded our last minute" (1.2.63, 101-3). Such is the tyrant's character. He has a boundary problem, exceeding his own and contracting or violating the boundedness of others. Theseus displays exactly this fault, insisting upon a relationship of intimacy with persons over whom he has absolute power.[45] Both the kinsmen and both the Amazons are *less than subjects* in Theseus's dukedom. They are captives, prisoners of war, lives to be disposed of by decrees. This specifically political circumstance does not register in readings of the play that are concerned with individualistic or exclusively private meanings of love and sexuality. Hippolyta and Emilia are captive soldiers, Amazons to be domesticated by Theseus's phallic power; Palamon and Arcite were combatants near death when Theseus ordered "All our surgeons / Convent in their behoof . . . we had rather have 'em / Prisoners to us than death!" (1.4.30-37). Theseus's comportment towards all four combines domination with desire, aggression with affection and admiration, as he blurs personal inclination with political office. All of their fates will originate in Theseus's imagination and will be effected by the mechanisms of his political power. None will be motivated by individual "growth."

Theseus functions as an unreliable but absolute political ruler. In the first scene of the play, Theseus is urged to take revenge. Hippolyta, queen of the Amazons, joins the other queens in a position commonly used to address him: she is on her knees (1.1.86).[46] Theseus at first protests the queens' insistence upon kneeling ("Pray you, kneel not" and "O no knees, none, widow" [1.1.54, 74]). But after Theseus has once refused them, the widows ask Hippolyta to "Lend us a knee" and Emilia "O help now! / Our cause cries for your knee" (1.1.96, 199-200). When the spectacle of the kneeling ladies finally affects Theseus, "All the Ladies rise" (1.1.207-5).

This is not the only time an extravagant display of kneeling deference indexes Theseus's tyrannical capriciousness as a ruler. When Arcite and Palamon are discovered dueling and an enraged Theseus orders both shall die, he is besieged by another wave of entreaties, this time not for revenge, but for forbearance. Lacking princely probity, he appears not to know which is appropriate to a given case. When he decides to let the kinsmen duel first and then kill the winner, the ladies resort to their knees, again, in supplication, with Emilia proclaiming "I will be woman and have pity. / My knees shall grow to th'ground but I'll get mercy / . . . the powers of all women will be with us" (3.6.191-94). As the sisters beg to no avail, even Pirithous enters the fray: "Nay, then, I'll in too" (3.6.201). Their combined and repeated conjurings for mercy finally cause Theseus to relent, only to produce a more arbitrary decree.

Theseus's disposition of the problem that Palamon and Arcite raise enmeshes an innocent bystander: the single-by-choice Emilia. In a mode of reasoned counsel, Emilia urges him to take back his oath to execute the kinsmen. "That oath was rashly made, and in your anger; / Your reason will not hold it" (3.6.227-28). Further, she reminds him of a prior oath made to her "of more authority . . . / Not made in passion neither, but good heed" (3.6.231-32). By this oath Theseus had promised to fulfill any reasonable request of Emilia's, and she proclaims "I tie you to your word now" (3.6.236). Emilia on her knees has presented Theseus with a morally serious challenge. In asking him to stand firm to his "word" and to be ruled in his rule-making by reason, Emilia mobilizes all the humanist principles of good rule by reason against the inconstant, wavering rule by passion or anger associated with the tyrant. Here Emilia distinguishes herself from the madness and unreason variously displayed by the kinsmen, Theseus, and the Jailer's mad daughter. She asks Theseus to banish both the kinsmen and to make them "swear . . . never more / To make me their contention, or to know me" (3.6.251-53). Thus, framed within a demonstration of marked moral clarity in Renaissance terms, Emilia's one request is that these kinsmen, without violence, should leave her alone.

Instead of heeding her reasonable request, Theseus offers her a choice that entails exactly the degree of involvement and responsibility from which she has just sought to be relieved. When she refuses to implicate herself in Theseus's process of "justice," ("for me, a hair shall never fall of these men" [3.6.287]) Theseus improvises. He decides to permit the duel, execute the loser, and give her to the winner. Death is a fate the kinsmen had already undertaken to risk, so instead of punishment there is now a prospect of reward. In violating his word, Theseus casually, as if his attention has already lapsed, transgresses the known, stated desire of Emilia, who seconds earlier was hunting with him as an equal. Only Emilia, who has lowered her body and raised her voice for mercy, has been punished by the end of the whole transaction.[47] Emilia is arbitrarily thrust out of the role of a reasoning interlocutor and into the role of a silent item of booty in the decree Theseus establishes unilaterally and in violation of "reason." Theseus's autocratic conduct suggests a wavering, divided mind, but one nevertheless possessed of final authority. Emilia's consent, of course, is never given.

While Theseus's treatment of Emilia illustrates the brutality of his thought, it highlights the equivocal position in which all the characters subject to his power find themselves. Theseus's injection of marriage here is important, for, as Rose notes, "marrying Emilia is never an explicit concern [even] of the kinsmen, who quarrel only over the right to love her."[48] In this sense, Theseus is in fact imposing marriage upon everyone else, as an expression of his control over them. Marriage, as an element of *his* imagination, is instituted as an act of Theseus's political power. Arcite upon his "victory" tells Emilia "To buy you I have lost what's dearest to me / Save what is bought" (5.3.112-13). Palamon, swept by Arcite's demise into "victory," reflects on the paradox "that we should things desire which do cost us / The loss of our desire! That naught could buy dear love but loss of dear love!" (5.4.110-12). Thus Palamon and Arcite equate the passions of friendship and love, while in Theseus's regime the two forms are set in a life-and-death struggle. As a consequence, both kinsmen articulate mixed evaluations of the "fate" Theseus has wrought for them. Subjection to passionate desire, subjection to absolute power; both place Palamon and Arcite as well as Emilia under a tyranny of false choices, in the thrall of others' imperatives.

On the other hand, as the only politically unsubordinated character, Theseus is able to make choices he considers consistent with maintaining what he calls "our human title" (1.1.233). Despite the fact that Theseus uses language suggesting a view that Rose terms "the heroics of marriage," in which marriage is seen as a definitional watershed in human identity, it is precisely the prospective threat posed to his "human title" by marriage that moves Theseus to defer it. He goes to war instead, claiming "As we are man, / Thus should we do; being sensually subdued, / We lose our human title" (1.1.231-33). While he can compel or defer his own marriage, his compulsion of connections among other characters represents for them a constraint inconsistent with that "human title" as volitional freedom or self-disposition. When Emilia, facing the prospect of the duel and its results, announces "I am extinct" (5.3.20) and, given to the victor, laments "Is this winning?" (5.3.138) it is clear that the right to freely choose one's affective association is an expression of self-ownership and integrity. But for all these characters, Theseus's unlimited authority cancels their self-possession. Theseus holds "title" to their lives.

IV. Emilia's Choice

Emilia is the dramatic counterweight to Theseus as well as his political victim. While Emilia is the only figure in the drama capable of what Weller describes as a "conscious articulation" of desire (for chastity and the company of women), criticism has neglected and misread her to an astonishing degree.[49] Roberts argues that "the Amazonian Emilia comes closer to being a simple allegorical figure than any of the men. Like Hippolyta, she remains curiously static, seeming more a projection of a male problem than an interesting dramatic character."[50] But Emilia's unwavering consistency is a sign of valued self-knowledge in a play (and a period) where inconstant desires and shifting appetites are deeply stigmatized, and her "persuasion" for women in itself offers a check to the male process of "projection." Rose describes Emilia quite misleadingly as the "remote superior lady" of courtly love tradition.[51] But rather than being remote or superior, Emilia articulates an actual rebuttal of the Petrarchan system, asserting resistance to the gender roles within courtly love. Rose places her along with Palamon and Arcite as "three ambivalent narcissists, for whom love becomes an isolated, compulsive experience."[52] On the contrary, Emilia's version of love is emphatically homosocial, and her impending marriage is compelled, not "compulsive." Rose asks, "Is she merely a passive victim in regard to choosing a mate, or is she unwilling to assert her prerogative as a subject and make a choice?"[53] This is an impossible question because Emilia has done nothing if not actively articulate her choice, throughout the drama, as a matter of her virgin "faith." To the exceptions taken against her "persuasion" for "true love 'tween maid and maid," she equably replies with model tolerance "I am not / Against your faith, yet I continue mine" (1.3.91, 81, 96-97).

Indeed, Emilia's *"prerogative* as a subject" is exactly what is canceled by Theseus's unbounded power over her. The drama traces this brutal cancellation of individual prerogative, which it connects to the political issue of "human title." The figure of Emilia in particular resists a construction of the play as focusing "exclusively on the conflicts of private life, conceived of as a separate domain" from the public sphere.[54] Instead, in juxtaposing the unboundedness of Theseus's absolute power with Emilia's articulated choice and its final subjection to Theseus's authority, the play actually expresses a longing for a form of life—public *or* private—from which the subordinating power of tyranny is absent. There, the individual might experience freedom of association as a means to self-fulfillment and Montaigne's "jovissance."[55] While *The Two Noble Kinsmen* associates marriage with tyranny and compulsion, its representation of female "chastity" is coextensive with a full-blown argument for a female homosociality in pursuit of "jovissance." Emilia's advocacy carries more poetic and political weight than the weaker and tainted male friendships in the drama.

Emilia's association with reason and wisdom, her sense of moderation, and the manner in which she intelligently takes part in efforts to persuade Theseus to mercy all combine with the absence of any hint of monstrosity to code this Amazon astonishingly positively. As Bawcutt notices, "Emilia is shown as a serious and intelligent girl."[56] Her seriousness is clear from her attempt to restrain Theseus from rash oaths and from her firm advocacy of the rule of reason. Exhibiting the Renaissance virtues of probity and "decorum," she is a proponent of both martial severity (1.1.128) and compassion (3.6.239, 242) when either is appropriate. All of these positions are morally serious; here they are propounded in a female voice. Only Emilia questions Theseus's illegitimate manner of rule.

In this same voice, Emilia sounds a critique of the gender mechanics of courtly love. In Emilia, the "female beloved" speaks up to announce that she has a critical consciousness that does not consent, exposing the Petrarchan system *as* "projection." When Palamon and Arcite are caught dueling, Arcite pleads with Theseus: "Duke, ask that lady / Why she is fair, and why her eyes command me / . . . to love her" (3.6.168-70). Hippolyta similarly blames Emilia's face: "that face of yours / Will bear the curses . . . of after ages / For these lost cousins" (3.6.186-88). The follower of Diana finally responds, "in my face, dear sister, I find no anger to 'em, nor no ruin"; instead, she argues, "the misadventure of their own eyes kill 'em" (3.6.188-90). This rejoinder is a fresh yet practical analysis of the Petrarchan situation from the "beloved's" point of view; in another play, perhaps, it would be a comic moment. After horrified pleading against her implication in the violence of the duel—"Shall anything that loves me perish for me?" (3.6.241)—Emilia continues to protest the Petrarchan role she is accorded through the balance of the play. She laments "that my unspotted youth must now be soiled / With blood of princes and my chastity / Be made the altar" of death (4.2.59-61). She prefers that "neither for my sake should fall," (4.2.69) but also hopes in her address to Diana that "If well inspired, this battle shall confound / Both these brave knights" and she might "continue in [Diana's] band" (5.1.166-67, 162). She refuses to be an inspirational presence at the combat itself, exclaiming "O, better never born, / Than minister to such a harm!" (5.3.65-66). Thus *The Two Noble Kinsmen* offers a woman who, rather than being remote and silent or exercising "a fundamental aloofness," is articulate and in the fray, repudiating continually the gender and affective roles graven in the Petrarchan system.[57]

What is the form of *frauendienst* that Emilia offers instead? She provides a fully developed articulation of an Amazonian position, situating herself affectively and socially among women alone. She not only connects chastity with a female associational preference; her idea of her reputation and her identity is drawn from and maintained within the company of women. Emilia's

first speech would be perfectly unremarkable if made by a male knight. The Third Queen, invoking virginity, has called upon Emilia to be the queen's advocate. In high contrast with Theseus, Emilia responds: "No knees to me. / What woman I may stead that is distressed / Does bind me to her" (1.1.35-37). Emilia's performance of chivalric service results in a specifically female loyalty, and this first exchange links virginity with bonds between women. Emilia describes herself as "a natural sister of our sex" (1.1.125).

Emilia's sisterhood, according to Hippolyta, rises to the level of a "persuasion," and we begin to hear its history. Emilia makes a case for same-sex affective primacy—even though she begins by assuring Hippolyta that "reason" supports that Theseus will place his marriage to her above his friendship with Pirithous.[58] When Emilia begins to recount the history of her youthful friendship, Hippolyta knows immediately what is coming: "'Twas Flavina," she interjects (1.3.54). As Waith ironically notes, "it appears that women, *pace* Montaigne, are also capable of such ideal relationships."[59] Indeed, the celebratory reminiscence proceeds in the profound language of Montaigne's most emotional passages: "I,"

> And she I sigh and spoke of were things innocent,
> Loved for we did, and like the elements
> That know not what, nor why, yet do effect
> Rare issues by their operance, our souls
> Did so to one another.
>
> (1.3.59-64)

Emilia here echoes the sense of sublimity and mystery with which Montaigne supplements Ciceronian rhetoric, suggesting an imperative not only within the soul but also beyond it, driving it without its conscious involvement.[60] Interestingly, Emilia's narrative does not suggest that likeness was the source of the friendship. Instead, sameness seems to have been, in a way, its goal, as the two copy one another, adopting the other's patterns and striving for resemblance. Flowers, bodily ornament—conventional female signs—are circulating, here, between women themselves. Even the casual actions and careless habits of dress of one become the serious ambition of the other:

> The flower that I would pluck
> And put between my breasts—O, then but beginning
> To swell about the blossom—She would long
> Till she had such another, and commit it
> To the like innocent cradle, where phoenix-like
> They died in perfume; on my head no toy
> But was her pattern; her affections—pretty,
> Though happily her careless wear—I followed
> For my most serious decking.
>
> (1.3.66-74)

Emilia brings her rapturous but delicately erotic lines to a close with a rhetorical turn, offering that "this rehearsal" has an "end." She concludes with the proposition that "true love 'tween maid and maid may be / More than in sex dividual" (1.3.81-82). The final locution is unusual, and it is clear that Emilia's is a dramatic proclamation, ushered in by a transport of passion, as she discloses in conceding that her "rehearsal" is "old emportment's bastard" (1.3.80).[61] Hippolyta's first comment is to tell Emilia "you're out of breath" before she reflects on Emilia's "high-speeded pace" to convert a declaration for homosociality into one against heterosexuality. She surmises that Emilia "shall never . . . love any that's called man" (1.3.83-85).[62] Emilia is sure she shall not, and the events of the play support this statement. On the death of Arcite she acknowledges him as a "right good man," still saying nothing about love (5.4.97).

The language used to describe Emilia's position here is based on notions of choice, conviction, or "determynacion"; her position is not centered in acts or in essences, but is articulable as a faith or a profession. It further rises to the level of an argument, proposing its thesis. In Hippolyta and Emilia's final exchange on the subject of Emilia's "rehearsal," Hippolyta calls Emilia's position an "appetite," a "persuasion," and Emilia refers to it as a kind of doctrine, a "faith" (1.3.89, 91, 97). The scope of this "faith" extends beyond particular friendships or object choice narrowly construed; Emilia invariably evaluates situations in terms of a world view markedly centered on a female standard. When the others commend Arcite at the tournament, Emilia says "Believe / His mother was a wondrous handsome woman; / His face methinks goes that way" (2.4.19-21). When Theseus vows that Palamon and Arcite must die, Emilia fears becoming the "scorn of women": "the goodly mothers that have groaned for these, / And all the longing maids that ever loved 'em, / If your vow stand, shall curse me" (3.6.250, 245-47). Trying to choose one of the kinsmen in order to avoid violence between them, Emilia strangely links Arcite's beauty with homosexual models and Palamon's looks to his mother. She compares Arcite to Ganymede and his brow to Juno's. As for Palamon, his melancholy appearance is "as if he had lost his mother" (4.2.28). All the affective links in this speech exceed the scope of heterosexual models. But Emilia remains "guiltless of election," either between the kinsmen or for marriage, in her long address to Diana. Instead, she entreats Diana to give her to whichever man loves her best "or else grant / The file and quality I hold I may / Continue in thy band" (5.1.160-62).

The address to Diana highlights the question of jurisdiction that Theseus has been shown to confound. For Emilia's appeal to Diana finds her with an undetermined husband already appointed to her. Nevertheless, Emilia still holds out the possibility that she will be given to neither kinsman. Strangely, the servant of Diana, rather than betraying her oath of chastity or falling in love, is instead separated from her mistress by a decree of the civil power; no impulse of "nature" has eroded her vows. The play dramatizes the degree to which Diana's mythic power is eclipsed by Theseus's absolute sovereignty. On the verge of her betrothal to the unknown victor, Emilia describes herself as "bride-habited, / But maiden-hearted" (5.1.150-51). This split in subjectivity results not from her ambivalence, but instead arises as a wound to subjectivity that results from Theseus's power to compel. Emilia's "faith" retreats to the interior realm of the heart under Theseus's authority to compel her body into marriage.

In considering the construction of the "heart" as an interiority produced for Emilia by the regime of marriage in the public sphere, there is one scene-within-a-scene that appears to be completely neglected in criticism. For Emilia's recollection of friendship with Flavina, though passionate, is not the only evidence the drama offers regarding expressions of Emilia's "prerogative" in contexts free of Theseus's control. While the Flavina story of a past love is nostalgic, there is one episode in *The Two Noble Kinsmen* in which our "maiden-hearted" heroine is "merry-hearted" in the play's present tense. In the scene so much considered for the collapse of friendship between Palamon and Arcite, where from their prison window they observe (but, like the criticism, do not hear) Emilia and her Woman, the two women engage in a rich exchange. This exchange and its location suggests that serious female association is linked to a proprietary space and is not just a matter for nostalgia. The trajectory of this suggestive exchange is obscured by interlineation with Palamon and Arcite's dialogue. Perhaps performance could make it very clear. Quoting the extracted conversation in full will reveal its intriguing teleology:

EMILIA: This garden has a world of pleasures in't.
What flower is this?
WOMAN: 'Tis called narcissus, madam.
EMILIA: That was a fair boy, certain, but a fool
To love himself; were there not maids enough?
Or were they all hard-hearted?
WOMAN: They could not be to one so fair.
EMILIA: Thou wouldst not.
WOMAN: I think I should not, madam.
EMILIA: That's a good wench;
But take heed to your kindness, though.
WOMAN: Why, madam?
EMILIA: Men are mad things.
Canst thou work such flowers in silk, wench?
WOMAN: Yes.
EMILIA: I'll have a gown full of 'em and of these.
This is a very pretty colour; will't not do
Rarely upon a skirt, wench?

WOMAN: Dainty, madam.
EMILIA: Of all flowers,
Methinks a rose is best . . .
It is the very emblem of a maid;
For when the west wind courts her gently,
How modestly she blows, and paints the sun
With her chaste blushes! When the north
     comes near her,
Rude and impatient, then, like chastity,
She locks her beauties in her bud again,
And leaves him to base briars.
WOMAN: Yet, good madam,
Sometimes her modesty will blow so far
She falls for it; a maid,
If she have any honour, would be loath
To take example by her.
EMILIA: Thou art wanton.
The sun grows high, let's walk in. Keep these
     flowers;
We'll see how near art can come near their
     colours.
I am wonderous merry-hearted, I could laugh
     now.
WOMAN: I could lie down now, I am sure.
EMILIA: And take one with you?
WOMAN: That's as we bargain, madam.
EMILIA: Well, agree then.
                                    (2.1.172-7)

Like Donne's lovers' chamber, like Palamon and Arcite's prison, "this garden" in which the women are alone "has a world of pleasures in't." The garden, a proprietary female space, composes a plenitude. The reflections on Narcissus, a possible commentary on the validity of Palamon and Arcite's friendship, introduce the concept of "hard-heartedness" in maids' response to men. Emilia proceeds to warn her "wench" to limit the "kindness" she shows to them, since "men are mad things." (This judgment is being confirmed simultaneously by Palamon and Arcite's descent into the "madness" of love).[63] Emilia's question "were there not maids enough?" assumes a certain dramatic irony as well, in its identification of maids as objects of love. The conversational shift to silk weaving incorporates and echoes two elements already seen in Emilia's Flavina narrative: flowers and dress, blossoms and patterns, suggesting the intimacy of women in a dressing chamber. The references to work and art in producing the silk gown strengthen the sense of plenitude, showing that the feminine space inhabited by the women is a creative economy.[64] Ironically, this "world of pleasures" is perfectly consistent with the urgings of conduct books that women, in the quarters presumably not set aside for their pleasure, should engage in useful pursuits like sewing and embroidery.

Emilia and her Woman continue their commentary on flowers, oblivious of being observed, as Emilia proposes the rose as the "very emblem of a maid" on account of its chastity. It is now the Woman's turn to warn the Lady: the rose is an unsafe metaphor, risky for a "maid," because it eventually opens and falls. Here the exchange takes perhaps its most interesting and unexpected turn. Emilia, having raised the issue of "hard-heartedness" in connection with a warning against unchastity (as an over-kindness to men), now teases the Woman, "Thou art wanton." On this note she proposes that they withdraw into their quarters with "Let's walk in." The suddenly "wondrous merry-hearted" Emilia feels she could laugh; the Woman's response that she could "lie down" completes the allusion to a card game called "laugh and lie down" that both the Penguin and Oxford annotations consider a proverbial expression with sexual meanings.[65] Sexual meanings indeed, but this bantering conversation begs the question of just what sort of sexual meanings are in play. The familiarity of the usages "thou" and "wench," the "merry" flirtatious tone of the otherwise markedly serious Emilia, and the by now obvious inference that Emilia, at least, cannot be referring to a sexual "bargain" with a man—all these converge to suggest that these final lines refer to a sexual encounter between Emilia and her Woman. The ambiguity of the lines— are they hypothetical? Do they refer to some (future) "bargain" with a "mad" man?—is substantially dispelled by Emilia's "now" and her imperative tense in "Well, agree then." One is left with a sense that an "agreement" is concluded, that, indeed, may already have been established ("That's as we bargain, madam").

V. Conclusion

The Two Noble Kinsmen's Emilia, then, offers a rebuttal to Renaissance commonplaces about female friendship's impossibility. She appears on stage with a marked preference for her own sex, a preference that places homoerotics squarely within the scope of female friendship. The status of "Emilia's choice" with respect to her impending forced marriage is unknowable, but its location in a proprietary female space suggests that it is likely to be unaffected.[66] While Emilia's probable sexual transaction with her Woman diverges from Montaigne's model—in admitting sexuality, in traversing class lines, and in the element of "bargaining" it contains—it nevertheless suggests a form of female association that fits smoothly with conventional Renaissance patterns of female household seclusion or governance. Although domestic and interior spaces are widely associated with women, they are never investigated as the plural, female community which, in the larger households so often described, they must always have been. In the character of Emilia, as she becomes quieter and quieter under Theseus's ducal prerogative, the possibilities and nuances inherent in the Renaissance configuration of the (noble) female household just make it into articulation; they are obscured but reconstructable as a fragmented scene-within-a-scene. Emilia's "Let's walk in" gestures towards a Renaissance space in which female "chastity" finds expression as a feminine economy, a social arrangement of women "among themselves."[67] This zone is constructed as a space beyond political tyranny, at least for a time.

Strikingly, in *The Two Noble Kinsmen,* the great figure of this resistance to tyrannical power is not the paradigmatic friendship-gendered-male so popular with writers of the period. Instead, friendship's partisan is a lady knight who revises the definitional prejudices of the male model regarding both gender and sexuality. In effect, Emilia's advocacy constitutes a "friendship theory" that does Montaigne one better: by embodying Montaigne's penultimate criterion of *volitional* association, Emilia shows how his effort to exclude women and sexual love from the field of friendship actually limits the sense of real choice that he exalts when he claims "our voluntarie choice and libertie hath no production more properly her owne, than that of affection and amitie."[68] Emilia's case argues that the preemption of self-specified, affective association is a political act in violation of reason.

An Amazon as the voice of reasoning autonomy and the critique of absolutism? It appears that Shakespeare and Fletcher here were perfectly capable of overriding gender conventions and sexual silences, motivated by a need to effectively trope opposition to the intrusive power of tyrants, of absolute monarchy, of persons possessed of "greatness." Chastity, pluralized, strengthened as female friendship, and linked to a proprietary zone of affectionate autonomy, offers the only contest in the play to political subjugation and unreasonable rule. The fabulous intensity with which "chastity" is urged for women in the Renaissance context was, no doubt, predominantly a device of control and authority. But perhaps a part of the reason "chastity" absorbs so much interest and attention is the way it, in turn, could metaphorize anxious (male) relations to sovereign political power, to the unreviewable strength of those "appointed" to rule. *The Two Noble Kinsmen* raises this possibility even as it deploys a fully-articulated Amazonian position as the gendered, homoerotic voice of individual prerogative under siege. What it shows is that even the strongest conventions regarding gender and sexuality could rewrite themselves when governed by a stronger urgency: the frightening blend of personal and political power embodied in the Renaissance conception of authority.

Notes

This essay is part of a larger project entitled *Soveraigne Amitie: Friendship and the Political Imagination in Renaissance Texts.* I thank Janel Mueller for her engagement in this conversation and for access to her transcriptions of the speeches of Elizabeth I; Lauren Berlant and Josh Scodel for their helpful comments on earlier drafts; and Jonathan Goldberg for his reactions to this essay.

[1] Michel de Montaigne, "Of Friendship," in *The Essayes of Montaigne: John Florio's Translation,* ed. J. I. M. Stewart (New York: Modern Library Editions, 1933), 147. For Cicero's treatment of women and friendship, see *De Amicitia* in *De Senectute, De Amicitia, De Divinatione,* tr. W. A. Falconer (Cambridge: Harvard Univ. Press, Loeb Classical Library, 1923), xiii, 46 (156-57).

[2] Rebecca Bushnell argues that "the tyrant's love of pleasure, his impulse to shift shapes, and his improper sovereignty often generate the accusation that he is, in effect, 'feminized'" (*Tragedies of Tyrants: Political Thought and Theater in the English Renaissance* [Ithaca: Cornell Univ. Press, 1990], 9). Bushnell also discusses the classical sources of these gender associations and their implications for the Renaissance stage (20-25).

[3] Montaigne, 150.

[4] Though Montaigne's explicit discussion of sexuality in "De l'amitié" excludes it from the sphere of true friendship, Constance Jordan convincingly argues that Montaigne's account of friendship is specifically, though complicatedly, homoerotic ("Sexuality and volition in 'Sur des vers de Virgile'," forthcoming in *Montaigne Studies*).

[5] William Shakespeare and John Fletcher, *The Two Noble Kinsmen,* ed. Eugene M. Waith (Oxford: Clarendon Press, 1989), 1.1.233. Subsequent references are to this edition.

[6] Jacques Derrida, "The Politics of Friendship," *The Journal of Philosophy* 85 (1988), 634.

[7] Louis Montrose argues that "invariably, the Amazons are relocated just within the receding boundary of *terra incognita,*" and are commonly configured in "an anti-culture that precisely inverts European norms of political authority, sexual license, marriage practices, and inheritance rules" ("*A Midsummer Night's Dream* and the Shaping Fantasies of Elizabethan Culture: Gender, Power, Form" in *Rewriting the Renaissance: The Discourses of Sexual Difference in Early Modern Europe,* ed. Margaret Ferguson, Maureen Quilligan, and Nancy Vickers [Chicago: Univ. of Chicago Press, 1986], 71).

[8] William Shakespeare, *A Midsummer Night's Dream,* in *The Complete Works of Shakespeare,* ed. David Bevington (New York: Harper Collins, 1992), 1.1.78.

[9] For a summary of this debate and its application to the Renaissance context, see Claude J. Summers's well-annotated discussion in "Homosexuality and Renaissance Literature, or the Anxieties of Anachronism," *South Central Review* (1992): 2-23. For specific considerations of sexuality in the Renaissance, compare Bruce Smith, *Homosexual Desire in Shakespeare's*

England: A Cultural Poetics (Chicago: Univ. of Chicago Press, 1991) and Alan Bray, *Homosexuality in Renaissance England* (London: Gay Men's Press, 1982).

[10] As to the role of sexuality in "chaste" female association, the presence or absence of sexual acts would be even less dispositive than it would have been for males. Janel Mueller has suggested a basis for gender asymmetry in conceiving homoeroticism, referencing "theological traditions that tended to ignore lesbianism . . . in contrast to what was viewed as the far graver perversion of male-male sexual relations" ("Troping Utopia: Donne's Brief for Lesbianism in 'Sapho to Philenis'," in *Sexuality and Gender in Early Modern Europe,* ed. James Grantham Turner [Cambridge: Cambridge Univ. Press, 1993], 195). Valerie Traub compares the asymmetry of regulated female heterosexuality and undiscussed female homoerotics to suggest the possibility that "the nature of [women's] erotic contacts did not invite sexual interpretation . . . that such behavior did not threaten the basis of the social contract—the open lineage family" (*Desire and Anxiety: Circulations of Sexuality in Shakespearean Drama* [London: Routledge, 1992], 108). Female homoeroticism, then, is not inconsistent with the chastity centrally concerned with heterosexual transgressions that would threaten certainty of lineage and property.

[11] The spectrum of views on historical approaches to sexuality extends between these two "poles," whose representatives are taken to be John Boswell and Michel Foucault. Boswell's *Christianity, Social Tolerance, and Homosexuality,* on the one hand, is often characterized as "essentialist" in its effort to trace a history of homosexuality; volume one of Foucault's influential *History of Sexuality* has inspired much scholarship in a "constructivist" mode (see Summers, 20 n. 7, and Traub, 103). Both Boswell and Foucault, however, attempted to moderate these characterizations. Boswell concludes that "most of the current spectrum of belief [about what homosexuality is] appears to have been represented in previous societies. . . . Both realists and nominalists must lower their voices" ("Revolutions, Universals, Categories," *Salmagundi* 58-59 [1982-1983], 112-13). In an interview, Foucault commented specifically on Boswell's methodology, characterizing it as, in effect, non-essentialist and claiming that Boswell's emphasis on how people conceived the meanings of their own behaviors is essential to an archaeology of sexuality ("Sexual Choice, Sexual Act," in *Foucault Live,* ed. Sylvère Lotringer, tr. J. Johnston [New York: Columbia Univ. Press, Semiotext(e) Foreign Agents Series, 1989], 211-31).

[12] The terms are Foucault's in "Friendship as a Way of Life," rept. in *Foucault Live,* 203-9. Foucault's interview in *Le Gai Pied* reveals an emphasis on this sense of choice and innovation which is not often associated with his work. He offers a notion of (modern) homosexuality/friendship as "a way of life" involving invention, improvisation and communicative experimentation not far from the sense of choice and articulate persuasion to be found in *The Two Noble Kinsmen.*

[13] Jonathan Goldberg, *Sodometries: Renaissance Texts, Modern Sexualities* (Stanford: Stanford Univ. Press, 1992), xiv-xv, 4, and following.

[14] Goldberg argues that in Renaissance England "there was . . . no recognition of homosexuality *per se,* no terms to identify a homosexual except within a seditious behavior that knew no limits" and that "sodomy" was not visible unless linked "with the much more visible signs of social disruption represented by unorthodox religious or social positions" ("Sodomy and Society: the Case of Christopher Marlowe," in *Staging the Renaissance: Reinterpretations of Elizabethan and Jacobean Drama,* ed. David Scott Kastan and Peter Stallybrass [New York: Routledge, 1991], 75-76).

[15] Illustrative of this sense are Ben Jonson's lines in "To Penshurst": "Thy lady's noble, fruitfull, chast withall, / His children thy great lord may call his own" (*Ben Jonson: The Complete Poems,* ed. George Parfitt [New Haven: Yale Univ. Press, 1975], 97).

[16] Elizabeth I, "Queen Elizabeth's First Speech to the House of Commons, February 10, 1559," *The Speeches and Other Documents By and To Elizabeth I, Relating to the Parliaments of 1559, 1563, and 1566: Issues of Her Marriage and Limitation of the Succession,* ed. and trancer. Janel Mueller, a transcription of the British Library's Lansdowne MS 94, Art.14, fol.29r-v.

[17] Philippa Berry, *Of Chastity and Power: Elizabethan Literature and the Unmarried Queen* (New York: Routledge, 1989), 18.

[18] For female narcissism, see Berry, 41, 67, and 188 n.76. These formulations derive from Irigarayan theory (as above and Introduction, 166 n.1). Compare this analysis to Traub, who notes the limitedness of narcissism as a model of early modern (female) homoerotics (104).

For the sense of female community as a biological or religious genealogy see Berry, 82. This formulation emphasizes a female tradition at a distance in time rather than as a companionate present. Barbara Lewalski's concept of "female community" as she uses that phrase to consider Amelia Lanier's *Salve Deus Rex Judeorum* (1611), similarly casts female association as a "community" or tradition of "good women" throughout religious history rather than as a social present ("Imagining Female Community: Aemelia Lanyer's Poems," in *Writing Women in Jacobean England* [Cambridge: Harvard Univ. Press, 1993], 213-41).

For the female sphere, see Berry's discussion of Spenser's "April Eclogue," 78-80.

[19] Berry, xi, 123, 124, 132.

[20] Leonard Barkan details the reception history of this mythical encounter in "Diana and Actaeon: The Myth as Synthesis," *English Literary Renaissance* 10 (1980): 317-59.

[21] *The Metamorphoses,* tr. Frank Justus Miller (Cambridge: Harvard Univ. Press, Loeb Classical Library, 1916), 134-35, book III, lines 155-57.

[22] Goldberg's observation regarding access to Elizabeth I might easily be applied to Ovid's Diana: "It was literally true that access to the queen's body was in the hands of a small number of women; no approach to her privy chamber without passing by the female guard. These women are the only people we can be sure were intimate with the queen's body" (*Sodometries,* 47).

[23] Nancy Vickers, in her effective arraignment of Petrarchan technique, observes that "in *The Metamorphoses,* [Diana] is surrounded by protective nymphs, but Petrarch makes no mention of either her company or of Actaeon's" ("Diana Described: Scattered Woman and Scattered Rhyme," *Critical Inquiry* 7 [1981], 268).

[24] For "company" and "sweet troop" see John Lyly, *Gallathea and Midas,* ed. Anne Begor Lancashire (Lincoln: University of Nebraska Press, 1969), (I.ii.12), 11. For "band" see V.1.162.

[25] Peter Stallybrass considers the regulatory function of the "enclosure" of the female body in Bakhtinian terms, arguing that the ideal woman is "rigidly 'finished': her signs are the enclosed body, the closed mouth, the locked house" in "Patriarchal Territories: The Body Enclosed" (*Rewriting the Renaissance,* 127). See also Lorna Hutson, *The Usurer's Daughter: Male Friendship and Fictions of Women in Sixteenth-Century England* (New York: Routledge, 1994) in which Hutson discusses the sixteenth-century role of Xenophon's *Oeconomicus* in constructing masculinity through the confinement of women (17-51).

[26] Georgiana Zeigler, "My Lady's Chamber: Female Space, Female Chastity in Shakespeare," *Textual Practice* 4 (1990), 73.

[27] Zeigler, 75, 77, 86.

[28] The metaphor of Diana and company was appropriated as a means for imagining female literary community. The dedicatory sonnet to Elizabeth Cary's *The Tragedy of Mariam* employs this metaphor of female relations structured by (mutual) service to Diana. Cary dedicates the play to another woman, addressing her as "Diana's Earthly Deputess," calling her "my Phoebe" and describing her as "Luna-like, unspotted, chaste, divine." Cary presents the play as a votaress' offering: her play is "consecrated to . . . Diana" (*The Tragedy of Mariam the Fair Queen of Jewry,* ed. Barry Weller and Margaret Ferguson [Berkeley: Univ. of California Press, 1994], 66, lines 8, 10, 13-14).

[29] Both G. R. Proudfoot (*"Henry VIII, The Two Noble Kinsmen,* and the Apochryphal Plays," in *Shakespeare: Select Bibliographical Guides,* ed. Stanley Wells [London: Oxford Univ. Press, 1973]) and Paul Bertram (*Shakespeare and "The Two Noble Kinsmen"* [New Brunswick: Rutgers Univ. Press, 1965]) offer summaries of the authorship debates. In general, Fletcher is accorded the greater part of the play, with Act I, substantial parts of Act V, and scattered scenes attributed to Shakespeare. See also Mary Beth Rose, *The Expense of the Spirit: Love and Sexuality in Renaissance Drama* (Ithaca: Cornell Univ. Press, 1988), 213 and accompanying note.

[30] *The Two Noble Kinsmen,* ed. N. W. Bawcutt (London: Penguin, 1977), 9. Hereafter cited parenthetically in the text by act, scene and line.

[31] Rose, 222.

[32] Barry Weller, *"The Two Noble Kinsmen,* The Friendship Tradition, and the Flight from Eros" in *Shakespeare, Fletcher, and "The Two Noble Kinsmen,"* ed. Charles II. Frey (Columbia: Univ. of Missouri Press, 1989), 108.

[33] Rose, 224, 223. In pursuing the subtitle of her book, "Love and Sexuality in English Renaissance Drama," Rose has no index entry or discussion of friendship as either oppositional to or included in "love and sexuality"; her indexing of homosexuality refers only to James I.

[34] Rose describes this transition as an official shift of "moral prestige" from celibacy to marriage (4).

[35] Mueller, 184, 194-96. Paula Blank has disagreed with Mueller's claim that Donne's poem represents a fully utopian moment, arguing instead that the poetic structure of comparison, of sameness, ultimately fails in the poem in a way consistent with Donne's poetry in general ("Comparing Sappho to Philaenis: John Donne's Homopoetics," *PMLA* 110 [1995], 359). But while Blank's concern is to show how the poem *fits* into Donne's poetic practice, Mueller's contextualization takes on a different project—placing Donne's "imagining" against a backdrop of virtual silence on female homoeroticism.

[36] James Holstun, "'Will you rent our ancient love asunder?': Lesbian Elegy in Donne, Marvell, and Milton," *ELH* 54 (1987): 835-67.

[37] Rose, 216 and Weller, 101.

[38] Jeanne Roberts, "Crises of Male Self-Definition in *The Two Noble Kinsmen,*" in Frey, 138.

[39] The "knot of love" here, ("so true, so long, . . . so deep") directly incorporates the language and cadence of Montaigne's "knot" of friendship "so hard, so fast, so durable" (199) that women had not the strength to perform it. Here, the women have the power to appreciate it; Emilia, of course, will go on to describe her experience of it, despite Montaigne's theory.

[40] "Wee sought one another before we had seene one another, and by the reports we heard of one another; . . . we embraced one another by our names" (Montaigne, 149).

[41] Cary, 92.

[42] Montaigne, 148.

[43] A number of critics have noted the degree to which Palamon and Arcite's love for Emilia is a figuration of a primary love for each other. See, for example, Weller, 96, and Roberts, 141. While I emphasize here the measurement of failure in this friendship in terms of classically-derived doctrine, their warm affectivity survives both their disclaimers of love for each other and their murderous oaths. See, for example, act 3, scene 2, in which they promise "no mention of this woman, 'twill disturb us," (I.15) and the scene where they lovingly dress each other for combat (3.6). This would be a textbook case of "homosociality" as Eve Sedgwick originally specified it, in which love (even if murderous) codes passionate relations between men (see Eve Kosofsky Sedgwick, *Between Men: English Literature and Male Homosocial Desire* [New York: Columbia Univ. Press, 1985]).

[44] Weller, 93.

[45] D'Orsay Pearson describes as a "critical myth" the notion that Theseus represented the ideal Renaissance prince, a reasonable man and an equitable ruler. Instead, he argues, Theseus's "Renaissance image as an unnatural, perfidious, and unfaithful father and lover far outweighed . . . his accomplishment in organizing the *demes* of Athens . . . or his reputation as an icon of the virtues of friendship" ("Unkinde Theseus: A Study in Renaissance Mythography," *English Literary Renaissance* 4 [1974], 276).

[46] In *A Midsummer Night's Dream,* Theseus had proclaimed "Hippolyta, I woo'd thee with my sword, / And won thy love doing thee injuries" (I.1.16-17).

[47] Rose considers Theseus's command that one kinsman must die as a "pointed deviation from Chaucer"

that "emphasizes the harsh, arbitrary, human irrationality of the monarch's decree." She does not address the matter of any cruelty here towards Emilia (219). Compare Theseus's similarly harsh decree in *A Midsummer Night's Dream,* in which Hermia, in insisting on her own choice of a husband, violates her father's authority; Theseus, escalating the threat there too, offers a dilemma inversely related to Emilia's: Hermia must choose "either to die the death or to abjure / For ever the society of men" (I.1.65-66).

[48] Rose, 220.

[49] Weller, 103.

[50] Roberts, 141.

[51] Rose, 219.

[52] Rose, 222.

[53] Rose, 222.

[54] Rose, 216.

[55] Montaigne, 147.

[56] Baweutt, 24.

[57] Weller, 96.

[58] Weller interestingly argues that Hippolyta too may be unsure of herself in this respect. "In rebuking Emilia's praise of single sex friendship, [Hippolyta] also seems to rebuke something in herself that Emilia's words have sympathetically evoked" (99).

[59] Waith, 55.

[60] "In the amitie I speake of, [mindes] entermixe and confound themselves one in another. . . . If a man urge me to tell wherefore I loved him, I feel it cannot be expressed, but by answering; because it was he, because it was myself. . . . There is beyond all my discourse . . . I know not what inexplicable and fatall power" (Montaigne, 149).

[61] The Oxford English Dictionary defines "dividual" as an adjective describing something "that is or may be divided or separated from something else; separate, distinct, particular," citing first a 1598 use, interestingly, in Florio and second this appearance in *The Two Noble Kinsmen*. The sense of the phrase would thus be that a love composed of "maid and maid" can exceed (for example, in strength) a love composed of separable or distinguishable sexes.

[62] Almost comically, Pirithous will repeatedly observe, with admiration, that Palamon and Arcite are "men"

in a series of one line speeches. Observing Arcite in the tournament: "Upon my soul, a proper man" (II.iv.16), upon the duel, "O heaven, what more than man is this!" (III.vi.156-57), and "These are men!" (III.vi.265).

[63] The Diana/Acteon myth is also directly relevant here. As Palamon and Arcite observe Emilia and her Woman in a private moment, they too are stricken and transformed in a change that will lead to death.

[64] This scene, in envisioning a female sphere as a plenitude, echoes the sense of self-sufficient female economy Mueller establishes in Donne's poem and is suggestive of the sense of place or actualization that appears to be (the only thing) lacking in Donne's powerful envisioning of lesbian economy (200-2).

[65] Bawcutt, 195; Waith, 115.

[66] For the spatial and affective arrangements of the noble household, particularly in reference to distances of both kinds between wives and their husbands, see Laurence Stone, *The Family, Sex and Marriage in England, 1500-1800* (New York: Harper, 1979), 81.

[67] Luce Irigaray, "Commodities Among Themselves," in *This Sex Which Is Not One,* tr. Catherine Porter (Ithaca: Cornell Univ. Press, 1985), 192-97.

[68] Montaigne, 146.

Source: "Emilia's Argument: Friendship and 'Human Title' in *The Two Noble Kinsmen*," in *ELH*, Vol. 64, No. 3, Fall, 1997, pp. 657-82.

Patterns of Consolation in Shakespeare's Sonnets 1-126

Emily E. Stockard, *Florida Atlantic University*

Since their mysterious publication in 1609, Shakespeare's *Sonnets* have resisted a variety of attempts to place an ordering construct on them.[1] This essay offers readers a purchase on what strikes many as a bewildering collection of poems. I will suggest that many of the sonnets can be understood as belonging to the tradition of Renaissance consolatory literature. Further, Shakespeare's rhetorical strategies of consolation place the sequence in the tradition of Renaissance skeptical thought. My approach to the *Sonnets* is unusual in that I consider individual poems in their surrounding contexts when, with the exception perhaps of the "procreation sonnets" (sonnets 1-17), it is more common to see them in isolation. In previous readings of the *Sonnets,* certain poems have been picked out for extensive treatment; many more have been ignored, perhaps rightfully so. But my approach does not require consideration of the relative literary merits of various sonnets; rather I will look at a sonnet's relation to those that surround it in order to point out patterns of argument that take form when individual sonnets are considered in their place in the sequence.

Although my primary objective in this essay is to identify the patterns of thought that the sequence as a whole displays, I do not want to suggest that these patterns can account for every sonnet. Nevertheless, despite the vexed question of the order of the *Sonnets,* Shakespeare's sequence has more cohesion than is generally acknowledged. For example, the many linked pairs and triads among Shakespeare's poems give evidence of a greater degree of organic unity than found in either Sidney's *Astrophil and Stella* or Spenser's *Amoretti*— the two major sonnet sequences contemporary with Shakespeare's.[2] In addition to explicit verbal links within small groups of sonnets, larger groups of poems share thematic concerns (the "procreation sonnets" being the example most often acknowledged). Obviously, many of the poems share the subject of mutability, primarily of beauty, life, and love. Less obviously, the sonnets cohere in their manner of argumentation, and it is this rhetorical consistency that is my focus. By its nature my study will draw attention to the large number of formally and thematically linked poems in Shakespeare's sequence. But I will focus most explicitly on the patterned rhetorical strategies by which many of the sonnets seek consolation for the problems posed by intractable reality, a reality no less intractable for being incorporated into a fictional construct.[3] In its attempt to grapple with reality, Shakespeare's sonnet sequence shares characteristics that Joel Altman finds in Renaissance drama. Altman asserts that

Renaissance tragedies and comedies reveal the inadequacy of invention before the "facts" of life. . . . Invention is variously characterized as persuasive power, poetic conceit, witty double-talk, imaginative capability, incantatory rite . . . but regardless of its local coloration, one can trace through the canon a growing anxiety about the capacity of wit, in its fullest sense, to master ultimate reality.[4]

The sonnets that I will look at also bring an array of inventive tools to the task of mastering the "'facts' of life." Shakespeare undertakes a search for ways to think about mutability that afford some consolation—but these methods ultimately fail.

An episode in *Richard II* demonstrates Shakespeare's interest both in the topos of consolation and, what is more important for my argument about the *Sonnets,* in the illusory or self-deceptive nature of consolatory thought. Early in the play, John of Gaunt suggests a variety of ways by which his son can console himself after being banished by Richard. All depend upon Bolingbroke's ability to think in a way that belies the reality of his punishment:

> Think not the king did banish thee,
> But thou the king. . . .
> Go, say I sent thee forth to purchase honor,
> And not, the king exiled thee; or suppose
> Devouring pestilence hangs in our air
> And thou art flying to a fresher clime.
> Look what thy soul holds dear, imagine it
> To lie that way thou goest, not whence thou
>   com'st.

Bolingbroke resolutely rejects Gaunt's suggestion that imaginative thinking will relieve the pain of his punishment:

> O, who can hold a fire in his hand
> By thinking on the frosty Caucasus?
> Or cloy the hungry edge of appetite
> By bare imagination of a feast?
> Or wallow naked in December snow
> By thinking on fantastic summer's heat?[5]

Shakespeare's *Sonnets* display in a more complex form the types of consoling strategies that Gaunt urges his son to accept. The sequence lacks the overt skeptical voice that would correspond to Bolingbroke's, but the patterns in the search for consolation themselves suggest in a covertly skeptical fashion the limitations of "bare imagination."[6]

Although the notion of consolation as expressed in the English literary tradition is usually connected to Chaucer and his use of Boethius's *Consolation of Philosophy,* I prefer to place Shakespeare's methods of consolation in the context of Montaignian skeptical thought. The methods of consolation exhibited in the *Sonnets* are the same strategies that Montaigne attributes to his own mind. Doubting the efficacy of the mind's pursuit of truth, Montaigne describes his tendency to use ideas for his own purposes, to deceive himself, to rationalize, to explain. In "Of Experience," he tells of the workings of his mind, including both its powers and its limitations. During a severe attack of kidney stones, his mind finds good reasons for him to suffer:

> [It] tells me that it is for my own good that I have the stone; that buildings of my age must naturally suffer some leakage. It is time for them to begin to grow loose and give way. It is common necessity. . . . [It tells me that] company should console me, since I have fallen into the commonest ailment of men of my time of life. On all sides I see them afflicted with the same type of disease, and their society is honorable for me, since it preferably attacks the great; it is essentially noble and dignified.[7] (836)

With sentences that could describe the self-deceptive methods of thought that Gaunt recommends, Montaigne calls upon these powers of his mind to "flatter" his imagination:

> Now I treat my imagination as gently as I can, and would relieve it, if I could, of all trouble and conflict. We must help it and flatter it, and fool it if we can. My mind is suited to this service; it has no lack of plausible reasons for all things. If it could persuade as well as it preaches, it would help me out very happily. (836)

The ability of the mind to invent strategies for relieving the imagination outstrips its ability successfully to persuade; however, Montaigne explains that his mind works on, undaunted by this failure:

> By such arguments, both strong and weak, I try to lull and beguile my imagination and salve its wounds, as Cicero did his disease of old age. If they get worse tomorrow, tomorrow we shall provide other ways of escape. (839)

Montaigne's obsessive search for comforting ways to view his illness mirrors that of Shakespeare's persona, who also creates consolations in response to a painful reality.[8] Like Montaigne's essays, Shakespeare's sonnet sequence implicitly calls into question the purpose and efficacy of mental effort. Both Shakespeare and Montaigne imply the skeptical view that momentary and illusory comfort, rather than truth, is the aim of thought.

This essay will track through the subsequence of sonnets 1-126, examining the different strategies of consolation that Shakespeare employs. Because similar methods tend to appear in clusters of sonnets, and because I want to point out the progression of these rhetorical strategies, I have divided the essay into six sections and organized it sequentially.[9] The name of each section refers to the strategy of consolation that dominates the particular group of poems noted in parentheses. At the end of the essay, I will briefly place the first subsequence (1-126) in relation to the second subsequence (127-154), where the search for consolation appears in an exaggerated and specifically sexual form.

Conventional Consolation (Sonnets 1-18)

In the course of sonnets 1-18 Shakespeare shifts the argument from one very conventional consolation for the mutability of beauty to another. This shift is the first instance of an argumentative strategy typical of the first subsequence: when a consoling argument fails to satisfy, Shakespeare's speaker alters the terms of the problem of mutability so as to derive a new means of comfort. The earliest sonnets in this group make the consolatory argument that the beauty of the young man whom the poems address will live on in his offspring. The speaker often aims this argument directly at the youth, who does not realize that fathering a child will provide his only consolation for old age and death. Shakespeare's argument for the consolatory aspect of procreation gradually gives way to a second consolatory argument—that the young man's beauty will be preserved in the poet's verse. After the first seventeen sonnets, sonnet 18 fundamentally changes the terms of the problem of mutability so that only the poet's art can defend the youth against the ravages of time.

This shift from procreative to poetic consolation for the mutability of beauty signals a primary alteration in the reality to which the sonnets respond. The poems of this group show the speaker coming to love the beautiful young man in whom he at first has expressed only an abstract interest. Like others, he wants beauty to regenerate itself. The speaker's initial stake in the argument for procreation appears in the first two lines of the first sonnet: "From fairest creatures we desire increase, / That thereby beauty's rose might never die."[10] The argument for the natural means of reproducing beauty depends upon the assumption that one example of a beautiful species can substitute for another—that the beautiful child duplicates the once-beautiful parent. But the love of the particular beautiful individual comes to replace the more generalized love of beauty which had prompted the speaker's desire for "fairest creatures" to reproduce themselves. He first announces his love when, in the couplet of sonnet 10, he asks the youth to "Make thee another self for *love of me.*" When the speaker begins to love the young man, procreation, the consolation first offered for lost beauty, no longer suffices.

The procreative argument makes its last appearance in sonnets 15-17, a triad which introduces instead the poet's power to immortalize the young man whom he has come to love. In these poems Shakespeare sets the two conventional methods for defeating mutability, procreation and poetry, in competition with each other, and describes each method metaphorically in terms of the other.[11] The recourse to metaphor and the competing arguments suggest that neither method provides sufficient consolation. Sonnet 15 makes the first argument for poetic immortality. The speaker sets out the familiar observation of beauty's rapid and certain decay. But instead of urging procreation, the couplet announces, "And all in war with time for love of you, / As he takes from you, I *engraft* you new." Paradoxically, to advocate verse as a means of immortality, the speaker uses a metaphor from the natural realm. Immediately after this proclamation of the power of verse to confer immortality, sonnet 16 reverts to the procreative argument, which the speaker claims is superior. He asks,

> But wherefore do not you a mightier way
> Make war upon this bloody tyrant time?
> And fortify yourself in your decay
> With means more blessed than my barren
>   rhyme?

Having declared verse "barren," the speaker concludes by using a metaphor from the realm of art to commend procreation: "And you must live, *drawn* by your own sweet skill." Given the defects of nature and of art, each must be portrayed as the other. The third sonnet (17) in this triple group explicitly announces dissatisfaction with both methods of consolation and repairs their defects with the argument that poetry and procreation can bolster each other in the fight against mutability. The speaker begins, "Who will believe my verse in time to come / If it were filled with your most high deserts?" and goes on to claim that his verse will "be scorned, like old men of less truth than tongue, / And your true rights be termed a poet's rage / And stretchèd meter of an antique song." The couplet solves the problem by explaining how both the youth and the poet's verse can achieve immortality: "But were some child of yours alive that time, / You should live twice in it and in my rhyme." The young man's beauty will live on in verse and in his progeny, and the child's beauty will validate the poetry.

A fundamental change in the sequence occurs after sonnet 17: the argument for procreation ceases. Sonnet 18 shifts the terms of the problem of mutability so that poetry alone can provide the solution. Here Shakespeare defines mutability as an inherent imperfection in nature and argues for the superior ability of verse to render the youth's beauty eternal. Procreation, after all, simply recreates mutable beauty; poetry captures forever the "golden time" of the young man. The first two lines of sonnet 18 claim that the young man's

beauty surpasses that of nature—that he is "more lovely and more temperate" than a summer's day. This argument for the youth's exceptional beauty proves to be a misdirection; the sonnet goes on to claim the superiority of art over nature and to define nature's primary flaw as that of mutability: "Rough winds do shake the darling buds of May, / And summer's lease hath all too short a date." Presumably, the young man's beauty shares this flaw of nature, since "every fair from fair sometime declines." But when mutability is defined as a flaw, the "eternal lines" of poetry can be said to make verse superior to nature's "changing course."

By offering his poetry as a means of consolation for the young man's loss of beauty, the poet establishes the link between the two men that comes to dominate the subsequence. This connection will prove to be both the occasion for his future sadness and the means of future consolations. The speaker's love for the young man, discovered in the course of inventing a general consolation for the decay of beauty, becomes the source of specific rather than generalized sorrow. In Montaignian fashion, this new source of sorrow requires new strategies of consolation, which the speaker constructs not for the young man but for himself. At the same time, the very occasion of sadness—the connection between the lover and his beloved—becomes the fundamental assumption upon which many later consoling arguments depend.

Neoplatonic Consolation (Sonnets 22-42)

The manipulation of the Neoplatonic commonplace that lovers share identities provides the dominant strategy of consolation among those sonnets numbered 22-42. Concern with the mutability of love replaces the concern with the mutability of beauty. Because the speaker loves an individual, the problem that occupies most of the remaining subsequence is how to maintain that love and how to find consolation for its possible loss. Consolation is necessary because, in spite of the frequent arguments that the lovers are fundamentally united by their love, the sonnets portray both implicitly and explicitly the betrayal of that love. The following quotation from Marsilio Ficino's *Commentary on Plato's Symposium,* with its argument that lovers freely share identities, explains the idea that the sonnets in this group both depend upon and undermine:

> Whenever two men embrace each other in mutual affection, this one lives in that; that one, in this. Such men exchange themselves with each other; and each gives himself to the other in order to receive the other.... Certainly this one has himself, but in that one. That one also possesses himself, but in this one. Certainly while I love you loving me, I find myself in you thinking about me, and I recover myself, lost by myself through my own negligence, in you, preserving me. You do the same in me. (55-56)[12]

Shakespeare's speaker invokes Neoplatonic doctrine not because it illustrates the truth about the love between him and his beloved, but because he wishes to exploit the capacity of this doctrine to establish a consoling union between the two lovers.

Sonnet 22 provides an example of the speaker's presuming upon the conventions of Neoplatonic love. Shakespeare bases the poem's argument on the Ficinian description of the inner similarity between lovers. But although it invokes this Neoplatonic commonplace, the sonnet suggests not the unity of the lovers, but the speaker's fear that he will lose his beloved:

> My glass shall not persuade me I am old
> So long as youth and thou are of one date,
> But when in thee time's furrows I behold,
> Then look I death my days should expiate.
> For all that beauty that doth cover thee
> Is but the seemly raiment of my heart,
> Which in thy breast doth live, as thine in me.
> How can I then be elder than thou art?
> O therefore love, be of thyself so wary
> As I not for myself, but for thee will
> Bearing thy heart, which I will keep so chary
> As tender nurse her babe from faring ill.
> 　Presume not on thy heart when mine is slain,
> 　Thou gav'st me thine not to give back again.

The sonnet begins with a playfully literal invocation of the conventional idea that lovers possess each other's hearts. The fact of this inner connection between the two men explains why the speaker can flatter himself that he shares his beloved's youth. His possession of the young man's heart, he argues, extends to the youth's outward appearance as well. This exchange of hearts prompts the speaker to explain to his beloved that because each lover lives in the other, each must bear himself carefully. In arguing that lovers preserve each other, Shakespeare echoes a tenet of Neoplatonism that Ficino explicitly states: "the lover removes himself from himself and gives himself to the beloved. Therefore the beloved takes care of him as his own possession. For one's things are always the dearest to one" (57).

Though based on the convention of mutual dependence, nonetheless this sonnet entirely undermines the Neoplatonic leverage of its argument. The speaker argues that, owing to the Neoplatonic merging of the two hearts, if he is slain, his beloved will lose his heart as well. But the appropriation of the language of courtly love reveals his fear of being "slain" by one who does not requite his love. Death occasioned by unrequited love also finds its explanation according to Neoplatonic theory: "the beloved does not love the lover. There the lover is completely dead. For he neither lives in himself . . . nor does he live in the beloved, since he is rejected by him" (Ficino, 55). In the Ficinian terms that the speaker invokes, the threat of death applies not

to both lover and beloved, as Shakespeare's speaker suggests, but to the lover alone. The couplet's warning is predicated on mutual love; but should the youth withdraw his love, Neoplatonic union would cease to exist, thus subverting the basis on which the threat depends. The hypothetical death of the youth (which would result from that of his lover) could not then be accounted for by a Neoplatonic exchange of hearts, as the speaker argues. And so the couplet of sonnet 22 undermines the fact of mutual love that its argument assumes.

The arguments of nearby sonnets also depend upon and undercut the notion of mutual identity. Sonnet 24 treats a Neoplatonic account of love with open skepticism. The speaker constructs an elaborate Neoplatonic conceit to describe the unity between him and his beloved: the "true image" of the beloved "in my bosom's shop is hanging still, / That hath his windows glazed with thine eyes." A Ficinian interpretation of this sonnet is possible if we assume a Platonic vocabulary, according to which the "true image" indicates an essence, not just an outward appearance. This reading suggests that, since the lovers are a composite being, each gains knowledge of himself by looking at his image in the other: "Mine eyes have drawn thy shape, and thine for me / Are windows to my breast." But the curtly stated skepticism of the couplet overturns this Neoplatonic ideal by reverting to the notion that the lover's eye paints only the visually apprehended surface of things: "Yet eyes this cunning want to grace their art; / They draw but what they see, know not the heart." This conclusion undermines even the possibility of mutual understanding, much more so the mutual or composite existence described by Ficino.[13]

The separation of the speaker from his beloved comes to the foreground in sonnets 33-35 and 40-42. These two triads openly accuse the young man of committing breaches of fidelity in love, with the second triad pointedly accusing him of sexual betrayal with a woman whom the speaker loves. Both triads manipulate the assumption of Neoplatonic unity in order to absolve the beloved of a fault, to work out a method of forgiveness, and to effect a consoling reconciliation between the lovers. Sonnet 35 arrives at the consoling thought that, although the lover has been betrayed, his own implication in that betrayal links him with his beloved. The speaker acknowledges his habitual forgiveness of the young man to be a vice; his use of consolatory strategies to mitigate the beloved's infidelity makes him an accessory to the offense. With deliberate irony, the lover succeeds in uniting himself with his beloved by placing himself in league with the "sweet thief" who has betrayed him. Finally however, this consolatory union of the two, depending as it does upon the speaker's self-betrayal, subverts itself. The subversion of Neoplatonic consolatory technique will culminate in sonnet 42, the final poem of the second triad and the final sonnet of this group.

Sonnets 40-42 describe a love triangle, once again working out a reconciliation with the young man by excusing his actions. Again the consolation obtained for betrayal in love depends upon the argument for an essential similarity between the two men. But in this triad the lover finds it increasingly difficult to create excuses for the young man, and explicitly labels the final instance of Neoplatonic consolation in this group of poems as "flattery." The first and second sonnets of the triad (40 and 41), while working toward a method of forgiveness, specifically acknowledge the fact of sexual infidelity. In order to salvage some shred of consolation for the inescapable fact that the man and the woman whom he loves have betrayed him, the lover creates in sonnet 42 an elaborate excuse that depends upon the commonplace that the two men are essentially the same person. Although critics have readily acknowledged the specious argumentation in this sonnet, they have not recognized that the poem represents the most obvious example of its kind, exaggerating the characteristics found in others of this group.[14] Here, more explicitly than elsewhere, Shakespeare sets about to manipulate Neoplatonic conceptions of love in order to construct what the speaker knows to be an empty excuse for his lovers' betrayal of him and a cold consolation for himself:

> That thou hast her, it is not all my grief,
> And yet it may be said I loved her dearly;
> That she hath thee is of my wailing chief,
> A loss in love that touches me more nearly.
> Loving offenders, thus I will excuse ye:
> Thou dost love her, because thou know'st I
>   love her,
> And for my sake ev'n so doth she abuse me,
> Suff'ring my friend for my sake to approve
>   her.
> If I love thee, my loss is my love's gain,
> And losing her, my friend hath found that
>   loss;
> Both find each other, and I lose both twain,
> And both for my sake lay on me this cross.
>   But here's the joy, my friend and I are one;
>   Sweet flatt'ry, then she loves but me alone.

Because the sonnet is by no means transparent, let me first give a straight-faced summary of the Neoplatonic argument that Shakespeare both makes and at the same time thoroughly undermines. After taking account of his grief at the loss of both of his lovers to each other, the speaker realizes that, given the Neoplatonic relation between himself and his male friend, both his lovers can be excused. Since the speaker and the young man are one, it stands to reason that they would love the same person; understandably, the youth duplicates the speaker's love for the woman. Similarly, because the woman recognizes the mutual identity of the speaker and his friend, she loves the friend as she loves the speaker. The love of the man and woman for each other proves their love for the speaker. In addition, the mutual identity of the speaker and his friend makes it impossible for him to lose the love of either. The young man may transfer his love from the speaker to the woman, but the speaker claims to be happy that the young man has gained what he has lost. By a similar process, the speaker regains the loss of the woman's love because she loves his surrogate self. The couplet sums up the consolations afforded by Neoplatonic theory: (1) the speaker and the young man share a Neoplatonic mutual existence in their love; and (2) because the two men cannot be said to be separate people, the speaker can argue "she loves but me alone."

But the bitter insistence with which the speaker undermines this Neoplatonic excuse cannot be ignored. The expansive magnanimity of the line, "Loving offenders, thus I will excuse ye," calls attention to the elaborate artificiality of his forgiveness. Stripped of its Neoplatonic assumptions, the second quatrain implies that the young man and the woman love each other with willful malice towards the speaker: the youth loves the woman "because thou know'st I love her." By loving the young man, "ev'n so doth she abuse me." The repetition of the phrase "for my sake" underscores the irony with which the speaker views his hollow claim that his lovers' betrayal of him proves their love for him. No longer able to sustain his specious argument, by the end of the third quatrain the speaker refutes the idea that Neoplatonic unity of the lovers prevents his losses in love: "Both find each other, and I lose both twain." The two betrayers love each other, not him. They gain; he loses. The couplet abruptly reasserts the Neoplatonic paradox, but it affords him only the false "joy" of what he knows to be "sweet flatt'ry." If any joy can be found in this argument it is in the perverse pleasure the speaker takes in his bitter parody of Neoplatonic pieties. Nevertheless, in spite of the obvious failure here of Neoplatonic thought to account for the circumstances of the speaker's love, other strategies of consolation in subsequent groups of sonnets will also depend upon the assumption of the lovers' essential unity.

Absence and the Consolation of Alternation (Sonnets 43-56)

The breach between the speaker and the young man, explicitly described in sonnet 42, drives the lover to adjust his consolatory strategy according to the reality of a separation that he can no longer deny. Connected sonnets find consolation in the alternating states of mind provoked in the speaker by the beloved's absence or presence. Finally, as in the previous group of poems, other sonnets within this group undermine the illusions upon which the consolations depend.

Sonnets 44 and 45 both lament the unbridgeable distance between the lovers, working as a pair to find consolation in the lack of consolation itself. Sonnet 44 explains sorrow in physiological terms; as in the Neo-platonic sonnets, the two lovers share one being, but here that being consists of one set of elements (earth, water, air, and fire) that suffer division during times of absence. In these terms, the very fact of inconsolable sorrow proves the lovers' unity and the strength of their love. The second sonnet of the pair (45) explains how the combination of the four elements can provide a brief moment of joy in the midst of sorrow at the beloved's absence. The "present-absent" elements, air and fire (the speaker's sighs and desires), travel between the two lovers, and so provide a brief moment of completeness—the only comfort afforded during the beloved's absence: "I joy, but then no longer glad, / I send them back again, and straight grow sad." This pair of sonnets explains the production of a brief moment of joy; but the primary consolation derives from the fact that inconsolable sorrow is treated as an indication of the lovers' fundamental union.

Two other pairs of sonnets produce more satisfying but also more deceptive methods of consoling for absence. The first pair (46 and 47) describes a consolatory league formed between the lover's eye and heart. The speaker alternates between two states of delight, one caused by gazing on the absent beloved's picture, one created by the heart's "thoughts of love." Sight and memory alternately provide satisfaction by producing the illusion of the beloved's presence. Sonnets 50 and 51 invent what is perhaps a less self-deceptive method of controlling absence: the lover himself undertakes a journey away from his beloved. The metaphorical level of the poem suggests that the journey away from the beloved constitutes the lover's unsuccessful attempt to abandon one who appears to have abandoned him. This journey, however, brings satisfaction only in the imagined return to be described in sonnet 51. The next sonnet will use precisely the same strategy of consolation whereby a separation between the two men is necessary to the lover's appreciation of their reunion.

Sonnet 52 provides the most successful (because most comforting) consolation based on alternating separation and reunion. Rather than regarding absence as an occasion for sorrow, the speaker argues that absence invests the beloved's presence with additional value. This understanding allows the lover to alternate between hopeful anticipation and eventual triumph at the beloved's return.

> So am I as the rich, whose blessed key
> Can bring him to his sweet up-locked treasure,
> The which he will not every hour survey,
> For blunting the fine point of seldom pleasure.
> Therefore are feasts so solemn and so rare,
> Since seldom coming, in the long year set,
> Like stones of worth they thinly placèd are,

> Or captain jewels in the carcanet.
> So is the time that keeps you as my chest,
> Or as the wardrobe which the robe doth hide
> To make some special instant special blest,
> By new unfolding his imprison'd pride.
>   Blessèd are you, whose worthiness gives scope,
>   Being had to triumph, being lacked to hope.

The argument in this sonnet has much in common with Gaunt's instructions to Bolingbroke to think of his "sullen" journey as a foil for the "precious jewel" of his homecoming (*Richard II*, I.iii.265, 267). But the comparison breaks down because Bolingbroke is to undertake a literal journey of limited duration from which he wishes to return. Shakespeare's speaker, on the other hand, has no such assurances that the young man will return from his metaphorical journey—an event upon which the consolation of alternation ultimately depends. The metaphors presuppose the fact of that return and so misrepresent the speaker's situation. The purposefully rationed pleasures of looking at one's treasure, celebrating feast days, and wearing occasional garments all come rarely but inevitably, and their enjoyment depends upon the precondition of possession. For in spite of the comparisons drawn in this sonnet, the speaker "lacks" the object of his desire in a more radical way than those who enhance their pleasure by limiting it.

The final poem in this group, sonnet 56, reveals the illusory nature of a state of happiness founded entirely upon the speaker's wishful thinking. Phrased as a series of commands, it instructs the youth to preserve the consolation of alternation that the lover has already constructed in this group of sonnets. Comparing their love to cycles characterized by inevitability (those of appetite, of seasons, and of sea-faring men), the speaker urges the young man to participate in the renewal of their love. If the young man accepts the vision of love that the poet offers, inevitably he will renew the force of his affections.[15] The couplet again emphasizes the consolation (found in sonnet 52) of "seldom pleasure": "winter, which being full of care, / Makes summer's welcome, thrice more wished, more rare." But unlike the summer's return, the return of the absent lover is not inevitable—as the lover's need to urge it implies. The assumption upon which the "consolation of alternation" depends does not square with reality.

Death and the Algebra of Consolation (Sonnets 62-74)

The consolations for the beloved's absence ultimately fail because they depend upon the eventual reunion of the two lovers—a reality that Shakespeare's speaker cannot control. Unable to reformulate reality, the lover reformulates his argumentative terms: he defines absence in its most extreme form—death.[16] In its redefinition of absence, this group of sonnets again displays

Shakespeare's argumentative tactic of shifting the terms of the problem posed in the sonnets immediately preceding. The shift in focus from absence to death offers advantages in the effort to find consolation. Death is an ultimate absence from which no return can be expected; it is also an inevitable absence that neither the lover nor the beloved can control. When death causes absence, the beloved cannot be said to refuse to return to his lover.[17] In addition, this shift in the formulation of the problem of absence does allow the lover a measure of control. He can invent consoling ways to think about the inevitable fact of death.[18]

The title of this section refers not only to the primary subject of this group of poems, but also to the method by which Shakespeare uses the fact of death to create consolations. Some sonnets operate like an algebraic equation with two variables, each of which can be solved in terms of the other.[19] Typically the speaker sets up two difficulties, one being the problem of death, and solves one problem in terms of the other. A feature of this group of sonnets is that Shakespeare does not necessarily distinguish which difficulty has greater weight—loss of life or loss of love.

To create consolations both for death and by means of death, in sonnets 66-68 Shakespeare sets both the lover's and the beloved's death in a satirical context whereby consolation for one problem lies in another. Yet another form of mutability, the decay of society, allows Shakespeare's speaker to find solace in and for his own death and the youth's. The speaker's argument that escape from this world is to be desired allows him to find a consolation *in* death: it brings an end to life in an intolerable world. Conversely, the consolation *for* death is that the world is an intolerable place.

The satirical context that Shakespeare establishes in sonnet 66 emphasizes death's desirability rather than its inevitability. Here the speaker cries for "restful death," and catalogues the conventional ills of society that provoke him. After giving instances of misplaced rewards, misplaced authority, and talents and virtues that go unrecognized, he declares, "Tir'd with all these, from these would I be gone, / Save that to die, I leave my love alone." By satirizing society's ills the speaker finds consolation not *for* his death but *in* his death; that is, death provides an escape from the world he abhors. The only reason the lover finds to live is that dying will separate him from his beloved, whom he refuses to abandon alone in a dreadful world.

The social satire in the following two sonnets (67-68) aligns the two men by finding the youth similarly unsuited to live in the world. Both poems present a world diminished from a former, more perfect age to which the youth properly belongs. The consolation provided by death in these two poems is that it allows

the speaker to establish the youth's virtue. Sonnet 67 asks a series of rhetorical and satirical questions which the couplet answers:

> Ah wherefore with infection should he live,
> And with his presence grace impiety,
> That sin by him advantage should achieve,
> And lace itself with his society?
> Why should false painting imitate his cheek,
> And steal dead seeing of his living hue?
> Why should poor beauty indirectly seek
> Roses of shadow, since his rose is true?
> Why should he live, now nature bankrout is,
> Beggared of blood to blush through lively veins?
> For she hath no exchequer now but his,
> And, proud of many, lives upon his gains.
> O him she stores, to show what wealth she had,
> In days long since, before these last so bad.

The rhetorical questions move from indicting society to complaining against art to exposing nature's flaws. The couplet explains nature's plan: the youth lives so that she can boast an example of her past wealth. As the questions shift from implying a morally corrupt society to suggesting a natural world in decline, the word *live* takes on a less figurative and an increasingly literal meaning. In the first two quatrains, the speaker demands why the youth should have to suffer in a society that feeds off his beauty. But in the context of the natural rather than the moral world, the final quatrain seems to ask a more radical question—the reason for the young man's physical existence itself. And it is that physical existence for which the couplet accounts: in him nature exhibits the superior beauty of an earlier time—a physical beauty which in the course of the sonnet becomes invested with moral significance.

Shakespeare continues in sonnet 68 to exploit the connection between the moral and natural realms, here manipulating a satire of human vanity in order to establish the youth's morality. The specific object of satire is the use of wigs to disguise aging. The young man's mutable beauty signifies the moral rectitude absent in a world that extends beauty past its natural termination. To portray growing old and dying as morally desirable acts, Shakespeare contrasts the beauty that is true (because it dies) to false beauty (because unnaturally prolonged). One who extends his period of beauty by robbing the grave deprives sepulchers of their right to the "golden tresses of the dead," "[r]obbing [the] old to dress his beauty new." By contrast, the young man is truly virtuous because truly beautiful: "in him those holy antique hours are seen, / Without all ornament, itself and true." The youth's moral superiority, as defined in this sonnet, results not from his choice to act virtuously, but from the fact that his beauty is natural rather than the product of art. This very fact proves the youth's virtue and proves dying to be a virtuous act. The speaker's argument solves two problems, each in terms of the other: he finds death itself virtuous and so provides himself with a consolation *for* death, and he finds the youth's inevitable death to be evidence of his virtue, a consolation *in* death.

Sonnets 71-74 shift the focus of the sequence from the young man's death to that of the speaker.[20] The lover anticipates his own death and instructs the youth to react to that event in a fashion that provides consolation. These four sonnets comprise two pairs that make contradictory arguments. In sonnets 71 and 72 the speaker argues that his death should cause the young man's love to decay; in sonnets 73 and 74 he argues that his death should cause that love to increase. The arguments of the first pair provide the speaker with two consolations in death; imagining the scenario of his own death (1) allows him to assume that his beloved will be grief-stricken, and (2) allows him to argue that there is a good reason for the beloved to cease loving him. Both sonnets urge the youth to stop loving, as the couplet of sonnet 71 puts it, "Lest the wise world should look into your moan, / And mock you with me after I am gone."

While sonnets 71 and 72 both create reasons for the youth to cease loving the speaker, at least publicly, sonnets 73 and 74 contradict and so call into question the sincerity of that argument. They argue that the lover's approaching death should increase the love between the two men. At the same time that the lover searches for a consoling way to view his death, he also uses his death to strengthen the youth's affection for him.

> That time of year thou mayst in me behold,
> When yellow leaves, or none, or few do hang
> Upon those boughs which shake against the
> cold,
> Bare ruined choirs, where late the sweet birds
> sang.
> In me thou seest the twilight of such day,
> As after sunset fadeth in the west,
> Which by and by black night doth take away,
> Death's second self, that seals up all in rest.
> In me thou seest the glowing of such fire,
> That on the ashes of his youth doth lie,
> As the death-bed whereon it must expire,
> Consumed with that which it was nourished
> by.
> This thou perceiv'st, which makes thy love
>   more strong,
> To love that well which thou must leave ere
>   long.

The progression of imagery suggests a movement towards increasingly consolatory ways to perceive old age. The imagery becomes warmer and more intimate, until in the image of the still-warm, "glowing" fire,

Shakespeare unites the present ("the glowing"), past ("the ashes of his youth"), and future (the unspecified time the fire "must expire"). This image of death may provide the speaker with some solace, but the sonnet is specifically addressed to the youth, and the couplet's lesson might be addressed to either man. Following on three quatrains that counsel the youth to look at the speaker in a certain way, the lesson seems most obviously directed at the young man. Knowledge of the speaker's approaching death should "make thy love more strong, / To love that well which thou must leave ere long." But it is the lover, not the beloved, who is described as leaving. Stephen Both attempts to clear up this confusion by pointing out that "leave" can mean either "depart from" or "give up, forego" (260). According to this reading, the couplet asserts that the love of both should increase for that which they will soon lose. Once again the passage of time, which in this sonnet leads specifically to death, provides a possibility for increased love between the two lovers. Death provides the speaker with an occasion to argue that the love between the two should increase; and the consolation *for* death is that it will strengthen their love before death occurs.

Last in the group, sonnet 74 describes yet another way by which death can create a consoling union between the lovers. To achieve this, Shakespeare gives unconventional treatment to two standard topoi of Renaissance literature: the ability of verse to confer immortality and the conflict between body and soul. As in previous sonnets (71 and 72), the speaker asks to be forgotten. But in this case he refers specifically to his body, which is "Too base of thee to be remembered." The poet's spirit, which "is thine, the better part of me," resides in his poetry and so remains with the young man on earth. As the couplet explains, "The worth of that is that which it contains, / And that is this, and this with thee remains." This version of a poetic solution to the problem of mutability is unconventional in that it depends for its success upon the continued life of an audience of one, not upon the future generations that are usually assumed in this sort of claim to immortality. The traditional, medieval Christian antagonism of body and spirit is also used unconventionally. The lover's spirit does not gain immortal life in heaven but gains renewed life on earth, where it is united with the beloved.[21] The effort to confer Neoplatonic unity on the lovers takes precedence over the claim that verse confers immortality. In the final poem of this group, as in others, the speaker gains a consolation both *for* his death (he will remain united with his beloved's spirit) and *in* his death (death provides him a chance to unite with his beloved).

The Consolation of Isolation (Sonnets 87-93)

Having addressed the loss of love by redefining absence as death, Shakespeare's speaker once again redefines the terms of his argument. This short but closely linked string of poems anticipates not death but abandonment, and the lover finds good reasons for the anticipated farewell as well as good reasons for the beloved to hate him. But his consolatory techniques prove unsatisfactory, and the final two sonnets of this group locate the ultimate consolation for loss of love in the speaker's isolation from reality. He states that he will live in a self-deceiving world of illusion, never acknowledging the lost love.[22] These poems reveal the speaker's desperate state and so explain his willingness to accept a consolation that he knows to be based on an illusion.

Sonnets 87-91 prepare for the lover's decision to live in a state of self-deception. The speaker relies on typical argumentative strategies, finding a way to unite himself with his beloved and using one loss to console for another—strategies that meet with almost immediate failure. For example, in the conclusion of sonnet 90 the speaker invites abandonment as a cure for other sorrows:

> But in the onset come; so shall I taste
> At first the very worst of fortune's might,
> And other strains of woe, which now seem
>   woe,
> Compared with loss of thee will not seem so.

Sonnet 91, in which the speaker admits the cost of losing his beloved, implies the ineffectual nature of such consolations. After listing pleasures others have, the lover claims, "And having thee, of all men's pride I boast; / Wretched in this alone, that thou mayst take / All this away, and me most wretched make."

In order to insulate himself against this complete misery, the lover resorts in the next two poems to a strategy of redefinition. The argumentative terms of sonnet 92 prevent, by definition, loss of the beloved during the speaker's life. This strategy for creating a consolation does not depend upon the immortalizing powers of poetry, or upon the Neoplatonically conceived love between the two men, or upon any possible form of union that the speaker might imagine. Instead, the speaker consoles himself by means of an argument that equates the loss of love with the loss of his life. Given this definition, he can argue that he will not lose his beloved during his lifetime:

> But do thy worst to steal thyself away,
> For term of life thou art assured mine,
> And life no longer than thy love will stay,
> For it depends upon that love of thine.
> Then need I not to fear the worst of wrongs,
> When in the least of them my life hath end.
> Thou canst not vex me with inconstant mind,
> Since that my life on thy revolt doth lie.
> O what a happy title do I find,

> Happy to have thy love, happy to die!
> But what's so blessed-fair that fears no blot?
> Thou mayst be false, and yet I know it not.

Shakespeare's speaker defines life as the time during which he possesses the youth's love. Thus he creates for himself a state of rest and stability, free from the vexations of the youth's inconstancy and from the fear of literal death. But the couplet points out the flaw in this scheme: the lover may not know of the youth's falsity in love. As the next sonnet points out, however, consolation lies in the possibility that objective truth can be ignored. The lover can choose to hide in the "reality" of his subjective world. Willful self-deception provides the speaker with his consolatory defense against the wretched state of being abandoned by the young man.

In the final sonnet of this group (93), the speaker manipulates the assumed connection between outer beauty and inner virtue to explain how he will necessarily remain, "Like a deceived husband," ignorant of his beloved's falsity:

> . . . heav'n in thy creation did decree,
> That in thy face sweet love should ever dwell,
> Whate'er thy thought or thy heart's workings
>   be,
> Thy looks should nothing thence but
>   sweetness tell.
> How like Eve's apple doth thy beauty grow,
> If thy sweet virtue answer not thy show.

The speaker argues that his beloved's outer appearance does not provide the expected evidence of his inner state. The young man may hate him, but that hatred will go unrecognized. Furthermore, the lover is willing to be misled into thinking his beloved to be virtuous. The speaker's ultimate consolation in the face of a reality that he cannot control is to ignore it. But the couplet, with its mention of "Eve's apple," betrays the speaker's awareness that this consolation depends upon succumbing to the temptation of being willingly deceived.

Infidelity: the Consolation of Mutability (Sonnets 113-125)

Following this attempt to deny reality, Shakespeare shifts the terms of reality itself in a fundamental way. This change, coming in the final group of poems in the first subsequence, provides a final solution to the problem of the loss of love. Throughout much of the subsequence, the speaker has been seeking consolations for the mutability of the young man's love. At the conclusion of the subsequence, however, mutability comes to the speaker's aid: the mutability of his own love for the young man provides him with the ultimate answer to his insoluble problem. This shift in reality brings about a corresponding shift in the object of the speaker's consolatory arguments. No longer does he formulate for himself consoling explanations and responses to the young man's actions. Consolations for the decay of the young man's love become unnecessary because the speaker's own love for him has altered. Instead, the lover applies his ingenuity to the task of putting forth the most consoling explanations and justifications possible for his own actions.[23] The speaker need not console himself by means of his arguments; rather he constructs his consoling rationalizations for the benefit of the young man whom he insists that he loves still.

As usual, the consolatory arguments depend upon paradox. Sonnets 113 and 114 explain, in a variety of ways, how a seeming lapse in love actually signifies strength of affection. The speaker seeks to console his beloved with the flattering argument that the very strength of his love for the young man has caused him to commit an act of betrayal. According to sonnet 113, his mind's eye is so occupied by love for the youth that it transforms everything that comes before it into the image of the beloved: "if it see the rud'st or gentlest sight, . . . it shapes them to your feature." Falsity in love results from the extreme degree to which the image of the youth occupies the lover's "most true mind."

Sonnets 117-119 continue the lover's quest to produce a consolatory if paradoxical explanation for his infidelity by reconciling infidelity with constancy in love.[24] These poems find consolation in two ways: by explaining how infidelity can lead to the recognition of truth and by pointing to the benefits of the speaker's faults. The couplet of sonnet 117 defends inconstancy in love with the rationalization that "I did strive to prove / The constancy and virtue of your love." In sonnets 118 and 119, Shakespeare uses the metaphor of poison to explain both the cause and the effect of the lover's infidelity. Sonnet 118 describes poison-taking as a preventive measure administered unnecessarily:

> As to prevent our maladies unseen,
> We sicken to shun sickness when we purge—
> Ev'n so, being full of your ne'er-cloying
>   sweetness,
> To bitter sauces did I frame my feeding;
> And sick of welfare found a kind of meetness
> To be diseased ere that there was true
>   needing.

After perversely choosing "to be diseased," the speaker realizes his error: "But thence I learn and find the lesson true, / Drugs poison him that so fell sick of you." The error of infidelity has had the consoling effect of teaching the speaker the value of his beloved. The sestet of the next sonnet (119), where the lover describes his misapprehension as a "madding fever," identifies not simply a lesson learned, but the gains made:

> O benefit of ill, now I find true
> That better is by evil still made better;
> And ruined love when it is built anew
> Grows fairer than at first, more strong, far
>   greater.
> So I return rebuked to my content,
> And gain by ills thrice more than I have
>   spent.

In concluding the subsequence, Shakespeare's speaker vows the absolute truth of his love for the young man by making paradoxical arguments to the effect that change does not in fact exist. He effects a consoling reconciliation between mutability and eternity by defining truth as the constant principle that resides in fluctuating appearances. Sonnet 123 refutes the charge of changeability in love by means of the argument that human beings are incapable of perceiving the unchanging truth that they embody. Essentially the speaker claims that change does not occur—that the human definition of change is based on limited human perspective. He begins ("No! Time, thou shalt not boast that I do change") and ends by defying the power of time:

> Thy registers and thee I both defy,
> Not wond'ring at the present, nor the past;
> For thy records, and what we see, doth lie,
> Made more or less by thy continual haste.
> This I do vow, and this shall ever be,
> I will be true despite thy scythe and thee.

The lover embraces the rationale that we see flux—the diminishment and enlargement that occurs over a period of time—and mistake this change for the truth. Eternal principles, he contends, hold true always and remain separate from time's effects. Since this is the case, the last line ("I will be true despite thy scythe and thee") provides a statement of definition rather than a statement of intent. According to the definition of change that he has invented in this sonnet, the speaker will by definition "be true."

As the culminating poem of this group, sonnet 125 combines the argumentative aims of sonnets 117-123 to create a consolation of quasireligious dimensions. Sonnets 117-121 portray the lover's attempts to excuse himself of guilt; in sonnets 122 and 123 the lover asserts that time cannot destroy love. In sonnet 125 the lover combines these arguments by distancing himself from time-servers and by locating the beloved's heart as the only place, set apart as it is from such "pitiful thrivers," where the unfaithful lover can receive absolution from his guilt.[25] He argues paradoxically that he is a "true soul" even though his fidelity has been discredited. Having confessed his sins, the lover escapes the control of those who would inform on him:

> Were't ought to me I bore the canopy,
> With my extern the outward honoring,

Or laid great bases for eternity,
Which proves more short than waste or
   ruining?
Have I not seen dwellers on form and favor
Lose all and more by paying too much rent
For compound sweet forgoing simple savor,
Pitiful thrivers, in their gazing spent?
No, let me be obsequious in thy heart,
And take thou my oblation, poor but free,
Which is not mixed with seconds, knows no
   art,
But mutual render, only me for thee.
  Hence, thou suborned informer! A true soul
  When most impeached stands least in thy
    control.

After describing the error of those who attend to the external appearance of things, the speaker proclaims his intention to serve his beloved. The two lovers will perform a mutual act involving freely offered sacrifice, presumably to atone for sins they have in common. Stephen Booth points out that elements of the diction recall Holy Communion, a ceremony that "not only commemorates Christ's oblation on the cross, but is itself a 'sacrifice'" (429). Moreover, the final two lines of the poem imply an act of confession—an act that frees the speaker from guilt. Yet the inscrutable terms of this religious ceremony and the insistence upon the beloved's heart for its location make this religion a very private one.

Conclusion

In the very earliest sonnets, before the development of a specific love attachment, the speaker portrays the youth's beauty as an individual instance of beauty in general, and the subsequence returns to that perspective in its final poem (126). In this last poem, however, the lover accepts conditions of mutability that he has earlier been at such pains to deny. His warnings of inevitable death recall sonnets 1-17, which instructed the youth to battle time by procreating and proposed ways by which the poet could immortalize the young man. But here the speaker makes no such proposals; this twelve-line poem lacks the final two lines where, in the sonnet, the speaker often constructs his consolations. By the end of this subsequence, mutability has proved to be the speaker's ally rather than a foe to be defeated. Instead of seeking consolations for the destruction of beauty, the final three couplets simply warn the young man of nature's inevitable defeat at the hands of time.

She keeps thee to this purpose, that her skill
May time disgrace and wretched minute kill.
Yet hear her, O thou minion of her pleasure;
She may detain but not still keep her treasure.
Her audit, though delayed, answered must be,
And her quietus is to render thee.

Presumably, as in the first few sonnets in the sequence, Shakespeare's speaker again views the youth simply as one example of the general principle of mutable beauty. And so the subsequence returns full circle.

The group of sonnets that concludes the first subsequence works to show a consolation for mutability *in* mutability—a consolation made available not by the speaker's own effort of thought, but by shifts in reality. The speaker does not intend that his love for the unfaithful young man should itself prove to be mutable; rather, in the group of poems that concludes the subsequence, he denies this to be the case, arguing paradoxically that evidence of his love's mutability signifies its strength and that mutability does not exist. Shakespeare, however, constructs the sequence so as to demonstrate the consolation provided by the waning of the speaker's love, and in the final sonnet of the first subsequence the speaker accepts the consolation that changing reality provides. The contrast between the two subsequences will underscore the consolation that mutability can and does supply in the first subsequence. In the second subsequence (127-154), much to the speaker's dismay, no such consolation is forthcoming.

While the speaker insistently seeks comforting states of mind in the first subsequence, the consolations sought in the second subsequence are often specifically sexual. Further, while the self-deception of the first subsequence is usually implicit, in his demands for sexual consolation Shakespeare's speaker openly requests to be deceived. The couplet of one of the most familiar of Shakespeare's sonnets (138) directly states this paradoxical acceptance of self-deception: "Therefore I lie with her, and she with me, / And in our faults by lies we flattered be." The sestet of sonnet 152 admits the speaker's perjured state:

For I have sworn deep oaths of thy deep
  kindness,
Oaths of thy love, thy truth, thy constancy,
And to enlighten thee gave eyes to blindness,
Or made them swear against the thing they
  see,
  For I have sworn thee fair: more perjured
  eye,
  To swear against the truth so foul a lie.

Nevertheless, this admission proves ineffectual in the speaker's effort to break his habit of seeking sexual consolation, and the final two sonnets describe him as suffering from an incurable disease. Sonnet 154 describes the creation of a "cool well" to which "men diseased" come for cure. This final poem of the sequence concludes, "but I, my mistress' thrall, / Came there for cure, and this by that I prove: / Love's fire heats water, water cools not love." Although in the first subsequence the speaker looks for ways to defeat mutability, that very mutability at last rescues him from the love that drives his compulsive search for consolation. By the end of the second subsequence the speaker longs, but apparently in vain, to be released from the state of immutable love which he had earlier sought.

In his sonnets Shakespeare constructs a fictional world that operates according to the tenets of Montaignian skepticism. The fiction of the sequence comprises two parts: (1) the speaker's mental search for satisfactory strategies of consolation, and (2) the "events" or "realities" that prompt the successive stages of this Montaignian search. Because, as Montaigne argues, the mind's arguments for alleviating sorrow never achieve perfect persuasion, consolation must finally reside in the way that Shakespeare controls the "events" of his fictional construct and not in his persona's argumentation. In the first subsequence the speaker obsessively seeks comfort for his unrequited love, but consolation comes only when the facts of the speaker's situation change and his love for the young man proves to be mutable. In the second subsequence, with no such source of comfort forthcoming, the concluding sonnets complain of the speaker's incurable disease. A final comparison of the sonnet sequence to *Richard II* emphasizes the skeptical quality of the sonnets—the sense of "the inadequacy of invention before the 'facts' of life" that Joel Altman finds in Renaissance drama (3). The dramatic character Bolingbroke successfully accomplishes his own consolation not by mental effort alone, a strategy that he emphatically rejects, but by rearranging the "facts" of his life—by returning from banishment to reclaim his inheritance. Richard, on the other hand, left to the mercy of Bolingbroke's alteration of reality, can be seen as a counterpart to the sonnets' passive speaker, consoled by neither his thoughts nor his actions. When imprisoned by the usurper, only another shift in external reality will rescue Richard from his sorrow. Unable to escape and resolved to "hammer out" the thoughts that fail to content him, the king concludes: "Nor I, nor any man that but man is, / With nothing shall be pleased, / Till he be eas'd with being nothing" (V.v.39-41). As in the sonnet sequence, mutability—here in the shape of the king's death—brings final contentment.

Notes

[1] Margreta de Grazia argues that readers necessarily apply a "structuring system" to the sonnets, "whether it be inscribed in the edition itself or taken for granted." She describes the rewordings and added rubrics of the early editions in "Locating and Dislocating the 'I' in Shakespeare's *Sonnets,*" in *William Shakespeare: His World, His Work, His Influence,* vol. 2, ed. John Andrews (New York: Charles Scribner's Sons, 1985), 443. Reorderings by Robert Witt, *Of Comfort and Despair: Shakespeare's Sonnet Sequence* (Salzburg: Universitat

Salzburg, 1979); and S. C. Campbell, *Only Begotten Sonnets: A Reconstruction* (London: Bell and Hyman, 1978), have been guided by the "structuring system" of Neoplatonic thought.

[2] I say this despite Spenser's numerological ordering. See Alastair Fowler's study *Triumphal Forms* (Cambridge: Cambridge University Press, 1970).

[3] In *The Birth of the Modern Mind: Self-Consciousness, and the Invention of the Sonnet* (Oxford: Oxford University Press, 1989), 3-4, Paul Oppenheimer credits a lawyer, Giacomo da Lentino (1188-1240), with the invention of the sonnet. Giacomo "saw logic as a method that might well reach beyond the usual—an arrangement of clauses, a statement of a problem, *rhetorica*—into a resolution of emotional problems. . . . If an emotional problem were to be resolved within a mere fourteen lines, and in isolation, it would have to be resolved in a particular way: by the poet and the poem themselves, and within the mind of the poet. There was no one else, no outside, no audience" (24). In the sonnet, "[emotional problems] might now actually be resolved, or provisionally resolved, through the logic of a form that turned expression inward, to a resolution in the abiding peace of the soul itself, or if one were not so certain of the existence of the soul, in reason. Reason, after all, was perceived as a manifestation of God's mind and of divine love."

[4] *The Tudor Play of Mind: Rhetorical Inquiry and the Development of Elizabethan Drama* (Berkeley: University of California Press, 1978), 321-22.

[5] *William Shakespeare: The Complete Works,* Alfred Harbage, ed. (New York: Viking Press, 1969), I.iii.279-87, 294-99. Further references to *Richard II* will be cited parenthetically.

[6] J. B. Leishman very tentatively broaches the possibility of self-deception in the *Sonnets,* remarking that "perhaps even in many of Shakespeare's most wholehearted sonnets, where his friend appears as the archetype of all other beauties, there may be some element of recognised, though loved, illusion, some willingness to be what Swift call 'well deceived.'" *Themes and Variations in Shakespeare's Sonnets* (London: Hutchinson of London, 1963), 213.

[7] *The Complete Works of Montaigne,* ed. Donald Frame (Stanford: Stanford University Press, 1967). All further quotations by Montaigne come from this edition and will be noted in the text.

[8] The interest in consolatory thought demonstrated by Shakespeare and Montaigne has ample precedent in the Italian Renaissance. In *Sorrow and Consolation in Italian Humanism* (Princeton: Princeton University Press, 1991), George McClure charts the shift in four-

teenth- and fifteenth-century consolations from a religious to a secular and psychological focus. Throughout this essay I will call attention to parallels between the examples of consolation cited by McClure and the strategies employed by Shakespeare.

[9] The groups into which I have divided the sequence are consistent with those identified by A. Kent Hieatt, Charles W. Hieatt, and Anne Lake Prescott in their computerized effort to date the *Sonnets,* "When Did Shakespeare Write *Sonnets* 1609?" *SP* 88 (1991): 69-109.

[10] All references to the *Sonnets* come from *Shakespeare's Sonnets,* ed. Stephen Booth (New Haven: Yale University Press, 1977).

[11] In this triad, Shakespeare participates in a traditional debate over the best means of securing immortality. McClure reports an argument made by a bereaved father, Giovanni Conversini da Ravenna, for the superiority of procreation to art. In *De consolatione de obitu filii* (1401), Conversini writes, "Truly, no thing, edifice, work, or fame is more personal and immediate to anyone and more mirrors and resembles the author than a child born of oneself. . . . Indeed, in the face of the son there shines the image of the father, in his mores the father's virtue, in his studies the father's glory. All those single works of mortals are produced from art and represent a dead image of the creator. A son, however, a gift of nature, represents the parent as a live image, so that a son, viewed as your likeness and effigy, assures that you are acknowledged, seen, recognized, and remembered" (*Sorrow and Consolation,* 111).

[12] Sears Jayne, trans. (Dallas: Spring Publications, 1985). Unless otherwise specified, all further quotations by Ficino come from this edition and will be cited in the text.

[13] Although sonnets 22 and 24 undermine the consoling claim that the lovers share an essential identity, the speaker persists in assuming that unity as a given. For example, sonnets 36 and 39 address in turn two social difficulties posed by the very fact of the lovers' spiritual union: (1) the beloved is tainted by his association with the lover, and (2) the young man is unable to receive the honor that belongs to him alone. Ostensibly, the speaker argues in both sonnets that he and his beloved must conduct their lives separately. But both poems can also be seen as providing consoling ways to explain or rationalize an estrangement between the two men.

[14] See Hilton Landry, *Interpretation in Shakespeare's Sonnets* (Berkeley: University of California Press, 1963); and *A New Variorum Edition of Shakespeare: The Sonnets,* vol. 1, ed. Hyder Rollins (Philadelphia: J. B. Lippincott Company, 1944).

[15] Martha Lifson cites this sonnet's couplet as one that employs "rhetoric as consolation, here for the fading of love's force. . . . We see the poet self-consciously choosing the metaphors in order to effect what he wants, in order to establish the inevitable arrival of summer which as the seasons go always follows winter," "The Rhetoric of Consolation: Shakespeare's Couplets," *Assays: Critical Approaches to Medieval and Renaissance Texts* 11 (1982): 104-5.

[16] Donne's "A Valediction Forbidding Mourning," a poem in which the speaker consoles his beloved in preparation for his absence, first formulates their parting metaphorically as a death.

[17] Inevitability is one of the traditional consolations for death, along with "the shortness and misery of life, the varieties of fortune, the benefits of death" (McClure, *Sorrow and Consolation,* 127). The most obvious example of this emphasis on the inescapable fact of mutability is sonnet 64, which simply catalogues instances of inevitable destruction so as to provide a consolation for death.

[18] The first sonnets in this group (62 and 63) reiterate positions found earlier in the subsequence. As in the procreation sonnets, the lover writes of aging and of the end of beauty. The couplet of 62 offers an explanation for the lover's inability to see his own aging. In doing so it asserts the Neoplatonic unity of the two men: "Tis thee, myself, that for myself I praise,/Painting my age with beauty of thy days." In the next sonnet (63) inevitable death allows the speaker to unite with his beloved. It describes the time when "my love shall be as I am now,/With time's injurious hand crushed and o'erworn." Predictably enough, it is the poet's verse that will provide the means of preservation. The two lovers are, therefore, joined both by a common fate and by poetry, the instrument of their immortality.

[19] An explicit articulation of this type of consolation occurs in the Earl of Surrey's early sixteenth-century poem, "Prisoned in Windsor." After cataloguing the vanished pleasures of his boyhood at Windsor, Surrey recalls the death of his friend Henry Fitzroy, the king's son with whom he shared those days. The poem concludes, "And with remembrance of the greater grief/To banish the less, I find my chief relief." By remembering Fitzroy's death, his greater sorrow, Surrey finds relief from the less significant woes that attend his imprisonment.

[20] Although focusing on sonnet 73, John Coldewey also examines sonnets 71-74 as a group and notes that they mark "an important moment of transition, a time when thought of death turns to thought about poetic inspiration." He pinpoints sonnet 73 as "a pivotal point at which the poet emphasizes not only his own body's frailty, but also the frailty of the poetic endeavor."

"'Bare ru'ind quires': Sonnet 73 and Poetry, Dying," *PQ* 67 (1988): 7.

[21] In *Sorrow and Consolation,* McClure cites an instance of this Neoplatonic belief in "the eternal communion between souls that death facilitates." In a letter written to console his family for the death of his brother, Anselmo, Ficino reports a vision in which his brother explains that "The nature of bodies is such that two are not in one identical place, and that no one can be in more than one place at a time. And to the same condition are subjected the souls that are enclosed in bodies. But the soul free from earthly bonds, through the power of indivisible essence, is whole throughout the world and in every part of the time far away and seldom and only briefly nearby—I am present with yours; and, there not being impediments of place, time, or distance, the soul and the other are reduced into one nature. Therefore, do not search for me outside of yourselves, because I am alive in you and I think as you yourselves." Thus, McClure concludes, "the bereaved must look only into their own souls, where the souls of the departed can be found ever present" (145).

[22] Michael Cameron Andrews calls sonnets 87-96 the "estrangement sonnets," and describes the progression of sonnets 87-92 from self-protection to emotional blackmail to utter abjection to a confession of pain and vulnerability to an ingenious dispensing with the truth. "Sincerity and Subterfuge in Three Shakespearean Sonnet Groups," *SQ* 33 (1982): 320-22.

[23] Only in sonnets 120 and 121 does the speaker admit guilt, and then in a qualified way. The lover finds consolation for his infidelity by establishing shared guilt. In sonnet 120 the speaker remembers the young man's past infidelity and argues that it should prompt the youth to forgive him for his similar offense. The following sonnet (121) instead invokes the general guilt of mankind. This sin makes others unfit to judge the speaker.

[24] The famous sonnet 116 ("Let me not to the marriage of true minds admit impediments") begs the question of infidelity in love, simply declaring that true love exists and defining it as unchanging. Jane Roessner argues that sonnets 110-114 expose "the ways in which the sonnets themselves have attempted" to disguise the decay of the friend's love (333). In order to assert unchanging love, sonnet 116 must exclude from its definition of love "all traces of real people in real time, in real space" and replace them "with a landscape and time and person of his own creations, whose essential quality is their absolute lack of relation to real things." "The Coherence and Context of Shakespeare's Sonnet 116," *JEGP* 81 (1981): 341.

[25] Thomas Greene focuses on examples in the sequence of "pitiful thrivers," and tracks them through the progression of sonnets 123-125. He suggests that these sonnets repress pain and guilt, but adds, "Yet a purely cynical reading would strain out that element of real wishing which is also present." "'Pitiful Thrivers': Failed Husbandry in the Sonnets," *Shakespeare and the Question of Theory,* ed. Patricia Parker and Geoffrey Hartman (New York: Methuen, 1985), 239-40.

Source: "Patterns of Consolation in Shakespeare's Sonnets 1-126," in *Studies in Philology*, Vol. XCIV, No. 4, Fall, 1997, pp. 465-93.

Cumulative Index to Topics

The Cumulative Index to Topics identifies the principal topics of discussion in the criticism of each play and non-dramatic poem. The topics are arranged alphabetically by play. Page references indicate the beginning page number of each essay containing substantial commentary on that topic. A parenthetical reference after a play indicates which volumes discuss the play extensively.

Topic Index

279, 283, 406, 413; **25:** 235; **28:** 339

characterization **20:** 12, 318, 324, 329, 353, 363, 367, 374, 387; **28:** 339; **29:** 101, 109, 146, 155, 165

Christian elements **3:** 194, 239, 260, 269, 275, 286, 293, 297, 318; **20:** 203, 206, 210, 256, 262, 289, 291, 294

combat scenes **22:** 365

dagger scene (Act III, scene i), staging of **20:** 406

evil **3:** 194, 208, 231, 234, 239, 241, 267, 289; **20:** 203, 206, 210, 374

free will versus fate **3:** 177, 183, 184, 190, 196, 198, 202, 207, 208, 213; **13:** 361

innocence **3:** 234, 241, 327

Jacobean culture, relation to **19:** 330; **22:** 365

Lady Macbeth

　ambition **3:** 185, 219; **20:** 279, 345

　characterization **20:** 56, 60, 65, 73, 140, 148, 151, 241, 279, 283, 338, 350, 406, 413; **29:** 109, 146

　childlessness **3:** 219, 223

　good and evil, combined traits of **3:** 173, 191, 213; **20:** 60, 107

　inconsistencies **3:** 202; **20:** 54, 137

　influence on Macbeth **3:** 171, 185, 191, 193, 199, 262, 289, 312, 318; **13:** 502; **20:** 345; **25:** 235; **29:** 133

　psychoanalytic interpretation **20:** 345

　as sympathetic figure **3:** 191, 193, 203

language and imagery **3:** 170, 193, 213, 231, 234, 241, 245, 250, 253, 256, 263, 271, 283, 300, 302, 306, 323, 327, 338, 340, 349; **13:** 476; **16:** 317; **20:** 241, 279, 283, 367, 379, 400; **25:** 235; **28:** 339; **29:** 76, 91; **42:** 258

laws of nature, violation of **3:** 234, 241, 280, 323; **29:** 120

letter to Lady Macbeth **16:** 372; **20:** 345; **25:** 235

Macbeth

　characterization **20:** 20, 42, 73, 107, 113, 130, 146, 151, 279, 283, 312, 338, 343, 379, 406, 413; **29:** 139, 152, 155, 165

　courage **3:** 172, 177, 181, 182, 183, 186, 234, 312, 333; **20:** 107

　disposition **3:** 173, 175, 177, 182, 186; **20:** 245, 376

　imagination **3:** 196, 208, 213, 250, 312, 345; **20:** 245, 376

　as "inauthentic" king **3:** 245, 302, 321, 345

　inconsistencies **3:** 202

　as Machiavellian villain **3:** 280

　manliness **20:** 113; **29:** 127, 133

　psychoanalytic interpretation **20:** 42, 73, 238, 376

　Richard III, compared with **3:** 177, 182, 186, 345; **20:** 86, 92; **22:** 365

　as Satan figure **3:** 229, 269, 275, 289, 318

　self-awareness **3:** 312, 329, 338; **16:** 317

　as sympathetic figure **3:** 229, 306, 314, 338; **29:** 139, 152

Macduff **3:** 226, 231, 253, 262,; **25:** 235; **29:** 127, 133, 155

madness **19:** 330

major tragedies, relation to Shakespeare's other **3:** 171, 173, 213,

Malcolm **25:** 235

manhood **3:** 262, 309, 333; **29:** 127, 133

Marxist criticism **42:** 229

moral lesson **20:** 23

murder scene (Act II, scene ii) **20:** 175

religious, mythic, or spiritual content **3:** 208, 269, 275, 318; **29:** 109

Neoclassical rules **3:** 170, 171, 173, 175; **20:** 17

nightmarish quality **3:** 231, 309; **20:** 210, 242

Porter scene (Act II, scene iii) **3:** 173, 175, 184, 190, 196, 203, 205, 225, 260, 271, 297, 300; **20:** 283

primitivism **20:** 206, 213

providential order **3:** 208, 289, 329, 336

psychoanalytic interpretation **3:** 219, 223, 226

regicide **16:** 317, 328 248, 275, 312

retribution **3:** 194, 208, 318

sexual anxiety **16:** 328; **20:** 283

sleepwalking scene (Act V, scene i) **3:** 191, 203, 219; **20:** 175

staging issues **13:** 502; **20:** 12, 17, 32, 64, 65, 70, 73, 107, 113, 151, 175, 203, 206, 210, 213, 245, 279, 283, 312, 318, 324, 329, 343, 345, 350, 353, 363, 367, 374, 376, 379, 382, 387, 400, 406, 413; **22:** 365; **32:** 212

structure **16:** 317; **20:** 12, 245

supernatural grace versus evil or chaos **3:** 241, 286, 323

theatricality **16:** 328

time **3:** 234, 246, 283, 293; **20:** 245

topical allusions or content **13:** 361; **20:** 17, 350; **29:** 101

treason and punishment **13:** 361; **16:** 328

violence **20:** 273, 279, 283

witches and supernaturalism **3:** 171, 172, 173, 175, 177, 182, 183, 184, 185, 194, 196, 198, 202, 207, 208, 213, 219, 229, 239; **16:** 317; **19:** 245; **20:** 92, 175, 213, 279, 283, 374, 387, 406, 413; **25:** 235; **28:** 339; **29:** 91, 101, 109, 120

Measure for Measure (Volumes 2, 23, 33)

ambiguity **2:** 417, 420, 432, 446, 449, 452, 474, 479, 482, 486, 495, 505

Angelo

　anxiety **16:** 114

　authoritarian portrayal of **23:** 307

　characterization **2:** 388, 390, 397, 402, 418, 427, 432, 434, 463, 484, 495, 503, 511; **13:** 84; **23:** 297; **32:** 81; **33:** 77

　hypocrisy **2:** 396, 399, 402, 406, 414, 421; **23:** 345, 358, 362

　repentance or pardon **2:** 388, 390, 397, 402, 434, 463, 511, 524

autobiographical elements **2:** 406, 410, 414, 431, 434, 437

Barnardine **13:** 112

bed-trick **13:** 84

characterization **2:** 388, 390, 391, 396, 406, 420, 421, 446, 466, 475, 484, 505, 516, 524; **23:** 299, 405; **33:** 77

Christian elements **2:** 391, 394, 399, 421, 437, 449, 466, 479, 491, 511, 522

comic form **2:** 456, 460, 479, 482, 491, 514, 516; **13:** 94, 104; **23:** 309, 326, 327

death, decay, and nature's destructiveness **2:** 394, 452, 516; **25:** 12

displacement **22:** 78

Duke

　as authoritarian figure **23:** 314, 317, 347; **33:** 85

　characterization **2:** 388, 395, 402, 406, 411, 421, 429, 456, 466, 470, 498, 511; **13:** 84, 94, 104; **23:** 363, 416; **32:** 81; **42:** 1

　dramatic shortcomings or failure **2:** 420, 429, 441, 479, 495, 505, 514, 522

　godlike portrayal of **23:** 320

　noble portrayal of **23:** 301

　speech on death (Act III, scene i) **2:** 390, 391, 395

Elbow **22:** 85; **25:** 12

Elbow, Mistress **33:** 90

Elizabethan betrothal and marriage customs **2:** 429, 437, 443, 503

Elizabethan culture, relation to **2:** 394, 418, 429, 432, 437, 460, 470, 482, 503

feminist interpretation **23:** 320

good and evil **2:** 432, 452, 524; **33:** 52, 61

homosexuality **42:** 1

immortality **16:** 102

inconsistency between first and second halves **2:** 474, 475, 505, 514, 524

Isabella **2:** 388, 390, 395, 396, 397, 401, 402, 406, 409, 410, 411, 418, 420, 421, 432, 437, 441, 466, 475, 491, 495, 524; **16:** 114; **23:** 278, 279, 280, 281, 282, 296, 344, 357, 363, 405; **28:** 102; **33:** 77, 85

judicial versus natural law **2:** 446, 507, 516, 519; **22:** 85; **33:** 58, 117

justice and mercy **2:** 391, 395, 399, 402, 406, 409, 411, 416, 421, 437, 443, 463, 466, 470, 491, 495, 522, 524; **22:** 85; **33:** 52, 61, 101

language and imagery **2:** 394, 421, 431, 466, 486, 505; **13:** 112; **28:** 9; **33:** 69

Lucio **13:** 104

marriage **2:** 443, 507, 516, 519, 524, 528; **25:** 12; **33:** 61, 90

as medieval allegory or morality play **2:** 409, 421, 443, 466, 475, 491, 505, 511, 522; **13:** 94

metadramatic elements **13:** 104

misgovernment **2:** 401, 432, 511; **22:** 85

misogyny **23:** 358;

moral seriousness, question of **2:** 387, 388, 396, 409, 417, 421, 452, 460, 495; **23:** 316, 321

Neoclassical rules **2:** 387, 388, 390, 394; **23:** 269

politics **23:** 379

power **13:** 112; **22:** 85; **23:** 327, 330, 339, 352; **33:** 85

as "problem play" **2:** 416, 429, 434, 474, 475, 503, 514, 519; **16:** 102; **23:** 313, 328, 351

psychoanalytic interpretations **23:** 331, 332, 333, 334, 335, 340, 355, 356, 359, 379, 395

Puritanism **2:** 414, 418, 434

rebirth, regeneration, resurrection, or immortality **13:** 84; **16:** 102, 114; **23:** 321, 327, 335, 340, 352; **25:** 12

resolution **2:** 449, 475, 495, 514, 516; **16:** 102, 114

sexuality **13:** 84; **16:** 102, 114; **23:** 321, 327, 335, 340, 352; **25:** 12; **33:** 85, 90, 112

social aspects **23:** 316, 375, 379, 395

sources **2:** 388, 393, 427, 429, 437, 475; **13:** 94

spectacle **42:** 258

Topic Index

Topic Index

Topic Index

ISBN 0-7876-1987-6

9 780787 619879

90000